MAXWELL'S
HANDBOOK FOR
R D A

RESOURCE DESCRIPTION & ACCESS

ALA Editions purchases fund advocacy, awareness, and accreditation programs for library professionals worldwide.

MAXWELL'S HANDBOOK FOR R|D|A®

RESOURCE DESCRIPTION & ACCESS

Explaining and Illustrating RDA: Resource
Description and Access Using MARC 21

ROBERT L. MAXWELL

An imprint of the American Library Association
CHICAGO   2013

ROBERT L. MAXWELL is a senior librarian at the Harold B. Lee Library, Brigham Young University, where he has chaired the Special Collections and Formats Catalog Department and catalogs special collections and classics materials. He won the ALA Highsmith Library Literature Award for 2002 for the book *Maxwell's Guide to Authority Work* (2002) and is the author of a number of other books on cataloging published by ALA. He has taught cataloging at Brigham Young University and the University of Arizona School of Information Resources and Library Science and has chaired the Bibliographic Standards Committee of the Rare Books and Manuscripts Section of the Association of College and Research Libraries (ACRL). He has been a voting member of the ALCTS Committee on Cataloging: Description and Access, the body responsible for developing official ALA positions on additions to and revisions of RDA. In addition to an MLS from the University of Arizona, he holds a JD from Brigham Young University and a PhD in classical languages and literatures from the University of Toronto.

© 2013 by the American Library Association. Any claim of copyright is subject to applicable limitations and exceptions, such as rights of fair use and library copying pursuant to Sections 107 and 108 of the US Copyright Act. No copyright is claimed for content in the public domain, such as works of the US government.

Printed in the United States of America

17 16 15 14 13   5 4 3 2 1

Extensive effort has gone into ensuring the reliability of the information in this book; however, the publisher makes no warranty, express or implied, with respect to the material contained herein.

ISBN: 978-0-8389-1172-3 (paper).

Library of Congress Cataloging-in-Publication Data

Maxwell, Robert L., 1957–
    Maxwell's handbook for RDA: resource description and access : explaining and illustrating RDA: resource description and access using MARC 21 / Robert L. Maxwell.
       pages   cm
    Includes bibliographical references and index.
    ISBN 978-0-8389-1172-3 (alk. paper)
    1. Resource description & access—Handbooks, manuals, etc. 2. Descriptive cataloging—Standards—Handbooks, manuals, etc. I. Title. II. Title: Maxwell's handbook for RDA. III. Title: Handbook for RDA.
    Z694.15.R47M39 2014
    025.32—dc23
                                             2013035124

Text design by Kim Thornton in Gotham and Minion Pro.
Composition by Dianne M. Rooney.

♾ This paper meets the requirements of ANSI/NISO Z39.48-1992 (Permanence of Paper).

CONTENTS

PREFACE

HEN THE FIRST EDITION OF MAXWELL'S HAND-
book for AACR2, the predecessor of this *Handbook for RDA*,
was issued, the Anglo-American Cataloguing Rules, 2nd edition (AACR2), was new and untried.[1] Most catalogers were
familiar with the first edition of the Anglo-American Cataloging Rules (AACR1), introduced in 1967; many had used
the preceding cataloging code, the ALA 1949 rules. All were
apprehensive about the possible effect the new cataloging
code would have on existing library catalogs and cataloging practices. Exactly the
same situation exists at the time of the introduction of *RDA: Resource Description
and Access.* If anything, the level of apprehension may be even higher because RDA's
development process was much more open than AACR2's had been, and implementation has been a bit more haphazard, with many libraries embracing RDA early on
and others holding back.

Maxwell's Handbook for RDA, therefore, has been designed to assist experienced
catalogers as well as library school students in the application of the most commonly
used RDA guidelines for descriptions of entities and resources, and the creation of
access points.

Although the bedrock cataloging principles on which RDA is based are similar to
those of AACR2, many modifications have been made, both in the guidelines themselves and in the policy decisions of the major national libraries and cooperative

cataloging programs. And as RDA is gradually implemented and more and more cat-alogers gain experience using the new code, their experience is influencing revision of RDA and the policy decisions. These revisions are happening at a great rate at the moment. Although this is expected to settle down as we begin using the new code, the pace of change just now is unsettling.

A major philosophical change has occurred in the shift from AACR2 to RDA, emphasizing the importance of cataloger judgment. While cataloger judgment was important in AACR2 as well, choice of AACR2 options were mostly prescribed by policy documents such as the Library of Congress's Rule Interpretations. Although a similar document exists for RDA, the Library of Congress-Program for Cooperative Cataloging Policy Statements (see discussion in chapter 1), it is far less extensive and a conscious effort has been made to avoid making policy decisions where uniformity of practice was not completely needed. Since catalogers, as human beings, tend to want to be told what to do in cataloging situations, this new emphasis on personal decision making is uncomfortable to some, but in fact it can be very liberating, allow-ing individuals to make judgments based on the needs of local and other users of the database. It also allows experimentation and practice with new ways of doing things, both of which can only be good for both users and the cataloging community as we move forward.

RDA is format-agnostic and does not require either ISBD or MARC structures. This *Handbook,* however, was written with the assumption that most catalogers, for the near future at least, will continue to encode cataloging information using the MARC formats, and follow ISBD structures. Some significant changes in the MARC format have taken place in preparation for implementation of RDA.[2] This *Handbook* makes full use of these new and revised MARC provisions.

In the immediate predecessor to this *Handbook,* the policy decisions of the four major Anglo-American national libraries were taken into account.[3] Because most of these important libraries had not yet published their decisions at the time of this writing, only the Library of Congress-Program for Cooperative Cataloging decisions were used in this edition of *Maxwell's Handbook for RDA.* Future editions will note the other agencies' decisions as they are published.

The basic premises of the *Handbooks* for AACR2 remain the same in *Maxwell's Handbook for RDA.* The editors of RDA include frequent examples to illustrate the rules; these examples are not given in MARC format nor are they given in full catalog description format. In fact, the examples only illustrate the specific element being described. Catalogers as well as library school students may find these examples mys-tifying in their brevity. The present text therefore attempts not only to explain the guidelines, but also to give full cataloging examples to illustrate each guideline dis-cussed. Furthermore, experience teaching cataloging has demonstrated that one of the most difficult concepts for beginning catalogers is the translation of a title page (or other source) into a catalog description. Therefore, in as many instances as possible and whenever relevant, a transcription of the title page or other source material has been included with examples of bibliographic records. The source material for authority records may be deduced from the source consulted elements, which are recorded in 670 fields.

Like its predecessors, the structure of this *Handbook* is based on the structure of the code itself. Because RDA is organized based on the structure of Functional Requirements for Bibliographic Records (FRBR)[4] rather than that of the International Standard Bibliographic Description (ISBD)[5] as AACR2 was (see discussion in chapter 1), many catalogers will find this confusing until they become used to the new code. As an aid to catalogers accustomed to AACR2, a set of appendixes has been included based on format (book, manuscript, motion picture, etc.) and organized in AACR2/MARC order.

Maxwell's Handbook for RDA is designed as a supplement to, not a substitute for, the text of *RDA: Resource Description and Access*. It is assumed that the reader will have the latest version of RDA at hand, either via the RDA Toolkit or in print.[6] In addition, the *Handbook's* provisions and examples will need to be updated as RDA itself changes and as the policies of agencies such as the Library of Congress and the Program for Cooperative Cataloging evolve. It must be emphasized that this *Handbook* is not meant as a self-help manual for beginning catalogers, although with more and more library schools dropping cataloging requirements (or cataloging course work altogether), it is probably inevitable that it will be so used. It is therefore designed to address problems beginners often find puzzling. It is my hope that the following pages may serve as a helpful introduction and a guide to *RDA: Resource Description and Access*.

Many individuals contributed in various ways to *Maxwell's Handbook for RDA*. First and foremost, many thanks must be given to Judith Kuhagen, of the Library of Congress and secretary to the Joint Steering Committee, for prompt and helpful responses to questions about RDA and LC practice. Judy was always helpful, always courteous, always willing to discuss issues and matters on which policy had not been settled, and she went far beyond the call of duty when she agreed to continue fielding questions even after she had retired from the Library of Congress. I am extremely grateful for her help.

A number of other people helped with specific issues. These include John Attig and Barbara Tillett, both Joint Steering Committee members who willingly answered questions of all kinds; Dave Reser of the Library of Congress on MARC issues and other LC policy issues; Kathy Glennan, Janet Bradford, and others from the Music Library Association on music issues; Ed Jones on serial issues; Cory Nimer on archival issues; members of the Brigham Young University Catalog Departments on whom I practiced; and many others.

Thanks also to the capable editors at ALA Editions, whose superb editing skills always make a better book, particularly Christopher Rhodes, Patrick Hogan, Alison Elms, Helayne Beavers, and indexer Christine Karpeles.

I am also grateful to Robert Murdoch, Assistant University Librarian for Collection Development and Technical Services at the Harold B. Lee Library, Brigham Young University, as well other members of the administration of the Lee Library, for encouraging me to complete the *Handbook* and allowing me time away from my regular duties for its final preparation.

I am very grateful to my mother, Margaret F. Maxwell, who was the author of the original *Handbook for AACR2*. She made it possible for me to continue the *Maxwell's Handbook* series and contributed to *Maxwell's Handbook for RDA* through her constant encouragement and willingness to read and comment on some of the chapters.

Finally, thanks to an understanding wife, Mary Ann Maxwell, whose title transitioned from "AACR2 widow" to "RDA widow," at least in the final stages of manuscript preparation, but sportingly decided she wanted to learn RDA at the same time as I did; and to my children, Carrie, Rachel, William, and David. As always, I dedicate this book to them.

Robert L. Maxwell
Harold B. Lee Library
Brigham Young University
Provo, Utah

NOTES

1. Margaret F. Maxwell, *Handbook for AACR2* (Chicago: American Library Association, 1980).

2. The examples in this *Handbook* reflect coding practice as of Fall 2013. Details of MARC coding are constantly changing, not the least because of RDA developments. Full details of the MARC formats are available at www.loc.gov/marc.

3. *Maxwell's Handbook for AACR2: Explaining and Illustrating the Anglo-American Cataloguing Rules through the 2003 Update* (Chicago: American Library Association, 2004).

4. IFLA Study Group on the Functional Requirements for Bibliographic Records, "User Tasks," ch. 6 in *Functional Requirements for Bibliographic Records Final: Report* (Munich: K. G. Sauer, 1998), 79–92. Also available at www.ifla.org/en/publications/functional-requirements-for-bibliographic-records.

5. ISBD Review Group, *ISBD: International Standard Bibliographic Description*, consolidated ed., IFLA Series on Bibliographic Control, vol. 44 (Berlin: De Gruyter, 2011).

6. Information about both the online and the print versions of RDA is available at www.rdatoolkit.org.

CHAPTER 1

INTRODUCTION

URING THE THREE DECADES THAT FOLLOWED THE 1978 publication of the second edition of the Anglo-American Cataloguing Rules (AACR2), the library cataloging environment and landscape have changed in important ways. Although the Machine-Readable Cataloging (MARC) format was in use at the time of its publication, AACR2 was primarily designed to produce cataloging in card format. Indeed, the first two editions of the predecessor to this *Handbook, Maxwell's Handbook for AACR2,* barely mentioned MARC, and all examples were given in card format.[1] AACR2 was revised regularly, but database and digital technologies began to change the way libraries, museums, and archives collected resources, and how information about those resources was organized and maintained.

As an exercise to take stock of progress and look to the future, the Joint Steering Committee for the Revision of AACR (JSC) sponsored the International Conference on the Principles and Future Development of AACR, held in Toronto in 1997.[2] After that meeting, the JSC set an ambitious agenda to implement many of the ideas emanating from the conference.

By the middle of the next decade it became evident that tinkering with AACR2 was not sufficient and a replacement was necessary. Work on this project began in 2004, and over the next five years drafts were circulated to the constituent bodies of the JSC (The American Library Association; The Australian Committee on

Cataloguing; the British Library; the Canadian Committee on Cataloguing; CILIP: the Chartered Institute of Library and Information Professionals [formerly the (British) Library Association]; and the Library of Congress).[3] Comments were received as well from interested parties worldwide, including other European national libraries.

By June 2009 the JSC, now called the Joint Steering Committee for Development of RDA, delivered the full text of the new guidelines, titled *RDA: Resource Description and Access,* to the publishers. RDA was published online one year later as the principal part of the RDA Toolkit in June 2010.[4]

RDA is based on two particularly important documents, Functional Requirements for Bibliographic Records (FRBR) and the *Statement of International Cataloguing Principles.* This introduction will briefly discuss each of these documents. Additionally, it will discuss the International Standard Bibliographic Description (ISBD), the MARC format (in general terms), cooperative cataloging programs and policies, as well as some general issues about RDA itself, including implementation issues.

FRBR

During the 1990s the International Federation of Library Associations and Institutions (IFLA) commissioned a new look at the bibliographic universe. The result was Functional Requirements for Bibliographic Records, or FRBR, published in 1998.[5] FRBR was joined by a companion volume, Functional Requirements for Authority Data, or FRAD, published in 2009.[6] FRAD is an expansion of FRBR and adds a number of entities not found in FRBR. There is also an extension of FRBR called Functional Requirements for Subject Authority Data, approved in 2010.[7] In this *Handbook,* "FRBR" refers to this suite of three related documents.

FRBR is not a cataloging code. It is a conceptual model of the bibliographic universe based on a database modeling technique called "entity-relationship," first introduced in the 1970s.[8] The entity-relationship model is widely used in database design, but until recently has not been used extensively in library databases. This model may be used to define a specific database universe that is divided into specific entities linked by specific relationships.

An *entity* is something that can be distinctly identified within the context of the database. For example, a business database might define as entities "customers," "employees," "managers," "stores," "suppliers," etc. A genealogical database might define as entities "persons," "places," "events."

A *relationship* is an association between two or more entities. A business database might define a relationship between a particular store and an employee. A genealogical database might define a "father-child" relationship between a male person and his children.

In this model, entities and relationships are defined by *attributes*. An attribute is a characteristic that may identify instances of entities or relationships. For example, one of the attributes of a person is his or her birth date; other possible attributes for persons might be where they live, their profession, marital status, and so forth. Entity-relationship databases are designed with the entities, relationships, and attributes needed for the purpose of the database. A personnel database might need to define many attributes and relationships for persons (e.g., Social Security Number, gender, marital status, position in the company, salary, etc.). A bibliographic database would not define all possible attributes and relationships for "person," just those needed for the purposes of the database, such as name, possibly birth and death dates, relationship to works the person created, etc.

RDA, which is based on FRBR, defines entities, relationships, and attributes (attributes are called "elements" in RDA). Most cataloging under RDA consists of describing the attributes of the different FRBR entities and recording the relationships between these entities.

In a database based on FRBR principles, an instance of an entity (for example, a person) would be described one time only, and then that description would be linked to as many other entities (for example, works, other persons, related corporate bodies, etc.) as needed. This contrasts with the current MARC structure, where information about an entity such as a person might be recorded in an authority record, but then is often repeated over and over in bibliographic records.

The entities in the FRBR model are divided into three groups. The first group is defined as "the products of intellectual or artistic endeavor" and consists of four entities:

> **WORK:** a distinct intellectual or artistic creation[9]
> **EXPRESSION:** the intellectual or artistic realization of a *work* in some form (e.g., alpha-numeric or musical notation)
> **MANIFESTATION:** the physical embodiment of an *expression* (e.g., a print publication)
> **ITEM:** a single exemplar or instance of a *manifestation* (i.e., a copy)

The relationships between these entities are shown in figure 1.1. In the figures in this chapter, entities are shown as rectangles, relationships as diamonds, and attributes (when shown) as ovals, all linked by lines.

The novel *Gone with the Wind* is an example of a *work*, a distinct intellectual creation by a person, Margaret Mitchell.

When a work takes on a form it is said to be realized and becomes an *expression*. *Gone with the Wind* exists in many expressions. When Mitchell first wrote the text of *Gone with the Wind* in manuscript form it became an expression. When this text was first published in revised form in 1936 it became another expression of the same work. This first published expression was translated into German in 1937, creating

Figure 1.1. Relationship Between FRBR Group 1 Entities

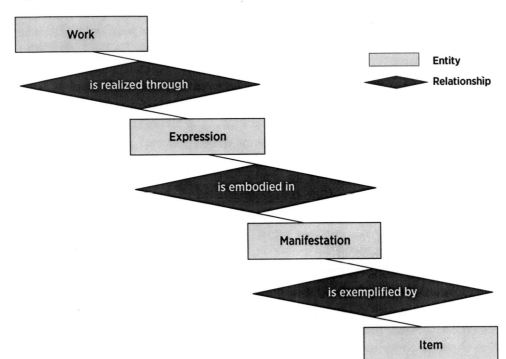

yet another expression of the same work. These are all expressions in text form. This work has also been recorded as various audiobooks. Each recording is a new "spoken word" expression of the work.

Expression is still an abstract concept. "Text" and "spoken word" are abstract forms, but they begin to become concrete when they are put into a "carrier," the container housing the information. For example, a spoken word recording of *Gone with the Wind* might be presented on different carriers, such as cassette tape, compact disc, long-playing record, or streaming audio. Presentation of an expression on a particular carrier is called "physical embodiment" of the expression and the result is called a *manifestation*. The text of *Gone with the Wind* was published in 1936 by Macmillan. This is one manifestation of that expression. The identical text was published in 2006 by Scribner. This is the same expression as the first, but a different manifestation.

Generally a manifestation is produced in multiple identical (or nearly identical) copies, although manifestations can exist with only a single copy. Individual copies of a manifestation are called *items*. Individual copies of the 1936 manifestation owned by a library are items.

The relationships between some specific Group 1 entity instances related to *Gone with the Wind* are shown in figure 1.2.

Figure 1.2. Relationship Between FRBR Group 1 Entities (Gone with the Wind)

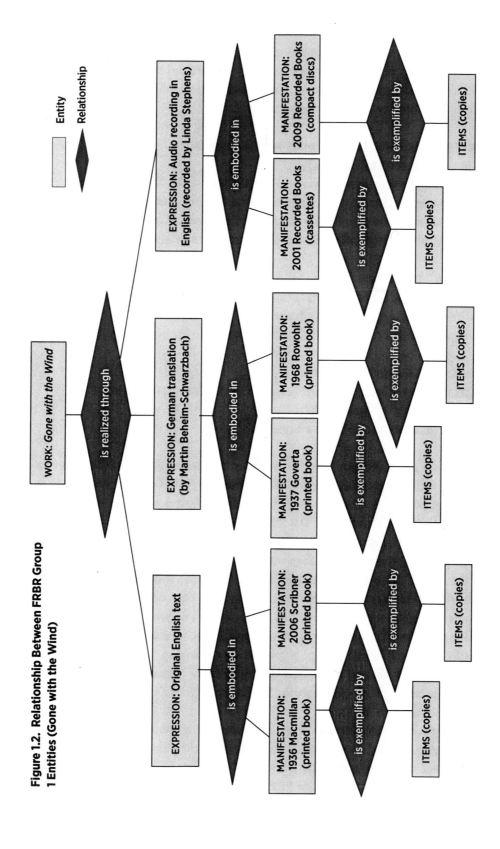

The second group of FRBR entities includes those that are capable of creating or having other relationships (such as production or ownership) to the Group 1 entities. The FRBR model defines three: person, family, and corporate body. The three entities here are defined much as would be expected:

PERSON: an individual or an identity established by an individual (either alone or in collaboration with others)

FAMILY: two or more persons related by birth, marriage, adoption, civil union, or similar legal status, or who otherwise present themselves as a family

CORPORATE BODY: an organization or group of individuals or organizations that is identified by a particular name and that acts, or may act, as a unit

FRBR Group 3 entities are entities that can be subjects of works, expressions, manifestations, or items. Any of the entities in Groups 1 and 2 can be the subject of a work—for example, a person entity, from Group 2, might be the subject of a biography. Beyond Groups 1 and 2, Group 3 defines four other entities:

CONCEPT: an abstract notion or idea

OBJECT: a three-dimensional artifact or a naturally occurring object

EVENT: an action or occurrence

PLACE: a location identified by a name

FRBR defines a set of attributes for each entity in the model. Because it is not a cataloging code, FRBR does not define how the information is to be recorded. For example, "name of person" is one of the attributes of the person entity in FRBR. FRBR defines this attribute as follows: "The name of a *person* is the word, character, or group of words and/or characters by which the *person* is known," and points out that a person may be known by more than one name, and that libraries normally select one of the names as a uniform heading (FRBR 4.6.1). But it does not tell us how to form the data to be recorded in this element, and if we are one of the libraries that wants to select one as a uniform heading, it does not tell us how to make that choice. That is the province of a cataloging code, such as RDA. RDA also defines entity attributes (called "elements" in RDA), but because it is a cataloging code it also informs us how to record the data, and in the case of the "name of person" attribute, it tells us how to choose between competing forms. See figure 1.3 for an example of an instance of an entity showing its attributes.

Any entity can be linked to any other entity through a specified relationship link. For example, figure 1.4 shows the relationship between the person described in figure 1.3 and various works, four that she created and five that she is the subject of. In an entity-relationship database based on FRBR, each of these works would be described

Figure 1.3. Attributes

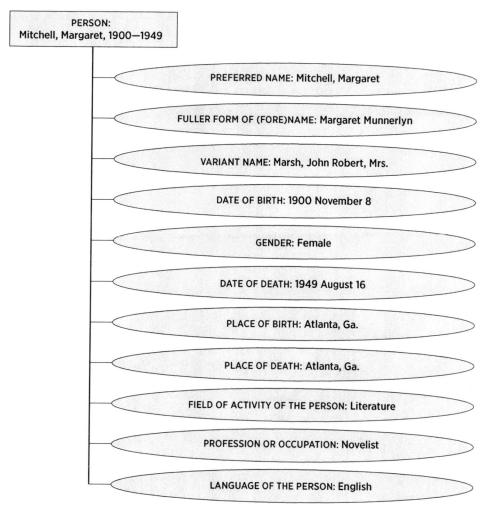

only once and then would be linked to descriptions of expressions, manifestations, and items as seen in figure 1.2. Similarly, each of the works shown in figure 1.4 might be linked to other entities such as persons, families, or corporate bodies, or related works. For example, *Road to Tara,* one of the works linked to Margaret Mitchell through a subject relationship link, would be linked to the description of its author, Anne Edwards, through a creator link. Figure 1.5 shows how different works can be related to each other.

The organization of RDA is based on FRBR. This is very different from the organization of RDA's predecessor, AACR2. The first half of RDA gives instructions for recording the attributes of the entities. RDA chapters 1 through 7 cover the Group 1 entities (work, expression, manifestation, and item); chapters 8 through 11 cover

Figure 1.4. Relationship Between FRBR Entities (Person to Work)

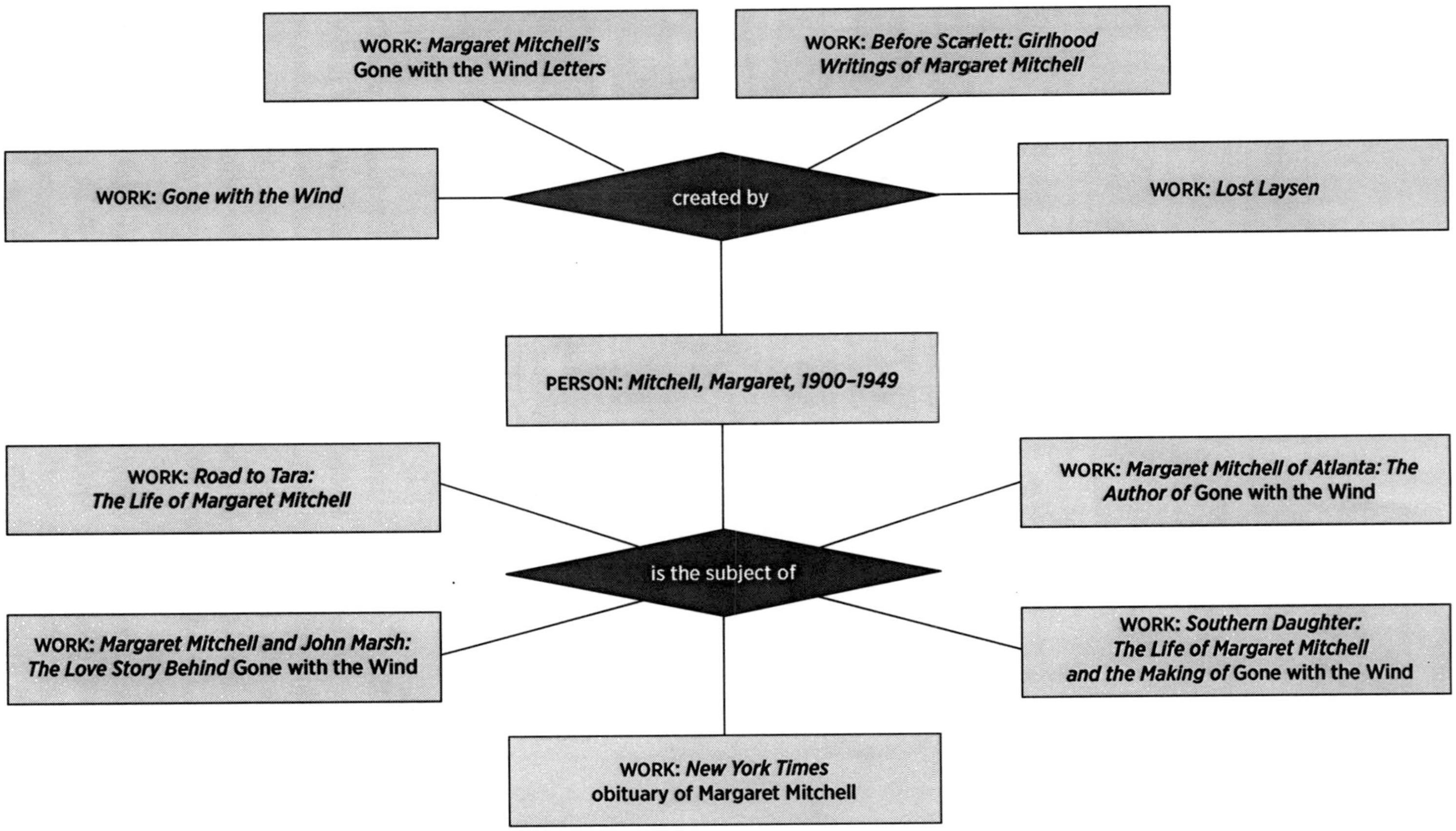

PERSON: *Mitchell, Margaret, 1900–1949*

created by

- WORK: *Before Scarlett: Girlhood Writings of Margaret Mitchell*
- WORK: *Lost Laysen*
- WORK: *Margaret Mitchell's Gone with the Wind Letters*
- WORK: *Gone with the Wind*

is the subject of

- WORK: *Margaret Mitchell of Atlanta: The Author of Gone with the Wind*
- WORK: *Southern Daughter: The Life of Margaret Mitchell and the Making of Gone with the Wind*
- WORK: *New York Times* obituary of Margaret Mitchell
- WORK: *Road to Tara: The Life of Margaret Mitchell*
- WORK: *Margaret Mitchell and John Marsh: The Love Story Behind Gone with the Wind*

Figure 1.5. Relationship Between FRBR Entities (Work to Work)

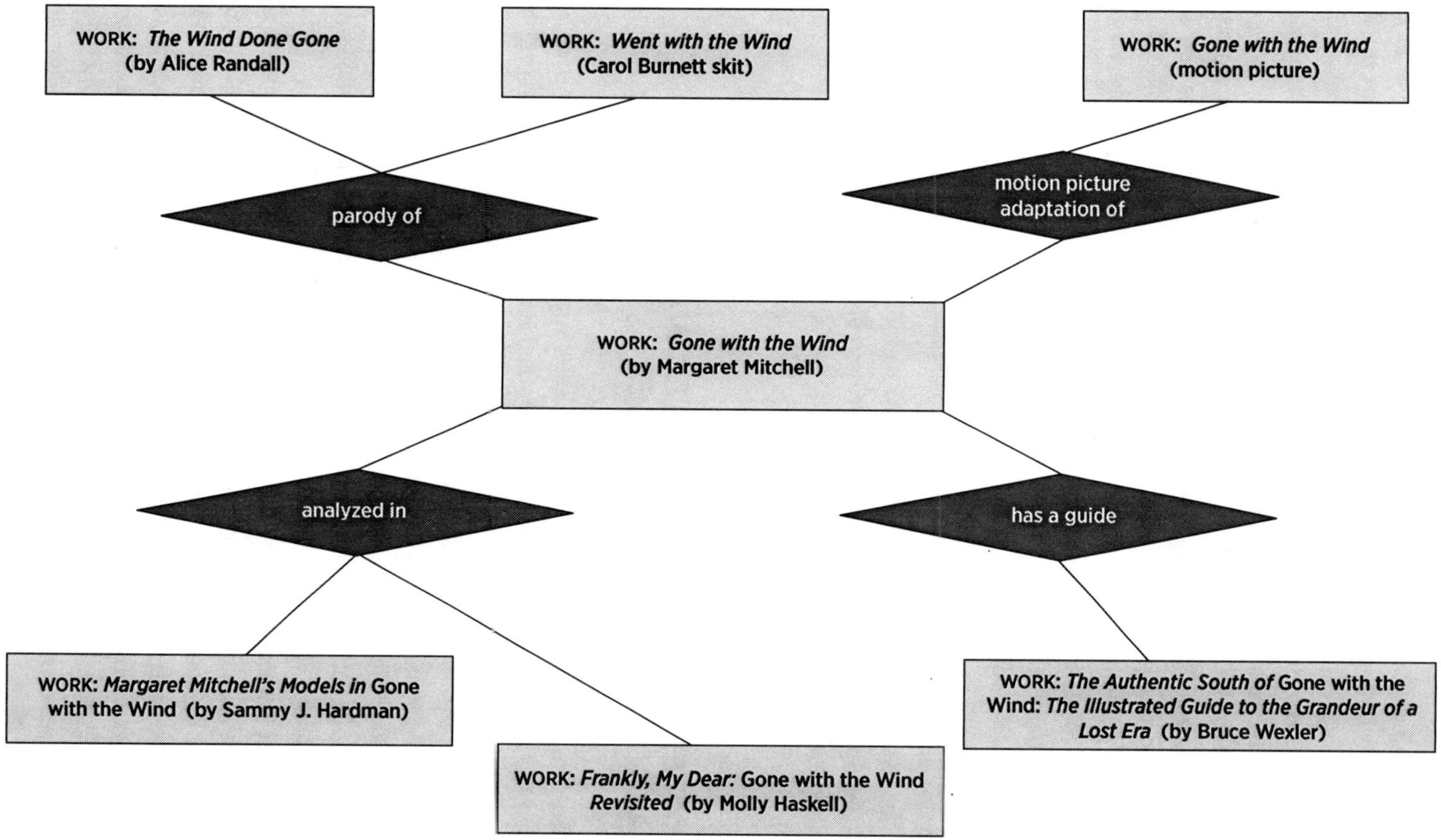

WORK: *Gone with the Wind* (motion picture)

motion picture adaptation of

has a guide

WORK: *The Authentic South of Gone with the Wind: The Illustrated Guide to the Grandeur of a Lost Era* (by Bruce Wexler)

WORK: *Went with the Wind* (Carol Burnett skit)

WORK: *Gone with the Wind* (by Margaret Mitchell)

WORK: *Frankly, My Dear: Gone with the Wind Revisited* (by Molly Haskell)

WORK: *The Wind Done Gone* (by Alice Randall)

parody of

analyzed in

WORK: *Margaret Mitchell's Models in Gone with the Wind* (by Sammy J. Hardman) the Group 2 entities (person, family, and corporate body); and chapters 12 through 16 cover the Group 3 entities (concept, object, event, and place). Of this third group, only the place entity is worked out in the current version of RDA. Instructions for describing concepts, objects, and events will be developed later, but placeholder chapters have been included in RDA for them.

Most of the RDA chapters on describing the attributes of entities are organized in a similar way. They all begin with a section describing the purpose and scope of the chapter, and general guidelines pertinent to the entity. The bulk of each chapter consists of guidelines for describing specific entity attributes. The chapter ends with guidelines for constructing access points for the entity. Understanding this FRBR-based structure is important to understanding RDA. This organization represents a philosophical shift away from AACR2, with its emphasis on creating access points to an emphasis instead on *describing* entities, with almost incidental information on creating access points.

The second half of RDA (chapters 17 through 37) gives instructions for recording relationships between the entities that have been described following the instructions in chapters 1 through 16.

STATEMENT OF INTERNATIONAL CATALOGUING PRINCIPLES

When the Anglo-American Cataloguing Rules appeared in 1967, the code was heralded as a new departure in cataloging, a unified set of rules based on principle rather than on the enumeration of specific problems. And indeed this was the case. The 1967 rules, like the 1978 second edition (AACR2), were based on the *Statement of Principles* Adopted at the International Conference on Cataloguing Principles, Paris, October 1961.[10] This brief statement, usually referred to as the Paris Principles, served the worldwide cataloging community well for half a century. Most cataloging codes published after 1961 were based on it.

At about the same time as the development of RDA, IFLA convened a series of meetings called the IFLA Meetings of Experts on an International Cataloguing Code. The charge of these meetings was to develop a new set of international cataloging principles to replace the Paris Principles. Meetings took place between 2003 and 2007 in Frankfurt, Germany; Buenos Aires, Argentina; Cairo, Egypt; Seoul, South Korea; and Pretoria, South Africa, where advice was taken from regional cataloging experts. The final document, titled *Statement of International Cataloguing Principles*, was published in 2009.[11]

The general principles as enumerated in section 2 of the Statement are:

2.1. *Convenience of the user.* Decisions taken in the making of descriptions and controlled forms of names for access should be made with the user in mind.

2.2. *Common usage.* Vocabulary used in descriptions and access should be in accord with that of the majority of users.

2.3. *Representation.* Descriptions and controlled forms of names should be based on the way an entity describes itself.

2.4. *Accuracy.* The entity described should be faithfully portrayed.

2.5. *Sufficiency and necessity.* Only those data elements in descriptions and controlled forms of names for access that are required to fulfill user tasks and are essential to uniquely identify an entity should be included.

2.6. *Significance.* Data elements should be bibliographically significant.

2.7. *Economy.* When alternative ways exist to achieve a goal, preference should be given to the way that best furthers overall economy (i.e., the least cost or the simplest approach).

2.8. *Consistency and standardization.* Descriptions and construction of access points should be standardized as far as possible. This enables greater consistency, which in turn increases the ability to share bibliographic and authority data.

2.9. *Integration.* The descriptions for all types of materials and controlled forms of names of all types of entities should be based on a common set of rules, insofar as it is relevant.

The Statement further stipulates that the rules in a cataloging code should be defensible and not arbitrary, recognizing that the principles may contradict each other in specific situations and advising that a defensible, practical solution be taken when this happens. It states that the most important, overriding principle is convenience of the user.

Section 3 of the Statement embraces the FRBR model, stating that a cataloging code should take into account the entities, attributes, and relationships in the bibliographic universe, listing the FRBR entities.

Section 4 of the Statement states that the database should enable the user to:

4.1. *find* bibliographic resources by searching for attributes or relationships

4.2. *identify* a bibliographic resource (i.e., confirm that the described entity is the same as the entity searched for)

4.3. *select* a bibliographic resource that is appropriate to the user's needs (i.e., choose between resources that have been identified in the previous step)

4.4. *acquire* the item or *obtain access* to it

4.5. *navigate* within the database and beyond

These closely reflect the "user tasks" enumerated in Section 6 of FRBR.

Additionally, the Statement discusses bibliographic description and access points, calling for internationally agreed-upon standards for description and for the formation of controlled and uncontrolled access points following these same standards.

Although the Statement was in development at the same time as RDA, it "informs the cataloguing principles used throughout RDA" (RDA 0.4.1) and is reflected in the objectives and principles delineated in RDA 0.4. As is the case with the Statement, the principle of user convenience is of paramount importance in RDA, as shown by the constant exhortation to the cataloger to make decisions based on whether a particular action will help the user find, identify, select, or gain access to the resource or entity. For example, RDA instructs the cataloger to record variant titles for a resource if they "are considered important for identification or access" (RDA 2.3.6.3), or to record a relationship to a distributor "if considered important for access" (RDA 21.4.1.3), or to record the regional encoding of a DVD "if considered important for identification or selection" (RDA 3.19.6.3). In all these cases decisions are left to the judgment of the cataloger, but that judgment is to be based on the principle of user convenience.

INTERNATIONAL STANDARD BIBLIOGRAPHIC DESCRIPTION (ISBD)

Building on the Paris Principles, IFLA sponsored another international meeting of cataloging experts in 1969 that called for the creation of standards to regularize the form and content of bibliographic descriptions. This project resulted in the International Standard Bibliographic Description (ISBD), which is still under development. The primary purpose of ISBD was to promote "universal bibliographic control," that is, basic cataloging data for all published resources in all countries provided in a mutually agreed-upon form. The first standard, an ISBD for monographic publications, appeared in 1971. Numerous standards for various formats followed, culminating in the recently published "consolidated edition."[12]

ISBD prescribed essential pieces of information that were to appear in bibliographic descriptions, the order in which this information was to be given, and a system of arbitrary punctuation that must be used. This was to facilitate international exchange of data as well as to permit quick identification of the elements of a description even if the catalog or database user was unfamiliar with the language of the description.

The descriptive cataloging rules in AACR2 Part I were firmly based on ISBD, and the text was organized around the structure of ISBD, unlike RDA, which is organized around the structure of FRBR. Although it acknowledges the influence of ISBD on its development (RDA 0.2), RDA does not prescribe ISBD formatting, and particularly does not require ISBD punctuation, as AACR2 did. However, recognizing that most cataloging agencies would continue to follow the ISBD structure, at least for the near future, RDA includes instructions for ISBD presentation in Appendix D.1, which gives ISBD elements in order and links them to relevant RDA elements. Examples and instructions in this *Handbook* follow ISBD structure and punctuation.

MACHINE-READABLE CATALOGING (MARC)

RDA does not prescribe any particular presentation format, but for the near future (at least) most libraries will continue to catalog using the MARC format.[13] RDA recognizes this and was designed to be compatible with MARC descriptions, although it is clearly looking forward to a more FRBR-based structure of the information. The RDA Toolkit includes MARC-to-RDA and RDA-to-MARC mappings as an aid to catalogers who continue to use MARC (see the Tools menu). All cataloging examples in this *Handbook* are given in MARC, and specifics about particular fields are given in the following chapters as they become relevant. The MARC record also includes some fields that are not explained in this *Handbook*. Only MARC fields that contain data currently called for by RDA are included (the figures, therefore, generally contain no "fixed fields," fields defined for classification numbers or subjects, or other non-RDA elements).[14]

When the application of the computer to library tasks began in the early 1960s, cataloging was one of the obvious candidates for automation. The computer could not simply digest a catalog record in card format, however, and generate a sensible result. Furthermore, the possibilities of access to computerized records far surpassed access to the traditional card catalog, but only if the records were systematically coded so that the machine could distinguish, for example, between a title and an author, or between a series and a subject heading. Thus various systems of encoding bibliographic data developed around the world.

In addition to improved access to the records within catalogs, computerization of cataloging also opened the possibility of shared cataloging. Large international databases (e.g., OCLC and Skyriver) appeared, containing catalog records contributed by member libraries for most of the world's current publications and a large percentage of earlier works. Such projects require standardization of the cataloging format used by the various libraries. MARC developed in different ways in different countries, and although there is still no single internationally accepted format, the formats are becoming reconciled so that the goal of easily exchangeable cataloging records around the world can be realized. The mechanism for worldwide transmission of data, the Internet, is well established and has become a catalyst for more serious efforts at standardization than took place in the past.

The Library of Congress (LC) was one of the first organizations to develop a machine-readable format for catalog records, and this format evolved into what is currently called "MARC 21," but referred to simply as "MARC" throughout this *Handbook.* MARC is used almost universally throughout the United States, Canada, and the United Kingdom. It is also widely used in other countries. Use of a single standard greatly enhances the ease of information exchange.

The MARC catalog description is divided into "fields," which in turn are divided into "subfields." These correspond to various aspects of the description. The fields are all numbered with a three-digit numeric "tag." Although not all numbers are used, there is a theoretical possibility of up to 1,000 fields (from 000 to 999). Following a field tag in a MARC record are two numeric digits called "indicators." Each of these may either be blank or may contain a number. The coding of the indicators normally instructs the system to manipulate the data in some way (e.g., for display or indexing purposes). Following the indicators are the subfields, which contain the actual RDA cataloging data (known in RDA as "elements"). Each subfield is preceded by a delimiter mark (in this *Handbook* shown by a double dagger, "‡") and a single letter or number, which tells what type of subfield is being used or what element it corresponds to. This system can obviously become extremely complex, but it is organized in a logical fashion and incorporates a system of mnemonics that is very helpful.

There are two major formats within MARC, the bibliographic format and the authority format.[15] The bibliographic format contains descriptions of resources collected by libraries. The authority format contains descriptions of persons, families, corporate bodies, geographic entities, works, expressions, and subjects. This bibliographic versus authority organization creates an uneasy fit with RDA and FRBR, but until a replacement for MARC becomes available it will be used to encode RDA records.

In the following discussion and throughout this *Handbook,* the letter *X* in a field tag represents any number from 0 to 9. For example, 1XX can represent 100, 110, 130, etc.; X11 can represent 111, 711, 811, etc.

MARC BIBLIOGRAPHIC FORMAT

The MARC bibliographic format is used to describe bibliographic resources of the type owned or accessed by libraries or archives. These roughly correspond to the FRBR manifestation and item entity. It is often said that in shared databases such as OCLC, bibliographic records are used to describe manifestations. However, although manifestation-related elements are indeed recorded there, bibliographic format records may in fact contain information about any of the FRBR entities. Although RDA was designed to allow encoding RDA descriptions in MARC records, MARC records were not designed with RDA in mind, and so the correspondence between RDA and MARC, particularly in the bibliographic format, is imperfect.

The theoretically possible 1,000 MARC tags are divided into groups of 100.

> **0XX** fields comprise mainly control fields and record various types of identification and classification numbers. A common field from this group found in this *Handbook* is the 020 field, where the International Standard Book Number (ISBN) is recorded.
>
> **1XX** fields record the principal creator of the work embodied in the resource, including persons, families, and corporate bodies. Additionally, AACR2 practice for the 130 field (title main entry) will continue under RDA, although there is no concept of title main entry in RDA. 130 may be used to identify a work embodied in a resource that has no identifiable creator.

In current MARC practice there is never more than one 1XX field in a record.

> **2XX** fields contain title, edition, and publication information. The most common of these are the 245 field, the title and statement of responsibility, and the 246 field, where variations on the title are recorded. Other 2XX fields include the 250 field, where edition information is recorded, and the 264 field, where publication information is recorded.
>
> **3XX** fields, which may be repeated, mainly contain elements related to the description of the manifestation, including physical description (e.g., extent and dimensions), carrier type, and digital file characteristics. It also contains some expression-related elements.
>
> **490** fields contain transcriptions of series statements found on the resource; the 490 field may be paired with an 8XX field if indexing of the series is desired.
>
> **5XX** fields contain various types of notes.
>
> **6XX** fields contain subject access points. Because RDA does not yet address subject access, these fields are not generally found in the cataloging examples in this *Handbook*.
>
> **7XX** fields contain added access points to the record, which may include authorized access points for coauthors, illustrators, translators, related works, etc.
>
> **8XX** fields contain authorized access points for series (see 490, above). Additionally, the 856 field contains the URL link for an electronic resource.
>
> **9XX** fields are locally defined fields; each library may define these as it wishes in accordance with its own policies. Except for the 490 field, in MARC the

number 9 in other positions also means "locally defined": X9X fields (e.g., 590) are reserved for local use as well.

In addition to the division of the 1,000 numbers into ten blocks, certain mnemonic devices exist that cross these blocks. In the 1XX, 4XX, 6XX, 7XX, and 8XX fields, the second and third digits of the tag have parallel meanings. The most common of these used in this *Handbook* follow:

X00 signifies a person or family. For example, a 100 field contains the authorized access point for a person or family who is the principal creator of the resource.

X10 signifies a corporate body. For example, a 710 field contains the authorized access point for a corporate body related to the resource.

X11 signifies a meeting or event. A 111 field contains the authorized access point for a meeting or event considered the principal creator of the resource.

X30 signifies a work not linked to a creator (e.g., an anonymous work). A 730 field may contain the authorized access point for a work related to the resource, or a work contained in the resource.

MARC AUTHORITY FORMAT

The tag/indicator/subfield structure of the MARC authority format is the same as that of the bibliographic format, but the organization is different. The MARC authority format is used to record descriptions of persons, families, corporate bodies, geographic entities, works, expressions, and subjects.

0XX fields comprise mainly control fields and record various types of identification numbers and codes. 0XX authority fields are not commonly found in this *Handbook,* but 010, the Library of Congress Control Number, is an example of an identifier—a core element for all these entities. Another field that is commonly found in the *Handbook* is 046, which contains coded dates related to the entity being described.

1XX fields contain the authorized access point for the entity being described. This is the form that will be used in bibliographic records to create links between the resource being described and other entities. Under Program for Cooperative Cataloging (PCC) policy there can be only one authorized access point per entity, and so there will never be more than one 1XX field in a PCC authority record.

There is only one **2XX** authority field, 260 ("complex see reference") and it is not used in this *Handbook.*

3XX fields are used to record the attributes of entities. For example, the 375 field may be used to record a person's gender. Previous to RDA, 3XX fields were not commonly used in MARC authority records. They are extensively used in this *Handbook*.

4XX fields contain variant access points, forms of the entity's name that differ from the authorized access point recorded in 1XX and that the cataloger thinks might be used to find the entity. In current systems, information recorded in these fields generally directs the user to the authorized access point.

5XX fields contain links to other entities that are related to the entity described in the authority record. The forms found in 5XX fields always correspond to forms found in the 1XX fields of other MARC authority records.

6XX fields contain notes of various kinds.

7XX fields contain other types of links. These fields are not used in this *Handbook*. The most common **8XX** field is the 856 field, which may be used to record a URL.

As in the bibliographic format, **9XX** fields are locally defined fields; each library may define these as it wishes in accordance with its own policies. The number 9 in other positions also means "local." For example, 090 is commonly used to record a call number used only by a particular library.

The same mnemonic devices within the second and third digits of the tag numbers that exist in the bibliographic format also exist in the authority format (e.g., X00 represents a tag for a person or family, whether in an authority 100, 400, or 500 field). For details see the last part of the section above on the MARC bibliographic format.

COOPERATIVE CATALOGING PROGRAMS

Cooperative cataloging programs have been in place in the United States for decades and have ranged from nationwide programs primarily designed to assist the Library of Congress in the production of cards for its card distribution program to local or statewide consortia that share cataloging responsibilities. The rise of mutually accepted record interchange standards, that is, the MARC formats, has greatly facilitated these efforts.

Program for Cooperative Cataloging (PCC)

The most successful of these programs to date is the Program for Cooperative Cataloging, or PCC. The PCC began in 1995 as a result of planning that had taken place earlier in the decade. It currently has four components: NACO (Name Authority

Cooperative Program); SACO (Subject Authority Cooperative Program); BIBCO (Bibliographic Record Cooperative Program); and CONSER (Cooperative Online Serials Program).

The most important goals of the PCC are to make more authoritative records (both bibliographic and authority records) available for sharing by all libraries, and to develop mutually acceptable standards for record creation.

In 2012 there were over 800 libraries and other institutions participating in at least one of the component programs of the PCC. Collectively, these libraries produced nearly 209,000 new name authority records, over 12,000 new series authority records, approximately 2,500 new subject authority records, and over 75,000 new bibliographic records.

Participating libraries are located in all parts of the world. The majority are in the United States, but there are also participants in Argentina, Australia, Brazil, Canada, England, Hong Kong, Ireland, Italy, Lithuania, Mexico, New Zealand, Scotland, South Africa, Wales, and many other countries. The PCC is truly an international effort.

The PCC maintains a web page at www.loc.gov/aba/pcc/, where further details about the program can be found.

Such a large cooperative effort requires that policies be made that can be followed by all participants. RDA introduced a greater degree of cataloger judgment than AACR2, and in many instances it does not matter that every cataloger make the same choices, even in a cooperative cataloging program. But in some cases it does matter, and for these cases PCC, in cooperation with the Library of Congress, has created an evolving set of policies known as the Library of Congress-Program for Cooperative Cataloging Policy Statements, or LC-PCC PSs. These policy statements may be found under the Resources tab in the RDA Toolkit, and links to the LC-PCC PSs are also given at relevant points in RDA itself.

The LC-PCC PS document is a hybrid that combines LC's own internal policy decisions with policy decisions that apply to PCC. These decisions are not always the same, so it is important to pay attention to the labels that appear with each policy statement. Whether each applies to LC, PCC, or both, is clearly marked at the beginning of each statement. For example, at the time of this writing LC-PCC PS 7.10 (April 2010), Summarization of the Content, is marked "CORE ELEMENT FOR LC." This means LC catalogers are required to include a summarization in certain instances, but other PCC catalogers are not. Similarly, LC-PCC PS 7.10.1.3 (January 2013) is marked "LC practice," which indicates that LC catalogers should follow the policy when creating summaries, but others are not bound by it, although they may follow it if they think it makes sense. On the other hand, LC-PCC PS 2.3.3 (September 2012), Parallel Title Proper, is labeled "CORE ELEMENT FOR LC/PCC," which means both LC and PCC catalogers are required to include the element. LC-PCC

PS 9.3.2.3 (July 2012), Recording Date of Birth, is marked "LC practice/PCC practice," which means both LC and PCC catalogers should follow the practice listed for including a date of birth as part of the access point for a person. This is an example of a policy where it is important that everyone follow the same practice because it affects the indexing of the shared authority file.

Non-PCC catalogers are free to follow these policy statements or not. Many will follow them, because for the most part they make sense and are based on sound judgment. Significant LC-PCC PSs are cited in this *Handbook* where relevant. Because RDA is newly implemented and the policies are in flux at this time, the date of each policy is included here with its citation. Catalogers should always check the LC-PCC PS itself for the most up to date information.

GENERAL RDA ISSUES

Core Elements

AACR2 1.0D allowed the cataloger to choose between three levels of detail in cataloging description when applying AACR2. The first level was brief cataloging, and only included the most essential elements. The second level included many more elements than the first, but did not require every possible AACR2 cataloging element. Third-level descriptions included elements from every rule that applied to the item being cataloged. All three levels were used in AACR2, but most catalogers opted for second-level descriptions.

RDA does not define levels of description. Instead RDA 0.6 designates certain elements (e.g., the FRBR entity attributes) to be core. "Core" designation means that the element is required in a description if it is applicable to the resource or entity being described, and if it is readily ascertainable. The cataloger is also required to "include any additional elements that are required in a particular case to differentiate" the resource or entity from others with similar attributes. Inclusion of other elements is at the discretion of the cataloger who should use judgment based on the needs of the database user and the policies of the cataloging agency.

The core elements are all listed in RDA 0.6, and are also repeated in general chapters dealing with groups of entities (for example, core elements applicable to persons, families, or corporate bodies are listed in 8.3). The cataloger is not expected to memorize these lists, however. All core elements are also clearly labeled in the guidelines that deal specifically with them. For example, type of family, an attribute of the family entity, is core. The guidelines for this element display as follows:

10.3 Type of Family
> **CORE ELEMENT**
>> **10.3.1 Basic Instructions on Recording Type of Family**
>>> **10.3.1.1 Scope**

In contrast, "family history" is not a core element. It displays as follows:

10.8 Family History
> **10.8.1 Basic Instructions on Recording Family History**
>> **10.8.1.1 Scope**

Certain elements are core only under certain circumstances. For example, the guidelines at 2.9.2 read:

2.9.2 Place of Distribution
> **CORE ELEMENT**
> *Place of distribution is a core element for a resource in a published form if the place of publication is not identified. If more than one place of distribution appears on the source of information, only the first recorded is required.*
>> **2.9.2.1 Scope**

This means the place of distribution element is required, but only if a place of publication has not been recorded. These elements are coming to be known in cataloging jargon as "core if" elements.

The core elements are intended to support the FRBR user tasks (mentioned above during the discussion of the *Statement of International Cataloguing Principles*). The database should allow the user to find, identify, select, and gain access to resources. The core elements were selected because they were thought to support these tasks, particularly "identify" and "select."

There are surprisingly few core elements compared with the rich data that can be recorded in an RDA description. This *Handbook* tends to push RDA to the limit and includes many more elements in descriptions shown in the figures than are called for by RDA's core requirements. Catalogers and cataloging agencies will have differing opinions as to the utility of many of the elements but they are encouraged to explore the possibilities of the non-core elements as ways to help their users navigate our bibliographic universe and discover the resources they need.

MOVING TARGET

One of the issues this *Handbook* has had to deal with is the "moving target" nature of RDA at this early stage. Just as AACR2 was, RDA is being revised on a regular schedule by the JSC. Major revisions are currently occurring on an annual basis; the first set of revisions was published in April 2012. The RDA Toolkit contains an update history, found at the bottom of the text under the RDA tab. Links to this history are also found at relevant places in the guidelines themselves. For example, RDA 9.15 (field of activity of a person) and 9.16 (profession or occupation of a person) were clarified in the April 2012 revision, and 9.15 was changed from a core to a non-core element. Links at RDA 9.15 and 9.16 (a blue rectangle that says "2012/04") take the reader to the previous wording and a brief summary of the change.

This is a convenient way of showing what has changed and when. As catalogers gain experience using RDA, rough edges are being smoothed out, and even large sections are being revised. It is expected that this will occur regularly for the next several years, after which the revision process may settle down to a less frenetic pace.

Another group of changes occur as well that are not as evident. These are called "fast track" changes, and include correction of typographical errors as well as other changes that are considered minor, such as the addition of new relationship designators in appendixes I through L. These changes are not marked or found in the update history, and unlike the major changes which are incorporated into RDA on an annual basis, the fast track changes can be incorporated at any time during the RDA Toolkit's monthly updates.

As mentioned above during the discussion of the LC-PCC PSs, LC and PCC policy for application of RDA is also in considerable flux as catalogers gain experience using the code.

Two important revisions took place just as this *Handbook* was being prepared for publication. First, the JSC approved a number of significant revisions at its November 2012 meeting, to be published around July 2013. The *Handbook* has attempted to take these changes into account, but because the revised text had not yet been officially published at the time of writing it is important that catalogers verify the final text in these areas before proceeding. Additionally, a long-term project to improve the readability of the guidelines began in 2011. The first revised texts were incorporated into RDA in December 2012, to be followed by others during 2013. These revised guidelines were not intended to change the outcome of application of the instructions, and so should not affect the guidance given in the *Handbook;* however, RDA quotations may differ in some instances between the *Handbook* and the current text of RDA found online.

In short, every effort has been made to keep this *Handbook* accurate as of its publication date, but because of the "moving target" problem the *Handbook* must always be used in tandem with RDA and the policy statements themselves in order to follow the most current practices.

NOTES

1. Margaret F. Maxwell, *Handbook for AACR2* (Chicago: American Library Association, 1980); Margaret F. Maxwell, *Handbook for AACR2, 1988 Revision* (Chicago: American Library Association, 1989).

2. The proceedings were published as *The Principles and Future of AACR: Proceedings of the International Conference on the Principles and Future Development of AACR, Toronto, Ontario, Canada, October 23–25, 1997,* Jean Weihs, ed. (Chicago: American Library Association, 1998).

3. The Deutsche Nationalbibliothek joined the JSC in 2012.

4. The RDA Toolkit resides at www.rdatoolkit.org.

5. IFLA Study Group on the Functional Requirements for Bibliographic Records, *Functional Requirements for Bibliographic Records, Final Report* (Munich: K. G. Saur, 1998); also available in PDF or HTML format at www.ifla.org/publications/functional -requirements-for-bibliographic-records.

6. IFLA Working Group on Functional Requirements and Numbering of Authority Records, *Functional Requirements for Authority Data: A Conceptual Model.* IFLA Series on Bibliographic Control, vol. 34 (Munich: K. G. Saur, 2009).

7. IFLA Working Group on the Functional Requirements for Subject Authority Records, *Functional Requirements for Subject Authority Data (FRSAD): A Conceptual Model,* www.ifla.org/files/assets/classification-and-indexing/functional-requirements -for-subject-authority-data/frsad-final-report.pdf.

8. For a comprehensive overview of FRBR, see Robert L. Maxwell, *FRBR: A Guide for the Perplexed* (Chicago: American Library Association, 2008).

9. All entity definitions are based on those found in RDA, which may differ slightly from FRBR.

10. The definitive text of the Paris Principles is International Conference on Cataloguing Principles, Paris, 1961, *Statement of Principles,* annotated edition with commentary and examples by Eva Verona (London: IFLA Committee on Cataloguing, 1971).

11. IFLA Cataloguing Section and IFLA Meetings of Experts on an International Catal- oguing Code, *Statement of International Cataloguing Principles.* IFLA Series on Bib- liographic Control, vol. 37 (Munich: K. G. Saur, 2009). Also available in English and numerous other languages at www.ifla.org/publications/statement-of-international -cataloguing-principles.

12. ISBD Review Group, *ISBD: International Standard Bibliographic Description,* consolidated ed. IFLA Series on Bibliographic Control, vol. 44 (Berlin: De Gruyter, 2011). Information about the history of ISBD was taken from the introduction to this document, xi–xvii.

13. On the Library of Congress's initiative to develop a replacement for MARC, see LC's Bibliographic Framework Transition Initiative page at www.loc.gov/marc/transition.

14. For complete information on MARC 21 coding, see www.loc.gov/marc.

15. MARC 21 also includes three other formats: holdings, classification, and community information. These formats are not discussed in this *Handbook.*

CHAPTER 2

DESCRIBING MANIFESTATIONS AND ITEMS

Instructions for recording the attributes of the *manifestation* and *item* entities are found in RDA chapters 1 through 4.

MARC CODING

HE *MANIFESTATION* AND *ITEM* ENTITIES ARE CURrently described in library catalogs in the MARC 21 bibliographic format.[1] In contrast to the MARC authority record, in which one can reasonably refer, for example, to a record describing a "person entity," a "corporate body entity," or a "work entity," the MARC bibliographic record contains much more than descriptive elements for the manifestation and item. As seen in chapters 7 and 8 of this *Handbook* (in the discussion of RDA chapter 7), some of the elements of the work and expression entities are currently recorded in bibliographic records rather than authority records. Additionally, the bibliographic record may contain links to any of the other FRBR entities (person, family, corporate body, concept, object, place, or event) in the form of authorized access points (including subject access points), and occasionally descriptive information about these other entities finds its way into the bibliographic record (e.g., a biographical note in an archival description about the creator of the records). To add to the confusion, sometimes item information is recorded in a separate kind of MARC record called a "holdings record" rather than in the bibliographic record. This confusing situation is due to the fact that the MARC record structure was not designed with FRBR or RDA in mind.

Examples of bibliographic records in the figures in this chapter are reasonably fully cataloged, although for space reasons sometimes certain elements or authorized access points have been omitted, and subject access points will not be included at all. However, because the bibliographic record may contain elements describing many FRBR entities, there is potential for confusion because this chapter of the *Handbook* is titled "Describing Manifestations and Items." To demonstrate the distinction, elements of bibliographic records that describe manifestations or items have been italicized in figures 2.1 through 2.4. Unitalicized elements in these figures relate to RDA instructions for describing other entities or non-RDA elements of the record. In an entity-relationship database structure, where the entities are given separate descriptions linked to each other by relationships, the italicized elements in the figures are probably the only elements that would appear in the description of a manifestation (or item).

RDA bibliographic records are identified by the value "i" or "c" in leader position 18 (labeled "Desc" in the OCLC fixed field display) and the presence of "‡e rda" in the 040 field (see figure 2.1a). The code "i" in leader position 18 means ISBD punctuation conventions have been followed in the description; "c" means ISBD punctuation has been omitted at the end of a subfield, a practice followed by some European libraries. Examples in this *Handbook* follow North American practice by including full ISBD punctuation. In contrast, an AACR2 bibliographic record may be recognized by the presence of value "a" in leader position 18 and no special coding in 040 (see figure 2.1b).[2] For space reasons, RDA coding is assumed in further figures in this chapter and is not explicitly shown. Other MARC coding issues will be discussed as they occur later in the chapter.

Figure 2.1a. RDA Coding

Visual Materials		Rec stat	c	Entered 20110128		Replaced 20110601161346.2		
Type	g	Elvl	I	Srce	d	Audn	Ctrl	Lang	eng
BLvl	m	Form		Gpub		Time	094	MRec	Ctry	cau
Desc	**i**	TMat	v	Tech	I	DtSt	t	Dates	2010, 2010

040	‡a UBY ‡b eng **‡e rda** ‡c UBY
245 04	‡a *The nature of existence :* ‡b *feature documentary.*
264 1	‡a *Beverly Hills, California :* ‡b *Walking Shadows,* ‡c *[2010]*
264 4	‡c *©2010*
300	‡a *1 videodisc (approximately 94 min.) :* ‡b sound, color ; ‡c *4 3/4 in.*
336	‡a two-dimensional moving image ‡2 rdacontent
337	‡a *video* ‡2 rdamedia
338	‡a *videodisc* ‡2 rdacarrier
346	‡b *NTSC* ‡2 rda

347	‡a *video file* ‡b *DVD video* ‡e *region 1* ‡2 rda
500	‡a *Title from disc label.*
508	‡a Director, Roger Nygard; producers, Roger Nygard and Paul Tarantino.
511 0	‡a Featuring: Orson Scott Card, Richard Dawkins, Ann Druyan, Daniel Gilbert, Irvin Kershner, Larry Niven, King Arthur Pendragon, Sri Sri Ravi Shankar, Brother Jed Smock, Leonard Susskind, Julia Sweeney.
511 0	‡a Musical score by Billy Sullivan.
521 8	‡a MPAA rating: Not rated.
520	‡a Roger Nygard roams the globe to interview spiritual leaders, scientists, and artists who have influenced, inspired, or startled humanity.
700 1	‡a Nygard, Roger, ‡d 1962- ‡e film director, ‡e film producer.
700 1	‡a Tarantino, Paul, ‡e film producer.
700 1	‡a Sullivan, Billy, ‡d 1962- ‡e composer.
710 2	‡a Walking Shadows (Firm), ‡e film producer.

Figure 2.1b. AACR2 coding

Visual Materials		Rec stat		c		Entered 20110128		Replaced 20110601161346.2		
Type	g	Elvl	I	Srce	d	Audn		Ctrl	Lang	eng
BLvl	m	Form		Gpub		Time	094	MRec	Ctry	cau
Desc	**a**	TMat	v	Tech	I	DtSt	s	Dates	2010,	
040	‡a UBY ‡c UBY									
245 04	‡a The nature of existence ‡h [videorecording] : ‡b feature documentary.									
...										

GENERAL GUIDELINES ON RECORDING ATTRIBUTES OF MANIFESTATIONS AND ITEMS

The guidelines in RDA chapter 1 apply to all elements described in chapters 2 through 4.

1.1. TERMINOLOGY. *Manifestation* is defined in RDA 1.1.5 as "the physical embodiment of an expression of a work." This means the physical form the expression of a work has taken. For example, Homer's *Odyssey* is a work. It has been realized through several different expressions ("the intellectual or artistic realization of a work"), including an English translation by Alexander Pope. This expression has itself been "embodied" several times, including a 1931 publication by the Limited Editions Club and a 2003 publication by Wildside Press. Each of these is a manifestation of this particular expression of the *Odyssey* (see figures 2.2 and 2.3). Note that the 100/240 field combination in these two descriptions is identical. This is because both manifestations are linked to the same expression of the work. Similarly, because that expression has a relationship with a particular translator, Alexander Pope, the same added access point for Pope is found in both bibliographic records. In an entity-relationship database structure, Pope would be clearly linked to the description of the expression, not to that of the manifestation, but in the current MARC structure the FRBR entity to which Pope is linked is somewhat ambiguous. For more information about creating relationship links in MARC bibliographic records, see chapter 9 of this *Handbook*.

Figure 2.2. Manifestation

100	0	‡a Homer, ‡e author.
240	10	‡a Odyssey. ‡l Greek ‡s (Pope)
245	14	‡a *The Odyssey of Homer /* ‡c *translated by Alexander Pope ; with an introduction by Carl Van Doren.*
264	1	‡a *Haarlem :* ‡b *Printed by Joh. Enschedé en Zonen for the members of the Limited Editions Club,* ‡c *1931.*
300		‡a *xiv, 548 pages ;* ‡c *31 cm*
336		‡a text ‡2 rdacontent
337		‡a *unmediated* ‡2 rdamedia
338		‡a *volume* ‡2 rdacarrier
500		‡a *"Of this edition ... , designed by J. van Krimpen, fifteen hundred copies have been printed ... by Joh. Enschedé en Zonen, Haarlem, Holland. Each copy is signed by the designer."--Colophon.*
590		‡a *Library copy is number 797.*
700	1	‡a Pope, Alexander, ‡d 1688-1744, ‡e translator.

Figure 2.3. Manifestation

020		‡a *9781587156755*
100	0	‡a Homer, ‡e author.
240	10	‡a Odyssey. ‡l Greek ‡s (Pope)
245	14	‡a *The Odyssey of Homer /* ‡c *Alexander Pope, translator ; with an introduction by Theodore Alois Buckley.*
264	1	‡a *Doylestown, Pennsylvania :* ‡b *Wildside Press,* ‡c *[2003]*
300		‡a *388 pages ;* ‡c *24 cm*
336		‡a text ‡2 rdacontent
337		‡a *unmediated* ‡2 rdamedia
338		‡a *volume* ‡2 rdacarrier
700	1	‡a Pope, Alexander, ‡d 1688-1744, ‡e translator.

Title page

The Odyssey of Homer
Alexander Pope, Translator
With an introduction by Theodore Alois Buckley

WILDSIDE PRESS
Doylestown, Pennsylvania

Item is defined in RDA 1.1.5 as "a single exemplar or instance of a manifestation." This follows the FRBR definition (FRBR 3.2.4). *Item* usually corresponds to the informal notion of a copy. When we say that a library owns a copy of Pope's translation of the *Odyssey,* in FRBR terms we might mean it owns one item (the copy numbered 797) of a particular manifestation (the 1931 publication by Limited Editions Club) of a particular expression (Pope's 1725 English-language translation) of a particular work (Homer's *Odyssey*). (The RDA elements dealing with *item* will be discussed later in this chapter.) Most bibliographic records do not record attributes of items because in most cases all the items in a manifestation are identical, including the copy in the library's collection. Figure 2.2 does include information about an item—the fact that the library's copy is number 797 of a numbered edition (see the 590 field). This is an example of an item-specific carrier characteristic (RDA 3.21).

1.3. CORE ELEMENTS. As explained in greater detail in chapter 1, RDA identifies certain elements as "core" throughout the code. The core elements were chosen because they were attributes and relationships thought to support FRBR and FRAD user tasks, listed in RDA 1.2 ("Functional Objectives and Principles").[3] RDA entity descriptions should contain, at a minimum, all core elements that are applicable and readily ascertainable as well as any other elements that might be required to differentiate one entity from another (see RDA 0.6.1). Inclusion of other elements is not required, and is at the discretion of the cataloger or cataloging agency (such as an individual library, or cooperative organizations such as the Program for Cooperative Cataloging [PCC]).

Agencies may develop requirements that go beyond RDA core. The Library of Congress (LC) and the Program for Cooperative Cataloging, for example, have designated certain elements that are not core in RDA to be core for their own catalogers. Information about LC and PCC decisions are found in Library of Congress-Program for Cooperative Cataloging Policy Statements (LC-PCC PSs), found under the Resources tab of the RDA Toolkit.

Core elements for all entities and relationships are given in RDA 0.6. They are also given separately in the chapter(s) devoted to each entity or relationship. Core elements for the manifestation and item entities are found in RDA 0.6.2 and again in

RDA 1.3. This information is also listed with each element's instruction. For example, RDA 2.3, title, which is a core element for manifestations, reads as follows:

> **2.3**
>> **Title**
>> **CORE ELEMENT**
>> *The title proper is a core element. Other titles are optional.*
>> **2.3.1 Basic Instructions on Recording Titles**
>>> **2.3.1.1 Scope**

Conversely, 3.5, dimensions, which is not a core element, reads as follows:

> **3.5 Dimensions**
>> **3.5.1 Basic Instructions on Recording Dimensions**
>>> **3.5.1.1 Scope**

The core elements for the manifestation entity are:

Title proper
Statement of responsibility
    Statement of responsibility relating to title proper (if more than one, only the first recorded is required)
Edition statement
    Designation of edition
    Designation of a named revision of an edition
Numbering of serials
    Numeric and/or alphabetic designation of first issue or part of sequence (for first or only sequence)
    Chronological designation of first issue or part of sequence (for first or only sequence)
    Numeric and/or alphabetic designation of last issue or part of sequence (for last or only sequence)
    Chronological designation of last issue or part of sequence (for last or only sequence)
Production statement
    Date of production (for a resource in an unpublished form)
Publication statement
    Place of publication (if more than one, only the first recorded is required)
    Publisher's name (if more than one, only the first recorded is required)
    Date of publication
Distribution statement

Place of distribution (for a published resource, if place of publication not identified; if more than one, only the first recorded is required)

Distributor's name (for a published resource, if publisher not identified; if more than one, only the first recorded is required)

Date of distribution (for a published resource, if date of publication not identified)

Manufacture statement

Place of manufacture (for a published resource, if neither place of publication nor place of distribution identified; if more than one, only the first recorded is required)

Manufacturer's name (for a published resource, if neither publisher nor distributor identified; if more than one, only the first recorded is required)

Date of manufacture (for a published resource, if neither date of publication, date of distribution, nor copyright date identified)

Copyright date (if neither date of publication nor date of distribution identified)

Series statement

Title proper of series

Numbering within series

Title proper of subseries

Numbering within subseries

Identifier for the manifestation

Identifier for the manifestation (if more than one, prefer an internationally recognized identifier if applicable)

Carrier type

Extent (only if the resource is complete or if the total extent is known)

Note that many of these core elements are only core if certain other conditions are met (e.g., the copyright date element is only core if neither a date of publication nor a date of distribution has been identified).

There are no core elements for the item entity.

Core designation means that the element must be recorded (if applicable and readily ascertainable) in the description of the manifestation.

For the sake of illustration, the figures in this book will usually include many elements beyond the core elements. See figure 2.4a for an example of a description of a manifestation that contains only core elements (recall that only italicized elements pertain to the manifestation; the 336 field contains a core element relating to the expression); figure 2.4b is an example of a description of the same manifestation containing elements beyond core. It is evident that the RDA core for the description of a manifestation can be minimal. Cataloging agencies may want their catalogers to include more elements, such as fuller statements of responsibility and dimensions (fields 245 and 300 in figure 2.4b). When making decisions about inclusion of non-core elements in entity descriptions, agencies need to think about possible future uses of the data. Many non-core elements such as encoding format (e.g., DVD video versus Blu-ray; see figure 2.4b, 347 field) or regional encoding (figure 2.4b, 347 field) may be useful as limiters to searches or as initial searches for records, but only if agencies apply them consistently in their databases.

Figure 2.4a. Core Elements

024	1	‡a *097363581468*
245	10	‡a *Hugo* / ‡c *Paramount Pictures and GK Films present a GK Films/Infinitum NIHL production.*
264	1	‡a *Hollywood, CA* : ‡b *Paramount Pictures,* ‡c 2012.
300		‡a *1 videodisc*
336		‡a two-dimensional moving image ‡2 rdacontent
338		‡a *videodisc* ‡2 rdacarrier

Figure 2.4b. Elements and Relationship Links beyond Core

024	1	‡a *097363581468*
028	42	‡a *35814* ‡b Paramount Pictures
028	42	‡a *11111023276* ‡b Paramount Pictures
130	0	‡a Hugo (Motion picture)
245	10	‡a *Hugo* / ‡c *Paramount Pictures and GK Films present a GK Films/Infinitum NIHL production ; produced by Graham King, Tim Headington, Martin Scorsese, Johnny Depp ; screenplay by John Logan ; directed by Martin Scorsese.*
264	1	‡a *Hollywood, CA* : ‡b *Paramount Pictures,* ‡c 2012.
264	4	‡c ©2011
300		‡a *1 videodisc* (126 min.) : ‡b sound, color ; ‡c *4 3/4 in.*
336		‡a two-dimensional moving image ‡2 rdacontent
337		‡a *video* ‡2 rdamedia
338		‡a *videodisc* ‡2 rdacarrier
344		‡h Dolby digital 5.1 ‡2 rda
346		‡b NTSC ‡2 rda
347		‡a video file ‡b DVD video ‡e region 1 ‡2 rda
380		‡a Motion picture.
500		‡a Based on the book "The invention of Hugo Cabret" by Brian Selznick.
518		‡a Originally produced as a motion picture in 2011.

500	‡a Bonus features: Shoot the moon: the making of Hugo; previews.
508	‡a Director of photography, Robert Richardson; editor, Thelma Schoonmaker; music, Howard Shore.
511 1	‡a Ben Kingsley, Sacha Baron Cohen, Asa Butterfield, Chloe Grace Moretz, Ray Winstone, Emily Mortimer, Christopher Lee.
520	‡a An orphan boy living a secret life in the walls of a Paris train station is caught up in a magical, mysterious adventure that could put all of his secrets in jeopardy.
521 8	‡a CHV rating: PG.
500	‡a Widescreen.
546	‡a English with dubbed French or Spanish dialogue; French or Spanish subtitles; English audio description; closed-captioned.
700 1	‡a Scorsese, Martin, ‡e film director, ‡e film producer.
...	

1.4. LANGUAGE AND SCRIPT. Cataloging agencies generally choose a language that they will use when creating descriptions, both for authority and bibliographic records. This is referred to in RDA as "the language and script preferred by the agency creating the data" (see RDA 0.11.2). For example, most U.S. libraries, including the Library of Congress, prefer English, but Library and Archives Canada has two preferred languages, French and English; they may create records using either language, or both.

The language preferred by the agency is familiarly known as the "language of cataloging." This does *not* mean the language of the resource being cataloged; rather, it means the language of the catalog *record*. The language of cataloging is recorded in bibliographic records in subfield ‡b of the 040 field (see figure 2.1). The language is recorded as a code, found the MARC Code List for Languages (see www.loc.gov/marc/languages/langhome.html). The code for English is "eng."

RDA 1.4 tells us which elements are to be recorded in the language and script of the resource, and which are to be recorded in the language preferred by the agency, that is, the language of the catalog record. For example, title proper is listed. This means the title proper is to be recorded in the description in the language and script it appears in, not translated into the language of the catalog record. Elements not listed in 1.4 are to be recorded in the language and script preferred by the agency— English language and roman script for most U.S. libraries, which is also the language preferred in this *Handbook*.

Recording information in the *script* in which it appears was for many years impossible in MARC, which at first only supported roman script. A number of other scripts are now supported, and these may be used to record or transcribe information in the elements listed in RDA 1.4. However, in North American practice, information recorded in non-roman scripts will always be accompanied by a parallel romanized element, following the optional addition listed in RDA 1.4 (see LC-PCC PS 1.4 option, July 2012). For an example, see figure 2.5, where title, statement of responsibility, and publication statement elements were recorded in Greek script and then romanized in parallel MARC fields. In this case the place of publication needed to be supplied by the cataloger. Although place of publication is one of the elements listed in 1.4 to be recorded in the language and script of the resource, later in the guideline the cataloger is instructed, "When information is supplied in an element listed at 1.4, record the supplied element in the most appropriate language and script." In this case the cataloger decided it was "appropriate" to record the place in English, but it might instead have been recorded in Greek. Note that other elements in the description are recorded in the English language and roman script.

Figure 2.5. Language and Script of the Resource

```
020      ‡a 9789603065517
100 1    ‡a Card, Orson Scott, ‡e author.
240 10   ‡a Ultimate Iron Man. ‡l Greek
245 10   ‡a Ultimate Iron Man : ‡b τα πρώτα βήματα / ‡c σενάριο, Orson Scott Card ; μολύβι,
         Andy Kubert & Mark Bagley ; μελάνι, Danny Miki, Batt, Jesse Delperdang, Jon Dell
         ; χρώμα, Richard Isanove, Dave McCaig, Laura Martin ; για την ελληνική γλώσσα,
         υπεύθυνη έκδοσης Μαρθα Ψυχακη ; μετάφραση Πάναγιώτης Αρκουδέας.
245 10   ‡a Ultimate Iron Man : ‡b ta prōta vēmata / ‡c senario, Orson Scott Card ; molyvi,
         Andy Kubert & Mark Bagley ; melani, Danny Miki, Batt, Jesse Delperdang, Jon Dell
         ; chrōma, Richard Isanove, Dave McCaig, Laura Martin ; gia tēn hellēnikē glōssa,
         hypeuthynē ekdosēs Martha Psychakē ; metaphrasē Panagiōtēs Arkoudeas.
264  1   ‡a [Athens] : ‡b Anubis Εκδοσεις Graphic Novels, ‡c [2006]
264  1   ‡a [Athens] : ‡b Anubis Ekdoseis Graphic Novels, ‡c [2006]
264  4   ‡c ©2006
300      ‡a 1 volume (unpaged) : ‡b chiefly color illustrations ; ‡c 26 cm
336      ‡a text ‡2 rdacontent
336      ‡a still image ‡2 rdacontent
337      ‡a unmediated ‡2 rdamedia
338      ‡a volume ‡2 rdacarrier
700 1    ‡a Kubert, Andy, ‡d 1962- ‡e illustrator.
700 1    ‡a Bagley, Mark, ‡d 1957- ‡e illustrator.
700 1    ‡a Psychakē, Martha, ‡e translator.
700 1    ‡a Arkoudeas, Panagiōtēs, ‡e translator.
700 1    ‡i Translation of: ‡a Card, Orson Scott. ‡t Ultimate Iron Man.
```

Title page

ULTIMATE IRON MAN™

ΤΑ ΠΡΩΤΑ ΒΗΜΑΤΑ

σενάριο, Orson Scott Card

μολύβι, ANDY KUBERT & MARK BAGLEY

μελάνι, DANNY MIKI, BATT, JESSE DELPERDANG, JON DELL

χρώμα, RICHARD ISANOVE, DAVE MCCAIG, LAURA MARTIN

για την ελληνική γλώσσα, υπεύθυνη έκδοσης ΜΑΡΘΑ ΨΥΧΑΚΗ

μετάφραση ΠΑΝΑΓΙΩΤΗΣ ΑΡΚΟΥΔΕΑΣ

In an effort to look archaic or classical, typographers sometimes design presentations of titles with premodern forms of capital letters. This particularly affects "I," which can stand for "i" or "j"; "V," which can stand for "u" or "v"; and "VV," which can stand for "w." When converting uppercase characters I, V, or VV to lower case when following the capitalization conventions of RDA appendix A, record:

j   for consonants (IVS = jus)
i   for vowels (ITER = iter)
v   for consonants (VOX = vox)
u   for vowels (HISTORIARVM = historiarum)
w   for consonantal uu or vv (VVINDOVV = window)

(See LC-PCC PS 1.4, October 2012) (see figure 2.6).

Figure 2.6. Transcription of U/V

100 1	‡a Hülsen, Christian, ‡d 1858-1935, ‡e author.
240 10	‡a Forum Romanum. ‡l English
245 10	‡a The Roman forum : ‡b its history and its monuments / ‡c Ch. Huelsen ; translated from the 2nd German edition by Jesse Benedict Carter.
264 1	‡a Rome : ‡b Loescher & Co. (Bretschneider and Regenberg) ; ‡a New York : ‡b G.E. Stechert & Co., ‡c 1906.
300	‡a xi, 259 pages : ‡b illustrations ; ‡c 17 cm
336	‡a text ‡2 rdacontent
336	‡a still image ‡2 rdacontent
337	‡a unmediated ‡2 rdamedia
338	‡a volume ‡2 rdacarrier
504	‡a Includes bibliographical references (pages 241-248).
700 1	‡a Carter, Jesse Benedict, ‡d 1872-1917, ‡e translator.

Title page

CH. HUELSEN

———

The
ROMAN FORVM
ITS HISTORY AND ITS MONUMENTS

———

TRANSLATED FROM THE 2ND GERMAN EDITION
BY
JESSE BENEDICT CARTER

———

With 5 plates and 139 illustrations in the text.

ROME
LOESCHER & Cº.
(Bretschneider and Regenberg)
1906

NEW YORK: G.E. STECHERT & Co.

1.6. CHANGES REQUIRING A NEW DESCRIPTION. This important guideline affects resources that change over time. There are three such kinds of resources:

1. Multipart monographs, defined in the RDA Glossary as "a resource issued in two or more parts (either simultaneously or successively) that is complete or intended to be completed within a finite number of parts." These parts may not be issued all at once but rather over a period of time, and later parts may exhibit changes.
2. Serials, defined in the RDA Glossary as "a resource issued in successive parts, usually bearing numbering, that has no predetermined conclusion." These by definition exist over time and may change.
3. Integrating resources, defined in the RDA Glossary as "a resource that is added to or changed by means of updates that do not remain discrete but are integrated into the whole." Again, by definition integrating resources exist over time and may change.

If the cataloger who is dealing with a multipart monograph, a serial, or an integrating resource discovers that a change has occurred (e.g., the title changes), the question arises whether to describe the change in the same description as that created when describing earlier parts of the resource, or whether the change is great enough that a new description (i.e., in current practice, a new MARC bibliographic record) is needed. This is really a question of whether the change is so significant that a new work or expression has come into existence, or whether it is so minor that the new part is just considered part of the original work. For this reason RDA 1.6, which deals with the question of description of manifestations, is closely related to RDA 6.1.3, changes affecting the identification of the work, discussed in chapter 7.

1.6.1. MULTIPART MONOGRAPHS. In the case of multipart monographs only two types of changes warrant a new description:

1. A change in mode of issuance. This means the multipart monograph changes to a serial or an integrating resource.
2. A change in media type. Media types are listed in RDA 3.2. If a multipart monograph begins as one type of media and somewhere along the way changes to another (e.g., its first parts are issued as paper-based books [unmediated media type] and at a certain point parts begin instead to be issued on CD-ROM computer discs [computer media type]), a new description should be made for the changed parts.

Other types of changes to multipart monographs do not require a new description. The description (including the title, statement of responsibility, and publisher elements) is based on the first or earliest part. Changes are described elsewhere in the record if considered important for identification or access.

Note that a change in the title of a multipart monograph does not trigger the creation of a new description. Instead, the new title is simply recorded in the original description as a later title proper (see RDA 2.3.2.12.1). Similarly, a change in the creator does not trigger a new description. Rather, the creator of a later part or parts is simply linked to the original description as an additional creator. In the current environment this is done by giving the new creator an added access point in a 7XX field of the bibliographic record (see RDA 18.4.2.1).

Volume 1 of K. S. B. Keats-Rohan's *Domesday People* was published in 1999. When volume 2 was issued in 2002, the title changed to *Domesday Descendants*. This title change does not require a new bibliographic description. The new title is recorded instead as a later title proper (see figure 2.7).

Figure 2.7. Change in Title of a Multipart Monograph

020	‡a 085115722X (volume 1 : acid-free paper)
020	‡a 0851156633 (volume 2 : acid-free paper)
100 1	‡a Keats-Rohan, K. S. B., ‡d 1957- ‡e author.
245 10	‡a Domesday people : ‡b a prosopography of persons occurring in English documents, 1066-1166 / ‡c compiled by K.S.B. Keats-Rohan.
246 1	‡i Volume 2 has title proper: ‡a Domesday descendants

264 1 ‡a Woodbridge, Suffolk : ‡b The Boydell Press, ‡c 1999-2002.

300   ‡a 2 volumes : ‡b map ; ‡c 25 cm.

336   ‡a text ‡2 rdacontent

336   ‡a cartographic image ‡2 rdacontent

337   ‡a unmediated ‡2 rdamedia

338   ‡a volume ‡2 rdacarrier

504   ‡a Includes bibliographical references and indexes.

505 0 ‡a I. Domesday book -- II. Pipe rolls to Cartae Baronum.

Title page of Volume I

DOMESDAY PEOPLE
A Prosopography of Persons Occurring
in English Documents 1066-1166
I. Domesday Book

compiled by
K.S.B. Keats-Rohan

THE BOYDELL PRESS

Title page of Volume II

DOMESDAY DESCENDANTS
A Prosopography of Persons Occurring
in English Documents 1066-1166
II. Pipe Rolls to *Cartae Baronum*

K.S.B. Keats-Rohan

THE BOYDELL PRESS

The multipart monograph titled *Piano technic* will be discussed in chapter 7 of this *Handbook* in the context of the identification of the work (see chapter 7 at RDA 6.1.3.1, with figure 7.7). This resource was published over a period of six years and the original creator died before the work was completed. The final three volumes were written by a different person. This, however, does not trigger a new bibliographic description. Information about the new author is simply added to the description in a note and he is linked to the description using an added access point (see figure 2.8).

1.6.2. SERIALS. A number of circumstances warrant a new description for serials. The first two, change in mode of issuance and change in media type, are the same as for multipart monographs. Serials, however, have three other conditions under which

Figure 2.8. Change in Responsibility for a Multipart Monograph

100 1	‡a McArtor, Marion Emmett, ‡d 1915-1956, ‡e composer.
245 10	‡a Piano technic / ‡c studies by Marion McArtor ; selected and correlated by Frances Clark ; edited by Louise Goss.
264 1	‡a Evanston, Illinois : ‡b Summy-Birchard Publishing Company, ‡c [1954-1960]
264 4	‡c ©1954-©1960
300	‡a 6 volumes ; ‡c 28 cm.
336	‡a notated music ‡2 rdacontent
336	‡a text ‡2 rdacontent
337	‡a unmediated ‡2 rdamedia
338	‡a volume ‡2 rdacarrier
490 0	‡a Frances Clark library for piano students
500	‡a "David Kraehenbuehl ... was commissioned to write the music for Books 4, 5 and 6 of the Piano Technic series."--Preface to Book 4.
546	‡b Staff notation.
700 1	‡a Kraehenbuehl, David, ‡d 1925-1997, ‡e composer.

Title page of Book 1

Piano Technic
Book 1
Frances Clark Library for Piano Students
Studies by Marion McArtor
Selected and correlated by Frances Clark
Edited by Louise Goss
Summy-Birchard Publishing Company · Evanston, Illinois
©1954 by Summy-Birchard Publishing Company

Title page of Book 4

Piano Technic
Book 4
Frances Clark Library for Piano Students
Music by David Kraehenbuehl
Planned and correlated by Frances Clark
Edited by Louise Goss
Summy-Birchard Publishing Company · Evanston, Illinois
©1960 by Summy-Birchard Publishing Company

a new description will be required: major change in the title proper of the serial, change in responsibility for the serial, and change in edition statement. Major change in title proper or change in responsibility are considered great enough changes to the original work that a new work has been created (see RDA 6.1.3.2). Change in edition statement is a change that indicates the creation of a new expression. In any of these cases a new bibliographical description will be needed.

1.6.2.2. CHANGE IN MEDIA TYPE OF A SERIAL. A change in media type requires a new description. The most common such change is a change from a printed version of a serial to an online version. The *Bryn Mawr Classical Review* is an example (see figure 2.9).

Figure 2.9a. Change in Media Type (Serial)

022 0	‡a 1055-7660
245 00	‡a Bryn Mawr classical review.
264 1	‡a Bryn Mawr, PA : ‡b Thomas Library, Bryn Mawr College, ‡c [1990-1998].
300	‡a 9 volumes ; ‡c 22 cm
310	‡a At least 8 times a year, ‡b June 1997-1998
321	‡a Six no. a year, ‡b 1990-May 1997
336	‡a text ‡2 rdacontent
337	‡a unmediated ‡2 rdamedia
338	‡a volume ‡2 rdacarrier
362 1	‡a Began with volume 1, number 1 (November 1990); ceased with volume 9, number 8 (December 1998)
530	‡a Issued also and continued in an online format.
588	‡a Description based on: Volume 1, number 1 (November 1990); title from cover.
588	‡a Latest issue consulted: Volume 9, number 8 (December 1998).
710 2	‡a Thomas Library (Bryn Mawr College)
776 08	‡i Online version: ‡t Bryn Mawr classical review ‡x 1063-2948

Figure 2.9b. Change in Media Type (Serial)

022 0	‡a 1063-2948
130 0	‡a Bryn Mawr classical review (Online)
245 10	‡a Bryn Mawr classical review.
246 1	‡i Listserv name: ‡a BMCR-L
246 1	‡i Also known as: ‡a BMCR
264 1	‡a Bryn Mawr, PA : ‡b Thomas Library, Bryn Mawr College
300	‡a 1 online resource
310	‡a Irregular
336	‡a text ‡2 rdacontent
337	‡a computer ‡2 rdamedia
338	‡a online resource ‡2 rdacarrier
347	‡a text file ‡b HTML ‡2 rda

```
362 1    ‡a Began with reviews for 1990.

530      ‡a Issued also in a print format.

500      ‡a Available via Internet, electronic mail, RSS feed, and Twitter. For email, RSS feed,
         and Twitter subscription go to: http://bmcr.brynmawr.edu/subscribe.html.

515      ‡a Individual articles are numbered 94.1.1-98.06.30, 1998.07.01-

588      ‡a Description based on: volume 1 (1990); title from title screen (viewed on April 16,
         2012).

588      ‡a Latest issue consulted: "2012.04.27"

710 2    ‡a Bryn Mawr College.

776 08   ‡i Print version: ‡t Bryn Mawr classical review ‡x 1055-7660

856 40   ‡u http://bibpurl.oclc.org/web/3018 ‡u http://ccat.sas.upenn.edu/bmcr
```

1.6.2.3. MAJOR CHANGE IN THE TITLE PROPER OF A SERIAL. A major change in the title proper of a serial is considered enough to create a new work, and therefore a new description is required. RDA 2.3.2.13.1 defines what is meant by a major change:

i) The addition, deletion, change, or reordering of any of the first five words (the first six words if the title begins with an article) unless the change belongs to one or more of the categories listed under minor changes (see RDA 2.3.2.13.2).

ii) The addition, deletion, or change of any word after the first five words (the first six words if the title begins with an article) that changes the meaning of the title or indicates a different subject matter.

iii) A change of name for a corporate body included anywhere in the title if the changed name is for a different corporate body.

The British Flute Society sponsored a journal called *Pan* for many years. In the preliminary matter of volume 29, no. 1, the editor announced that the Society had been thinking about renaming the journal and had decided to call it *Flute,* although the name *Pan* would continue to be used for a few issues in conjunction with the new name. This is a major change in title, and so a new record is required (see figure 2.10).

Figure 2.10a. Change in Title (Serial)

```
022 0    ‡a 1360-1563

130 0    ‡a Pan (British Flute Society)

245 10   ‡a Pan.

246 1    ‡l Masthead title: ‡a Journal of the British Flute Society

264   1  ‡a [Rochester, Kent] : ‡b British Flute Society

300      ‡a 28 volumes : ‡b color illustrations ; ‡c 22 cm

310      ‡a Quarterly
```

336	‡a text ‡2 rdacontent
337	‡a unmediated ‡2 rdamedia
338	‡a volume ‡2 rdacarrier
362 1	‡a Began with v. 1, no. 1 (April 1983); ceased with vol. 28, no. 3 (September 2009).
500	‡a "The journal of the British Flute Society"--Masthead.
588	‡a Description based on surrogate of: Volume 18, no. 3 (September 1999); title from cover.
588	‡a Latest issue consulted: Volume 28, no. 3 (September 2009).
710 2	‡a British Flute Society, ‡e sponsoring body.
785 00	‡a Flute (British Flute Society) ‡x 2045-4074

Figure 2.10b. Change in Title (Serial)

022 0	‡a 2045-4074
130 0	‡a Flute (British Flute Society)
245 10	‡a Flute.
264 1	‡a [England] : ‡b British Flute Society
300	‡a volumes : ‡b color illustrations ; ‡c 25 cm
310	‡a Quarterly
336	‡a text ‡2 rdacontent
337	‡a unmediated ‡2 rdamedia
338	‡a volume ‡2 rdacarrier
362 1	‡a Began with volume 29, number 1 (March 2010)
588	‡a Description based on: volume 29, number 1 (March 2010); title from title page.
588	‡a Latest issue consulted: volume 29, no. 1 (March 2010)
710 2	‡a British Flute Society, ‡e issuing body.
780 00	‡t Pan (British Flute Society) ‡x 1360-1563

1.6.2.4. CHANGE IN RESPONSIBILITY FOR A SERIAL. This guideline is a little trickier than the guideline about serial title changes (RDA 1.6.2.3). The cataloger is instructed to create a new description if "there is a change in responsibility that requires a change in the identification of the serial as a work," referring to RDA 6.1.3.2. What sorts of changes in responsibility require a change in the identification of the work? To answer this we need to consider how authorized access points for works are created.

As discussed in chapter 7 of this *Handbook*, in RDA the authorized access point for a work is created either by combining the authorized access point for the person, family, or corporate body responsible for the work (i.e., the creator of the work) with the preferred title of the work; or by giving the preferred title alone (see RDA 6.27

and accompanying discussion in chapter 7 of this *Handbook*). This applies to serials as well as any other kind of work.

RDA 19.2 describes the circumstances under which persons, families, or corporate bodies can become creators of works. In the case of persons and families, the scope under which they can be the creator of a serial is quite limited (see RDA 19.2.1.1.3). A person or family may be considered the creator if they are "responsible for the serial as a whole, not an individual issue or a few issues." Corporate bodies may be considered creators of serials (and other works) if they are responsible for issuing a work that falls in to one of the categories listed under RDA 19.2.1.1.1. Briefly, these are:

a. works of an administrative nature dealing with any of the following aspects of the body itself:
    i) its internal policies, procedures, finances, or operations,
    ii) its officers, staff, or membership, or
    iii) its resources
b. works that record the collective thought of the body
c. works that record hearings conducted by corporate bodies
d. works that report the collective activity of a conference, an expedition, or an event
e. certain works that result from the collective activity of a performing group
f. certain cartographic works
g. certain legal works
h. named individual works of art by two or more artists acting as a corporate body

If a person, family, or corporate body is the creator of a serial under RDA 19.2, then the authorized access point for the serial is created by combining the authorized access point for the creator with the preferred title of the serial (see chapter 7 of this *Handbook*). A common example of this is an annual report, which is a work of an administrative nature dealing with the operations of a corporate body. The authorized access point for the Annual report of the Agricultural Experiment Station, Michigan State University is formed:

Michigan State University. ‡b Agricultural Experiment Station. ‡t Annual report of the Agricultural Experiment Station, Michigan State University

The title was shortened to "Annual report" in 1989. Under RDA 2.3.2.13.2iii, the deletion of the name of a corporate body is considered a minor change, and so a new record was not required and the authorized access point does not change, even though the new title is much shorter than the old one. The new title is simply noted in the description (see the 246 field in figure 2.11a).

Figure 2.11a. Change in Responsibility (Serial)

022	‡a 0361-5715
110 2	‡a Michigan State University. ‡b Agricultural Experiment Station.
210 0	‡a Annu. rep. Agric. Exp. St. Mich. State Univ.
222 0	‡a Annual report of the Agricultural Experiment Station, Michigan State University
245 10	‡a ... annual report of the Agricultural Experiment Station, Michigan State University.
246 1	‡i Issues for 1989-2010 have title: ‡a Annual report
264 1	‡a East Lansing, Michigan : ‡b Agricultural Experiment Station
300	‡a volumes : ‡b illustrations ; ‡c 28 cm.
310	‡a Annual
336	‡a text ‡2 rdacontent
337	‡a unmediated ‡2 rdamedia
338	‡a volume ‡2 rdacarrier
362 0	‡a -2010.
490 1	‡a SR
588	‡a Description based on: 1984; title from cover.
588	‡a Latest issue consulted: 2010.
785 00	‡a Michigan State University. AgBioResearch. ‡t Annual report
830 0	‡a Special report (Michigan State University. Agricultural Experiment Station)

Figure 2.11b. Change in Responsibility (Serial)

110 2	‡a Michigan State University. ‡b AgBioResearch.
245 10	‡a .. annual report.
246 3	‡a AgBioResearch annual report
246 3	‡a MSU AgBioResearch annual report
246 3	‡a Michigan State University AgBioResearch annual report
264 1	‡a East Lansing, Michigan : ‡b AgBioResearch, Michigan State University, ‡c 2011-
300	‡a volumes : ‡b color illustrations ; ‡c 28 cm.
310	‡a Annual
336	‡a text ‡2 rdacontent
337	‡a unmediated ‡2 rdamedia
338	‡a volume ‡2 rdacarrier
362 1	‡a Began in 2011.
490 1	‡a SR
588	‡a Description based on: 2011; title from cover.
588	‡a Latest issue consulted: 2011.

780 00 ‡a Michigan State University. Agricultural Experiment Station. ‡t Annual report of the Agricultural Experiment Station, Michigan State University ‡x 0361-5715

830 0 ‡a SR (Michigan State University. AgBioResearch)

Front Cover

Michigan State University
AgBioResearch
2011 Annual Report

Back cover

Michigan State University
SR-131/January 2012

When a corporate body changes its name, in cataloging theory the corporate body with the previous name ceases to exist and a new corporate body, with a new name, is born. A corporate body name change is an example of a change in responsibility for a serial. The Agricultural Experiment Station changed its name to AgBioResearch in 2011. Responsibility for the annual report has changed, which is a change that "requires a change in the identification of the serial as a work" even though the title ("Annual report") did not change (RDA 1.6.2.4). The authorized access point for the "new" serial is:

Michigan State University. ‡b AgBioResearch. ‡t Annual report

This is the form that might be found in an authority record for the work, if an authority record existed. In terms of the corresponding bibliographic record, the creator is recorded in the 110 field and the preferred title in 240 or 245. The description of the original serial will contain "Michigan State University. ‡b Agricultural Experiment Station" in the 110 field. When the responsible corporate body changed, a new description was required, with "Michigan State University. ‡b AgBioResearch" recorded in the 110 field (see figure 2.11b).

RDA 1.6.2.4 also applies to cases where a change in responsibility affects the entity used as an addition to an authorized access point for a serial work. The United Nations Special Unit on Palestinian Rights published a journal called *Bulletin*. This work does not fall into any of the categories RDA 19.2.1.1.1, so the Special Unit is not considered the creator of the work, and the authorized access point would be based on the preferred title alone, "Bulletin." However, because more than one journal titled *Bulletin* exists, following RDA 6.27.1.9 something needs to be added as a qualifier to the preferred title. In this case the most logical qualifier to add is the name of the issuing body. The authorized access point for this journal is:

Bulletin (United Nations. Special Unit on Palestinian Rights)

In 1982 the Special Unit on Palestinian Rights changed its name to Division for Palestinian Rights. *Bulletin* continued to be published with no change in title. However, because this change affects the name of the entity chosen to qualify the title in the authorized access point for the work, a new description (and authorized access point) is required (see figure 2.12).

Figure 2.12a. Change in Responsibility (Serial)

130 0	‡a Bulletin (United Nations. Special Unit on Palestinian Rights)
245 10	‡a Bulletin / ‡c United Nations, Special Unit on Palestinian Rights.
264 1	‡a [New York] : ‡b Special Unit on Palestinian Rights, ‡c 1978-1982.
300	‡a 5 volumes : ‡b illustrations ; ‡c 28 cm
310	‡a Twelve numbers a year, ‡b 1979-1982
321	‡a Quarterly, ‡b 1978
336	‡a text ‡2 rdacontent
336	‡a still image ‡2 rdacontent
337	‡a unmediated ‡2 rdamedia
338	‡a volume ‡2 rdacarrier
362 0	‡a No. 1 (June 1978)-volume V, no. 5/6 (May/June 1982).
515	‡a Issues for June 1978-September/October 1979 lack volume numbering but constitute volume 1, no. 1-volume 2, no. 9/10.
515	‡a Some numbers issued combined; none published November-December 1979.
588	‡a Description based on: No. 1 (June 1978); title from caption.
588	‡a Latest issue consulted: Volume V, no. 5/6 (May/June 1982)
710 2	‡a United Nations. ‡b Special Unit on Palestinian Rights, ‡e issuing body.
785 00	‡t Bulletin (United Nations. Division for Palestinian Rights)

Figure 2.12b. Change in Responsibility (Serial)

130 0	‡a Bulletin (United Nations. Division for Palestinian Rights)
245 00	‡a Bulletin / ‡c United Nations, Division for Palestinian Rights.
264 1	‡a [New York] : ‡b Division for Palestinian Rights, ‡c 1982-
300	‡a volumes : ‡b illustrations ; ‡c 28 cm
336	‡a text ‡2 rdacontent
336	‡a still image ‡2 rdacontent
337	‡a unmediated ‡2 rdamedia
338	‡a volume ‡2 rdacarrier
310	‡a Twelve numbers a year
362 0	‡a Volume V, no. 7 (July 1982)-

515	‡a Issue for Jan. 1985 called volume VII, no. 1 but constitutes volume VIII, no. 1.
588	‡a Description based on: Volume V, no. 7 (July 1982); title from cover.
588	‡a Latest issue consulted: Volume XXXV, no. 1 (January 2012)
710 2	‡a United Nations. ‡b Division for Palestinian Rights, ‡e issuing body.
780 00	‡t Bulletin (United Nations. Special Unit on Palestinian Rights)

1.6.2.5. CHANGE IN EDITION STATEMENT (OF A SERIAL). A new description is required if a changed (or different) edition statement appears "indicating a significant change to the scope or coverage of a serial."

The cataloger must exercise caution when faced with wording on a serial publication that appears to be an edition statement. RDA 2.5.2.1 states that the presence of a word such as "edition" or "issue" is evidence that such a statement is a designation of edition, but this may not be the case with a serial. Such words are often simply indicative of numbering of the parts of the serial, and are recorded as such following RDA 2.6 (see also RDA 2.5.2.5). For example, the individual volumes in *Who's Who of American Women* refer to themselves as "First edition," "Second edition," etc. This is simply numbering (see figure 2.13).

On the other hand, if the statement indicates "a significant change to the scope or coverage of a serial," it is probably a true edition statement and should be recorded; it also triggers a new description. The new serial is either a completely different work or

Figure 2.13. "Edition" = Numbering

022	‡a 0270-2940 ‡y 0083-9841
210 0	‡a Who's who Am. women ‡b (1959)
222 0	‡a Who's who of American women ‡b (1959)
245 00	‡a Who's who of American women.
264 1	‡a Chicago, Illinois : ‡b Marquis-Who's Who, ‡c 1958-1964.
300	‡a 3 volumes ; ‡c 28 cm
310	‡a Biennial
336	‡a text ‡2 rdacontent
337	‡a unmediated ‡2 rdamedia
338	‡a volume ‡2 rdacarrier
362 0	‡a 1st edition (1958-1959)-3rd edition (1964-1965).
500	‡a First and second editions also called volume 1-2.
588	‡a Description based on: First edition (1958-1959); title from title page.
588	‡a Latest issue consulted: Third edition (1964-1965)
785 00	‡t Who's who of American women and women of Canada ‡x 0270-2800

Title page

Who's Who of American Women
A Biographical Dictionary of Notable
Living American Women
Volume 1 (1958-1959)
First Edition
Marquis—Who's Who
Chicago 11, Illinois

---

a new expression. An example is the Polish edition of the popular magazine *Fantasy & Science Fiction*. This edition is not a translation of the American edition, although it does contain translations of some matter that appeared in the American edition. Its contents are, however, quite different from its American cousin (see figure 2.14).

Figure 2.14. Edition Statement Triggers New Description

022	‡a 1897-4325
130 0	‡a Fantasy & science fiction (Edycja Polska)
245 10	‡a Fantasy & science fiction.
246 3	‡a Fantasy and science fiction
250	‡a Edycja Polska.
264 1	‡a Warszawa : ‡b Powergraph Sp. z o.o., ‡c 2010-
300	‡a volumes : ‡b illustrations ; ‡c 21 cm
310	‡a Quarterly
336	‡a text ‡2 rdacontent
337	‡a unmediated ‡2 rdamedia
338	‡a volume ‡2 rdacarrier
362 1	‡a Began with: Nr 1 (zima 2010).
588	‡a Description based on: Nr 1 (zima 2010); title from cover.
588	‡a Latest issue consulted: surrogate of Nr 4 (jesień 2010).
775 0	‡t Fantasy & science fiction ‡x 1095-8258

Cover of Nr 1

Fantasy & Science Fiction
EDYCJA POLSKA   ZIMA

1.6.3. INTEGRATING RESOURCES. Unlike multipart monographs and serials, integrating resources are described based on the *latest* iteration. Therefore, generally speaking, rather than make a new description when an integrating resource changes we simply update the existing description. However, there are four circumstances where a new description will be made. The first two, change in mode of issuance and change in media type, are the same as with multipart monographs or serials: if an integrating resource changes to a multipart monograph or a serial, create a new description for the new resource; if an integrating resource changes media type (e.g., changes from a printed paper resource to an online resource), create a new description. There are two other circumstances: the re-basing of the resource, and a change in edition statement.

1.6.3.3. RE-BASING OF AN INTEGRATING RESOURCE. Integrating resources are so named because changes occur through updates that are not discrete, but are integrated into the whole. Examples include loose-leaf publications for which the publisher may send out updated replacement pages from time to time. Sometimes, however, the publisher reissues the entire resource at once, incorporating all the changes that have been made since the previous resource was first issued. This is called "re-basing." If this happens, rather than updating the description of the existing integrating resource, the cataloger instead creates a new description for the re-based integrating resource (see figure 2.15). This can get quite complex. For detailed advice on how to handle re-based integrating resources, see LC-PCC PS 1.6.3.3 (February 2010).

Figure 2.15. Re-based Integrating Resource

245 00	‡a Business and commercial litigation, 2007 / ‡c Kenneth A. Kroot, Joseph L. Kish, general editors ; chapter authors, Michael T. Beirne [and twenty-four others].	
264 31	‡a Springfield, IL : ‡b Illinois Institute for Continuing Legal Education, ‡c 2007-	
300	‡a volumes (loose-leaf) : ‡b illustrations, forms ; ‡c 30 cm + ‡e 1 CD-ROM (4 3/4 in.)	
336	‡a text ‡2 rdacontent	
337	‡a unmediated ‡2 rdamedia	
338	‡a volume ‡2 rdacarrier	
500	‡a Includes index.	
500	‡a "This handbook replaces all previous editions of Business and commercial litigation."	
588	‡a Description based on: 2007; title from title page.	
700 1	‡a Kroot, Kenneth A., ‡e editor of compilation.	
700 1	‡a Kish, Joseph L., ‡e editor of compilation.	
700 1	‡a Beirne, Michael T., ‡e author.	
710 2	‡a Illinois Institute for Continuing Legal Education, ‡e publisher.	

Title page

BUSINESS AND
COMMERCIAL LITIGATION
Kenneth A. Kroot
Joseph L. Kish
General Editors
2007
Chapter authors:

Michael T. Beirne	Joseph L. Kish
Joseph G. Bisceglia	Kenneth A. Kroot
J. Blazejowski	Jeffrey J. Mayer
Richard C. Bollow	Michael S. Mayer
Robert L. Byman	Jeanah Park
Gia F. Colunga	Brian A. Rosenblatt
J. Timothy Eaton	William J. Ryan
Daniel T. Graham	Gregory J. Scandaglia
H. Roderic Heard	Sara Stertz
William N. Howard	Daniel J. Voelker
James H. Kallianis, Jr.	Charlotte L. Wager
Brent E. Kidwell	Susan L. Walker

Michelle L. Wolf-Boze
IICLE
This handbook replaces all previous editions of BUSINESS AND COMMERCIAL LITIGATION.
ILLINOIS INSTITUTE FOR CONTINUING LEGAL EDUCATION
2395 West Jefferson
Springfield, IL 62702

1.6.3.4. CHANGE IN EDITION STATEMENT (OF AN INTEGRATING RESOURCE). If an edition statement appears that indicates a significant change in the scope or coverage of an integrating resource, create a new description instead of updating the existing description. In the case of figure 2.16, *Trial Objections* was completely rewritten by a new author, as indicated by the edition statement "Third edition."

Figure 2.16. Changed Edition Statement in Integrating Resource

---

020   ‡a 1580120180

100 1   ‡a Dunn, R. Rogge, ‡e author.

245 10   ‡a Trial objections / ‡c Rogge Dunn ; production editor, Ben Ritter.

250   ‡a Third edition.

264 31   ‡a Costa Mesa, CA : ‡b James Publishing, ‡c [2001]-

300	‡a 1 volume (loose-leaf) ; ‡c 23 cm + ‡e CD-ROM (4 3/4 in.)
310	‡a Updated annually
336	‡a text ‡2 rdacontent
337	‡a unmediated ‡2 rdamedia
338	‡a volume ‡2 rdacarrier
500	‡a Revised edition of: Trial objections / by Mark A. Dumbroff. Second edition, 1995.
588	‡a Description based on: Third edition through revision 14 (9/09); title from title page.

1.7. TRANSCRIPTION. It is important to pay attention to terms used in RDA; one of the more important distinctions is that between an instruction to transcribe and an instruction to record. When RDA tells us to "transcribe" something, it means copy exactly what you see, with certain exceptions as listed in RDA 1.7. When RDA tells us to "record" an element, it means to record the information following whatever instructions are given, but this does not necessarily result in an exact reproduction of the information as it appears in the source. Thus, for example, we are instructed to "transcribe" a title as it appears (RDA 2.3.1.4) but to "record" numerals elsewhere in the form preferred by the agency (RDA 1.8.2).

Information recorded in elements in RDA 2.4 that specify transcribing should be reproduced exactly as to wording and spelling, but not necessarily as to capitalization and punctuation. Unless permitted by a particular guideline, do not omit words. Do not abbreviate or correct the spelling of any words.

1.7.2. CAPITALIZATION. When a designer lays out a title page or other published source he or she makes decisions about capitalization of words (including internal capitalization) based on design considerations rather than considerations of bibliographic usage or style. See, for example, the title pages reproduced with figures 2.6, 2.7, and 2.15. Traditional cataloging and bibliographic practice is not to reproduce this capitalization. RDA 1.7.2 instructs us to apply the instructions in RDA appendix A when transcribing information. These reflect traditional cataloging practice and so will be familiar to catalogers used to AACR2. Generally, capitalize the first word of a title proper, alternative title, parallel title, or quoted title (a title embedded within other text); other words in English language titles are given in lower case. Proper names are capitalized according to normal English practice (see RDA A.2). Guidelines for other elements are also given in RDA appendix A, as well as guidelines for capitalization in other languages such as German, which differ from the English guidelines. For an example of conversion of uppercase letters to lowercase in a transcription of both a title and publication statement, see figure 2.6 (in the discussion above at RDA 1.4).

RDA, however, gives two alternatives to this traditional practice (see 1.7.1 alternatives). If the cataloging agency has in-house guidelines for capitalization, etc., these may be followed instead of appendix A. An example of an in-house guideline might be to follow *The Chicago Manual of Style*. The *Chicago Manual*'s somewhat complex guidelines call for capitalization of the first and last words in titles, and all other "major words," that is, nouns, pronouns, verbs, adverbs, and some conjunctions.[4] If following the *Chicago Manual* as an in-house guideline, the cataloger would have transcribed the title of figure 2.6 as follows:

245 10 ‡a The Roman Forum : ‡b Its History and Its Monuments

The Library of Congress and the Program for Cooperative Cataloging in-house guideline for capitalization encourages catalogers to follow RDA appendix A, but permits a "take what you see" approach, at the discretion of the cataloger (LC-PCC PS 1.7.1, first alternative, September 2012). A cataloger following the "take what you see" approach might instead have transcribed the title and statement of responsibility of figure 2.6 as follows:

245 10 ‡a The ROMAN FORVM : ‡b ITS HISTORY AND ITS MONUMENTS / ‡c TRANSLATED FROM THE 2ND GERMAN EDITION BY JESSE BENEDICT CARTER.

RDA's second alternative is to take without modification data created by another agency or data derived from a digital source of information using scanning, copying, or downloading. If such a source had been available for the information recorded in figure 2.6, application of this second alternative might have produced a result similar to the "take what you see" version shown immediately above. The LC and PCC policy for this second alternative is generally to accept data derived from digital sources (such as ONIX publisher data), but make any adjustments to the data (e.g., supplying punctuation) judged appropriate (LC-PCC PS 1.7.1, second alternative, July 2012).

This *Handbook* follows the capitalization guidelines of RDA appendix A throughout, but the two alternative practices are perfectly legitimate in RDA and catalogers will encounter descriptions following all three practices.

1.7.3. PUNCTUATION. Punctuation that appears on the source should generally be transcribed, but punctuation missing from the source may be added for clarity. Some clarifying punctuation has been added to the transcription of the other title information (field 245 subfield ‡b) of figure 2.7. In previous cataloging practice certain substitutions were made: ellipses (. . .) were replaced with a dash (--) and square brackets were replaced with parentheses (see AACR2 1.1B1). These are transcribed exactly as found in RDA (see figure 2.17). The title proper in this figure would have been transcribed as follows in previous cataloging practice:

245 14 ‡a Ein Spatz in der Hand--

Figure 2.17. Transcription of Punctuation

100 1	‡a Lander, Jeannette, ‡d 1931- ‡e author.
245 14	‡a Ein Spatz in der Hand ... : ‡b Sachgeschichten / ‡c Jeannette Lander.
250	‡a Erste Auflage.
264 1	‡a Frankfurt am Main : ‡b Insel, ‡c 1973.
300	‡a 107 pages ; ‡c 20 cm
336	‡a text ‡2 rdacontent
337	‡a unmediated ‡2 rdamedia
338	‡a volume ‡2 rdacarrier

Title page

Jeannette Lander
Ein Spatz in der Hand . . .
Sachgeschichten

Insel

Colophon

Insel Verlag Frankfurt am Main
Erste Auflage 1973
Druck: Kösel, Kempten
Printed in Germany

Under AACR2 practice for serial title transcription, if a date, name, number, etc., appeared in the title and it varied from issue to issue it was omitted and replaced by the mark of omission (ellipsis) except if it appeared at the beginning of the title, in which case the mark of omission was left out (see AACR2 12.1B7). The practice is the same in RDA, except the mark of omission is given even at the beginning of the title (see RDA 2.3.1.4, Date, name, number, etc., that varies from issue to issue). See figure 2.11b for an example. In previous cataloging practice this title proper would have been recorded:

245 10 ‡a Annual report.

RDA does not require the use of ISBD punctuation (e.g., space-colon-space between title proper and other title information, space-slash-space before the first statement of responsibility, etc.). However, recognizing that most catalogers will continue to incorporate ISBD punctuation conventions into bibliographic data, RDA gives a summary of ISBD presentation in appendix D.1. This *Handbook* follows ISBD punctuation conventions.

1.7.8. ABBREVIATIONS. In elements where RDA instructs the cataloger to transcribe, do not abbreviate any words. For instance, in a change from previous cataloging practice, RDA 2.8.1.4 instructs us to transcribe places of publication and publishers' names in the form in which they appear on the source. Figure 2.8 is an example of this. In previous cataloging practice, the publication area would have been recorded:

> 260   ‡a Evanston, Ill. : ‡b Summy-Birchard Pub. Co., ‡c c1954-c1960.

On the other hand, *do* reproduce abbreviations that appear in sources that are to be recorded in transcribed elements. In figure 2.15, the abbreviation "IL" appears on the source, and so it is so transcribed in the Place of Publication element (MARC field 264, subfield ‡a).

1.7.9. INACCURACIES. In a departure from previous cataloging practice, formulations such as "[sic]" or "[i.e. . . .]" will *not* be interpolated into a transcription to signal or correct a misspelling (see figure 2.18). The title proper of this manifestation would have been recorded as follows in AACR2:

> 245 10 ‡a Habeus [sic] corpus and detentions at Guantanamo Bay

Figure 2.18. Transcription of Inaccuracies

110 1	‡a United States. ‡b Congress. ‡b House. ‡b Committee on the Judiciary. ‡b Subcommittee on the Constitution, Civil Rights, and Civil Liberties.
245 10	‡a Habeus corpus and detentions at Guantanamo Bay : ‡b hearing before the Subcommittee on the Constitution, Civil Rights, and Civil Liberties of the Committee on the Judiciary, House of Representatives, One Hundred Tenth Congress, first session, June 26, 2007.
246 3	‡a Habeas corpus and detentions at Guantanamo Bay
264 1	‡a Washington : ‡b U.S. Government Printing Office, ‡c 2009.
264 2	‡a Washington, DC : ‡b For sale by the Superintendent of Documents, U.S. Government Printing Office
300	‡a iii, 129 pages ; ‡c 24 cm
336	‡a text ‡2 rdacontent

337	‡a unmediated ‡2 rdamedia
338	‡a volume ‡2 rdacarrier
504	‡a Includes bibliographical references.
500	‡a "Serial no. 110-152."

Title page

HABEUS CORPUS AND DETENTIONS
AT GUANTANAMO BAY

―――

HEARING
BEFORE THE
SUBCOMMITTEE ON THE CONSTITUTION,
CIVIL RIGHTS, AND CIVIL LIBERTIES
OF THE
COMMITTEE ON THE JUDICIARY
HOUSE OF REPRESENTATIVES
ONE HUNDRED TENTH CONGRESS
FIRST SESSION
June 26, 2007
Serial no. 110-152
Printed for the use of the Committee on the Judiciary
U.S. GOVERNMENT PRINTING OFFICE
WASHINGTON : 2009
For sale by the Superintendent of Documents, U.S. Government Printing Office
Mail: Stop IDCC, Washington, DC

1.8. NUMBERS EXPRESSED AS NUMERALS OR AS WORDS. In contrast to RDA 1.7, which consists of instructions for *transcribing* information, RDA 1.8 is about *recording* information in elements that are not transcribed elements. The guidelines apply *only* to the elements listed in RDA 1.8.1, none of which are transcribed elements. Guidelines under RDA 1.8, which in some cases result in recording a different form of the number from that found in the source, do *not* apply to transcribed elements such as the title proper. If a number expressed as a word, a roman numeral, or an arabic numeral is found in a title proper, it should be transcribed exactly as it is found.

1.8.2. FORM OF NUMERALS. When recording numerals in elements listed in RDA 1.8.1, they are to be recorded in the form preferred by the agency creating the data. An agency might have, for instance, a policy that roman numerals are always to be recorded as arabic numerals. This was generally the rule in AACR2 (see AACR2 C2B). Or the policy of the agency might be to apply the alternative guideline in RDA 1.8.2 and record numerals in the form in which they appear. This is the Library of Congress's policy (LC-PCC PS 1.8.2, February 2010).

To illustrate, the date of publication is one of the elements listed under RDA 1.8.1. Under AACR2 practice, a roman numeral would have been converted to an arabic numeral before recording it as the date of publication. Under RDA the treatment of the numeral depends on the policy of the cataloging agency. The title page of the book cataloged in figure 2.19 gives its date of publication as a roman numeral. When following the Library of Congress's policy this numeral is recorded as found. An agency that prefers to convert roman numerals to arabic in these elements would have recorded the publication elements as follows:

264   1 ‡a Mount Vernon, New York : ‡b The Press of A. Colish, ‡c 1977.

Both are correct under RDA practice.

Figure 2.19. Form of Numerals

100 1	‡a Stillwell, Margaret Bingham, ‡d 1887-1984, ‡e author.
245 10	‡a Rhythm and rhymes : ‡b the songs of a bookworm / ‡c by Margaret B. Stillwell.
250	‡a Keepsake edition.
264 1	‡a Mount Vernon, New York : ‡b The Press of A. Colish, ‡c MDCCCCLXXVII [1977]
264 4	‡c ©1977
300	‡a xii, 97 pages : ‡b illustrations ; ‡c 24 cm
336	‡a text ‡2 rdacontent
337	‡a unmediated ‡2 rdamedia
338	‡a volume ‡2 rdacarrier
500	‡a Limited edition of 500 copies.
590	‡a L. Tom Perry Special Collections copy signed by the author.

Title page

Rhythm and Rhymes
The Songs of a Bookworm
By Margaret B. Stillwell
Mount Vernon, New York
MDCCCCLXXVII

Verso of title page
Copyright © 1977, Margaret B. Stillwell
From The Press of A. Colish,
Mount Vernon, New York

1.9. DATES. Because dates are usually given as numbers, when recorded in elements that do not call for transcription, dates follow the same guidelines as other numbers in RDA 1.8. RDA 1.9 gives guidelines for forms to use when supplying dates in certain elements (dates of production, publication, distribution, or manufacture), rather than recording information found on the resource. Two things should be noted. First, the fact that the date was supplied rather than found in the resource must be clearly indicated. There are a number of ways this could be done, but the most common practice is to enclose the supplied information in square brackets, as shown for supplied dates of publication in 264 fields in figures 2.1, 2.3, 2.5, 2.8, and 2.16. Second, abbreviations are not used, in contrast to AACR2 practice (see RDA examples under 1.9.2.5).

1.11. FACSIMILES AND REPRODUCTIONS. For treatment of facsimiles and reproductions, see the appendix at the end of this chapter.

IDENTIFYING MANIFESTATIONS AND ITEMS

RDA chapter 1 included guidelines (such as transcription) that applied to all elements in chapters 2 through 4. Chapter 2 gives specific guidelines for recording information about attributes of manifestations and items.

2.1. BASIS FOR IDENTIFICATION OF THE RESOURCE. RDA chapter 2 begins with two sections of guidelines for choosing sources of information to use in describing a resource. RDA is less prescriptive than previous cataloging codes on this issue, relying to some extent instead on the judgment of the cataloger.

RDA 2.1 has two sections, "Comprehensive Description" and "Analytical Description." The instructions are slightly different depending on which type of description is being made. A comprehensive description is a description of a resource as a whole (e.g., a book published in one volume, an encyclopedia published in twenty-five volumes, or a complete or ongoing run of a serial). An analytical description is a description of a part of a resource (e.g., a chapter in a book, an article in a serial publication, a single volume of a multivolume monograph). Because analytical description is much less commonly done than comprehensive description, this *Handbook* will not discuss it in depth (but see below in this chapter at 2.3.2.9 and this *Handbook's* appendix L), but the cataloger should be aware of the distinction here in the guidelines about choosing a source.

2.1.2.1. GENERAL GUIDELINES. The basic guideline is to choose a source of information identifying the resource as a whole. More detailed guidelines will be given in 2.2 on choosing a "preferred source of information," but this basic guideline should always be kept in mind in case of ambiguity as to which to choose when there are several available sources. Does one of the sources apply to the resource as a whole?

This is usually easy enough to determine if the resource was issued as a single unit, but what about a resource issued in more than one part, such as a multivolume encyclopedia, a serial, or a kit? RDA 2.1.2.3 tells us to choose one of the following "as appropriate":

a. If the parts of a resource issued as a set are unnumbered or numbering does not establish an order, choose a source identifying the resource as a whole, preferring a source with a collective title.
b. If the parts are sequentially numbered, choose the lowest numbered part available as the source.
c. If the parts are unnumbered or not sequentially numbered, choose the part issued first.
d. If there is no source of information identifying the resource as a whole but one has a title identifying the predominant content, use that source.
e. If none of these work, treat all the parts as a collective source of information.

Examples of "b," a resource with sequentially numbered parts, include a multivolume monograph (the first volume would be chosen as the basis for identification of the resource: see figures 2.7 and 2.8) or a serial publication (the first available issue would be chosen: see figures 2.9 through 2.14, paying special attention to 2.11a, in which the description was based on the 1984 issue, which was the first issue available to the cataloger but probably not the first issue of the serial publication). An example of "c" is an unnumbered series; the basis of identification of such a series would be the earliest publication in the series.

RDA instructs the cataloger to identify the part used as the basis of the description if it is not the first part. In North American serials practice the issue or part used is always identified, whether it is the first issue or part, or a later issue or part (see figures 2.9 through 2.14, first 588 field).

In contrast to a monograph or serial publication issued in more than one part, the basis of identification for an integrating resource, no matter how many parts it has, is the *current* iteration of the resource as a whole. The basis of the description should always be noted in a 588 field (see figures 2.15 and 2.16).

To summarize: the basis for the description of a monograph or serial should generally be the first available part; the basis for the description of an integrating resource is the most current iteration of the resource as a whole.

2.2. SOURCES OF INFORMATION. If RDA 2.1 tells us which source to choose as the basis of identification for a resource, RDA 2.2 tells us *where* in that source to look for the information.

2.2.2. PREFERRED SOURCE OF INFORMATION. The "preferred source of information" is the source catalogers use to obtain information for the purpose of transcribing or recording in a bibliographic description. Sometimes the same information is presented more than once in different ways in a resource. For example, the title proper may appear with slightly different wording on the title page, the verso of the title page, the half-title, the front cover, the spine, the back cover, or the colophon. RDA 2.2.2 gives guidelines to help the cataloger choose one of these sources. One reason a cataloging code is concerned with this is our shared cataloging environment. In the current cataloging environment, before cataloging a resource from scratch, it is customary to search a cataloging database such as OCLC to see if someone else has already cataloged it. When attempting to match an existing record to the resource in hand the cataloger needs to be able to predict which part of the resource was used, for example, to transcribe the title information. If everyone is expected to use the title page when cataloging a book, I can confidently try to match the wording of the title of the book I have in my hand against title transcriptions (in MARC 245 fields) in existing records without worrying that another cataloger might instead have transcribed the title there as it appeared on, for example, the cover, where it might differ from the title page presentation. If I find a record that matches the title on my title page, and other information such as publisher, date, pagination, and size match, then I can with some confidence assume that the record I found is a record for the same book as the one in my hand. If it were not for the concept of "preferred source of information" I could not be confident this was the case.

Choose the preferred source first by choosing the source that will be the basis for the description (e.g., the first volume of a multivolume monograph, see 2.1 above); then look at the "presentation format" (e.g., a printed volume, a motion picture) and follow the instructions in 2.2.

RESOURCES CONSISTING OF ONE OR MORE PAGES, LEAVES, SHEETS, OR CARDS (OR IMAGES OF ONE OF MORE PAGES, LEAVES, SHEETS, OR CARDS). RDA 2.2.2.2 may hold the record for longest section title. Generally speaking this section discusses printed materials such as books, or images of printed materials such as microform or digital images. For such materials the "preferred source of information" is the title page (or title sheet, or title card). If the resource does not have a title page/sheet/card, then the preferred source of information is the first of the following that bears a title:

a. a cover or jacket issued with the resource
b. a caption (a page at the beginning of the resource that bears its title and is also the first page of its text or music)
c. a masthead (a statement somewhere near the beginning of a serial publication that states the title, ownership, editors, etc.)

    d. a colophon (a statement, usually at the end of the resource, that gives information about the title, author, publisher, printer, date of publication/printing, or other information)

If none of these sources bears a title, then look for another source within the resource that bears a title; if there are more than one, choose one in which the information is "formally presented."

2.2.2.3. RESOURCES CONSISTING OF MOVING IMAGES. The preferred source of information for a resource consisting of moving images is the title frame or frames, or the title screen or screens. A title frame is the section of a film that contains text such as the title, director, cast, etc. It usually appears at the beginning of the resource, but may also appear at the end (or both places). A title screen is a data display in a digital resource that includes the title of the resource and may also give other data relating to the publication. As an alternative, RDA allows a label permanently affixed to the resource (*not* the container) that bears a title as the preferred source of information.

If the resource does not have a title frame or screen, then first apply the alternative (use a label permanently affixed to the resource, but not the container), or embedded textual metadata that contains a title. If that still does not produce a preferred source of information, for tangible resources (e.g., a DVD) use a container or accompanying material, or an internal source (e.g., a disc menu).

2.2.2.4. OTHER RESOURCES. For all other resources, prefer sources that formally present a collective title over sources that list titles of the individual contents. For tangible resources, choose either text on the resource or label that is permanently affixed to the resource (excluding accompanying material such as a booklet, or a container), or an internal source such as a title screen. If neither of these can be used, a container or accompanying material may be used. For online resources, use the textual content of the resource or embedded textual metadata that contains a title.

2.2.4. OTHER SOURCES OF INFORMATION. This guideline is important because if information from outside the resource itself is recorded in certain listed elements this must be indicated, either by a note or by bracketing the information. This information is repeated later in chapter 2 in the instructions for individual elements under the subheading "Sources of Information." Pay attention, however, to the exception listed at the very end of the guideline. If the resource is of a type that does not normally carry formal identifying information (for example, a photograph, a rock, or an archival collection), nothing needs to be done (e.g., bracketing) to indicate that the information recorded came from outside the resource (see figure 2.20).

Figure 2.20. Unbracketed Devised Title

245 00	‡a Stomach of a frog, tangential section.
264 0	‡c 2010
300	‡a 1 microscope slide : ‡b stained ; ‡c 3 x 8 cm
336	‡a three-dimensional form ‡2 rdacontent
337	‡a microscopic ‡2 rdamedia
338	‡a microscope slide ‡2 rdacarrier
500	‡a Made by Robert Morgan Craig.
500	‡a Ten microns; stained with Zenker's stain.
700 1	‡a Craig, Robert Morgan.

2.3. TITLE. A title is one or more words or characters that names a resource or a work. A resource might have many titles associated with it, and many kinds of titles are listed under RDA 2.3.

2.3.1.4. RECORDING TITLES. Titles are to be *transcribed* following the transcription guidelines of 1.7, discussed above.

It is permissible to abridge a title by omitting words *only* if this can be done without loss of essential information. If words are omitted this should be indicated by ellipses (...), and none of the first five words should ever be omitted. Catalogers should use care and judgment in abridging a title, particularly the title proper. Only in rare instances is it appropriate to abbreviate the title proper. In the nineteenth century and earlier, title pages were often crowded with extraneous information, because they often doubled as an advertisement that was printed as a broadside and distributed separately. But even in these instances, the title proper was generally concise. "Other title information" is more likely to be overly lengthy and in need of abridgment than is the title proper (see figure 2.21).

Figure 2.21. Abridgement of Title

100 1	‡a Frost, John, ‡d 1800-1859, ‡e author.
245 10	‡a Border wars of the West : ‡b comprising the frontier wars of Pennsylvania, Virginia, Kentucky, Ohio, Indiana, Illinois, Tennessee, and Wisconsin ... / ‡c by John Frost, LL.D.
264 1	‡a New York ; ‡a Auburn : ‡b Miller, Orton & Mulligan, ‡c 1856.
300	‡a 608 pages : ‡b illustrations ; ‡c 24 cm
336	‡a text ‡2 rdacontent

336	‡a still image ‡2 rdacontent
337	‡a unmediated ‡2 rdamedia
338	‡a volume ‡2 rdacarrier
500	‡a Added title page, engraved, in color.

Title page

Border Wars of the West: comprising the
Frontier Wars of Pennsylvania, Virginia, Kentucky,
Ohio, Indiana, Illinois, Tennessee, and Wisconsin;
and embracing
Individual Adventures among the Indians,
and exploits of
Boone, Kenton, Clark, Logan, Brady, Poe, Morgan,
the Whetzels, and other border heroes of the west.
By John Frost, LL.D.
With Numerous Engravings.
New York and Auburn:
Miller, Orton & Mulligan   1856

If the title on an issue of a serial includes a date, number, or name that varies from issue to issue, omit the date, number, or name, and indicate the omission by ellipses (...). For examples, see figure 2.11a, where the issue used as the basis of the description had the title "1984 annual report of the Agricultural Experiment Station, Michigan State University," and figure 2.11b.

2.3.1.5. NAMES OF PERSONS, FAMILIES, AND CORPORATE BODIES. The title is usually different from the name of the person, family, or body responsible for the item, but this is not always the case, as seen in figures 2.22 and 2.23. Transcribe the title information as it appears in the preferred source.

Figure 2.22. Title Proper the Name of a Corporate Body

028 02	‡a 19129-2 ‡b Atlantic
110 2	‡a Led Zeppelin (Musical group), ‡e creator.
245 10	‡a Led Zeppelin.
264 1	‡a New York : ‡b Atlantic, ‡c [1994]
264 4	‡c ℗1971
300	‡a 1 audio disc ; ‡c 4 3/4 in. + ‡e 1 booklet (8 unnumbered pages)
336	‡a performed music ‡2 rdacontent
337	‡a audio ‡2 rdamedia
338	‡a audio disc ‡2 rdacarrier

344 ǂa digital ǂb optical ǂg stereo ǂ2 rda

347 ǂa audio file ǂb CD audio ǂ2 rda

511 0 ǂa Jimmy Page, Robert Plant, John Bonham, John Paul Jones, Memphis Minnie.

518 ǂa Recorded at Headley, Grange, Hampshire; Island Studios, London; and Sunset Sound, Los Angeles, Calif.

530 ǂa Also issued as analog disc and cassette.

505 0 ǂa Black dog (4:55) -- Rock and roll (3:40) -- The battle of evermore (5:38) -- Stairway to heaven (7:55) -- Misty mountain hop (4:39) -- Four sticks (4:49) -- Going to California (3:36) -- When the levee breaks (7:08).

Disc label

Led Zeppelin

1. Black Dog (4:55)
2. Rock and Roll (3:40)
3. The Battle of Evermore (5:38)
4. Stairway to Heaven (7:55)
5. Misty Mountain Hop (4:39)
6. Four Sticks (4:49)
7. Going to California (3:36)
8. When the Levee Breaks (7:08)

Produced by Jimmy Page
℗1971 Atlantic
Made in USA

Atlantic
19129-2
(250 008)
1120141D

Figure 2.23. Title Proper the Name of a Corporate Body

111 2 ǂa Conference on the Acquisition of Material from Africa ǂd (1969 : ǂc University of Birmingham)

245 1 ǂa Conference on the Acquisition of Material from Africa : ǂb University of Birmingham, 25th April 1969 / ǂc reports and papers compiled by Valerie Bloomfield.

264 1 ǂa Zug, Switzerland : ǂb Inter Documentation Company AG, ǂc [1969]

264 4 ǂc ©1969

300 ǂa vii, 154 pages ; ǂc 21 cm

336 ǂa text ǂ2 rdacontent

337   ǂa unmediated ǂ2 rdamedia

338   ǂa volume ǂ2 rdacarrier

500   ǂa At head of title: Standing Conference on Library Materials on Africa.

700 1   ǂa Bloomfield, Valerie, ǂe editor of compilation.

710 2   ǂa Standing Conference on Library Materials on Africa, ǂe sponsoring body.

Title page

Standing Conference on Library Materials on Africa

Conference
on the Acquisition of Material from Africa
University of Birmingham 25th April 1969
Reports and Papers compiled by Valerie Bloomfield

Inter Documentation Company AG Zug Switzerland

Transcribe a title exactly as found even if a name of an author, publisher, etc., appears in it, so long as the name is an integral part of the title (for example, linked to the title by a case ending) (see figure 2.24). On the other hand, if a name simply appears *before* a title and is not integrally linked to the title, it is not considered part of the title and will not be transcribed with it. See figure 2.17. "Jeannette Lander" is not an integral part of the title and is transcribed instead as the statement of responsibility.

Figure 2.24. Title Proper Includes Statement of Responsibility

100 1   ǂa Téramond, Béhotéguy de, ǂe author.

240 10   ǂa 300 recettes culinaires pour maigrir (par la méthode des basses-calories). ǂl English

245 10   ǂa Béhotéguy de Téramond's low-calorie French cookbook : ǂb with season-by-season diet menus / ǂc illustrations by Dorothy Ivens.

246 30   ǂa Low-calorie French cookbook

264 1   ǂa New York : ǂb Grosset & Dunlap, Publishers, ǂc [1964]

300   ǂa 224 pages : ǂb illustrations ; ǂc 25 cm

336   ǂa text ǂ2 rdacontent

337   ǂa unmediated ǂ2 rdamedia

338   ǂa volume ǂ2 rdacarrier

500   ǂa Translation of: 300 recettes culinaires pour maigrir (par la méthode des basses-calories).

500   ǂa Includes index.

Title page

Béhotéguy de Téramond's
Low-Calorie
French Cookbook
with Season-by-Season Diet Menus
Illustrations by Dorothy Ivens

Grosset & Dunlap • Publishers
New York
Verso of title page
Copyright © 1964 Editions Pallas
First published in France under the title:
"300 Recettes Culinaires pour Maigrir
(par la Méthode des Basses-Calories),"
Editions de la Pensée Moderne, éditeurs, Paris

2.3.1.6. INTRODUCTORY WORDS, ETC. Introductory words such as "Walt Disney presents
. . ." that are not intended to be part of the title often precede the titles of films, sound
recordings, and websites. Do not transcribe these words as part of the title proper (see
figure 2.25). If the form that includes the introductory words is considered important
for identification of, or access to, the resource, record it as a variant title.

Figure 2.25. Introductory Words

024	1	‡a 876964003568
028	42	‡a 10356 ‡b Magnolia Home Entertainment
245	10	‡a Freakonomics / ‡c Chad Troutwine presents, in association with Cold Fusion Media, a Green Film Company Production ; produced by Chad Troutwine, Chris Romano, Dan O'Meara.
264	1	‡a Los Angeles, California : ‡b Magnolia Home Entertainment, ‡c [2011].
264	4	‡c ©2011
300		‡a 1 videodisc (93 min.) : ‡b sound, color ; ‡c 4 3/4 in.
336		‡a two-dimensional moving image ‡2 rdacontent
337		‡a video ‡2 rdamedia
338		‡a videodisc ‡2 rdacarrier
344		‡h Dolby digital 5.1 ‡2 rda
346		‡b NTSC ‡2 rda
347		‡a video file ‡b DVD video ‡e region 1 ‡2 rda
380		‡a Motion picture.
500		‡a Based on the book "Freakonomics" by Steven D. Levitt and Stephen J. Dubner.

546	‡a In English, with optional subtitles in Spanish; closed-captioned.
518	‡a DVD release of the 2010 motion picture.
520	‡a Documentary based on the book about incentives-based thinking; examines human behavior through case studies.
521 8	‡a MPAA rating: PG-13.
500	‡a Wide screen (1.78:1)
546	‡a English with dubbed French or Spanish dialogue; French or Spanish subtitles; English audio description; closed-captioned.
700 1	‡i Motion picture adaptation of (work): ‡a Levitt, Steven D. ‡t Freakonomics.
700 1	‡a Dubner, Stephen J.
700 1	‡a Troutwine, Chad, ‡d 1968- ‡e film producer.
700 1	‡a Romano, Chris, ‡d1978- ‡e film producer.
700 1	‡a O'Meara, Dan, ‡e film producer.
710 2	‡a Cold Fusion Media, ‡e film producer.
710 2	‡a Green Film Company, ‡e film producer.

Title frames

Chad Troutwine Presents
In Association With Cold Fusion Media
A Green Film Company Production
FREAKONOMICS
BASED ON THE BOOK BY STEVEN D. LEVITT AND STEPHEN J. DUBNER
CO PRODUCERS
RAFI CHAUDRY   PETER CERBIN   HILARY CARR
CO EXECUTIVE PRODUCERS
STEPHEN J. DUBNER   STEVEN D. LEVITT
EXECUTIVE PRODUCERS
MICHAEL ROBAN   PAUL FIORE   JAY RIFKIN   DAMON MARTIN
EXECUTIVE PRODUCER SETH GORDON
PRODUCED BY
CHAD TROUTWINE   CHRIS ROMANO   DAN O'MEARA

Container

SIX ROGUE FILMMAKERS EXPLORE THE HIDDEN SIDE OF EVERYTHING
FREAKONOMICS
THE MOVIE
©2011 Magnolia Home Entertainment
Distributed by Magnolia Home Entertainment,
2222 South Berrington Avenue, Los Angeles, California 90064

2.3.2. TITLE PROPER. The title proper element is core in an RDA record. It is defined as "the chief name of a resource (i.e., the title normally used when citing the resource)." If more than one title proper appears in the resource, record the one found in the preferred source of information (see discussion above at 2.2.2).

Transcribe the title proper just as it appears on the preferred source of information. In MARC bibliographic records the title proper is recorded in subfield ‡a of the 245 field (see figures throughout this chapter). The 245 field serves double duty in the MARC record. First, it records and displays the title proper, other title information, and statement of responsibility, all transcribed from the resource itself. Second, it gives database users *access* to all parts of the field, but particularly to the title proper through keyword or browse searching, if the 245 field is indexed. This is important because a title search is one of the principal methods of finding a resource.

An alternative title (a second title introduced by "or" or the equivalent in another language, e.g., *Hans Brinker, or, The silver skates*) is part of the title proper, and so is included in the same subfield ‡a as the first title. However, because it is a second title, its first word is capitalized following RDA appendix A.4.1. Indexed access is given to the alternative title by transcribing it (minus any initial article) in the 246 field (see figure 2.26). See below under 2.3.6, Variant Title, for information on coding the 246 field.

Figure 2.26. Alternative Title

028 32	‡a NOV170665 ‡b Novello
130 0	‡a How cold the wind doth blow.
245 10	‡a How cold the wind doth blow, or, The unquiet grave : ‡b for solo voice : from the collection Folk songs from Sussex (1912) collected by W. Percy Merrick / ‡c with piano accompaniment and optional violin obligato by Ralph Vaughan Williams.
246 30	‡a Unquiet grave
264　1	‡a London : ‡b Novello, ‡c [2011]
264　4	‡c ©2011
300	‡a 1 score (6 pages) ; ‡c 30 cm
336	‡a notated music ‡2 rdacontent
337	‡a unmediated ‡2 rdamedia
338	‡a volume ‡2 rdacarrier
500	‡a Vaughan Williams composed the accompaniment for this song, which was taken from W. Percy Merrick's 1912 collection, Folk songs from Sussex (some of the verses were taken from the collection). No separate violin part is provided for this edition.
546	‡b Staff notation.
700 1	‡a Vaughan Williams, Ralph, ‡d 1872-1958, ‡e arranger of music.
700 1	‡a Merrick, W. Percy, ‡e compiler.
730 0	‡a Folk songs from Sussex (Collection)

2.3.2.6. COLLECTIVE TITLE AND TITLES OF INDIVIDUAL CONTENTS. Sometimes the preferred source of information includes a collective title together with individual titles for works included in the resource. In this case, the collective title serves as the title proper. The individual titles, because they are neither the title proper of the resource, other title information, nor statement of responsibility, are omitted but may be listed instead as authorized access points for the individual works or in a structured description (a contents note) following RDA 25.1. Keyword access to the titles of individual works as they appear in the resource may be available through their presence in the 505 field, depending on the indexing of the system, and keyword and browse access to controlled forms of the title is given by recording the authorized access point for the works in 7XX fields (see figure 2.27).

Figure 2.27. Title Proper—Collective and Individual Titles

020	‡a 033033560X
100 1	‡a Dexter, Colin, ‡e author.
245 14	‡a The third Inspector Morse omnibus / ‡c Colin Dexter.
264 1	‡a London : ‡b Pan Books, ‡c 1994.
300	‡a 530 pages : ‡b illustrations, maps ; ‡c 20 cm
336	‡a text ‡2 rdacontent
336	‡a still image ‡2 rdacontent
336	‡a cartographic image ‡2 rdacontent
337	‡a unmediated ‡2 rdamedia
338	‡a volume ‡2 rdacarrier
505 0	‡a Last bus to Woodstock -- The wench is dead -- The jewel that was ours.
700 12	‡i Contains (work): ‡a Dexter, Colin. ‡t Last bus to Woodstock.
700 12	‡i Contains (work): ‡a Dexter, Colin. ‡t Wench is dead.
700 12	‡i Contains (work): ‡a Dexter, Colin. ‡t Jewel that was ours.

Title page

The Third
Inspector Morse
Omnibus

Last Bus to Woodstock
The Wench is Dead
The Jewel That Was Ours

Colin Dexter

Pan Books
In Association With Macmillan London

2.3.2.8. OTHER ELEMENTS RECORDED AS PART OF THE TITLE PROPER

2.3.2.8.1. TYPE OF COMPOSITION, MEDIUM OF PERFORMANCE, KEY, ETC. Determination of the length of the title proper can be a problem in music cataloging, because so many pieces of music are given titles consisting of a generic term (the name of a type of composition, such as "symphony" or "concerto") followed by a medium of performance (e.g., "for flute"), key (e.g., "in B flat"), opus number (e.g., "no. 3"), etc. In such a case, all of this information is included as part of the title proper (see figure 2.28). On the other hand, if the title is not generic (e.g., "Don Giovanni"), or consists of a generic term modified by a nongeneric adjective (e.g., "The Pastoral Symphony"), any mention of medium of performance, key, etc., on the source will be treated as other title information (see figure 2.29).

Figure 2.28. Generic Title Proper (Music)

020		‡a 0793542022
02	32	‡a HL00120015 ‡b Hal Leonard
100	1	‡a Starer, Robert, ‡e composer.
240	10	‡a Sonatas, ‡m piano, ‡n no. 3
245	10	‡a Sonata for piano, no. 3 / ‡c Robert Starer.
264	1	‡a Milwaukee, WI : ‡b MCA Music Publishing, ‡c [1994]
264	2	‡b Hal Leonard
264	4	‡c ©1994
300		‡a 1 score (23 pages) ; ‡c 31 cm
336		‡a notated music ‡2 rdacontent
337		‡a unmediated ‡2 rdamedia
338		‡a volume ‡2 rdacarrier
546		‡b Staff notation.
500		‡a Title from cover.

Cover

Robert Starer
Sonata for Piano, No. 3
A publication of MCA Music Publishing
A division of MCA Inc.
7777 W. Bluemound Rd., Milwaukee, WI 53213
Distributed by Hal Leonard

Foot of first page of music
© Copyright 1994 by MCA Music Publishing, A Division of MCA Inc.

Figure 2.29. Nongeneric Title Proper (Music)

028	32	‡a K 163 ‡b Keturi Musikverlag
100	1	‡a Baumann, Herbert, ‡d 1925- ‡e composer.
245	10	‡a Sonata serena : ‡b für Hackbrett (oder Marimba/Xylophon) und Harfe (ersatzweise Klavier) / ‡c Herbert Baumann.
250		‡a Faksimile-Ausgabe.
264	1	‡a Rimsting/Chiemsee : ‡b Keturi Musikverlag, ‡c [1993]
264	4	‡c ©1993
300		‡a 1 score (24 pages) + 1 part (11 pages) ; ‡c 30 cm
336		‡a notated music ‡2 rdacontent
337		‡a unmediated ‡2 rdamedia
338		‡a volume ‡2 rdacarrier
546		‡b Staff notation.
500		‡a Title from cover.

Cover

Herbert Baumann
Sonata Serena
für Hackbrett (oder Marimba/Xylophon)
und Harfe (ersatzweise Klavier)
Faksimile-Ausgabe
Keturi Musikverlag
Höhenweg 36, D-8219 Rimsting/Chiemsee

Foot of first page of music

© Copyright 1993 by Keturi Musikverlag, D-83251 Rimsting/Chiemsee
Alle Rechte vorbehalten

2.3.2.8.2. SCALE. The title of a cartographic resource sometimes includes information about the scale. Although the scale statement is given formally as part of the scale element (RDA 7.25), it will still be transcribed as part of the title proper if appropriate (see figure 2.30).

Figure 2.30. Scale as Part of Title Transcription

020		‡a 0851523625 (paper)
020		‡a 0851523633 (cloth)
110	2	‡a John Bartholomew and Son, ‡e cartographer.
245	10	‡a Bartholomew one inch map of the Lake District.
250		‡a Revised.
255		‡a Scale 1:63,360. 1 in. to 1 mile.

264	1	‡a Edinburgh : ‡b John Bartholomew & Son Ltd, ‡c 1971.
300		‡a 1 map : ‡b color ; ‡c 70 x 82 cm, folded to 21 x 12 cm
336		‡a cartographic image ‡2 rdacontent
337		‡a unmediated ‡2 rdamedia
338		‡a sheet ‡2 rdacarrier
500		‡a Relief shown by gradient tints.

Information from map

Bartholomew One Inch Map of the Lake District
Revised 1971   Scale 1:63360—1 inch to the mile
© John Bartholomew & Son Ltd, Edinburgh
SBN 85152 362 5 paper
85152 363 3 cloth

2.3.2.9. RESOURCE LACKING A COLLECTIVE TITLE. Most items that include a number of separate works have a collective title on the chief source of information. Such materials present no problem for the cataloger (see above at 2.3.2.6). But some resources simply list a number of separate titles, with or without their authors, on the preferred source of information. Other resources do not list the titles in any one source, but separately throughout the resource (e.g., on separate title pages). As noted in RDA 1.5, the cataloger has a choice: create a comprehensive description for the resource as a whole (RDA 1.5.2), or create separate (analytical) descriptions for each part (RDA 1.5.3). In some cases where there is no collective title, creating a separate (analytical) description for each part might be the simpler solution. In that case, simply choose a preferred source of information for each part and use that to record the title proper (see figures 2.31a and 2.31b for analytical descriptions of two sides of a map with separate titles).

Figure 2.31a. Resource without a Collective Title—Analytical Description

110	2	‡a National Geographic Society (U.S.). ‡b Cartographic Division, ‡e cartographer.
245	14	‡a The earth's fractured surface / ‡c produced by the Cartographic Division, National Geographic Society ; John F. Shupe, chief cartographer.
255		‡a Scale 1:48,000,000. 1 in. = 758 miles. At equator ; ‡b Winkel tripel projection ‡c (W 180°--E 180°/N 90°--S 90°).
264	1	‡a Washington, D.C. : ‡b National Geographic Society, ‡c 1995.
300		‡a 1 map : ‡b color ; ‡c 51 x 83 cm, folded to 23 x 15 cm
336		‡a cartographic image ‡2 rdacontent
337		‡a unmediated ‡2 rdamedia
338		‡a sheet ‡2 rdacarrier

500		‡a "April 1995."
500		‡a Relief shown by satellite imagery, gradient tints, and spot heights. Depth shown by satellite imagery, shading, and soundings.
500		‡a Includes text, indexed ancillary map showing major plates, and indexes to earthquakes and volcanic eruptions.
501		‡a Issued with (on verso): Living on the edge / produced by the Cartographic Division, National Geographic Society.
700	1	‡a Shupe, John F., ‡e cartographer.

Information from map

The Earth's Fractured Surface
Produced by the Cartographic Division
National Geographic Society
Gilbert M. Grosvenor, President and Chairman
William L. Allen, editor, National Geographic Magazine
John F. Shupe, chief cartographer
Washington, D.C., April 1995
Winkel Tripel Projection
Scale 1:48,000,000 or 1 inch = 758 miles
at the equator

Figure 2.31b. Resource without a Collective Title—Analytical Description

110	2	‡a National Geographic Society (U.S.). ‡b Cartographic Division, ‡e cartographer.
245	10	‡a Living on the edge : ‡b [West Coast of the United States] / ‡c produced by the Cartographic Division, National Geographic Society ; John F. Shupe, chief cartographer.
255		‡a Scale 1:2,380,000. 1 in. = 38 miles ; ‡b Albers conic equal-area projection, standard parallels 20°30' and 45°30'.
264	1	‡a Washington, D.C. : ‡b National Geographic Society, ‡c 1995.
300		‡a 1 map : ‡b color ; ‡c sheet 57 x 93 cm, folded to 23 x 15 cm
336		‡a cartographic image ‡2 rdacontent
337		‡a unmediated ‡2 rdamedia
338		‡a sheet ‡2 rdacarrier
500		‡a "April 1995."
500		‡a Relief shown by satellite imagery, gradient tints, and spot heights. Depth shown by satellite imagery, shading, and soundings.
500		‡a Includes text, cross section, 2 graphs, and 5 ancillary maps.
501		‡a Issued with (on verso): The earth's fractured surface / produced by the Cartographic Division, National Geographic Society.
700	1	‡a Shupe, John F., ‡e cartographer.

Information from map

Living on the Edge
Produced by the Cartographic Division
National Geographic Society
Gilbert M. Grosvenor, President and Chairman
William L. Allen, editor, National Geographic Magazine
John F. Shupe, chief cartographer
Washington, D.C., April 1995
Albers Conic Equal-Area Projection, Standard Parallels 20°30' and 45°30'
Scale 1:2,380,000 or 1 inch = 38 miles
Elevations in feet, soundings in fathoms

Figure 2.31c. Resource without a Collective Title—Comprehensive Description

110 2 ‡a National Geographic Society (U.S.). ‡b Cartographic Division, ‡e cartographer.

245 14 ‡a The earth's fractured surface ; ‡b Living on the edge : [West Coast of the United States] / ‡c produced by the Cartographic Division, National Geographic Society ; John F. Shupe, chief cartographer.

255 ‡a Scale 1:48,000,000. 1 in. = 758 miles. At equator ; ‡b Winkel tripel projection ‡c (W 180°--E 180°/N 90°--S 90°).

255 ‡a Scale 1:2,380,000. 1 in. = 38 miles ; ‡b Albers conic equal-area projection, standard parallels 20°30' and 45°30'.

264 1 ‡a Washington, D.C. : ‡b National Geographic Society, ‡c 1995.

300 ‡a 2 maps on 1 sheet : ‡b both sides, color ; ‡c sheet 57 x 93 cm, folded to 23 x 15 cm

336 ‡a cartographic image ‡2 rdacontent

337 ‡a unmediated ‡2 rdamedia

338 ‡a sheet ‡2 rdacarrier

500 ‡a "April 1995."

500 ‡a Relief shown by satellite imagery, gradient tints, and spot heights. Depth shown by satellite imagery, shading, and soundings.

500 ‡a Includes text, indexed ancillary map showing major plates, indexes to earthquakes and volcanic eruptions, cross section, 2 graphs, and 5 ancillary maps.

700 1 ‡a Shupe, John F., ‡e cartographer.

710 22 ‡a National Geographic Society (U.S.). ‡b Cartographic Division. ‡t Earth's fractured surface.

710 22 ‡a National Geographic Society (U.S.). ‡b Cartographic Division. ‡t Living on the edge.

RDA 2.3.2.9 gives guidance for choosing a title proper when creating a comprehensive description for such resources. If the titles of the parts appear on a single source of information, transcribe them as they appear there. For ISBD punctuation in this case, see RDA appendix D.1.2.2. If all the parts are by the same person, family, or corporate body, separate the titles proper of the parts by semicolons. Precede the second title (including a connecting word or phrase) by subfield ‡b (see figure 2.32).

Figure 2.32. Resource without a Collective Title—Comprehensive Description

100 1	‡a Martineau, Harriet, ‡d 1802-1876, ‡e author.
245 10	‡a Feats on the fjord ; ‡b and, Merdhin / ‡c by Harriet Martineau.
264 1	‡a London ; ‡a Toronto : ‡b J.M. Dent & Sons Ltd ; ‡a New York : ‡b E.P. Dutton & Co., ‡c 1910.
300	‡a xi, 239 pages : ‡b illustrations ; ‡c 18 cm.
336	‡a text ‡2 rdacontent
336	‡a still image ‡2 rdacontent
337	‡a unmediated ‡2 rdamedia
338	‡a volume ‡2 rdacarrier
490 0	‡a Everyman's library. For young people
504	‡a Includes bibliographical references (page viii).
700 12	‡a Martineau, Harriet, ‡d 1802-1876. ‡t Merdhin.

Title page

Feats on the Fjord and Merdhin by
Harriet Martineau
London & Toronto
Published by J.M. Dent
& Sons Ltd & in New York
by E.P. Dutton & Co.

If the resource does not have a single source of information showing all the titles, the sources identifying the individual parts may be treated as a collective source of information (see RDA 2.1.2.2). In this case, record the titles in the order in which they appear in the resource. The maps described in figure 2.31c are an example. Because there is no particular order in which the parts appear, the cataloger must arbitrarily choose one of the parts to record first.

If the parts are by different persons, families, or corporate bodies, each part is recorded with its own statement of responsibility (if there is one). Following RDA D.1.2.2 for ISBD punctuation, separate each group of data by a full stop (period). Do not insert any subfield coding after the first statement of responsibility (subfield ‡c).

Figure 2.33a is an example of a comprehensive description of a resource lacking a collective title with parts by different persons. This resource was issued in a "dos-à-dos" binding where two works are printed together back to back—literally—so that the reader has to turn the book over after reading one work in order to read the other. As with the maps described in figure 2.31c, the cataloger must arbitrarily choose one to record first in the MARC record. And like the maps, the cataloger might decide in the end that analytical descriptions of the two works are simpler than a comprehensive description (see figure 2.33b).

Figure 2.33a. Resource without a Collective Title—Comprehensive Description

245	04	‡a The hard way up / ‡c by A. Bertram Chandler. The veiled world / by Robert Lory.
264	1	‡a New York : ‡b Ace Books, ‡c [1972]
300		‡a 162, 116 pages ; ‡c 18 cm.
336		‡a text ‡2 rdacontent
337		‡a unmediated ‡2 rdamedia
338		‡a volume ‡2 rdacarrier
490	1	‡a Ace double
500		‡a Two novels issued together, bound opposite each other so that each begins from the outer cover of the book.
700	12	‡a Chandler, A. Bertram, ‡d 1912-1984. ‡t Hard way up.
700	12	‡a Lory, Robert. ‡t Veiled world.
830	0	‡a Ace double-novel books

Title page

THE HARD WAY UP
by A. Bertram Chandler

ACE BOOKS
New York, N.Y.

Title page on opposite side of book

THE VEILED WORLD
by Robert Lory

ACE BOOKS
New York, N.Y.

Figure 2.33b. Resource without a Collective Title—Analytical Descriptions

100	1	‡a Chandler, A. Bertram, ‡d 1912-1984, ‡e author.
245	14	‡a The hard way up / ‡c by A. Bertram Chandler.
264	1	‡a New York : ‡b Ace Books, ‡c [1972]
300		‡a 162 pages ; ‡c 18 cm.
336		‡a text ‡2 rdacontent
337		‡a unmediated ‡2 rdamedia
338		‡a volume ‡2 rdacarrier
490	1	‡a Ace double
501		‡a With: The veiled world / by Robert Lory.
830	0	‡a Ace double-novel books

100	1	‡a Lory, Robert, ‡e author.
245	14	‡a The veiled world / by Robert Lory.
264	1	‡a New York : ‡b Ace Books, ‡c [1972]
300		‡a 116 pages ; ‡c 18 cm.
336		‡a text ‡2 rdacontent
337		‡a unmediated ‡2 rdamedia
338		‡a volume ‡2 rdacarrier
490	1	‡a Ace double
501		‡a With: The hard way up / by A. Bertram Chandler.
830	0	‡a Ace double-novel books

2.3.2.10. RESOURCE WITH NO TITLE. Title proper is a core element in RDA, so the cataloger must record something in this element. If no title appears anywhere in the resource, the cataloger may either find a title for the resource in another source, or devise a title.

If a title if found in another source, simply record it as found. If the resource is of a type that normally would carry a title (such as a printed book), the cataloger must indicate that the information was taken from outside the resource (see RDA 2.2.4). In North American practice this is done by enclosing the supplied title in square brackets. A note should be recorded in a MARC 500 field to indicate the source of the title (see figure 2.34).

Figure 2.34. Supplied Title

100	1	‡a Pratt, Orson, ‡d 1811-1881, ‡e author.
245	10	‡a [Tracts] / ‡c by Orson Pratt, one of the twelve apostles of the Church of Jesus Christ of Latter-day Saints and president of said Church throughout Great Britain and all European countries.
264	1	‡a Liverpool ; ‡a London : ‡b L.D.S. Book and Star Depôt, ‡c 1856-1857.
300		‡a 128 pages ; ‡c 20 cm
336		‡a text ‡2 rdacontent
337		‡a unmediated ‡2 rdamedia
338		‡a volume ‡2 rdacarrier
500		‡a Published without a title page; title supplied from Flake, C.J. Mormon bibliography, 6548.
510	4	‡a Flake, C.J. Mormon bibliography, ‡c 6548
505	0	‡a The true faith -- True repentance -- Water baptism -- The Holy Spirit -- Spiritual gifts -- Necessity for miracles -- Universal apostacy -- Latter-day kingdom.

Caption title on page 1

CHAPTER I.

THE TRUE FAITH

Printing Along Fold in Each Signature

By Orson Pratt, one of the Twelve Apostles of the Church of Jesus Christ of Latter-day Saints and President of said Church throughout Great Britain and all European countries. Liverpool: 42, Islington. London: L.D.S. Book and Star Depôt, 35 Lewis Street, [each signature has a different date]

2.3.2.11. RECORDING DEVISED TITLES. In the absence of a title in the resource itself, the cataloger may devise a title if none can be found in any other source. Under the guidelines of 2.3.2.11, the title should describe the resource's nature, its subject, or both. North American catalogers following LC-PCC policy will record this title in English (LC-PCC PS 2.3.2.11, February 2010).

The devised title in figure 2.20 describes the nature of the resource, the stomach of a frog. The devised title in figure 2.35 describes both the nature of the resource (a gold lamella) and the subject of the text contained in it. Neither of these resources is of the type that normally carries identifying information, so the title proper is not bracketed (see RDA 2.2.4, exception), and no note is made indicating that the title has been devised.

Figure 2.35. Devised Title

245	00	‡a Gold lamella with a Greek inscription containing good wishes for the deceased Heraklianus.
264	0	‡c between 1st and 3rd centuries.
300		‡a 1 sheet ; ‡c 30 x 55 mm
336		‡a text ‡2 rdacontent
337		‡a unmediated ‡2 rdamedia
338		‡a sheet ‡2 rdacarrier
340		‡a gold
500		‡a Lamellae, small pieces of metal on which an inscription appears, range in date from the second century BC through the Roman Period and are found in tombs from Palestine. They were buried with the deceased, placed on the forehead.
500		‡a The inscription is on one side of the lamella only.
500		‡a Text of inscription: θαρσει, Ἡρακλιανε, ουδὶς αθανατος.
500		‡a Text of inscription: tharsei, Hērakliane, oudis athanatos.
500		‡a Translation of inscription: Cheer up, Heraklianus, nobody's immortal.
546		‡a Greek.
561		‡a Acquired as a donation from David H. Swingler of Oxnard, California. Purchased by Swingler between 1983 and 1985 from Royal Athena Gallery in New York. Provenance unknown.
581		‡a Blumell, Lincoln H., "A gold lamella with a Greek inscription in the Brigham Young University collection," Zeitschrift für Papyrologie und Epigraphik 177 (2011) 166-168.

2.3.2.11.1. DEVISED TITLES FOR MUSIC. When devising a title for music include, as applicable, the medium of performance, numeric designation, key, or other distinguishing characteristics of the work or expression (see figure 2.36).

Figure 2.36. Devised Title Proper (Music)

100	1	‡a Bowles, Paul, ‡d 1910-1999, ‡e composer.
245	10	‡a [Songs for medium voice and piano] / ‡c Paul Bowles.
264	1	‡a [Place of publication not identified] : ‡b [Publisher not identified], ‡c [2011]
300		‡a 1 score (28 pages in various pagings) ; ‡c 28 cm
336		‡a notated music ‡2 rdacontent
337		‡a unmediated ‡2 rdamedia
338		‡a volume ‡2 rdacarrier
382		‡a medium voice ‡a piano
546		‡b Staff notation.

500	‡a Title supplied by cataloger.
500	‡a All songs reprinted with permission of the composer.
505 0	‡a In the woods -- Farther from the heart -- Once a lady was here -- April fool baby -- My sister's hand in mine -- Secret words.

2.3.2.11.2. DEVISED TITLES FOR CARTOGRAPHIC RESOURCES. Always identify the area covered and subject portrayed, if applicable, when devising a title for a cartographic resource. In figure 2.37 the title for the set of maps was devised by the cataloger based on a letter from the issuing body accompanying the resource.

Figure 2.37. Devised Title Proper (Cartographic Resource)

110 1	‡a Arizona. ‡b Office of the State Climatologist, ‡e cartographer.
245 10	‡a [Climatology maps of Arizona] / ‡c prepared under the direction of the State Climatologist, the Laboratory of Climatology, Arizona State University.
255	‡a Scale 1:1,000,000 and approximately 1:3,000,000 ; ‡b Lambert conformal conic projection.
264　1	‡a [Phoenix, Arizona] : ‡b Available from ARIS, ‡c 1975.
300	‡a 16 maps on 5 sheets : ‡b color ; ‡c 23 x 20 cm and 81 x 64 cm.
336	‡a cartographic image ‡2 rdacontent
337	‡a unmediated ‡2 rdamedia
338	‡a sheet ‡2 rdacarrier
490 1	‡a Cooperative publication / Arizona Resources Information System ; ‡v no. 5
500	‡a Title devised by cataloger based on cover letter from Arizona Resources Information System.
505 0	‡a [1] National Weather Service stations as of March 1975 -- [2] Evaporation and evapotranspiration -- [3] Arizona precipitation -- [4] Solar energy -- [5] Arizona temperatures.
710 2	‡a Arizona State University. ‡b Laboratory of Climatology, ‡e cartographer.
710 2	‡a Arizona Resources Information System, ‡e publisher.
830　0	‡a Cooperative publication (Arizona Resources Information System) ; ‡v no. 5.

2.3.2.11.4. DEVISED TITLES FOR ARCHIVAL RESOURCES AND COLLECTIONS. RDA 2.3.2.11.4 is a very brief résumé of archival cataloging practice as found in *Describing Archives: A Content Standard,* or DACS, published by the Society of American Archivists.[5] DACS 2.3 calls for the title element to include two parts: the name of the creator(s) or collector(s), and the nature of the archival unit (e.g., "papers") being described. Although RDA 2.3.2.11.4 only mentions including the name of the creator or collector, indicating the nature of the resource is included under the general guideline at 2.3.2.11. For an example, see figure 2.38.

Figure 2.38. Devised Title Proper (Archival Resource)

100	1	‡a Camp, Walter Mason, ‡d 1867-1925, ‡e creator.
245	14	‡a The Walter Mason Camp papers.
264	0	‡c 1905-1925
300		‡a 3 linear ft. ‡a (8 boxes)
336		‡a text ‡2 rdacontent
336		‡a still image ‡2 rdacontent
336		‡a cartographic image ‡2 rdacontent
337		‡a unmediated ‡2 rdamedia
338		‡a volume ‡2 rdacarrier
545		‡a Railway engineer, editor, and historian of the Indian wars of the U.S. Plains, 1864-1890. Camp researched the Indian wars from 1890 to 1925, conducting interviews with surviving Indian and White participants; his heaviest activity was from 1900 to 1920.
520		‡a The collection consists of correspondence, interview notes, general research and field notes, drafts of writings, photographs, maps, news clippings and miscellaneous research and reference materials created and collected by Camp, and pertaining to the Indian Wars of the plains (1864-1890). The bulk of the collection consists of correspondence (1908-1923), interviews, general research and field notes (1890-1924). Chief interviewees and correspondents were officers, enlisted men, and Indian scouts of the U.S. 7th Cavalry, and the Indians who fought at the Battle of Little Bighorn. Significant information on other battles is also present in the papers, including the following: Slim Buttes, Washita, Beecher Island, Wounded Knee, Wagon Box, Adobe Walls, Rosebud, Redwater Creek, Platte Bridge and Red Buttes, Nez Perce Campaign, Hayfield Fight, Dull Knife Fight, Fetterman Massacre, Conner-Cole Expedition and the Battle of Buffalo Wallow.
530		‡a Microfilmed copies available; ‡d MSS FM 5.
561		‡a Custody assumed by Camp's widow in 1925; sold to William Carey Brown in 1933, who organized and apparently misplaced some of the papers. Some materials were added by Brown and Robert Ellison. Some of the materials were removed from the collection by Brown; these are now at the University of Colorado Library. The bulk of the papers went to Ellison; on his death, most of these went to the Lilly Library and the Denver Public Library; the remaining papers were purchased by Fred Rosenstock.
541		‡c Gift and purchase; ‡a Fred Rosenstock; ‡d 1968-1981.
506		‡a Use of the original Camp interview notes and notes is restricted. Only those scholars requiring access in order to authenticate a particular note or to verify a transcription will be allowed to use them and then only under the supervision of the curator of manuscripts. All others must use the microfilmed copies found in box 8 of the collection.

555 0	‡a Finding aid available in the repository and online. ‡u http://files.lib.byu.edu/ead/ XML/MSS57.xml
524	‡a The Walter Mason Camp Papers, ca. 1890-1925.
581	‡a Camp, Walter Mason. Custer in '76 : Walter Camp's notes on the Custer fight / edited by Kenneth Hammer. -- Provo, Utah : Brigham Young University Press, 1976.
852	‡a L. Tom Perry Special Collections, Harold B. Lee Library, Brigham Young University, ‡e Provo, Utah 84602.

2.3.2.12. RECORDING CHANGES IN THE TITLE PROPER. Guidelines for changes that require a new description, including changes in the title proper, are given in RDA 1.6. See above under 1.6 for a full discussion.

2.3.3. PARALLEL TITLE PROPER. Sometimes a resource repeats the title proper in other languages (the resource may or may not contain text matching the languages of the titles). If this is the case, the first title on the preferred source of information is usually regarded as the title proper. Succeeding repetitions of this title in other languages are usually regarded as parallel titles.

Guidelines in RDA for parallel titles are somewhat different than in previous cataloging practice. Under AACR2 parallel titles had to appear on the chief source of information (roughly equivalent to RDA's preferred source of information). Under RDA guidelines, parallel titles can be taken from any source within the resource. AACR2 had fairly elaborate rules for which parallel titles to transcribe and which to omit. In RDA the various parallel title elements are not core, and so it is left to the cataloger's judgment or the cataloging agency's policy whether or not to record them. Under LC-PCC policy parallel titles proper are core, and so LC or PCC catalogers will record them (LC-PCC PS 2.3.3, September 2012).

Parallel titles proper are recorded following the same instructions as other titles under RDA 2.3.1. They are recorded in the MARC 245 field, and are separated from the title proper and from one another by space-equal sign-space. The first parallel title is preceded by subfield ‡b unless subfield ‡b or subfield ‡c have already occurred. Some common patterns are:

> 245 ... ‡a Title proper = ‡b Parallel title proper / ‡c statement of responsibility.
>
> 245 ... ‡a Title proper = ‡b Parallel title proper 1 = Parallel title proper 2 / ‡c statement of responsibility.
>
> 245 ... ‡a Title proper = ‡b Parallel title proper : other title information / ‡c statement of responsibility.

245 ... ‡a Title proper : ‡b other title information = Parallel title proper : parallel other title information / ‡c statement of responsibility.

245 ... ‡a Title proper / ‡c statement of responsibility = Parallel title proper / parallel statement of responsibility.

Direct access to a parallel title is given by recording it in a 246 field (see figure 2.39). See below under 2.3.6, Variant Title, for information about coding the 246 field.

Figure 2.39. Parallel Title

110 2	‡a Metropolitan Toronto Central Library. ‡b Languages Centre.
245 10	‡a Spanish books = ‡b Libros en español : a catalogue of the holdings of the Languages Centre, Metropolitan Toronto Central Library.
246 31	‡a Libros en español
264 1	‡a [Toronto, Ontario] : ‡b Metropolitan Toronto Library Board, ‡c 1974.
300	‡a 299 pages ; ‡c 27 cm
336	‡a text ‡2 rdacontent
337	‡a unmediated ‡2 rdamedia
338	‡a volume ‡2 rdacarrier
546	‡a Preliminary matter in English and Spanish.
500	‡a Includes index.

Title page

Spanish Books
Libros en Español
A Catalogue of the Holdings of the
Languages Centre
Metropolitan Toronto Central Library

Metropolitan Toronto Library Board
1974

Parallel information is often given for other title information and statements of responsibility as well. If so, under ISBD ordering, elements in the same language are kept together (see the patterns above and RDA D.1.2.1). For example, the map cataloged in figure 2.40 has a parallel statement of responsibility as well as a parallel title proper; the kit cataloged in figure 2.41 has parallel other title information as well as a parallel title proper.

Figure 2.40. Parallel Title with Statement of Responsibility

110	2	‡a Trigonometrical Survey (South Africa), ‡e cartographer.
245	10	‡a Suidelike Afrika / ‡c Driehoeksmeting = Southern Africa / Trigonometrical Survey.
246	31	‡a Southern Africa
250		‡a Derde uitgawe = ‡b Third edition.
255		‡a Scale 1:2,500,000 ; ‡b Albers equal area projection, standard parallels 18° South and 32° South ‡c (E10°--E37°/S17°--S36°).
264	1	‡a Pretoria : ‡b Die Staatsdrukker, ‡c 1972.
264	3	‡c 1977.
300		‡a 1 map : ‡b color ; ‡c 96 x 68 cm.
336		‡a cartographic image ‡2 rdacontent
337		‡a unmediated ‡2 rdamedia
338		‡a sheet ‡2 rdacarrier
490	1	‡a T.S.O. misc. ; ‡v 4793
500		‡a Relief shown by contours and color.
500		‡a Base map: Trigonometrical Survey, 1962.
546		‡a Includes glossary in Afrikaans, English, and Portuguese.
810	2	‡a Trigonometrical Survey (South Africa). ‡t T.S.O. misc. ; ‡v 4793.

Information from map face

Suidelike Afrika
Derde Uitgawe 1972
1:2 500 000
Albers se vlaktroue projeksie,
standaard parallele 18° Suid en 32° Suid.
Herdruk En Uitgegee Deur Die Staatsdrukker,
Privaatsak X85, Pretoria, 1977.

Driehoeksmeting
Trigonometrical Survey
T.S.O. Misc. 4793

Southern Africa
Third Edition 1972
1:2 500 000
Albers equal-area projection,
standard parallels
18° South and 32° South.
Reprinted and Published by the
Government Printer
Private Bag X85, Pretoria 1977

Figure 2.41. Parallel Title with Other Title Information

245	00	‡a 5 children : ‡b a cultural awareness sound filmstrip program for early childhood = 5 niños : un programa bilingüe para la primera enseñanza.
246	3	‡a Five children
246	31	‡a 5 niños
246	3	‡a Cinco niños
264	1	‡a New York, N.Y. : ‡b Scholastic, ‡c [1974]
300		‡a 5 filmstrips, 5 audiocassettes, 2 teacher's guides, 1 wall chart ; ‡c in container 21 x 22 x 5 cm
336		‡a still image ‡a spoken word ‡a text ‡2 rdacontent
337		‡a projected ‡a audio ‡a unmediated ‡2 rdamedia
338		‡a audiocassette ‡a filmstrip ‡a volume ‡a sheet ‡2 rdacarrier
546		‡a Sound recordings in Spanish; text on filmstrips in Spanish; teacher's guides in English.
521	1	‡a 003-008.
530		‡a Also available with sound discs.
520		‡a Teaches children to appreciate cultural differences.
505	0	‡a Vaquero = Cowboy (56 frames) -- Mira mira Marisol = Mira mira Marisol (46 frames) -- Feliz cumpleaños, Howard = Happy birthday, Howard (66 frames) -- Hijo del pescador = Fisherman's son (61 frames) -- La carta de Sara = Sara's letter (56 frames).
710	2	‡a Scholastic Inc., ‡e publisher.

Box cover

5 Children
A Cultural Awareness Sound Filmstrip Program
for Early Childhood

5 Niños
Un Programa Bilingüe para la Primera Enseñanza

Vaquero
Mira Mira Marisol
Feliz Cumpleaños, Howard
Hijo del Pescador
La Carta de Sara

Produced by Scholastic
50 West 44th Street, New York, N.Y. 10036

The website cataloged in figure 2.42 has a title proper and four parallel titles proper. These are all found in different sources in the resource, but there is a sequence as shown by the order of the language links on each page. Remember that because parallel title proper is not core, the cataloger is not required to record any of them, but if in the cataloger's judgment they are useful for identification of or access to the resource, any or all of them may be recorded.

Figure 2.42. Multiple Parallel Titles

110 1	‡a Switzerland. ‡b Bundesrat, ‡e author.
245 14	‡a Der Schweizerische Bundesrat = ‡b Le Conseil fédéral suisse = Il Consiglio federale svizzero = Il Cussegl federal svizzer = The Swiss Federal Council.
246 31	‡a Conseil fédéral suisse
246 31	‡a Consiglio federale svizzero
246 31	‡a Cussegl federal svizzer
246 31	‡a Swiss Federal Council
264 1	‡a [Switzerland] : ‡b Schweizerische Eidgenossenschaft, ‡c [2007]-
264 4	‡c ©2007
300	‡a 1 online resource
336	‡a text ‡2 rdacontent
336	‡a still image ‡2 rdacontent
337	‡a computer ‡2 rdamedia
338	‡a online resource ‡2 rdacarrier
347	‡a text file ‡b HTML ‡2 rda
500	‡a Official website of the Swiss Bundesrat.
856 40	‡u http://www.admin.ch/br/sitemap/index.html?lang=de

Title screen of German language section

Schweizerische Eidgenossenschaft   Der Schweizerische Bundesrat
Confédération suisse
Confederazione Svizzera
Confederaziun svizra
Startseite | Übersicht | Kontakt | Glossar

                                         Deutsch | Français | Italiano | Rumantsch | English

Sometimes a source of information in a resource presenting a translated work gives the original title as well as the title of the translation. This is regarded in RDA as a parallel title even if no text in the language of the parallel title is included in the resource (under previous cataloging practice such a title was only considered a parallel title if the resource included "all or some of the text in the original language," cf. AACR2 1.1D3). The title page of the book cataloged in figure 2.43 includes the original French title *Contes Drolatiques,* but the text is entirely in English. Following RDA 2.3.2.4, the English title is chosen as the title proper and following RDA 2.3.3 the French title is recorded as a parallel title. Under AACR2, the French title would not have been considered a parallel title because none of the text of the resource is in French.

Figure 2.43. Parallel Title Not Corresponding to Any Text in the Resource

100	1	‡a Balzac, Honoré de, ‡d 1799-1850, ‡e author.
240	10	‡a Contes drolatiques. ‡l English
245	10	‡a Droll stories = ‡b Contes drolatiques / ‡c by Honoré de Balzac ; illustrated by Gustave Doré.
246	31	‡a Contes drolatiques
264	1	‡a [Place of publication not identified] : ‡b The Bibliophilist Society, ‡c [between 1920 and 1930?]
300		‡a xxxii, 650 pages : ‡b illustrations ; ‡c 26 cm
336		‡a text ‡2 rdacontent
336		‡a still image ‡2 rdacontent
337		‡a unmediated ‡2 rdamedia
338		‡a volume ‡2 rdacarrier
700	1	‡a Doré, Gustave, ‡d 1832-1883, ‡e illustrator.

Title page

CONTES DROLATIQUES

Droll Stories

by

Honore de Balzac

ILLUSTRATED BY GUSTAVE DORE

THE BIBLIOPHILIST SOCIETY

2.3.4. OTHER TITLE INFORMATION. Other title information is, as its name implies, information about the title or resource aside from the title itself, or, in RDA's definition, "information that appears in conjunction with, and is subordinate to, the title proper of a resource." Unlike parallel titles, which may be recorded if found anywhere in the resource, other title information must be taken from the same source as that chosen for the title proper. It is to be transcribed in the same way as the title proper: exactly as to order, wording, and spelling, but not necessarily following the capitalization and punctuation found in the source (see discussion above at 1.7, 1.7.2, and 1.7.3). In MARC ISBD presentation, other title information recorded in the 245 field is separated from the title proper or other instances of other title information by space-colon-space and preceded by subfield ‡b unless subfields ‡b or ‡c have already appeared (see figure 2.1 and others throughout this chapter; note also figures 2.26, which has two sets of other title information but only one subfield ‡b; figure 2.31c, in which subfield ‡b has already occurred and so is not repeated with the other title information; and figures 2.39 and 2.41, which show the coding of other title information following parallel titles).

Other title information is not a core element and therefore might not be recorded at all. Most catalogers used to AACR2 cataloging will probably continue to record other title information (which has been identified as a core element for the Library of Congress, see LC-PCC PS 2.3.4, April 2010); it should always be recorded if in the judgment of the cataloger the information will help the catalog user find, identify, or select the resource.

In serials cataloging practice, other title information is generally not recorded, because it often varies from issue to issue. AACR2 practice was to record other title information for serials "if considered to be important" (AACR2 12.1E1), and always to record it if an acronym appeared with the full form of the title (the acronym was considered other title information), or if a statement of responsibility naming the responsible entity was an integral part of the other title information (e.g., "newsletter of the Somerset and Dorset Family History Society"). These certainly may be recorded as other title information in an RDA record, but it is not required. For an example of not recording other title information in a serial record, see figure 2.13. Words or phrases conveying only information about currency of contents ("including amendments through 2011") or frequency of updating ("updated daily") should not be considered other title information but should rather be recorded in the frequency element (RDA 2.14).

Lengthy other title information may be abridged using the mark of omission (...) to show where parts have been omitted. Do not omit any of the first five words (see RDA 2.3.1.4, which applies to all titles, including other title information) (see figure 2.21). Alternatively, lengthy other title information pertaining to the bibliographic history of the resource may more appropriately be recorded as a quoted note (see figure 2.44).

If other title information includes a name that would normally be treated as part of a statement of responsibility, but is an integral part of the other title information, record it with the other title information (see RDA 2.3.1.5). The preposition "of" (and its equivalent in other languages) with a name is considered in traditional cataloging practice to be "integral" and so is transcribed in the other title information element when it appears with other title information (see figure 2.45).

Figure 2.44. Other Title Information Recorded as Note

020	‡a 0030206618
100 1	‡a Schulz, Charles M., ‡e author.
245 10	‡a How long, Great Pumpkin, how long? / ‡c by Charles M. Schulz.
264 1	‡a New York : ‡b Holt, Rinehart and Winston, ‡c 1977.
300	‡a 1 volume (unpaged) : ‡b all illustrations ; ‡c 26 cm.
336	‡a text ‡2 rdacontent
336	‡a still image ‡2 rdacontent
337	‡a unmediated ‡2 rdamedia
338	‡a volume ‡2 rdacarrier
490 1	‡a Peanuts parade paperbacks ; ‡v 16
500	‡a "Cartoons from You're the guest of honor, Charlie Brown, and, Win a few, lose a few, Charlie Brown."
590	‡a Brigham Young University copy from the Chad Flake collection, donated by Chad Flake.
830 0	‡a Peanuts parade ; ‡v 16.

Title page

Peanuts Parade 16
How Long, Great Pumpkin, How Long?
Cartoons from You're the Guest of Honor, Charlie Brown
and Win a Few, Lose a Few, Charlie Brown
by Charles M. Schulz
Holt, Rinehart and Winston / New York

Figure 2.45. Statement of Responsibility Integral to Other Title Information

100 1	‡a Doré, Gustave, ‡d 1832-1883, ‡e artist.
245 12	‡a A Doré treasury : ‡b a collection of the best engravings of Gustave Doré / ‡c edited and with an introduction by James Stevens.
264 1	‡a [New York] : ‡b Bounty Books, ‡c [1970]
264 4	‡c ©1970
300	‡a ix, 246 pages : ‡b chiefly illustrations ; ‡c 32 cm
336	‡a text ‡2 rdacontent
336	‡a still image ‡2 rdacontent
337	‡a unmediated ‡2 rdamedia
338	‡a volume ‡2 rdacarrier
700 1	‡a Stevens, James, ‡e editor.

Title page

A Doré Treasury
A Collection of the Best Engravings
of Gustave Doré
edited and with an introduction by
James Stevens

Bounty Books
A Division of Crown Publishers, Inc.

2.3.4.5. SUPPLYING OTHER TITLE INFORMATION FOR CARTOGRAPHIC RESOURCES. In an exception to the "record what you see" philosophy of RDA, if the title proper or other title information of a cartographic resource do not include any indication of the geographic area covered or the subject of the resource, the cataloger may supply this information as other title information (note this is not a core element). Anything the cataloger supplies should be enclosed in brackets, following current MARC practice (see figure 2.31b). This provision is at variance with the principle of representation (see RDA 0.4.3.4). However, the objective of responsiveness to user needs (RDA 0.4.2.1) overrides other principles,[6] and in this case including this information as other title information clearly helps the user find, identify, and select the resource.

2.3.5. PARALLEL OTHER TITLE INFORMATION. Like any other title information, parallel other title information is not core; and it should be recorded only if it appears in the same source as the corresponding parallel title proper or, if there isn't a corresponding parallel title proper, the same source as the title proper. There are a few permutations of how this is recorded in the MARC record. If there is a corresponding parallel title proper, it should be recorded with that title (see figure 2.41). If there is no corresponding parallel title proper, simply record parallel other title information in the order in which it appears. The parallel other title information is preceded by space-equal sign-space (see figure 2.46).[7]

Figure 2.46. Parallel Other Title Information

020	‡a 9788885065178
100 1	‡a Verdi, Giuseppe, ‡d 1813-1901, ‡e composer.
240 10	‡a Traviata (Sketches)
245 13	‡a La traviata : ‡b schizzi e abbozzi autografi = autograph sketches and drafts / ‡c Giuseppe Verdi ; a cura di Fabrizio Della Seta = edited by Fabrizio Della Seta.
264 1	‡a Parma : ‡b Ministero per i beni e le attività culturali, Comitato nazionale per le celebrazioni verdiane : ‡b Istituto nazionale di studi verdiani, ‡c [2000]

300	‡a 2 volumes ; ‡c 43 cm
336	‡a notated music ‡2 rdacontent
336	‡a text ‡2 rdacontent
337	‡a unmediated ‡2 rdamedia
338	‡a volume ‡2 rdacarrier
546	‡a Commentaries in Italian and English.
546	‡b Staff notation.
504	‡a Includes bibliographical references.
700 1	‡a Della Seta, Fabrizio, ‡e editor.
710 2	‡a Istituto di studi verdiani, ‡e publisher.
710 2	‡a Comitato nazionale per le celebrazioni verdiane, ‡e publisher.

Title page

GIUSEPPE VERDI
LA TRAVIATA
Schizzi e abbozzi autografi
Autograph sketches and drafts
a cura di
edited by
Fabrizio Della Seta

MINISTERIO PER I BENI E LE ATTIVITÀ CULTURALI
COMITATO NAZIONALE PER LE CELEBRAZIONI VERDIANE
ISTITUTO NAZIONALE DI STUDI VERDIANI

2.3.6. VARIANT TITLE. The title proper is taken from the preferred source of information of the resource, as described above. In a book, for instance, this is the title page. A variant title will sometimes appear elsewhere in the resource, on the spine or cover of a book, for example. Because some library users are likely to search for the resource using a variant title, variants may be recorded, especially if they are different enough from the title proper that they would file in a different place in the database's alphabetic index, or would give different access through keyword searching from a search on the title proper. The variant title element is not core in RDA, and so it is left to the cataloger's judgment whether recording a variant title would help a user find or identify a resource. If so, it should be recorded.

Title variations within the resource itself (RDA 2.3.6.1a) are recorded in and indexed from the 246 field. The indicators in this field may be used to generate notes automatically. If the cataloger wants the system to generate a note as well as index the variant title, the first indicator should be set to "1." If the cataloger simply wishes the title to be indexed without also generating a display, the first indicator should be set to "3."

The second indicator specifies the type of variant and generates various types of notes (usually with the first indicator set to "1"):

"0" generates the display "Portion of title: [title]"
"1" generates "Parallel title: [title]"
"2" generates "Distinctive title: [title]"
"3" generates "Other title: [title]"
"4" generates "Cover title: [title]"
"5" generates "Added title page title: [title]"
"6" generates "Caption title: [title]"
"7" generates "Running title: [title]"
"8" generates "Spine title: [title]"

A 5XX note should *not* be included in addition to a correctly coded 246 field in the above cases. If the variant title falls outside of these cases, the cataloger may create whatever note is appropriate by leaving the second indicator blank. The field then begins with subfield ‡i, which contains the wording of the note, then subfield ‡a, which contains the variant title. Subfield ‡a is indexed. Because the 246 field does not contain provisions for non-filing characters, initial articles must be dropped. Do not end this field with a full stop.

Figure 2.47 is an example of the use of the 246 field. Significantly different titles from that of the title page of this photography book (which in fact has nothing to do with astronomy) appear on the spine and the cover; if no provision is made for this and the database user types in a search using the spine or cover title he or she will not find the resource. Therefore, the cataloger adds two 246 fields for the variant titles, which will index. The coding will generate the following in the display of the resource description:

Cover title: Easy guide to southern stars
Spine title: Aukland project

Figure 2.47. Variant Title

020	‡a 9781934435267
100 1	‡a Gossage, John R., ‡e photographer.
245 10	‡a Southern stars : ‡b a guide to the constellations visible in the southern hemisphere / ‡c by John Gossage ; with a preface by John Tebbutt.
246 14	‡a Easy guide to southern stars

246 18 ‡a Aukland project
264 1 ‡a Santa Fe : ‡b Radius Books, ‡c [2011]
264 2 ‡a New York, NY : ‡b D.A.P./Distributed Art Publishers
264 4 ‡c ©2011
300 ‡a 2 volumes : ‡b color illustrations ; ‡c 31 cm
336 ‡a still image ‡2 rdacontent
336 ‡a text ‡2 rdacontent
337 ‡a unmediated ‡2 rdamedia
338 ‡a volume ‡2 rdacarrier

Title page
SOUTHERN STARS
A GUIDE TO THE CONSTELLATIONS VISIBLE IN THE SOUTHERN HEMISPHERE
BY JOHN GOSSAGE
With Preface by John Tebbutt, F.R.A.S., of Windsor Observatory, N.S.W.
WITH A MINIATURE STAR ATLAS
RADIUS BOOKS, SANTA FE

Front cover
AN EASY GUIDE TO SOUTHERN STARS

Spine
THE AUKLAND PROJECT

Colophon
Copyright © 2011 RADIUS BOOKS
All photographs copyright ©2011 John Gossage
RADIUS BOOKS 227 E. Palace Ave., Suite W, Santa Fe, NM 87501
Available through
D.A.P./DISTRIBUTED ART PUBLISHERS, 155 Sixth Ave., 2nd Floor, New York, NY 10013
ISBN 13: 978-1-934435-26-7

Field 246 is also used for different titles for which no note is necessary (e.g., for alternative titles or parallel titles). In such cases, the first indicator is coded "3"; this tells the system not to generate a note. The second indicator is "0" for portions of the title (see figures 2.24 and 2.26), "1" for parallel titles (see figures 2.39 through 2.43), and is left blank for other variations that need indexing. For example, the title of the film illustrated in figure 2.48 is given consistently as "The book of Jer3miah" but clearly many library users will attempt to find this resource using the title "The book of Jeremiah." This artificial variant is recorded in a 246 field. For another example of an artificial variant, see figure 2.14.

Figure 2.48. Artificial Variant Title

245 04	‡a The book of Jer3miah. ‡n Season one / ‡c created by Jeff Parkin ; executive producers, Jeff Parkin, Jared Cardon ; directed by Jeff Parkin.
246 3	‡a Book of Jeremiah. ‡n Season one
264 1	‡a [Provo, Utah] : ‡b Tinder Transmedia, ‡c [2012]
264 4	‡c ©2012
300	‡a 1 videodisc (approximately 213 min.) : ‡b sound, color ; ‡c 4 3/4 in.
336	‡a two-dimensional moving image ‡2 rdacontent
337	‡a video ‡2 rdamedia
338	‡a videodisc ‡2 rdacarrier
346	‡b NTSC ‡2 rda
347	‡a video file ‡b DVD video ‡e region 1 ‡2 rda
500	‡a Title from disc label.
508	‡a Head writer, Lyvia Martinez.
511 1	‡a Jared Shores, Jeff Blake, Becca Ingram, Camee Anderson Faulk, Richie Uminsky, Christopher Davis, Jordan Lance Strain.
511 0	‡a Musical score by Ben Carson and Alan Williams.
520	‡a When college freshman Jeremiah Whitney accepts the charge of a mysterious Mesoamerican box, it makes him the target of a terrifying conspiracy.
700 1	‡a Parkin, Jeff, ‡d 1965- ‡e film producer, ‡e film director.
700 1	‡a Cardon, Jared, ‡e film producer.
700 1	‡a Martinez, Lyvia, ‡e screenwriter.

An important kind of artificial variant is the correction of a misspelled word in the title that would affect a user's access to the resource. Under RDA 1.7.9, misspelled words in the title proper are transcribed as found in the source, but if considered important for identification or access, a corrected form is recorded as a variant title (see figure 2.18).

2.3.9. KEY TITLE; 2.3.10. ABBREVIATED TITLE. The key title is a unique title assigned to a serial in conjunction with the ISSN. It is often identical to the title proper, but may be qualified to differentiate it from other identical titles. If found on a serial resource or in another record for the serial, it should be recorded in the 222 field. The first indicator is blank; the second gives the number of non-filing characters in order to give the system instructions to disregard articles in sorting. A second field, 210, records the "abbreviated title." This consists of a title using abbreviated forms of the words in the key title. The first indicator is "1" if the cataloger wishes to index the abbreviated key title; otherwise it is "0." Because key title and abbreviated title are assigned by an ISSN Network national center, and never by catalogers at other institutions, catalogers do not need to worry about producing these titles. However, they should always be recorded if they are known (see figures 2.11a and 2.13).

2.4. STATEMENT OF RESPONSIBILITY. A statement of responsibility is a word or phrase identifying persons, families, or corporate bodies responsible for the intellectual or artistic content of a resource. A statement of responsibility may include, in addition to or instead of names of authors or creators of works, the names of persons, families, or bodies having other responsibility for the resource, such as editors, translators, writers of prefaces, illustrators, etc.

The first statement of responsibility relating to the title proper is core (required). Others may be recorded as well if the cataloger judges them to be important for identification or access.

2.4.1.4. RECORDING STATEMENTS OF RESPONSIBILITY. The statement of responsibility is separated from the title proper and other title information (if any) in a MARC record by space-slash-space. Subfield ‡c appears immediately after the slash. There are generally no further subfields in the 245 field. The statement of responsibility is always recorded in this position (following the title proper and other title information) even if this means transposing the statement when it appears before the title on the source of information (see figures 2.6, 2.17, 2.28, 2.29, and 2.46).

The statement of responsibility is transcribed exactly as it appears in the source of information. Do not add words such as "by" or "and" unless these appear in the source. But if these do appear, transcribe them as you see them. That is, "and" must be transcribed as "and"; the ampersand "&" will be transcribed as "&" (see figure 2.49). Do not abbreviate any word in a statement of responsibility unless it is abbreviated in the source, in which case transcribe it just as it appears.

Figure 2.49. Statement of Responsibility

```
100 1   ‡a Foeken, D., ‡e author.
245 10  ‡a Tied to the land : ‡b household resources and living conditions of labourers on
        large farms in Trans Nzoia District, Kenya / ‡c Dick Foeken & Nina Tellegen.
264  1  ‡a [Aldershot, England] : ‡b Avebury, ‡c [1994]
264  4  ‡c ©1994
300     ‡a xii, 152 pages : ‡b illustrations, maps ; ‡c 24 cm.
336     ‡a text ‡2 rdacontent
336     ‡a still image ‡2 rdacontent
```

336	‡a cartographic image ‡2 rdacontent
337	‡a unmediated ‡2 rdamedia
338	‡a volume ‡2 rdacarrier
490 1	‡a African Studies Centre research series ; ‡v 1
504	‡a Includes bibliographical references (pages 155-157).
700 1	‡a Tellegen, Nina, ‡e author.
830 0	‡a African Studies Centre research series ; ‡v 1.

Title page

African Studies Centre
Research Series
1/1994
Tied to the land
Household resources and living conditions of
labourers on large farms in Trans Nzoia District,
Kenya
Dick Foeken & Nina Tellegen

Avebury

Generally do not leave out words or otherwise abridge statements of responsibility. However, RDA optionally allows words to be omitted if this does not entail "loss of essential information." This guideline refers to words such as titles, initials, qualifications, etc., that AACR2 1.1F7 required to be omitted. If following the optional omission, do not indicate the omission by using the mark of omission (...); just silently omit the information. This *Handbook* shows both practices. For a fully transcribed statement of responsibility, see figure 2.21. For an example following the optional omission, see figure 2.47.

Statements of responsibility are included in serial records if present on the source, particularly if they name a corporate body that is also the issuing body (not just the publisher) (see figure 2.50). However, statements identifying an editor are only recorded if the editor is "considered to be an important means of identifying the serial," meaning he or she edited the serial for all or nearly all of its existence. Because the editor usually changes during a serial's existence, statements identifying an editor are generally not recorded. A statement of responsibility naming an editor appears on the verso of the cover of the serial cataloged in figure 2.50, but it will not be recorded in the description.

Caution: before recording persons, families, or corporate bodies found on the source as a statement of responsibility, make sure the phrase really *is* a statement of responsibility. Sometimes a person's name is included on the source simply because

Figure 2.50. Statement of Responsibility for Serial

022 0	‡a 1540-7063
245 10	‡a Integrative and comparative biology / ‡c the Society for Integrative and Comparative Biology.
264 1	‡a McLean, VA : ‡b The Society for Integrative and Comparative Biology, ‡c [2002]-
300	‡a volumes : ‡b illustrations ; ‡c 26 cm
310	‡a Six issues yearly
336	‡a text ‡2 rdacontent
336	‡a still image ‡2 rdacontent
337	‡a unmediated ‡2 rdamedia
338	‡a volume ‡2 rdacarrier
362 1	‡a Began with Volume 42, number 1 (February 2002)
588	‡a Description based on: Volume 42, number 1 (February 2002); title from cover.
588	‡a Latest issue consulted: Volume 51, number 4 (October 2011).
710 2	‡a Society for Integrative and Comparative Biology, ‡e issuing body.
780 00	‡a American zoologist ‡x 0003-1569

Cover

Integrative and
Comparative Biology

The Society for Integrative and Comparative Biology

Formerly American Zoologist
Volume 42 Number 1
February 2002

Verso of Cover

John S. Edwards, Editor
University of Washington
Copyright © 2002 by the Society for Integrative and Comparative Biology

---

he or she happens to head an agency responsible for publication or production of the resource. In the resource cataloged in figure 2.51, Weldon P. Shofstall has no responsibility for the work, and is only named because he heads the Department of Education.

2.4.1.5. STATEMENT NAMING MORE THAN ONE PERSON, ETC. RDA instructs the cataloger to "record a statement of responsibility naming more than one person, etc., as a single statement." This simple statement masks a major change from AACR2 practice,

Figure 2.51. Named Person Not Part of a Statement of Responsibility

245 04	‡a The Myers Demonstration Library : ‡b an ESEA Title III project.	
264 1	‡a Phoenix : ‡b Arizona Department of Education, ‡c [1971]	
300	‡a 1 volume (unpaged) ; ‡c 28 cm	
336	‡a text ‡2 rdacontent	
336	‡a still image ‡2 rdacontent	
337	‡a unmediated ‡2 rdamedia	
338	‡a volume ‡2 rdacarrier	
500	‡a Title from cover.	
710 1	‡a Arizona. ‡b Department of Education.	

Title page

> The Myers Demonstration Library
> An ESEA Title III Project
> Arizona
> Department of Education
> W.P. Shofstall, Ph.D., Superintendent

which limited the number of names that could be recorded in a single statement of responsibility to three (AACR2 1.1F5). This was informally referred to as "the rule of three." There is no such limitation in RDA. The basic guideline is to record all the names (see figure 2.52; note that this figure also illustrates the optional omission of "inessential" information of RDA 2.4.1.4). RDA recognizes that there are limits to the amount of information that can be recorded, however, and this guideline includes an option to omit names if more than three names appear in the statement. Simply leave any but the first off and summarize what was omitted (see figure 2.15). RDA's abandonment of the rule of three marks an important step forward in giving access to persons, families, or corporate bodies that would formerly have been entirely omitted from descriptions of resources, and this *Handbook* encourages catalogers to record all names found in most cases rather than following the optional omission.

Figure 2.52. Multiple Names in Statement of Responsibility

020	‡a 0412453002
100 1	‡a Gross, Trevor, ‡e author.
245 10	‡a Introductory microbiology / ‡c Trevor Gross, Jane Faull, Steve Ketteridge and Derek Springham.
250	‡a First edition.
264 1	‡a London : ‡b Chapman & Hall University & Professional Division, ‡c 1995.

300	‡a xiv, 414 pages : ‡b illustrations ; ‡c 25 cm
336	‡a text ‡2 rdacontent
336	‡a still image ‡2 rdacontent
337	‡a unmediated ‡2 rdamedia
338	‡a volume ‡2 rdacarrier
500	‡a Includes index.
590	‡a Brigham Young University copy water damaged.
700 1	‡a Faull, Jane, ‡e author.
700 1	‡a Ketteridge, Steve, ‡e author.
700 1	‡a Springham, Derek, ‡e author.

Title page

Introductory Microbiology

Trevor Gross
Principal Lecturer, Department of Biological Sciences,
The Manchester Metropolitan University

Jane Faull
Department of Biology, Birbeck College, University of London

Steve Ketteridge
Staff Development Officer, Queen Mary and Westfield College, University of London

and

Derek Springham
Queen Mary and Westfield College, University of London

Chapman & Hall
University and Professional Division
London Glasgow Weinheim New York Tokyo Melbourne Madras

2.4.1.6. MORE THAN ONE STATEMENT OF RESPONSIBILITY. If there are multiple statements of responsibility given in a resource, the cataloger *may* record them (remember only the first is core) in the order they are found. Separate statements by space-semicolon-space. For examples, see figures 2.2, 2.3, 2.5, 2.6, and others throughout this chapter.

2.4.1.7. CLARIFICATION OF ROLE. If the relationship between the person, family, or corporate body named in a statement of responsibility and the resource is not clear, the cataloger may add a word or phrase in square brackets (see figure 2.53). Caution:

this is only done if the relationship is genuinely unclear. In most cases statements are recorded as is, even if there is no accompanying wording (e.g., "by"). In the case of figure 2.53, the word was added to make clear that Arnold is not the author or artist that created the pictures and stories.

Figure 2.53. Clarification of Role

020	‡a 0486220419
245 00	‡a Pictures and stories from forgotten children's books / ‡c [selected] by Arnold Arnold.
264 1	‡a New York : ‡b Dover Publications, Inc., ‡c [1969]
264 4	‡c ©1969
300	‡a viii, 170 pages : ‡b illustrations ; ‡c 21 x 23 cm.
336	‡a text ‡2 rdacontent
336	‡a still image ‡2 rdacontent
337	‡a unmediated ‡2 rdamedia
338	‡a volume ‡2 rdacarrier
490 1	‡a Dover pictorial archive series
504	‡a Includes bibliographical references.
700 1	‡a Arnold, Arnold, ‡e editor of compilation.
830 0	‡a Dover pictorial archive series.

Title page

Pictures and Stories from
Forgotten Children's Books
By Arnold Arnold
Dover Publications, Inc., New York

2.4.1.8. NOUN PHRASES OCCURRING WITH A STATEMENT OF RESPONSIBILITY. This RDA guideline represents a simplification of earlier cataloging practice. Under AACR2 1.1F12 the cataloger had to figure out whether a noun phrase was "indicative of the nature of the work" or not. If it was, the phrase was recorded as part of other title information. If, instead, it was "indicative of the role" of the entity named, the phrase was recorded as part of the statement of responsibility. Under RDA any noun or noun phrase that occurs with a statement of responsibility will be recorded with the statement of responsibility. See figures 2.8 (where "studies" would have been considered other title information in AACR2) and 2.23 (where "reports and papers" would have been other title information).

2.4.1.9. NO PERSON, FAMILY, OR CORPORATE BODY NAMED IN THE STATEMENT OF RESPONSIBIL-ITY. Statements that would be considered statements of responsibility for the resource if a person, family, or corporate body were named are recorded. As an example of this, no one is explicitly named in the statement of responsibility recorded in figure 2.54. Caution: a source may contain a phrase that seems somewhat like a statement of responsibility but is not. In figure 2.21 the foot of the title page includes the statement "with numerous engravings." This is not a statement of responsibility because it simply gives information about the content; it does not specify or imply any kind of responsibility. Because it is also not a title, it is not recorded in the title or statement of responsibility elements. If the information is considered important for identification or access (this will be rare), it may be recorded in a note.

Figure 2.54. Unnamed Bodies in Statement of Responsibility

245 00	‡a General education in school and college / ‡c a committee report by members of the faculties of Andover, Exeter, Lawrenceville, Harvard, Princeton, and Yale.
264 1	‡a Cambridge, Massachusetts : ‡b Harvard University Press, ‡c 1953.
300	‡a v, 142 pages ; ‡c 22 cm
336	‡a text ‡2 rdacontent
337	‡a unmediated ‡2 rdamedia
338	‡a volume ‡2 rdacarrier

Title page

General Education
in School and College
A Committee Report
By Members of the Faculties of
Andover, Exeter, Lawrenceville,
Harvard, Princeton, and Yale
Harvard University Press
Cambridge, Massachusetts
1953

2.4.2. STATEMENT OF RESPONSIBILITY RELATING TO TITLE PROPER.

2.4.2.2. SOURCES OF INFORMATION. In a change from previous cataloging practice, statements of responsibility can be taken from anywhere in the resource itself without bracketing. For example, the statement of responsibility about the translator in figure 2.55 was taken from the verso of the title page, and would have been bracketed under AACR2. Statements of responsibility can also be taken from other sources, but this would be rare. In RDA, only statements taken from outside the resource need to be bracketed.

Figure 2.55. Statement of Responsibility from Verso of Title Page

020		‡a 9781402052347
020		‡a 1402052340
100	1	‡a Weizsäcker, Carl Friedrich, ‡c Freiherr von, ‡d 1912-2007, ‡e author.
240	10	‡a Aufbau der Physik. ‡l English
245	14	‡a The structure of physics / ‡c by Carl Friedrich von Weizsäcker ; edited, revised and enlarged by Thomas Görnitz and Holger Lyre ; translated into English by Helmut Biritz.
264	1	‡a Dordrecht, The Netherlands : ‡b Springer, ‡c [2006]
264	4	‡c ©2006
300		‡a xxxiii, 360 pages : ‡b illustrations ; ‡c 25 cm.
336		‡a text ‡2 rdacontent
336		‡a still image ‡2 rdacontent
337		‡a unmediated ‡2 rdamedia
338		‡a volume ‡2 rdacarrier
490	1	‡a Fundamental theories of physics ; ‡v volume 154
504		‡a Includes bibliographical references (pages 347-352) and index.
700	1	‡a Görnitz, Thomas, ‡e editor.
700	1	‡a Lyre, Holger, ‡e editor.
700	1	‡a Biritz, Helmut, ‡e translator.
830	0	‡a Fundamental theories of physics ; ‡v v. 154.

Title page

The Structure of Physics
by Carl Friedrich von Weizsäcker
edited, revised and enlarged by
Thomas Görnitz, University of Frankfurt, Germany
and
Holger Lyre, University of Bonn, Germany

Springer

Title page verso

Published by Springer,
P.O. Box 17, 3300 AA Dordrecht, The Netherlands
Original version: *Aufbau der Physik,* Hanser Verlag, Munich, 1985.
Translated into English by Helmut Biritz, Georgia Institute of Technology, School of Physics, Atlanta, USA.
©2006 Springer

Series title page
Fundamental Theories of Physics
An international book series on the fundamental theories of physics: their clarification, development, and application.
Editor: Alwyn Van der Merwe, University of Denver, U.S.A.

2.4.3. PARALLEL STATEMENT OF RESPONSIBILITY RELATING TO TITLE PROPER. Just as resources may exhibit parallel titles proper and parallel other title information, they may also exhibit parallel statements of responsibility. A parallel statement of responsibility is a statement of responsibility that is in a language or script different from that recorded in a statement of responsibility related to the title proper. This element is not core, and should be recorded only if it appears in the same source as the corresponding parallel title proper, or, if there isn't a corresponding parallel title proper, the same source as the title proper. As with parallel other title information, there are a few variations on how this is recorded in the MARC record. If there is a corresponding parallel title proper, it should be recorded with that title (see figure 2.40). If there is no corresponding parallel title proper, simply record a parallel statement of responsibility in the order in which it appears. The parallel statement of responsibility is preceded by space-equal sign-space (see figure 2.46). The resource cataloged in figure 2.46 exhibits a special problem: the name "Fabrizio Della Seta" is intended to be read with both statement of responsibility phrases, but only appears once on the title page. RDA 1.7.7, "Letters or Words Intended to Be Read More Than Once," deals with this problem. Simply repeat the name as appropriate in the transcription.

2.5. EDITION STATEMENT. In the book world, one definition of edition is "the whole number of copies printed from the same set of types and issued at the same time."[8] This is the most traditional definition of the term, and as such it sounds somewhat like the FRBR definition of manifestation. However, this is not the only meaning of "edition." When we say that a text exists in different editions, we mean that the original text has been revised in some way and issued again. "Edition" in this sense corresponds in many ways to the FRBR expression entity. So the much-used word "edition" unfortunately does not correspond to any FRBR entity exactly. However, the term "edition statement" *does* correspond to a FRBR entity, the manifestation. An edition statement is a word or group of words appearing in a resource (manifestation) identifying the edition to which the resource belongs, and it can refer to "edition" in either sense discussed above.

Recall that an expression can be embodied in many manifestations. If one of the senses of "edition" roughly corresponds to the definition of expression, then the same edition may be said to exist in numerous manifestations. Those manifestations may, however, have different edition *statements* describing the same edition. One may say "First edition"; another might say "1st edition"; another might say "Edition the first"; another manifestation might not have any statement at all. This is how edition *statement* is an attribute of manifestation—because edition statements for the same edition might differ between manifestations, this is one method we can use to differentiate between manifestations.

2.5.1.4. RECORDING EDITION STATEMENTS. Just as with titles, an edition statement is to be transcribed exactly as to wording and spelling, but not necessarily as to capitalization and punctuation (see discussion of RDA 1.7, above). This represents a significant change from previous cataloging practice. Under AACR2 words were abbreviated if they appeared in the AACR2 abbreviations appendix (appendix B) and numerals were also modified according to AACR2's appendix C. Thus, an edition statement that read "Second edition" on the source would be recorded "2nd ed." This will not be done in RDA. This same edition statement will be transcribed exactly as it appears, "Second edition." On the other hand, if abbreviations appear in the resource, copy them exactly as you see them. Most of the examples for RDA 2.5.1.4 include abbreviated words, and this may mislead the unwary. It must be assumed that all of these statements with abbreviations appeared that way on the source. For examples, see 250 fields in figures 2.14, 2.16, 2.17, and others throughout this chapter. For an example of an edition statement consisting of a single word, see figure 2.30.

The cataloger is required to record a designation of edition as found, but a statement such as "35th impression" or "9th printing" may generally be ignored, because it usually simply means that more copies of the resource have been made. Unless a cataloger is working in a specialized environment (for example, a library which collects all printings of a particular author's works and needs to distinguish between them) such a statement would only be recorded if the cataloger knew that there *was* some significant difference, either in content or format, between one printing or impression and another.

2.5.2. DESIGNATION OF EDITION. The designation of edition element is usually the first part of the edition statement (which may include other parts, such as a statement of responsibility). If it appears in a resource, it must be recorded, because the element is designated as core. The designation of edition is transcribed in subfield ‡a of the 250 field of the MARC record.

2.5.2.1. SCOPE. Printers and publishers have no regard for the cataloger's convenience in their use of bibliographical terminology. Even when the publisher uses the word "edition" or its equivalent in another language, the cataloger cannot assume that the work in hand is indeed different from other issues of the work. This is especially true in regard to many French and Latin American publications; RDA 2.5.2.1 states that in some languages "the same term or terms may be used to designate both edition and printing. A statement detailing the number of copies printed is not a designation of edition." RDA then gives a list of tips that may help to determine if these slippery words really are a "designation of edition." However, the cataloger is not required be an expert on all the vagaries of publishing practices worldwide, much less to compare copies to verify the validity of an edition statement. If you simply cannot decide, take the word "edition" or its equivalent at face value and record it as a designation of edition.

Music title pages frequently use the word "edition" to indicate the arrangement or form of the work, as "edition for 2 pianos," in figure 2.56. Such statements are designations of edition. For another designation of edition in a music description, see figure 2.57.

Figure 2.56. Designation of Edition

024 2	‡a M003027920	
028 22	‡a H.S. 2287 ‡b H. Sikorski	
100 1	‡a Prokofiev, Sergey, ‡d 1891-1953, ‡e composer.	
240 10	‡a Concertos, ‡m piano, 1 hand, orchestra, ‡n op. 53, ‡r B major; ‡o arranged	
245 10	‡a Konzert Nr. 4 für Klavier (linke hand) und Orchester, B-Dur, opus 53 / ‡c Sergej Prokofjew = Concerto no. 4 for piano (left hand) and orchestra, B-flat major, opus 53 / Sergei Prokofiev.	
250	‡a Ausgabe für 2 Klaviere / ‡b von Anatoli Wedernikow = Edition for 2 pianos / by Anatoly Vedernikov.	
264 1	‡a Hamburg ; ‡b Musikverlag Hans Sikorski ; ‡a London : ‡b Boosey & Hawkes Music Publishers ltd. ; ‡a New York : ‡b G. Schirmer Inc., ‡c [1995]	
264 4	‡c ©1995	
300	‡a 1 score (55 pages) ; 32 cm.	
336	‡a notated music ‡2 rdacontent	
337	‡a unmediated ‡2 rdamedia	
338	‡a volume ‡2 rdacarrier	
490 1	‡a Sikmuz	
500	‡a Duration: approximately 24 min.	
546	‡b Staff notation.	
700 1	‡a Vedernikov, Anatoliĭ, ‡e editor.	
830 0	‡a Sikmuz.	

Title page

Sergej Prokofjew	Sergei Prokofiev
Konzert Nr. 4	Concerto No. 4
für Klavier (linke Hand)	for Piano (left hand)

und Orchester	and Orchestra
B-Dur opus 53	B flat major Opus 53
Ausgabe für 2 Klaviere	Edition for 2 Pianos
von Anatoli Wedernikow	By Anatoly Vedernikov

Boosey & Hawkes Music Publishers Ltd., London
G. Schirmer Inc., New York

MUSIKVERLAG HANS SIKORSKI, HAMBURG

Foot of first page of music

©1995 by Musikverlag Hans Sikorski, Hamburg

H.S. 2287

Back cover

ISMN M-003-02792-0   edition sikorski

Figure 2.57. Designation of Edition

028 32 ‡a 042 ‡b Comus Edition

100 1 ‡a Richardson, Alan, ‡d 1904-1978,‡e composer.

245 10 ‡a Sussex lullaby : ‡b for viola (or cello) and piano / ‡c Alan Richardson.

250 ‡a Revised edition / ‡b prepared by John White.

264 1 ‡a Colne, Lancashire, Great Britain : ‡b Comus Edition, ‡c [1995]

264 4 ‡c ©1995

300 ‡a 1 score (7 pages) + 2 parts ; ‡c 30 cm

336 ‡a notated music ‡2 rdacontent

337 ‡a unmediated ‡2 rdamedia

338 ‡a volume ‡2 rdacarrier

500 ‡a Viola and cello parts printed on opposite sides of a single leaf.

546 ‡b Staff notation.

500 ‡a Duration: approximately 3 min.

700 ‡a White, John, ‡d 1938- ‡e editor.

Title page

Cat. no. 042
Alan Richardson
Sussex Lullaby
for Viola (or Cello) and Piano

Revised edition prepared by John White

Comus Edition, Heirs House Lane, Colne, Lancashire, Great Britain

Foot of first page of music

© Copyright 1995 Comus Edition

The definition of "edition" is quite inclusive in the case of electronic resources, and because many commercially produced electronic resources are either new versions of older resources or anticipate future versions, a designation of edition will almost always be present. Words within a statement, such as "edition," "issue," "release," "level," "update," or most commonly, "version" (often abbreviated to "v"), are evidence that the statement is a designation of edition. A word standing alone without the presence of such a word may also be a designation of edition. For example, the word "Wii" in figure 2.58 designates "a particular format" (RDA 2.5.2.1e). Unusual statements, or a number standing alone, may also constitute edition statements. In the latter case, a bracketed word such as "[Version]" should be added (see RDA 2.5.2.3 with figure 2.59).

Figure 2.58. Designation of Edition—Format

```
024 1    ‡a 834656084554
028 52   ‡a RVL P SJQE ‡b GameMill
245 00   ‡a Jewel quest trilogy.
250      ‡a Wii.
264  1   ‡a Edina, MN : ‡b GameMill Entertainment, Inc., ‡c [2010]
264  4   ‡c ©2010
300      ‡a 1 computer disc : ‡b sound, color ; ‡c 4 3/4 in. + ‡e 1 instruction booklet (7 pages
         : illustrations ; 18 cm)
336      ‡a computer program ‡2 rdacontent
336      ‡a text ‡2 rdacontent
336      ‡a still image ‡2 rdacontent
337      ‡a computer ‡2 rdamedia
338      ‡a computer disc ‡2 rdacarrier
338      ‡a volume ‡2 rdacarrier
347      ‡a program file ‡b DVD-ROM ‡2 rda
538      ‡a System requirements: Nintendo Wii.
500      ‡a Title from disc label.
521 8    ‡a ESRB rating: Everyone 10+ (violent references, alcohol and tobacco reference).
520      ‡a "Collect jewels, travel to exotic locations to unlock secrets, and restore balance to
         the Earth with a mystical Mah Jong experience!"--Container.
505 0    ‡a Jewel Quest -- Jewel Quest mysteries -- Mahjong Quest.
500      ‡a "Game developed by iWin Software, Inc."--Container.
710 2    ‡a GameMill Entertainment, Inc., ‡e publisher.
710 2    ‡a iWin Software, Inc.
```

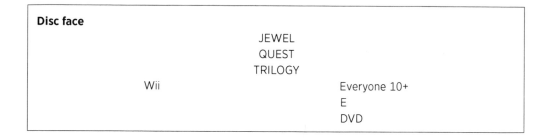

Figure 2.59. Designation of Edition—Number Standing Alone

245	00	‡a ArcGIS Desktop.
246	3	‡a ArcGIS Desktop 10
250		‡a [Version] 10.
264	1	‡a Redlands, CA : ‡b ESRI, ‡c [2010]
264	4	‡c ©2010
300		‡a 4 DVD-ROMs ; ‡c 4 3/4 in. + ‡e 1 booklet (16 cm)
336		‡a computer program ‡2 rdacontent
337		‡a computer ‡2 rdamedia
338		‡a computer disc ‡2 rdacontent
347		‡a program file ‡b DVD-ROM ‡2 rda
500		‡a Accompanying booket entitled: ArcGIS Desktop Tips and Shortcuts.
520		‡a Contains integrated applications that are intended to be used with ArcView, ArcEditor, and ArcInfo in order to do comprehensive mapping and geographical analysis.
505	0	‡a ArcGIS Desktop -- ArcGIS Desktop Tutorial Data -- ArcReader -- ArcInfo Workstation.
500		‡a Title from disc face.
710	2	‡a Esri (Redlands, Calif.), ‡e publisher.

2.5.2.2. SOURCES OF INFORMATION. A designation of edition may be taken from any source within the resource itself, although if one is found in the same source as the title proper, that designation will be preferred over other versions of the same designation that might be found elsewhere. Previous cataloging practice was somewhat more rigid about places within a resource that could be used to provide edition information without bracketing. In RDA an edition statement is bracketed only if it comes from outside the resource itself, and this will be rare.

2.5.2.4. DESIGNATION OF EDITION IN MORE THAN ONE LANGUAGE OR SCRIPT. If a resource contains a designation of edition in more than one language, record the designation that matches the language of the title proper. Figure 2.40 includes such a statement. The title proper on the map is Afrikaans; therefore the Afrikaans-language edition statement is recorded rather than the English-language statement (concerning the parallel designation of edition, see below at 2.5.3; see also figure 2.56).

2.5.2.5. STATEMENTS INDICATING REGULAR REVISION OR NUMBERING. The cataloger must be cautious about statements in serials that seem to be designations of edition. Sometimes these are simply statements of frequency or numbering. See the discussion of this problem above at 1.6.2.5.

2.5.2.6. DESIGNATION OF EDITION INTEGRAL TO TITLE PROPER, ETC. Sometimes designations of edition are presented as an integral part of the title proper, other title information, or statement of responsibility. If this occurs, transcribe the information there and do not repeat it in the Designation of Edition element. See figure 2.60, where the designation of edition "re-edition" is integral to other title information.

Figure 2.60. Edition Statement Integral to Other Title Information

020	ǂa 9783110212242
100 1	ǂa Kockelmann, Holger, ǂe author.
245 10	ǂa Praising the goddess : ǂb a comparative and annotated re-edition of six demotic hymns and praises addressed to Isis / ǂc Holger Kockelmann.
264 1	ǂa Berlin : ǂb Walter de Gruyter, ǂc [2008]
264 4	ǂc ©2008
300	ǂa ix, 131 pages : ǂb illustrations ; ǂc 25 cm.
336	ǂa text ǂ2 rdacontent
337	ǂa unmediated ǂ2 rdamedia
338	ǂa volume ǂ2 rdacarrier
490 1	ǂa Archiv für Papyrusforschung und verwandte Gebiete. Beiheft ; ǂv 15
500	ǂa Originally presented as the author's thesis (master's)--University of Oxford, 2001.
504	ǂa Includes bibliographical references (pages 107-131) and indexes.
830 0	ǂa Archiv für Papyrusforschung und verwandte Gebiete. ǂp Beiheft ; ǂv 15.

Title page

Praising the Goddess
A Comparative and Annotated Re-Edition
of Six Demotic Hymns and Praises
Addressed to Isis
by
Holger Kockelmann

Note that the words "the 2nd German edition" in the statement of responsibility shown in figure 2.6, although an edition statement, is *not* an edition statement related to the resource in hand and so will be recorded as part of the statement of responsibility, not the designation of edition.

2.5.3. PARALLEL DESIGNATION OF EDITION. Just as titles proper, other title information, and statements of responsibility sometimes appear on a resource in more than one language, so do designations of edition. Because this element is not core, it is not required to transcribe a parallel designation of edition; but if the cataloger judges it useful it may be recorded following the designation edition, separated by space-equal sign-space (see figures 2.40 and 2.56).

2.5.4. STATEMENTS OF RESPONSIBILITY RELATING TO THE EDITION. Occasionally an edition statement is followed by a statement of responsibility pertaining only to the edition in hand (e.g., it may name a reviser, an illustrator, or someone who has performed some other function just for the particular edition). If this is the case, such a statement of responsibility may be transcribed (note that this element is not core), following space-slash-space, as part of the edition area. Precede the statement of responsibility by subfield ‡b. In transcribing this statement of responsibility, follow all applicable rules for transcription, punctuation, spacing, etc., as given in RDA 1.7 (see figure 2.57).

Sometimes a resource contains a statement of responsibility that relates to the edition but no designation of edition. Such statements are recorded as statements of responsibility relating to the title proper (see figure 2.55).

2.5.6. DESIGNATION OF A NAMED REVISION OF AN EDITION. Sometimes an edition statement includes a statement naming a revision of the edition named in the designation of edition. If so, this should be recorded after the designation of edition, separated by a comma (see figure 2.61).

Figure 2.61. Named Revision of an Edition

110 2 ‡a National Institute of Standards and Technology (U.S.), ‡e author.

245 10 ‡a Codes for the identification of federal and federally assisted organizations : ‡b recommendations of the National Institute of Standards and Technology / ‡c William C. Barker, Hildegard Ferraiolo.

250 ‡a Version 1.0, January 2006 edition.

264 1 ‡a Gaithersburg, MD : ‡b U.S. Department of Commerce, Technology Administration, National Institute of Standards and Technology, ‡c 2006.

300 ‡a 1 online resource (102 pages)

336 ‡a text ‡2 rdacontent

337 ‡a computer ‡2 rdamedia

338 ‡a online resource ‡2 rdacarrier

347 ‡a text file ‡b PDF ‡2 rda

490 1 ‡a NIST special publication. ; ‡v 800-87

500 ‡a Title from PDF title page.

700 1 ‡a Barker, William C. ‡q (William Curt), ‡e author.

700 1 ‡a Ferraiolo, Hildegard, ‡e author.

830 0 ‡a NIST special publication. ; ‡v 800-87.

856 40 ‡u http://purl.access.gpo.gov/GPO/LPS69959

PDF title page

NIST
National Institute of
Standards and Technology
Technology Administration
U.S. Department of Commerce

Special Publication 800-87
Version 1.0
January 2006 edition

Codes for the Identification of Federal and Federally Assisted Organizations
Recommendations of the National Institute of Standards and Technology

William C. Barker
Hildegard Ferraiolo

2.6. NUMBERING OF SERIALS. Numbering of serials is defined in RDA 2.6.1.1 as "the identification of each of the issues or parts of a serial." It is somewhat odd that the element is called "*numbering* of serials" because this identification can consist of non-numeric data such as letters or "any other character" or combination of letters, characters, and numerals, and may include a caption such as "volume," "number" or "issue" if present in the source. The element as a whole includes both numbering and chronological designations for the issues of the serial.

This element is designated as core, but because the information must be taken from the first or last issue or part of the serial, it is only recorded if that issue or part is available (see RDA 2.6.1.2 and the guidelines listed there for the various numbering sub-elements). "Available" in this context means that either the cataloger has actual access to the issues or parts, or has reliable information about them, e.g., an RDA record cataloged by another institution which did have access to the issues or parts, or images of the issues or parts. If this information is not available the element is normally omitted, although RDA 2.2.4 does allow information to be taken from other sources. If such information is used in this element it should be bracketed, but most serials catalogers would instead give the information in a note (see below under 2.20.5.3).

2.6.1.4. RECORDING NUMBERING OF SERIALS. This instruction is somewhat complex because it combines two practices, "recording" a number following RDA 1.8, but "transcribing" other words or characters exactly as they appear in the resource. As a reminder, RDA 1.8 says to "record numerals in the form preferred by the agency creating the data," which may be different from that found in the resource. For example, an agency might prefer always to use arabic rather than roman numerals; or indeed the form preferred by the agency might be the form in which it appears on the resource (see RDA 1.8.2 alternative). The latter is the preference of the Library of Congress (LC-PCC PS 1.8.2, February 2010).

The numbering of serials element is recorded in MARC bibliographic field 362 with the first indicator coded "0." MARC calls this "formatted style."

2.6.2–2.6.5. NUMERIC, ALPHABETIC, AND/OR CHRONOLOGICAL DESIGNATION. Four sub-elements—the numeric/alphabetic designation of the first or last part, and the chronological designation of the first or last part—will be treated together here because the instructions are the same for each. Remember, however, that the source for each is the first or last issue or part as appropriate. Catalogers may not record inferred information (e.g., obtained by deducing information about the first issue from a later issue).

Both numeric/alphabetic and chronological designations are recorded in subfield ‡a of the 362 field. If both are recorded together, the numeric/alphabetic designation is recorded first and the chronological designation follows in parentheses (see figures 2.12a and 2.13). If a designation relating to the first part or issue is recorded alone, it is followed by a dash (see figure 2.12b). If a designation relating to the last part or issue is recorded alone, it is preceded by a dash (see figure 2.11a). If designations relating to both the first and last part or issue are recorded, they are separated by a dash (see figures 2.12a and 2.13).

These figures illustrate some issues about recording these designations in RDA. In figure 2.12a, the first issue of *Bulletin* has the designation "No. 1"; the last has the designation "Volume V, no. 5/6." These are recorded exactly as they appear, even though this means the styles of the two designations are different.

Figure 2.13 illustrates the application of RDA 1.8.3, "numbers expressed as words." RDA 1.8.3 tells us to substitute numerals for numbers expressed as words. The first and last issues of this serial had "first edition" and "third edition." Following 1.8.3 these are rendered "1st edition" and "3rd edition." Note that the instructions in 1.8 apply only to a limited set of RDA elements, including the elements being discussed here. RDA 1.8 does *not* apply to any of the edition statement elements and sub-elements (RDA 2.5), so if these words had been recorded as an edition statement rather than numbering (see discussion above under 1.6.2.5) they would have remained spelled out.

Alternative instructions. Each of the sub-elements described in RDA 2.6.2–2.6.5 contains an alternative to make a note on the numbering following RDA 2.20.5.3 rather than recording this information in the numbering of serials element. This note is a less formal way of recording the same information as found in the numbering of serials element (RDA 2.6). LC and PCC will generally follow the alternative instruction in each case (see LC-PCC PSs for RDA 2.6.2.3–2.6.5.3, September 2012). Following the alternative satisfies the core requirement of RDA 2.6. For information on how to apply the alternative, see below under 2.20.5.

2.7. PRODUCTION STATEMENT. The production statement element is used in descriptions of unpublished resources. There is no guidance in RDA about the difference between "unpublished" and "published." "Publication" usually means to issue copies of a resource to the public, whether for free distribution or for sale. This often refers to printed copies, but this is not required. RDA ultimately leaves the question of whether a resource is published or not to the cataloger's judgment. Note that all online resources (e.g., Internet resources) are considered published (see RDA 2.8.1.1 as revised July 2013). This would include reproductions of unpublished resources such as theses or manuscripts.

If a cataloger determines that a resource is unpublished, RDA 2.7, Production Statement, applies to its description. There are three basic sub-elements: place of production, producer's name, and date of production. Of these, only date of production is core, so in most cases this is the only part of the production statement that will be recorded, although if the place and producer are known they may also be recorded. The production statement element is recorded in the MARC bibliographic 264 field with the second indicator coded "0."

2.7.2. PLACE OF PRODUCTION. If it appears in the resource or is otherwise known, the place of production of an unpublished resource may be recorded in subfield ‡a of the MARC 264 field. If the name of the place appears in the resource it should be transcribed as is. If it is taken from another source it should be bracketed. In the document described in figure 2.62, "The Observatory," that is, the Royal Observatory of which the author was the founder, is identified as the place it was written. The cataloger was able to infer from this the place of production, but because it is not explicitly stated in the resource it is recorded in brackets. Because the place of production element is not core, however, in most cases it is omitted from descriptions of unpublished resources (see figure 2.63).

Figure 2.62. Place of Production

100	1	‡a Flamsteed, John, ‡d 1646-1719, ‡e author.
245	14	‡a The description and uses of an instrument for finding [th]e true places of [th]e sun & Jupitor with the eclipses of [Jupiter]'s satellites and their configurations at all times / ‡c by John Flamsteed.
264	0	‡a [Greenwich, London, England] : ‡b [John Flamsteed], ‡c 1685 August 4.
300		‡a 23 pages, bound (35 lines) : ‡b illustrations ; ‡c 21 cm
336		‡a text ‡2 rdacontent
336		‡a still image ‡2 rdacontent
337		‡a unmediated ‡2 rdamedia
338		‡a volume ‡2 rdacarrier
340		‡a vellum ‡d holograph
500		‡a Dated at end: The Observatory August [th]e 4th of 1685.
500		‡a Written at Greenwich, England.

Figure 2.63. Place of Production Omitted

100	1	‡a Rallison, Janette, ‡d 1966-‡e author.
245	10	‡a Janette Rallison manuscripts.
264	0	‡c 2007-2009.
300		‡a 1.5 linear ft. ‡a (3 boxes)
336		‡a text ‡2 rdacontent
337		‡a unmediated ‡2 rdamedia
338		‡a sheet ‡2 rdacarrier
351		‡a Organization within the boxes and folders represents the original order in which materials were received.
506		‡a Open for public research.
520	2	‡a Collection includes manuscripts of works written by Janette Rallison between 2007 and 2009.
541		‡c Donated; ‡a Janette Rallison; ‡d 2010 ‡e (A2010.04.231)
561		‡a The materials were maintained by the creator, Janette Rallison, until April, 2010, when the materials were donated to Brigham Young University.
852		‡a L. Tom Perry Special Collections, Harold B. Lee Library, Brigham Young University, ‡e Provo, Utah 84602.

2.7.4. PRODUCER'S NAME. If the name of the producer of an unpublished resource appears on the resource or is known to the cataloger, it may be recorded in sub-field ‡b of the MARC 264 field, separated from the place of production element (if present) by space-colon-space. A name appearing in the resource should be transcribed exactly as it appears. If it is supplied by the cataloger from another source, it should be bracketed. In the case of the document described in figure 2.62, although John Flamsteed's name appears, the document doesn't actually state that Flamsteed (rather than, e.g., a secretary) produced the document. The cataloger assumed that the document was handwritten by Flamsteed and therefore recorded his name in brackets. Producer's name is not core, so in most cases it is omitted from descriptions of unpublished resources (see figure 2.63).

2.7.6. DATE OF PRODUCTION. Unlike the place of production and producer's name elements, the date of production element is core and is therefore required in RDA descriptions of unpublished materials. This element is recorded in subfield ‡c of the MARC 264 field. If preceding elements (place of production or producer's name) have been recorded, the date of production element is preceded by a comma. The date of production may appear in the source (see figure 2.62), but information about this element can be taken from any source and therefore will not be bracketed even if the cataloger does not find it in the resource and must instead supply it (see figure 2.63). Note that this is different from the procedure with published resources (see below under 2.8.6).

2.8. PUBLICATION STATEMENT. The three basic elements of the publication statement are place of publication, publisher's name, and date of publication. All three are core in RDA and so must be recorded in RDA descriptions of published materials. The publication statement element is recorded in the MARC bibliographic 264 field with the second indicator coded "1."

2.8.1.4. RECORDING PUBLICATION STATEMENTS. The RDA guidelines call for transcribing places of publication and publishers' names exactly as they appear on the source of information. This represents a change from previous cataloging practice, which often omitted information or abbreviated words.

2.8.2. PLACE OF PUBLICATION. This element is core, but if more than one place appears in the resource only one is required (see below under 2.8.2.4). Place of publication is transcribed exactly as it appears, in subfield ‡a of the 264 field with the second indicator coded "1" (see figures throughout this chapter).

2.8.2.2. SOURCES OF INFORMATION. The cataloger can find information about the place of publication of a resource basically anywhere, but preference is given to the source where the publisher's name was found (see below under 2.8.4.2); next, the cataloger may look elsewhere in the resource. If the cataloger finds no place of publication in the resource and instead records information found outside the resource being cataloged it should be bracketed (see figures 2.10, 2.37, 2.39, and others throughout this chapter).

2.8.2.3. RECORDING PLACE OF PUBLICATION. The place name should be recorded exactly as found in the source of information (see RDA 2.8.1.4). In contrast to previous cataloging practice, do not abbreviate words (see figures 2.1, 2.3, and others in this chapter). On the other hand, if a place name appears as an abbreviation in the resource, record it in that form (see figures 2.4 and 2.9a, and others in this chapter). Optionally, if the place name appears without its larger jurisdiction, the larger jurisdiction may be added in brackets if it is thought to be important for identification or access. This might be the case where there are more than one place with the same name (see figure 2.64).

Figure 2.64. Larger Place Supplied

020	‡a 0921243219
100 1	‡a Carman, Bliss, ‡d 1861-1929.
245 10	‡a Bliss Carman's letters to Margaret Lawrence, 1927-1929 / ‡c edited by D.M.R. Bentley ; assisted by Margaret Maciejewski.
264 1	‡a London [Ontario] : ‡b Canadian Poetry Press, ‡c 1995.
300	‡a xxi, 162 pages : ‡b portraits ; ‡c 23 cm.
336	‡a text ‡2 rdacontent
336	‡a still image ‡2 rdacontent
337	‡a unmediated ‡2 rdamedia
338	‡a volume ‡2 rdacarrier
490 1	‡a Post-Confederation poetry
504	‡a Includes bibliographical references.
700 1	‡a Lawrence, Margaret, ‡e addressee.
700 1	‡a Bentley, D. M. R., ‡e editor.
700 1	‡a Maciejewski, Margaret, ‡e editor.
830 0	‡a Post-Confederation poetry.

Title page

Bliss Carman's Letters
to
Margaret Lawrence
1927-1929

Edited by D.M.R. Bentley
Assisted by Margaret Maciejewski

LONDON · CANADIAN POETRY PRESS · 1995

This guideline to record information exactly as it appears "on the source of information" presumably includes sources outside the resource being described, so RDA records might record abbreviated words here even when bracketed (meaning the information has been supplied by the cataloger). Because this point is somewhat ambiguous, however, this *Handbook* recommends not using abbreviations when supplying information. Additionally, RDA gives no guidance on fullness (should the cataloger supply "London" or "London, England"?) (see figures 2.39 and 2.45), or language or script (should the cataloger supply information in the same language or script as other sub-elements of the publication sub-element?) (see figure 2.5), instead leaving this to the cataloger's judgment.

2.8.2.4. MORE THAN ONE PLACE OF PUBLICATION. In contrast to AACR2's somewhat complex rule about recording multiple places of publication, RDA's is quite simple: record the place names in the order found in the resource (see figures 2.21, 2.32, and 2.34). If in addition to multiple places there are multiple publishers, and specific places are associated with specific publishers, the places should be recorded in the MARC record in conjunction with their appropriate publisher(s):

 264 1 ‡a Place A : ‡b Publisher A ; ‡a Place B : ‡b Publisher B . . .

For examples, see figures 2.6, 2.32, and 2.56.

Remember that only the first place recorded is core, so RDA does not require recording of all place names.

2.8.2.6. PLACE OF PUBLICATION NOT IDENTIFIED IN THE RESOURCE. If a place of publication is not found in the resource, the cataloger should attempt to supply the information, in brackets in current MARC practice. The name of a city should be supplied if possible, or if not, the name of a country. If the cataloger has a pretty good idea but is not sure, a question mark should follow the name of the place. For examples of supplied places of publication, see figures 2.5, 2.10, and others in this chapter. If it is not possible to supply a place of publication, record instead "Place of publication not identified" (see figures 2.36 and 2.43). This is a change from previous cataloging practice, which recorded "S.l." in such cases.

2.8.4. PUBLISHER'S NAME. This element is core, but as with the place of publication element, if more than one publisher's name appears in the resource only one is required (see below under 2.8.4.5). It is recorded in subfield ǂb of the 264 field with the second indicator coded "1," and follows its corresponding place of publication, separated from it by space-colon-space (see figures throughout this chapter).

2.8.4.2. SOURCES OF INFORMATION. The cataloger can find information about the publisher of a resource basically anywhere, but preference is given to the source where the title proper was found; if the publisher's name is not found there, the cataloger may next look elsewhere in the resource. If the cataloger finds no publisher's name in the resource and instead records information found outside the resource being cataloged, it should be bracketed in current MARC practice.

Not all resources have a conventionally arranged title page or other preferred source of information. The title page of a book usually includes the name of the publisher near the bottom of the page. However, sometimes the title page lacks such information. In these cases, if a corporate body is named at the top of the page and no publication information is found elsewhere, it may be regarded as the publisher.

The person or body issuing a so-called privately printed resource—a commercial publisher, a private press, or a person or group for whom it was printed—may be treated as the publisher (see LC-PCC PS 2.8.1.1, January 2013) (see figure 2.19). In the absence of evidence to the contrary, a government printer or printing office is recorded as the publisher (see LC-PCC PS 2.8.1.1, January 2013) (see figure 2.18).

2.8.4.3. RECORDING PUBLISHERS' NAMES. The publisher's name is transcribed exactly as it appears, without shortening or abbreviating. Optionally, the cataloger may omit levels in the publisher's corporate hierarchy that are not required to identify the publisher (see RDA 2.8.1.4). For example, in figure 2.28, "a division of MCA Inc." was omitted, and in figure 2.45 "a division of Crown Publishers, Inc." was omitted. On the other hand, the cataloger chose to include the entire hierarchy in figure 2.46. LC and PCC will generally not omit levels in corporate hierarchy (LC-PCC PS 2.8.1.4, September 2012).

2.8.4.4. STATEMENT OF FUNCTION. A word or phrase accompanying a name may be transcribed if it clarifies the function of the entity, unless the phrase merely states that the entity published the resource. This instruction is carried over from previous practice, but will probably be used less now that the MARC 264 field makes clear distinctions between publishers, manufacturers, and distributors. The phrase in figure 2.2 is an example of recording statements of function; alternately, the printer could have been given in a manufacturer's statement, but in this case the whole phrase seemed grammatically inseparable. For an example where a phrase was not transcribed (because it merely stated a publishing function), see figure 2.28.

2.8.4.5. MORE THAN ONE PUBLISHER. In contrast to AACR2's rather complex rule about recording multiple publishers, RDA's is quite simple: record publishers' names in the order found in the resource (see figure 2.46). If there are multiple places as well, and specific places are associated with specific publishers, the places should be recorded in the MARC record in conjunction with their appropriate publisher(s):

   264   1   ‡a Place A : ‡b Publisher A ; ‡a Place B : ‡b Publisher B . . .

For examples, see figures 2.6, 2.32, and 2.56.

    Remember that only the first publisher recorded is core, so RDA does not require recording of all publishers' names.

2.8.4.7. NO PUBLISHER IDENTIFIED. If the publisher is not identified in the resource, it may be identified in other sources. As noted above at 2.8.2.2, if information about the publisher is taken from outside the resource, in current MARC practice it is recorded in square brackets. The book cataloged in figure 2.65 is a reprint, and the only clue in the book itself about the publisher is the phrase "Nabu public domain reprints" on the verso of the title page. Some research on the Internet reveals that this series is published by Nabu Press, located in Charleston, South Carolina. If, on the other hand, no information can be found about the publisher, record "Publisher not identified" in this element (see figure 2.36). This is a change from previous cataloging practice, which recorded "s.n." in such cases.

Figure 2.65. Supplied Publisher

020	‡a 9781171688969
245 04	‡a The complete story of the Galveston horror / ‡c written by the survivors ; edited by John Coulter.
264 1	‡a [Charleston, South Carolina] : ‡b [Nabu Press], ‡c [2010]
300	‡a 386 pages : ‡b illustrations ; ‡c 25 cm.
336	‡a text ‡2 rdacontent
337	‡a unmediated ‡2 rdamedia
338	‡a volume ‡2 rdacarrier
490 1	‡a Nabu public domain reprints

500	‡a "Incidents of the awful tornado, flood and cyclone disaster, personal experiences of survivors, horrible looting of dead bodies and the robbing of empty homes, pestilence from so many decaying bodies unburied, barge captains compelled by armed men to tow dead bodies to sea, millions of dollars raised to aid the suffering survivors, President McKinley orders Army rations and Army tents issued to survivors and orders U.S. Troops to protect the people and property, tales of the survivors from Galveston adrift all night on rafts, acts of valor, United States soldiers drowned, great heroism, great vandalism, great horror, a second Johnstown flood, but worse, hundreds of men, women and children drowned, no way of escape, only death! Death! Everywhere!"—Title page of original publication.
500	‡a "List of identifications": pages 362-386.
534	‡p Facsimile reprint. Originally published: ‡c New York : United Publishers of America, 1900.
700 1	‡a Coulter, John, ‡e editor of compilation.
830 0	‡a Nabu public domain reprints.

Title page

The Complete Story
OF THE
Galveston Horror.
Written by the Survivors.

Incidents of the awful tornado, flood and cyclone disaster, personal experiences of survivors, horrible looting of dead bodies and the robbing of empty homes, pestilence from so many decaying bodies unburied, barge captains compelled by armed men to tow dead bodies to sea, millions of dollars raised to aid the suffering survivors, President McKinley orders Army rations and Army tents issued to survivors and orders U.S. Troops to protect the people and property, tales of the survivors from Galveston adrift all night on rafts, acts of valor, United States soldiers drowned, great heroism, great vandalism, great horror, a second Johnstown flood, but worse, hundreds of men, women and children drowned, no way of escape, only

Death! Death! Everywhere!
Edited by John Coulter, Formerly of the N.Y. Herald
Fully Illustrated with Photographs
UNITED PUBLISHERS OF AMERICA

Title page verso
Nabu public domain reprints

2.8.6. DATE OF PUBLICATION. The third principal part of the publication statement is the date of publication element. This element is core, meaning it must be present in an RDA record for a published resource (for an exception, see 2.8.6.5, below). It is recorded in subfield ‡c of the 264 field with the second indicator coded "1," and is separated from a preceding element by a comma (see figures throughout this chapter).

The date of publication is the date (usually a year) that copies of a resource were first issued to the public. Such a date is may be explicitly given in a statement such as "Published in 2011 by Orbit" on the verso of the title page. A date coinciding with an edition statement (e.g., "Third edition 2011") is usually a date of publication. A date at the foot of the title page in a book is normally also considered the date of publication, even in the absence of an explicit statement.

Note that copyright dates or printing dates are *not* dates of publication, although they may coincide with the date of publication. A printing date represents the date of an impression. An impression consists of all of the copies of a publication run at one time from a set of photographic plates, type, etc. Frequently, if the publication sells well, the publisher will decide at a later date to run more copies from the same plates or forms of type. Customarily, although not always, a second run of a publication will be referred to as a "second impression" or "second printing." This information will usually be printed, possibly along with a date, on the title page or its verso, or in the book's colophon. Generally speaking, succeeding impressions or printings are identical to the first; in most cases catalogers treat them as copies of the first impression and the date of a later impression is not considered a new date of publication as long as the publisher has not changed. The book cataloged in figure 2.66 is an example. Except for the verso of the title page, this book is a photographic reprint of the 1889 edition. Because it is a book in relatively high demand, it has been reprinted in this way every few years. The date of publication for any of these impressions should be recorded as 1889. If a library feels it is important to record which printing it has, the cataloger may include a note in a 590 field such as "The library's copy is the 2002 impression." Alternately, the cataloger may record "2002" as a date of manufacture (see below at 2.10.6). For an example, see figure 2.40. In most cases, however, the printing date is simply ignored in the description of the manifestation. This is so that in our shared-cataloging environment libraries may use the same bibliographic record no matter which printing they happen to have in their collection. If an explicit date of manufacture is recorded in a bibliographic record, it restricts use of that record to copies with the same date of manufacture, limiting its usefulness for shared cataloging.

Figure 2.66. Printing Date not a Publication Date

020	‡a 0199102066
100 1	‡a Liddell, Henry George, ‡d 1811-1898, ‡e author.
245 13	‡a An intermediate Greek-English lexicon : ‡b founded upon the seventh edition of Liddell and Scott's Greek-English lexicon.
250	‡a First edition.
264 1	‡a Oxford : ‡b The Clarendon Press, ‡c 1889.
300	‡a 910 pages ; ‡c 23 cm
336	‡a text ‡2 rdacontent

```
337       ‡a unmediated ‡2 rdamedia
338       ‡a volume ‡2 rdacarrier
700 1     ‡a Scott, Robert, ‡d 1811-1887, ‡e author.
```

Title page

An Intermediate
Greek-English Lexicon
Founded upon
the Seventh Edition of
Liddell and Scott's
Greek-English Lexicon
Oxford
At the Clarendon Press

Verso of title page

Oxford University Press, Great Clarendon Street, Oxford OX2 6DP
Oxford New York
Aukland Bangkok Buenos Aires Cape Town Chennai
. . .
São Paolo Shanghai Singapore Taipei Tokyo Toronto
with an associated company in Berlin
Impression of 2002
First edition 1889

Like a printing date, a copyright date is not a date of publication. "Copyright" denotes certain rights granted to the creator of a work (or other owner of the copyright) for a limited time, and the copyright date is the year these rights begin, which may or may not coincide with the publication date of a resource. Copyright date may not be substituted for date of publication in RDA, as it could in AACR2 (on the copyright date element see below under 2.11).

2.8.6.2. SOURCES OF INFORMATION. Information about the date of publication can be found anywhere, but preference is given to the source where the title proper was found. If no date of publication is found in that source, the cataloger next looks elsewhere in the resource. If the cataloger finds no date of publication in the resource a date may be supplied, either from a source outside the resource being cataloged (e.g., a record for the resource created by a bookseller such as amazon.com), or inferred from information in the resource such as a copyright date or date of manufacture. Supplied dates should be bracketed in current MARC practice.

2.8.6.3. RECORDING DATE OF PUBLICATION. This guideline instructs the cataloger to record the date of publication following RDA 2.8.1, which in turn instructs the cataloger to follow 1.8 for numbers (including dates). RDA 1.8.2 says to record numerals "in the form preferred by the agency creating the data." An agency could, for example, decide only to record numerals as arabic numerals; if a date appears in roman numerals, the numeral would be converted to arabic rather than transcribed. Alternatively, the policy of the agency could be to record numerals in the form in which they appear on the source (i.e., transcribe). This is the Library of Congress's policy (see LC-PCC PS 1.8.2, first alternative, February 2010). If following this alternative, the agency may also add an equivalent numeral in another form in square brackets. For example, an agency might choose always to record numerals in the form found on the source, but always add an arabic equivalent, for example:

> 264   1 . . . ‡c MMII [2002]

This *Handbook* generally follows the alternative, to transcribe a date of publication in the form in which it appears (see figure 2.19).

2.8.6.5. MULTIPART MONOGRAPHS, SERIALS, AND INTEGRATING RESOURCES. For these resources, record the publication date of the first part and that of the last part (if it has ended or been completed). According to RDA 2.8.6.2, this information should be found on the first or last part. If these parts are not available the information may be supplied, but as with other kinds of resources, in current MARC practice supplied dates are recorded in square brackets. If the dates are not available and cannot be supplied, do not record anything in this element.

For examples, see figures 2.7, 2.8, 2.9, and others throughout this chapter.

2.8.6.6. DATE OF PUBLICATION NOT IDENTIFIED IN A SINGLE-PART RESOURCE. If the date of publication is not identified in the resource, it may be identified in other sources or supplied by the cataloger. As noted above at 2.8.6.2, if information about the date of publication is taken from outside the resource or inferred, in current MARC practice it is recorded in square brackets. The book cataloged in figure 2.65 is a reprint, and no date of publication appears in it. However, the resource's description on amazon .com gives the year of publication, which is recorded in this element.

Best practices have not entirely evolved yet, but as of this writing most RDA catalogers infer that a copyright date corresponds to the publication date and will supply the same date in square brackets for the date of publication. The book cataloged in figure 2.60, for example, had no publication date, but showed "©2008" on the verso of the title page. The cataloger therefore supplied "[2008]" in square brackets as the publication date in the first 264 field. If the cataloger feels unsure about this, a question mark may be added: "[2008?]." Once the date of publication has been recorded, as in figure 2.60, no further dates are required. However, in this case the cataloger also recorded the copyright date in the second 264 field. This is entirely optional.

A copyright date on a resource lacking a date of publication is probably the most common situation catalogers will encounter, and it is a fairly good guess that the date to supply as the date of publication is the same as the copyright date. Catalogers should be more cautious with resources that lack both a publication date and a copyright date. Distribution and printing dates are certainly evidence that can be weighed, but other evidence should be considered if possible: is there a dated preface or introduction? Was a record found for a manifestation of the work with an earlier date of publication, but with otherwise identical attributes? Does a bookseller such as amazon.com or Barnes & Noble give a date of publication?

RDA directs us to follow 1.9.2 for the form of supplied dates. They are to be recorded as follows:

Actual year known..[2003]
Either one of two consecutive years...............[1971 or 1972]
Probable year..[1969?]
Probable range of years....................................[between 1970 and 1979?]
Earliest possible date known ....[not before August 21, 1492]
Latest possible date known.............................[not after 1850]
Earliest/latest possible date known.................[between August 12, 1899 and March 2, 1900]

The following are some examples of conversion of AACR2-style supplied dates to the RDA forms:

AACR2	*RDA*
[ca. 1960] *becomes*	[1960?], *or something like* [between 1958 and 1962]
[188-] *becomes*	[between 1880 and 1889]
[17--] *becomes*	[between 1700 and 1799]
[not after Sept. 10, 1495] *becomes*	[not after September 10, 1495]

If no information can be found about the date of publication, the cataloger may record "date of publication not identified" in this element. This is a change from AACR2 cataloging practice, which required a date to be supplied:

    264   1   ‡a New York : ‡b Sear Publishing Company, ‡c [date of publication not identified]

However, it seems likely that catalogers will use this formulation only rarely. At the very least the cataloger knows that the manifestation was published before the date of cataloging:

264 1 ‡a New York : ‡b Sear Publishing Company, ‡c [not after January 20, 2013]

If a publication date is supplied, the RDA core requirement is satisfied. However, if "date of publication not identified" is recorded instead, the date of distribution becomes core and must be recorded if present on the resource or if it can be supplied. If neither a publication date nor a date of distribution is available, then copyright date becomes core and must be recorded if it appears in the resource or is known from another source. If none of these three dates is available, the date of manufacture becomes core and must be recorded if it appears in the resource or is known from another source.

2.9. DISTRIBUTION STATEMENT. The three basic elements of the distribution statement are place of distribution, distributer's name, and date of distribution. The elements of the distribution statement are not core, but if any of the three elements of the publication statement are not available and therefore have not been recorded, the corresponding element in the distribution statement becomes core and if available must be recorded in records for published resources. The distribution statement element is recorded in the MARC bibliographic 264 field with the second indicator coded "2."

Guidelines for sources of information and recording the elements of the distribution statement are the same as for the publication statement, and will not be repeated here. For examples of distribution statement elements, see figures 2.18, 2.28, and 2.47. In all of these cases the distribution statement was not core because all the elements of the publication statement had been recorded. In the cataloger's judgment, inclusion of the distribution statement in these cases enhanced the library user's ability to find or identify the resource.

2.10. MANUFACTURE STATEMENT. The three basic elements of the manufacture statement are place of manufacture, manufacturer's name, and date of manufacture. The elements of the manufacture statement are not core, but if any of the three elements of the publication statement—or lacking that, the same elements in the distribution statement, or for the date element, a copyright date—are not available and therefore have not been recorded, the corresponding element in the manufacture statement becomes core. If available the manufacture statement must be recorded in records for published resources. The manufacture statement element is recorded in the MARC bibliographic 264 field with the second indicator coded "3."

Guidelines for sources of information and recording the elements of the manufacture statement are the same as for the publication and distribution statements and will not be repeated here. For an example of a manufacture statement, see figure 2.67, which shows a record for an early printed book that lacks a publication date, but has a date of printing.

Figure 2.67. Manufacture Statement

100	1	‡a Bracciolini, Poggio, ‡d 1380-1459, ‡e author.
245	10	‡a Modus epistolandi co[m]pendiosissimus et facillimus / ‡c a Pogio Florentino compositus.
246	3	‡a Modus epistolandi compendiosissimus et facillimus
246	3	‡a Modus epistolandi copendiosissimus et facillimus
246	1	‡i Title from colophon: ‡a Epistolandi modus domini Pogij oratoris atq[ue] poet[a] e excellentissimi
246	3	‡a Epistolandi modus domini Pogij oratoris atque poetae excellentissimi
264	1	‡a Venundatur Parrhisiis in vico Sancti Jacobi : ‡b ab Alexandro Aliatte e regione diui Benedicti, ‡c [date of publication not identified]
264	3	‡a [Place of manufacture not identified] : ‡b Impressus impensis Alexandri Aliatt[a]e, ‡c vltima Martij MDV [1505 March 31]
300		‡a 8 unnumbered pages ; ‡c 19 cm (4to)
336		‡a text ‡2 rdacontent
337		‡a unmediated ‡2 rdamedia
338		‡a volume ‡2 rdacarrier
500		‡a Signature: A⁴.
520		‡a Brief essay on epistolary style including examples of letters by classical writers (Cicero and Ovid) and contemporary humanists such as Gaspar Veronensis.
590		‡a Brigham Young University copy bound in modern dark brown mottled calf with two concentric frames of triple blind rules, small gilt floral ornaments at the outer corners of the central frame.
700	1	‡a Aliate, Alexander, ‡d active 1497-1507, ‡e bookseller.

Title page

Modus epistolandi cõpendiosissimus et fa-
cillimus a Pogio florentino compositus.

Colophon

Epistolandi modus domini Pogij Oratoris atq$_3$ Poetaę
excellentissimi Finitur. Impressus impensis Alexandri
Aliattę. vltima martij .M.D.V.

2.11. COPYRIGHT DATE. A copyright date is the date on which a copyright on a work begins, and may be found in resources in several forms, including a year following the symbol © (e.g., "©2013"), or with the word spelled out (e.g., "copyright 2013"), or a combination (e.g., "copyright © 2013"). In the nineteenth century, copyright date was often given in resources as a phrase such as "Entered according to Act of Congress, March 27, 1850, by Spencer Kemble, in the Clerk's Office of the District Court of the United States for the Eastern District of Pennsylvania." A phonogram date is also a copyright date, the date the copyright on a recording begins. It is usually found on resources as a year following the symbol ℗ (e.g., "℗2013").

Copyright date is core if no date of publication or date of distribution has been identified in the description of the resource. As discussed above under 2.8.6.6, in current RDA practice the cataloger will almost always supply a publication date when one is not present on the resource, so the copyright date element will rarely be core. However, the cataloger may wish to record it, for example, if the copyright date is significantly different from the date of publication. Another reason might be to show evidence for an inferred date of publication. Copyright date is recorded in subfield ‡c of the 264 field, with the second indicator coded "4."

2.11.1.3. RECORDING COPYRIGHT DATES. No matter what the form the copyright date takes in the resource, it is always recorded in RDA as a date (usually a year) following the symbol ©. For example, the long nineteenth-century phrase asserting copyright shown above would be recorded:

    264 4 ©1850

Phonogram dates are always recorded as a date (usually a year) following the symbol ℗. For an example, see figure 2.22.

If more than one copyright or phonogram date is found in a single-part resource, generally record only the latest date. However, if multiple copyright dates apply to various aspects of a resource (e.g., a copyright date for the text accompanying a compact disc and a phonogram date for the recording), more than one may be recorded using separate 264 fields. Descriptions of resources issued in more than one part may record the latest copyright or phonogram dates associated with the first and the last part. In this case a single 264 field is used and the symbol is repeated (see figure 2.8).

For other examples of the copyright date element, see figures 2.1a, 2.4b, 2.5, and others throughout this chapter. Note that a copyright date will never stand alone in RDA, but will always be found in conjunction with at least one other 264 field, that designated for the publication statement.

2.12. SERIES STATEMENT. "Series" is defined in RDA as "A group of separate resources related to one another by the fact that each resource bears, in addition to its own title proper, a collective title applying to the group as a whole. The individual resources may or may not be numbered." (RDA Glossary). The collective title referred to in the definition is called the series statement.

2.12.1.4. RECORDING SERIES STATEMENTS. The series statement is to be transcribed exactly as it appears as to wording and spelling but not necessarily as to capitalization and punctuation, in the same way as other transcribed elements (see above at 1.7). It is recorded in the MARC bibliographic 490 field, with the first indicator coded "1" if the library indexes the series, and "0" if it does not. If the first indicator is coded "1," the description of the resource will always contain a MARC 8XX field in addition to the 490 field. The 8XX field contains the authorized access point for the series, which indexes. Because series are regarded as works in FRBR and RDA, authorized access points for series are formed following the guidelines for authorized access points for works (see chapter 7).

The Library of Congress does not currently create authorized access points for series and so new LC original cataloging will always record the series statement in 490 with first indicator coded "0" and no 8XX field. Catalogers who encounter these records in OCLC or elsewhere may update them to include an authorized access point if desired.

In current cataloging practice a number of phrases found on resources that might appear to be series statements are not considered so. For example, publishers often put words prominently on books designating broad categories such as "Science Fiction" or "Romance Novels." These are usually simply guides to help bookstores organize the resources and are not regarded as series. Similarly, phrases giving the name of an in-house editor or publisher such as "A Tom Doherty Associates book" are not generally considered series statements. For a full treatment of these "series-like phrases," see LC-PCC PS 2.12 (September 2012) under "series or phrases."

2.12.1.5. RESOURCE IN MORE THAN ONE SERIES. If a resource belongs to more than one series, each is recorded in a separate 490 field. Be careful, however. Sometimes what appear to be two series statements are actually the statement of a main series and its subseries. These are recorded together in a single 490 field (see figure 2.32).

2.12.2. TITLE PROPER OF SERIES. The title proper of a series is defined as "the chief name of a series," parallel to the definition of title proper in 2.3.2. It is recorded in subfield ‡a of the 490 field.

2.12.2.2. SOURCES OF INFORMATION. Because series titles proper may appear in more than one place in different forms within a given resource, RDA prescribes an order of preference. The cataloger should look first on the series title page, a page apart from the main title page that shows the series title proper and normally includes other information about the series, such as the name of the editor of the series or a numeric designation. If a series title proper is found there, transcribe it. Ignore other presentations of the series.

If the resource does not have a series title page, or the series in question is not found there, look elsewhere in the resource for the series title proper. If more than one presentation is found, use judgment in deciding which will be most useful in identifying or accessing the resource, and record that form. RDA also permits series information to be taken from outside the resource itself (RDA 2.12.2.2c). This is only rarely done, but if it is, in current MARC practice the information found should be recorded in square brackets.

See figure 2.68 for an example of a resource including a series title proper given in different forms. In this example, the phrase "The Modern Library" appears on the title page and its verso. The series title page, however, reads "The Modern Library of the world's best books." The cataloger will record the form found on the series title page.

Figure 2.68. More than One Form of Series Title

100 0	‡a Thomas, ‡c Aquinas, Saint, ‡d 1225?-1274, ‡e author.	
245 10	‡a Introduction to Saint Thomas Aquinas / ‡c edited, with an introduction, by Anton C. Pegis.	
264 1	‡a New York : ‡b Random House, ‡c [1948]	
300	‡a xxx, 690 pages ; ‡c 19 cm.	
336	‡a text ‡2 rdacontent	
337	‡a unmediated ‡2 rdamedia	
338	‡a volume ‡2 rdacarrier	
490 0	‡a The modern library of the world's best books	
504	‡a Includes bibliographical references (pages 682-690).	
700 1	‡a Pegis, Anton C. ‡q (Anton Charles), ‡d 1905-1978, ‡e editor.	

Verso of title page

Copyright, 1948, by Random House, Inc.
Random House is the publisher of
The Modern Library

Series title page

The Modern Library
of the world's best books

Title page

Introduction to
Saint Thomas Aquinas
Edited, with an Introduction, by
Anton C. Pegis
President, Pontifical Institute of
Mediaeval Studies, Toronto
The Modern Library • New York

Figure 2.44 is another example of a resource that includes variant forms of the series statement. The title page for Schulz's *How Long, Great Pumpkin, How Long?* lists the series as "Peanuts Parade 16." The book's cover calls it "A Peanuts Parade Book." Facing the title page is a page headed "Peanuts Parade Paperbacks" that gives, in addition to the series title, a list of titles of books in the series with their numbering. According to the definition, this page constitutes the series title page and will be chosen for transcription in the series title proper. The two other forms of the series title proper are not transcribed anywhere in the description (but note that a different form of the series title was chosen as the authorized access point for the series in the 830 field, probably because of different presentations on books in the series).

2.12.2.3. RECORDING TITLE PROPER OF SERIES. Transcribe the title proper of the series exactly as it appears as to wording and spelling, but not necessarily as to capitalization and punctuation. Do not abbreviate words unless they appear abbreviated in the resource (see figure 2.40).

If numbering is grammatically embedded in the series title, it is so transcribed. Do not transpose the numbering to the series numbering sub-element of the statement (see figure 2.69).

Figure 2.69. Series Numbering within Series Title Proper

020	‡a 9781574413076
100 1	‡a Gamble, Stephen, ‡d 1963- ‡e author.
245 10	‡a Dennis Brain : ‡b a life in music / ‡c Stephen Gamble, William C. Lynch.
264 1	‡a Denton, Texas : ‡b University of North Texas Press, ‡c [2011]
300	‡a x, 384 pages : ‡b illustrations ; ‡c 24 cm.
336	‡a text ‡2 rdacontent
336	‡a still image ‡2 rdacontent
337	‡a unmediated ‡2 rdamedia
338	‡a volume ‡2 rdacarrier
490 1	‡a Number 7 in the North Texas lives of musicians series
504	‡a Includes bibliographical references (pages 362-369).
700 1	‡a Lynch, William C., ‡d 1943- ‡e author.
830 0	‡a North Texas lives of musicians series ; ‡v no. 7.

Title page

DENNIS BRAIN
A LIFE IN MUSIC
STEPHEN GAMBLE
WILLIAM C. LYNCH
Number 7 in the North Texas Lives of Musicians Series

University of North Texas Press
Denton, Texas

Verso of title page

All text ©2011 Stephen Gamble and William C. Lynch. All rights reserved.
Dennis Brain: A Life in Music is Number 7 in the North Texas Lives of Musicians Series

---

2.12.3. PARALLEL TITLE PROPER OF SERIES. A parallel title of a series is a presentation of the series title proper in another language or script. If a series parallel title appears in a resource, it may be transcribed in the 490 field following the title proper in its own subfield ‡a. Series parallel titles are separated from the title proper and other parallel titles by space-equal sign-space (see figure 2.70). The parallel title proper of series element is not core, and so it is not required to record it in an RDA record.

Figure 2.70. Parallel Title Proper of Series

020	‡a 9789074461740 (paperback)
020	‡a 9074461743 (paperback)
100 1	‡a Nelis, Jan, ‡e author.
245 10	‡a From ancient to modern : ‡b the myth of romanità during the ventennio fascista : the written imprint of Mussolini's cult of the 'Third Rome' / ‡c Jan Nelis.
264 1	‡a Bruxelles ; ‡a Roma : ‡b Belgisch Historisch Instituut te Rome, ‡c 2011.
300	‡a 242 pages ; ‡c 24 cm.
336	‡a text ‡2 rdacontent
337	‡a unmediated ‡2 rdamedia
338	‡a volume ‡2 rdacarrier
490 0	‡a Institut Historique Belge de Rome études = ‡a Belgisch Historisch Instituut te Rome studies, ‡x 0073-8530 ; ‡v 1
500	‡a Based on a fully re-worked version of the author's doctoral thesis--Ghent University, 2006.
504	‡a Includes bibliographical references (pages 173-242).
710 2	‡a Institut historique belge de Rome, ‡e issuing body.

Title page

From ancient to modern:
the myth of *romanità*
during the *ventennio fascista*
The written imprint of Mussolini's cult of the 'Third Rome'
Jan Nelis

Bruxelles - Brussel - Roma
Belgisch Historisch Instituut te Rome
Institut Historique Belge de Rome
Istituto Storico Belga di Roma
2011

Title page verso

©2011 IHBR – BHIR
ISSN 0073-8530
ISBN 978-90-74461-74-0

Series title page

INSTITUTE HISTORIQUE BELGE DE ROME
ÉTUDES
BELGISCH-HISTORISH INSTITUUT TE ROME
STUDIES
I

2.12.4. OTHER TITLE INFORMATION OF SERIES. Record other title information associated with the series statement only if it significantly helps identify the series. This is very rare. If other title information is included in the series statement, it follows the same transcription rules as the title proper and is recorded in the same subfield ‡a as the series title proper, but separated from the title proper by space-colon-space. Unlike the 245 field, there is no subfield coding for other title information in the MARC 490 field. See figure 2.71 for an example of a series statement that includes other title information. Conversely, the series title page in figure 2.55 gives extensive other title information for the series "Fundamental theories of physics." This other title information does not contribute to the identification of the series, and is not recorded.

Figure 2.71. Series Other Title Information

---

020   ‡a 0405044593

100 1   ‡a Gilman, Charlotte Perkins, ‡d 1860-1935, ‡e author.

245 14 ‡a The living of Charlotte Perkins Gilman : ‡b an autobiography / ‡c by Charlotte Perkins Gilman.

250   ‡a Reprint edition.

264   1 ‡a New York : ‡b Arno Press, ‡c 1972.

300   ‡a xxxviii, 341 pages : ‡b illustrations ; ‡c 23 cm.

336   ‡a text ‡2 rdacontent

336   ‡a still image ‡2 rdacontent

337   ‡a unmediated ‡2 rdamedia

338   ‡a volume ‡2 rdacarrier

490 1   ‡a American women : images and realities

534   ‡p Reprint. Originally published: ‡c New York ; London : D. Appleton-Century Compani Incorporated, 1935.

830   0 ‡a American women : images and realities.

Title page

The Living of
Charlotte Perkins Gilman
An Autobiography
by
Charlotte Perkins Gilman
Arno Press
New York • 1972

Series title page

American Women
Images and Realities
Advisory Editors
Annette K. Baxter
Leon Stein

2.12.6. STATEMENT OF RESPONSIBILITY RELATING TO SERIES. Statements of responsibility associated with the series statement are generally transcribed only if they are considered necessary for identification of the series. Statements of responsibility naming series editors, for example, are almost never recorded (see the series title page of the book illustrated in figure 2.71, which shows the statement of responsibility "advisory editors, Annette K. Baxter, Leon Stein").

If recorded, a statement of responsibility associated with a series statement is recorded in subfield ‡a of the 490 field, separated from the title proper of the series and other title information (if any) by space-slash-space.

Sometimes the series title proper is so general, vague, or commonly used that an accompanying statement of responsibility will normally be considered necessary for identification of the series. The series title proper "Selected documents" is an example (see figure 2.72; see also figure 2.37).

If, as sometimes happens, all of the parts of a series are by the same author, a statement of responsibility may be included as part of the series area if it appears in

Figure 2.72. Series Statement of Responsibility

245 00 ǂa Human rights.

264 1 ǂa [Washington, D.C.] : ǂb The Department of State, Bureau of Public Affairs, Office of Public Communication, ǂc 1978.

264 2 ǂa Washington, D.C. : ǂb For sale by the Superintendant of Documents, U.S. Government Printing Office

300   ǂa 63 pages ; ǂc 27 cm.

336   ǂa text ǂ2 rdacontent

337   ǂa unmediated ǂ2 rdamedia

338   ǂa volume ǂ2 rdacarrier

490 1 ǂa Selected documents / Bureau of Public Affairs, Office of Public Communication ; ǂv no. 5 (revised)

490 1 ǂa Department of State publication ; ǂv 8961. ǂa General foreign policy series ; ǂv 310

500   ǂa Caption title.

500   ǂa At head of title: The Department of State.

710 1 ǂa United States. ǂb Department of State.

830   0 ǂa Selected documents (United States. Department of State. Bureau of Public Affairs) ; ǂv no. 5, revised.

830   0 ǂa Department of State publication ; ǂv 8961.

830   0 ǂa Department of State publication. ǂp General foreign policy series ; ǂv 310.

Title page

The Department
of State

Selected Documents No. 5 (Revised)
Bureau of Public Affairs Office of Public Communication

Human Rights

Series statement on last page

Department of State Publication 8961
General Foreign Policy Series 310
Released November 1978
Office of Public Communication
Bureau of Public Affairs
For Sale by the Superintendent of Documents, U.S. Government Printing Office
Washington, D.C. 20402

conjunction with the series title and if in the judgment of the cataloger it is considered necessary for the identification of the series (see figure 2.73).

Figure 2.73. Series Statement of Responsibility

100 1	‡a Dunnett, Dorothy, ‡e author.
245 14	‡a The ringed castle / ‡c by Dorothy Dunnett.
264 1	‡a New York : ‡b Popular Library, ‡c [1971]
300	‡a 640 pages ; ‡c 18 cm.
336	‡a text ‡2 rdacontent
337	‡a unmediated ‡2 rdamedia
338	‡a volume ‡2 rdacarrier
490 1	‡a The Lymond chronicle / by Dorothy Dunnett ; ‡v V
520	‡a Lymond leaves Tudor England to journey to Muscovy, where he becomes advisor to the half-mad czar and finds himself caught up in the intrgues of medieval Russia, while his enemies at home continue to conspire against him.
700 1	‡i Sequel to: ‡a Dunnett, Dorothy. ‡t Pawn in Frankincense.
700 1	‡i Sequel: ‡a Dunnett, Dorothy. ‡t Checkmate.
800 1	‡a Dunnett, Dorothy. ‡t Lymond chronicles ; ‡v 5th.

Title page

THE RINGED CASTLE
BY DOROTHY DUNNETT

POPULAR LIBRARY · NEW YORK

Series title page

THE LYMOND CHRONICLE
by Dorothy Dunnett

THE GAME OF KINGS
QUEENS' PLAY
THE DISORDERLY KNIGHTS
PAWN IN FRANKINCENSE
THE RINGED CASTLE
CHECKMATE
Available in paperback exclusively from Popular Library

Back cover

THE LYMOND CHRONICLE V
THE RINGED CASTLE

Sometimes, as with a statement of responsibility for a work, the statement of responsibility is joined grammatically to the title proper. If this is the case, transcribe it as it appears (see figure 2.74).

Figure 2.74. Series Statement of Responsibility Inseparable from Title Proper

020	‡a 0701204486
100 1	‡a Woolf, Virginia, ‡d 1882-1941, ‡e author.
245 12	‡a A reflection of the other person / ‡c editor, Nigel Nicolson ; assistant editor, Joanne Trautmann.
264 1	‡a London : ‡b The Hogarth Press, ‡c 1978.
300	‡a xxi, 442 pages : ‡b portraits ; ‡c 24 cm.
336	‡a text ‡2 rdacontent
337	‡a unmediated ‡2 rdamedia
338	‡a volume ‡2 rdacarrier
490 0	‡a The letters of Virginia Woolf ; ‡v vol IV
504	‡a Includes bibliographical references and index.
700 1	‡a Nicolson, Nigel, ‡e editor.
700 1	‡a Banks, Joanne Trautmann, ‡d 1941-2007, ‡e editor.

Title page

A REFLECTION
OF THE OTHER PERSON
The Letters of Virginia Woolf
Volume IV: 1929-1931
Editor: Nigel Nicolson
Assistant Editor: Joanne Trautmann

1978
THE HOGARTH PRESS
LONDON

Series title page

THE LETTERS OF VIRGINIA WOOLF
Vol I. The Flight of the Mind (1888-1912)
Vol II. The Question of Things Happening (1912-22)
Vol III. A Change of Perspective (1923-28)
Vol IV. A Reflection of the Other Person (1929-31)

2.12.8. ISSN OF SERIES. ISSN is an identifier assigned by an ISSN registry to a serial. Because most series are serials, they may have an ISSN assigned to them. If an ISSN applicable to a series appears within a resource in the series or is otherwise known, it may be recorded exactly as it appears in the source, including internal hyphenation. ISSN is recorded in subfield ‡x of the MARC 490 field, following the series title proper, other title information (if any), and statement of responsibility (if any). It is separated from preceding elements by a comma (see figure 2.70). If the ISSN is taken from outside the resource, it should be enclosed in square brackets. In the MARC record the letters "ISSN" are not transcribed. Local systems may display subfield ‡x of the 490 field as "ISSN:".

ISSN of series is not a core element. However, LC and PCC have declared it to be core for their cataloging (LC-PCC PS 2.12.8, July 2012).

2.12.9. NUMBERING WITHIN SERIES. If a series is numbered, the number is recorded as part of the series statement in the MARC 490 field. It is separated from preceding elements by space-semicolon-space and subfield ‡v. Numbering includes an accompanying caption such as "volume," if there is one. If no caption appears with the number, the cataloger should not create one (see, e.g., figures 2.70 and 2.73).

2.12.9.2. SOURCES OF INFORMATION. Numbering can be taken from any source within the resource. It does not need to appear with the series title proper, although if it does not, the cataloger should use caution to be sure the numbering in fact applies to the series. Unlike other elements within the series statement, there is no preferred hierarchy of sources. This *Handbook* recommends, however, that if the numbering appears in the same source as the title proper of the series, it be recorded as found there rather than in a form found somewhere else (see figure 2.74, where the numbering appears in different forms on the series title page and the main title page).

2.12.9.3. RECORDING NUMBERING WITHIN SERIES. Numbering is to be recorded "as it appears" on the source. This means captions are to be transcribed exactly as they appear, not abbreviated as they often were in previous cataloging practice. In figure 2.55 the caption appears as "volume" and in figure 2.74 it appears as "vol" (no period); in both cases the caption is recorded exactly as it appears. The number itself should be recorded as instructed in RDA 1.8, which basically calls for numerals to be recorded "in the form preferred by the agency." This *Handbook* follows the Library of Congress's preference of recording numerals in the form in which they appear on the source of information (LC-PCC PS 1.8.2, first alternative, February 2010). In figures 2.73 and 2.74, the numeral appears as a roman numeral, and is so recorded in this element. In previous cataloging practice these would have been converted to arabic numerals.

2.12.10–2.12.17. SUBSERIES. Sometimes a main series may have a number of subordinate parts. If so, the title of the main series is recorded first in the MARC 490 field, followed by its series numbering, if any. If the main series is numbered, it is separated from the subseries by a period and repeated subfield ‡a. If it is not numbered, the subseries title proper follows the title proper of the main series in the same subfield ‡a as the main series title proper, from which it is separated by a period. For an example of a subseries with an unnumbered main series, see figures 2.32 and 2.60. For an example of a subseries with a numbered main series, see figure 2.72 (second 490 field).

2.13. MODE OF ISSUANCE. Mode of issuance is defined as "a categorization reflecting whether a resource is issued in one or more parts, the way it is updated, and its intended termination." Although not core in RDA, it is core for LC and PCC (LC-PCC PS 2.13, July 2012), and the MARC format also requires specification of the mode of issuance.

There are four possible modes of issuance given in RDA: the resource was issued as a single unit, as a multipart monograph, as a serial, or as an integrating resource. The information for this element is recorded in MARC leader byte 07 ("bibliographic level"), which is labeled BLvl in the OCLC fixed field display. Coding is as follows:

Single unit ....m (monograph)
                                                                    a (monographic component part)
Multipart monograph...m (monograph)
                                                                    a (monographic component part)
Serial ....s (serial)
                                                                    b (serial component part)
Integrating resource..i (integrating resource)

For an example, see figure 2.1, in which BLvl is coded "m" because the resource is a monograph issued as a single unit. Current MARC coding practice does not distinguish between the single unit and the multipart monograph modes of issuance.

2.14. FREQUENCY. Frequency refers to the intervals at which parts of a serial or updates to an integrating resource are issued. It is not a core element in RDA but is core for LC and PCC (LC-PCC PS 2.14, July 2012).

2.14.1.3. RECORDING FREQUENCY. Frequency is recorded by giving one of the terms listed in RDA 2.14.1.3 in subfield ‡a of the MARC bibliographic 310 field (current frequency) or 321 (former frequency). For examples, see figures 2.9b, 2.10, 2.11, 2.12a, 2.13, and 2.14.

If none of the terms is appropriate, make a note under 2.20.12 instead (see below).

2.15. IDENTIFIER FOR THE MANIFESTATION. This element is defined as "a character string associated with a manifestation that serves to differentiate that manifestation from other manifestations." Although there are numerous types of identifiers for manifestations, the most common for books is the ISBN (International Standard Book Number), and for serials is the ISSN (International Standard Serial Number). Also included for music are publisher's and plate numbers, and the International Standard Music Number (ISMN).

The Identifier for the manifestation element is core, and so if the resource has one and the cataloger is aware of it, it should be recorded. (Note that catalogers are not required to do research beyond the resource in hand to discover if a resource has an identifier.)

2.15.1.2. SOURCES OF INFORMATION. Information about this element can be found anywhere. Identifiers appear on resources, but also, for example, at publishers' websites and in publishers' catalogs.

2.15.1.4. RECORDING IDENTIFIERS FOR MANIFESTATIONS. According to RDA, identifiers are to be recorded in accordance with their "display format." ISBN, for example, is intended to include dashes at certain points within the number. MARC, however, requires that the ISBN be recorded without dashes.

National agencies assign blocks of ISBNs to publishers, who in turn assign individual ISBNs to individual resources. ISBN was not used before 1970, but resources published before then may have had ISBNs assigned to them retrospectively by publishers, especially when they reprinted titles. In 2007 ISBN changed from a ten-digit code to a thirteen-digit code, but resources published during a transition period of several years may show both. ISBN is recorded in the MARC bibliographic 020 field without internal dashes. For examples, see figures 2.3, 2.5, 2.16, and others throughout this chapter. If the resource gives both the ten-digit and thirteen-digit ISBN, record both (see figure 2.55).

ISSN is an eight-digit numeral used to identify serial publications. An international committee is responsible for the standard. It is recorded in the MARC bibliographic 022 field, including an internal dash between the fourth and fifth digits. For examples, see figures 2.9 through 2.14, and figure 2.50.

ISMN is an identifier for printed music. ISMN is recorded in subfield ‡a of the MARC bibliographic 024 field, with the first indicator coded "2." Do not include any internal dashes. For an example, see figure 2.56. Note that as of January 1, 2008, ISMN changed from a ten-character to a thirteen-character identifier. Current practice is to code thirteen-character ISMNs in the 024 field with the first indicator coded "3."

A universal product code may be recorded in subfield ‡a of the MARC 024 field with the first indicator coded "1." See figures 2.4 and 2.25 for examples.

Publishers' catalog numbers often appear on motion picture resources such as DVDs. These may be recorded as an identifier. Record these numbers in subfield ‡a of the MARC bibliographic 028 field with the first indicator coded 4. Record the publisher's name (often the production company) in subfield ‡b. For an example, see figure 2.4b.

2.15.1.5. MORE THAN ONE IDENTIFIER FOR THE MANIFESTATION. If a resource is issued in more than one part there may be an identifier for the resource as a whole as well as identifiers for the individual parts. When creating a description for the resource as a whole, at a minimum record the identifier for the whole (if one exists). However, the optional addition instructs catalogers to record all identifiers, both that for the whole resource as well as identifiers for individual parts. Because identifiers such as ISBN are commonly used to find resources, it only makes sense for catalogers to record all identifiers available (see figure 2.7). RDA also has an alternative guideline allowing for recording a span of identifiers rather than all the individual identifiers. Current practice is not to follow this alternative, but instead record separately all identifiers (see LC-PCC PS 2.15.1.5, alternative, September 2012).

2.15.1.7. QUALIFICATION. If a resource has more than one identifier of the same type (e.g., an ISBN for a paperback and another for a hardback when the cataloger wishes to consider both formats the same manifestation and thus use the same description for both), record in parentheses a word that differentiates between the identifiers (see figure 2.30). Identifiers may also be qualified to specify the type of binding even if there is only one (see figure 2.70).

2.15.2 PUBLISHER'S NUMBER FOR MUSIC. A publisher's number is usually a catalog number used by the publisher to identify its publications. On a score it usually appears on the title page or the cover. On a sound recording it can appear anywhere, but is often found on the back or the spine of the case, or printed on the disc itself. Publisher's numbers for scores are recorded in subfield ‡a of the 028 field, with the first indicator coded "3"; the source of the number (usually the publisher's name) is recorded in subfield ‡b (see figures 2.26, 2.28, and 2.29). For sound recordings, record publisher's number in subfield ‡a of the 028 field, with the first indicator coded "0"; record the source of the number in subfield ‡b (see figure 2.22). For both scores and sound recordings, if the second indicator is coded "2" the system may be programmed to generate a label such as "Publisher's number."

2.15.3. PLATE NUMBER FOR MUSIC. A plate number is a number that appears at the bottom of each page of a music score. Plate numbers may be recorded as identifiers for the manifestation, although they often reappear in republications reproducing the same printing plates. If found in a resource, a plate number is recorded in subfield ‡a of the MARC 028 field with the first indicator coded "2." The source of the plate number (usually the name of the publisher) is recorded in subfield ‡b. If the second indicator is coded "2," the system may be programmed to generate a label such as "Plate number." Figure 2.56 shows an example of a plate number.

2.17. CUSTODIAL HISTORY OF ITEM. This element records the provenance of a resource. Provenance is the history of the ownership of a resource. Recording this information might not be important for most library materials, but for certain types of resources it is crucial to know the custodial history. The custodial history of item element is used most frequently in libraries for archival or manuscript materials, for which it is important to know who has had custody of the resource in as much detail as possible. Record custodial history in subfield ‡a of the MARC 561 field. For examples, see figures 2.35, 2.38, and 2.63.

2.18. IMMEDIATE SOURCE OF ACQUISITION OF ITEM. This element is really a subset of that described in 2.17. It records the last link in the chain of ownership of a resource or artifact, the source from which the library acquired the item. Libraries may prefer to keep this information private, using nonpublic acquisition records to keep track of this information. If a library wishes to include this element in a MARC bibliographic record, it is recorded in a 541 field (see figures 2.38 and 2.63).

2.20. NOTE ON MANIFESTATION OR ITEM. The subsections of RDA 2.20 give detailed instructions for a variety of notes that may appear in RDA descriptions of manifestations or items. Unlike AACR2, which prescribed a certain order for the appearance of notes, in RDA notes may appear in any order. The cataloger should use his or her best judgment, ordering notes in a logical and helpful manner. No notes are core (required) in RDA.

2.20.2. NOTE ON TITLE. A note may be made giving the source of the title proper if it did not come from the normal preferred source for the type of resource. The element is most commonly recorded in a MARC 500 field, but in certain cases another field is used. For example, in figure 2.1 the title proper of the film was taken from the disc label rather than the preferred source (the title frame). Similarly, in figure 2.51 the title of the book was found on the cover, not the preferred source. If the cataloger supplies the title a note such as that in figures 2.34, 2.36, or 2.37 may be made.

It is typical to record this element for digital resources (see 500 fields in figures 2.58, 2.59, and 2.61). In CONSER practice a note is always given explaining the source of a serial title, often as part of the "description based on" note in the 588 field (see figures 2.9 through 2.14, and figure 2.50). This practice is also followed for integrating resources (see figures 2.15 and 2.16).

2.20.2.4. TITLE VARIATIONS, INACCURACIES, AND DELETIONS. This element covers a number of situations, including cases where the title on some issues or parts of a serial or multipart monograph differ slightly from the form chosen as the title proper. If the difference is not considered important for access, simply make a note such as:

500   ‡a Title varies slightly.

A note may also be made if the title proper contains an inaccuracy. In figure 2.18 the first word was misspelled. In the cataloging shown in the figure the cataloger did not feel it was important to display a note, although an added access point for the title was given. If the cataloger had wanted to create a note it might have been recorded as follows, generating the note from the 246 field:

246   1   ‡i Title should read: ‡a Habeas corpus and detentions
            at Guantanamo Bay

On variant titles, see also 2.3.6, above.

2.20.3. NOTE ON STATEMENT OF RESPONSIBILITY. The cataloger may make a note on persons, families, or corporate bodies not named in a statement of responsibility in the description that have intellectual or artistic responsibility for the content of the resource (see figure 2.20). Note that in AACR2 such notes were required if a person or corporate body was to be given as an added access point. RDA does not require access points to be justified in the description, so the note described in 2.20.3 is not required.

A common note of this type is the "at head of title" note, which records a name not transcribed in a statement of responsibility that appears at the top of the title page. Usually this is the name of a corporate body appearing in this position whose relationship to the work is not certain, but for whom an added access point should be given because of its prominent position on the title page (see figures 2.23 and 2.72).

The note in figure 2.8 gives information about the composer of books 4 through 6 of a multipart monograph, who was not mentioned in the statement of responsibility based on the first book. Similarly, the note in figure 2.26 gives fuller details about the role of the composer and the origin of the work than is contained in the formal statement of responsibility.

2.20.5. NOTE ON NUMBERING OF SERIALS. As seen above under 2.6, the note on numbering of serials is an alternative, less formal way of recording the same information as that recorded in the numbering of serials element (RDA 2.6). RDA 2.6 is a core element, but it contains an alternative guideline to record the numbering information as a note, which satisfies the core requirement. LC and PCC will generally follow the alternative (see LC-PCC PSs for RDA 2.6.2.3–2.6.5.3, September 2012).

As discussed at 2.6, the sources of information for the numbering of serials element are quite restrictive: the information must come from the first or last issue or part of the serial, and so if the cataloger does not have access to either of these issues or parts, the element generally cannot be recorded. In contrast, although the note on numbering of serials element records the same information, that is, information about the first or last issue or part of a serial, information for this note may be taken from any source, so if the cataloger knows the information it may be recorded even if the first or last issue or part are not available.

The note described in 2.20.5.3 is recorded in MARC bibliographic records in the 362 field with the first indicator coded "1." This is referred to in MARC as an "unformatted note." Wording is not prescribed, but the examples given at RDA 2.20.5.3 are typical of current cataloging practice. Numbers, letters, or other characters, captions, and chronological designations may be transcribed as found. If the information recorded includes both numbering and a chronological designation, it may be recorded in the same way as the numbering of serials element in 2.6, that is, the numbering recorded first and the chronological designation following in parentheses, but this is not required. For examples in this *Handbook,* see figures 2.9, 2.10, 2.11b, and 2.14. Notes for complex or irregular numbering (2.20.5.4) and period covered (2.20.5.5) are recorded in a MARC 515 field:

> 515 ‡a Issues for August 1973–December 1974 also called v. 1, no. 7–v. 2, no. 12.
>
> 515 ‡a Report year ends June 30.

For an example, see figure 2.9b.

2.20.7. NOTE ON PUBLICATION STATEMENT. If clarification or expansion of information recorded in the publication statement would be helpful for identification or access, the cataloger may make a note. In figure 2.75 the publication statement has been transcribed exactly as it appears, as required by RDA 2.8. It is a reasonable assumption that many database users would recognize neither the place nor the publisher, so a note is given clarifying the facts. This type of note may be used more in RDA than in previous cataloging practice. Under AACR2 1.4C2 the publication statement might have been given:

> 260 ‡a Novi Eboraci [New York] : ‡b Sumptibus Duttonis, ‡c 1960.

The bracketed interpolation in the place of publication element, which is not permitted in RDA records, would have made the note less necessary.

Another example of this kind of note is a quoted phrase from the resource giving the publication date in greater detail than that given in the publication statement. See figure 2.31 ("April 1995").

Figure 2.75. Note on Publication Statement

100 1	‡a Milne, A. A. (Alan Alexander), ‡d 1882-1956, ‡e author.
240 10	‡a Winnie-the-Pooh. ‡l Latin
245 10	‡a A.A. Milnei Winnie ille Pu : ‡b liber celeberrimus omnibus fere pueris puellisque notus / ‡c nunc primum de Anglico sermone in Latinum conversus auctore Alexandro Lenardo.
246 30	‡a Winnie ille Pu
264 1	‡a Novi Eboraci : ‡b Sumptibus Duttonis, ‡c MCMLX [1960]
300	‡a 121 pages : ‡b illustrations, map ; ‡c 19 cm
336	‡a text ‡2 rdacontent
336	‡a still image ‡2 rdacontent
336	‡a cartographic image ‡2 rdacontent
337	‡a unmediated ‡2 rdamedia
338	‡a volume ‡2 rdacarrier
500	‡a Translation of: Winnie-the-Pooh.
500	‡a Published in New York by Dutton.
500	‡a Map on endpapers.
700 1	‡a Lenard, Alexander, ‡e translator.

Title page

A.A. Milnei
Winnie ille Pu
Liber celeberrimus omnibus fere
pueris puellisque notus
nunc primum de anglico sermone
in Latinum conversus
auctore Alexandro Lenardo
Novi Eboraci: Sumptibus Duttonis
MCMLX

2.20.12. NOTE ON FREQUENCY. This note is related to the frequency element (see above at 2.14), which requires terms describing the frequency of serials or integrating resources to be taken from a list. If no 2.14 term is appropriate to the resource being described, a less formal note can be given following 2.20.12. There is in fact little difference in the MARC record between these two elements. Both are recorded in subfield ‡a of the MARC bibliographic 310 field (current frequency) or 321 (former frequency). For examples, see figures 2.9a (which includes both former and current frequency), 2.16 (an integrating resource), and 2.50.

2.20.13. NOTE ON ISSUE, PART, OR ITERATION USED AS THE BASIS FOR IDENTIFICATION OF THE RESOURCE. Because resources that exist over time, such as serials, multipart monographs, and integrating resources, may exhibit differences between parts or iterations, catalogers may record information differently depending on which part or iteration they are consulting. This can cause confusion for others trying to decide if a particular record applies to the resource they have in hand. The note described in 2.20.13 is meant to remedy this by instructing the cataloger to identify the issue or part used as the basis for the description. In North American cataloging practice it is usually worded "Description based on: . . ." and is recorded in the MARC 588 field. This note has long been required in PCC CONSER records for serials and will continue to be required in RDA records. For examples, see figures 2.9 through 2.14, and figure 2.50. It is also required for multipart monographs if the description is based on a part other than the first.

2.20.13.5. DATE OF VIEWING OF AN ONLINE RESOURCE. The date on which online resources were seen should be given because they change (or, for that matter, disappear) so readily. The note is usually combined with the source of title note (see figure 2.76). For an example of this note in an online serial, see figure 2.9b.

Figure 2.76. Date of Viewing

110	1	‡a Illinois.
240	10	‡a Laws, etc.
245	10	‡a Laws of Illinois.
264	1	‡a Macomb, Illinois : ‡b Western Illinois University Libraries, ‡c [2010?]
300		‡a 1 online resource
336		‡a text ‡2 rdacontent
337		‡a computer ‡2 rdamedia
338		‡a online resource ‡2 rdacarrier
347		‡a text file ‡b HTML ‡2 rda
588		‡a Title from home page (viewed May 29, 2012).
505	0	‡a Prior to statehood -- Northwest Territory -- Indiana Territory -- Illinois Territory -- The road to Illinois statehood -- Illinois state constitution -- The state of Illinois [laws]
520		‡a Contains digitized laws of Illinois from 1787 to the present and Indiana Territory from 1801 to 1809. Also includes United States government publications concerning Illinois statehood and materials on the Illinois Constitutional Conventions.

710 2   ‡a Western Illinois University. ‡b University Libraries, ‡e editor of compilation.
856 40 ‡u http://www.wiu.edu/libraries/govpubs/illinois_laws/

DESCRIBING CARRIERS

RDA chapter 1 included guidelines (such as transcription) that applied to all elements in chapters 2–4. Chapter 2 gave specific guidelines for recording information about attributes of manifestations and items. Chapter 3 contains more guidelines for recording information about attributes of manifestations and items, those attributes that describe the carrier of the resource.

As defined in the RDA glossary, a carrier is "a physical medium in which data, sound, images, etc., are stored," and it may include a container that is an integral part of the resource. "Physical" encompasses not only what is conventionally considered physical, but also electronic media. The carrier for a text, for example, might be ink printed on paper, bound into a codex or rolled into a scroll. Or, it might be contained in a digital medium such as a computer disc or an online web page, or the text might be carried by a microform carrier such as microfiche or microfilm. RDA chapter 3 tells how to describe these carriers.

3.1.1. SOURCES OF INFORMATION. The description of the carrier is based on what the cataloger can ascertain from the resource itself, including accompanying material or a container. This information can be augmented by evidence found in any source (e.g., a description of a book with unnumbered pages that gives an accurate count).

3.1.2. MANIFESTATIONS AVAILABLE IN DIFFERENT FORMATS. In terms of MARC, this guideline basically instructs the cataloger to create separate bibliographic records for resources that are available in different formats (i.e., an expression of a work that is available in different carriers, such as a film available in a film reel, a videocassette, and a videodisc such as DVD).

3.1.3. FACSIMILES AND REPRODUCTIONS. For treatment of facsimiles and reproductions, see the appendix to this chapter.

3.1.4. RESOURCES CONSISTING OF MORE THAN ONE CARRIER TYPE. In contrast to 3.1.2, which gives guidelines for dealing with an expression of a work that exists in manifestations distinguished from each other by the fact that they exist in different formats, RDA 3.1.4 refers to the situation where the content of a single resource is contained in more than one carrier. The resource described in figure 2.22, for example, consists of a compact disc and an accompanying booklet, a commonly encountered situation (see also figure 2.58 and 2.59). The kit described in figure 2.41 is contained in several parts consisting of four carrier types. RDA gives three options for dealing with this situation.

3.1.4.1. RECORDING ONLY CARRIER TYPE AND EXTENT OF EACH CARRIER. Following this option, only the carrier type or types (RDA 3.3, MARC 338 field[s]) and extent for each type of carrier (RDA 3.4, MARC 300 field[s]) are recorded. The description of the kit in figure 2.41 is an example of this approach. The extent of the filmstrips, audiocassettes, teacher's guides, and wall chart are all given in a 300 field; the corresponding carrier types are recorded in the 338 field. Dimensions of the individual units are not given (the dimensions recorded in the description are the dimensions for the container, the optional addition given in RDA 3.1.4.1). Alternately, separate extent statements for each unit could have been recorded in separate 300 fields, and the separate carrier types could have been recorded in separate 338 fields. Either method conveys the same information.

3.1.4.2. RECORDING CARRIER TYPE, EXTENT, AND OTHER CHARACTERISTICS OF EACH CARRIER. If more detail is desired, "other characteristics" (i.e., any of the elements given in RDA 3.5–3.19) for each carrier can be recorded in addition to carrier type(s) and extents. This is the approach taken with the resource described in figure 2.58. This resource consists of a computer disc and a booklet. Each is fully described: "other characteristics" in this instance include the dimensions of each unit (RDA 3.5, recorded in the 300 field) and the digital file characteristics of the computer disc (RDA 3.19, recorded in the 347 field).

As mentioned with 3.1.4.1, the extent statements and other characteristics for each unit of figure 2.58 could have been given in separate 300 fields:

300 ‡a 1 computer disc : ‡b sound, color ; ‡c 4 3/4 in.
300 ‡a 1 instruction booklet (7 pages) : ‡b illustrations ; ‡c 18 cm

Figure 2.58 instead uses a technique in which one component is treated as the predominant component and the other component(s) as accompanying material. Accompanying material is recorded in subfield ‡e of the MARC bibliographic 300 field (see LC-PCC PS 3.1.4, October 2012, for details on using this technique). Either technique (separate extent statements, or predominant component plus accompanying material) conveys the same information.

3.1.4.3. RECORDING PREDOMINANT CARRIER TYPE AND EXTENT IN GENERAL TERMS. If it is not thought important to record the individual carriers, the predominant carrier type and its extent can be recorded and the rest summarized as "various pieces." This is the approach taken with the silver pitcher set described in figure 2.77.

Figure 2.77. Various Pieces

245	00	ǂa Silver pitcher set.
264	0	ǂc [1885?]
264	3	ǂa [New Bedford, Massachusetts] : ǂf Pairpoint Mfg. Co.
300		ǂa 1 pitcher, various pieces ; ǂc 12 x 8 x 8 cm-50 x 38 x 30 cm in box 55 x 40 x 35 cm
336		ǂa three-dimensional form ǂ2 rdacontent
337		ǂa unmediated ǂ2 rdamedia
338		ǂa object ǂ2 rdacarrier
340		ǂa silver
520	2	ǂa Quadruple-plated silver set with foliage ornamentation manufactured by Pairpoint Manufacturing Co. of New Bedford, Massachusetts. The set includes a pitcher with a hinged lid, stand, underplate, and goblet.
561		ǂa Set was originally owned by Karl G. Maeser, whose family donated the item to the Brigham Young University Alumni Association. It was later transferred to the BYU Honors Association, which donated it to the library in 2007.
700	1	ǂa Maeser, Karl G., ǂe former owner.
710	2	ǂa Pairpoint Manufacturing Co., ǂe manufacturer.

3.1.5. ONLINE RESOURCES. The carrier type for a remote-access online resource is to be recorded as "online resource." This will appear both in the extent (300 field) and the carrier type (338 field) elements (see figures 2.9b, 2.42, and 2.76). If the online resource is complete and has a recordable extent (e.g., a digital copy of a printed book), record it in parentheses as part of the extent statement (see figure 2.61).

3.2. MEDIA TYPE. Media type, an element new in RDA, is a broad term categorizing the general type of device (if any) required to use the information contained in the resource. It is to be recorded using one of the terms in the list found with RDA 3.2.1.3.

Media type is not a core element in RDA, but it is core for LC and PCC, and the general practice has been to record the element (cf. LC-PCC PS 3.2, October 2012).

Media type is recorded in subfield ǂa of the MARC bibliographic 337 field. In MARC, the field must include information about the source of the term. For RDA records, therefore, the field should always end with "ǂ2 rdamedia" (meaning the term came from RDA's vocabulary). For examples, see all the figures in this chapter.

The basic guideline in RDA 3.2 is to record all the media types applicable to the resource. RDA 3.2.1.3 has an alternate guideline, however, that allows the cataloger to record one or more of the types that apply to the predominant or most substantial parts of the resource and not record the others. This *Handbook* has generally not applied this alternative guideline.

3.3. CARRIER TYPE. Carrier type is actually a subset of media type—each carrier type term has one, and only one, corresponding media-type term. It is a term that categorizes the format of the carrier housing the resource. Carrier type is to be recorded using one of the terms in the list found with RDA 3.3.1.3.

Carrier type is a core element, meaning it is required in RDA descriptions of manifestations (e.g., MARC bibliographic records).

Carrier type is recorded in subfield ‡a of the MARC bibliographic 338 field. In MARC, the field must include information about the source of the term. For RDA records, therefore, the field should always end with "‡2 rdacarrier" (meaning the term came from RDA's vocabulary). For examples, see all the figures in this chapter.

The basic guideline in RDA 3.3 is to record all the carrier types applicable to the resource. RDA 3.3.1.3 has an alternate guideline, however, that allows the cataloger to record one or more of the types that apply to the predominant or most substantial parts of the resource and not record the others. This *Handbook* has generally not applied this alternative guideline.

3.4. EXTENT. Extent refers to the number of units or subunits that make up a resource. For example, the resource described in figure 2.30 consists of one map, and so the extent is recorded as "1 map" (300 field). In earlier drafts of RDA this simple pattern was meant to be applied to all kinds of resources, so the extent of a book would have been "1 volume," normally with the addition of subunits, e.g., "1 volume (395 pages)." It was eventually decided that this represented too great a break with past cataloging practice, particularly for texts, and so a somewhat complex set of guidelines was devised with separate guidelines for certain types of resources, some of which depart to a greater or lesser extent from the basic guideline for recording extent.

The extent element is core in RDA, meaning it is required in an RDA description of a manifestation, unless the resource is incomplete or the total extent is unknown.

3.4.1.3. RECORDING EXTENT. Extent is recorded in subfield ‡a of the MARC bibliographic 300 field. It may also appear in subfield ‡e if the cataloger is using the accompanying material technique (see discussion above at 3.4.1.2). See examples throughout this chapter. With some exceptions noted below, record extent by giving the number of units and a term from the list of carrier types in 3.3.1.3 (in the singular or plural as appropriate). The extent element for the documentary film recorded in figure 2.1a was recorded by giving the number of units ("1") and the carrier type corresponding to the unit from 3.3.1.3 ("videodisc"). (The parenthetical extension in subfield ‡a of the 300 field in 2.1a is not part of the extent element; it is the duration element [see RDA 7.22]. Mingling these two separate elements in a single MARC subfield is a problem related to MARC, not RDA.)

3.4.1.3 ALTERNATIVE. Terms outside the list given in 3.3.1.3 may be used to describe the type of unit for resources that do not fall under the exceptions listed in 3.4.2 through 3.4.6 under two circumstances: (1) the carrier is not on the list at 3.3.1.3; or (2) the agency creating the description prefers to use an alternative term.

The figures in this chapter generally follow the basic instruction to use terms from the list in 3.3.1.3. The resource described in figure 2.41 includes filmstrips and audiocassettes, both of which have appropriate terms in 3.3.1.3, but it also includes teachers' guides and a wall chart, for which no term is found. These terms may be recorded in extent elements. Similarly, the term "pitcher" does not appear in the list in 3.3.1.3, but is appropriate for use in an extent statement of figure 2.77 because no term listed there is appropriate.

Figure 2.59 is an example of the application of the 3.4.1.3 alternative. In this case there is no question that the term "computer disc," which appears in 3.3.1.3, is appropriate for describing the carrier of the resource, but the agency preferred to use a term in common use, DVD-ROM. Contrast figure 2.59 with 2.58, where the term "computer disc" was used. Either approach is acceptable in RDA, but the cataloger should consider the overall use in the database. In the shared cataloging environment we work in today, it is likely that most extent elements in RDA records will follow the basic guideline of recording terms from 3.3.1.3. Will it really be useful to have a few miscellaneous records in the database using alternative terms? This *Handbook* generally uses terms taken from 3.3.1.3.

3.4.1.7. NUMBER OF SUBUNITS. If a unit being described in an extent statement has an ascertainable number of subunits, and the subunits are considered important for identification or selection of the resource, record them in parentheses following the term for the unit. Subunits may include files or images in a computer resource, pages of a digitized book, frames in a video collection of still images, and many other things. Kinds of subunits are not limited to those listed in the subsections of 3.4.1.7. For examples, see figure 2.22 (extent element in 300 subfield ‡e) and figures 2.26, 2.28, 2.29, 2.56, 2.57, and 2.61.

Remember that not everything that appears in parentheses following a recorded extent is a record of subunits. See the discussion of figure 2.1a above at 3.4.1.3. Figure 2.44 is another example.

3.4.1.10. INCOMPLETE RESOURCE. When describing a resource that is not complete (e.g., a multipart monograph or a serial) or a resource for which the total number of units is not known, RDA gives the cataloger two choices: either record the term that describes the type of unit without recording a number (e.g., "volumes") or, following the alternate guideline, do not record the extent at all. This *Handbook* follows the basic guideline (see figures 2.10b, 2.11, 2.12b, 2.14, 2.15, and 2.50). The LC policy is only to apply the alternative to serials, not to multipart monographs or integrating resources (LC-PCC PS 3.4.1.10, alternative, February 2010).

3.4.1.11. COMPREHENSIVE DESCRIPTION OF A COLLECTION. RDA offers three ways of recording the extent element when describing a collection: either give the number of items, containers, or volumes (3.4.1.11.1); the amount of storage space (3.4.1.11.2); or simply follow the general guidelines for extent and record the number of units and a term describing the type of unit (3.4.1.11.3).

The first two alternatives can be combined (see the optional additions to 3.4.1.11.1 and 3.4.1.11.2), and they are usually in archival cataloging. RDA calls for the storage space statement to be given first, then the number of containers in parentheses (3.4.1.11.2 optional addition). For examples, see figures 2.38 and 2.63. RDA calls for recording the amount of storage space in metric units, but has an alternative to record the amount in the system of measurement preferred by the agency. The Library of Congress, and most North American libraries and archives, will record the amount of storage space in terms of inches, cubic inches, feet, or cubic feet (LC-PCC PS 3.4.1.11.2, alternative, February 2010).

3.4.1.12. ANALYTICAL DESCRIPTION OF A PART. When describing a part of a larger resource, if it is possible to follow one of the instructions for extent in 3.4.1.3 to 3.4.1.10 (or the exceptions listed in 3.4.1.3, RDA 3.4.2–3.4.6), do so. For example, if a cataloger chooses to create a record for a single volume of a multipart monograph, the extent would be recorded following 3.4.5. However, if the part being described is at a particular place within a larger resource (e.g., an article in a book), record the "position of the part within the larger resource." See figure 2.78 for an example.

Figure 2.78. Analytical Description

```
100 1   ‡a Card, Orson Scott, ‡e author.
240 10  ‡a Missed. ‡l French
245 10  ‡a Jamais trop loin / ‡c auteur: Orson Scott Card ; traducteur: Pierre-Alexandre
        Sicart ; dessin & couleur: Éric Hérenguel.
264  1  ‡a Toulon : ‡b Soleil Press, ‡c 2011.
300     ‡a pages 79-82 : ‡b color illustrations, color portrait ; ‡c 30 cm
336     ‡a text ‡2 rdacontent
336     ‡a still image ‡2 rdacontent
337     ‡a unmediated ‡2 rdamedia
338     ‡a volume ‡2 rdacarrier
700 1   ‡a Sicart, Pierre-Alexandre, ‡d 1975- ‡e translator.
```

```
700 1    ‡a Hérenguel, Éric, ‡d 1966- ‡e illustrator.
773 0    ‡t Lanfeust mag., ‡g no 139 (Février 2011)
```

3.4.2. EXTENT OF CARTOGRAPHIC RESOURCE. The extent of a cartographic resource follows the same general pattern given in 3.4.1—that is, the number of units together with a term naming the units—but unlike 3.4.1, the term is not chosen from the carrier type list in 3.3.1.3. Instead, use one of the special terms for cartographic resources listed in 3.4.2.2. For examples, see figures 2.30, 2.31, and 2.40.

3.4.2.3. MORE THAN ONE CARTOGRAPHIC UNIT ON ONE OR MORE SHEETS. If a cartographic resource consists of more than one unit and each is on a separate sheet, RDA instructs the cataloger to follow 3.4.2.2, e.g., "4 maps." But if the number of sheets differs from the number of units, we are to record both the number of units and the number of sheets. A sheet is defined in the RDA glossary as "a flat piece of thin material." This material is most commonly paper. Do not forget that a sheet has two sides; therefore it is possible, and in fact quite common, for two maps to be printed on either side of one sheet. This is the case in the description shown in figure 2.31c. It is also possible to have more than one map on the same side of a sheet, as is the case with the resource described in figure 2.37. Conversely, it is possible for a single map to be printed on more than one sheet (e.g., "1 map on 2 sheets").

3.4.2.5. ATLASES. Atlases share characteristics of both text and cartographic material, so in RDA the extent element for an atlas records information about both aspects. When describing an atlas, record "1 atlas" followed by the number of volumes or pages in parentheses, following the guidelines for extent of text in RDA 3.4.5 (see figure 2.79).

Figure 2.79. Atlas

```
110 2    ‡a National Geographic Society (U.S.), ‡e cartographer.
245 10   ‡a National Geographic visual atlas of the world.
246 3    ‡a Visual atlas of the world
255      ‡a Scales differ.
264  1   ‡a Washington, D.C. : ‡b National Geographic Society, ‡c [2009]
300      ‡a 1 atlas (416 pages) : ‡b color illustrations, color maps ; ‡c 43 cm
336      ‡a cartographic image ‡2 rdacontent
336      ‡a still image ‡2 rdacontent
336      ‡a text ‡2 rdacontent
337      ‡a unmediated ‡2 rdamedia
```

338	‡a volume ‡2 rdacarrier
500	‡a Relief shown by shading and spot heights.
504	‡a Includes bibliographical references (pages 412-414) and indexes.
505 0	‡a World -- North America -- South America -- Europe -- Asia -- Africa -- Australia and Oceania -- Antarctica -- Oceans -- Space -- Flags and facts -- Appendix -- Index.

Title page

National Geographic
Visual
Atlas of the World

NATIONAL GEOGRAPHIC
WASHINGTON, D.C.

3.4.3. EXTENT OF NOTATED MUSIC. Like the extent of cartographic resources, the extent element for notated music follows the same general pattern given in 3.4.1, that is, the number of units together with a term naming the units, but the terms for notated music come from RDA 7.20.1.3. The number of volumes or pages is specified in parentheses following the term naming the unit(s), following the instructions in RDA 3.4.5. For examples, see figures 2.26, 2.28, 2.36, and 2.56. If the resource consists of a score as well as a set of parts, both are recorded in the extent element. Figure 2.57 shows how this is done in a single MARC bibliographic 300 field. Alternately, this element could have been recorded as two separate 300 fields:

300   ‡a 1 score (7 pages) ; ‡c 30 cm
300   ‡a 2 parts ; ‡c 30 cm

3.4.4. EXTENT OF STILL IMAGE. The extent element for a still image follows the general guidelines of 3.4.1, that is, give the number of units together with a term describing the units. However, the terms are taken from the list in 3.4.4.2 instead of from the list of carrier types (see figure 2.80). Note that some of these terms represent a change from previous cataloging practice. Instead of AACR2's "art original" use "collage," "drawing," "icon," "painting," or "print." Instead of "art print" or "art reproduction," use "print."

Figure 2.80. Extent of Still Image

100 1   ‡a Kershisnik, Brian Thomas, ‡d 1962- ‡e artist.
245 10 ‡a Sleeping Apostles / ‡c Kershisnik.

264	0	‡c 2011.
300		‡a 1 print : ‡b black and white ; ‡c 92 x 71 cm
336		‡a still image ‡2 rdacontent
337		‡a unmediated ‡2 rdamedia
338		‡a sheet ‡2 rdacarrier
340		‡a paper ‡c ink ‡d monoprint ‡e mat board
500		‡a Title and statement of responsibility from handwritten caption.
500		‡a Printed on sheet 98 x 76 cm.
520		‡a Monoprint depicting the three Apostles who fell asleep while Jesus was in Gethsemane.

3.4.5. EXTENT OF TEXT. Text, along with a few other content types, is noted as an exception to the basic extent guidelines for treating extent in 3.4.1 (see 3.4.1.3, exceptions). Of these content types, text departs the farthest from the basic guideline. However, like the extent statements for other content types, extent of text is recorded in the MARC bibliographic 300 field, subfield ‡a.

The guidelines for extent of text apply to the "print on paper" (or other physical medium such as plastic or cloth) format. Resources with text contained in other media such as microform or digital media are covered by the guidelines of 3.4.1.

Extent of text guidelines are divided between guidelines for resources consisting of a single unit and resource consisting of more than one unit.

3.4.5.2. SINGLE VOLUME WITH NUMBERED PAGES, LEAVES, OR COLUMNS. This guideline distinguishes between volumes numbered in terms of pages, leaves, or columns. There is a subtle but important difference between these provisions and the equivalent in AACR2 2.5B1 that makes a difference to recording extent.

AACR2 described a volume in terms of pages if it was "a volume with leaves *printed* on both sides." RDA describes a volume in terms of pages if it is *numbered* in terms of pages.

AACR2 described a volume in terms of leaves if it was "a volume with leaves *printed* on only one side." RDA describes a volume in terms of leaves if it is *numbered* in terms of leaves.

Both AACR2 and RDA describe a volume in terms of columns if the volume has more than one column to the page and the columns are numbered.

The difference between the AACR2 and RDA definitions make a difference to the extent statement. In RDA a volume is described in terms of pages if consecutive page numbers appear on both sides of the leaves; in AACR2 a volume was described in terms of pages if the leaves were printed on both sides, whether consecutive page numbers appeared on both sides or on only one side. In RDA a volume is described in terms of leaves if the leaves are numbered on one side only, whether printing appears on one or both sides of the leaf; in AACR2 a volume was described in terms of leaves if printing appeared on only one side of the leaf.

The AACR2 treatment of pages and leaves occasionally caused rather strange extent statements, such as:

48 [i.e. 96] p.

This represented a book in which each of its 48 leaves was numbered on one side, but printing appeared on both sides of the leaves; therefore AACR2 required that the book be described in terms of pages. But because "48 p." gave a false impression of the extent of the item, a correction had to be added. RDA sensibly records the extent statement for this book in terms of leaves:

48 leaves

The exception in 3.4.5.2 for updating loose-leaf resources is a practical solution to the problem of recording the extent of an integrating resource, which is liable to change over time. For an example, see figure 2.16. Further guidelines for loose-leaf resources can be found in LC-PCC PS 3.4.1.10, January 2013, and LC-PCC PS 0.0, September 2012.

When recording the extent of a single volume, record the last numbered page, leaf, or column in each sequence. "Sequence" refers to consecutive runs of numbers, not to the form of the numerals. A book whose pages are numbered i–xxx and then 1–500 is said to have two sequences; however, a book whose pages are numbered i–xxx and then 31–500 has only one sequence, because the only change has been from roman to arabic numerals in the same sequence. Hence, the pagination of the first book would be recorded "xxx, 500 pages," but the second would simply be recorded "500 pages." Note that "pages" is spelled out. This represents a change from previous cataloging practice, where the word would have been abbreviated "p." in the extent statement. For examples, see figure 2.2 and others throughout this chapter.

3.4.5.3. SINGLE VOLUME WITH UNNUMBERED PAGES, LEAVES, OR COLUMNS. If a resource has no numbered pages, leaves, or columns, RDA gives the cataloger three choices. Either (a) count all the pages, leaves, or columns, and record them in the form "8 unnumbered pages" (see figure 2.67); (b) give an approximate count if the number is not readily ascertainable (see figure 2.81); or (c) simply record "1 volume (unpaged)" (see figures 2.5, 2.44, and 2.51).

If following the first method (recording an exact count), give the extent in terms of pages if the leaves are printed or written on both sides, or in terms of leaves if the leaves are printed or written on only one side. Except for early printed books, do not

Figure 2.81. Page Count Estimate

245	00	‡a [Tibetan sutra].
264	1	‡a [Tibet?] : ‡b [Publisher not identified], ‡c [between 1700 and 1799?]
300		‡a approximately 400 pages : ‡b illustrations ; ‡c 57 x 19 cm
336		‡a text ‡2 rdacontent
336		‡a still image ‡2 rdacontent
337		‡a unmediated ‡2 rdamedia
338		‡a volume ‡2 rdacarrier
500		‡a Title supplied by cataloger.
500		‡a Block book containing an 18th century Vajrayana Buddhist sutra. Unbound paper leaves between two wooden boards. Each section begins with a mantra page printed in red ink with woodcuts of the gods.

count every page in a volume. In general cataloging begin the count with the first page or leaf containing either printing or illustration; end it with the last such page or leaf (see figure 2.82). Most catalogers would not count pages for items longer than 100 pages, but this is entirely the cataloger's decision. Library of Congress catalogers will usually choose the third method ("1 volume (unpaged)") of recording the extent of a volume with no numbered pages, leaves, or columns (LC-PCC PS 3.4.5.3, October 2012).

Figure 2.82. Unpaged Book

100	1	‡a Wakoski, Diane, ‡e author.
245	14	‡a The ice queen / ‡c Diane Wakoski ; illustrations by Margaret Prentice.
264	1	‡a [Tuscaloosa, Alabama] : ‡b Parallel Editions, ‡c 1994.
300		‡a 31 unnumbered pages : ‡b illustrations (some color) ; ‡c 34 cm
336		‡a text ‡2 rdacontent
336		‡a still image ‡2 rdacontent
337		‡a unmediated ‡2 rdamedia
338		‡a volume ‡2 rdacarrier
500		‡a "This limited edition book was designed and produced by Eileen Wallace, Steve Miller, Paula Marie Gourley, Timothy Geiger, Shari DeGraw and Inge Bruggeman in the MFA in the Book Arts Program at the University of Alabama"--Colophon.
500		‡a Two color illustrations on double leaves.
500		‡a Edition limited to 70.
590		‡a Brigham Young University copy is number 11, signed by author.
700	1	‡a Prentice, Margaret, ‡e illustrator.

Title page

The Ice Queen
Diane Wakoski

Illustrations by Margaret Prentice
Parallel Editions 1994

3.4.5.3.2. INESSENTIAL MATTER. Books published in the second half of the nineteenth century often included a several-page list of other books issued by the publisher. The book illustrated in figure 2.83 has such a list on three unnumbered pages following page 460. Inessential matter such as publishers' advertisements are to be disregarded in the pagination of the volume in general cataloging (note that in rare materials cataloging, including early printed resources, these pages may be counted).

Figure 2.83. Inessential Matter

---

100 1 ‡a Bishop, Frederick, ‡e author.

245 14 ‡a The illustrated London cookery book : ‡b containing upwards of fifteen hundred first-rate receipts selected with great care, and a proper attention to economy ... : combined with useful hints on domestic economy ... / ‡c by Frederick Bishop.

264 1 ‡a London : ‡b [Publisher not identified], ‡c MDCCCLIII [1852]

264 3 ‡a London : ‡b J. Haddon

300 ‡a xxxi, 460 pages : ‡b illustrations (some folded) ; ‡c 23 cm

336 ‡a text ‡2 rdacontent

336 ‡a still image ‡2 rdacontent

337 ‡a unmediated ‡2 rdamedia

338 ‡a volume ‡2 rdacarrier

500 ‡a Includes index.

500 ‡a Added engraved title page.

Printed title page

The
Illustrated London
Cookery Book,
containing upwards of
fifteen hundred first-rate receipts
selected with great care, and a proper attention to economy;
and embodying all the latest improvements in the culinary art:
accompanied by important remarks and counsel on the
arrangement and well-ordering of the kitchen,

combined with
useful hints on domestic economy.
The whole based on many years' constant practice and experience;
and addressed to
Private Families as well as the Highest Circles.
By Frederick Bishop.
Late cuisinier to St. James's Palace, Earl Grey, the Marquis of Stafford,
Baron Rothschild, Earl Norbury, Captain Duncombe, and
Many of the first families in the Kingdom.
Profusely illustrated with engravings on wood.
London: 227, Strand.
MDCCCLII.

Engraved title page

The
Illustrated
London Cookery
Book
&
Complete Housekeeper.
250 engravings.
London: 227, Strand.

3.4.5.5. MISLEADING NUMBERING. The cataloger will record the last number in a sequence unless that leaves a "completely false impression" of the extent of the resource. If the last number does give a completely false impression, the cataloger will record the number as it appears, but then add "that is" with the correct number. For example, in figure 2.84, the book's pagination began numbering in duplicate part way through the sequence. Because of the nature of the duplication, it was judged clearer to apply 3.4.5.5 (misleading numbering) than 3.4.5.12 (duplicated paging).

Figure 2.84. Misleading Numbering

020	‡a 2251013814
100 1	‡a Cicero, Marcus Tullius, ‡e author.
245 10	‡a De l'invention / ‡c Cicéron ; texte établi et traduit par Guy Achard.
250	‡a Première édition.
264 1	‡a Paris : ‡b Les Belles Lettres, ‡c 2002.
300	‡a 244, that is, 422 pages ; ‡c 20 cm.
336	‡a text ‡2 rdacontent
337	‡a unmediated ‡2 rdamedia
338	‡a volume ‡2 rdacarrier
490 1	‡a Collection des Universités de France, ‡x 0184-7155

504 ‡a Includes bibliographical references and indexes.

546 ‡a French and Latin on facing pages (pages 55-234 numbered in duplicate); commentary in French.

700 12 ‡a Cicero, Marcus Tullius. ‡t De inventione. ‡l French ‡s (Achard)

700 12 ‡a Cicero, Marcus Tullius. ‡t De inventione. ‡l Latin ‡s (Achard)

700 1 ‡a Achard, Guy, ‡e editor, ‡e translator.

830 0 ‡a Collection des universités de France.

Title page

COLLECTION DES UNIVERSITÉS DE FRANCE
publiée sous le patronage de l'ASSOCIATION GUILLAUME BUDÉ

CICÉRON
DE L'INVENTION
texte établi et traduit
par Guy Achard
Professeur à l'Université de Lyon III

PARIS
LES BELLES LETTRES
2002

3.4.5.7. PAGES, ETC., NUMBERED AS PART OF A LARGER SEQUENCE. Sometimes a publication may be an extract from a larger work. Inclusive paging is given for such a publication. A common example is an offprint (see figure 2.85). This is similar to the treatment of the extent of an analytical description of a part (see above at 3.4.1.12, with figure 2.78).

Figure 2.85. Offprint

---

100 1 ‡a Bühler, Curt F. ‡q (Curt Ferdinand), ‡d 1905-1985, ‡e author.

245 10 ‡a Some aspects of the collecting of incunabula in America / ‡c by Curt F. Bühler.

264 1 ‡a [New York] : ‡b [Bibliographical Society of America], ‡c 1975.

300 ‡a pages 445-448 ; ‡c 23 cm

336 ‡a text ‡2 rdacontent

337 ‡a unmediated ‡2 rdamedia

338 ‡a volume ‡2 rdacarrier

580 ‡a Offprint from Papers of the Bibliographical society of America, volume sixty-nine (1975).

787 1 ‡t Papers of the Bibliographical Society of America.

3.4.5.8. COMPLICATED OR IRREGULAR PAGING, ETC. RDA offers three ways to deal with a volume that has complex paging, foliation, or columns. (1) Record the total number of pages, leaves, or columns, followed by "in various pagings," "in various foliations," or "in various numberings." This requires the cataloger to count (or at least add up) the pages, leaves, or columns; this does not work if the volume switches between pages, leaves, or columns. For an example, see figure 2.36. (2) Record the complex paging, foliation, or columns exactly as they appear. This is the approach of figure 2.86. (3) Record "1 volume (various pagings)." This is the easiest approach and is the approach Library of Congress catalogers will normally follow (see LC-PCC PS 3.4.5.8, September 2012).

Figure 2.86. Complicated Paging

020	ǂa 0824074491
100 1	ǂa Reeds, Karen, ǂe author.
245 10	ǂa Botany in medieval and Renaissance universities / ǂc Karen Meier Reeds.
264 1	ǂa New York : ǂb Garland Publishing, Inc., ǂc 1991.
300	ǂa xix, 316 pages, pages 519-542, 260-273, 10 pages of plates : ǂb illustrations ; ǂc 24 cm.
336	ǂa text ǂ2 rdacontent
336	ǂa still image ǂ2 rdacontent
337	ǂa unmediated ǂ2 rdamedia
338	ǂa volume ǂ2 rdacarrier
490 1	ǂa Harvard dissertations in the history of science
502	ǂb Ph. D. ǂc Harvard University ǂd 1975
500	ǂa "Annex: 'Renaissance humanism and botany,' Annals of science 33 (1976), 519-542, 'Publishing scholarly books in the sixteenth century,' Scholarly publishing, April 1983, 259-274."
504	ǂa Includes bibliographical references (pages 261-283) and index.
830 0	ǂa Harvard dissertations in the history of science

Title page

Botany in
Medieval and
Renaissance Universities
Karen Meier Reeds

Garland Publishing, Inc.
New York & London 1991

3.4.5.9. LEAVES OR PAGES OF PLATES. Record plates in terms of pages or leaves following the pattern "25 leaves of plates" or "15 pages of plates." If the plates are numbered on one side only, record in terms of leaves; if the plates are numbered on both sides, record in terms of pages. See figure 2.86 for an example.

Generally disregard an unnumbered sequence of plates, unless the unnumbered sequence constitutes a substantial part of the resource or an unnumbered sequence includes plates that are referred to in a note. Describe unnumbered sequences of plates in terms of pages if they are printed on both sides, and in terms of leaves if they are printed on one side. In figure 2.87 the cataloger determined that the plates constituted a substantial part of the resource.

Figure 2.87. Unnumbered Plates

020	‡a 9789004188822
111 2	‡a Colloque international sur les études isiaques ‡n (4th : ‡d 2008 : ‡c Liège, Belgium)
245 10	‡a Isis on the Nile : ‡b Egyptian gods in Hellenistic and Roman Egypt : proceedings of the IVth International Conference of Isis Studies, Liège, November 27-29, 2008 : Michel Malaise in honorem / ‡c edited by Laurent Bricault and Miguel John Versluys.
246 30	‡a Proceedings of the IVth International Conference of Isis Studies
264 1	‡a Leiden ; ‡a Boston : ‡b Brill, ‡c 2010.
300	‡a xxviii, 293 pages, 68 unnumbered pages of plates : ‡b illustrations ; ‡c 25 cm.
336	‡a text ‡2 rdacontent
336	‡a still image ‡2 rdacontent
337	‡a unmediated ‡2 rdamedia
338	‡a volume ‡2 rdacarrier
490 1	‡a Religions in the Graeco-Roman world ; ‡v volume 171
546	‡a In English, French, and German.
504	‡a Includes bibliographical references (pages xi-xiv) and index.
700 1	‡a Bricault, Laurent, ‡e editor of compilation.
700 1	‡a Versluys, M. J., ‡e editor of compilation.
700 1	‡a Malaise, Michel, ‡e author, ‡e honoree.
830 0	‡a Religions in the Graeco-Roman world ; ‡v v. 171.

Title page

Isis on the Nile
Egyptian Gods in Hellenistic and Roman Egypt
Proceedings of the IVth International Conference of Isis Studies
Liège, November 27-29, 2008

Michel Malaise in honorem
edited by Laurent Bricault and Miguel John Versluys

BRILL
LEIDEN · BOSTON
2010

The type of paper used for printing has nothing to do with whether a leaf is a plate or not. The important thing to watch for is that "plate" material must be outside the regular numbering of the book. A plate does not form part of the original physical makeup of the folded signatures or gatherings that make up the book. A plate *interrupts* the regular sequence of pagination of the book. Plates may be gathered together in one place in the book, or they may be scattered through the book.

3.4.5.10. FOLDED LEAVES. For an example, see figure 2.88.

Figure 2.88. Folded Leaves

020		‡a 0792304284
100	1	‡a Ziegler, Peter A., ‡e author.
245	10	‡a Evolution of Laurussia : ‡b a study in late Palaeozoic plate tectonics / ‡c by Pieter A. Ziegler.
264	1	‡a Dordrecht ; ‡a Boston ; ‡a London : ‡b Kluwer Academic Publishers, ‡c [1989]
264	4	‡c ©1989
300		‡a viii, 102 pages, 13 folded leaves of plates : ‡b illustrations (some color) ; ‡c 27 cm
336		‡a text ‡2 rdacontent
336		‡a still image ‡2 rdacontent
337		‡a unmediated ‡2 rdamedia
338		‡a volume ‡2 rdacarrier
500		‡a "Designated publication no. 0163 of the International Lithosphere Programme."
500		‡a "Published with the co-operation of and on behalf of the Royal Geological and Mining Society of the Netherlands (K.N.G.M.G.)."
504		‡a Includes bibliographical references (pages 79-102).

Title page

Evolution of Laurussia
A Study in Late Palaeozoic Plate Tectonics
by Pieter A. Ziegler

> Geological-Paleontological Institute,
> University of Basel, Switzerland
> (formerly Shell Internationale Petroleum Maatschappij B.V.,
> The Hague, The Netherlands)
> Designated publication no. 0163 of the International Lithosphere Programme.
> Published with the co-operation of and on behalf of
> the Royal Geological and Mining Society of the Netherlands (K.N.G.M.G.)
> Kluwer Academic Publishers
> Dordrecht / Boston / London

3.4.5.14. SINGLE SHEET. Use "1 sheet" to record the extent of a single sheet. This replaces AACR2's "1 broadside" (see figure 2.89).

Figure 2.89. Single Sheet

245 00	‡a Poesia = ‡b Poetry : Friday, March 17, 7:30 p.m., El Pueblo Community Center, 6th and Irvington : mecha dance following poetry, 9:00 p.m. / ‡c Fernando Tápia, Chocolate Brown, Marta Bermudez, Miguel Mendez, Elena Parra, Aristeo Brito ; a Campo-El Pueblo/Gonzalez co-production.	
246 31	‡a Poetry	
264 1	‡a [Tucson, Arizona] : ‡b Campo-El Pueblo/Gonzalez, ‡c [1978]	
300	‡a 1 sheet : ‡b illustration ; ‡c 44 x 28 cm	
336	‡a text ‡2 rdacontent	
336	‡a still image ‡2 rdacontent	
337	‡a unmediated ‡2 rdamedia	
338	‡a sheet ‡2 rdacarrier	
700 1	‡a Tápia, Fernando.	
700 1	‡a Brown, Chocolate.	
700 1	‡a Bermudez, Marta.	
700 1	‡a Mendez, Miguel.	
700 1	‡a Parra, Elena.	
700 1	‡a Brito, Aristeo.	

Broadside

> Poesia/Poetry
> fernando tápia
> chocolate brown
> marta bermudez
> miguel mendez
> elena parra
> aristeo brito
> Friday, March 17, 7:30 p.m.

> El Pueblo Community Center
> 6th and Irvington
> Mecha dance following poetry, 9:00 p.m.
> A Campo-El Pueblo/Gonzalez Co-Production

3.4.5.15. SINGLE PORTFOLIO OR CASE. A portfolio is a container for holding loose materials, usually consisting of two covers joined at the back. A case is a somewhat more substantial container, usually enclosed on all four sides; like a portfolio it is used for holding loose materials. Record "1 portfolio" or "1 case" (see figure 2.90).

Figure 2.90. Case

100 1	‡a Porter, Eliot, ‡d 1901-1990, ‡e photographer.
245 10	‡a Glen Canyon / ‡c Eliot Porter.
264 1	‡a New York : ‡b Daniel Wolf Press, Inc., ‡c [1980]
264 4	‡a ‡c ©1980
300	‡a 1 case (4 unnumbered pages, 10 photographs in folders) : ‡b color illustrations ; ‡d 65 x 54 cm
336	‡a still image ‡2 rdacontent
336	‡a text ‡2 rdacontent
337	‡a unmediated ‡2 rdamedia
338	‡a sheet ‡2 rdacarrier
500	‡a Each print is 41 x 32 cm, mounted on 4-ply board, with photographer's signature on verso and portfolio stamp on recto of mount.
500	‡a "This portfolio has been published in an edition of 250 copies. The ten photographs of Glen Canyon, Utah are dye-transfer prints and were selected by the artist and printed under his supervision by Berkey K & L, New York. The portfolio was designed by Eleanor Morris Caponigro and printed letterpress from Centaur types on Arches Cover by Michael & Winifred Bixler, Boston. The cases were made by Moroquain, Inc., New York."--Colophon.
505 0	‡a Coyote Gulch, Escalante River, August 17, 1971 -- Cliff, Moonlight Creek, San Juan River, May 23, 1962 -- Reflections in pool, Indian Creek, Escalante River, September 22, 1965 -- Redbud in bloom, Hidden Passage, Glen Canyon, April 10, 1963 -- Green reflections in stream, Moqui Creek, Glen Canyon, September 2, 1962 -- Amphitheater, Davis Gulch, Escalante basin, May 12, 1965 -- Escalante River outwash, Glen Canyon, September 2, 1962 -- Tamarisk and grass, river's edge, Glen Canyon, August, 1961 -- Waterslide from above, Long Canyon, September 21, 1965 -- Dungeon Canyon, Glen Canyon, August 29, 1961.
590	‡a BYU copy is no. 48 of 250, signed by Eliot Porter.
700 1	‡a Bixler, Michael, ‡e printer.
700 1	‡a Bixler, Winifred, ‡e printer.
710 2	‡a Arjomari Prioux S.A., ‡e papermaker.
710 2	‡a Daniel Wolf Press, ‡e publisher.

3.4.5.16. MORE THAN ONE VOLUME. Record the extent of a monographic resource consisting of more than one volume by giving the total number of physical volumes and using the term "volumes." For examples, see figures 2.7, 2.8, 2.46, and 2.47. Record the extent of a completed serial resource by giving the number of *bibliographical* volumes, not physical volumes. "Bibliographical volumes" refers to the terms the serial uses to describe itself. If the last volume of a completed serial calls itself "volume 35" and it began with volume 1, record "35 volumes" no matter how many physical volumes the serial is bound into (see figures 2.9a, 2.10a, 2.12a, and 2.13).

Note that the earlier cataloging practice of combining physical and bibliographical volumes in this statement (e.g., "3 v. in 5") is not followed in RDA. Simply record the total number of physical volumes (for monographs) or bibliographic volumes (for serials).

If the resource is incomplete, either record "volumes" without a number or do not record the extent element at all. See discussion above at 3.4.1.10.

3.4.5.17. CONTINUOUSLY PAGED VOLUMES. Sometimes a multivolume resource is continuously paged, that is, a sequence of page numbers crosses from one volume to the next. In this case, follow the statement about the number of volumes with the pagination, foliation, or columniation following in parentheses. For an example, see figure 2.91. Optionally, the pagination, etc., can be omitted. The Library of Congress will apply 3.4.5.17 to multipart monographs, but will omit pagination, etc., for serials and integrating resources (see LC-PCC PS 3.4.5.17, October 2012).

Figure 2.91. Continuously Paged Volume

020	‡a 9781611460667 (volume 1)
020	‡a 9781611461008 (volume 2)
100 1	‡a Greene, John C., ‡d 1946- ‡e author
245 10	‡a Theatre in Dublin, 1745-1820 : ‡b a history / ‡c John C. Greene.
264 1	‡a Bethlehem [Pennsylvania] : ‡b Lehigh University Press ; ‡a Lanham, Maryland : ‡b Rowman & Littlefield, ‡c [2011]
300	‡a 2 volumes (708 pages) : ‡b illustrations ; ‡c 29 cm
336	‡a text ‡2 rdacontent
337	‡a unmediated ‡2 rdamedia
338	‡a volume ‡2 rdacarrier
504	‡a Includes bibliographical references and index.

Title page

THEATRE IN DUBLIN, 1745-1820
A History

Volume 1

John C. Greene

LEHIGH UNIVERSITY PRESS
Bethlehem

3.4.5.19. UPDATING LOOSE-LEAFS. For a multivolume updating loose-leaf, record the number of volumes followed by "loose-leaf" in parentheses. The extent of figure 2.15 is based on this guideline, but because the resource is incomplete, no number is recorded (see RDA 3.4.5.16). For further information about treatment of loose-leaf resources, see LC-PCC PS 3.4.5.19 (October 2012).

3.4.6. EXTENT OF THREE-DIMENSIONAL FORM. The extent element for a three-dimensional form follows the general guidelines of 3.4.1, that is, give the number of units together with a term describing the units. However, the terms are taken from the list in 3.4.6.2 instead of the list of carrier types. Note some of these terms represent a change from previous cataloging practice. Instead of AACR2's "art original" or "art reproduction," use a specific term such as "sculpture." If none of the terms listed in 3.4.6 is appropriate to the object, the cataloger may use another term. See figure 2.77.

3.5. DIMENSIONS. The size of the carrier of the manifestation being cataloged is part of its description. Sometimes the size of the container is also recorded. The information should be taken directly from the resource itself.

The dimensions element is not core in RDA, but the Library of Congress has made it core for all resources other than serials and online electronic resources (see LC-PCC PS 3.5, May 2012).

3.5.1.3. RECORDING DIMENSIONS. Dimensions are generally recorded in centimeters, rounded up to the next whole centimeter. However, other systems of measurement may be used if preferred by the cataloging agency. The Library of Congress will use inches for discs (audio, video, and computer) and audio carriers (such as cassettes), but will use centimeters for all other kinds of resources (see LC-PCC PS 3.5.1.3, September 2011, and LC-PCC PS 3.5.1.4.4, February 2010). Other agencies may use metric measurements for all kinds of resources if they wish.

Dimensions are recorded in subfield ‡c of the MARC bibliographic 300 field. Punctuation at the end of this field can be somewhat tricky in RDA for the uninitiated when applying ISBD punctuation, which most North American catalogers will continue to do for the foreseeable future. In a change from previous cataloging codes (but in step with other standards), RDA considers "cm" and "mm" to be symbols, not abbreviations (and so they do not end with a period). When recorded within a field these symbols are generally not followed by a period, but punctuation at the end of a field depends on ISBD conventions.

In ISBD punctuation each area before the note area (Area 7) is separated from the previous area by full stop (period)-space-dash-space (. --). In North American practice, the note area began a new paragraph on the card, and so did not have this preceding punctuation. In MARC coding, the full stop is not automatically provided; the cataloger must manually insert it at the end of a field preceding a new ISBD area. The physical description area (Area 5), recorded in MARC 300, normally ends with the dimensions element, and thus normally ends with "cm" or "mm." If the series area (Area 6) is present in the record, in ISBD conventions it is preceded by full stop-space-dash-space, requiring a period to be input at the end of the 300 field.

What does all this mean? In current RDA practice, if the 300 field ends with "cm" or "mm," a period is added if a series statement (490) is present. Otherwise, the field will not end with a period. This seems a rather convoluted and silly distinction, but it's easy enough to apply. Contrast figure 2.91 (no period at the end of the 300 field, because no series statement in 490 was recorded) with figure 2.87 (period at the end of the 300 field, because a series statement was recorded in 490).

3.5.1.4. DIMENSIONS OF CARRIER. Because carriers vary in their nature, there are separate guidelines for different kinds of carriers. Find the 3.5.1.4 sub-rule corresponding to the carrier being described and follow its instructions.

3.5.1.4.1. CARDS. Record the height × the width of an individual card. Figure 2.92 illustrates the dimensions of a flash card; figure 2.93 illustrates the dimensions of a microopaque.

Figure 2.92. Extent of a Card

```
100 1    ‡a Brown, Esther, ‡e author.
245 10   ‡a Parts and wholes / ‡c by Esther Brown.
264   1  ‡a Boston, Massachusetts : ‡b Teaching Resources Corporation, ‡c [1973]
264   4  ‡c ©1973
300      ‡a 69 flash cards : ‡b color ; ‡c 10 x 8 cm + ‡e 1 guide.
336      ‡a still image ‡2 rdacontent
336      ‡a text ‡2 rdacontent
337      ‡a unmediated ‡2 rdacarrier
338      ‡a card ‡2 rdamedia
490 0    ‡a Language skills
```

520   ‡a Designed to develop an understanding of the relationship of parts to wholes.

500   ‡a Catalog no. 84-310.

710 2   ‡a Teaching Resources Corporation, ‡e publisher.

Back of card

Parts and Wholes

Guide title page

Guide
Language Skills Development
Parts and Wholes
Picture Cards
by Esther Brown
Teaching Resources Corporation
100 Boylston Street, Boston, Massachusetts 02116

Container

Language Skills
Parts and Wholes
Catalog no. 84-310

Figure 2.93. Extent of a Card

100 1   ‡a Georgi, Charlotte, ‡e author.

245 10   ‡a Twenty-five years of Pulitzer prize novels, 1918-1943 : ‡b a content analysis / ‡c by Charlotte Georgi.

264   1 ‡a Rochester, New York : ‡b University of Rochester Press for Association of College and Research Libraries, ‡c 1958.

300   ‡a 4 microopaques (103 frames) ; ‡c 8 x 13 cm

336   ‡a text ‡2 rdacontent

337   ‡a microform ‡2 rdamedia

338   ‡a microopaque ‡2 rdacarrier

490 1   ‡a ACRL microcard series ; ‡v no. 96

502   ‡b M.S.L.S. ‡c University of North Carolina ‡d 1956

504   ‡a Includes bibliographical references (frames 67-69).

500   ‡a Microcard: UR-58 RL 22.

830   0 ‡a ACRL microcard series ; ‡v no. 96

Frame 1

UR-58
RL 22
Micro Card

Frame 2

Twenty-five years of Pulitzer prize novels, 1918-1943:
a content analysis by Charlotte Georgi
A thesis submitted to the Faculty of the University of North Carolina
in partial fulfillment of the requirements for the degree of
Master of Science in the School of Library Science
Chapel Hill 1956

3.5.1.4.3. CASSETTES. Most cassettes record the length × the height of the face of the cassette; audiocassettes also record the width of the tape (see figure 2.94). For information about other kinds of cassettes, see details in 3.5.1.4.3.

Figure 2.94. Extent of a Cassette

020		‡a 9781433228377
028	02	‡a 5180 ‡b Blackstone Audio
100	1	‡a Card, Orson Scott, ‡e author.
245	10	‡a Treason / ‡c by Orson Scott Card.
250		‡a Unabridged.
264	1	‡a [Ashland, Oregon] : ‡b Blackstone Audio, Inc., ‡c [2010]
264	4	‡c ℗2010
300		‡a 8 audiocassettes (approximately 10 hr., 30 min.) ; ‡c 3 7/8 x 2 1/2 in., 1/8 in. tape
336		‡a spoken word ‡2 rdacontent
337		‡a audio ‡2 rdamedia
338		‡a audiocassette ‡2 rdacarrier
344		‡a analog ‡b magnetic ‡c 1 7/8 ips ‡g stereo ‡2 rda
511	0	‡a Read by Stefan Rudnicki.
520		‡a Lanik Mueller's birthright as heir to planet Treason's most powerful rulership will never be realized. He is a "rad" (radical regenerative) who can regenerate injured flesh and trade extra body parts to the Offworld oppressors for iron. On a planet without hard metals or the means of escape, iron offers the promise of freedom through the chance to build a spacecraft. But it is a promise which may never be fulfilled, as Lanik uncovers a conspiracy beyond his imagination.
700	1	‡a Rudnicki, Stefan, ‡d 1945- ‡e voice actor.
710	2	‡a Blackstone Audio, Inc., ‡e publisher.

Cassette label

Treason
by Orson Scott Card
(5180) (p)2010 by Blackstone Audio, Inc.

Cass.	Side
1	1

3.5.1.4.4. DISCS. Record the diameter of the disc. LC practice is to record this in inches (see figures 2.1 [a DVD], 2.58 [a computer disc], and 2.95 [an LP]).

Figure 2.95. Extent of a Disc

028 02 ‡a RTS-2 ‡b Varèse Sarabande

245 00 ‡a Beyond the sound barrier.

264　1 ‡a North Hollywood, CA : ‡b Varèse Sarabande, ‡c [1980]

300　　 ‡a 1 audio disc ; ‡c 12 in.

336　　 ‡a performed music ‡2 rdacontent

337　　 ‡a audio ‡2 rdamedia

338　　 ‡a audio disc ‡2 rdacarrier

344　　 ‡a analog ‡c 33 1/3 rpm ‡g stereo ‡h dbx encoded ‡2 rda

490　1 ‡a DBX recording technology showcase series ; ‡v volume 2

511　0 ‡a London Symphony Orchestra; Morton Gould and Lee Holdridge, conductors.

505　0 ‡a Windjammer theme / Gould -- Tribute to a badman suite / Rozsa -- Princess Leia theme / Williams -- Tango / Gould -- Russian sailors' dance / Gliere -- Lazarus and his beloved suite / Holdridge -- Boy with goldfish suite / Tanner, Siu, Elliott.

700　1 ‡a Gould, Morton, ‡d 1913-1996, ‡e conductor.

700　1 ‡a Holdridge, Lee, ‡d 1944- ‡e conductor.

710　2 ‡a London Symphony Orchestra, ‡e performer.

830　　0 ‡a DBX recording technology showcase series ; ‡v v. 2.

Disc label

VARÈSE SARABANDE
Manufactured under license from dbx, inc. Made in U.S.A.
BEYOND THE SOUND BARRIER

RTS-2	dbx
Stereo Side 1	encoded disc

dbx - RECORDING TECHNOLOGY SHOWCASE SERIES
Volume 2
[contents of side 1]

3.5.1.4.5. FILMSTRIPS AND FILMSLIPS. A filmslip is a short filmstrip, sometimes mounted to lie flat instead of being rolled, as a filmstrip generally is. Record the width of the film in millimeters (mm) (see figures 2.96 [filmslip] and 2.97 [filmstrip]).

Figure 2.96. Filmslip

245 00	‡a Different kinds of plants / ‡c collaborator, Illa Podendorf ; produced by Encyclopaedia Britannica Films.
264 1	‡a [Wilmette, Illinois] : ‡b Encyclopaedia Britannica Films, ‡c [1963]
300	‡a 1 filmslip (14 frames) : ‡b color ; ‡c 35 mm + ‡e 1 student guide
336	‡a still image ‡2 rdacontent
337	‡a projected ‡2 rdamedia
338	‡a filmslip ‡2 rdacarrier
490 0	‡a Plants around us
500	‡a Filmslip and student guide in plastic envelope 28 x 13 cm.
520	‡a Describes differences among plants, including size, age, and color.
700 1	‡a Podendorf, Illa, ‡e collaborator.
710 2	‡a Encyclopaedia Britannica Films, inc., ‡e producer.

Title frame

Plants Around Us

Different Kinds of Plants
Collaborator: Illa Podendorf,
The University of Chicago Laboratory School

Produced by Encyclopaedia Britannica Films
©1963 by Encyclopaedia Britannica Films
Copyright and all rights of reproduction,
including by television, reserved.

Figure 2.97. Filmstrip

245 00	‡a Walt Disney's Kidnapped / ‡c adapted from the Walt Disney motion picture version of the novel by Robert Louis Stevenson ; produced by Encyclopaedia Britannica Films in cooperation with Walt Disney Productions and in collaboration with Paul A. Witty ; Oscar E. Sams, producer.
246 30	‡a Kidnapped
264 1	‡a [Wilmette, Illinois] : ‡b Encyclopaedia Britannica Films, ‡c [1960]
300	‡a 1 filmstrip (54 frames) : ‡b color ; ‡c 35 mm.
336	‡a still image ‡2 rdacontent

337	‡a projected ‡2 rdamedia
338	‡a filmstrip ‡2 rdacarrier
490 0	‡a Walt Disney famous stories retold
520	‡a David Balfour's perilous venture to claim his inheritance from a villainous and miserly Scottish uncle.
730 0	‡i Adaptation of (work): ‡a Kidnapped (Motion picture : 1960)
710 2	‡a Walt Disney Productions, ‡e producer.
710 2	‡a Encyclopaedia Britannica Films, inc., ‡e producer.

Frame 1

Encyclopaedia Britannica Films
presents

Frame 2

Walt Disney
Famous Stories Retold
a series of filmstrips

Frame 3

Walt Disney's
Kidnapped
adapted from the Walt Disney motion picture version
of the novel by Robert Louis Stevenson
© MCMLX by Walt Disney Productions
Copyright and all rights of reproduction, including by television, reserved

Frame 4

Produced by
Encyclopaedia Britannica Films
in cooperation with
Walt Disney Productions
and in collaboration with
Paul A. Witty, Ph.D., Northwestern University
Oscar E. Sams, producer.

3.5.1.4.6. FLIPCHARTS. A flipchart is a set of charts or pictures hinged at the top so that information may be presented in logical sequence. Record the height × width of the flipchart (see figure 2.98).

Figure 2.98. Flipchart

100 1	‡a Bergwall, Charles, ‡e author.
245 10	‡a Vicalog : ‡b Eye Gate visual card catalog / ‡c conceived and designed by Charles Bergwall and Sherwin S. Glassner.

264	1	‡a Jamaica, N.Y. : ‡b Eye Gate House, Inc., ‡c [between 1960 and 1969]
300		‡a 1 flipchart (6 sheets) : ‡b black and white ; ‡c 22 x 36 cm
336		‡a text ‡2 rdacontent
336		‡a still image ‡2 rdacontent
337		‡a unmediated ‡2 rdamedia
338		‡a volume ‡2 rdacarrier
340		‡k double sided ‡2 rda
500		‡a 2 heavy cardboard sheets with 4 transparencies hinged at the top.
500		‡a Shows the parts of a catalog card.
700	1	‡a Glassner, Sherwin S., ‡e author.
710	2	‡a Eye Gate House, inc., ‡e publisher.

Cover sheet

Vicalog
Eye Gate Visual Card Catalog
Another Eye Gate Audio Visual Product
Eye Gate House, Inc.
146-01 Archer Ave., Jamaica 35, N.Y.

Instructions for using "Vicalog"
[text]
Conceived and designed by Charles Bergwall
and Sherwin S. Glassner

3.5.1.4.7. MICROFICHES. Dimensions of microfiches are recorded height × width of the microfiche. They are almost always 11 × 15 cm (see figure 2.99).

Figure 2.99. Microfiche

100	1	‡a Thimmes, Pamela Lee, ‡e author.
245	10	‡a Convention and invention : ‡b studies in the Biblical sea-storm type scene / ‡c by Pamela Lee Thimmes.
264	1	‡a Ann Arbor, MI : ‡b University Microfilms International, ‡c 1990, ©1990.
300		‡a 4 microfiches (vi, 326 leaves) ; ‡c 11 x 15 cm
336		‡a text ‡2 rdacontent
337		‡a microform ‡2 rdamedia
338		‡a microfiche ‡2 rdacarrier
340		‡d typescript (microform copy)
500		‡a "90-26505"--Microfiche header.
502		‡b Ph.D. ‡c Vanderbilt University ‡d 1990

504 ‡a Includes bibliographical references (leaves 310-326).

776 08 ‡i Reproduction of (manifestation): ‡a Thimmes, Pamela Lee. ‡t Convention and invention. ‡d 1990

3.5.1.4.8. OVERHEAD TRANSPARENCIES. An overhead transparency is a transparent image, either mounted or unmounted, designed for use on an overhead projector. Record height × width of the transparency, excluding a frame or mount (see figure 2.100).

Figure 2.100. Overhead Transparency

245 00 ‡a Africa / ‡c collaborators, Nadine I. Clark, Herbert S. Lewis ; producers, Weking Schroeder, Penelope Wilmot ; produced by Encyclopaedia Britannica Films in cooperation with Compton's Pictured Encyclopedia.

264 1 ‡a Chicago, Illinois : ‡b Encyclopaedia Britannica Educational Corporation, ‡c [1963]

264 4 ‡c ©1963

300 ‡a 16 overhead transparencies : ‡b some color ; ‡c 22 x 22 cm

336 ‡a still image ‡2 rdacontent

337 ‡a projected ‡2 rdamedia

338 ‡a overhead transparency ‡2 rdacarrier

500 ‡a Teacher's guide on envelope.

500 ‡a With plastic frame, 27 x 26 cm.

521 2 ‡a Junior and senior high schools.

505 0 ‡a unit 1. The land (8 transparencies) -- unit 2. The people (3 transparencies) -- unit 3. Africa, past and present (5 transparencies).

500 ‡a Series 30040.

700 1 ‡a Clark, Nadine I., ‡e collaborator.

700 1 ‡a Lewis, Herbert S., ‡e collaboraor.

710 2 ‡a Encyclopaedia Britannica Films, inc., ‡e producer.

710 2 ‡a Compton's Pictured Encyclopedia (Firm), ‡e producer.

Transparency

Series: Africa   Unit I: The Land
Encyclopaedia Britannica Educational Corporation
425 North Michigan Avenue • Chicago, Illinois 60611
©1963 by Encyclopaedia Britannica Educational Corporation

Envelope

Series 30040 Africa
Unit I, 8 transparencies
The Land

> Produced by Encyclopaedia Britannica Films
> in cooperation with Compton's Pictured Encyclopedia
> Collaborators: Nadine I. Clark, Herbert S. Lewis
> Producers: Weking Schroeder, Penelope Wilmot

3.5.1.4.9. REELS. The basic guideline for reels is to record the diameter of the reel and the width of the film or tape. For an example of an audiotape reel, see figure 2.101 (remember that North American practice is to record dimensions for audio resources in inches); for an example of a microfilm reel, see figure 2.102.

Figure 2.101. Audiotape Reel

245 00	‡a Examples from Engramelle / ‡c a research project by George Houle.	
246 30	‡a Engramelle	
264 0	‡a [Stanford, California] : ‡b [George Houle], ‡c [1978 or 1979]	
300	‡a 1 audiotape reel ; ‡c 7 in., 1/4 in.	
336	‡a performed music ‡2 rdacontent	
337	‡a audio ‡2 rdamedia	
338	‡a audiotape reel ‡2 rdacarrier	
344	‡a analog ‡c 7 1/2 ips ‡f 4 track ‡2 rda	
500	‡a Computer recreation of the performance of ornamentation and notes inégales in 18th-century French music, derived from the instructions for mechanical-organ cylinders in Marie-Dominique-Joseph Engramelle's La tonotechnie (1775).	
500	‡a Title from label on tape.	
500	‡a "Computer simulations executed at CCRMA."	
500	‡a Tape accompanies: Performance of French music of the eighteenth century : articulation, notes inégales and ornamentation / George Houle.	
700 1	‡a Houle, George, ‡e programmer.	
700 1	‡a Jaffe, David A. ‡q (David Aaron), ‡d 1955- ‡e composer.	
700 1	‡a Fields, Matthew H., ‡d 1961- ‡e composer.	
700 1	‡i Augments (work): ‡a Engramelle, Joseph. ‡t Tonotechnie.	
700 1	‡i Supplement to (work): ‡a Houle, George. ‡t Performance of French music of the eighteenth century.	

Figure 2.102. Microfilm Reel

245 00	‡a Frank Leslie's boys' and girls' weekly.
264 1	‡a [Washington, D.C.] : ‡b Library of Congress Photoduplication Service, ‡c 1969.
300	‡a 11 microfilm reels : ‡b illustrations ; ‡c 10 cm, 35 mm

310	ǂa Weekly
336	ǂa text ǂ2 rdacontent
337	ǂa microform ǂ2 rdamedia
338	ǂa microfilm reel ǂ2 rdacarrier
340	ǂo negative ǂ2 rda
362 1	ǂa Began with Volume 1, no. 1 (October 13, 1866); ceased with Volume 36, no. 905 (February 9, 1884).
500	ǂa "An illustrated journal of amusement, adventure, and instruction."
588	ǂa Description based on: Volume 1, no. 1 (October 13, 1866); title from title frame.
588	ǂa Latest issue consulted: Volume 36, no. 905 (February 9, 1884).
700 1	ǂa Leslie, Frank, ǂd 1821-1880.
776 08	ǂi Reproduction of (manifestation): ǂt Frank Leslie's boys' and girls' weekly ǂd New York : Frank Leslie, 1866-1884

Frame 1

START

Frame 2

Frank Leslie's boys' and girls' weekly
New York
Shelf no. 20365 (AP 200.F65)

Frame 3

[reproduction of LC card]
Microfilmed 1969, Library of Congress Photoduplication Service

Frame 4

October 13, 1866 thru April 25, 1868
(reel 1)

3.5.1.4.10. ROLLS. Libraries usually store microfilm on reels, but if microfilm or other film is not stored on a reel, record only the gauge (width) of the film (see figure 2.97 for a filmstrip roll).

3.5.1.4.11. SHEETS. The dimensions of sheets are given height × width of the sheet, excluding a frame (see figures 2.35 and 2.89; see also 3.5.3). If the sheet is issued folded but intended to be used unfolded, record both the dimensions unfolded and the dimensions folded (see figures 2.30 and 2.31; see also 3.5.2).

3.5.1.4.12. SLIDES. Record height × width. See figures 2.20 and 2.103.

Figure 2.103. Slide

245 00	‡a German painting of the twentieth century.
264 1	‡a East Providence, Rhode Island : ‡b Herbert E. Budek Company Inc., ‡c [1962]
300	‡a 122 slides : ‡b color ; ‡c 5 x 5 cm + ‡e 1 commentary.
336	‡a still image ‡2 rdacontent
337	‡a projected ‡2 rdamedia
338	‡a slide ‡2 rdacarrier
500	‡a In flat plastic holders (28 x 23 cm) punched for insertion in 3-ring binder.
520	‡a Chronological development of German painting from the beginning of the century to the post-war period of the 1950s. The works of Kubin, Kokoschka, Kandinsky, Klee, etc.

First slide in set 1

GERMAN PAINTING
OF THE
TWENTIETH CENTURY
Set 1

Last slide in set 1

THE END
Copyright 1962, by
Herbert E. Budek Company Inc.

3.5.1.4.13. THREE-DIMENSIONAL FORMS. Record the dimensions of the object itself. Generally give height × width × depth. If the object is in a container, optionally record the container's dimensions as well (see figure 2.77).

3.5.1.4.14. VOLUMES. Dimensions are recorded in centimeters, except for resources measuring less than ten centimeters, which are measured in millimeters. For a book, measure the height of the cover. Fractions of a centimeter are rounded up to the next centimeter (see figures throughout this chapter). Give both height and width if the width is less than half the height or is greater than the height (see figures 2.53 and 2.81).

3.5.1.5. DIMENSIONS OF CONTAINER. If it is considered important, the dimensions of a container may be recorded, either in lieu of, or in addition to, the dimensions of the carrier itself (see figure 2.77).

3.5.1.6. RESOURCES CONSISTING OF MORE THAN ONE CARRIER. If the resource consists of more than one carrier, but all carriers are the same type and the same size, record the dimensions of only one of them (see figures 2.92 through 2.94, 2.99, and 2.100 through 2.103). Note the exception for unbound texts. The Tibetan sutra in figure 2.81 is an example.

If the carriers are of the same type but differ in size, record the dimensions of the smallest and the largest, separated by a hyphen (see figure 2.77). If the carriers are all of two sizes, record both separated by "and" (see figure 2.37).

3.5.2.2. RECORDING DIMENSIONS OF MAPS, ETC. Dimensions for maps generally follow the same guidelines as other materials, except that the dimensions of a map are recorded measured within the "neat lines" (the innermost of a series of lines that frame the map), *not* the edges of the paper (see figures 2.30, 2.31, 2.37, and 2.40). If the map is irregularly shaped, has no neat lines, or bleeds off the edge, record the dimensions of the map itself, or if that is not possible, record the height and width of the sheet. In this case, include the word "sheet" with the dimensions (see figures 2.31c and 2.104).

Figure 2.104. Sheet Size of Map Measured

110	2	‡a Tulsa Metropolitan Area Planning Commission.
245	10	‡a Existing land use, 1964 : ‡b [in Tulsa, Oklahoma] / ‡c Tulsa Metropolitan Area Planning Commission.
255		‡a Scale approximately 1:140,000.
264	1	‡a [Tulsa, Oklahoma] : ‡b Tulsa Metropolitan Area Planning Commission, ‡c 1965.
300		‡a 1 map : ‡b color ; ‡c sheet 48 x 40 cm
336		‡a cartographic image ‡2 rdacontent
337		‡a unmediated ‡2 rdamedia
338		‡a sheet ‡2 rdacarrier

Information from map

October, 1965   Scale in Miles
Tulsa Metropolitan Area Planning Commission
Existing Land Use—1964

3.5.2.3. MAPS, ETC., ON MORE THAN ONE SHEET OF DIFFERING SIZES. If the sheets are of two different sizes, record both (see figure 2.37).

3.5.2.6. MAP, ETC., ON FOLDED SHEET. For a map designed to be folded, include the dimensions of the folded map as well as the dimensions of the sheet (see figures 2.30 and 2.31).

3.5.3.2. RECORDING DIMENSIONS OF STILL IMAGES. The guidelines for recording the dimensions of a still image are generally the same as for sheets (see 3.5.1.4.11), except the cataloger is to record "the measurements of the pictorial area" rather than measure to the edge of the sheet (see figure 2.80).

3.6. BASE MATERIAL. Base material, the physical material a resource is composed of, may be recorded if considered important. It may be recorded in a number of places in the MARC bibliographic record, including subfield ‡b of the 300 field, subfield ‡a of the 340 field, or in a general note (500 field). Because 340 subfield ‡a is defined specifically for base material and the other two are more general, this *Handbook* recommends recording this information there (see figure 2.35, where the base material of the sheet is gold; figure 2.62, where the base material is vellum; figure 2.77, where the base material of the object is silver; and figure 2.80, where the base material of the print is paper). If a more narrative approach is needed under 3.6.1.4, it should be recorded in a 500 field.

3.7. APPLIED MATERIAL. Applied material, the physical or chemical substance applied to the base material of the resource, may be recorded if considered important. Like base material (3.6), it may be recorded in a number of places in the MARC bibliographic record, including subfield ‡b of the 300 field, subfield ‡c of the 340 field, or in a general note (500 field). Because 340 subfield ‡c is defined specifically for the applied material element and the other two are more general, this *Handbook* recommends recording this information there (see figure 2.80, which was printed using ink). If a more narrative approach is needed under 3.7.1.4, it should be recorded in a 500 field.

3.8. MOUNT. If a still image is mounted the material may be recorded using this element if it is considered important. Like base material (3.6) and applied material (3.7), it may be recorded in a number of places in the MARC bibliographic record, including subfield ‡b of the 300 field, subfield ‡e of the 340 field, or in a general note (500 field). Because subfield 340 ‡e is defined specifically for the mount element and the other two are more general, this *Handbook* recommends recording this information there (see figure 2.80, mounted on mat board). If a more narrative approach is needed under 3.8.1.4, it should be recorded in a 500 field.

3.9. PRODUCTION METHOD. The production method, or the process used to produce the resource, may be recorded if it is considered important. With art prints the process will normally be considered important. For example, the production method of the print illustrated in figure 2.80 is monoprint, a print process in which an image is painted in ink on a block and then printed. The production method element can be recorded in subfield ‡b of the 300 field, subfield ‡d of the 340 field, or subfield ‡a of a 500 field. Because 340 subfield ‡d is defined specifically for the production method element and the other two are more general, this *Handbook* recommends recording this information there (see figure 2.80, monoprint). If a more narrative approach is needed under 3.9.1.4, it should be recorded in a 500 field. For an example of production method recorded for a manuscript (RDA 3.9.2), see figures 2.62 and 2.99.

3.11. LAYOUT. The layout of a resource (the arrangement of the text, images, tactile notation, etc.) may be recorded if considered important for identification or selection. Layout is recorded in subfield ‡b of the 300 field, subfield ‡k of the 340 field, or subfield ‡a of a 500 field. Because 340 subfield ‡k is defined specifically for the layout element and the other two are more general, this *Handbook* recommends recording this information there (see figure 2.98; "‡2 rda" indicates that the vocabulary is prescribed by RDA). If more detail is wanted, record this information in a general note in a 500 field.

3.11.1.3. CARTOGRAPHIC IMAGES. The layout of a cartographic image is considered important for identification or selection (the element is core for the Library of Congress; see LC-PCC PS 3.11.1.3, October 2012). In traditional cataloging practice it is recorded in subfield ‡b of the 300 field. For an example, see figure 2.31c. Alternately, the new MARC 340 subfield ‡k could be used to record this element ("‡2 rda" indicates that the vocabulary is prescribed by RDA):

> 340 ‡k both sides ‡2 rda

It remains to be seen which method will be used by the cartographic cataloging community for RDA descriptions. However, because 340 subfield ‡k is specifically designed for layout information, it seems to be a better place to record layout than 300 subfield ‡b, which is much more general in nature.

3.11.1.3. TACTILE TEXT. The layout of tactile text (e.g., Braille) may be recorded if considered important for identification or selection. Until recently it has been recorded in subfield ‡b of the 300 field. The new MARC 340 subfield ‡k may also be used to record this element ("‡2 rda" indicates that the vocabulary is prescribed by RDA) (see figure 2.105). Note in this example that "jumbo braille" is considered part of the font size element, not the tactile text element (see below at 3.13).

Figure 2.105. Layout of Tactile Text

100 1	‡a Byrd, Elizabeth, ‡e author.
245 14	‡aThe famished land : a novel of the Irish potato famine.
264 1	‡a [Washington, D.C.] : ‡b Division for the Blind and Physically Handicapped, Library of Congress, ‡c 1975.

264   3   ‡a [Full Sutton, England] : ‡b HMP, transcribing agency

300   ‡a 6 volumes ; ‡c30 cm

336   ‡a tactile text ‡2 rdacontent

337   ‡a unmediated ‡2 rdamedia

338   ‡a volume ‡2 rdacarrier

340   ‡k single sided ‡n jumbo braille ‡2 rda

546   ‡b Contracted braille.

506   ‡a Availability restricted to those meeting the eligibility criteria of the holding agency.

520   ‡a A love story set in Ireland during the years of the potato famine. Moira McFlaherty and her big family live happily in a small village where she dreams of the day she will marry her childhood sweetheart. When the famine comes, her courage sustains the family.

3.12. BOOK FORMAT. Frequently recorded in descriptions of early printed books, book format is a description of the makeup of the signatures or gatherings in the book. In traditional book production several pages were printed on a large sheet of paper, which was folded one or more times to create a gathering of several pages. If the sheet was folded once this created four pages on two leaves; if it was folded twice, this created eight pages on four leaves; if it was folded three times, this created sixteen pages on eight leaves; and so on. Several gatherings were produced and these gatherings were then sewn together to form the book. The book format is determined by examining the binding and deducing how many times (or how) the sheets were folded. It is beyond the scope of this book to go into this in great detail, but basically, if the sheets were folded once (forming two leaves), this is called folio; if folded twice (forming four leaves), this is called quarto (4to); and if folded three times (forming eight leaves), this is called octavo (8vo). In conventional rare materials cataloging, format is recorded in parentheses immediately following the dimensions of the book, in subfield ‡c of the 300 field (see figure 2.67, a book in quarto format). A new subfield in the 340 field was recently approved for book format, 340 subfield ‡m. It remains to be seen whether this will be adopted for rare materials cataloging, but because it is a subfield specifically assigned to book format (which 300 subfield ‡c is not), it seems like a good idea:

340   ‡m 4to ‡2 rda

3.13. FONT SIZE. Font size may be recorded if it is considered important for identification or selection. One instance where font size is generally considered important for identification or selection is large print versions of resources. This element may be recorded in subfield ‡b of the 300 field, in a general note (500 field), or in subfield ‡n of the 340 field. Because subfield ‡n of the 340 field is specifically designed to record font size and the other two options are not, this *Handbook* recommends recording the information there, with subfield "‡2 rda" indicating that the vocabulary is prescribed by RDA (see figures 2.105 and 2.106).

Figure 2.106. Font Size

020	‡a 0739442023
100 1	‡a Clark, Mary Higgins, ‡e author.
245 10	‡a Nighttime is my time / ‡c Mary Higgins Clark.
250	‡a Doubleday large print home library edition.
264 1	‡a New York : ‡b Simon & Schuster, ‡c [2004]
300	‡a viii, 576 pages ; ‡c 22 cm
336	‡a text ‡2 rdacontent
337	‡a unmediated ‡2 rdamedia
338	‡a volume ‡2 rdacarrier
340	‡n large print ‡2 rda
520	‡a Narrowly escaping an abduction attempt, a young woman wonders if serial kidnappings taking place throughout the country are related, a suspicion that compels her to join the investigation and pit herself against a dangerous adversary.

3.14. POLARITY. Polarity refers to the colors and tones of an image. A positive image is a normal image. A negative image is the inversion of the tones of a positive image, so that light areas are dark and dark areas light, and colors are reversed. Recording the polarity of an image may be considered important for film, including microform, particularly if it is negative. Polarity may be recorded in subfield ‡b of the 300 field, in a general note in a 500 field, or in 340 subfield ‡o. This *Handbook* recommends using the 340 field because the 340 subfield ‡o is specifically designed to record polarity, with subfield "‡2 rda" indicating that the vocabulary is prescribed by RDA (see figure 2.102).

3.16. SOUND CHARACTERISTIC. The sound characteristic element records details about the encoding of the sound of a resource. The element may be recorded in various spots in MARC, including MARC 300 subfield ‡b, MARC 500 subfield ‡a, or MARC 344. The MARC 344 field was designed specifically for encoding the RDA sound characteristic element, and will be used in this *Handbook*.

3.16.2. TYPE OF RECORDING. Record "analog" or "digital." Record the type of recording in MARC 344 subfield ‡a (see figure 2.22, 2.94, and 2.95).

3.16.3. RECORDING MEDIUM. Record "magnetic," "magneto-optical," or "optical" if considered important. Record the recording medium in MARC 344 subfield ‡b (see figures 2.22 and 2.94).

3.16.4. PLAYING SPEED. If considered important for identification or selection, record the playing speed of the resource in subfield ‡c of the 344 field. Playing speed for analog discs is generally considered important for identification or selection (see figure 2.95). Playing speed for cassettes is not usually recorded if it is the standard 1⅞ inches per second, but has been recorded in figure 2.94 to show an example.

3.16.7. TAPE CONFIGURATION. Record the number of tracks on an audiotape in MARC 344 subfield ‡f (see figure 2.107).

Figure 2.107. Tape Configuration

028 02	‡a 010 12201 ‡b Motivational Programming Corp.	
245 10	‡a Genesis of a novel : ‡b a documentary on the writing regimen of Georges Simenon.	
264 1	‡a Tucson, Arizona : ‡b Motivational Programming Corporation, ‡c [1969]	
264 4	‡c ℗1969	
300	‡a 1 sound cassette (24 min.) ; ‡c 3 7/8 x 2 1/2 in., 1/8 in. tape	
336	‡a spoken word ‡2 rdacontent	
337	‡a audio ‡2 rdamedia	
338	‡a audiocassette ‡2 rdacarrier	
344	‡a analog ‡b magnetic ‡f 2 track ‡g mono ‡2 rda	
490 0	‡a 20th century European authors	
520	‡a An account of the development of Georges Simenon's book, Le président.	
504	‡a Bibliography on container.	
700 1	‡a Simenon, Georges, ‡d 1903- ‡t Président.	
710 2	‡a Motivational Programming Corporation, ‡e publisher.	

Cassette label

010 12201
Genesis of a novel
A documentary on the writing regimen of Georges Simenon
Motivational Programming Corporation
512 Transamerica Building, Tucson, Arizona 85701

3.16.8. CONFIGURATION OF PLAYBACK CHANNELS. Record "mono," "stereo," "quadra-phonic," or "surround" in MARC 344 subfield ‡g if considered important for identification or selection (see figures 2.22, 2.94, 2.95, 2.97, and 2.107).

3.16.9. SPECIAL PLAYBACK CHARACTERISTIC. If a resource's audio uses an equalization system, noise reduction system, etc., this may be recorded in MARC 344 subfield ‡h if considered important for identification or selection (see figure 2.95). Although RDA specifically refers to audio recordings, it may be appropriate to record this information for other resources with audio characteristics, such as a video recording (see figures 2.4b and 2.25).

3.18. VIDEO CHARACTERISTIC. Technical specifications relating to the video imaging encoding are recorded in this element.

3.18.2 VIDEO FORMAT. The standard used to encode an analog video may be recorded using this element. Record the information in subfield ‡a of the MARC bibliographic 346 field (see figure 2.108).

Figure 2.108. Video Format

245 00	‡a Governance in the academic library / ‡c a program presented under the auspices of the Committee on Academic Status of the Association of College and Research Libraries.
264 1	‡a Chicago : [Committee on Academic Status of the Association of College and Research Libraries], ‡c 1974.
264 2	‡b Distributed by ACRL
300	‡a 1 videocassette (approximately 40 min.) : ‡b sound, black and white ; ‡c 3/4 in.
336	‡a two-dimensional moving image ‡2 rdacontent
337	‡a video ‡2 rdamedia
338	‡a videocassette ‡2 rdacarrier
346	‡a Sony U-Matic, UC-60
500	‡a Participants: David Laird, Jane Flener, Ellsworth Mason, Stuart Forth, and Frederick Duda; moderator, Eldred Smith.
520	‡a Patterns of administration in academic libraries, a panel discussion.
710 2	‡a Association of College and Research Libraries. ‡b Committee on Academic Status, ‡e sponsoring body.

3.18.3. BROADCAST STANDARD. Broadcast standard describes the system used to format a video when broadcast on television. Record broadcast standard in MARC bibliographic field 346, subfield ‡b (see figures 2.1a, 2.4b, 2.25, and 2.48).

3.19. DIGITAL FILE CHARACTERISTIC. Technical specifications relating to the digital encoding of the resource are recorded in this element.

3.19.2. FILE TYPE. Record the type of data in a resource using the MARC 347 field, subfield ‡a. See figures 2.1a, 2.4b, 2.25, 2.48 (video files), figures 2.9b, 2.61, 2.76 (text files), figure 2.22 (audio file), figures 2.58, 2.59 (program files), and figure 2.109 (image file).

Figure 2.109. File Type (Image Files)

100 1	‡a Stafford, James E., ‡e cartographer.
245 10	‡a Surface water resource map of Wyoming : ‡b streamflows and storage / ‡c by James E. Stafford and Tomas Gracias ; digital cartography by James E. Stafford, Tomas Gracias, and Robin W. Lyons ; map editing and design by Richard W. Jones.
246 1	‡i Title in upper right margin: ‡a Surface water resources map of Wyoming
250	‡a Version 1.0.
255	‡a Scale 1:500,000 ; ‡b transverse Mercator projection ‡c (W 111°--W 104°/N 45°--N 41°).
264 1	‡a Laramie, Wyoming : ‡b Wyoming State Geological Survey, ‡c 2009.
300	‡a 1 CD-ROM : ‡b color ; ‡c 4 3/4 in.
336	‡a cartographic image ‡2 rdacontent
336	‡a text ‡2 rdacontent
337	‡a computer ‡2 rdamedia
338	‡a computer disc ‡2 rdacarrier
347	‡a image file ‡b TIFF ‡b JPEG ‡2 rda
352	‡a raster
490 0	‡a MS ; ‡v 91
538	‡a System requirements: Pentium class or equivalent; 64MB RAM; MS Windows 98**/ NT/2000/XP; ArcReader 92; Adobe Adobe Acobat Reader; computer with image-viewing software; for .shp, .lyr, or .mxd files, GIS software.
500	‡a Relief shown by contours and spot heights.
500	‡a Includes text, tables of rivers/creeks/lakes/reservoirs, and river and geologic maps of Wyoming.
504	‡a Includes bibliographical references.
700 1	‡a Gracias, Tomas, ‡e cartographer.
700 1	‡a Lyons, Robin W., ‡e cartographer.
700 1	‡a Jones, Richard W. ‡q (Richard Warren), ‡e editor.
710 2	‡a Wyoming State Geological Survey, ‡e issuing body.

3.19.3. ENCODING FORMAT. Record the encoding format of the digital content of a resource in subfield ‡b of the MARC 347 field. See figures 2.1a, 2.4b, 2.25, and 2.48 (DVD video); figures 2.9b and 2.76 (HTML); figure 2.22 (CD audio), figure 2.61 (PDF); figures 2.58 and 2.59 (DVD-ROM); and figure 2.109 (JPEG, TIFF).

3.19.6. REGIONAL ENCODING. Regional encoding is a code telling the database user which region of the world for which a DVD has been encoded. This is an important element for selection. Regional encoding is recorded in the MARC 347 field, subfield ‡e (see figures 2.1a, 2.4b, 2.25, and 2.48).

3.19.8. DIGITAL REPRESENTATION OF CARTOGRAPHIC CONTENT. Details about the digital encoding of geospatial information in a cartographic resource is recorded using this element in subfield ‡a of the MARC 352 field (see figure 2.109).

3.20. EQUIPMENT OR SYSTEM REQUIREMENT. If a resource has equipment or system requirements beyond what is obvious for the type of carrier or file, record this information using this element in subfield ‡a of the 538 field. There is no prescribed vocabulary or format (see figure 2.109, which does not mention the requirement of a CD-ROM drive because that would presumably be obvious from the type of carrier).

Attributes of the Item

3.21. ITEM-SPECIFIC CARRIER CHARACTERISTIC. An item-specific carrier characteristic is anything specific to the item (copy) being described that does not apply to other items in the same manifestation. This information is recorded in a note, usually referred to as a local note. Local notes are usually recorded in a MARC bibliographic 590 field. Alternately, they can be recorded in nearly any appropriate field, as long as the field ends with ‡5 and the library's MARC symbol, which transforms the field into a local field. For example, the item specific carrier characteristic element in figure 2.82, recorded in a 590 field, might have instead been recorded as:

> 500 ‡a Brigham Young University copy is number 11, signed by the author.
> ‡5 UPB

Because most catalog records now exist in a shared cataloging environment, this *Handbook* recommends that the item specific carrier characteristic element name the library rather than use the generic "Library's copy . . ." of the RDA examples. It may be obvious to the cataloger which library the note applies to, but it is probably not going to be obvious to later viewers of the record, especially if seen outside the context of the local catalog database.

Item-specific carrier characteristic information can include information like the number of the library's copy of a limited edition (see figures 2.2 and 2.82), the fact that the library's copy is autographed or inscribed (see figure 2.19), or that the library's copy is damaged in some way (see figure 2.52). The custodial history of item element discussed above at 2.17 is also an item-specific carrier characteristic, and may be recorded in general cataloging if thought significant (see figure 2.44, here recorded in 590 rather than 561). Other examples of the item-specific carrier characteristic element might include a description of the binding (particularly if it is in disrepair), marginal notations or highlighting, or notation of missing parts from the library's copy.

3.21.2. ITEM-SPECIFIC CARRIER CHARACTERISTIC OF EARLY PRINTED RESOURCE. There is really no difference between RDA 3.21.2 and 3.21.1; the same kind of information can be recorded in either type of note. However, the presence of 3.21.2 in RDA highlights the fact that catalogers are much more prone to describe item-specific information for early printed resources. See the 590 note in figure 2.67, which describes the binding of the book in detail.

3.22. NOTE. This element covers any note that provides additional information relating to all the copies in a manifestation, or to an item. As such it covers a lot of territory. Some examples in this chapter include figures 2.2, 2.19, and 2.82 (number of copies produced in the manifestation); figures 2.21 and 2.83 (presence of an engraved title page in addition to the printed title page); figure 2.35 (a description of the format of the manifestation); figure 2.67 (signatures of an early printed resource); figure 2.77 (description of the pieces); figure 2.84 (duplicated paging not described in the extent element); and figures 2.96 and 2.103 (note about the housing of the manifestation).

3.22.4. NOTE ON DIMENSIONS OF MANIFESTATION. If significant information about the dimensions of the manifestation were not recorded in the dimensions element, they may be recorded in a note (see figures 2.80 and 2.90).

Providing Acquisition and Access Information

Chapter 4 continues the suite of chapters in RDA devoted to recording the attributes of manifestations and items.

4.2 TERMS OF AVAILABILITY. Terms of availability is defined as "the conditions under which the publisher, distributor, etc., will normally supply a resource or the price of a resource." This information was once frequently recorded with the standard number, but because prices change most catalogers will not record information about this element (see LC-PCC PS 4.2.1.3, September 2011). If desired, this information may be recorded in subfield ‡c of the 020 field following the ISBN:

> 020   ‡a 0877790086 : ‡c $10.00

If there is no known ISBN associated with the resource, terms of availability may be recorded in 020 without the ISBN:

> 020   ‡c For sale ($450.00) or rent ($45.00)

4.3. CONTACT INFORMATION. Contact information is information about an organization from which the resource may be obtained. This element is frequently used for archival resources, and records the name and address of the archives. In archival cataloging, MARC bibliographic field 852 is generally used for this element (see figures 2.38 and 2.63). Alternatively, the 270 field might be used, particularly for non-archival resources:

> 270   ‡a Harold B. Lee Library, Brigham Young University, ‡b Provo, ‡c Utah ‡e 84602

4.4. RESTRICTIONS ON ACCESS. If there are any limitations placed on access to the resource, they should be plainly described in the record. This sort of information is recorded in the MARC bibliographic 506 field (see figure 2.105). This element can also be recorded where there are no restrictions on access, if users might expect restrictions (see figure 2.63).

4.5. RESTRICTIONS ON USE. In some cases there are no restrictions on access, but there are restrictions on use. These should also be plainly described in the record. Like the restrictions on access element, the restrictions on use element are recorded in the MARC bibliographic 506 field (see figure 2.38).

4.6. UNIFORM RESOURCE LOCATOR. A uniform resource locator (URL) is the address of a remote access resource. It is recorded in the MARC bibliographic 856 field. The field has been designed so that the local system (if it is adequately programmed) can allow the user to go directly to the resource by clicking on the link in the database record. At the least, it should display so that the user can copy the address and approach the resource through a different program.

The 856 field can serve as a locator for many types of electronic resources, including "in-house" resources that may reside on the library's local network. Examples in this *Handbook* are for electronic resources located at World Wide Web sites on the Internet. For information about other uses of the 856 field, see the documentation

in *MARC 21 Format for Bibliographic Data* (www.loc.gov/marc/bibliographic/bd856
.html).

The first indicator in an 856 field is in nearly all cases "4." The second indicator
identifies the relationship between the electronic resource at the location recorded
in the 856 field and the item described in the catalog record. If the record describes
the resource, the second indicator is "0." If the location is for a version of the resource
(e.g., the record is for a printed book and the 856 location is for a digital copy of
the book), the second indicator is "1." If the location is for a related resource (e.g., a
publisher's description of the book), the second indicator is "2." All 856 fields in this
chapter have indicators "40." The URL must be recorded *exactly* (this is critical) in
subfield ‡u (see figures 2.9b, 2.42, 2.61, and 2.76).

URLs can be recorded in many other fields beside 856. For example, see the 500
field in figure 2.9b and the 555 field in figure 2.38.

NOTES

1. Full information about *MARC 21 Format for Bibliographic Data* is available at
   www.loc.gov/marc/bibliographic/ecbdhome.html.

2. Pre-AACR2 authority records are identified by "d" in 008 position 10 for "AACR2
   compatible heading," "b" for AACR1, and "a" for earlier rules.

3. IFLA Study Group on the Functional Requirements for Bibliographic Records,
   "User Tasks," ch. 6 in *Functional Requirements for Bibliographic Records Final: Report*
   (Munich: K. G. Sauer, 1998), 79–92. Also available at www.ifla.org/en/publications/
   functional-requirements-for-bibliographic-records. FRAD is an extension of FRBR;
   see IFLA Working Group on Functional Requirements and Numbering of Authority Records, *Functional Requirements for Authority Data: A Conceptual Model.* IFLA
   Series on Bibliographic Control, vol. 34 (Munich: K. G. Saur, 2009).

4. *The Chicago Manual of Style Online,* 8.157, accessed 7 June 2013, www.chicago
   manualofstyle.org/16/ch08/ch08_sec157.html.

5. *Describing Archives: A Content Standard* (Chicago: Society of American Archivists,
   2007).

6. See *Statement of International Cataloguing Principles* 2, "the highest [principle] is the
   convenience of the user" at www.ifla.org/files/cataloguing/icp/icp_2009-en.pdf.

7. On the ISBD punctuation for this situation, see *International Standard Bibliographic
   Description,* consolidated ed. (Berlin: DeGruyter Saur, 2011), s.v. section 1, Title and
   Statement of Responsibility Area, prescribed punctuation, with examples at 1.3.4.7.4.
   RDA appendix D.1 does not cover all possible situations.

8. Definition from the *Oxford English Dictionary* online, accessed June 7, 2013, s.v. "edition," www.oed.com.

FACSIMILES AND REPRODUCTIONS

MOST LIBRARIES OWN MANY REPRINT EDITIONS OF BOOKS, AND libraries may increasingly acquire them from the proliferation of reprint publishers, including so-called print-on-demand publishers, many of which simply print and bind public domain books that have been digitized for collections such as Google Books (books.google.com) or the Internet Archive (www.archive.org). Libraries also own other kinds of facsimiles or reproductions, including microform reproductions. Additionally, libraries commonly give access through their catalog to digital facsimiles of resources such as books and scores. Therefore, it is important that catalogers understand how to deal with these resources.

RDA's basic guideline for facsimiles and reproductions is 1.11, which states, "When describing a facsimile or reproduction, record the data relating to the facsimile or reproduction in the appropriate element. Record any data relating to the original manifestation as an element of a related work or related manifestation, as applicable." Basically, the guideline stipulates that the record must describe the resource in hand (i.e., the facsimile or reproduction). Information pertaining to the original resource will be provided by notes or linking fields.

The RDA provisions are basically the same as AACR2's on the matter of facsimiles and reproductions. The Library of Congress and most North American libraries, however, did not follow the stipulations of AACR2 for "reproductions of previously existing materials that are made for preservation purposes," that is, most facsimiles and reproductions, including photocopies, microform, reproductions published on demand (e.g., by University Microfilms International), and digital reformatting of previously existing materials. For such resources, bibliographic data were transcribed as for the original work; details relating to the reproduction were recorded in note. This resulted in records that appeared at first glance to represent the original resource.

It is not clear whether or not this practice will continue under RDA, but the initial policies for early implementers of RDA were to apply RDA as written, and this is the practice followed in this *Handbook*. North American catalogers should watch for developments in LC and PCC policy.[1]

This appendix will cover print reproductions, microform reproductions, and online (digital) reproductions.

PRINT REPRODUCTIONS

In the most straightforward situation, the publisher creates a new title page for the reprint that uses its own imprint, sometimes rewording the title, and usually also reprinting the original title page, as in figure 2.110. In this case the title and statement of responsibility and publication elements are transcribed from the new title page (see RDA 2.3.2.3). The cataloger will ignore the original title page for most purposes, although in this case the original makes it clear that the phrase "A visit from St. Nicholas" is an alternative title, so it will be recorded in a 246 field. A formal note pertaining to the original publication is recorded in a 534 field. This field contains what is known as a structured description of the related manifestation (see RDA 27.1.1.3).

Figure 2.110. Reprint—New Title Page

020	‡a 0486227979 (paperback)
020	‡a 0486220834 (cloth)
100 1	‡a Moore, Clement Clarke, ‡d 1779-1863, ‡e author.
245 14	‡a The night before Christmas : ‡b (A visit from St. Nicholas) / ‡c Clement C. Moore ; with a life of Moore by Arthur N. Hosking.
246 30	‡a Visit from St. Nicholas
264 1	‡a New York : ‡b Dover Publications, Inc., ‡c 1971.
300	‡a 16 unnumbered pages, 36 pages : ‡b illustrations ; ‡c 16 cm.
336	‡a text ‡2 rdacontent
336	‡a still image ‡2 rdacontent
337	‡a unmediated ‡2 rdamedia
338	‡a volume ‡2 rdacarrier
490 0	‡a Dover books for children
520	‡a An important Christmas Eve visitor pays a call.
500	‡a "Facsimile of the original 1848 edition."

534	‡p Facsimile of: ‡t A visit from St. Nicholas / by Clement C. Moore. ‡c New York : Henry M. Onderdonk, 1848.
504	‡a "Bibliography of the works of Clement Clarke Moore": pages 34-36.
700 1	‡a Hosking, Arthur Nicholas, ‡d 1874- ‡e author of introduction, etc.

Title page of facsimile

The Night Before Christmas
(A Visit from St. Nicholas)
Clement C. Moore
Facsimile of the Original 1848 Edition
With a Life of Moore by
Arthur N. Hosking
Dover Publications, Inc.
New York

Title page of original

A Visit from St. Nicholas
by Clement C. Moore, LL.D.
With Original Cuts,
designed and engraved by Boyd.
New York:
Henry M. Onderdonk
1848.

Sometimes the original title page is reproduced as the title page of the reprint edition, with the reprint publisher's imprint added to it. Such is the case with the example shown in figure 2.111. In this example, "1891" at the bottom of the title page is reproduced from the original. It should be ignored in the transcription.

Figure 2.111. Reprint—
Original Title Page Reprinted with New Publisher Information

020	‡a 1897853424 (paperback)
100 1	‡a Moore, A. W. ‡q (Arthur William), ‡d 1853-1909, ‡e author.
245 14	‡a The folk-lore of the Isle of Man : ‡b being an account of its myths, legends, superstitions, customs, & proverbs / ‡c collected from many sources, with a general introduction and with explanatory notes to each chapter by A.W. Moore, M.A.
264 1	‡a Felinfach [Wales] : ‡b Llanerch publishers, ‡c 1994.
300	‡a xii, 192 pages : ‡b illustrations ; ‡c 21 cm
336	‡a text ‡2 rdacontent
336	‡a still image ‡2 rdacontent

337 ‡a unmediated ‡2 rdamedia

338 ‡a volume ‡2 rdacarrier

534 ‡p Facsimile reprint. Originally published: ‡c Douglas, Isle of Man : Brown & Son, 1891.

Title page

The
Folk-Lore
of the
Isle of Man,
Being an Account of Its
Myths, Legends, Superstitions,
Customs, & Proverbs,
Collected from many sources; with a General Introduction;
and with Explanatory Notes to Each Chapter;
by
A.W. Moore, M.A.;
Author of "Manx Names," &c.
Facsimile reprint 1994 by Llanerch publishers,
Felinfach. ISBN 1 897853 42 4
1891

Often a publisher will reproduce the original title page exactly, adding its own imprint information in another place, such as the verso of the title page, as in figure 2.112. Again, the imprint of the original is *not* transcribed in the 264 field, even though no other publication data appear on the title page. It will be recorded in a note.

Figure 2.112. Reprint—Original Title Page Reprinted Unchanged

020 ‡a 1899373004

100 1 ‡a Harris, Walter, ‡d 1686-1761, ‡e author.

245 14 ‡a The history and antiquities of the city of Dublin : ‡b from the earliest acounts / ‡c compiled ... by the late Walter Harris, Esq. ; with an appendix containing an history of the cathedrals of Christ-Church and St. Patrick, the university, the hospitals and other public buildings ; also two plans, one of the city as it was in the year 1610 ..., the other as it is at present ...

264 1 ‡a Ballynahinch, County Down, Northern Ireland : ‡b Davidson Books, ‡c 1994.

300 ‡a 509 pages : ‡b illustrations (some folded), maps ; ‡c 21 cm.

336 ‡a text ‡2 rdacontent

336 ‡a still image ‡2 rdacontent

336 ‡a cartographic image ‡2 rdacontent

337   ‡a unmediated ‡2 rdamedia

338   ‡a volume ‡2 rdacarrier

534   ‡p Facsimile reprint. Originally published: ‡c Dublin : Printed for Laurence Flinn and James Williams, MDCCLXVI [1766].

Title page

The
History and Antiquities
of the City of Dublin,
from the earliest acounts:
compiled from
Authentick Memoirs, Offices of Record, Manuscript
Collections, and other unexceptionable Vouchers.
By the late Walter Harris, Esq;
with an
Appendix,
Containing,
An History of the Cathedrals of Christ-Church and
St. Patrick, the University, the Hospitals and other Public Buildings.
Also two Plans, one of the City as it was in the Year 1610,
being the earliest extant; the other as it is at Present, from
the accurate Survey of the late Mr. Rocque; with several
other Embellishments.
Dublin:
Printed for Laurence Flinn, in Castle-street;
and James Williams, in Skinner-row
M DCC LXVI.

Verso of title page

This is an exact photolithographic facsimile of the first
and only edition of 1766.
The maps and plans are reproduced to the same size
as the originals
ISBN 1-899373-00-4
Printed and published, 1994 by Davidson Books
Ballynahinch, County Down, Northern Ireland BT24 8QD

In some cases a publisher will reprint an item and provide little or no information about the reprint itself. Here, too, the reprint information is recorded in the publication area. An example of this situation may be seen in figure 2.65, a print-on-demand publication. In the case of figure 2.113, the name of the reprint publisher, the University of Notre Dame Press, appears only on the back cover. A new preface has been added, which claims that this is a "new, second edition" (although, in fact, no changes have been made) and states that the book has been out of print "for some three-score years." Given publishing practices of the period, this book probably would have been in print until at least the mid-1930s; in addition, the book arrived as a new book in the library in 1995, sixty years later. The cataloger is thus justified in estimating a publication date of 1995.

Figure 2.113. Reprint—Original Title Page Reprinted Unchanged

020	‡a 0268011095
100 1	‡a O'Dea, John, ‡e author.
245 10	‡a History of the Ancient Order of Hibernians and Ladies' Auxiliary / ‡c by John O'Dea.
246 14	‡a History of the Ancient Order of Hibernians in America and Ladies' Auxiliary
250	‡a New, second edition.
264 1	‡a Notre Dame, Indiana : ‡b University of Notre Dame Press, ‡c [1995?]
300	‡a 3 volumes (1505 pages) ; ‡c 22 cm
336	‡a text ‡2 rdacontent
337	‡a unmediated ‡2 rdamedia
338	‡a volume ‡2 rdacarrier
534	‡p Facsimile reprint. Originally published: ‡c Philadelphia : Published by authority of the A.O.H., 1923.
504	‡a Includes bibliographical references and indexes.

Title page to volume 1

History
of the
Ancient Order of Hibernians
and Ladies' Auxiliary
by
John O'Dea
Volume 1
Published by authority of the
National Board of the A. O. H.
1923

The most difficult case is that of a publisher attempting to reproduce an original in every detail. There may be nothing at all in the item identifying the publisher or the date of publication. In figure 2.114, the resource has been scrupulously reproduced, including a simulation of the original binding. The library's copy came with a publisher's advertisement telling about the facsimile, but a copy of this book could easily arrive in the collection without this small slip of paper. The cataloger is still required to describe the facsimile, not the original, in the publication, extent, and dimensions elements.

Figure 2.114. Reprint—Original Title Page Reprinted Unchanged

130	0	‡a Book of Mormon.
245	14	‡a The Book of Mormon / ‡c an account written by the hand of Mormon, upon plates taken from the plates of Nephi ... ; [translated] by Joseph Smith, Junior.
264	1	‡a [Salt Lake City, Utah] : ‡b [Deseret Book Company], ‡c [1980]
300		‡a 588 pages ; ‡c 20 cm
336		‡a text ‡2 rdacontent
337		‡a unmediated ‡2 rdamedia
338		‡a volume ‡2 rdacarrier
500		‡a "Deseret Book Company ... produce[d] this limited facsimile edition on the 150th anniversary of the publication of the Book of Mormon"--Publisher's prospectus laid in.
534		‡p Facsimile reprint. Originally published: ‡c Palmyra [New York] : Printed by E.B. Grandin, for the Author, 1830.
700	1	‡a Smith, Joseph, ‡c Jr., ‡d 1805-1844, ‡e translator.

Title page

The
Book of Mormon:
An Account Written by the Hand of Mormon,
upon Plates Taken from the Plates of Nephi.
Wherefore it is an abridgment of the Record of the People of Nephi;
and also of the Lamanites;
written to the Lamanites, which are a remnant of the House of Israel;
and also to Jew and Gentile;
written by way of commandment, and also by the spirit of Prophesy and of Revelation.
Written, and sealed up, and hid up unto the Lord, that they might not be destroyed;
to come forth by the gift and power of God unto the interpretation
thereof by the gift of God

...

By Joseph Smith, Junior,
Author and Proprietor.
Palmyra:
Printed by E.B. Grandin, for the Author.
1830.

MICROFORM REPRODUCTIONS

RDA treats microform reproductions in exactly the same way as any other reproduction, that is, describe the reproduction, and give information about the original in a note or link. For an example of a microfilm reproduction of a serial resource, see figure 2.102. Note the publication, extent, and dimensions elements (264 and 300 fields), and record publication data for the microfilm and information about its physical description. Under pre-RDA Library of Congress and North American practices, the information in these elements would have been based on the original (following AACR2 conventions):

260 ‡a New York : ‡b F. Leslie, ‡c 1866-1884.
300 ‡a 36 v. : ‡b ill. ; ‡c 32-41 cm.

Figure 2.102 uses a link in a 776 field to describe the relationship of the microform to the original rather than the note in a 534 field seen in figures 2.110 to 2.114. Either technique can be used.

ONLINE (DIGITAL) REPRODUCTIONS

Online digital reproductions pose a particular problem in a shared MARC cataloging environment. Technically speaking, each time an organization produces a digital reproduction of an existing resource a new manifestation is created, and under traditional cataloging practice this would require a new catalog record to describe it. However, with the proliferation of digitization projects it was soon discovered that this could create a confusing mass of records for what was thought by most to be identical content, and so it was thought desirable that a single bibliographic record should be used for all iterations of an online reproduction of a resource. So-called provider-neutral policies were implemented by the Program for Cooperative Cataloging and OCLC with guidelines for creating these records.[2]

For an example of a provider-neutral monograph record, see figure 2.115, describing the same resource that was described in 2.65 for a print-on-demand version, and with which 2.115 may be contrasted.

The provider-neutral description is recorded partly based on the original resource, and so does not follow RDA guidelines as set forth in RDA 1.11. Title, statement of responsibility, and publication elements, etc., are recorded based on the original.

Extent should be recorded "1 online resource" with the extent of the original given in parentheses (see the 300 field of figure 2.115). Details normally recorded in 300 subfield ‡b, such as illustrative content, are recorded based on the content of the resource. Do not give dimensions.

Figure 2.115. Provider-Neutral Record

245 04		‡a The complete story of the Galveston horror / ‡c written by the survivors ; edited by John Coulter.
264	1	‡a [Place of publication not identified] : ‡b United Publishers of America, ‡c [1900]
264	4	‡c ©1900
300		‡a 1 online resource (386 pages) : ‡b illustrations
336		‡a text ‡2 rdacontent
337		‡a computer ‡2 rdamedia
338		‡a online resource ‡2 rdacarrier
347		‡a text file ‡b PDF ‡2 rda
500		‡a "Incidents of the awful tornado, flood and cyclone disaster, personal experiences of survivors, horrible looting of dead bodies and the robbing of empty homes, pestilence from so many decaying bodies unburied, barge captains compelled by armed men to tow dead bodies to sea, millions of dollars raised to aid the suffering survivors, President McKinley orders Army rations and Army tents issued to survivors and orders U.S. Troops to protect the people and property, tales of the survivors from Galveston adrift all night on rafts, acts of valor, United States soldiers drowned, great heroism, great vandalism, great horror, a second Johnstown flood, but worse, hundreds of men, women and children drowned, no way of escape, only death! Death! Everywhere!"—Title page of original publication.
500		‡a "List of identifications": pages 362-386.
588		‡a Description based on online resource; title from PDF title page (viewed June 21, 2012).
700 1		‡a Coulter, John, ‡e editor of compilation.
776 08		‡i Print version: ‡t The complete story of the Galveston horror. ‡d [Place of publication not identified] : United Publishers of America, [1900] ‡w (OCoLC)770864
856 40		‡3 Internet Archive ‡u http://www.archive.org/details/completestoryofg00coulrich
856 40		‡3 HathiTrust Digital Library ‡u http://catalog.hathitrust.org/api/volumes/oclc/770864.html
856 40		‡3 Heritage Quest ‡u http://persi.heritagequestonline.com/hqoweb/library/do/books/results/shortcitation?urn=urn:proquest:US;glhbooks;Genealogy-glh32495880;-1;-1;&letter=T

Digital reproduction of title page

The Complete Story
OF THE
Galveston Horror.
Written by the Survivors.
Incidents of the awful tornado, flood and cyclone disaster, personal experiences of survivors, horrible looting of dead bodies and the robbing of empty homes, pestilence from so many decaying bodies unburied, barge captains compelled by armed men to tow dead bodies to sea, millions of dollars raised to aid the suffering survivors, President McKinley orders Army rations and Army tents issued to survivors and orders U.S. Troops to protect the people and property, tales of the survivors from Galveston adrift all night on rafts, acts of valor, United States soldiers drowned, great heroism, great vandalism, great horror, a second Johnstown flood, but worse, hundreds of men, women and children drowned, no way of escape, only
Death! Death! Everywhere!
Edited by John Coulter, Formerly of the N.Y. Herald
Fully Illustrated with Photographs
UNITED PUBLISHERS OF AMERICA

Content type depends on the content type of the resource. In the case of figure 2.115, it is "text." Media type is "computer" and carrier type is "online resource."

If a series statement is present for the original and it applies to all iterations of the online version, record it as usual in a 490 field.

Notes about the original may be included as appropriate. A note detailing the source of the description (RDA 2.20.13 and 2.20.2.3) is required, recorded in a 588 field.

Access points may be given in 7XX fields as appropriate. A link to the original manifestation is given in a 776 field, using the relationship designator "Print version:".

Finally, URLs leading to any digital reproduction of the resource are given in 856 fields, as long as the URLs are general and not institution specific. Information about the digitizing or holding agency may be given in subfield ‡3 of the 856 field.

NOTES

1. A Library of Congress discussion paper of this issue, "Reconsidering the Cataloging Treatment of Reproductions," April 29, 2010, is available at www.loc.gov/aba/pcc/reports/reproductions.pdf.

2. *Program for Cooperative Cataloging (PCC) Provider Neutral E-Resource MARC Record Guidelines,* www.loc.gov/aba/pcc/scs/documents/PCC-PN-guidelines.html.

CHAPTER 3

DESCRIBING PERSONS

Instructions for recording the attributes of the *person* entity
are found in RDA chapters 8 and 9.

MARC CODING

HE *PERSON* ENTITY IS CURRENTLY DESCRIBED IN
library catalogs in the MARC 21 authority format.[1] RDA
records for persons are identified by the value "z" in the 008
field position 10 (labeled "Rules" in the OCLC fixed field display) and the presence of "‡e rda" in the 040 field (see figure
3.1a). In contrast, an AACR2 authority record may be recognized by the presence of value "c" in 008 position 10 and
no special coding in 040 (see figure 3.1b).[2] For space reasons,
RDA coding is assumed in further figures in this chapter and
is not explicitly shown. Other MARC coding issues will be discussed as they occur
later in the chapter.

Figure 3.1a. RDA Coding (OCLC Style)

Rec stat	c	Entered	19800725		Replaced 20110930071248.0			
Type	z	Upd status	a	Enc lvl	n	Source		
Roman		Ref status	a	Mod rec		Name use		a
Govt agn		Auth status	a	Subj	a	Subj use		a
Series	n	Auth/ref	a	Geo subd	n	Ser use		b
Ser num	n	Name	a	Subdiv tp	n	**Rules**		**z**

010	‡a n 80072514
046	‡f 17310602 ‡g 18020522
040	‡a DLC ‡b eng **‡e rda** ‡c DLC ‡d DLC ‡d PPi-MA ‡d UPB
100 1	‡a Washington, Martha, ‡d 1731-1802
370	‡a New Kent County (Va.) ‡b Mount Vernon (Va.) ‡2 naf
375	‡a female
377	‡a eng
400 1	‡a Dandridge, Martha, ‡d 1731-1802
400 1	‡a Custis, Martha, ‡d 1731-1802
670	‡a Martha Washington's benediction, 1948
670	‡a Britannica online, 9 August 2011 ‡b (Martha Washington, née Martha Dandridge, also called Martha Custis (1749-1759), born June 2, 1731, New Kent County, Virginia; died May 22, 1802, Mount Vernon, Virginia; American first lady and wife of George Washington)

Figure 3.1a. RDA Coding (LC style)

008	800725n| azannaabn |a aaa
010	‡a n 80072514
046	‡f 17310602 ‡g 18020522
040	‡a DLC ‡b eng **‡e rda** ‡c DLC ‡d DLC ‡d PPi-MA ‡d UPB
100 1	‡a Washington, Martha, ‡d 1731-1802
370	‡a New Kent County (Va.) ‡b Mount Vernon (Va.) ‡2 naf
375	‡a female
377	‡a eng
400 1	‡a Dandridge, Martha, ‡d 1731-1802
400 1	‡a Custis, Martha, ‡d 1731-1802
670	‡a Martha Washington's benediction, 1948
670	‡a Britannica online, 9 August 2011 ‡b (Martha Washington, née Martha Dandridge, also called Martha Custis (1749-1759), born June 2, 1731, New Kent County, Virginia; died May 22, 1802, Mount Vernon, Virginia; American first lady and wife of George Washington)

Figure 3.1b. AACR2 Coding (OCLC Style)

Rec stat	c	Entered	19800725		Replaced	20110930071248.0	
Type	z	Upd status	a	Enc lvl	n	Source	
Roman		Ref status	a	Mod rec		Name use	a
Govt agn		Auth status	a	Subj	a	Subj use	a
Series	n	Auth/ref	a	Geo subd	n	Ser use	b
Ser num	n	Name	a	Subdiv tp	n	**Rules**	**c**

```
010      ‡a n 80072514
040      ‡a DLC ‡b eng ‡c DLC ‡d DLC ‡d PPi-MA ‡d UPB
100 1    ‡a Washington, Martha, ‡d 1731-1802
400 1    ‡a Dandridge, Martha, ‡d 1731-1802
400 1    ‡a Custis, Martha, ‡d 1731-1802
670      ‡a Martha Washington's benediction, c1948
670      ‡a Britannica online, 9 Aug. 2011 ‡b (Martha Washington, née Martha Dandridge,
         also called Martha Custis (1749-1759), b. June 2, 1731, New Kent County, Virginia;
         d. May 22, 1802, Mount Vernon, Virginia; American first lady and wife of George
         Washington)
```

Figure 3.1b. AACR2 Coding (LC Style)

```
008      800725n| acannaabn |a aaa
010      ‡a n 80072514
040      ‡a DLC ‡b eng ‡c DLC ‡d DLC ‡d PPi-MA ‡d UPB
100 1    ‡a Washington, Martha, ‡d 1731-1802
400 1    ‡a Dandridge, Martha, ‡d 1731-1802
400 1    ‡a Custis, Martha, ‡d 1731-1802
670      ‡a Martha Washington's benediction, c1948
670      ‡a Britannica online, 9 Aug. 2011 ‡b (Martha Washington, née Martha Dandridge,
         also called Martha Custis (1749-1759), b. June 2, 1731, New Kent County, Virginia;
         d. May 22, 1802, Mount Vernon, Virginia; American first lady and wife of George
         Washington)
```

8.1. TERMINOLOGY. *Person* is defined in RDA as "an individual or an identity established by an individual (either alone or in collaboration with one or more other individuals)" (RDA 8.1.2). This definition was deliberately written broadly to include human beings, personae such as pseudonyms or stage names, fictitious characters (e.g., Kermit the Frog) and nonhuman entities such as animal actors (e.g., Shamu).[3] The last two categories represent an expansion of previous cataloging practice, which did not recognize fictitious or nonhuman entities as persons. Previous to RDA, fictitious and nonhuman person entities were established in the *Library of Congress Subject Headings* authority file and used only for subject access. Under RDA they may be established in the LC/NACO Authority File if the form is needed as an access point in an RDA bibliographic record.

This expansion may seem a bit strange at first, but it is not as far-fetched as it sounds. For example, the film *Free Willy* featured a male orca named Keiko. In the AACR2 bibliographic record for this film the human actors are given added access points, but the real star, Keiko, is not even mentioned. If he had been, it would have had to be as a subject—but the film is not about the actor Keiko. A library user searching for films featuring the actor Keiko, knowing indexing practices for human actors (that is, not indexed in subject fields), might well attempt a search for Keiko and find nothing. This is not helpful. Figure 3.2 shows how this might look in an RDA context.

Figure 3.2a. Animal Actor as Person (Authority Record)

046	‡f 1976- ‡g 2003-12-12 ‡2 edtf
100 0	‡a Keiko, ‡d approximately 1976-2003
368	‡c Orca whale
373	‡a Marineland (Ont.)
374	‡a Actors ‡2 lcsh
375	‡a male
670	‡a Free Willy, 1993: ‡b credits (Keiko as Willy)
670	‡a Wikipedia, 3 August 2011 ‡b (Keiko; born approximately 1976, died December 12, 2003; male orca actor who starred in the film Free Willy; captured near Iceland in 1979, later sold to Marineland in Ontario; performed in parks in North America)

Figure 3.2b. Animal Actor as Person (Abbreviated Bibliographic Record)

245 00	‡a Free Willy / ‡c Warner Bros. in association with Le Studio Canal+, Regency Enterprises and Alcor Films.
...	
700 0	‡a Keiko, ‡d approximately 1976-2003, ‡e actor.

8.3. CORE ELEMENTS. As explained in greater detail in chapter 1, RDA identifies certain elements as "core" throughout the code. The core elements were chosen because they were attributes and relationships thought to support FRBR and FRAD user tasks.[4] RDA entity descriptions should contain, at a minimum, all core elements that are applicable and readily ascertainable as well as any other elements that might be required to differentiate one entity from another (see RDA 0.6.1). Inclusion of other elements is not required, and is at the discretion of the cataloger or cataloging agency (such as an individual library, or cooperative organizations such as the Program for Cooperative Cataloging [PCC]).

Agencies may develop requirements that go beyond RDA core. The Library of Congress (LC) and PCC, for example, have designated certain elements that are not core in RDA to be core for their own catalogers. Information about LC and PCC decisions are found in Library of Congress-Program for Cooperative Cataloging Policy Statements (LC-PCC PSs), found under the Resources tab of the RDA Toolkit.

Core elements for all entities and relationships are given in RDA 0.6. They are also given separately in the chapter(s) devoted to each entity or relationship. Core elements for the person entity are found in RDA 0.6.4 and again in RDA 8.3. This information is also listed with each element's instruction. For example, RDA 9.2, name of the person, which is a core element, reads as follows:

> 9.2 Name of the Person
> CORE ELEMENT
> *Preferred name for the person is a core element. Variant names for the person are optional.*
> 9.2.1. Basic Instructions on Recording Names of Persons
>   9.2.1.1 Scope

Conversely, 9.8, place of birth, which is not a core element, reads as follows:

> 9.8 Place of Birth
> 9.8.1 Basic Instructions on Recording Place of Birth
>   9.8.1.1 Scope

The core elements for the person entity are:

> Preferred name for the person
> Title of the person (certain kinds of titles, see 9.4)
> Date of birth and/or death of the person
> Other designation associated with the person
> Profession or occupation (for a person whose name consists of a phrase or appellation not conveying the idea of a person)
> Identifier for the person

In addition, the following are core if the person's name is the same or similar to that of another person:

> Title of the person (other than the kinds in the base core)
> Fuller form of name
> Profession or occupation
> Period of activity of the person

Please note that core designation means that the element must be recorded (if applicable and readily ascertainable) in the description for the person. It does *not* mean that it must be included as part of the authorized access point for the person. For example, date associated with the person is a core element. This means that, if known, a person's birth and/or death date must be recorded somewhere in the description. It does not mean that RDA requires the date to be part of the access point (see further, below, in the discussion of RDA 9.3).

For the sake of illustration, the figures in this book will usually include many elements beyond the core elements. See figure 3.3a for an example of a description of a person that contains only core elements; figure 3.3b is an example of a description of the same person containing elements beyond core. It is evident that the RDA core for the description of a person can be minimal. Cataloging agencies will undoubtedly want their catalogers to include more elements, such as, at the least, variant names and sources consulted (fields 400 and 670 in figure 3.3b). In making decisions about inclusion of non-core elements in entity descriptions, agencies need to think about possible future uses of the data. Many non-core elements, such as gender, language, places associated with the person, and occupation will be useful as limiters to searches or as initial searches for records (e.g., a person who wants to find Spanish-speaking female authors), but only if agencies apply them consistently in their databases.

Figure 3.3a. Core Elements

010	‡a n 50035187
046	‡f 19250527 ‡g 20081026
100 1	‡a Hillerman, Tony

Figure 3.3b. Elements beyond Core

010	‡a n 50035187
046	‡f 19250527 ‡g 20081026
100 1	‡a Hillerman, Tony
370	‡a Sacred Heart (Okla.)
370	‡e Albuquerque (N.M.) ‡2 naf
374	‡a Authors ‡a Journalists ‡a Educators ‡2 lcsh
375	‡a male
377	‡a eng
400 1	‡a Hillerman, Anthony Grove
670	‡a Kilroy was there, 2004: ‡b title page (Tony Hillerman)
670	‡a New York times, via WWW, October 27, 2008 ‡b (Tony Hillerman; born Anthony Grove Hillerman, May 27, 1925, Sacred Heart, Okla.; died Sunday [October 26, 2008], Albuquerque, aged 83; his lyrical, authentic, and compelling mystery novels set among the Navajos of the Southwest blazed innovative trails in the American detective story)

8.4. LANGUAGE AND SCRIPT. One of the basic principles of RDA is that of representation: "The data describing [an entity] should reflect the [entity's] representation of itself" (RDA 0.4.3.4). It is therefore no surprise that RDA 8.4 calls for recording names in the language and script in which they appear. This would mean that the preferred name of a person who uses Chinese would be recorded in Chinese script; a Greek-speaker's name would be recorded in Greek script; an English-speaker's name in Latin script (see figure 3.4a). RDA 8.4 includes an alternative, however: "Record a transliterated form of the name either as a substitute for, or in addition to, the form that appears on the source." LC and PCC will continue to record a form transliterated following the ALA-LC Romanization Tables as the preferred name for names appearing in non-Latin scripts (LC-PCC PS 8.4, alternative, February 2010).[5] Non-Latin script forms may be included in the record as variant access points. Including non-Latin variant access points is a relatively recent practice and NACO policies have not been fully developed. Until they are, catalogers may record non-Latin script variant access points in 4XX fields, but should include a 667 field reading "Non-Latin script reference(s) not evaluated" (see figure 3.4b).

Figure 3.4a. Name Appearing in Non-Latin Script (RDA Basic Guideline)

046	ǂf 1957
100 1	ǂa Βλαβιανός, Χάρης, ǂd 1957-
374	ǂa Poets ǂ2 lcsh
375	ǂa male
377	ǂa gre
400 1	ǂa Vlavianos, Charēs, ǂd 1957-
670	ǂa Pōlētēs thaumatōn, 1985: ǂb title page (Χάρης Βλαβιανός) cover (born 1957; studied in England; poet)

Figure 3.4b.
Name Appearing in Non-Latin script (RDA Alternative: LC/NACO Practice)

046	ǂf 1957
100 1	ǂa Vlavianos, Charēs, ǂd 1957-
374	ǂa Poets ǂ2 lcsh
375	ǂa male
377	ǂa gre
400 1	ǂa Βλαβιανός, Χάρης, ǂd 1957-
667	ǂa Non-Latin script reference not evaluated.
670	ǂa Pōlētēs thaumatōn, 1985: ǂb title page (Χάρης Βλαβιανός) cover (born 1957; studied in England; poet)

8.5.2. CAPITALIZATION. RDA calls for faithful recording of a person's usage in matters such as abbreviation, hyphenation, and diacritical marks (see RDA 8.5). RDA 8.5.2 calls for capitalization of names of persons to follow RDA appendix A.2. Generally, capitalize each surname or forename; capitalize other words associated with the name following the usage of the language involved (see, e.g., figure 3.1). However, appendix A.2.1 instructs us to follow the capitalization of the commonly known form for names with unusual capitalization. For an example, see figure 3.5.

Figure 3.5. Capitalization of Personal Names with Unusual Usage

046	ǂf 19520925
100 1	ǂa hooks, bell, ǂd 1952-
370	ǂa Hopkinsville (Ky.) ǂ2 naf
373	ǂa City University of New York ǂ2 naf ǂs 1994
374	ǂa Social critic
374	ǂa Educators ǂa Authors ǂ2 lcsh
375	ǂa female
377	ǂa eng
400 0	ǂa bell hooks, ǂd 1952-
400 1	ǂa Watkins, Gloria Jean, ǂd 1952-
670	ǂa Teaching critical thinking, 2010: ǂb title page (bell hooks; other words on title page capitalized conventionally)
670	ǂa Contemporary authors online, 30 August 2011 ǂb (bell hooks; born Gloria Jean Watkins, September 25, 1952, in Hopkinsville, Kentucky; social critic, educator, writer; teaches at City University of New York since 1994)

8.8. SCOPE OF USAGE. This RDA element allows the cataloger to specify the type of work associated with a name when a person uses more than one (as in the case of pseudonyms). For example, Charles Lutwidge Dodgson wrote mathematical works under his real name and children's works under the name Lewis Carroll. The scope of usage element may be used to explain this. The element may also define the scope of usage within cataloging practice or rules. For example, the form Dodgson, Charles Lutwidge, 1832-1898, may not be used in subject fields according to the rules of the *Library of Congress Subject Headings Manual* (LCSH). The scope of usage element is recorded in the MARC 667 field (see figure 3.6).

Figure 3.6. Scope of Usage

046	ǂf 18320127 ǂg 18980114
100 1	ǂa Dodgson, Charles Lutwidge, ǂd 1832-1898
370	ǂa Daresbury (England) ǂb Guildford (England) ǂ2 naf

373	‡a Christ Church (University of Oxford) ‡a Church of England ‡2 naf
374	‡a Authors ‡a Mathemeticians ‡a Deacons--Church of England ‡2 lcsh
375	‡a male
377	‡a eng
400 1	‡a Dodgson, C. L. ‡q (Charles Lutwidge), ‡d 1832-1898
400 0	‡a D. C. L., ‡d 1832-1898
500 1	‡w r ‡i Alternate identity: ‡a Carroll, Lewis, ‡d 1832-1898
667	‡a Name used in mathematical works.
667	‡a SUBJECT USAGE: This heading not valid for use as a subject. Works about this person are entered under Carroll, Lewis, 1832-1898.
670	‡a Euclid and his modern rivals, 1879: ‡b title page (Charles L. Dodgson)
670	‡a The new belfry of Christ Church, Oxford, 1872: ‡b title page (D.C.L.)
670	‡a OCLC, 1 November 2011 ‡b (access point: Dodgson, Charles Lutwidge, 1832-1898; usage: Charles Lutwidge Dodgson, C.L. Dodgson, Charles L. Dodgson, D.C.L.)
670	‡a Comtemporary authors online, 1 November 2011 ‡b (Lewis Carroll, known as Dodgson, Charles L.; Dodgson, Charles Lutwidge; born January 27, 1832, in Daresbury, Cheshire, England; died January 14, 1898, in Guildford, Surrey, England; teacher of mathematics at Christ Church, Oxford; deacon in Church of England, 1861)

8.9. DATE OF USAGE. The date of usage element allows recording of a date or range of dates associated with the use of the preferred name of the person. This information may be important if the person has changed his or her name or uses more than one name. This element is recorded in the MARC 667 field (see figure 3.7).

Figure 3.7. Date of Usage

046	‡f 19290728 ‡g 19940519
100 1	‡a Onassis, Jacqueline Kennedy, ‡d 1929-1994
370	‡a Southampton (N.Y.) ‡b New York (N.Y.) ‡2 naf
374	‡a First lady
374	‡a Editors ‡2 lcsh
375	‡a female
377	‡a eng
400 1	‡a Kennedy, Jacqueline Bouvier, ‡d 1929-1994
400 1	‡a Bouvier, Jacqueline, ‡d 1929-1994
400 1	‡a Kennedy, Jackie, ‡d 1929-1994
400 1	‡a Onassis, Jackie, ‡d 1929-1994

667	‡a This person used the name Jacqueline Bouvier until her marriage to John F. Kennedy on September 12, 1953; she used Jacqueline Bouvier Kennedy from her marriage to Kennedy until her marriage to Aristotle Onassis on October 20, 1968; she used Jacqueline Kennedy Onassis from her marriage to Onassis until her death in 1994.
670	‡a Jackie, 1998: ‡b title page (Jackie) cover (Jackie Kennedy) page 4 (Jackie Onassis)
670	‡a Washington post, May 20, 1994: ‡b page A1 (Jacqueline Kennedy Onassis, died May 19, 1994, 10:15PM, New York, N.Y.) page A20 (Jacqueline Bouvier Kennedy Onassis, born July 28, 1929, Southampton, N.Y., daughter of John Bouvier; married John F. Kennedy, September 12, 1953) page 6 (married Aristotle Onassis, 1968)
670	‡a New York times, October 21, 1968: ‡b page 1 (married Aristotle Socrates Onassis 20 October 1968 on the island of Skorpios)

8.10. STATUS OF IDENTIFICATION. RDA instructs us to record the level of authentication of the data identifying the entity. The possible levels are "fully established," "provisional," and "preliminary." "Fully established" means the data are sufficient to fully establish the authorized access point. "Provisional" means the data are insufficient to establish the authorized access point. "Preliminary" means the data were recorded without the described resource in hand.

In nearly all cases NACO catalogers are expected to fully establish authorized access points in authority records in the LC/NACO Authority File. Provisional records are allowed, however, if the cataloger has inadequate information about the entity to fully establish the authorized access point. For example, a cataloger might need to establish a name, but the only evidence for the form appears in a language or script that the cataloger does not know well enough to ensure choosing the correct form for the authorized access point. This does not happen very often with names of persons.

NACO participants will almost never create preliminary records, but they do exist in the authority file, sometimes the result of a machine-driven project to populate the file from access points on bibliographic records. If NACO participants encounter preliminary records, they should upgrade them to fully established records if they are making other changes to the record by evaluating and, if appropriate, changing the authorized access point in light of the resource in hand and other evidence that might be available.[6]

This information is coded in the MARC authority record in field 008 position 33, which is labeled in the OCLC display as "Auth status." Fully established records contain "a" in this position. Provisional records contain "c" in this position, and preliminary records contain "d." See figure 3.1 for an example.

8.11. UNDIFFERENTIATED NAME INDICATOR. If more than one person uses the same name and no additional information can be found to distinguish them, RDA permits the same authorized access point to be used for them all (see RDA 8.6, 8.11, and 9.19.1.1). This is a solution that should only be used as a last resort, if the cataloger is unable after reasonable research to find any information that can distinguish the descriptions of the persons.

An authority record containing such an authorized access point is called an "undifferentiated name record." The record for an undifferentiated name is marked in two ways that make it easily recognizable. The first is the undifferentiated name indicator described in RDA 8.11. This is not a core element in RDA, but it is required for records in the LC/NACO Authority File.

In the MARC record, the undifferentiated name indicator is given as a code. Field 008/32 ("undifferentiated personal name") is coded "b." This position is labeled "Name:" in the OCLC fixed field display (see figure 3.8).

Figure 3.8. Undifferentiated Personal Name

Rec stat	c	Entered	19940613		Replaced 20120212102623.0		
Type	z	Upd status	a	Enc lvl	n	Source	
Roman		Ref status	n	Mod rec		Name use	a
Govt agn		Auth status	a	Subj	a	Subj use	a
Series	n	Auth/ref	a	Geo subd	n	Ser use	b
Ser num	n	**Name**	**b**	Subdiv tp	n	Rules	z

100 1	‡a Baker, Barbara	
670	‡a [Author of All colour book of stamps]	
670	‡a All colour book of stamps, 1974: ‡b title page (Barbara Baker)	
670	‡a [Author of Feel good]	
670	‡a Feel good, 1994: ‡b title page (Barbara Baker)	
670	‡a [Compiler of September 11, 2001 remembered]	
670	‡a September 11, 2001 remembered, 2002, 1966: ‡b title page (compiled by Barbara Baker)	

LC/NACO practice also includes another, perhaps more obvious, indication that the record is for an undifferentiated name. The record will contain a 100 field, just like any other authority record for a personal name, but each individual included in the record will receive at least two 670 fields. The first of these will be given in the format "[Author (etc.) of (title)]." The second will be a 670 field in normal format for the work being cataloged (see details on 670 fields below under 8.12). Each person covered by the authorized access point will have a similar pair of 670 fields. If it can be determined that other works are by one of the persons already covered in the record, additional 670 fields for these may be added under the appropriate bracketed 670 field.

Best practices have yet to develop for RDA undifferentiated records, but because the record represents multiple individuals, it seems unlikely that many elements beyond core will be included in the description because most of these elements serve to distinguish one person from another. If the cataloger has enough information to record non-core element information about a person it is probable that he or she has enough information to create an RDA description for the person separate from the undifferentiated name record.

The undifferentiated name technique is available in RDA only for descriptions of persons. It may not be used for families, corporate bodies, or other entities such as works or expressions.

The authorized access point "Baker, Barbara" (figure 3.8) is for an undifferentiated name, representing three persons. No information is known about any of these women that would help the cataloger distinguish the names, and so they will share a single authorized access point (with the result that the works of all three will be interfiled within the same access point in the index of bibliographic records), and their description will be stored in a single authority record. Note that it is much easier to differentiate names in RDA than in previous codes, for example, by using a person's occupation. In the case of Barbara Baker we do not have this information.

If a cataloger later discovers further information about one of the names on an undifferentiated name record that allows it to be distinguished from the others, a new authority record should be made for the person including the newly distinguished authorized access point, and the forms in corresponding bibliographic records should be corrected. The 670 fields in the original undifferentiated name record corresponding to the new authorized access point will also be removed. A 667 field is included in the new record such as the following:

667   ‡a Formerly on undifferentiated name record: n 86016735

For a two-year period in the late 1980s, the Library of Congress experimented with streamlining this procedure, issuing a ruling that these records should have 670 fields for no more than three persons. If the authorized access point represented more, no additional 670 fields were added (beyond those for the third), and a 667 field was added containing the note "Record covers additional persons." This policy was rightly found to be unworkable, and has been discontinued. Undifferentiated personal name records should now contain 670 pairs for all persons represented by the authorized access point, no matter how many there are. If an older record is encountered with the 667 field described above, however, the 667 field should be retained because it represents the missing 670 fields.

8.12. SOURCE CONSULTED. Just as the author of a scholarly paper justifies his or her assertions by citing sources (usually in footnotes), so the creator of an RDA description for a person in an authority record must justify access points by citing where the information came from. In MARC authority work, this is done using the 670 field.[7] The source consulted element is not core in RDA, but at least one instance, that of the resource in hand that generated the need for a new authorized access point, is required in LC/NACO practice.

There is no prescribed format for style or punctuation within the field, but a customary practice among NACO catalogers has arisen which is described here; there is usually no reason to depart from this practice. Subfield ‡a contains the title proper of the work cited. If the title proper is very general (such as "Complete works"), it may be preceded by the preferred name of the creator of the work.[8] If the title is very long it may be shortened by omitting words after the first four or five. Abbreviation of words in the title and elsewhere in the source consulted element is permitted, but RDA in general discourages abbreviation and the cataloger must ensure that persons consulting the record are able to identify the resource being cited. Examples in this *Handbook* avoid abbreviation. The title is followed by the publication date, as found in the 264 field of the bibliographic record for the cited source. A colon customarily closes this subfield if a specific location within the source is cited in subfield ‡b. Subfield ‡b begins with this location and then contains the information found in the source. This information is contained within parentheses. Although ‡b is not repeated, several sets of parentheses may be found in this section if information from more than one place in the work is cited. To summarize, the customary format for the 670 field is as follows:

> 670 ‡a Title proper, publication date: ‡b location of data (data) location of other data (data)

For example:

> 670 ‡a Child of the dark, 1962: ‡b title page (Carolina Maria de Jesus) page 9 (born 1913, Sacramento, Minas Gerais, Brazil)

The first instance of the source consulted element in the record should cite the work being cataloged that generated the need for the authorized access point. If no other sources give additional information about the authorized access point, this may be the only instance of the element in the record. Subfield ‡b of the 670 field contains the name exactly as given in the work. See figure 3.3b. If the name is not found in the source, subfield ‡b contains "(name not given)." This wording is only used with the required source consulted element for the resource being cataloged. Other sources that do not give information about the person would not be cited in 670 fields.

If the name is given in a language that uses case (e.g., Latin, Greek, or German), cite it exactly as given. Do not convert it in the source consulted element to the nominative case, although the access points should all be formed in the nominative case. In figure 3.9, for example, the source contains the Latin form "Alexandri Olivar." The forename is transcribed in the 670 field exactly as it appears in the item, in the genitive case ("Alexandri"); however, when it is given as a variant access point in a 400 field, it is converted to the nominative case ("Alexander").

Figure 3.9. Name in Language Using Case

100 1	‡a Olivar, Alexandre
375	‡a male
377	‡a spa ‡a lat
400 1	‡a Olivar, Alexander
400 1	‡a Olivar, Alejandro
670	‡a Sancti Petri Chrysologi Collectio sermonum, 1982 : ‡b volume 3, title page (Alexandri Olivar)
670	‡a Catàleg dels manuscrits de la Biblioteca del Monestir de Montserrat, 1977: ‡b title page (Alexandre Olivar)
670	‡a OCLC, November 15, 2011 ‡b (access point: Olivar, Alexandre; usage: Alexandre Olivar; Alejandro Olivar; Alexandri Olivar)

Additional instances of the source consulted element may be necessary if more information is needed to justify the form chosen for an access point than that found in the resource being cataloged. This happens, for instance, when it is necessary to distinguish the authorized access point from an identical access point for a different person or entity already in the authority file. Additional instances of the source consulted element show where additional information was found. Figure 3.1, for example, shows where the cataloger determined that Martha Washington was born in 1731 and died in 1802.

Figure 3.1 also shows two other customary citation practices:

1. The first 670 field has no subfield ‡b. Subfield ‡b is unnecessary in this instance because the information about the form of the name was found in the title proper itself.
2. If the 670 field cites a print source that lists names in alphabetical order or a digital source, no location need be given in ‡b, and in such cases it is customary not to follow the title proper with a colon. In other cases, the location in the source must be cited. Normally this is by page number, or a customary term. Some examples of these include: "title page," "title page verso," "jacket,"

and "colophon." Citations to the cover of a book use the following wordings: "cover" means the front cover, "page 2 of cover" means the inside of the front cover, "page 3 of cover" means the inside of the back cover, and "page 4 of cover" means the back cover. For examples see the figures throughout this chapter.

When recording data in the source consulted element (subfield ‡b of 670), it is probably better to err on the side of too much rather than too little. Names are recorded exactly as found in the source, as are birth and death dates. Include, and do not abbreviate or translate, titles or other terms associated with the name. Even though these may not be needed to form an access point, they may come in handy later on if an otherwise identical name needs to be added to the authority file and something is needed to resolve the conflict.

NACO catalogers are required to search their utility, for example, OCLC or SkyRiver, for information about the authorized access point. The cataloger searches for information both about access points used in the database for the name and the name's usage as found in transcribed elements in the records (the most common of these is the 245 field, which includes the title and statement of responsibility). If information is found, and if it adds to information already cited in other instances of the source consulted element (e.g., other 670 fields), it should be recorded in an additional 670 field. The format is as follows:

670   ‡a OCLC, [date consulted] ‡b (access point(s): [data]; usage: [data])

or

670   ‡a SkyRiver, [date consulted] ‡b (access point(s): [data]; usage: [data])

For example, cataloging the book *Nascita di Cristo: poema* by Pellegrino Gaudenzi, the cataloger must create an authorized access point for the author. The source consulted element for the work cataloged will be recorded as follows:

670   ‡a Nascita di Cristo, 1797: ‡b title page (Pellegrino Gaudenzi)

Searching OCLC yields three records for this author, all with the access point "Pellegrino, Gaudenzi, 1749-1784." Only one of the records shows usage of the name in a 245 field: "Gaudenzi Pellegrino." The source consulted element for the OCLC information will be recorded:

670   ‡a OCLC, June 23, 2011 ‡b (access point: Gaudenzi, Pellegrino, 1749-1784; usage: Pellegrino Gaudenzi)

For the authority record for this person, see figure 3.10.

Figure 3.10. Citing OCLC Information

046	ǂf 1749 ǂg 1784
100 1	ǂa Gaudenzi, Pellegrino, ǂd 1749-1784
374	ǂa Poets ǂ2 lcsh
375	ǂa male
377	ǂa ita
670	ǂa Nascita di Cristo, 1797: ǂb title page (Pellegrino Gaudenzi)
670	ǂa OCLC, June 23, 2011 ǂb (access point: Gaudenzi, Pellegrino, 1749-1784; usage: Pellegrino Gaudenzi)

In most cases NACO catalogers are not required to go beyond searching their database (which may be a utility such as OCLC, or a catalog such as the Library of Congress catalog) to find information, unless it is necessary to resolve a conflict. Because different databases are involved, containing different records and thus different information, a NACO cataloger at an OCLC library might in certain cases arrive at a different authorized access point than a NACO cataloger at a SkyRiver library or a cataloger at the Library of Congress. This is to be expected and is permissible under RDA. Once the access point has been authorized in the LC/NACO Authority File, that form should be used by all catalogers who use the file, regardless of which database they work in.

Libraries in general and catalog departments in particular tend to keep in-house files of information about local persons and entities that is recorded nowhere else. This information may be cited in authority records in the following format:

670   ǂa [MARC symbol for the library] files, [date consulted] ǂb (data)

For instance, the Brigham Young University library (MARC symbol: UPB) keeps information about the death of prominent local persons. In figure 3.11, the final source consulted element records in field 670 the information the library has kept about the death date of Milton R. Hunter.

Figure 3.11. Local Files

046	ǂf 1902 ǂg 1975
100 1	ǂa Hunter, Milton R. ǂq (Milton Reed), ǂd 1902-1975
375	ǂa male
377	ǂa eng
378	ǂq Milton Reed

670	‡a "... thy word is truth," 1957: ‡b title page (Milton R. Hunter; Council of Seventy) page 7, etc. (Mormon elder)
670	‡a LC data base, 2 May 1986 ‡b (access point: Hunter, Milton Reed, 1902- ; usage: Milton R. Hunter)
670	‡a UPB files, January 15, 1993 ‡b (died 1975)

Catalogers often get information directly from the author or someone close to the author, such as a publisher. This information is cited in a 670 field with the wording "Letter from . . . , [date]," "Phone call to . . . , [date]," "E-mail correspondence with . . . , [date of the exchange]," etc. See, for example, figure 3.12.

Figure 3.12. Citing a phone call

046	‡f 19120313 ‡g 19960107
100 1	‡a Maxwell, W. LeGrand ‡q (William LeGrand), ‡d 1912-1996
374	‡a Musicians ‡2 lcsh
375	‡a male
377	‡a eng
378	‡q William LeGrand
400 1	‡a Maxwell, William LeGrand, ‡d 1912-1996
400 1	‡a Maxwell, LeGrand, ‡d 1912-1996
670	‡a Modulations, interludes and aids for organists, 1978: ‡b title page (W. LeGrand Maxwell)
670	‡a Phone call to author's son, 23 January 1996 ‡b (full name William LeGrand Maxwell; preferred form W. LeGrand Maxwell; also known as LeGrand Maxwell; born 13 March 1912, died 7 January 1996)

The ready availability of online sources of data has brought about a revolution in methods to find information about persons. Catalogers now have at their fingertips the ability to determine birth and death dates and a host of other useful information. Any online resource may be cited, but it is not current practice to include the Uniform Resource Locator (URL) (the Internet address). Though the URL is without a doubt useful information, because URLs change so frequently it is considered counter-productive to include them in the source consulted element. Any Internet page can be cited, however, if information is found about an access point from one. The suggested form is:

> 670 ‡a Name of the page (etc.), via WWW, [date consulted] ‡b [location within the page if appropriate] (data)

If it is clear from the name of the resource that it is online, it is not necessary to include "via WWW." Because the URL is generally not cited in a 670 field it is good practice to give enough information here that the site can easily be found again using an Internet search engine. For examples, see figures 3.1, 3.2, 3.3b, 3.5, and others throughout this chapter. Note that ‡u (for URL) has been defined for use in many MARC authority record fields, so more URLs are now being cited than previously.

The source consulted element should contain all relevant information found when the cataloger was consulting the source, including information that may go beyond that needed to form an access point. This is often important because later users of the authority record will use this information to decide if the authorized access point in the authority record is the same as that needed for the new bibliographic record. For example, the cataloger who receives a work on trees in New Zealand by Ann Phillips will find in the LC Name Authority File (LCNAF) several persons by this exact name, including "Phillips, Ann," "Phillips, Ann, 1930- ," and "Phillips, Ann, 1953-" (see figure 3.13).

Figure 3.13. Supplemental Information

100 1	‡a Phillips, Ann
373	‡a New Zealand Tree Crops Association ‡2 naf
374	‡a Research scientist
375	‡a female
377	‡a eng
670	‡a Make money from woodturning, 1994: ‡b title page (Ann Phillips) page 155 (former research scientist; member New Zealand Tree Crops Association)
675	‡a New Zealand national bibliography, 1981-82; ‡a New Zealand Books in Print, 1986-94; ‡a Who's who in New Zealand, 1978

046	‡f 1930
100 1	‡a Phillips, Ann, ‡d 1930-
370	‡a England ‡2 naf
372	‡a Children's literature ‡2 lcsh
374	‡a Novelists ‡2 lcsh
375	‡a female
377	‡a eng
670	‡a The multiplying glass, 1981: ‡b title page (Ann Phillips)
670	‡a A haunted year, 1994: ‡b title page (Ann Phillips) jacket (born and raised in England)
670	‡a British national bibliograpy, 1992 ‡b (Phillips, Ann, 1930- [entry for A haunted year])

046	‡f 19531109
100 1	‡a Phillips, Ann, ‡d 1953-
372	‡a Music ‡2 lcsh
374	‡a Editors ‡2 lcsh
375	‡a female
377	‡a eng
670	‡a Rudiments of music, 1999: ‡b title page (Ann Phillips, compiler/editor)
670	‡a Phone call to publisher February 5, 2002 ‡b (born November 9, 1953)

It is completely irrelevant to the formation of the access point itself that the person represented by the first authority record is a former research scientist and member of the New Zealand Tree Crops Association, that the person described on the second record is a novelist born and raised in England, or that the third Ann Phillips is a compiler/editor. Strictly speaking, all that was necessary to create the authority record was the citation of the usage in the work, "Ann Phillips," and citations justifying the addition of date of birth to the second and third authorized access points. However, the creators of all three records included supplemental information, perhaps sensing that this was a common name likely to cause problems of identification later. Because of this foresight, the cataloger of the book on trees in New Zealand knows that the correct authorized access point is "Phillips, Ann," and not one of the others. Additionally, including the RDA elements that contain this information in the record (in 3XX MARC fields) makes it easier to find the supplemental information at a glance, rather than searching through 670 fields, as was required in AACR2 authority records.

Supplemental information about the person or entity used for identification rather than formulation of an access point should be given in the source consulted element as briefly as possible in the language of the cataloging agency, even if the original source gives the information in another language. See, for example, figure 3.14. The entry for Lanskoy in the *Dictionnaire de Biographie Française* reads "LANSKOY (ANDRÉ), peintre [Moscou 31 mars 1902 – Paris 22 août 1976] . . ." In the source consulted element, the name is copied as found, but all other information is translated into English.

Figure 3.14. Supplemental Information Given in English

046	‡f 19020331 ‡g 19760822
100 1	‡a Lanskoy, André, ‡d 1902-1976
370	‡a Moscow (Russia) ‡b Paris (France) ‡2 naf
374	‡a Painters ‡2 lcsh
375	‡a male

670   ‡a André Lanskoy, 1960

670   ‡a Dictionnaire de biographie française, 1933- : ‡b fasc. 122, page 803 (Lanskoy, André; painter, born Moscow March 31, 1902; died Paris August 22, 1976)

In addition to citing information found in various sources in 670 fields, it is sometimes useful to cite works that were checked in which information was *not* found. The obvious reason for this is to save the next cataloger the trouble of checking those sources again in the future should a conflict need to be resolved. Figure 3.13, the Ann Phillips case, is a good example. Of the three authorized access points, a check of the dates the records were created in the LCNAF reveals that the authorized access point without dates was the last created. Because the same name, "Phillips, Ann" was already in use by several other persons than the author of *Make Money from Woodturning*, the cataloger clearly wanted to find more information about this Ann Phillips, and so checked a number of sources to try to find qualifiers or birth/death dates. This being a fairly common name, it seems likely that more persons named Ann Phillips will create resources that need cataloging, requiring that they be distinguished from those already established. Because the cataloger who established the authorized access point for the New Zealander was unable to find any qualifying data for the name, this authorized access point, "Phillips, Ann" will be the authorized access point that future persons named Ann Phillips will have to be distinguished from. Further research is likely to concentrate on getting more information about the Ann Phillips already established without dates, if no dates or other qualifying information can be found for a future Ann Phillips. Therefore, the creator of the authority record for "Phillips, Ann" included a 675 field citing every reference source he or she checked in trying to find more information about the author, so that the future cataloger who must distinguish others with the same name won't waste time looking in the same sources.

The final paragraph of RDA 8.12.1.3 deals with this situation, saying to record the phrase "No information found" following the citation for the source consulted. In the MARC format the 675 field is used to record such information. Because the sources listed in a 675 field by definition are sources in which information was not found, the addition of the RDA phrase is not necessary, and is not included in current practice.

The cataloger should use judgment in adding 675 fields to authority records; it is not necessary to include one for every source consulted. The format of this non-repeatable field is as follows:

675   ‡a Source, date; ‡a Source, date; ‡a Source, date [etc.]

8.13. CATALOGUER'S NOTE. The cataloguer's note element contains information about the person represented by the authorized access point that might be helpful to persons using the authority record. The cataloguer's note element is not core in RDA, but it is core for the LC and PCC in certain situations.[9]

This element is normally addressed to other catalogers, and does not cite data, but rather explains something that might not otherwise be understood. For example, a contemporary author may have used several pseudonyms, but not all of them have been used in bibliographic records. The 667 field for the basic record might contain a list of the unused pseudonyms. Another common use of this element in name authority records is to give instructions about subject use, because most, but not all, names can be used as subject headings (for an example, see figure 3.6).

Catalogers are called upon to make judgments about the identity of persons they are dealing with. Even if the cataloger is not sure, he or she must make a decision about whether to identify a particular name on the resource being cataloged with the same name in other resources. If the cataloger simply cannot decide, a note to this effect can be made in the authority record. The most common wording of this note is: "Cannot identify with . . ." For example, in figure 3.15, the cataloger of *Sensibility: A Poem* (Edinburgh, 1789) could not decide whether the Thomas Hall named on the title page was the same person as "Hall, Thomas, active 18th century-19th century," whose name had already been established in the authority file, and who also wrote poetry. Therefore, he or she made a new authorized access point for the author of *Sensibility,* but including in the cataloguer's note element the possibility that they might, after all, be the same person.

Figure 3.15. "Cannot Identify with" Note

046	ǂs 1789
100 1	ǂa Hall, Thomas, ǂd active 1789
374	ǂa Poets ǂ2 lcsh
375	ǂa male
377	ǂa eng
667	ǂa Cannot identify with Hall, Thomas, active 18th century-19th century
670	ǂa Sensibility : a poem, 1789: ǂb title page (Thomas Hall, author of Benevolence and other poems)

The cataloger of the recording "Gambler's Life" including trombonist Al Hall was unsure that this was the same Al Hall who also played bass, but concluded in the end that they were identical. Because he or she was not entirely sure, however, a cataloguer's note element was included in the record to show the cataloger's thinking process. See figure 3.16.

A variant on this note, for situations where the cataloger is certain of the facts of the situation, is worded "Not the same as: _____." Such a note should be used sparingly, and only when there is a real possibility of confusion. If separate authority records have been created it is assumed they are for separate persons or entities, and so adding a note to one stating that it does not represent the same person or entity as another is somewhat redundant.

Figure 3.16. Tentative Identification

046	ǂf 19150318 ǂg 19880118
100 1	ǂa Hall, Al, ǂd 1915-1988
370	ǂa Jacksonville (Fla.) ǂb New York (N.Y.) ǂe Philadelphia (Pa.) ǂ2 naf
372	ǂa Jazz ǂ2 lcsh
374	ǂa Double bassists ǂa Cellists ǂa Tubists ǂa Trombonists ǂ2 lcsh
375	ǂa male
400 1	ǂa Hall, Alfred Wesley, ǂd 1915-1988
667	ǂa Bassist and trombonist judged to be the same person.
670	ǂa Mr. Wilson, 1955?: ǂb container (Al Hall, bass)
670	ǂa Reclams Jazzführer, 1990 ǂb (Hall, Al (Alfred Wesley); born March 18, 1915, Jacksonville, Florida; died January 18, 1988, New York; bassist; raised in Philadelphia; played cello and tuba, starting on bass in 1932)
670	ǂa Gambler's life, 1974: ǂb container (Al Hall, trombone)

Figure 3.17 shows a 667 note that users of the LC/NACO Authority File may encounter but will never make themselves. There have been various large projects by the Library of Congress to populate the LCNAF with the contents its manual authority files, and frequently this has involved machine generation of records with little direct human intervention. These records are identified by the 667 note "Machine-derived authority record." Once in the file they may be manipulated and updated just like any other authority record.

Figure 3.17. Machine-Derived Authority Record

100 1	ǂa Prescott, John, ǂd 1959-
667	ǂa Machine-derived authority record.
670	ǂa LCCN 92-760047: Prescott, J. Sonata for tuba and piano opus 23, 1990?: ǂb (usage: John Prescott)

STRUCTURE OF CHAPTER 9. RDA chapter 9, "Identifying Persons," follows the same structure as most of the other chapters in the "Recording Attributes" parts of RDA (RDA sections 1 through 4). It begins with a section on the purpose and scope of the chapter (RDA 9.0) and then proceeds to general guidelines on identifying persons, including sources that may be consulted for information about persons (RDA 9.1). It then treats, one by one, the various elements and sub-elements of the person entity that are recognized by RDA, giving instructions on where to get information about the element or sub-element, and how to record that information. This section is the heart of chapter 9, and occupies the bulk of it (RDA 9.2–9.18). The chapter ends with a final section on constructing access points for persons (RDA 9.19). It is crucial to understand this structure. Catalogers used to AACR2 chapter 22, which is chiefly about creating an access point (heading) for a person, may be misled into thinking that the guidelines about recording elements, and particularly wording about core elements, constitute instructions about how to construct the access point for the person, when in fact this central section gives instructions for recording the *information* in the record or description for the person. In the entity-relationship or linked-data database structure RDA anticipates, we will be creating descriptions of persons that exist independently from, but are linked to, other entities such as works that they may have a relationship to. In such an environment bibliographic records with formal access points might not exist, but the elements contained in the description of the person will be essential.

9.2. Name of the Person

GENERAL GUIDELINES

9.2.1. BASIC INSTRUCTIONS ON RECORDING NAMES OF PERSONS. "Name of the person" is defined in RDA 9.2.1 as "a word, character, or group of words and/or characters by which a person is known." A single individual can have more than one name. One of those names will be chosen under RDA as the preferred name; others may be included in the description as variant names.

9.2.2. PREFERRED NAME FOR THE PERSON. Preferred name is a core element in RDA, meaning any description of a person entity must include this element. It is defined as "the name or form of name chosen to identify the person. It is also the basis for the authorized access point representing that person." A single human being may have more than one identity (for example, in the case of pseudonyms); in RDA each of these is considered a separate entity, and so a separate description will be created for each identity, each having its own preferred name (see below under 9.2.2.8).

9.2.2.4. RECORDING THE PREFERRED NAME. Preferred names for persons are recorded in subfields ‡a, ‡b, and sometimes ‡c of the 100 field of authority records in the form prescribed generally in RDA 9.2.2.4. If the name consists, as most do, of more than one part, the first element is "that part of the name under which the person would normally be listed in authoritative alphabetic lists," followed by other parts of the name.

An exception is made if a person's preference is known to be different from this; this exception is applied very rarely. Naturally, because name forms can be complex, RDA gives more specific guidelines. Details are found in RDA 9.2.2.9–9.2.2.26 (see below).

CHOOSING THE PREFERRED NAME

If a person is known by more than one form of the same name, or by more than one name (for example, a birth name, a nickname, and a married name), RDA 9.2.2.2 gives us guidance for choosing one of these as the preferred name. We are to choose, in priority order:

1. A name found in preferred sources of information in resources associated with the person
2. A name found in other formal statements found in those same resources
3. A name found in any other source

However, this somewhat mechanical exercise is tempered by 9.2.2.3, which states that we are to choose the name "by which the person is commonly known" as the preferred name. This relates to one of the bedrock principles of cataloging theory, that of representation. As stated in RDA 0.4.3.4,

> the name or form of name chosen as the preferred name for a person, family, or corporate body should be (a) the name or form of name most commonly found in resources associated with that person, family, or corporate body, or (b) a well-accepted name or form of name in the language and script preferred by the agency creating the data.

Why is this? Because the database will present the preferred name in displays and indexes, and the form chosen should be the one most likely to be the one library users will use when attempting to find resources associated with the person. RDA 9.2.2.2 is a "default"—it is expected that in most cases the name found in preferred sources of information in resources associated with the person is the one most library users will expect to find in the database, but the cataloger must make this decision on the basis of all available evidence, and if he or she determines that another form is the "commonly known" form, that is the form that should be chosen as the preferred name.

The preferred name may be a person's legal name, but more likely it will be another form—few people actually use their full, legal name except in the most formal of situations. So, for example, we will choose religious name "Teresa" for works by and about the prominent nun known as Mother Teresa rather than her given name "Agnes (or Agnese) Gonscha Bojaxhiu," because that is how she is commonly known. We will choose the nickname "Bill Clinton" rather than "William Jefferson Clinton," because that is how the president is commonly known. We will choose the initialism

"P. G. Wodehouse" rather than spelled out "Pelham Grenville Wodehouse," because that is how the author is commonly known.

How does this work in practice? As noted above, by default we are to determine the preferred form from the "preferred sources of information in resources associated with the person" (RDA 9.2.2.2a). Preferred sources of information are found in RDA 2.2.2, and are discussed more fully in the chapter on describing manifestations and items. The preferred source of information for a book is the title page; therefore the title page of a book is considered strong evidence that a name printed on it is the "commonly known" version of the name. This is not limited to the title pages of items published within the author's lifetime. Thus, if the cataloger sees on the title page of the 1994 HarperTrophy edition of *The Lion, the Witch, and the Wardrobe* the author's name in the form "C. S. Lewis," that is taken as strong evidence of how the author's name is commonly known, and, in the absence of evidence to the contrary, this will be the form used as the basis for the preferred name, even though the cataloger may know that the author's full name is Clive Staples Lewis. In figure 3.18, the preferred name "Lewis, C. S." appears in subfield ‡a of the 100 field. Subfields ‡q "(Clive Staples)" and ‡d "1898-1963" are not part of the preferred name and will be discussed below under 9.5 and 9.3.

Figure 3.18. Preferred Name

046	‡f 18981129 ‡g 19631122
100 1	‡a Lewis, C. S. ‡q (Clive Staples), ‡d 1898-1963
370	‡a Belfast (Northern Ireland) ‡2 naf
374	‡a Authors ‡a Scholars ‡2 lcsh
375	‡a male
377	‡a eng
378	‡q Clive Staples
400 1	‡a Lewis, Clive Staples, ‡d 1898-1963
400 1	‡a Lewis, Jack, ‡d 1898-1963
670	‡a The lion, the witch and the wardrobe, 1994: ‡b t.p. (C.S. Lewis)
670	‡a C.S. Lewis, his letters to children, c1985: ‡b t.p. (C.S. Lewis) text (known as Jack Lewis; Clive Staples Lewis)
670	‡a Oxford Dictionary of National Biography ‡b (Lewis, Clive Staples; writer and scholar; born in Belfast on 29 November 1898; died 22 November 1963)

9.2.2.5. DIFFERENT FORMS OF THE SAME NAME. In many cases there is evidence that a person used many forms of the same name. For example, take the case of Robert F. Kennedy. Most title pages displaying his name use the form "Robert F. Kennedy," but some use the form "Robert Kennedy," some use "Bobby Kennedy," as he was popularly known, one simply calls him "Senator Kennedy," and another "RFK." These are four variants on the same name ("Robert F. Kennedy," "Robert Kennedy," "Senator Kennedy," "RFK") and one different name ("Bobby Kennedy"). The variants on the same name are said to differ in "fullness."

The basic guideline is to choose the form most commonly found as the preferred name. If no form is deemed to be more commonly found than the others, the latest form is chosen; if the cataloger is unsure of the latest form, the fullest form is chosen. "Fullness" is not defined in RDA. In earlier cataloging practice it referred to the number of parts to the name, not the length of the individual parts. "Robert F. Kennedy" and "RFK" were considered equal in fullness, each form having three parts, but "RFK" was a fuller form than "Robert Kennedy," because the latter only has two parts. Because RDA does not define the term, it is up to the cataloger to judge what constitutes a fuller form. In this case a search of the OCLC database shows that "Robert F. Kennedy" clearly predominates in title pages (based on transcriptions in MARC 245 fields), and so that form is chosen as the preferred name (see figure 3.19).

Figure 3.19. Different Forms of the Same Name

046	ǂf 19251120 ǂg 19680606
100 1	ǂa Kennedy, Robert F. ǂq (Robert Francis), ǂd 1925-1968
370	ǂa Brookline (Mass.) ǂb Los Angeles (Calif.) ǂc United States ǂ2 naf
374	ǂa Politicians ǂa Attorneys general ǂ2 lcsh
375	ǂa male
377	ǂa eng
378	ǂq Robert Francis
400 1	ǂa Kennedy, Bobby, ǂd 1925-1968
400 0	ǂa RFK, ǂd 1925-1968
400 1	ǂa Kennedy, ǂc Senator, ǂd 1925-1968
670	ǂa Robert Francis Kennedy, 1983
670	ǂa RFK, 2003: ǂb container (Robert F. Kennedy)
670	ǂa Wikipedia, September 5, 2011 ǂb (Robert F. Kennedy; Robert Francis "Bobby" Kennedy; born November 20, 1925 in Brookline, Mass.; died June 6, 1968 in Los Angeles; also referred to by his initials RFK; an American politician, a Democratic senator from New York, and a noted civil rights activist. Younger brother of President John F. Kennedy and acted as one of his advisors during his presidency. From 1961 to 1964, he was the U.S. Attorney General)
670	ǂa OCLC, September 5, 2011 ǂb (access points: Kennedy, Robert F., 1925-1968; Kennedy, Robert Francis, 1925-1968; usage: Robert F. Kennedy; Bobby Kennedy; RFK; Senator Kennedy; Robert Kennedy)

9.2.2.6. DIFFERENT NAMES FOR THE SAME PERSON. In contrast to RDA 9.2.2.5, different forms of the same name, sometimes a person is known by different names. Robert F. Kennedy is an example of this. "Robert" and "Bobby" are not different forms of the same name, they are different names (note that the nickname "Bobby" can be used both for persons named "Robert" and persons named "Roberta"), and so "Robert F. Kennedy" and "Bobby Kennedy" are different names. If the person has not changed his name from one to the other, and the two names do not represent different identities, then the preferred name is "the name by which the person is clearly most commonly known" (see figure 3.19).

9.2.2.7. CHANGE OF NAME. Unless a person has more than one identity (as in the case of pseudonyms), when a person changes his or her name the latest form is chosen as the preferred name unless there is reason to believe that the person will remain better known by the earlier name. Robert F. Kennedy's sister-in-law was originally known as Jacqueline Bouvier and published as a newspaper reporter under this name. When she married she changed her surname to Kennedy and at her second marriage changed her name again to Jacqueline Kennedy Onassis, the latest form that she used. Because she was well known under that name and there is no reason to believe she will remain better known by one of the earlier names, that name is chosen as the basis for her preferred name (see figure 3.7).

9.2.2.8. INDIVIDUALS WITH MORE THAN ONE IDENTITY. Sometimes persons create separate identities for themselves, as in the case of pseudonyms or stage names. In contrast to AACR2, which had a somewhat complicated procedure depending on whether the person was considered a contemporary author or not, RDA treats these cases more simply: "If an individual has more than one identity, choose the name associated with each identity as the preferred name for that identity." Thus, if a person uses more than one name (a real name and one or more pseudonyms), the cataloger will choose a preferred name for each identity, and each identity will receive a separate description (in the current environment, this means separate authority records). The identity most commonly associated with any given work by the person will be linked to the description of the work by a "creator" relationship link (see RDA 6.27.1.7 and 19.2.1.3).

This is a change from AACR2. Under AACR2, the form "Dodgson, Charles Lutwidge, 1832-1898" (see figure 3.6) would have been given as the "main entry" for all mathematical works by this person, even if some of them had been published under his alter ego Lewis Carroll, because of AACR2's treatment of separate bibliographic identities. In RDA, whichever identity is most commonly associated with a given work will be the one linked to the work via the "creator" relationship.

Cases of individuals with more than one identity are varied and can become quite complex, and exist for all types of resources, from printed books to recorded music to audio-visual materials. Practice in the LC/NACO Authority File varies according to three broad categories: (a) persons whose bibliographic identity is only a pseudonym and never use their real name as a creator or contributor to a resource (i.e., they in fact only have one identity), (b) persons who have two identities (who either use their real name and one pseudonym, or do not use their real name but use two pseudonyms), and (c) persons who have three or more identities (one of which may or may not be the person's real name).

In the first case, which is the exception written into RDA 9.2.2.8, the pseudonym is given as the preferred name and the person's real name is given as a variant. Because there is really only one identity, only one authority record is made. John Wayne is an example. Although his real name is known, the only name associated with any resource as a creator or contributor is "John Wayne" (see figure 3.20).

Figure 3.20. Single Identity (Pseudonym)

046	‡f 19070526 ‡g 19790611
100 1	‡a Wayne, John, ‡d 1907-1979
374	‡a Actors ‡2 lcsh
375	‡a male
377	‡a eng
400 1	‡a Morrison, Marion Michael, ‡d 1907-1979
400 1	‡a Wayne, Duke, ‡d 1907-1979
670	‡a The films of John Wayne, 1970
670	‡a Encyclopædia Britannica, 1992 ‡b (Wayne, John; byname Duke, original name Marian Michael Morrison; born May 26, 1907; died June 11, 1979)

In the second case, persons who have two identities, two preferred names are chosen and two authority records are created. They are linked using 500 fields, and the relationship may be specified using the relationship designators "alternate identity" or "real identity" (see RDA K.2.1). Charles Dodgson (figure 3.6) and Lewis Carroll are an example of this case (see figure 3.21).

Figure 3.21. Two Identities

046	‡f 18320127 ‡g 18980114
100 1	‡a Carroll, Lewis, ‡d 1832-1898
370	‡a Daresbury (England) ‡b Guildford (England) ‡2 naf
372	‡a Children's literature ‡2 lcsh
373	‡a Christ Church (University of Oxford) ‡a Church of England ‡2 naf
374	‡a Authors ‡a Mathemeticians ‡a Deacons--Church of England ‡2 lcsh

375	‡a male
377	‡a eng
500 1	‡w r ‡i Real identity: ‡a Dodgson, Charles Lutwidge, ‡d 1832-1898
667	‡a Name used in children's works.
670	‡a Lewis Carroll and Alice, 1832-1982, 1982
670	‡a OCLC, 1 November 2011 ‡b (access point: Carroll, Lewis, 1832-1898; usage: Lewis Carroll)
670	‡a Comtemporary authors online, 1 November 2011 ‡b (Lewis Carroll, known as Dodgson, Charles L.; Dodgson, Charles Lutwidge; born January 27, 1832, in Daresbury, Cheshire, England; died January 14, 1898, in Guildford, Surrey, England; teacher of mathematics at Christ Church, Oxford; deacon in Church of England, 1861)

RDA doesn't treat the third case, more than two identities, any differently from the second, but for practical reasons LC/NACO policy has a different procedure for recording the relationships between the identities. The cataloger first chooses one of the identities as the "basic" identity. The MARC record for this identity will include 500 fields linking the record to those of all the other identities, but they are coded "‡w nnnc" in order to suppress their display. The basic record will also contain a 663 field with the text "For works of this author entered under other names, search also under [list of names]." All other authority records created for this person's identities will contain a single 500 field linking to the record for the basic identity, again coded "‡w nnnc," and a 663 field with the text "Works by this author are entered under the name used in the item. For a listing of other names used by this author, search also under [authorized access point of the basic identity]."

The result of this procedure will be that the user who searches for the basic identity will be provided with a list of the names of all the identities; the user searching for one of the other identities will not be given all the names, but will instead be directed to the record for the basic identity for the list. The purpose of this is simplification of authority database maintenance. Under the LC/NACO procedure, whenever a new identity is used by an person, a new authority record will be created for the identity, with a 500 and a 663 field linking back to the record for the basic identity, and the record for the basic identity will be modified by the addition of the new name to its 663 field and one new 500 field. The alternative, revising the records for each of the person's identities to reflect the addition of a new identity, could quickly become quite complex; the LC/NACO procedure, although somewhat less helpful to the catalog user, is sensible and less prone to error on the part of the cataloger. An example of such an author is Orson Scott Card, who writes principally under his real name, but also uses several pseudonyms. Figure 3.22 gives the authority records necessary for this complex situation.

Figure 3.22. More than Two Identities

a. The basic record

100 1	‡a Card, Orson Scott
372	‡a Science fiction ‡a Fantasy fiction ‡2 lcsh
374	‡a Authors ‡2 lcsh
375	‡a male
377	‡a eng
500 1	‡w nnnc ‡a Bliss, Frederick
500 1	‡w nnnc ‡a Green, Bryan
500 1	‡w nnnc ‡a Gump, P. Q.
500 1	‡w nnnc ‡a Walley, Byron
663	‡a For works of this author entered under other names, search also under ‡b Bliss, Frederick, ‡b Green, Bryan, ‡b Gump, P.Q., ‡b Walley, Byron
670	‡a A storyteller in Zion, 1993: ‡b title page (Orson Scott Card)
670	‡a Sunstone, volume 20, no. 1 (April 1997): ‡b page 18 (Frederick Bliss and P.Q. Gump are pseudonyms used by Orson Scott Card in Sunstone)
675	‡a Friend, October 1977: page 38 (Byron Wally) ‡a The rag mission, 1979 (Bryan Green)

b. The other records

100 1	‡a Bliss, Frederick
500 1	‡w nnnc ‡a Card, Orson Scott
663	‡a Works by this author are entered under the name used in the item. For a listing of other names used by this author, search also under ‡b Card, Orson Scott
670	‡a Sunstone, volume 20, no. 1 (Apr. 1997): ‡b page 18 (Frederick Bliss and P.Q. Gump are pseudonyms used by Orson Scott Card in Sunstone)

100 1	‡a Green, Bryan
500 1	‡w nnnc ‡a Card, Orson Scott
663	‡a Works by this author are entered under the name used in the item. For a listing of other names used by this author, search also under ‡b Card, Orson Scott
670	‡a The rag mission, 1979 ‡b (Bryan Green; pseudonym used by Orson Scott Card)

100 1	‡a Gump, P. Q.
500 1	‡w nnnc ‡a Card, Orson Scott
663	‡a Works by this author are entered under the name used in the item. For a listing of other names used by this author, search also under ‡b Card, Orson Scott
670	‡a Sunstone, volume 20, no. 1 (April 1997): ‡b p. 18 (Frederick Bliss and P.Q. Gump are pseudonyms used by Orson Scott Card in Sunstone)

100 1	‡a Walley, Byron	
500 1	‡w nnnc ‡a Card, Orson Scott	
663	‡a Works by this author are entered under the name used in the item. For a listing of other names used by this author, search also under ‡b Card, Orson Scott	
670	‡a Friend, Oct. 1977: ‡b page 38 (Byron Wally; pseudonym used by Orson Scott Card)	

Sometimes two or more authors work together and publish under a shared or joint pseudonym. In this case, rather than an individual with more than one identity, we have an identity associated with more than one individual. The case of shared identities is not mentioned specifically in RDA's guidelines on dealing with multiple identities, but the situation is covered by the definition of "person" in RDA 8.1.2: "The term person refers to an individual or an identity established by an individual (either alone or in collaboration with one or more other individuals)." Thus the general guidelines for dealing with persons apply to joint pseudonyms: "choose the name by which the person [i.e., the shared identity] is commonly known" (RDA 9.2.2.3).

LC/NACO practice is to create a record for each entity: one for the pseudonym and one for each real name, if the persons wrote under their real names—as is the case with Bill Miller and Bob Wade, who wrote under the joint pseudonym Whit Masterson (see figure 3.23). Notes recorded in the 663 field will display to the public when the user searches under the authorized access point displayed in the 100 field. The 500 fields are coded with "‡w nnnc," which suppresses their display because the information is instead displayed from the 663 field. For details, see *Descriptive Cataloging Manual Z1* under 663.

Figure 3.23. Joint Pseudonym

a. The record for the pseudonym

100 1	‡a Masterson, Whit
374	‡a Authors ‡2 lcsh
377	‡a eng
500 1	‡w nnnc ‡a Miller, Bill, ‡d 1920-1961
500 1	‡w nnnc ‡a Wade, Bob, ‡d 1920-
663	‡a Joint pseudonym of Bill Miller and Bob Wade. For works of these authors written under their own or other names, search also under: ‡b Miller, Bill, 1920-1961 ‡b Wade, Bob, 1920-
670	‡a Touch of evil: ‡b title page (Whit Masterson)
670	‡a American authors and books, 1962 ‡b (Miller, Bill, 1920-1961; wrote with Bob Wade under pen names: Wade Miller; Whit Masterson; Dale Wilmer)

b. The records for the real identities

046	‡f 1920 ‡g 1961
100 1	‡a Miller, Bill, ‡d 1920-1961
374	‡a Authors ‡2 lcsh
375	‡a male
377	‡a eng
500 1	‡w nnnc ‡a Masterson, Whit
500 1	‡w nnnc ‡a Miller, Wade
500 1	‡w nnnc ‡a Wilmer, Dale
663	‡a For works of this author written in collaboration with Bob Wade, search also under: ‡b Miller, Wade, ‡b Masterson, Whit, ‡b Wilmer, Dale
670	‡a Murder, queen high, 1949: ‡b title page (Bill Miller)
670	‡a American authors and books, 1962 ‡b (Miller, Bill, 1920-1961; wrote with Bob Wade under pen names: Wade Miller; Whit Masterson; Dale Wilmer)

046	‡f 19200608
100 1	‡a Wade, Bob, ‡d 1920-
370	‡a San Diego (Calif.) ‡2 naf
374	‡a Authors ‡2 lcsh
375	‡a male
377	‡a eng
500 1	‡w nnnc ‡a Masterson, Whit
500 1	‡w nnnc ‡a Miller, Wade
500 1	‡w nnnc ‡a Wilmer, Dale
663	‡a For works of this author written in collaboration with Bill Miller, search also under: ‡b Miller, Wade, ‡b Masterson, Whit, ‡b Wilmer, Dale
670	‡a Murder, queen high, 1949: ‡b title page (Bob Wade)
670	‡a American authors and books, 1962 ‡b (Miller, Bill, 1920-1961; wrote with Bob Wade under pen names: Wade Miller; Whit Masterson; Dale Wilmer)
670	‡a lmdb.com, 10 September 2011 ‡b (Robert Allison Wade, born June 8, 1920 in San Diego, California; wrote with Bill Miller under pseudonym Whit Masterson)

RECORDING NAMES CONTAINING ONE OR MORE SURNAMES

9.2.2.9. GENERAL GUIDELINES. Once we have chosen the preferred name for the person, RDA instructs us to manipulate the form of the name in order to record it in the description of the entity (in the MARC authority format environment, the preferred name is recorded in subfields ‡a, ‡b, and ‡c of the 100 field; names with surnames are coded first indicator "1"). Generally, the surname is to be recorded as the first part of the preferred name, even if, as is usually the case with western languages, in normal order the surname comes last. So "C.S. Lewis" is recorded as "Lewis, C. S." (see figure 3.18). Some manipulation takes place even with a name from a language where the surname normally comes first: a comma is placed after the surname. "Mao Zedong" is recorded "Mao, Zedong." RDA has been criticized for continuing these practices, but their strength in the Anglo-American cataloging tradition is such that this manipulation of name forms remains in the code.

In the case of C. S. Lewis, note the spacing. RDA 8.5.6.1 calls for a space between "C." and "S." when *recording* the preferred name. This contrasts with RDA's guidelines for *transcribing* separate letters or initials found in RDA 1.7.6: "transcribe the letters without spaces between them." "C.S. Lewis" would be transcribed without spaces between the initials, for example, in a statement of responsibility.

If a person is known by a surname alone, that is how the preferred name is recorded even if it is known that the person has forenames. For example, the performer Teller does not use his forenames (Raymond Joseph) and does not use a title (such as "Mr. Teller"). His preferred name is "Teller" (see figure 3.24).

Figure 3.24. Surname Only

046	‡f 19480214
100 1	‡a Teller, ‡d 1948-
370	‡a Philadelphia (Pa.) ‡2 naf
373	‡a Penn & Teller ‡2 naf
374	‡a Actors ‡a Authors ‡2 lcsh
375	‡a male
377	‡a eng
400 1	‡a Teller, Raymond Joseph, ‡d 1948-
400 1	‡a Teller, NFN, ‡d 1948-
510 2	‡w r ‡i Group member of: ‡a Penn & Teller
670	‡a Cruel tricks for dear friends, 1989: ‡b title page (Teller)
670	‡a Imdb.com, 18 November 2011 ‡b (Teller; producer, writer, actor; born Raymond Joseph Teller February 14, 1948 in Philadelphia, Pennsylvania; driver's licence reads NFN Teller, meaning "no first name." Part of the acting duo Penn & Teller)

Terms of address (Dr., Mrs., Miss) are omitted unless the name consists only of a surname (and the person uses a term of address) or the person is identified only by a partner's name and a term of address.

9.2.2.9.1. SURNAME REPRESENTED BY AN INITIAL. If the person's surname is represented only by an initial, and at least one forename is given in full, the initial is regarded as a surname and is inverted to the beginning of the form when recording the preferred name (see figure 3.25).

Figure 3.25. Surname Represented by an Initial

046	‡f 1960~ ‡2 edtf
100 1	‡a B., Patricia
370	‡e Montréal (Québec) ‡2 naf
374	‡a Students ‡2 lcsh
375	‡a female
377	‡a fre
400 0	‡a Patricia B.
670	‡a Esthétique pour Patricia, 1980: ‡b title page (Patricia B.) page 4 of cover ("jeune étudiante inscrite en lettres à l'université") page 7 etc. (20 years old; lives in Montréal)

9.2.2.9.2. PART OF THE NAME TREATED AS A SURNAME. Some individuals are identified by made-up names that do not actually contain a surname. Malcolm X is one such individual. "X" is not an initial standing for a surname (see 9.2.2.9.1). However, "X" identifies this person and functions as if it were a surname. It is therefore treated as a surname and recorded as the first part of the preferred name (see figure 3.26).

Figure 3.26. Part of the Name Treated as a Surname

046	‡f 19250519 ‡g 19650221
100 1	‡a X, Malcolm, ‡d 1925-1965
370	‡a Omaha (Neb.) ‡b New York (N.Y.) ‡2 naf
373	‡a Black Muslims $2 lcsh
375	‡a male
377	‡a eng
400 0	‡a Malcolm X, ‡d 1925-1965
400 1	‡a Little, Malcolm, ‡d 1925-1965
400 0	‡a Hajj Malik el-Shabazz, ‡d 1925-1965
670	‡a The autobiography of Malcolm X, 1965.
670	‡a Britannica online, 9 September 2011 ‡b (Malcolm X, original name Malcolm Little, Muslim name el-Hajj Malik el-Shabazz (born May 19, 1925, Omaha, Nebraska, U.S.; died February 21, 1965, New York, New York), African American leader and prominent figure in the Nation of Islam)

9.2.2.9.3. PERSONS KNOWN BY A SURNAME ONLY. This guideline applies to persons who identify themselves by their surname and a term of address (e.g., Mrs. Oliphant) (see figure 3.27). This was a common practice particularly in the eighteenth and nineteenth centuries for women authors, Mrs. Oliphant being a typical example. The preferred name consists of the surname, with the term in subfield ‡c. Caution: do not use this guideline for persons of nobility whose title is recorded as the preferred name. A title of nobility is not regarded as a surname. For such persons, see RDA 9.2.2.14.

Figure 3.27. Persons Known by a Surname Plus Title

046	‡f 18280404 ‡g 1897
100 1	‡a Oliphant, ‡c Mrs. ‡q (Margaret Oliphant Wilson), ‡d 1828-1897
374	‡a Novelists ‡2 lcsh
375	‡a female
377	‡a eng
378	‡q Margaret Oliphant Wilson
400 1	‡a Oliphant, Margaret Oliphant Wilson, ‡d 1828-1897
670	‡a Agnes, 1866: ‡b title page (Mrs. Oliphant)
670	‡a British writers, supplement 10, 2004 ‡b (Mrs. Oliphant; Oliphant, Margaret Oliphant Wilson; British novelist born April 4, 1828 in Wallyford, Scotland; died 1897)

9.2.2.9.4. MARRIED PERSON IDENTIFIED ONLY BY A PARTNER'S NAME. The most common application of this guideline is to a married woman who chooses to identify herself by her husband's name plus the term of address "Mrs." (or the equivalent in other languages). The preferred name will be the name by which she identifies herself plus the title. Not including the title as part of the preferred name would be misleading. For an example, see figure 3.28.

Figure 3.28. Married Person Identified Only by a Partner's Name

046	‡f 19040611 ‡g 20010525
100 1	‡a Scott, Chester, ‡c Mrs., ‡d 1904-2001
370	‡a Luther (Mich.) ‡b Chatham (Ill.) ‡2 naf
375	‡a female
377	‡a eng
400 1	‡a Merritt, Marguerite, ‡d 1904-2001
400 1	‡a Scott, Marguerite, ‡d 1904-2001
670	‡a Mrs. Chester Scott memoir (University of Illinois at Springfield Norris L Brookens Library Archives/Special Collections), 1987: ‡b title page (Scott, Mrs. Chester

(Marguerite Merritt) born 1904) preface (Mrs. Chester Scott was born on June 11, 1904 in Luther, Michigan; graduated from Albion College in 1926 with a major in home economics; married Chester Scott in 1929, lived in Chicago; now lives in Chatham, Illinois)

670   ‡a Social Security death index, 7 September 2011 ‡b (Marguerite Scott, born 11 June 1904, died 25 May 2001; residence at death: Chatham, Illinois)

9.2.2.9.5. WORDS, ETC., INDICATING RELATIONSHIP FOLLOWING SURNAMES. In an important change from previous cataloging practice, in RDA words indicating family relationships such as "Jr.," "fils," "III," etc., are considered part of the preferred name and so will always be recorded (if the person uses or is known by the term). Previously such terms were only treated as part of the name if the name was Portuguese. Practice remains slightly different for Portuguese names and for names in other languages. If the term occurs in a Portuguese name it is recorded as part of the surname (in the MARC format in subfield ‡a). In other languages the term is recorded immediately following the person's forename(s) (in the MARC format in subfield ‡c) (see figure 3.29).

Figure 3.29. Words Indicating a Family Relationship

046	‡f 19090616 ‡g 19790717
100 1	‡a Brown, Hiram S., ‡c Jr. ‡q (Hiram Staunton), ‡d 1909-1979
370	‡a Brooklyn (New York, N.Y.) ‡b Chestertown (Md.) ‡2 naf
374	‡a Motion picture producers and directors ‡2 lcsh
375	‡a male
377	‡a eng
378	‡q Hiram Staunton
670	‡a Mysterious Doctor Satan, 1940: ‡b credits (producer, Hiram S. Brown, Jr.)
670	‡a IMDB, June 7, 2011 ‡b (Hiram S. Brown Jr.; Hiram Staunton Brown Jr.; film producer; born June 16, 1909 in Brooklyn, New York, N.Y.; died July 17, 1979 in Chestertown, Md.)
678 0	‡a Hiram S. Brown, Jr. (1909-1979) was an American film producer.

9.2.2.10. COMPOUND SURNAMES. A compound surname is a surname consisting of two or more proper names. RDA instructs us to record preferred names containing compound surnames in the same way as any other name containing a surname: record the entire surname as the first part of the preferred name followed by a comma, followed by the rest of the name (see RDA 9.2.2.9). However, there are some rather large exceptions to the basic guideline:

1. If the person prefers another part of the surname to be listed first, that is how the preferred name should be recorded. Only rarely will the cataloger have information about the person's preference.

2. If the person's preference is unknown, the preferred name should be recorded as reference sources in the person's language or country of residence list it. The cataloger should be cautious, however. Some reference sources, such as the *Dictionary of National Biography*,[10] enter all persons in a uniform style (in this case, under the last element of the name) regardless of personal preference. Listings in such sources are not definitive for the RDA form of the preferred name.

3. If neither the person's preference is known nor is the name found in an appropriate reference source, the preferred form should be recorded according to the usage for the person's country as specified in *Names of Persons: National Usages for Entry in Catalogues*.[11]

4. Finally, if the person's country is not covered in *Names of Persons*, the cataloger is instructed to record the first part of the surname as the first element (coming full circle back to the basic guideline in RDA 9.2.2.9).

The difficulty with compound surnames is not so much knowing how to record the preferred name as it is recognizing whether the name includes a compound surname at all, rather than just forenames that have the appearance of surnames. If the name does not, in fact, include a compound surname, RDA 9.2.2.10, with its elaborate provisions and exceptions, does not apply at all. The decision about whether a name contains a compound surname or not requires experience and familiarity with the language of the person and of the name.

How can the cataloger tell if the name includes a compound surname? Here are some clues:

1. RDA gives one piece of advice in the introduction to the guideline: "Take regular or occasional initializing of a part preceding a surname as an indication that that part is not used as part of the surname." Coretta Scott King's name sometimes appears as Coretta S. King. This person's name does not contain a compound surname even though "Scott King" potentially might be one (see figure 3.30).

Figure 3.30. Simple Surname

046	‡f 19270427 ‡g 20060130
100 1	‡a King, Coretta Scott, ‡d 1927-2006
370	‡a Heiberger (Ala.) ‡b Rosarito (Tijuana, Baja California, Mexico) ‡2 naf

375	‡a female
377	‡a eng
670	‡a My life with Martin Luther King, Jr., 1969: ‡b title page (Coretta Scott King)
670	‡a New York times WWW site, February 1, 2006 ‡b (Coretta Scott King; born Coretta Scott, April 27, 1927, Heiberger, Alabama; died Monday [January 30, 2006], Rosarito, Mexico, aged 78)

2. Does the name contain a hyphen between two parts of the name that have the appearance of surnames? Names such as Chris Wallace-Crabbe contain compound surnames (see figure 3.31).

Figure 3.31. Hyphenated Surname

046	‡f 19340506
100 1	‡a Wallace-Crabbe, Chris, ‡d 1934-
370	‡a Richmond (Vic.) ‡2 naf
374	‡a Poets ‡2 lcsh
375	‡a male
377	‡a eng
400 1	‡a Crabbe, Chris Wallace-, ‡d 1934-
400 1	‡a Wallace-Crabbe, Christopher Keith, ‡d 1934-
400 1	‡a Crabbe, Christopher Keith Wallace-, ‡d 1934-
670	‡a The thing itself, and other poems, 2007: ‡b title page (Chris Wallace-Crabbe)
670	‡a Dictionary of literary biography, 2004: ‡b volume 289 (Chris Wallace-Crabbe; born Christopher Keith Wallace-Crabbe in Richmond, Melbourne, on 6 May 1934; Australian poet)

3. Does the name contain a conjunction? Spanish compound surnames often (but not always) contain the conjunction "y" between the parts of the surname, for example, Emilio Cotarelo y Mori (see figure 3.32). A conjunction between parts of a compound surname may occur in other languages as well.

Figure 3.32. Surname with Conjunction

046	‡f 1857 ‡g [1935,1936] ‡2 edtf
100 1	‡a Cotarelo y Mori, Emilio, ‡d 1857-1935 or 1936
374	‡a Authors ‡a Historians ‡a Critics ‡2 lcsh
375	‡a male
377	‡a spa
400 1	‡a Mori, Emilio Cotarelo y, ‡d 1857-1935 or 1936

670	‡a Actrices españolas en el siglo XVIII, 2007: ‡b title page (Emilio Cotarelo y Mori)
670	‡a World biographical information system, 15 September 2011 ‡b (Cotarelo y Mori, Emilio; born 1857; died 1935 or 1936; writer, historian, critic)

4. Is there typographical evidence? If the name appears in a reference source or on a title page as David LLOYD GEORGE, the name probably contains a compound surname. If the name appears like this:

David

Lloyd George

the name "Lloyd George" might be compound, although this is less likely and further research would be prudent.

5. Is the person referred to in the resource being cataloged or a reference source by surname alone, without forenames? A sentence such as "In his lifetime, Vaughan Williams eschewed all honours with the exception of the Order of Merit which was conferred upon him in 1938" indicates that the name Ralph Vaughan Williams contains a compound surname (see figure 3.33).

Figure 3.33. Unhyphenated Compound Surname

046	‡f 18721012 ‡g 19580826
100 1	‡a Vaughan Williams, Ralph, ‡d 1872-1958
370	‡a Down Ampney (England)
370	‡b London (England) ‡2 naf
374	‡a Composers ‡a Teachers ‡a Authors ‡a Conductors (Music) ‡2 lcsh
375	‡a male
377	‡a eng
400 1	‡a Williams, Ralph Vaughan, ‡d 1872-1958
670	‡a Wassail song, 1913: ‡b caption (Ralph Vaughan Williams)
670	‡a Grove music online, 13 June 2011 ‡b (Vaughan Williams, Ralph; born Down Ampney, Gloucs., 12 Oct 1872; died London, 26 Aug 1958. English composer, teacher, writer and conductor)

Once the cataloger has determined that a name contains a compound surname he or she can apply RDA 9.2.2.10. If usage is known, it should be followed in recording the preferred name. For example, in addition to containing the conjunction "y," an important clue that the surname is compound is that Emilio Cotarelo y Mori is found in World Biographical Information System entered under "Cotarelo y Mori, Emilio" (see figure 3.32). Similarly, Serafín Alvarez Quintero appears under "Alvarez Quintero" in the Spanish-language encyclopedia *Enciclopedia Hispanica*[12] (see figure 3.34).

Figure 3.34. Reference Source for Compound Surname

046	‡f 18721012 ‡g 19580826
100 1	‡a Álvarez Quintero, Serafín, ‡d 1871-1938
372	‡a Comedy ‡a Drama ‡2 lcsh
374	‡a Dramatists ‡2 lcsh
375	‡a male
377	‡a spa
400 1	‡a Quintero, Serafín Álvarez, ‡d 1871-1938
670	‡a El ojito derecho, 2007: ‡b title page (Serafín y Joaquín Álvarez Quintero)
670	‡a Hispánica, 2003: ‡b micropedia, page 41 (Álvarez Quintero, Serafín, 1871-1938, Spanish author of comedy and drama)

If usage is not known the cataloger should follow the national usage given in *Names of Persons*. Usage for compound surnames in English and most other western languages is to record the entire compound surname as the beginning of the preferred name (see figures 3.31 through 3.34). The major exception is Portuguese. Usage for Portugal, Brazil, and other Portuguese-speaking countries is to begin the preferred name with the last part of the surname (see figure 3.35). If the Portuguese compound surname is followed by a word indicating family relationship (e.g., Filho, Pai, Júnior, Neto, or Sobrinho), it is recorded immediately after the surname as discussed above with RDA 9.2.2.9.5 (see figure 3.36). Be wary of Portuguese names consisting of two or more words not themselves surnames. Do not separate the parts of names such as "Castelo Branco, Camilo" or "Espirito Santo, Vicente Antonio de."

Figure 3.35. Portuguese Compound Surname

100 1	‡a Belato, Neyta Oliveira
373	‡a Universidade de Ijuí. Equipe Interdisciplinar do Programa de Desenvolvimento Municipal
374	‡a College teachers ‡2 lcsh
375	‡a female
377	‡a por
400 1	‡a Oliveira Belato, Neyta
670	‡a Planejamento participativo, 1987: ‡b title page (Neyta Oliveira Belato) page 4 of cover (Professora e membro da Equipe Interdisciplinar do Programa de Desenvolvimento Municipal da Universidade de Ijui (RS))

Figure 3.36. Portuguese Compound Surname with Word Indicating Relationship

100 1	‡a Leite Sobrinho, João Benedito Pereira
375	‡a male
377	‡a por
400 1	‡a Pereira Leite Sobrinho, João Benedito
400 1	‡a Sobrinho, João Benedito Pereira Leite
670	‡a Região noroeste do Estado de Mato Grosso, 1992: ‡b page 5 (João Benedito Pereira Leite Sobrinho)

Special care should be taken with Anglo-American names of women that have the appearance of compound surnames. It is not uncommon for a woman to give her birth (or other) surname before her husband's surname in formal presentations of her name, but unless the names are hyphenated this is not normally intended as a compound surname. Examples already seen include Jacqueline Kennedy Onassis, whose surname is not "Kennedy Onassis" (see figure 3.7) and Coretta Scott King, whose surname is not "Scott King" (see figure 3.30). Similarly, beginning in the nineteenth century, it was common for boys to be given their mother's birth surname as a second forename. For example, the first President Bush's full name is George Herbert Walker Bush. "Walker" is his mother's birth surname, but "Walker Bush" is not a compound surname.

If the nature of a surname that appears to be compound is uncertain and a decision cannot be made following the suggestions above, do not spend great amounts of time puzzling over it. Make a decision one way or the other about the preferred name and record the other form as a variant name (see below under 9.2.3, variant name for the person).

9.2.2.11. SURNAMES WITH SEPARATELY WRITTEN PREFIXES. The guiding principle governing this guideline is the same as that for 9.2.2.10 (compound surnames): record a name with a separately written prefix beginning with the part most commonly used as the first part in alphabetical listings in the person's language or country. RDA appendix F provides specific guidance for a number of languages to help catalogers who are unsure of national customs governing entry in the various languages. Guidelines are applied to surnames that include a separately written prefix consisting of an article, a preposition, or a combination of the two. RDA appendix F has drawn extensively on information contained in *Names of Persons*. For languages not covered in RDA, see *Names of Persons*. Caution: the guidelines are to be applied according to the language of the *person*, not the language of the surname.

If a person writes in more than one language, base the name on the language of most of the person's works. In case of uncertainty, catalogers in the United States who wish to follow the LC Policy Statement for RDA 9.2.2.11 (February 2010) will apply the instructions for English if that is one of the languages. If uncertainty remains, the cataloger should not spend time puzzling over the decision, but using judgment should choose one form for the preferred name, recording the other form as a variant name (see below under 9.2.3, variant name for the person).

English. Record the prefix as the first part of the preferred name (see figure 3.37).

Figure 3.37. English: Prefix Recorded First

046	‡f 19061213 ‡g 19961215
100 1	‡a Van der Post, Laurens
370	‡a Philippolis (South Africa) ‡b London (England) ‡2 naf
374	‡a Authors ‡a Explorers ‡a Conservationists ‡2 lcsh
375	‡a male
377	‡a eng
400 1	‡a Der Post, Laurens Van
400 1	‡a Post, Laurens Van der
400 1	‡a Van der Post, Jan
670	‡a Yet being someone other, 1982: ‡b title page (Laurens van der Post)
670	‡a Contemporary authors (online), January 30, 2007 ‡b (Laurens (Jan) van der Post; born December 13, 1906, Philippolis, South Africa; died December 15, 1996, London, England; writer, explorer, conservationist)

French. Record the prefix as the first part of the preferred name if the prefix consists of an article alone (le, la, les) or of a contraction of a preposition and an article (du, des) (see figure 3.38). If the prefix consists of a preposition (de) and an article (la, l'), record the article as the first part of the preferred name (see figure 3.39). If the French surname includes the preposition "de" with no article, record the part of the name following the preposition as the first part of the preferred name (see figure 3.40). The article in French, as well as a contraction of an article and preposition (des, du), is capitalized in a proper name (see RDA appendix A.40.3).

Figure 3.38. French: Preposition Contracted with Article

046	‡f 19110506 ‡g 19931221
100 1	‡a Des Cars, Guy
370	‡a Paris (France) ‡b Paris (France) ‡2 naf
372	‡a Detective and mystery stories ‡2 lcsh
374	‡a Authors ‡2 lcsh
375	‡a male

377	‡a fre
378	‡q Guy Augustin Marie Jean de la Pérusse
400 1	‡a Cars, Guy Des
670	‡a L'entremetteuse, 2009: ‡b title page (Guy Des Cars)
670	‡a Wikipedia, 17 May 2010 ‡b (Guy des Cars; Guy Augustin Marie Jean de la Pérusse des Cars was a French author who specialized in detective stories. He was born on 6 May 1911 in Paris and died on 21 December 1993 in the same city)

Figure 3.39. French: Preposition with Article

046	‡f 1621-07-08? ‡g 1695-04-13 ‡2 edtf
100 1	‡a La Fontaine, Jean de, ‡d 1621-1695
370	‡a Chateau-Thierry (France) ‡b Paris (France) ‡2 naf
374	‡a Poets ‡2 lcsh
375	‡a male
377	‡a fre
400 1	‡a Fontaine, Jean de La, ‡d 1621-1695
400 1	‡a De La Fontaine, Jean, ‡d 1621-1695
670	‡a Fables, 2010: ‡b title page (Jean de La Fontaine)
670	‡a Britannica online, 6 June 2011 ‡b (Jean de La Fontaine, born July 8?, 1621, Château-Thierry, France; died April 13, 1695, Paris, poet)

Figure 3.40. French: Preposition Alone

046	‡f 17990520 ‡g 18500818
100 1	‡a Balzac, Honoré de, ‡d 1799-1850
370	‡c France ‡2 naf
374	‡a Novelists ‡a Dramatists ‡2 lcsh
375	‡a male
377	‡a fre
400 1	‡a De Balzac, Honoré, ‡d 1799-1850
670	‡a Le père Goriot, 2011: ‡b title page (Honoré de Balzac)
670	‡a Wikipedia, 1 July 2010 ‡b (Honoré de Balzac, born 20 May 1799, died 18 August 1850; French novelist and playwright)

German. Treatment of German surnames with prefix follows almost the same pattern as that for French. Record the prefix as the first part of the preferred name if the prefix is an article (der, die, das) or a contraction of a preposition and an article (am, aus'm, vom, zum, zur) (see figure 3.41). For all other German surnames with prefix, record part following the prefix as the first part of the preferred name (see figure 3.42).

Figure 3.41. German: Preposition Contracted with Article

046	‡f 1939
100 1	‡a Vom Brocke, Bernhard, ‡d 1939-
375	‡a male
377	‡a ger
400 1	‡a Brocke, Bernhard vom, ‡d 1939-
670	‡a Forschung im Spannungsfeld von Politik und Gesellschaft, c1990: ‡b title page (Bernhard vom Brocke) jacket (Dr. phil.; born 1939)

Figure 3.42. German: Preposition Alone

046	‡f 18860522
100 1	‡a Hentig, Werner-Otto von, ‡d 1886-
400 1	‡a Von Hentig, Werner-Otto, ‡d 1886-
374	‡a Diplomats ‡2 lcsh
375	‡a male
377	‡a ger
670	‡a Werner Otto von Hentig, 1971
670	‡a Das deutsche Reich von 1918 bis heute, 1933: ‡b page 511 (Von Hentig, Otto; born 22 May 1886; jurist, attache to Peking, consul to Constantinople, Teheran, and numerous other capitals)

Italian. Record the prefix of an Italian name as the first part of the preferred name (see figure 3.43). Consult reference sources for medieval or early modern names, which ordinarily did not include an actual surname; the prefix was often part of a byname (e.g., Leonardo da Vinci).

Figure 3.43. Italian name with prefix

046	‡f 18630512 ‡g 19380301
100 1	‡a D'Annunzio, Gabriele, ‡d 1863-1938
400 1	‡a Annunzio, Gabriele d', ‡d 1863-1938
400 1	‡a Nuncius, Gabriel, ‡d 1863-1938
370	‡a Pescara (Italy) ‡b Gardone Riviera (Italy) ‡2 naf
374	‡a Authors ‡2 lcsh
375	‡a male
377	‡a ita
670	‡a Laudi del cielo, del mare, della terra e degli eroi, 1903-1904: ‡b title page of each volume (Gabriele d'Annunzio) colophon of each volume (Gabriel Nuncius)
670	‡a New Grove, 2nd edition ‡b (D'Annunzio, Gabriele; born March 12, 1863, Pescara, died March 1, 1938, Gardone Riviera; Italian writer)

Portuguese. Record the part of the surname following the prefix as the first part of the preferred name (see figure 3.44).

Figure 3.44. Portuguese Name with Prefix

100 1	‡a Santos, António Furtado dos	
375	‡a male	
377	‡a por	
400 1	‡a Furtado dos Santos, António	
400 1	‡a Dos Santos, António Furtado	
670	‡a Portugal. Código penal (anotado), 1983: ‡b title page (António Furtado dos Santos)	

Spanish. If the prefix consists of an article alone, the article is recorded as the first part of the preferred form (see figure 3.45). This is quite rare in Spanish surnames. In all other cases, record the part of the name following the prefix as the first part of the preferred name (see figure 3.46). Note that the guideline states that if the prefix consists of an article *only,* the recorded form begins with the article. Thus, if the name includes an article (el, la, lo, los, las) *and* a preposition (de), the part of the name following the prefixes will be recorded as the first part of the preferred name.

Figure 3.45. Spanish Name: Article Alone

100 1	‡a La Calle, Pedro
375	‡a male
377	‡a spa
400 1	‡a Calle, Pedro La
670	‡a Canción de cuna, 1996: ‡b caption (Pedro La Calle)

Figure 3.46. Spanish Name with Prefix

046	‡f 1913 ‡g 1972
100 1	‡a Maza, Francisco de la, ‡d 1913-1972
374	‡a College teachers ‡a Historians ‡2 lcsh
375	‡a male
377	‡a spa
400 1	‡a De la Maza, Francisco, ‡d 1913-1972
400 1	‡a La Maza, Francisco de, ‡d 1913-1972
670	‡a Francisco de la Maza, 1996
670	‡a World biographical information system, 6 March 2011 ‡b (Maza, Francisco de la; born 1913; died 1972; professor, historian)

If the surname has a prefix and it is not an article or preposition (or combination of the two), the prefix should be recorded as the first part of the preferred name (see figure 3.47).

Figure 3.47. Prefix Other than Article or Preposition

100 1	‡a Santo Domingo, Isabella
375	‡a female
377	‡a spa
400 1	‡a Domingo, Isabella Santo
670	‡a Los caballeros las prefieren brutas, 2004: ‡b title page (Isabella Santo Domingo)

RECORDING NAMES CONTAINING A TITLE OF NOBILITY

When the cataloger encounters a person with a title of nobility, he or she will usually have to choose the preferred name between at least two different names: the person's personal name (consisting of given name[s] and surname[s]) and the person's title of nobility. This choice is made following the guidelines in RDA 9.2.2.6. The RDA guidelines on recording names containing a title of nobility come into play only if, after applying 9.2.2.6, the cataloger concludes the person is more commonly known by the title than by the family name.

9.2.2.14. GENERAL GUIDELINES ON RECORDING NAMES CONTAINING A TITLE OF NOBILITY.

These guidelines, which should be compared to RDA 9.4.1.5, depend on RDA 9.2.2.6; that is, the preferred name should be based on the name by which the person is commonly known. If a nobleman or -woman uses title rather than family name in his or her works or is so listed in appropriate reference sources, the first part of the preferred name for such an individual should be the proper name in the title of nobility rather than the family name. Check reference sources to identify the individual's rank and personal name accurately.

The formula for recording the preferred name is fairly simple to follow:

> [Proper name in the title of nobility], [personal (family) name in direct order], [term of rank in the language in which it was conferred]

The personal name portion of the preferred name should exclude unused forenames. The cataloger can determine how the personal name commonly appears (and thus discover which forenames are "used") by checking preferred sources of information of the person's works or by consulting reference sources.

Sequential numbers (e.g., "2nd Earl of") are not used with a title of nobility in the preferred name; in case two or more of the bearers of such a title have the same personal name, they should be distinguished in the same fashion as other persons with identical names, by recording dates of birth and death or other distinguishing information (RDA 9.3–9.6, 9.15–9.16).

One nobleman better known by his title than by his personal name is the Duke of Wellington. He is generally referred to in resources as "The Duke of Wellington," not "Arthur Wellesley," his personal name. The *Encyclopaedia Britannica*[13] indexes him under his title, followed by his personal name and dates.[14] The preferred form of his name begins with the proper name in the title of nobility, followed by the personal name in direct order, then the term of rank. The proper name in the title and the personal name are recorded in a single subfield ‡a in MARC field 100. The term of rank, as a title, is placed in subfield ‡c of the MARC field (see figure 3.48).

Figure 3.48. Title of Nobility

046	‡f 17690501 ‡g 18520914
100 1	‡a Wellington, Arthur Wellesley, ‡c Duke of, ‡d 1769-1852
368	‡d Duke of Wellington
370	‡a Dublin (Ireland) ‡b Walmer (England) ‡2 naf
374	‡a Prime ministers ‡2 lcsh
374	‡a Army commander
375	‡a male
377	‡a eng
400 1	‡a Wellesley, Arthur, ‡c Duke of Wellington, ‡d 1769-1852
670	‡a The iron Duke of Wellington, 1999
670	‡a Encyclopaedia Britannica, 2002 ‡b (Wellington, Arthur Wellesley, 1st duke of; Prime minsister of Great Britain; born May 1, 1769, Dublin, Ireland; died September 14, 1852, Walmer Castle, Kent, England; British army commander during the Napoleonic Wars)

Very often the application of RDA 9.2.2.14 for persons whose preferred name is based on a title of nobility, such as the Duke of Wellington, results in a form that seems to violate the spirit of general guideline 9.2.2.3, that the cataloger choose as the basis for the preferred name "the name by which the person is commonly known." Often the name in nobility (Duke of Wellington, for example) is the only name found in chief sources of information of that person's works. Nonetheless, RDA 9.2.2.14 directs the cataloger to add the personal name (forename[s] and family surname) in direct order (e.g., Arthur Wellesley) followed by the term of rank (e.g., Duke of). Application of this rule to the Duke of Wellington results in the somewhat artificial form "Wellington, Arthur Wellesley, Duke of," despite the fact that "Duke of Wellington" is the form of name by which he is commonly known.

The cataloger should be aware that certain British titles below the rank of baron and certain other titles for persons of other countries are simply terms of honor (e.g., "Sir," "Dame," "Lord," or "Lady"). The preferred name for these persons will be based on the family name, not the term of honor.

The preferred name for noble persons of other countries follows the same pattern as that used for British nobility (follow, however, the guidelines of RDA appendix A for capitalization of the title) (see figure 3.49).

Figure 3.49. Title of Nobility

046	‡f 1810 ‡g 1861
100 1	‡a Cavour, Camillo Benso, ‡c conte di, ‡d 1810-1861
368	‡d Conte di Cavour
370	‡a Turin (Italy) ‡b Turin (Italy) ‡2 naf
374	‡a Finance ministers ‡2 lcsh
375	‡a male
377	‡a ita
400 1	‡a Benso, Camillo, ‡c conte di Cavour, ‡d 1810-1861
670	‡a Discorso, 1852: ‡b title page (conte Camillo Benso di Cavour, ministro di finanze intorno al trattato di commercio colla Francia)
670	‡a Dell'imposta sulla rendita in Inghilterra e sul capitale degli Stati Uniti : lettere di Emilio Broglio al conte di Cavour, 1856
670	‡a I nostri grandi, 1933: ‡b page 470 (Camillo Cavour; born Torino, 1810; died Torino, 1861)

For further treatment of titles of nobility, see the discussion below with RDA 9.4.1.5.

RECORDING NAMES THAT DO NOT CONTAIN A SURNAME OR TITLE OF NOBILITY

Although the majority of names North American catalogers will deal with contain a surname, there are a number of types of names that do not, and guidelines for recording them are found in RDA 9.2.2.18–9.2.2.26.

9.2.2.18. GENERAL GUIDELINES. RDA gives no guidelines for determining whether a name contains a surname or not. This is left to the cataloger's judgment. However, if the nature of the name is ambiguous, the cataloger is to apply RDA 9.2.2.9.2, that is, treat the name as if it contains a surname and record the supposed surname as the first part of the preferred name.

RDA 9.2.2.18 instructs us to check reference sources for names that do not contain a surname or title of nobility, and record as the first part of the preferred name the element under which the name is listed in those reference sources. If the name is not found in reference sources, follow the guidelines in RDA 9.2.2.18–9.2.2.26.

Cher is an example of a person with a name that does not contain a surname or title of nobility. Cher is not a pseudonym—it is a nickname for the performer's given name; but she chooses not to be known by her surname. A good reference source for performers is the Internet Movie Database (www.imdb.com). IMDb lists this person simply as "Cher" (see figure 3.50).

Figure 3.50. Person Known by Given Name

046	ǂf 19460520
100 0	ǂa Cher, ǂd 1946-
370	ǂa El Centro (Calif.) ǂ2 naf
373	ǂa Sonny & Cher ǂ2 naf
374	ǂa Actresses ǂa Film directors ǂ2 lcsh
375	ǂa female
377	ǂa eng
400 1	ǂa LaPiere, Cherilyn Sarkisian, ǂd 1946-
510 2	ǂw r ǂi Group member of: ǂa Sonny & Cher
670	ǂa Jacobs, L. Cher, 1975
670	ǂa IMDB.com, 5 May 2012 ǂb (Cher; actress, director; born Cherilyn Sarkisian LaPiere May 20, 1946, in El Centro, California; was member of Sonny & Cher)
678 0	ǂa Cher (1946-) is an American singer and actress.

The name is recorded in MARC X00 subfield ǂa, with the first indicator coded "0." Words or phrases denoting place of origin, occupation, or other characteristics (except the word "Saint," see 9.2.2.18.1) that are commonly associated with the name are considered an integral part of the name and will be recorded as part of the preferred name. These words or phrases are recorded in subfield ǂc (see figure 3.51). Roman numerals associated with a given name are also considered an integral part of the name, and are recorded as part of the preferred name in subfield ǂb (see figure 3.52).

Figure 3.51. Forename with Characteristic Word

100 0	ǂa Billy, ǂc the Kid
374	ǂa Outlaws ǂ2 lcsh
375	ǂa male

```
377        ‡a eng
400 1      ‡a McCarty, William Henry
400 1      ‡a Antrim, Henry
400 1      ‡a McCarty, Billy
400 1      ‡a Antrim, William Henry
670        ‡a History of Billy the Kid, 1920
670        ‡a Antrim is my stepfather's name, 1993: ‡b CIP title page (Billy the Kid) galley
           (born William Henry McCarty; called both Henry Antrim and Billy McCarty by
           his contemporaries; also called William Henry Antrim; stepfather's surname was
           Antrim)
```

Figure 3.52. Forename with Roman Numeral

```
046        ‡f 19200518 ‡g 20050402
100 0      ‡a John Paul ‡b II, ‡c Pope, ‡d 1920-2005
370        ‡a Wadowice (Poland) ‡b Rome (Italy) ‡2 naf
368        ‡d Pope
374        ‡a Church official
375        ‡a male
377        ‡a lat ‡a pol
400 1      ‡a Wojtyła, Karol Józef, ‡d 1920-2005
400 0      ‡a Johannes Paulus ‡b II, ‡c Pope, ‡d 1920-2005
670        ‡a The way to Christ, 1984: ‡b title page (Karol Wojtyła (Pope John Paul II))
670        ‡a Britannica online, 13 August 2012 ‡b (Blessed John Paul II, Latin Johannes Paulus,
           original name Karol Józef Wojtyła (born May 18, 1920, Wadowice, Poland—died
           April 2, 2005, Vatican City; beatified May 1, 2011; feast day October 22), the
           bishop of Rome and head of the Roman Catholic Church (1978-2005), the first
           non-Italian pope in 455 years and the first from a Slavic country)
```

9.2.2.21. NAMES CONSISTING OF INITIALS, SEPARATE LETTERS, OR NUMERALS. If a person consistently uses initials, separate letters, or numerals for identification, the initials, separate letters, or numerals, in direct order, will be used as the preferred name. If the name includes typographic devices (ellipses, asterisks, etc.), include them if they appear as part of a multi-letter abbreviation of a name; omit them if they follow single letter initials. Thus the preferred name of the abbé de B . . . is "B., abbé de," rather than "B . . . , abbé de."

It is helpful to make some attempt to find the identity of the author by looking in dictionaries of pseudonyms, anonyms, etc. In the example shown in figure 3.53, Sharp's *Handbook of Pseudonyms and Personal Nicknames* gives the information that

"A.L.O.E." stands for "A Lady of England" and that the initials are the pseudonym of Charlotte Maria Tucker.

Figure 3.53. Separate Letters

046	‡f 18210508 ‡g 18931202
100 0	‡a A. L. O. E., ‡d 1821-1893
374	‡a Authors ‡2 lcsh
375	‡a female
377	‡a eng
400 1	‡a E., A. L. O., ‡d 1821-1893
400 1	‡a Tucker, Charlotte Maria, ‡d 1821-1893
400 0	‡a Lady of England, ‡d 1821-1893
670	‡a The robber's cave, 2004: ‡b title page (A.L.O.E.)
670	‡a Sharp, H.S. Handbook of pseudonyms and personal nicknames, 1972: ‡b p. 1020 (Tucker, Charlotte Maria; A.L.O.E. (A Lady of England))
670	‡a Dictionary of national biography, 9 July 2003 ‡b (born 8th May 1821, died 2nd Dec. 1893)

9.2.2.22. NAMES CONSISTING OF A PHRASE. Sometimes a person may disguise his or her identity by using a phrase for identification. Following the general principles of RDA 9.2.3, if this is the appellation by which the person is commonly known, this phrase will be used for the preferred name. If the phrase or appellation does not contain a forename, or consists of a forename preceded by a term other than a term of address or title, it will be recorded in direct order. An example is "Old Sleuth" (see figure 3.54).

Figure 3.54. Person Known by Phrase

046	‡f 1839? ‡g 1898 ‡2 edtf
100 0	‡a Old Sleuth, ‡d 1839?-1898
374	‡a Authors ‡2 lcsh
375	‡a male
377	‡a eng
400 1	‡a Halsey, Harlan Page, ‡d 1839?-1898
670	‡a Jack the Juggler, or, The boy hypnotist, 1895: ‡b title page (Old Sleuth)
670	‡a Literature online, 4 May 2012 ‡b (Old Sleuth = Harlan Page Halsey, 1839?-1898)

9.2.2.23. FORENAME OR FORENAMES PRECEDED BY A TERM OF ADDRESS, ETC. If a person uses a forename and no surname plus a term of address or a title of position or office, record the preferred name beginning with the forename, followed by the word or phrase. The author of *The Boy's Book of Sports and Games* identifies himself as Uncle John. The preferred name for this person will be "John, Uncle" (see figure 3.55). Note that 9.2.2.23 refers to a person using a forename (and no surname) plus term of address, etc. For a person who uses a surname (and no forename) plus term of address, see RDA 9.2.2.9.3.

Figure 3.55. Person Known by a Forename Preceded by a Term of Address

100 0	‡a John, ‡c Uncle
374	‡a Authors ‡2 lcsh
375	‡a male
377	‡a eng
400 0	‡a Uncle John
670	‡a The boy's book of sports and games, 1851: ‡b title page (Uncle John)

9.2.2.25. CHARACTERIZING WORD OR PHRASE. This is deceptively similar to the situation in 9.2.2.22. RDA 9.2.2.22 treats in part a "phrase or appellation that does not contain a forename" and 9.2.2.25 treats a "characterizing word or phrase." What is the difference? Appellation is another word for name; in 9.2.2.22 it refers to a name that is in the form of a phrase, like "Old Sleuth" (see figure 3.54). A "characterizing word or phrase" is a word or phrase that describes an individual, such as "a physician" or "the daughter of a Wesleyan minister." Appellations are clearly intended to be names, and as such are similar to pseudonyms. Characterizing words or phrases normally appear on resources as ways to preserve the anonymity of an author, and are not usually intended by the person to be a name.

If a person is known only by a characterizing word or phrase, the word or phrase is treated as a name for purposes of identification in the database. There is no alternative if we want to give access to resources associated with such a person. Record the word or phrase in direct order, omitting initial articles, as the preferred name. Capitalize according to the rules for the language in appendix A (see figure 3.56).

Figure 3.56. Person Known by a Characterizing Word or Phrase

100 0	‡a Private Citizen for Truth and Accountability
377	‡a eng
670	‡a Bush on 9/11: ‡b title frame (created by a private citizen for truth and accountability)

However, because characterizing words or phrases are not intended to be names, and indeed so-called names such as "a military chaplain" are confusing to users of the database, RDA 9.2.2.25 instructs us that if the person is known by a real name or another name, that form should instead be chosen as the basis for the preferred name, and the characterizing word or phrase should be recorded as a variant (see figure 3.57). Because of this reasonable preference in RDA (which follows the preference of earlier cataloging practice), it is uncommon that a characterizing word or phrase would be used as the preferred name for a person whose identity is known.

Figure 3.57. Person Known by a Characterizing Word or Phrase and by Real Name

046	‡f 1703 ‡g 1791
100 1	‡a Wesley, John, ‡d 1703-1791
375	‡a male
377	‡a eng
400 0	‡a Lover of Mankind, and of Common Sense, ‡d 1703-1791
670	‡a The desideratum, or, Electricity made plain and useful, 1790: ‡b title page (by a lover of mankind, and of common sense; printed and sold .. at the Rev. Mr. Wesley's preaching-houses in town and country)
670	‡a English short title catalogue, via WWW, 20 November 2011 ‡b (A lover of mankind, and of common sense, is John Wesley, 1703-1791)

RECORDING VARIANT NAMES

9.2.3. VARIANT NAME FOR THE PERSON. Once the preferred name has been chosen, it will be recorded as described above in the description of a person entity (in a 100 field in the MARC authority format). In current systems, the preferred name is how the name will appear in displays such as database indexes and in bibliographic records. But what if the person has gone by more than one form of name or a different name altogether? One of the fundamental justifications for authority work is that by nature names change or appear in different forms. Librarians, following RDA guidelines, choose certain forms to be preferred names, but the average library user does not know these guidelines and so is likely to attempt catalog searches using forms that were not chosen as the preferred name. The cataloger needs to help such users to find their way to resources associated with the person. This is done by recording variant names in the description of the person entity, and is governed by RDA 9.2.3.

Before continuing, it is important to understand that variant names are *not* core in RDA. No provision under 9.2.3 is labeled as core, and therefore no recording of variant names is required in RDA. This means that whether to record variants or not is left to the judgment of the cataloger. It remains to be seen whether the Library of

Congress or the Program for Cooperative Cataloging will create policy statements or declare that recording certain variant names is core in records created under their auspices. Meanwhile, catalogers should consider whether recording a variant name will be helpful to the user of the database. If so, the variant probably should be recorded.

Variant names of persons are recorded in 400 fields in the MARC authority format. How they display depends on how the library's system is set up, but they are intended to display to the public similarly to the following, when a user does a search on a variant (using, for example, a display generated by the description in figure 3.51):

McCarty, William Henry
    search under
    Billy, the Kid

Alternately, the database could automatically re-execute the search so that the user who searched for McCarty would be presented with resources linked to the preferred name Billy, the Kid. This would be particularly useful when the user is performing keyword rather than browse searches against the database.

Here are some points to consider when deciding whether (and how) to include variant names in the description of the person.

What is already in the database? The cataloger should search the database he or she is using (for example, the LC/NACO Authority File) to avoid conflicts (i.e., identical forms). A variant name should not be added that would conflict with an existing preferred name. If the variant would conflict, the form must be differentiated in some way. For example, see figure 3.28. Mrs. Chester Scott was also known as Marguerite Scott, as we learn from the Social Security Death Index. Therefore, a variant form should be recorded for "Scott, Marguerite." However, there is already an established personal name "Scott, Marguerite" in the LC/NAF. Therefore, the variant name form recorded in the description for Mrs. Chester Scott must be differentiated. In this case, this can be done by the addition of Mrs. Scott's birth and death dates. (On ways to differentiate names, see below under 9.3–9.6 and 9.16.)

If no way is found to differentiate the variant name, it is permitted under NACO policy to change the preferred name already in the database by qualifying it if some way to do so can be found. If no way can be found to change the existing name form so that it will be different from the new variant name, the variant name may be added to the new description in a 500 field, which would generate a display such as the following when a user searches using the variant:

Scott, Marguerite
    search also under
    Scott, Charles, Mrs.

This means that both "Scott, Marguerite" and "Scott, Charles, Mrs." are valid preferred names, but they represent different persons, so the user must determine which one he or she wants.

Variant names, then, should not conflict with already existing preferred names. However, under NACO policy, variant names can "conflict" with (i.e., be identical to) other *variant* names. For example, Carlos Visca, author of *Los Ideales y Formas de la Aventura en la Edad Media* (1963), sometimes identifies himself as "C. V."; the author of *General Hints for the Revision of a Parliamentary Representation* (1830) identifies himself as "Civis" but also "C. V." "C. V." is recorded as a variant name on each description, and might display as follows when used in a search against the database:

C. V.

> *search under*
> Civis
> Visca, Carlos

The catalog user then needs to choose which "C. V." is wanted.

Catalogers should consider any variant as a potential form to record in the description of the person. Specific types of variants will be discussed below. Earlier cataloging practice discouraged recording of two categories of variants: variants that did not affect the primary elements of a name and variants of variants.

In earlier cataloging practice, the primary elements of a personal name were defined as all elements to the left of the comma and the first element to the right of the comma. In figure 3.11, for example, the primary elements are "Hunter, Milton." Recording of variants in which the primary elements were identical was discouraged. In the case of figure 3.11, there are two different forms of the name, "Milton R. Hunter," and "Milton Reed Hunter," and the latter is a variant of the first. However, because "Hunter, Milton Reed" had identical primary elements to "Hunter, Milton R.," the variant "Hunter, Milton Reed" would not have been recorded.

The reasoning behind this guideline (and it was never a hard rule) was that in index displays forms with identical primary elements would generally display next to each other, and so the inclusion of such variants was not thought to be helpful to the user. In the case of Hunter, a display such as the following might appear when the user made a search if both forms were recorded:

1. Hunter, Mildred Picston Bowers, 1913-
2. Hunter, Milton R. (Milton Reed), 1902-1975
3. Hunter, Milton Reed, 1902-1975
4. Hunter, Miriam C.
5. Hunter, Mollie, 1922-

It was thought that the user of the database would easily find records associated with Milton R. Hunter even in the absence of the variant form "Hunter, Milton Reed, 1902-1975."

RDA has no restriction against the recording of forms with identical primary elements; the cataloger must judge if recording such a variant would be helpful. Consideration should be given to index displays, but also to other factors such as the abilities of the library system when keyword searches are performed. For example, if Hunter's authorized access point had not included the word "Reed" but had instead been recorded "Hunter, Milton R., 1902-1975," it might be sensible to record the variant "Hunter, Milton Reed, 1902-1975" so that keyword searches would produce correct results if the user did a search on "Milton Reed Hunter."

Earlier cataloging practice also discouraged the recording of "variants of variants." For example, see figure 3.31, Wallace-Crabbe, Chris, 1934-. One type of variant that is usually recorded is rearrangement of complex names such as those with compound surnames. The first variant in this record, "Crabbe, Chris Wallace-, 1934-," is a variant of this type. This person also has a variant name form: in addition to "Chris Wallace-Crabbe," the basis of the preferred name, he is also known as "Christopher Keith Wallace-Crabbe." This variant form is recorded second in this description. The third variant form, "Crabbe, Christopher Keith Wallace-, 1934-," is a rearrangement of the second recorded variant. This is known as a "variant of a variant," and such forms were discouraged in earlier cataloging practice. RDA has no such restriction and whether to record the variant or not is left to the cataloger's judgment, who should consider whether recording the variant would be useful and helpful to users of the database.

Another earlier cataloging practice was "matching" variants to the authorized access point (the preferred name plus cataloger additions such as fuller forms and dates). This meant that if the authorized access point included dates, all the variant forms should include dates; but if the authorized access point did not include dates, variant forms could not in most cases include dates. There were also somewhat complicated guidelines that variant forms should "match" the authorized access point in terms of fuller forms as well. RDA has no such restrictions, and again, the form of the variant access points is left to the cataloger's judgment.

9.2.3.3. GENERAL GUIDELINES. In most cases, variant names should be recorded following the same guidelines as if they had been chosen as the preferred name. This applies to guidelines on such matters as capitalization, diacritical marks, etc., given in RDA 8.5, and guidelines for form and order of the name given in RDA 9.2.2.4 and 9.2.2.9–9.2.2.26. The second variant recorded in figure 3.31, for example, is formed following the guidelines for compound surnames in RDA 9.2.2.10. In addition, there are a number of specific instructions given in 9.2.3.4–9.2.3.10, some of which may call for recording other types of variants. A few of these will be discussed here.

9.2.3.4. REAL NAME. If the preferred name is not the person's real name, and the person does not use his or her real name as a creator or contributor, the real name should be recorded as a variant if known. Figure 3.20 is an example of this. The person commonly known as John Wayne never used his real name, Marion Michael Morrison, in resources he created or contributed to. The real name is recorded as a variant name. This recorded variant could create the following user display in the database:

> Morrison, Marion Michael, 1907-1979
>   *search under*
>   Wayne, John, 1907-1979

Another example of this type of variant name is found in figure 3.5.

In contrast, if the preferred name is not the person's real name, and the person *does* also use his or her real name as a creator or contributor, the person is said to have more than one identity. In this case, the person's real name is not recorded in the description as a variant name. RDA 9.2.2.8 applies and both names are given as preferred names in separate descriptions. In this case the names are linked by the inclusion of 500 fields in the MARC record. See, for examples, figures 3.6, 3.21, 3.22, and 3.23. This MARC mechanism might formulate a user display such as the following:

> Carroll, Lewis, 1832-1898
>   *search also under*
>   Real identity: Dodgson, Charles Lutwidge, 1832-1898

9.2.3.7. EARLIER NAME OF PERSON. If a person has changed his or her name, earlier forms of the name are recorded as variant names. An example is Jacqueline Kennedy Onassis (see figure 3.7). Mrs. Onassis was well known by Jacqueline Bouvier Kennedy, as well as by Jacqueline Bouvier, so these two forms are recorded as variants:

> Kennedy, Jacqueline Bouvier, 1929-1994
>   *search under*
>   Onassis, Jacqueline Kennedy, 1929-1994

Another case where a person commonly changes his or her name is when he or she takes a new name for religious reasons, as when entering a convent or becoming an ecclesiastical official. When Karol Józef Wojtyła became pope he changed his name to John Paul II. Following RDA 9.2.2.7, the latest form, John Paul II, is chosen as the basis of the preferred form. Karol Józef Wojtyła will be recorded as a variant (see figure 3.52):

> Wojtyła, Karol Józef, 1920-2005
> *search under*
> John Paul II, Pope, 1920-2005

It has not been the normal practice to record earlier names for persons whose earlier names were not associated with resources as a creator or contributor. Catalogers do not normally, for example, record as a variant name the birth name of a woman who did not begin publishing until after her marriage unless she was well known under the earlier name or the earlier name form appears in a reference source (such as a genealogical database). RDA 9.2.3.7, however, has no restrictions of this sort. The decision about recording earlier names as variants is left to the cataloger's judgment: will recording the name be helpful to users of the database?

9.2.3.9. ALTERNATIVE LINGUISTIC FORM. See figure 3.9 for an example of the application of this guideline. The Catalan form of this person's name, Alexandre Olivar, was chosen as the basis of the preferred name. However, the name also appears in Latin and Spanish forms. These are recorded as variant names:

> Olivar, Alejandro
> *search under*
> Olivar, Alexandre

Similarly, in figure 3.4b, the form of the name in a different script from that preferred by the agency is recorded as a variant name:

> Βλαβιανός, Χάρης, 1957-
> *search under*
> Vlavianos, Charēs, 1957-

9.2.3.10. OTHER VARIANT NAME. RDA 9.2.3.10 allows the cataloger to record any kind of variant found, "as required." The examples to RDA 9.2.3.10 give numerous types of variants, but the list is not closed. Other types of variants than those found in the examples are possible. As usual, the cataloger should use judgment: will recording the variant help the user navigate the database?

The following are some examples of types of variant names already seen in this chapter.

Different Name. Tony Hillerman (see figure 3.3) goes by a nickname. His official name is Anthony Grove Hillerman. This name may be recorded as a variant name. It could display in a database as follows:

> Hillerman, Anthony Grove
> *search under*
> Hillerman, Tony

Other examples of different names as variants are found in figures 3.16, 3.18, 3.19, 3.20, and elsewhere. This is a very common type of variant and in most cases it makes sense to record different names as variants.

Difference in Fullness. Sometimes the variant is based on a difference in the fullness of the name. For example, in figure 3.12, the preferred name was based on the name "W. LeGrand Maxwell." This person was also known as "William LeGrand Maxwell" and "LeGrand Maxwell." Both these variant names differ from the preferred name only in fullness. If the cataloger thinks recording these variant names would be useful to catalog users, they should be recorded:

> Maxwell, William LeGrand, 1912-1996
> *search under*
> Maxwell, W. LeGrand (William LeGrand), 1912-1996

Other examples of difference in fullness include figure 3.18 (Lewis, C. S. versus Lewis, Clive Staples) and figure 3.19 (Kennedy, Robert F. versus RFK). Most catalogers would consider such variants worth recording, but thought should be given to the "primary elements" issue discussed above.

Rearrangement of Parts of the Name. This type of variant is not so much a variant name as it is a rearrangement of a form already recorded as a preferred or variant name. It is thought to be helpful to library users, who may not know the sometimes arcane rules about which part of a multipart surname will appear at the beginning of the preferred name, to direct them to the preferred form by rearranging the name into various other forms and recording those forms as variants. This is normally done by taking the form already in the description and moving another part to the front, followed by the remainder of the name in the same order as the original form. There are three common situations where this is done: with compound surnames, with surnames that include a separately written prefix, and with persons who have a title of nobility.

Figure 3.31 shows a name containing a compound surname. The variant is formed by rotating the first part of the preferred name, "Wallace-" to the end. The rest of the name remains in the same order:

> Crabbe, Chris Wallace-, 1934-
> > *search under*
> > Wallace-Crabbe, Chris, 1934-

This is done with each part of the surname, if there are more than two. Conjunctions (such as "y" in some Spanish compound surnames) are not normally rotated to the front to create variants (see figure 3.32), but no instruction forbidding this variant is given in RDA. If the cataloger feels such a variant would be useful, it may be made. Consideration should be given to the fact, however, that very few such variants have been recorded in databases such as the LC/NACO Authority File under previous cataloging practice.

Other examples of variants created by rearrangement of compound surname forms are figures 3.33 through 3.36.

Laurens Van der Post (see figure 3.37) has a surname with a separately written prefix. The surname actually has three parts. Following the RDA guidelines for such names one form is chosen as the preferred name, and rearranged forms may be recorded as variant names for the other two possibilities:

> Post, Laurens Van der
> > *search under*
> > Van der Post, Laurens

> Der Post, Laurens Van
> > *search under*
> > Van der Post, Laurens

Other examples include figures 3.38 through 3.47.

Name forms that include a title of nobility formed following RDA 9.2.2.14 include a second name, the person's personal or family name. The preferred name is re-arranged by rotating the personal surname to the front to create a variant, as seen in figure 3.48:

> Wellesley, Arthur, Duke of Wellington, 1769-1852
> > *search under*
> > Wellington, Arthur Wellesley, Duke of, 1769-1852

Figure 3.49 is another example.

Phrase Names. As seen above, if a person is identified by a characterizing word or phrase, and the person's actual identity is known, the preferred name will normally be based on the person's real name, not the characterizing word or phrase. In such cases, the characterizing word or phrase is recorded as a variant name (see figure 3.57):

Lover of Mankind, and of Common Sense, 1703-1791
    search under
    Wesley, John, 1703-1791

Figure 3.5 is an example of an ambiguous name. The name by which this person identifies herself, "bell hooks," might be a phrase name. The cataloger in this case instead decided that the name had the appearance of a forename and surname and so recorded the preferred name as "hooks, bell" (see RDA 9.2.2.22). Because the name is somewhat ambiguous, however, the name in the form of a phrase is recorded as a variant (see final sentence in RDA 9.2.2.22):

bell hooks, 1952-
    search under
    hooks, bell, 1952-

Similar examples include figure 3.26 and figure 3.55 (see RDA 9.2.2.23).

Inverted Forms of Initials. In traditional cataloging practice, a variant form is recorded for names consisting solely of initials by rotating the final initial to the front and treating it as though it were a surname (see figure 3.53). Although this sort of variant is shown in the examples to RDA 9.2.3.10, the cataloger should consider how useful recording this variant would be. It seems unlikely that most catalog users would search for a name using such a form:

E., A. L. O., 1821-1893
    search under
    A. L. O. E., 1821-1893

OTHER IDENTIFYING ATTRIBUTES

RDA 9.2 contains extensive guidelines about choosing and recording preferred and variant names in descriptions of persons. RDA 9.3.9.18 contains guidelines for recording other attributes of persons that may be useful for identifying the person or differentiating the person from another person with the same name. Remember: RDA 9.3.9.18 is concerned only with recording information in elements of the description of the person, *not* with creation of the authorized access point for the person. Some of the information recorded in these elements may be included in the authorized access point, but much will not and nearly all of the elements can be recorded independently of access points in the MARC record.

9.3. DATE ASSOCIATED WITH THE PERSON. The date associated with the person element records a significant date associated with a person, including birth and death dates. Date of birth and death are core, meaning that if the cataloger knows the information, he or she should record the element in the description of the person. This does not necessarily mean the date needs to be a part of the authorized access point for the person, although if it is its presence in that form satisfies the core requirement. However, the basic field intended for recording this element in MARC is the 046 field. Date of birth is recorded in subfield ‡f, date of death in ‡g, and period of activity in subfields ‡s (start period) and ‡t (end period).

According to the MARC documentation for the 046 field, dates are recorded according to the ISO document *Representations of Dates and Times* (ISO 8601) in the pattern yyyy, yyyy-mm, or yyyymmdd.[15] For example, December 1, 1922, would be recorded 19221201; March 2011 would be recorded 2011-03. This pattern is called the "basic format" in ISO 8601. ISO 8601 also has an extended format, in which dates are recorded in the pattern yyyy-mm-dd (e.g., 1922-12-01). The MARC format documentation prefers the basic format when recording dates in ISO format.

The ISO standard is useful for simple dates, but does not provide for uncertain or approximate dates. If ISO is not specific enough for the situation, another standard can be used as long as subfield ‡2 specifies the standard. The Library of Congress is developing a standard called the Extended Date/Time Format (EDTF) for this purpose, which may be used in unusual situations.[16]

Neither of these standards corresponds to the date formats given in the examples to RDA, but catalogers recording the date element in MARC 046 fields should follow one of the two. The forms found in the RDA examples should be used in access points.

The following table shows the RDA forms recorded in either ISO or EDTF format. If a form is available in the ISO 8601 column, it should be used. Please note that because the EDTF format is under development at the time of this writing and is subject to change, catalogers should consult the format itself.

The examples in RDA only show date forms as they would appear in access points, but it is possible to record the information in the element much more specifically. If the cataloger knows the exact birth date of the person is June 2, 1731, the information should be recorded in MARC 046 using the ISO format as 17310602, even though the date in the access point will be the year only (1731) (see figure 3.1). Most of the

RDA FORM (used in MARC X00 subfield ‡d)	ISO 8601 FORM (used in MARC 046)	EDTF FORM (used in MARC 046 if ISO form unavailable)
1974	1974	1974
1816?	—	1816?
65 A.D.	0065	0065
828 or 829	—	[0828,0829]
approximately 931	—	0931~
361 B.C.	-0360 (note there is a difference of one because the B.C. system has no year zero)	-0360
1647 or 1648	—	[1647,1648]
1936 May 5	19360505	1936-05-05
19th century	18	18
13th century-14th century	12/13	12/13
7th century B.C.	-06	-06
1st century B.C.-1st century A.D.	-00/00	-00/00
—	—	Uncertain month: 2004-06?-11 2010-05?
—	—	Uncertain day: 2004-06-11?
—	—	Uncertain year: 2004?-06-11

figures in this chapter include a date associated with the person element recorded in MARC 046. Most are straightforward, but a few show unusual situations.

In figure 3.2, the EDTF format must be used because the date of birth is approximate. MARC 046 can be repeated, but if more than one date is included in a single 046, as here, and the field is tagged as being in EDTF format (‡2 edtf), all the dates must be given in EDTF format, which explains the hyphens in the death date form in ‡g.

Figure 3.15 shows period of activity of the person. This type of date is recorded in ‡s (start period) and ‡t (end period) if there are two dates.

In figure 3.32 the person's death date is not exact, but is known to be one of two years.

Figure 3.39 shows the format when the exact day of birth is uncertain. Note, again, that all dates in the 046 field are given in EDTF format.

Figure 3.54 shows an uncertain year of birth.

Because this element is core, the information should be recorded if known. Routine use of the 046 field to record this information is strongly encouraged because its location and format are more predictable and more easily machine-understandable than forms found in the authorized access point.

9.3.2. DATE OF BIRTH. The examples in RDA for dates may be confusing because they are shown out of context. Date of birth is recorded in subfield ‡f of the 046 field. Recording this information in 046 is straightforward because the 046 field has specific subfields denoting what type of date is being recorded (birth date, death date, start of a period, etc.). However, if the information is being recorded in an access point, a signal must be supplied by the cataloger as to whether the date is a birth, death, or some other type of date, because all dates in access points for persons are recorded in subfield ‡d of X00 fields. RDA does not specify what sort of signal is to be used. The usual signal that a date represents a birth date is the presence of the word "born" before the date or a hyphen after the date:

> Quiamco, Antoine, born 1910

or

> Quiamco, Antoine, 1910-

These conventions are well known and easily understood by database users. For consistency, LC and PCC have issued a policy statement with RDA 9.3.2.3 (July 2012) to use a hyphen after the date of birth, rather than using the term "born" with the date, in access points. This represents a change from AACR2 practice, where if the cataloger knew only the birth date, the name was established with the form "b. 1910" if it was thought the person had died, but with the form "1910-" if it was thought he or she was still alive. This inevitably brought inconsistency into the database because the form was determined by the arbitrary fact of when the name was established. The rule of thumb was that if the person had been born more than approximately 100 years before the date the name was being established, the "b. 1881" form was used; otherwise the form with the hyphen was used. Under the current policy, all birth dates will be recorded in access points with the hyphen. See figures 3.42 and 3.50.

9.3.3. DATE OF DEATH. Date of death is recorded in subfield ‡g of the 046 field. In access points, the usual signal that a date represents a death date is the presence of the word "died" or a hyphen before the date:

> Zöpfel, David, died 1563

or

> Zöpfel, David, -1563

LC and PCC have issued a policy statement with RDA 9.3.3.3 (July 2012) to use a hyphen before the date of death, rather than the term "died" with the date, in access points (see figure 3.58).

Figure 3.58. Death Date

046	‡g 20060526
100 0	‡a Monguito, ‡d -2006
370	‡a Manguito (Cuba)
370	‡b New York (N.Y.) ‡2 naf
372	‡a Salsa (Music) ‡2 lcsh
374	‡a Singers ‡a Composers ‡a Band directors ‡2 lcsh
375	‡a male
377	‡a spa
400 1	‡a Quian, Ramón, ‡d -2006
400 0	‡a El Único, ‡d -2006
400 0	‡a Único, ‡d -2006
670	‡a Salsa, 2010: ‡b container (Monguito)
670	‡a Descarga.com, September 22, 2010 ‡b (Monguito "El Unico"; b. Ramón Quian, Manguito, Matanzas Province, Cuba; d. May 26, 2006, New York City; Afro-Cuban sonero (extemporising salsa singer), composer, bandleader, producer; dubbed "El Unico" (The Unique))

9.3.4. PERIOD OF ACTIVITY OF THE PERSON. This type of date refers to a single date or a range of dates giving the period in which a person was active. These dates are recorded in subfield ‡s (start period) and ‡t (end period) of the 046 field. If there is only one date, it is recorded in subfield ‡s. As with birth and death dates, RDA does not specify the label that should be used with this date in access points. In previous cataloging practice, the label was "fl.," but that abbreviation is not permitted in RDA. Some examples in RDA use the term "flourished." LC-PCC PS 9.3.4.3 (October 2010) instructs catalogers to use the term "active" as the label before the first date (e.g., Xie,

He, active 479-501). Century dates, which were used in previous (AACR2) practice without a label (e.g., Rivas, Manuel Antonio de, 18th cent.) should also be preceded by the term "active" (e.g., Rivas, Manuel Antonio de, active 18th century).

In previous practice, period of activity dates were only used if the dates preceded the twentieth century. RDA does not include this restriction (see figure 3.59). In RDA, the element is labeled core only "when needed to distinguish a person from another person with the same name." They may be used in access points even if there is no need to distinguish (RDA 9.19.1.5), but LC-PCC PS 9.19.1.5 (October 2012) instructs catalogers that a term indicating period of activity should be included in access points only if there is no other way to distinguish two identical forms.

Figure 3.59. Period of Activity

046	‡s 1918
100 1	‡a Keil, Ernst, ‡d active 1918
374	‡a Military captain
374	‡a College teachers ‡2 lcsh
375	‡a male
377	‡a ger
667	‡a Not the same as: Keil, Ernst; Keil, Ernst, 1816-1878; Keil, Ernst-Edmund; Keil, Ernst-Edmund, 1928-
670	‡a Wehrmacht und Erziehung, 1918: ‡b title page (Professor Ernst Keil, Hauptmann)

How does the cataloger determine the period of activity of the person? Reference sources are always a good bet, and if reference sources consistently give the same or similar dates for the period of activity, those dates should be used. If the only evidence is the resource in hand, the publication year may be the date chosen. A search of a database such as OCLC may show other publications by the person which could expand the period of activity. Be careful, though: resources do get published after people die. It is probably wiser to only use dates of publication of first editions or printings of resources.

9.4. TITLE OF THE PERSON. This element includes many kinds of titles but specifically excludes terms of address that simply indicate gender or marital status (e.g., Mr. or Mrs.). This element is defined as a word or phrase indicative of (1) royalty, (2) nobility, (3) ecclesiastical rank or office, (4) a term of address for a person of religious vocation, or (5) another term indicative of rank, honor, or office. Categories 1 to 4 are core; category 5 is core if needed to distinguish between persons with the same name. RDA 9.4.1.7 (high ecclesiastical officials) and 9.4.1.8 (other persons of religious vocation) exclude persons whose names contain surnames from application of this guideline, although such terms may be recorded as an element of the description even if such a person's name does include a surname.

Record the titles covered by RDA 9.4 in subfield ‡d of a 368 field. Additionally, unlike the date associated with the person element, in many cases RDA 9.4 titles—especially those listed as core—must be included in the authorized access point for the person (see RDA 9.19.1.2). When recorded as part of an access point, the title of the person element is recorded in X00 subfield ‡c *after* the full preferred or variant name, but before dates associated with the person.

9.4.1.4. TITLES OF ROYALTY. Because royal persons are almost invariably known by given name, not surname, correlate this guideline with provisions of RDA 9.2.2.20 that cover recording persons whose name does not contain a surname. RDA 9.4.1.4 only guides treatment of the title itself. According to RDA 9.2.2.20 and 9.2.2.5.2, the name will be recorded as it appears in reference sources and will include any roman numerals, recorded in X00 subfield ‡b, appearing with the name in these sources.

We are instructed to record the title and the name of the state or people in the language preferred by the agency (English for LC and PCC catalogers, see LC-PCC PS 9.4.1.4.1–9.4.1.4.3, October 2012). The resulting phrase is recorded in X00 subfield ‡c. Do not include the word "saint" (see RDA 9.19.1.2 exception). AACR2 22.16A2 instructed catalogers not to add epithets associated with the name of a person with the highest royal status within a state. This instruction is not in RDA, so forms of the name found with epithets should be considered.

The preferred name for the Prussian king Frederick the Great illustrates provisions of the guideline. His preferred name is to be chosen according to the form found in reference sources. *Encyclopaedia Britannica* (2002) lists him as king of Prussia, and gives his name as "Frederick II, byname Frederick the Great, German Friedrich der Grosse." In this case the cataloger judged that "Frederick II" was the more common form. The title is recorded in English. Record as variants forms not chosen for the preferred name (see figure 3.60).

Figure 3.60. Royal Person

046	‡f 17120124 ‡g 17860817
100 0	‡a Frederick ‡b II, ‡c King of Prussia, ‡d 1712-1786
368	‡d King of Prussia
374	‡a Heads of state ‡2 lcsh
370	‡a Berlin (Germany) ‡b Potsdam (Germany) ‡c Prussia (Kingdom) ‡2 naf
375	‡a male
377	‡a ger
400 0	‡a Friedrich ‡b II, ‡c King of Prussia, ‡d 1712-1786

400 0	‡a Frederick, ‡c the Great, ‡d 1712-1786
400 0	‡a Friedrich, ‡c der Grosse, ‡d 1712-1786
670	‡a Friedrich II. von Preussen im Geschichtsbild ... 1983
670	‡a Encyclopaedia Britannica, 2002 ‡b (Frederick II, King of Prussia, byname Frederick the Great, German Friedrich der Grosse; born January 24, 1712, Berlin; died August 17, 1786, Potsdam)

9.4.1.4.2. CONSORTS OF ROYAL PERSONS. An appropriate title in the preferred language of the cataloging agency, as well as the phrase "consort of" and the name of the ruler, will be given for consorts of rulers. Prince Philip, Duke of Edinburgh and consort of Queen Elizabeth II of Great Britain, is an example of such a person. The *Encyclopedia Americana* (2001) lists him as "Philip, Duke of Edinburgh and consort of Elizabeth II, Queen of the United Kingdom of Great Britain and Northern Ireland." He is also referred to in the article as "Prince Philip, the duke of Edinburgh." Thus, he has two titles, Prince and Duke of Edinburgh. The cataloger should choose his higher title, Prince, to add to the preferred name (see figure 3.61).

Figure 3.61. Consort of Royal Person

046	‡f 19210610
100 0	‡a Philip, ‡c Prince, consort of Elizabeth II, Queen of Great Britain, ‡d 1921-
368	‡d Prince, consort of Elizabeth II, Queen of Great Britain
368	‡d Duke of Edinburgh
370	‡a Kerkyra (Greece) ‡c Great Britain ‡2 naf
375	‡a male
377	‡a eng
400 1	‡a Edinburgh, Philip, ‡c Duke of, ‡d 1921-
400 0	‡a Philip, ‡c Duke of Edinburgh, ‡d 1921-
400 1	‡a Mountbatten, Philip, ‡d 1921-
670	‡a The evolution of human organisations, 1967: ‡b title page (His Royal Highness the Prince Philip, Duke of Edinburgh, K.G.)
670	‡a Encyclopedia Americana, 2001 ‡b (Philip, Duke of Edinburgh and consort of Elizabeth II, Queen of the United Kingdom of Great Britain and Northern Ireland; also known by the surname Mountbatten; born June 10, 1921, Corfu, Greece)

9.4.1.5. TITLES OF NOBILITY. Names that include titles of nobility have already been discussed above at RDA 9.2.2.14. However, application of 9.2.2.14 is only to persons who use their title *rather than surname* in resources with which they are associated, or are listed under title in reference sources. If applicable, 9.2.2.14 will result in the proper name of the title of nobility being recorded as the first part of the preferred name. But the stipulations of 9.2.2.14 do not apply to all persons who hold a title of nobility. (1) Some people are clearly known by their family name, even though their title of nobility might be listed as well in resources associated with the person; and (2) some peoples' titles are never (or rarely) used in resources associated with them. In either of these cases, RDA 9.4.1.5 must be considered.

In both cases, because the title of the person element is core, the title needs to be recorded in the description of the person, if known. Record it in a MARC 368 field, subfield ‡d. In the first case, the title is also recorded as an addition to the preferred name, in X00 subfield ‡c, between the preferred name and dates (if any).

Mary Anne Disraeli, who received the title Viscountess Beaconsfield after her marriage to the British prime minister Benjamin Disraeli, is an example. She is better known as Mary Anne Disraeli than as the Viscountess Beaconsfield, and is so listed in reference sources. She is not a person who uses her title rather than her surname. However, resources associated with her also closely associate her with her title. Her preferred name is recorded as Disraeli, Mary Anne, but under RDA 9.4.1.5 her title will be recorded as well, including in the authorized access point. A variant name will be recorded beginning with the proper name in the title of nobility (see figure 3.62).

Figure 3.62. Title of Nobility Added to Authorized Access Point

046	‡f 17921111 ‡g 18721215
100 1	‡a Disraeli, Mary Anne, ‡c Viscountess Beaconsfield, ‡d 1792-1872
368	‡d Viscountess Beaconsfield
370	‡a Exeter (England) ‡b Hughenden Valley (England) ‡2 naf
375	‡a female
377	‡a eng
400 1	‡a Beaconsfield, Mary Anne Disraeli, ‡c Viscountess, ‡d 1792-1872
400 1	‡a Evans, Mary Ann, ‡d 1792-1872
670	‡a Mr Disraeli's "rattle", 2004: ‡b page 2 of cover, etc. (Mrs Disraeli; Mary Anne Evans; Viscountess Beaconsfield; m. John Wyndham Lewis, and subsequently Benjamin Disraeli)
670	‡a Oxford dictionary of national biography, via WWW, November 15, 2004 ‡b (Disraeli (née Evans; other married name Lewis), Mary Anne, Viscountess Beaconsfield; born Exeter, November 11, 1792; died Hughenden, December 15, 1872)

Francis Bacon was knighted in 1603, ennobled in 1618 as Baron Verulam, and in 1620 or 1621 given the title Viscount Saint Alban. He was already well known as an author before receiving these titles and his printed works only mention his titles, of course, after he received them toward the end of his life. After his death the vast majority of resources refer to him as "Francis Bacon" or "Sir Francis Bacon," and do not refer to him by either of his titles. RDA 9.4.1.5 instructs us to record the information about his titles of nobility, but the exception listed at the end of RDA 9.19.1.2 (instructions about creation of the authorized access point) tells us to "add a title of nobility only if the title . . . commonly appears with the name in resources associated with the person . . ." The title will not be added to the authorized access point for Francis Bacon. Variant names will be recorded based on the titles (see figure 3.63).

Figure 3.63. Title of Nobility Not Added to Authorized Access Point

046	‡f 15610122 ‡g 16260409
100 1	‡a Bacon, Francis, ‡d 1561-1626
368	‡d Viscount Saint Alban ‡s 1620
368	‡d Baron Verulam ‡s 1618
370	‡a London (England) ‡b London (England) ‡2 naf
374	‡a Lawyers ‡a Statesmen ‡a Philosophers ‡2 lcsh
375	‡a male
377	‡a eng ‡a lat
400 1	‡a Saint Alban, Francis Bacon, ‡c Viscount, ‡d 1561-1626
400 1	‡a St. Albans, Francis Bacon, ‡c Viscount, ‡d 1561-1626
400 1	‡a Verulam, Francis Bacon, ‡c Baron, ‡d 1561-1626
670	‡a The essays of Francis Bacon, 2010
670	‡a Britannica online, academic edition, 15 September 2011 ‡b (Francis Bacon, Viscount Saint Alban, also called (1603-18) Sir Francis Bacon (born January 22, 1561, York House, London, England; died April 9, 1626, London), lord chancellor of England (1618-21); became Baron Verulam in 1618 and created Viscount St. Albans in 1620/21; lawyer, statesman, philosopher, and master of the English tongue)
678 0	‡a Sir Francis Bacon (1561-1626) was an English lawyer, statesman, and philosopher, and was also known as Baron Verulam and Viscout Saint Alban.

Dealing with titles of nobility requires a great deal of judgment on the part of the cataloger. In summary, if a person is commonly known by a title of nobility, the preferred name is based on the title, as with the Duke of Wellington (figure 3.48). If a person does not use the title rather than his or her surname or is more commonly known by family name, but is also known by his or her title of nobility, the preferred name is based on the family name, but the title of nobility is added after the preferred name in the authorized access point, as with Mary Anne Disraeli (figure 3.62). If a person with a title of nobility is commonly known by his or her family name and is not known by his or her title, the title is recorded in the description, but is not included in the authorized access point, as with Francis Bacon (figure 3.63).

9.4.1.6. POPES. The title "Pope" is recorded in descriptions of persons who became pope. Since this element is core, it is a required addition in the authorized access point for the person. John Paul II is an example (see figure 3.52).

9.4.1.7. BISHOPS, ETC. This guideline applies only to high ecclesiastical officials *whose preferred name does not include a surname*. In such cases, record the person's highest title, if possible in the language preferred by the cataloging agency (English for libraries following the Library of Congress's policy). Because this element is core, it must be recorded if known and must be included in the authorized access point for the person.

The Greek Orthodox Archbishop of America was born Demetrios Trakatellis, but when he was enthroned as Archbishop he dropped his surname and became known simply as Demetrios, which is how his preferred name will appear. His title will be recorded and included in the preferred name (see figure 3.64).

Figure 3.64. Ecclesiastical Title Added to Authorized Access Point

046	‡f 19280201
100 1	‡a Demetrios, ‡c Archbishop of America, ‡d 1928-
368	‡d Archbishop of America ‡s 19990918
368	‡d Exarch of the Atlantic and Pacific Oceans
370	‡a Thessalonikē (Greece) ‡2 naf
371	‡z Archdiocese address: ‡a 8-10 East 79th St. ‡b New York ‡c N.Y. ‡e 10021
373	‡a Orthodoxos Ekklēsia tēs Hellados ‡2 naf
373	‡a Greek Orthodox Archdiocese of North and South America ‡2 naf
375	‡a male
377	‡a eng ‡a gre
400 1	‡a Trakatellis, Demetrios, ‡d 1928-
667	‡a Not the same as Trakatellis, Demetrios n 85157936
670	‡a Divine liturgy celebrated by His Eminence Archbishop Demetrios, 1999
670	‡a Greek Orthodox Archdiocese of America, via WWW, 15 September 2011 ‡b (Archbishop Demetrios; Primate of the Greek Orthodox Church in America, Exarch of the Atlantic and Pacific Oceans, Chairman of the Holy Eparchial Synod of Bishops; consecrated as Bishop of Vresthena September 17, 1967; elevated to Metropolitan August 20, 1991; enthroned as Archbishop of America September 18, 1999; born Demetrios Trakatellis in Thessaloniki, Greece on February 1, 1928; Archdiocese headquarters: 8-10 East 79th St., New York, N.Y. 10021)

RDA 9.4.1.7 does not apply to persons whose preferred name includes a surname. Although information about such a person's ecclesiastical office may be recorded in the description, the title will not be included in authorized access points for persons whose preferred name includes a surname. See, for example, figure 3.65. Although Cardinal Newman consistently used his ecclesiastical title in his later writings, and although he is commonly known as Cardinal Newman, the fact that his name includes a surname means that his ecclesiastical title will not be included in the authorized access point. Information about the title may be recorded elsewhere in the record.

Figure 3.65. Ecclesiastical Title Not Added to Authorized Access Point

046	ǂf 18010221 ǂg 18900811
100 1	ǂa Newman, John Henry, ǂd 1801-1890
368	ǂd Cardinal
370	ǂa London (England) ǂb Birmingham (England) ǂ2 naf
373	ǂa Oratory of St. Philip Neri (Birmingham, England) ǂ2 naf
374	ǂa Theologians ǂ2 lcsh
375	ǂa male
377	ǂa eng
670	ǂa Apologia pro vita sua & six sermons, 2008: ǂb title page (John Henry Cardinal Newman)
670	ǂa Oxford dictionary of national biography, via WWW, 15 April 2012 ǂb (Newman, John Henry; theologian and cardinal; born 21 February 1801 in London; died 11 August 1890 at the Birmingham Oratory)

9.4.1.8. OTHER PERSONS OF RELIGIOUS VOCATION. This guideline applies only to persons of religious vocation *whose preferred name does not include a surname*. The person's title is recorded in the language in which it was conferred or the language of the country in which the person resides. Include initials used to denote a Christian religious order that regularly appear with the person's name. If his or her secular name is known, it should be recorded as a variant name (see figure 3.66). The title may be recorded as an element in the description in MARC 368 subfield ǂd, but it should also be included in the authorized access point for the person (see RDA 9.19.1.2). RDA 9.4.18 does *not* apply to a person whose preferred name includes a surname. Do not add a title to the authorized access point for such a name.

Figure 3.66. Religious Title Added to Authorized Access Point

046	ǂf 18661027 ǂg 1939
100 1	ǂa Cuthbert, ǂc Father, O.S.F.C., ǂd 1866-1939
368	ǂd Father, O.S.F.C.

370	‡a Brighton (England) ‡2 naf
374	‡a Friars ‡a Authors ‡2 lcsh
375	‡a male
377	‡a eng
400 1	‡a Hess, Lawrence Anthony, ‡d 1866-1939
670	‡a The Capuchins, 1929: ‡b title page (Father Cuthbert, O.S.F.C.)
670	‡a Catholic authors, 1948: ‡b pages 179-180 (Father Cuthbert, O.S.F.C., born Lawrence Anthony Hess in Brighton, England October 27, 1866; Capuchin friar and prolific writer, particularly on St. Francis of Assisi; died of pneumonia in 1939)

9.5. FULLER FORM OF NAME. The fuller form of name element records:

1. the full form of a part of a name represented only by an initial or abbreviation in the form chosen as the preferred name, *or*
2. a part of the name not included in the form chosen as the preferred name (RDA 9.5.1.1).

Note that the second part is an expansion on what was permitted in previous cataloging codes. In AACR2, fuller forms that included a part of the name not included in the form chosen for the preferred name were permitted only if a cataloger needed to differentiate one name from another. In RDA there is no restriction.

Caution: a fuller form must expand the name recorded, not a similar name. In figure 3.16, "Alfred Wesley" is *not* a fuller form of "Al" because "Al" and "Alfred" are different names—"Al" is not an abbreviation of "Alfred." Similarly, "Christopher Keith" is not a fuller form of "Chris" in figure 3.31. On the other hand, in figure 3.38, "Guy Augustin Marie Jean de la Pérusse" is a fuller form of "Guy."

There are currently no RDA instructions for recording fuller forms of variant names, but they are permitted in variant access points (see RDA 9.19.1.2.1, second paragraph).

Not only are there two different definitions of fuller form in RDA 9.5.1.1, RDA 9.5.1.3 divides recording practice for the element between:

a. the fuller form of the second part of a name that is inverted (i.e., the part that follows the comma, usually forenames), and
b. the fuller form of the part recorded at the beginning of the preferred name (i.e., the part that precedes the comma, usually a surname; but also included is the complete preferred name if the name is not inverted, e.g., a name that does not include a surname).

These fuller forms are recorded separately. Usually either the fuller form of the part of the name after the comma or the fuller form of the part before the comma is recorded. If it is necessary to record the fuller forms of both parts, they are recorded as a single element.

Fuller form of name is listed as a core element when needed to differentiate one person from another with the same name. It may also be recorded as an element of the description even if not needed to differentiate.

The fuller form of name element is recorded in subfield ‡q of the MARC authority format 378 field (see figure 3.67). A fuller form may be recorded in 378 whether it appears as part of the authorized access point or not (see figure 3.38).

Figure 3.67. Fuller Form

046	‡f 19060529 ‡g 19640117
100 1	‡a White, T. H. ‡q (Terence Hanbury), ‡d 1906-1964
370	‡a Bombay (India) ‡2 naf
374	‡a Authors ‡2 lcsh
375	‡a male
377	‡a eng
378	‡q Terence Hanbury
400 1	‡a White, Terence Hanbury, ‡d 1906-1964
400 1	‡a Aston, James, ‡d 1906-1964
670	‡a Mistress Mashan's repose, 1946: ‡b title page (T.H. White)
670	‡a Contemporary authors online, 16 September 2011 ‡b (T(erence) H(anbury) White; known as: White, T. Hanbury; Aston, James; White, T.H.; British writer; born May 29, 1906 in Bombay, India; died at sea on board the S.S. Exeter January 17, 1964)

If included as part an access point, a fuller form is enclosed in parentheses following subfield ‡q. No parentheses are used when recording a fuller form as an element in a 378 field. Fuller forms are always recorded in direct order, never inverted. There are several patterns:

1. Fuller form of forenames:

100 1	‡a Hunter, Milton R. ‡q (Milton Reed)
378	‡q Milton Reed

100 1	‡a Fox, Daniel ‡q (Daniel Bryan)
378	‡q Daniel Bryan

2. Fuller forms of surnames:

    100 1   ‡a Ramírez A., Jorge ‡q (Ramírez Aljure)

    378   ‡q Ramírez Aljure

    100 1   ‡a Sánchez, Alberto ‡q (Sánchez Vizcaíno)

    378   ‡q Sánchez Vizcaíno

3. Fuller forms of both forenames and surnames:

    100 1   ‡a González P., M. A. ‡q (Marco Antonio González Pastor)

    378   ‡q Marco Antonio González Pastor

    100 1   ‡a F. Gomez, H. ‡q (Helena Fernán-Gomez)

    378   ‡q Helena Fernán-Gomez

4. Fuller forms of non-inverted names:

    100 0   ‡a H. D. ‡q (Hilda Doolittle)

    378   ‡q Hilda Doolittle

    100 0   ‡a D. A. F. ‡q (Davide Antonio Fossati)

    378   ‡q Davide Antonio Fossati

5. Fuller forms of names with a separable prefix:

    100 1   ‡a Freitas, J. Garcia de ‡q (José Garcia)

    378   ‡q José Garcia

    100 1   ‡a Aalderen, H. J. van ‡q (Herman Jan)

    378   ‡q Herman Jan

6. Fuller forms of names represented only by a surname and a title:

    100 1   ‡a Achilles, Dr. ‡q (Alexander)

    378   ‡q Alexander

    100 1   ‡a Barwell, Mrs. ‡q (Louisa Mary)

    378   ‡q Louisa Mary

This last type of form might not seem to follow from the definition and guidelines for fuller forms, but it represents traditional cataloging practice; the names "Alexander" and "Louisa Mary" are at least part of fuller forms of "Achilles" and "Barwell," because these persons' full names are "Alexander Achilles" and "Louisa Mary Barwell." On the other hand, a woman's name is *not* a fuller form of her husband's name, so in cases like Mrs. Chester Scott (see figure 3.28), do not record the fuller form element in a 378 field and do not add a fuller form to the access point. "Marguerite Scott" is not a fuller form of "Chester Scott":

Scott, Chester, Mrs., 1904-2001

not

Scott, Chester, Mrs. (Marguerite Scott), 1904-2001

9.6. OTHER DESIGNATION ASSOCIATED WITH THE PERSON. This is a fairly broadly defined element and includes a number of subcategories. Within these subcategories, only designations for Christian saints and spirits are core.

This element is recorded in subfield ‡c of the MARC authority format 368 field. The core sub-elements (Saint and Spirit) are also recorded as a required part of the access point, in X00 subfield ‡c. Because of MARC coding guidelines, other information may either precede or follow the word "Saint," or may precede the word "(Spirit)," in the same subfield. The other, non-core, sub-elements may be recorded in the 368 field, but are only included in an access point when needed to distinguish it from the authorized access point of another person with the same name.

The categories listed in 9.6.1.6–9.6.1.9 are new to RDA in 2013. Because best practices have not yet been established, they are not discussed in this *Handbook*. However, see figure 3.2a, where the real nonhuman entities element (9.6.1.8) was recorded as an element of the description but not as a part of the authorized access point. If the element had been included in the access point it would have appeared as:

100 0 ‡a Keiko ‡c (Orca whale), ‡d approximately 1976-2003

9.6.1.4. SAINTS. The preferred name of a saint will be chosen and recorded according to appropriate guidelines in RDA 9.2. The word "Saint" is recorded in 368 subfield ‡c and is added following the name in subfield ‡c of the authorized or variant access point (see figure 3.68), *unless* the person was a pope, emperor, empress, king, or queen, in which case, see RDA 9.19.1.2. Caution: RDA 9.2.2.9.6, 9.2.2.14, and 9.2.2.18 may be misunderstood in this context. These guidelines read "Do not include the term Saint as part of the name of a canonized person . . . Record the term as a designation associated with the person." This simply means the word "Saint" is not a part of the person's preferred or variant names. The element is still recorded and added to the access point after the preferred name has been recorded there.

Figure 3.68. Saint

```
046      ‡f 19020109 ‡g 19750626
100 1    ‡a Escrivá de Balaguer, Josemaría, ‡c Saint, ‡d 1902-1975
368      ‡c Saint
```

370	‡a Spain ‡b Rome (Italy) ‡2 naf
375	‡a male
400 1	‡a De Balaguer, Josemaría Escrivá, ‡c Saint, ‡d 1902-1975
400 1	‡a Balaguer, Josemaría, Escrivá de, ‡c Saint, ‡d 1902-1975
670	‡a Mons. Josemaría Escrivá de Balaguer y el Opus Dei, 1982
670	‡a Favors of Saint Josemaría Escrivá, 2004: ‡b E-CIP data sheet (canonized by Pope John Paul II on Oct. 6, 2002)
670	‡a Saint Josemaria Escriva, via WWW, 19 September 2011 ‡b (born in Spain 9 January 1902; died Rome 26 June 1975)

A word or phrase may be added following the word "Saint" (still in subfield ‡c) and preceding dates (if any) to distinguish between two saints with identical names. This may be done even if dates are available. Determine uniqueness of saints' names by checking reference sources such as Holweck's *Biographical Dictionary of the Saints.*[17] The phrase "Bishop of Jerusalem" was added to the example shown in figure 3.69 because "Cyril, Saint, Patriarch of Alexandria" and "Cyril, Saint, Apostle of the Slavs" are already found in the authority file.

Figure 3.69. Saint

046	‡f 0313~ ‡g 0386 ‡2 edtf
100 0	‡a Cyril, ‡c Saint, Bishop of Jerusalem, ‡d approximately 313-386
368	‡d Saint ‡d Bishop of Jerusalem
370	‡f Jerusalem ‡2 naf
375	‡a male
377	‡a grc
400 0	‡a Cyrillus, ‡c Saint, Bishop of Jerusalem, ‡d approximately 313-386
670	‡a Cyril of Jerusalem And Nemesius of Emesa, 2006
670	‡a Brill's new Pauly online, 13 August 2011 ‡b (Cyrillus, of Jerusalem, Bishop; born ca. AD 313; died 386)

9.6.1.5. SPIRITS. Purported communications from spirits are related to resources associated with them just as any other entity would be. Preferred name is chosen and recorded following the guidelines of RDA 9.2. If the spirit is supposed to have been a real person, follow RDA guidelines and establish the name of that person (if not already in the authority file). Record "Spirit" in 368 subfield ‡c and add "(Spirit)" in subfield ‡c to the complete authorized access point for the spirit (see figure 3.70). If the name established for the living person includes dates, common cataloging practice is to retain them for the spirit (see figure 3.71).

Figure 3.70. Spirit

100 0	‡a Beloved Bob ‡c (Spirit)
368	‡c Spirit
377	‡a eng
670	‡a The "I AM" discourses, 1987: ‡b title page (Beloved Bob; ascended master youth) page vii (these dictations were given through ... Guy W. Ballard, pen name Godfré Ray King)

Figure 3.71. Spirit

100 0	‡a Diana, ‡c Princess of Wales, ‡d 1961-1997 ‡c (Spirit)
368	‡c Spirit ‡d Princess of Wales
377	‡a eng
670	‡a Channeled letters from Princess Diana, 1997

9.7. GENDER. The person's gender may be recorded as an RDA element. In the MARC record, gender is recorded in the 375 field. RDA 9.7.1.3 instructs us to use the terms "male," "female," or "not known," although other terms such as "transsexual" may also be used. See figures throughout this chapter for examples. Consistent recording of gender in records for persons could prove extremely helpful (in tandem with other RDA elements) to users of the database who are interested in finding resources associated with, for example, women authors from Australia who lived during the 20th century.

9.8-9.11. PLACE. The RDA place elements are recorded in the MARC 370 field. In LC/ NACO practice, place names are recorded in RDA place elements using the authorized access point for the place. The cataloger should check the LC/NACO Authority File for the authorized access point. Record in the 370 field the form found in the 151 field of the place's authority record. Indicate that the form was found in the Authority File by recording "‡2 naf" at the end of the field. If the place has not been established, record a form that would be chosen as the authorized access point if it had been established (for details, see RDA chapter 16 and chapter 6 of this *Handbook*). In that case, do not record a source in subfield ‡2.[18]

Certain place names cannot be established in the LC/NACO Authority File because of LC subject policies, but are found instead in LCSH. These names can be recorded in RDA place elements as well, but the source must be specified as "‡2 lcsh." Common examples of this are non-jurisdictional places or extinct cities. LCSH forms are recorded exactly as found (see figures 3.72 and 3.73). When recording geographic names from both files in the same record, segregate them into separate 370 fields, one for names from the LC/NACO Authority File (or names that are not established) and one for names from LCSH (see figure 3.73).

Figure 3.72. Place Element Recorded from LCSH

100 1	‡a Bell, Derena A.
370	‡a Star Valley (Wyo. and Idaho) ‡2 lcsh
373	‡a Brigham Young University ‡2 naf
375	‡a female
377	‡a eng
670	‡a I know that my Savior loves me, 2010: ‡b t.p. (Derena A. Bell) jacket (Derena A. Bell, born in Star Valley, Wyoming; graduate of Brigham Young University with degree in interior design)

Figure 3.73. Place Element Recorded from LCSH

046	‡f -0383 ‡g -0321
100 0	‡a Aristotle
370	‡f Stagira (Greece)
370	‡b Chalkis (Extinct city) ‡2 lcsh
374	‡a Philosophers ‡2 lcsh
375	‡a male
377	‡a grc
670	‡a Moral psychology and human action in Aristotle, 2011
670	‡a Brill's new Pauly online, 8 March 2011 ‡b (Aristotle, son of Nicomachus, of Stagira, Philosopher and natural scientist, born 384 BC in Stagira; died in Chalcis in 322 BC)

RDA contains no instructions for cases where the place names associated with persons have changed over time as it does for places associated with corporate bodies (see RDA 11.3.3.4). For example, the city Kurt Redel was born in was known as Breslau, Germany at the time of his birth in 1918 (see figure 3.74). In 1945 the city became part of Poland and its name was changed to Wrocław. In the spirit of 11.3.3.4, this *Handbook* recommends recording the place name in use at the time of the event in the person's life, in Redel's case, Breslau.

Figure 3.74. Change in Name of Place Associated with the Person

046	‡f 19181008
100 1	‡a Redel, Kurt, ‡d 1918-
370	‡a Breslau (Germany) ‡2 naf

373	‡a Kammer-Orchester Pro Arte (Munich, Germany) ‡2 naf
374	‡a Conductors (Music) ‡a Flutists ‡2 lcsh
375	‡a male
670	‡a The Salzburg symphonies, 1963: ‡b labels (Kurt Redel, conductor)
670	‡a Three duos brillants, [1994?]: ‡b label (Kurt Redel) container (flute; also conductor who founded Orchestre Pro Arte de Munich)
670	‡a Wikipedia, 28 December 2011 ‡b (Kurt Redel, born 8 October 1918 in Breslau, Silesia, now Wrocław, Poland, is a German flutist and conductor)

Recording information in the RDA place elements is helpful for finding persons associated with resources. Patron queries such as "I'm interested in reading books by politicians from France" can be answered if the data have been recorded in a consistent and predictable way throughout the database.

9.8. PLACE OF BIRTH. The place of birth element is recorded in MARC field 370, subfield ‡a, following the guidelines discussed above under 9.8–9.11. For examples of the place of birth element, see figures 3.1, 3.3, 3.6, and others throughout this chapter.

9.9. PLACE OF DEATH. The place of death element is recorded in MARC field 370, subfield ‡b, following the guidelines discussed above under 9.8–9.11. For examples of the place of death element, see figures 3.1, 3.6, 3.73, and others throughout this chapter.

9.10. COUNTRY ASSOCIATED WITH THE PERSON. This element is useful for persons who are closely associated with a country but were not born or did not die there. Prince Philip, the husband of Queen Elizabeth II, is an example (see figure 3.61). He was born in Greece but is much more closely associated with Great Britain. The country associated with the person element is recorded in MARC field 370, subfield ‡c, following the guidelines discussed above under 9.8–9.11.

9.11. PLACE OF RESIDENCE, ETC. The place of residence, etc., element is recorded in MARC field 370, subfield ‡e, following the guidelines discussed above under 9.8–9.11. See, for example, figure 3.3. If a person is associated with a place but it is not clear that he or she in fact resided there, record this in subfield ‡f instead of ‡e. For example, Saint Cyril (figure 3.69) was Bishop of Jerusalem, but it is not clear whether he actually lived in the city or not. Similarly, Aristotle is associated with the Greek town of Stagira (see figure 3.73).

9.12. ADDRESS OF THE PERSON. Any address associated with a person may be recorded in this element. This includes street address, e-mail address, and URLs associated with the person. This element is recorded in the MARC 371 field: the address is recorded in subfield ‡a, city in subfield ‡b, intermediate jurisdiction (e.g., state or province) in subfield ‡c, country in subfield ‡d, and postal code in subfield ‡e. If recording an e-mail address, use subfield ‡m; use subfield ‡u for URLs associated with the person. An explanatory note may be recorded in subfield ‡z. Unlike the other RDA place elements, the address of the person element is not recorded formally from the established form of a place name. Simply record the information as found (see figure 3.64).

Before recording information in this element, which is not core, caution should be taken for privacy issues. Recording information not found in freely available public sources, particularly about a person's home address, may not be appropriate.

9.13. AFFILIATION. Affiliation is an association between a person and a group. The scope note given in 9.13.1.1 defines "group" broadly, covering associations through employment, membership, cultural identity, etc. RDA 9.13.1.3 instructs the cataloger to record the preferred names of such groups in this element. The name need not be established in the authority file, but if it is there, use the established form. If it has not been established, determine what the preferred name for the group would be and record that form.

The affiliation element is recorded in the MARC authorities format 373 field subfield ‡a. The period during which the person was affiliated with the group can be recorded using subfield ‡s (start period) and subfield ‡t (end period). If recording a form found in the LC/NACO Authority File, do not include subfield coding except subfield ‡a and include "‡2 naf" in the field. Some groups are established as subjects, not names. These can also be recorded in this element. If recording a form found in the LCSH subject authority file, do not include subfield coding except subfield ‡a and include "‡2 lcsh" in the field (see figure 3.26). For other examples of the affiliation element, see figures 3.2, 3.5, 3.6, 3.13, and others in this chapter.

9.14. LANGUAGE OF THE PERSON. The language of the person element refers to the language the person uses when writing or otherwise creating resources (for example, when creating a spoken word recording). It does not refer to every language the person knows. In cases where the person is a translator it might be a good idea to record both the language of the work(s) translated as well as the language of the translation. However, RDA does not prescribe this and there are as yet no agency policy decisions, so this remains a matter for the cataloger's judgment.

The language of the person element is recorded in the MARC authorities format 377 field subfield ‡a (language code) or subfield ‡l (language term). Current practice is to record the MARC language code as found in the *MARC Code List for Languages* (www.loc.gov/marc/languages/langhome.html) rather than a language term. For examples, see figures throughout this chapter.

Consistent recording of the language of the person element will be very useful to database users who want to find a set of persons based on language (e.g., all science fiction authors who write in Russian).

9.15–9.16. FIELD OF ACTIVITY OF THE PERSON; PROFESSION OR OCCUPATION. Field of activity of the person is defined as a "field of endeavour, area of expertise, etc., in which a person is engaged or was engaged." This definition should be carefully compared with the definition of the profession or occupation element in RDA 9.16, "a person's vocation or avocation." The difference between these elements became confusing in the original publication of RDA because the examples given in 9.15.1.3 for fields of activity were in fact not fields of activity (e.g., poetry), but professions or occupations (e.g., poet). These were corrected in April 2012.

Field of activity is a concept describing what the person does or is interested in. It does not have to relate to the person's profession (e.g., what the person is paid to do). Abstract nouns or noun phrases such as "poetry," "music criticism," "classical languages and literature," or "science fiction" are examples of descriptions of a person's field of activity. More concrete nouns such as "trees" can also describe a field of activity.

Words or phrases describing a person's occupation usually represent instances of a class of persons, such as "poet," "music critic," "professor," or "author." They may correspond directly to a field of activity—the field of activity of a "music critic" is "music criticism"—or they may not—the field of activity of a "professor" might be "classical languages and literature." As with field of activity, the profession or occupation element does not necessarily have to relate to a person's job (what the person is paid to do).

These elements are quite useful for identifying persons with the same or similar names (see, e.g., figure 3.13). The evolving best practice prefers recording terms from controlled vocabularies in these elements, if such terms are available. A commonly used vocabulary is *Library of Congress Subject Headings*. If a term from a controlled vocabulary is used its MARC source code should be recorded with it in subfield ‡2 (e.g., ‡2 lcsh, or ‡2 dot for the U.S. Department of Labor's *Dictionary of Occupational Titles*).[19] If no controlled term is found, uncontrolled terms may also be recorded. This *Handbook* records both types of terms. There is no question that these elements will be useful, if consistently applied, for database users who are looking for groups of persons such as "music critics who speak Arabic."

A person, of course, can have more than one field of activity and occupation, and so the elements can be repeated.

The RDA field of activity of the person element (9.15) is recorded in the MARC authorities format 372 field subfield ‡a. If a person's association with a field of activity has an identifiable beginning and end, these dates can be recorded in subfield ‡s (start) and ‡t (end). For examples, see figures 3.13, 3.34, and 3.38.

The RDA profession or occupation element (9.16) is recorded in the MARC authorities format 374 field subfield ‡a. If a person's association with a profession or occupation has an identifiable beginning and end, these dates can be recorded in subfield ‡s (start) and ‡t (end). For examples, see figures 3.2 through 3.4 and others in this chapter.

The profession or occupation element is core under two circumstances: (1) if the name consists of a phrase or appellation not conveying the idea of a person, and (2) if needed to distinguish one person from another with the same name. It can be recorded as an element in a 374 field even if not core, but it is only recorded as part of the authorized access point for the person if it is core. There is a slight change for the access point in RDA from previous cataloging practice. Under AACR2, procedures for the addition of what it called "distinguishing terms" differed depending on whether the name was entered under given name or surname, sometimes recording the term in parentheses, and sometimes not. In RDA no distinction is made: the term is always added in parentheses following the preferred name in subfield ‡c.

Figure 3.75 illustrates both of these core circumstances. The name "3x3is9" does not convey the idea of a person, and so the profession or occupation element becomes core and must be recorded (in MARC field 374). Additionally, because the person's real name is known, it will be recorded as a variant name. However, there is another "Bryan, Chris" in the database. Since there is no other information available to distinguish these persons (e.g., fuller forms or dates), the same term recorded in the 374 field will be used to distinguish the form of the variant name from the preferred name of the other Chris Bryan.

Figure 3.75. Profession or Occupation

100 0	‡a 3x3is9 ‡c (Musician)
374	‡a Musicians ‡2 lcsh
375	‡a male
377	‡a eng
400 0	‡a Three Times Three is Nine ‡c (Musician)
400 1	‡a Bryan, Chris ‡c (Musician)
670	‡a Musicworks 101, 2008: ‡b liner notes (3x3is9) page 48 (3x3is9 = stage name of Chris Bryan)

9.17. BIOGRAPHICAL INFORMATION. A short biographical sketch of the person may be recorded in this element. This element might be well suited to public displays that would give brief information about the person to the user of the database. Best practices have not evolved, but it is recommended that information recorded in this element be limited to pertinent information that might help in identifying the person.

Biographical information is recorded in subfield ‡a of the MARC authorities format 678 field, with the first indicator coded "0." For examples, see figures 3.29 and 3.63.

9.18. IDENTIFIER FOR THE PERSON. An identifier for the person is a character string uniquely associated with the person (or the record representing the person). This is a core element. In the LC/NACO Authority File the identifier is the Library of Congress Control Number, recorded in the 010 field. In most cases the cataloger does not need to record information in this element, as it is automatically generated by the database system. For this reason, the identifier for the person element has not been included in most figures in this book; as examples, the element is included with figures 3.1 and 3.3.

ACCESS POINTS

One of the objectives governing RDA is that the data should enable the user to find all resources associated with a particular person (RDA 0.4.2.1). In our current MARC database environment this is done through the formulation and use of authorized access points representing entities such as persons, corresponding to what previous cataloging practice called "headings." These access points are embedded in bibliographic records for resources associated with the person and serve as links between a particular bibliographic record and all other bibliographic records that contain the identical access point. In many systems, the access point in the bibliographic record is also linked to its corresponding authority record.

The user of the database finds all resources associated with a particular person by learning what the authorized access point is for that person and then querying the database for instances of the authorized access point indexed as a creator or contributor, or as a subject.

For this to succeed, the authorized access point must be consistent (i.e., always used in the same form) and unique to the person (i.e., more than one person should not share the same access point). The data describing a person must be sufficient to differentiate that person from other persons with the same name (RDA 0.4.3.1).

When two persons in the database have identical names, a "conflict" exists that must be resolved in the authorized access point. Given the important principle of representation upon which the preferred name is based (see RDA 0.4.3.4: an entity should be represented as it represents itself or as it is commonly known), it is not unusual that preferred names for different persons would be identical. Authorized access points for persons with identical preferred names are differentiated from each other by the addition of other elements such as fuller forms or dates of birth and death.

9.19. CONSTRUCTING ACCESS POINTS TO REPRESENT PERSONS. Once the elements discussed above in 9.2–9.18 have been recorded it is a relatively simple, even mechanical, matter to construct an access point for the person. In fact, it is hoped that given the mechanical nature of creating the access point from elements that have been separately recorded, it might be possible for future systems to create authorized access points "on the fly" that contain only those elements needed to differentiate between persons in a given database.

9.19.1. AUTHORIZED ACCESS POINT REPRESENTING A PERSON. The authorized access point for a person is constructed using the 100 field in the MARC authority record. This form is recorded in bibliographic records using the 100, 600, or 700 fields. Coding of subfields is the same in authority and bibliographic records. The authorized access point is constructed with three parts: (a) the preferred name, (b) additions required in all cases, and (c) additions required in case of conflict.

Preferred Name. Begin with the preferred name as already recorded following the procedures outlined in RDA 9.2.2 (see discussion above). Preferred name is recorded in subfields ‡a, ‡b, and ‡c of the 100 MARC authority field.

Some examples of preferred name recorded in figures in this chapter include:

figure 3.1	100 1	‡a **Washington, Martha**
figure 3.2	100 0	‡a **Keiko**
figure 3.11	100 1	‡a **Hunter, Milton R.**
figure 3.24	100 1	‡a **Teller**
figure 3.25	100 1	‡a **B., Patricia**
figure 3.27	100 1	‡a **Oliphant,** ‡c **Mrs.**
figure 3.29	100 1	‡a **Brown, Hiram S.,** ‡c **Jr.**
figure 3.48	100 1	‡a **Wellington, Arthur Wellesley,** ‡c **Duke of**
figure 3.51	100 0	‡a **Billy,** ‡c **the Kid**
figure 3.52	100 0	‡a **John Paul** ‡b **II**
figure 3.61	100 0	‡a **Philip**

Additions Required in All Cases. Next, add to the authorized access point, in this order, information already recorded in certain elements (all of which are labeled core):

9.19.1.2a. Title of royalty (see 9.4.1.4) or title of nobility (unless the title does not commonly appear with the person's name) (see 9.4.1.5)

9.19.1.2b. The term "Saint" (unless the access point is for a pope, emperor, empress, king, or queen) (see 9.6.1.4)

9.19.1.2c. Title of religious rank (for persons without surname) (see 9.4.1.6–9.4.1.8)

9.19.1.2d. The term "Spirit" (see 9.6.1.5)

. . .

9.19.1.2h. Profession or occupation (if the name does not convey the idea of a person) (see 9.16)

The elements listed under 9.19.1.2e and 9.19.1.2g are not based on core elements and are only added to the authorized access point in case of conflict with another authorized access point.[20]

Some examples of these required additions recorded in figures in this chapter include:

figure 3.52	100 0	‡a John Paul ‡b II, ‡c **Pope**
figure 3.61	100 0	‡a Philip, ‡c **Prince, consort of Elizabeth II, Queen of Great Britain**
figure 3.62	100 1	‡a Disraeli, Mary Anne, ‡c **Viscountess Beaconsfield**
figure 3.64	100 0	‡a Demetrios, ‡c **Archbishop of America**
figure 3.68	100 1	‡a Escrivá de Balaguer, Josemaría, ‡c **Saint**
figure 3.70	100 0	‡a Beloved Bob ‡c **(Spirit)**
figure 3.75	100 0	‡a 3x3is9 ‡c **(Musician)**

Additions Required in Case of Conflict. Next, if the authorized access point as formed so far is identical to another access point already in the database, add date of birth or death (9.19.1.3); fuller form of name (9.19.1.4); period of activity or profession or occupation (9.19.1.5); a term indicating a person named in a sacred scripture or an apocryphal book (9.19.1.2e); the term "Fictitious character," "Legendary character," etc. (9.19.1.2f); a term indicating another type, species, or breed (9.19.1.2g); a term of rank, honor, or office (9.19.1.6); or another designation (9.19.1.7).

Optionally, fuller forms, dates, or terms of rank, honor, or office can be added even if it is not necessary to distinguish between otherwise identical access points. North American practice has long been to add birth and death dates if they are known (the option existed under AACR2 as well). LC and PCC will continue this practice under RDA (see LC-PCC PS 9.19.1.3, option, May 2013). LC-PCC policy for fuller forms is to include a fuller form in the authorized access point if the fuller form represents an initial or abbreviation in the preferred name and the cataloger considers it important for identification. Unused forenames or surnames should only be included if needed to distinguish one access point from another (see LC-PCC PS 9.19.1.4, option, January 2013). A term of rank, honor, or office may be added if the cataloger considers it important for identification (see LC-PCC PS 9.19.1.6, option, May 2013).

In current MARC practice, access points are constructed as follows:[21]

1. The preferred name (9.19.1.1) comes first. This appears in X00 subfields ‡a, ‡b, and ‡c. The preferred name includes words or numbers indicating relationship (e.g., "Jr.," "III," etc.).
2. Fuller form (9.19.1.4) follows the preferred name. This appears in parentheses in X00 subfield ‡q.

3. Dates (9.19.1.3 *or* 9.19.1.5, not both) appear following a comma in X00 subfield ‡d. In the access point the date must be formatted as instructed in 9.3.1.3 (see discussion above of RDA 9.3). The date element *always* comes last in the access point for a person unless the term "(Spirit)" is being added.

4. The preceding three elements are the most common elements in an access point for a person. The following elements, if present, generally appear between the fuller form and any dates, with the exception of "(Spirit)," which always comes last.

5. Title or other designation (9.19.1.2) appear in X00 subfield ‡c. Punctuation varies depending on the situation.

6. Other term of rank, honor, or office (9.19.1.7) appears following a comma, in X00 subfield ‡c.

7. Profession or occupation (9.19.1.5) is used only if fuller form or birth/death dates are not available to distinguish, or the addition of fuller form or birth/death dates are not enough to distinguish, or the name does not convey the idea of a person (see 9.19.1.2). This appears in parentheses in X00 subfield ‡c.

Other designation (9.19.1.8) appears in parentheses in X00 subfield ‡c.

Some examples of additions required in case of conflict or optionally added according to the cataloger's judgment include:

figure 3.2	100 0	‡a Keiko, ‡d **approximately 1976-2003**
figure 3.11	100 1	‡a Hunter, Milton R. ‡q **(Milton Reed), ‡d 1902-1975**
figure 3.27	100 1	‡a Oliphant, ‡c Mrs. ‡q **(Margaret Oliphant Wilson), ‡d 1828-1897**
figure 3.29	100 1	‡a Brown, Hiram S., ‡c Jr. ‡q **(Hiram Staunton), ‡d 1909-1979**
figure 3.52	100 0	‡a John Paul ‡b II, ‡c Pope, ‡d **1920-2005**
figure 3.58	100 0	‡a Monguito, ‡d **-2006**
figure 3.59	100 1	‡a Keil, Ernst, ‡d **active 1918**

9.19.2. VARIANT ACCESS POINT REPRESENTING A PERSON. Variant access points are constructed in much the same way as authorized access points, except a variant access point is based on a variant name for the person rather than the preferred name. Variant access points for a person are constructed using the 400 field in the MARC authority record.

Variant access point forms are never recorded in bibliographic records, only in authority records. Instead, if a user constructs a search using a variant access point, a display similar to the following directing the user to the authorized access point should be triggered from the authority record:

Hillerman, Anthony Grove
search under
Hillerman, Tony

Alternately, the system could re-execute the user's search automatically.[22]

The instructions for variant access points differ slightly from those for the authorized access point by requiring, in addition to the variant name, additions from 9.19.1.2–9.19.1.7 only "if they are considered to be important for identification." Discussion below assumes such additions are considered to be important for identification but bear in mind: some of these additions are listed as core elements, so designated by the authors of RDA because they supported (among others) the FRBR user task to *identify* the entity (see RDA 0.6.1). By definition core elements are considered important for identification. Other additions are not required unless the variant access point conflicts with an authorized access point in another description.

Variant name. Begin with the variant name as already recorded following the procedures outlined in RDA 9.2.3 (see discussion above). The variant name is recorded in subfields ‡a, ‡b, and ‡c of the 400 MARC authority field.

Examples of variant names recorded in figures in this chapter include:

figure 3.3	400	1	‡a Hillerman, Anthony Grove
figure 3.4b	400	1	‡a Βλαβιανός, Χάρης
figure 3.52	400	0	‡a Johannes Paulus ‡b II

Addition of Elements Designated as Core. Although not required, it is strongly recommended to add elements designated as core to variant access points. These include, in order, elements listed in 9.19.1.2 (see discussion above).

Examples of such additions recorded in figures in this chapter include:

figure 3.52	400	0	‡a Johannes Paulus ‡b II, ‡c **Pope**
figure 3.68	400	1	‡a De Balaguer, Josemaría Escrivá, ‡c **Saint**
figure 3.75	400	0	‡a Three Times Three is Nine ‡c **(Musician)**

Additions Required in Case of Conflict with an Authorized Access Point, or to Be Added if Considered Important for Identification. Next, if the variant access point as formed so far is identical to another authorized access point already in the database, add date of birth or death (9.19.1.3), fuller form of name (9.19.1.4), or period of activity or profession or occupation (9.19.1.5). (Note that under LC/NACO policy, variant access points may be identical to other variant access points in the LC/NACO Authority File.) Optionally, fuller forms and dates can be added even if it is not necessary to distinguish between otherwise identical access points. North American practice has long been to add fuller forms and birth and death dates if they are known, but in RDA practice this is being left up to the cataloger's judgment. Usually, but not always, these additions will be the same elements added to the authorized access point.

Some examples of additions required in case of conflict recorded in figures in this chapter include:

figure 3.4b   400 1   ‡a Βλαβιανός, Χάρης, ‡d **1957-**
figure 3.6   400 1   ‡a Dodgson, C. L. ‡q **(Charles Lutwidge)**, ‡d **1832-1898**
figure 3.75   400 1   ‡a Bryan, Chris ‡c **(Musician)**

APPENDIX F. ADDITIONAL INSTRUCTIONS ON NAMES OF PERSONS. RDA appendix F contains special guidelines for names in certain languages or scripts. Most of the information in appendix F corresponds to treatment given in the IFLA work discussed above, *Names of Persons: National Usages for Entry in Catalogues,* which should be consulted if the cataloger encounters a name in a language not covered in appendix F or elsewhere in RDA. Because they are fairly common in North American databases, the treatment of Roman names will be discussed here.

APPENDIX F.8. ROMAN NAMES. A Roman of classical times whose name "has become well established in a form in the language preferred by the agency creating the data" will be searched in reference sources in that language (English for those following the Library of Congress Policy Statement corresponding to F.8.1 [February 2010]). The preferred name will be based on the form most commonly used in such sources.

Ovid is entered as "Ovidius Naso, Publius" in *Brill's New Pauly,* but is referred to throughout the article as "Ovid." The *Britannica Academic Edition Online,* the *Encyclopedia Americana,* and the *Oxford Classical Dictionary*[3] all list him under "Ovid," with the added information that the Latin form of his name is Publius Ovidius Naso. Each of these sources also gives his dates and other information about him. Preferred name will be "Ovid" (see figure 3.76).

Figure 3.76. Roman Name

046	‡f -00420320 ‡g 0017
100 0	‡a Ovid, ‡d 43 B.C.-17 A.D.
370	‡a Sulmona (Italy) ‡b Constanța (Romania) ‡2 naf
374	‡a Poets ‡2 lcsh
375	‡a male
377	‡a lat
400 1	‡a Ovidius Naso, Publius, ‡d 43 B.C.-17 A.D.
400 1	‡a Naso, Publius Ovidius, ‡d 43 B.C.-17 A.D.
670	‡a Two thousand years of solitude : exile after Ovid, 2012

670	‡a Publii Ovidii Nasonis de tristibus libri V, 2005
670	‡a Brill's new Pauly, 28 January 2012 ‡b (Ovidius Naso, Publius; Ovid; poet born in Sulmo 20 March 43 B.C.; died in exile at Tomi in AD 17)
670	‡a Britannica academic edition, online, 28 January 2012 ‡b (Ovid; full Latin name Pubius Ovidius Naso; born March 20, 43 BCE in Sulmo (now Sulmona, Italy); died 17 CE, Tomis, Moesia (now Constanța, Romania))

Preferred and variant Latin names, as with all languages that decline nouns, should be recorded in the nominative case only, not necessarily in the case in which they appear in the source (see discussion above under 8.12, with figure 3.9). No reference should be made from the genitive form of Ovid's name (Publii Ovidii Nasonis, see the second 670 field in figure 3.76).

RDA 9.2.2.5.2 also deals with Latin forms of names, instructing the cataloger to choose the form most commonly found in reference sources as the preferred name, but in case of doubt to choose the Latin form for persons who were active before A.D. 1400. In most cases this guideline will not conflict with the instructions in appendix F.8 for Roman names, but 9.2.2.5.2 refers chiefly to medieval Latin and Greek authors, not to persons of the classical period. The names of Romans who lived before approximately the fifth century A.D. should be established according to appendix F.8.

NOTES

1. Full information about MARC 21 authority format is available at www.loc.gov/marc/authority/ecadhome.html.

2. Pre-AACR2 authority records are identified by "d" in 008 position 10 for "AACR2 compatible heading," "b" for AACR1, and "a" for earlier rules.

3. RDA 9.0 explicitly mentions fictitious entities as within the scope of "person," and was expanded in November 2012 to explicitly include real nonhuman entities.

4. IFLA Study Group on the Functional Requirements for Bibliographic Records, "User Tasks," ch. 6 in *Functional Requirements for Bibliographic Records Final: Report* (Munich: K. G. Sauer, 1998), 79–92. Also available at www.ifla.org/en/publications/functional-requirements-for-bibliographic-records. FRAD is an extension of FRBR; see IFLA Working Group on Functional Requirements and Numbering of Authority Records, *Functional Requirements for Authority Data: A Conceptual Model.* IFLA Series on Bibliographic Control, vol. 34 (Munich: K. G. Saur, 2009).

5. For the ALA-LC Romanization Tables, see www.loc.gov/catdir/cpso/roman.html.

6. Information about NACO authentication level procedures for preliminary and provisional access points is available in the Library of Congress's *Descriptive Cataloging*

Manual Z1 at 008/33. This document is available at www.loc.gov/catdir/cpso/z1andlcguidelines.html.

7. Source information about certain elements may be recorded directly in the element's MARC field itself, in subfield ‡v, rather than in a 670 field. This technique is available for the 046 and 370–378 fields. This method has not yet found much favor in practice and is not used in this book.

8. Under older authority practice, a form of the preferred name of the creator of the work was always included in the 670 field before the title proper, so the cataloger will encounter early records with 670 fields formed in this way.

9. *Descriptive Cataloging Manual* Z1 at 667. This document is available at www.loc.gov/catdir/cpso/z1andlcguidelines.html.

10. *Dictionary of National Biography* (London: Oxford University Press, 1921–22).

11. *Names of Persons: National Usages for Entry in Catalogues,* 4th revised and enlarged edition (Munich: K. G. Saur, 1996). This work has been digitized and is available at www.ifla.org/files/cataloguing/pubs/names-of-persons_1996.pdf.

12. *Enciclopedia Hispanica* (Barcelona: Editorial Barsa Planeta, 2003).

13. *Encyclopædia Britannica* (Chicago: Encyclopædia Britannica, 2002).

14. The *Dictionary of National Biography* lists all individuals under family name. Therefore, it is not a good source for determining the preferred entry of a British nobleman or -woman. The *Encyclopedia Americana* (Danbury, CT: Grolier, 1994) and *Encyclopædia Britannica* list members of the British nobility under title when they are best known by title, or under family name when they are best known by it. *Who's Who* is another source of information for living British noblemen and -women.

15. Information about ISO 8601 is available at dotat.at/tmp/ISO_8601-2004_E.pdf.

16. The draft document is available at www.loc.gov/standards/datetime/pre-submission.html.

17. Holweck, F. G. *Biographical Dictionary of the Saints* (Detroit: Omnigraphics, 1990).

18. See the Library of Congress's *Descriptive Cataloging Manual* Z1 at 370—Associated Place (November 2013). Previous to Fall 2013 a different practice for recording place names in 370 was followed, so catalogers will encounter records that do not follow the procedure described here.

19. Occupational term source codes are available at www.loc.gov/standards/sourcelist/occupation.html. Lists of more general sources of controlled vocabularies are available at www.loc.gov/standards/sourcelist.

20. This describes cataloging practice as of the July 2013 RDA revision. The core and other issues remain under discussion by the Joint Steering Committee, however, so catalogers should consult the latest documentation.

21. Information about order of elements in access points for persons is available in the Library of Congress's *Descriptive Cataloging Manual* Z1 at 100—Personal Name.

22. Some systems allow the user to choose between sets of alternative authorized access points. For example, a database in Quebec might allow its users to prefer to search French authorized access points rather than English authorized access points. Such systems are beyond the scope of this book.

23. *The Oxford Classical Dictionary,* 3rd rev. ed. (Oxford: Oxford University Press, 2003).

CHAPTER 4

DESCRIBING FAMILIES

Instructions for recording the attributes of the *family* entity
are found in RDA chapters 8 and 10.

ECOGNITION OF *FAMILY* AS AN ENTITY THAT MAY be considered in descriptive cataloging is a new concept with RDA. Families could not, for example, be given as main or added entries in AACR2 cataloging. The archival cataloging community, however, has long acknowledged families as creators of and contributors to resources in their cataloging standard, *DACS,* and its predecessor, *APPM.*[1] RDA guidelines are partially based on the experience of the archival cataloging community, but RDA family names may be used as appropriate in any context, not just in archival cataloging.

Families can be creators of or contributors to a wide variety of resources. They can create records that might find their way into an archival collection, such as the *Ida Boyd Reid Collection on the Boyd Family* (see figure 4.1). They can create serial publications such as the *Felsenstein Family Newsletter* (see figure 4.2). They can collectively write monographs such as *The Herman & Elsa Rentschler Family Cookbook* (see figure 4.3). They can create Internet resources such as the *Hassall Family Website* (see figure 4.4) and the *Osmond Family Blog* (see figure 4.5). They may be related to resources by publishing them, performing them, owning them, and in many other ways.

Figure 4.1a. Family Creator of Records—RDA Coding (OCLC Style)

Rec stat	c	Entered	19800725			Replaced	20110930071248.0	
Type	z	Upd status	a	Enc lvl	n	Source		c
Roman		Ref status	a	Mod rec		Name use		a
Govt agn		Auth status	a	Subj	n	Subj use		b
Series	n	Auth/ref	a	Geo subd	n	Ser use		b
Ser num	n	Name	n	Subdiv tp	n	**Rules**		**z**

010	‡a no2011105126
040	‡a UPB ‡b eng **‡e rda** ‡c UPB ‡d UPB
100 3	‡a Boyd (Family : ‡g Boyd, John David, 1839-1917)
376	‡a Family ‡b Boyd, John David, 1839-1917
500 1	‡w r ‡i Progenitor: ‡a Boyd, John David, ‡d 1839-1917
667	‡a SUBJECT USAGE: This heading is not valid for use as a subject; use a family name heading from LCSH.
670	‡a Ida Boyd Reid collection on the Boyd family, 1839-1996 ‡b (family established by John David Boyd (1839-1917); surname of family members consistently given as Boyd)

Figure 4.1b. Family Creator of Records—RDA Coding (LC Style)

008	110708n| aznnnabbn |a ana c
010	‡a no2011105126
040	‡a UPB ‡b eng **‡e rda** ‡c UPB ‡d UPB
100 3	‡a Boyd (Family : ‡g Boyd, John David, 1839-1917)
376	‡a Family ‡b Boyd, John David, 1839-1917
500 1	‡w r ‡i Progenitor: ‡a Boyd, John David, ‡d 1839-1917
667	‡a SUBJECT USAGE: This heading is not valid for use as a subject; use a family name heading from LCSH.
670	‡a Ida Boyd Reid collection on the Boyd family, 1839-1996 ‡b (family established by John David Boyd (1839-1917); surname of family members consistently given as Boyd)

Figure 4.2. Family Creator of Serial

100 3	‡a Felsenstein (Family : ‡g Felsenstein, Noah Abraham, 1813-1885)
376	‡a Family ‡b Felsenstein, Noah Abraham, 1813-1885
400 3	‡a פלזנשטיין (Family : ‡g Felsenstein, Noah Abraham, 1813-1885)
500 1	‡w r ‡i Progenitor: ‡a Felsenstein, Noah Abraham, ‡d 1813-1885

667	‡a SUBJECT USAGE: This heading is not valid for use as a subject; use a family name heading from LCSH.
667	‡a Non-Latin script reference not evaluated.
670	‡a Felsenstein family newsletter, 2002: ‡b volume 1, issue 2 caption (Felsenstein family) page 7 (Reb Noach Avrohom Felsenstein, progenitor of the Felsenstein family; lived in Fuerth, Germany with his wife Hannah and twelve children. Most of the family escaped Nazi Europe by emigrating to England. Family members now live in North America, Argentina, England, France, Spain, New Zealand, and Israel.)
670	‡a Felsenstein.org.il, 27 September 2011 ‡b (Noah Abraham Felsenstein; בן יצחק נח אברהם; born 10 July 1813 in Bruk, Germany; married Hannah Weissman 29 March 1852; died 29 July 1885 in Fuerth, Germany)
670	‡a MyHeritage.com, 27 September 2011 ‡b (Hebrew script form of family name פלזנשטיין)
678	‡a The Felsenstein Family descends from Noah Abraham Felsenstein and his wife Hannah, who lived in Germany. Most of the family escaped Nazi Europe by emigrating to England. Family members now live in North America, Argentina, England, France, Spain, New Zealand, and Israel.

Figure 4.3. Family Creator of Monograph

100 3	‡a Rentschler (Family : ‡c Saline, Mich.)
370	‡f Saline (Mich.) ‡2 naf
376	‡a Family ‡b Rentschler, Herman, 1895-1973 ‡b Rentschler, Elsa, 1894-1980 ‡b Retschler, Emanuel, 1864-
400 3	‡a Rentschler (Family : ‡g Rentschler, Emauel, 1864-)
400 3	‡a Rentschler (Family : ‡g Rentschler, Herman, 1895-1973)
400 3	‡a Rentschler (Family : ‡g Rentschler, Elsa, 1894-1980)
500 1	‡w r ‡i Progenitor: ‡a Rentschler, Emanuel, ‡d 1864-
500 1	‡w r ‡i Progenitor: ‡a Rentschler, Herman, ‡d 1895-1973
500 1	‡w r ‡i Progenitor: ‡a Rentschler, Elsa, ‡d 1894-1980
667	‡a SUBJECT USAGE: This heading is not valid for use as a subject; use a family name heading from LCSH.
670	‡a The Herman & Elsa Rentschler family cookbook : celebrating the centennial of the Rentschler farmhouse, 2006: ‡b cover (published by Saline Area Historical Society)
670	‡a Saline Area Historical Society, via WWW, 25 April 2012 ‡b (Rentschler family cookbook; inspired by 100th anniversary of the Emanuel Rentschler Farmhouse near Saline, Michigan; recipes contributed by family members)

Figure 4.4. Family Creator of Website

046	ǂs 1798
100 3	ǂa Hassall (Family : ǂd 1798- : ǂc Australia)
370	ǂc Australia ǂ2 naf
376	ǂa Family ǂb Hassall, Rowland, 1768-1820
400 3	ǂa Hassall (Family : ǂg Hassall, Rowland, 1768-1820)
500 1	ǂw r ǂi Progenitor: ǂa Hassall, Rowland, ǂd 1768-1820
667	ǂa SUBJECT USAGE: This heading is not valid for use as a subject; use a family name heading from LCSH.
670	ǂa The Hassall family website, via WWW, 18 February 2012 ǂb (Hassall family, Hassall of Australia; "The Hassall family site provides information on the Hassall family in Australia"; descendants of Rowland Hassall, who emigrated from England to Australia in 1796, first to Tahiti and arriving in Australia in 1798)

Figure 4.5. Family Creator of a Blog

046	ǂs 1944
100 3	ǂa Osmond (Family : ǂd 1944- : ǂg Osmond, Olive, 1925-2004)
376	ǂa Family ǂb Osmond, Olive, 1925-2004 ǂb Osmond, George, 1917-2007
400 3	ǂa Osmond (Family : ǂd 1944- : ǂg Osmond, George, 1917-2007)
500 1	ǂw r ǂi Progenitor: ǂa Osmond, Olive, ǂd 1925-2004
500 1	ǂw r ǂi Progenitor: ǂa Osmond, George, ǂd 1917-2007
510 2	ǂw r ǂi Founded organization: ǂa Osmonds (Musical group)
510 2	ǂw r ǂi Founded organization: ǂa Osmond brothers
667	ǂa SUBJECT USAGE: This heading is not valid for use as a subject; use a family name heading from LCSH.
670	ǂa Osmond family blog, 28 September 2011 ǂb (first organized by Alan Osmond, but contributed to by all members of the Osmond family)
670	ǂa Wikipedia, 28 September 2011 ǂb (The Osmonds, American family musical group; members of the family include descendants of Olive Osmond (1924-2004) and George Osmond (1917-2007); members perform in singing groups including The Osmonds; Donny & Marie; and The Osmonds--The Second Generation)
670	ǂa FamilySearch, 28 September 2011 ǂb (Olive & George Osmond, married 1 December 1944 in Salt Lake City, Utah)
678	ǂa Utah family prominent in the entertainment business, including the singing groups The Osmonds; Donny & Marie; and The Osmonds--The Second Generation.

MARC Coding. The *family* entity is currently described in library catalogs in the MARC 21 authority format.[2] RDA records for families are identified by the value "z" in the 008 field position 10 (labeled "Rules" in the OCLC fixed field display) and the presence of "‡e rda" in the 040 field (see figure 4.1). In contrast, an AACR2 authority record is recognized by the presence of value "c" in 008 position 10 and no special coding in 040.[3] However, because recognition of family as an entity is new with RDA, there are no AACR2 authority records for families. For space reasons, RDA coding is assumed in figures in this chapter and is not explicitly shown except in figure 4.1. Other MARC coding issues will be discussed as they occur later in the chapter.

Subject Practice. Because family names were not used for descriptive cataloging under AACR2, the Library of Congress has for many years established family names as subject headings in *Library of Congress Subject Headings.* These were for general family groups, not specific families, and were formed differently from family name access points in RDA. It is reasonable to assume that in the future RDA family name access points will be available for use in both descriptive and subject access points so that families will not arbitrarily have different access points depending on whether they are related to the resource as a creator or as a subject. As of this writing, however, the Library of Congress has requested that RDA family name forms not be used in subject (MARC 600) fields in bibliographic records. For this reason, current practice in the LC/NACO Authority File is to include a cataloguer's note directing that the authorized access point not be used in subject access points (see figures throughout this chapter):

> 667   ‡a SUBJECT USAGE: This heading is not valid for use as a subject; use a family name heading from LCSH.

Users of this *Handbook* should be aware of possible changes to this policy and follow whatever policy is in place at the time.

8.1. TERMINOLOGY. *Family* is defined in RDA as "two or more persons related by birth, marriage, adoption, civil union, or similar legal status, or who otherwise present themselves as a family" (RDA 8.1.2). Catalogers do not need to make judgments: if a group presents itself as a family, it is a family for purposes of RDA. Note, however, that the term encompasses larger groups such as dynasties, clans, and royal houses.

Contrast should be made with an organization related to a family, which if named is a corporate body (see RDA 8.1.3). For example, the Hoopes Family Organization runs a website and produces a newsletter. This corporate body has a formal name, has officers and directors, and is a distinct entity from the Hoopes Family, which includes all descendants of Joshua Hoopes, who immigrated to the United States from England in 1683 (see figures 4.6 and 4.7). Similarly, a singing group named after a family, such as The Osmonds, is a corporate body; the related Osmond family, which sometimes performs together, is composed of family members both within and outside the singing group (see figures 4.5 and 4.8).

Figure 4.6. Family organization

046	‡s 1970
110 2	‡a Hoopes Family Organization
410 2	‡a Hoopes Family Org.
500 3	‡w r ‡i Founding family: ‡a Hoopes (Family : ‡d 1683- : ‡g Hoopes, Joshua, 1645-1723)
670	‡a Newsletter (Hoopes Family Organization). Newsletter, Mar. 1989: ‡b title page (Hoopes Family Organization, Inc.; Hoopes Family Org., Inc.)
670	‡a The official Hoopes Family Organization newsletter website, 13 March 2011 ‡b (organization related to descendants of Joshua Hoopes, who immigrated to America from England in 1683; Hoopes Family Organization, Inc., formed in 1970)

Figure 4.7. Family Related to Family Organization

046	‡s 1683
100 3	‡a Hoopes (Family : ‡d 1683- : ‡g Hoopes, Joshua, 1645-1723)
370	‡c United States ‡2 naf
376	‡a Family ‡b Hoopes, Joshua, 1645-1723
500 1	‡w r ‡i Progenitor: ‡a Hoopes, Joshua, ‡d 1645-1723
510 2	‡w r ‡i Founded organization: ‡a Hoopes Family Organization
	‡a SUBJECT USAGE: This heading is not valid for use as a subject; use a family name heading from LCSH.
670	‡a The official Hoopes Family Organization newsletter website, 13 March 2011 ‡b (organization related to descendants of Joshua Hoopes, who immigrated to America from England in 1683; Hoopes Family Organization, Inc., formed in 1970)

Figure 4.8. Family Musical Group

046	‡s 1971˜ ‡2 edtf
110 2	‡a Osmonds (Musical group)
370	‡c United States ‡2 naf
377	‡a eng
368	‡a Musical group

372	‡a Popular music
500 3	‡w r ‡i Founding family: ‡a Osmond (Family : ‡d 1944- : ‡g Osmond, Olive, 1925-2004)
510 2	‡w r ‡i Predecessor: ‡a Osmond Brothers
670	‡a The Osmonds, 1975
670	‡a Wikipedia, 28 September 2011 ‡b (The Osmonds, American family musical group; began as The Osmond Brothers in 1958; name changed to the Osmonds around 1971)

8.3. CORE ELEMENTS. As explained in greater detail in chapter 1, RDA identifies certain elements as "core" throughout the code. The core elements were chosen because they were attributes and relationships thought to support FRBR and FRAD user tasks.[4] RDA entity descriptions should contain, at a minimum, all core elements that are applicable and readily ascertainable, as well as any other elements that might be required to differentiate one entity from another (see RDA 0.6.1). Inclusion of other elements is not required, and is at the discretion of the cataloger or cataloging agency (such as an individual library, or cooperative organizations such as the Program for Cooperative Cataloging [PCC]).

Agencies may develop requirements that go beyond RDA core. The Library of Congress (LC) and the PCC, for example, have designated certain elements that are not core in RDA to be core for their own catalogers. Information about LC and PCC decisions are found in the Library of Congress-Program for Cooperative Cataloging Policy Statements (LC-PCC PSs), found under the Resources tab of the RDA Toolkit.

Core elements for all entities and relationships are given in RDA 0.6. They are also given separately in the chapter(s) devoted to each entity or relationship. Core elements for the family entity are found in RDA 0.6.4 and again in RDA 8.3. This information is also listed with each element's instruction. For example, RDA 10.2, name of the family, which is a core element, reads as follows:

> **10.2 Name of the Family**
> **CORE ELEMENT**
> *Preferred name for the family is a core element. Variant names for the family are optional.*
> **10.2.1. Basic Instructions on Recording Names of Families**
> > **9.2.1.1 Scope**
> > . . .

Conversely, 10.7, hereditary title, which is not a core element, reads as follows:

10.7 Hereditary Title
   10.7.1 Basic Instructions on Recording Hereditary Titles
      10.7.1.1 Scope

    . . .

The core elements for the family entity are:

    Preferred name for the family
    Type of family
    Date associated with the family
    Identifier for the family

In addition, the following are core if the family's name is the same as or similar to that of another family:

    Place associated with the family
    Prominent member of the family

Please note that core designation means that the element must be recorded (if applicable and readily ascertainable) in the description for the family. It does *not* mean that it must be included as part of the authorized access point for the family. For example, identifier for the family is a core element. This means that the identifier (in NACO practice, the Library of Congress Control Number) must be recorded in the description. It does not mean that RDA requires the identifier to be part of the access point.

    For the sake of illustration, the figures in this book will usually include many elements beyond the core elements. See figure 4.9a for an example of a description of a family that contains only core elements; figure 4.9b is an example of a description of the same family containing elements beyond core. It is evident that the RDA core for a family description can be fairly minimal. Cataloging agencies will undoubtedly want their catalogers to include more elements, such as, at the least, variant names and sources consulted (fields 400 and 670), and as long as the LC policy is in place, the subject usage note (fields 667 throughout this chapter).

Figure 4.9a. Core Elements

010	‡a no2010196583
046	‡s 1811
100 3	‡a Spanjaard (Family : ‡d 1811-)
376	‡a Family

Figure 4.9b. Elements beyond Core

010	‡a no2010196583
046	‡s 1811
100 3	‡a Spanjaard (Family : ‡d 1811-)
370	‡c Netherlands ‡f Borne (Netherlands) ‡2 naf
	‡a Family ‡b Spanjaard, Salomon Jacob, 1783-1861 ‡b Gelder, Sara David van, 1793-1882
500 1	‡w r ‡i Progenitor: ‡a Spanjaard, Salomon Jacob, ‡d 1783-1861
500 1	‡w r ‡i Progenitor: ‡a Gelder, Sara David van, ‡d 1793-1882
510 2	‡w r ‡i Founded organization: ‡a Berith Salom (Organization)
667	‡a SUBJECT USAGE: This heading is not valid for use as a subject; use a family name heading from LCSH.
670	‡a Berith Salom, via WWW, December 2, 2010 ‡b (website for descendants of Salomon Jacob Spanjaard and Sarah David van Gelder; Berith Salom (literally 'the alliance of Salomon') is a family association founded in 1861 during the celebration of 50 years of their marriage)
670	‡a OCLC, viewed December 3, 2010 ‡b (usage: Salomon Jacob Spanjaard (1783-1861); usage: Sara David van Gelder (1793-1882))

8.4. LANGUAGE AND SCRIPT. One of the basic principles of RDA is that of representation: "The data describing [an entity] should reflect the [entity's] representation of itself" (RDA 0.4.3.4). It is therefore no surprise that RDA 8.4 calls for recording names in the language and script in which they appear. This would mean that the preferred name of a family that uses Chinese would be recorded in Chinese script, a Greek-speaking family's name would be recorded in Greek script, and an English-speaking family's name would be recorded in Latin script. RDA 8.4 includes an alternative, however: "Record a transliterated form of the name either as a substitute for, or in addition to, the form that appears on the source." LC and NACO will continue to record a form transliterated following the ALA-LC Romanization Tables as the preferred name for names appearing in non-Latin scripts.[5] Non-Latin script forms may be included in the record as variant access points. Including non-Latin variant access points is a relatively recent practice, and NACO policies have not been fully developed. Until they are, catalogers may record non-Latin script variant access points in 4XX fields, but should include a 667 field reading "Non-Latin script reference(s) not evaluated" (see figure 4.2).

8.10. STATUS OF IDENTIFICATION. RDA instructs us to record the level of authentication of the data identifying the entity. The possible levels are "fully established," "provisional," and "preliminary." For a full discussion of this element, see chapter 3 under 8.10.

8.11. UNDIFFERENTIATED NAME INDICATOR. The undifferentiated name technique, using the same access point for two or more different entities with the same name, is only available in RDA for descriptions of persons, not families.

8.12. SOURCE CONSULTED. Just as the author of a scholarly paper justifies his or her assertions by citing sources (usually in footnotes), so the creator of an RDA description for a family in an authority record must justify access points by citing where the information came from. In MARC authority work, this is done using the 670 field.[6] The source consulted element is not core in RDA, but at least one instance—that of the resource in hand that generated the need for a new authorized access point—is required in LC/NACO practice. Examples of 670 fields are found in figures throughout this chapter. For a full discussion of LC/NACO practice in the source consulted element, see chapter 3 under 8.12.

8.13. CATALOGUER'S NOTE. The cataloguer's note element contains information about the family represented by the authorized access point that might be helpful to persons using the authority record. The cataloguer's note element is not core in RDA, but it is core for the Library of Congress in certain situations (see *Descriptive Cataloging Manual* Z1 at 667).[7] Usage of the cataloguer's note element in descriptions of families is developing. The most common use of this note in current practice for descriptions of families is the subject usage note described above and shown in 667 fields in figures throughout this chapter. For an example of a different type of cataloguer's note, see the second 667 field in figure 4.2.

STRUCTURE OF CHAPTER 10. RDA chapter 10, "Identifying Families," follows the same structure as most of the other chapters in the parts of RDA that cover recording attributes (RDA sections 1 through 4). It begins with a section on the purpose and scope of the chapter (RDA 10.0) and then proceeds to general guidelines on identifying families, including sources that may be consulted for information about families (RDA 10.1). It then treats, one by one, the various elements and sub-elements of the family entity that are recognized by RDA, giving instructions on where to get information about the element or sub-element, and how to record that information. This section is the heart of chapter 10, and occupies the bulk of it (RDA 10.2–10.9). The chapter ends with a final section on constructing access points for families (RDA 10.10). It is crucial to understand this structure. Catalogers used to AACR2 Part II, which is chiefly about forming access points (headings), may be misled into thinking that the guidelines about recording elements, and particularly wording about core elements, constitute instructions about how to construct the access point for the family. In fact, this central section gives instructions for recording the *information* in the record or description for the family. In the entity-relationship or linked-data database structure RDA anticipates, we will be creating descriptions of families that exist independently from, but are linked to, other entities such as works that they may have a relationship to. In such an environment bibliographic records with formal access points might not exist, but the elements contained in the description of the family will be essential.

10.2. Name of the Family

GENERAL GUIDELINES

10.2.1. BASIC INSTRUCTIONS ON RECORDING NAMES OF FAMILIES. "Name of the family" is defined in RDA as "a word, character, or group of words and/or characters by which a family is known." A family can have more than one name. One of those names will be chosen under RDA as the preferred name; others may be included in the description as variant names.

10.2.2. PREFERRED NAME FOR THE FAMILY. Preferred name is a core element in RDA, meaning any description of a family entity must include this element. It is defined as "the name or form of name chosen as the basis for the authorized access point representing that family."

CHOOSING THE PREFERRED NAME

If a family is known by more than one form of the same name, or by more than one name, RDA 10.2.2.2 gives us guidance for choosing one of these as the preferred name. We are to choose, in priority order:

1. A name found in preferred sources of information in resources associated with the family
2. A name found in other formal statements found in those same resources
3. A name found in any other source

However, this somewhat mechanical exercise is tempered by 10.2.2.3, which states that we are to choose the name "by which the family is commonly known" as the preferred name. This is particularly important with family names, which may not have a form agreed on by all members of the family, and relates to one of the bedrock principles of cataloging theory, that of representation. As stated in RDA 0.4.3.4,

> the name or form of name chosen as the preferred name for a person, family, or corporate body should be: (a) the name or form of name most commonly found in resources associated with that person, family, or corporate body, or (b) a well-accepted name or form of name in the language and script preferred by the agency creating the data.

RDA 10.2.2.3 also suggests that the name might not appear as a formal family name in any source. "The name chosen can be the surname (or equivalent) used by members of the family." It does not need to be presented formally as a family name (for example, "The Johnson Family").

In our current environment it is necessary to choose and record a preferred name because the database will present the preferred name in displays and indexes, and the form chosen should be the one most likely to be the one library users will use when attempting to find resources associated with the family. RDA 10.2.2.2 is a "default"—it is expected that in most cases the name found in preferred sources of information in resources associated with the family is the one most library users will expect to find in the database, but the cataloger must make this decision on the basis of all available evidence. If he or she determines that another form is the "commonly known" form, that is the form that should be chosen as the preferred name.

Preferred sources of information are found in RDA 2.2.2, and are discussed more fully in the chapter on describing manifestations and items. The preferred source of information for a book, for example, is the title page; therefore the title page of a book is considered strong evidence that a name printed on it is the "commonly known" version of the name (see RDA 2.2.2.2). For families, preferred sources in books might be most relevant when the name is related to the resource as a subject. Families as creators and contributors are more commonly associated with non-book materials such as archival collections or websites, although they certainly can create or contribute to printed materials, including monographs (as in figure 4.3, where the name appears on the title page) and serials (as in figure 4.2, where the name was chosen from the caption of a newsletter).

The preferred source for most archival collections is any source of information within the collection itself (see RDA 2.2.2.4). The collection related to the Boyd family (see figure 4.1) has no formal source of information, but the surname of family members is consistently given as "Boyd" throughout the records.

The preferred source of information for an updating website such as a blog, which is an integrating resource, is a source of information "identifying the current iteration of the resource as a whole" that "contains a title" (RDA 2.1.2.4 and 2.2.2.4). The opening pages of "The Hassall family website" and "The Osmond family blog" are examples of such sources (see figures 4.4 and 4.5).

10.2.2.5. DIFFERENT FORMS OF THE SAME NAME. Although family names are somewhat simpler than names of persons because they usually consist only of surnames, these surnames can exhibit different forms just as names of persons can. RDA refers discussion of this problem to 9.2.2.5, the treatment of different forms of the same name of a person. For a full discussion see chapter 3 in this *Handbook* under 9.2.2.5.

An example of a family with different forms of the same name is the Chamborant family, which maintains a genealogy website (see figure 4.10). The title of the website gives the form Chamborant, and this is the most common form of the name given there, but there are also variants. This family name varies in fullness (some of its members bear compound surnames, including Belloc de Chamborant) and spelling (variants include Camborentum and Champhorant). The preferred name is chosen according to the guidance in 9.2.2.5, which is to choose the most commonly found name as the preferred name in the case of differences in fullness, or the form found in the first resource received in the case of spelling. For either category in this case, the form chosen will be the form found in the title of the website, Chamborant. Other forms will be recorded as variant names.

Figure 4.10. Variant Forms of Name

046	‡s 11
100 3	‡a Chamborant (Family : ‡d 11th century- : ‡c France)
370	‡c France ‡2 naf
376	‡a Family
400 3	‡a Belloc de Chamborant (Family : ‡d 11th century- : ‡c France)
400 3	‡a De Chamborant (Family : ‡d 11th century- : ‡c France)
400 3	‡a Camborent (Family : ‡d 11th century- : ‡c France)
400 3	‡a Camborentum (Family : ‡d 11th century- : ‡c France)
400 3	‡a Champhorant (Family : ‡d 11th century- : ‡c France)
667	‡a SUBJECT USAGE: This heading is not valid for use as a subject; use a family name heading from LCSH.
670	‡a Chamborant.fr, 3 December 2012 ‡b (Chamborant; Belloc de Chamborant; family founded in the 11th century residing chiefly in France, mainly in March, Poitou and Limousin; variant names: Camborent, Camborentum, Champhorant)

10.2.2.6. DIFFERENT NAMES FOR THE SAME FAMILY. Sometimes a family is known by more than one name, but has not changed its name. For example, a number of Acadian families of the eighteenth century bore nicknames in addition to their "real" name (see figure 4.11). If a family is known by more than one name, the commonly known form is chosen as the preferred name, and other names are recorded as variant names.

Figure 4.11. Different Names for the Same Family

046	‡s 1671
100 3	‡a Benoit (Family : ‡d 1671- : ‡g Benoist, Martin, 1643-1748)
376	‡a Family ‡b Benoist, Martin, 1643-1748
400 3	‡a Benoist (Family : ‡d 1671- : ‡g Benoist, Martin, 1643-1748)
400 3	‡a Labrière (Family : ‡d 1671- : ‡g Benoist, Martin, 1643-1748)
500 1	‡w r ‡i Progenitor: ‡a Benoist, Martin, ‡d 1643-1748

667	ǂa SUBJECT USAGE: This heading is not valid for use as a subject; use a family name heading from LCSH.
670	ǂa The Benoit family, via WWW, 10 September 2011 ǂb (descendants of Martin Benoist dit Labrière [family nickname] and Marie Chaussegros, who emigrated from France for North America in 1671)

10.2.2.7. CHANGE OF NAME. Sometimes a family changes its name, for a variety of reasons. In the case of the House of Windsor, the family changed its name from Saxe-Coburg and Gotha because of anti-German sentiment in England during World War I (see figure 4.12). Families sometimes change their names after immigration to a new country. For example, the Carpenter family of Carpenter's Station, Kentucky, was originally known as the Zimmerman family, but the name changed at approximately the time of the U.S. Revolutionary War (see figure 4.13).

Figure 4.12. Change of Name

046	ǂs 19170717
100 3	ǂa Windsor (Royal house : ǂd 1917- : ǂc Great Britain)
370	ǂc Great Britain ǂ2 naf
376	ǂa Royal house
500 3	ǂw a ǂa Saxe-Coburg and Gotha (Royal house : ǂd 1901-1917 : ǂc Great Britain)
667	ǂa SUBJECT USAGE: This heading is not valid for use as a subject; use a family name heading from LCSH.
670	ǂa The women of Windsor, 2006: ǂb page 20 (proclamation issued 17 July 1917 by George V "declaring that the Name of Windsor is to be borne by His Royal House and Family and relinquishing the use of all German Titles and Dignities" including the name Saxe-Coburg and Gotha)
670	ǂa Britannica academic edition, 5 September 2011 ǂb (house of Windsor, formerly (1901-17) Saxe-Coburg-Gotha, or Saxe-Coburg and Gotha, the royal house of the United Kingdom, which succeeded the house of Hanover on the death of its last monarch, Queen Victoria, on Jan. 22, 1901)

Figure 4.13. Change of Name

046	ǂs 1780
100 3	ǂa Carpenter (Family : ǂd 1780- : ǂc Carpenter's Station, Ky.)
370	ǂf Carpenter's Station (Ky.)
376	ǂa Family
500 3	ǂw a ǂa Zimmerman (Family : ǂg Zimmerman, George, 1740-1779)
500 1	ǂw r ǂi Progenitor: ǂa Zimmerman, George, ǂd 1740-1779
667	ǂa SUBJECT USAGE: This heading is not valid for use as a subject; use a family name heading from LCSH.

> 670   ‡a The Carpenters of Carpenter's Station, Kentucky, 2001 ‡b (Carpenter family, founder of Carpenter's Station, Kentucky, in 1780; descendants of Swiss immigrant George Zimmerman, who arrived in Philadelphia in 1746; family changed its name to Carpenter some time around the Revolutionary War)

RDA 10.2.2.7 tells us to chose the new name as the preferred name "for resources associated with that name." This means that separate descriptions are created for the families associated with each name, the same as RDA's treatment of change of name of a corporate body (RDA 11.2.2.6). In other words, when a family changes its name, a new entity is created. Contrast the treatment of change of family name to change of name of a person (RDA 9.2.2.7), where one description is made for the person, with the latest form of the name normally chosen as the preferred name and earlier forms recorded as variant names.

Recording the Preferred Name. Preferred names for families are recorded in MARC authority records in subfield ‡a of the 100 field, with the first indicator coded "3," in the form prescribed generally in RDA 10.2.2.4. The preferred name begins with the part of the name that "would normally be listed [first] in authoritative alphabetic lists" in the family's language or country. An exception is made if it is known that the family's preference is different. Both of these instructions can be problematic for families that have spread internationally. Which country or language? Who speaks for the family's preference? The cataloger may need to use judgment and rely on the principle of representation: which form is the most commonly known for the family?

Recording family names is generally easier than recording personal names because most family names consist only of a surname, not a combination of a forename and a surname, and so cataloging practice for family names does not involve inverting forms and deciding which part comes first. In general, a family name is recorded in direct order, as found.

10.2.2.8. SURNAMES. Most family names are based on surnames, and most often only have one element, but compound family names and family names with separately written prefixes also exist. These are treated according to the instructions for personal names in RDA 9.2.2.10–9.2.2.12.

An example of a family with a compound name is the Bowes-Lyon family (see figure 4.14). As with other family names, the preferred name is recorded in direct order. Compound family names are more easily recognized than compound surnames of persons, because with a family name there is rarely a question whether part of the name might be a forename. For a full discussion of compound names, see chapter 3 of this *Handbook* at 9.2.2.10.

Family names with separately written prefixes are treated in the same way as names of persons whose surnames include a separately written prefix. Begin the preferred name of this type with the part most commonly used as the first part in alphabetical

Figure 4.14. Compound Name

100 3	‡a Bowes-Lyon (Family : ‡c Great Britain)	
370	‡c Great Britain ‡2 naf	
376	‡a Family ‡c Earls of Strathmore and Kinghorne	
400 3	‡a Lyon, Bowes- (Family : ‡c Great Britain)	
400 3	‡a Strathmore and Kinghorne, ‡c Earls of (Family : ‡c Great Britain)	
667	‡a SUBJECT USAGE: This heading is not valid for use as a subject; use a family name heading from LCSH.	
670	‡a Bowes, Lyon, and Bowes-Lyon family papers, 16th-20th century	
670	‡a The official website of the British monarchy, 3 April 2012 ‡b (Queen Elizabeth the Queen Mother, born Elizabeth Angela Marguerite Bowes-Lyon; The Bowes-Lyon family is descended from the royal house of Scotland)	
670	‡a [UK] National Register of Archives, via WWW, 3 April 2012 ‡b (Bowes-Lyon family; title Earl of Strathmore and Kinghorne in family since 1677)	
678	‡a British noble family descended from the royal house of Scotland, possessing the title Earl of Strathmore and Kinghorne. Queen Elizabeth II of Great Britain is a member of the Bowes-Lyon family through her mother Elizabeth Angela Marguerite Bowes-Lyon.	

listings in the family's language or country. RDA appendix F provides specific guidance for a number of languages to help catalogers who are unsure of national customs governing entry in the various languages.

Figures 4.15 and 4.16 are contrasting examples for how this works in practice. According to RDA 9.2.2.11 and appendix F.11, the names of English-speaking families record the prefix as the first element (e.g., Van Buren); the names of Dutch-speaking families, however, record the part following the prefix as the first element unless the prefix is "ver" (e.g., Gogh). The prefix is simply dropped from the preferred form of the family name. For a full discussion of names with separately written prefixes, see chapter 3 of this *Handbook* at 9.2.2.11.

Figure 4.15. Name with Separately Written Prefix

100 3	‡a Van Buren (Family : ‡c Los Altos, Calif.)
370	‡f Los Altos (Calif.) ‡2 naf
376	‡a Family
400 3	‡a Buren (Family : ‡c Los Altos, Calif.)
667	‡a SUBJECT USAGE: This heading is not valid for use as a subject; use a family name heading from LCSH.
670	‡a Van Buren family home page, 4 October 2011 ‡b (Welcome to the Van Buren family of Los Altos, California, home page)

Figure 4.16. Name with Separately Written Prefix

100 3	‡a Gogh (Family : ‡g Gogh, Vincent van, 1820-1888)
376	‡a Family ‡b Gogh, Vincent van, 1820-1888
400 3	‡a Van Gogh (Family : ‡g Gogh, Vincent van, 1820-1888)
667	‡a SUBJECT USAGE: This heading is not valid for use as a subject; use a family name heading from LCSH.
670	‡a Van Gogh letters collection, 1872-1890 ‡b (collection of letters between Vincent van Gogh and his family)

10.2.3. VARIANT NAME FOR THE FAMILY. Just as with persons, families are known by different names or different forms of the same name. One of these forms is chosen, as described above, as the preferred name, and in current systems the preferred name is how the name will appear in displays such as database indexes and bibliographic records. But if the family is known by other names, these will be recorded in the description if in the judgment of the cataloger this would be helpful for identification or access (note that RDA 10.2.3, variant name for the family, is not a core element).

Variant names of families are recorded in 400 fields in the MARC authority format, with the first indicator coded "3." How they display depends on how the library's system is set up, but they are intended to display to the public similarly to the following, when a user does a search on a variant (using, e.g., a display generated by the description in figure 4.11):

> Labrière (Family : 1671- : Benoist, Martin, 1643-1748)
> > *search under*
> > Benoit (Family · 1671- : Benoist, Martin, 1643-1748)

Alternately, the database could automatically re-execute the search so that the user who searched for the Labrière family would be presented with resources linked to the preferred name Benoit. This would be particularly useful when the user is performing keyword rather than browse searches against the database.

For a fuller discussion of recording variant names, including comments on cataloger judgment in deciding whether to record a variant or not, see chapter 3 of this *Handbook* under 9.2.3.

10.2.3.3. GENERAL GUIDELINES. In most cases, variant names should be recorded following the same guidelines as if they had been chosen as the preferred name. This applies to guidelines on such matters as capitalization, diacritical marks, etc., given in RDA 8.5. In addition to recording different names as variants (see figure 4.11) there are a number of specific instructions given in 10.2.3.4–10.2.3.6.

10.2.3.4. ALTERNATIVE LINGUISTIC FORM OF NAME. Alternative linguistic forms may be recorded as variant names. These include different language forms (see figure 4.10, which records a Latin form of this French family's name), different scripts (see figure 4.2, which records a Hebrew script version of the family's name), and different spellings (see figures 4.10 and 4.11):

> Camborentum (Family : 11th century- : France)
>> *search under*
>> Chamborant (Family : 11th century- : France)

> פלזנשטיין (Family : Felsenstein, Noah Abraham, 1813-1885)
>> *search under*
>> Felsenstein (Family : Felsenstein, Noah Abraham, 1813-1885)

10.2.3.5. HEREDITARY TITLE. If a family has a hereditary title it may be recorded as an element of the description (see below under 10.7). The title may also be recorded as a variant name by recording the proper name in the title first, followed by a comma, and then the term of rank in the plural. For an example, see figure 4.14, the Bowes-Lyon family, which possesses the hereditary title "Earl of Strathmore and Kinghorne." The variant name is "Strathmore and Kinghorne, Earls of":

> Strathmore and Kinghorne, Earls of (Family : Great Britain)
>> *search under*
>> Bowes-Lyon (Family : Great Britain)

10.2.3.6. OTHER VARIANT NAME. Other types of variants may also be recorded if the cataloger judges them necessary. This includes variants beginning with parts of the name not chosen to begin the preferred name. Shown in the RDA examples to this guideline are variants based on names that have separable prefixes. Figures 4.15 and 4.16 include this sort of variant:

> Buren (Family : Los Altos, Calif.)
>> *search under*
>> Van Buren (Family : Los Altos, Calif.)

> Van Gogh (Family : Gogh, Vincent van, 1820-1888)
>> *search under*
>> Gogh (Family : Gogh, Vincent van, 1820-1888)

A type of variant name not explicitly included in 10.2.3.6 that a cataloger may want to record is a variant based on manipulation of a compound family name, as seen in figure 4.14. This parallels treatment of variant names of persons (see chapter 3 of this *Handbook* at 9.2.3.10):

> Lyon, Bowes- (Family : Great Britain)
> *search under*
> Bowes-Lyon (Family : Great Britain)

OTHER IDENTIFYING ATTRIBUTES

RDA 10.2 contains guidelines about choosing and recording preferred and variant names in descriptions of families. RDA 10.3–10.9 contain guidelines for recording other attributes of families that may be useful for identifying the family or differentiating the family from another family with the same name. Remember that RDA 10.3–10.9 are concerned only with recording information in elements of the description of the family, *not* with creation of the authorized access point for the family. Some of the information recorded in these elements may be included in the authorized access point, but much will not and nearly all of the elements can be recorded independently of access points in the MARC record.

10.3. TYPE OF FAMILY. This element is a categorization describing the family. Words such as "Family," "Clan," "Royal house," or "Dynasty" may be used. The list given in RDA 10.3 is not closed and other terms may be used, particularly if none of the four apply. If one of the terms given in RDA does apply to the family, however, it should be used.

The type of family element is core and is recorded in subfield ‡a of the 376 field. The term is also included in all access points associated with the description. It is recorded there in parentheses immediately after the preferred or variant name. Examples will be found in all figures in this chapter. The most common term used in this element will be "Family," but other terms can be used when appropriate. Figure 4.12 shows a description of a royal house. For a description of a clan, see figure 4.17.

Figure 4.17. Clan

046	‡s 07
100 3	‡a Doyle (Clan : ‡d 8th century- : ‡c Ireland)
370	‡c Ireland ‡2 naf
376	‡a Clan
400 3	‡a O DubhGhaill (Clan : ‡d 8th century- : ‡c Ireland)
400 3	‡a DubhGhaill (Clan : ‡d 8th century- : ‡c Ireland)
400 3	‡a Doyel (Clan : ‡d 8th century- : ‡c Ireland)
400 3	‡a O'Doyle (Clan : ‡d 8th century- : ‡c Ireland)

| 667 | ‡a SUBJECT USAGE: This heading is not valid for use as a subject; use a family name heading from LCSH. |
| 670 | ‡a The Doyle Clan home page, 15 August 2011: ‡b ("The Clann O DubhGhaill/ Clan Doyle exists to promote and strengthen a mutual interest and fellowship throughout the world between all persons bearing the family name of Doyle, Doyel, O'Doyle, or their relatives"; includes descendants of the Irish Clann O DubhGhaill, which originated during the 8th century Viking invasions of Ireland; the O DubhGhaill/Doyle Clan Gathering is convened regularly at Wexford Town, County Wexford in Ireland) |

10.4. DATE ASSOCIATED WITH THE FAMILY. This element records a significant date or dates associated with the family. Because families exist over time, it is most likely that this element will include a range of dates, either open (for families that continue to exist) or closed (for families that are extinct or groupings that represent only a set period). The element is listed in RDA as core, but is very frequently unknown or impossible to determine. Because the element is core, however, the cataloger should make at least some effort to attempt to determine dates for the family. In figure 4.5, for example, it only took a few seconds to check FamilySearch.org to find the marriage date of the ancestor couple. In addition to this site there are numerous other online genealogical resources that may give easy access to significant dates for families.

RDA does not define what it means by "a significant date," nor does it say what the dates given in the example under 10.4.1.3 represent. The question to answer is, "when did this entity begin and end?" There are many types of dates that might be recorded. For a family group based on an ancestor or ancestral couple, the beginning date might be the marriage date of the couple, or the birth date of their first child, or the date of emigration of the ancestor to a new country. For example, in figure 4.9, the Spanjaard family website defines the family as descendants of a couple that married in 1811. This is given as the starting date for the family. Because the family is still in existence, no ending date is recorded. The date of the Benoit family (see figure 4.11) is based on the date of the ancestor's emigration from France to North America in 1671. The date in the family described in figure 4.13 is based on the founding of a town named after the family.

Dates for royal houses or dynasties are normally easier to determine than those of more ordinary families because information about these families is readily accessible in reference sources. The starting date of the House of Windsor can be determined to the exact day (perhaps even the hour!)—the date of the proclamation of George V changing the name of the family (see figure 4.12).

In early RDA records for families in the LC/NACO Authority File, dates associated with the family have in some cases have been determined by the date of the earliest and latest materials in a collection. This strains the notion of "significant" and seems too limiting to define a family by the dates of materials in a collection of documents created by the family. What if the family later adds other materials to the collection? What if parts of the family's records are in a different repository (as is the case with the Bowes-Lyon family)? Although best practices have not evolved yet, it seems better to try to find other significant dates to identify the family, if possible.

The date in this element is recorded as a year, or even a specific day if that information is available. Dates can be vaguer than this, however. The cataloger discovered that the Chamborant family dates to eleventh-century France, but could not find anything more specific (see figure 4.10). The date recorded for the Doyle clan is based on more or less legendary stories about the first ancestors arriving in Ireland in the eighth century (see figure 4.17).

If no date(s) can be determined for the family, none need be recorded. If this element is present in the description, the information is recorded in the 046 MARC field. Subfield ‡s contains the beginning date; subfield ‡t contains an end date (if any). If the element has been recorded, it should also be included in access points for the family. This part of the access point is recorded in X00 fields immediately following the type of family element, separated from it by space-colon-space and preceded by subfield ‡d. In the access point only the year (or century) is recorded, even if a date recorded in the element (046 field) is more specific. For examples, see figures 4.10 and 4.17, discussed in the previous paragraph. For fuller information about recording dates in RDA descriptions, see chapter 3 of this *Handbook* at 9.3.

10.5. PLACE ASSOCIATED WITH THE FAMILY. This element records either a place where the family lives or a place that is associated with the family in some other way (for example, an ancestral homeland). The element is core if needed to distinguish the family from another family with the same name, but as with any element may be recorded even if not needed to distinguish the name if the cataloger feels this would help identify or contextualize the family.

RDA place elements for families are recorded in the MARC 370 field, in subfield ‡c (associated country), subfield ‡e (place of residence), or subfield ‡f (other associated place). These subfields are repeatable (or, alternately, the entire 370 field is repeatable), allowing multiple places to be recorded if necessary.

In LC/NACO practice, place names are recorded in RDA place elements in the same form that would be used as the authorized access point for the place.[8] For a fuller discussion, see chapter 3 of this *Handbook* at 9.8–9.11.

In figure 4.3 the family group is descended from a couple who lived on a farm near Saline, Michigan, in the nineteenth century. The element is recorded in 370 subfield ‡f because, although this was the place of residence of the couple, it is no longer the place of residence of the family, which has spread throughout the United States. On the other hand, the Hassall family (figure 4.4) is defined as family members who live in Australia (an associated country), so in this case the information is recorded in subfield ‡c. Sometimes the distinction between subfield ‡e (place of residence) and subfield ‡f (other place) can be a little ambiguous and perhaps the subfield decision is not crucial. The Hoopes family (figure 4.7) defines itself as descendants of a seventeenth-century immigrant to America, but by now family members might live elsewhere. Similarly, it is not clear with the Van Buren family what "of Los Altos, California" might mean—do they all live in Los Altos (see figure 4.15)? Very likely subfield ‡f will be used with most families established more than a generation before, because family members probably live in various places. More important than which subfield is chosen is that the information be recorded.

Place may also be added to access points for the family if needed to differentiate the family name from another, or if the cataloger believes it would help identify or contextualize the family. In addition to figures already mentioned in this section, see figures 4.10, 4.12, 4.13, 4.14, and 4.17 for examples. Note, however, that the place associated with the family element may be recorded in 370 without including it in the access point (see figure 4.7).

10.6. PROMINENT MEMBER OF THE FAMILY. This element records a well-known individual who is a member of a family. "Well-known" is not defined in RDA. It can certainly include persons who are well-known in the normal sense of the phrase (see, e.g., figure 4.16, the Gogh family, which records Vincent van Gogh in this element) but more commonly it is a person or persons around whom the family is centered. Probably most family groupings derive from an ancestor or ancestor couple. Such persons would be prominent members of the family for purposes of this element. In figure 4.2, for example, the Felsenstein family is defined as descendants of Noah Abraham Felsenstein. Other examples include the Rentschler family (figure 4.3), the Hassall family (figure 4.4), and the Hoopes family (figure 4.7).

The prominent member of the family element is recorded in subfield ‡b of the 376 field in the MARC authority format with no other subfield coding. Subfield ‡b is repeatable (or, alternately, the entire 376 field is repeatable), allowing multiple names to be recorded if necessary.

The name should be recorded as instructed in 9.19.1 (the instructions for constructing the authorized access point for a person). In LC/NACO practice, this means the person's name should be established in the LC/NACO Authority File and the form found in the 100 field of the authority record for the person should be recorded (without internal subfield coding) in the 376 field of the record for the family. See the figures already cited in this section as well as others in this chapter.

Descriptions of families may record more than one prominent member. For example, the Osmond family (figure 4.5), defines itself as descendants of Olive and George Osmond, who are both recorded in the 376 field of this record. This particular family has quite a few well-known members, including Donny and Marie Osmond, who might also have been recorded in this element.

The name of a prominent member of the family may also be added to access points for the family if needed to differentiate the family name from another, or if the cataloger believes it would help identify or contextualize the family. See the figures already mentioned in this section. In contrast to the element itself, however, in which multiple names may be recorded, only one name may be added to an access point. If it would be useful in the cataloger's judgment to give other names in access points, they may be given as part of variant access points. In the case of figure 4.5, for example, the Osmond family consists of the children, grandchildren, and great-grandchildren of Olive and George Osmond. In the cataloger's judgment the family is slightly better known as descendants of Olive Osmond, so her name is added to the authorized access point, but a form with George's name added is recorded as a variant access point.

It is possible to record a prominent member of the family element in the description of a family and not include the person's name in the access point. See, for example, figure 4.4. In this case the cataloger felt the family was better identified by the fact that they lived in Australia than by the name of the ancestor who immigrated to that country.

RDA does not restrict the number of additions to the access points, but it may be better practice to add either a place associated with the family or a prominent member of the family, rather than both, particularly if the core "date associated with the family" has already been added (see figures 4.5, 4.10 through 4.13, and 4.17).

It is worth noting briefly here that descriptions of persons who are prominent family members can also be linked to descriptions of families by recording the authorized access point for the person(s) in 500 fields in the family record. This is particularly appropriate for ancestors, where the link may include the relationship term "progenitor." See figures 4.1 through 4.3, and others throughout this chapter.

10.7. HEREDITARY TITLE. If the family possesses a hereditary title (e.g., a title of nobility) that is inherited by family members, it may be recorded as an element in the record. For example, the title Earl of Strathmore and Kinghorne is always held by a member of the Bowes-Lyon family. The title is recorded in subfield ‡c of the 376 MARC authority field, in direct order in the plural form. See figure 4.14.

10.8. FAMILY HISTORY. This element, which includes information pertaining to the history of the family, may be recorded in the 678 MARC authority field. The family history element might be well suited to public displays to give brief information about the family to the user of the database. Best practices have not evolved, but it is recommended that information recorded in this element be limited to pertinent information that might help in identifying the family. For examples, see figures 4.5 and 4.14.

10.9. IDENTIFIER FOR THE FAMILY. An identifier for the family is a character string uniquely associated with the family (or the record representing the family). This is a core (i.e., required) element. In the LC/NACO Authority File the identifier is the Library of Congress Control Number, recorded in the 010 field. In most cases the cataloger does not need to record information in this element, as it is automatically generated by the database system. For this reason, the identifier for the family element has not been included in most figures in this book; as examples, the element is included with figures 4.1 and 4.9.

ACCESS POINTS

One of the objectives governing RDA is that the data should enable the user to find all resources associated with a particular family (RDA 0.4.2.1). In our current MARC database environment, this is done through the formulation and use of authorized access points representing entities such as families, corresponding to what previous cataloging practice called "headings." These access points are embedded in bibliographic records for resources associated with the family, and serve as links between a particular bibliographic record and all other bibliographic records that contain the identical access point. In many systems the access point in the bibliographic record is also linked to its corresponding authority record.

The user of the database finds all resources associated with a particular family by learning what the authorized access point is for that family and then querying the database for instances of the authorized access point indexed as a creator or contributor, or as a subject.

In order for this to work, the authorized access point must be consistent (i.e., always used in the same form) and unique to the family (i.e., more than one family should not share the same access point). The data describing a family must be sufficient to differentiate that family from other families with the same name (RDA 0.4.3.1).

When two families in the database have identical names, a "conflict" exists that must be resolved in the authorized access point. Given the important principle of representation upon which the preferred name is based (see RDA 0.4.3.4: an entity should be represented as it represents itself or as it is commonly known), it is not at all unusual that preferred names for different families would be identical. Authorized access points for families with identical preferred names are differentiated from each other by the addition of other elements such as dates, places, or the name of a prominent family member.

10.10. CONSTRUCTING ACCESS POINTS TO REPRESENT FAMILIES. Once the elements discussed above in 10.2–10.9 have been recorded it is a relatively simple, even mechanical, matter to construct an access point for the family. In fact, it is hoped that given the mechanical nature of creating the access point from elements that have been separately recorded, it might be possible for future systems to create authorized access points "on the fly" containing only those elements needed to differentiate between families in a given database.

10.10.1. AUTHORIZED ACCESS POINT REPRESENTING A FAMILY. The authorized access point for a family is constructed using the 100 field in the MARC authority record, with the first indicator coded "3." This form is recorded in bibliographic records using the 100, 600, or 700 fields (also with first indicator coded "3"). Coding of subfields is the same in authority and bibliographic records. The authorized access point is constructed with three parts: (a) the preferred name, (b) additions required in all cases, and (c) additions required in case of conflict.

Preferred name. Begin with the preferred name as already recorded following the procedures outlined in RDA 10.2.2 (see discussion above). Preferred name is recorded in subfield ‡a of the 100 MARC authority field.

Some examples of preferred name recorded in figures in this chapter include:

figure 4.1   100 3   ‡a **Boyd**
figure 4.2   100 3   ‡a **Felsenstein**
figure 4.12   100 3   ‡a **Windsor**
figure 4.15   100 3   ‡a **Van Buren**
figure 4.17   100 3   ‡a **Doyle**

Additions Required in All Cases. Next, add to the authorized access point, in this order, information already recorded in certain elements (which are labeled core):

a. Type of family (10.3). This follows the name and an opening parenthesis.
b. Date associated with the family (10.4). This follows the type of family, space-colon-space, and subfield ‡d. A date recorded in the access point should be no more specific than the year, even if more detailed dating has been recorded in the 046 field. Remember that this element is core, but may be omitted if the information is unknown.

Some examples of these required additions recorded in figures in this chapter include:

figure 4.1   100 3   ‡a Boyd (**Family** . . .
figure 4.5   100 3   ‡a Osmond (**Family** : ‡d **1944-** . . .
figure 4.12   100 3   ‡a Windsor (**Royal house** : ‡d **1917-** . . .
figure 4.15   100 3   ‡a Van Buren (**Family** . . .
figure 4.17   100 3   ‡a Doyle (**Clan** : ‡d **8th century-** . . .

Additions Required in Case of Conflict. Next, if the authorized access point as formed so far is identical to another access point already in the database, add either or both of the following elements:

  a. Place associated with the family (10.5). This follows the preceding element by space-colon-space and subfield ‡c. Follow the instructions in RDA 16.2.2.4, using the second form type, for example, "Budapest, Hungary," not "Budapest (Hungary)." If the place name appears in the list of abbreviated place names in RDA appendix B.11, it should be abbreviated in this part of the authorized access point as well.

  b. Prominent member of the family (10.6). This follows the preceding element by space-colon-space and subfield ‡g.

These elements may optionally be added if the addition assists in the identification of the family, even if not needed to distinguish the name from another. This *Handbook* has taken the position that the addition does in most cases assist in identification, and so one of the elements has been added except in figure 4.9. RDA does not forbid adding all possible elements, but this *Handbook* recommends that the cataloger choose either a place associated with the family or a prominent member of the family, whichever is judged to identify the family the best, and not add both.

Finally, close the authorized access point by adding a closing parenthesis.

Some examples of additions required in case of conflict or optionally added according to the cataloger's judgment include:

figure 4.1	100 3	‡a Boyd (Family : ‡g **Boyd, John David, 1839-1917)**
figure 4.2	100 3	‡a Felsenstein (Family : ‡g **Felsenstein, Noah Abraham, 1813-1885)**
figure 4.5	100 3	‡a Osmond (Family : ‡d 1944- : ‡g **Osmond, Olive, 1925-2004)**
figure 4.12	100 3	‡a Windsor (Royal house : ‡d 1917- : ‡c **Great Britain)**
figure 4.15	100 3	‡a Van Buren (Family : ‡c **Los Altos, Calif.)**
figure 4.17	100 3	‡a Doyle (Clan : ‡d 8th century- : ‡c **Ireland)**

10.10.2. VARIANT ACCESS POINT REPRESENTING A FAMILY. Variant access points are constructed in much the same way as authorized access points, except a variant access point is based on a variant name for the family rather than the preferred name, or has different qualifying elements. Variant access points for a family are constructed using the 400 field in the MARC authority record, with the first indicator coded "3."

Variant access point forms are never recorded in bibliographic records, only in authority records. Instead, if a user constructs a search using a variant access point, a display similar to the following directing the user to the authorized access point should be triggered from the authority record:

> O'Doyle (Clan : 8th century- : Ireland)
> *search under*
> Doyle (Clan : 8th century- : Ireland)

Alternately, the system could re-execute the user's search automatically.[9]

The instructions for variant access points differ slightly from those for the authorized access point by requiring, in addition to the variant name, only the addition of type of family (dates associated with the family are required for the authorized access point, but not for variant access points). Dates, place, or name of a prominent member of the family are added "if considered important for identification." Discussion below assumes that such additions are considered to be important for identification, but this is entirely a matter for the cataloger's judgment. As discussed in chapter 3 of this book at 9.2.3, variant access points in descriptions of different persons do not need to be distinguished from each other in current LC/NACO policy, so conflict with another variant access point need not be an important factor in this decision. On the other hand, a variant access point in one description should not conflict with an *authorized* access point in another.

Variant name. Begin with the variant name as already recorded following the procedures outlined in RDA 9.2.3 (see discussion above). The variant name is recorded in subfield ‡a of the 400 MARC authority field, with first indicator coded "3."

Some examples of variant name recorded in figures in this chapter include:

figure 4.2	400 3	‡a פלונשטיין
figure 4.10	400 3	‡a **Belloc de Chamborant**
figure 4.11	400 3	‡a **Benoist**
figure 4.14	400 3	‡a **Lyon, Bowes-**
figure 4.16	400 3	‡a **Van Gogh**

Type of Family. Next, add the type of family following an opening parenthesis. Some examples of this required addition include:

figure 4.2	400 3	‡a פלונשטיין **(Family** . . .
figure 4.16	400 3	‡a Van Gogh **(Family** . . .
figure 4.17	400 3	‡a DubhGhaill **(Clan** . . .

Additions Required in Case of Conflict with an Authorized Access Point, or to Be Added if Considered Important for Identification. The date associated with the family element, the place associated with the family element, or the prominent member of the family element may be added to variant access points if considered important for identification or in order to avoid conflict with an authorized access point. Close the access point by adding a closing parenthesis. Examples include:

figure 4.2   400 3   ‡a פלזנשטיין (Family : ‡g **Felsenstein, Noah Abraham, 1813-1885)**

figure 4.10   400 3   ‡a Belloc de Chamborant (Family : ‡d **11th century-** : ‡c **France)**

figure 4.11   400 3   ‡a Benoist (Family : ‡d **1671-** : ‡g **Benoist, Martin, 1643-1748)**

figure 4.14   400 3   ‡a Lyon, Bowes- (Family : ‡c **Great Britain)**

figure 4.16   400 3   ‡a Van Gogh (Family : ‡g **Gogh, Vincent van, 1820-1888)**

figure 4.17   400 3   ‡a DubhGhaill (Clan : ‡d **8th century-** : ‡c **Ireland)**

RDA 10.2.3.5 instructs us to record a hereditary title associated with the family as a variant name. An example of this is:

figure 4.14   400 3   ‡a Strathmore and Kinghorne, ‡c Earls of (Family : ‡c Great Britain)

Variant access points may also be created based on the preferred name, but with different qualifying elements, if in the judgment of the cataloger this aids in identification of the family. Examples in this chapter include:

figure 4.3   400 3   ‡a Rentschler (Family : ‡g Rentschler, Herman, 1895-1973) (authorized access point qualified by a place associated with the family)

figure 4.4   400 3   ‡a Hassall (Family : ‡g Hassall, Rowland, 1768-1820) (authorized access point qualified by a place associated with the family)

figure 4.5   400 3   ‡a Osmond (Family : ‡d 1944- : ‡g Osmond, George, 1917-2007) (authorized access point qualified by the name of a different prominent member of the family)

NOTES

1. *Describing Archives: A Content Standard* (Chicago: Society of American Archivists, 2007); *Archives, Personal Papers, and Manuscripts,* 2nd ed. (Chicago: Society of American Archivists, 1989).

2. Full information about MARC 21 authority format is available at www.loc.gov/marc/authority/ecadhome.html.

3. Pre-AACR2 authority records are identified by "d" in 008 position 10 for "AACR2 compatible heading," "b" for AACR1, and "a" for earlier rules.

4. IFLA Study Group on the Functional Requirements for Bibliographic Records, "User Tasks," ch. 6 in *Functional Requirements for Bibliographic Records Final: Report* (Munich: K. G. Sauer, 1998), 79–92. Also available at www.ifla.org/en/publications/functional-requirements-for-bibliographic-records. FRAD is an extension of FRBR; see IFLA Working Group on Functional Requirements and Numbering of Authority Records, *Functional Requirements for Authority Data: A Conceptual Model.* IFLA Series on Bibliographic Control, vol. 34 (Munich: K. G. Saur, 2009).

5. For the ALA-LC Romanization Tables, see www.loc.gov/catdir/cpso/roman.html.

6. Source information about certain elements may be recorded directly in the element's MARC field itself, in subfield ‡v, rather than in a 670 field. This technique is available for the 046 and 370–378 fields. This method has not yet found much favor in practice and is not used in this book.

7. The *Descriptive Cataloging Manual* Z1 is available at www.loc.gov/catdir/cpso/z1andlcguidelines.html.

8. See the *Descriptive Cataloging Manual* Z1 at 370—Associated Place (November 2013). Previous to Fall 2013 a different practice for recording place names in 370 was followed, so catalogers will encounter records that do not follow the procedure described here.

9. Some systems allow the user to choose between sets of alternative authorized access points. For example, a database in Quebec might allow its users to prefer to search French authorized access points rather than English authorized access points. Such systems are beyond the scope of this book.

CHAPTER 5

DESCRIBING CORPORATE BODIES

Instructions for recording the attributes of the *corporate body* entity are found in RDA chapters 8 and 11.

MARC CODING

HE *CORPORATE BODY* ENTITY IS CURRENTLY described in library catalogs in the MARC 21 authority format.[1] RDA records for corporate bodies are identified by the value "z" in the 008 field position 10 (labeled "Rules" in the OCLC fixed field display) and the presence of "‡c rda" in the 040 field (see figure 5.1a). In contrast, an AACR2 authority record may be recognized by the presence of value "c" in 008 position 10 and no special coding in 040 (see figure 5.1b).[2] For space reasons, RDA coding is assumed in further figures in this chapter and is not explicitly shown. Other MARC coding issues will be discussed as they occur later in the chapter.

Figure 5.1a. RDA Coding (OCLC Style)

Rec stat	c	Entered	19800624			Replaced 20110319074927.0	
Type	z	Upd status	a	Enc lvl	n	Source	
Roman		Ref status	a	Mod rec		Name use	a
Govt agn		Auth status	a	Subj	a	Subj use	a
Series	n	Auth/ref	a	Geo subd	n	Ser use	b
Ser num	n	Name	n	Subdiv tpm	n	**Rules**	**z**

010	‡a n 80055753
046	‡s 1973
040	‡a DLC ‡b eng **‡e rda** ‡c DLC ‡d DLC ‡d VtMiM-Mu ‡d UPB
110 2	‡a Kronos Quartet
368	‡a String quartets ‡2 lcsh
370	‡e San Francisco (Calif.) ‡2 naf
410 2	‡a Kronos Performing Arts Association
410 2	‡a KPAA
670	‡a Music of Warren Benson, 1981: ‡b label (Kronos Quartet)
670	‡a Kronos Quartet, via WWW, 17 September 2011 ‡b (The Kronos Quartet/Kronos Performing Arts Association (KPAA) is a non-profit organization based in San Francisco. The mission of Kronos is to continually re-imagine the string quartet experience. Kronos fulfills its mission through commissioning, performing, presenting, recording and publishing contemporary music, and collaborating with, mentoring and encouraging other artists; founded in 1973.)

Figure 5.1a. RDA Coding (LC Style)

008	800624n| a**z**annaabn |a ana
010	‡a n 80055753
046	‡s 1973
040	‡a DLC ‡b eng **‡e rda** ‡c DLC ‡d DLC ‡d VtMiM-Mu ‡d UPB
110 2	‡a Kronos Quartet
368	‡a String quartets ‡2 lcsh
370	‡e San Francisco (Calif.) ‡2 naf
410 2	‡a Kronos Performing Arts Association
410 2	‡a KPAA
670	‡a Music of Warren Benson, 1981: ‡b label (Kronos Quartet)
670	‡a Kronos Quartet, via WWW, 17 September 2011 ‡b (The Kronos Quartet/Kronos Performing Arts Association (KPAA) is a non-profit organization based in San Francisco. The mission of Kronos is to continually re-imagine the string quartet experience. Kronos fulfills its mission through commissioning, performing, presenting, recording and publishing contemporary music, and collaborating with, mentoring and encouraging other artists; founded in 1973.)

Figure 5.1b. AACR2 Coding (OCLC Style)

Rec stat	c	Entered	19800624			Replaced	20110319074927.0
Type	z	Upd status	a	Enc lvl	n	Source	
Roman		Ref status	a	Mod rec		Name use	a
Govt agn		Auth status	a	Subj	a	Subj use	a
Series	n	Auth/ref	a	Geo subd	n	Ser use	b
Ser num	n	Name	n	Subdiv tp	n	**Rules**	**c**

010	‡a n 80055753
040	‡a DLC ‡b eng ‡c DLC ‡d DLC ‡d VtMiM-Mu ‡d UPB
110 2	‡a Kronos Quartet
410 2	‡a Kronos Performing Arts Association
410 2	‡a KPAA
670	‡a Music of Warren Benson, 1981: ‡b label (Kronos Quartet)
670	‡a Kronos Quartet, via WWW, 17 Sept. 2011 ‡b (The Kronos Quartet/Kronos Performing Arts Association (KPAA) is a non-profit organization based in San Francisco. The mission of Kronos is to continually re-imagine the string quartet experience. Kronos fulfills its mission through commissioning, performing, presenting, recording and publishing contemporary music, and collaborating with, mentoring and encouraging other artists; founded in 1973.)

Figure 5.1b. AACR2 Coding (LC Style)

008	800624n| a**c**annaabn |a ana
010	‡a n 80055753
040	‡a DLC ‡b eng ‡c DLC ‡d DLC ‡d VtMiM-Mu ‡d UPB
110 2	‡a Kronos Quartet
410 2	‡a Kronos Performing Arts Association
410 2	‡a KPAA
670	‡a Music of Warren Benson, 1981: ‡b label (Kronos Quartet)
670	‡a Kronos Quartet, via WWW, 17 Sept. 2011 ‡b (The Kronos Quartet/Kronos Performing Arts Association (KPAA) is a non-profit organization based in San Francisco. The mission of Kronos is to continually re-imagine the string quartet experience. Kronos fulfills its mission through commissioning, performing, presenting, recording and publishing contemporary music, and collaborating with, mentoring and encouraging other artists; founded in 1973.)

8.1. TERMINOLOGY. *Corporate body* is defined in RDA as "an organization or group of persons and/or organizations that is identified by a particular name and that acts, or may act, as a unit." This definition should be carefully considered. For purposes of the cataloging database, a corporate body only exists if:

a. it is an organization or group of persons
b. it is identified by a particular name
c. it acts (or may act) as a unit

If any of these is absent, no corporate body exists. Consider, for example, the following title page:

THE UTAH BILL

———

A Plea for Religious Liberty.

———

SPEECH OF
Hon. W. H. Hooper
OF UTAH,
Delivered in the House of Representatives, March 23, 1870,
TOGETHER WITH THE
REMONSTRANCE
Of the Citizens of Salt Lake City, in Mass Meeting, held March 31, 1870,
to the Senate of the United States

———

WASHINGTON, D.C.
Gibson Brothers, Printers.
1870

The citizens of Salt Lake City are a group of persons that acted (they created a "remonstrance"), but they are not identified by a particular name. No corporate body exists, and so no RDA description will be created for the citizens of Salt Lake City to link them to this document.

On the other hand, the Kronos Quartet consists of four string players that have a particular name and that act as a unit (see figure 5.1).

RDA 11.0 reemphasizes the requirement that a corporate body must have a particular name and further defines "particular name": "the words referring to it are a specific appellation rather than a general description." "Citizens of Salt Lake City" is a general description; "The Kronos Quartet" is a specific appellation.

RDA 11.0 also elaborates somewhat on the definition in 8.1, clarifying that the definition includes conferences and events such as athletic contests and expeditions. Most surprisingly to many, vessels such as ships and spacecraft are corporate bodies. The crew is identified with the ship, and as a body is considered capable of creation of works such as the ship's log (see figure 5.2). None of this is new to cataloging theory. The same types of entities were considered corporate bodies in earlier cataloging codes (compare AACR2 21.1B1).

Figure 5.2. Spacecraft as Corporate Body

046	‡s 1969
110 2	‡a Apollo 11 (Spacecraft)
368	‡a Spacecraft
370	‡c United States ‡2 naf
372	‡a Outer space--Exploration. ‡2 lcsh
377	‡a eng
500 1	‡w r ‡i Group member: ‡a Armstrong, Neil, ‡d 1930-
500 1	‡w r ‡i Group member: ‡a Aldrin, Buzz
670	‡a Apollo 11 mission commentary, 1969
670	‡a Britannica academic edition, 18 October 2011 ‡b (Apollo 11, U.S. spaceflight during which commander Neil Armstrong and lunar module pilot Edwin ("Buzz") Aldrin, Jr., on July 20, 1969, became the first people to land on the Moon. Launched July 16, 1969; returned July 24, 1969)

8.3. CORE ELEMENTS. As explained in greater detail in chapter 1, RDA identifies certain elements as "core" throughout the code. The core elements were chosen because they were attributes and relationships thought to support FRBR and FRAD user tasks.[3] RDA entity descriptions should contain, at a minimum, all core elements that are applicable and readily ascertainable as well as any other elements that might be required to differentiate one entity from another (see RDA 0.6.1). Inclusion of other elements is not required, and is at the discretion of the cataloger or cataloging agency (such as an individual library, or cooperative organizations such as the Program for Cooperative Cataloging [PCC]).

Agencies may develop requirements that go beyond RDA core. The Library of Congress (LC) and PCC, for example, have designated certain elements that are not core in RDA to be core for their own catalogers. Information about LC and PCC decisions are found in Library of Congress-Program for Cooperative Cataloging Policy Statements (LC-PCC PSs), found under the Resources tab of the RDA Toolkit.

Core elements for all entities and relationships are given in RDA 0.6. They are also given separately in the chapter(s) devoted to each entity or relationship. Core elements for the corporate body entity are found in RDA 0.6.4 and again in RDA 8.3. This information is also listed with each element's instruction. For example, RDA 11.2, name of the corporate body, which is a core element, reads as follows:

> **11.2 Name of the Corporate Body**
> **CORE ELEMENT**
> *Preferred name for the corporate body is a core element. Variant names for the corporate body are optional.*

> 11.2.1. Basic Instructions on Recording Names of Corporate Bodies
>> 11.2.1.1 Scope
>>
>> . . .

Conversely, 11.8, language of the corporate body, which is not a core element, reads as follows:

> 11.8 Language of the Corporate Body
>> 11.8.1 Basic Instructions on Recording Languages of the Corporate Body
>>> 11.8.1.1 Scope
>>>
>>> . . .

The core elements for the corporate body entity are:

> Preferred name for the corporate body
> Location of conference, etc.
> Date associated with the corporate body
> Associated institution (for conferences, etc., if the institution's name provides better identification than the local place name or if the local place name is unknown or cannot be readily determined)
> Number of a conference, etc.
> Other designation associated with the corporate body (for a body whose name does not convey the idea of a corporate body)
> Identifier for the corporate body

In addition, the following are core if the corporate body's name is the same or similar to that of another corporate body:

> Location of headquarters
> Associated institution
> Other designation associated with the corporate body

Please note that core designation means that the element must be recorded (if applicable and readily ascertainable) in the description for the corporate body. It does *not* mean that it must be included as part of the authorized access point for the corporate body. For example, "date associated with the corporate body" is a core element. This means that, if known, dates associated with the corporate body must be recorded somewhere in the description. It does not mean that RDA requires the date to be part of the access point (see further, below, in the discussion of RDA 11.4).

For the sake of illustration, the figures in this book will usually include many elements beyond the core elements. See figure 5.3a for an example of a description of a corporate body that contains only core elements; figure 5.3b is an example of a description of the same corporate body containing elements beyond core. It is evident that the RDA core for the description of a corporate body can be fairly minimal. Cataloging agencies will undoubtedly want their catalogers to include more elements, such as, at the least, variant names and sources consulted (fields 410 and 670 in figure 5.3b). In making decisions about inclusion of non-core elements in entity descriptions, agencies need to think about possible future uses of the data. Many non-core elements, such as location of headquarters, language, address, and field of activity will be useful as limiters to searches or as initial searches for records (e.g., a library user who wants to find works by or about Spanish papermakers), but only if agencies apply them consistently in their databases.

Figure 5.3a. Core Elements

010	‡a no2011160339
046	‡s 1698
110 2	‡a Guarro Casas

Figure 5.3b. Elements beyond Core

010	‡a no2011160339
046	‡s 1698
110 2	‡a Guarro Casas
368	‡a Papermaking firm
370	‡e Barcelona (Spain) ‡2 naf
372	‡a Papermaking ‡2 lcsh
373	‡a ArjoWiggins Appleton ‡2 naf
377	‡a spa
410 2	‡a Guarro (Papermaking firm)
500 1	‡w r ‡i Founder: ‡a Guarro, Ramon
670	‡a Westergard, J. Oddballs, 2011: ‡b colophon (Guarro paper)
670	‡a Guarro Casas, via WWW, 10 October 2011 ‡b (Guarro Casas S.A.; papermaker in Barcelona, Spain for 300 years; founded in 1698 by Ramon Guarro in La Torre de Claramunt in Capellades (Catalonia); became a member of the Arjowiggins group in the 1990s)

8.4. LANGUAGE AND SCRIPT. One of the basic principles of RDA is that of representation: "The data describing [an entity] should reflect the [entity's] representation of itself" (RDA 0.4.3.4). It is therefore no surprise that RDA 8.4 calls for recording names in the language and script in which they appear. This would mean that the preferred name of a corporate body that uses Japanese would be recorded in Japanese script; the name of a body using Greek would be recorded in Greek script; the name of a body using English would be recorded in Latin script (see figure 5.4a). RDA 8.4 includes an alternative, however: "Record a transliterated form of the name either as a substitute for, or in addition to, the form that appears on the source." LC and NACO will continue to record a form transliterated following the ALA-LC Romanization Tables as the preferred name for names appearing in non-Latin scripts.[4] Non-Latin script forms may be included in the record as variant access points. Including non-Latin variant access points is a relatively recent practice and NACO policies have not been fully developed. Until they are, catalogers may record non-Latin script variant access points in 4XX fields, but should include a 667 field reading "Non-Latin script reference(s) not evaluated" (see figure 5.4b).

Figure 5.4a. Name Appearing in Non-Latin Script (RDA Basic Guideline)

110 2	‡a 日外アソシエーツ
370	‡c Japan ‡e Tokyo (Japan) ‡2 naf
377	‡a jpn
410 2	‡a Nichigai Asoshiētsu
670	‡a Sakuhinmei kara hikeru Nihon jidō bungaku zenshū annai, 2006: ‡b title page (日外アソシエーツ = Nichigai Asoshiētsu; in Tokyo)

Figure 5.4b.
Name Appearing in Non-Latin Script (RDA Alternative: LC/NACO Practice)

110 2	‡a Nichigai Asoshiētsu
370	‡c Japan ‡e Tokyo (Japan) ‡2 naf
377	‡a jpn
410 2	‡a 日外アソシエーツ
667	‡a Non-Latin script reference not evaluated.
670	‡a Sakuhinmei kara hikeru Nihon jidō bungaku zenshū annai, 2006: ‡b title page (日外アソシエーツ = Nichigai Asoshiētsu; in Tokyo)

8.5.2. CAPITALIZATION. RDA calls for faithful recording of a corporate body's usage in matters such as abbreviation, hyphenation, and diacritical marks (see RDA 8.5). However, current RDA 8.5.2 calls for standardization of capitalization of names of corporate bodies, following RDA appendix A.2. Generally, for English-language corporate bodies, capitalize each word except articles, prepositions, or conjunctions; for other languages, capitalize words in the name following the usage of the language involved (see figure 5.3). When capitalizing, routinely convert letters following the initial letter to lowercase, even though corporate logos or other presentations of the name are given in all capitals (for example, the website of the corporate body illustrated in figure 5.3 shows the name as GUARRO CASAS). However, if a corporate name exhibits unusual capitalization (such as internal capitalization of letters within a word), follow the capitalization practice of the body (see figure 5.5).

Figure 5.5. Unusual Capitalization

046	‡s 2000-01
110 2	‡a FedEx Corporation
368	‡a Shipping firm
370	‡e Memphis (Tenn.) ‡2 naf
372	‡a Shipping ‡2 lcsh
377	‡a eng
410 2	‡a FedEx (Firm)
510 2	‡w r ‡i Predecessor: ‡a FDX Corporation
670	‡a Annual report, 2001: ‡b title page (FedEx Corporation, Memphis, TN) page 2 of cover (FedEx)
670	‡a FedEx Corporation, via WWW, 5 May 2012 ‡b (Company founded as Federal Express in 1971; the corporation was created in 1998 as FDX Corporation and became FedEx Corporation in January 2000. Headquarters in Memphis, Tenn.)
678 1	‡a This company was founded in 1971 as Federal Express; the corporation was created in 1998 as FDX Corporation and became FedEx Corporation in January 2000.

8.5.6. SPACING. Because it would be unreasonable to expect discernment of specific spacing conventions of corporate bodies from typographic presentations, RDA 8.5.6.2 instructs catalogers to regularize spacing for corporate bodies. Separate letters and initialisms are recorded without spaces between them, whether the body uses full stops after the letters or not (see figure 5.6).

Figure 5.6. Spacing of Initialism

046	‡s 1990
110 2	‡a MADD Canada
370	‡c Canada ‡e Oakville (Ont.) ‡2 naf
371	‡a 2010 Winston Park Drive ‡a Suite 500 ‡b Oakville ‡c Ontario ‡e L6H 5R7 ‡m info@madd.ca
372	‡a Non-profit organization with a mission to stop impaired driving and support its victims.
377	‡a eng ‡a fre
410 2	‡a Mothers Against Drunk Driving (Organization)
410 2	‡a Mères contre l'alcool au volant (Organization)

670	‡a The heart of the matter, [2001]: ‡b cassette label (MADD Canada)
670	‡a MADD Canada web page, 4 August 2011 ‡b (MADD Canada, madd; Mothers Against Drunk Driving; Les mères contre l'alcool au volant; headquarters Oakville, Ontario; formed in 1990; 2010 Winston Park Drive, Suite 500 Oakville, Ontario L6H 5R7; info@madd.ca; Telephone - (905) 829-8805, 1-800-665-6233; Fax: (905) 829-8860)
670	‡a OCLC, 19 June 2012 ‡b (usage: MADD Canada, MADD)

On the other hand, do not add spaces between words where the corporate body does not. Following the usage of the bodies, the words contained in "ExxonMobil" and "Lucasfilm" should not be separated (see figures 5.7 and 5.8). Regarding these two figures, note also the contrasting capitalization practices of the bodies, which will be respected.

Figure 5.7. Spacing

046	‡s 1999
110 2	‡a ExxonMobil Chemical (Firm)
368	‡a Firm
370	‡e Houston (Tex.) ‡2 naf
371	‡a 13501 Katy Freeway ‡b Houston ‡c TX ‡e 77079-1398 ‡d USA
372	‡a Chemical manufacture
377	‡a eng
410 2	‡a ExxonMobil Chemical Company
510 2	‡w a ‡a Exxon Chemical Company
670	‡a Vistalon elastomers, 2002: ‡b cover (ExxonMobil Chemical) colophon, etc. (ExxonMobil Chemical Company; Houston, Tex.; division of Exxon Mobil Corporation; Esso Chemical Company became Exxon Chemical Company in 1973; following merger of Exxon Corp. and Mobil Corp. in 1999, many chemical operations of each company combined and the Exxon Chemical Company changed to ExxonMobil Chemical Company; 13501 Katy Freeway, Houston, TX 77079-1398, USA; (281)870-6050)

Figure 5.8. Spacing

046	‡s 2003
110 2	‡a Lucasfilm Animation (Firm)
368	‡a Firm
372	‡a Animation (Cinematography) ‡2 lcsh
377	‡a eng
510 2	‡w r ‡i Hierarchical superior: ‡a Lucasfilm, Ltd.

670	‡a Star wars : the clone wars, [2008], 2008: ‡b title frame (Lucasfilm Animation)
670	‡a Lucasfilm Ltd. home page, 18 June 2012 ‡b (Lucasfilm Animation; founded 2003; digital animation studio)

8.5.7. ABBREVIATIONS. Follow the abbreviation practice of the corporate body. If it regularly abbreviates certain words in its name, record the abbreviation. Do not abbreviate a word that is not abbreviated by the body. This includes the word "Department," which was routinely abbreviated in previous U.S. cataloging practice, even though contrary to AACR2 (see figure 5.9). Always follow the usage of the body, however—sometimes the body abbreviates this word (see figure 5.10).

Figure 5.9. Abbreviation

046	‡s 1789
110 1	‡a United States. ‡b Department of State
370	‡c United States ‡2 naf
372	‡a Diplomacy ‡2 lcsh
377	‡a eng
410 1	‡a United States. ‡b Office of the Secretary of State
410 1	‡a United States. ‡b Secretary of State
670	‡a United States foreign policy 1971: a report of the Secretary of State, 1972
670	‡a Patterns of global terrorism, 1990, 1991: ‡b cover (United States Department of State) page 2 of cover (Office of the Secretary of State)
670	‡a U.S. Department of State website, 9 January 2012 ‡b (created in 1789)

Figure 5.10. Abbreviation

046	‡s 1995
110 2	‡a Radio Dept. (Musical group)
368	‡a Musical groups ‡2 lcsh
370	‡f Lund (Sweden) ‡2 naf
372	‡a Popular music ‡2 lcsh
377	‡a swe ‡a eng
410 2	‡a Radioavdelningen (Musical group)
670	‡a Marie Antoinette, 2006: ‡b container (Radio Dept.)
670	‡a The Radio Dept. website, 6 March 2011 ‡b (band formed in 1995 in Lund, Sweden, named Radioavdelningen ("The Radio Department" in Swedish); produces recordings using the English name Radio Dept.)

8.10. STATUS OF IDENTIFICATION. RDA instructs us to record the level of authentication of the data identifying the entity. The possible levels are "fully established," "provisional," and "preliminary." "Fully established" means the data are sufficient to fully establish the authorized access point. "Provisional" means the data are insufficient to establish the authorized access point. "Preliminary" means the data were recorded without the described resource in hand.

In nearly all cases, NACO catalogers are expected to fully establish authorized access points in authority records in the LC/NACO Authority File. Provisional records are allowed, however, if the cataloger has inadequate information about the entity to fully establish the authorized access point. For example, RDA 11.2.2.5.2 stipulates that a form in the official language of the body is to be chosen as the preferred name. If a cataloger needs to establish the name of a corporate body, but the only evidence for the form appears in a language that is not the official language of the body and the cataloger suspects a form does exist in the official language, the cataloger may establish the name at a provisional level of authentication using the evidence at hand (see figure 5.11). If evidence of the form in the body's official language appears later, the preferred name can be changed and the description coded as fully established.

Figure 5.11. Provisional Record

008	position 33 coded "c."
110 2	‡a Université de Genève. ‡b Generative Grammar Group
370	‡e Geneva (Switzerland) ‡2 naf
372	‡a Generative grammar ‡2 lcsh
377	‡a fre ‡a eng
410 2	‡a Université de Genève. ‡b Département de linguistique. ‡b Generative Grammar Group
667	‡a Could not establish in the vernacular.
670	‡a Generative grammar in Geneva, journal home page, viewed June 29, 2004: ‡b (University of Geneva, Department of Linguistics, Generative Grammar Group)

If the authorized access point for a subordinate corporate body is formed as a subdivision of a higher body (see discussion at 11.2.2.13–11.2.2.29, below), the status of identification element in the description of the subordinate body should not be a higher level than that of the description of the higher body. That is, if the authorized access point for the higher body was established in a provisional record, any records for subordinate bodies with access points formed as a subdivision of the higher body should also be coded as provisional.

NACO participants will almost never create preliminary records, but they do exist in the authority file, sometimes as the result of a machine-driven project to populate the file from access points on bibliographic records. If NACO participants encounter preliminary records, they should upgrade them to fully established records if they are making other changes to the record by evaluating and, if appropriate, changing the authorized access point in light of the resource in hand and other evidence that might be available.[5]

This information is coded in the MARC authority record in field 008 position 33, which is labeled in the OCLC display as "Auth status." Fully established records contain "a" in this position. Provisional records contain "c" in this position, and preliminary records contain "d." See figure 5.1 for an example.

8.11. UNDIFFERENTIATED NAME INDICATOR. The undifferentiated name technique, using the same access point for two or more different entities with the same name, is only available in RDA for descriptions of persons, not corporate bodies.

8.12. SOURCE CONSULTED. Just as the author of a scholarly paper justifies his or her assertions by citing sources (usually in footnotes), so the creator of an RDA description for a corporate body in an authority record must justify access points by citing where the information came from. In MARC authority work, this is done using the 670 field.[6] The source consulted element is not core in RDA, but at least one instance, that of the resource in hand that generated the need for a new authorized access point, is required in LC/NACO practice. Examples of 670 fields are found in figures throughout this chapter. For a full discussion of LC/NACO practice in the source consulted element, see chapter 3 under 8.12.

8.13. CATALOGUER'S NOTE. The cataloguer's note element contains information about the corporate body represented by the authorized access point that might be helpful to persons using the authority record. The cataloguer's note element is not core in RDA, but it is core for the Library of Congress in certain situations (see *Descriptive Cataloging Manual* Z1).[7] A common use of this element is to notify the cataloger that a form cannot be used as a subject under the *Library of Congress Subject Headings Manual* (LCSH) policy. For example, corporate forms for government and religious officials are not used as subject access points (see figure 5.12). For examples of other types of cataloguer's notes, see figures 5.4b and 5.11. For a fuller treatment of the cataloguer's note element, see chapter 3 of this *Handbook* under 8.13.

Figure 5.12. Cataloguer's Note

046	‡s 19781022 ‡t 20050402
110 2	‡a Catholic Church. ‡b Pope (1978-2005 : John Paul II)
500 0	‡a John Paul ‡b II, ‡c Pope, ‡d 1920-2005
667	‡a SUBJECT USAGE: This heading is not valid for use as a subject. Works about this person are entered under John Paul II, Pope, 1920-2005.

670	‡a Encyklika Redemptor hominis Ojca Świętego Jana Pawła II, 1979: ‡b t.p. (Ojca Świętego Jana Pawła II)
670	‡a Catholic directory, 1979: ‡b page 5 (John Paul II, inaugurated Pope 22 October 1978)
670	‡a New York times, via WWW, 8 April 2005: ‡b obituary dated 3 April 2005 (Pope John Paul II died 2 April 2005, at Vatican City)

STRUCTURE OF CHAPTER 11. RDA chapter 11, "Identifying Corporate Bodies," follows the same structure as most of the other chapters in the "Recording Attributes" parts of RDA (RDA sections 1 through 4). It begins with a section on the purpose and scope of the chapter (RDA 11.0) and then proceeds to general guidelines on identifying corporate bodies, including sources that may be consulted for information about corporate bodies (RDA 11.1). It then treats, one by one, the various elements and sub-elements of the corporate body entity that are recognized by RDA, giving instructions on where to get information about the element or sub-element, and how to record that information. This section is the heart of chapter 11, and occupies the bulk of it (RDA 11.2–RDA 11.12). The chapter ends with a final section on constructing access points for corporate bodies (RDA 11.13). It is crucial to understand this structure. Catalogers used to AACR2 chapter 24, which is chiefly about creating an access point (heading) for a corporate body, may be misled into thinking that the guidelines about recording elements, and particularly wording about core elements, constitute instructions about how to construct the access point for the corporate body; in fact this central section gives instructions for recording the *information* in the record or description for the corporate body. In the entity-relationship or linked-data database structure RDA anticipates, we will be creating descriptions of corporate bodies that exist independently from, but are linked to, other entities such as works that they may have a relationship to. In such an environment bibliographic records with formal access points might not exist, but the elements contained in the description of the corporate body will be essential.

11.2. Name of the Corporate Body

GENERAL GUIDELINES

11.2.1. BASIC INSTRUCTIONS ON RECORDING NAMES OF CORPORATE BODIES. "Name of the corporate body" is defined in RDA as "a word, character, or group of words and/or characters by which a corporate body is known." A corporate body can be known by more than one name. One of these names will be chosen under RDA as the preferred name; others may be recorded in the description as variant names.

11.2.2. PREFERRED NAME FOR THE CORPORATE BODY. Preferred name is a core element in RDA, meaning any description of a corporate body entity must include this element. It is defined as "the name or form of name chosen as the basis for the authorized access point representing that body." Unlike persons (for example, in the case of pseudonyms), corporate bodies may not have more than one identity. Treatment of a corporate body that changes its name is also different from that of a person who changes his or her name. Except in the case of pseudonyms, when a person changes his or her name, that person is still considered the same entity, and so the changed name is simply reflected in the description for the person already existing in the authority file. By contrast, when a corporate body changes its name a new description is created. See further discussion below under 11.2.2.6.

CHOOSING THE PREFERRED NAME

If a corporate body is known by only one name, that name should be chosen as its preferred name. Lucasfilm Animation is an example (see figure 5.8). However, it is rare that no variants or different names exist. If a corporate body is known by more than one form of the same name, RDA 11.2.2.2 gives us guidance for choosing one of these as the preferred name. We are to choose, in priority order:

1. A name found in preferred sources of information in resources associated with the corporate body
2. A name found in other formal statements found in those same resources
3. A name found in any other source

However, this somewhat mechanical exercise is tempered by 11.2.2.3, which states that we are to choose the name "by which the corporate body is commonly identified" as the preferred name. This relates to one of the bedrock principles of cataloging theory, that of representation. As stated in RDA 0.4.3.4,

> the name or form of name chosen as the preferred name for a person, family, or corporate body should be: (a) the name or form of name most commonly found in resources associated with that person, family, or corporate body, or (b) a well-accepted name or form of name in the language and script preferred by the agency creating the data.

RDA 11.2.2.2 is a "default"—it is expected that in most cases the name found in preferred sources of information in resources associated with the corporate body is the one most library users will expect to find in the database, but the cataloger must make this decision on the basis of all available evidence, and if he or she determines that another form is the "most commonly known" form, that is the form that should be chosen as the preferred name.

RDA does not define "resources associated with the corporate body." Previous cataloging practice preferred "items issued by the body" as the source for the body's preferred name (see AACR2 24.1A). "Resources associated with the body" includes more than "items issued by the body." However, in keeping with the principle of representation—that entities should be described using terms they use to describe themselves—it seems wise to continue to consult resources issued by the corporate body if possible and give these resources greater weight when deciding how the body is "commonly identified."

The preferred name might be the corporate body's formal, legal name as registered in its foundational documents. On the other hand, for cataloging purposes the term "corporate body" includes much more than legally incorporated entities, and even for a legally incorporated entity another name might more commonly be found in resources associated with the body. The cataloger is not required to do legal research to discover the name of a body, but is only expected to consult resources associated with the body, such as the resource he or she is cataloging, which might be an annual report or minutes of meetings—or for that matter a book or film about the body. Another important resource associated with the body is the body's home page, which normally gives the body's name as the body wishes itself to be represented. Although there is no requirement to do research, it is quite easy to do an Internet search on the name of a corporate body, and it makes sense to undertake this rather minimal effort when establishing the name of a corporate body.

11.2.2.5. DIFFERENT FORMS OF THE SAME NAME. In many cases there is evidence that a corporate body uses many forms of the same name. "IBM"/"International Business Machines" and "NATO"/"North Atlantic Treaty Organization" are examples of a bodies that are known both by a full name and an initialism. "Nabisco"/"National Biscuit Company" and "Unesco"/"United Nations Educational, Scientific, and Cultural Organization" are examples of acronyms and fuller forms. Sometimes the words in the name are given in different order. "Educational and Cultural Organization of the United Nations" is a form sometimes used by Unesco. Bodies often have forms of their names in different languages (see figure 5.6). RDA 11.2.2.5 gives guidance for choosing one of these forms as the preferred name.

The basic guideline is to choose, in this order:

1. A form found in the preferred source of information.
2. If more than one form is found in the preferred source of information, a form "presented formally."
3. If no form is "presented formally," choose the most commonly found form. This will probably entail looking at sources beyond the preferred source of information of any particular resource.

4. If the most commonly found form cannot be determined, choose a brief form such as an initialism or acronym, as long as that form will differentiate the body from others with similar names.
5. If none of these apply, choose the name found in reference sources or the official form.

The decision about a corporate body's preferred name should not be made in a vacuum, based only on information from the resource being cataloged. Although extra research is not required by RDA, NACO catalogers are at least expected to check their database (e.g., OCLC) for evidence about the entity. As already noted, it is also not unreasonable to expect catalogers to check the body's home page, if one exists. Once all the evidence is in, the cataloger should apply 11.2.2.5.

Key to application of RDA 11.2.2.5 is the concept of preferred sources. Preferred sources of information refer to particular sources within specific physical formats. These sources are described in RDA 2.2.2. The preferred source of information for a book, for example, is the title page, with alternative sources listed in case there is no title page or in case the information does not appear on the title page. The preferred source for a moving image is the title frame(s) or screen(s); in case there is no title frame or screen, alternative sources are title-bearing labels permanently affixed to the resource or metadata embedded with the resource. The preferred source for other resources are a label bearing a title permanently affixed to the resource, or metadata embedded with the resource; or any other source within the resource itself (see RDA 2.2.2 for details).

Because the title transcription also comes from the preferred source in both AACR2 and RDA records, transcriptions of titles found in 245 fields of AACR2 or RDA MARC catalog records in databases such as OCLC are suitable surrogates for preferred sources and may be used in choosing the preferred name for a corporate body. Forms found in the 260 field (publication information) are not reliable. Although publication information usually comes from preferred sources, in AACR2 records the names of publishers were often shortened rather than transcribed.

MADD Canada (figure 5.6) is an example of how this works in practice. The cassette label, a preferred source of *The Heart of the Matter,* gives the form MADD Canada. The body's website prominently displays a logo with the word "madd" plus a red maple leaf, but the metadata in the header reads "MADD Canada," and "MADD Canada" appears several times on the home page. The logo is probably more formally presented than the other forms on the page. Elsewhere in the site "Mothers Against Drunk Driving" and "Les mères contre l'alcool au volant" appear. An OCLC search shows usage of both MADD Canada and MADD, but the MADD usage comes from unreliable 260 fields, whereas MADD Canada is found in 245 title transcriptions. The following forms of the body's name were found:

madd [plus red maple leaf]
MADD Canada
MADD
Mothers Against Drunk Driving
Les mères contre l'alcool au volant

Because MADD Canada was found in preferred sources, and in addition is clearly the most prominent form, it is chosen as the preferred name. Other forms may be recorded as variant names.

The corporate body described in figure 5.13 is another example. The name American Philosophical Society appears on the title pages (preferred sources) of resources associated with the body. Elsewhere in these resources the forms "APS" and "American Philosophical Society, Held at Philadelphia, for Promoting Useful Knowledge" are found. The body's website formally presents both APS and American Philosophical Society. Because the form "American Philosophical Society" is the form most commonly found in preferred sources, it is chosen as the preferred name.

Figure 5.13. Preferred Name from Preferred Source

046	‡s 1743
110 2	‡a American Philosophical Society
370	‡e Philadelphia (Pa.) ‡2 naf
377	‡a eng
410 2	‡a American Philosophical Society, Held at Philadelphia, for Promoting Useful Knowledge
410 2	‡a APS
670	‡a The universal Bach, 1986: ‡b title page (American Philosophical Society) title page verso (APS)
670	‡a A catalogue of portraits and other works in the possession of the American Philosophical Society, 1961: ‡b half title (American Philosophical Society, Held at Philadelphia, for Promoting Useful Knowledge)
670	‡a American Philosophical Society, via WWW, 18 October 2011 ‡b (APS, American Philosophical Society; founded by Benjamin Franklin in 1743)

The Educational Resources Information Center also calls itself ERIC (see figure 5.14). The name is usually presented both ways on preferred sources. Both forms are given prominently on the body's website. Working through 11.2.2.5, neither name is presented more formally than the other. It is also not clear which is the most commonly found form. In this case RDA instructs the cataloger to choose a brief form ("ERIC"). However, that form will not differentiate the body from others. There are several corporate bodies that use the initialism ERIC. The fuller form will be chosen as the preferred name and "ERIC" will be recorded as a variant name.

Figure 5.14. Preferred Sources Show Two Forms

046	ǂs 1966
110 2	ǂa Educational Resources Information Center
370	ǂe Washington (D.C.) ǂ2 naf
377	ǂa eng
410 2	ǂa ERIC
410 1	ǂa United States. ǂb Educational Resources Information Center
410 2	ǂa United States. ǂb Office of Educational Research and Improvement. ǂb Educational Resources Information Center
670	ǂa Gender bias and fairness, 1990: ǂb label on title page (U.S. Department of Education, Office of Educational Research and Improvement, Educational Resources Information Center (ERIC))
670	ǂa How to use ERIC, 1972: ǂb title page (U.S. Department of Health, Education, and Welfare, National Institute of Education, Educational Resources Information Center)
670	ǂa A pocket guide to ERIC, fall 1995: ǂb title page (Educational Resources Information Center, National Library of Education, Office of Educational Research and Improvement, U.S. Department of Education) page 1 (ERIC, established in 1966) page 11 (Federal sponsor: U.S. Department of Education, National Library of Education, Office of Educational Research and Improvement; Washington, DC)
670	ERIC, Educational Resources Information Center, via WWW, 10 June 2012

In contrast to ERIC, Unesco is a corporate body that commonly uses a brief form if its name on its publications, and the brief form is adequate to differentiate the body from others (see figure 5.15).

Figure 5.15. Preferred Sources Show Two Forms

046	ǂs 19461104
110 2	ǂa Unesco
410 2	ǂa United Nations. ǂb Unesco
410 2	ǂa United Nations Educational, Scientific, and Cultural Organization
410 2	ǂa Educational and Cultural Organization of the United Nations
410 2	ǂa United Nations. ǂb Educational, Scientific, and Cultural Organization
410 2	ǂa Organisation des Nations Unies pour l'éducation, la science et la culture
410 2	ǂa Organización de las Naciones Unidas para la Educación la Ciencia y la Cultura
670	ǂa Proposed Educational and Cultural Organization of the United Nations, 1945
670	ǂa Address by Mr. Amadou-Mahtar M'Bow, Director-General of the United Nations Educational Scientific and Cultural Organization (Unesco), 1980
670	ǂa General conference of the United Nations Educational, Scientific and Cultural Organisation : project for a Unesco Educational Centre, 1946

670	‡a UNESCO/United Nations Educational, Scientific and Cultural Organisation, via WWW, 3 February 2012 ‡b (constitution of UNESCO signed 16 November 1945, came into force 4 November 1946)
670	‡a La crise de l'Unesco (Organisation des Nations Unies pour l'éducation, la science et la culture), 1991
670	‡a Premio Internacional Simón Bolivar, 1979: ‡b title page (Unesco, Organización de las Naciones Unidas para la Educación la Ciencia y la Cultura)

Sometimes the brief form of the name used by a corporate body in its publications is the same as the name of another organization. ERIC was an example of this, but there was really only one other choice for the preferred name. RDA, however, instructs the cataloger in such cases to "choose the form found in reference sources, or the official form." The National Research Council of Canada sometimes is so listed in resources associated with it; it also appears as "National Research Council." The brief form is not sufficient to identify the body, because there is another organization of the same name based in Washington, DC. *World of Learning*[8] gives the official form of the Canadian body as National Research Council of Canada. This is the form, rather than the brief form, that will be chosen as the preferred name (see figure 5.16).

Figure 5.16. Preferred Sources Show Two Forms

110 2	‡a National Research Council of Canada
370	‡c Canada ‡2 naf
377	‡a eng
410 2	‡a National Research Council (Canada)
670	‡a Annotated bibliography on building for disabled persons, 1971: ‡b title page (National Research Council)
670	‡a Coatings for exterior metal, 1967: ‡b title page (National Research Council of Canada)

11.2.2.5.1. VARIANT SPELLINGS. The RDA guideline, which is to use the spelling found in the first resource received, is sensible and does not require the cataloger to predict variants. Once the form has been chosen and established in the authority file, it should be used even if other resources are later received with a different spelling. Encyclopaedia Britannica, Inc., is an example (see figure 5.17). Another example of a variant spelling is substitution of a spelled-out word for an abbreviation or symbol. The name of the German music publisher Breitkopf & Härtel usually appears with the ampersand, but sometimes appears as Breitkopf und Härtel (see figure 5.18).

Figure 5.17. Variant Spelling

110 2	‡a Encyclopaedia Britannica, Inc.
370	‡e Chicago (Ill.) ‡2 naf
372	‡a Encyclopedia production
377	‡a eng
410 2	‡a Encyclopædia Britannica, Inc.
670	‡a Britannica instant research system, 1994: ‡b user's guide title page verso (Encyclopaedia Britannica, Inc., Chicago, IL)
670	‡a Britannica atlas, 1982: ‡b title page verso (Encyclopædia Britannica, inc.)

Figure 5.18. Variant Spelling

110 2	‡a Breitkopf & Härtel
368	‡a Music publishers ‡2 lcsh
370	‡e Wiesbaden (Germany) ‡2 naf
372	‡a Music publishing ‡2 lcsh
377	‡a ger
410 2	‡a Breitkopf und Härtel
670	‡a Concerto for piano and orchestra in C major, 2011: ‡b title page (Breitkopf & Härtel, Wiesbaden)
670	‡a Breitkopf und Härtel in Paris, 1990

Variant spellings due to orthographic reform are also treated under RDA 11.2.2.5.1. The Library of Congress has issued a policy statement on variants caused by orthographic reform (LC-PCC PS 11.2.2.5.1, October 2012). If the first resource received for a corporate body located in a country where orthographic reform has taken place gives the name in the old orthography, the name is established using that form. A variant access point is made in the reformed orthography. If a resource is subsequently received showing the name in the reformed orthography, the preferred name is changed to the new form and the old spelling is given as a variant. This is a slight modification to RDA 11.2.2.5.1, which as written would keep the name spelled as found on the first resource received as the preferred name.

The Museum der Deutschen Binnenschifffahrt is an example of a name affected by orthographic reform. The 1996 German spelling reform called for tripling of some double consonants. Binnenschiffahrt became Binnenschifffahrt. The first resource received had the form Museum der Deutschen Binnenschiffahrt, and so the name was so established (see figure 5.19a). Later a resource was received with the form Museum der Deutschen Binnenschifffahrt. The preferred name was changed to the new spelling (see figure 5.19b).

**Figure 5.19a. Variant Spelling Caused by Orthographic Reform
(First Resource Received)**

110 2	‡a Museum der Deutschen Binnenschiffahrt
368	‡a Museums ‡2 lcsh
370	‡e Duisburg (Germany) ‡2 naf
377	‡a ger
410 1	‡a Duisburg (Germany). ‡b Museum der Deutschen Binnenschiffahrt
410 2	‡a Museum der Deutschen Binnenschifffahrt
410 2	‡a Museum of German Inland Shipping
670	‡a Tyros, Hafenstadt Phöniziens, 1985: ‡b t.p. (Museum der Deutschen Binnenschiffahrt, Duisburg-Ruhrort)
670	‡a M:AI Museum für Architektur und Ingenieurkunst, via WWW, 9 May 2009 ‡b (Museum of German Inland Shipping)

**Figure 5.19b. Variant Spelling Caused by Orthographic Reform
(Resource Received with New Spelling)**

110 2	‡a Museum der Deutschen Binnenschifffahrt
368	‡a Museums ‡2 lcsh
370	‡e Duisburg (Germany) ‡2 naf
377	‡a ger
410 1	‡a Duisburg (Germany). ‡b Museum der Deutschen Binnenschifffahrt
410 2	‡w nne ‡a Museum der Deutschen Binnenschiffahrt
410 2	‡a Museum of German Inland Shipping
670	‡a Tyros, Hafenstadt Phöniziens, 1985: ‡b t.p. (Museum der Deutschen Binnenschiffahrt, Duisburg-Ruhrort)
670	‡a M:AI Museum für Architektur und Ingenieurkunst, via WWW, 9 May 2009 ‡b (Museum of German Inland Shipping)
670	‡a Museum der Deutschen Binnenschifffahrt, Duisburg-Ruhrort, 2010

11.2.2.5.2. MORE THAN ONE LANGUAGE FORM OF THE NAME. When the name of a corporate body appears in resources associated with it in different languages, the name in the official language of the body is chosen as the preferred name. In countries such as Canada or South Africa, where there is more than one official language, NACO contributors should use the English-language form if one of the languages is English (LC-PCC PS 11.2.2.5.2, October 2012). The National Library of South Africa—which has eleven official languages, including English—is such a body (see figure 5.20). If English is not one of the languages, choose the most commonly found form.

Figure 5.20. Language Variant

110 2	‡a National Library of South Africa
368	‡a Libraries ‡2 lcsh
370	‡c South Africa ‡e Pretoria (South Africa) ‡2 naf
377	‡a eng ‡a afr ‡a nbl ‡a nso ‡a sot ‡a ssw ‡a tsn ‡a tso ‡a ven ‡a xho ‡a zul
410 1	‡a South Africa. ‡b National Library
410 2	‡a Nasionale Biblioteek van Suid-Afrika
410 2	‡a Laeborari ya Setjhaba ya Afrika Borwa
410 2	‡a Layiburari ya Rixaka ya Afrika-Dzonga
... [variant access points for the seven other language variants]	
670	‡a Quarterly bulletin of the National Library of South Africa, Sept. 1999.
670	‡a National Library of South Africa, via WWW, 7 August 2011 ‡b (English: National Library of South Africa, Afrikaans: Nasionale Biblioteek van Suid-Afrika; Sesotho: Laeborari ya Setjhaba ya Afrika Borwa; Xitsonga: Layiburari ya Rixaka ya Afrika-Dzonga; IsiXhosa: Ithala leeNcwadi likaZwelonke loMzantsi Afrika; Tshivenda: Laiburari ya Lushaka ya Afurika Tshipembe; SiSwati: Umtapo weTincwadzi waVelonkhe waseNingizimu Afrika; Setswana: Laeborari ya Bosetshaba ya Aferika Borwa; Sepedi: Bokgobapuku bja setshaba bja Afrika Borwa; IsiZulu: Umtapo woLwazi kaZwelonke eNingizimu Afrika; IsiNdebele: Ibulungelo leeNcwadi lesiTjhaba leSewula Afrika)

Figures 5.6 and 5.15 also show bodies that have more than one official language, but in each of those cases a name common to all the languages was chosen as the preferred name.

11.2.2.5.3. INTERNATIONAL BODIES. Choose a name in the language preferred by the cataloging agency for an international body, if one exists. Catalogers following LC policy (including NACO catalogers) will choose English forms (LC-PCC PS 11.2.2.5.3, October 2012). One such body, The International Federation of Library Associations and Institutions (IFLA), uses several languages, including English. The English-language form will be chosen for the LC/NACO preferred form (see figure 5.21).

Figure 5.21. International Body

046	‡s 19760823
110 2	‡a International Federation of Library Associations and Institutions
370	‡e Hague (Netherlands) ‡2 naf
377	‡a eng ‡a fre ‡a ger ... *[codes for other languages of the body]*
410 2	‡a IFLA

410 2 ‡a Fédération internationale des associations de bibliothécaires et des bibliothèques

410 2 ‡a Internationaler Verband der Bibliothekarischen Vereine und Institutionen

... *[variant access points for other language variants]*

‡a Bowker annual, 1977: ‡b (name expanded from International Federation of Library Associations with adoption of new constitution on Aug. 23, 1976; expanded to include libraries & library schools; to be designated by acronym IFLA).

670 ‡a Names of persons, 1977: ‡b title page (International Federation of Library Associations and Institutions)

670 ‡a Division of Special Libraries. Newsletter, July 1981: ‡b title page (International Federation of Library Associations and Institutions, Fédération internationale des associations de bibliothécaires et des bibliothèques, Internationaler Verband der Bibliothekarischen Vereine und Institutionen; IFLA)

670 ‡a IFLA, via WWW, 21 October 2011 ‡b (international body representing the interests of library and information services and their users; originally founded in 1927 as International Federation of Library Associations in Edinburgh, Scotland; headquarters in The Hague, Netherlands, at the Royal Library of the Netherlands)

11.2.2.5.4. CONVENTIONAL NAME. If a body is well known by a name other than its official name, as evidenced by forms found in reference sources in its own language, that name (the "conventional name") is chosen as the preferred name. RDA has many exceptions to this guideline, however.

Ancient and International Bodies. This exception is limited to bodies of ancient origin or international in character whose names have become well established in a form in the language preferred by the cataloging agency. LC/NACO catalogers will follow the LC-PCC PS and choose an English form as the preferred name, if one exists. Check English-language reference sources to determine the name when in doubt.

The Council of Trent is such a body. It is listed in the *Encyclopedia Americana* and the *New Catholic Encyclopedia*[9] as "Council of Trent." The preferred name for this body will be the one found in these sources because it is an English-language form. If RDA 11.2.2.5.4 had been applied without the exception for ancient and international bodies, the preferred form would have been the conventional name in the body's own language, Latin. Instead, this form will be recorded as a variant name (see figure 5.22). Note that as in all languages that decline nouns, Latin preferred and variant names should be recorded in the nominative case only, not necessarily in the case in which they appear in the source. In this case, the Latin variant is recorded as "Concilium Tridentinum," not "Concilii Tridentini" (as the name appears on the title page).

Figure 5.22. Ancient and International Body

046	‡s 15451213 ‡t 15631204
111 2	‡a Council of Trent ‡d (1545-1563 : ‡c Trento, Italy)
368	‡a Councils and synods ‡2 lcsh
370	‡e Trento (Italy) ‡2 naf
377	‡a lat
411 2	‡a Concilium Tridentinum ‡d (1545-1563 : ‡c Trento, Italy)
410 2	‡a Catholic Church. ‡b Council of Trent ‡d (1545-1563 : ‡c Trento, Italy)
410 2	‡a Catholic Church. ‡b Concilium Tridentinum ‡d (1545-1563 : ‡c Trento, Italy)
670	‡a Acta genuina s.s. oecumenici Concilii Tridentini, 1874
670	‡a New Catholic encyclopedia, 2003 ‡b (Council of Trent; 19th ecumenical council, opened at Trent 13 December 1545, closed 4 December 1563; main object was to respond to Protestant movement and to reform the Church)

Religious Orders and Societies. The preferred name of such bodies is the conventional name ("best-known form of the name") in the language preferred by the cataloging agency if such a name exists. The Library of Congress has issued a policy statement, which should be followed by contributors to the LC/NACO Authority File, that the preferred language is English (LC-PCC PS 11.2.2.5.4, October 2012). The Redemptorists are such a body. Although they originated in Italy, the conventional English form should be chosen as the preferred name rather than a form in Italian. *Britannica Academic Edition*[10] lists them as "Redemptorists," and also as "Congregation of the Most Holy Redeemer," as well as "C. SS. R." The title page of the resource cited in figure 5.23 has a Latin form. The forms not chosen for the preferred name are recorded as variant names.

Figure 5.23. Religious Order or Society

046	‡s 1732
110 2	‡a Redemptorists
368	‡a Religious communities ‡2 lcsh
410 2	‡a Congregation of the Most Holy Redeemer
410 2	‡a C. SS. R.
410 2	‡a Congregatio SS. Redemptoris
410 2	‡a Congregatio Sanctissimi Redemptoris
670	‡a Documenta authentica facultatum et gratiarum spiritualium quas Congregationi SS. Redemptoris S. Sedes concessit, 1903
670	‡a Britannica academic edition, 21 October 2011 ‡b (Redemptorists, Congregation of the Most Holy Redeemer, C. SS. R.; community of Roman Catholic priests founded in 1732; originally in Scala, Italy, but now spread worldwide)

Governments. If the name of a government appears in varying forms, use the conventional name rather than the official name. Thus, the cataloger will use "France" rather than "République Française." A word of caution: because a government is regarded as a corporate body, if its name changes, following 11.2.2.6 the cataloger will use the name appropriate to the resource being cataloged. The practice of choosing the conventional name as the preferred name for governments will be discussed more fully in chapter 6, "Describing Geographic Entities."

Conferences, Congresses, Meetings, etc. This guideline is directed to choosing among varying names of conferences. The thrust of the guideline is to choose the more specific name if there is more than one choice. Prefer, in order:

1. A form that includes the name of a body associated with the conference
2. A form in which the conference name is entered subordinately to another body
3. A specific name for the conference rather than the general name for a series of conferences the conference may be a part of

An example of the third category is Hot Quarks, which is the specific name of the conference which was also the fourth Workshop for Young Scientists on the Physics of Ultrarelativistic Nucleus-nucleus Collisions (see figure 5.24). For more on preferred names of conferences, see the discussion below under 11.2.2.11.

Figure 5.24. Specific Name of Conference

046	‡s 20100621 ‡t 20100626
111 2	‡a Hot Quarks (Workshop) ‡d (2010 : ‡c La Londe-les-Maures, France)
368	‡a Congresses and conventions ‡2 lcsh
370	‡e La Londe les Maures (France) ‡2 naf
411 2	‡a HQ '10 ‡d (2010 : ‡c La Londe-les-Maures, France)
411 2	‡a Workshop for Young Scientists on the Physics of Ultrarelativistic Nucleus-nucleus Collisions ‡n (4th : ‡d 2010 : ‡c La Londe-les-Maures, France)
670	‡a Hot Quarks 2010, 2011, viewed on April 25, 2011 ‡b main home page (Hot Quarks 2010; HQ '10) title page of ebook (Hot Quarks 2010) preface (The 4th Workshop for Young Scientists on the Physics of Ultrarelativistic Nucleus-nucleus Collisions (Hot Quarks 2010) was held in La Londe-Les-Maures, France, from June 21-26, 2010)

Local Places of Worship. It may seem strange to treat a place of worship, normally a building, in the chapter in which RDA treats corporate bodies. This is done because frequently the name of the building is the same as the name of the body that occupies it. Record as the preferred name of the place of worship the name as it appears in preferred sources of resources associated with it. If the name varies, use the predominant form. If there is no predominant form, choose a name according to order of preference as given. Cologne Cathedral is an example of a place of worship with variant names. It is commonly known in English as Cologne Cathedral and in German as Kölner Dom; its official name is Hohe Domkirche zu Köln. Kölner Dom is the form found most frequently in resources most closely associated with the body, including its own website, and that form will be chosen as the preferred name (see figure 5.25).

Figure 5.25. Local Place of Worship

046	‡s 1248
110 2	‡a Kölner Dom
370	‡e Cologne (Germany) ‡2 naf
377	‡a ger
410 2	‡a Cologne Cathedral
410 2	‡a Hohe Domkirche zu Köln
670	‡a Steine für den Kölner Dom, 2004
670	‡a Cologne Cathedral, 1985
670	‡a Der Kölner Dom, via WWW, 21 October 2011 ‡b (Der Kölner Dom; Cologne Cathedral; Catholic place of worship; official name: Hohe Domkirche zu Köln; current Gothic cathedral begun in 1248)

For further discussion of access points for places of worship, see below under 11.13.1.2 and 11.13.1.3.

Different Names. A type of variant not found in RDA for corporate bodies is *different names* (the scope of 11.2.2.5 is different forms of the *same* name). Sometimes a body is known by different names at the same time. Often these are nicknames, but sometimes there are simply different names used for the body. For example, the St. Louis Southwestern Railway Company was also known as Southwestern Lines and as the Cotton Belt Railway Company. These are not different forms of the same name, but are different names. Although this situation is not specifically covered in RDA, we can fall back on the basic principle of representation (RDA 0.4.3.4) and choose the name most commonly found in resources associated with the corporate body as the preferred name (see figure 5.26).

Figure 5.26. Different Names

110 2	‡a St. Louis Southwestern Railway Company
368	‡a Railroad companies ‡2 lcsh
370	‡f Texas ‡f Missouri ‡f Oklahoma ‡2 naf
377	‡a eng

410	2	ǂa Saint Louis Southwestern Railway Company
410	2	ǂa Southwestern Lines
410	2	ǂa Cotton Belt Railway Company
410	2	ǂa St. Louis Southwestern Railway Company of Texas
670		ǂa Agreement between St. Louis Southwestern Railway Company and System Federation No. 45, Railway Employes' Dept., A.F. of L.-C.I.O., 1977
670		ǂa Museum of the Great Plains for Southwestern Lines tariff book, 1935 ǂb (Southwestern Lines; also called Cotton Belt Railway Company, St. Louis Southwestern Railway Company, St. Louis Southwestern Railway Company of Texas; served Texas, Missouri, Okla.)

11.2.2.6. CHANGE OF NAME. RDA takes the same position that the previous cataloging code took, that is, that a corporate body that has changed its name is a new and different entity. This is a theoretically sound position. Corporate bodies do not change their names capriciously. Normally a corporate body changes its name because it wants to pursue a new direction, or it wants a fresh image. Often name changes occur when bodies emerge from a merger as a new entity. RDA 11.2.2.6 does not really belong with RDA guidelines for choosing the preferred name of a body. The section is just reminding us that if a corporate body changes its name, the new name is to be chosen as the preferred name for use with resources associated with the new name. In other words, a new description is made for a separate entity from the one that used the previous name.

The Library of Congress and Program for Cooperative Cataloging have given helpful guidance in their policy statement to 11.2.2.6 (October 2012) regarding what constitutes a new name. If minor differences are found in the presentation of the name, including

1. representation of words, for example, abbreviations or acronyms versus spelled-out forms; changes of spelling, etc.
2. changes of prepositions, articles, or conjunctions, and/or
3. changes in punctuation

the cataloger should consider this a minor change and not a true change of name.

Remember also that a corporate body sometimes is known by more than one name at the same time (see above under 11.2.2.5.4, Different Names). This also does not constitute a name change for purposes of 11.2.2.6.

When a corporate body changes its name, create a new description (authority record) for the new body. Because the bodies are related, the previous and the new descriptions should be linked using 5XX fields. See, for example, figure 5.7, Exxon Mobil Chemical (Firm). This name was created when the parent body of Exxon

Chemical Company, Exxon, merged with Mobil. The previous body's description is linked to the new description in the MARC 21 format by recording its preferred name in a 510 field; the preferred name of the new firm will, conversely, be recorded in the description of previous firm in the same way, in a 510 field.

The relationship between the two bodies can be specified by coding or by the inclusion of a relationship designator. The 510 field in figure 5.7 uses coding. The code "a" in the first position of subfield ‡w means the name that follows is the earlier name. Code "b" in the same position means that the name that follows is the later name. This is meant to produce a public display something like the following, when a library user searches under "ExxonMobil Chemical (Firm)":

> ExxonMobil Chemical (Firm)
> *search also under the earlier name*
> Exxon Chemical Company

This coding is an older MARC practice, shown here only as an example. In current practice, the relationship designators from RDA appendix K.4.3 should be used instead. This would be coded as follows in a MARC 21 record:

> 510 2   ‡w r ‡i Predecessor: ‡a Exxon Chemical Company

This would display something like:

> ExxonMobil Chemical (Firm)
> *search also under*
> Predecessor: Exxon Chemical Company

The relationship designators in RDA appendix K allow the cataloger to bring out a much richer variety of relationships than those inherent in the MARC coding of subfield ‡w, and catalogers should use them instead of following the old coding practice (see *Descriptive Cataloging Manual* Z1 at 510).

Recording the Preferred Name—General Guidelines

Preferred names for most corporate bodies are recorded in subfields ‡a or ‡b of the 110 field of authority records with first indicator coded "2," in the form prescribed generally in RDA 11.2.2.4. The preferred name of a jurisdiction (e.g., "United States") is recorded in the 151 field when standing alone, or in the 110 field with the first indicator coded "1" when standing as the parent body of a subordinate body recorded

as a subdivision. The preferred names of most meetings or other events are recorded
in the 111 field with the first indicator coded "2." The preferred name of a meeting or event name that is recorded as a subdivision of the authorized access point
of another corporate body is recorded in subfield ‡b of the 110 field, following the
preferred name of the corporate body (see discussion of subordinate bodies, below,
under 11.2.2.13–11.2.2.29).

Most names of corporate bodies are recorded as found, in direct order. Sometimes
elements are added or removed, however, and sometimes the name of the body is
recorded subordinately to that of another body.

11.2.2.7. NAMES CONSISTING OF OR CONTAINING INITIALS. Follow the usage of the body if
it uses an initialism in its name. Include full stops if the body uses them; do not add
them if the body does not. MADD Canada and Unesco are examples (see figures 5.6
and 5.15). If the cataloger believes database users might search for the name using
full stops, a variant form with full stops may be recorded in the description.

11.2.2.8. INITIAL ARTICLES. Articles at the beginning of a corporate body's name are
included as part of the preferred name recorded in the 1XX field. However, an alternative guideline, followed by LC and PCC (LC-PCC PS 11.2.2.8, alternative, October
2012), instructs the cataloger to omit the article. This alternative stems from filing
needs but conflicts with the principle of representation (information about an entity
should appear as the entity itself presents it). All examples in this *Handbook* follow
LC-PCC practice and omit initial articles. Examples include The Kronos Quartet (figure 5.1) and The Radio Dept. (figure 5.10).

11.2.2.10. TERMS INDICATING INCORPORATION AND CERTAIN OTHER TERMS. In most instances,
adjectival terms or abbreviations indicating incorporation will be omitted from the
preferred name of a corporate body (see Guarro Casas, figure 5.3, whose full name
includes "S.A.," a Spanish term indicating incorporation).

If such a term is integral to the name or is necessary to make it clear that the name
is that of a corporate body, however, include the term (see figure 5.17, Encyclopaedia
Britannica, Inc., whose name without the term is the name of a work). If the term
indicating incorporation cannot be omitted, follow the punctuation and capitalization customarily used by the corporate body, either including or omitting the comma
preceding the term, as appropriate.

Note that the term "Company" is not an adjectival term indicating incorporation
and should not be omitted from a corporate body's name if it is present (see figure 5.26).

Omit from the names of ships prefixes such as "U.S.S." or "R.M.S." (see figure
5.27). It is not customary to record a form of the name with the prefix as a variant
name, particularly for common prefixes such as "U.S.S.," "S.S.," or "H.M.S.," but if the

cataloger feels it would be helpful to users of the database he or she may record it. In the case of figure 5.27, the cataloger recorded the variants because the prefix was somewhat unusual outside of Australia.

Figure 5.27. Omission of Ship's Prefix

046	‡s 1940
110 2	‡a Bendigo (Corvette)
368	‡a Corvette
370	‡c Australia ‡2 naf
377	‡a eng
410 2	‡a H.M.A.S. Bendigo
410 2	‡a HMAS Bendigo
670	‡a H.M.A.S. Bendigo, corvette, 1995: ‡b p. 5 (keel of HMAS Bendigo was laid down in the Cockatoo dockyards, Sydney, 1940)

11.2.2.11. NUMBER OR YEAR OF CONVOCATION OF A CONFERENCE, ETC. This guideline instructs us to manipulate the name of a meeting or event that we have already found and selected as the preferred name using the procedure described above under 11.2.2.3–11.2.2.5. The names that the cataloger found in preferred sources for the workshop illustrated in figure 5.24 were "Hot Quarks 2010" and "HQ '10." The cataloger chose the spelled-out form as the preferred name. RDA instructs us to omit the year from the name when recording it, leaving "Hot Quarks."

Previous cataloging practice omitted from the preferred name of a meeting or event words indicating frequency, in addition to the number and date. RDA does not omit words indicating frequency, so such words remain part of the preferred name of RDA corporate bodies. Take, for example, the name "100th American Library Association Annual Conference, June 1981" (figure 5.28). The number "100th" and "June 1981" (date) are omitted, leaving "American Library Association Annual Conference" (see discussion below under 11.2.2.14 for treatment of the meeting as a subordinate body). Under previous practice, "Annual" would also have been omitted (cf. AACR2 24.7A1).

Figure 5.28. Frequency of Conference Part of Preferred Name

046	‡s 198106
110 2	‡a American Library Association. ‡b Annual Conference ‡n (100th : ‡d 1981 : ‡c San Francisco, Calif.)
368	‡a Congresses and conventions ‡2 lcsh
370	‡e San Francisco (Calif.) ‡2 naf

---

373   ‡a American Library Association ‡2 naf

377   ‡a eng

670   ‡a Hearings held at the 100th American Library Association Annual Conference, June 1981, San Francisco, California, 1982

11.2.2.12. NAMES FOUND IN A NON-PREFERRED SCRIPT. In this guideline, we are instructed to use a transliteration scheme chosen by our cataloging agency if we need to transliterate a name written in a script not used by the agency. Libraries contributing to the LC/NACO Authority File will use the ALA-LC Romanization Tables discussed above under 8.4. This guideline applies to authorized access points only if the agency is applying the alternative in RDA 8.4. The basic RDA guideline is to record names in the language and script in which they appear on the source, but the alternative allows a transliterated form to be recorded as a substitute for the form appearing on the source. See the discussion above under 8.4 with figure 5.4b.

RDA has an alternative to 11.2.2.12 under which if, in addition to a vernacular script form, a transliterated form is also found on the source, that form may be chosen as the preferred name rather than a form systematically transliterated following the agency's adopted transliteration table. Under the LC-PCC policy this alternative is not applied (LC-PCC PS 11.2.2.12, alternative, October 2012). However, if the found transliterated form differs significantly from the systematically transliterated form, the found form may be recorded in the description as a variant name.

Recording the Preferred Name—Subordinate Bodies

In many respects the guidelines governing corporate bodies are analogous to those for personal authors. But in one important respect corporate bodies are unlike personal authors: corporate bodies may have subdivisions, units subordinate or related in some way to the parent body. When dealing with a subordinate body, one of two options is open to the cataloger:

1. If the subordinate body has a distinctive name that is sufficient to identify it in the database, its preferred name will generally be recorded according to the basic instructions discussed above (usually just as it is found) (RDA 11.2.2.13).
2. If the name of the subordinate body or its type falls into one of the categories discussed below, the subordinate body's preferred name will be formed as a subdivision of the authorized access point representing the body to which it is subordinate (RDA 11.2.2.14, 11.2.2.18–11.2.2.29).

In a simplification from previous cataloging codes, which treated subordinate bodies differently depending on whether they were government or nongovernment bodies, the general guidelines of RDA 11.2.2.13–11.2.2.15 cover most subordinate bodies. However, some guidelines covering special cases remain, in RDA 11.2.2.16–11.2.2.29.

11.2.2.13. GENERAL GUIDELINES ON RECORDING NAMES OF SUBORDINATE AND RELATED BODIES. This guideline is actually only a restatement of the general guideline for choosing and recording preferred names for all corporate bodies (11.2.2.3–11.2.2.4). If a subordinate body has a distinctive, self-sufficient name that is consistently used in resources associated with it, record it directly under that name. The Student Society for Ancient Studies, at Brigham Young University, has such a name (see figure 5.29). Note in this case the parenthetical qualifier, made under the provisions of 11.13.1.4 optional addition (see discussion below). The qualifier is not a part of the preferred name, but an addition to the preferred name.

Figure 5.29. Preferred Name of Subordinate Body

110 2	‡a Student Society for Ancient Studies (Brigham Young University)
370	‡e Provo (Utah) ‡2 naf
373	‡a Brigham Young University ‡2 naf
377	‡a eng
410 2	‡a Brigham Young University. ‡b Student Society for Ancient Studies
670	‡a Studia antiqua (Provo, Utah), fall 2001: ‡b title page (Student Society for Ancient Studies, Brigham Young University)

If the preferred name of a subordinate body is recorded directly under its own name, 11.2.2.13 instructs us to record as a variant the name of the body as a subdivision of the authorized access point of the parent organization; in the case of figure 5.29, a display generated from the second 410 field might appear:

> Brigham Young University. Student Society for Ancient Studies
> *search under*
> Student Society for Ancient Studies (Brigham Young University)

Note that recording of variant names in RDA descriptions of corporate bodies is not core (i.e., not required) even though the last paragraph of 11.2.2.13 is stated as an instruction. The cataloger should record the variant name if according to his or her judgment the variant would be helpful to the user of the database. Because database users do not know the RDA guidelines for subordinate bodies and therefore might conclude that a subordinate body's name is always recorded following the name of its parent body, in this case the variant form is clearly helpful and should be recorded.

11.2.2.14. SUBORDINATE AND RELATED BODIES RECORDED SUBORDINATELY. This guideline enumerates eighteen types of subordinate bodies that are to be recorded as subdivisions of the authorized access point of the higher body. These types have their origin in the 2009 *Statement of International Cataloguing Principles* 6.3.4.3.2, which calls for recording the name of a corporate body following that of a higher body "when the corporate name implies subordination, or subordinate function, or is insufficient to identify the subordinate body."[11]

If the name of the subordinate body is to be recorded as a subdivision of the authorized access point of the higher body under the stipulations of RDA 11.2.2.14, and it includes the name of the higher body (including abbreviations of the name), omit the name of the higher body from the subdivision unless the result would not make sense.

The name of the parent body is recorded in subfield ‡a of the 110 field exactly as found in its own description (authority record); the name of the subordinate body is recorded in subfield ‡b.

11.2.2.14.1. BODY WHOSE NAME IMPLIES IT IS PART OF ANOTHER (TYPE 1). A subordinate body whose name includes a word such as "department," "division," or some other word implying that the body is a component part of something else will be recorded as a subdivision of the authorized access point of the higher body. Do not repeat the name of the higher body or any words that link the lower to the higher body.

Figure 5.30 is a description of a Type 1 body, a subordinate body whose name contains the word "department." The State of Virginia's Department of Historic Resources is another example (see figure 5.31).

Figure 5.30. Subordinate Body—Type 1

110 2	‡a American Museum of Natural History. ‡b Department of Library Services
368	‡a Libraries ‡2 lcsh
373	‡a American Museum of Natural History ‡2 naf
377	‡a eng
670	‡a Catalog of the American Museum of Natural History film archives, 1987: ‡b title page (Department of Library Services)

Figure 5.31. Subordinate Body—Type 1

110 1	‡a Virginia. ‡b Department of Historic Resources
370	‡e Richmond (Va.) ‡2 naf

377	‡a eng
670	‡a An archaeological reconnaissance survey of Craig County, 1991: ‡b title page (Virginia Department of Historic Resources, Richmond)

Previous cataloging policy in North America abbreviated the word "Department" in access points for corporate bodies, but this is no longer the case under RDA. Do not abbreviate the word unless it is abbreviated in presentations of the name in resources associated with the body.

11.2.2.14.2. BODY WHOSE NAME IMPLIES ADMINISTRATIVE SUBORDINATION (TYPE 2). If the name of a body is worded in such a fashion that it implies administrative subordination to a higher body, its name will be recorded as a subdivision of the authorized access point of the higher body, so long as the name of the higher body is needed to identify the subordinate (for an example, see figure 5.32). A good rule of thumb for a decision about whether or not the name of the higher body is required for the identification of the subordinate body is if the name of the commission, committee, etc., is made up simply of generic words signifying its function or if it has a distinctive name. The Commission on Obscenity and Pornography (figure 5.33) needs the name of the higher body for identification.

Figure 5.32. Subordinate Body—Type 2

110 2	‡a Chartered Institute of Environmental Health. ‡b National Pest Advisory Panel
373	‡a Chartered Institute of Environmental Health ‡2 naf
377	‡a eng
410 2	‡a NPAP
410 2	‡a National Pest Advisory Panel
670	‡a Pest minimisation, 2009: ‡b back cover (National Pest Advisory Panel, Chartered Institute of Environmental Health; NPAP)

Figure 5.33. Subordinate Body—Type 2

046	‡s 1969 ‡t 1970
110 1	‡a United States. ‡b Commission on Obscenity and Pornography
368	‡a Government investigations ‡2 lcsh
377	‡a eng
410 2	‡a Commission on Obscenity and Pornography
670	‡a The report of the Commission on Obscenity and Pornography, 1970
670	‡a Wikipedia, 18 May 2012 ‡b (President's Commission on Obscenity and Pornography; organized in 1969, published its report in 1970)

The Library of Congress has issued a supplementary list of words in English, French, and Spanish that normally imply administrative subordination, in addition to "committee" and "commission" as given under RDA 11.2.2.14.2. If a subordinate body's name includes one of the words on the following lists, it is probably a "Type 2" body (LC-PCC PS 11.2.2.14.2, May 2013).

English

administration	board	office
administrative . . . (e.g.,	bureau	panel
administrative office)	directorate	secretariat
advisory . . . (e.g.,	executive	service
advisory panel)	. . . group (e.g., work	task force
agency	group)	working party
authority	inspectorate	

French

administration	commissariat	inspection
agence	commission	mission
bureau	délégation	office
cabinet	direction	secrétariat
comité	groupe de . . .	service

Spanish

administración	delegación	jefatura
agencia	diputación	junta
asesoría	dirección	negociado
comisaría	directoria	oficina
comisión	fiscalía	secretaría
comité	gabinete	secretariado
consejería	gerencia	servicio
coordinación	grupo de . . .	superintendencia

These are not closed lists. There may be other words in English, French, or Spanish that "normally imply administrative subordination." This will require the cataloger's judgment.

11.2.2.14.3. BODY WHOSE NAME IS GENERAL IN NATURE OR MERELY INDICATES A GEOGRAPHIC, CHRONOLOGICAL, OR NUMBERED OR LETTERED SUBDIVISION OF A PARENT BODY (TYPE 3). Some subordinate or related bodies have names so general that the name of a higher body is needed for identification. Often such bodies do no more than indicate a geographic, chronological, or numbered or lettered subdivision of a higher body. "Friends of the Libraries" is an example (see figure 5.34). Record the preferred name of such a body as a subdivision of the authorized access point for the higher body. On the other hand, when this body changed its name to "Friends of the USC Libraries," the new name became distinctive enough that it is recorded directly, not subordinately (see the 510 field for the later name in figure 5.34).

Figure 5.34. Subordinate Body—Type 3

110 2	‡a University of Southern California. ‡b Friends of the Libraries
373	‡a University of Southern California ‡2 naf
377	‡a eng
510 2	‡w r ‡i Successor: ‡a Friends of the USC Libraries
670	‡a Coranto, 1963- : ‡b volume 1, no. 1 title page (Friends of the Libraries, University of Southern California)
675	‡a Remebering Noel Coward, 1981: title page (Friends of the USC Libraries)

Names such as "Research Center," "Library," or "Technical Laboratory" are also examples of general names that should be recorded as a subdivision of the authorized access point for the higher body. See figure 5.35 for an example. Figure 5.35 actually involves two such bodies—the library, a "Type 3" body is subordinate to another "Type 3" body, the North Western Regional Office.

Figure 5.35. Subordinate Body—Type 3

110 1	‡a Great Britain. ‡b Department of Industry. ‡b North Western Regional Office. ‡b Library
368	‡a Libraries ‡2 lcsh
377	‡a eng
670	‡a Statistics: a guide to sources available in the North West Regional Office Library, 1977: ‡b title page (within the Department of Industry)

11.2.2.14.4. BODY WHOSE NAME DOES NOT CONVEY THE IDEA OF A CORPORATE BODY AND DOES NOT CONTAIN THE NAME OF THE HIGHER BODY (TYPE 4). Occasionally the name of a subordinate unit does not suggest the idea that it is a corporate body at all. Referring to the examples in RDA, "Science, Technology, and Business" and "Economics and Research" sound like concepts or processes rather than names of organized units of an institution or corporation. Their preferred names will be recorded as subdivisions following the authorized access point of the higher body to which they belong. Figure 5.36, a description of a subordinate body that calls itself "Corporate Grants," is an example. This name sounds like a set of gifts given by a corporation, not the name of a corporate body. In figure 5.37 the name of the body, "Strategic Planning" sounds more like a description of a process than the name of a corporate body.

Figure 5.36. Subordinate Body—Type 4

110 2	‡a Apple Computer, Inc. ‡b Corporate Grants
370	‡e Cupertino (Calif.) ‡2 naf
373	‡a Apple Computer, Inc. ‡2 naf
377	‡a eng
410 2	‡a Apple Corporate Grants
670	‡a The way we give, 1984-1985: ‡b page 1, etc. (Corporate Grants; Apple Corporate Grants; the Apple Computer department which administers the company's giving programs, located in Cupertino, Calif.)

Figure 5.37. Subordinate Body—Type 4

110 1	‡a Western Australia. ‡b Main Roads Department. ‡b Strategic Planning
377	‡a eng
670	‡a Culway report, 1991: ‡b cover (Strategic Planning, Main Roads Department, WA)

11.2.2.14.5. UNIVERSITY FACULTY, SCHOOL, COLLEGE, INSTITUTE, LABORATORY, ETC., WHOSE NAME SIMPLY INDICATES A PARTICULAR FIELD OF STUDY (TYPE 5). As with the names covered by Type 3, those covered by Type 5 would be incomplete, ambiguous, or insufficient to identify the subordinate unit if they were recorded independently of the parent body. Type 5 is limited to names of higher education bodies that simply are descriptive of the field of study (see figure 5.38).

Figure 5.38. Subordinate Body—Type 5

110 2	‡a Brigham Young University--Hawaii Campus. ‡b Institute for Polynesian Studies
370	‡e Laie (Hawaii) ‡2 naf
373	‡a Brigham Young University--Hawaii Campus ‡2 naf
377	‡a eng
410 2	‡a Institute for Polynesian Studies
670	‡a Islands, plants and Polynesians, 1991: ‡b title page (Institute of Polynesian Studies, Brigham Young University--Hawaii Campus, Laie, Hawaii)

11.2.2.14.6. NONGOVERNMENTAL BODY WHOSE NAME INCLUDES THE ENTIRE NAME OF THE HIGHER OR RELATED BODY (TYPE 6). Caution: "Type 6" only applies to nongovernment bodies. If the subordinate body's name as it appears in resources associated with it includes the *entire* name of the higher body, it will be recorded as a subdivision of the authorized access point of the higher body. The "entire name of the higher body" means its preferred name, *excluding* additions made by the cataloger, such as qualifiers, etc. (see LC-PCC PS 11.2.2.14.6, May 2013). The name of the higher body is not repeated as part of the subdivision: "University of Michigan. Library," not "University of Michigan. University of Michigan Library" (see figure 5.39).

Figure 5.39. Subordinate Body—Type 6

110 2	‡a University of Michigan. ‡b Library
368	‡a Libraries ‡2 lcsh
370	‡e Ann Arbor (Mich.) ‡2 naf
371	‡a 818 Hatcher South ‡b Ann Arbor ‡c Michigan ‡e 48109-1190
373	‡a University of Michigan ‡2 naf
377	‡a eng
410 2	‡a MLibrary
410 2	‡a University of Michigan. ‡b MLibrary
670	‡a Collection analysis project, 1983: ‡b volume 1, title page (University of Michigan Library)
670	‡a MLibrary [University of Michigan Library website], 24 October 2011 ‡b (MLibrary, University of Michigan Library, 818 Hatcher South, Ann Arbor, Michigan 48109-1190)

In contrast, the government body that calls itself the Ontario Geological Survey is also an example of a name that includes the full name of the its higher body, "Ontario." Remember, however, that 11.2.2.14.6 does not apply to government bodies, so although the body's name includes "Ontario," its preferred name is not recorded as a subdivision of the authorized access point for the government (see figure 5.40).

Figure 5.40.
Subordinate Government Body Recorded Directly Under Its Own Name

110 2	‡a Ontario Geological Survey
368	‡a Geological surveys ‡2 lcsh
410 1	‡a Ontario. ‡b Geological Survey
410 1	‡a Ontario. ‡b Division of Mines. ‡b Geological Survey
410 2	‡a OGS
670	‡a The Geology and ore deposits of the Sudbury structure, 1984: ‡b title page (Ontario Geological Survey) spine (OGS)

Note two of the examples under RDA 11.2.2.13, the guideline for recording a subordinate body directly under its own name. "BBC Symphony Orchestra" is not a name that includes the entire name of the body ("British Broadcasting Corporation" is its preferred name, not "BBC") and therefore does not fall under Type 6. See also the example "Harvard Law School." As with BBC, the name of the Law School does not include the *entire* name of the higher body ("Harvard University"). Therefore, these subordinate bodies are recorded directly under their own names; a variant form is recorded, however, from the name of the higher body with the lower body entered subordinately. For further guidance on the meaning of "entire name," see LC-PCC PS 11.2.2.14.6 (October 2012).

11.2.2.14.7. MINISTRY OR SIMILAR MAJOR EXECUTIVE AGENCY (TYPE 7). The preferred name of a top-level executive agency in a government will be recorded as a subdivision of the authorized access point for the government, regardless of whether its name includes words such as "department," "ministry," "administration," or not. However, names of most such agencies do include such terms; in most cases, these agencies are also examples of 11.2.2.14.1 (Type 1), having names that imply that the body is a part of another. The Alberta Ministry of Energy is an example of a Type 7 subordinate body (figure 5.41).

Figure 5.41. Subordinate Body—Type 7

110 1	‡a Alberta. ‡b Ministry of Energy
368	‡a Executive departments ‡2 lcsh
377	‡a eng
670	‡a Energy : annual report, 2009-2010: ‡b cover page 4 (Ministry of Energy) page 3 (this annual report of the Ministry of Energy contains the Minister's accountability statement)

11.2.2.14.8. GOVERNMENT OFFICIAL OR A RELIGIOUS OFFICIAL (TYPE 8). See discussion below under 11.2.2.18 and 11.2.2.25–11.2.2.29.

11.2.2.14.9. LEGISLATIVE BODY (TYPE 9). The names of legislative bodies are recoded subordinately to their government. The Conseil de Paris is such a body (see figure 5.42). Note here the application of the general guideline introducing 11.2.2.14: the name of the government (here, the phrase "de Paris") is omitted. See also the discussion of RDA 11.2.2.19, legislative bodies, below.

Figure 5.42. Subordinate Government Body—Type 9

110 1	‡a Paris (France). ‡b Conseil
368	‡a Legislative bodies ‡2 lcsh
377	‡a fre
410 2	‡a Conseil de Paris
670	‡a Mémoire de M. le préfet de Paris au Conseil de Paris, 1971
670	‡a Wikipedia.fr, 13 January 2012 ‡b (Conseil de Paris, deliberative assembly composed of the Mayor of Paris, who presides, and 163 counselors)

11.2.2.14.11. COURT (TYPE 11). The names of courts are recorded subordinately to their jurisdiction. See discussion at 11.2.2.21, below.

11.2.2.14.14. DELEGATION TO AN INTERNATIONAL OR INTERGOVERNMENTAL BODY (TYPE 11). Delegations to international bodies are discussed below under 11.2.2.24.

11.2.2.15. DIRECT OR INDIRECT SUBDIVISION. Sometimes a subordinate corporate body that is to be recorded under 11.2.2.14 as a subdivision of a higher body is part of a whole chain or hierarchy of bodies, each dependent on the one above it. Recording the preferred name of the lowest link of the chain, the most subordinate of the subordinate units, can present problems. Sometimes it is necessary to give the entire hierarchy, as in the "Bibliography and Indexes Committee" example under 11.2.2.15 in RDA (the first example after "but"). This is known as "indirect subdivision." In the example, each of the elements in the hierarchy depends directly on the one above it: "Bibliography and Indexes Committee" is a Type 1 name, "History Section" is a Type 3 name, "Resources and Technical Services Division" is a Type 1 name. The committee's name is meaningless without the name of the section to which it is attached, and the section's name is meaningless without the name of the division; the division has a name that implies subordination and so it must be attached to that of the parent organization, American Library Association.

But as the above example demonstrates, such a practice often results in a very long authorized access point. More important, over the years the intervening bodies between the first and last link of the hierarchy may change, or control of the subordinate agency may be shifted from one higher body to another. When this happens, if all of the links in the hierarchy have been included in the authorized access point, the authorized access point for the subordinate body may need to be changed. Such a change often means extensive recataloging. RDA 11.2.2.15 offers a good solution to the problem. Record the subordinate body's name as a subdivision of the first larger body that can be recorded directly under its own name. Leave out the intermediate units as long as the name of the subordinate body has not been, or is unlikely to be, used by another body within the organization. If all intermediate units are omitted, this is known as "direct subdivision." Figure 5.43 is a good example of this practice. The hierarchy for this body is:

> American Library Association
> Association for Library Collections & Technical Services
> Cataloging and Classification Section
> Committee on Cataloging: Description and Access
> Interactive Multimedia Guidelines Review Task Force

Figure 5.43. Direct Subdivision

110 2	‡a Association for Library Collections & Technical Services. ‡b Interactive Multimedia Guidelines Review Task Force
373	‡a Association for Library Collections & Technical Services. Committee on Cataloging: Description and Access ‡2 naf
377	‡a eng
410 2	‡a Association for Library Collections & Technical Services. ‡b Committee on Cataloging: Description and Access. ‡b Interactive Multimedia Guidelines Review Task Force
670	‡a Guidelines for bibliographic description of interactive multimedia, 1994: ‡b title page (The Interactive Multimedia Guidelines Review Task Force; Committee on Cataloging: Description and Access, Cataloging and Classification Section, Association for Library Collections & Technical Services)

The lowest element of this hierarchy that is recorded directly under its own name is "Association for Library Collections & Technical Services," so that is where the preferred name for the subordinate body begins. All the bodies below it fall under one of the types of RDA 11.2.2.14. The name "Interactive Multimedia Guidelines Review Task Force" is not likely to be used by any other body that is subordinate to the Association for Library Collections & Technical Services. Therefore, the preferred name will be "Association for Library Collections & Technical Services. Interactive Multimedia Guidelines Review Task Force."

The subordinate body illustrated in figure 5.37 calls itself "Strategic Planning." It is likely that many bodies within the government of Western Australia will, at one point or another, have a subordinate body with this name or a similar name because this is a common activity. Following the instructions in 11.2.2.15, the lowest unit in the hierarchy that will distinguish between the bodies is interposed, "Main Roads Department." For a similar example, see figure 5.35.

The subordinate body illustrated in figure 5.44 exists within the following hierarchy:

New Zealand
Ministry of Agriculture and Fisheries
MAF Biosecurity Authority
Animal Biosecurity

Figure 5.44. Direct Subdivision

110 1	ǂa New Zealand. ǂb Animal Biosecurity
377	ǂa eng
410 1	ǂa New Zealand. ǂb MAF Biosecurity Authority. ǂb Animal Biosecurity
670	ǂa Biosecurity, August 1, 1999 ǂb title page (MAF Biosecurity Authority) page 3 (Animal Biosecurity comprises the animal health component of the former MAF Regulatory Authority Animal Health and Welfare Group)

The subordinate body's name, "Animal Biosecurity" (which incidentally is a good example of a Type 4 name), is extremely unlikely to be used by any other agency within the New Zealand government. Therefore its preferred name is recorded directly as a subdivision of New Zealand, omitting the two intervening levels of hierarchy. The variant name recorded in the 410 field of figure 5.44 follows the instruction in the last sentence of 11.2.2.15.

If the cataloger has omitted some of the connecting links in a hierarchy in recording a preferred name, the final paragraph of 11.2.2.15 ("Variant names . . .") hints that a variant name may be recorded that includes at least the immediately superior body. Although 11.2.2.15 is a sensible guideline, the user of the catalog cannot be expected to know which intermediate bodies have been dropped, and so help may be given in the form of a variant access point based on the variant name. Although variant name is not a core element in RDA and therefore not required, this variant seems particularly helpful to the user who is trying to navigate the often complex world of subordinate corporate bodies in the database. The description for the Interactive Multimedia Guidelines Review Task Force (figure 5.43) should contain a variant access point including the immediately superior body in a 410 field, as shown. It may display:

> Association for Library Collections & Technical Services. Committee on Cataloging: Description and Access. Interactive Multimedia Guidelines Review Task Force
> > *search under*
> > > Association for Library Collections & Technical Services. Interactive Multimedia Guidelines Review Task Force

11.2.2.16. JOINT COMMITTEES, COMMISSIONS, ETC. The preferred name for a joint committee will be recorded directly under its own name if it is made up of representatives of two or more *separate, independent* corporate bodies. A joint committee sponsored the publication in the example shown in figure 5.45.

Figure 5.45. Joint Committee

110 2	‡a Joint Committee of the American Library Association and the National Education Association
373	‡a American Library Association ‡a National Education Association of the United States ‡2 naf
377	‡a eng
410 2	‡a American Library Association. ‡b Joint Committee of the American Library Association and the National Education Association
410 2	‡a National Education Association of the United States. ‡b Joint Committee of the American Library Association and the National Education Association
670	‡a By way of introduction : a book list for young people, 1938: ‡b title page (Joint Committee of the American Library Association and the National Education Association)

Variant names may be recorded for each of the corporate bodies involved in the joint committee, with the name of the joint committee as subdivision. The message generated from the first 410 field of the description shown in figure 5.45 may display:

> American Library Association. Joint Committee of the American Library Association and the National Education Association
> > *search under*
> > Joint Committee of the American Library Association and the National Education Association

A similar message may display from a variant access point beginning with National Education Association.

If the bodies making up a joint committee are themselves subordinate to a single larger body, the preferred name of the joint committee will be recorded as a subdivision of the authorized access point for the larger body. For example, the many joint committees within the American Library Association are recorded as subdivisions of "American Library Association." See also the last example in RDA 11.2.2.16.

11.2.2.18. GOVERNMENT OFFICIALS. It may seem odd to consider a government official as a corporate body, but the authorized access point for this type of corporate body is used to identify the creator of official communications or proclamations that come out over the signature of a government official but represent the position of the government (see RDA 19.2.1.1.2 and 6.31). The corporate body entity for a government official is a separate entity from the person entity (the individual holding the office), so in addition to the official's description as a corporate body, he or she will also have a separate description as a person, recorded as described in RDA chapters 8 and 9 (see chapter 3 of this *Handbook*), and the two descriptions will be linked by recording relationship information (see RDA chapters 30 and 32, with chapter 29). This is currently accomplished in MARC authority records by recording the related entity in a 5XX field. The relationship information recorded in figure 5.46 might appear to the user of the database as follows:

> Reagan, Ronald
> > *search also under*
> > Incumbent of: United States. President (1981-1989 : Reagan)
> > Incumbent of: California. Governor (1967-1975 : Reagan)

and

> California. Governor (1967-1975 : Reagan)
> > *search also under*
> > Incumbent: Reagan, Ronald

Figure 5.46a. Governor

046	‡s 1967 ‡t 1975
110 1	‡a California. ‡b Governor (1967-1975 : Reagan)
368	‡a Heads of state ‡2 lcsh
370	‡f California ‡2 naf
377	‡a eng
500 1	‡w r ‡i Incumbent: ‡a Reagan, Ronald
667	‡a SUBJECT USAGE: This heading is not valid for use as a subject. Works about this person are entered under Reagan, Ronald.
670	‡a California's blueprint for national welfare reform, 1974: ‡b title page (Governor Ronald Reagan)
	‡a Britannica academic edition online, 23 February 2012 ‡b (Ronald Reagan, governor of California from 1967-1975)

Figure 5.46b. Description of the Individual

046	‡f 19110206 ‡g 20040605
100 1	‡a Reagan, Ronald
370	‡a Tampico (Ill.) ‡b Bel Air (Los Angeles, Calif.) ‡2 naf
374	‡a Actors ‡a Politicians ‡a Heads of state ‡2 lcsh

375	ǂa male
377	ǂa eng
378	ǂq Ronald Wilson
510 1	ǂw r ǂa Incumbent of: ǂa United States. ǂb President (1981-1989 : Reagan)
510 1	ǂw r ǂa Incumbent of: ǂa California. ǂb Governor (1967-1975 : Reagan)
670	ǂa The official Ronald Wilson Reagan quote book, 1980
670	ǂa Britannica academic edition online, 23 February 2012 ǂb (Ronald W. Reagan, in full Ronald Wilson Reagan; born Feb. 6, 1911, Tampico, Ill.; died June 5, 2004, Bel Air, Los Angeles, Calif.; film actor, 40th president of the United States (1981-1989), governor of California (1967-1975))
678 0	ǂa Ronald Reagan (1911-2004) was an American politician and actor. He served as president of the United States (1981-1989) and governor of California (1967-1975)

11.2.2.18.1 HEADS OF STATE, HEADS OF GOVERNMENT, ETC. This guideline includes heads of state (governors as well as sovereigns and presidents) and heads of government (prime ministers, etc.). The preferred name begins with the authorized access point for the jurisdiction (MARC 110 field, subfield ǂa) followed by the official's title (after a full stop, in subfield ǂb) in the language preferred by the cataloging agency, English for most North American catalogers. In cases where the title varies with the gender of the incumbent (e.g., King versus Queen), a general term should be used if available (e.g., Sovereign). Otherwise the choice of term is left up to the judgment of the cataloger. In practice, however, if a series of corporate body names of this type has already been created in the authority file, the cataloger should choose for the title the term that has been used for other incumbents of the office.

The preferred name as formed without qualification represents all incumbents of the office as a group. If a specific incumbent needs to be identified we are instructed to add to the preferred name, in parentheses, the years of incumbency and, after space-colon-space, a brief form of the incumbent's name, which may be a surname or another form of the name. Figure 5.46a shows the preferred name of Ronald Reagan in his official capacity of Governor of California. It also shows how to record the relationship information between the corporate body and person entities for this individual using a MARC 500 field. Consider carefully the cataloguer's note element recorded in the 667 field of this description (see discussion above under 8.13). Authorized access points for government officials as corporate bodies are not used as subject access points under LC subject policy, and so all descriptions of this type will include this note.

Figure 5.46b illustrates the description of Ronald Reagan as a person entity. Note that because Reagan was a government official on two separate occasions, the person description is linked to two different corporate body descriptions as shown in the MARC 510 fields.

It is possible for an office to have more than one incumbent simultaneously. If this is the case, two names will be added to the end of the preferred name. The joint sovereignship of William and Mary is an example (see figure 5.47).

Figure 5.47. Joint Incumbents

046	‡s 1689 ‡t 1694
110 1	‡a England and Wales. ‡b Sovereign (1689-1694 : William and Mary)
368	‡a Heads of state ‡2 lcsh
370	‡c England and Wales ‡2 naf
377	‡a eng
500 0	‡w r ‡i Incumbent: ‡a William ‡b III, ‡c King of England, ‡d 1650-1702
500 0	‡w r ‡i Incumbent: ‡a Mary ‡b II, ‡c Queen of England, ‡d 1662-1694
667	‡a SUBJECT USAGE: This heading is not valid for use as a subject. Works about these persons are entered under William III, King of England, 1650-1702; Mary II, Queen of England, 1662-1694.
670	‡a By the King and Queen, a declaration requiring all officers and soldiers to observe strict discipline, and for payment of quarters, 1691
670	‡a Oxford dictionary of national biography, 4 October 2011 ‡b (William and Mary reigned over England and Wales from 1689-1694)

Heads of governments are recorded in the same way as heads of state. This includes the case of nations where the head of government is different from the head of state (see figure 5.48), and also heads of other governments such a states, provinces, and cities (see figure 5.49).

Figure 5.48. Head of Government

046	‡s 20070517 ‡t 20120516
110 1	‡a France. ‡b Prime Minister (2007-2012 : Fillon)
368	‡a Head of government
368	‡a Prime ministers ‡2 lcsh
370	‡c France ‡2 naf
377	‡a fre
500 1	‡w r ‡i Incumbent: ‡a Fillon, François
667	‡a SUBJECT USAGE: This heading is not valid for use as a subject. Works about this person are entered under Fillon, François.

670 ‡a Rapport sur l'évolution de l'économie nationale et sur les orientations des finances publiques présenté [devant l'Assemblée nationale] au nom de M. François Fillon, Premier ministre, 2009

670 ‡a Premier ministre, portail du gouvernement, 19 May 2012 ‡b (François Fillon, b. 4 March 1954 in Le Mans (Sarthe); prime minister since 2007)

670 ‡a Wikipedia, 21 November 2012 ‡b (François Fillon; François Charles Armand Fillon; born 4 March 1954; Prime Minister of France from 17 May 2007 to 16 May 2012)

Figure 5.49. Mayor

046 ‡s 19510507 ‡t 19550502

110 1 ‡a Tucson (Ariz.). ‡b Mayor (1951-1955 : Emery)

368 ‡a Mayors ‡2 lcsh

370 ‡f Tucson (Ariz.) ‡2 naf

377 ‡a eng

500 1 ‡w r‡i Incumbent: ‡a Emery, Fred, ‡c Jr., ‡d 1906-1983

667 ‡a SUBJECT USAGE: This heading is not valid for use as a subject. Works about this person are entered under Emery, Fred, Jr., 1906-1983.

670 ‡a A city in action, 1951 to 1955, 1955: ‡b (City of Tucson, Office of the Mayor) preface (Fred Emery, Mayor)

670 ‡a Tucson city mayors and council members, via WWW, 6 June 2011 ‡b (Fred Artemas Emery, Jr., mayor May 7, 1951-May 2, 1955)

670 ‡a New York times obituary, 26 October 1983 ‡b (Fred Emery, Jr., died Friday [21 October 1983] at age 77; mayor of Tucson 1951-1955)

670 ‡a Social Security death index, 26 October 2011 ‡b (b. 17 Jan 1906; d. Oct. 1983; residence at death: Tucson, Arizona)

Previous to April 2012, the preferred name of a head of government was formed slightly differently from that of a head of state: the title of a head of government was recorded in the official language of the jurisdiction. As of the April 2012 revision of RDA, the preferred name of a head of government is formed in exactly the same way as that of a head of state: the title is recorded in the language preferred by the cataloging agency (English for libraries following LC-PCC policy). In figure 5.48, the title is recorded in English. Under previous practice the authorized access point would have been formed:

France. Premier ministre (2007-2012 : Fillon)

As with heads of state, the relationship between the head of government as corporate body and the incumbent as person is recorded using MARC 5XX.

11.2.2.18.5. OTHER OFFICIALS. The preferred corporate name for an official who is not head of a jurisdiction of the types listed in 11.2.2.18.1–11.2.2.18.4 is the preferred name for the agency he or she represents. In other words, preferred corporate names for officials below the head of jurisdiction level do not include dates and names of incumbents. In figure 5.9, for example, the work cited in the first 670 field, a report by the Secretary of State, is for purposes of RDA considered to be created by the Department of State, which also serves as the preferred name for the Secretary of State. Because users of the database probably do not know this distinction between different types of government officials, it is helpful to record a variant name for the office of Secretary of State formed in the same way as government officials in 11.2.2.18.1–11.2.2.18.4 (see the second 410 field of figure 5.9). This may display to the user as follows:

> United States. Secretary of State
> *search under*
> United States. Department of State

11.2.2.19. LEGISLATIVE BODIES. The preferred name of a legislative body is recorded as a subdivision of the authorized access point of the jurisdiction for which it legislates. For example:

> 110 1   ‡a United States. ‡b Congress

If the legislature has more than one chamber, the preferred name of the chamber is recorded as a subdivision of the authorized access point for the legislature:

> 110 1   ‡a United States. ‡b Congress. ‡b Senate

As with any other name, the preferred name for a chamber of the legislature is based on the most common form found in resources associated with the body. However, the preferred name for the U.S. House of Representatives, by Library of Congress policy, will continue to use the conventional name "House" rather than "House of Representatives" (LC-PCC PS 11.2.2.19.1, May 2013). See figure 5.50.

Figure 5.50. Legislative Body

046	‡s 1789
110 1	‡a United States. ‡b Congress. ‡b House
368	‡a Legislative bodies ‡2 lcsh
370	‡c United States ‡e Washington (D.C.) ‡2 naf
377	‡a eng
410 1	‡a United States. ‡b House

410 1   ‡a United States. ‡b House of Representatives

670   ‡a Final report of the Select Subcommittee to Investigate the United States Role in Iranian Arms Transfers to Croatia and Bosnia, 1997: ‡b title page (U.S. House of Representatives)

670   ‡a United States House of Representatives, via WWW, 11 October 2011 ‡b (the House assembled for the first time in New York in 1789, then in Philadelphia in 1790, then in Washington, D.C. in 1800)

11.2.2.19.2. LEGISLATIVE COMMITTEES AND SUBORDINATE UNITS. This guideline applies to subordinate units of all legislative bodies except U.S. legislative bodies (for which, see 11.2.2.19.2 exception). The preferred name of a legislative committee or other subordinate unit is recorded as a subdivision of the authorized access point for the legislature or chamber (see figure 5.51).

Figure 5.51. Non-U.S. Subcommittee

110 1   ‡a Canada. ‡b Parliament. ‡b House of Commons. ‡b Sub-Committee on Human Rights and International Development

370   ‡c Canada ‡2 naf

377   ‡a eng ‡a fre

410 1   ‡a Canada. ‡b Parliament. ‡b House of Commons. ‡b Standing Committee on Foreign Affairs and International Trade. ‡b Sub-Committee on Human Rights and International Development

410 1   ‡a Canada. ‡b Parliament. ‡b House of Commons. ‡b Sous-comité des droits de la personne et du développement international

670   ‡a Conflict, Human rights and Democracy in Colombia: a Canadian agenda, 2002: ‡b title page (House of Commons, Canada, Standing Committee on Foreign Affairs and International Trade, Sub-Committee on Human Rights and International Development)

670   ‡a Conflit, droits de la personne et démocratie en Colombie: un programme d'action canadien, 2002: ‡b title page (Chambre des Communes, Canada, Comité permanent des affaires érangères et du commerce international, Sous-comité des droits de la personne et du développement international)

11.2.2.19.2 *EXCEPTION*. LEGISLATIVE SUBCOMMITTEES OF THE UNITED STATES CONGRESS. Legislative subcommittees of the U.S. Congress (and, under LC policy, subcommittees of U.S. state legislatures as well as other legislative subordinate bodies, LC-PCC PS 11.2.2.19.2 exception, May 2013) are treated differently from such bodies in other countries, whose preferred names are recorded directly as a subdivision of the authorized access point for the legislature or chamber under the general provisions of 11.2.2.19.2. The preferred name of a U.S. legislative subcommittee or subordinate body is recorded as a subdivision of the authorized access point for the *committee* to which it is subordinate (see figure 5.52).

Figure 5.52. US Subcommittee

110 1	‡a United States. ‡b Congress. ‡b House. ‡b Committee on Foreign Affairs. ‡b Subcommittee on Human Rights and International Organizations
370	‡c United States ‡2 naf
377	‡a eng
410 1	‡a United States. ‡b Congress. ‡b House. ‡b Subcommittee on Human Rights and International Organizations Trade
670	‡a Protection of whales, 1981: ‡b t.p. (Subcommittee on Human Rights and International Organizations of the Committee on Foreign Affairs, House of Representatives)

To better visualize the distinction, if the Canadian subcommittee illustrated in figure 5.51 had been recorded according to the 11.2.2.19.2 exception (U.S. bodies), its preferred name would have included the name of the Standing Committee on Foreign Affairs and International Trade:

> Canada. Parliament. House of Commons. Standing Committee on Foreign Affairs and International Trade. Sub-Committee on Human Rights and International Development

Conversely, if the U.S. subcommittee illustrated in figure 5.52 had been recorded according to the general guideline given in 11.2.2.19.2 (non-U.S. bodies), its preferred name would have omitted the name of the Committee on Foreign Affairs:

> United States. Congress. House. Subcommittee on Human Rights and International Organizations

Because database users cannot be expected to know or understand this distinction, a variant name should be recorded with or without the higher committee's name, as appropriate. This is recorded in a 410 field of the description, as seen in the two figures.

11.2.2.19.3. SUCCESSIVE LEGISLATURES. If the legislature of a jurisdiction meets successively and the successive legislatures are numbered, the ordinal number of the legislature and the inclusive years of the legislature are added in parentheses to the preferred name for the legislature as shown in figure 5.53. In U.S. cataloging practice previous to RDA this guideline was only applied to the U.S. Congress, but the LC policy that governed this was not carried over into the LC policy statements for RDA. RDA 11.2.2.19.3 may be applied to any legislature, as appropriate.

Figure 5.53. Successive Legislature

046	‡s 2011
110 1	‡a Canada. ‡b Parliament ‡n (41st, 1st session : ‡d 2011-)
368	‡a Legislative bodies ‡2 lcsh
370	‡c Canada ‡2 naf
377	‡a eng ‡a fre
410 1	‡a Canada. ‡b Parlement ‡n (41st, 1st session : ‡d 2011-)
670	‡a Here for all Canadians : stability, prosperity, security : speech from the throne to open the first session of the Forty-first Parliament of Canada, June 3, 2011, 2011
670	‡a Ici pour tous les Canadiens et Canadiennes : stabilité, prosperité, securité : discours du trône ouvrant la première session de la quarante-et-unième législature du Canada, le 3 juin 2011, 2011

11.2.2.21.1. CIVIL AND CRIMINAL COURTS. This guideline stipulates that the preferred name of a court is to be recorded as a subdivision of the authorized access point for the governmental jurisdiction whose authority it exercises. In the example shown in figure 5.54, the United States Supreme Court is recorded as a subdivision of the United States because its authority extends to the entire country.

Figure 5.54. Court

046	‡s 17890924
110 1	‡a United States. ‡b Supreme Court
368	‡a Courts ‡2 lcsh
370	‡c United States ‡2 naf
377	‡a eng
410 2	‡a Supreme Court of the United States
670	‡a United States Supreme Court reports, lawyers' edition, 1991
670	‡a Supreme Court of the United States, via WWW, 3 April 2011 ‡b (The Supreme Court of the United States was created by authority of the Judiciary Act of September 24, 1789 (1 Stat. 73). It was organized on February 2, 1790.)

11.2.2.24. DELEGATIONS TO INTERNATIONAL AND INTERGOVERNMENTAL BODIES. The rules governing preferred names and authorized access points for delegations have changed frequently over the years, most recently in 1998. The preferred name for a delegation has been recorded as a subdivision of the authorized access point for the country represented since AACR1 rule 86. This was a change from ALA 1949 rule 79, which formulated a conference heading with the name of the delegation as a subheading following the name of the conference for such a group.[12] Under ALA 1949 rule 79, the preferred name for the example shown in figure 5.55 would have been recorded:

> Inter-American Conference for the Maintenance of Peace, Buenos Aires, 1936.
>   Delegation from the United States of America

Figure 5.55. Delegation to International Conference

046	19361201 ‡t 19361223
110 1	‡a United States. ‡b Delegation (Inter-American Conference for the Maintenance of Peace (1936 : Buenos Aires, Argentina))
368	‡a Delegation
370	‡c United States ‡2 naf
377	‡a eng
410 2	‡a United States. ‡b Delegation to the Inter-American Conference for the Maintenance of Peace
670	‡a Report of the delegation of the United States of America to the Inter-American Conference for the Maintenance of Peace, 1937: ‡b t.p. (Buenos Aires, Argentina, December 1-23, 1936)

This collocated all the delegations in a single place in the index, but the form was misleading because delegations are subordinate bodies to their own country, not to the conference. RDA 11.2.2.24, as well as its predecessors AACR2 24.26 and AACR1 rule 86, represents a return to 1908 rules.

Record the preferred name of a delegation representing a country as a subdivision of the authorized access point for the country. The subdivision should be recorded in the language of the country represented.

Application of 11.2.2.24 requires a fair amount of cataloger's judgment. The cataloger in the case illustrated by figure 5.55 decided that the name of the delegation was ambiguous (if indeed it had a formal name) and so applied the provision to record "Delegation" with a qualifier to distinguish this delegation from others. On the other hand, the cataloger could have decided that the name of the delegation was "The Delegation of the United States of America to the Inter-American Conference for the Maintenance of Peace," in which case the preferred name would be recorded (omitting "of the United States of America" as instructed) "United States. Delegation to the Inter-American Conference for the Maintenance of Peace." Because the name of the delegation is somewhat unclear, this form is recorded in the description as a variant name.

Previous cataloging practice (e.g., AACR2 24.26) called for a general explanatory reference from the name of the conference to bring together in the catalog all of the names of the various delegations. Under this practice the name of the conference would have been be recorded, with a general name for the delegations given as a subdivision. This would have displayed something like this:

Inter-American Conference for the Maintenance of Peace, Buenos Aires (1936 : Buenos Aires, Argentina). Delegations
> *Delegations to the Inter-American Conference for the Maintenance of Peace are entered under the name of the nation followed by the name of the delegation, e.g., United States. Delegation (Inter-American Conference for the Maintenance of Peace (1936 : Buenos Aires, Argentina)); Mexico. Delegación (Inter-American Conference for the Maintenance of Peace (1936 : Buenos Aires, Argentina))*

Explanatory references such as this one were never implemented in the LC/NACO Authority File, and instructions for an explanatory reference for delegations to international bodies are not present in RDA.

11.2.2.25–11.2.2.29. SUBORDINATE RELIGIOUS BODIES. Subordinate religious bodies generally follow the same guidelines as other subordinate bodies. Special guidelines are given here for councils, religious officials, hierarchical organizations within a religious body, and Papal diplomatic missions.

Like government officials at the top level (see discussion of RDA 11.2.2.18, above), a religious official acting in an official capacity can be treated as a corporate body to identify the creator of official communications that represent the official policy of the religious body. RDA 11.2.2.26 instructs us to record as the preferred name of this body the title of the official, as a subdivision of the authorized access point for the religious jurisdiction. Like the treatment of top government officials, the incumbent of an office can be specified by adding the dates of incumbency and a brief form of his or her name in parentheses (see figure 5.12).

Caution: this procedure is available *only* for top government and religious officials. It cannot be used with officials of other corporate bodies (e.g., preferred names such as "General Electric Company. Chief Executive Officer (1981-2001 : Welch)" are not permitted).

Recording Variant Names

11.2.3. VARIANT NAME FOR THE CORPORATE BODY. Just as with persons and families, corporate bodies may be known by different names or different forms of the same name. One of these forms is chosen, as described above, as the preferred name, and in current systems the preferred name is how the name will appear in displays such as database indexes and bibliographic records. But if the body is known by other names, these will be recorded in the description if in the judgment of the cataloger this would be helpful for identification or access (note that RDA 11.2.3, variant name for the corporate body, is not a core element).

Variant names for most corporate bodies are recorded in subfields ‡a or ‡b of the 410 field of authority records, with the first indicator coded "2." If the variant name is for a jurisdiction (e.g., "Frankreich"), the variant is recorded in the 451 field when standing alone, or in 410 with the first indicator coded "1" when the jurisdiction stands as the parent body of a subordinate body recorded as a subdivision. Variant names for most meeting or event names are recorded in subfield ‡a of the 411 authority field with first indicator coded "2." Meeting or event names that are recorded as subordinate to another corporate body are recorded in subfield ‡b of the 410 field, following the preferred name of the corporate body.

How variant names display depends on how the library's system is set up, but they are intended to display to the public similarly to the following, when a user does a search on a variant (using, for example, a display generated by the description in figure 5.1):

> Kronos Performing Arts Association
> *search under*
> Kronos Quartet

Alternately, the database could automatically re-execute the search so that the user who searched for Kronos Performing Arts Association would be presented with resources linked to the preferred name Kronos Quartet. This would be particularly useful when the user is performing keyword rather than browse searches against the database.

For a fuller discussion of recording variant names, including thoughts on cataloger judgment in deciding whether to record a variant or not, see chapter 3 of this *Handbook* under 9.2.3.

11.2.3.3. GENERAL GUIDELINES. In most cases, variant names should be recorded following the same guidelines as though they had been chosen as the preferred name. This applies to guidelines on such matters as capitalization, diacritical marks, etc., given in RDA 8.5.

Regarding subordinate bodies, if the preferred name has been recorded subordinately a variant may be recorded with the direct form, and conversely, if the preferred name has been recorded directly a variant may be recorded formed subordinately— *if the name might reasonably sought in that form*. Figures 5.15, 5.22, and 5.29 are examples of preferred names recorded directly with subordinately formed variant names.

> United Nations. Unesco
>> *search under*
>> Unesco

Figures 5.32, 5.33, and 5.38 are examples of the reverse: the preferred name is recorded in subordinate form, with the direct form recorded as a variant name.

> National Pest Advisory Panel
>> *search under*
>> Chartered Institute of Environmental Health. National Pest Advisory
>> Panel

Figures 5.30 (Department of Library Services), 5.34 (Friends of the Libraries), 5.36 (Corporate Grants), and 5.39 (Library) are cases where it is probable that the name would not reasonably be sought in that form, so variants are not recorded.

There are a number of other specific instructions given in 11.2.3.4–11.2.3.7.

Reminder: The variant name element is not core in RDA and so in all cases recording of variant names is at the discretion and good judgment of the cataloger, as far as RDA is concerned. Agencies such as the Library of Congress or the Program for Cooperative Cataloging may issue policy statements requiring the recording of certain variants.

11.2.3.4. EXPANDED NAME. Sometimes corporate bodies are known both by a full name and by an acronym or initialism based on that name. If the acronym or initialism is recorded as the preferred name, the full form may be recorded as a variant name. The preferred name chosen for "Unesco" is the initialism. The spelled-out form "United Nations Educational, Scientific, and Cultural Organization" is recorded as a variant name (see figure 5.15).

> United Nations Educational, Scientific, and Cultural Organization
>> *search under*
>> Unesco

This guideline also applies to expansion of abbreviations. If the preferred name of the body contains an abbreviation and if, in the judgment of the cataloger, a database search using an expanded form of the word would cause the library user to be unable to find the name (i.e., the difference would affect access), a variant with the word spelled out should be recorded. RDA does not specify what affects access, but traditionally if the abbreviated word is within the first five or six words of the name a variant name is recorded with the word spelled out. Figure 5.26, "St. Louis Southwestern Railway Company" is an example:

> Saint Louis Southwestern Railway Company
> > *search under*
> > St. Louis Southwestern Railway Company

11.2.3.5. ACRONYM/INITIALISM/ABBREVIATED FORM. This is the reverse of guideline 11.2.3.4. If the preferred name of the body is a full form and the body also uses an acronym, initialism, or abbreviated form, the shorter form may be recorded as a variant. The preferred name chosen for "Educational Resources Information Center" is the spelled-out form. The body is also known as "ERIC," which is recorded as a variant name (see figure 5.14):

> ERIC
> > *search under*
> > Educational Resources Information Center

If it will make a difference in searching the database, a second variant "E.R.I.C." may be made. Conversely, if the acronym or initialism was recorded (either as a preferred name or a variant name) with full stops, a variant may be recorded without full stops (see figure 5.56):

> ZEF Spiritual Convention (1st : 1975 : Aijal, India)
> > *search under*
> > Z.E.F. Spiritual Convention (1st : 1975 : Aijal, India)

Figure 5.56. Variant Form of Initialism

046	‡s 19750312 ‡t 19750319
111 2	‡a Z.E.F. Spiritual Convention ‡n (1st : ‡d 1975 : ‡c Aijal, India)
368	‡a Congresses and conventions ‡2 lcsh
370	‡e Aijal (India) ‡2 naf
377	‡a lus
411 2	‡a ZEF Spiritual Convention ‡n (1st : ‡d 1975 : ‡c Aijal, India)
411 2	‡a Zoram Evangelical Fellowship Spiritual Convention ‡n (1st : ‡d 1975 : ‡c Aijal, India)
670	‡a Z.E.F. Spiritual Convention vawi khatna Dawrpui Veng Biakin, 12-19 March 1975, 1975: ‡b title page (First Z.E.F. Spiritual Convention; held in Aijal) p. i (Zoram Evangelical Fellowship Spiritual Convention)

RDA gives no guidance on when to do this, leaving it up to the judgment of the cataloger in the context of the database. Traditionally, variants of forms recorded *with* full stops have been recorded without the full stops, but a variant was not made if the recorded form did not have full stops in the first place. This is because the vast majority of corporate names with acronyms or initialisms do not include full stops, and it is expected that users will omit full stops when searching.

Use caution in applying this guideline. The cataloger should not make up variants just because a word in the name can be abbreviated. Variant names of this type should be recorded based on usage of the body as reflected in resources associated with it. For example, all the words in the name "National Library of South Africa" (figure 5.20) are commonly abbreviated. The cataloger should not record a made-up abbreviated form such as "Nat'l Lib. of S.A." unless the form is found in a resource associated with the library. This contrasts with 11.2.3.4, which calls for expansion of abbreviations if they would affect access even if the spelled-out form is not found in resources associated with the body.

11.2.3.6. ALTERNATIVE LINGUISTIC FORM OF NAME. A variant name may be recorded if there are alternate linguistic forms of the name. This includes different language forms (see figures 5.15, 5.21 through 5.23, and 5.51), different scripts (see figure 5.4), and different spellings (see figure 5.19b):

> Layiburari ya Rixaka ya Afrika-Dzonga
> > *search under*
> > National Library of South Africa

> 日外アソシエーツ
> > *search under*
> > Nichigai Asoshiētsu

> Museum der Deutschen Binnenschiffahrt
> > *search under*
> > Museum der Deutschen Binnenschifffahrt

11.2.3.7. OTHER VARIANT NAME. This guideline allows the cataloger to record essentially any variant he or she finds and believes would be helpful to the user of the database. Included are different names (see figures 5.1, 5.23, and 5.26), general name of a series of conferences when the preferred name of one of the conferences is different (see figure 5.24); variants on direct versus indirect subdivision (see figures 5.40, 5.43, 5.44, 5.50, 5.51, and 5.52):

Cotton Belt Railway Company
search under
St. Louis Southwestern Railway Company

Workshop for Young Scientists on the Physics of Ultrarelativistic Nucleus-nucleus Collisions (4th : 2010 : La Londe-les-Maures, France)
search under
Hot Quarks (Workshop) (2010 : La Londe-les-Maures, France)

New Zealand. MAF Biosecurity Authority. Animal Biosecurity
search under
New Zealand. Animal Biosecurity

A variant name customarily recorded for corporate bodies is a shorter form based on a surname when the name of the body begins with the full name of a person. Although there is no evidence that the shorter form Kennedy Medical Center ever appears in resources associated with the John F. Kennedy Medical Center, a hospital in Liberia, this form may be recorded as a variant name (see figure 5.57).

Figure 5.57. Variant Name: Shorter Form of Associated Personal Name

110 2	‡a John F. Kennedy Medical Center (Monrovia, Liberia)
368	‡a Hospitals ‡2 lcsh
370	‡e Monrovia (Liberia) ‡2 naf
377	‡a eng
410 2	‡a Kennedy Medical Center (Monrovia, Liberia)
670	‡a The John F. Kennedy Medical Center, 1986: ‡b t.p. (John F. Kennedy Medical Center, Monrovia, Liberia, West Africa)

Other Identifying Attributes

RDA 11.2 contains guidelines about choosing and recording preferred and variant names in descriptions of corporate bodies. RDA 11.3–11.12 contain guidelines for recording other attributes of corporate bodies that may be useful for identifying the corporate body or differentiating it from another corporate body with the same name. Reminder: RDA 11.3–11.12 are concerned only with recording information in elements of the description of the corporate body, *not* with creation of the authorized access point for the corporate body. Some of the information recorded in these elements may be included in the authorized access point, but much will not and nearly all of the elements can be recorded independently of access points in the MARC record.

11.3–11.5, 11.7. ELEMENTS THAT MAY BE USED TO DISTINGUISH CORPORATE BODIES. All of the elements listed between RDA 11.3 and 11.12 may be useful for identifying and contextualizing corporate bodies, but four elements in particular are used to distinguish corporate bodies that have the same name. These are place associated with the corporate body (11.3), date associated with the corporate body (11.4), associated institution (11.5), and other designation associated with the corporate body (11.7). One of these elements, date (11.4) is labeled core in all cases; the others are labeled core "when needed to distinguish a corporate body from another corporate body with the same name." This language does not mean that all four elements must be used if "needed" to distinguish bodies with the same name. Instead, the cataloger should use judgment to decide which of the four elements would best distinguish the bodies; once that decision has been made, then the chosen element is the one that is "needed," and hence that one becomes core.

The cataloger may judge which element best distinguishes the bodies by asking the question "what is the difference between these bodies?" If the principal difference is the location of the bodies, then place is probably the best element to use (see discussion below under 11.3). If the difference has to do with time period, then dates are probably the best (see below under 11.4). If the difference has to do with association with different institutions that is probably the best element to use (see below under 11.5). If none of those are appropriate, then something else (other designation) may be used (see below under 11.7). Once the cataloger has decided the best element to use to distinguish the bodies, then that element is the one that is "needed" and it becomes core.

11.3. PLACE ASSOCIATED WITH THE CORPORATE BODY. This element is core for places associated with conferences, meetings, or other events, meaning if known the place of the meeting must be recorded as an element of the description. This requirement is qualified, however: if the meeting is better identified by the name of an institution, recording the name of the institution rather than the local place satisfies the core requirement (see below under 11.5, associated institution).

Place is core in the description of other corporate bodies only if it is needed to distinguish one corporate body from another with the same name, but as with any element it may be recorded even if not needed to distinguish the name if the cataloger feels this would help identify or contextualize the body.

RDA place elements for corporate bodies are recorded in the MARC 370 field, in subfield ‡c (associated country), subfield ‡e (place of headquarters) or subfield ‡f (other associated place). These subfields are repeatable (or, alternately, the entire 370 field is repeatable), allowing multiple places to be recorded if necessary.

In LC/NACO practice, place names are recorded in RDA place elements in the same form that would be used as the authorized access point for the place.[13] For a fuller discussion, see chapter 3 of this *Handbook* at 9.8–9.11.

Figures 5.24 and 5.56 illustrate two cases where the place associated with the corporate body element is core. In these cases the place has been recorded both in the description (370 field) and in the access points (X11 subfield ‡c).

The place element is core in figure 5.57 for another reason. This John F. Kennedy Medical Center is a hospital in Liberia. There is another John F. Kennedy Medical Center, a hospital in Edison, New Jersey. As discussed in the previous section, place associated with the corporate body is core "when needed to distinguish a corporate body from another corporate body with the same name," but the core requirement comes after the choice has been made of which element to use to distinguish the bodies. In the case of the John F. Kennedy Medical Centers, both are hospitals, so "other designation" (e.g., "Hospital") would not be helpful to distinguish them; neither are dates or associated institutions. Asking the question "what makes these two bodies different?" the cataloger concludes that the difference is that they are in different places. Therefore, in this instance, the place name is "needed" to distinguish the two bodies, and thus becomes core.

In figure 5.4 the corporate body is associated with Japan, and its headquarters are located in Tokyo. In this case the cataloger chose to record both the associated country (370 subfield ‡c) and the headquarters location (370 subfield ‡e). Figure 5.20 also shows this; the National Library of South Africa's headquarters is Pretoria, but it serves the nation as a whole.

Radio Dept., the Swedish musical group, was originally formed in Lund, Sweden, but it is not clear that the body is still located there (see figure 5.10). The cataloger in this instance chose to code the place in 370 subfield ‡f, defined fairly ambiguously as "other associated place."

Figure 5.34 does not record a place—although the location of the University of Southern California is easy enough to discover, it is not clear that that place would also be the headquarters of the Friends of the Library. On the other hand, it is clear that the University of Michigan Library is located in Ann Arbor, Michigan (figure 5.39).

11.3.3.4. CHANGE OF NAME OF JURISDICTION OR LOCALITY. If the name of a jurisdiction has been recorded in the place associated with the corporate body element, and that name has changed, record the latest name of the jurisdiction that was in use during the lifetime of the body. This means that if the preferred name for a place changes the descriptions of corporate bodies that have recorded this element should be revised, and authorized access points that have used the place name as a qualifier (whether to distinguish from another body with the same name or for any other reason) must change. The access point must always be qualified with this latest form. Optionally, earlier names of the jurisdiction may be recorded as elements (in MARC 370) in addition to the latest name.

For example, the name of the city of Pietersburg, South Africa, was officially changed to Polokwane in 2005. The Hugh Exton Photographic Museum had previously been established in the authority file as "Hugh Exton Photographic Museum (Pietersburg, South Africa)." The museum remained in existence after the change of the city's name. "Polokwane, South Africa" will be recorded in the place associated with the corporate body element recorded in the 370 field of the authority record and the qualifier in the authorized access point will be changed to "Polokwane, South Africa" (see figure 5.58). This figure also displays the optional addition, retaining the earlier name in 370. (Note that when an already-established form is changed, the original form is usually retained as a variant name, with coding "nne" in subfield ‡w. This code means the field contains an earlier established form of the heading. See the second 410 field of the post-2005 record.)

Figure 5.58. Change of Place Name Requiring Description Revision

Pre-2005 Record

110 2	‡a Hugh Exton Photographic Museum (Pietersburg, South Africa)
368	‡a Museums ‡2 lcsh
370	‡e Pietersburg (South Africa) ‡2 naf
372	‡a Photography ‡2 lcsh
377	‡a eng
410 2	‡a Exton Photographic Museum (Pietersburg, South Africa)
670	‡a Memories of Pietersburg, 1990: ‡b title page (Hugh Exton Photographic Museum)

Post-2005 Record

110 2	‡a Hugh Exton Photographic Museum (Polokwane, South Africa)
368	‡a Museums ‡2 lcsh
370	‡e Pietersburg (South Africa) ‡e Polokwane (South Africa) ‡2 naf
372	‡a Photography ‡2 lcsh
377	‡a eng
410 2	‡a Exton Photographic Museum (Polokwane, South Africa)
410 2	‡w nne ‡a Hugh Exton Photographic Museum (Pietersburg, South Africa)
670	‡a Memories of Pietersburg, 1990: ‡b title page (Hugh Exton Photographic Museum)
670	‡a Hugh Exton Photographic Museum, via WWW, 29 October 2011 ‡b (in Polokwane, South Africa; collection of 23,000 historic photographs taken between 1892 and 1945 by photographer Hugh Exton)

The Conference on Local Government held in Pietersburg in 1994, on the other hand, no longer existed when the place name changed. The latest name of the place in use during the short lifetime of this body was Pietersburg. Therefore this element will remain "Pietersburg, South Africa" in the description of the Conference (see figure 5.59).

Figure 5.59. Change of Place Name *Not* Requiring Description Revision

046	‡s 19941029
111 2	‡a Conference on Local Government ‡d (1994 : ‡c Pietersburg, South Africa)
368	‡a Congresses and conventions ‡2 lcsh
370	‡e Pietersburg (South Africa) ‡2 naf
377	‡a eng
670	‡a Local government, ‡b title page (Conference on Local Government) page 7 (held at the Library Gardend (Pietersburg) October 29, 1994

11.4. DATE ASSOCIATED WITH THE CORPORATE BODY. This element is defined as a significant date or range of dates associated with a corporate body. For a conference, meeting, or event, it is the date or range of dates on which the event was held. For other corporate bodies it includes dates such as the date the body was founded. Because corporate bodies exist over time, it is most likely that this element will include a range of dates, either open (for corporate bodies that continue to exist) or closed (for corporate bodies that have ceased to exist).

This element is core for a conference, etc., or when needed to distinguish a corporate body from another with the same name. Whether core or not, if the cataloger knows the information, he or she may record the element in the description of the corporate body. This does not necessarily mean the date will also to be a part of the authorized access point for the corporate body.

The basic field intended for recording this element in MARC is the 046 field. The earliest date associated with the body (e.g., the beginning of a conference or the founding of a company) is recorded in subfield ‡s; an ending date is recorded in subfield ‡t. For fuller information about recording dates in RDA descriptions, see chapter 3 of this *Handbook* at 9.3.

The instruction at 11.4.1.3 says to "record a date associated with a corporate body by giving the year or span of years." This instruction seems misplaced. It applies to recording a date in an access point. RDA catalogers do not limit themselves to recording the year or years when recording the information in the 046 field, if more specific information (e.g., month and day) is available. See, for example, figures 5.5, 5.12, 5.15, and others.

In addition to being core on its own, the date associated with the corporate body element is, with place, associated institution, and "other designation," one of the elements that can be used to distinguish corporate bodies that have the same name. If the difference between the bodies has to do with time period rather than place or associated institution, date is probably the best element to use. Yale College is an example. Founded in 1718, Yale College became Yale University in 1887. Simultaneously another body called Yale College was created, which became the undergraduate liberal arts school of Yale University. These two separate bodies have the same name, share the same location, and have the same associated institution. But they do differ chronologically, so date may be used to distinguish them (see figure 5.60).

Figure 5.60. Date Element Used to Distinguish Bodies with the Same Name

046	‡s 1718 ‡t 1887
110 2	‡a Yale College (1718-1887)
370	‡e New Haven (Conn.) ‡2 naf
510 2	‡w r ‡i Predecessor: ‡a Collegiate School (New Haven, Conn.)
510 2	‡w r ‡i Successor: ‡a Yale University
670	‡a Biographical record of the Class of 1850 of Yale College, 1901
670	‡a Phone call to Yale University Library Manuscripts and Archives, 21 March 2000 ‡b (Collegiate School changed its name to Yale College in 1718; Yale College changed its name to Yale University in 1887; since 1887, the name Yale College has referred to the undergraduate liberal arts school of Yale University)

046	‡s 1887
110 2	‡a Yale College (1887-)
370	‡e New Haven (Conn.) ‡2 naf
410 2	‡a Yale University. ‡b Yale College
670	‡a Yale College programs of study, 1999: ‡b page ii (Yale College is the oldest and largest school of Yale University, which comprises also the Graduate School of Arts and Sciences as well as ten professional schools)
670	‡a Phone call to Yale University Library Manuscripts and Archives, 21 March 2000 ‡b (Yale College changed its name to Yale University in 1887; since 1887, the name Yale College has referred to the undergraduate liberal arts school of Yale University)

11.4.2. DATE OF CONFERENCE, ETC. The date or dates of a conference or other event should be recorded. Information about these dates can be taken from any source; catalogers are not limited to information published, for example, with the proceedings of a conference. Information about dates is frequently available from the event's website. The stipulations about recording specific dates if necessary to distinguish between two or more conferences (RDA 11.4.3.2) are specifically geared toward access points. This is not the form such dates would be recorded in an 046 field (see full details in chapter 3 of this *Handbook* at 9.3). For examples of dates of conferences, etc., see figures 5.22, 5.24, 5.56, and 5.59. In these figures, contrast the treatment of the element as recorded in 046 fields and the dates recorded in the authorized access point for the body.

11.4.3. DATE OF ESTABLISHMENT. If known, the date of establishment of a corporate body should be recorded. For examples, see figures 5.1 through 5.3 and others throughout this chapter.

11.4.4. DATE OF TERMINATION. If the corporate body is no longer in existence and the date the body was terminated or dissolved is known, this information should be recorded. This includes dissolution of a corporate body because its name has changed. In this case the date of termination of the original body would closely coincide with the date of establishment of the new body. For examples of the date of termination element, see figures 5.12, 5.22, 5.24, 5.33, 5.46, and others throughout this chapter. For an example of date of termination coinciding with a name change of the body, see figure 5.61 (FDX Corporation), and compare this figure with figure 5.5 (FedEx Corporation).

Figure 5.61. Date of Termination

046	‡s 1998 ‡t 19991231
110 2	‡a FDX Corporation
368	‡a Shipping firm
370	‡e Memphis (Tenn.) ‡2 naf
372	‡a Shipping ‡2 lcsh
377	‡a eng
410 2	‡a FDX
510 2	‡w r ‡i Predecessor: ‡a Federal Express Corporation
510 2	‡w r ‡i Successor: ‡a FedEx Corporation
670	‡a Annual report, 1999: ‡b t.p. (FDX Corporation; FDX)
670	‡a FedEx Corporation, via WWW, 5 May 2012 ‡b (Company founded as Federal Express in 1971; the corporation was created in 1998 as FDX Corporation and became FedEx Corporation in January 2000. Headquarters in Memphis, Tenn.)
678 1	‡a This company was founded in 1971 as Federal Express; the corporation was created in 1998 as FDX Corporation and became FedEx Corporation in January 2000.

11.5. ASSOCIATED INSTITUTION. This element records information about an institution commonly associated with the corporate body. It is recorded in the MARC authority 373 field, subfield ‡a.

The associated institution element is core for descriptions of conferences or other events if the name of the institution provides better identification of the event than a local place name or the local place name is unknown. In previous cataloging practice, if a conference or event is associated with an institution other than one that is simply a venue (such as a hotel or an airport), the associated institution element was usually chosen as core over the place associated with the corporate body element. However, the choice is completely the cataloger's judgment. In the case of the Third International Workshop on Nude Mice, held at Montana State University, Bozeman, the cataloger decided that the conference was better identified in the authorized access point by "Montana State University (Bozeman, Mont.)," the authorized access point for the associated institution, than it would have been by the place name "Bozeman, Mont." (see figure 5.62). As for recording the elements themselves, note that in an RDA description we are not required to choose one over the other. Both elements may be recorded, the place in MARC 370 and the associated institution in MARC 373.

Figure 5.62. Associated Institution Core

046	‡s 19790906 ‡t 19790909
111 2	‡a International Workshop on Nude Mice ‡n (3rd : ‡d 1979 : ‡c Montana State University (Bozeman, Mont.))
377	‡a eng
368	‡a Congresses and conventions ‡2 lcsh
370	‡e Bozeman (Mont.) ‡2 naf
372	‡a Nude mouse ‡2 lcsh
373	‡a Montana State University (Bozeman, Mont.) ‡2 naf
670	‡a Proceedings of the Third International Workshop on Nude Mice, Montana State University, Bozeman, Montana, September 6-9, 1979, 1982

The element is core for other corporate bodies if something is needed to distinguish the corporate body from another with the same name, and the institution's name provides better identification than other elements such as a local place name or date. There are a number of university marching bands that call themselves "Cougar Marching Band." The name of the university identifies these bands much better than a local place name would (see figure 5.63). Again, however, the cataloger is required to make a choice only for the form in the authorized access point. Both elements may be recorded within the description.

This element may be recorded even in cases where it is not core. Guarro Casas, in figure 5.3, is not a conference or event, nor does its name need to be distinguished from another corporate body's name, but the cataloger has the information that Guarro Casas is associated with the Arjowiggins group, and so recorded the element in a 373 field. See also figures 5.30 through 5.45.

RDA 11.5.1.3 instructs the cataloger to record the preferred name of the associated institution in this element. The name need not be established in the authority file, but if it is there, use the established form. If it has not been established, determine what the preferred name for the institution would be and record that form.

Figure 5.63. Associated Institution Core to Distinguish

110 2	‡a Cougar Marching Band (University of Houston)
368	‡a Bands (Music) ‡2 lcsh
370	‡e Houston (Tex.) ‡2 naf
373	‡a University of Houston ‡2 naf
410 2	‡a University of Houston. ‡b Cougar Marching Band
670	‡a The Cougar band-aid : the official paper of the Cougar Marching Band, 1979

110 2	‡a Cougar Marching Band (Washington State University)
368	‡a Bands (Music) ‡2 lcsh
370	‡e Pullman (Wash.) ‡2 naf
373	‡a Washington State University ‡2 naf
410 2	‡a Washington State University. ‡b Cougar Marching Band
410 2	‡a WSU Cougar Marching Band
670	‡a WSU Cougar Marching Band pregame, 2006
670	‡a Cougar Marching Band, via WWW, 3 November 2011 ‡b (associated with Washington State University, Pullman, Wash.)

110 2	‡a Cougar Marching Band (Brigham Young University)
368	‡a Bands (Music) ‡2 lcsh
370	‡e Provo (Utah) ‡2 naf
373	‡a Brigham Young University ‡2 naf
410 2	‡a Brigham Young University. ‡b Cougar Marching Band
670	‡a Go mighty tubas!, 2002 ‡b (name not given)
670	‡a BYU bands-Cougar Marching Band, via WWW, September 11, 2006

The associated institution element is recorded in the MARC authorities format 373 field subfield ‡a. The period during which the body was affiliated with the group can be recorded using subfield ‡s (start period) and subfield ‡t (end period). If recording a form found in the LC/NACO Authority File, do not include subfield coding except subfield ‡a and include "‡2 naf" in the field. Some groups are established as subjects, not names. These can also be recorded in this element. If recording a form found in the LCSH subject authority file, do not include subfield coding except subfield ‡a and include "‡2 lcsh" in the field. For examples of the associated institution element see figure 5.62 and other figures in this chapter.

11.6. NUMBER OF A CONFERENCE, ETC. This core element is used only with conference or meeting names. In the current MARC implementation the element can only be recorded as part of an access point, in X11 subfield ‡n. It is recorded as an ordinal numeral. See figures 5.24 (411 field) and 5.62 for examples.

11.7. OTHER DESIGNATION ASSOCIATED WITH THE CORPORATE BODY. This element is defined as core if the body has a name that does not convey the idea that it is a corporate body (RDA 11.7.1.4). Otherwise it is core if needed to distinguish between corporate bodies with the same name (RDA 11.7.1.5 and 11.7.1.6). "Needed" has been discussed above: if corporate bodies with the same name are encountered, the cataloger decides between place, date, associated institution, and "other designation" which element best distinguishes the two bodies; once that has been decided the chosen element becomes "needed" and core.

The "other designation" can be any word, phrase, an abbreviation indicating legal status (such as "Inc."), or any other term that the cataloger deems useful to differentiate the bodies from other entities with the same name.

11.7.1.4. NAMES NOT CONVEYING THE IDEA OF A CORPORATE BODY. If in the cataloger's judgment a name does not convey the idea that the entity is a corporate body, a word or phrase should be recorded to clarify the nature of the entity. The element is recorded in MARC authority field 368, subfield ‡a. For example, because "Apollo 11" does not convey the idea of a corporate body, in figure 5.2 the term "Spacecraft" was recorded. Under provisions for creation of authorized access points (RDA 11.13.1.2), it was also added as a qualifier to the body's preferred name. For another example of a vessel, see figure 5.27. Similarly, the names "ExxonMobil Chemical" (figure 5.7), "Lucasfilm Animation" (figure 5.8), and "Radio Dept." (figure 5.10) were not thought to be names conveying the idea of a corporate body, so the cataloger recorded the element.

"Encyclopaedia Britannica" (figure 5.17) is another example of a name that does not convey the idea that it represents a corporate body. However, the body uses a term of incorporation with its name, "Inc." Under the stipulations of 11.2.2.10 this term would be omitted, but an exception is made if the term is needed to make clear that the name is that of a corporate body. The preferred name for this body will be "Encyclopaedia Britannica, Inc."; this form of the name does convey the idea of a corporate body.

The name illustrated in figure 5.24, "Hot Quarks," is also a name that does not convey the idea of a corporate body (in this case the name of a meeting). The term "Workshop" was chosen as a qualifier. Note that in this case there are two parenthetical qualifiers. The first is recorded because the name does not convey the idea of a corporate body. The second is required by the guidelines for meeting names.

It is not necessary to record the element in the case of preferred names that have been recorded as subdivisions of the authorized access points of their parent bodies under 11.2.2.14.4 because their name did not convey the idea of a corporate body. See figures 5.36 ("Corporate Grants"), 5.37 ("Strategic Planning"), and 5.44 ("Animal Biosecurity").

The decision of whether the name conveys the idea of a corporate body or not is entirely the cataloger's judgment, but the Library of Congress has issued a policy statement with the instruction that a *preferred* name that consists solely of an initialism or acronym does not convey the idea of a corporate name (LC-PCC PS 11.7.1.4, October 2012). The other designation element should be recorded when describing these corporate bodies. An example is "D.E.P.T.H." (figure 5.64). Because a British library created the description of this corporate body in the authority file, the "other designation" "Organisation" is recorded with British spelling. RDA does not prescribe a particular spelling convention, and once the entity has been described in an authority record the form chosen should be used by other agencies using the file.

Figure 5.64. Name Not Conveying the Idea of a Corporate Body

110 2	‡a D.E.P.T.H. (Organisation)
368	‡a Organisation
370	‡e Ilford (London, England) ‡2 naf
372	‡a Diabetes--Prevention ‡a Diabetes--Treatment ‡2 lcsh
371	‡a 7 Spurway Parade ‡a Woodford Avenue ‡b Ilford ‡c Essex ‡e IG2 6UU ‡d United Kingdom
410 2	‡a DEPTH (Organisation)
410 2	‡a Diabetes, Education, Prevention, Treatment, Health (Organisation)
670	‡a Newsletter, winter 1991: ‡b title page (D.E.P.T.H., Diabetes, Education, Prevention, Treatment, Health)
670	‡a Trade TOD, Trade of the Day, via WWW, 12 July 2011 ‡b (Diabetes, Education, Prevention, Treatment, Health; 7 Spurway Parade, Woodford Avenue, Ilford, Essex, IG2 6UU, United Kingdom, telephone +44 (0)20 8551 6263)

11.7.1.5. TYPE OF JURISDICTION. The description of jurisdiction names is mainly covered in RDA chapter 16, but because jurisdictions are corporate bodies, provision is made here for distinguishing between two jurisdictions with the same name. This sub-element is recorded in MARC authority field 368, subfield ‡b. For an example, see figure 5.65. There are several jurisdictional entities called "Washington" as well as a number of other corporate bodies, such as "Washington (Battleship : BB-47)." All of these entities must be distinguished from each other. Most of the other jurisdictional names can be distinguished by a higher jurisdiction's name, but that is not possible with the State of Washington, which is instead distinguished by its type of jurisdiction.

Figure 5.65. Type of Jurisdiction

043	‡a n-us-wa
151	‡a Washington (State)
368	‡b State
670	‡a Washington State energy code, chapter 51-11 WAC, 2009

Names of jurisdictions and other places are described in detail in chapter 6 of this *Handbook*, "Describing Geographic Entities."

11.7.1.6. OTHER DESIGNATION. This sub-element, recorded in 368 subfield ‡c, allows the cataloger to choose essentially any term that makes sense to distinguish between bodies with the same or similar names. For example, there are a number of churches with the same or similar names, all related to Mormonism, descended from the church organized by Joseph Smith in 1830. After Smith's death many went their separate ways but retained church organizations. Some of these call themselves "The Church of Christ." They are not local congregations, so a local place name cannot be used to distinguish them; instead another designation will be used. See figure 5.66 for two of these churches.

Figure 5.66. Other Designation

110 2	‡a Church of Christ (Temple Lot)
368	‡c Temple Lot
377	‡a eng
670	‡a Zion's advocates, May 1922: ‡b title page (Church of Christ (Temple Lot))
670	‡a Encyclopedia of American religion, 1978 ‡b (Church of Christ (Temple Lot) formed in 1852 as offshoot of Church of Jesus Christ of Latter-day Saints)

110 2	‡a Church of Christ (Whitmerites)
368	‡c Whitmerites
377	‡a eng
410 2	‡a Church of Christ (David Whitmer)
670	‡a The solution of the Mormon problem, 1926: ‡b title page (Church of Christ)
670	‡a Divergent paths of the Restoration, 2001: ‡b page 102 (Church of Christ (David Whitmer); pages 102-103 (In the late 1840s William E. McLellin attempted to form a new church under the name Church of Christ which advocated David Whitmer as the rightful president and prophet of the Mormon church. However, this movement failed to obtain Whitmer's support. In 1875, Whitmer did form a successful church, also called the Church of Christ. In 1925, John J. Snyder (who led the church after Whitmer's death) and the remaining members united with the Church of Christ (Temple Lot)).

11.8. LANGUAGE OF THE CORPORATE BODY. This element refers to the language the body uses in its communications. The language of the corporate body element is recorded in the MARC authorities format 377 field subfield ‡a (language code) or subfield ‡l (language term). Current practice is to record the MARC language code as found in the *MARC Code List for Languages* (www.loc.gov/marc/languages/langhome.html) rather than a language term. For examples, see figures throughout this chapter.

Consistent recording of the language of the corporate body element will be very useful to database users who want to find a set of corporate bodies based on language (e.g., all bodies using Afrikaans in South Africa).

11.9. ADDRESS OF THE CORPORATE BODY. This element may be used to record the address of the corporate body's headquarters or offices, or general e-mail addresses for the body, or URLs of the body's home page(s). The address of the corporate body element is recorded in the MARC 371 field; the address is recorded in subfield ‡a, city in subfield ‡b, intermediate jurisdiction (e.g., state or province) in subfield ‡c, country in subfield ‡d, and postal code in subfield ‡e. If recording an e-mail address, use subfield ‡m; use subfield ‡u for URLs associated with the corporate body. An explanatory note may be recorded in subfield ‡z. Unlike the other RDA place elements, the address of the corporate body element is not recorded formally from the established form of a place name. Simply record the information as found (see figures 5.6, 5.7, 5.39, and 5.64).

Catalogers need not go out of their way to find this information, particularly for corporate bodies that no longer exist. However, if a cataloger is consulting a body's official website it is usually a simple matter to discover an address.

11.10. FIELD OF ACTIVITY OF THE CORPORATE BODY. The scope of this element is quite broad, defined as "a field of business in which a corporate body is engaged, its area of competence, responsibility, jurisdiction, etc." The element is recorded in MARC authority field 372, subfield ‡a. Information can be recorded in narrative style, as shown in the examples to RDA 11.10.1.3 and figure 5.6, or as words or short phrases, as seen in figures 5.3b, 5.5, and others throughout this chapter. The evolving best practice is to record terms from controlled vocabularies when possible. When such a term is recorded, also record ‡2 and the code for the thesaurus (e.g. "‡2 lcsh").[14] Recording information in this element might be particularly useful for corporate bodies whose names do not convey any information about their field of activity, such as D.E.P.T.H. (figure 5.64).

11.11. CORPORATE HISTORY. This element is a recorded as a narrative containing information about the corporate body. It is geared toward historical information about the body, but can include other information as well. The corporate history element is especially useful for corporate bodies that have a history of name changes, mergers, or other complex issues (see figure 5.67).

Figure 5.67. Corporate History

046	‡s 1935 ‡t 1949
110 2	‡a Paramount Pictures, Inc.
368	‡a Motion picture studios ‡2 lcsh
372	‡a Motion pictures--Distribution ‡a Motion pictures--Production and direction ‡2 lcsh
377	‡a eng
510 2	‡w r ‡i Predecessor: ‡a Paramount Publix Corporation
510 2	‡w r ‡i Product of a split: ‡a Paramount Pictures Corporation
510 2	‡w r ‡i Product of a split: ‡a United Paramount Theatres
510 2	‡w r ‡i Hierarchical subordinate: ‡a Paramount Productions
670	‡a Dipsy gypsy, 1941: ‡b credits (Paramount Pictures, Inc.)
670	‡a International motion picture almanac, 1982 ‡b (Paramount Pictures, Inc. formed in 1935; formerly known as Paramount Publix Corporation [1930-1935]; name changed back to Paramount Pictures Corporation in 1949 [also used from 1914-1918])
678 1	‡a Paramount Pictures, Inc. was formed in 1935 out of a reorganization of Paramount Publix Corporation. The company was divided in 1949 in a court-ordered separation of its motion picture production/distribution units and its movie theater chain. The production and distribution division was reorganized as Paramount Pictures Corporation, and the theaters as United Paramount Theatres.

Record the corporate history element in subfield ‡a of MARC authority field 678 with the first indicator coded "1." For other examples, see figures 5.5 and 5.61.

11.12. IDENTIFIER FOR THE CORPORATE BODY. An identifier for the corporate body is a character string uniquely associated with the corporate body (or the record representing the corporate body). This is a core (i.e., required) element. In the LC/NACO Authority File the identifier is the Library of Congress Control Number, recorded in the 010 field. In most cases the cataloger does not need to record information in this element, as it is automatically generated by the database system. For this reason, the identifier for the corporate body element has not been included in most figures in this book; as examples, the element is included with figures 5.1 and 5.3.

Access Points

One of the objectives governing RDA is that the data should enable the user to find all resources associated with a particular corporate body (RDA 0.4.2.1). In our current MARC database environment this is done through the formulation and use of authorized access points representing entities such as corporate bodies, corresponding to what previous cataloging practice called "headings." These access points are embedded in bibliographic records for resources associated with the corporate body and serve as links between a particular bibliographic record and all other bibliographic records that contain the identical access point. In many systems the access point in the bibliographic record is also linked to its corresponding authority record.

The user of the database finds all resources associated with a particular corporate body by learning what the authorized access point is for that body and then querying the database for instances of the authorized access point indexed as a creator or contributor, or as a subject.

In order for this to work the authorized access point must be consistent (i.e., always used in the same form) and unique to the corporate body (i.e., more than one body should not share the same authorized access point). The data describing a corporate body must be sufficient to differentiate that body from other bodies with the same name (RDA 0.4.3.1).

When two corporate bodies in the database have identical names, a "conflict" exists that must be resolved in the authorized access point. Given the important principle of representation upon which the preferred name is based (see RDA 0.4.3.4: an entity should be represented as it represents itself or as it is commonly known), and given naming practices of corporate bodies, it is not unusual that preferred names for different corporate bodies would be identical. Authorized access points for corporate bodies with identical preferred names are differentiated from each other by the addition of parenthetical "qualifiers" containing a local place associated with the corporate body, dates associated with the body, associated institutions, or some other designation.

11.13. CONSTRUCTING ACCESS POINTS TO REPRESENT CORPORATE BODIES. Once the elements discussed above in 11.2–11.12 have been recorded it is a relatively simple matter to construct an access point for the corporate body. The goal of allowing systems to create authorized access points "on the fly" containing only those elements needed to differentiate between entities in a given database by drawing on elements recorded elsewhere in the description has been mentioned before (see discussion in chapter 3, at 9.19, and in chapter 4, at 10.10). Constructing access points for corporate bodies in this way might be more difficult than constructing access points for persons or families. There are at least three problems:

1. The human cataloger chooses the best element to use as a qualifier in the authorized access point from an array of elements (see discussion of elements that may be used to distinguish corporate bodies at 11.3–11.5 and 11.7, above).
2. It is possible and in fact desirable to record *all* these elements within the body of the description.
3. Authorized access points for corporate bodies often contain qualifiers for reasons other than differentiation from another corporate body with the same name.

Thus it would be difficult for a system to determine when to add a qualifying element to an access point, and which element to add. It therefore seems less likely that future systems might be able satisfactorily to create authorized access points for corporate bodies without some sort of human intervention, unless a method were created in MARC for the cataloger to designate a particular element as the preferred qualifier to be used if needed.

11.13.1. AUTHORIZED ACCESS POINT REPRESENTING A CORPORATE BODY. The authorized access point for most corporate bodies is constructed using the 110 field in the MARC authority record, with the first indicator coded "2." Authorized access points for corporate bodies that are also jurisdictions, such as "Tucson (Ariz.)" are recorded in the 151 field when standing alone, or in the 110 field with the first indicator coded "1" when standing as the parent body of a subordinate body recorded as a subdivision. Authorized access points for most meetings or other events are coded in the 111 field with the first indicator coded "2." A meeting or event name that is recorded as a subdivision of the authorized access point of another corporate body is recorded in subfield ‡b of the 110 field.

The form recorded in any of these 1XX fields is recorded in bibliographic records using the 110/111, 610/611/651, or 710/711 fields. Coding of subfields is the same in authority and bibliographic records. The authorized access point is constructed with three parts: (a) the preferred name, (b) additions required in all cases, and (c) additions required in case of conflict.

When a place name is used as one of these additions, follow the instructions in RDA 16.2.2.4, using the second form type, for example, "Budapest, Hungary," not "Budapest (Hungary)." If the place name appears in the list of abbreviated place names in RDA appendix B.11, it should be abbreviated in this part of the authorized access point as well.

Preferred Name. Begin with the preferred name as already recorded following the procedures outlined in RDA 11.2.2 (see discussion above). Preferred name is recorded in subfields ‡a or ‡b of the appropriate MARC authority field.

Some examples of preferred name recorded in figures in this chapter include:

figure 5.1	110	2	‡a **Kronos Quartet**
figure 5.2	110	2	‡a **Apollo 11**
figure 5.10	110	2	‡a **Radio Dept.**
figure 5.12	110	2	‡a **Catholic Church. ‡b Pope (1978-2005 : John Paul II)**
figure 5.17	110	2	‡a **Encyclopaedia Britannica, Inc.**
figure 5.22	111	2	‡a **Council of Trent**
figure 5.28	110	2	‡a **American Library Association. ‡b Annual Meeting**
figure 5.29	110	2	‡a **Student Society for Ancient Studies**
figure 5.47	110	1	‡a **England and Wales. ‡b Sovereign (1689-1694 : William and Mary)**
figure 5.65	151		‡a **Washington**

Additions Required in All Cases. There are three additions required in all cases when applicable:

a. 11.13.1.2. If the preferred name for the body does not convey the idea of a corporate body, add an appropriate designation to the authorized access point as a qualifier (the designation is discussed above under 11.7.1.4). For catalogers following the Library of Congress Policy Statements, including contributors to the LC/NACO Authority File, the designation is in English (LC-PCC PS 11.13.1.2, February 2010).

Some examples of this required addition recorded in figures in this chapter include:

figure 5.2	110	2	‡a Apollo 11 **(Spacecraft)**
figure 5.10	110	2	‡a Radio Dept. **(Musical group)**
figure 5.24	111	2	‡a Hot Quarks **(Workshop)** . . .
figure 5.27	110	2	‡a Bendigo **(Corvette)**
figure 5.64	110	2	‡a D.E.P.T.H. **(Organisation)**

b. 11.13.1.8. If the corporate body is a meeting or event, the number (if applicable), date, and location of the event are added to the authorized access point. In the access point the date is recorded as the year only, even if a more specific date has been recorded in the 046 field.

Examples of this required addition recorded in figures in this chapter include:

figure 5.22	111	2	‡a Council of Trent ‡d **(1545-1563 : ‡c Trento, Italy)**
figure 5.24	111	2	‡a Hot Quarks (Workshop) ‡d **(2010 : ‡c La Londe-les-Maures, France)**
figure 5.28	110	2	‡a American Library Association. ‡b Annual Conference ‡n **(100th : ‡d 1981 : ‡c San Francisco, Calif.)**

figure 5.56 111 2 ‡a Z.E.F. Spiritual Convention ‡n **(1st : ‡d 1975 : ‡c Aijal, India)**

figure 5.59 111 2 ‡a Conference on Local Government ‡d **(1994 : ‡c Pietersburg, South Africa)**

figure 5.62 111 2 ‡a International Workshop on Nude Mice ‡n **(3rd : ‡d 1979 : ‡c Montana State University)**

Note carefully the required addition of the place name to the "Council of Trent" example in figure 5.22. Previous cataloging practice did not repeat the place name in the qualifier if it was already present in the name of the conference (cf. AACR2 24.7B4). In RDA authorized access points for conferences or events the place is added to the qualifier even if it is present in the name.

    c. Place associated with the corporate body in certain cases (11.13.1.3). If the body is (i) a local chapter of higher body and its preferred name is recorded subordinately, (ii) a local church, or (iii) a radio or television station and the preferred name consists solely or principally of its call letters, place is added as a qualifier unless the place name appears in the body's preferred name. St. Mary at Hill, a church in London, is an example (see figure 5.68).

Note that this example includes two qualifiers; the first is added because "St. Mary at Hill" does not convey the idea of a corporate body; the second is added because of the instruction in 11.13.1.3. If two qualifiers are needed, they are separated by space-colon-space, as shown in this figure. Contrast St. Mary at Hill with Kölner Dom, figure 5.25, which does not add a qualifier because the name of the place is a part of the body's preferred name. For an example of application of this guideline to a radio station, see figure 5.69.

Figure 5.68. Place Name as Qualifier for Local Church

110 2	‡a St. Mary at Hill (Church : London, England)
368	‡a Church
370	‡e London (England) ‡2 naf
377	‡a eng
410 2	‡a Saint Mary at Hill (Church : London, England)
670	‡a The medieval records of a London city church (St. Mary at Hill) A.D. 1430-1559, 1987

Figure 5.69. Place Name as Qualifier for Radio Station

110 2	‡a WGBH (Radio station : Boston, Mass.)
368	‡a Radio stations ‡2 lcsh
370	‡e Boston (Mass.) ‡2 naf
377	‡a eng
410 2	‡a 89.7 WGBH (Radio station : Boston, Mass.)
670	‡a A chance to grow, 1967: ‡b title page (WGBH, Boston)
670	‡a WGBH homepage, 13 December 2011 ‡b (89.7 WGBH)

Additions required in case of conflict. If the authorized access point as formed so far is identical to another access point already in the database, add one of the following five elements (the cataloger chooses which element best distinguishes the bodies):

a. Place associated with the body (11.13.1.3). The form of the place in the qualifier is its authorized form as outlined in 16.2.2.4, second paragraph. If the name of the place changes, or a corporate body moves from one location to another, the qualifier giving the place is revised in existing authorized access points. Optionally, place may be added as a qualifier even if not needed to distinguish between bodies with the same name, if the addition assists in the identification of the body.

Examples in this chapter include:

figure 5.57 110 2 ‡a John F. Kennedy Medical Center (**Monrovia, Liberia**)
figure 5.58 110 2 ‡a Hugh Exton Photographic Museum (**Polokwane, South Africa**)

b. Associated institution (11.13.1.4). An associated institution should be recorded in the qualifier in its authorized form. Optionally, associated institution may be added as a qualifier even if not needed to distinguish between bodies with the same name, if the addition assists in the identification of the body.

Examples in this chapter include:

figure 5.29 110 2 ‡a Student Society for Ancient Studies (**Brigham Young University**)
figure 5.55 110 1 ‡a United States. ‡b Delegation (**Inter-American Conference for the Maintenance of Peace (1936 : Buenos Aires, Argentina)**)
figure 5.63 110 2 ‡a Cougar Marching Band (**University of Houston**)

    c. Date associated with the body (11.13.1.5). Normally, only record the year(s) in this qualifier rather than a more specific date. Optionally, date(s) may be added as a qualifier even if not needed to distinguish between bodies with the same name, if the addition assists in the identification of the body.

An example from this chapter is:

> *figure 5.60*   110 2   ‡a Yale College **(1718-1887)**
>   110 2   ‡a Yale College **(1887-)**

    d. Type of jurisdiction (11.13.1.6). This qualifier is only used with names of jurisdictions. There is no option to add this qualifier unless it is needed to distinguish between jurisdictions with the same name.

An example from this chapter is:

> *figure 5.65*   151   ‡a Washington **(State)**

    e. Other designation associated with the body (11.13.1.7). This qualifier is added if none of the other possible qualifiers is sufficient or appropriate to distinguish between corporate bodies with identical names. Optionally, such a designation may be added as a qualifier even if not needed to distinguish between bodies with the same name, if the addition assists in understanding the nature and purpose of the body.

An example from this chapter is:

> *figure 5.66*   110 2   ‡a Church of Christ **(Temple Lot)**
>   110 2   ‡a Church of Christ **(Whitmerites)**

11.13.2. VARIANT ACCESS POINT REPRESENTING A CORPORATE BODY. Variant access points are constructed in much the same way as authorized access points, except a variant access point is based on a variant name for the corporate body rather than the preferred name. Variant access points for a corporate body are constructed using the 410, 411, or 451 field in the MARC authority record in the same way as described above at 11.13.1 for the 110, 111, or 151 field.

    Variant access point forms are never recorded in bibliographic records, only in authority records. Instead, if a user constructs a search using a variant access point, a display similar to the following directing the user to the authorized access point should be triggered from the authority record:

Cologne Cathedral
> *search under*
> Kölner Dom

Alternately, the system could re-execute the user's search automatically.[15]

The instructions for variant access points differ slightly from those for the authorized access point by requiring, in addition to the variant name, additions from 11.13.1.2–11.13.1.8 only "if necessary."

What makes an addition "necessary" isn't explained. However, traditional cataloging practice has deemed it necessary to make a qualifying addition to a variant name if it conflicts with a form already established as an *authorized* access point for another entity; but it is not deemed necessary to make a qualifying addition to a variant name if it conflicts with a *variant* access point for another entity. For example, there are dozens of corporate bodies that, in addition to a spelled-out form of their name, use the initialism "CBC," including California Banksite Company, Canadian Broadcasting Corporation, Commonwealth Business Council, and Cumbria Bird Club. Each of these will record a variant access point as follows:

410 2   ‡a CBC

According to traditional cataloging practice, it is not "necessary" to add anything as a qualifier to this variant access point, even though it will be identical to variant access points found in numerous other entity descriptions. As a result, if a user searches the database using "CBC," a message such as the following may display:

CBC
> *search under*
> California Banksite Company
> Canadian Broadcasting Corporation
> Commonwealth Business Council
> Cumbria Bird Club

On the other hand, if a variant name for a corporate body is identical to the authorized access point for another, traditional cataloging practice deems it "necessary" to add something to the variant name to differentiate it from the authorized access point for the other body. For example, there are two bodies with similar preferred names, "Roxburghe Club," a club in London, and "Roxburghe Club of San Francisco." The Roxburghe Club of San Francisco is sometimes known simply as "The Roxburghe Club," so this is a variant name for the body (see figure 5.70). However, the variant name conflicts with the authorized access point for the London club. This is a case, then, where it is "necessary" to make a qualifying addition to the variant name:

> 410 2 ‡a Roxburghe Club (San Francisco, Calif.)

not

> 410 2 ‡a Roxburghe Club

Figure 5.70. Variant Name Conflicts with Authorized Access Point

046	‡s 18120616
110 2	‡a Roxburghe Club
368	‡a Clubs ‡2 lcsh
370	‡e London (England) ‡2 naf
377	‡a eng
667	‡a Do not confuse with Roxburghe Club of San Francisco
670	‡a The rules and regulations, Roxburghe Club, 1870
670	‡a The Roxburghe Club, via WWW, 15 March 2012 ‡b (bibliophilic society founded 16 June 1812 at a dinner previous to the sale of the library of John, Duke of Roxburghe)

046	‡s 19280403
110 2	‡a Roxburghe Club of San Francisco
368	‡a Clubs ‡2 lcsh
370	‡e San Francisco (Calif.) ‡2 naf
377	‡a eng
410 2	‡a Roxburghe Club (San Francisco, Calif.)
670	‡a The Roxburghe Club of San Francisco : the first three years, 1931
670	‡a Online Archive of California, Roxburghe Club Collection, 15 March 2012 ‡b (The Roxburghe Club was formed in San Francisco on April 3, 1928 and was named in honor of the original Roxburgh Club of England)

Some additions to corporate body names, however, are made for reasons other than differentiation, including additions to names not conveying the idea of a corporate body, the addition of number, date, and location of conferences, and the addition of place in certain cases (such as to access points for local churches) (see above in the discussion of 11.13.1). Discussion below assumes such additions are "necessary." Other additions are not required unless the variant access point conflicts with an authorized access point in another description.

Variant Name. Begin with the variant name as already recorded following the procedures outlined in RDA 11.2.3 (see discussion above). The variant name is recorded in subfields ‡a or ‡b of the 410 MARC authority field, or subfield ‡a of the MARC 411 or 451 field.

Examples of variant names recorded in figures in this chapter include:

figure 5.1	410	2	‡a **Kronos Performing Arts Association**
figure 5.4a	410	2	‡a **日外アソシエーツ**
figure 5.9	410	1	‡a **United States. ‡b Secretary of State**
figure 5.10	410	2	‡a **Radioavdelningen**
figure 5.11	410	2	‡a **Université de Genève. ‡b Département de linguistique. ‡b Generative Grammar Group**

"Necessary" Additions. Necessary additions to variant names in access points include:

a. Additions required to differentiate the variant from the authorized access point of another body (11.13.1.3–11.13.1.7)
b. Additions to variant names that do not convey the idea of a corporate body (11.13.1.2)
c. Additions to variant names that represent conferences or events (11.13.1.8)
d. Additions of place names to the variant names of certain types of corporate bodies (11.13.1.3)

Examples of such additions recorded in figures in this chapter include:

Differentiation:

figure 5.16	410	2	‡a National Research Council **(Canada)**
figure 5.66	410	2	‡a Church of Christ **(David Whitmer)**
figure 5.70	410	2	‡a Roxburghe Club **(San Francisco, Calif.)**

Names that do not convey the idea of a corporate body:

figure 5.3b	410	2	‡a Guarro **(Papermaking firm)**
figure 5.6	410	2	‡a Mothers Against Drunk Driving **(Organization)**
figure 5.10	410	2	‡a Radioavdelningen **(Musical group)**
figure 5.64	410	2	‡a Diabetes, Education, Prevention, Treatment, Health **(Organisation)**
figure 5.68	410	2	‡a Saint Mary at Hill **(Church** : London, England)
figure 5.69	410	2	‡a 89.7 WGBH **(Radio station** : Boston, Mass.)

Conferences or events:

| *figure 5.22* | 410 | 2 | ‡a Catholic Church. ‡b Council of Trent ‡d **(1545-1563** : ‡c **Trento, Italy)** |

figure 5.24	411	2	‡a Workshop for Young Scientists on the Physics of Ultrarelativistic Nucleus-nucleus Collisions ‡n **(4th : ‡d 2010 : ‡c La Londe-les-Maures, France)**
figure 5.56	411	2	‡a Zoram Evangelical Fellowship Spiritual Convention ‡n **(1st : ‡d 1975 : ‡c Aijal, India)**

Place names for certain types of corporate bodies:

figure 5.68	410	2	‡a Saint Mary at Hill (Church : **London, England**)
figure 5.69	410	2	‡a 89.7 WGBH (Radio station : **Boston, Mass.**)

NOTES

1. Full information about MARC 21 authority format is available at www.loc.gov/marc/authority/ecadhome.html.

2. Pre-AACR2 authority records are identified by "d" in 008 position 10 for "AACR2 compatible heading," "b" for AACR1, and "a" for earlier rules.

3. IFLA Study Group on the Functional Requirements for Bibliographic Records, "User Tasks," ch. 6 in *Functional Requirements for Bibliographic Records Final: Report* (Munich: K. G. Sauer, 1998), 79–92. Also available at www.ifla.org/en/publications/functional-requirements-for-bibliographic-records. FRAD is an extension of FRBR; see IFLA Working Group on Functional Requirements and Numbering of Authority Records, *Functional Requirements for Authority Data: A Conceptual Model.* IFLA Series on Bibliographic Control, vol. 34 (Munich: K. G. Saur, 2009).

4. For the ALA-LC Romanization Tables, see www.loc.gov/catdir/cpso/roman.html.

5. Information about NACO authentication level procedures for preliminary and provisional access points is available in the Library of Congress's *Descriptive Cataloging Manual* Z1 at 008/33. This document is available at www.loc.gov/catdir/cpso/z1andlcguidelines.html.

6. Source information about certain elements may be recorded directly in the element's MARC field itself, in subfield ‡v, rather than in a 670 field. This technique is available for the 046 and 370–378 fields. This method has not yet found much favor in practice and is not used in this book.

7. *Descriptive Cataloging Manual* Z1 at 667. This document is available at www.loc.gov/catdir/cpso/z1andlcguidelines.html.

8. *World of Learning* (London: Allen & Unwin, 1947–).

9. *Encyclopedia Americana* (Danbury, CT: Grolier, 1994); *New Catholic Encyclopedia,* 2nd ed. (New York: Thomson-Gale; Washington, DC: Catholic University of America, 2003).

10. *Britannica Academic Edition* (Chicago: Encyclopædia Britannica).

11. The *Statement of International Cataloguing Principles* is available at www.ifla.org/files/
cataloguing/icp/icp_2009-en.pdf. Section 6.3.4.3.2, in turn, is based on Paris Principle
9.61. See also International Conference on Cataloguing Principles, Paris, 1961, *Statement of Principles,* annotated edition with commentary and examples by Eva Verona
(London: IFLA Committee on Cataloguing, 1971).

12. *A.L.A. Cataloging Rules for Author and Title Entries,* 2nd ed., ed. Clara Beetle
(Chicago: American Library Association, 1949), 135.

13. See *Descriptive Cataloging Manual* Z1 at 370—Associated Place (November 2013).
Previous to Fall 2013 a different practice for recording place names in 370 was
followed, so catalogers will encounter records that do not follow the procedure
described here.

14. Codes for thesauri are available at www.loc.gov/standards/sourcelist.

15. Some systems allow the user to choose between sets of alternative authorized access
points. For example, a database in Quebec might allow its users to prefer to search
French authorized access points rather than English authorized access points. Such
systems are beyond the scope of this book.

CHAPTER 6

DESCRIBING GEOGRAPHIC ENTITIES

Instructions for recording the attributes of the *place* entity are found in RDA chapter 16, with some information in chapter 11, "Identifying Corporate Bodies." The as yet undeveloped chapter 12 is also intended to give general guidance for describing the *place* entity.

MARC CODING

HE *PLACE* ENTITY IS CURRENTLY DESCRIBED IN library catalogs in the MARC 21 authority format.[1] RDA records for places are identified by the value "z" in the 008 field position 10 (labeled "Rules" in the OCLC fixed field display) and the presence of "‡e rda" in the 040 field (see figure 6.1a). In contrast, an AACR2 authority record may be recognized by the presence of value "c" in 008 position 10 and no special coding in 040 (see figure 6.1b).[2] For space reasons, RDA coding is assumed in further figures in this chapter and is not explicitly shown. Other MARC coding issues will be discussed as they occur later in the chapter.

Figure 6.1a. RDA Coding (OCLC Style)

Rec stat	c	Entered	19800725	Replaced	20110930071248.0	
Type	z	Upd status	a	Enc lvl	n	Source
Roman		Ref status	b	Mod rec		Name use	a
Govt agn		Auth status	a	Subj	a	Subj use	a
Series	n	Auth/ref	a	Geo subd	n	Ser use	b
Ser num	n	Name	n	Subdiv tp	n	**Rules**	**z**

010	‡a n 79076156
040	‡a DLC ‡b eng **‡e rda** ‡c DLC ‡d DLC ‡d NIC ‡d DLC-ON ‡d WaU ‡d DLC ‡d OCoLC ‡d WaU ‡d OCoLC
151	‡a Moscow (Russia)
368	‡b City
370	‡c Russia ‡2 naf
451	‡a Москва (Russia)
451	‡a Moskva (Russia)
451	‡w nne ‡a Moscow (R.S.F.S.R.)
667	‡a Non-Latin script reference not evaluated.
670	‡a An historical account and description of the City of Moscow, 1813
670	‡a Kratkiĭ putevoditel', 1957: ‡b title page (Москва)
670	‡a GEONet, 5 April 2009 ‡b (Moscow (Conventional); capital of Russia; variants: Moskva, Москва ; 55°45'08"N 037°36'56"E)

Figure 6.1a. RDA Coding (LC Style)

008	790824n| a**z**annaabn |b ana
010	‡a n 79076156
040	‡a DLC ‡b eng **‡e rda** ‡c DLC ‡d DLC ‡d NIC ‡d DLC-ON ‡d WaU ‡d DLC ‡d OCoLC ‡d WaU ‡d OCoLC
151	‡a Moscow (Russia)
368	‡c City
370	‡c Russia ‡2 naf
451	‡a Москва (Russia)
451	‡a Moskva (Russia)
451	‡a Moscow (R.S.F.S.R.) ‡w nne
667	‡a Non-Latin script reference not evaluated.
670	‡a An historical account and description of the City of Moscow, 1813
670	‡a Kratkiĭ putevoditel', 1957: ‡b title page (Москва)
670	‡a GEONet, 5 April 2009 ‡b (Moscow (Conventional); capital of Russia; variants: Moskva, Москва ; 55°45'08"N 037°36'56"E)

Figure 6.1b. AACR2 Coding (OCLC Style)

Rec stat	c	Entered	19800725		Replaced 20110930071248.0		
Type	z	Upd status	a	Enc lvl	n	Source	
Roman		Ref status	b	Mod rec		Name use	a
Govt agn		Auth status	a	Subj	a	Subj use	a
Series	n	Auth/ref	a	Geo subd	n	Ser use	b
Ser num	n	Name	n	Subdiv tp	n	**Rules**	**c**

010	‡a n 79076156
040	‡a DLC ‡b eng ‡c DLC ‡d DLC ‡d NIC ‡d DLC-ON ‡d WaU ‡d DLC ‡d OCoLC ‡d WaU ‡d OcoLC
151	‡a Moscow (Russia)
451	‡a Москва (Russia)
451	‡a Moskva (Russia)
451	‡a Moscow (R.S.F.S.R.) ‡w nne
667	‡a Non-Latin script reference not evaluated.
670	‡a An historical account and description of the City of Moscow, 1813
670	‡a Kratkiĭ putevoditel′, 1957: ‡b title page (Москва)
670	‡a GEONet, 5 April 2009 ‡b (Moscow (Conventional); capital of Russia; variants: Moskva, Москва ; 55°45'08"N 037°36'56"E)

Figure 6.1b. AACR2 Coding (LC Style)

008	790824n| acannaabn |b ana
010	‡a n 79076156
040	‡a DLC ‡b eng ‡c DLC ‡d DLC ‡d NIC ‡d DLC-ON ‡d WaU ‡d DLC ‡d OCoLC ‡d WaU ‡d OCoLC
151	‡a Moscow (Russia)
451	‡a Москва (Russia)
451	‡a Moskva (Russia)
451	‡a Moscow (R.S.F.S.R.) ‡w nne
667	‡a Non-Latin script reference not evaluated.
670	‡a An historical account and description of the City of Moscow, 1813
670	‡a Kratkiĭ putevoditel′, 1957: ‡b title page (Москва)
670	‡a GEONet, 5 April 2009 ‡b (Moscow (Conventional); capital of Russia; variants: Moskva, Москва ; 55°45'08"N 037°36'56"E)

General Guidelines

Place names are used to represent governments and jurisdictions (RDA 11.2.2.5.4); in addition, many government bodies are entered subordinately to such place names (RDA 11.2.2.14–11.2.2.24). Place names are also used to record certain elements of work entity descriptions (RDA 6.5), person entity descriptions (RDA 9.8–9.11), family entity descriptions (RDA 10.5), and corporate body entity descriptions (RDA 11.3). Additionally, place names are used in access points to differentiate family names (RDA 10.10.1.4) and corporate names (RDA 11.3.3, 11.13.1.2) from other entities with the same name. RDA chapter 16 gives guidance about the forms of name that should be used in all these cases.

Chapter 16 is quite short, in part because it does not deal yet with place names that do not represent governments (e.g., lakes, mountains, deserts, and other non-jurisdictional places). Because governments are corporate bodies, many of the relevant guidelines for describing these places are found in chapter 11.

Non-jurisdictional place names, such as archaeological sites, parks, lakes, mountains, valleys, and the like, are not established in the LC/NACO Authority File, but may be needed to record an element in an RDA record for a person, family, or corporate body as noted above. The form of non-jurisdictional place names is governed by the *Library of Congress Subject Headings Manual,* and is beyond the scope of this book.[3]

RDA chapter 12 is intended to be the chapter giving general guidelines for recording the attributes of the place entity. This chapter has not been written yet. Much of the information in chapter 8, "General Guidelines on Recording Attributes of Persons, Families, and Corporate Bodies," can be applied to the place entity, however, and these guidelines will be discussed here in the context of geographic entities.

8.3. CORE ELEMENTS. No elements have as yet been identified as core in RDA for the place entity. However, because jurisdictional places are corporate bodies, three core elements for corporate bodies apply to them as well. These are: preferred name (RDA 11.2.2), date associated with the corporate body (RDA 11.4), and identifier (RDA 11.2), as well as other designation associated with the corporate body to distinguish the place from other entities with the same name (RDA 11.7).

8.4. LANGUAGE AND SCRIPT. One of the basic principles of RDA is that of representation: "The data describing [an entity] should reflect the [entity's] representation of itself" (RDA 0.4.3.4). It is therefore no surprise that RDA 8.4 calls for recording names in the language and script in which they appear. This would mean that the preferred name of a jurisdiction that uses Russian would be recorded in Cyrillic script, a Japanese-speaking jurisdiction's name would be recorded in Japanese script, and an English-speaking jurisdiction's name in Latin script. RDA 8.4 includes an alternative, however: "Record a transliterated form of the name either as a substitute for, or in addition to, the form that appears on the source." LC and NACO will continue to record a form transliterated following the ALA-LC Romanization Tables as the preferred name for names appearing in non-Latin scripts.[4] Non-Latin script forms may be included in the record as variant access points. Including non-Latin variant access points is a relatively recent practice, and NACO policies have not been fully developed. Until they are, catalogers may record non-Latin script variant access points in 4XX fields, but should include a 667 field reading "Non-Latin script reference(s) not evaluated" (see figure 6.1).

8.10. STATUS OF IDENTIFICATION. RDA instructs us to record the level of authentication of the data identifying the entity. The possible levels are "fully established," "provisional," and "preliminary." For a full discussion of this element, see chapter 3 of the *Handbook* under 8.10.

8.11. UNDIFFERENTIATED NAME INDICATOR. The undifferentiated name technique, using the same access point for two or more different entities with the same name, is only available in RDA for descriptions of persons, not places.

8.12. SOURCE CONSULTED. Just as the author of a scholarly paper justifies his or her assertions by citing sources (usually in footnotes), so the creator of an RDA description for a place in an authority record must justify access points by citing where the information came from. In MARC authority work, this is done using the 670 field.[5] The source consulted element is not core in RDA, but at least one instance, that of the resource in hand that generated the need for a new authorized access point, is required in LC/NACO practice.

In addition, LC/NACO practice also requires research beyond the resource in hand when establishing a place entity (see LC-PCC PS 16.2.2.2, January 2013). This extra research will always generate a second source consulted element in descriptions of place entities. NACO catalogers should chose the preferred name based on the form found in the following online reference sources:

1. For places in the United States: the United States Board on Geographic Names (BGN) Geographic Names Information System (GNIS) (http://geonames .usgs.gov/pls/gnispublic).
2. For places in Australia: Geoscience Australia, place name search (www.ga.gov .au/map/names/).
3. For places in Canada: Natural Resources Canada's Canadian Geographical Names Data Base (http://geonames.nrcan.gc.ca/search/search_e.php).
4. For places in Great Britain: The Ordnance Survey Gazetteer of Great Britain (http://leisure.ordnancesurvey.co.uk).
5. For places in New Zealand: Land Information New Zealand's New Zealand Geographic Placenames Database (www.linz.govt.nz/placenames/find-names/ index.aspx or www.linz.govt.nz/placenames/find-names/macrons/index.aspx).
6. For other names: consider the form found in the resource in hand together with the form found on the GEOnet Names Server (GNS) (http://earth-info .nga.mil/gns/html/index.html).

The conventional citation for research on U.S. names from the Board of Geographic Names database is:

670 ‡a BGN, [date consulted] ‡b (data, including latitude and longitude as found)

or

670 ‡a GNIS, [date consulted] ‡b (data, including latitude and longitude as found)

For an example, see figure 6.2.

Figure 6.2. Required Research for a Name in the United States

151	‡a Fayette (Iowa)
368	‡b Town
370	‡c United States ‡f Iowa ‡f Fayette County (Iowa) ‡2 naf
670	‡a Pictorial souvenir album of the City of Fayette, Iowa, U.S.A., 1898
670	‡a BGN, June 16, 2010 ‡b (Fayette, Fayette County, Iowa, populated place, 42°50'31"N 91°48'07"W)

The conventional citation for research in the GEOnet names server is:

670 ‡a GEOnet, [date consulted] ‡b (data, including latitude and longitude as found)

For an example, see figure 6.3.

Figure 6.3. Required Research in GEOnet

151	‡a Ouagadougou (Burkina Faso)
368	‡b City
370	‡c Burkina Faso ‡2 naf
451	‡a Ouagadouga (Burkina Faso)
451	‡a Wagadugu (Burkina Faso)
670	‡a Index des voies de la ville de Ouagadougou, 1997
670	‡a GEOnet, August 23, 2010 ‡b (Ouagadougou; variants: Ouagadouga, Wagadugu; capital of Burkina Faso, 12°22'13"N 001°31'29"W)

Examples of 670 fields are found in figures throughout this chapter. For a full discussion of LC/NACO practice in the source consulted element, see chapter 3 under 8.12.

8.13. CATALOGUER'S NOTE. The cataloguer's note element contains information about the place represented by the authorized access point that might be helpful to persons using the authority record. The cataloguer's note element is not core in RDA, but it is core for the Library of Congress in certain situations (see *Descriptive Cataloging Manual* Z1 at 667).[6] The most common use of this note for descriptions of places is a subject usage note for cases where the jurisdiction has changed its name. In Library of Congress subject practice, only the latest form of the name is used in most cases (see the *Subject Headings Manual* at H708), and catalogers are informed that a given place name cannot be used as a subject by the cataloguer's note element (see figure 6.4). For an example of a different type of cataloguer's note, see the 667 field in figure 6.1.

Figure 6.4. Cataloguer's Note

046	ǂs 1964 ǂt 19800418
151	ǂa Southern Rhodesia
368	ǂb Country
551	ǂw r ǂi Predecessor: ǂa Rhodesia and Nyasaland
551	ǂw r ǂi Successor: ǂa Zimbabwe
667	ǂa SUBJECT USAGE: This heading is not valid for use as a subject. Works about this place are entered under Zimbabwe.
670	ǂa Agreement between the Government of the Republic of South Africa and the Government of Southern Rhodesia for the avoidance of double taxation, 1965
670	ǂa Standard encyclopedia of Southern Africa, 1974: ǂb volume 9, page 324 (from 1953 to 1963 Southern Rhodesia was part of the Federation of Rhodesia and Nyasaland)
670	ǂa GEOnet, January 21, 2011 ǂb (Zimbabwe, Republic of; variant: Southern Rhodesia; 19°00′00″S 29°00′00″E)

STRUCTURE OF CHAPTER 16. RDA chapter 16, "Identifying Places," brief though it is, follows the same structure as most of the other chapters in the "Recording Attributes" parts of RDA (RDA sections 1 through 4). It begins with a section on the purpose and scope of the chapter (RDA 16.0) and then proceeds to general guidelines on identifying places, including sources that may be consulted for information about places (RDA 16.1). It then treats, one by one, the various elements and sub-elements of the place entity that are recognized by RDA, giving instructions on where to get information about the element or sub-element, and how to record that information. In this undeveloped chapter there are only two such elements, name of the place and identifier for the place (RDA 16.2–16.3). When this chapter is more fully developed there will undoubtedly be guidelines for recording other elements (such as dates associated with the place, as seen in the 046 field of figure 6.4, or other places associated with the jurisdiction, as seen in the 370 field of figure 6.2 and elsewhere in this chapter). The chapter ends with a final section on constructing access points for places (RDA 16.4).

16.2. Name of the Place

GENERAL GUIDELINES

16.2.1. BASIC INSTRUCTIONS ON RECORDING NAMES OF PLACES. "Name of the place" is defined in RDA as "word, character, or group of words and/or characters by which a place is known." A single place can have more than one name. One of those names will be chosen under RDA as the preferred name; others may be included in the description as variant names.

16.2.2. PREFERRED NAME FOR THE PLACE. The preferred name of other entities is a core element in RDA, meaning any description of the entity must include this element. Although core elements have not yet been defined for the place entity, it is reasonable to expect that preferred name will be core here as well. Additionally, because jurisdictions are corporate bodies, preferred names of this type of place are core under 11.2.2. Preferred name for the place is defined as

> the name or form of name chosen to identify a place. The preferred name is
> also used: a) as the conventional name of a government, etc.; b) as an addition
> to the name of a family, a corporate body, a conference, etc.; c) to record a place
> associated with a person, family, or corporate body.

16.2.2.4. RECORDING THE PREFERRED NAME. Preferred names for places are recorded in subfield ‡a of the 151 field of authority records in the form prescribed generally in RDA 16.2.2.4.

In addition they may be recorded in a parenthetical qualifier in an access point for a family name, the name of a corporate body, or the preferred title of a work. Geographic qualifiers to the preferred names of families are recorded in subfield ‡c of the 100 field (see discussion in chapter 4 of this *Handbook* at 10.10.1). Geographic qualifiers to the preferred names of corporate bodies are recorded without special subfield coding in subfield ‡a or ‡b of the 110 field, or in subfield ‡c of the 111 field (see discussion in chapter 5 of this *Handbook* at 11.13.1). Geographic qualifiers to preferred titles of works are recorded without special subfield coding (see discussion in chapter 7 of this *Handbook* at 6.27.1.9). When recording a place name in a parenthetical qualifier in an access point, follow the instructions in RDA 16.2.2.4, using the second form type, for example, "Budapest, Hungary," not "Budapest (Hungary)." If the place name appears in the list of abbreviated place names in RDA appendix B.11, it should be abbreviated in this part of the authorized access point as well.

Preferred names of places are also recorded in place-related elements in the descriptions of persons, families, corporate bodies, and works. Such elements are recorded in the MARC authorities 370 field. See discussion in chapter 3 at 9.8–9.11 (persons); in chapter 4 at 10.5 (families); in chapter 5 at 11.3 (corporate bodies); and in chapter 7 at 6.5 (works).

For further discussion of RDA 16.2.2.4, see below under Additions to the Preferred Name, following the discussion of 16.2.2.8.

CHOOSING THE PREFERRED NAME

If a place is known by more than one form of the same name, or by more than one name, RDA 16.2.2.3 gives us guidance for choosing one of these as the preferred name. We are to choose a form of the name in the language preferred by the agency, if there is one; and if not, a form of the name in the official language of the jurisdiction in which the place is located. RDA 16.2.2.4 stipulates that an initial article found with the name is part of the preferred name. However, an alternative guideline, followed in current LC-PCC cataloging practice, instructs the cataloger to omit the article unless the name is supposed to file under the article (e.g., "Los Angeles").

The approach to choosing the preferred name for jurisdictions differs somewhat from that used with other corporate bodies, where preference is given to forms found in preferred sources of information in resources associated with the corporate body (see RDA 11.2.2.2a). In the case of place names, preference is given instead to forms found in reference sources (see 16.2.2.2). Sources to be used by catalogers in the LC/NACO Authority File have been discussed above under 8.12 (source consulted element). Both approaches support the basic principle that we choose the most commonly known form of an entity's name as the preferred name (see RDA 0.4.3.4, discussion of the principle of representation). By following a slightly different approach in chapter 16 from that of chapter 11, RDA takes the stand that the most commonly known form for place names—that is, the form most users will use when searching for the jurisdiction in library databases—is more likely to be that found in reference sources than that found in preferred sources of information in resources associated with the jurisdiction.

16.2.2.6. DIFFERENT LANGUAGE FORMS OF THE NAME. We are instructed here to choose as the preferred name a form in the language preferred by the agency. The language preferred by the Library of Congress and the Program for Cooperative Cataloging is English (LC-PCC PS 16.2.2.6, October 2012). Figure 6.1 shows evidence for two forms of the name, Moscow and Москва. The English form, Moscow, is chosen as the preferred name.

16.2.2.7. CHANGE OF NAME. Governments or jurisdictions (i.e., corporate bodies) are usually identified by a place name. If the name of such a place changes, the new name is chosen as the preferred name for use with resources associated with that name, just as with any other corporate body. In 1980 the government known by the name Southern Rhodesia was overthrown and the new government changed the nation's name to Zimbabwe. A new description was made, and the preferred name Zimbabwe began to be used for resources associated with the new nation. The two descriptions are linked by 551 "search also under" fields, as seen by the second 551 field in figure 6.4. Use relationship designators appropriate to corporate bodies from appendix K to show the relationship between jurisdictions. The relationship designator is recorded in subfield ‡i of the 551 field; "‡w r" must also be present (a MARC requirement).

The two records taken together might produce a message such as the following when a user performs a search on "Southern Rhodesia":

> Southern Rhodesia
> > *search also under*
> > Successor: Zimbabwe

Note carefully that 16.2.2.7 applies to the names of governments or jurisdictions as established (16.2.2.7a), as well as these same names when used as additions (qualifiers) to family and corporate names (16.2.2.7b). This means that if the name of the place changes, not only should the new name be used with resources associated with it (see RDA 11.2.2.6), but the new name may also need to replace the old name in qualifying additions to preferred names of families and corporate bodies (see RDA 11.3.3.4). For a discussion of this see chapter 5 at 11.3.3.4, with figures 5.58 and 5.59.

OMISSIONS FROM THE PREFERRED NAME

16.2.2.8. PLACE NAMES FOR JURISDICTIONS. If the first part of the place name is a term indicating a type of jurisdiction ("City," "Commonwealth," "County," "State"), omit the term (and a preposition if necessary) unless the place is commonly listed under the term. "Commonwealth of Massachusetts" is recorded as "Massachusetts." Conversely, "District of Columbia" is recorded as "District of Columbia," not "Columbia," because the place is always listed under "District." Some cases are less clear and the cataloger will need to use judgment. "Ciudad Juárez," given as an example under 16.2.2.8.1, is known and listed both as "Ciudad Juárez" and "Juárez." The basic principle calling for the most commonly known form to be chosen as the preferred name requires a decision by the cataloger. In this case, the cataloger choosing the examples for RDA decided that "Ciudad Juárez" was the most commonly known form.

The town illustrated in figure 6.2, Fayette (Iowa), exemplifies this procedure. The source given in the first source consulted element (670 field) gives the name as "City of Fayette." "City of" is omitted from the preferred name as recorded in the description. Because this is a routine omission, the form including the type of jurisdiction is not normally recorded as a variant name in the description; for example, figure 6.2 does not include a 451 field with "City of Fayette (Iowa)." This is left up to the judgment of the cataloger, however.

Although it is omitted from the preferred name of most places, type of jurisdiction may be recorded as an element of the description in a MARC 368 field, subfield ‡b (see most figures in this chapter).

Sometimes the omission of the type of jurisdiction from the preferred name means the preferred name will conflict with another preferred name. In this case 16.2.2.8.2 refers us back to 11.7.1.5, which, with 11.13.1.6, instructs us to distinguish the two names by an addition to the qualifier. For example, in the eastern United States distinct civil jurisdictions with the same name frequently coincide with each other. In Bedford County, Pennsylvania, there is a town that calls itself Bedford, a separate jurisdiction called "Township of Bedford," and another that calls itself "Borough of Bedford." These are listed separately in the Geographic Names Information System (GNIS), and separate descriptions have been created for each in the LC/NACO Authority File. The preferred names are distinguished from each other by the addition of the type of jurisdiction to the qualifier for the township and the borough (see figure 6.5).

Figure 6.5a. Type of Jurisdiction Omitted

151	‡a Bedford (Pa.)
368	‡b Town
370	‡c United States ‡f Pennsylvania ‡f Bedford County (Pa.) ‡2 naf
451	‡a Fort Bedford (Pa.)
451	‡a Manor of Bedford (Pa.)
551	‡w r ‡i Predecessor: ‡a Raystown (Pa.)
670	‡a Welcome home celebration, Bedford, Pa., July 4th, 1919, in honor of all Bedford County participants of all U.S. wars, 1919
670	‡a GNIS, July 23, 2011 ‡b (Bedford, populated place in Pennsylvania, county seat, 40°01'07"N, 78°30'14"W, named in honor of John Russell, the fourth Duke of Bedford; variant names: Camp Raystown, Fort Bedford, Manor of Bedford, Raystown, Raystown)
670	‡a Bedford County history, via WWW, July 23, 2011 ‡b (Town of Raystown settled in about 1751; Fort Bedford erected there in 1758; the place was referred to as Raystown until 1758; after that it was referred to as Bedford (or variants on Bedford))

Figure 6.5b. Type of Jurisdiction Added to Qualifier

151	‡a Bedford (Pa. : Borough)
	‡b Borough
370	‡c United States ‡f Pennsylvania ‡f Bedford County (Pa.) ‡2 naf
670	‡a FIRM, flood insurance rate map, Borough of Bedford, Pennsylvania, Bedford County, 1988 : ‡b map recto (Borough of Bedford, Pennsylvania, Bedford County)
670	‡a GNIS, July 23, 2011 ‡b (Borough of Bedford, civil jurisdiction in Pennsylvania, 39°59'08"N, 78°29'15"W)

Figure 6.5c. Type of Jurisdiction Added to Qualifier

151	‡a Bedford (Pa. : Township)
368	‡b Township
370	‡c United States ‡f Pennsylvania ‡f Bedford County (Pa.) ‡2 naf
670	‡a FIRM, flood insurance rate map, Township of Bedford, Pennsylvania, Bedford County, 1989 : ‡b map recto (Township of Bedford, Pennsylvania, Bedford County)
670	‡a GNIS, July 23, 2011 ‡b (Township of Bedford, civil jurisdiction in Pennsylvania, 40°00'02"N, 78°32'29"W)

ADDITIONS TO THE PREFERRED NAME

Although chapter 16 guidelines apply only to geographic names that represent jurisdictions (corporate bodies), jurisdictions are treated differently from most other corporate bodies in one respect. RDA 16.2.2.4 instructs us, for most preferred names of jurisdictions, to include as a qualifying addition the preferred name of the larger place in which it is located (if the name of the larger place appears in appendix B.11, the applicable abbreviation is used instead of the preferred name). This form is placed in parentheses, just like any other qualifier (see figure 6.1). Unlike for most other corporate bodies, where such an addition is made only if the preferred name of the body is the same as that of another entity, the qualifier is added to most place names whether the name of the place conflicts with that of another entity or not.

There are a few important exceptions to this guideline. The instruction to add a qualifier does not apply to countries and a few other jurisdictions (see below, under 16.2.2.9 and 16.2.2.10).

The final paragraph of 16.2.2.4 gives instructions for how a place name that has been qualified is to be recorded in qualifiers to the preferred names of other entities. Rather than enclose the name of the larger jurisdiction in parentheses, as is the practice when establishing the place per se, the name of the larger jurisdiction in these cases is preceded instead by a comma. If the name of the larger jurisdiction appears in appendix B, it is abbreviated:

Preferred Name	*Qualifier*
Paris (France)	. . . (Paris, France)
Mexico City (Mexico)	. . . (Mexico City, Mexico)
Ontario (Calif.)	. . . (Ontario, Calif.)
Budapest (Hungary)	. . . (Budapest, Hungary)
Toronto (Ont.)	. . . (Toronto, Ont.)

As discussed above, preferred names of places are used in parenthetical qualifiers of all kinds throughout RDA, including qualifying additions to family names, corporate body names, and preferred titles of works. They are also used when recording place-related elements for works, persons, families, and corporate bodies (i.e., in MARC 370 fields). In LC/NACO practice, if a place name is to be used as a qualifier in an access point of another entity, it must first be established in the LC/NACO Authority File so that it will be clear what the preferred name of the place is. If a place is to be recorded as an element in the description of another entity (e.g., in the place of birth element for a person, RDA 9.8) the form should also be based on the established form of the place, but in current LC/NACO practice a place can be recorded in such an element even if it has not yet been formally established. In that case the cataloger should determine what the preferred name would be if it had been established and so record it.

16.2.2.9. PLACES IN AUSTRALIA, CANADA, THE UNITED STATES, THE FORMER U.S.S.R., OR THE FORMER YUGOSLAVIA. RDA 16.2.2.9 and 16.2.2.10 constitute a number of exceptions to the general guideline of 16.2.2.4 ("Record as part of the name of a place . . . the name of the larger place in which it is located . . ."). Do *not* qualify the name of a state or province in Australia, Canada, the United States, or a country that was a constituent republic in the former U.S.S.R. or Yugoslavia, by adding the name of a larger place. For example, within the United States "Arizona" stands without a qualifier (see figure 6.6).

Figure 6.6. Qualifier Omitted

151	‡a Arizona
368	‡b State
370	United States ‡2 naf
670	‡a 2012-2016 Arizona's five-year transportation facilities construction program, 2011
670	‡a Wikipedia, April 19, 2011 ‡b (Arizona; State of Arizona; 34°N 112°W)
675	‡a GNIS, June 16, 2012

A place below the state, republic, province, etc., level in one of the countries covered by 16.2.2.9 is qualified by the name of the state, republic, province, etc., in which it is located. The town of Fayette in figure 6.2 is qualified by "Iowa." If the name of the state, republic, province, etc., appears in RDA appendix B.11 (abbreviations of certain geographic names), it should be abbreviated in the qualifier (see figure 6.5a).

16.2.2.10. ENGLAND, NORTHERN IRELAND, SCOTLAND, AND WALES. Under the first version of AACR2 (1978) catalogers were instructed to add the name of a county to names of places in England, Wales, or the Republic of Ireland. For catalogers outside of the British Isles, this rule was difficult to apply and led to access points that were cumbersome and less than helpful to library users. The rule was modified under later versions of AACR2 and has been brought into RDA as guideline 16.2.2.10. The jurisdiction names England, Northern Ireland, Scotland, and Wales are not qualified. Places within these jurisdictions are qualified by the name of the jurisdiction (see figures 6.7 and 6.8).

Figure 6.7. England, Northern Ireland, Scotland, or Wales

046	‡t 1536
046	‡s 19990701
151	‡a Wales
368	‡b Country
451	‡a Cymru
667	‡a Authorized access point for Wales valid as a jurisdiction before 1536 and after 1 July 1999 only. Between 1536 and 1 July 1999, use "(Wales)" as qualifier for places (16.2.2.4) and for nongovernment bodies (11.13.1.3) only.
670	‡a Report on the proposed education (Wales) measure = Adroddiad ar y mesur arfaethedig ynghylch addysg (Cymru), 2011
670	‡a Ordnance Survey gazetteer of Great Britain, 17 June 2009 ‡b (Wales)
678	‡a In 1536 Wales was united with England to form England and Wales. In 1707 Scotland was united with England and Wales to form Great Britain. Subsequent to a referendum held in 1998, devolution into an autonomous entity within the United Kingdom became effective 1 July 1999 with the state opening of the Welsh National Assembly in Cardiff by Queen Elizabeth II.

Figure 6.8. Place within England, Northern Ireland, Scotland, or Wales

151	‡a Cwmllynfell (Wales)
368	‡b Villages ‡2 lcsh
370	‡c Wales ‡2 naf

670	‡a Hanes eglwys Cwmllynfell, 1935
670	‡a Ordnance Survey gazetteer of Great Britain, 17 June 2009 ‡b (Cwmllynfell, Wales, 2 miles ESE of Brynamman)

16.2.2.12. PLACES IN OTHER JURISDICTIONS. For places not covered by 16.2.2.9 and 16.2.2.10, add the name of the country, for example, Moscow (Russia) or Ouagadougou (Burkina Faso) (see figures 6.1 and 6.3). This is a restatement of the instruction already given in 16.2.2.4.

16.2.2.13. PLACES WITH THE SAME NAME. If the addition of the larger place under 16.2.2.9– 16.2.2.11 is not sufficient to distinguish identical place names, RDA first instructs us to try to distinguish the names by including as part of the name a word or phrase that is commonly used to distinguish them. An example is the two Frankfurts in Germany (see figure 6.9). If this is not possible, make further additions to the qualifier, either by adding the type of jurisdiction to the qualifier as discussed above under 16.2.2.8 (with figure 6.5), or by qualifying by the name of an intermediate place (such as a county name), if that is more appropriate (cf. LC-PCC PS 16.2.2.13, May 2013). RDA does not specify which level of "smaller place" to use other than that it be "appropriate." For the places illustrated by figure 6.10, catalogers chose to qualify one of the many French Beauforts by the name of the French region (Nord-Pas-de-Calais), and another by the name of the French département (Hérault).

Figure 6.9. Conflict Resolved by Addition of Phrase

151	‡a Frankfurt am Main (Germany)
368	‡b City
370	‡c Germany ‡f Hesse (Germany) ‡2 naf
451	‡a Frankfort (Germany)
451	‡a Frankfurt (Germany)
670	‡a Frankfurts alte Brücke, 2010
670	‡a GEONet, 22 November 2011 ‡b (Frankfurt, Frankfurt am Main, Frankfort; populated place in Hessen, Germany, 50°07'00"N 8°41'00"E)

151	‡a Frankfurt an der Oder (Germany)
368	‡b City
370	‡c Germany ‡f Brandenburg, Germany
451	‡a Frankfurt (Germany)
670	‡a Frankfurt (Oder) und das Land Lebus, 2005
670	‡a GEONet, 22 November 2011 ‡b (Frankfurt, Frankfurt an der Oder; populated place in Brandenburg, Germany, 52°21'00"N 14°33'00"E)

Figure 6.10. Conflict Resolved by Expansion of Qualifier

151	‡a Beaufort (Nord-Pas-de-Calais, France)
368	‡b Town
370	‡c France ‡f Nord-Pas-de-Calais (France) ‡2 naf
670	‡a Les habitants de Beaufort de 1619 à 1905, 2006?: ‡b v. 1, p. 6 (Beaufort in canton d'Hautmont, arrondissement d'Avesnes sur Helpe, département du Nord)
670	‡a GEOnet, 13 November, 2008 ‡b (Beaufort; populated place, 50°13'N 3°57'48"E; in Nord-Pas-de-Calais; other populated places in France named Beaufort)

151	‡a Beaufort (Hérault, France)
368	‡b Commune
370	‡c France ‡f Hérault (France) ‡2 naf
451	‡a Beaufort (Languedoc-Roussillon)
670	‡a Précis chronologique d'histoire de Beaufort dans l'Hérault, 2001: ‡b page 115 (commune de Beaufort; canton d'Olonzac, arr. de Béziers)
670	‡a GEOnet, 13 November 2008 ‡b (Beaufort; populated place, 43°17'49"N 2°45'22"E; in Languedoc-Roussillon; other populated places in France named Beaufort)

16.2.2.14. PLACES WITHIN CITIES, ETC. Named city sections may be established. The preferred name of such a place is qualified by the name of the city, even if it does not conflict with another name. Hollywood is an example (see figure 6.11).

Figure 6.11. City Section

151	‡a Hollywood (Los Angeles, Calif.)
368	‡b Neighborhoods ‡2 lcsh
370	‡c United States ‡f Los Angeles (Calif.) ‡2 naf
410 2	‡a Los Angeles (Calif.). ‡b Hollywood
667	‡a SUBJECT USAGE: This heading is not valid for use as a geographic subdivision.
670	‡a Facts about Hollywood, U.S.A., 1947
670	‡a GNIS, 13 December 2011 ‡b (Hollywood, community in Los Angeles, California, 34°05'54"N 118°19'36"W)

16.2.3. VARIANT NAME FOR THE PLACE. As with other entities, places are known by different names or different forms of the same name. One of these forms is chosen, as described above, as the preferred name, and in current systems the preferred name is how the name will appear in displays such as database indexes and bibliographic records. But if the place is known by other names, these will be recorded in the description if in the judgment of the cataloger this would be helpful for identification or access.

Variant names of places are recorded in 451 fields in the MARC authority format. How they display depends on how the library's system is set up, but when a user does a search on a variant (using, for example, a display generated by the description in figure 6.1), they are intended to display to the public similarly to the following:

Moskva (Russia)
    search under
    Moscow (Russia)

Alternately, the database could automatically re-execute the search so that the user who searched for Moskva would be presented with resources linked to the preferred name Moscow. This would be particularly useful when the user is performing key-word rather than browse searches against the database.

For a fuller discussion of recording variant names, including thoughts on cataloger judgment in deciding whether to record a variant or not, see chapter 3 of this *Handbook* under 9.2.3.

16.2.3.3. GENERAL GUIDELINES. In most cases, variant names should be recorded following the same guidelines as if they had been chosen as the preferred name. This applies to the guidelines on such matters as capitalization, diacritical marks, etc., given in RDA 8.5. There are a number of specific instructions given in 16.2.3.4–16.2.3.8.

16.2.3.4. INITIAL ARTICLES. If the preferred name begins with an initial article, a variant omitting the initial article may be recorded as a variant (see figure 6.12). Conversely, if the alternative to 16.2.2.4 was followed and the initial article was omitted, a variant that includes the initial article may be recorded.

Figure 6.12. Variant without Initial Article

151	‡a Los Angeles (Calif.)
368	‡b City
370	‡c United States ‡f California ‡2 naf
451	‡a Pueblo de Nuestra Señora la Reina de los Angeles de Porciuncula (Calif.)
451	‡a LA (Calif.)
451	‡a L.A. (Calif.)
451	‡a Angeles (Calif.)
670	‡a Los Angeles, improbable city, 1979: ‡b title page (Los Angeles; El Pueblo de Nuestra Señora la Reina de los Angeles de Porciuncula)
670	‡a The official web site of the City of Los Angeles, July 23, 2011 ‡b (City of Los Angeles; LA; L.A.)
670	‡a GNIS, July 23, 2011 ‡b (Los Angeles, populated place in California, 34°03'08"N 118°14'37"W)

16.2.3.5. EXPANDED NAME. If the preferred form of the name contains an abbreviation or initialism and this would affect access, the spelled-out form may be recorded as a variant (see figure 6.13):

> Sant'Angelo d'Ischia (Italy)
> > *search under*
> > S. Angelo d'Ischia (Italy)

Figure 6.13. Variant Expanded Name

151	‡a S. Angelo d'Ischia (Italy)
368	‡b Villages ‡2 lcsh
370	‡c Italy ‡f Ischia (Italy) ‡2 naf
451	‡a Sant'Angelo d'Ischia (Italy)
670	‡a International Conference on Environment Protection (2nd : 1988 : S. Angelo d'Ischia (Italy)). 2nd International Conference ... c1988: ‡b title page (S. Angelo, Ischia (NA) Italy)
670	‡a Napoli e dintorni, 1976: ‡b page 395 (S. Angelo d'Ischia, a small village of fishermen, commune of Ischia, province of Naples)
675	‡a GEONet, 2 February 2009

16.2.3.6. INITIALISM/ABBREVIATED FORM. Conversely, if the preferred form of the name is a spelled-out form but the place is also known by an initialism or abbreviated form, record the initialism or abbreviated form as a variant name (see figure 6.12):

> L.A. (Calif.)
> > *search under*
> > Los Angeles (Calif.)

16.2.3.7. ALTERNATIVE LINGUISTIC FORM OF NAME. This type of variant comprises different forms of the same name. These include different language forms (see figures 6.7 and 6.12), different scripts (see figure 6.1), and different spellings (see figure 6.9):

> Cymru
> > *search under*
> > Wales

> Pueblo de Nuestra Señora la Reina de los Angeles de Porciuncula (Calif.)
> > *search under*
> > Los Angeles (Calif.)

> Москва (Russia)
> > *search under*
> > Moscow (Russia)

> Frankfort (Germany)
> > *search under*
> > Frankfurt am Main (Germany)

16.2.3.8. OTHER VARIANT NAME. This final guideline allows the cataloger to record any other variant that he or she deems helpful to the user of the database. The most common such variant is a different name, as is the case with Bedford, Pennsylvania, which has also been known as Fort Bedford and Manor of Bedford (see figure 6.5a):

> Manor of Bedford (Pa.)
> > *search under*
> > Bedford (Pa.)

Care should be taken to distinguish different names used at the same time, which are recorded as variant names, from cases where a jurisdiction changes its name. As discussed above with 16.2.2.7, when a jurisdiction changes its name a new description is made for the new entity, and the two descriptions are linked together using 551 fields in the MARC authority record. Bedford, which changed its name from Raystown, is an example. The 551 link is intended to display similarly to the following:

> Raystown (Pa.)
> > *search also under the later name*
> > Bedford (Pa.)

RDA 16.2.3.8 also recommends a reference to the preferred name for a city section to a variant giving the name formulated as a subdivision of the city. This makes sense, because the city section is jurisdictionally subordinate to the city, and database users who are aware of cataloging practices for subordinate bodies might attempt to find the city section using this form (see also LC-PCC PS 16.2.2.13, October 2012). For an example, see figure 6.11:

> Los Angeles (Calif.). Hollywood
> > *search under*
> > Hollywood (Los Angeles, Calif.)

As discussed above under 16.2.2.7, sometimes it is necessary to change the form of an already established preferred name. Moscow (Russia) (figure 6.1) is an example. This place had been established as "Moscow (R.S.F.S.R.)." But when the larger jurisdiction

changed its name from "Russian Soviet Federated Socialist Republic" to "Russia,"
this required a change in most qualifiers that contained the old name (abbreviated
according to appendix B.11 to "R.S.F.S.R."). To help users who may be used to the old
form of the preferred name, that form is added to the description as a variant name
after the form of the preferred name has been changed. The coding "‡w nne" in the
MARC 451 field indicates that the form in that field is an earlier established form of
the authorized access point, no longer valid:

> Moscow (R.S.F.S.R.)
> *search under*
> Moscow (Russia)

In addition to being helpful to human users of the database who need to learn the
new form of the name, the practice of including the former authorized access point
as a specially coded variant access point allows for automated update of forms in
bibliographic records from the old to the new form.

16.3. IDENTIFIER FOR THE PLACE. This section of chapter 16 was not completed for the
initial release of RDA, but identifiers should still be used with descriptions of place
entities. An identifier for the place is a character string uniquely associated with the
place (or the record representing the place). The element is core (i.e., required) for
all other entity descriptions, and should be included in LC/NACO Authority File
records for places. In the LC/NACO Authority File, the identifier is the Library of
Congress Control Number, recorded in the 010 field. In most cases the cataloger
does not need to record information in this element, as it is automatically generated
by the database system. For this reason, the identifier for the place element has not
been included in most figures in this book; as an example, the element is included
with figure 6.1.

SELECTED ELEMENTS FOR CORPORATE BODIES THAT MAY BE RECORDED IN DESCRIPTIONS OF JURISDICTIONAL PLACES

11.3. PLACE ASSOCIATED WITH THE CORPORATE BODY. This element is required for most
jurisdictions; most are qualified by the name of a larger place (see RDA 16.2.2.4 and
discussion, above). The place element for jurisdictions may be recorded in the MARC
370 field, in subfield ‡c (associated country) or subfield ‡f (other associated place).
These subfields are repeatable (or, alternately, the entire 370 field is repeatable), allowing multiple places to be recorded if necessary.[7] See figures throughout this chapter
for examples.

11.3.3.4. CHANGE OF NAME OF JURISDICTION OR LOCALITY. If the name of a larger place has been recorded in the place associated with the corporate body element, and that name has changed, record the latest name that was in use during the lifetime of the jurisdiction being described. This means that if the preferred name for a place changes the descriptions of jurisdictions that have recorded this element should be revised, and authorized access points that have used the place name as a qualifier must change. For an example, see figure 6.1, Moscow (Russia). This element (and qualifier) were previously recorded "R.S.F.S.R."

11.4. DATE ASSOCIATED WITH THE CORPORATE BODY. This element is defined as a significant date or range of dates associated with a jurisdiction. It includes dates such as the date the jurisdiction was founded. Because jurisdictions exist over time, this element may include a range of dates, either open (for jurisdictions that continue to exist) or closed (for jurisdictions that have ceased to exist).

This element is core, meaning that if the cataloger knows the information, he or she should record the element in the description of the jurisdiction. The basic field intended for recording this element in MARC is the 046 field. The earliest date associated with the jurisdiction (e.g., its founding date) is recorded in subfield ‡s; an ending date is recorded in subfield ‡t. For fuller information about recording dates in RDA descriptions, see chapter 3 of this *Handbook* at 9.3. For examples of dates associated with a jurisdiction, see figures 6.4 and 6.7.

11.7. OTHER DESIGNATION ASSOCIATED WITH THE CORPORATE BODY. This element is core if needed to distinguish between jurisdictions with the same name (RDA 11.7.1.5 and 11.7.1.6). The "other designation" can be any word or phrase, but with jurisdictions the most commonly used "other designation" is type of jurisdiction.

11.7.1.5. TYPE OF JURISDICTION. Type of jurisdiction is recorded in MARC authority field 368, subfield ‡b. See examples throughout this chapter. For an example where type of jurisdiction is core (because more than one jurisdiction has the same name), see figure 6.5. The evolving best practice for recording this information as an element (in a 368 field) is to use controlled vocabulary terms. The most common of these controlled vocabularies is *Library of Congress Subject Headings* (LCSH). LCSH is not very rich in terms for types of jurisdiction, so controlled terms have not been used extensively in this chapter. However, see figures 6.8, 6.11, and 6.13. If recording terms from controlled vocabularies, also record the code for the vocabulary in subfield ‡2.[8]

11.7.1.6. OTHER DESIGNATION. Occasionally type of jurisdiction is not sufficient to differentiate between places with the same name. In this case another designation may be used, and is recorded in MARC 368 subfield ‡c. There are two countries that go by the name Congo. One has been qualified by the name of its capital city, the other by its type of government (see figure 6.14).

Figure 6.14. Other Designation

046	‡s 19600815
151	‡a Congo (Brazzaville)
368	‡b Republics ‡2 lcsh
368	‡c Brazzaville
451	‡a République populaire du Congo
451	‡a People's Republic of the Congo
451	‡a Republic of the Congo
670	‡a Annuaire artistique de la République populaire du Congo, année 1980: ‡b t.p. (Brazzaville, R.P.C.)
670	‡a Treaty with the People's Republic of the Congo ... 1991
670	‡a Britannica online, 15 May 2010 ‡b (Republic of the Congo; often called Congo (Brazzaville) with its capital added parenthetically to distinguish it from neighboring Democratic Republic of the Congo; colony of France from 1891; became a republic within the French Community in 1958 and acquired complete political independence August 15, 1960)
670	‡a GEOnet, 12 November 2012 ‡b (independent political entity; Republic of the Congo, République du Congo; Congo; République populaire du Congo; 01°00'00"S 015°00'00"E)

046	‡s 1960-07 ‡t 1971-10
046	‡s 1977-05
151	‡a Congo (Democratic Republic)
368	‡b Republics ‡2 lcsh
368	‡c Democratic Republic
451	‡a Congo (Kinshasa)
451	‡a République démocratique du Congo
451	‡a Democratic Republic of the Congo
551	‡a Belgian Congo ‡w a
551	‡a Zaire
670	‡a Britannica online, 15 May 2010 ‡b (République Démocratique du Congo, Democratic Republic of the Congo; often called Congo (Kinshasa) to distinguish it from Congo (Brazzaville); gained independence from Belgium July 1960; from October 1971-May 1997 known as the Republic of Zaire; from May 1997- the name Democratic Republic of the Congo was reinstated)
670	‡a GEOnet, 12 November 2012 ‡b (independent political entity; Democratic Republic of the Congo; République Démocratique du Congo; Zaire; 00°00'00"S 025°00'00"E)

ACCESS POINTS

One of the objectives governing RDA is that the data should enable the user to find all resources associated with a particular entity (RDA 0.4.2.1), including places or jurisdictions. In our current MARC database environment this is done through the formulation and use of authorized access points representing entities such as places, corresponding to what previous cataloging practice called "headings." These access points are embedded in bibliographic records for resources associated with the place and serve as links between a particular bibliographic record and all other bibliographic records that contain the identical access point. In many systems the access point in the bibliographic record is also linked to its corresponding authority record.

The user of the database finds all resources associated with a particular place (including jurisdictions) by learning what the authorized access point is for that place and then querying the database for instances of the authorized access point indexed as a creator or contributor, or as a subject.

In order for this to work, the authorized access point must be consistent (i.e., always used in the same form) and unique to the place (i.e., more than one place should not share the same access point). The data describing a place must be sufficient to differentiate that place from other places with the same name (RDA 0.4.3.1).

When two places in the database have identical names, a "conflict" exists that must be resolved in the authorized access point. Given the important principle of representation upon which the choice of preferred name is based (see RDA 0.4.3.4: an entity should be represented as it represents itself or as it is commonly known), it is not uncommon that conflicts should arise because the names of many places are identical. Preferred names for places with identical names are differentiated from each other by the addition of other elements such a larger place or a type of jurisdiction, as discussed above.

16.4. CONSTRUCTING ACCESS POINTS TO REPRESENT PLACES. Like 16.3, this section was left incomplete at the first release of RDA, but the cataloger is referred to 11.13.1.1 for access points for jurisdictions, which is the general guideline for creation of access points for corporate bodies.

In practice, however, authorized and variant access points for a place use the exact form of the preferred or variant name, including omissions and additions as prescribed in 16.2. This differs somewhat from construction of access points for other entities, where additions may be made to the form chosen as the preferred name. Presumably a similar procedure will be followed when chapter 16 is developed, but in the meantime enough guidelines have been given to allow catalogers to create descriptions and access points for places.

NOTES

1. Full information about MARC 21 authority format is available at www.loc
   .gov/marc/authority/ecadhome.html.

2. Pre-AACR2 authority records are identified by "d" in 008 position 10 for "AACR2
   compatible heading," "b" for AACR1, and "a" for earlier rules.

3. The *Subject Headings Manual* is available in the Library of Congress product *Cataloger's Desktop*, desktop.loc.gov. See especially sections H690–H1055.

4. For the ALA-LC Romanization Tables, see www.loc.gov/catdir/cpso/roman.html.

5. Source information about certain elements may be recorded directly in the element's
   MARC field itself, in subfield ‡v, rather than in a 670 field. This technique is available
   for the 046 and 370–378 fields. This method has not yet found much favor in practice
   and is not used in this book.

6. The *Descriptive Cataloging Manual* is available at www.loc.gov/catdir/cpso/
   z1andlcguidelines.html.

7. See *Descriptive Cataloging Manual* Z1 at 370--Associated Place (November 2013).
   Previous to Fall 2013 a different practice for recording place names in 370 was
   followed, so catalogers will encounter records that do not follow the procedure
   described here.

8. Codes are available at www.loc.gov/standards/sourcelist.

CHAPTER 7

DESCRIBING WORKS

Instructions for recording the attributes of the *work* entity
are found in RDA chapters 5, 6, and 7.

MARC CODING

HE *WORK* ENTITY IS CURRENTLY DESCRIBED IN
library catalogs in the MARC 21 authority and bibliographic
formats.[1] RDA authority records for works are identified by
the value "z" in the 008 field position 10 (labeled "Rules" in the
OCLC fixed field display) and the presence of "‡e rda" in the 040
field (see figure 7.1a). In contrast, an AACR2 authority record
may be recognized by the presence of value "c" in 008 position 10
and no special coding in 040 (see figure 7.1b).[2] For space reasons,
RDA coding is assumed in further figures in this chapter and is
not explicitly shown. Other MARC coding issues will be discussed as they occur later in
the chapter.

Figure 7.1a. RDA Coding (OCLC Style)

Rec stat	c	Entered	19860303		Replaced	20110806074811.0	
Type	z	Upd status	a	Enc lvl	n	Source	
Roman		Ref status	a	Mod rec		Name use	a
Govt ag	n	Auth status	a	Subj	a	Subj use	a
Series	n	Auth/ref	a	Geo subd	n	Ser use	b
Ser num	n	Name	n	Subdiv tp	n	**Rules**	**z**

010		ǂa n 85138792
040		ǂa DLC ǂb eng **ǂe rda** ǂc DLC ǂd DLC ǂd IAhCCS ǂd WaU
046		ǂk 1968
130	0	ǂa Planet of the apes (Motion picture : 1968)
380		ǂa Motion pictures ǂ2 lcsh
430	0	ǂa Monkey planet (Motion picture)
500	1	ǂi Motion picture adaptation of (work): ǂa Boulle, Pierre, ǂd 1912-1994. ǂt Planète des singes ǂw r
500	1	ǂi Film director: ǂa Schaffner, Franklin J. ǂw r
530	0	ǂi Remade as (work): ǂa Planet of the apes (Motion picture : 2001) ǂw r
530	0	ǂi Sequel: ǂa Beneath the planet of the apes (Motion picture) ǂw r
530	0	ǂi Prequel: ǂa Rise of the planet of the apes ǂw r
670		ǂa Planet of the apes, 2004
670		ǂa Internet movie database, January 24, 2011 ǂb (Planet of the apes (1968), directed by Franklin J. Schaffner; also known as Monkey planet; also lists Planet of the apes (2001), directed by Tim Burton)
670		ǂa Wikipedia, August 5, 2011 ǂb (Planet of the apes (1968 American science fiction film); based on the novel La planète des singes by Pierre Boulle; followed by sequel Beneath the Planet of the apes (1970); Rise of the Planet of the apes (2011), primarily a prequel to the 1968 film)

Figure 7.1a. RDA Coding (LC Style)

008		860303n| a**z**annaabn |a ana
010		ǂa n 85138792
040		ǂa DLC ǂb eng **ǂe rda** c DLC ǂd DLC ǂd IAhCCS ǂd WaU
046		ǂk 1968
130	0	ǂa Planet of the apes (Motion picture : 1968)
380		ǂa Motion pictures ǂ2 lcsh
430	0	ǂa Monkey planet (Motion picture)
500	1	ǂw r ǂi Motion picture adaptation of (work): ǂa Boulle, Pierre, ǂd 1912-1994. ǂt Planète des singes
500	1	ǂw r ǂi Film director: ǂa Schaffner, Franklin J.
530	0	ǂw r ǂi Remade as (work): ǂa Planet of the apes (Motion picture : 2001)
530	0	ǂw r ǂi Sequel: ǂa Beneath the planet of the apes (Motion picture)
530	0	ǂw r iǂ Prequel: ǂa Rise of the planet of the apes
670		ǂa Planet of the apes, 2004
670		ǂa Internet movie database, January 24, 2011 ǂb (Planet of the apes (1968), directed by Franklin J. Schaffner; also known as Monkey planet; also lists Planet of the apes (2001), directed by Tim Burton)

670   ‡a Wikipedia, August 5, 2011 ‡b (Planet of the apes (1968 American science fiction film); based on the novel La planète des singes by Pierre Boulle; followed by sequel Beneath the planet of the apes (1970); Rise of the planet of the apes (2011), primarily a prequel to the 1968 film)

Figure 7.1b. AACR2 Coding (OCLC Style)

Rec stat	c	Entered	19860303			Replaced 20110806074811.0	
Type	z	Upd status	a	Enc lvl	n	Source	
Roman		Ref status	a	Mod rec		Name use	a
Govt agn		Auth status	a	Subj	a	Subj use	a
Series	n	Auth/ref	a	Geo subd	n	Ser use	b
Ser num	n	Name	n	Subdiv tp	n	**Rules**	**c**

010   ‡a n 85138792

040   ‡a DLC ‡b eng ‡c DLC ‡d DLC ‡d IAhCCS ‡d WaU

130 0 ‡a Planet of the apes (Motion picture : 1968)

430 0 ‡a Monkey planet (Motion picture)

670   ‡a Planet of the apes, 2004

670   ‡a Internet movie database, January 24, 2011 ‡b (Planet of the apes (1968), directed by Franklin J. Schaffner; also known as Monkey planet; also lists Planet of the apes (2001), directed by Tim Burton)

670   ‡a Wikipedia, August 5, 2011 ‡b (Planet of the Apes (1968 American science fiction film); based on the novel La planète des singes by Pierre Boulle; followed by sequel Beneath the Planet of the Apes (1970); Rise of the Planet of the apes (2011), primarily a prequel to the 1968 film)

Figure 7.1b. AACR2 Coding (LC Style)

008   860303n| a**c**annaabn |a ana

010   ‡a n 85138792

040   ‡a DLC ‡b eng ‡c DLC ‡d DLC ‡d IAhCCS ‡d WaU

130 0 ‡a Planet of the apes (Motion picture : 1968)

430 0 ‡a Monkey planet (Motion picture)

670   ‡a Planet of the apes, 2004

670   ‡a Internet movie database, January 24, 2011 ‡b (Planet of the apes (1968), directed by Franklin J. Schaffner; also known as Monkey planet; also lists Planet of the apes (2001), directed by Tim Burton)

670   ‡a Wikipedia, August 5, 2011 ‡b (Planet of the apes (1968 American science fiction film); based on the novel La planète des singes by Pierre Boulle; followed by sequel Beneath the planet of the apes (1970); Rise of the planet of the apes (2011), primarily a prequel to the 1968 film)

5.1. TERMINOLOGY. *Work* is defined in RDA as "a distinct intellectual or artistic creation." The term "work" is also used in RDA to refer to aggregate works (including series or serials) as well as to parts of works. This definition has been discussed more fully in chapter 1. Darwin's *On the Origin of the Species* is an example of a work (see figure 7.2). This well-known work has been realized in a number of expressions, including an audio recording by David Case (see figure 7.3). Description of the *expression* entity, "the intellectual or artistic realization of a work in the form of alpha-numeric, musical or choreographic notation, sound, image, object, movement, etc., or any combination of such forms," will be discussed in chapter 8.

Figure 7.2. Work

046	‡k 1859
100 1	‡a Darwin, Charles, ‡d 1809-1882. ‡t On the origin of species
380	‡a Scientific work
400 1	‡a Darwin, Charles, ‡d 1809-1882. ‡t Origin of species
400 1	‡a Darwin, Charles, ‡d 1809-1882. ‡t Darwin's Origin of species
400 1	‡a Darwin, Charles, ‡d 1809-1882. ‡t On the origin of species by means of natural selection, or, The preservation of favoured races in the struggle for life
670	‡a A concordance to Darwin's Origin of species, first edition, 1981
670	‡a Nineteenth-century liturature criticism, vol. 57, 1997 ‡b (On the origin of species by means of natural selection, or, The preservation of favoured races in the struggle for life; referred to elsewhere in article by title On the origin of species; first published 1859)

Figure 7.3. Expression

046	‡k 1992
100 1	‡a Darwin, Charles, ‡d 1809-1882. ‡t On the origin of species. ‡l English. ‡h Spoken word ‡s (Case)
336	‡a spoken word ‡2 rdacontent
377	‡a eng
400 1	‡a Darwin, Charles, ‡d 1809-1882. ‡t Origin of species
500 1	‡w r ‡i Voice actor: ‡a Case, David
670	‡a The origin of species, 2006 ‡b (unabridged edition; read by David Case)
670	‡a OCLC, 13 March 2010 ‡b (David Case recording first published 1992; recordings by others have also been published)

RDA 5.1.4 defines authorized access point as

> the standardized access point representing an entity, [and then explains that] the authorized access point representing a work or expression is constructed by combining (in this order): a) the authorized access point representing a person, family, or corporate body responsible for the work, if appropriate; b) the preferred title for the work; c) other elements as instructed at 6.27–6.31.

This sounds deceptively like the AACR2 concept of a uniform title heading. It is important to understand that AACR2 uniform titles are *not* the same as RDA authorized access points for works or expressions.

The AACR2 concept of uniform title was developed as a means of collocating resources to help users of the catalog discover related materials that might have different titles. Although AACR2 speaks in terms of a "uniform title for a work" (e.g., AACR2 25.2A), AACR2 and the concepts underlying it were established long before the theoretical foundation of FRBR.[3] In terms of FRBR, AACR2 uniform titles can represent works, expressions, and even in some cases manifestations (for example, uniform titles for the Bible: see AACR2 25.18A13, which prescribes the addition of the year of publication to the uniform title). Furthermore, AACR2 uniform titles represent these three entities in a very imprecise way. The same uniform title can represent different entities, and different instances of the same entity. For example, the AACR2 uniform title

> Homer. Iliad

represents the work "Iliad" but it also represents all expressions of the Iliad in its original language (Greek), of which there are many. The AACR2 uniform title

> Homer. Iliad. English

represents all English translations of the Iliad. These are separate expressions. The AACR2 uniform title

> Homer. Iliad. English & Greek

represents all resources that contain at least one expression of the Iliad in English and at least one expression of the Iliad in Greek. The AACR2 uniform title:

> Homer. Iliad. Polyglot

represents all resources that contain expressions of this work in at least three languages.

This imprecision is inherent in the AACR2 concept of uniform title because its purpose was not to identify works or expressions, but rather to bring together related resources.

In contrast, the primary purpose of an RDA authorized access point for a work or expression is to identify the work or expression embodied in a resource. A secondary result of this sort of access point is to bring together related resources in a manner similar to AACR2's uniform title, but there is no provision in RDA for an undifferentiated access point for works or expressions as there is for the person entity (where it is permitted to use the same access point for more than one person if nothing can be found to differentiate them). Thus, if there is more than one translation of a work in the same language—that is, separate expressions—or more than one type of content (e.g., text versus spoken word), in RDA the authorized access points for these expressions should be different. An authorized access point such as "Homer. Iliad. English" does not make sense in an RDA context because there are many translations, so we would expect access points such as "Homer. Iliad. English (Pope)" and "Homer. Iliad. English (Lattimore)." Or, referring again to figure 7.3, there are many expressions of *On the Origin of Species* in its original language, English, including many text versions and numerous recordings by different readers. In an AACR2 context, these might all have been represented by the single uniform title:

> Darwin, Charles, 1809-1882. On the origin of species

In an RDA context, this form represents the work (which might be used when needed as a subject, for example), but more is required in order to represent the expression. In the case of figure 7.3, David Case's recording is differentiated from other expressions of the work by the addition of its language, its content type, and its narrator. This will be discussed in greater detail in chapter 8 of this *Handbook*.

One reason RDA envisions separate access points for individual works and expressions is that RDA is looking beyond MARC to an entity-relationship database structure based on FRBR. In such a structure, works and expressions will have separate descriptions linked to other FRBR entities as appropriate. The entity-relationship structure cannot work if an expression description represents many expressions, because the system requires clear and precise linking between the FRBR entity descriptions. Having distinct access points in MARC records is a step in the direction of this kind of a database structure, and will facilitate later conversion of MARC databases to the new structure. It also brings the benefit of greater precision to MARC records themselves, which can only benefit users of the database.

5.3. CORE ELEMENTS. As explained in greater detail in chapter 1, RDA identifies certain elements as "core" throughout the code. The core elements were chosen because they were attributes and relationships thought to support FRBR and FRAD user tasks.[4] RDA entity descriptions should contain, at a minimum, all core elements that are applicable and readily ascertainable, as well as any other elements that might be required to differentiate one entity from another (see RDA 0.6.1). Inclusion of other elements is not required, and is at the discretion of the cataloger or cataloging agency (such as an individual library, or cooperative organizations such as the Program for Cooperative Cataloging [PCC]).

Agencies may develop requirements that go beyond RDA core. The Library of Congress (LC) and PCC, for example, have designated certain elements that are not core in RDA to be core for their own catalogers. Information about LC and PCC decisions are found in Library of Congress-Program for Cooperative Cataloging Policy Statements (LC-PCC PSs), found under the Resources tab of the RDA Toolkit.

Core elements for all entities and relationships are given in RDA 0.6. They are also given separately in the chapter(s) devoted to each entity or relationship. Core elements for the work entity are found in RDA 0.6.3 and again in RDA 5.3. This information is also listed with each element's instruction. For example, RDA 6.2, title of the work, which is a core element, reads as follows:

> **6.2 Title of the Work**
> **CORE ELEMENT**
> ***Preferred title for the work is a core element. Variant titles for the work are optional.***
> 6.2.1. Basic Instructions on Recording Titles of Works
> > 6.2.1.1 Scope
> > . . .

Conversely, 6.7, history of the work, which is not a core element, reads as follows:

> **6.7 History of the Work**
> 6.7.1 Basic Instructions on Recording the History of the Work
> > 6.7.1.1 Scope
> > . . .

The core elements for the work entity are:

> Preferred title for the work
> Identifier for the work

In addition, the following are core if the preferred title for the work is the same or similar to that of another work:

Form of work
Date of work
Place of origin of the work
Other distinguishing characteristic of the work

The following elements are core for musical works without distinctive titles; they are also core for musical works with distinctive titles if needed to differentiate a work from another with the same title:

Medium of performance
Numeric designation
Key

If the work is a bilateral treaty the following element is core for both signatories:

Signatory for a treaty, etc.

Note that the creator of a work is not given as a core attribute. This is because the creator of a work is a person, family, or corporate body, and as such is a separate entity from the work entity; the creator of the work is not an attribute of the work. However, the principal or first-named creator *is* in fact given in RDA 0.6.6 as a core *relationship* to the work, meaning that relationship must be recorded in RDA descriptions. The entity description for the creator of the work will be linked to the description for the work, optionally using a relationship designation specifying the type of relationship.

RDA 5.3, referring to RDA 6.7.1, calls for preceding the preferred title of the work by the authorized access point for the creator *when constructing the authorized access point* for the work. This is *not* the same as recording the creator as an attribute of the work. It *is*, however, a description of how the relationship between the work and its creator is recorded in our current MARC environment, where the links between entities are created by access points. In a MARC authority record for a work, the relationship between the work and its creator is shown by the combination of the authorized access point for the work's creator with its preferred title in the authorized access point for the work.

Please note that core designation means that the element must be recorded (if applicable and readily ascertainable) in the description for the work. It does *not* mean that it must be included as part of the authorized access point for the work. For example, identifier for the work (RDA 6.8) is a core element. This means that the identifier (in NACO practice, the Library of Congress Control Number) must be recorded in the description. It does not mean that RDA requires the identifier to be part of the access point.

For the sake of illustration, the figures in this book will usually include many elements beyond the core elements. See figure 7.4a for an example of a description of a work that contains only core elements (marked in bold); figure 7.4b is an example of a description of the same work containing elements beyond core. (Note that the personal name in the 100 field is not an attribute of the work, but constitutes the link between the work and its creator, which is a core relationship.) It is evident that the RDA core for the description of a work can be fairly minimal. Cataloging agencies will undoubtedly want their catalogers to include more elements, including at least variant titles and sources consulted (fields 400 and 670 in figure 7.4b). In making decisions about inclusion of non-core elements in entity descriptions, agencies need to consider possible future uses of the data. Many non-core elements such as form of work or date will be useful as limiters to searches or as initial searches for records (e.g., a person who wants to find poems by American authors written in the twentieth century), but only if agencies apply them consistently in their databases.

Figure 7.4a. Core Elements

010	ǂa **no2011076912**
100 1	ǂa Barks, Coleman. ǂt **Understanding of the question**

Figure 7.4b. Elements beyond Core

010	ǂa no2011076912
046	ǂk 1995
100 1	ǂa Barks, Coleman. ǂt Understanding of the question
380	ǂa Poems ǂ2 aat
400 1	ǂa Barks, Coleman. ǂt Ruminations
400 1	ǂa Barks, Coleman. ǂt Why doesn't a soul fly when it hears the call?
670	ǂa Ruminations, 2011: ǂb colophon (An understanding of the question, first published in 1995) first line of text (Why doesn't a soul fly when it hears the call?)

5.4. LANGUAGE AND SCRIPT. One of the basic principles of RDA is that of representation: "The data describing [an entity] should reflect the [entity's] representation of itself" (RDA 0.4.3.4). It is therefore no surprise that RDA 5.4 calls for recording titles in the language and script in which they appear. This would mean that the preferred title of a work written Chinese would be recorded in Chinese script, a Russian work would be recorded in Cyrillic script, and an English work would be recorded in Latin script (see figure 7.5a). RDA 5.4 includes an alternative, however: "Record a transliterated form of the title either as a substitute for, or in addition to, the form that appears on the source." LC and PCC will continue to record a form transliterated following the ALA-LC Romanization Tables as the preferred name for names appearing in non-Latin scripts.[5] Non-Latin script forms may be included in the record as variant access points. Including non-Latin variant access points is a relatively recent practice and PCC policies have not been fully developed. Until they are, catalogers may record non-Latin script variant access points in 4XX fields, but should include a 667 field reading "Non-Latin script reference(s) not evaluated" (see figure 7.5b).

Figure 7.5a. Title Appearing in Non-Latin Script (RDA Basic Guideline)

046	‡k 1957
100 1	‡a Пастернак, Борис, ‡d 1890-1960. ‡t Доктор Живаго
380	‡a Novels ‡2 aat
400 1	‡a Пастернак, Борис, ‡d 1890-1960. ‡t Doktor Zhivago
530 0	‡w r ‡i Adapted as a motion picture (work): ‡a Doctor Zhivago (Motion picture : 1965)
530 0	‡w r ‡i Adapted as a motion picture (work): ‡a Doctor Zhivago (Motion picture : 2002)
670	‡a Доктор Живаго, 1957
670	‡a IMDB.com, 30 January 2009 ‡b (Boris Pasternak's novel Doctor Zhivago adapted as two films, one made in 1965 and the other in 2002)

Figure 7.5b.
Title Appearing in Non-Latin script (RDA Alternative: LC/NACO practice)

046	‡k 1957
100 1	‡a Pasternak, Boris, ‡d 1890-1960. ‡t Doktor Zhivago
380	‡a Novels ‡2 aat
400 1	‡a Pasternak, Boris, ‡d 1890-1960. ‡t Доктор Живаго
530 0	‡w r ‡i Adapted as a motion picture (work): ‡a Doctor Zhivago (Motion picture : 1965)
530 0	‡w r ‡i Adapted as a motion picture (work): ‡a Doctor Zhivago (Motion picture : 2002)
667	‡a Non-Latin script reference not evaluated.
670	‡a Doktor Zhivago, 1957: ‡b title page (Доктор Живаго)
670	‡a IMDB.com, 30 January 2009 ‡b (Boris Pasternak's novel Doctor Zhivago adapted as two films, one made in 1965 and the other in 2002)

5.7. STATUS OF IDENTIFICATION. RDA instructs us to record the level of authentication of the data identifying the entity. The possible levels are "fully established," "provisional," and "preliminary." If an authorized access point for a work begins with the authorized access point for the creator, the status of identification element for the work description should not be at a higher level than that of the description of the creator. That is, if the authorized access point for the creator was established in a provisional record, any work records based on that access point should also be coded as provisional. For a full discussion of this element, see chapter 3 of this *Handbook* under 8.10.

5.8. SOURCE CONSULTED. Just as the author of a scholarly paper justifies his or her assertions by citing sources (usually in footnotes), so the creator of an RDA description for a work in an authority record must justify access points by citing where the information came from. In MARC authority work, this is done using the 670 field.[6] The source consulted element is not core in RDA, but at least one instance, that of the resource in hand that generated the need for a new authorized access point, is required in LC/NACO practice. Examples of 670 fields are found in figures throughout this chapter. For a full discussion of LC/NACO practice in the source consulted element, see chapter 3 of this *Handbook* under 8.12.

5.9. CATALOGUER'S NOTE. The cataloguer's note element contains information about the work represented by the authorized access point that might be helpful to persons using the authority record. The cataloguer's note element is not core in RDA, but it is core for the Library of Congress in certain situations (see *Descriptive Cataloging Manual* Z1 at 667).[7] A common use of the cataloguer's note element in descriptions of works is a note giving details about a series. For example, if a subtitle could be interpreted as the title proper of a series or as a subseries, it may be recorded in the cataloguer's note element and as a variant title (see figure 7.6). For an example of a different type of cataloguer's note, see the 667 field in figure 7.5b.

Figure 7.6. Cataloguer's Note

046		ǂk 2008
130	0	ǂa Sozomena (Berlin, Germany)
370		ǂg Berlin (Germany) ǂ2 naf
373		ǂa Walter de Gruyter & Co. ǂ2 naf
380		ǂa Series (Publications) ǂa Monographic series ǂ2 lcsh
430	0	ǂa Studies in the recovery of ancient texts
642		ǂa vol. 2 ǂ5 DPCC ǂ5 ICU
643		ǂa Berlin ǂa New York ǂb Walter de Gruyter
644		ǂa f ǂ5 ICU
645		ǂa t ǂ5 DPCC ǂ5 ICU
646		ǂa s ǂ5 ICU
667		ǂa Subtitle: Studies in the recovery of ancient texts

670   ‡a Poems in context, 2008: ‡b series title page (Sozomena : studies in the recovery of ancient texts, edited on behalf of the Herculaneum Society, vol. 2)

670   ‡a De Gruyter website, 26 November 2011 ‡b (first volume published 2008)

STRUCTURE OF CHAPTERS 6 AND 7. RDA chapter 6, "Identifying Works and Expressions," and chapter 7, "Describing Content," follow much the same structure as most of the other chapters in the "Recording Attributes" parts of RDA (RDA sections 1–4). Chapter 6 begins with a section on the purpose and scope of the chapter (RDA 6.0) and then proceeds to general guidelines on identifying works, including sources that may be consulted for information about works (RDA 6.1.1). It then treats, one by one, the various elements and sub-elements of the work entity that are recognized by RDA, giving instructions on where to get information about the element or sub-element, and how to record that information. This section, along with a similar section on expressions, is the heart of chapter 6, and occupies the bulk of it (RDA 6.2–6.26). Chapter 7 is a supplementary chapter to chapter 6, which gives details about elements of work and expression entity descriptions related to content.

Chapter 6 ends with a final section on constructing access points for works (RDA 6.27–6.31). It is crucial to understand this structure. Catalogers accustomed to AACR2 chapter 25, which is chiefly about creating an access point (heading) for a uniform title, may be misled into thinking that the guidelines about recording elements, and particularly wording about core elements, constitute instructions about how to construct the access point for the work, when in fact the central section of chapter 6 and all of chapter 7 give instructions for recording the *information* in the description for the work. In the entity-relationship or linked-data database structure RDA anticipates, we will be creating descriptions of works that exist independently from, but are linked to, other entity descriptions such as for persons or expressions that they may have a relationship to. In such an environment, bibliographic records with formal access points might not exist, but the elements contained in the description of the work will be essential.

One point to remember when looking at chapters 6 and 7 is that in our current MARC database structure, which contains bibliographic, authority, and holding records, elements treated in RDA chapter 6 are recorded in the MARC authority format (and some may also appear in bibliographic records), whereas elements treated in RDA chapter 7 are only recorded in the MARC bibliographic format. This *Handbook* will treat these elements in the same order as they appear in RDA, and therefore this chapter will continue with a section about description of the work entity in MARC authority records, and will conclude with a section about description of the work entity in MARC bibliographic records.

RDA chapters 6 and 7 include information about both works and expressions. For simplicity, this *Handbook* will treat work and expression separately. This chapter will cover RDA elements related to the work entity; chapter 8 will cover elements related to the expression.

6.1.3. CHANGES AFFECTING THE IDENTIFICATION OF A WORK. One of the characteristics of some works is that they can develop over time. One of the attributes listed in FRBR for the work entity is "intended termination," defined as "a reflection of whether the work has been conceived as having a finite end or whether it is intended to continue indefinitely" (FRBR 4.2.5). Works intended to continue indefinitely have a characteristic that most works having a finite end do not: they can undergo change during their lifetime. The two changes that are bibliographically significant for works are (1) changes in responsibility for the work and (2) changes in the title of the work. The question RDA 6.1.3 addresses is whether a change is significant enough to signal the existence of a new, different work, or if the change is minor and continuing parts of the resource remain part of the original work. RDA 6.1.3 treats changes somewhat differently depending on the resource's mode of issuance (multipart monograph, serial, or integrating resource).

6.1.3.1. WORKS ISSUED AS MULTIPART MONOGRAPHS. Normally if responsibility for a work published as a multipart monograph changes somewhere along the line, the original author is still considered the principal creator of the work as a whole, including the parts with changed responsibility (see RDA 18.4.2.1). In other words, RDA does not consider this change to signal the existence of a new work. For example, the work *Piano Technic* was published in six volumes over a period of six years. The creator of the first three volumes was Marion McArtor. By the time volume four was published, however, McArtor had died and his name disappears from the title page, replaced by that of a new creator, David Kraehenbuehl. According to RDA, this remains the same work, and would be covered by the same work description (see figure 7.7).

Figure 7.7. Change in Multipart Monograph: Same Work

Authority record for the work (might not be created in the current MARC environment)

046	‡k 1953 ‡l 1960
100 1	‡a McArtor, Marion Emmett, ‡d 1915-1956. ‡t Piano technic
380	‡a Musical studies
400 1	‡a Kraehenbuehl, David, ‡d 1925-1997. ‡t Piano technic
670	‡a Piano technic, 1954-1960: ‡b volume 1-3 title page (studies by Marion McArtor) volume 4-6 title page (music by David Kraehenbuehl)

Bibliographic record

100 1	‡a McArtor, Marion Emmett, ‡d 1915-1956, ‡e composer.
245 10	‡a Piano technic / ‡c studies by Marion McArtor ; selected and correlated by Frances Clark ; edited by Louise Goss.
...	
700 1	‡a Kraehenbuehl, David, ‡d 1925-1997, ‡e composer.

However, the result is different according to RDA 6.1.3.1 if:

1a. the mode of issuance of a multipart monograph changes (e.g., it changes to a serial or integrating resource, cf. 1.6.1.1), or

1b. its media type changes (e.g., from text on paper to an audio version, cf. 1.6.1.2), and

2. there is a change in responsibility for the work (i.e., the principal creator changes and this is reflected in the authorized access point of the work).

The difference here is that, in addition to a change in responsibility for the work, there is also a change either in mode of issuance or in media type. In this case RDA considers the resulting resource to be a new work, which would be reflected in a different access point for the new work and a new work description for the changed portions of the resource. This is a rare occurrence.

6.1.3.2. WORKS ISSUED AS SERIALS. A change in responsibility for a serial that affects the authorized access point for the work (6.1.3.2.1), or a major change in the title proper of a serial (6.1.3.2.2), creates a resource that is considered a new work in RDA. The *Newsletter* of the Midwest Inter-Library Center is an example of 6.1.3.2.1. The contents of the *Newsletter* deal almost entirely with the policies, procedures, and operations of the center. Therefore, under the provisions of RDA 19.2.1.1.1a, the center is considered the creator of the *Newsletter* and the authorized access point for the work would include the authorized access point for the center. In 1966 the Midwest Inter-Library Center changed its name to the Center for Research Libraries. The *Newsletter* continued, still dealing with the internal policies, etc., of the body. This change affects the authorized access point of the serial, and therefore under 6.1.3.2.1 a new work has been created, which would have its own description (see figure 7.8).

Figure 7.8. Change in Responsibility for Serial: New Work

Authority record for the first work (might not be created in the current MARC environment)

046	‡k 1949 ‡l 1964
110 2	‡a Midwest Inter-Library Center. ‡t Newsletter
373	‡a Midwest Inter-Library Center ‡2 naf
380	‡a Newsletters ‡2 lcsh
510 2	‡w r ‡i Continued by (work): ‡a Center for Research Libraries. ‡t Newsletter
670	‡a Newsletter, 1949-1964: ‡b title page (Midwest Inter-Library Center)
675	‡a Newsletter, 1965-1980: ‡b title page (Center for Research Libraries)

Bibliographic record for the first work

...	
110 2	‡a Midwest Inter-Library Center, ‡e author.
245 10	‡a Newsletter / ‡c issued by the Midwest Inter-Library Center.
...	
785 00	‡a Center for Research Libraries. ‡t Newsletter, ‡x 0008-9087
...	

Under 6.1.3.2.2, if the serial undergoes a major change in its title proper (see RDA 2.3.2.13.1 for criteria for "major change") a new work is deemed to be created, which generates a new description. In the current MARC environment, this is normally handled for most serials by manipulation of bibliographic records, but it could also be handled by authority records for the works, which would be closer to the anticipated entity-relationship database structure (see figure 7.9).

Figure 7.9. Change in Serial Title: New Work

Authority record for the first work (might not be created in the current MARC environment)

022	‡a 0449-329X
046	‡k 1967 ‡l 1970
130 0	‡a Journal of typographic research
380	‡a Periodicals ‡2 lcsh
530 0	‡w r ‡i Continued by (work): ‡a Visible language
670	‡a Journal of typographic research, 1967-1970
675	‡a Visible language, 1971-

Bibliographic record for the first work

```
...
022      ‡a 0449-329X
245 04   ‡a The journal of typographic research.
...
785 00   ‡a Visible language, ‡x 0022-2224
...
```

Changes of this kind to series, which may be a type of serial, are handled in the current environment through the authority record structure. As with other serials, RDA deems a new work to be created—necessitating a new description—if there is a change in responsibility that affects the authorized access point of a series (see figure 7.10, where the body responsible for "Bulletin" changed its name from Commonwealth Forestry Bureau to Forestry and Timber Bureau) or a major change in title of a series (see figure 7.11, where the title of the series changed from "Paper" to "Crime Prevention Unit series" to "Crime detection and prevention series").

Figure 7.10. Change in Responsibility for Series: New Work

```
022        ‡a 0067-1452
046        ‡k 1931 ‡l 1945
050   4    ‡a SD110 ‡b .A33 ‡s FU
130   0    ‡a Bulletin (Australia. Commonwealth Forestry Bureau)
373        ‡a Australia. Commonwealth Forestry Bureau ‡2 naf
380        ‡a Series (Publications) ‡a Monographic series ‡2 lcsh
410   1    ‡a Australia. ‡b Commonwealth Forestry Bureau. ‡t Bulletin
530   0    ‡w r ‡i Continued by (work): ‡a Bulletin (Australia. Forestry and Timber Bureau)
642        ‡a no. 25 ‡5 DPCC ‡5 FU
643        ‡a Canberra ‡b Commonwealth Forestry Bureau
644        ‡a f ‡5 FU
645        ‡a t ‡5 DPCC ‡5 FU
646        ‡a c ‡5 FU
670        ‡a The vegetative reproduction of forest trees, 1939: ‡b title page (Bulletin /
           Commonwealth Forestry Bureau)
675        ‡a Branching and flowering characteristics of Monterey pine, 1960: ‡b title page
           (Bulletin; Forestry and Timber Bureau)
```

Figure 7.11. Change in Series Title: New Work

046		‡k 1992 ‡l 1994
130	0	‡a Crime Prevention Unit series
380		‡a Series (Publications) ‡a Monographic series ‡2 lcsh
642		‡a paper no. 37 ‡5 DLC
643		‡a London ‡b Home Office Police Research Group
644		‡a f ‡5 DLC
645		‡a t ‡5 DLC
646		‡a s ‡5 DLC
530	0	‡w r ‡i Continues (work): ‡a Paper (Great Britain. Home Office. Crime Prevention Unit)
530	0	‡w r ‡i Continued by (work): ‡a Crime detection and prevention series
667		‡a In 1992 when the Police Research Group was established and administration of the Crime Prevention Unit was transferred to it, the series, Paper, changed its name to the Crime Prevention Unit series.
670		‡a Theft and loss from UK libraries, 1992: ‡b title page (Crime Prevention Unit series, paper no. 37)
670		‡a OCLC, January 15, 2012 ‡b (titles in series "Paper (Great Britain. Home Office. Crime Prevention Unit)" issued 1984-1992; titles in series "Crime Prevention Unit series" issued 1992-1994; "Crime detection and prevention series" issued 1994-1998)

Where changes produce new works, the descriptions of the works are linked in MARC authority records through 5XX "search also" references or in MARC bibliographic records through 76X-78X linking fields. Authority record linkings may produce a display such as the following to the user of the database:

Crime Prevention Unit series
   search also under the earlier title
   Paper (Great Britain. Home Office. Crime Prevention Unit)
   search also under the later title
   Crime detection and prevention series

Note that not all series are serials. Series in which a single author creates all the works are multipart monographs. Examples include C. S. Lewis's *Narnia Chronicles* and J. R. R. Tolkien's *Lord of the Rings*. Changes in such series are governed by RDA 6.1.3.1, "Works Issued as Multipart Monographs." For example, Anne McCaffrey wrote a number of novels with the series title "The Dragonriders of Pern." Toward the end of her life she cowrote the books with her son Todd, and after her death in 2011, Todd McCaffrey continued to write books in the series himself. This is a change in responsibility for the work (the series) and if this series had been a serial a new description (and new authorized access point) would have been required (RDA 6.1.3.2.1). But because this type of series is a multipart monograph, RDA 6.1.3.1 governs. No new description or authorized access point is needed. Similarly, when the title of a multipart monograph series changes a new description is not required.

For further discussion of the distinction between series that are serials and those that are multipart monographs, see the appendix on series at the end of this chapter.

6.1.3.3. WORKS ISSUED AS INTEGRATING RESOURCES. A change in responsibility for an integrating resource that affects the authorized access point for the work (6.1.3.3.1), or a change in the title proper of an integrating resource (6.1.3.3.2), does *not* create a resource that is deemed to be a new work in RDA. Instead, the description of the original work is updated by revising the authorized access point to reflect the new creator or the new title. In the integrating resource illustrated in figure 7.12, a blog, the work was initially described in January 2011 using the title that appeared at the time, "Pour une littérature corse." By November 29, 2011, the title had changed to "Pour une littérature (et autres arts) corse(s)." The description was changed by changing the authorized access point (in the MARC 130 field), and adding the former title as a variant (in a new MARC 430 field).

Figure 7.12. Change in Title of Integrating Resource: Same Work

Description before title change

130	0	‡a Pour une littérature corse (Blog)
380		‡a Blogs ‡2 lcsh
430	0	‡a Pourunelittératurecorse (Blog)
430	0	‡a Blog Pour une littérature corse
430	0	‡a Blog Pourunelittératurecorse
430	0	‡a Pourunelitteraturecorse.blogspot.com
670		‡a Éloge de la littérature corse, par quelques-uns de ses lecteurs, [2010], ©2010: ‡b title page (blog Pour une littérature corse) cover (blog Pourunelittératurecorse)
670		‡a Google search, January 3, 2011 ‡b (pourunelitteraturecorse.blogspot.com; title: Pour une littérature corse)

Description after title change

130	0	‡a Pour une littérature (et autres arts) corse(s) (Blog)
380		‡a Blogs ‡2 lcsh
430	0	‡w nne ‡a Pour une littérature corse (Blog)
430	0	‡a Pourunelittératurecorse (Blog)

430	0	‡a Blog Pour une littérature corse
430	0	‡a Blog Pourunelittératurecorse
430	0	‡a Pourunelitteraturecorse.blogspot.com
670		‡a Éloge de la littérature corse, par quelques-uns de ses lecteurs, [2010], ©2010: ‡b title page (blog Pour une littérature corse) cover (blog Pourunelittératurecorse)
670		‡a Google search, January 3, 2011 ‡b (pourunelitteraturecorse.blogspot.com; title: Pour une littérature corse)
670		‡a pourunelitteraturecorse.blogspot.com, 29 November 2011 ‡b main page (Pour une littérature (et autres arts) corse(s); "Ce blog est destiné à accueillir des points de vue (les vôtres, les miens) concernant les oeuvres corses et particulièrement la littérature corse (écrite en latin, italien, corse, français, etc.)") header (Pour une littérature (et autres arts) corse(s))

Work Descriptions in Authority Records

6.2. TITLE OF THE WORK. Title of the work is defined as "a word, character, or group of words and/or characters by which a work is known." Works are often known by many titles. One of these will be chosen as the preferred title for the work. Others may be recorded as variant titles.

RECORDING THE TITLE

How work titles are recorded in MARC authority records depends on whether the work has a recognized creator or not. This will be covered in more detail in this *Handbook's* chapter 9, "Relationships." Briefly, a person, family, or corporate body can be the creator of a work, that is, can be deemed "responsible for the creation of a work" (RDA 19.2.1). RDA chapter 19 also notes that a work can have more than one creator, and that these creators may play the same role (e.g., two authors who collaborate) or different roles (e.g., a collaboration between a composer and a lyricist).

Titles of works that have recognized creators are recorded in MARC authority fields following the authorized access point for the creator. If the creator is a person or family, the title is recorded in subfield ‡t of a 100, 400, or 500 field with indicators as appropriate for the situation (see discussion in chapters 3 and 4 of this *Handbook*); if the creator is a general corporate body, the title is recorded in subfield ‡t of a 110, 410, or 510 field with indicators as appropriate for the situation (see discussion in chapter 5); if the creator is a meeting, conference, etc., the title is recorded in subfield ‡t of a 111, 411, or 511 field, with first indicator "2." See figures 7.2 and 7.8 for examples.

For fuller discussion of the creator segment of these fields, see below under 6.27.

Some works do not have recognized creators, either because the creator is unknown (see RDA 6.27.1.8), because responsibility for the work is deemed too diffuse in the case of certain collaborative works (e.g., motion pictures, see RDA 6.27.1.3), or because the work is an aggregate work, a compilation of works by different creators (see RDA 6.27.1.4). The titles of such works are recorded in MARC authority fields 130, 430, or 530. The second indicator is a "non-filing indicator" (meaning the number of characters the system should skip when filing the title), and potentially could be coded with any number from 0 to 9, but in LC-PCC practice this indicator is always coded "0" (see discussion at 6.2.1.7). See figure 7.1 for an example.

6.2.1.4. CAPITALIZATION. The capitalization of a work title is manipulated if necessary from the form in which it was found. Preferred and variant titles should be recorded in the work descriptions (i.e., MARC authority records) following the instructions in RDA appendix A.3. This contrasts with RDA instructions for recording titles in manifestation descriptions (i.e., MARC bibliographic records), where various capitalization styles may be employed depending on the policies of the cataloging agency (see RDA 2.3.1.4 along with 1.7.1). Appendix A has a number of sets of capitalization guidelines dependent on the language of the title, but by and large A.3 calls for the first word of a title to be capitalized, with other words capitalized according to the usage of the language (for example, in English, only proper nouns are capitalized, whereas in German all nouns are capitalized). For example, the title of the work in figure 7.1 appeared in the resource as "PLANET OF THE APES." This title was chosen as the preferred title and is recorded in the description of the work as "Planet of the apes."

Premodern Forms of Letters. Sometimes, in an effort to look archaic or classical, typographers design presentations of titles in resources with premodern forms of capital letters. This particularly affects I, which can stand for "i" or "j"; V, which can stand for "u" or "v"; and VV, which can stand for "w." For example, the 2008 film of the Bolshoi Ballet production of Khachaturian's *Spartacus* presents the title "SPARTACVS" on all the packaging and in the opening credits. When the letters are converted to lower case according to the convention of appendix A.3, should this be recorded "Spartacvs" or "Spartacus"? This problem is not addressed in RDA, but LC-PCC PS 6.2.2.8 (July 2012) instructs catalogers to use "i" for vowels, "j" for consonants, "u" for vowels, "v" for consonants, and "w" for VV. The preferred title of the film will be recorded "Spartacus" (see figure 7.13).

Figure 7.13. Premodern Forms of Letters

```
046      ‡k 2008
130   0  ‡a Spartacus (Motion picture : 2008)
370      ‡g Paris (France) ‡2 naf
380      ‡a Motion pictures ‡2 lcsh
430   0  ‡a Spartacvs (Motion picture : 2008)
```

500 1	‡w r ‡i Motion picture adaptation of (work): Khachaturi͡an, Aram Ilʹich, ‡d 1903-1978. ‡t Spartak
500 1	‡w r ‡i Film director: ‡a MacGibbon, Ross, ‡d 1955-
500 1	‡w r ‡i Choreographer: ‡a Grigorovich, I͡Urii͡ Nikolaevich, ‡d 1927-
670	‡a Spartacus, 2008: ‡b opening credits (Bel Air Media, Paris, State Academic Bolshoi Theatre of Russia, in association with France 2, BBC, Decca Music Group, present SPARTACVS .. music, Aram Khachaturian, choreography, Yuri Grigorovich) container (SPARTACVS)
670	‡a imdb.com, 3 May 2010 ‡b (Spartacus; filmed in Paris, France, released 28 October 2008 in Russia; directed by Ross MacGibbon)

6.2.1.7. INITIAL ARTICLES. In a 2012 RDA revision, the previous guideline to omit initial articles from titles of works was rescinded. Following the principle of representation (RDA 0.4.3.4), RDA now prefers titles to be recorded as found, including initial articles. However, recognizing that MARC as currently implemented would have difficulty producing traditional filing order if the new RDA guideline were immediately implemented, an alternative that allows omission of initial articles is included with 6.2.1.7. Until difficulties with the MARC database structure are worked out, LC and PCC practice will be to apply the alternative. Initial articles are omitted from the form of a preferred or variant title as recorded in the description unless the title should file under the article (as when the title begins with the name of a person or place). For example, the title illustrated in figure 7.4 was found as "An understanding of the question," but is recorded as "Understanding of the question." For another example, see figure 7.9. As a convenience, RDA gives a list of initial articles in a number of common languages in appendix C.

Care must be taken not to apply this list mechanically. Many word forms that can be articles in one context may be some other type of word in another. For example, the French word "un" does mean "as," the indefinite article, but it also means "one," a number. RDA 6.2.1.7 calls for the form "un" to be omitted from the beginning of a title only if it is the indefinite article, not if it is the number.

6.2.1.9. ABBREVIATIONS. This guideline refers to appendix B.3, which forbids the manipulation of found titles by abbreviation of words in them. The title should be transcribed exactly as found (with the exception of capitalization and initial articles, as noted above). If an abbreviation appears in the title as found, it is so transcribed, but words found in full form should not be abbreviated.

6.2.2. PREFERRED TITLE OF THE WORK. This element is core, meaning it is required in the description of a work. The preferred title is the form chosen as the basis for the authorized access point for the work.

CHOOSING THE PREFERRED TITLE

6.2.2.4. WORKS CREATED AFTER 1500. Often the cataloger will find more than one title associated with a work. RDA instructs us to choose the preferred title for modern works (a) from titles in the original language of the work, or (b) as found in resources embodying the work or reference sources. This is an application of the principle of representation (RDA 0.4.3.4), under which the most commonly known title for a work is chosen as the preferred title, with one caveat: the preferred title is the most commonly known title *in the original language of the work,* which is not necessarily the most commonly known title to users of the database.

The RDA stipulation to choose a title from forms found in "resources embodying the work or in reference sources" is so all-inclusive as to be almost meaningless. The cataloger must weigh the evidence and make a judgment: which form (in the original language) is the best known or most common?

Most work descriptions in this chapter's figures have English preferred titles because the original language of the work was English. Boris Pasternak's novel (seen in figure 7.5) is an example of a preferred title in another language. The title of this work as it appears in its original language, Russian, is Доктор Живаго; under LC/NACO policy a romanized form will be recorded as Doktor Zhivago, but the preferred title is still based on the Russian title, not a title in English.

Some works are not based in the written word, and as such there might be no title associated with them in a resource embodying the work. This category includes most works of art. The preferred title of these works will be based on the form most commonly found in reference sources, giving preference to sources in the language of users of the database (English-language reference sources for contributors to the LC/NACO Authority File; cf. LC-PCC PS 6.2.2.4 and 6.2.2.5 [January 2013]). Leonardo's Last Supper is an example. There is no title embodied in the resource itself (the fresco), but "The Last Supper" is clearly the most commonly known title for this work in English (see figure 7.14).

Figure 7.14. Preferred Title from Reference Sources

046	‡k 1495⁻ ‡l 1497 ‡2 edtf
100 0	‡a Leonardo, ‡c da Vinci, ‡d 1452-1519. ‡t Last supper
370	‡g Milan (Italy) ‡2 naf
373	‡a Santa Maria delle Grazie (Church : Milan, Italy) ‡2 naf
380	‡a Mural paintings (Visual works) ‡2 aat
400 0	‡a Leonardo, ‡c da Vinci, ‡d 1452-1519. ‡t Cenacolo

400 0	‡a Leonardo, ‡c da Vinci, ‡d 1452-1519. ‡t Ultima cena
400 0	‡a Leonardo, ‡c da Vinci, ‡d 1452-1519. ‡t Dernier souper
400 0	‡a Leonardo, ‡c da Vinci, ‡d 1452-1519. ‡t Cène
670	‡a Leonardo, c1999: ‡b t.p. (L'ultima cena)
670	‡a Le dernier souper et ses anges copieurs, c1993
670	‡a Oxford art online, 16 June 2010 ‡b (Leonardo da Vinci: Last Supper (begun c. 1495, completed 1497), tempera mural, S Maria delle Grazie, Milan)
670	‡a Leonardo : il Cenacolo svelato = the Last Supper unveiled = la Cène dévoilée, 2011
678	‡a Fresco depicting the Last Supper as told in the Gospel of John, begun about 1495 by Leonardo da Vinci in the monastery of Santa Maria delle Grazie in Milan, Italy.

If it is unclear which title is the best known or most common, or if for some reason it is not possible to choose a title in the original language, the title proper of the first published edition should be chosen. RDA also addresses the situation where the work is published with different titles simultaneously (perhaps in different countries). In this case, RDA very practically instructs us to choose the title proper of the first resource received (see figure 7.15).

Figure 7.15. Choice of Title (Simultaneous Publication)

046	‡k 1935
100 1	‡a Christie, Agatha, ‡d 1890-1976. ‡t Death in the air
380	‡a Novels ‡2 aat
380	‡a Detective and mystery stories ‡2 lcsh
400 1	‡a Christie, Agatha, ‡d 1890-1976. ‡t Death in the clouds
670	‡a Death in the air, 1935
670	‡a Death in the clouds, 1935

The cataloger should not spend excessive amounts of time making this decision. There may be more than one title that could be chosen and hair-splitting reasoning is not necessary. Choose one of the titles as quickly as possible; once a preferred title has been chosen variants that were not chosen can be recorded in the description, and these will lead the database user to the preferred title.

If the title includes an alternative title, RDA instructs the cataloger to omit the alternative title. The title of the Maurice Sendak classic *Higglety Pigglety Pop!, or, There Must Be More to Life* includes an alternative title that will be omitted from the preferred title for the work (see figure 7.16).

Figure 7.16. Alternative Title Omitted

046	‡k 1967
100 1	‡a Sendak, Maurice. ‡t Higglety pigglety pop
380	‡a Short stories ‡a Children's stories ‡2 lcsh
400 1	‡a Sendak, Maurice. ‡t There must be more to life
670	‡a Higglety pigglety pop!, or, There must be more to life, 1967

In a change of practice from AACR2, statements of responsibility and introductory phrases that are part of the title will no longer be routinely omitted from preferred titles for works. However, because the preferred title is usually based on the title proper of a manifestation, the instructions for recording manifestation titles are relevant. RDA 2.3.1.5 says that if a title includes a name that would normally be treated as part of a statement of responsibility, but is an integral part of the title (e.g., connected by a case ending), it is to be recorded as part of the title. RDA 2.3.1.6 instructs us to omit "words that serve as an introduction and are not intended to be part of the title." This requires the cataloger to decide whether the words are intended to be part of the title.

Under previous practice the introductory phrase "This is the story of" would have been omitted from the preferred title for the work "This is the story of Faint George who wanted to be a knight." Likely in RDA it would be retained because the phrase was probably intended to be part of the title (see figure 7.17). On the other hand, the phrase "Metro-Goldwyn-Mayer presents," appearing in the film credits as "Metro-Goldwyn-Mayer presents The honeymoon machine," was undoubtedly not intended to be part of the title, and so is omitted (see figure 7.18; for another example, see figure 7.13). For an example of a statement of responsibility that probably would have been omitted from the preferred title for the work under previous rules, see figure 7.19.

Figure 7.17. Introductory Phrase Retained

046	‡k 1957
100 1	‡a Barry, Robert E. ‡t This is the story of Faint George who wanted to be a knight
380	‡a Children's stories ‡2 lcsh
400 1	‡a Barry, Robert E. ‡t Faint George who wanted to be a knight
670	‡a This is the story of Faint George who wanted to be a knight, 1957

Figure 7.18. Introductory Phrase Not Retained

046	‡k 1961
130 0	‡a Honeymoon machine (Motion picture)
380	‡a Motion pictures ‡2 lcsh

500 1	ǂw r ǂi Film director: ǂa Thorpe, Richard, ǂd 1896-1991
670	ǂa The honeymoon machine, 2011: ǂb credits (Metro-Goldwyn-Mayer presents The honeymoon machine)
670	ǂa IMDB.com, 12 July 2012 ǂb (The honeymoon machine; comedy directed by Richard Thorpe released 16 August 1961)

Figure 7.19. Statement of Responsibility Retained

046	ǂk 1998
100 1	ǂa Burningham, John. ǂt John Burningham's France
380	ǂa Travel literature ǂ2 aat
400 1	ǂa Burningham, John. ǂt France
670	ǂa John Burningham's France, 1998

6.2.2.5. WORKS CREATED BEFORE 1501. RDA has separate guidelines for choice of preferred title based on when the work was created. This stems from the principle of representation (RDA 0.4.3.4): the preferred title should in general be the most commonly known one. RDA deems titles for modern works (post-1500) to be most commonly known by forms found in resources embodying the work or reference sources, including sources contemporary with the work. RDA considers the commonly known form of titles of premodern works (those created before 1501) to be forms found in modern reference sources, not sources contemporary with the work. This is undoubtedly correct.

Most works created before 1501 exist in many varying versions, editions, etc., with almost as many variant titles. The cataloger is to identify the best-known title, using modern reference works, if possible, in the language of the original work.

Some of these works are known to be the responsibility of a particular creator. The preferred titles of such works are recorded following the authorized access point for the creator, just as with modern works (see figure 7.20).

Figure 7.20. Pre-1501 Work

046	ǂk 1314 ǂl 1321
100 0	ǂa Dante Alighieri, ǂd 1265-1321. ǂt Divina commedia
380	ǂa Epics ǂa Poems ǂ2 aat
400 0	ǂa Dante Alighieri, ǂd 1265-1321. ǂt Divine comedy
500 0	ǂw r ǂi Contains (work): ǂa Dante Alighieri, ǂd 1265-1321. ǂt Inferno
500 0	ǂw r ǂi Contains (work): ǂa Dante Alighieri, ǂd 1265-1321. ǂt Purgatorio
500 0	ǂw r ǂi Contains (work): ǂa Dante Alighieri, ǂd 1265-1321. ǂt Paradiso
670	ǂa Appunti sparsi per un commento alla Divina commedia, 1977

670 ‡a Islam and the Divine comedy, 1977

670 ‡a Literature resource center (online), 15 April 2010 ‡b (Divine comedy, Divina commedia, in three parts, Inferno, Purgatorio, and Paradiso; Inferno completed 1314, Paradiso completed in 1321)

Many works created before 1501 have no known author. Of these, many epics, poems, romances, tales, plays, chronicles, etc., have been retold, reprinted, published, translated, etc., many times in many versions over the centuries. Catalogers have given the name "anonymous classic" to the genre. Because anonymous classics find a place (usually in translation) even in small general libraries, the cataloger should know how to deal with such works.

By definition, anonymous works do not have a relationship link to a creator. Therefore in the MARC authority format the preferred title for such a work is recorded in a 130 field without the name of a creator. An example of such a work is the Old French poem La Chanson de Roland. This poem is known as *The Song of Roland* in English, but the most commonly known French title in modern resources is *La Chanson de Roland;* therefore, that form is chosen as the preferred title (see figure 7.21).

Figure 7.21. Pre-1501 Work

130 0 ‡a Chanson de Roland

380 ‡a Chansons de geste ‡2 lcsh

430 0 ‡a Song of Roland

670 ‡a La chanson de Roland, 2010

670 ‡a The new Oxford companion to literature in French, 1995: ‡b page 705-706 (Roland, La Chanson de; Song of Roland; medieval French chanson de geste)

Classical and Byzantine Greek Works. The guideline for choosing the preferred title for a work in classical or Byzantine Greek is an exception to the general rule of choosing a title in the original language of the work, but this, again, is based on the principle of representation, under which we are to choose the most commonly known title. Following the instructions in the exception produces a title that is most likely to be searched by a database user looking for a classical or Byzantine Greek work: choose a well-established title in the language preferred by the agency (English for contributors to the LC/NACO Authority File), and if there is no such title, a Latin title. Only if there is no Latin title are we instructed to choose a title in the original language, Greek. This simply reflects the way people search for these works. An example is Homer's *Odyssey.* Most English-speaking database users will search under that title rather than the Latin title *Odyssea* or the Greek title *Odysseia* (much less the title in Greek script, Ὀδύσσεια) (see figure 7.22). On the other hand, Sophocles' play *Oedipus*

Rex is better known by its Latin title than any English title, and it is unlikely that many database users would search for it using its Greek title *Oidipous Tyrannos* (see figure 7.23). The comic play *Katomyomachia* (literally "The cat and mouse battle") by the Byzantine writer Theodore Prodromos is not well-known by an English or a Latin title, so in this case the Greek form is chosen as the preferred title (see figure 7.24).

Figure 7.22. Pre-1501 Work (Classical Greek Exception)

100 0	‡a Homer. ‡t Odyssey
380	‡a Epics ‡a Poems ‡2 aat
400 0	‡a Homer. ‡t Odyssea
400 0	‡a Homer. ‡t Homeri Odyssea
400 0	‡a Homer. ‡t Odysseia
400 0	‡a Homer. ‡t Ὀδύσσεια
667	‡a Non-Latin script reference not evaluated.
670	‡a Homeri Odyssea, 1909-
670	‡a Brill's new Pauly online, 23 August 2009 ‡b (Odyssey; Ὀδύσσεια)

Figure 7.23. Pre-1501 Work (Classical Greek Exception)

046	‡k -04
100 0	‡a Sophocles. ‡t Oedipus Rex
380	‡a Plays (Document genre) ‡2 aat
400 0	‡a Sophocles. ‡t Oidipous Tyrannos
400 0	‡a Sophocles. ‡t Οἰδίπους τύραννος
400 0	‡a Sophocles. ‡t Oedipus the King
667	‡a Non-Latin script reference not evaluated.
670	‡a Sophokleous Oidipous Tyrannos, 1978
670	‡a Brill's new Pauly online, 23 August 2009 ‡b (Oedipus Rex; Οἰδίπους τύραννος)
670	‡a Oedipus the King, 2009

Figure 7.24. Pre-1501 Work (Byzantine Greek Exception)

100 1	‡a Prodromus, Theodore. ‡t Katomyomachia
380	‡a Plays (Document genre) ‡2 aat
400 1	‡a Prodromus, Theodore. ‡t Κατομυομαχία
667	‡a Non-Latin script reference not evaluated.
670	‡a Katomyomachia, 1955: ‡b title page (Κατομυομαχία)

One problem in dealing with older works such as those treated in 6.2.2.5 is the question of exactly what constitutes the work. When is a version an expression of the work and when is it a completely different work? Take, for example, the anonymous classic *Mother Goose,* a collection of traditional nursery rhymes and tales. No one knows the author of most of the poems and the collection varies with the edition, but it can be said to be an aggregate work. Following the general guidelines of 6.2.2.5, we choose a generally accepted title in the language of the original as found in modern sources as the preferred title, "Mother Goose" (see figure 7.25).

Figure 7.25. Pre-1501 Aggregate Work

130	0	‡a Mother Goose
380		‡a Poems ‡a Fairy tales ‡a Nursery rhymes ‡2 aat
430	0	‡a Nursery rhymes
430	0	‡a Book of nursery songs and rhymes
430	0	‡a Mother Goose nursery rhymes
430	0	‡a Real Mother Goose
670		‡a A book of nursery songs and rhymes, 1969
670		‡a Mother Goose nursery rhymes, 1958
670		‡a The real Mother Goose, 1945
670		‡a Wikipedia, October 7, 2010 ‡b (Mother Goose, imaginary author of traditional collection of fairy tales and nursery rhymes dating from the middle ages and later, published as Mother Goose or Mother Goose rhymes; title Nursery rhymes dates from the 19th century)

6.2.2.7. MANUSCRIPTS AND MANUSCRIPT GROUPS. Manuscripts pose special problems because the physical manuscript itself can be considered a work (analogous to an art object) separate from the intellectual content contained in the manuscript, which is also a work. The physical manuscript and the work contained in it therefore usually have separate work descriptions and separate authorized access points. An example of the distinction between the preferred title for the text and that for the manuscript as a physical entity is the manuscript called *The Book of Kells,* which contains a distinct expression of a work, the Gospels in Latin (see figure 7.26).

Figure 7.26. Named Manuscript

Description of the manuscript

130	0	‡a Book of Kells
373		‡a Trinity College (Dublin, Ireland). Library ‡2 naf
380		‡a Manuscripts ‡2 lcsh

410	2	‡a Trinity College (Dublin, Ireland). ‡b Library. ‡k Manuscript. ‡n A.1.6
410	2	‡a Trinity College (Dublin, Ireland). ‡b Library. ‡k Manuscript. ‡n 58
430	0	‡a Kells, Book of
430	0	‡a Codex Cenannensis
530	0	‡a Bible. ‡p Gospels. ‡l Latin. ‡s Book of Kells
667		‡a Authorized access point represents the manuscript as a physical entity, including its decoration. For textual contents of the manuscript use: Bible. Gospels. Latin. Book of Kells. [date, as appropriate].
670		‡a The Book of Kells, c1990: ‡b t.p. (The Book of Kells; ms. 58 in the Library of Trinity College, Dublin)
670		‡a E-mail correspondence with Bernard Meehan, keeper of mss. at Trinity College, Nov. 30, 2000 ‡b (shelfmark changed from A 1 6 to 58 in 1900)
670		‡a Evangeliorum quattuor Codex Cenannensis, 1950-1951

Description of the expression of the work contained in the manuscript

130	0	‡a Bible. ‡p Gospels. ‡l Latin. ‡s Book of Kells
380		‡a Sacred scripture
530	0	‡a Book of Kells
667		‡a Authorized access point represents the textual content of the physical manuscript. For the manuscript as a physical entity, including its decoration, use: Book of Kells.
667		‡a DESCRIPTIVE USAGE: Bible authorized access points used in descriptive portions of the record are analytical, i.e., they need to contain data elements in RDA 6.30.3.2 as applicable.

Exceptionally, in the MARC environment a physical manuscript and the work contained in it may share the same authorized access point if the work has no title or is known by the same title as the physical manuscript, and there is no creator that may be linked to the work (see discussion at LC-PCC PS 6.2.2.7, January 2013).

AACR2 25.13, on which RDA 6.2.2.7 is based, gave instructions for choosing the preferred title for a manuscript as well as, in certain cases, the work contained within the manuscript. RDA 6.2.2.7, unfortunately, is written only in terms of the work contained within the manuscript. The Library of Congress Policy Statement for 6.2.2.7 includes an extensive gloss on the RDA guideline, giving instructions for naming the manuscript. This section of the *Handbook* is based on the Library of Congress policy statement.

The preferred title for a manuscript is selected, in this order of preference, from (1) the name of the physical manuscript, or, if there is no name for the manuscript, (2) a devised title beginning with the authorized access point for the repository where the physical manuscript is housed. This corresponds to RDA 6.2.2.7b and 6.2.2.7c.

The LC-PCC PS advises the cataloger to "consider the name of the physical manuscript to be the name used by the repository or scholars or the name found in reference sources, not a 'name' devised only for the edition in hand." The Book of Kells has
such a name (figure 7.26). The Dead Sea scrolls qualify as an example of a manuscript
group that has come to be identified in reference sources by a name. Use this name as
the preferred title for the group (see figure 7.27).

Figure 7.27. Manuscript Group

130	0	‡a Dead Sea scrolls
370		‡g Dead Sea Region (Israel and Jordan) ‡2 lcsh
380		‡a Manuscript group
430	0	‡a Judean scrolls
430	0	‡a מגילות ים המלח
430	0	‡a Megilot Yam ha-melaḥ
667		‡a Authorized access point is for the collection of manuscripts in Hebrew, Aramaic, and Greek; for the works contained in the physical manuscripts, use the authorized access point for the individual works.
667		‡a Non-Latin script reference not evaluated.
670		‡a The Dead Sea scrolls, 2011
670		‡a Hymns from the Judean scrolls, 1950
670		‡a מגילות ים המלח = The Dead Sea scrolls, 1950

Most manuscripts do not acquire a name by which they are commonly known. If
the name of the manuscript cannot be determined, construct an access point beginning with the authorized access point for the *current* repository that holds the manuscript, followed in subfield ‡k by the term "Manuscript," followed by the repository's
preferred designation for the manuscript:

> ‡a [authorized access point of repository]. ‡k Manuscript. ‡n [repository's
> preferred designation for the manuscript].

This designation is usually numeric and often includes some sort of prefix. If similar
manuscripts from the same repository have already been established in the authority
file, the numbering and prefix pattern of already-established authorized access points
should be followed, even if the resource being cataloged has a variant form of the
designation. If it is thought to be useful, the cataloger may give a variant access point
using the variant form of the designation.

An example is the papyrus manuscript containing the Egyptian text *Instructions of
'Onchsheshonqy.* The manuscript itself has no name. One of the resources being cataloged gives the repository designation for the manuscript "P. BM 10508" on the title

page. The current repository of this manuscript is the British Library. A search of the authority file shows that a pattern has been established for the repository designation for this category of manuscript in the British Library: "Papyrus [number]." That pattern is followed in the preferred title for this manuscript (see figure 7.28).

Figure 7.28. Devised Title for Manuscript

046	‡k -03
110 2	‡a British Library. ‡k Manuscript. ‡n Papyrus 10508
373	‡a British Library ‡2 naf
380	‡a Manuscripts (Papyri) ‡2 lcsh
410 2	‡a British Library. ‡k Manuscript. ‡n P. BM 10508
410 2	‡w nne ‡a British Museum. ‡k Manuscript. ‡n Papyrus 10508
667	‡a Authorized access point for the physical manuscript; for the work contained in the physical manuscript, see n 84094115 (Instructions of 'Onchsheshonqy)
670	‡a British Museum Department of Egyptian & Assyrian Antiquities Catalogue of demotic papyri in the BM, 1939-1955: ‡b volume 2 (The Instructions of 'Onchsheshonqy (British Museum Papyrus 10508))
670	‡a Instructions of 'Onchsheshonqy. Ger. Die Lehre des Anchscheschonqi (P. BM 10508), 1984: ‡b p. 143 (British Museum Papyrus 10508)
670	‡a Wikipedia, list of ancient Egyptian papyri, 21 January 2011 ‡b (British Museum papyrus 10508; 4th century BC or later; contains Instruction of Ankhsheshonq)

The requirement that authorized access points of this type be based on the *current* repository means that if a manuscript changes hands or if the repository's name changes (i.e., becomes a new corporate body under RDA principles), the authorized access point for the manuscript will be changed. Figure 7.28 is an example. In 1973 the British Library separated from the British Museum. Previous to this date the preferred title of the manuscript was "British Museum. Manuscript. Papyrus 10508." After 1973 the British Museum no longer owned the manuscript, so the preferred title was changed to the form in the 110 field of figure 7.28. Because the title had previously been established with another form, the previous authorized access point was changed to a variant access point, as seen in the second 410 field of figure 7.28. The coding "‡w nne" means that the form had previously been an authorized access point.

Descriptions of manuscripts should include a cataloguer's note element explaining the relationship between the manuscript and the work contained in it. An example of this element may be seen in the 667 field of figure 7.28. Earlier cataloging practice was to include formal "search also under" links between the records in 5XX fields. Current practice omits those links except for the Bible and liturgical works (see figure 7.26), but in a future entity-relationship database structure formal links of some sort for all these related work descriptions will probably be necessary.

6.2.2.9. RECORDING THE PREFERRED TITLE FOR A PART OR PARTS OF A WORK. RDA 5.1.2, as noted above, defines the term "work" to include components of works. Therefore parts are treated as though they were a complete work for purposes of identification and access, and thus can have a preferred title just as the work as a whole can. Identification of and access to parts is particularly important when the parts have been published separately. RDA 6.2.2.9 gives guidance for choosing and recording a preferred title for a part or parts of a work.

6.2.2.9.1. ONE PART. If a part of a work has a distinctive title that will be selected as its preferred title, the preferred title is not recorded subordinately to the main title of the work, although such a form may be given as a variant title. Jonathan Swift's *Voyage to Lilliput* is an example. The account of Captain Gulliver's adventures among the Lilliputians is the first part of a work commonly known as *Gulliver's Travels*. Because the part has a distinctive title by which it has become commonly known, that title will be chosen as the preferred title for the part (see figure 7.29).

Figure 7.29. Part of a Work with Distinctive Title

046	‡k 1726
100 1	‡a Swift, Jonathan, ‡d 1667-1745. ‡t Voyage to Lilliput
380	‡a Novels ‡2 lcsh
400 1	‡a Swift, Jonathan, ‡d 1667-1745. ‡t Lemuel Gulliver's voyage to Lilliput
400 1	‡a Swift, Jonathan, ‡d 1667-1745. ‡t Adventures of Capt. Gulliver, in a voyage to the Islands of Lilliput
400 1	‡a Swift, Jonathan, ‡d 1667-1745. ‡t Gulliver's travels. ‡n Part 1, ‡p Voyage to Lilliput
670	‡a Lemuel Gulliver's voyage to Lilliput, 1727
670	‡a The adventures of Capt. Gulliver, in a voyage to the Islands of Lilliput, 1796
670	‡a Gulliver's Travels. Part I. The voyage to Lilliput, 1805
670	‡a A voyage to Lilliput, 1858
670	‡a Literature criticism online, 3 August 2009 ‡b (A voyage to Lilliput, first part of Gulliver's travels, first published 1726)

RDA 6.2.2.9 applies not only to parts of single works, but also to parts within aggregate works such as multipart monographs or series. The same principle applies: if the part has a distinctive title, that title is selected as the preferred title for the work. The part may be linked to the whole series or multipart monograph using a variant access point. Orson Scott Card's *Tales of Alvin Maker* is an example of a whole work (a multipart monograph), each of whose parts may be handled in such a fashion. See figure 7.30 for descriptions of both the work as a whole and of one of the parts.

Figure 7.30. Part of a Work with Distinctive Title

Description of the whole

046	‡k 1987
100 1	‡a Card, Orson Scott. ‡t Tales of Alvin Maker
380	‡a Novels ‡2 aat
380	‡a Series (Publications) ‡2 lcsh
380	‡a Multipart monograph
430 0	‡a Tales of Alvin Maker
500 1	‡w r ‡i Contains (work): ‡a Card, Orson Scott. ‡t Seventh son
500 1	‡w r ‡i Contains (work): ‡a Card, Orson Scott. ‡t Red prophet
500 1	‡w r ‡i Contains (work): ‡a Card, Orson Scott. ‡t Prentice Alvin
...	
642	‡a v. II ‡5 UPB
643	‡a New York ‡b T. Doherty Associates
644	‡a f ‡5 UPB
645	‡a t ‡5 UPB
646	‡a s ‡5 UPB
670	‡a Red prophet, 1988: ‡b series title page (volume II of the Tales of Alvin Maker; Seventh son listed as the first novel in the series)
670	‡a Seventh son, 1987

Description of the part

046	‡k 1988
100 1	‡a Card, Orson Scott. ‡t Red prophet
380	‡a Novels ‡2 aat
400 1	‡a Card, Orson Scott. ‡t Tales of Alvin Maker. ‡n Volume II, ‡p Red prophet
500 1	‡w r ‡i Contained in (work): ‡a Card, Orson Scott. ‡t Tales of Alvin Maker
670	‡a Red prophet, 1988: ‡b series title page (volume II of the Tales of Alvin Maker)

If the part does not have a distinctive title, a general term such as a chapter or book number, or a general division (such as "preface"), will be chosen as the preferred title of the part. This is recorded in the access point subordinately to the preferred title of the work (see RDA 6.27.2.1). Single books from Homer's works, which usually do not have a distinct title, are frequently published separately. An example is the 2002 publication of Book 1 of the *Iliad* by the University of Michigan Press. The preferred title for the part is "Book 1" (see figure 7.31). The form of the designation is based on the form found in the resource being cataloged (in this case, "Book 1"). In practice, however, if other similar parts of the same work have already been established in the authority file, subsequent catalogers will use the designation that has already been used. Once the pattern of "Book 1" has been established, it will be followed for other books. For example, one publication of book 9 of the *Iliad* has in the title the designation "Liber IX." Because the pattern has already been established to use the form "Book 1," the preferred title for Liber IX will also be "Book 9" (see figure 7.31).

Figure 7.31. Part of a Work without a Distinctive Title

100 0	ǂa Homer. ǂt Iliad. ǂn Book 1
380	ǂa Epics ǂa Poems ǂ2 aat
670	ǂa Iliad, Book 1, 2002

100 0	ǂa Homer. ǂt Iliad. ǂn Book 9
380	ǂa Epics ǂa Poems ǂ2 aat
400 0	ǂa Homer. ǂt Homeri Iliadis liber IX
400 0	ǂa Homer. ǂt Iliad. ǂn Liber IX
670	ǂa Homeri Iliadis liber IX, 1661

The final paragraph of 6.2.2.9.1 contains an exception for serials and integrating resources which instructs the cataloger to record both the designation and the title as the preferred title for a part, if the part is identified by both. This applies to preferred titles of monographic series, which are serials (see figure 7.32). This paragraph should not be applied, however, to parts of multipart monograph series, which are not serials (e.g., *Red Prophet*, figure 7.30). On the distinction between these two types of series, see the discussion in the appendix on series at the end of this chapter.

Figure 7.32. Serial Part Identified by Designation and Title

130 0	ǂa Islamic history series. ǂn Part II, ǂp Rightly guided caliphs
380	ǂa Series (Publications) ǂa Monographic series ǂ2 lcsh
430 0	ǂa Rightly guided caliphs
642	ǂa 2 ǂ5 DPCC ǂ5 ICU
643	ǂa Riyadh ǂb International Islamic Publishing House
644	ǂa f ǂ5 ICU
645	ǂa t ǂ5 DPCC ǂ5 ICU
646	ǂa s ǂ5 ICU
670	ǂa 'Umar ibn al-Khaṭṭâb, 2007: ǂb t.p. (Islamic history series. Part II, The rightly guided caliphs)

6.2.2.9.2. TWO OR MORE PARTS. RDA deals with this in two ways, depending on how the parts are arranged.

Consecutive Parts. If the selection is a sequence of two or more consecutively numbered parts, the preferred title is the designation of the parts followed by the inclusive number of the parts. The designation is to be recorded in the singular. Although this may seem strange, the purpose of this stipulation is so that the same designation will be recorded whether a resource consists of a single part or of multiple parts. In figure 7.31, a single part of the *Iliad* is designated using the term "Book [number]." Resources containing consecutively numbered parts of the *Iliad* will also use the same term, in the singular: "Book [number-number]" (see figure 7.33).

Figure 7.33. Consecutively Numbered Parts of a Work

100 0	‡a Homer. ‡t Iliad. ‡n Book 1-6
380	‡a Epics ‡a Poems ‡2 aat
400 0	‡a Homer. ‡t First six books of Homer's Iliad
670	‡a The first six books of Homer's Iliad, 1858.

Unnumbered or Nonconsecutive Parts. If the selection consists of unnumbered or nonconsecutive parts, RDA instructs the cataloger to record a preferred title for each part (see figure 7.34, first bibliographic record and authority record). This seems to be a very user-centered practice, and more helpful than the AACR2 practice of simply using "Selections" when there are more than two or three works. RDA does, however, give an alternative: "Selections" may be used as the preferred title for the parts instead of (or in addition to) recording the preferred title for each part (see figure 7.34, second bibliographic record and authority record). This might be an appropriate procedure to follow if there are a large number of parts. It is also the only procedure available if the selected parts consist of extracts that cannot be identified easily, as in the compilation of miscellaneous quotations from *Poor Richard's Almanack,* published by Blue Mountain Arts in 1975 (see figure 7.35). On the qualifier to "Selections," see below under 6.6.

Figure 7.34. Nonconsecutively Numbered Parts of a Work

Bibliographic record listing all the parts

100 1	‡a Shakesepare, William, ‡d 1564-1616, ‡e author.
245 10	‡a Of imagination all compact : ‡b four sonnets / ‡c by William Shakespeare.
...	
505 0	‡a Sonnet LXXIII. That time of year thou mayest in me behold -- Sonnet XCVII. How like a winter hath my absence been -- Sonnet CXVI. Let me not to the marriage of true minds -- Sonnet CXVII. Accuse me thus: that I have scanted all.

500   ‡a "Printed by Grabhorn-Hoyem ... for Jeremiah Donovan"--Statement on verso of each broadside.

...

700 12 ‡a Shakesepare, William, ‡d 1564-1616. ‡t Sonnets. ‡n 73.

700 12 ‡a Shakesepare, William, ‡d 1564-1616. ‡t Sonnets. ‡n 97.

700 12 ‡a Shakesepare, William, ‡d 1564-1616. ‡t Sonnets. ‡n 116.

700 12 ‡a Shakesepare, William, ‡d 1564-1616. ‡t Sonnets. ‡n 117.

Bibliographic record following 6.2.2.9.2's alternative guideline

100 1   ‡a Shakesepare, William, ‡d 1564-1616, ‡e author.

240 10 ‡a Sonnets. ‡k Selections (Donovan)

245 10 ‡a Of imagination all compact : ‡b four sonnets / ‡c by William Shakespeare.

...

505 0   ‡a Sonnet LXXIII. That time of year thou mayest in me behold -- Sonnet XCVII. How like a winter hath my absence been -- Sonnet CXVI. Let me not to the marriage of true minds -- Sonnet CXVII. Accuse me thus: that I have scanted all.

500   ‡a "Printed by Grabhorn-Hoyem ... for Jeremiah Donovan"--Statement on verso of each broadside.

...

Authority record for one of the parts

100 1   ‡a Shakesepare, William, ‡d 1564-1616. ‡t Sonnets. ‡n 73

380   ‡a Sonnets ‡2 lcsh

400 1   ‡a Shakesepare, William, ‡d 1564-1616. ‡t That time of year thou mayest in me behold

500 1   ‡w r ‡i Contained in (work): ‡a Shakesepare, William, ‡d 1564-1616. ‡t Sonnets. ‡k Selections (Donovan)

670   ‡a Of imagination all compact : four sonnets, 1971 ‡b (first line of sonnet: That time of year thou mayest in me behold)

Authority record for the collection

100 1   ‡a Shakesepare, William, ‡d 1564-1616. ‡t Sonnets. ‡k Selections (Donovan)

380   ‡a Sonnets ‡2 lcsh

381   ‡a Donovan

400 1   ‡a Shakesepare, William, ‡d 1564-1616. ‡t Of imagination all compact

500 1   ‡w r ‡i Contains (work): ‡a Shakesepare, William, ‡d 1564-1616. ‡t Sonnets. ‡n 73

500 1   ‡w r ‡i Contains (work): ‡a Shakesepare, William, ‡d 1564-1616. ‡t Sonnets. ‡n 97

500 1	‡w r ‡i Contains (work): ‡a Shakesepare, William, ‡d 1564-1616. ‡t Sonnets. ‡n 116	
500 1	‡w r ‡i Contains (work): ‡a Shakesepare, William, ‡d 1564-1616. ‡t Sonnets. ‡n 117	
670	‡a Of imagination all compact : four sonnets, 1971: ‡b verso of broadsides (printed by Grabhorn-Hoyem ... for Jeremiah Donovan)	

Figure 7.35. Extracts

100 1	‡a Saunders, Richard, ‡d 1706-1790. ‡t Poor Richard. ‡k Selections (Blue Mountain Arts)
373	‡a Blue Mountain Arts (Firm) ‡2 naf
380	‡a Quotations ‡2 lcsh
400 1	‡a Saunders, Richard, ‡d 1706-1790. ‡t Poor Richard's quotations
670	‡a Poor Richard's quotations, 1975 ‡b (published by Blue Mountain Arts)

6.2.2.10. RECORDING THE PREFERRED TITLE FOR A COMPILATION OF WORKS. If a compilation of works is known by a distinctive title, that title is used as the preferred title for the compilation. A common application of this guideline is to collections of poems or short stories, which are often published under a distinctive title, if the collection remains known by that title. Walt Whitman published a collection of his poetry under the title *Leaves of Grass.* Individual poems within the collection, such as "Song of Myself" and "I Sing the Body Electric," are themselves works. Because the collection has a distinctive title, its preferred name is "Leaves of grass" (see figure 7.36).

Figure 7.36. Compilation with Distinctive Title

100 1	‡a Whitman, Walt, ‡d 1819-1892. ‡t Leaves of grass
380	‡a Poems ‡2 aat
400 1	‡a Whitman, Walt, ‡d 1819-1892. ‡t Walt Whitman's Leaves of grass
500 1	‡w r ‡i Contains (work): ‡a Whitman, Walt, ‡d 1819-1892. ‡t Song of myself
500 1	‡w r ‡i Contains (work): ‡a Whitman, Walt, ‡d 1819-1892. ‡t I sing the body electric
...	
670	‡a Leaves of grass, 1860
670	‡a Walt Whitman's Leaves of grass, 2009

Most often compilations do not have distinctive titles by which they have become well known. In such cases the preferred title for the compilation will be a cataloger-devised title (referred to in RDA as a "conventional collective title"), formed following the instructions in 6.2.2.10.

6.2.2.10.1. COMPLETE WORKS. The conventional collective title "Works" is used for a compilation that purports to be the complete works of a person, family, or corporate body. This includes compilations published during the lifetime of the author, even though the author may create other works after the publication. There may be many compilations of the works of an author. For cataloging purposes these may all be considered the same aggregate work, although they may represent many different expressions of that aggregate work.[8] Therefore the title "Works" itself would probably never need to be qualified to distinguish it from another aggregate work with the same title. For an example, see figure 7.37.

Figure 7.37. Complete Works

100 0	‡a Persius. ‡t Works
380	‡a Poems ‡2 aat
400 0	‡a Persius. ‡t A. Persi Flacci Saturarum liber
400 0	‡a Persius. ‡t Saturarum liber
400 0	‡a Persius. ‡t Satires
670	‡a A. Persi Flacci Saturarum liber, 1956
670	‡a Satires, 1998

6.2.2.10.2. COMPLETE WORKS IN A SINGLE FORM. If the resource being cataloged consists of a collection purporting to be a creator's complete works in a single form, the preferred title is a term naming the form. But what if the creator only worked in one form? Should 6.2.2.10.1 or 6.2.2.10.2 apply? RDA is ambiguous. In AACR2 practice, following LC policies, the rule for complete works in a single form (AACR2 25.10, equivalent to RDA 6.2.2.10.2) was only applied if the creator worked in more than one form (for example, poetry, short stories, and essays). If the creator worked in only one form, the rule for "Works" (AACR2 25.8, equivalent to RDA 6.2.2.10.1) was applied. Thus, although Persius only wrote poems, the collective title for a compilation of his poems was "Works," not "Poems" (see figure 7.37). This is an area in RDA that perhaps needs further clarification; until then it might be wise to continue the practice of applying 6.2.2.10.2 only to creators who worked in more than one form.

A list of eight terms is provided with 6.2.2.10.2. Terms from this list should be used if appropriate. However, the list is not closed. Other appropriate terms may be used if needed for a form not included in the list. Albrecht Dürer, for example, created works in many forms: in addition to his prose writing he also created paintings, woodcut prints, and engravings. A collection titled *The Complete Woodcuts of Albrecht Dürer* can be assigned the preferred title "Woodcuts" (see figure 7.38).

Figure 7.38. Complete Works in a Single Form

100 1	‡a Dürer, Albrecht, ‡d 1471-1528. ‡t Woodcuts
380	‡a Woodcuts (Prints) ‡2 aat
400 1	‡a Dürer, Albrecht, ‡d 1471-1528. ‡t Complete woodcuts of Albrecht Dürer
670	‡a The complete woodcuts of Albrecht Dürer, 1936

6.2.2.10.3. OTHER COMPILATIONS OF TWO OR MORE WORKS. Resources frequently contain two or more works, but not the complete works, of an author. RDA deals with this problem in the same way as it deals with unnumbered or nonconsecutive parts under 6.2.2.9.2 (see above). RDA instructs us to record the preferred title for each of the works in the compilation, no matter how many there are. In the bibliographic record, this means including an added access point for each work in the compilation; for the authority file, this means an authority record representing each work, containing its authorized access point. For example, *The Best of Rumpole* contains seven short stories by John Mortimer. Applying the main part of 6.2.2.10.3, the bibliographic record for this resource would contain an added access point for each of these seven works, and these authorized access points would be authorized by corresponding records in the authority file (see figure 7.39, first bibliographic record). This gives better controlled access to the individual works than was allowed under previous cataloging practice, which can only be of benefit to the users of the database.

Figure 7.39. Compilation of Two or More Works

Bibliographic record listing all of the works

100 1	‡a Mortimer, John, ‡d 1923-2009, ‡e author.
245 14	‡a The best of Rumpole / ‡c by John Mortimer.
...	
505 0	‡a Rumpole and the younger generation -- Rumpole and the showfolk -- Rumpole and the tap end -- Rumpole and the bubble reputation -- Rumpole a la carte -- Rumpole and the children of the devil -- Rumpole on trial.
...	
700 12	‡a Mortimer, John, ‡d 1923-2009. ‡t Rumpole and the younger generation.
700 12	‡a Mortimer, John, ‡d 1923-2009. ‡t Rumpole and the showfolk.
700 12	‡a Mortimer, John, ‡d 1923-2009. ‡t Rumpole and the tap end.
700 12	‡a Mortimer, John, ‡d 1923-2009. ‡t Rumpole and the bubble reputation.
700 12	‡a Mortimer, John, ‡d 1923-2009. ‡t Rumpole a la carte.
700 12	‡a Mortimer, John, ‡d 1923-2009. ‡t Rumpole and the children of the devil.
700 12	‡a Mortimer, John, ‡d 1923-2009. ‡t Rumpole on trial.

Bibliographic record following 6.2.2.10.3's alternative guideline

100 1	‡a Mortimer, John, ‡d 1923-2009, ‡e author.
240 10	‡a Short stories. ‡k Selections (The best of Rumpole)
245 14	‡a The best of Rumpole / ‡c by John Mortimer.
...	
505 0	‡a Rumpole and the younger generation -- Rumpole and the showfolk -- Rumpole and the tap end -- Rumpole and the bubble reputation -- Rumpole a la carte -- Rumpole and the children of the devil -- Rumpole on trial.
...	

Authority record for one of the works

100 1	‡a Mortimer, John, ‡d 1923-2009. ‡t Rumpole and the younger generation
380	‡a Short stories ‡2 lcsh
500 1	‡w r ‡i Contained in (work): ‡a Mortimer, John, ‡d 1923-2009. ‡t Short stories. ‡k Selections (Rumpole of the Bailey)
500 1	‡w r ‡i Contained in (work): ‡a Mortimer, John, ‡d 1923-2009. ‡t Short stories. ‡k Selections (The best of Rumpole)
670	‡a The best of Rumpole, 1993: ‡b title page verso (Rumpole and the younger generation, first published 1978 in the anthology Rumpole of the Bailey)

Authority record for the collection

100 1	‡a Mortimer, John, ‡d 1923-2009. ‡t Short stories. ‡k Selections (The best of Rumpole)
380	‡a Short stories ‡2 lcsh
381	‡a The best of Rumpole
400 1	‡a Mortimer, John, ‡d 1923-2009. ‡t Best of Rumpole
500 1	‡w r ‡i Contains (work): ‡a Mortimer, John, ‡d 1923-2009. ‡t Rumpole and the younger generation
500 1	‡w r ‡i Contains (work): ‡a Mortimer, John, ‡d 1923-2009. ‡t Rumpole and the showfolk
500 1	‡w r ‡i Contains (work): ‡a Mortimer, John, ‡d 1923-2009. ‡t Rumpole and the tap end
500 1	‡w r ‡i Contains (work): ‡a Mortimer, John, ‡d 1923-2009. ‡t Rumpole and the bubble reputation
500 1	‡w r ‡i Contains (work): ‡a Mortimer, John, ‡d 1923-2009. ‡t Rumpole a la carte
500 1	‡w r ‡i Contains (work): ‡a Mortimer, John, ‡d 1923-2009. ‡t Rumpole and the children of the devil
500 1	‡w r ‡i Contains (work): ‡a Mortimer, John, ‡d 1923-2009. ‡t Rumpole on trial
670	‡a The best of Rumpole, 1993

However, the authors of RDA realized there was probably a limit to how many access points could reasonably be included in a bibliographic record, and so, as for RDA 6.2.2.9.2, an alternative guideline is provided for recording a preferred title for the compilation itself, rather than (or in addition to) preferred titles for each of the individual works in the compilation. This is done by first recording the collective title that would be appropriate to the compilation, followed by the term "Selections." For an example, see the second bibliographic record and second authority record in figure 7.39. Catalogers accustomed to AACR2 practice must give special attention to the wording of the alternative: the term "Selections" *follows* an appropriate conventional collective title in RDA, it never stands alone. So if the appropriate conventional collective title is "Works," a compilation that includes some, but not all, of the works of a person, family, or corporate body would be given the preferred title "Works. Selections" (see figure 7.40). This preferred title is also used for resources that contain extracts or quotations (see figure 7.41). On the qualifier to "Selections," see below under 6.6.

Figure 7.40. Selected Works

100 1	‡a Pratchett, Terry. ‡t Works. ‡k Selections (The city watch trilogy)
380	‡a Novels ‡2 aat
381	‡a The city watch trilogy
400 1	‡a Pratchett, Terry. ‡t City watch trilogy
500 1	‡w r ‡i Contains (work): ‡a Pratchett, Terry. ‡t Guards! Guards!
500 1	‡w r ‡i Contains (work): ‡a Pratchett, Terry. ‡t Men at arms
500 1	‡w r ‡i Contains (work): ‡a Pratchett, Terry. ‡t Feet of clay
670	‡a The city watch trilogy, 1999 ‡b (contains Guards! Guards! ; Men at arms ; Feet of clay)

Figure 7.41. Selected Works

100 1	‡a Pratchett, Terry. ‡t Works. ‡k Selections (Briggs)
380	‡a Quotations ‡2 lcsh
381	‡a Briggs
400 1	‡a Pratchett, Terry. ‡t Wit and wisdom of Discworld
500 1	‡w r ‡i Compiler: ‡a Briggs, Stephen, ‡d 1951-
670	‡a The wit and wisdom of Discworld, 2007: ‡b cover (favorite quotations from the famous Discworld universe, compiled by Stephen Briggs)

Compilations of two or more works by different creators is handled in a similar way, but without the alternative "Selections" guideline (see RDA 6.27.1.4).

6.2.3. VARIANT TITLE FOR THE WORK. Just as with other entities, works may be known by different names (i.e., titles) or different forms of the same name (i.e., title). One of these titles is chosen, as described above, as the preferred title, and in current systems the preferred title, as a part of the authorized access point, is how the work will be represented in displays such as database indexes and bibliographic records. However, if the work is known by other titles, these will be recorded in the description if in the judgment of the cataloger this would be helpful for identification or access (note that RDA 6.2.3, variant title for the work, is not a core element).

Variant titles of works are recorded in 400, 410, 411, or 430 fields in the MARC authority format, parallel to the way preferred titles are recorded (see above at Recording the Title, following 6.2). How they display depends on how the library's system is set up, but they are intended to display to the public similarly to the following, when a user does a search on a variant (using, for example, a display generated by the description in figure 7.1):

> Monkey planet (Motion picture)
> > *search under*
> Planet of the apes (Motion picture : 1968)

Alternately, and perhaps better, the database could automatically re-execute the search so that the user who searched for *Monkey Planet* would be presented with resources linked to the preferred title. This would be particularly useful when the user is performing keyword rather than browse searches against the database.

For a fuller discussion of recording variants, including thoughts on cataloger judgment in deciding whether to record a variant or not, see this *Handbook's* chapter 3 under 9.2.3.

6.2.3.3. GENERAL GUIDELINES. In most cases, variant titles should be recorded following the same guidelines as though they had been chosen as the preferred title. This applies to guidelines on such matters as capitalization, diacritical marks, etc., given in RDA 6.2.1. Any title that is different from the title recorded as the preferred title may be recorded as a variant title. However, RDA instructs the cataloger to record a variant title appearing on a manifestation of the work "only if it differs significantly from the preferred title and the work itself might reasonably be sought under that title." This good advice refers to recording variant titles in the description of the work (in contrast to a description of a manifestation or an expression). Minor variants can be recorded in the record for the manifestation (in current practice, in the bibliographic record). Variants of titles in languages other than the work's original language might more appropriately be recorded in a description of the expression (i.e., an authority record) than the description of the work, though practice varies. The question the cataloger should ask is "would a user search for a *work* using this title?" A database user is unlikely to search for Shakespeare's work *Merry Wives of Windsor* using the French-language variant "Joyeuses commères de Windsor" found in a 2004 manifestation of the work, even though that is a major variant, so that variant probably should not recorded with the *work* description, although it might appropriately be recorded with the description of the expression. A good rule of thumb may be to record in the description of the work major variants associated with expressions of the work in its original language.

6.2.3.4. ALTERNATIVE LINGUISTIC FORM OF TITLE FOR THE WORK. Alternative linguistic forms may be recorded as variant titles. These include forms of the title in different languages. Despite the preceding suggestion about not recording in work descriptions forms in languages different from that of the original, in some cases such variants are appropriately recorded. Because of RDA guidelines, sometimes the preferred title is not a title in the original language of the work. In these cases it is appropriate to record a variant in a different language from that of the preferred title, particularly a title in the original language (see figures 7.22 and 7.23):

> Sophocles. Οἰδίπους Τύραννος
> > *search under*
> > Sophocles. Oedipus Rex

Although it has not been routine in past cataloging practice to include a variant in the language of users of the catalog for preferred titles that are not in that language, recording such variants is not forbidden by RDA. If in the judgment of the cataloger these variants would be helpful to users of the database they may be included in the description of the work *if justified by warrant* (i.e., a title in the language of users of the catalog has been found in a resource associated with the work) (see figures 7.20, 7.21, and 7.23):

> Song of Roland
> > *search under*
> > Chanson de Roland

Sometimes manifestations of the original expression of a work bear parallel titles, or the work itself was created in multiple languages. In such cases variants in the different languages may appropriately be recorded in the work description. This sometimes occurs in film credits, as in the 2007 film *Like Stars on Earth* (see figure 7.42):

Taare zameen par (Motion picture)
> *search under*
> Like stars on Earth (Motion picture)

Figure 7.42. Alternative Linguistic Form

046		‡k 2007
130	0	‡a Like stars on Earth (Motion picture)
380		‡a Motion pictures ‡2 lcsh
430	0	‡a तारे ज़मीन पर (Motion picture)
430	0	‡ تارے زمین پر a (Motion picture)
430	0	‡a Taare zameen par (Motion picture)
500	1	‡w r ‡i Film director: ‡a Khan, Aamir, ‡d 1965-
670		‡a Like stars on Earth, 2007: ‡b opening credits (Like stars on Earth = तारे ज़मीन पर = تارے زمین پر ; produced and directed by Aamir Khan) container (Taare zameen par)

If the work is not textual, as is the case of an art object or a physical manuscript considered as an object (as contrasted with the textual work contained in the manuscript), it may be appropriate to include different language forms as variants in the description of the work (see figures 7.14, 7.26, and 7.27):

Leonardo, ‡c da Vinci, ‡d 1452-1519. ‡t Cenacolo
> *search under*
> Leonardo, ‡c da Vinci, ‡d 1452-1519. ‡t Last supper

Megilot Yam ha-melaḥ
> *search under*
> Dead Sea scrolls

The category "alternate linguistic forms" also includes different scripts (see figures 7.5b, 7.22 through 7.24, 7.27, and 7.42) and different spellings (see figures 7.12 and 7.13):

Pasternak, Boris, 1890-1960. Доктор Живаго
> *search under*
> Pasternak, Boris, 1890-1960. Doktor Zhivago

Spartacvs (Motion picture : 2008)
> *search under*
> Spartacus (Motion picture : 2008)

6.2.3.5. OTHER VARIANT TITLE FOR THE WORK. This guideline gives the cataloger license to record almost any other variant title found, bearing in mind the caveat given in the exception to 6.2.3.3. If a variant title would help the users of a given database find a work, or users might reasonably be expected to search for a work using the variant, it probably should be recorded. Some examples of variants already encountered in this chapter include:

Different titles (see figures 7.1, 7.4b, 7.15, 7.25, and 7.27; figure 7.31, second description; figure 7.33; and figures 7.35 through 7.38):

> Barks, Coleman. Ruminations
>> *search under*
>> Barks, Coleman. Understanding of the question

Variations on the same title (see figures 7.2, 7.17, and 7.19):

> Darwin, Charles, 1809-1882. Darwin's Origin of species
>> *search under*
>> Darwin, Charles, 1809-1882. On the origin of species

Subtitles that might be mistaken for titles (see figure 7.6):

> Studies in the recovery of ancient texts
>> *search under*
>> Sozomena (Berlin, Germany)

Alternative titles (see figure 7.16):

> Sendak, Maurice. There must be more to life
>> *search under*
>> Sendak, Maurice. Higglety pigglety pop

First line of an untitled poem (see figure 7.34):

> Shakespeare, William, 1564-1616. That time of year thou mayest in me behold
>> *search under*
>> Shakespeare, William, 1564-1616. Sonnets. 73

Title formed as subdivision of larger work (see figure 7.29 and figure 7.30, second description):

Swift, Jonathan, 1667-1745. Gulliver's travels. Part 1, Voyage to Lilliput
search under
Swift, Jonathan, 1667-1745. Voyage to Lilliput

Title recorded independently of the larger work (see figure 7.32):

Rightly guided caliphs
search under
Islamic history series. Part II, Rightly guided caliphs

Relationships to different creators (note that these variants do not stem from a variant title) (see figure 7.7):

Kraehenbuehl, David, 1925-1997. Piano technic
search under
McArtor, Marion Emmett, 1915-1956. Piano technic

Different formulations of the preferred title due to RDA guidelines (see figures 7.10, 7.26, and 7.28):

Australia. Commonwealth Forestry Bureau. Bulletin
search under
Bulletin (Australia. Commonwealth Forestry Bureau)

Trinity College (Dublin, Ireland). Library. Manuscript. A.1.6
search under
Book of Kells

OTHER IDENTIFYING ATTRIBUTES

6.3. FORM OF WORK. Form of work, defined as "a class or genre to which a work belongs," corresponds to the FRBR attribute of the same name (FRBR 4.2.2). It is a core element in RDA when needed to differentiate a work from another entity with the same name or title, but it can certainly be recorded in other cases if in the cataloger's judgment the presence of the element would help the database user find or identify the work. Remember that recording the form of work element in the description of the work does *not* necessarily mean it will be part of the authorized access point.

The RDA definition of form of work is quite vague, and best practices have not yet been developed. The words and phrases given with 6.3 as examples are all very broad categories but narrower terms are not forbidden (e.g., "Silent film" versus the broader "Motion picture"). A best practice is emerging to use terms from controlled vocabularies if possible. The *Library of Congress Subject Headings* (LCSH) and *Art and Architecture Thesaurus* (AAT) are good sources of terms to describe form of work.[9]

The form of work attribute of the work entity should be contrasted with three other form-related attributes in RDA.

Content type (RDA 6.9.1) is an attribute of the expression and corresponds to the FRBR attribute "form of expression" (FRBR 4.3.2). Content type reflects "the fundamental form of communication in which the content is expressed," such as "still image," "text," or "two-dimensional moving image." An artwork might have as its form of work "painting" and the content type of one of its expressions "still image." Words recording this element are drawn from a controlled vocabulary found in RDA 6.9.1.

Two attributes of the manifestation are related to its form: media type (RDA 3.2) and carrier type (RDA 3.3). Media type is a general term reflecting the type of intermediation needed to use the resource, such as "audio," "video," or "unmediated." The closely related carrier type reflects the storage medium and housing of the resource, such as "audiocassette," "videodisc," or "volume." Both of these elements are recorded using controlled vocabularies.

Catalogers need to think about the form elements for work, expression, and manifestation, and make sure words recorded in the form of work element are not terms that in fact describe the expression or manifestation rather than the work. It might be helpful to remember that the terms chosen to record this element need to apply equally to *all* expressions and manifestations of the work. Thus if the cataloger is dealing with an audiobook of a work of fiction, the term "audio novel" would not be appropriate as the form of work, because the same work might also exist in a printed text expression. Instead, the more general term "novel" should be used.

Form of work is recorded in MARC authority field 380. The word, or first word of a phrase, is customarily capitalized. If a term is recorded from a controlled vocabulary, the vocabulary's code should be recorded in subfield ‡2 (e.g., "‡2 lcsh" or "‡2 aat").[10] Examples may be seen in most of the figures in this chapter.

The term is recorded exactly as found in the controlled vocabulary, even though that may be plural. If no controlled term is found, form of work is generally recorded in the singular, but if the element is for an aggregate work, a plural term may be appropriate. More than one form can be recorded if appropriate (see figure 7.25).

6.4. DATE OF WORK. Date of work, defined as "the earliest date associated with a work," is a core element if needed to differentiate a work from another entity with the same name or title, but, like the form of work element, it can be recorded in other cases, if in the cataloger's judgment the presence of the element would help the database user find or identify the work. Remember that recording the date of work element in the description of the work does *not* necessarily mean it will be part of the authorized access point.

Date of work is recorded in the MARC authorities 046 field. Subfield ‡k contains the beginning date; subfield ‡l contains an end date (if there is one). Recording a year in these subfields is normally straightforward, but some situations may require more complex coding (e.g., figures 7.14 and 7.23). For fuller information about recording dates in RDA descriptions, see chapter 3 of this *Handbook* at 9.3.

The definition given in 6.4.1.1 implies that only one date may be recorded, the earliest one associated with a work, but 6.4.1.3 clarifies that a range of dates may be recorded. This may be appropriate for a work that exists over time (such as a serial or multipart monograph), or a work that was created over an identifiable period (see figures 7.7 through 7.9 and others in this chapter).

The date of the work theoretically should be the date the creator first produced the work, which might be long before its publication. If this information is known it should be recorded in the date of work element. For example, it is known that the composer Debussy first composed the flute solo piece *Syrinx* in 1913, although it was not published until 1927 (see figure 7.43).

Figure 7.43. Date of Work

046	‡k 1913
100 1	‡a Debussy, Claude, ‡d 1862-1918. ‡t Syrinx
370	‡g Paris (France) ‡2 naf
380	‡a Music ‡2 lcsh
382	‡a flute
384 0	‡a D♭ major
400 1	‡a Debussy, Claude, ‡d 1862-1918. ‡t Flûte de Pan
670	‡a La flûte de Pan, ou, Syrinx, 1992?
670	‡a Grove music online, 24 June 2010 ‡b (Syrinx; composition by Debussy for solo flute first created in 1913 with title La flûte de Pan for Louis Fleury who first performed it in Paris the same year; published in 1927 with title Syrinx)
678	‡a Composition for solo flute created by Claude Debussy in 1913 with title La flûte de Pan for Louis Fleury who performed it in Paris the same year. It was first published in 1927, with the title Syrinx.

However, catalogers normally will not have this kind of detailed information. In the absence of information about when the person, family, or corporate body created the work, the date of its first publication or release may be recorded instead (see most of the figures in this chapter).

6.5. PLACE OF ORIGIN OF THE WORK. Place of origin of the work, defined as "the country or other territorial jurisdiction from which a work originated," is a core element if needed to differentiate a work from another entity with the same name or title, but, like the form of work and date of work elements, it can be recorded in other cases if in the cataloger's judgment the presence of the element would help the database user find or identify the work. Remember that recording the place of origin of the work element in the description of the work does *not* necessarily mean it will be part of the authorized access point.

The place of origin element is recorded in the MARC authorities 370 field, subfield ‡g. The subfield is repeatable (or, alternately, the entire 370 field is repeatable), allowing multiple places to be recorded if necessary. In LC/NACO practice, place names are recorded in RDA place elements in the same form that would be used as the authorized access point for the place.[11] For a fuller discussion, see chapter 3 of this *Handbook* at 9.8–9.11.

A work's place of origin is recorded in work descriptions less often than the form or date of the work, because the place of origin is usually less closely associated with a work in the minds of users of the database and therefore is less likely to be helpful in identifying or finding works. However, it is occasionally useful to distinguish works from other entities with the same name or title. In figure 7.6, for example, the location of the publisher was used to distinguish this series title from other works with the same title. The cataloger decided it was best distinguished in the access point by its place of origin (Berlin, Germany) although its form (Series) or publisher (Walter de Gruyter), or even its beginning date (2008) would also have been possible choices. The beauty of treating these attributes as elements of the record is that they can all be recorded, as in figure 7.6.

The place of origin of the work element might also be usefully recorded when a work is strongly associated with its place of origin, even if it is not needed to distinguish. The original of da Vinci's mural "The Last Supper" is fixed in place in the church of Santa Maria delle Grazie in Milan. This is a case where it is quite appropriate to record this element in the description of the work (see figure 7.14). Similarly, the Dead Sea Scrolls are strongly associated with their place of origin, the region around the Dead Sea, even though they are no longer located there (see figure 7.27).

This RDA element does not originate as a FRBR attribute (cf. FRBR 4.2). RDA defines the element narrowly, so that it applies only to the place of origin. Many works have other places strongly associated with them. As currently defined this place-related element does not include such places. For example, Dublin, Ireland cannot be recorded as an element of the work description for the Book of Kells, even though that place is extremely closely associated with that famous manuscript (see figure 7.26).

6.6. OTHER DISTINGUISHING CHARACTERISTIC OF THE WORK. This element is defined as "a characteristic other than form of work, date of work, or place of origin of the work that serves to differentiate a work" from another entity with the same name or title. It is core in those cases where it is needed to differentiate. Strictly speaking, by this definition the element only exists in cases of conflict, but in the spirit of the other elements and RDA as a whole it is permissible to record the element even when not needed to differentiate.

As noted above at 6.2.2.10.1, an author's works may be compiled more than once. These compilations may be considered to be the same aggregate work, and so the preferred title "Works" probably does not need to be qualified to distinguish it from another aggregate work by the author with the same preferred title. This may also be said of other conventional collective titles such as "Plays" or "Correspondence," because these identify aggregate works that purport to be the complete works of the author in a particular form.

The same cannot be said, however, for collections that do not claim to be complete, and therefore may include the term "Selections" as part of their preferred title. Different compilations of selections from a particular author will invariably be different aggregate works. If more than one such collection has been produced they will more than likely share the same preferred title, which means that they will have to be differentiated by qualifying the authorized access point.

For example, selections from Shakespeare's *Sonnets* have been compiled many times. Application of the alternative instruction in 6.2.2.10.3 gives them all the preferred title "Sonnets. Selections." Since these compilations are different aggregate works, something must be included in the description to distinguish them. This could be any of the "core if" elements: form of work (RDA 6.3), date of work (RDA 6.4), place of origin of the work (RDA 6.5), or other distinguishing characteristic of the work (RDA 6.6). In the case of selections, other distinguishing characteristic is often the most helpful. In figure 7.34 the characteristic chosen to distinguish this compilation of some of the sonnets from others is the surname of the compiler (see the authority record for the collection in figure 7.34; see also the 240 field in the alternative bibliographic record in the same figure). For other examples, see figures 7.35 and 7.39 through 7.41, which distinguish by using the publisher of the compilation, its title proper, or its compiler.

The other distinguishing characteristic of the work element is usually recorded in the MARC authorities 381 field, in subfield ‡a. However, if the "other distinguishing characteristic" is a corporate body, the information is recorded instead in the 373 field. Record the preferred name of the body in 373. The name need not be established in the authority file, but if it is there, use the established form. If it has not been established, determine what the preferred name for the group would be and record that form. If recording a form found in the LC/NACO Authority File, do not include subfield coding except subfield ‡a and include "‡2 naf" in the field.

Various types of "other distinguishing characteristics" exemplified in this chapter and used to differentiate between conflicting titles include the name of a corporate body (see figures 7.10 and 7.35), a title (see figures 7.39 [second authority record] and 7.40), and the surname of a person, usually a compiler or editor of an aggregate work (see figures 7.34 [second authority record] and 7.41). Additionally, this element (an associated corporate body) was recorded in figures 7.6, 7.8, 7.14, 7.26, and 7.28 even though not needed to differentiate.

6.7. HISTORY OF THE WORK. Brief details related to the history of the work may be recorded in this element. This element might be well suited to public displays that would give brief information about the work to the user of the database. Best practices have not evolved, but it is recommended that information recorded in this element be limited to pertinent information that might help in identifying the work.

The RDA Toolkit suggests that this element can be coded either in the 665 or the 678 MARC authority field. This *Handbook* recommends using 678, with the first indicator coded blank. For examples, see figures 7.14 and 7.43.

6.8. IDENTIFIER FOR THE WORK. An identifier for the work is a character string uniquely associated with the work (or the record representing the work). This is a core (i.e., required) element. In the LC/NACO Authority File the identifier is the Library of Congress Control Number, recorded in the 010 field. In most cases the cataloger does not need to record information in this element, as it is automatically generated by the database system. For this reason, the identifier for the work element has not been included in most figures in this book; as examples, the element is included with figures 7.1 and 7.4.

ELEMENTS OF MUSICAL WORKS

When RDA was initially planned it was hoped that the general guidelines could be written to apply to all types of resources with few or no special rules giving different treatment to certain categories. One of the basic principles for the formulation of cataloging codes as outlined in the new *Statement of International Cataloguing Principles* is that "the descriptions for all types of materials and controlled forms of names of all types of entities should be based on a common set of rules, insofar as it is relevant."[12] However, as work progressed it was found that integration of all the guidelines for three categories of resources—music, legal materials, and religious works—was not possible, at least not for the original release of RDA. There are, therefore, special guidelines for these three categories of works and expressions. However, the special guidelines do not tell the cataloger everything he or she needs to know about describing such works and expressions. If the general guidelines are adequate for a particular issue, a special guideline is not repeated. For example, there is no special guideline for date of a musical work. This element can certainly be recorded in the description of a musical work, but because there are no special music-related details, the cataloger will follow the general guideline found in 6.4.

6.14. TITLE OF A MUSICAL WORK. This element is defined as "a word, character, or group of words and/or characters by which a musical work is known." As with any work, a title by which a musical work is known can be either a preferred title, chosen and recorded according to the guidelines of RDA 6.14.2, or a variant title, chosen and recorded according to the guidelines of RDA 6.14.3. Preferred and variant titles are recorded in the MARC format in subfield ‡t of X00, X10, and X11 access point fields if they have a specific creator, or subfield ‡a of X30 access point fields if they do not. Preferred titles are recorded in 1XX fields and variant titles in 4XX fields.

6.14.2.1–6.14.2.3. PREFERRED TITLE FOR A MUSICAL WORK. Preferred titles for musical works are chosen in a similar manner to those of other works.[13] For musical works created after 1500, the preferred title will be the best known title in the language in which it was originally presented as found in "resources embodying the work or reference sources." Note that the "language in which [the title] was [originally] presented" is not necessarily the composer's native language. Usually the preferred title will be the composer's original title, but if another title in the same language has become better known it should be chosen. Works that predate 1500 follow the same procedure, but modern sources are preferred. If in the judgment of the cataloger the result of this choice is "very long," a brief title may be chosen from reference sources.

When choosing the preferred title for a musical work it is good practice to check reference sources such as thematic catalogs or *New Grove* (now part of "Oxford Music Online," www.oxfordmusiconline.com) for forms of the title (again, in the language in which the title was originally presented), especially for the works of well-known or prolific composers.[14]

Applying these guidelines to *Syrinx* (figure 7.43), the cataloger may discover that "the composer's original title in the language in which it was presented" (i.e., French) is "La flûte de Pan." However, the work has become better known in French publications as "Syrinx," and so that title is chosen as the preferred title (see the first exception to 6.14.2.3).

The exception under 6.14.2.3 for numbered sequences may be somewhat confusing. If the title of a musical work includes the name of a type of composition (e.g., symphony, concerto, sonata), and that type of composition is also cited in its own numbered sequence in lists of the composer's works, the name of the type of composition is chosen as the preferred title rather than the more specific name of the work.

Mozart wrote a large number of piano concertos, which are numbered sequentially. One of the concertos has the title "Krönungs-Konzert" ("Coronation Concerto" in English). Because this title (a) contains a word naming a type of composition ("Konzert"), and (b) the composer's compositions of that type (piano concertos) are

Figure 7.44. Composition in Numbered Sequence

046	‡k 17880224
100 1	‡a Mozart, Wolfgang Amadeus, ‡d 1756-1791. ‡t Concertos, ‡m piano, orchestra, ‡n K. 537, ‡r D major
370	‡g Vienna (Austria) ‡2 naf
380	‡a Concertos ‡2 lcsh
382	‡a piano ‡a orchestra
383	‡c K. 537 ‡d Köchel6 ‡2 mlati
383	‡a no. 26
384 0	‡a D major
400 1	‡a Mozart, Wolfgang Amadeus, ‡d 1756-1791. ‡t Krönungs-Konzert
400 1	‡a Mozart, Wolfgang Amadeus, ‡d 1756-1791. ‡t Coronation concerto
400 1	‡a Mozart, Wolfgang Amadeus, ‡d 1756-1791. ‡t Concertos, ‡m piano, orchestra, ‡n no. 26, ‡r D major
670	‡a Piano concerto in D major, K. 537, 1996
670	‡a Concerto in D major (Coronation concerto) for pianoforte and orchestra, K. 537, 1964
670	‡a Klavier-Konzert Nr. 26 D dur (Krönungs-Konzert) K.V. 537, 1965
670	‡a Oxford music online, 3 May 2012 ‡b (Piano concerto, Köchel no. 537, Breitkopf edition no. 26; in D major; composed in Vienna, 24 February 1788; also known as Coronation)

cited as a numbered sequence (this concerto is no. 26), the preferred title will be "Concertos" (on the matter of choosing a plural English word for this type of composition, see 6.14.2.5) (see figure 7.44).

On the other hand, J. S. Bach wrote hundreds of cantatas. Although Bach's complete works have been numbered, there is no numbered sequence of the cantatas themselves (their assigned numbers are from the numbering sequence of Bach's works as a whole). Most of these cantatas have specific names, such as "Kaffee-Kantate" (known in English as "The Coffee Cantata"). This title does contain a work naming a type of composition ("Kantate"), but because Bach's works of this type are not cited in their own numbered sequence, the preferred title will be "Kaffee-Kantate" (see figure 7.45).

Figure 7.45. Composition Not in a Numbered Sequence

046	‡k 1734
100 1	‡a Bach, Johann Sebastian, ‡d 1685-1750. ‡t Kaffee-Kantate
380	‡a Cantatas ‡2 lcsh
382	‡a soprano ‡a tenor ‡a bass ‡a orchestra
383	‡c BWV 211 ‡d Wohlfarth ‡2 mlati

400 1	‡a Bach, Johann Sebastian, ‡d 1685-1750. ‡t Cantatas, ‡n BWV 211
400 1	‡a Bach, Johann Sebastian, ‡d 1685-1750. ‡t Kaffeekantate
400 1	‡a Bach, Johann Sebastian, ‡d 1685-1750. ‡t Coffee cantata
400 1	‡a Bach, Johann Sebastian, ‡d 1685-1750. ‡t Cantate du café
400 1	‡a Bach, Johann Sebastian, ‡d 1685-1750. ‡t Schweigt stille, plaudert nicht
500 1	‡w r ‡i Librettist: ‡a Henrici, Christian Friedrich, ‡d 1700-1764
670	‡a Jagdkantate, 1997: ‡b label (Kaffeekantate : BWV 211) container (Kaffee-Kantate = Coffee-cantata = Cantate du café) back of container (Schweigt stille, plaudert nicht)
670	‡a Oxford music online, 14 February 2010 ‡b (Schweigt stille, plaudert nicht (Coffee Cantata), BWV 211 (composed 1734, for soprano, tenor, bass, and orchestra), text by Picander [Christian Friedrich Henrici]).

6.14.2.4. RECORDING THE PREFERRED TITLE FOR A MUSICAL WORK. If 6.14.2.1–6.14.2.3 were all that was needed to choose and record the preferred title for a musical work, special rules in RDA for these works would not have been necessary. However, in traditional cataloging practice—incorporated into RDA—preferred titles of musical works are frequently severely manipulated from the form in which they are found in resources embodying the work or in reference sources. This is partly due to a sense that because music is an abstract language it is less tied to written titles than are text-based works, which results in willingness to be freer in recording preferred titles. More importantly, however, this manipulation allows titles, when presented as authorized access points, to file in a logical, hierarchical manner, which is an expectation of the community that uses these preferred titles the most.

Begin with the title chosen as described under 6.14.2.1–6.14.2.3:

1. Remove any statement of medium of performance. For example, in figure 7.46, the title selected under 6.14.2.3 would be "Sonata for piano, no. 3." Remove "for piano," leaving "Sonata no. 3." Remove "voor fluit, altviool en piano" from the title shown in figure 7.47, leaving "Trio, 1992."

Figure 7.46. Medium of Performance

046	‡k 1994
100 1	‡a Starer, Robert. ‡t Sonatas, ‡m piano, ‡n no. 3
380	‡a Sonatas ‡2 lcsh
382	‡a piano
383	‡a no. 3
670	‡a Sonata for piano, no. 3, 1994

Cover

Robert Starer
Sonata for Piano, No. 3
A publication of MCA music publishing
A division of MCA Inc.
7777 W. Bluemound Rd., Milwaukee, WI 53213
Distributed by Hal Leonard

Foot of first page of music

© Copyright 1994 by MCA Music Publishing, A Division of MCA Inc.

Figure 7.47. Medium of Performance

046	ǂk 1992
100 1	ǂa Otten, Ludwig. ǂt Trios, ǂm piano, flute, viola
380	ǂa Trios ǂ2 lcsh
382	ǂa piano ǂa flute ǂa viola
670	ǂa Trio voor fluit, altviool en piano, 1992

Title page

Ludwig Otten
Trio
voor fluit, altviool en piano
1992

Donemus Amsterdam

2. Remove the name of the key. The title selected under 6.14.2.3 in figure 7.48 would be "Konzert Nr. 4 für Klavier (linke Hand) und Orchester, B-Dur, opus 53." Remove the medium of performance ("für Klavier (linke Hand) und Orchester") and the key ("B-Dur"), leaving "Konzert Nr. 4, opus 53."

Figure 7.48. Key

046	ǂk 1931
100 1	ǂa Prokofiev, Sergey, ǂd 1891-1953. ǂt Concertos, ǂm piano, 1 hand, orchestra, ǂn op. 53, ǂr B♭ major
380	ǂa Concertos ǂ2 lcsh
382	ǂa piano, 1 hand ǂa orchestra
383	ǂa no. 4 ǂb op. 53
384 0	ǂa B♭ major

400 1	‡a Prokofiev, Sergey, ‡d 1891-1953. ‡t Konzert Nr. 4 für Klavier (linke Hand) und Orchester, B-Dur, opus 53
670	‡a Konzert Nr. 4 für Klavier (linke Hand) und Orchester, B-Dur, opus 53 = Concerto No. 4 for Piano (left hand) and Orchestra, B flat major Opus 53, [1995], ©1995
670	‡a New Grove ‡b (op. 53. Piano concerto no. 4, B♭, left hand, 1931)

Title page

Sergej Prokofjew	Sergei Prokofiev
Konzert Nr. 4	Concerto No. 4
für Klavier (linke Hand)	for Piano (left hand)
und Orchester	and Orchestra
B-Dur opus 53	B flat major Opus 53
Ausgabe für 2 Klaviere	Edition for 2 Pianos
von Anatoli Wedernikow	By Anatoly Vedernikow

Boosey & Hawkes Music Publishers Ltd., London
G. Schirmer Inc., New York

MUSIKVERLAG HANS SIKORSKI, HAMBURG

Foot of first page of music

©1995 by Musikverlag Hans Sikorski, Hamburg

3. Remove the serial, opus, and thematic index number(s). For definitions of these terms see below under 6.16. The partially manipulated example from figure 7.48 becomes "Konzert" by removing "Nr. 4" and "opus 53." The title in figure 7.46, already shortened to "Sonata no. 3," becomes "Sonata."

4. Remove other numbers unless they are an integral part of the title (i.e., grammatically connected to the rest of the title). "Six songs from A Shropshire lad," figure 7.49, becomes "Songs from A Shropshire lad."

Figure 7.49. Number

046	‡k 1911
100 1	‡a Butterworth, George, ‡d 1885-1916. ‡t Songs from A Shropshire lad
380	‡a Songs ‡2 lcsh
382	‡a voice ‡a piano
500 1	‡w r ‡i Musical setting of (work): ‡a Housman, A. E. ‡q (Alfred Edward), ‡d 1859-1936. ‡t Shropshire lad
670	‡a Six songs from A Shropshire lad, [1911]
670	‡a Oxford music online, 15 April 2011 ‡b (6 songs from A Shropshire lad, composition by George Butterworth (1911), setting of poems by A.E. Housman for solo voice and piano)

<table>
<tr><td colspan="2">Cover</td></tr>
</table>

Cover

GEORGE BUTTERWORTH
Six Songs from "A Shropshire Lad"
(A.E. Housman)
Price 12s. 6d.

Galliard Limited   Galaxy Music Corporation
London   New York

5. Remove a date of composition present in the title. The title in figure 7.47, which has already been reduced to "Trio, 1992," becomes "Trio."

6. Remove adjectives and epithets not part of the original title of the work. "The famous Salve Regina," figure 7.50, becomes "Salve Regina."

Figure 7.50. Adjective Not Part of Original Title

046	ǂk 1736
100 1	ǂa Hasse, Johann Adolf, ǂd 1699-1783. ǂt Salve Regina, ǂm mezzo-soprano, string orchestra, ǂr A major
380	ǂa Antiphons (Music) ǂ2 lcsh
382	ǂa mezzo-soprano ǂa string orchestra
384 0	ǂa A major
400 1	ǂa Hasse, Johann Adolf, ǂd 1699-1783. ǂt Famous Salve Regina
530 0	ǂw r ǂi Musical setting of (work): ǂa Salve regina (Antiphon)
670	ǂa The famous Salve Regina, [1740]
670	ǂa Oxford music online, 8 July 2011 ǂb (Salve regina, in A major, antiphon for mezzo-soprano and string orchestra, first published 1736 in Venice, then in London in 1740)

Title Page

The famous Salve Regina
composed by Sigr. Hasse
London.
Printed for & Sould by J. Walsh Musicall Instrument maker in Ordinary to his Majesty at the Golden Harp & Ho boy in Catherine Street near, Summers et house in the Strand

7. Remove an initial article if following the alternative guideline to 6.2.1.7. "The Death of Klinghoffer" (figure 7.51) becomes "Death of Klinghoffer." Initial articles should be removed whether or not they appear in the nominative case in languages that distinguish by case. The Liszt work titled "Dem Andenken Petőfis" (literally "To the memory of Petőfi") is recorded "Andenken Petőfis," even though this is not grammatically correct German (see figure 7.52).

Figure 7.51. Initial article

```
046      ǂk 1989 ǂl 1991
100 1    ǂa Adams, John, ǂd 1947- ǂt Death of Klinghoffer (Opera)
380      ǂa Operas ǂ2 lcsh
383      ǂb op. 2
500 1    ǂw r ǂi Librettist: ǂa Goodman, Alice
530   0  ǂw r ǂi Adapted as a motion picture (work): ǂa Death of Klinghoffer (Motion picture)
670      ǂa The death of Klinghoffer, 1994: ǂb t.p. (The death of Klinghoffer : an opera in two
         acts with prologue)
670      ǂa Oxford music online, 10 June 2012 ǂb (The Death of Klinghoffer (op. 2 of John
         Adams; libretto by Alice Goodman), 1989-1991, based on the events surrounding
         the hijacking of the cruise ship Achille Lauro in 1985; first performed in Brussels,
         19 March 1991)
```

Figure 7.52. Initial article

```
046      ǂk 1877
100 1    ǂa Liszt, Franz, ǂd 1811-1886. ǂt Andenken Petöfis
380      ǂa Music ǂ2 lcsh
382      ǂa piano
383      ǂc LW. A279
383      ǂc S. 195
400 1    ǂa Liszt, Franz, ǂd 1811-1886. ǂt Petőfi szellmének
400 1    ǂa Liszt, Franz, ǂd 1811-1886. ǂt Petőfis Geiste gewidmet
400 1    ǂa Liszt, Franz, ǂd 1811-1886. ǂt To the spirit of Petőfi
400 1    ǂa Liszt, Franz, ǂd 1811-1886. ǂt Dem Andenken Petöfis
500 1    ǂw r ǂi Based on (work): ǂa Liszt, Franz, ǂd 1811-1886. ǂt Holt költő szerelme
670      ǂa Dem Andenken Petöfis : Melodie von Franz Liszt, 1877
670      ǂa 16 magyar rhapsodia, 1959: ǂb title page (Petőfi szellmének = Petőfis Geiste
         gewidmet = To the spirit of Petőfi) preface (for piano; composed in 1877; uses
         same themes as A holt költő szerelme; later augmented and included in Magyar
         történelmi arcképek; also arranged by Liszt for piano 4-hands)
670      ǂa Oxford music online, July 18, 2010 ǂb (Dem Andenken Petöfis; composed in
         1877; based on Des toten Dichters Liebe (Holt költő szerelme); later used as no.
         6 in Historische ungarische Bildnisse; also exists in piano 4-hand version, Dem
         Andenken Petöfis/Petöfi szellemének; first performed in Budapest 28 February
         1877; LW. A279; S. 195)
```

6.14.2.5. PREFERRED TITLE CONSISTING SOLELY OF THE NAME OF ONE TYPE OF COMPOSITION.
This provision is probably the least intuitive of all the provisions for recording the preferred title of a musical work, and its application often results in a preferred title that bears little resemblance to "the composer's original title in the language in which it was presented" (cf. 6.14.2.3). However, it does result in collocation of similar works in a logical and hierarchical manner, which might otherwise be separated because their titles differ.

If after the application of 6.14.2.3 (choosing a preferred title) and 6.14.2.4 (recording a preferred title by removing certain elements from the title as found) there remains nothing but the name of a type of composition, 6.14.2.5 instructs us to record the "accepted form" of the name in the language preferred by the agency (English for contributors to the LC/NACO Authority File, cf. LC-PCC PS 6.14.2.5, January 2013). The name is to be recorded in the plural unless the composer wrote only one work of the type.[15]

For example, in figure 7.53, the title chosen as "the composer's original title in the language in which it was presented" under 6.14.2.3 was "Symphonie no. 3, F dur für grosses Orchester, op. 76." Application of 6.14.2.3 removes the serial number ("no. 3"), the key ("F dur"), the medium of performance ("für grosses Orchester"), and the opus number ("op. 76"), leaving a title that "consists solely of the name of one type of composition," "Symphonie." The accepted form of this type of composition in English is "Symphony." Because Dvořák wrote more than one composition of this type, the preferred title is recorded "Symphonies."

Figure 7.53.
Preferred Title Consisting Solely of the Name of One Type of Composition

046	‡k 18750615 ‡l 18760723
100 1	‡a Dvořák, Antonín, ‡d 1841-1904. ‡t Symphonies, ‡n no. 5, op. 76, ‡r F major
380	‡a Symphonies ‡2 lcsh
382	‡a orchestra
383	‡a no. 5
383	‡a no. 3
383	‡b op. 76
383	‡b op. 24
383	‡c B. 54 ‡d Burghauser ‡2 mlati
383	‡c S. 32
384 0	‡a F major
400 1	‡a Dvořák, Antonín, ‡d 1841-1904. ‡t Symphonies, ‡n no. 3, op. 76, ‡r F major
670	‡a Symphony no. 5 in F major, op. 76, 1990.

> 670 ‡a Symphonie no. 3, F dur für grosses Orchester, op. 76, 1888: ‡b first page of music (Dritte Symphonie, F dur, op. 76)
>
> 670 ‡a Oxford music online, 13 December 2011 ‡b (Symphony no. 5, in F major, op. 76, composed 15 June-23 July 1875; first published in Berlin in 1888 as Symphony no. 3, first performance Prague, 25 March 1879; revised in 1887; once known as op. 24; Burghauser 54, Šourek 32)

Other examples of the application of this guideline include figure 7.46 ("Sonata for piano, no. 3" becomes "Sonatas"), figure 7.47 ("Trio voor fluit, altviool en piano" becomes "Trios"), and figure 7.48 ("Konzert Nr. 4 für Klavier (linke Hand) und Orchester, B-Dur, opus 53" becomes "Concertos"). A special case is shown in figure 7.44. The preferred title chosen in this case under 6.14.2.3 might have been "Krönungs-Konzert," which would not have been reduced solely to "Konzert" under the application of 6.14.2.4. However, as explained above with the "numbered sequence" exception to 6.14.2.3, if the title of a musical work includes the name of a type of composition, and that type of composition is also cited in its own numbered sequence in lists of the composer's works, the name of the type of composition is chosen as the preferred title rather than the more specific name of the work. Mozart's concertos are listed in a numbered sequence, so "Krönungs-Konzert" becomes "Concertos."

The stipulation that the name be recorded in the plural unless the composer wrote only one work of the type raises two issues. First, the language in 6.14.2.5, "one type of composition," does not include medium of performance. So the question is not whether the composer wrote, for example, more than one flute sonata, but whether he or she wrote more than one sonata of any kind. Second, the stipulation requires the cataloger to do some research to find this fact out, and it also requires changing the preferred title if the work's preferred title is first established in the singular and the composer later composes another work of the same type.

In order to reduce the amount of research needed to make this determination, the Library of Congress has instructed its catalogers to choose between singular and plural as follows:

1. If the composer is dead, reference sources should be consulted.
2. If the composer is alive, the singular should be chosen for the preferred title unless the work being cataloged bears a serial number, including the number 1 (e.g., "Sonata for violoncello and piano no. 2," or "String quintet no. 1 in F major"). The assumption is that if a serial number is included with the title, either there are other compositions of the same type or the composer intends to create others. No further research is required (LC-PCC PS 6.14.2.5, January 2013).

For an example of this sort of preferred title recorded in the singular, see figure 7.54.

Figure 7.54.
Preferred Title Consisting Solely of the Name of One Type of Composition

100 1	‡a Polar, Octavio, ‡d 1856-1942. ‡t Minuet, ‡m piano, ‡n op. 15
380	‡a Minuets ‡2 lcsh
382	‡a piano
383	‡b op. 15
670	‡a Ureta, A. Música clásica peruana. El romanticismo, 1995: ‡b container (Minueto para piano, op. 15)

6.14.2.7. RECORDING THE PREFERRED TITLE FOR A PART OR PARTS OF A MUSICAL WORK. RDA 6.14.2.7 is based on 6.2.2.9. It deals with the publication of only a part, rather than the whole, of a musical work. The preferred title for the part is independent of the preferred title for the whole work, but in the MARC authority record it is recorded as a subdivision of the preferred title for the whole.

If the part is identified by a number, the number is recorded as the preferred title for the part, in subfield ‡n of the MARC 100 field:

> 100 1 ‡a Brahms, Johannes, ‡d 1833-1897. ‡t Ungarische Tänze. ‡n **Nr. 5**

If the part is identified by a title, that title is recorded as the preferred title in subfield ‡p of the MARC 100 field:

> 100 1 ‡a Verdi, Giuseppe, ‡d 1813-1901. ‡t Aïda. ‡p **Celeste Aïda**

> 100 1 ‡a Beethoven, Ludwig van, ‡d 1770-1827. ‡t Symphonies, ‡n no. 1, op. 21, ‡r C major. ‡p **Andante cantabile con moto**

Generally, if the part is designated both by a title and a number, prefer the title. See, however, the second paragraph of 6.14.2.7.1.3 and 6.14.2.7.1.4 for exceptions.

If a resource contains more than one part of a work, follow the instructions given in 6.14.2.7.2. These instructions are generally the same as the instructions of 6.2.2.9.1 (see above). This means that musical works are always identified separately, not grouped as other works can be under 6.2.2.9.2. An alternative guideline allowing the use of "Selections" exists. However, if the composer uses the name "Suite" for a group of works, use that term rather than "Selections" (see figure 7.55).

Figure 7.55. Suite

046	‡k 1945
100 1	‡a Copland, Aaron, ‡d 1900-1990. ‡t Appalachian spring. ‡p Suite
380	‡a Suites ‡2 lcsh
382	‡a orchestra
670	‡a Appalachian spring : Ballet for Martha : suite, version for 13 instruments, [1972], 1972
670	‡a Oxford music online, February 2, 2011 ‡b (Appalachan Spring; ballet by Copland composed 1943-1944; suite created 1945)

6.14.2.8. COMPILATIONS OF MUSICAL WORKS. Preferred titles for compilations of musical works are formulated in the same way as those of 6.2.2.10. However, music preferred title practice includes a number of conventional collective titles for broad media that do not exist for other types of materials. The examples under 6.14.2.8 list many such conventional collective titles. These lists are not exclusive. They are meant to be examples on which the cataloger may pattern conventional collective titles to fit compilation of musical works in the resource being described.

6.14.3. VARIANT TITLE FOR A MUSICAL WORK. Variant titles for musical works are recorded in exactly the same way and for the same reasons as those of other works. See discussion above under 6.2.3.

6.15. MEDIUM OF PERFORMANCE. The medium of performance element is core when needed to differentiate a musical work from another with the same title, but it is useful to record this element even in cases where it is not needed to differentiate. Recording the element in the description of the work does not necessarily mean it will become a part of the authorized access point for the work. The element is defined as the "instrument, instruments, voice, voices, etc., for which a musical work was originally conceived." It is recorded in subfield ‡a of the MARC authority 382 field. If there is more than one medium of performance the element may be repeated, either by repeating the entire MARC field or by repeating subfield ‡a in a single 382 field.[16]

6.15.1.3. RECORDING MEDIUM OF PERFORMANCE. RDA instructs the cataloger to record the medium of performance in a particular order. This instruction is geared toward creating a predictable order in the authorized access point for the musical work and may be less important when recording media in an element of the description. Various proposals have been formulated to de-emphasize the order in the element; however, until RDA is so revised, media should be recorded in the 382 field in the order listed in RDA 6.15.1.3. Standard combinations of instruments, individual instruments, and voices are listed in 6.15.1.5–6.15.1.13. Terms describing medium of performance recorded in descriptions of musical works in the LC/NACO Authority File should be in English whenever possible.

RDA 6.15.1.6 offers a choice of names for a few individual instruments. LC policy specifies using English horn, contrabassoon, and timpani in three of these cases. This is the same policy as existed under AACR2. In a change of LC practice introduced with RDA, however, catalogers should now record "cello" rather than "violoncello" (the LC/NACO practice prior to RDA) (see LC-PCC PS 6.15.1.6, January 2013).

Examples of this element are found in figures 7.43 through 7.50 and 7.52 through 7.55.

6.16. NUMERIC DESIGNATION OF A MUSICAL WORK. This element is core when needed to differentiate a musical work from another with the same title, but may usefully be recorded even if not needed to differentiate. The element is recorded in the MARC authorities 383 field; serial numbers are recorded in subfield ‡a, opus numbers in subfield ‡b, and thematic index numbers in subfield ‡c. A code identifying the thematic index may be recorded in subfield ‡d; the name of a publisher associated with an opus number may be recorded in subfield ‡e. Neither of these sub-elements is called for by RDA, but they are clearly useful.

Unusually for RDA, prefixes such as "opus" or "number" are abbreviated when recording information in this element. If the word appears in RDA appendix B.7–10, the abbreviation should be recorded instead recording a spelled-out form (see figures 7.44, 7.46, and 7.48).

A serial number is a number within a sequence assigned to an individual composer's works of a particular type (e.g., sonatas, symphonies, and concertos), in the same medium of performance (e.g., for piano, for string orchestra, etc.).

An opus number is a sequential (but not necessarily chronological) numbering of a composer's works, often created by the composer or his or her publisher. Opus numbers are sometimes assigned to groups of works, resulting in numberings such as "op. 3, no. 4."

A thematic index or catalog is a numbered bibliography that lists details of a composer's works that includes a musical quotation from each work, usually consisting of the first few notes of the piece (called the "incipit").

Any serial and opus numbers that are found may be recorded (see figures 7.44, 7.46, and 7.48). If different publishers (or others) have assigned conflicting serial or opus numbers, both may be recorded in separate 383 fields (see figure 7.53). In the case of conflicting opus numbers, the publisher associated with a particular opus number may be recorded with the element (in subfield ‡e).

As an aid to standardization, the Music Library Association (MLA) has developed a list of standard thematic catalog codes and abbreviations that should be used when recording thematic index numbers in records for musical works of certain composers. This list is found at http://bcc.musiclibraryassoc.org/BCC-Historical/BCC2011/

Thematic_Indexes.htm. Additionally, instructions for thematic index usage are given in the 667 fields of authority records in the LC/NACO Authority File for all composers appearing in the MLA list. If a thematic index from the list is cited in the numeric designation of a musical work element, the abbreviation given in the MLA list should be used as a prefix to the number recorded in 383 subfield ‡c, the code given in the list should be recorded in 383 subfield ‡d, and the field should end with "‡2 mlati" (identifying the source of the abbreviation and code). For examples, see figures 7.44 and 7.45.

Thematic index numbers from catalogs not on the MLA list may also be recorded in this element. It is recommended that prefixes to the numbers be recorded as found in works lists in *New Grove* (or its electronic version, "Oxford Music Online"). Thematic catalogs for Franz Liszt, for example, were not found in the MLA list at the time of publication of this *Handbook*. Prefixes recorded in the 383 fields shown in figure 7.52 follow *New Grove*.

6.17. KEY. Key is determined by the adherence of a musical work (or a part of a musical work) to the note pattern of a major or minor scale. Not all musical works have an identifiable key. Although musical works frequently change keys within themselves, tonal works usually have a principal key, normally the key in which a movement begins and ends.

Key is core in RDA if needed to differentiate a work from another entity with the same name, but even if there is no need to differentiate it is useful to record the information if known. In the description of a musical work this element records the *original* key of the composition.

In previous cataloging practice it was important for the cataloger to be able to discern the key of a musical work because in certain cases it was required to state the key in the authorized access point for the work even if the key was not given in the title of the work. This requirement has been weakened somewhat in RDA. The key element is to be recorded in the description of a work if the information is readily available in a reference source, if the key appears in the composer's original title or in the title proper of its first manifestation, or if it is apparent from the resource described. "Apparent" is not defined and could depend on the cataloger's ability (or lack thereof) to identify the key by looking at the music.

The key is designated by its pitch name (a capital letter between A and G modified with a flat sign [♭] or sharp sign [♯] if appropriate) and its mode, that is, major or minor. Key is recorded in the MARC authority 384 field, subfield ‡a. The original key is to be recorded in descriptions of musical works. This is shown in the MARC record by coding the first indicator "0." Examples in this chapter include figures 7.43, 7.44, 7.48, 7.50, and 7.53.

ELEMENTS OF LEGAL WORKS

Generally speaking, legal works follow the same principles and guidelines as other works and they should be described following those principles and guidelines. RDA 6.19–6.22 give a few guidelines that are specific to legal works, but for other descriptive elements catalogers should follow the guidelines found in RDA 6.2–6.8. For example, there is no specific element called "history of a legal work," but this information may be recorded in the description of a legal work following the guidelines of RDA 6.7.

6.19. TITLE OF A LEGAL WORK. This element is defined as "a word, character, or group of words and/or characters by which a legal work is known." As with any work, a title by which a legal work is known can be either a preferred title, chosen and recorded according to the guidelines of RDA 6.19.2, or a variant title, chosen and recorded according to the guidelines of RDA 6.19.3. Preferred and variant titles are recorded in the MARC format in subfield ‡t of X00, X10, and X11 access point fields if they have a specific creator, or subfield ‡a of X30 access point fields if they do not. Preferred titles are recorded in 1XX fields and variant titles in 4XX fields.

6.19.2.1–6.19.2.3. PREFERRED TITLE FOR A LEGAL WORK. Preferred titles for legal works are chosen in a similar manner to those of other works. For legal works created after 1500 the preferred title will be the best known title as found in "resources embodying the work or reference sources." Works predating 1500 follow the same procedure but modern sources are preferred. The principal difference between preferred titles of many legal works and those of other kinds of works is the use of two conventional collective titles used with legal works, "Laws, etc." and "Treaties, etc."

6.19.2.4. RECORDING THE PREFERRED TITLE FOR A LEGAL WORK. In general, the titles of legal works are recorded just as the titles of other works. However, capitalization conventions are in some cases different from those of other titles. RDA refers the cataloger to 6.2.1, which refers us to appendix A on matters of capitalization. RDA A.18, Names of Documents, tells us to "capitalize the formal, or conventional, name of a document such as a charter, constitution, legislative act, pact, plan, statement of policy, or treaty." This means that unlike other titles, where normally only the first word is capitalized, all nouns, adjectives, verbs, etc., of the formal name of a law or treaty will be capitalized. Because the preferred title of a law is based on its official or citation title (i.e., a formal name) (see below under 6.19.2.5.2), this means that in most cases this convention will be followed.

6.19.2.5. MODERN LAWS, ETC.

6.19.2.5.1. COMPILATIONS. The conventional collective title "Laws, etc." is used as the preferred title for general collections of laws of a jurisdiction (see figure 7.56). Such collections are aggregate works, and in most cases different collections will contain different aggregations of the laws; therefore, in most cases, each collection will be a separate aggregate work from other collections of the laws of a jurisdiction. Because such collections are very common, the effect of using the preferred title "Laws, etc." is to create a situation where different works frequently have the same preferred title. RDA deals with this by including elements in the description such as date of a legal work (RDA 6.20) or other distinguishing characteristic of a legal work (RDA 6.21) to differentiate the works, as well as by including qualifiers and other elements in the authorized access points for these works (see 6.29).

Figure 7.56. Laws, etc.

046	‡k 1867
110 1	‡a Canada. ‡t Laws, etc. (Statutes of Canada)
380	‡a Statutes ‡2 lcsh
381	‡a Statutes of Canada
410 1	‡a Canada. ‡t Statutes of Canada
670	‡a Statutes of Canada, 1867

6.19.2.5.2. SINGLE LAWS, ETC. The preferred title of a single law or enactment is based on the title of the law, preferably its official short title or citation title (see figure 7.57). This may be the same as the title proper (see figure 7.58).

Figure 7.57. Single Laws

046	‡k 2010
110 1	‡a United States. ‡t Patient Protection and Affordable Care Act
380	‡a Law
410 1	‡a United States. ‡t Act Entitled The Patient Protection and Affordable Care Act
410 1	‡a United States. ‡t Public Law 111-148
410 1	‡a United States. ‡t 2010 Health Care Act
670	‡a RIA's complete analysis of the tax and benefits provisions of the 2010 Health Care Act as amended by the 2010 Health Care Reconciliation Act, 2010.
670	‡a An act entitled The Patient Protection and Affordable Care Act: ‡b citation title, 124 Stat. 119 (Patient Protection and Affordable Care Act)

Figure 7.58. Single Laws

046	‡k 2002
110 1	‡a India. ‡t Prevention of Terrorism Act, 2002
380	‡a Law
410 1	‡a India. ‡t Act No. 15 of 2002
670	‡a The Prevention of Terrorism Act, 2002 (Act No. 15 of 2002), 2002: ‡b citation title, p. 62 (Citation title, Prevention of Terrorism Act, 2002)

6.19.2.7. ONE TREATY, ETC. Treaties are agreements between two or more governments. They pose special problems for catalogers because of their nature and because of the way in which they are drawn up. After representatives of the various governments at a treaty conference have met, they draw up an agreement, which is then signed. The representatives then return to their own countries, where the treaty is ratified by the government. The treaty is next published by the government under a title that it creates, naming itself, of course, in first place on the title page. Each governing body involved does this, resulting in a number of different versions of the document. Although the text of the document should be the same, the title pages will vary. Which form would be chosen as the preferred title? Because of this problem, cataloging rules since ALA 1949 rule 88A have called for the use of the conventional collective title "Treaties, etc." as the preferred title, even for single treaties. This remains true in RDA (see figure 7.59).

Figure 7.59. Treaty between Two Parties

046	‡k 20100601
110 1	‡a Russia (Federation). ‡t Treaties, etc. ‡g European Union, ‡d 2010 June 1
370	‡g Rostov-na-Donu (Russia) ‡2 naf
380	‡a Treaties ‡2 lcsh
410 2	‡a European Union. ‡t Treaties, etc. ‡g Russia (Federation), ‡d 2010 June 1
430 0	‡a Agreement between the Government of the Russian Federation and the European Union on the protection of classified information ‡d (2010)
670	‡a Agreement between the Government of the Russian Federation and the European Union on the protection of classified information, signed 1 June 2010 in Rostov-on-Don, Russia, 2010

Because nearly all treaties will have the same preferred title, they fall under the category of works with titles that conflict with the titles of other works. Their descriptions will need to be differentiated from each other by the inclusion of elements such as date (RDA 6.20) or another distinguishing characteristic (RDA 6.21); in addition access points for treaties need to be differentiated from each other (see 6.29.1.15).

RDA 6.19.2.7 has an exception to the use of "Treaties, etc." as the preferred title for a treaty. As will be seen in the discussion below at 6.29.1.15, the authorized access point for a treaty begins with the authorized access point representing the government named first in resources embodying the treaty. If the first signatory to a multilateral treaty cannot be ascertained, the preferred title for the treaty is "the name by which the treaty is known." In the example given in the RDA 6.19.2.7 exception, *Agreement Establishing the World Trade Organization,* the signatories were not listed and are unknown, so it was impossible to include the authorized access point for a government at the beginning of the authorized access point for the treaty. This RDA guideline descends from AACR2 25.16B2, where a treaty was entered under title if there were four or more parties to the treaty. This in turn was related to AACR2's so-called rule of three, where "main entry" under an individual entity was not allowed if responsibility was too diffuse. In contrast, under RDA 6.29.1.15 the authorized access point for the first listed party to the treaty is included at the beginning of the authorized access point for the treaty, regardless of how many parties are listed. Therefore it is likely that many fewer authorized access points for treaties will be given as the title alone in RDA than under AACR2, and that the exception to 6.19.2.7 will be invoked only rarely. In nearly all cases the preferred title for a treaty will be "Treaties, etc."

6.19.3. VARIANT TITLE FOR A LEGAL WORK. Variant titles for legal works are recorded in exactly the same way and for the same reasons as those of other works. See discussion above under 6.2.3. One provision specific to legal works, 6.19.3.6, instructs the cataloger to record the title proper of the resource being described as a variant title when the preferred title is a conventional collective title (see figure 7.56). Recording this variant may produce a user display such as the following:

Canada. Statutes of Canada
search under
Canada. Laws, etc. (Statutes of Canada)

6.20. DATE OF A LEGAL WORK. This element, defined as the earliest date associated with a legal work, is core if needed to differentiate a work from another work with the same title, but may be recorded whether needed to differentiate or not. The element is recorded in the MARC authorities 046 field. Subfield ‡k contains the date. As currently written, RDA does not allow for recording a later date associated with a legal work (e.g., the last date for laws of differing dates in a compilation or the ending date of the time period a law was in force). However, such later dates associated with a legal work might also be useful information to record in the description.

Recording a year in the 046 field is normally straightforward, but some situations may require more complex coding. The form given with the examples to RDA

6.20.3.3, date of signing of a treaty, is not the form recorded as an element in MARC (in an 046 field). The examples show how the information is to be recorded in an access point for a treaty. But compare how the date of the treaty is recorded in the date of a legal work element (046) and in the access point for the treaty (110 subfield ‡d) in figure 7.59. See figures 7.56 through 7.58 for other examples of the date of a legal work element. For fuller information about recording dates in RDA descriptions, see chapter 3 of this *Handbook* at 9.3.

6.21. OTHER DISTINGUISHING CHARACTERISTIC OF A LEGAL WORK. This element is based on RDA 6.6, "Other Distinguishing Characteristic of the Work," and for the most part the information is recorded in the same way as for nonlegal works. The element is normally recorded in the MARC authorities 381 field, or in the 373 field if the "other distinguishing characteristic" is the name of an associated institution such as a publisher. The form of the corporate body's name recorded in 373 should be its authorized form as found in the LC/NACO Authority File if the name has been established. If the name is found in the LC/NACO Authority File "‡2 naf" is recorded in the field.

Like the date of the work and signatory to a treaty, etc., elements, the other distinguishing characteristic of a legal work is core when needed to differentiate a legal work from another entity with the same name or title. Because the conventional collective titles "Laws, etc." and "Treaties, etc." are used so often with legal works this situation will arise frequently. The core language does not mean that all three elements become core with works that have the same title. Rather, whichever of the three is most appropriate should be chosen by the cataloger to differentiate the works. In practice, "other distinguishing characteristic of a legal work" is recorded only if other differentiating elements have failed to differentiate adequately.

An example is the case where two governments have concluded separate treaties on the same day (see figure 7.60). As already seen, the preferred title of both treaties will be "Treaties, etc." Recording the date will not differentiate them, nor will listing the signatories, because they are the same. A word or words from the title proper of the treaties as published should be recorded as the other distinguishing characteristic of a legal work element.

Figure 7.60. Other Distinguishing Characteristic

046	‡k 19250224
110 1	‡a United States. ‡t Treaties, etc. ‡g Canada, ‡d 1925 February 24 (Boundary)
380	‡a Treaties ‡2 lcsh
381	‡a Boundary
410 1	‡a Canada. ‡t Treaties, etc. ‡g United States, ‡d 1925 February 24 (Boundary)
430 0	‡a Defining boundary between United States and Canada ‡d (1925)

670   ‡a Defining boundary between United States and Canada, 1925: ‡b page 1 (treaty concluded on February 24, 1925; to define more accurately at certain points and to complete the boundary between the United States and Canada and to maintain the demarcation of that boundary)

---

046   ‡k 19250224

110 1   ‡a United States. ‡t Treaties, etc. ‡g Canada, ‡d 1925 February 24 (Lake of the Woods)

380   ‡a Treaties ‡2 lcsh

381   ‡a Lake of the Woods

410 1   ‡a Canada. ‡t Treaties, etc. ‡g United States, ‡d 1925 February 24 (Lake of the Woods)

430 0 ‡a Concerning regulation of level of Lake of the Woods ‡d (1925)

670   ‡a Concerning regulation of level of Lake of the Woods, 1925: ‡b page 1 (treaty concluded February 24, 1925)

"Laws, etc." is generally used for compilations and will usually require recording an "other distinguishing characteristic." The cataloger should record an appropriate designation for the compilation in this element, which will usually be the title proper of the compilation's first manifestation, or a commonly used brief title (see figure 7.56). Other possibilities include the name of an editor or publisher if the compilation is better known by that designation.

Certain conventions have risen in North American practice that will be carried forward into RDA for U.S. jurisdictions at the state level. For laws enacted by a state legislature at its annual session(s), record "Session laws" in this element (LC-PCC PS 6.29.1.32, February 2010) (see figure 7.61). For most states, record "Compiled statutes" in this element for compilations of codified legislation (LC-PCC PS 6.29.1.32, January 2013, with exceptions for California, Louisiana, and Texas) (see figure 7.62).

Figure 7.61. Other Distinguishing Characteristic (Session Laws)

046   ‡k 1990

110 1   ‡a Colorado. ‡t Laws etc. (Session laws : 1990-)

380   ‡a Laws

410 1   ‡a Colorado. ‡t West's Colorado legislative service

670   ‡a West's Colorado legislative service, 1990, no. 1

Figure 7.62. Other Distinguishing Characteristic (Compiled Statutes)

046   ‡k 1988

110 1   ‡a Utah. ‡t Laws, etc. (Compiled statutes : 1988-)

```
380      ‡a Statutes ‡2 lcsh
410 1    ‡a Utah. ‡t Utah code unannotated
670      ‡a Utah code unannotated, 1988
```

6.22. SIGNATORY TO A TREATY, ETC. A signatory to a treaty is normally a government that has formally signed a treaty and agrees to adhere to its terms. Signatories to treaties are to be recorded in the form "prescribed in chapter 11.2.2," meaning in the same form as the authorized access point for the signatory.

The MARC authority format does not currently have a specific field for this element. We are instead instructed in the RDA to MARC authority mapping in the RDA Toolkit to record a signatory as part of an access point for the treaty, in subfield ‡g of 110 or 410. This can work for bilateral treaties, which add the name of a signatory to the authorized access point for the treaty, but only if a variant access point is given as instructed under 6.29.3.3. In figures 7.59 and 7.60 each signatory is recorded in the description in either subfield ‡g of 110 or subfield ‡g of 410. But access points for treaties between more than two parties do not contain the name of any signatory as an addition to the access point (see 6.29.1.33, "If there is more than one party on the other side, add only the date, earlier date, or earliest date of signing"). Until MARC addresses this problem, this *Handbook* recommends recording the signatories to a multilateral treaty in the MARC 667 field (see figure 7.63).

Figure 7.63. Signatories to a Multilateral Treaty

```
046      ‡k 19921007
110 1    ‡a Canada. ‡t Treaties, etc. ‡d 1992 Oct. 7
380      ‡a Treaties ‡2 lcsh
410 1    ‡a United States. ‡t Treaties, etc. ‡d 1992 Oct. 7
410 1    ‡a Mexico. ‡t Treaties, etc. ‡d 1992 Oct. 7
43   0   ‡a North American Free Trade Agreement ‡d (1992)
430  0   ‡a NAFTA ‡d (1992)
430  0   ‡a Accord de libre-échange nord américain ‡d (1992)
430  0   ‡a Tratado de Libre Comercio de América del Norte ‡d (1992)
667      ‡a Signatories: Canada ; United States ; Mexico
670      ‡a The North American Free Trade Agreement, 1992: ‡b preamble (signatories: The
         Government of Canada, the Government of the United Mexican States and the
         Government of the United States of America)
670      ‡a NAFTA website, 12 December 2011 ‡b (English title: North American Free Trade
         Agreement; French title: L'Accord de libre-échange nord américain; Spanish title:
         Tratado de Libre Comercio de América del Norte)
```

ELEMENTS OF RELIGIOUS WORKS

In general, religious works follow the same principles and guidelines as other works and they should be described following those principles and guidelines. RDA 6.23 gives guidelines for recording the titles of religious works, which differ somewhat from the general guidelines for recording titles of works, but for other descriptive elements catalogers should follow the guidelines found in RDA 6.2–6.8. For example, there is no specific element called "form of a religious work," but this information may be recorded in the description of a religious work following the guidelines of RDA 6.3.

6.23. TITLE OF A RELIGIOUS WORK. The title of a religious work element is defined as "a word, character, or group of words and/or characters by which a religious work is known." As with any work, a title by which a religious work is known can be either a preferred title, chosen and recorded according to the guidelines of RDA 6.23.2, or a variant title, chosen and recorded according to the guidelines of RDA 6.23.3. Preferred and variant titles are recorded in the MARC format in subfield ‡t of X00, X10, and X11 access point fields if they have a principal creator, or subfield ‡a of X30 access point fields if they do not. Preferred titles are recorded in 1XX fields and variant titles in 4XX fields.

6.23.2.1– 6.23.2.3. PREFERRED TITLE FOR A RELIGIOUS WORK. Because of the complex nature of religious works as a category, instructions on how to choose and record the preferred title differ depending on the type of religious work (see RDA 6.23.2.5–6.23.2.8).

6.23.2.4. RECORDING THE PREFERRED TITLE. In general, the titles of religious works are recorded in the same way as the titles of other works. However, capitalization conventions are in some cases different from those of other titles. RDA refers the cataloger to 6.2.1, which refers us to appendix A on matters of capitalization. Appendix A.17.6 tells us to "capitalize the name of a creed or confession"; and A.17.8 to "capitalize the title of a sacred scripture." This means unlike other titles, where normally only the first word is capitalized, all nouns, adjectives, verbs, etc., of titles of these types of religious work will be capitalized.

6.23.2.5. SACRED SCRIPTURES. Although nowhere defined in RDA, "sacred scripture" usually refers to a text regarded as authoritative or holy by a religious body, or of particular importance to its religious tradition. Often sacred scripture has been formally canonized by the religious body; the canon for that body is a collection of books accepted by it as sacred or authoritative scripture.

The preferred title for sacred scripture is the title by which it is most commonly identified in reference sources in the language preferred by the cataloging agency, preferring reference sources that deal with the religious group to which the scripture belongs, if available. This means that contributors to the LC/NACO Authority File should consult English-language reference sources dealing with the religious group when choosing the preferred name of a work that presents itself as sacred scripture (LC-PCC PS 6.23.2.5, January 2013). An example of such a reference source is *Encyclopaedia of the Qur'ān,* but such sources also include editions of the scripture itself, which commonly give the title as *The Qur'ān* (see figure 7.64).

Figure 7.64. Sacred Scripture

130	0	‡a Qur'ān
380		‡a Sacred scripture
430	0	‡a Quran
430	0	‡a Koran
430	0	‡a قرآن
430	0	‡a Ḳur'ān
667		‡a Non-Latin script references not evaluated.
670		‡a The Qur'an (Oxford world's classics), 2009
670		‡a Three translations of the Koran (al-Qur'an) side by side, 2009
670		‡a Encyclopaedia of the Qur'ān, 2001
670		‡a Encyclopaedia of Islam, Second edition, online, September 2, 2010 ‡b (al-Ḳur'ān)
670		‡a Wikipedia, September 2, 2010 ‡b (Quran; Qur'an (Arabic: القرآن al-Qur'ān, literally "the recitation"; also sometimes transliterated as Qur'ān, Koran, Alcoran or Al-Qur'ān) is the central religious text of Islam)

6.23.2.6. APOCRYPHAL BOOKS. An apocryphal book is a work that presents itself as sacred scripture, or that a religious tradition holds (or once held) as sacred scripture, but that another religious tradition considers non-scriptural, and indeed may consider false or heretical (thus, from the point of view of that tradition, the work is "apocryphal"). Because the distinction between sacred scripture and apocryphal books is so judgment laden, RDA does not require the cataloger to decide whether a text is "sacred scripture" or "apocryphal." The guideline for choosing and recording the preferred title is the same for both categories: choose a title commonly found in sources in the language preferred by the cataloging agency (see figure 7.65).

Figure 7.65. Apocryphal Book

046		‡k 0090 ‡l 02
130	0	‡a Gospel of Thomas (Infancy Gospel)
380		‡a Apocryphal infancy Gospels ‡2 lcsh
430	0	‡a Thomas Gospel of the Infancy

430	0	‡a De infantia Iesu evangelium Thomae
667		‡a Not same as Gospel of Thomas (Coptic Gospel)
670		‡a The apocryphal New Testament, 1924: ‡b page 49 (Gospel of Thomas)
670		‡a New Catholic encyclopedia, 1981: ‡b volume 2, page 405 (Thomas Gospel of the Infancy; it has nothing in common with the Gnostic Gospel of Thomas)
670		‡a De infantia Iesu evangelium Thomae, 2010: ‡b page 201 (apparently a compilation of stories that once circulated independently) page 205 (composed no earlier than 90 AD or later than the early 3rd century; earliest versions in Syriac, Latin, Georgian, Ethiopic; not clear what the original language was; ascribed to "Thomas the Israelite" or "Thomas the Ismaelite," sometimes identified with the apostle Thomas)

RDA does separate out one category of apocryphal book for treatment elsewhere: the books of the Bible accepted as sacred scripture in the Catholic and Orthodox canon, but called "The Apocrypha" by Protestants. Guidelines for "The Apocrypha" are found in 6.23.2.9.4.

6.23.2.7. THEOLOGICAL CREEDS, CONFESSIONS OF FAITH, ETC. For this type of religious work, choose a "well-established" title in the language preferred by the cataloging agency (see figure 7.66); if there is no such title, use a title in the original language of the work (see figure 7.67).

Figure 7.66. Confession of Faith

046		‡k 155905
130	0	‡a Gallic Confession
370		‡g Paris (France) ‡2 naf
380		‡a Creeds ‡2 lcsh
430	0	‡a Gallican Confession
430	0	‡a Confessio Gallicana
430	0	‡a Confession de foy faicte d'un commun accord par les François qui désirent vivre selon la pureté de l'Evangile de nostre Seigneur Jesus Christ
430	0	‡a Confession of Faith of La Rochelle
670		‡a Das Glaubensbekenntniss der französisch-reformirten Kirche (Confessio Gallicana) vom Jahre 1559, 1885.
670		‡a Oxford encyclopedia of the Reformation, 1996: ‡b v. 2, p. 156 (Gallic Confession; adopted at the first national synod of the Reformed Churches of France, in Paris, May 1559; generally called the Confession of Faith of La Rochelle after the the 7th national synod (La Rochelle, 1571) designated it the official confession of the church)

670	‡a New Schaff-Herzog encyclopedia, 1908-1914: ‡b volume 4, page 423 (Gallican Confession; title on first published edition: Confession de foy faicte d'un commun accord par les François qui désirent vivre selon la pureté de l'Evangile de nostre Seigneur Iesus Christ)

Figure 7.67. Creed

130	0	‡a Shahada
380		‡a Creeds ‡2 lcsh
430	0	‡a Shahadah
430	0	‡a شهادة
667		‡a Non-Latin script references not evaluated.
670		‡a The shahada : declaration of faith, 1994
670		‡a The encyclopedia of Islam (Brill online), 2 August 2010 ‡b (Shahāda; in religious sense, shahāda denotes the Islamic profession of faith, the act of declaring "There is no god but God, and Muhammad is the Messenger of God")
670		‡a The Oxford encyclopedia of the modern Islamic world, 1995 ‡b (Shahādah. The Islamic witness of faith is "There is no god but God, and Muḥammad is the Apostle of God"; recitation of the shahādah (literally "witness") is the first of the five pillars of Islam)
670		‡a Wikipedia, September 8, 2008 ‡b (Shahada. The Shahada (Arabic: الشهادة) is the Islamic creed. The Shahada is the Muslim declaration of belief in the oneness of God and acceptance of Muhammad as his prophet. The declaration reads: "La illaha ill Allah, Muhammadur Rasul Allah" [romanized] which is translated into "There is no God but Allah, Muhammad is the Messenger of Allah" in English; Shahadah)

6.23.2.8. LITURGICAL WORKS. Choice of preferred title for liturgical works depends on the guidelines for formation of the access point for the work under RDA 6.30.1.5. In most cases the authorized access point for a liturgical work begins with the authorized access point for the church or denominational body it applies to, followed by the title of the work. Returning to 6.23.2.8, if the name of the body is given in the language of the cataloging agency (English for contributors to the LC/NACO Authority File), the preferred title for the work is "a well-established title in that language" (see figure 7.68). Otherwise a brief title in the language of the liturgy is chosen (see figure 7.69). (But note a few exceptions in RDA for Roman Catholic and Jewish liturgical works.)

Figure 7.68. Liturgical Work

046	‡k 1993
110 2	‡a Presbyterian Church (U.S.A.). ‡t Book of common worship (1993)
380	‡a Liturgical work
670	‡a To glorify God, 1999: ‡b p. ix (Book of common worship (1993) of the Prebyterian Church (USA))

670 ‡a Wikipedia, December 20, 2011 ‡b (The Book of Common Worship of 1993 is the fifth liturgical book of the Presbyterian Church (USA), created because of the reunion of the United Presbyterian Church (USA) and the Presbyterian Church (US))

Figure 7.69. Liturgical Work

046 ‡k 1980
110 2 ‡a Suomen evankelis-luterilainen kirkko. ‡t Kirkkokäsikirja
380 ‡a Liturgical work
410 2 ‡a Suomen evankelis-luterilainen kirkko. ‡t Suomen Evankelisluterilaisen Kirkon kirkkokäsikirja
410 2 ‡a Suomen evankelis-luterilainen kirkko. ‡t Manuale
670 ‡a Suomen Evankelisluterilaisen Kirkon kirkkokäsikirja, 1980.
670 ‡a Wikipedia (Finnish), 3 March 2012 ‡b (Kirkkokäsikirja; Latin title Manuale; containing the Breviary, the Gradual, and the Mass)

6.23.2.9. PARTS OF THE BIBLE. The aggregate work called the Bible is a collection of works regarded as sacred scripture by many religious bodies and traditions. Under 6.23.2.5 the preferred title for this religious work is the title by which it is commonly identified in reference sources in the language of the cataloging agency. For contributors to the LC/NACO Authority File, who will use English-language reference sources, this results in the preferred title "Bible." RDA 6.23.2.9 gives guidelines for dealing with the individual works within the collection, as well as for parts of those individual works.

6.23.2.9.1. TESTAMENTS. The biblical collection is commonly divided into three sections, known in Protestant traditions as "Old Testament," "New Testament," and "Apocrypha." Catholic and Orthodox traditions do not recognize the "Apocrypha" division, instead including most of those works in the Old Testament. Jewish tradition does not recognize the New Testament at all, and refers to the collection as "Tanakh" or "Hebrew Bible." When RDA was under development there was a much discussion about how to refer to these divisions of the Bible. In the end RDA continued the practice of AACR2, following the Protestant divisions "Old Testament," "New Testament," and "Apocrypha." In a significant change from AACR2, however, abbreviations will not be used for the preferred titles of these divisions.

Preferred titles of parts of the Bible are recorded as subdivisions following "Bible," the preferred title for the collection as a whole. "Old Testament" and "New Testament" are the preferred titles for those divisions of the Bible, and resources containing one or the other will be cited in the database as:

Bible. Old Testament

or

Bible. New Testament

(see figure 7.70). On "Apocrypha," see 6.23.2.9.4.

Figure 7.70. Old Testament

130	0	‡a Bible. ‡p Old Testament
380		‡a Sacred scripture
430	0	‡a Old Testament
430	0	‡a Bible. ‡p Tanakh
430	0	‡a Tanakh
430	0	‡a Bible. ‡p Hebrew Bible
430	0	‡a Hebrew Bible
667		‡a DESCRIPTIVE USAGE: Bible authorized access points used in descriptive portions of the record are analytical, i.e., they need to contain data elements in RDA 6.30.3.2 as applicable.
670		‡a A brief introduction to the Old Testament, 2012
670		‡a Tanakh, 1999
670		‡a The Hebrew Bible and its interpreters, 1990

6.23.2.9.2. BOOKS. For cataloging agencies using English as their preferred language, RDA specifies that the preferred title for a book within the Bible is the brief citation form of the book's title as found in the Authorized (King James) Version. This preferred title will be recorded directly as a subdivision of the preferred title of the collection as a whole, "Bible" (see figure 7.71). This is a change from previous cataloging practice, which interposed "O.T." (for Old Testament) or "N.T." (for New Testament) between "Bible" and the preferred title of the individual book.

Figure 7.71. Individual Book within the Bible

130	0	‡a Bible. ‡p Mark
380		‡a Sacred scripture
430	0	‡a Mark (Book of the New Testament)
430	0	‡a Bible. ‡p New Testament. ‡p Mark
667		‡a DESCRIPTIVE USAGE: Bible authorized access points used in descriptive portions of the record are analytical, i.e., they need to contain data elements in RDA 6.30.3.2 as applicable.
670		‡a A theology of Mark, 2012

6.23.2.9.3. GROUPS OF BOOKS. The list of groups of books of the Bible commonly identified by a group name given under 6.23.2.9.3 includes all of the groups that can be gathered in this manner. Do *not* add to this list. Like individual books, the preferred name for each grouping is recorded directly as a subdivision of the preferred title "Bible" without following the former practice of interposing "O.T." or "N.T."

6.23.2.9.4. APOCRYPHA. Like the divisions "Old Testament" and "New Testament," the preferred title for the Apocrypha is "Apocrypha," recorded as a subdivision to the preferred title "Bible":

> 130 0 ‡a Bible. ‡p Apocrypha

Works found within the third Protestant traditional division of the Bible, the Apocrypha, are treated slightly differently from works found within the Old and New Testaments. Instead of recording their preferred title directly as a subdivision to the preferred name "Bible," preferred titles of works within the Apocrypha are recorded as a further subdivision of the form recorded for "Apocrypha" (see figure 7.72). The English-language preferred titles for the individual books are listed within RDA 6.23.2.9.4.

Figure 7.72. Individual Book within the Apocrypha

130	0	‡a Bible. ‡p Apocrypha. ‡p Bel and the Dragon
380		‡a Sacred scripture
430	0	‡a Bel and the Dragon
430	0	‡a Bible. ‡p Bel and the Dragon
667		‡a DESCRIPTIVE USAGE: Bible authorized access points used in descriptive portions of the record are analytical, i.e., they need to contain data elements in RDA 6.30.3.2 as applicable.
670		‡a Bel and the Dragon, 1897

6.23.2.9.5. SINGLE SELECTIONS. This guideline follows the general principles underlying preferred titles for parts of other works. If the single selection is commonly identified by a distinctive title of its own, choose that title as the preferred title, recorded directly (see figure 7.73). If the selection is not so identified, the preferred title for the selection is the name of the book plus inclusive chapter and verse numbers as appropriate (see figure 7.74).

Figure 7.73. Named Selection

130	0	‡a Magnificat
380		‡a Sacred scripture
430	0	‡a Bible. ‡p Luke I, 46-55

430	0 ‡a Mariae Cantica
667	‡a DESCRIPTIVE USAGE: Bible authorized access points used in descriptive portions of the record are analytical, i.e., they need to contain data elements in RDA 6.30.3.2 as applicable.
670	‡a The Magnificat within the context and framework of Lukan theology, [1986], ©1986.
670	‡a Mariae Cantica vulgo Magnificat, 1550

Figure 7.74. Unnamed Selection

130	0 ‡a Bible. ‡p Apocrypha. ‡p Ecclesiasticus XXXIX, 12-35
380	‡a Sacred scripture
667	‡a DESCRIPTIVE USAGE: Bible authorized access points used in descriptive portions of the record are analytical, i.e., they need to contain data elements in RDA 6.30.3.2 as applicable.
670	‡a Full of praise, 1999: ‡b t.p. (Sir 39, 12-35)

6.23.2.9.6. TWO OR MORE SELECTIONS. If a resource contains two or more discrete selections from the Bible, each selection is "identified separately." In other words, in a bibliographic record, there will be one authorized access point given for each selection.

6.23.2.9.7. OTHER SELECTIONS FROM THE BIBLE. This guideline applies to Bible selections not covered in 6.23.2.9.5 and 6.23.2.9.6. The version of RDA in effect before 2013 instructed the cataloger to use "the most specific title" applicable. There was no provision in the RDA guidelines for biblical preferred titles and authorized access points with the conventional collective title "Selections" (as is available for other kinds of works, see RDA 6.2.2.9.2). Thus, the preferred title "Bible. Old Testament" would have been assigned to Mortimer J. Cohen's *Pathways Through the Bible: Classic Selections from the Tanakh,* even though it only contains parts of the Tanakh. This was a change from previous cataloging practice, which would have included the conventional collective title "Selections" with the preferred title for the Old Testament. The 2013 revisions restored the use of "Selections" in this situation (e.g., "Bible. Old Testament. Selections").

6.23.2.19. PARTS OF OTHER SACRED SCRIPTURES. Parts of other sacred scriptures are treated similarly to parts of the Bible. The preferred title for the part is recorded as a subdivision of the preferred title for the scripture as a whole (see figure 7.75). This represents a change from earlier cataloging practice, which usually cited the title for the part alone, not as a subdivision of the preferred title for the scripture as a whole.

Figure 7.75. Other Sacred Scripture

130	0	‡a Pearl of Great Price. ‡p Book of Moses
380		‡a Sacred scripture
430	0	‡a Book of Moses
670		‡a A study of the changes in the contents of the Book of Moses from the earliest available sources to the current edition, 1958
670		‡a Encyclopedia of Mormonism, 1992 ‡b (Book of Moses; extract of several chapters from Genesis in the Joseph Smith translation of the Bible; constitutes one of the texts of the Pearl of Great Price)

6.23.3. VARIANT TITLE FOR A RELIGIOUS WORK. Variant titles for religious works are recorded in exactly the same way and for the same reasons as those of other works. See discussion above at 6.2.3.

ACCESS POINTS

One of the objectives governing RDA is that the data should enable the user to find all resources associated with a particular work (RDA 0.4.2.1). In our current MARC database environment this is done through the formulation and use of authorized access points representing entities such as works, corresponding to what previous cataloging practice called "headings." These access points are embedded in bibliographic records for resources associated with the work and serve as links between a particular bibliographic record and all other bibliographic records that contain the identical access point. In many systems the access point in the bibliographic record is also linked to its corresponding authority record.

The user of the database finds all resources associated with a particular work by learning what the authorized access point is for that work, and then querying the database for instances of the authorized access point indexed as a work or as a subject.

In order for this to function properly, the authorized access point must be consistent (i.e., always used in the same form) and unique to the work (i.e., more than one work should not share the same access point). The data describing a work and its relationship to its creator must be sufficient to differentiate that work from other works with the same title (RDA 0.4.3.1).

When two works in the database have identical titles and are related to the same creator (if there is an explicit relationship link to a creator), a "conflict" exists that must be resolved in the authorized access point. It is somewhat unusual, though not unknown, for a creator to be related to two works with the same title. However, it is not unusual for works that are not explicitly related to a creator (for example, a motion picture) to have identical titles. Authorized access points for works not related to a creator that have identical preferred titles, or, for works related to a creator that have both the same creator and identical preferred titles, are differentiated from each other by the addition of other elements such the work's form, its date, place of origin, or another distinguishing characteristic. Musical, legal, and religious works may also receive other specialized additions.

6.27.1.2. WORKS CREATED BY ONE PERSON, FAMILY, OR CORPORATE BODY. The authorized access point for a work created by one person, family, or corporate body is constructed using the 100, 110, or 111 field of the MARC authority record. The preferred title, including any parenthetical qualifier, is recorded in subfield ‡t.

A person, family, or corporate body that is responsible for the intellectual or artistic content of a work is considered to be its creator. A creator can work alone or be jointly responsible with other creators of a work. The idea of a person as creator is fairly intuitive. Families, new to Anglo-American descriptive cataloging practice with RDA, can also create works, including a collection of family records, a family newsletter, or a family blog. Corporate bodies are considered to be creators under certain circumstances defined in RDA 19.2.1.1.1. These circumstances are familiar to AACR2 catalogers (cf. AACR2 21.1B2), and include corporate bodies that issue works of an administrative nature dealing with the body itself, works that record the collective thought or activity of the body, and certain cartographic and legal works (see more detailed discussion in this *Handbook's* chapter 9, "Recording Relationships").

It is relatively simple to create the access point for a work with one creator. Begin with the exact form of the authorized access point for the creator (as described in chapters 3 through 5 of this *Handbook*); add a period (unless the creator's authorized access point ends with an open date, cf. LC-PCC PS 1.7.1.1f, January 2013) and subfield ‡t; and add the preferred title for the work chosen as described above in this chapter. See figures 7.2, 7.8, and others throughout this chapter.

If a work appears to be created by one person, family, or corporate body, but that creator is unknown or uncertain, see RDA 6.27.1.8.

6.27.1.3. COLLABORATIVE WORKS. The authorized access point for a work created by more than one person, family, or corporate body is generally constructed using the 100, 110, or 111 field of the MARC authority record. The preferred title, including any parenthetical qualifier, is recorded in subfield ‡t. In some cases (discussed below) the authorized access point for this type of work does not begin with the authorized access point of a creator. In these cases the authorized access point is recorded in the MARC authority 130 field, with the preferred title, including any parenthetical qualifier, in subfield ‡a.

Before proceeding it is necessary to discuss the RDA concept of principal responsibility for a collaborative work, which is crucial to the instructions for creating an authorized access point for such a work. The relevant RDA guideline is the language about core in 19.2, "Creator." This guideline is in the RDA section dealing with recording relationships of works to persons, families, and corporate bodies. Recording the relationship of the *principal* creator to the work is core in RDA (i.e., required). In the MARC authority database structure, this relationship link is made by giving the access point for the creator at the beginning of the access point for the work. The link is made in the MARC bibliographic database structure by recording the access point for the principal creator in a 1XX field of the bibliographic record.

One creator may be named in resources embodying a collaborative work as the main creator of the work. This is the principal creator. More often, however, principal responsibility for a collaborative work is not indicated. In such cases, the first-named creator is considered the principal creator of the work. In previous cataloging practice, if there were more than three creators of a collaborative work, none of them was considered the principal creator (the so-called rule of three). This is no longer the case in RDA. In RDA it does not matter how many creators are named in a resource embodying a collaborative work. What we are looking for is either the one that is explicitly shown in the resource to be the principal creator, or the one named first. Recording the relationship of the work to this person, family, or corporate body is core (required).

Once principal responsibility has been determined it is relatively simple to create the access point for a collaborative work. Begin with the exact form of the authorized access point (as described in chapters 3 through 5 of this *Handbook*) for the creator with principal responsibility; add a period (unless that creator's authorized access point ends with an open date, cf. LC-PCC PS 1.7.1.1f, January 2013) and subfield ‡t; and add the preferred title for the work chosen as described above in this chapter. See figure 7.7 for a resource with two creators. An example of a resource with four creators is *The Penguin Guide to Recorded Classical Music* (see figure 7.76).

Figure 7.76. Collaborative Work

046	‡k 2007
100 1	‡a March, Ivan. ‡t Penguin guide to recorded classical music
380	‡a Reference work
400 1	‡a Greenfield, Edward. ‡t Penguin guide to recorded classical music
400 1	‡a Layton, Robert, ‡d 1930- ‡t Penguin guide to recorded classical music
400 1	‡a Czajkowski, Paul. ‡t Penguin guide to recorded classical music
430　0	‡a Penguin guide to recorded classical music
670	‡a The Penguin guide to recorded classical music, 2007: ‡b title page (Ivan March, Edward Greenfield, Robert Layton and Paul Czajkowski)

There is an alternative guideline to creating the authorized access point by combining the authorized access point for the principal creator with the preferred title of the work. The alternative instructs the cataloger to create the authorized access point by combining the authorized access points for *all* the creators with the preferred title for the work. The authorized access point shown in figure 7.76 would appear as follows if applying the alternative guideline:

> 100 1   ‡a March, Ivan; ‡a Greenfield, Edward; ‡a Layton, Robert, ‡d 1930- ;‡a Czajkowski, Paul. ‡t Penguin guide to recorded classical music

The alternative guideline is not followed in LC/NACO practice (see LC-PCC PS 6.27.1.3, January 2013).

RDA 6.27.1.3 lists a few exceptions to the basic guideline. If one or more of the creators of a collaborative work is a corporate body (under 19.2.1.1.1) and in addition there are one or more persons or families who are also creators of the collaborative work, the corporate body will be considered the principal creator and the authorized access point for the work will be constructed by combining the authorized access point for the corporate body and the preferred title of the work. The work described in figure 7.77, *Catalogue of the Library of Thomas Jefferson,* was created by E. Millicent Sowerby. However, because the catalog was issued by the Library of Congress, and it is a work dealing with the library's resources (see 19.2.1.1.1.a.iii), the library is also considered a creator, making this a collaborative work. Under the main guideline to 6.27.1.3, Sowerby would probably be judged the principal creator of the work. However, under the exception, if one of the creators of a collaborative work is a corporate body, that body becomes the principal creator.

Figure 7.77. Collaborative Work Involving a Corporate Body

046	‡k 1952 ‡l 1959
110 2	‡a Library of Congress. ‡t Catalogue of the library of Thomas Jefferson
380	‡a Library catalogs ‡2 lcsh
400 1	‡a Sowerby, E. Millicent ‡q (Emily Millicent). ‡t Catalogue of the library of Thomas Jefferson
670	‡a Catalogue of the library of Thomas Jefferson, 1952-1959 ‡b (issued by Library of Congress; author: E. Millicent Sowerby)

If the collaborative work is a motion picture, its authorized access point is constructed using the preferred title of the work alone (without the inclusion of an authorized access point for a creator). The rationale behind this exception seems to be that the creation of most motion pictures is too diffuse to assign principal creator status to one person, family, or corporate body. Authorized access points of this sort are recorded in the MARC authority field 130. For examples, see figures 7.1, 7.13, 7.18, and 7.42.

Note that the exception for motion pictures is found in an RDA guideline treating collaborative works. Motion pictures can, like any other work, be the work of a single creator. If so, the exception under 6.27.1.3 does not apply. The authorized access point for such a work will be constructed by combining the authorized access point for the creator with the preferred title of the work. Gerald McDermott is the sole creator of the motion picture *Arrow to the Sun*. He wrote the script of the motion picture, designed and drew the animated cartoons, and directed and produced the entire film. The authorized access point for this work will be constructed by combining the authorized access point for McDermott with the preferred title of the work (in this case, qualified to distinguish it from the book by McDermott with the same title) (see figure 7.78).

Figure 7.78. Motion Picture with a Single Creator

046	‡k 1973
100 1	‡a McDermott, Gerald. ‡t Arrow to the sun (Motion picture)
380	‡a Motion pictures ‡2 lcsh
500 1	‡w r ‡i Adapted as (work): ‡a McDermott, Gerald. ‡t Arrow to the sun (Children's book)
670	‡a Arrow to the sun, 1973

6.27.1.4. COMPILATIONS OF WORKS BY DIFFERENT PERSONS, FAMILIES, OR CORPORATE BODIES. A compilation of works by different creators is considered in FRBR and RDA to be a work separate from the works contained in it. This kind of work is called an aggregate work, and like other works, may have a preferred title. The authorized access point for an aggregate work is the preferred title for the compilation alone. This would normally be the most commonly found collective title (a title that applies to the compilation as a whole) found on manifestations of the aggregate work. But if the compilation does not have a collective title, there is no evidence to use in choosing a preferred title. In that case, RDA prefers that no authorized access point be created for the compilation. Instead, a separate authorized access point should be created for each work in the compilation. Alternatively, an authorized access point for the compilation may be created based on a title for the compilation devised by the cataloger. This procedure has obvious drawbacks and will not normally be followed in LC/NACO practice (see LC-PCC PS 6.27.1.4, January 2013).

The authorized access point for a compilation of works by different creators is recorded in the MARC authority format field 130. Examples include figures 7.6 and 7.9 through 7.11, all serials or series. A monographic example is an anthology of science fiction short stories published in 1998 under the title *Legends* (see figure 7.79).

Figure 7.79. Compilation of Works by Different Creators

046	‡k 1998
130 0	‡a Legends (Anthology)
380	‡a Short stories ‡a Anthologies ‡2 lcsh
381	‡a Anthology
500 1	‡w r ‡i Compiler: ‡a Silverberg, Robert
670	‡a Legends, 1998: ‡b title page (edited by Robert Silverberg)

6.27.1.5. ADAPTATIONS AND REVISIONS. RDA 6.27.1.5 requires the cataloger to make a judgment: is the resource in hand a new work derived from another work, or is it simply a revision of an existing work? If the resource is a new work, the authorized access point is constructed by combining the authorized access point for the adaptor or reviser (who is the creator of the new work) plus the preferred title for the adaptation or revision. If the resource is judged to be simply a revision of an existing work, the authorized access point is the same as the authorized access point for the existing work (as formed under 6.27.1.2–6.27.1.4), because it *is* the same work.

The decision is left up to the cataloger, but RDA gives some guidance. If the nature and content of the resource in hand is "substantially" changed from that of an existing work, *and* the resource is presented as the work of the adaptor or reviser, the new resource is considered a different work, although it has a derivative relationship to the earlier work. If, on the other hand, the new resource is presented simply as a new edition or version of a previously existing work, it is a new expression of the same work.

RDA is not as prescriptive as previous cataloging codes in defining the point at which change becomes substantial enough for the new resource to be considered a new work. In traditional Anglo-American practice, the following changes are considered substantial enough to give rise to a new work.

New Work
(Authorized Access Point Different from That of the Preexisting Work)

- A paraphrase or rewrite
- An adaptation for children
- An adaptation of a literary work in a different literary form or genre
- An adaptation of an artwork in a different medium
- A parody
- A revision of a text for which the original author is no longer considered responsible, as evidenced by presentations of the author's name in resources embodying the work

- An abridgement if extensive rewriting is involved
- A motion picture version of a literary work
- A free transcription of a musical work, a variation on a musical theme, or a paraphrase in the general style of another musical work

In traditional Anglo-American practice, the following revisions are *not* considered substantial enough to give rise to a new work. Instead, the revised version is considered a different expression of the same work.

New Expression of the Same Work
(Authorized Access Point Based on That of the Preexisting Work)

- A revision of a text for which the original author is considered responsible, as evidenced by presentations of the author's name in resources embodying the work
- An abridgement, if extensive rewriting is not involved
- A translation
- The addition of dubbing or subtitling to a film
- "Colorizing" a black-and-white film
- A photographic reproduction of an artwork
- A reproduction of an artwork in the same medium as the original
- A transcription or an arrangement of a musical work, including addition of parts or accompaniment
- A recording of a musical work

The science fiction author Orson Scott Card wrote a short story titled "Ender's Game" in 1977. In 1985 he published a revised version of the short story as a novel, also titled *Ender's Game*. This is an example of an adaptation of a literary work in a different literary form, resulting in a new work under RDA 6.27.1.5. The short story and the novel are different works, which will have different authorized access points. The authorized access point for the revised version (the novel) will begin with the authorized access point "representing the person . . . responsible for the adaptation or revision," Orson Scott Card, and will conclude with the preferred title for the adaptation, "Ender's game." In this case, because the creator of the original is the same as the creator of the adaptation and the title did not change, this procedure results in identical authorized access points for the two works. Under RDA 6.27.1.9, if the access point of one work is the same as that of a different work, a term is added to the preferred title as a qualifier (see further discussion below). In this case, the preferred titles are disambiguated by addition of the form of the work (see figure 7.80). In 1994 the author revised the novel, issuing an "author's definitive edition." Under 6.27.1.5 this does not constitute a substantial change. The "author's definitive edition" is simply a new expression of the same work, and the authorized access point for the work will remain the same.

Figure 7.80. Adaptation—Different Work

046	‡k 1977
100 1	‡a Card, Orson Scott. ‡t Ender's game (Short story)
380	‡a Short stories ‡2 lcsh
500 1	‡w r ‡i Novelization (work): ‡a Card, Orson Scott. ‡t Ender's game (Novel)
670	‡a Ender's game, 1977 ‡b (short story published in Analog 97, no. 8 (Aug. 1977))

046	‡k 1985
100 1	‡a Card, Orson Scott. ‡t Ender's game (Novel)
380	‡a Novels ‡2 aat
500 1	‡w r ‡i Novelization of (work): ‡a Card, Orson Scott. ‡t Ender's game (Short story)
670	‡a Ender's game, 1985
670	‡a Ender's game, 1994: ‡b cover (Author's definitive edition)

Leonardo da Vinci's "Last Supper" (see figure 7.14) has been copied innumerable times. If a copy involves a change in medium (as nearly all do), under 6.27.1.5 it is considered a new work, no matter how faithful the copy. An example is Rudolf Stang's 1858 engraving (see figure 7.81). On the other hand, a photograph of the mural is considered a new expression rather than a new work; therefore, if described in an RDA database, it would share the same work authorized access point as the original expression. Similarly, a plaster reproduction of Michelangelo's "David" sold to tourists in Florence is considered an expression of the same work as the original, because its medium did not change.

Figure 7.81. Reproduction—Different Work

046	‡k 1858
100 1	‡a Stang, Rudolf, ‡d 1831-1927. ‡t Last supper
380	‡a Engravings (Prints) ‡2 aat
500 1	‡w r ‡i Based on (work): ‡a Leonardo, ‡c da Vinci, ‡d 1452-1519. ‡t Last supper
670	‡a Rudolf Stang's Stich des Abendmahles von Leonardo da Vinci, 1889
670	‡a ArtStor, 30 December 2011 ‡b (copy of Leonardo da Vinci's Last Supper by Rudolf Stang, engraving created in 1858)
670	‡a Museum Boppard, 30 December 2011 ‡b (Rudolf Stang achieved his height of fame with his reproduction of 'The Last Supper' by Leonardo da Vinci)

6.27.1.6. COMMENTARY, ANNOTATIONS, ILLUSTRATIVE CONTENT, ETC., ADDED TO A PREVIOUSLY EXISTING WORK. RDA 6.27.1.5 dealt with *changes* to an existing work. RDA 6.27.1.6 deals with *additions* to an existing work. These additions include commentary, notes, and illustrations, and are of such a nature that they might be considered a separate work on their own, related to the previously existing work. RDA 6.27.1.6 deals with resources that include both the previously existing work and the addition. This is an example of an aggregate work. Although there is always the option of considering the work and the addition to be separate works (with two separate authorized access points linking the works to the description of the resource), the resource also presents an aggregate work that can have its own description and authorized access point.

If the presentation of the resource (e.g., the wording on a title page) implies that the entity responsible for the addition is the creator of the work as a whole, the authorized access point is constructed by combining the authorized access point for the creator of the addition with the preferred title for the work as a whole (see figure 7.82). If, on the other hand, the resource presents itself primarily as an edition of the previously existing work, the resource is treated as an expression of the previously existing work; the two use the same authorized access point (see figure 7.83).

Figure 7.82. Addition of Commentary—Different Work

046	‡k 2000
110 2	‡a Canon Law Society of America. ‡t New commentary on the Code of Canon Law
380	‡a Commentaries ‡2 aat
510 2	‡w r ‡i Commentary on (work): ‡a Catholic Church. ‡t Codex Juris Canoni (1983)
670	‡a New commentary on the Code of Canon Law, 2000: ‡b title page (commissioned by the Canon Law Society of America)

Figure 7.83. Addition of Commentary—Different Expression of Same Work

046	‡k 196110
111 2	‡a International Conference on Cataloguing Principles ‡d (1961 : ‡c Paris, France). ‡t Statement of principles
380	‡a Document
670	‡a International Conference on Cataloguing Principles (1961 : Paris, France). Report, 1963: ‡b page 91 (Statement of principles)
670	‡a Statement of principles adopted at the International Conference on Cataloguing Principles, Paris, October 1961, 1971: ‡b title page (with commentary and examples by Eva Verona)

6.27.1.8. WORKS OF UNCERTAIN OR UNKNOWN ORIGIN. All works have creators, but in many cases the creator is unknown. If the creator of a work is uncertain or unknown, the authorized access point for the work is the preferred title of the work alone (see figures 7.12, 7.21, 7.25, 7.26, and 7.65). If in such cases scholarly consensus exists on a probable creator for the work, however, the authorized access point for the work is constructed by combining the authorized access point for the probable creator with the preferred title for the work, following 6.27.1.2. An example is a painting titled "The Taking of Christ," housed in the National Gallery of Ireland. Attributed for centuries to Gerard van Honthorst, it is now universally accepted as the work of Caravaggio (see figure 7.84).

Figure 7.84. Work of Uncertain Origin

046	ǂk 1602
100 1	ǂa Caravaggio, Michelangelo Merisi da, ǂd 1573-1610. ǂt Taking of Christ
380	ǂa Oil paintings (Visual works) ǂ2 aat
400 1	ǂa Caravaggio, Michelangelo Merisi da, ǂd 1573-1610. ǂt Cattura di Cristo
400 1	ǂa Honthorst, Gerrit van, ǂd 1590-1656. ǂt Taking of Christ
670	ǂa Benedetti, S. Caravaggio, 1993: ǂb page 5 (Taking of Christ; painted for the Mattei family in 1602)
670	ǂa Caravaggio, 2004: ǂb title page (Cattura di Cristo)
670	ǂa Caravaggio's 'Taking of Christ,' a masterpiece rediscovered, in The Burlington magazine, vol. 135, no. 1088, November 1993: ǂb page 731-741 (previous to 1993 attributed to Gerrit van Honthorst, thought to have been a copy of an original by Caravaggio)

6.27.1.9. ADDITIONS TO ACCESS POINTS REPRESENTING WORKS. If an authorized access point for a work is identical to that of another entity, a word or phrase called a qualifier needs to be added to disambiguate them. This happens when works share the same preferred title *and* are linked to the same principal creator (as in figure 7.80), or when two works share the same preferred title and are not linked to any principal creator (i.e., the authorized access point is the preferred title alone) (see figure 7.1).

If the authorized access points for two works need to be disambiguated, the cataloger chooses the most appropriate qualifier from four of the core elements for the work: the form of the work, the date of the work, the place of origin of the work, or another term that can distinguish the works. The qualifier is recorded in parentheses, following the preferred title. If more than one addition is needed, it is separated from the first by space-colon-space (as in figure 7.1). On the frequent need to disambiguate authorized access points that include "Selections" as part of their preferred title, see discussion above at 6.6.

The cataloger decides the most appropriate qualifier by asking the question "what is it that makes these two works different?" In the case of "Planet of the Apes," for example, the date of production was chosen to distinguish this motion picture from others with the same title made at different times (see figure 7.1). In the case of *Sozomena* (figure 7.6), the place of origin of the work was chosen to disambiguate this series from a monographic anthology with the same title. The cataloger could have chosen instead another distinguishing characteristic, such as "(Series)" or the name of the publisher "(Walter De Gruyter)." The publisher's name was chosen to disambiguate the series title "Bulletin" in figure 7.10.

If qualifying using a place name, follow the instructions in RDA 16.2.2.4, using the second form type, for example, "Budapest, Hungary," not "Budapest (Hungary)." If the place name appears in the list of abbreviated place names in RDA appendix B.11, it should be abbreviated in this part of the authorized access point as well.

A work's authorized access point sometimes needs to be disambiguated from the authorized access point for another entity, such as a corporate body (see figure 7.85) or a place (see figure 7.86).

Figure 7.85. Disambiguation of a Work Title from a Corporate Body Name

046		‡k 1973
130	0	‡a Association for Scottish Literary Studies (Series)
380		‡a Series (Publications) ‡a Monographic series ‡2 lcsh
410	2	‡a Association for Scottish Literary Studies. ‡t Association for Scottish Literary Studies (Series)
642		‡a no. 2 ‡5 DLC
643		‡a Aberdeen ‡b Association for Scottish Literary Studies ‡d no. 20-
643		‡a Edinburgh ‡b Scottish Academic Press ‡d <no. 2>-no. 19
644		‡a f ‡5 DLC
645		‡a t ‡5 DLC
646		‡a s ‡5 DLC
670		‡a The poems of John Davidson, 1973: ‡b series title page (Association for Scottish Literary Studies no. 2)
670		‡a OCLC, 12 May 2012 ‡b (series title: Association for Scottish Literary Studies; first volume published 1973)

Figure 7.86. Disambiguation of a Work Title from a Place Name

046		‡k 2004
130	0	‡a Baltic Sea Region (Series)
380		‡a Series (Publications) ‡a Monographic series ‡2 lcsh
430	0	‡a Ostseeregion
642		‡a Bd. 1 ‡5 DPCC ‡5 DLC
643		‡a Berlin ‡b BWV, Berliner Wissenschafts-Verlag
644		‡a f ‡5 DLC

645	‡a t ‡5 DPCC ‡5 DLC
646	‡a s ‡5 DLC
667	‡a Subtitle: northern dimensions, European perspectives = nördliche Dimensionen, europäische Perspektiven
670	‡a International Winter School "Loss, Decline and Doom in the Baltic Sea Area" (2003 : Greifswald, Germany). Perceptions of loss, decline and doom in the Baltic Sea Region, 2004: ‡b series title page (The Baltic Sea Region = Die Ostseeregion)
670	‡a OCLC, January 12, 2011 ‡b (series title: Baltic Sea Region, Die Ostseeregion; first volume published 2004)

In summary, there are two aspects of a work that disambiguate it from other works: its relationship to a principal creator and its preferred title. If two works have the same preferred title but different principal creators, no further disambiguation is needed in the authorized access point. If two works have the same principal creator and the same preferred title, or have no principal creator and the same preferred title, a qualifier needs to be added to the authorized access point following the instructions of 6.27.1.9.

6.27.2. AUTHORIZED ACCESS POINT REPRESENTING A PART OR PARTS OF A WORK. The authorized access points for a part of a work is formed in the same way as the authorized access point for the whole work, that is, by combining the authorized access point for the creator (if any) with the preferred title of the part (recorded as instructed in RDA 6.2.2.9). For details and examples, see the discussion above with 6.2.2.9.

6.27.4. VARIANT ACCESS POINT REPRESENTING A WORK OR EXPRESSION. Variant access points for works are constructed in much the same way as authorized access points, except a variant access point is created by combining the authorized access point for the creator (if any) with a variant title for the work (RDA 6.2.3), rather than the preferred title.

Variant access point forms are never recorded in bibliographic records, only in authority records. Instead, if a user constructs a search using a variant access point, a display similar to the following directing the user to the authorized access point should be triggered from the authority record (e.g., figure 7.26):

> Kells, Book of
> *search under*
> Book of Kells

Alternately, the system could re-execute the user's search automatically. It would be particularly useful when a user is constructing a keyword search if the system redirected the user's search based on variant forms found in the authority record.

Under LC/NACO practice, a variant access point for a work should not conflict with (i.e., be identical to) the authorized access point of another work. If conflict arises, the variant access point should be qualified in some way. However, under the same practice a variant access point for a work may conflict with a *variant* access point of another work. In such cases the variant access points do not need to be qualified (see LC-PCC PS 6.27.4, January 2013).

For a full discussion of variant titles, see above under 6.2.3.

6.27.4.2. VARIANT ACCESS POINT REPRESENTING ONE OR MORE LIBRETTOS, LYRICS, OR OTHER TEXTS FOR MUSICAL WORKS. Under previous cataloging codes, librettos and song texts were treated similarly to RDA's treatment, that is, the author of the text was considered the principal creator of the work and the authorized access point for the work began with the authorized access point for the author. However, there was an alternate rule, followed in North American practice, that considered the composer of the musical work to be the principal creator of the libretto or song text, with a variant access point given for the author of the text (see AACR2 21.28A and its Library of Congress Rule Interpretation). This alternative guideline has been eliminated in RDA. The principal creator of a libretto and other text for a musical work is the author of the text. Do not confuse this with the instructions in 6.28.1.2, which is a guideline for creating the authorized access point for an aggregate work consisting of music *and* text. When considering the libretto or text as a work separate from the music, its authorized access point begins with the authorized access point for the author of the text.

RDA 6.27.4.2 calls for a variant access point created by combining the authorized access point for the composer of the musical work combined with the preferred title of the musical work, plus the term "Libretto," "Librettos," "Lyrics," "Text," or "Texts" as appropriate, plus another distinguishing term if needed. This *variant* access point is similar in form to the *authorized* access point for this type of work in previous cataloging practice (see figure 7.87; in previous cataloging practice the authorized access point began with the authorized access point for Mozart).

Figure 7.87. Libretto

046	‡k 1791
100 1	‡a Schikaneder, Emanuel, ‡d 1751-1812. ‡t Zauberflöte
380	‡a Librettos ‡2 lcsh
400 1	‡a Mozart, Wolfgang Amadeus, ‡d 1756-1791. ‡t Zauberflöte. ‡s Libretto
670	‡a The authentic Magic flute libretto, 2009
670	‡a Oxford music online, 3 January 2012 ‡b (Die Zauberflöte, libretto written by Emanuel Schikaneder for Mozart's opera in 1791)

6.27.4.3. VARIANT ACCESS POINT REPRESENTING A PART OF A WORK. As discussed above under 6.2.2.9, a part of a work may be identified by a distinctive title ("Voyage to Lilliput"), or by the preferred title for the work as a whole followed by a general term ("Part 1"), itself sometimes followed by a title for the part. The choice of which is used as the authorized access point for a part may be difficult for the average library user to predict; therefore, RDA 6.27.4.3 calls for recording variant access points constructed in ways that were not chosen for the authorized access point if the cataloger thinks these would be helpful in giving the user access to the resource. For example, a user looking for the first part of *Gulliver's Travels* might well look under that title rather than the preferred title for the part. It is therefore important for access to record this variant, which might give rise to a user display such as the following (see figure 7.29):

> Swift, Jonathan, 1667-1745. Gulliver's travels. Part 1, Voyage to Lilliput
> *search under*
> Swift, Jonathan, 1667-1745. Voyage to Lilliput

For fuller discussion of treatment of parts of works, see above beginning with 6.2.2.9.

6.27.4.4. VARIANT ACCESS POINT REPRESENTING A COMPILATION OF WORKS. The preferred title for a compilation of works is frequently a conventional collective title, as described above under 6.2.2.10. If so, this is a made-up title constructed according to cataloging guidelines which might not be obvious to the user. For example, the authorized access point for the Roman poet Persius's *Satires* is constructed using the preferred title "Works." It seems more than likely that a user might attempt to find this collection using the title "Satires," and so it would seem important for access to include this variant (see figure 7.37):

> Persius. Satires
> *search under*
> Persius. Works

ACCESS POINTS FOR MUSICAL WORKS

Authorized access points for musical works are based, like those of all other works, on the name of the creator if any and the preferred title of the work. However, because musical works are frequently aggregate works (e.g., music plus text), RDA has given some special guidelines about creating an access point for the aggregate work. In addition there are other guidelines specific to musical works.

6.28.1.2. MUSICAL WORKS WITH LYRICS, LIBRETTO, TEXT, ETC. This guideline treats works that include both music and words. RDA takes the position that the principal creator of this sort of aggregate work is the composer of the music, and so the authorized access point is constructed by combining the authorized access point for the composer of the music with the preferred title of the work. An example is figure 7.45, *Kafee-Kantate,* with music by J. S. Bach and words by Christian Friedrich Henrici. For another example, see figure 7.49.

6.28.1.4. MUSICAL WORKS COMPOSED FOR CHOREOGRAPHIC MOVEMENT. This guideline covers a particular type of work: music composed to accompany dance. Such music can, of course, be performed without performing the dance, but in order for it to be performed as intended a choreographer must contribute a choreography (instructions for the dance movement), which is a work in its own right. Different choreographies can be associated with such a musical work, and this can result in notably different performances. The choreography and the music are, therefore, extremely closely related works. However, RDA takes the sensible position that the principal creator of the *musical* work is the composer of the music. The authorized access point is constructed by combining the authorized access point for the composer with the preferred title for the work. See figure 7.88, Khachaturian's *Spartak,* and figure 7.13, a description of a related work, a motion picture derived from the ballet.

Figure 7.88. Ballet

```
046     ǂk 1950 ǂl 1954
100 1   ǂa Khachaturi͡an, Aram Ilʹich, ǂd 1903-1978. ǂt Spartak
380     ǂa Ballets ǂ2 lcsh
400 1   ǂa Khachaturi͡an, Aram Ilʹich, ǂd 1903-1978. ǂt Spartacus
400 1   ǂa Khachaturi͡an, Aram Ilʹich, ǂd 1903-1978. ǂt Спартак
530  0  ǂw r ǂi Adapted as a motion picture (work): ǂa Spartacus (Motion picture : 2008)
667     ǂa Non-Latin script reference not evaluated.
670     ǂa Спартак, 1954
670     ǂa Oxford Music Online, 7 May 2011 ǂb (Spartacus, Spartak; Ballet in four acts
        composed 1950-1954 by Khachaturian to a scenario by Nikolay Volkov; first
        choreographed by Leonid Jacobson (Leningrad, 1956). Khachaturian revised the
        score in 1968)
```

6.28.1.5. ADAPTATIONS OF MUSICAL WORKS. This guideline is related to RDA 6.27.1.5, Adaptations and Revisions. As seen above in the discussion of RDA 6.27.1.5, when a work is modified the cataloger must make a judgment: is the modification extensive enough that a new work is created, or is it simply a revision of an existing work (giving rise to a new expression of that work, not a new work)? RDA 6.28.1.5 is a guideline for the case where the adaptation is extensive enough that a new musical work is created. This includes free transcriptions, paraphrases, and arrangements where the harmony or musical style is changed, and performances involving substantial adaptation or improvisation. Application of this guideline requires judgment, and there may be cases where the cataloger is not sure if a new work has been created or the resource is simply a new expression of an existing work. In case of doubt, treat the resource as a new expression, applying 6.28.3.2–6.28.3.6.

The authorized access point for such works follows the general guideline: combine the authorized access point for the principal creator with the preferred title (or use the preferred title alone as appropriate). An example is Beethoven's variations on *Rule, Britannia*, based on music first composed by Thomas Augustine Arne (see figure 7.89). For an example of a new work created by a composer based on an earlier work of his own, see figure 7.52.

Figure 7.89. Adaptation of a Musical Work

Original work

046	ǂk 1740
100 1	ǂa Arne, Thomas Augustine, ǂd 1710-1778. ǂt Alfred. ǂp Rule, Britannia
380	ǂa Songs ǂ2 lcsh
400 1	ǂa Arne, Thomas Augustine, ǂd 1710-1778. ǂt Rule, Britannia
400 1	ǂa Arne, Thomas Augustine, ǂd 1710-1778. ǂt Grand ode in honour of Great Britain
400 1	ǂa Arne, Thomas Augustine, ǂd 1710-1778. ǂt When Britain first at heav'n's command
500 1	ǂw r ǂ i Musical variations (work): ǂa Beethoven, Ludwig van, ǂd 1770-1827. ǂt Variations sur le thème Rule Britannia
670	ǂa Alfred, 1981: ǂb page 143 (A grand ode in honour of Great Britain : When Britain first at heav'n's command) page 159 (Rule, Britannia)
670	ǂa Oxford music online, 28 January 2012 ǂb (musical setting of David Mallet and James Thomson's masque Alfred, first performed in 1740, later revised as an oratorio; the original work contained seven musical numbers including Rule, Britannia)

Adaptation

046	ǂk 1803
100 1	ǂa Beethoven, Ludwig van, ǂd 1770-1827. ǂt Variations sur le thème Rule Britannia
380	ǂa Variations ǂ2 lcsh
382	ǂa piano
383	ǂc WoO 79
384 0	ǂa D major

```
400 1   ‡a Beethoven, Ludwig van, ‡d 1770-1827. ‡t 5 variations on "Rule Britannia"
400 1   ‡a Beethoven, Ludwig van, ‡d 1770-1827. ‡t Five variations on "Rule Britannia"
400 1   ‡a Beethoven, Ludwig van, ‡d 1770-1827. ‡t Variations on "Rule Britannia"
400 1   ‡a Beethoven, Ludwig van, ‡d 1770-1827. ‡t Variations, ‡m piano, ‡n WoO 79, ‡r D
        major
500 1   ‡w r ‡i Musical variations based on (work): ‡a Arne, Thomas Augustine, ‡d 1710-
        1778. ‡t Alfred. ‡p Rule, Britannia
670     ‡a Variations pour le Pianoforte sur le thême Rûle Britannia,  N. 26, 1804
670     ‡a Oxford music online, 28 January 2012 ‡b (Five variations on 'Rule Britannia', D,
        Woo79; composed in 1803, published in Vienna in 1804)
```

6.28.1.7. CADENZAS. A cadenza is a piece of music inserted near the end of a concerto movement or an aria intended to display the virtuosity of the performer. It may be improvised by the performer, or more formally composed either by the composer of the original piece or by another composer. RDA takes the position that a cadenza is a related work, separate from the original musical work. Its authorized access point is constructed by combining the authorized access point for the composer of the cadenza with the preferred title of the cadenza (see figure 7.90).

Figure 7.90. Cadenza

```
046     ‡k 1902
100 1   ‡a Joachim, Joseph, ‡d 1831-1907. ‡t Kadenz zum Violin-Konzert op. 77 von
        Johannes Brahms
380     ‡a Cadenza
382     ‡a violin
384 0   ‡a D major
400 1   ‡a Joachim, Joseph, ‡d 1831-1907. ‡t Cadenza to the violin-concerto by Johannes
        Brahms, opus 77
400 1   ‡a Joachim, Joseph, ‡d 1831-1907. ‡t Cadenza for Brahms' violin concerto
500 1   ‡w r ‡i Cadenza composed for (work): ‡a Brahms, Johannes, ‡d 1833-1897. ‡t
        Concertos, ‡m violin, orchestra, ‡n op. 77, ‡r D major
670     ‡a Kadenz zum Violin-Konzert op. 77 von Johannes Brahms = Cadenza to the violin-
        concerto by Johannes Brahms, opus 77, 1902
670     ‡a Cadenza for Brahms' violin concerto, 1947
```

6.28.1.9. ADDITIONS TO ACCESS POINTS REPRESENTING MUSICAL WORKS WITH TITLES THAT ARE NOT DISTINCTIVE. Access points for musical works with distinctive titles are formed in the same way as access points for other works, that is, by combining the authorized access point for the creator (if any) with the preferred title. No further additions are necessary unless the access point conflicts with that of another work (in which case 6.28.1.10 is applied).

However, if the application of 6.14.2.3–6.14.2.6 leaves a title that is not "distinctive" (that is, the title is solely the name of one or more types of composition), RDA instructs us to add certain elements to the preferred title (if applicable) when recording the authorized access point, whether the access point conflicts with another or not.[17]

Medium of Performance. First add the medium of performance, as recorded in the medium of performance element (see discussion above at 6.15). In access points in MARC records, medium of performance is recorded in subfield ‡m, preceded by a comma. For examples, see figures 7.46 through 7.48, 7.50, and 7.54.

Medium of performance is not recorded as part of the access point if the medium is implied by the title. For example, "Symphonies" implies "orchestra" and so the medium of performance is not included in the access point, although it may be recorded in the medium of performance element in the MARC 382 field (see figure 7.53). If, on the other hand, a composer writes something called a symphony for organ, "organ" should be added to the access point, because "organ" is *not* implied by the title. Medium of performance is also omitted if the work is a set of compositions for different media or is part of a series with the same title but for differing media, the composer has not designated the medium, or if stating the medium would be so complex that another method of identifying the piece would be more useful.

Numeric Designation. If the work has a serial number, an opus number, or a thematic index number, add it as it has been recorded in the numeric designation element (see discussion above at 6.16). In access points in MARC records, a numeric designation is recorded in subfield ‡n, preceded by a comma. More than one type of number may be recorded with the access point, and a range of numbers may be recorded if appropriate. For examples, see figures 7.44, 7.45 (400 field), 7.46, 7.48, 7.53, and 7.54.

Key. If the original key of the composition has been identified following 6.17 (see discussion above), add it to the access point in subfield ‡r following a comma. For examples, see figures 7.44, 7.48, 7.50, and 7.53.

If these three elements are insufficient to distinguish between two or more works by the same composer, the cataloger may further add to the preferred title, in the following order: (a) the year of completion of the work, (b) the year of its first publication, or (c) any other identifying elements, such as place of composition, etc. This addition is recorded in parentheses. For example, Gary Schocker composed two sets of "dances" for flute duet and piano. These have been distinguished by the addition of the date of publication to the authorized access point (see figure 7.91).

Figure 7.91. Year of Composition Used to Distinguish

046	‡k 1993
100 1	‡a Schocker, Gary, ‡d 1959- ‡t Dances, ‡m piano, flutes (2) ‡n (1993)
380	‡a Music ‡2 lcsh
382	‡a piano, flutes (2)
400 1	‡a Schocker, Gary, ‡d 1959- ‡t Pieces, ‡m piano, flutes (2)
670	‡a Flautas fantasticas!, 2002: ‡b container (Three dances for two flutes and piano)
670	‡a Airborne, 1998: ‡b disc label (Three pieces for two flutes [i.e. 2 flutes and piano]) insert (3 dances for 2 flutes)
670	‡a Geroge Mason University WWW site, October 20, 2009: ‡b Performing arts; Archives; Spring 2006; Yuka Harimoto senior flute recital (Three dances for two flutes and piano; 1993)

6.28.1.10. ADDITIONS TO ACCESS POINTS REPRESENTING MUSICAL WORKS WITH DISTINCTIVE TITLES. The additions described in RDA 6.28.1.9 are prescriptive; that is, when the preferred title consists solely of a type or types of composition, the cataloger *must* add all of the prescribed elements that are available. RDA 6.28.1.10 addresses the situation where the preferred title is *not* solely a type or types of composition (as "Syrinx" [figure 7.43] or "Songs from A Shropshire lad" [figure 7.49]). In this case, all of the elements described in 6.28.1.9 *may* be added to the authorized access point, but *only* if they are needed to resolve a conflict between a work with the same or similar access point to another work. The preferred method is to add either the medium of performance (as instructed above with 6.28.1.9) or a descriptive word or phrase within parentheses (with no subfield coding). An example is John Adams' *Death of Klinghoffer*. "(Opera)" has been added to the authorized access point to distinguish the work from the composer's motion picture music with the same name (see figure 7.51). If neither medium of performance nor another distinguishing characteristic of the work resolves the conflict, add other elements as instructed in 6.28.1.10.1.

6.28.2. AUTHORIZED ACCESS POINT REPRESENTING A PART OR PARTS OF A MUSICAL WORK. RDA 6.28.2 is based on 6.27.2; it deals with the publication of only a part, rather than the whole, of a musical work. The authorized access points for a part of a musical work is formed in the same way as the authorized access point for the whole work, that is, by combining the authorized access point for the creator (if any) with the preferred title of the part (recorded as instructed in RDA 6.14.2.7). For details and examples, see the discussion above with 6.14.2.7.

6.28.4. VARIANT ACCESS POINT REPRESENTING A MUSICAL WORK OR EXPRESSION. Variant access points for musical works are recorded following the same principles as variant access points for other works (see discussion above with 6.27.4).

ACCESS POINTS FOR LEGAL WORKS

The process of forming access points for legal works generally follows the same principles as access points for other works, normally following the pattern of the authorized access point for the principal creator plus the preferred title for the legal work. In the case of laws, decrees, legislation, constitutions, treaties, etc., the principal creator is usually the jurisdiction governed by the laws (see RDA 19.2.1.1.1g).

6.29.1.2. LAWS GOVERNING ONE JURISDICTION. Construct the authorized access point by combining the authorized access point for the jurisdiction with the preferred title as chosen or formed under 6.19.2. The preferred title may be the title of the law (see figures 7.57 and 7.58) or the conventional collective title "Laws, etc." (see figure 7.56).

6.29.1.15. TREATIES, ETC., BETWEEN NATIONAL GOVERNMENTS. The authorized access point for a treaty between national governments is formed in most cases by combining the authorized access point for the government named first in the resource publishing the treaty (or in a reference source) with the preferred title for the treaty, which will generally be the conventional collective title "Treaties, etc." If the treaty is between a single government on one side and many on the other, the authorized access point begins with the authorized access point for the one government rather than the first named.

Routinely including the first-named jurisdiction in the authorized access point represents a change from previous cataloging practice, which did not include the jurisdiction in the access point if there were more than three signatories (see AACR2 21.35A2). This follows from RDA's more expansive view of the core creator relationship, under which the creator having principal responsibility or the first-named creator is recorded, no matter how many creators there are (see RDA 19.2). Previous cataloging codes took the position that when more than three creators were involved with a work, responsibility became too diffuse to assign any of them principal responsibility (this was one manifestation of the so-called rule of three).

For examples of authorized access points for treaties, see figures 7.59 and 7.60.

6.29.1.32. ADDITIONS TO ACCESS POINTS REPRESENTING LAWS, ETC. If the authorized access point for a law or collection of laws created under 6.29.1.2–6.29.1.6 is identical to that of another (as it nearly always will be if the conventional collective title "Laws, etc." is the preferred title), RDA instructs the cataloger to add the year of promulgation of the law as a qualifier. This may sometimes be the best qualifier for a law, but catalogers following LC policy, including contributors to the LC/NACO Authority File, need not feel bound by this excessively prescriptive instruction and instead may choose to qualify the authorized access point by a more suitable term or phrase, following RDA 6.27.1.9. Customary practice has been to qualify the conventional collective title "Laws, etc." with the published title of the collection (as shown in figure 7.56), and in many cases this may still be the best qualifier. However, catalogers may choose to add any of the distinguishing elements from 6.27.1.9, including the form of the work, the date of the work, the place of origin of the work, or another term or phrase. The LC policy statement does give explicit instructions for qualifying the authorized access points of collections of U.S. state laws. For examples, see figures 7.61 and 7.62.

6.29.1.33. ADDITIONS TO ACCESS POINTS REPRESENTING TREATIES, ETC. The conventional title "Treaties, etc." is nearly always chosen for a treaty or treaties (see RDA 6.19.2.7 and 6.19.2.8 and discussion, above) and so the access point for a treaty will usually be the same as that of other treaties. For this reason 6.29.1.33 instructs the cataloger routinely to add certain elements to the authorized access point.

If the treaty is between two parties, add the name of the other party to the treaty and the date of signing to the authorized access point (already constructed using the authorized access point for the first party and the preferred title "Treaties, etc.") (see figure 7.59). If there are more than two parties, only add the date of signing (see figure 7.63). Compilations of treaties are treated the same way, except that the authorized access point does not include a date of signing (because there is no one date of signing).

If more than one treaty between the parties is signed on the same date, these additions may not be enough to differentiate them. In this case, also add a term from the titles of the treaties to distinguish them (see figure 7.60 and discussion of 6.21, above).

6.29.3. VARIANT ACCESS POINT REPRESENTING A LEGAL WORK OR EXPRESSION. Variant access points for legal works are recorded in the same way as authorized access points for legal works, except they include variant titles for the work rather than the preferred title. Variant access points are recorded in MARC 4XX fields and may appear as follows to the user of the database (e.g., as generated from the 410 field of figure 7.61):

> Colorado. West's Colorado legislative service
> *search under*
> Colorado. Laws, etc. (Session laws : 1990-)

Any variant access point may be recorded if the cataloger believes it will help the user access the legal work. Typical variants include title proper of a compilation whose preferred title is a conventional title (see, e.g., figures 7.56, 7.59, and 7.60) and variant titles found in the resource(s) embodying the legal work (see figures 7.57 and 7.58). Descriptions for treaties generally include variant access points beginning with the authorized access point(s) for the party or parties not used as the first part of the authorized access point (see figures 7.59, 7.60, and 7.63):

> European Union. Treaties, etc. Russia (Federation), 2010 June 1
> *search under*
> Russia (Federation). Treaties, etc. European Union, 2010 June 1

ACCESS POINTS FOR RELIGIOUS WORKS

The normal pattern for forming an authorized access point for works is to combine the authorized access point for the principal creator (if any) with the preferred title of the work. This pattern is followed for religious works as well, but many religious works, such as sacred scripture, are not considered to have a principal creator and so their authorized access points are based on the preferred title alone. Certain types of religious works are detailed under 6.30.1. Authorized access points for all other kinds of religious works follow the general instructions for authorized access points for works under 6.27.1.

6.30.1.2. WORKS ACCEPTED AS SACRED SCRIPTURE. The authorized access point for a work accepted as sacred scripture by a religious group is based on the preferred title. Discussion of choosing the preferred title for sacred scripture is found above under 6.23.2.5. For an example, see figure 7.64. Although not mentioned in RDA 6.30, the authorized access point for an apocryphal book is formed the same way, based on the preferred title (see 6.23.2.6 above, with figure 7.65).

6.30.1.4. THEOLOGICAL CREEDS, CONFESSIONS OF FAITH, ETC. The authorized access point for this type of work is also based on its preferred title alone. For a discussion of how to choose the preferred title and examples, see above under 6.23.2.7, with figures 7.66 and 7.67.

6.30.1.5. LITURGICAL WORKS. The authorized access point for a liturgical work is formed by combining the authorized access point for the church or religious body to which the work pertains with the preferred title for the liturgical work. For a discussion of how to choose the preferred title and examples, see above under 6.23.2.8, with figures 7.68 and 7.69.

6.30.2. AUTHORIZED ACCESS POINT REPRESENTING A PART OR PARTS OF A RELIGIOUS WORK. The authorized access point for a part of a religious work is formed in the same way as that of any other work: combine the authorized access point for the work as a whole with the preferred title for the part.

6.30.2.2. PART OR PARTS OF A SACRED SCRIPTURE. The authorized access point for a part of a sacred scripture is formed in most cases by combining the authorized access point for the sacred scripture with the preferred title of the part. For discussion of how to choose the preferred title for the part, which can be somewhat complex, see above under 6.23.2.9–6.29.2.19, with figures 7.70 through 7.75. One exception to this pattern is single selections of sacred scripture commonly identified by a distinctive title, for which the authorized access point is the preferred title of the part (that is, not in combination with the authorized access point for the sacred scripture as a whole). See above under 6.23.2.9.5, with figure 7.73.

6.30.5. VARIANT ACCESS POINT REPRESENTING A RELIGIOUS WORK. A variant access point for a religious work may be recorded if the cataloger believes the variant would help the user of the database find the work. A variant access point is generally formed in the same way as an authorized access point, that is, the combination of the authorized access point for the principal creator of the work with the preferred title for the work.

Some examples of variant access points for religious works include:

Variation in script (see figure 7.64):

قرآن
> *search under*
> Qur'an

Different language (see figure 7.65):

> De infantia Iesu evangelium Thomae
> *search under*
> Gospel of Thomas (Infancy Gospel)

Different spelling (see figure 7.67):

> Shahadah
> *search under*
> Shahada

Variant title in the same language (see figure 7.66):

> Gallican Confession
> *search under*
> Gallic Confession

Variant formation of the access point (see figure 7.73):

> Bible. Luke I, 46-55
> *search under*
> Magnificat

Preferred title of the part as variant (see figure 7.75):

> Book of Moses
> *search under*
> Pearl of Great Price. Book of Moses

For a general discussion of variant titles, see above under 6.2.3.

WORK DESCRIPTIONS IN BIBLIOGRAPHIC RECORDS (RDA CHAPTER 7, DESCRIBING CONTENT)

As noted earlier in this chapter, RDA chapter 7 deals with the attributes of works that are in the current environment normally recorded in bibliographic records.

is possible that in a future cataloging environment all attributes of a work will be recorded in the same description rather than split between authority and bibliographic records.

7.2. NATURE OF THE CONTENT. This element is very similar to RDA 6.3, the form of work element, and this sort of information might be recorded in the 380 field of the authority record for the work. There might be a slight distinction in the somewhat greater detail found in the "graph plotting" and "spreadsheet" examples under 7.2.1.3 than would normally be recorded in a 6.3 form of work element, but the "field recording," "cross-cultural survey," and "Singspiel" examples might also be appropriately recorded as the form of work element.

In a MARC bibliographic record, this element is generally recorded in a note field such as 500. Alternately, in some cases this element might be recorded in a MARC bibliographic 380 field, just as in the authority record. For an example, see figure 7.92. When deciding whether to record this information in an authority record or a bibliographic record, remember that the authority record for a work applies to all expressions and manifestations of the work; a bibliographic record generally applies only to a single manifestation. Normally, if the information recorded in a bibliographic record is common to all expressions or manifestations of the work, in order to be consistent the same information should appear in all bibliographic records associated with the work, making it more efficient to record it once in the authority record instead. Figure 7.92 is an example where the nature of the content, "Play," might have been better recorded in the authority record for the work. On the other hand, in the current MARC environment it might be appropriate to record this type of information in a bibliographic record if the nature of the content of the work is not apparent from the information given elsewhere in the bibliographic record (see figure 7.93). Information recorded in this element may take the form of a quotation from the resource, as seen in figure 7.94.

Figure 7.92. Nature of Content

020	‡a 2760901971
100 1	‡a Tremblay, Michel, ‡d 1942- ‡e author.
245 10	‡a Marcel poursuivi par les chiens / ‡c Michel Tremblay.
264 1	‡a Montréal : ‡b Leméac, ‡c [1992]
300	‡a 69 pages ; ‡c 20 cm.
336	‡a text ‡2 rdacontent
337	‡a unmediated ‡2 rdamedia
338	‡a volume ‡2 rdacarrier
380	‡a Play

490 1   ‡a Théâtre ; ‡v 195

830   0   ‡a Collection Théâtre Leméac ; ‡v 195.

Figure 7.93. Nature of Content

020   ‡a 0842523294 (paperback : alkaline paper)

100 1   ‡a Angerhofer, Paul J., ‡d 1960- ‡e author.

245 10 ‡a In aedibus Aldi : ‡b the legacy of Aldus Manutius and his press / ‡c Paul J. Angerhofer, Mary Ann Addy Maxwell, Robert L. Maxwell ; with binding descriptions by Pamela Barrios.

264   1 ‡a Provo, Utah : ‡b Friends of the Harold B. Lee Library, Brigham Young University, ‡c 1995.

300   ‡a ix, 172 pages : ‡b illustrations, maps ; ‡c 28 cm

336   ‡a text ‡2 rdacontent

336   ‡a still image ‡2 rdacontent

336   ‡a cartographic image ‡2 rdacontent

337   ‡a unmediated ‡2 rdamedia

338   ‡a volume ‡2 rdacarrier

500   ‡a Catalog to accompany an exhibition at the Harold B. Lee Library.

504   ‡a Includes bibliographical references (pages 129-135) and indexes.

700 1   ‡a Maxwell, Mary Ann Addy, ‡d 1960- ‡e author.

700 1   ‡a Maxwell, Robert L., ‡d 1957- ‡e author.

700 1   ‡a Barrios, Pamela, ‡e author.

710 2   ‡a Harold B. Lee Library, ‡e sponsoring institution.

Figure 7.94. Nature of Content

100 1   ‡a Rheault, Charles A., ‡c Jr., ‡e author.

245 10 ‡a SP at 75 : ‡b the Society of Printers, 1955-1980 / ‡c Charles A. Rheault, Jr.

246 3   ‡a S.P. at 75

246 3   ‡a SP at seventy-five

264   1 ‡a Boston : ‡b The Society of Printers, ‡c 1981.

300   ‡a 114 pages : ‡b illustrations ; ‡c 25 cm

336   ‡a text ‡2 rdacontent

336   ‡a still image ‡2 rdacontent

337   ‡a unmediated ‡2 rdamedia

338   ‡a volume ‡2 rdacarrier

500   ‡a "This book is a record of the society in the period 1955-1980, and differs from its more historically-oriented predecessor, Printing as an art, by Ray Nash (Cambridge, 1955)"--Page 1.

500   ‡a 350 copies printed.

7.3. COVERAGE OF THE CONTENT. This element refers to the chronological or geographic coverage of the resource's content. Either aspect may be recorded in a MARC bibliographic 500 field; additionally, field 513 is available for chronological coverage and field 522 may be used for geographic coverage. The work illustrated in figure 7.95 is a report covering the period January 2004 through December 2005. In figure 7.96, the element shows geographic coverage not evident from the title of the resource.

Figure 7.95. Coverage of Content

100 1	‡a Williams, David, ‡e author.
245 10	‡a Expanded satellite-based mobile communications tracking system requirements / ‡c David Williams (Battelle), Derrick Vercoe, Peggy Erlandson, and Jennifer Wittpenn (QUALCOMM), and Amy Houser (FMCSA).
264　1	‡a Washington, DC : ‡b U.S. Department of Transportation, Federal Motor Carrier Safety Administration, ‡c [2006]
300	‡a 1 online resource (29 unnumbered pages) : ‡b color illustrations
336	‡a text ‡2 rdacontent
337	‡a computer ‡2 rdamedia
338	‡a online resource ‡2 rdacarrier
347	‡a text file ‡b PDF ‡2 rda
513	‡a Interim report; ‡b January 2004-December 2005.
500	‡a Title from title screen (viewed on November 10, 2011).
700 1	‡a Vercoe, Derrick, ‡e author.
700 1	‡a Erlandson, Peggy, ‡e author.
700 1	‡a Wittpenn, Jennifer, ‡e author.
700 1	‡a Houser, Amy, ‡e author.
856 4	‡u http://www.fmcsa.dot.gov/facts-research/research-technology/report/Mobile-Communications/mobile-communications-tracking-system-requirements.pdf

Figure 7.96. Coverage of Content

110 2	‡a NovoPrint USA, Inc., ‡e cartographer.
245 10	‡a Waterloo, Cedar Falls and vicinity, Iowa.
255	‡a Scale 1:40,055.
264　1	‡a [Milwaukee, Wisconsin?] : ‡b NovoPrint USA, ‡c [2009]
300	‡a 1 map : ‡b color ; ‡c 44 x 60 cm
336	‡a cartographic image ‡2 rdacontent
337	‡a unmediated ‡2 rdamedia
338	‡a sheet ‡2 rdacarrier
522	‡a Includes map of Black Hawk County.

7.4. COORDINATES OF CARTOGRAPHIC CONTENT. This work-related element records the coordinates of a map or atlas. It is generally only recorded if found on the resource, although if the cataloger knows the coordinates they may be recorded even if not found on the resource.

7.4.2. LONGITUDE AND LATITUDE. Longitude and latitude are recorded in MARC bibliographic field 255, subfield ‡c. The entire element is enclosed in parentheses in MARC ISBD presentation. Record the farthest extent found on the map for each of the four cardinal directions; follow the punctuation pattern shown in 7.4.2.3. For an example, see figure 7.97. Figure 7.97 also shows an alternate and somewhat more precise method of recording this same information, using coded forms of longitude and latitude in the 034 field. In 034 the westernmost coordinate is recorded in subfield ‡d, the easternmost in subfield ‡e, the northernmost in subfield ‡f, and the southernmost in subfield ‡g. The figure is recorded in the form "Hdddmmss" (hemisphere [N, S, E, or W], degrees, minutes, seconds).

Figure 7.97. Coordinates of Cartographic Content

034 1	‡a a ‡b 250000 ‡d W0852000 ‡e W0810400 ‡f N0344200 ‡g N0305200
110 2	‡a ADC (Firm), ‡e cartographer.
245 10	‡a Georgia road atlas & travel guide highway atlas : ‡b including Albany, Americus, Athens, Atlanta, Atlanta Downtown, Augusta, Brunswick, Columbus, Griffin, Macon, Rome, Savannah, Valdosta, Warner Robins & Waycross.
255	‡a Scale 1:250,000 ‡c (W 85°20'00"--W 81°04'00"/N 34°42'00"--N 30°52'00").
264 1	‡a [Alexandria, Virginia] : ‡b ADC the Map People, ‡c [2011]
300	‡a 1 atlas (xvi, 72 pages) : ‡b color maps ; ‡c 29 cm
336	‡a cartographic image ‡2 rdacontent
337	‡a unmediated ‡2 rdamedia
338	‡a volume ‡2 rdacarrier
500	‡a Title from cover.
500	‡a At head of title: ADC the Map People, by Kappa Map Group.
500	‡a Includes indexes.

7.7. INTENDED AUDIENCE. If a resource is created with a particular audience in mind (e.g., children or young adults), this information may be recorded in the intended audience element if the cataloger thinks it would help the user identify or select the resource. It is particularly common to record this element for juvenile materials (cf. LC-PCC PS 7.7, April 2010), but it is also commonly used to record the MPAA audience rating for a motion picture, which is important information to some library users.

As a practical matter, catalogers are not expected to figure out the intended audience just by looking at the resource. Information about the intended audience is generally recorded only if the information is stated on the resource or can easily be found in another source (e.g., for a motion picture, in the Internet Movie Database [www.imdb.com]). The intended audience element is recorded in the MARC bibliographic 521 field. The 521 field with the first indicator blank is intended to generate in the local system the term "Audience:" at the beginning of the note. First indicator "0" generates "Reading grade level:"; "1" generates "Interest age level:"; "2" generates "Interest grade level:"; "3" generates "Special audience characteristics:"; and "4" generates "Motivation/interest level:". If the first indicator is coded "8," no display constant will be generated. Because the first indicator is blank, the note generated from the 521 field of figure 7.98 is intended to display to the public as: "Audience: High school students." For an example of intended audience for a motion picture, see figure 7.99.

Figure 7.98. Intended Audience

100 1	‡a Roehm, A. Wesley, ‡e author.
245 14	‡a The record of mankind / ‡c A. Wesley Roehm, Morris R. Buske, Hutton Webster, Edgar B. Wesley.
264 1	‡a Boston : ‡b D.C. Heath and Company, ‡c [1956]
300	‡a vi, 754 pages : ‡b illustrations (some color) ; ‡c 24 cm
336	‡a text ‡2 rdacontent
337	‡a unmediated ‡2 rdamedia
338	‡a volume ‡2 rdacarrier
521	‡a High school students.
504	‡a Includes bibliographical references and index.
700 1	‡a Buske, Morris R., ‡d 1912-2005, ‡e author.
700 1	‡a Webster, Hutton, ‡d 1875-1955, ‡e author.
700 1	‡a Wesley, Edgar B. ‡q (Edgar Bruce), ‡d 1891-1980, ‡e author.

Figure 7.99. Intended Audience

245 00	‡a Forever strong / ‡c Picture Rock Entertainment presents a Go Films production in association with BNR Films ; a Ryan Little film ; produced by Adam Abel and Ryan Little ; written by David Pliler ; directed by Ryan Little.
264 1	‡a [Place of publication not identified] : ‡b [Publisher not identified], ‡c 2009.
264 2	‡a [Salt Lake City, Utah] : ‡b Excel Entertainment Group
264 4	‡c ©2009
300	‡a 1 videodisc (approximately 112 min.) : ‡b sound, color ; ‡c 4 3/4 in.

336	‡a two-dimensional moving image ‡2 rdacontent
337	‡a video ‡2 rdamedia
338	‡a videodisc ‡2 rdacarrier
344	‡h Dolby digital 5.1
346	‡b NTSC ‡2 rda
347	‡a video file ‡b DVD video ‡e all regions ‡2 rda
508	‡a Music by J. Bateman, Bart Hendrickson ; edited by John Lyde ; director of photography, T.C. Christensen.
511 1	‡a Gary Cole, Sean Faris, Penn Badgley, Sean Astin.
546	‡a English; optional English and Spanish subtitles.
521 8	‡a MPAA rating: PG-13.
520	‡a "Best friends and teammates Rick and Lars become bitter rivals when Rick's free-spirited lifestyle lands him in juvenile detention. There a concerned counselor and a national championship rugby coach recruit Rick for a new team and a new direction"--Container.
500	‡a Wide screen (16:9)
700 1	‡a Abel, Adam, ‡d 1976- ‡e film producer.
700 1	‡a Little, Ryan, ‡e film director, ‡e film producer.
700 1	‡a Pliler, David, ‡e screenwriter.
700 1	‡a Cole, Gary, ‡d 1956- ‡e actor.
700 1	‡a Faris, Sean, ‡e actor.
700 1	‡a Badgley, Penn, ‡d 1986- ‡e actor.
700 1	‡a Astin, Sean, ‡d 1971- ‡e actor.
710 2	‡a Picture Rock Entertainment, ‡e presenter.
710 2	‡a Go Films, ‡e production company.
710 2	‡a BNR Films, ‡e production company.
710 2	‡a Excel Entertainment Group, ‡e film distributor.

7.8. SYSTEM OF ORGANIZATION. This element is primarily used in archival cataloging, but may also be used to describe the organization or arrangement of other types of collections. The element is recorded in the MARC 351 field. For an example, see figure 7.100.

Figure 7.100. System of Organization

100 1	‡a Condie, Richard ‡q (Richard P.), ‡e creator.
245 10	‡a Richard Condie papers.
264 0	‡c approximately 1950-1970.
300	‡a 1.5 linear ft. ‡a (3 boxes)
300	‡a 4 linear ft. ‡a (4 cartons)
336	‡a text ‡2 rdacontent

336	‡a notated music ‡2 rdacontent
336	‡a still image ‡2 rdacontent
337	‡a unmediated ‡2 rdamedia
338	‡a volume ‡2 rdacarrier
338	‡a sheet ‡2 rdacarrier
351	‡a Arranged in 4 series: I. Richard Condie personal papers, approximately 1950-1970. 2. Richard Condie photographs, approximately 1950-1970. 3. Richard Condie press clippings, approximately 1950-1970. 4. Richard Condie choral music, approximately 1950-1970.
520 2	‡a Collection includes press clippings from national and local publications highlighting events in Condie's career, especially in relation to the Mormon Tabernacle Choir; photographs, books, and scores annotated and marked by Condie during performance or study; and other personal materials such as a typescript of an oral history given by Condie, approximately 1950-1970.
546	‡a Materials are in English.
852	‡a L. Tom Perry Special Collections, Harold B. Lee Library, Brigham Young University, ‡e Provo, Utah 84602.

7.9. DISSERTATION OR THESIS INFORMATION. This element records details about a resource that is a dissertation or thesis. Unlike previous cataloging practice, which recorded this information in a structured phrase, RDA simply calls for recording specific pieces of information as discrete sub-elements: the degree, the name of the granting institution, and the year in which the degree was granted. The dissertation or thesis information element is recorded in the 502 field.

Record the name of the degree in subfield ‡b of the 502 field. The information can be recorded directly as presented in the resource.

Record the name of the granting institution in subfield ‡c of the 502 field. Although this will be the name of a corporate body, it is not necessary to give the name in the same form as the authorized access point for the body. Simply record the name as it appears on the resource.

Record the year the degree was granted in subfield ‡d of the 502 field. Record the year as a numeral.

If the library desires, this coding can produce a traditional thesis statement in a note. The thesis information recorded in the 502 field shown in figure 7.101 could display to the public as follows:

Thesis (Ph. D.)--University of Michigan, 1971.

Figure 7.101. Dissertation or Thesis Information

100 1	‡a Maxwell, Margaret F., ‡d 1927- ‡e author.
245 10	‡a Anatomy of a book collector : ‡b William L. Clements and the Clements Library / ‡c by Margaret Nadine Finlayson Maxwell.

```
264   0   ǂc 1971.
300       ǂa viii, 420 leaves : ǂb color illustrations ; ǂc 28 cm
336       ǂa text ǂ2 rdacontent
336       ǂa still image ǂ2 rdacontent
337       ǂa unmediated ǂ2 rdamedia
338       ǂa volume ǂ2 rdacarrier
500       ǂa Typescript (photocopy).
500       ǂa Published as: Shaping a library : William L. Clements as collector. Amsterdam :
          Nico Israel, 1973.
500       ǂa Abstract (3 leaves) bound with copy.
502       ǂb Ph. D. ǂc University of Michigan ǂd 1971
504       ǂa Includes bibliographical references (leaves 412-419).
700   1   ǂi Adapted as (work): ǂa Maxwell, Margaret F., ǂd 1927- ǂt Shaping a library.
```

Dissertations and theses are often revised by the author and later published. This new resource is no longer the thesis or dissertation, and so the dissertation or thesis information element should not be recorded in the bibliographic record for the new resource. However, the new publication is clearly related to the original thesis, either as a new expression or as a new work, depending on the extent of the revision or adaptation (see discussion above under 6.27.1.5). In this case a note, recording a description of the thesis or an authorized access point for the related work or expression may be included in the bibliographic record for the new resource (see RDA 25.1.1.3 and 26.1.1.3). If a note is included, it is recorded in a 500 field (see figure 7.102).

Figure 7.102. Recording a Relationship to a Thesis

```
020       ǂa 9060726316
100   1   ǂa Maxwell, Margaret F., ǂd 1927- ǂe author.
245  10   ǂa Shaping a library : ǂb William L. Clements as collector / ǂc by Margaret Maxwell.
264   1   ǂa Amsterdam : ǂb Nico Israel, ǂc 1973.
300       ǂa 364 pages : ǂb illustrations ; ǂc 21 cm
336       ǂa text ǂ2 rdacontent
336       ǂa still image ǂ2 rdacontent
337       ǂa unmediated ǂ2 rdamedia
338       ǂa volume ǂ2 rdacarrier
500       ǂa Originally presented as the author's thesis (Ph. D.--University of Michigan) under
          the title: Anatomy of a book collector.
504       ǂa Includes bibliographical references (pages 348-356).
700   1   ǂi Adaptation of (work): ǂa Maxwell, Margaret F., ǂd 1927- ǂt Anatomy of a book
          collector.
```

NOTES

1. Full information about *MARC 21 Format for Authority Data* is available at www.loc.gov/marc/authority/ecadhome.html. Information about *MARC 21 Format for Bibliographic Data* is available at www.loc.gov/marc/bibliographic/ecbdhome.html.

2. Pre-AACR2 authority records are identified by "d" in 008 position 10 for "AACR2 compatible heading," "b" for AACR1, and "a" for earlier rules.

3. The idea of collocating translations under a uniform title goes back at least to Antonio Panizzi's 1841 *Rules for the Compilation of the Catalogue,* LI, "The works of translators are to be entered under the name of the original author . . ." and LII, "Translations are to be entered immediately after the original, generally with only the indication of the language into which the version has been made . . ." Panizzi's *Rules* are conveniently available in *Foundations of Cataloging: A Sourcebook,* ed. Michael Carpenter and Elaine Svenonius (Littleton, Colo.: Libraries Unlimited, 1985), 3–17.

4. IFLA Study Group on the Functional Requirements for Bibliographic Records, "User Tasks," ch. 6 in *Functional Requirements for Bibliographic Records Final: Report* (Munich: K. G. Sauer, 1998), 79–92. Also available at www.ifla.org/en/publications/functional-requirements-for-bibliographic-records. FRAD is an extension of FRBR; see IFLA Working Group on Functional Requirements and Numbering of Authority Records, *Functional Requirements for Authority Data: A Conceptual Model.* IFLA Series on Bibliographic Control, vol. 34 (Munich: K.G. Saur, 2009).

5. For the ALA-LC Romanization Tables, see www.loc.gov/catdir/cpso/roman.html.

6. Source information about certain elements may be recorded directly in the element's MARC field itself, in subfield ‡v, rather than in a 670 field. This technique is available for the 046 and 370–378 fields. This method has not yet found much favor in practice and is not used in this book.

7. *Descriptive Cataloging Manual* Z1 is available at www.loc.gov/catdir/cpso/z1andlcguidelines.html.

8. As of this writing, PCC policy is not entirely settled on this issue.

9. *Library of Congress Subject Headings* is available at http://id.loc.gov/authorities/subjects.html. *Art and Architecture Thesaurus* is available at www.getty.edu/research/tools/vocabularies/aat.

10. Codes for various thesauri are available at www.loc.gov/standards/sourcelist.

11. See *Descriptive Cataloging Manual* Z1 at 370--Associated Place (November 2013). Previous to Fall 2013 a different practice for recording place names in 370 was followed, so catalogers will encounter records that do not follow the procedure described here.

12. Principle 2.9, Integration, available at www.ifla.org/files/cataloguing/icp/icp_2009-en.pdf.

13. Although it was written for AACR2 cataloging, an excellent guide to understanding the principles and procedures underlying descriptions of musical works and expressions is Michelle Koth's *Uniform Titles for Music* (Lanham, MD: Scarecrow Press; Middleton, WI: Music Library Association, 2008). Much of Koth's information remains valid under RDA, as long as the reader bears in mind that AACR2 uniform titles are not equivalent to RDA access points for works and expressions (see discussion above under 5.1, Terminology).

14. *The New Grove Dictionary of Music and Musicians,* 2nd ed. (2001), *The New Grove Dictionary of Opera* (1992), and *The New Grove Dictionary of Jazz,* 2nd ed. (2002); now available online through subscription as "Oxford Music Online" (see www.oxfordmusiconline.com).

15. For a full discussion of English "accepted forms" to use, see Koth, *Uniform Titles for Music,* 43–50.

16. An excellent discussion of medium of performance in the context of AACR2 (but still relevant to RDA) is found in Koth, *Uniform Titles for Music,* 55–104.

17. *Types of Compositions for Use in Music Uniform Titles: A Manual for Use with AACR2 Chapter 25,* a useful guide to types of composition, is available at www.library.yale .edu/cataloging/music/types.htm.

SERIES AUTHORITY RECORDS

THE TERM "SERIES" IS DEFINED IN RDA AS "A GROUP OF SEPARATE resources related to one another by the fact that each resource bears, in addition to its own title proper, a collective title applying to the group as a whole. The individual resources may or may not be numbered." A series may be a serial or a multipart monograph.

If a series is issued with no predetermined conclusion, it is a serial. This type of series is called a monographic series. An example is the series called *Benjamins Translation Library*. This series publishes scholarly works, reference books, and text books related to translation and interpreting studies. The series will continue to publish indefinitely.

If a series is conceived with the intention of completion within a finite number of parts, it is a multipart monograph. Fiction series by a single author (such as C. S. Lewis's *Narnia Chronicles*) are considered multipart monographs. Such series do eventually come to an end.

In either case a series is an aggregate work that may be described just like any other work, as seen throughout this chapter.

Series have the same attributes as other works, and these may be recorded as described earlier in this chapter. These attributes include title (RDA 6.2), form (RDA 6.3), date (RDA 6.4), place of origin (RDA 6.5), other distinguishing characteristic (RDA 6.6), history of the work (RDA 6.7), and identifier (RDA 6.8). These elements have been thoroughly discussed already and that discussion will not be repeated here. Additionally, the distinction between series that are serials and series that are multipart monographs becomes important when a change of title or change of responsibility for the series occurs. This has been discussed above at 6.1.3.2.

However, series authority records have some peculiarities that will be discussed in this appendix. Examples of series descriptions in this chapter are shown in figures 7.6, 7.10, 7.11, 7.30, 7.32, 7.85, and 7.86.

In many ways an authority record for a series is exactly the same as for any other work. The authorized access point for a series (including the authorized access point for its principal creator, if any, combined with its preferred title) is recorded in a 130 field (if there is no principal creator) or in 100, 110, or 111 (if a principal creator is recorded). Variant access points are recorded in 4XX fields and relationships to other entities (usually other series) are recorded in 5XX fields. The source consulted element (RDA 5.8), including information found about the series, is recorded in 670 fields.

However, there are a number of MARC fields that are unique to series.

Series Numbering. The definition of series noted above mentions that a series may be numbered or unnumbered. Series numbering is an important element identifying the part in the series being described, and it is recorded after the authorized access point for the series for indexing purposes. It is important that numbering be recorded consistently so that the index will display instances of the series in numerical order. Therefore, the MARC series authority record has a field giving the form of numbering to be used. This is the 642 field, "series numbering example."

Instructions for recording the form of the series numbering are found in RDA 24.6 (Numbering of Part), discussed in detail in chapter 9 of this *Handbook.* The numbering of a part is to be recorded as found in the source, including any captions. However, the numbering is manipulated somewhat, not transcribed.

The number itself is to be recorded following RDA 1.8, that is, in the form preferred by the agency creating the data. For example, an agency could prefer to convert all roman numerals to arabic. The Library of Congress's preference is to record numerals in the form in which they appear (see LC-PCC PS 1.8.2 first alternative, February 2010). So a variety of practices could exist for the number itself.

As for "terms used as part of the numbering" (i.e., a caption), RDA 24.6.1.3 instructs us to abbreviate terms used as part of the numbering if the terms appear in appendixes B.7–10.

For example, the series numbering of the resource described in figure 7.30, which appears on the source as "volume II," could either be recorded "v. 2" or "v. II," depending on the agency's policy for form of the numeral. This is recorded in subfield ‡a of the 642 field in the authority record and this pattern will be followed in subfield ‡v of 8XX fields in bibliographic records. Because different libraries might have different preferences for the numeral, the MARC symbol for the library that will use the form is recorded in 642 subfield ‡5 in a shared authority file such as the LC/NACO Authority File. Following the pattern found with figure 7.30, the indexed form of the series for volume III of the same series would appear in a bibliographic record as follows:

800 1   ‡a Card, Orson Scott. ‡t Tales of Alvin Maker ; ‡v v. III.

RDA is written as though we will make this form of numbering decision every time we see a part of a series. As a practical matter, however, the decision is only made once, when the series is first described in an authority record. Thereafter catalogers should follow the pattern recorded in the 642 field, no matter how the numbering appears on the resource in hand. This ensures consistency in the index.

Note that the procedure for recording series numbering in the indexed field (8XX) is different from the procedure for *transcribing* the series statement in a 490 field, which is governed by RDA 2.3.1.7. For a fuller discussion of recording series numbering, see chapter 9 of this *Handbook* at 24.6.

Series Place and Publisher. As an aid to identifying the series, its place of publication and publisher or issuing body are recorded in a MARC 643 field: the place in subfield ‡a and the publisher in subfield ‡b. Controlled forms are not used, nor is ISBD punctuation given: simply record the information as it appears in subfields ‡a and ‡b of the 264 field of the bibliographic record. For examples, see figures 7.6, 7.10, 7.11, 7.30, 7.32, and 7.86. This field may be repeated if publication information changes during the course of a series's lifespan. See figure 7.85, which also shows a technique for detailing in subfield ‡d which publisher applies to which parts of the series.

This information could also be recorded in an RDA record in the place of origin of the work element (RDA 6.5, MARC 370) and the other distinguishing characteristic of the work element (RDA 6.6; here the other distinguishing characteristic would be the publisher, recorded as a corporate body in MARC 373). At the time of writing of this *Handbook,* however, this information will continue to be recorded in MARC 643.

Series Analysis Practice. Libraries can choose whether to analyze series (i.e., create a bibliographic record for each part in the series), not analyze them (i.e., create a serial record to represent the series as a whole, with no bibliographic records for the parts), or something in between. The library's decision on this matter is recorded in subfield ‡a of a 644 field in the series authority record. Record "f" if fully analyzing the series, "n" if not analyzing it, and "p" if analyzing part of it. The most commonly used code is "f." Details can be recorded in subfields ‡b and ‡d. Because different libraries will have differing practices, the library's MARC code is recorded in subfield ‡5. See the figures already mentioned in this appendix for examples.

Series Tracing Practice. Libraries can choose whether to trace (i.e., index) a series or not. The library's decision is recorded in subfield ‡a of a 645 field. Record "t" if tracing, or "n" if not. Details can be recorded in subfield ‡d. Because different libraries will have differing practices, the library's MARC code is recorded in subfield ‡5. See the figures already mentioned in this appendix for examples.

As a practical matter, the presence of "t" in this position means that the cataloger will transcribe the series statement in a bibliographic record in a 490 field with the first indicator coded "1," and record the authorized form of the series (which will index) in an 8XX field. The presence of "n" in this position means that the cataloger will transcribe the series statement in a bibliographic record in a 490 field with the first indicator coded "0," with no corresponding 8XX field. This means that the series will not index.

Series Classification Practice. Libraries have a number of choices when it comes to classification of individual parts of a series. They can keep the entire series together; they can keep the series within another, related series; or they can classify individual volumes separately in a call number that is appropriate to its subject matter. Decisions about classification are recorded in subfield ‡a of a 646 field. Record "s" if classifying individual parts in their own separate numbers, record "c" if classifying all volumes of a series together in the same number, or record "m" if classifying a series within another series. Details can be recorded in subfield ‡d. Because different libraries will have differing practices, the library's MARC code is recorded in subfield ‡5. See the figures already mentioned in this appendix for examples.

If the library classifies all volumes of a series together, the series authority record should also record the call number to be used. This information is recorded in an 050 field. For an example, see figure 7.10, which shows that all parts of the series will be classified in SD 110 .A33 plus the volume number.

Change in Series Title. As discussed above under 6.1.3, there are a number of changes that can occur with a work that develops over time (such as a series), and some of these changes affect how the series is treated. Of particular importance is a change in the title of the series. If a series is a serial and a major change in the title occurs, a new series is considered to have been created and a new series authority record will be created. If the series is a multipart monograph (e.g., a multipart work by a single author such as Tolkien's *Lord of the Rings*) and a title change occurs, a new series is *not* considered to have been created. Instead, the title change is noted in the authority record and may be given as a variant title for the series if considered important for identification or access. For full details, see 6.1.3, above; see also the discussion in chapter 2 of this *Handbook* at 1.6.2.3.

Series: Expression or Work? A series is an aggregate work, but as with any other work a series can exist in multiple expressions. For example, all the parts of the series might be translated into another language, or might be given in another format (e.g., a series originally presented as text might be later presented as an audiobook). For information about dealing with expressions, see chapter 8 of this *Handbook*.

DESCRIBING EXPRESSIONS

Instructions for recording the attributes of the *expression* entity are found in RDA chapters 5, 6, and 7.

MARC CODING

HE *EXPRESSION* ENTITY IS CURRENTLY DESCRIBED in library catalogs in the MARC 21 authority and bibliographic formats.[1] RDA authority records for expressions are identified by the value "z" in the 008 field position 10 (labeled "Rules" in the OCLC fixed field display) and the presence of "‡e rda" in the 040 field (see figure 8.1a). In contrast, an AACR2 authority record may be recognized by the presence of value "c" in 008 position 10 and no special coding in 040 (see figure 8.1b).[2] To conserve space, RDA coding is assumed in the figures in this chapter and is not explicitly shown. Other MARC coding issues will be discussed as they occur later in the chapter.

Figure 8.1a. RDA Coding (OCLC Style)

Rec stat	c	Entered	20021021		Replaced	20111026033134.0	
Type	z	Upd status	a	Enc lvl	n	Source	c
Roman		Ref status	a	Mod rec		Name use	a
Govt agn		Auth status	a	Subj	a	Subj use	a
Series	n	Auth/ref	a	Geo subd	n	Ser use	b
Ser num	n	Name	n	Subdiv tp	n	**Rules**	**z**

```
010      ‡a nr2002038978
040      ‡a UPB ‡b eng ‡e rda ‡c UPB ‡d UPB
046      ‡k 2001
100 1    ‡a Card, Orson Scott. ‡t Ender's shadow. ‡l French
336      ‡a text ‡2 rdacontent
377      ‡a fre
400 1    ‡a Card, Orson Scott. ‡t Stratégie de l'ombre
500 1    ‡i Translator: ‡a Mousnier-Lompré, Arnaud ‡w r
670      ‡a La stratégie de l'ombre, 2001: ‡b title page (traduit de l'Anglais par Arnaud
         Mousnier-Lompré)
```

Figure 8.1a. RDA Coding (LC Style)

```
008      021021n| azannaabn |a aaa c
010      ‡a nr2002038978
040      ‡a UPB ‡b eng ‡e rda ‡c UPB ‡d UPB
046      ‡k 2001
100 1    ‡a Card, Orson Scott. ‡t Ender's shadow. ‡l French
336      ‡a text ‡2 rdacontent
377      ‡a fre
400 1    ‡a Card, Orson Scott. ‡t Stratégie de l'ombre
500 1    ‡w r ‡i Translator: ‡a Mousnier-Lompré, Arnaud
670      ‡a La stratégie de l'ombre, 2001
```

Figure 8.1b. AACR2 Coding (OCLC Style)

Rec stat	c	Entered		20021021		Replaced 20111026033134.0	
Type	z	Upd status	a	Enc lvl	n	Source	c
Roman		Ref status	a	Mod rec		Name use	a
Govt agn		Auth status	a	Subj	a	Subj use	a
Series	n	Auth/ref	a	Geo subd	n	Ser use	b
Ser num	n	Name	n	Subdiv tp	n	**Rules**	**c**

```
010      ‡a nr2002038978
040      ‡a UPB ‡b eng ‡c UPB ‡d UPB
100 1    ‡a Card, Orson Scott. ‡t Ender's shadow. ‡l French
400 1    ‡a Card, Orson Scott. ‡t Stratégie de l'ombre
670      ‡a La stratégie de l'ombre, 2001
```

Figure 8.1b. AACR2 Coding (LC Style)

008	021021n| a̲cannaabn |a aaa c
010	‡a nr2002038978
040	‡a UPB ‡b eng ‡c UPB ‡d UPB
100 1	‡a Card, Orson Scott. ‡t Ender's shadow. ‡l French
400 1	‡a Card, Orson Scott. ‡t Stratégie de l'ombre
670	‡a La stratégie de l'ombre, 2001

5.1. TERMINOLOGY. *Expression* is defined in RDA as "the intellectual or artistic realization of a work in the form of alpha-numeric, musical or choreographic notation, sound, image, object, movement, etc., or any combination of such forms," with the additional information that the term may used to refer to aggregate expressions (including expressions of series or serials) as well as to parts of expressions. This definition has been discussed more fully in the discussion of RDA and FRBR in chapter 1 of this *Handbook*.

RDA 5.1.4 defines authorized access point as "the standardized access point representing an entity," and then explains that the authorized access point representing a work or expression is constructed by combining (in this order): a) the authorized access point representing a person, family, or corporate body responsible for the work, if appropriate; b) the preferred title for the work; c) other elements as instructed at 6.27–6.31.

This sounds deceptively like the AACR2 concept of a uniform title heading. It is important to understand that AACR2 uniform titles are not the same as RDA authorized access points for works or expressions, as was fully discussed in chapter 7 under 5.1.

5.3. CORE ELEMENTS. As explained in greater detail in chapter 1, RDA identifies certain elements as "core" throughout the code. The core elements were chosen because they were attributes and relationships thought to support FRBR and FRAD user tasks.[3] RDA entity descriptions should contain, at a minimum, all core elements that are applicable and readily ascertainable as well as any other elements that might be required to differentiate one entity from another (see RDA 0.6.1). Inclusion of other elements is not required, and is at the discretion of the cataloger or cataloging agency (such as an individual library, or cooperative organizations such as the Program for Cooperative Cataloging [PCC]).

Agencies may develop requirements that go beyond RDA core elements. The Library of Congress (LC) and PCC for example, have designated certain elements that are not core in RDA to be core for their own catalogers. Information about LC decisions are found in Library of Congress-Program for Cooperative Cataloging Policy Statements (LC-PCC PSs), found under the Resources tab of the RDA Toolkit.

Core elements for all entities and relationships are given in RDA 0.6. They are also given separately in the chapter(s) devoted to each entity or relationship. Core elements for the expression entity are found in RDA 0.6.3 and again in RDA 5.3. This information is also listed with each element's instruction. For example, RDA 6.9, content type, which is a core element for expressions, reads as follows:

> **6.9 Content Type**
> **CORE ELEMENT**
> **6.9.1. Basic Instructions on Recording Content Type**
> **6.9.1.1 Scope**
> . . .

Conversely, 7.15, illustrative content, which is not a core element, reads as follows:

> **7.15 Illustrative Content**
> **7.15.1 Basic Instructions on Recording Illustrative Content**
> **7.15.1.1 Scope**
> . . .

The core elements for the expression entity are:

> Identifier for the expression
> Content type
> Language of expression

Note that "title" is not listed as a core element for the expression. This is because RDA does not recognize title as an attribute of the expression entity, even though it is one of the attributes of expression in FRBR (see FRBR 4.3, 2009 edition).

In addition to the three elements that are always core for expression, the following are core if needed to differentiate between expressions of a work whose descriptions would otherwise be identical:

> Date of expression
> Other distinguishing characteristic of the expression

For expressions of cartographic works, the following are core in all cases if applicable and readily ascertainable:

Horizontal scale of cartographic content
Vertical scale of cartographic content

Note that core designation means that the element must be recorded (if applicable and readily ascertainable) in the description for the expression. It does *not* mean that it must be included as part of the authorized access point for the expression. For example, content type (RDA 6.9) is a core element. This means that the content type element must be recorded in the description. It does not mean that RDA requires the content type to be part of the access point, although in certain cases it may be.

For the sake of illustration, the figures in this book will usually include many elements beyond the core elements. See figure 8.2a for an example of a description of an expression that contains only core elements (marked in bold); figure 8.2b is an example of a description of the same expression containing elements beyond core. (Note that the personal name and title in the 100 field are not elements of the expression, but constitute the relationship link between the expression and its work.) It is evident that the RDA core for the description of an expression can be fairly minimal. Cataloging agencies will undoubtedly want their catalogers to include more elements, such as, at least, variant titles and sources consulted (fields 430 and 670 in figure 8.2b). In making decisions about inclusion of non-core elements in entity descriptions agencies need to think about possible future uses of the data. Many non-core elements such as accessibility content (e.g., presence of closed captioning or subtitles) or color content (color versus black and white) may be useful as limiters to searches or as initial searches for records (e.g., a person who wants to find black-and-white films with subtitles in French), but only if agencies apply them consistently in their databases.

Figure 8.2a. Core Elements

010	‡a n 83734335
100 1	‡a Lewis, C. S. ‡q (Clive Staples), ‡d 1898-1963. ‡t Chronicles of Narnia. ‡h **Spoken word** ‡s (**Caedmon (Firm)**)
336	‡a **spoken word** ‡2 rdacontent
373	‡a **Caedmon (Firm)** ‡2 naf
377	‡a **eng**

Figure 8.2b. Elements beyond Core

010	‡a n 83734335
046	‡k 1977 ‡l 1989
100 1	‡a Lewis, C. S. ‡q (Clive Staples), ‡d 1898-1963. ‡t Chronicles of Narnia. ‡h **Spoken word** ‡s (**Caedmon (Firm)**)

336	‡a **spoken word** ‡2 rdacontent
373	‡a **Caedmon (Firm)** ‡2 naf
377	‡a **eng**
430	0 ‡a Chronicles of Narnia. ‡h Spoken word ‡s (Caedmon (Firm))
500	1 ‡w r ‡i Voice actor: ‡a York, Michael, ‡d 1942-
642	‡a bk. 6 ‡5 UPB
643	‡a New York, New York ‡b Caedmon
644	‡a f ‡5 UPB
645	‡a t ‡5 UPB
645	‡a s ‡5 UPB
670	‡a The last battle, 1977 ‡b (audiobook abridged by Walter Hooper, read by Michael York)
670	‡a OCLC, 10 January 2010 ‡b (The chronicles of Narnia, audiobook series produced between 1977 and 1989 by Caedman, read by various actors including Michael York, Anthony Quayle, Claire Bloom, Ian Richardson)

5.7. STATUS OF IDENTIFICATION. RDA instructs us to record the level of authentication of the data identifying the entity. The possible levels are "fully established," "provisional," and "preliminary." All authorized access points for expressions begin with the authorized access point for a work. The status of identification element for an expression description depending on that work should not be at a higher level than that of the description of the work. That is, if the authorized access point for the work was established in a provisional description, any expression descriptions based on that access point should also be coded as provisional. For a full discussion of this element, see chapter 3 of this *Handbook* under 8.10.

5.8. SOURCE CONSULTED. Just as the author of a scholarly paper justifies his or her assertions by citing sources, so the creator of an RDA description for an expression in an authority record must justify access points by citing where the information came from. In MARC authority work, this is done using the 670 field.[4] The source consulted element is not core in RDA, but at least one instance, that of the resource in hand that generated the need for a new authorized access point, is required in LC/NACO practice. Examples of 670 fields are found in figures throughout this chapter. For a full discussion of LC/NACO practice in the source consulted element, see chapter 3 of this *Handbook* under 8.12.

5.9. CATALOGUER'S NOTE. The cataloguer's note element contains information about the expression represented by the authorized access point that might be helpful to persons using the authority record. The cataloguer's note element is not core in RDA, but it is core for the Library of Congress in certain situations (see *Descriptive Cataloging*

Manual Z1 at 667).[5] The most common use of the cataloguer's note element in current LC/NACO cataloging is likely for descriptions of expressions is the "Non-Latin script reference not evaluated" note, recorded in the 667 MARC authority field. A variant title in a non-Latin script may be recorded in the record for an expression, but because NACO policies have not yet been fully developed for this catalogers including a reference that has non-Latin script should include this note (see figure 8.3).

Figure 8.3. Cataloguer's Note

046	ǂk 2007
100 1	ǂa Rowling, J. K. ǂt Harry Potter and the prisoner of Azkaban. ǂl Arabic
336	ǂa text ǂ2 rdacontent
377	ǂa ara
400 1	ǂa Rowling, J. K. ǂt Hārī Būtir wa-sajīn Azkābān
400 1	ǂa Rowling, J. K. ǂt هاري بوتر وسجين ازكابان
500 1	ǂw r ǂi Translator: ǂa Muḥammad, Aḥmad Ḥasan
667	ǂa Non-Latin script reference not evaluated.
670	ǂa Hārī Būtir wa-sajīn Azkābān, 2007: ǂb t.p. (هاري بوتر وسجين ازكابان)

STRUCTURE OF CHAPTERS 6–7. RDA chapter 6, "Identifying Works and Expressions," and chapter 7, "Describing Content," follow much the same structure as most of the other chapters in the "Recording Attributes" parts of RDA (RDA sections 1 through 4). Chapter 6 begins with a section on the purpose and scope of the chapter (RDA 6.0) and then proceeds to general guidelines on identifying expressions, including sources that may be consulted for information about expressions (RDA 6.1.1). After a section on work-related attributes, chapter 6 then treats, one by one, the various elements and sub-elements of the expression entity that are recognized by RDA, giving instructions on where to get information about the element or sub-element, and how to record that information. This section, with the preceding section on works, is the heart of chapter 6, and occupies the bulk of it (RDA 6.2–6.26). Chapter 7 is a supplementary chapter to chapter 6, giving details about elements of expression entity descriptions related to content. Returning to chapter 6, the chapter ends with a final section on constructing access points for expressions (RDA 6.27–6.31). It is crucial to understand this structure. Catalogers used to AACR2 chapter 25, which is chiefly about creating an access point (heading) for a uniform title, may be misled into thinking that the guidelines about recording elements, and particularly wording about core elements, constitute instructions about how to construct the access point for the expression, when in fact the central section of chapter 6 and all of chapter 7 give instructions for recording the *information* in the description for the expression. In the entity-relationship or linked-data database structure RDA anticipates, we will be creating descriptions of expressions that exist independently from, but are linked to, other entities such as persons or works that they may have a relationship to. In such an environment bibliographic records with formal access points might not exist, but the elements contained in the description of the expression will be essential.

One point to remember when looking at chapters 6 and 7 is that in our current MARC database structure, which includes bibliographic, authority, and holding records, elements treated in RDA chapter 6 are generally recorded in the MARC authority format, and elements treated in RDA chapter 7 are generally recorded in the MARC bibliographic format. This *Handbook* treats these elements in the same order as they appear in RDA, and therefore this chapter will continue with a section about description of the expression entity in MARC authority records, and will conclude with a section about description of the expression entity in MARC bibliographic records.

RDA chapters 6 and 7 include information about both works and expressions. For simplicity, this *Handbook* will treat work and expression separately. This chapter will only cover RDA elements related to the expression entity; chapter 7 of this *Handbook* has covered elements related to the work, which should be used in tandem with this chapter. An understanding of how to describe works is assumed in this chapter.

6.9. CONTENT TYPE. The first element in RDA chapter 6 that pertains to the expression is content type, defined as "a categorization reflecting the fundamental form of communication in which the content is expressed and the human sense through which it is intended to be perceived." RDA's content type element corresponds to the FRBR "form of expression" attribute, defined there as "the means by which the work is realized (e.g., through alphanumeric notation, musical notation, spoken word, musical sound, cartographic image, photographic image, sculpture, dance, mime, etc.)."

Content type is a core element and is recorded in subfield ‡a of the MARC 336 field, in both the authority and bibliographic formats. The field should also include "‡2 rdacontent," showing the source of the term. Terms are drawn from a controlled vocabulary, a short list found in RDA 6.9.1.3. The cataloger may not record terms not found in the list. If no suitable term is available to describe the expression, record "other." For examples, see figures 8.2 and 8.3.

If the expression has more than one content type, all may be recorded either by repeating subfield ‡a in the 336 field or by repeating the entire field. Alternately the content type describing the predominant or most substantial part of the resource can be recorded, ignoring the others. Multiple content types are probably most frequently encountered in bibliographic records, particularly because resources described in bibliographic records may comprise more than one work or expression. A common example is an illustrated text. For example, *The Homer Encyclopedia* consists principally of text but also has many illustrations, including maps. This can all be recorded in the content type element (see figure 8.4).

Figure 8.4. Content Type (Bibliographic Record)

020	‡a 9781405177689
041 0	‡a eng ‡a grc
245 04	‡a The Homer encyclopedia / ‡c edited by Margalit Finkelberg.
264 1	‡a Chichester, West Sussex ; ‡a Malden, MA : ‡b Wiley-Blackwell, ‡c 2011.
300	‡a 3 volumes (I, 1072 pages) : ‡b illustrations, maps ; ‡c 26 cm
336	‡a text ‡2 rdacontent
336	‡a still image ‡2 rdacontent
336	‡a cartographic image ‡2 rdacontent
337	‡a unmediated ‡2 rdamedia
338	‡a volume ‡2 rdacarrier
546	‡a Chiefly in English, with some Greek.
504	‡a Includes bibliographical references and index.
700 1	‡a Finkelberg, Margalit, ‡e editor of compilation.

Content type is core, and so must always be recorded. Sometimes it is also used as a qualifier to distinguish between expressions with otherwise identical authorized access points. For an example, see subfield ‡h of the 100 field of figure 8.2.[6]

6.10. DATE OF EXPRESSION. Date of expression is core if needed to differentiate one expression from another, but may be recorded whether or not it is necessary. The element is recorded in the MARC authority 046 field; single dates are recorded in subfield ‡k. If a span of dates must be recorded, the closing date is recorded in subfield ‡l. For full information about coding dates in the 046 field, see chapter 3 of this *Handbook* under 9.3 (date associated with the person). For an example of the date of expression element, see figure 8.3.

If the date of expression is needed to differentiate one expression from another it may be recorded as part of the access point for the expression, in subfield ‡f. For example, one way to distinguish between various expressions of an author's complete works is to include the date of the expression in the access point. Anton Chekhov is an example of an author whose complete works have been published many times in different expressions (see figure 8.5).

Figure 8.5. Date of Expression Used to Distinguish

046	‡k 2010
100 1	‡a Chekhov, Anton Pavlovich, ‡d 1860-1904. ‡t Works. ‡f 2010
336	‡a text ‡2 rdacontent
377	‡a rus

400 1   ‡a Chekhov, Anton Pavlovich, ‡d 1860-1904. ‡t Sobranie sochineniĭ v pi͡atnadt͡sati tomakh

400 1   ‡a Chekhov, Anton Pavlovich, ‡d 1860-1904. ‡t Собрание сочинений в пятнадцати томах

667   ‡a Non-Latin script reference not evaluated.

670   ‡a Sobranie sochineniĭ v pi͡atnadt͡sati tomakh, 2010: ‡b (Собрание сочинений в пятнадцати томах)

The date of expression element should be carefully compared with the date of work element (RDA 6.4). The date of work element is also recorded in the 046 field, but when used to distinguish between otherwise identical authorized access points for works it is usually recorded in a parenthetical qualifier immediately following the preferred title with no special subfield coding. For an example, see figure 7.1.

6.11. LANGUAGE OF EXPRESSION. Language of expression is a core element. In authority records the element is recorded in subfield ‡a of the MARC 377 field; language of expression may also be recorded as part of the authorized access point for the expression, in subfield ‡l. When recording the element in field 377, use the code for the language(s) from the MARC Code List for Languages.[7] When recording the element as part of the authorized access point, catalogers following LC practice (including contributors to the LC/NACO Authority File) will use the spelled-out form of the name of the language in the MARC Code List for Languages (see LC-PCC PS 6.11.1.3, January 2013). See figures 8.2 and 8.5 for examples of the element recorded in the 377 field. For examples of the element also recorded as part of the authorized access point, see figures 8.1 and 8.3.

The language of expression element may also be recorded in bibliographic records using the MARC language code in the 008 field positions 35–37 (the fixed field labeled "Lang" in OCLC) and the MARC 041 fields. For example, *The Homer Encyclopedia* is chiefly in English, but also contains Greek (see figure 8.4). This is an example of an expression involving more than one language (RDA 6.11.1.4).

6.12. OTHER DISTINGUISHING CHARACTERISTIC OF THE EXPRESSION. This element may be used to distinguish one expression from another if content type, date, or language are not enough to distinguish, or another element is more appropriate. The element is usually recorded in the MARC authorities 381 field, in subfield ‡a. However, if the "other distinguishing characteristic" is a corporate body, the information is recorded instead in the 373 field. For example, because there are many spoken word expressions of *The Chronicles of Narnia*, content type alone is not enough to distinguish them from one another. The name of the publisher was chosen as an appropriate "other distinguishing characteristic" of this expression (see figure 8.2).

6.13. IDENTIFIER FOR THE EXPRESSION. An identifier for the expression is a character string uniquely associated with the expression (or the record representing the expression). This is a core (i.e., required) element. In the LC/NACO Authority File the identifier is the Library of Congress Control Number, recorded in the 010 field. In most cases the cataloger does not need to record information in this element, as it is automatically generated by the database system. For this reason, the identifier for the work element has not been included in most figures in this book; as examples, the element is included with figures 8.1 and 8.2.

ELEMENTS OF MUSICAL EXPRESSIONS

6.18. OTHER DISTINGUISHING CHARACTERISTIC OF THE EXPRESSION OF A MUSICAL WORK. Any of the general elements of expressions described above can be recorded for expressions of a musical works, but RDA also lists one element specific to expressions of musical works because it specifies language to be used in certain situations. The other distinguishing characteristic of the expression of a musical work element is recorded in subfield ‡a the MARC authority 381 field and may also appear in subfield ‡o of the authorized access point for the expression.

6.18.1.4. ARRANGEMENTS, TRANSCRIPTIONS, ETC. This guideline requires the cataloger to distinguish between "classical" and "popular" music, assuming that such a distinction can be made. It deals with an original work that has been changed, either by rewriting for another medium of performance or by simplification, whether by the original composer or by another. If the change is not significant enough to create a new work (see discussion in chapter 7 at 6.27.1.5) the result is a new expression of the original work, and under RDA principles should be distinguished from the original expression of the work. RDA specifies that the new expression is to be distinguished from the original by recording the word "arranged" in the description of the expression. For an example, see figure 8.6; note that the general other distinguishing characteristic of the expression element from 6.12 has also been recorded ("McDonald") to distinguish this arrangement from others of the same work.

Figure 8.6. Arrangement of a Musical Work

046	‡k 2010
100 1	‡a Wade, John Francis, ‡d 1711 or 12-1786. ‡t Adeste fideles; ‡o arranged ‡s (McDonald)
336	‡a notated music ‡2 rdacontent
377	‡a lat
381	‡a arranged

```
381      ‡a McDonald
500 1    ‡w r ‡i Arranger of music: ‡a McDonald, Marshall
670      ‡a Christmas classics for solo piano, 2010 ‡b (arranged by Marshall McDonald)
```

In the case of "popular" music, "arranged" is recorded only if an instrumental work has been arranged for voices or if a vocal work has been arranged for instruments.

6.18.1.6. VOCAL AND CHORUS SCORES. According to the RDA glossary, a vocal score is "a score showing all vocal parts, with the instrumental accompaniment either arranged for keyboard(s) or other chordal instrument(s) or omitted." A chorus score is

> a score of a work for solo voices and chorus showing only the parts for chorus, at least in those portions of the work in which the chorus sings, with the instrumental accompaniment either arranged for keyboard(s) or other chordal instrument(s) or omitted.

The distinction is that a vocal score will show, in addition to the chorus parts of a work, any solo vocal parts as well.

Record "Vocal score(s)" or "Chorus score(s)" in the MARC 381 field. This element may also appear in the authorized access point for the expression in subfield ‡s (see figure 8.7).

Figure 8.7. Vocal Score

```
046      ‡k 2010
100 1    ‡a Vaughan Williams, Ralph, ‡d 1872-1958. ‡t Wasps (Incidental music). ‡s Vocal
         score
336      ‡a notated music ‡2 rdacontent
377      ‡a eng
381      ‡a Vocal score
670      ‡a The wasps : performing edition for narrator, male voices and orchestra, 1909
```

ELEMENTS OF RELIGIOUS EXPRESSIONS

Only two elements relating to religious expression are mentioned in RDA, date and "other distinguishing characteristic," but other elements may be recorded in the description of an expression of a religious work, notably the content type, language, and identifier elements, which are core (see discussion above under 6.9, 6.11, and 6.13). Because there are no special instructions about these elements for religious expressions, the information about them is not repeated at 6.24–6.25.

6.24. DATE OF EXPRESSION OF A RELIGIOUS WORK. The date of the expression of a religious work is core if needed to differentiate one expression of the Bible from another, and may also be used to differentiate expressions of other religious works if needed. The element is defined as "the earliest date associated with an expression of a religious work." This will usually be the date of the earliest manifestation embodying that expression. The element is recorded in the MARC authority 046 field subfield ‡k.

6.24.1.4. THE BIBLE AND PARTS OF THE BIBLE. The language in this guideline, taken almost verbatim from AACR2 28.18A13, is problematic. AACR2 organized the Bible by version, and then by date of publication. This may have been a sensible arrangement, but it was not based on FRBR principles as RDA purports to be.

In RDA, as in AACR2, we are instructed to record "the year of publication" of the resource. In many (if not most) cases, however, the year of publication of a given Bible will not be the date of the expression, because most versions of the Bible have been reprinted many times after the initial publication of the version. The "year of publication" of the Bible in hand will be the date of its manifestation, but that date is not necessarily the date of its expression.

For example, the English expression of the Bible called "The New Revised Standard Version" was first published in 1989. The text of this popular version has been reprinted many times since then, including a 2011 publication by Hendrickson Publishers, a 2010 publication by Oxford University Press, a 2009 publication by Abingdon Press, and numerous others. All these manifestations contain the same text, and so all embody the same expression of the Bible. The date of this expression is 1989, not 2011, 2010, 2009, or another date of publication (see figure 8.8).

Figure 8.8.
Date of Expression of a Religious Work (Authority Record for the Expression)

046		‡k 1989
130	0	‡a Bible. ‡l English. ‡s New Revised Standard. ‡f 1989
337		‡a text ‡2 rdacontent
377		‡a eng
381		‡a New Revised Standard
430	0	‡a New Revised Standard Version Bible
430	0	‡a Bible. ‡l English. ‡s NRSV
530	0	‡w r ‡i Revision of: ‡a Bible. ‡l English. ‡s Revised Standard Version. ‡f 1946
670		‡a The New Revised Standard Version Bible with Apocrypha, pocket edition, 2006
670		‡a National Council of Churches, via WWW, 3 August 2011 ‡b (New Revised Standard Version; NRSV; first appeared in 1989; English translation sponsored by the National Council of Churches based on the Revised Standard Version and intended to be widely ecumenical; translated by a committee of 30 Protestant, Catholic, and Orthodox scholars)

The alternative guideline, which the Library of Congress will not apply (see LC-PCC PS 6.24.1.4, February 2010), is even more problematic. A facsimile reproduction does not contain two expressions of a work, but only one, and the date of the expression is normally the date of the original publication. Regarding the example given in the RDA 6.24.1.4 alternative, the 1534 publication of Luther's translation of the Bible and the 2002 facsimile reprint are two manifestations of the same German expression of the Bible, with 1534 as the date of the expression.

6.25. OTHER DISTINGUISHING CHARACTERISTIC OF THE EXPRESSION OF A RELIGIOUS WORK. This element is core if needed to distinguish one expression of a religious work from another. The element is recorded in subfield ‡a of MARC authority field 381.

6.25.1.4. THE BIBLE AND PARTS OF THE BIBLE. For most expressions of religious works, "other distinguishing characteristic" is the same as for any other work as described above under 6.12. The other distinguishing characteristic element for the Bible, however, is specified in RDA 6.25.1.4 as "the name of the version." In addition to recording this element in the 381 field, it may also appear as part of the authorized access point for the expression, in subfield ‡s.

We are instructed to "record a brief form" of the name of the version. In practice, this usually means the word "Version" is dropped from the name. The following list gives some of the commonly used English versions (see figure 8.8 for an example):

Rheims—Rheims New Testament (1582)
Douai—Douai Old Testament (1609-1610) with the Rheims New Testament
Authorized—King James Version (1611)
Revised—Revised Version (New Testament 1881, Old Testament 1885)
American Standard—American Standard Version (1901)
Revised Standard—Revised Standard Version (New Testament 1946, Old Testament 1962, Apocrypha 1957)
New Revised Standard—New Revised Standard Version (1989)
New English—New English Bible (New Testament 1961, Old Testament 1966)
Today's English—Today's English Version (1966)

Some versions are identified by the name of the translator. Use the translator's name in place of the name of the version if the expression is identified is by the translator (see figure 8.9). Some names commonly used as the "other distinguishing characteristic of the expression" of the Bible are:

Kleist-Lilly—New Testament by James A. Kleist and Joseph Lilly (1956)
Knox—translation by Ronald Knox (1955)
Moffatt—translation by James Moffatt (1926)

Montgomery—New Testament translation by Helen Barrett Montgomery (1924)

Lamsa—translation by George M. Lamsa (1933)

Phillips—New Testament translation by J. B. Phillips (1958)

Schonfield—New Testament translation by Hugh Schonfield (1955)

Smith-Goodspeed—Old Testament translation by J. M. Powis Smith; New Testament translation by Edgar Goodspeed

Figure 8.9. Version of the Bible

046		‡k 1540
130	0	‡a Bible. ‡p Psalms. ‡l English. ‡s Coverdale. ‡f 1540
337		‡a text ‡2 rdacontent
377		‡a eng
381		‡a Coverdale
430	0	‡a Psalter or boke of Psalmes
430	0	‡a Coverdale Psalter
500	1	‡w r ‡i Translator: ‡a Coverdale, Miles, ‡d 1488-1568
670		‡a The Psalter or boke of Psalmes, 1540
670		‡a The Oxford guide to The book of common prayer, 2006: ‡b page 146 (Coverdale Psalter; became part of The book of common prayer)

For further information about versions of the English Bible, see a Bible encyclopedia or dictionary, such as *The HarperCollins Bible Dictionary.*[8]

Another term can be substituted for the name of the version when the text is the original language, when the version is unknown, when it has been altered, when it cannot be identified by translator's name, or when more than two versions are involved. The use of the surname of the person who has altered the text as an alternative to use of name of version is analogous to using the name of a translator in place of version (see figure 8.10).

Figure 8.10. Version of the Bible

046		‡k 1867
130	0	‡a Bible. ‡l English. ‡s Smith. ‡f 1867
337		‡a text ‡2 rdacontent
377		‡a eng
381		‡a Smith
500	1	‡w r ‡i Editor: ‡a Smith, Joseph, ‡c Jr., ‡d 1805-1844
670		‡a The Holy Scriptures, translated and corrected by the spirit of revelation by Joseph Smith, Jr., the seer, 1867

ACCESS POINTS FOR EXPRESSIONS OF WORKS

One of the objectives governing RDA is that the data should enable the user to find all resources associated with a particular expression (RDA 0.4.2.1). In our current MARC database environment this is done through the formulation and use of authorized access points representing entities such as expressions, corresponding to what previous cataloging practice called "headings." These access points are embedded in bibliographic records for resources associated with the expression and serve as links between a particular bibliographic record and all other bibliographic records that contain the identical access point. In many systems, the access point in the bibliographic record is also linked to its corresponding authority record.

The user of the database finds all resources associated with a particular expression by learning what the authorized access point is for that expression and then querying the database for records containing instances of the authorized access point. Because the RDA authorized access point for an expression is based on the authorized access point for the work (see 6.27.3), the expression access point collocates with other expressions of the same work, which allows the user of the database to navigate more easily and find resources that he or she might not otherwise have known about.

In order for this to function properly, the authorized access point must be consistent (i.e., always used in the same form) and unique to the expression (i.e., more than one expression should not share the same access point). The data describing an expression should be sufficient to differentiate that expression from other entities with similar characteristics (RDA 0.4.3.1).

An RDA authorized access point for an expression is somewhat different from a uniform title access point created under the previous cataloging code, AACR2. AACR2's organizing principle was not based on the FRBR work and expression entities, so an AACR2 uniform title access point represents something different from an RDA authorized access point for a work or an expression. For example, a typical pattern for a translation in AACR2 was "Author. Title. Language," such as "Homer. Iliad. French." *The Iliad* has been translated into French many times, and each translation is a different expression of the original work. FRBR principles, which RDA follows, indicate that these expressions should be differentiated from each other. In the context of expression descriptions (also known as authority records in the MARC environment), this means that each expression would have its own description. Because authorized access points serve as links to specific expression descriptions, this means that, at least in the current MARC database structure, they need to be distinct from one another as well. RDA accomplishes this by adding qualifying data to access points if necessary to distinguish one expression from another.

In its initial implementation of RDA, the Library of Congress, perhaps for reasons of economy, has decided in most cases not to distinguish the authorized access point of one expression of a work within a given language from another (see LC-PCC PS

6.27.3, July 2012), instead using the same authorized access point to represent all the expressions in the language. This means their catalogers will not, for example, differentiate the authorized access point for one French translation of Shakespeare's *Hamlet* from that of other translations. Similarly, LC catalogers will not differentiate the authorized access point of one arrangement of a musical work from that of another arrangement, although these are clearly different expressions of the musical work.

This policy has the effect of creating a category of undifferentiated expression descriptions, a category that does not exist in RDA except for descriptions of persons (see RDA 8.11). RDA does not recognize undifferentiated expressions for good reason: it is looking forward to a database structure based on FRBR principles where expressions have separate descriptions and thus separate identifying elements (including authorized access points).

This policy is LC practice, which others are not required to follow; in fact, the same policy statement instructs LC catalogers to use differentiated access points for expressions if other catalogers have created an authority record for them in the LC/NACO Authority File. This *Handbook* will follow RDA as written by constructing unique authorized access points for expressions.

6.27.3. AUTHORIZED ACCESS POINT REPRESENTING AN EXPRESSION. The authorized access point for an expression begins with the authorized access point for a work constructed according to RDA 6.27.1 and 6.27.2 (see chapter 7 of this *Handbook* for details). The cataloger is then instructed to add one or more elements chosen from among elements which may have already been recorded in the description under preceding RDA guidelines. These are:

- The content type (see RDA. 6.9). This element is core and should always be present in the description of an expression. If chosen as part of the authorized access point, content type should be recorded there exactly as recorded as an element in the 336 field, except it will be capitalized if present in the authorized access point. The term is coded in subfield ‡h and is generally recorded following a period. For an example, see figure 8.2.
- The date of the expression (see RDA 6.10). If included in the authorized access point, date should be recorded only as a year or years, even though more detail might have been recorded in the 046 field. The date of the expression is coded following a period in subfield ‡f of the authorized access point. For an example, see figure 8.5.
- The language of the expression (see RDA 6.11). If included in the authorized access point, the name of the language is spelled out in the preferred language of the cataloging agency, English for participants in the Program for Cooperative Cataloging (e.g., "French," not "Français"). This form will be different

from that of the element as recorded in the 377 field, which is a code. The language of the expression is added to the access point following a period and subfield ‡l (see figures 8.1 and 8.3).

- A term indicating another distinguishing characteristic of the expression (see RDA 6.12). If such a term is included in the authorized access point, it is recorded there exactly as it was recorded as an element in the 381 or 373 field of the MARC authority record. This addition is recorded at the end of the authorized access point in parentheses, in subfield ‡s ("version") (see figure 8.2).

The elements given in 6.27.3 are not listed in priority order. The cataloger should choose whichever one best distinguishes between the conflicting access points, and whichever one would best identify the expression to the user of the database, who may only see the authorized access point as part of an index list, out of context from the record(s) it is attached to. As many elements may be included in the authorized access point for the expression as needed to distinguish it from that of another expression.

If a work exists only in its original expression, that is, it has never been translated, revised, reissued in a different format, etc., there is no need to differentiate this expression from any other expression. In this case, the authorized access point for the work may also be used as the authorized access point for its only expression—no addition would be "applicable." However, as soon as another expression appears this is no longer valid, and the access points need to be differentiated.

In the case of translations, the language element is customarily the first addition made to the authorized access point for an expression. If the work has been translated into a given language only once, that addition will be all that is necessary to accurately identify the expression (see figure 8.3). However, if more than one expression exists in the same language, another addition will need to be made. Because the translator is normally the major distinguishing characteristic between expressions in a single language, this *Handbook* recommends the addition of the translator's surname as "another distinguishing characteristic" (see figure 8.11) although another possibility might be the date of the expression.

Figure 8.11. Addition of Other Distinguishing Characteristic

046	‡k 1929
100 0	‡a Plato. ‡t Symposium. ‡l French ‡s (Robin)
337	‡a text ‡2 rdacontent
377	‡a fre
381	‡a Robin
400 0	‡a Plato. ‡t Banquet
500 1	‡w r ‡i Translator: ‡a Robin, Léon, ‡d 1866-1947
670	‡a Le banquet, 1929: ‡b title page (texte établi et traduit par Léon Robin)

It is somewhat unusual for a modern work to exist in more than one expression in its original language, but it can occur. For example, Orson Scott Card first published the novel *Ender's Game* in 1985, but reissued it with changed text in 1994 as the "author's definitive edition." The authorized access point for this new expression may be differentiated by the addition of the name of the edition (see figure 8.12). Alternately, the year of the expression could be used:

100 1 ‡a Card, Orson Scott. ‡t Ender's game (Novel). ‡l English. ‡f 1994

Figure 8.12. Addition of Other Distinguishing Characteristic

046	‡k 1994
100 1	‡a Card, Orson Scott. ‡t Ender's game (Novel). ‡l English ‡s (Author's definitive edition)
337	‡a text ‡2 rdacontent
377	‡a eng
381	‡a Author's definitive edition
670	‡a Ender's game, 1994: ‡a cover page 1 (Author's definitive edition)

If a new expression of a work is created in a different form from the original, the RDA content type is normally added to differentiate. For example, the original expression of C. S. Lewis's *Chronicles of Narnia* was a text in English. This popular work was transformed over a period of years by its publisher, Caedmon, to a spoken word expression, still in English. It makes sense to add the content type "Spoken word" to the authorized access point for this expression to distinguish it from the original text expression (see figure 8.2). Because *The Chronicles of Narnia* have been performed as an audiobook more than once, there is more than one spoken word expression of this work, so the authorized access point in figure 8.2 has been further qualified, in this case by the name of the publisher responsible for issuing the audiobook.

Classical works usually exist in multiple expressions in their original language because scholars trying to find the author's original intent constantly reissue new and presumably improved texts. This *Handbook* recommends that the surname of the editor be given as "another distinguishing characteristic" in this case (see figure 8.13).

Pre-RDA cataloging practice for collections purporting to be an author's complete works (using the preferred title "Works") has been to distinguish access points for different expressions by the addition of the year of the expression (see figure 8.5). However, choosing the date as an addition is not an RDA requirement and in many cases (perhaps in most cases) another distinguishing characteristic might more readily identify the expression than the date of its publication to the user of the database. How many users know that the popular *Riverside Shakespeare* edition of Shakespeare's

Figure 8.13. Addition of Other Distinguishing Characteristic

046	‡k 1965
100 0	‡a Apuleius. ‡t Metamorphoses. ‡t Latin ‡s (Robertson)
337	‡a text ‡2 rdacontent
377	‡a lat
381	‡a Robertson
500 1	‡w r ‡i Editor: ‡a Robertson, D. S. ‡q (Donald Struan), ‡d 1885-1961
670	‡a Les metamorphoses, 1965: ‡b (texte établi par D.S. Robertson)

works was first published in 1974, and could therefore pick it out when faced with an extremely long list of access points for different expressions of Shakespeare's works, all differentiated by date? The current authorized access point for this expression is:

> 100 1   ‡a Shakespeare, William, ‡d 1564-1616. ‡t Works. ‡f 1974

but a more easily identifiable access point might be:

> 100 1   ‡a Shakespeare, William, ‡d 1564-1616. ‡t Works ‡s (Riverside Shakespeare)

Take care that if adding the date of the expression to an authorized access point for an expression, the actual date of the expression is recorded. This may not be the same as the date of the manifestation being cataloged, which could simply be a reprint of (and thus the same expression as) an earlier publication.

6.27.4. VARIANT ACCESS POINT REPRESENTING A WORK OR EXPRESSION. Variant access points for expressions are constructed in much the same way as the authorized access point, except that a variant access point may be based on a variant title for the *work* and thus not begin with the authorized access point for the work (as the *authorized* access point for the expression always does).

Variant access point forms are never recorded in bibliographic records, only in authority records. Instead, if a user constructs a search using a variant access point, a display similar to the following directing the user to the authorized access point should be triggered from the authority record (for example, figure 8.1):

> Card, Orson Scott. Stratégie de l'ombre
> > *search under*
> > Card, Orson Scott. Ender's shadow. French

Alternately, the system could re-execute the user's search automatically. It would be particularly useful when a user is constructing a keyword search (perhaps just entering the French title) if the system redirected the user's search based on variant forms found in the authority record.

6.27.4.5. VARIANT ACCESS POINT REPRESENTING AN EXPRESSION. Although RDA does not recognize title as an attribute of the expression entity, it does recognize that certain variant titles for *works* are closely associated with a particular expression. The most common instance of this is when the title is for a translation of the original work. Variant access points are not core in RDA, but customary practice is to record the variant title of a work in a translated language as a variant access point to the authorized access point for that expression. Examples in this *Handbook* include figures 8.1, 8.3, 8.5, and 8.11:

> Plato. Banquet
> > *search under*
> > Plato. Symposium. French (Robin)

A variant access point may be recorded giving a title in a different script, as in figure 8.3:

> Rowling, J. K. هاري بوتر وسجين ازكابان
> > *search under*
> > Rowling, J. K. Harry Potter and the prisoner of Azkaban. Arabic

When describing an expression of a series with an access point that is constructed by combining the name of the creator with the preferred title, it is customary to record as a variant access point the preferred title alone (see figure 8.2b):

> Chronicles of Narnia. Spoken word (Caedmon (Firm))
> > *search under*
> > Lewis, C. S. (Clive Staples), 1898.1963. Chronicles of Narnia. Spoken word (Caedmon (Firm))

ACCESS POINTS FOR EXPRESSIONS OF MUSICAL WORKS

6.28.3. AUTHORIZED ACCESS POINT REPRESENTING A MUSICAL EXPRESSION. The authorized access point for an expression of a musical work, like that of other expressions, begins with the authorized access point for the work constructed according to RDA 6.28.1 and 6.28.2 (see chapter 7 of this *Handbook* for details). Many access points for musical expressions follow the general guidelines of RDA 6.27.3 and 6.27.4.5, described above. A few categories of musical expressions have special guidelines, however, and these are covered in 6.28.3.

6.28.3.2. ARRANGEMENTS, TRANSCRIPTIONS, ETC. Recording arrangements and transcriptions as part of the other distinguishing characteristics of the expression of a musical work element have already been discussed above at 6.18.1.4. If this element is to be recorded in the description of the expression under the guidelines found at 6.18.1.4, it should also be recorded in the authorized access point. The authorized access point for the work is followed by a semicolon and subfield ‡o, and then the word "arranged" is recorded.

Musical works are frequently arranged more than once. Each arrangement is a different expression of the musical work, and as such may receive its own description, which in turn would include its own unique authorized access point. As discussed above under "Access Points for Expressions of Works," for its initial implementation of RDA the Library of Congress has instructed its catalogers not to differentiate between these expressions, but rather use the same authorized access point (ending with "arranged") for all arranged expressions of a given musical work, although they will use distinctive authorized access points if they have been established in the LC/NACO Authority File by other catalogers. As also discussed above, this *Handbook* takes the position that it is more appropriate for expressions to have unique authorized access points that differentiate between them, and so this *Handbook* examples follow this practice. In the example shown in figure 8.6, the well-known tune "Adeste fideles" has been arranged countless times, each a different expression of the original work. In the case of figure 8.6, the authorized access point for this particular expression has been qualified by the addition of the surname of the arranger as an "other distinguishing characteristic of the expression" under 6.27.3d.

6.28.3.5. VOCAL AND CHORUS SCORES. Recording vocal and chorus scores as part of the other distinguishing characteristics of the expression of a musical work element has already been discussed above at 6.18.1.6. If this element is to be recorded in the description of the expression under the guidelines found at 6.18.1.6, it should also be recorded in the authorized access point. The authorized access point for the work is followed by a period and subfield ‡s, and then "Vocal score," "Vocal scores," "Chorus score," or "Chorus scores" is recorded (see figure 8.7).

6.30.3. AUTHORIZED ACCESS POINT REPRESENTING AN EXPRESSION OF A RELIGIOUS WORK. The authorized access point for an expression of a religious work, like that of other expressions, begins with the authorized access point for the work constructed according to RDA 6.30.1 and 6.30.2 (see chapter 7 of this *Handbook* for details). Many access points for expressions of religious works follow the general guidelines of RDA 6.27.3 and 6.27.4.5, described above. A few important categories of expressions of religious works have special guidelines, however, and these are covered in 6.30.3.

6.30.3.2. AUTHORIZED ACCESS POINT REPRESENTING AN EXPRESSION OF THE BIBLE. RDA instructs the cataloger to add three elements to the authorized access point for the Bible or part of the Bible as constructed following 6.30.1 or 6.30.2 (see discussion in chapter 7 of this *Handbook*), "as applicable." "As applicable" might be taken to mean "if needed to differentiate the access point of one expression of the Bible from another," but in traditional cataloging practice all three are added to the authorized access point if known whether needed for differentiation or not.

- The language of the expression (see RDA 6.11). The name of the language is spelled out in the preferred language of the cataloging agency, English for participants in the Program for Cooperative Cataloging (e.g., "French," not "Français"). This form will be different from that of the element as recorded in the 377 field, which is a code. The language of the expression is added to the access point following a period and subfield ‡l (see figures 8.8 through 8.10).
- A term indicating another distinguishing characteristic of the expression (see RDA 6.25). For expressions of the Bible, this is the name of the version or its equivalent (see discussion above at 6.25.1.4). This element is recorded in the authorized access point exactly as it was recorded as an element in the 381 field of the MARC authority record. This addition is recorded following the language element, a period, and subfield ‡s (see figures 8.8 through 8.10).
- The date of the expression (see RDA 6.24.1.4, including discussion above). The date should be recorded as a year or years alone, even though more detail might have been recorded in the 046 field. The date of the expression is recorded following the version element, a period, and subfield ‡f (see figures 8.8 through 8.10).

EXPRESSION ELEMENTS RECORDED IN BIBLIOGRAPHIC RECORDS (RDA CHAPTER 7, DESCRIBING CONTENT)

As noted earlier in this chapter, RDA chapter 7 deals with the attributes of expressions that are in the current environment normally recorded in bibliographic records. It is possible that in a future cataloging environment all attributes of an individual expression will be recorded in the same description rather than split between authority and bibliographic records.

7.10. SUMMARIZATION OF THE CONTENT. A brief summary may be included if it amplifies and clarifies the description of the resource. Summaries are particularly useful for descriptions of nonbook materials, as such items are often not easily accessible for browsing (see, for example, figures 8.14 and 8.15). Summaries are also frequently included as part of the description of popular fiction and children's literature (see, for example, figure 8.16).

Figure 8.14. Summarization of the Content

046		‡k 2011
245 04		‡a The fantastic flying books of Mr. Morris Lessmore / ‡c Moonbot Studios.
246 3		‡a Moonbot Studios presents The fantastic flying books of Mr. Morris Lessmore
264 1		‡a Shreveport, LA : ‡b Moonbot Studios, ‡c [2011]
300		‡a 1 online resource (15 min.) : ‡b sound, color
336		‡a two-dimensional moving image ‡2 rdacontent
337		‡a computer ‡2 rdamedia
338		‡a online resource ‡2 rdacarrier
347		‡a video file ‡2 rda
380		‡a Motion picture
546		‡a No dialogue; some text in French and English.
508		‡a Directors, William Joyce, Brandon Oldenburg; writer, William Joyce; producers, Alissa M. Kantrow, Lampton Enochs, Trish Farnsworth-Smith; editor, Eva Contis; music, John Hunter; senior animator, Jamil Lahham; animators, Beavan Blocker, John Durbin, Mike Klim, Stanley Moore, Dominic Pallotta, Mickey Sauls.
520		‡a Mr. Morris Lessmore is swept away by a hurricane reminiscent of Katrina to a world inhabited entirely by books.
700 1		‡a Joyce, William, ‡d 1957- ‡e author, ‡e film director.
...		
856 40		‡u http://vimeo.com/35404908
856 42		‡z Film may be downloaded from ‡u http://www.morrislessmore.com/?p=film

Figure 8.15. Summarization of the Content

100 1		‡a Moon, Alan R., ‡d 1952- ‡e author.
245 14		‡a Ticket to ride / ‡c Alan R. Moon.
264 1		‡a Los Altos, CA : ‡b Days of Wonder, ‡c [2009]
264 4		‡c ©2009
300		‡a 1 game (1 board, 225 train cars, 144 cards, 5 scoring markers) : ‡b cardboard, plastic, wood, color ; ‡c box 51 x 27 x 5 cm + ‡e 1 rules booklet.
336		‡a three-dimensional form ‡2 rdacontent
337		‡a unmediated ‡2 rdamedia
338		‡a other ‡2 rdacarrier
500		‡a For 2-5 players.
521		‡a Age 8 to adult.
520		‡a Players attempt to gain the most points by claiming train routes and connecting cities in the United States and Canada.

500	‡a Title from container.
586	‡a Spiel des Jahres (Germany), 2004
586	‡a Parents' Choice Foundatin Silver Honor, 2004
586	‡a As d'or, Jeu de l'année (France), 2005
586	‡a Juego del año (Spain), 2005
710 2	‡a Days of Wonder, Inc., ‡e publisher.

Figure 8.16. Summarization of the Content

020	‡a 9780007247912
100 1	‡a Seuss, ‡c Dr., ‡e author.
245 14	‡a The cat in the hat / ‡c by Dr. Seuss.
250	‡a 50th birthday edition.
264　1	‡a New York : ‡b HarperCollins Children's Books, ‡c [2007].
300	‡a 61 pages : ‡b color illustrations ; ‡c 24 cm
336	‡a text ‡2 rdacontent
336	‡a still image ‡2 rdacontent
337	‡a unmediated ‡2 rdamedia
338	‡a volume ‡2 rdacarrier
520	‡a A zany but well-meaning cat brings a cheerful, exotic, and exuberant form of chaos to a household of two young children one rainy day while their mother is out.
521	‡a Elementary school students.

The summarization of the content element is recorded in the MARC bibliographic 520 field. This field, with the first indicator blank, generates in the local system the label "Summary:" at the beginning of the element. The public display of this field in figure 8.16 will appear: "Summary: A zany but well-meaning cat brings a cheerful, exotic, and exuberant form of chaos to a household of two young children one rainy day while their mother is out."

This element is also used to describe archival collections. In this case the first indicator of the MARC 520 field is coded "2," which generates the label "Scope and content:" (see figure 8.17).

Figure 8.17. Scope of Content

100 1	‡a Billings, Lewis K. ‡q (Lewis Kevin), ‡d 1956- ‡e creator.
245 10	‡a Lewis K. Billings scrapbooks.
264　0	‡c 1997-2009.
300	‡a 12 linear ft. ‡a (12 cartons)

336	‡a text ‡2 rdacontent
337	‡a unmediated ‡2 rdamedia
338	‡a volume ‡2 rdacarrier
351	‡b Chronological.
506	‡a Open for public research.
520 2	‡a Contains scrapbooks that document Lewis K. Billings political campaign to be the mayor of Provo, of his terms in office, and of the 2002 Winter Olympics in Utah. Materials date from 1997 to 2009.
561	‡a Donated by Lewis K. Billings in 2011.
852	‡a L. Tom Perry Special Collections, Harold B. Lee Library, Brigham Young University, ‡e Provo, Utah 84602.

7.11. PLACE AND DATE OF CAPTURE. This element records the place and date associated with the "capture" of the content of a resource, meaning the place and date it was recorded or filmed. The information may be recorded as a free-text note in subfield ‡a of the 518 field (see figure 8.18), or more formally following the format of 7.11.2 and 7.11.3, in subfield ‡p (place of capture) and subfield ‡d (date of capture). The element may also be recorded in coded form in the 033 field (see the MARC documentation at www.loc.gov/marc/bibliographic/bd033.html for information about coding in the 033 field). Figure 8.19 formally records this element in both 033 and 518 fields.

Figure 8.18. Place and Date of Capture

041 1	‡a fre ‡j eng
046	‡k 2007
245 03	‡a Le premier cri.
264 1	‡a [Place of publication not identified] : ‡b Buena Vista Home Entertainment, ‡c 2008.
300	‡a 1 videodisc (96 min.) : ‡b sound, color ; ‡c 4 3/4 in.
336	‡a two-dimensional moving image ‡2 rdacontent
337	‡a video ‡2 rdamedia
338	‡a videodisc ‡2 rdacarrier
344	‡h Dolby digital 5.1
346	‡b PAL
347	‡a video file ‡b DVD video ‡e region 2 ‡2 rda
380	‡a Motion picture.
546	‡a French with optional English subtitles.
518	‡a Originally produced in France as a motion picture and released in 2007.
508	‡a Director, Gilles de Maistre; scenario, Marie-Claire Javoy; executive producer, Stéphanie Schorter-Champenier; producers, Miguel Courtois and Gilles de Maistre; cinematography, Gilles de Maistre.

500 ‡a Wide screen (1.85:1)

520 ‡a Film follows several women from various parts of the world as they give birth.

700 1 ‡a Maistre, Gilles de, ‡e film director, ‡e film producer, ‡e director of photography.

700 1 ‡a Javoy, Marie-Claire, ‡d 1964- ‡e screenwriter.

Figure 8.19. Place and Date of Capture

028 02 ‡a CDA67722 ‡b Hyperion

033 2 ‡a 20080806 ‡a 20080811 ‡b 5754 ‡c B8

041 0 ‡g eng ‡g fre ‡g ger ‡h eng

100 1 ‡a Haydn, Joseph, ‡d 1732-1809, ‡e composer.

240 10 ‡a Quartets, ‡m strings, ‡n H. III, 25-30

245 10 ‡a String quartets, op. 17 / ‡c Joseph Haydn.

264 1 ‡a London : ‡b Hyperion, ‡c [2009]

264 4 ‡c ℗2009

300 ‡a 2 audio discs ; ‡c 4 3/4 in.

306 ‡a 002539 ‡a 002609 ‡a 002242 ‡a 003250 ‡a 002206 ‡a 001837

336 ‡a performed music ‡2 rdacontent

337 ‡a audio ‡2 rdamedia

338 ‡a audio disc ‡2 rdacarrier

344 ‡a digital ‡b optical ‡g stereo ‡2 rda

347 ‡a audio file ‡b CD audio ‡2 rda

511 0 ‡a The London Haydn String Quartet (Catherine Manson, violin ; Margaret Faultless, violin; James Boyd, viola; Jonathan Cohen, cello).

518 ‡p St. George's, Brandon Hill, Bristol ‡d 2008 August 6-11

546 ‡a Program notes in English, German and French (15 pages) inserted in container.

505 0 ‡a No. 4 in C minor (25:39) -- No. 3 in E flat major (26:09) -- No. 2 in F major (22:42) -- No. 1 in E major (32:50) -- No. 5 in G major (22:06) -- No. 6 in D major (18:37).

710 3 ‡a London Haydn Quartet, ‡e performer.

7.12. LANGUAGE OF THE CONTENT. The language of the content element is similar to the language of expression element (see discussion above at 6.11). The language of expression element formally records the names of the language(s) in which a work is expressed. The language of the content element is less formal, and may be recorded as a free-text note in the 546 field. The language(s) of the primary content of the resource are always recorded in the language of expression element. If the language(s) of other content or other information about the language(s) are considered important for identification or selection, this may be recorded in the language of the content element. For example, the fact that a foreign language film has dubbing or subtitles may be important for selection to a person who does not know the primary language of the film (see figure 8.18). For other examples of this element, see figures 8.14 and 8.19.

7.13. FORM OF NOTATION. The form of notation element records information about the characters or symbols used to express the content, and should be recorded if it would help the user identify or select the resource. The element is core for LC and PCC for musical notation (LC-PCC PS 7.13.3, May 2012). The form of notation element is recorded in the MARC 546 field, subfield ‡b. Recording the element may be most useful if the form of notation is unexpected, for example, Turkish written in Arabic script (see figure 8.20), music expressed in an unusual notation (see figure 8.21), or when the text is expressed in a tactile notation such as Braille (see figure 8.22).

Figure 8.20. Script

100 0	‡a Ibn al-ʻArabī, ‡d 1165-1240, ‡e author.
245 10	‡a İlm-i Cifir şerhi ve havassı / ‡c Şeyh'ül Ekber Muhyiddin-i Arabi ; çeviren Uğur Bursalı, hazırlayan Mustafa Varlı.
264 1	‡a İstanbul : ‡b EsmaYayınları, ‡c [2000?]
300	‡a 180, 84 pages ; ‡c 20 cm
336	‡a text ‡2 rdacontent
337	‡a unmediated ‡2 rdamedia
338	‡a volume ‡2 rdacarrier
546	‡a Turkish ‡b in Arabic script.
700 1	‡a Bursalı, Uğur, ‡e translator.

Figure 8.21. Form of Musical Notation

100 1	‡a Cabezas, Estela, ‡e author.
245 10	‡a Música en colores : ‡b sistema audiovisual para la enseñanza de la música / ‡c Estela Cabezas.
264 1	‡a [Chile] : ‡b Ediciones Universitarias de Valparaiso : ‡b Universidad Catolica de Valparaiso, ‡c [1980]
264 4	‡c ©1980
300	‡a 1 score (169 pages) : ‡b illustrations, portraits ; ‡c 25 x 36 cm
336	‡a notated music ‡2 rdacontent
337	‡a unmediated ‡2 rdacontent
338	‡a volume ‡2 rdacontent
546	‡b Conventional staff and graphic notation.

Figure 8.22. Form of Tactile Notation

245	00	‡a George Washington Birthplace National Monument, Virginia / ‡c National Park Service, U.S. Department of the Interior.
264	1	‡a Harpers Ferry, WV : ‡b National Park Service, Harpers Ferry Center, ‡c [2010]
300		‡a 1 volume ; ‡c 28 cm
336		‡a tactile text ‡2 rdacontent
337		‡a unmediated ‡2 rdamedia
338		‡a volume ‡2 rdacarrier
500		‡a Title from cover.
546		‡b "This edition is a contracted (Grade II) braille transcription."
710	2	‡a Harpers Ferry Center (U.S.), ‡e publisher.

7.14. ACCESSIBILITY CONTENT. This element records information about content that assists those with visual or hearing impairments, including closed captioning and subtitles in the same language as the spoken content of the resource. It does not include subtitles in a language different from the primary language of the content, which are recorded in the language of the content element (see 7.12, above). If the information includes information about language (such as American sign language) the accessibility content element is recorded in the MARC 546 field. Otherwise it is recorded in the MARC 500 field (see second 546 field in figure 8.23).

Figure 8.23. Accessibility Content

041	1	‡a spa ‡j eng ‡j ger ‡j spa
245	03	‡a El último aplauso / ‡c Happinet Corporation presenta una producción de German Kral Filmproduktion, Happinet Corporation.
264	1	‡a [Buenos Aires, Argentina] : ‡b AVH, ‡c [2010]
264	4	‡c ©2010
300		‡a 1 videodisc (87 min.) : ‡b sound, color ; ‡c 4 3/4 in.
336		‡a two-dimensional moving image ‡2 rdacontent
337		‡a video ‡2 rdamedia
338		‡a videodisc ‡2 rdacarrier
344		‡h Dolby digital 5.1
346		‡b NTSC ‡2 rda
347		‡a video file ‡b DVD video ‡e region 4 ‡2 rda
380		‡a Motion picture.
546		‡a Spanish with optional English or German subtitles.
546		‡a Closed captioned in Spanish for the hearing impaired.
518		‡a An Argentine-German-Japanese coproduction released in 2009.

511 1   ‡a Cristina de los Ángeles, Inés Arce, Julio César Fernán, Abel Frías, Omar Garré, Orquesta Típica Imperial.

508   ‡a Editor, Ulrike Tortora; musical production, Luis Borda.

500   ‡a Anamorphic wide screen (1.78:1)

520   ‡a This documentary follows the lives of singers of tango from 1999 to today, showing the great classics of tango and tango generations represented by the Orquesta Tipica Imperial.

700 1   ‡a Kral, German, ‡d 1968- ‡e film director.

7.15. ILLUSTRATIVE CONTENT. According to FRBR, when an expression is accompanied by augmentations such as illustrations that are not integral to the intellectual or artistic realization of the work, these augmentations are considered separate expressions of their own separate works (FRBR 3.2.2). Thus, the text *Alice's Adventures in Wonderland* that is published with illustrations by John Tenniel would be considered by FRBR to be expressions of two works, the text and the illustrations. However, as a practical matter, illustrations accompanying a text are not usually given a separate work description from that of the text in library databases. RDA, therefore, takes the position that the presence or absence of illustrative content is an element related to the expression, and gives instructions for this element in the section of chapter 7 devoted to attributes of the expression. This may not seem intuitive to catalogers used to AACR2's placement of this information with the physical description (e.g., AACR2 2.5C), most of which is related in RDA to the manifestation and is now found in RDA chapter 3, "Describing Characters."

7.15.1.3. RECORDING ILLUSTRATIVE CONTENT. Illustrative content is recorded in subfield ‡b of the MARC 300 field, preceded by a colon. Use the words "illustration" or "illustrations" as appropriate (see figures 8.4 and 8.16). The RDA 7.15.1.3 alternative gives a list of other more specific terms that may be used. The Library of Congress generally will not record terms from this list (see LC-PCC PS 7.15.1.3, February 2010). However, one of the terms, "map(s)," is commonly used to show the presence of cartographic content in the resource (see figure 8.4). For an example using one of the other terms, see figure 8.21.

7.15.1.4. DETAILS OF ILLUSTRATIVE CONTENT. If more detail than that recorded following 7.15.1.3 is considered important for identification or selection of the resource, it is recorded as a free-text note in a MARC 500 field (see figure 8.24).

Figure 8.24. Details of Illustrative Content

100 1   ‡a Sexton, Tom, ‡d 1940- ‡e author.

245 10 ‡a Crows on bare branches / ‡c poems by Tom Sexton.

264	1	‡a Chestertown, New York : ‡b Chester Creek Press, ‡c [2008]
264	4	‡c ©2008
300		‡a 26 unnumbered pages : ‡b color illustrations ; ‡c 21 cm
336		‡a text ‡2 rdacontent
336		‡a still image ‡2 rdacontent
337		‡a unmediated ‡2 rdamedia
338		‡a volume ‡2 rdacarrier
500		‡a Limited edition of 50 signed and numbered copies.
500		‡a Printed letterpress and illustrated by the printer, Robert Walp, with six multi-color illustrations printed from woodcuts and polymer plates.
700	1	‡a Walp, Robert, ‡e illustrator.

7.16. SUPPLEMENTARY CONTENT. If a resource contains content such as a bibliography or index that supplements the primary content of the resource, this may be recorded if the cataloger believes the information would help the user identify or select the resource. When recording the presence of a bibliography or bibliographical references, record this element using a MARC 504 field. If not, use a 500 field.

North American cataloging practice has evolved standard language for recording this element. Although it is not required, most catalogers record the information following this practice. If a publication contains bibliographical citations in any form (including footnotes, etc.), record the following in a 504 field:

> 504   ‡a Includes bibliographical references.

However, if the publication contains a single bibliography, record the pagination:

> 504   ‡a Includes bibliographical references (pages 310-325).

Previous cataloging practice bracketed the beginning or ending page number if it was inferred by the cataloger because it did not actually appear on the source. LC and PCC practice in RDA is *not* to follow this bracketing convention. That is, record "(pages 310-325)," not "(pages [310]-325)" (see LC-PCC PS 1.7.1, Punctuation in Notes, section 3 [square brackets], January 2013).

If the publication contains an index or indexes to its own contents, record one of the following in a 500 field:

> 500   ‡a Includes index.
> 500   ‡a Includes indexes.

If a publication contains bibliographical references and an index or indexes, the information may be combined in a single 504 field, as in the following example:

504 ‡a Includes bibliographical references (pages 530-555) and indexes.

For an example of the supplementary content element in context, see figure 8.4.

7.17. COLOUR CONTENT. This element records the presence of color in the content of a resource. RDA considers this an attribute of the expression. It is usually recorded alongside information about illustrative content (see above at 7.15).

7.17.1.3. RECORDING COLOUR CONTENT. If the resource contains content in colors other than black and white or grey, record the information in subfield ‡b of the MARC 300 field, following a colon.

Despite the spelling of "colour" in the title of 7.17, RDA does not require any particular spelling of the word. U.S. catalogers will likely follow the Library of Congress and record "color" (LC-PCC PS 7.17.1.3, April 2010). However, this *Handbook* recommends that catalogers not change the spelling when using cataloging copy that recorded the word "colour." Note that generally the word "color" will be recorded, *not* "colored." "Colored" is reserved for the rare situation where the illustrations have been colored by hand.

For examples of this element, see figures 8.14, 8.15, 8.16, 8.18, 8.23, and 8.24.

The exceptions listed in 7.17.1.3 for still images, moving images, three-dimensional forms, and resources designed for persons with visual impairments are exceptional in the sense that they give more options for recording color content, including in some cases black and white, and specific colors. For more information see RDA 7.17.2–7.17.5; see figure 8.25 for a motion picture example.

Figure 8.25. Colour Content

130 0	‡a King of Kings (Motion picture : 1927)
245 14	‡a The king of kings / ‡c De Mille Pictures ; producer-director, Cecil B. DeMille ; story-screenplay, Jeanie Macpherson.
264 1	‡a United States : ‡b Pathé Exchange, ‡c 1927.
300	‡a 3 film reels (approximately 112 min., 4,032 ft.) : ‡b silent, black and white ; ‡c 16 mm
336	‡a two-dimensional moving image ‡2 rdacontent
337	‡a projected ‡2 rdamedia
338	‡a film reel ‡2 rdacarrier
508	‡a Chief photographer, Peverell Marley; assistant photographers, Fred Westerberg, Jacob A. Badaracco; art directors, Mitchell Leisen, Anton Grot; film editor, Frank Urson; 2nd assistant director, William J. Cowen, Roy Burns.
511 1	‡a H.B. Warner, Dorothy Cumming, Ernest Torrence, Joseph Schildkraut.

```
500    ‡a Full screen (1.33:1)
700 1  ‡a DeMille, Cecil B. ‡q (Cecil Blount), ‡d 1881-1959, ‡e film director, ‡e film
       producer.
710 2  ‡a DeMille Pictures Corporation, ‡e film producer.
```

7.17.1.4. DETAILS OF COLOUR CONTENT. If more detail than that recorded following 7.17.1.3 is considered important for identification or selection of the resource, it is recorded as a free-text note in a MARC 500 field (see figure 8.24).

7.18. SOUND CONTENT. If a resource (other than one that consists primarily of recorded sound) includes sound, record the word "sound" in this element. This element is recorded in subfield ‡b of the MARC bibliographic 300 field. For examples, see figures 8.14, 8.18, and 8.23. These are all descriptions of motion pictures. Note that the element is not recorded in figure 8.19. This recording of Haydn's string quartets is an example of a resource that "consists primarily of recorded sound" so it falls under the exception listed in the scope note in 7.18.1.1. If a motion picture is silent, record "silent" in this element instead of "sound" (see figure 8.25).

7.19. ASPECT RATIO. Aspect ratio, the ratio of the width to the height of a moving image, is important in descriptions of moving image materials because it can affect the type of playback equipment needed to view the resource. Record one of the following terms:

> full screen (if the ratio is less than 1.5:1)
> wide screen (if the ratio is 1.5:1 or greater)
> mixed (if there are multiple aspect ratios in same work)

In addition, record the ratio with the denominator (the figure after the colon) of 1, if the ratio is known. Aspect ratio is recorded in the MARC bibliographic 500 field. For examples, see figures 8.18 and 8.25. More details may also be recorded (see figure 8.23).

7.20. FORMAT OF NOTATED MUSIC. This element is defined as "the musical or physical layout of the content of a resource that is presented in the form of musical notation." The element should be recorded using terms from the list in 7.20.1.3 if appropriate, although other terms can be used if none of the listed terms is "appropriate or sufficiently specific" (see 7.20.1.4).

According to RDA appendix D, the RDA to MARC bibliographic mapping in the RDA Toolkit (D.2.1), the format of notated music element is recorded in the MARC bibliographic 500 field. However, this element is closely linked with RDA 3.4.3.2, recording extent of notated music, in which we are instructed to record the term(s) chosen under 7.20 in the extent statement (MARC bibliographic 300 field, subfield ‡a). In the current environment most catalogers will not record the term(s) for the format in a 300 field and then repeat them in a 500 field in order to record the format of notated music element (see figure 8.26, where the element is only recorded as part of the extent statement in 300 subfield ‡a). However, this might change in a non-MARC environment.

Figure 8.26. Format of Notated Music

```
028 32   ‡a 6071 ‡b Breitkopf & Härtel
028 22   ‡a 29828 ‡b Breitkopf & Härtel
041 0    ‡a ger ‡g ger ‡g eng
100 1    ‡a Brahms, Johannes, ‡d 1833-1897, ‡e composer.
240 10   ‡a Deutsches Requiem. ‡s Vocal score
245 14   ‡a Ein deutsches Requiem : ‡b nach Worten der Heiligen Schrift : für Soli, Chor
         und Orchester = A German requiem : on words from the Holy Scriptures : for soli,
         chorus and orchestra / ‡c Johannes Brahms ; Klavierauszug vom Komponisten =
         piano vocal score by the composer.
264  1   ‡a Wiesbaden  : ‡b Breitkopf & Härtel, ‡c 2010.
300      ‡a 1 vocal score (95 pages) ; ‡c 27 cm
336      ‡a notated music ‡2 rdacontent
337      ‡a unmediated ‡2 rdamedia
338      ‡a volume ‡2 rdacarrier
500      ‡a For solo voices (SBar), chorus (SATB), and orchestra; accompaniment arranged
         for piano.
546      ‡b Staff notation.
500      ‡a Duration: approximately 1 hr., 20 min.
500      ‡a Postface in German and English by Frank Reinisch.
700 1    ‡a Reinisch, Frank, ‡e author of afterword, colophon, etc.
```

Note also that two of the terms listed in 7.20, "vocal score" and "chorus score," might also have been recorded under 6.18.1.6 as part of the other distinguishing characteristic of the expression of a musical work element (see figure 8.26, with discussion above at 6.18.1.6).

7.21. MEDIUM OF PERFORMANCE OF MUSICAL CONTENT. This element may seem similar to the medium of performance element detailed in RDA 6.15. However, that element is an attribute of the *work* and describes the medium of performance for which a musical work was originally conceived. The medium of performance of musical content element (7.21) is an attribute of the *expression*. It is recorded in a MARC bibliographic 500 field, and is given as a free-text note. For an example, see figure 8.26. For the abbreviations used in this example, see appendix B.5.6.

7.22. DURATION. Duration measures the extent of a resource that extends over time. It is an attribute of the *expression* (see FRBR 4.3.8) and as such may be an element that helps distinguish one expression of a work from another—if the duration element is different in two resources they are likely different expressions. In RDA, duration is recorded for the specific playing or running time of a recorded expression; for an expression whose content type is notated music, duration is the expected performance time, which will nearly always be an approximation. Although not noted in RDA, duration might also be recorded, if the cataloger thinks it is important for selection or identification, for another type of resource that is expected to be performed—for example, a poem or possibly a play.

Duration may be recorded in a number of places in the MARC bibliographic format, including fields 300 subfield ‡a, 306 subfield ‡a, 500 subfield ‡a, or 505 subfield ‡a. It may be recorded either in terms of hours, minutes, and seconds (which are abbreviated following appendix B.5.3), or in the format "1:30:00" (for one hour, thirty minutes, zero seconds), as shown in the examples to 7.22.1.3. If recorded in the 306 field, the information is recorded following the pattern *hhmmss* (i.e., 002016 means twenty minutes, thirty seconds). Duration is routinely recorded if the resource states it, but it may also be recorded even if it is not stated but "readily ascertainable." For examples, see figures 8.14 (300 field), 8.18 (300 field), 8.19 (306 and 505 fields), 8.23 (300 field), 8.25 (300 field), and 8.26 (500 field).

7.23. PERFORMER, NARRATOR, AND/OR PRESENTER. Normally statements found on a resource about its creators or contributors are recorded in a statement of responsibility following the instructions in RDA 2.4. However, 2.4.1.1 lists several exceptions, including:

- statements identifying performers of music whose participation is confined to performance, execution, or interpretation
- statements identifying performers, narrators, and/or presenters

Instead of recording such statements in a statement of responsibility related to the title proper, they are to be recorded in the performer, narrator, and/or presenter element as instructed in 7.23. The element is not transcribed (though it may be quoted if the source gives a concise statement). Instead, information about the performers, narrators, or presenters is given by simply listing the names, together with information about what they did (if necessary).

This element is recorded in the MARC bibliographic 511 field. If recording information about the cast of a motion picture, the first indicator is coded "1"; the system may be programmed to display the label "Cast:" when this coding is found. For any other type of performer, etc., the indicator is coded "0," and information about the persons' roles will be included by the cataloger when recording the element.

The names of the principal performers (singers, readers, orchestra, cast, etc.) should be recorded. Performers who are not principal performers may also be recorded if, in the cataloger's judgment, their inclusion would be helpful to the user of the database. For an example recording performers in a musical sound recording, see figure 8.19. For examples recording the cast of a motion picture, see figures 8.23 and 8.25.

7.24. ARTISTIC AND/OR TECHNICAL CREDIT. As noted above in the discussion of RDA 7.23, statements found on a resource about its creators or contributors are normally recorded in a statement of responsibility following the instructions in RDA 2.4. However, 2.4.1.1 lists the following exception:

- statements identifying persons who have contributed to the artistic and/or technical production of a resource

Rather than transcribe such information in a statement of responsibility related to the title proper, record it in the artistic and/or technical credit element following the guidelines of 7.24. "Artistic and/or technical credit" is defined in RDA 7.24.1.1 as "a listing of persons, families, or corporate bodies making contributions to the artistic and/or technical production of a resource." These include many types of contributors, such as producers, directors, writers, composers, production designers, etc. The roles of these persons, families, or corporate bodies should be recorded as a "statement of function."

Record these names in the MARC bibliographic 508 field. For examples of this element in descriptions of films, see figures 8.14, 8.18, 8.23, and 8.25. The element can also be recorded in descriptions of other types of resources, such as sound recordings (see figure 8.27).

Figure 8.27. Artistic and/or Technical Credit

```
028 02  ‡a 87076-2 ‡b Anti-
100 1   ‡a Staples, Mavis, ‡e creator.
245 10  ‡a You are not alone / ‡c Mavis Staples.
264  1  ‡a Los Angeles, CA : ‡b Anti-, ‡c [2010]
264  4  ‡c ℗2010
300     ‡a 1 audio disc ; ‡c 4 3/4 in.
```

```
336     ‡a performed music ‡2 rdacontent
337     ‡a audio ‡2 rdamedia
338     ‡a audio disc ‡2 rdacarrier
344     ‡a digital ‡b optical ‡g stereo ‡2 rda
347     ‡a audio file ‡b CD audio ‡2 rda
511 0   ‡a Mavis Staples; with vocal and instrumental accompaniment.
508     ‡a Producer, Jeff Tweedy.
518     ‡a Recorded at the Wilco Loft, Chicago, Illinois.
505 00  ‡t Don't knock -- ‡t You are not alone -- ‡t Downward road -- ‡t In Christ there is no
        east or west -- ‡t Creep along Moses -- ‡t Losing you -- ‡t I belong to the band --
        ‡t Last train -- ‡t Only the Lord knows -- ‡t Wrote a song for everyone -- ‡t We're
        gonna make it -- ‡t Wonderful Savior -- ‡t Too close ; ‡t On my way to Heaven.
520     ‡a Mavis Staples delivers an album that pays homage to the original spiritual roots of
        the Staples Singers.
700 1   ‡a Tweedy, Jeff, ‡d 1967- ‡e producer.
```

7.25. SCALE. Scale is "the ratio of the dimensions of an image or three-dimensional form contained or embodied in a resource to the dimensions of the entity it represents."

7.25.1.3. RECORDING SCALE. RDA instructs us to record the scale as a representative fraction, no matter how the statement appears in the source. The ratio is 1:X (e.g., 1:250 means that one inch on the resource represents 250 inches on the object represented by the resource).

For graphic materials such as architectural drawings or three-dimensional artifacts, this element is recorded in the MARC bibliographic 507 field. In the set of architectural plans described in figure 8.28 the scale was given as "1/8 inch = 1 foot." This scale statement converts to the representative fraction "1:96" (there are 96 units of 1/8 inch each in a foot). Following the instructions in 7.25.5.3, the scale as given in the resource may be recorded as "additional scale information," abbreviating as instructed in appendix B.5.7.

Figure 8.28. Scale

```
245 00  ‡a MacKinnon's Café architectural plans, University Park, Pa.
264  0  ‡c 2000
300     ‡a 30 architectural drawings : ‡b color ; ‡c 28 x 44 cm
336     ‡a still image ‡2 rdacontent
337     ‡a unmediated ‡2 rdamedia
338     ‡a sheet ‡2 rdacarrier
```

507   ‡a Scale 1:96 ‡b 1/8 in. to 1 ft.

506   ‡a Unrestricted access.

545   ‡a MacKinnon's Café is located on the ground floor of the West Pattee Wing of
           Pattee Library next to the entrance to the wing. It was constructed within an
           existing area formerly part of the News and Microforms Library in 2000. The
           café is named for Don MacKinnon, a 1948 graduate of Penn State, who made a
           generous gift for its construction.

520 2   ‡a This collection consists of 30 architectural drawings of MacKinnon's Café at the
           Pennsylvania State University, University Park campus. Drawings include floor
           plans, ceiling plans, elevation drawings, and an artist's representation of what the
           interior might look like. The plans are dated "03-03-00" and "03-05-00." There are
           a total of five different drawings with multiple copies of each.

For cartographic resources, the scale element is recorded in subfield ‡a of the MARC bibliographic 255 field. If only a verbal scale is given, it must be converted to a representative fraction. A useful figure to know for this conversion is that one mile equals 63,360 inches. The scale statement "1:475,200" given as one of the examples to 7.25.1.3 was calculated by multiplying 63,360 by 7.5. Similarly, 7,096,320, in the scale statement of figure 8.29, is the product of 112 and 63,360. Additional scale information that appears on the resource may be recorded following 7.25.5.3. For a map this is recorded in the same 255 field as the basic scale statement, following the representative fraction and a period.

Figure 8.29. Conversion of Verbal Scale

110 2   ‡a H.M. Gousha Company, ‡e cartographer.

245 10   ‡a Road map of the United States.

246 1   ‡i Panel title: ‡a Touraide interstate travel guide

255   ‡a Scale 1:7,096,320. 1 in. to 112 miles. 1 in. to 179 km

250   ‡a 1977 edition.

264 1   ‡a San Jose, Calif. : ‡bThe H.M. Gousha Company, ‡c [1977]

300   ‡a 1 map : ‡b color ; ‡c 45 x 67 cm, folded to 23 x 10 cm

336   ‡a cartographic image ‡2 rdacontent

337   ‡a unmediated ‡2 rdamedia

338   ‡a sheet ‡2 rdacarrier

500   ‡a Relief shown by shading and spot heights.

500   ‡a Includes index to National Park properties and insets of Alaska and the Hawaiian
         Islands.

500   ‡a Directory of interstate retail facilities and mileage chart on verso.

500   ‡a Map distributed by Conoco Inc.

Information from map face

Road map of the
United States
Conoco

Scale in miles and kilometers
One inch 112 miles
One inch 179 kilometers

© The H.M. Gousha Company
Box 5227 – San Jose, Calif 95150

1977 edition

Information from map panel

Touraide˙
Interstate Travel Guide

Conoco

Sometimes, as in the map described in figure 8.30, a map includes a bar scale or a grid rather than a scale statement. Scale can be calculated by using a scale indicator (a device for measuring bar graphs and grids to convert them into a representative fraction) or a conversion formula. If no grid, bar graph, or verbal statement is found on a map, compare the map to another of known scale and give an approximate scale. Scale statements computed from a bar scale or grid, or estimated by comparison with another map of known scale, are preceded by "approximately."

Figure 8.30. Estimated Scale Statement

034	1	‡a a ‡b 1560000 ‡d W0803100 ‡e W0744100 ‡f N0421600 ‡g N0394300
110	2	‡a PRISM Climate Group, ‡e cartographer.
245	10	‡a Plant hardiness zone map, Pennsylvania / ‡c mapping by the PRISM Climate Group, Oregon State University ; ARS, Agricultural Research Service.
255		‡a Scale approximately 1:1,560,000 ‡c (W 80°31'--W 74°41'/N 42°16'--N 39°43').
264	1	‡a [Washington, D.C.] : ‡b [United States Department of Agriculture], ‡c [2012]
300		‡a 1 map : ‡b color ; ‡c 29 x 38 cm
336		‡a cartographic image ‡2 rdacontent
337		‡a unmediated ‡2 rdamedia
338		‡a sheet ‡2 rdacarrier

500	‡a Shows "Average annual extreme minimum temperature, 1976-2005" in both Fahrenheit and Celsius degrees.
500	‡a Includes color logos for the United States Department of Agriculture (USDA), the Agricultural Research Service (ARS), and Oregon State University.
710 1	‡a United States. ‡b Agricultural Research Service, ‡e sponsoring body.

Useful guidelines for the conversion of map scales to representative fractions are found in *Cartographic Materials,* appendix B.[9]

If no scale can be determined, record "Scale not given" (see figure 8.31). Scale is only recorded for digital resources if a scale statement is explicitly given in the resource. In other cases, record "Scale not given" (see figure 8.32). This sensible guideline recognizes the fact that the actual scale displayed for a digital resource is dependent on unpredictable factors such as screen resolution, projection settings, etc., and can often be varied or manipulated.

Figure 8.31. Scale Not Given

100	1	‡a Sgrooten, Christian, ‡d approximately 1525-1603, ‡e cartographer.
240	10	‡a Kaarten van de Nederlanden
245	10	‡a Christiaan Sgroten's Kaarten van de Nederlanden / ‡c in reproduktie uitgegeven onder auspicien van het Koninklijk Nederlandsch Aardrijkskundig Genootschap ; met een inleiding van S.J. Fockema Andreae en B. van 't Hoff.
255		‡a Scale not given.
264	1	‡a Leiden : ‡b E.J. Brill, ‡c 1961.
300		‡a 1 map on 21 sheets ; ‡c sheets 62 x 71 cm + ‡e 1 pamphlet, in portfolio 64 x 73 cm
336		‡a cartographic image ‡2 rdacontent
337		‡a unmediated ‡2 rdamedia
338		‡a sheet ‡2 rdacarrier
500		‡a Reprint. Originally published approximately 1573.
500		‡a Title from pamphlet.
504		‡a Pamphlet includes bibliographical references.
700	1	‡a Fockema Andreae, S. J. ‡q (Sybrandus Johannes), ‡d 1904-1968, ‡e editor.
700	1	‡a Hoff, Bert van 't, ‡d 1900-1979, ‡e editor.
710	2	‡a Koninklijk Nederlands Aardrijkskundig Genootschap, ‡e issuing body.

Figure 8.32. Scale Not Given (Digital Resource)

034	0	‡a a ‡d W0895000 ‡e W0893830 ‡f N0308030 ‡g N0300130
100	1	‡a Nayegandhi, Amar, ‡e cartographer.

245 10 ‡a EAARL coastal topography, Alligator Point, Louisiana, 2010 / ‡c Amar Nayeghandi, J.M. Bonisteel-Cormier, C.W. Wright, J.C. Brock, D.B. Nagle, Saisudha Vivekanandan, Xan Fredericks, and J.A. Barras.

255 ‡a Scale not given ; ‡b universal transverse Mercator projection ‡c (W 89°50'00"--W 89°38'30"/N 30°08'30"--N 30°01'30").

264 1 ‡a [Reston, Virginia] : ‡b U.S. Department of the Interior, U.S. Geological Survey, ‡c 2012.

300 ‡a 1 online resource (1 map) : ‡b color

336 ‡a cartographic image ‡2 rdacontent

337 ‡a computer ‡2 rdamedia

338 ‡a online resource ‡2 rdacarrier

347 ‡a data file ‡a image file ‡2 rda

490 1 ‡a Data series ; ‡v 665

500 ‡a Relief shown by gradient tints.

500 ‡a Title from HTML index page (viewed on March 23, 2012).

500 ‡a Includes location map.

710 2 ‡a Geological Survey (U.S.), ‡e sponsoring body.

830 0 ‡a Data series (Geological Survey (U.S.)) ; ‡v 655.

856 40 ‡u http://pubs.usgs.gov/ds/665/

7.25.1.4. MORE THAN ONE SCALE. Sometimes the scale used on a single item varies, especially on small-scale maps (those covering large areas). If this is the case, give the largest fraction followed by the smallest fraction, connecting the two by a hyphen (see figure 8.33).

Figure 8.33. More Than One Scale

110 2 ‡a Falk-Verlag, ‡e cartographer.

245 10 ‡a Frankfurt a. M., Offenbach / ‡c Falk.

246 3 ‡a Frankfurt am Main, Offenbach

246 18 ‡a Falkplan extra Frankfurt

250 ‡a 12. Auflag.

255 ‡a Scale 1:16,500-1:27,500 ; ‡b Hyperboloid projection

264 1 ‡a Stuttgart : ‡b Falk-Verlag, ‡c [1998?]

300 ‡a 1 map : ‡b color ; ‡c on sheet 75 x 103 cm, folded in cover 25 x 12 cm

336 ‡a cartographic image ‡2 rdacontent

337 ‡a unmediated ‡2 rdamedia

338 ‡a sheet ‡2 rdacarrier

546 ‡a Legend in German, English, and French.

If the main maps contained in a resource are drawn to more than one scale, use the statement "Scales differ" (see figure 8.34) Alternately, give more than one scale statement in separate 255 fields. This may be particularly appropriate if the projection or coordinates also differ (see figure 8.35). The Library of Congress will apply the alternative guideline only if there are no more than two scales (LC-PCC PS 7.25.1.4, February 2010).

Figure 8.34. Scales Differ

020		‡a 9788187460008
110	2	‡a Indian Map Service, ‡e cartographer.
245	10	‡a India road atlas / ‡c designed, cartographed & printed by Indian Map Service ; editors, R.P. Arya, Gayathri Arya, Anshuman Arya.
250		‡a Edition 2011.
255		‡a Scales differ.
264	1	‡a Jodhpur : ‡b Indian Map Service, [2011]
264	4	‡c ©2008
300		‡a 1 atlas (79 pages) : ‡b color illustrations, color maps ; ‡c 25 cm
336		‡a cartographic image ‡2 rdacontent
337		‡a unmediated ‡2 rdamedia
338		‡a volume ‡2 rdacarrier
500		‡a Includes index.
700	1	‡a Arya, R. P., ‡e editor.
700	1	‡a Arya, Gayathri, ‡e editor.
700	1	‡a Arya, Anshuman, ‡e editor.

Figure 8.35. Differing Scales Recorded Separately

110	2	‡a National Geographic Society (U.S.). ‡b Cartographic Division, ‡e cartographer.
245	14	‡a The earth's fractured surface ; ‡b Living on the edge : [West Coast of the United States] / ‡c produced by the Cartographic Division, National Geographic Society ; John F. Shupe, chief cartographer.
255		‡a Scale 1:48,000,000. 1 in. = 758 miles ; ‡b Winkel tripel projection ‡c (W 180°--E 180°/N 90°--S 90°).
255		‡a Scale 1:2,380,000. 1 in. = 38 miles ; ‡b Albers conic equal-area projection, standard parallels 20°30' and 45°30'.
265	1	‡a Washington, D.C. : ‡b National Geographic Society, ‡c 1995.
300		‡a 2 maps on 1 sheet : ‡b both sides, color ; ‡c sheet 57 x 93 cm folded to 23 x 15 cm
336		‡a cartographic image ‡2 rdacontent
337		‡a unmediated ‡2 rdamedia

338	‡a sheet ‡2 rdacarrier
500	‡a Relief shown by satellite imagery, gradient tints, and spot heights. Depth shown by satellite imagery, shading, and soundings.
500	‡a Includes text, indexed ancillary map showing major plates, indexes to earthquakes and volcanic eruptions, cross section, 2 graphs, and 5 ancillary maps.
700 1	‡a Shupe, John F., ‡e cartographer.
710 22	‡a National Geographic Society (U.S.). ‡b Cartographic Division. ‡t Earth's fractured surface.
710 22	‡a National Geographic Society (U.S.). ‡b Cartographic Division. ‡t Living on the edge.

7.25.3.3. RECORDING HORIZONTAL SCALE OF CARTOGRAPHIC CONTENT. Details of how to record this sub-element have already been discussed above. However, for some cartographic resources it would be inappropriate to record scale. Such resources include imaginary maps. Additionally, a pictorial "bird's-eye view" of an area is not drawn to an accurate scale. If no scale is stated on such an item, do not try to approximate one. Use the statement "Not drawn to scale" (see figure 8.36).

Figure 8.36. Not Drawn to Scale (Bird's-Eye View)

100 1	‡a Gross, Peter Alfred, ‡d 1849-1914, ‡e cartographer.
245 10	‡a Birds-eye view of Toronto, 1876 / ‡c designed, sketched, lithographed & published by P.A. Gross, Toronto, Ont.
255	‡a Not drawn to scale.
264 1	‡a Ottawa : ‡b Association of Canadian Map Libraries and Archives, ‡c 2000.
300	‡a 1 view : ‡b color ; ‡c 28 x 47 cm.
336	‡a cartographic image ‡2 rdacontent
337	‡a unmediated ‡2 rdamedia
338	‡a sheet ‡2 rdacarrier
490 1	‡a Canadian cities, bird's eye views = ‡a Villes du Canada, vues à vol d'oiseau
500	‡a Relief shown pictorially.
500	‡a Facsimile.
534	‡p Original version: ‡c Toronto : P.A. Gross, [1876].
500	‡a "Reproduction from an original in the National Archives of Canada."
500	‡a "Sponsored by Global Genealogy Supply, Milton, Ontario."
500	‡a Includes illustrations of buildings.
710 2	‡a Association of Canadian Map Libraries and Archives, ‡e publisher.
830 0	‡a Canadian cities, bird's eye views

Some maps, particularly those designed for tourists, are deliberately not drawn to scale, in order that certain areas or features may be highlighted. The same statement, "Not drawn to scale," is appropriate for such items (see figure 8.37).

Figure 8.37. Not Drawn to Scale

110	1	‡a Fern/Horn Endeavors, ‡e cartographer.
245	10	‡a Yellowstone National Park : ‡b panoramic hiking map.
255		‡a Not drawn to scale.
264	1	‡a Estes Park, Colorado : ‡b Fern/Horn Endeavors, ‡c [2000]
264	4	‡a ©2000
300		‡a 1 map : ‡b color ; ‡c 58 x 86 cm.
336		‡a cartographic image ‡2 rdacontent
337		‡a unmediated ‡2 rdamedia
338		‡a sheet ‡2 rdacarrier
490	1	‡a Trail tracks
500		‡a Relief shown pictorially.
500		‡a Includes index to trails.
830	0	‡a Trail tracks (Estes Park, Colo.)

Information from map

Yellowstone National Park
Panoramic Hiking Map
Trail Tracks ®
©2000
This map is for illustrative purposes only. Distances are not to scale.

7.25.5. ADDITIONAL SCALE INFORMATION. Supplemental information about scale that appears on the resource, including statements that do not appear as a representative fraction, may be recorded in this element. Depending on the resource, it is recorded either in MARC bibliographic field 255 (cartographic resources) or subfield b of MARC bibliographic field 507 (everything else). See discussion above at 7.25.1.3, with figures 8.28 and 8.29.

7.26. PROJECTION OF CARTOGRAPHIC CONTENT. Projection is the method used to represent the surface of the Earth or another sphere on a flat surface such as a sheet. If the resource includes a statement of projection, it may be transcribed, as it appears, in this element. The projection of cartographic content element follows the scale element, in subfield ‡b of the 255 field, preceded by space-semicolon-space. For examples, see figures 8.32, 8.33, and 8.35. Phrases concerning the meridians or parallels associated with the projection statement may also be recorded as part of this element (see figure 8.35).

7.27. OTHER DETAILS OF CARTOGRAPHIC CONTENT. This element calls for notes about the cartographic content that have not been recorded in other elements. Particularly common are notes giving details about how relief is shown on the resource (see figures 8.29, 8.32, 8.35, 8.36, and 8.37).

7.28. AWARD. If an expression of a work has received an award or prize, the information may be recorded in this element. The award element is recorded in the MARC bibliographic 586 field. If the expression has received more than one award, each is generally recorded in a separate field (see figure 8.15), or all may be recorded in a single field.

NOTES

1. Full information about *MARC 21 Format for Authority Data* is available at www.loc .gov/marc/authority/ecadhome.html. Information about *MARC 21 Format for Bibliographic Data* is available at www.loc.gov/marc/bibliographic/ecbdhome.html.

2. Pre-AACR2 authority records are identified by "d" in 008 position 10 for "AACR2 compatible heading," "b" for AACR1, and "a" for earlier rules.

3. IFLA Study Group on the Functional Requirements for Bibliographic Records, "User Tasks," ch. 6 in *Functional Requirements for Bibliographic Records Final: Report* (Munich: K. G. Sauer, 1998), 79–92. Also available at www.ifla.org/en/publications/ functional-requirements-for-bibliographic-records. FRAD is an extension of FRBR; see IFLA Working Group on Functional Requirements and Numbering of Authority Records, *Functional Requirements for Authority Data: A Conceptual Model.* IFLA Series on Bibliographic Control, vol. 34 (Munich: K. G. Saur, 2009).

4. Source information about certain elements may be recorded directly in the element's MARC field itself, in subfield ‡v, rather than in a 670 field. This technique is available for the 046 and 370–378 fields. This method has not yet found much favor in practice and is not used in this book.

5. *Descriptive Cataloging Manual* Z1 is available at www.loc.gov/catdir/cpso/ z1andlcguidelines.html.

6. As of this writing the Program for Cooperative Cataloging has asked that content type not be recorded in NACO authority records. It is assumed that this restriction will be lifted. Content type has been recorded in all authority records for expression in this book. Catalogers should follow the latest PCC guidelines.

7. MARC Code List for Languages, www.loc.gov/marc/languages/langhome.html.

8. *The HarperCollins Bible Dictionary,* rev. ed., Mark Allan Powell, ed. (New York: HarperCollins, 2011).

9. Anglo-American Cataloguing Committee for Cartographic Materials, *Cartographic Materials: A Manual of Interpretation for AACR2, 2002 Revision,* 2nd ed., Elizabeth Mangan, ed. (Chicago: American Library Association, 2003).

CHAPTER 9

RECORDING RELATIONSHIPS

ECORDING RELATIONSHIPS BETWEEN ENTITIES has been fundamental to cataloging since its beginnings, although the activity hasn't always been described in those terms. Relationship considerations underlie Cutter's famous objects of the catalog, which are that the catalog should:

1. Enable the user to find a book of which either the author, title, or subject is known;
2. Show the user what the library has by a given author, on a given subject, or in a given kind of literature; and
3. Assist in the choice of a book as to its edition or as to its character.[1]

In order to accomplish the first object, the catalog must be able to show the relationship between a book and an author or a title or a subject; to accomplish the second the catalog must be able to show the relationship between a person or a topic or a literary genre and works represented in the database; to accomplish the third, the catalog must be able to show the relationships between manifestations or expressions of a given work.[2]

Because relationships are so important, RDA devotes over half of its chapters (17 though 39) to guidelines for recording them, with an additional four appendixes also devoted to relationship issues (Appendixes I through L).

MARC Coding. Relationships are shown in several ways in MARC records. In a bibliographic record, access points are all links between the description of the resource and related entities such as persons, families, corporate bodies, works, and concepts; in short, any of the FRBR entities. Access points are recorded in 1XX (sometimes in combination with 240), 6XX, 7XX, and 8XX fields. Figure 9.1 illustrates how relationships appear in a bibliographic record. The record in this figure represents a manifestation of two expressions of a work titled "Psalmorum Davidis paraphrasis poetica." This resource has a relationship with a person, the creator of the work. This is shown by the presence of the author's authorized access point in the 100 field, and the field links this record with other records in the database containing the same authorized access point (see chapter 3 for information about forming the authorized access point for a person). As mentioned, this publication contains two expressions of the work, an edition of the original Latin expression and an expression in English. The relationship of this publication to these two expressions is shown by the first two 700 fields, the authorized access points for the two expressions (see chapter 8 for information about forming the authorized access point for an expression). These expressions were realized by a person, Roger Green. The relationship of the expressions to this person is shown by the presence of the third 700 field. This resource is a paraphrase of another work, the Psalms. The resource's relationship to this other work is shown by the presence of the 730 field, which also serves as a link to all other resources in the database that are also related to the Psalms (see chapter 7 for information about forming the authorized access point for a work). This work also has a relationship to other paraphrases of the Psalms, both in English and in Latin. Under current subject analysis practice, this relationship is shown by the two 630 fields in the record. The resource has a relationship to a series, "Travaux d'humanisme et Renaissance." This relationship is recorded in the 490 field and a link to other resources within the same series (i.e., with the same relationship) is made through the 830 field.

Figure 9.1. Relationships (Bibliographic Record)

020	‡a 9782600014458
100 1	‡a Buchanan, George, ‡d 1506-1582, ‡e author.
245 10	‡a Poetic paraphrase of the Psalms of David = ‡b Psalmorum Davidis paraphrasis poetica / ‡c George Buchanan ; edited, translated, and provided with introduction and commentary by Roger P.H. Green.
246 3	‡a Psalmorum Davidis paraphrasis poetica
264 1	‡a Genève : ‡b Librairie Droz, ‡c 2011.
300	‡a 640 pages ; ‡c 25 cm.
336	‡a text ‡2 rdacontent

337 ‡a unmediated ‡2 rdamedia

338 ‡a volume ‡2 rdacarrier

490 1 ‡a Travaux d'humanisme et Renaissance, ‡x 0082-6081 ; ‡v no CDLXXVI

504 ‡a Includes bibliographical references (pages 629-632) and index.

546 ‡a Text in Latin with parallel English translation; preface, introduction and commentary in English.

630 00 ‡a Bible. ‡p Psalms ‡v Paraphrases, English.

630 00 ‡a Bible. ‡p Psalms ‡v Paraphrases, Latin.

700 12 ‡a Buchanan, George, ‡d 1506-1582. ‡t Psalmorum Davidis paraphrasis poetica. ‡l English ‡s (Green)

700 12 ‡a Buchanan, George, ‡d 1506-1582. ‡t Psalmorum Davidis paraphrasis poetica. ‡l Latin ‡s (Green)

700 1 ‡a Green, Roger ‡q (Roger P. H.), ‡e editor, ‡e translator.

730 0 ‡i Paraphrase of (work): ‡a Bible. ‡p Psalms.

830 0 ‡a Travaux d'humanisme et Renaissance ; ‡v no 476.

Additionally, another relationship is discernible in this record. The resource has a relationship to its publisher, Librairie Droz. This type of relationship is typically simply recorded in subfield ‡b of the 264 field without making an explicit link using an added access point, although this could also be done.

Depending on the system, a given access point may link to the authority record for the entity, or if there is no authority record, it may simply link all the bibliographic records that share a relationship with the same entity. The system may do this by matching exact character strings, or by links created behind the scenes using identifiers.

MARC authority records also show relationships. Several relationships are shown in the authority records illustrated in figure 9.2, which are related to the resource described in figure 9.1. In the description of one of the expressions (figure 9.2a), the relationship of this expression to its work is shown in the record by the presence of the authorized access point for the work at the beginning of the 100 field, "‡a Buchanan, George, ‡d 1506-1582. ‡t Psalmorum Davidis paraphrasis poetica." This also links this expression description to the description of the work (see figure 9.2b, which contains the identical string). The relationship between the work and its author is shown in the work description (figure 9.2b) by the presence of the authorized access point for the person at the beginning of the 100 field, which is identical to the form found in the 100 field of the description of the person (figure 9.2c). In the MARC format these three authority records are linked by the forms found in their 100 fields.

Relationships in authority records are also shown through 5XX fields, commonly known as "see also" references. A form in 5XX always contains an authorized access

Figure 9.2. Relationships (Authority Records)

9.2a. Expression

046	‡k 2011
100 1	‡a Buchanan, George, ‡d 1506-1582. ‡t Psalmorum Davidis paraphrasis poetica. ‡l English ‡s (Green)
336	‡a text ‡2 rdacontent
377	‡a eng
381	‡a Green
400 1	‡a Buchanan, George, ‡d 1506-1582. ‡t Poetic paraphrase of the Psalms of David
500 1	‡w r ‡i Translator: ‡a Green, Roger ‡q (Roger P. H.)
670	‡a Poetic paraphrase of the Psalms of David, 2011: ‡b title page (edited and translated by Roger P.H. Green) page 9 (translated more than once into English since its original Latin publication)

9.2b. Work

046	‡k 1565
100 1	‡a Buchanan, George, ‡d 1506-1582. ‡t Psalmorum Davidis paraphrasis poetica
380	‡a Poem
400 1	‡a Buchanan, George, ‡d 1506-1582. ‡t Paraphrasis Psalmorum Davidi poetica
670	‡a Poetic paraphrase of the Psalms of David = Psalmorum Davidis paraphrasis poetica, 2011: ‡b page 9 (Psalmorum Davidis paraphrasis poetica, Paraphrasis Psalmorum Davidi poetica) page 13 (first printed late 1565 or early 1566)

9.2c. Person (Author of the Work)

046	‡f 15060201- ‡g 15820928 ‡2 edtf
100 1	‡a Buchanan, George, ‡d 1506-1582
370	‡a Killearn (Scotland) ‡b Edinburgh (Scotland) ‡2 naf
374	‡a Poet ‡a Historian ‡a Administrator
375	‡a male
377	‡a lat
670	‡a Poetic paraphrase of the Psalms of David = Psalmorum Davidis paraphrasis poetica, 2011: ‡b title page (George Buchanan)
670	‡a Oxford dictionary of national biography online, 8 July 2012 ‡b (Buchanan, George (1506-1582), poet, historian, and administrator, was born about 1 February 1506 at a farm called The Moss in Killearn parish, Stirlingshire; died 28 September 1582 in Edinburgh)

9.2d. Person (Translator of the Expression)

100 1	‡a Green, Roger ‡q (Roger P. H.)
372	‡a Humanities ‡a Latin language and literature
373	‡a University of Glasgow ‡2 naf ‡s 1995 ‡t 2008
374	‡a Professor
375	‡a male
377	‡a eng
378	‡q Roger P. H.
670	‡a International Congress of Neo-Latin Studies (10th : 1997 : Avila, Spain). Acta Conventus Neo-Latini Abulensis, 2000: ‡b CIP title page (Roger Green)
670	‡a Phone call to publisher, October 26, 1999: ‡b (Roger P.H. Green)
670	‡a George Buchanan, 2009: ‡b title page (Roger P.H. Green) page xiv (Roger Green; Professor of Humanity, University of Glasgow, 1995-2008)

point and links the authority record to another authority record with the same form in a 1XX field. In figure 9.2a the relationship between the expression and its translator is shown by the 500 field containing the authorized access point for Green, which is identical to the form found in the 100 field of Green's own authority record (figure 9.2d).

Other kinds of relationships are also found in authority records. For example, the expression described in figure 9.2a has a relationship to the English language, as shown in the 377 field, and the presence of this information in the record could be used to link this description to other English-language expressions. The places recorded in the 370 field of figure 9.2c could be used to link Buchanan's description with those of other persons associated with Killearn or Edinburgh, or the recording of the associated institution in the 373 field of figure 9.2d could be used to link this person with other persons associated with the University of Glasgow.

RECORDING PRIMARY RELATIONSHIPS BETWEEN WORK, EXPRESSION, MANIFESTATION, AND ITEM

CHAPTER 17. GENERAL GUIDELINES ON RECORDING PRIMARY RELATIONSHIPS. The so-called primary relationships are those between a work and its expression(s), manifestation(s), and item(s). These four entities are the FRBR Group 1 entities, the products of intellectual or artistic endeavor. The relationships between these entities is shown in figure 9.3 (as well as figure 1.1). A work, "a distinct intellectual or artistic creation," is said to be *realized through* one or more expressions (FRBR 3.2.1). An expression, the "realization of a work in the form of alpha-numeric, musical, or choreographic notation, sound, image, object, movement, etc." is said to be *embodied in* one or more manifestations (FRBR 3.2.2). A manifestation, "the physical embodiment of an expression of a work," is said to be *exemplified by* one or more items (FRBR 3.2.3). And finally, an item is "a single exemplar of a manifestation" (FRBR 3.2.4).

Figure 9.3. Primary Relationships

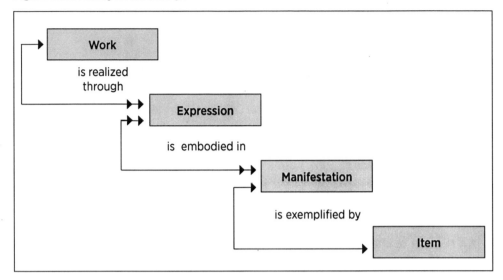

RDA chapter 17 gives instructions for recording the relationships between these primary entities. Unfortunately, these instructions are not very helpful in the MARC environment, and the LC policy statement for the chapter simply says "Do not apply chapter 17 in the current implementation scenario" (LC-PCC PS 17.0, January 2013). However, we do in fact record these relationships in the MARC environment; therefore, a brief discussion of this follows.

17.4.2. CONVENTIONS USED TO RECORD PRIMARY RELATIONSHIPS. RDA has three conventions for recording primary relationships: identifiers, authorized access points, and composite descriptions.

17.4.2.1. IDENTIFIER FOR THE WORK, EXPRESSION, MANIFESTATION, OR ITEM. An identifier is a character string uniquely associated with a work, expression, manifestation, or item. Recording identifiers has been discussed in chapter 7 (for works, at RDA 6.8); chapter 8 (for expressions, at RDA 6.13); and chapter 2 (for manifestations, at RDA 2.15).

Although there are many kinds of identifiers for works or expressions, in the current MARC environment the most commonly used identifiers are the Library of Congress Control Numbers (LCCNs) recorded in the 010 field of authority records representing works or expressions. In library implementations that link authority records to access points in bibliographic records, the LCCN corresponding to the authority record describing the work or expression may be embedded into the authorized access point recorded in a bibliographic record, usually in a way that is invisible to the user. This identifier serves as the link between the bibliographic record and the authority record and thus may be thought to record the relationship between the manifestation recorded in the bibliographic record and the expression or the work.

Identifiers for manifestations such as ISBNs or ISMNs are commonly recorded in MARC bibliographic records, but they are not used in the current MARC environment to record relationships (or create links) between manifestations and works, expressions, or items.

17.4.2.2. AUTHORIZED ACCESS POINT REPRESENTING THE WORK OR EXPRESSION. Authorized access points for works or expressions are used in the current MARC environment to show the relationship between a manifestation and a work or expression embodied in it, and between works and expressions. The presence of an authorized access point for a work or expression in a bibliographic record may record the relationship between the resource described and the work or expression in the resource.

In current RDA practice for MARC bibliographic records, an authorized access point for a work or an expression embodied in the manifestation being described is recorded in 1XX or 7XX fields.

If there is only one work or expression embodied in the manifestation, the current practice is to record its access point in a 1XX field and 240 field combination or a 130 field.

If under RDA 6.27–6.31 the authorized access point for a work would be constructed by combining the authorized access point for the creator with the preferred title of the work (see, e.g., 6.27.1.2), this authorized access point is recorded in the bibliographic record by giving the authorized access point for the creator in a 100, 110, or 111 field as appropriate, and giving the preferred title portion a 240 field. The first indicator of the 240 field tells the system whether to display the title. North American practice is generally to code this indicator "1" (display). The second indicator gives the number of nonfiling characters (the number of characters that the system should skip before beginning to file the title). If the preferred title is recorded without an initial article following the RDA 6.2.1.7 alternative, this indicator should be coded "0." Current North American practice is to follow the alternative, coding the indicator "0." The authorized access point for an expression based on such a work is recorded in the same way (see figure 9.4).

Figure 9.4. Authorized Access Point for Expression in Bibliographic Record

020	‡a 9781554537822
100 1	‡a Dubuc, Marianne, ‡d 1980- ‡e author.
240 10	‡a Au carnaval des animaux. ‡l English
245 10	‡a Animal masquerade / ‡c Marianne Dubuc.
264 1	‡a Toronto : ‡b Kids Can Press, ‡c [2012]

300	‡a 1 volume (unpaged) : ‡b color illustrations ; ‡c 19 cm
336	‡a text ‡2 rdacontent
336	‡a still image ‡2 rdacontent
337	‡a unmediated ‡2 rdamedia
338	‡a volume ‡2 rdacarrier
500	‡a English translation and editing by Yvette Ghione (see colophon).
520	‡a The animals attend a masquerade dressed as each other: the lion goes as an elephant, the elephant as a parrot, and the parrot as a turtle.
700 1	‡a Ghione, Yvette, ‡e translator, ‡e editor.

If under RDA 6.27–6.31 the authorized access point for a work would be constructed by using the preferred title alone (see, e.g., 6.27.1.4), this authorized access point is recorded in the bibliographic record in a 130 field. The authorized access point for an expression based on such a work is recorded in the same way. Figure 9.5 contains an authorized access point for the work embodied in this resource, recorded in subfield ‡a of the 130 field.

Figure 9.5. Authorized Access Point Representing a Work

130 0	‡a Saint Columbia (Hymn tune) ; ‡o arranged ‡s (Wilberg)
245 14	‡a The king of love my shepherd is : ‡b for mixed choir (SATB), two flutes, and harp or piano / ‡c Irish tune arranged by Mack Wilberg ; [words by] Henry Baker.
264 1	‡a [United States] : ‡b Oxford University Press, ‡c [2000]
300	‡a 1 score (8 pages) and 2 parts ; ‡c 27 cm
336	‡a notated music ‡2 rdacontent
337	‡a unmediated ‡2 rdamedia
338	‡a volume ‡2 rdacarrier
490 1	‡a Oxford sacred music
546	‡b Staff notation.
500	‡a Flute parts on pages 9 and 10.
500	‡a Caption title.
700 1	‡a Wilberg, Mack, ‡e arranger of music.
700 1	‡a Baker, H. W. ‡q (Henry Williams), ‡d 1821-1877, ‡a writer of added lyrics.
830 0	‡a Oxford sacred music.

Current practice is to explicitly record an access point for the work embodied in the manifestation described in the bibliographic record only if its preferred title differs from the title proper of the manifestation recorded in subfield ‡a of the 245 field. The authorized access point for the work embodied in the description in figure 9.6 is, in fact, "Bowerman, Bruce L. Essentials of business statistics" and could in theory be recorded in the record as:

    100   1 ‡a Bowerman, Bruce L.
    240 10 ‡a Essentials of business statistics

However, because the preferred title of the work is exactly the same as the title proper recorded in 245 subfield ‡a, most catalogers would not formally record the authorized access point for the work in a 100 and 240 field combination.

Figure 9.6. Recording the Work Embodied in the Resource

020	‡a 9780073401829
100 1	‡a Bowerman, Bruce L., ‡e author.
245 10	‡a Essentials of business statistics / ‡c Bruce L. Bowerman, Richard T. O'Connell, Emily S. Murphree, J.B. Orris, with major contributions by Steven C. Huchendorf, Dawn C. Porter, Patrick J. Schur.
250	‡a Fourth edition.
264 1	‡a New York, N.Y. : ‡b McGraw-Hill/Irwin, ‡c [2012]
300	‡a xxii, 665 pages : ‡b color illustrations ; ‡c 29 cm
500	‡a Includes bibliographical references (pages 657-658) and indexes.
700 1	‡a O'Connell, Richard T., ‡e author.
700 1	‡a Murphree, Emily, ‡e author.
700 1	‡a Orris, J. B., ‡e author.
700 1	‡a Huchendorf, Steven C., ‡e author.
700 1	‡a Porter, Dawn C., ‡e author.
700 1	‡a Schur, Patrick, ‡e author.

Title page

Bruce L. Bowerman
Miami University
Richard T. O'Connell
Miami University
Emily S. Murphree
Miami University
J.B. Orris
Miami University

Essentials of Business Statistics

FOURTH EDITION

with major contributions by
Steven C. Huchendorf
University of Minnesota
Dawn C. Porter
University of Southern California
Patrick J. Schur
Miami University

McGraw-Hill
Irwin

If there is more than one work or expression embodied in the manifestation, the current practice is to record access points for each in 700, 710, 711, or 730 fields as appropriate, with the second indicator coded "2" (meaning the resource contains the work or expression represented by the authorized access point). Access points coded in this way are called "analytic" access points, because they "analyze" all or part of the contents of the resource. Authorized access points for works or expressions may be recorded in 7XX fields with the second indicator coded blank, but this signifies that the authorized access point is for a *related* work or expression, not a work or expression embodied in the resource.

In figure 9.1, the manifestation with the title "Poetic paraphrase of the Psalms of David" is the embodiment of two particular expressions of a particular work. This is recorded by giving the authorized access points for the expressions the two 700 fields (the first two in this case) of the record. These authorized access points link the bibliographic record to the corresponding authority records because each is identical to the character string in the 100 field of the authority record (see figure 9.2); if either of the expressions has been published in other manifestations, the authorized access points would also link this publication to those.

Authorized access points also record the relationship between an expression and a work in another way. The authorized access point for an expression consists of the authorized access point for the work realized by the expression, followed by expression-related elements. In the case of figure 9.2a, a description of an expression, the authorized access point found in the 100 field up to subfield ‡l is identical to the authorized access point for the work (see the 100 field in figure 9.2b). Subfield ‡l ("English") and subfield ‡s ("(Green)") are elements that have been added to differentiate the authorized access point for this expression from that of other expressions of the same work. The relationship between the expression and the work is recorded, in the MARC authority environment, by the presence of the authorized access point for the work at the beginning of the 1XX field in the authority record for the expression.

17.4.2.3. COMPOSITE DESCRIPTION. A composite description is a description that combines elements of work, expression, manifestation, or item in the same description in such a way that the relationships are evident to the human observer of the record, if not to a machine. "Composite description" describes the current cataloging environment in which the bibliographic record often has elements describing many FRBR entities, including work, expression, manifestation, and item. In the case of the piece of music described in figure 9.5, the relationship between the manifestation and the expression is recorded in the transcription of the title and statement of responsibility as well as the expression authorized access point in 130, and their relationship to the work is recorded by the presence of the 130 field in this bibliographic record. The answer to the question "which expression of the musical work Saint Columbia is this?" is found in the 245 field and the 130 field: it is the expression (arrangement) for mixed choir, two flutes, and harp or piano, arranged by Mack Wilberg. We learn that this expression is in notated music (as opposed to a recording) by the recording of the extent (a manifestation element) in subfield ‡a of the 300 field, and of content type (an expression element) in the 336 field. Through all of these clues in the composite description we learn that this 2000 manifestation is related to a particular expression which, in turn, is related to a particular work.

RECORDING RELATIONSHIPS TO PERSONS, FAMILIES, AND CORPORATE BODIES

CHAPTER 18. GENERAL GUIDELINES ON RECORDING RELATIONSHIPS TO PERSONS, FAMILIES, AND CORPORATE BODIES ASSOCIATED WITH A RESOURCE. Chapter 17 covered recording the "primary relationships" within the FRBR Group 1 entities (work, expression, manifestation, item). These entities are referred to as "a resource" in RDA (see RDA 18.1.3). Chapters 18 through 22 cover recording the relationship between those Group 1 entities and the Group 2 entities, that is, those entities that are capable of responsibility for the creation of any of the Group 1 entities: persons, families, or corporate bodies.

18.3. CORE ELEMENTS. Core elements have been discussed extensively in the preceding chapters about describing entities. RDA 18.3 enumerates the relationships that are core, and as such perhaps should have been called "core relationships" rather than "core elements."

There are only two core relationships. The principal of these is the relationship of the work to its creator. If a single person, family, or corporate body is the creator of a work embodied in a resource, then he, she, or it has a relationship to that resource, and according to RDA that relationship must be recorded. In a MARC bibliographic record this relationship is recorded by giving the authorized access point for the creator in a 100 (person or family), 110 (corporate body), or 111 (meeting) field as appropriate. For an example, see figure 9.1.

If more than one person, family, or corporate body is the creator of a work of shared responsibility, only the relationship to the creator deemed to have principal responsibility is core. If no creator is explicitly shown to have principal responsibility (as is usually the case), then the first-named creator is deemed to have principal responsibility, and the relationship to this person, family, or corporate body is core. The relationship between the resource and the principal creator of the work is recorded by giving the authorized access point for that creator in a 100, 110, or 111 field, just as for resources with single creators (see figure 9.6).

In contrast to previous cataloging practice, it doesn't matter how many creators a work of shared responsibility has. The relationship to the principal or first-named creator is recorded in the 100, 110, or 111 fields whether there are two or twenty-five. In AACR2, if there were more than three creators, in most cases no one was recorded at all in 1XX. In AACR2's language, the description was "entered under title" (see AACR2 21.6C2). This practice will no longer be followed in RDA. If creators of a resource are known, the relationship to one of them will be recorded in 1XX. The textbook described in figure 9.6, a work of shared responsibility, has seven creators. None is designated as the principal creator, so the relationship to the first-named is recorded in the 100 field. In previous cataloging practice no one would have been recorded in a 100 field for this description.

Relationships to other creators are not core in RDA, but if they are recorded they are recorded by giving the authorized access point in a 700, 710, or 711 field as appropriate. if the number is manageable most catalogers will record relationships to all creators even if not core.

There is no limitation in RDA to the number of non-core creator relationships that may be recorded. In AACR2, if there were more than three creators only the relationship to the first-named was recorded in a 700, 710, or 711 field. All others were omitted from the bibliographic record entirely (see AACR2 21.6C2). In contrast, refer to the textbook recorded in figure 9.6, where the relationships to all of the non-core creators have been recorded in 700 fields.

Because these relationships are not core, there is no requirement that *all* must be recorded. If in the cataloger's judgment only some of the relationships are important (for example, perhaps some of the creators are associated with the library's parent institution and so would be of interest to local database users), those may be recorded and others not.

There is also no requirement that added access points correspond to names recorded in statements of responsibility or notes, as there was in AACR2 (see AACR2 21.29F). Following the option in RDA 2.4.1.5, the statement of responsibility recorded in figure 9.6 might have been abbreviated to "Bruce L. Bowerman [and six others]." Added access points for the unnamed creators could still be recorded in the RDA bibliographic record.

All works have at least one and possibly more creators, but sometimes the creators are unknown. In this case no relationship to a creator is recorded. In figure 9.5 the only persons related to this resource are related to the expression, not the work, and so no core relationship will be recorded in a 1XX field. (It is an oddity of the initial implementation of RDA that the access point for the work is recorded in 130. The field is called "main entry-uniform title" in the MARC bibliographic format, and there is no concept of main entry for title in RDA. 1XX fields in RDA are used for creators of works, but the work itself is not its own creator, and so it is strange that this field, rather than 730, should be used to record the relationship of the resource to the work, but that is the current practice, a holdover from AACR2 main entry practice.)

The second core relationship mentioned in 18.3 is a person, family, or corporate body associated with the work aside from the work's creator(s), *if* the access point for the person, family, or corporate body is used to construct the authorized access point for the work. This occurs only rarely, but one example would be a defendant in a trial, listed as an "other person associated with a work" in 19.3.2.6. According to 6.29.1.24, the authorized access point for the official proceedings of a trial is constructed by combining the authorized access point for the person or body prosecuted (i.e., the defendant) with the preferred title of the work. Returning to 18.3, this is an example of an "other person . . . associated with a work (if the access point representing that person . . . is used to construct the authorized access point representing the work)" and thus is core, that is, the relationship must be recorded. For an example, see figure 9.7.

Figure 9.7. Core Relationship to "Other Person" Related to Work

100 1	‡a Anthony, Susan B. ‡q (Susan Brownell), ‡d 1820-1906, ‡e defendant.
245 13	‡a An account of the proceedings on the trial of Susan B. Anthony on the charge of illegal voting at the presidential election in Nov., 1872 : ‡b and on the trial of Beverly W. Jones, Edwin T. Marsh and William B. Hall, the inspectors of elections by whom her vote was received.
264 1	‡a Rochester, N.Y. : ‡b Daily Democrat and Chronicle Book Print, 3 West Main St., ‡c 1874.
300	‡a vii, 212 pages ; ‡c 23 cm
336	‡a text ‡2 rdacontent
337	‡a unmediated ‡2 rdamedia
338	‡a volume ‡2 rdacarrier
710 1	‡a United States. ‡b Circuit Court (New York : Northern District)

18.4. RECORDING RELATIONSHIPS TO PERSONS, FAMILIES, AND CORPORATE BODIES ASSOCIATED WITH A RESOURCE. Two conventions for recording relationships to a resource are enumerated in 18.4.1, identifier and authorized access point. These have been discussed above at 17.4.2. The third convention mentioned under 17.4.2, the composite description, is not mentioned with 18.4. It is not clear why not. Composite descriptions, including MARC bibliographic records taken as a whole, can record relationships even in the absence of explicit identifiers or authorized access points. For example, in figure 9.8 the cataloger chose not to include added access points for persons related to the film such as the actors or producer. Their relationship to the resource *is* recorded, however, in the description by the inclusion of the statement of responsibility (245 field) and the credits and performer notes (508 and 511).

Figure 9.8. Composite Description

024 1	‡a 883316288849
245 00	‡a Sunday in New York / ‡c Metro-Goldwyn-Mayer presents a Seven Arts production ; screen play, Norman Krasna ; produced by Everett Freeman ; directed by Peter Tewksbury.
250	‡a Remastered edition.
264 1	‡a [Place of publication not identified] : ‡b [publisher not identified], ‡c [2011]
264 2	‡a Burbank, CA : ‡b Distributed by Warner Home Video
264 4	‡c ©2011
300	‡a 1 videodisc (105 min.) : ‡b sound, color ; ‡c 4 3/4 in.
336	‡a two-dimensional moving image ‡2 rdacontent
337	‡a video ‡2 rdamedia
338	‡a videodisc ‡2 rdacarrier
344	‡a digital ‡g mono ‡h Dolby
346	‡a NTSC
347	‡a video file ‡b DVD video ‡e all regions
380	‡a Motion picture.
490 1	‡a Archive collection
500	‡a full screen (1.33:1)
511 1	‡a Cliff Robertson, Jane Fonda, Rod Taylor, Robert Culp, Jo Morrow, Jim Backus, Peter Nero.
508	‡a Director of photography, Leo Tover; music, Peter Nero; editor, Fredric Steinkamp.
518	‡a Originally produced in the United States as a motion picture in 1963.
500	‡a Based on Norman Krasna's play of the same title.
520	‡a A sophisticated comedy concerning a young Albany girl's romantic misadventures with a man who she meets one rainy Sunday in New York. Complications result from the appearance of her airline-pilot brother and her home-town beau.
500	‡a Includes trailer.
700 1	‡i Motion picture adaptation of (work): ‡a Krasna, Norman. ‡t Sunday in New York.
830 0	‡a Archive collection.

18.4.1.2. AUTHORIZED ACCESS POINT REPRESENTING THE PERSON, FAMILY, OR CORPORATE BODY. The most commonly used convention for recording relationships of persons, families, or corporate bodies to resources is the inclusion of authorized access points in MARC bibliographic records. These authorized access points, which serve as *links* between resources and persons, families, or corporate bodies, are recorded in 100, 110, and 111 fields (principal creator) or 700, 710, and 711 fields (other persons, families, or corporate bodies associated with the resource).

The concept of principal creator is discussed below under 19.2. The authorized access point for the principal creator is recorded in a 1XX field in an RDA record. As it is a link to the *principal* creator, there is only one such field per record. There are three types of 1XX fields for creators:

100 Personal name (including family names)
110 Corporate name
111 Meeting name

Access points for other persons, families, and corporate bodies are recorded in 7XX fields. There may be many such fields in a bibliographic record. The same three types exist:

700 Personal name (including family names)
710 Corporate name
711 Meeting name

The following explanation of field coding has been limited to basic information. There are more subfields for each MARC field than those explained here. For further information, consult *MARC 21 Format for Bibliographic Data* at www.loc.gov/marc/bibliographic.

100 and 700 fields are used to record authorized access points for persons. The first indicator is coded "0" if the name of a person consists solely of a forename (see figure 9.9, 100 field) or "1" if the person's preferred name begins with a surname (see figure 9.1, 100 and 700 fields). The second indicator is normally blank (for the exception, see below at chapter 25, "Related Works," and chapter 26, "Related Expressions"). Some of the more commonly used subfields are subfield ‡a (preferred name), subfield ‡q (fuller form), subfield ‡c (title), and subfield ‡d (dates). Authorized access points for persons are constructed according to RDA chapter 9. See chapter 3 of this *Handbook* at 9.19 for more information.

Authorized access points for families are also recorded in 100 and 700 fields, but with the first indicator coded "3" (see figure 9.10, 100 field). The second indicator is normally blank (for the exception, see below at chapter 25, "Related Works," and chapter 26, "Related Expressions"). Commonly used subfields are subfield ‡a (preferred

Figure 9.9. Personal Name Consisting of Forename Alone

020	‡a 9783451325373
100 0	‡a Benedict ‡b XVI, ‡c Pope, ‡d 1927- ‡e interviewee.
245 10	‡a Licht der Welt : ‡b Der Papst, die Kirche und die Zeichen der Zeit / ‡c Benedikt XVI ; ein Gesprach mit Peter Seewald.
250	‡a 2. Auflage.
264 1	‡a Freiburg : ‡b Herder, ‡c [2010]
264 4	‡c ©2010
300	‡a 255 pages ; ‡c 21 cm
336	‡a text ‡2 rdacontent
337	‡a unmediated ‡2 rdamedia
338	‡a volume ‡2 rdacarrier
505 0	‡a Vorwort -- T. 1. Zeichen der Zeit -- T. 2. Das Pontifikat -- T. 3. Wo gehen wir hin? -- Anhang.
700 1	‡a Seewald, Peter, ‡e interviewer.

Figure 9.10. Family Name

100 3	‡a Chatman (Family : ‡c S.C.), ‡e author.
245 10	‡a Chatman's family reunion chronicle.
264 1	‡a Washington, DC : ‡b Dr. Emanuel D. Chatman, ‡c 2005-
310	‡a Annual
336	‡a text ‡2 rdacontent
337	‡a unmediated ‡2 rdamedia
338	‡a volume ‡2 rdacarrier
362 1	‡a Began with ed. 1 (July 1st, 2005).
588	‡a Description based on: Ed. 1 (July 1st, 2005); title from cover.
588	‡a Latest issue consulted: 7th edition (July 31, 2011).

name and type of family), subfield ‡d (date associated with the family), subfield ‡c (place associated with the family), and subfield ‡g (prominent member of the family). Authorized access points for families are constructed according to guidelines in RDA chapter 10. See chapter 4 of this *Handbook* at 10.10 for more information.

110 and 710 fields contain authorized access points for corporate bodies. The first indicator is "1" if the authorized access point begins with the authorized access point for a jurisdiction (e.g., a country or city) (see figure 9.11, 110 field), and "2" if it represents any other type of corporate body (see figure 9.12, 710 fields). The second indicator is normally blank (for the exception, see below at chapter 25, "Related Works,"

and chapter 26, "Related Expressions"). The basic name is recorded in subfield ‡a, and subordinate units in subfield ‡b.

Figure 9.11. Jurisdiction

110 1	‡a Utah. ‡b District Court (3rd District), ‡e creator.
245 10	‡a Utah District Court records of United States vs. George Reynolds.
264 0	‡c 1985.
300	‡a 1 reel of microfilm ‡a (0.15 linear ft.)
300	‡a 1 sound tape reel ‡a (0.15 linear ft.)
506	‡a Open for public research.
520 2	‡a Utah District Court Records of United States vs. George Reynolds is a microfilm copy from 1985, including papers and files in Case Nos. 1631 and 2148, United States vs. George Reynolds from the National Archives--Denver Branch. George Reynolds, an LDS Church official, was indicted for bigamy on 23 October 1874. Reynolds argued that polygamy was protected by the Free Exercise Clause of the First Amendment of the Constitution. The case is the first freedom of religion to issue from that court.
852	‡a L. Tom Perry Special Collections, Harold B. Lee Library, Brigham Young University, ‡e Provo, Utah 84602.

Figure 9.12. Corporate Body

024 1	‡a 822231171928
028 02	‡a LSO0719 ‡b LSO Live
100 1	‡a Britten, Benjamin, ‡d 1913-1976, ‡e composer.
245 10	‡a War requiem / ‡c Britten.
264 1	‡a [London] : ‡b LSO Live, ‡c [2012]
300	‡a 2 audio discs (83 min., 48 sec.) ; ‡c 4 3/4 in.
336	‡a performed music ‡2 rdacontent
337	‡a audio ‡2 rdamedia
338	‡a audio disc ‡2 rdacarrier
344	‡a digital ‡b optical ‡g stereo ‡2 rda
347	‡a audio file ‡b SACD ‡2 rda
546	‡a Sung in Latin and English.
500	‡a Title from container.
500	‡a Intersperses the text of the Requiem with poems by Wilfred Owen.
511 0	‡a Gianandrea Noseda ; London Symphony Orchestra ; Sabina Cvilak, soprano ; Ian Bostridge, tenor ; Simon Keenlyside, baritone ; Choir of Eltham College ; London Symphony Chorus.
518	‡a Recorded live 9 & 11 October 2011 at the Barbican, London.

500	‡a Program notes in English with French and German translations and sung text in Latin (with English translation) and English inserted in container (30 pages).
505 0	‡a Disc 1. Requiem aeternam -- Dies irae -- Offertorium. Disc 2. Sanctus -- Agnus Dei -- Libera me.
700 1	‡a Noseda, Gianandrea, ‡e conductor.
700 1	‡a Cvilak, Sabina, ‡d 1978- ‡e performer.
700 1	‡a Bostridge, Ian, ‡e performer.
700 1	‡a Keenlyside, Simon, ‡e performer.
700 1	‡i Basis for libretto: ‡a Owen, Wilfred, ‡d 1893-1918. ‡t Poems. ‡k Selections.
710 2	‡a London Symphony Orchestra, ‡e performer.
710 2	‡a Eltham College. ‡b Choir, ‡e performer.
710 2	‡a London Symphony Chorus, ‡e performer.

Meetings, expeditions, fairs, etc., are also corporate bodies, but their authorized access points are recorded in 111 or 711 in the MARC bibliographic format when based on the meeting's preferred name (see figure 9.13, 111 field). The first indicator is "2." The second indicator is normally blank (for the exception, see below at chapter 25, "Related Works," and chapter 26, "Related Expressions"). The preferred name is recorded in subfield ‡a, date in subfield ‡d, location in subfield ‡c, and number in subfield ‡n. Authorized access points for meetings that are subordinate to other corporate bodies are recorded in 110 and 710 fields as described in the previous paragraph (see figure 9.14, 110 field).

Figure 9.13. Meeting

020	‡a 9783110239676 (hardcover : alk. paper)
111 2	‡a International Summer School in Coptic Papyrology ‡n (1st : ‡d 2006 : ‡c Vienna, Austria), ‡e author.
245 10	‡a Koptische dokumentarische und literarische Texte : ‡b First International Summer School in Coptic Papyrology 2006 in der Papyrussammlung der Österreichischen Nationalbibliothek / ‡c herausgegeben von Monika R.M. Hasitzka.
246 30	‡a First International Summer School in Coptic Papyrology 2006 in der Papyrussammlung der Österreichischen Nationalbibliothek
264 1	‡a Berlin ; New York : ‡b De Gruyter, ‡c [2011]
264 4	‡c ©2011
300	‡a x, 104 pages ; ‡c 30 cm + ‡e 1 booklet (16 pages of plates) in pocket.
336	‡a text ‡2 rdacontent
337	‡a unmediated ‡2 rdamedia
338	‡a volume ‡2 rdacarrier
490 1	‡a Corpus papyrorum Raineri Archiducis Austriae ; ‡v Band 31

504	‡a Includes bibliographical references and index.
700 1	‡a Hasitzka, Monika R. M., ‡e editor of compilation.
710 2	‡a Österreichische Nationalbibliothek. ‡b Papyrussammlung, ‡e sponsoring body.
830 0	‡a Corpus papyrorum Raineri Archiducis Austriae ; ‡v Bd. 31.

Figure 9.14. Meeting

020	‡a 9788190383448
110 2	‡a North East India Geographical Society. ‡b Annual Academic Session ‡d (2008 : ‡c Guwahati, India), ‡e author.
245 10	‡a North-East India, geo-environmental issues / ‡c editor, Sujit Deka.
264 1	‡a Guwahati : ‡b EBH Publishers (India), ‡c [2008]
300	‡a xviii, 317 pages : ‡b illustrations, maps ; ‡c 22 cm
336	‡a text ‡2 rdacontent
337	‡a unmediated ‡2 rdamedia
338	‡a volume ‡2 rdacarrier
500	‡a "Department of Geography, Pandu College."
520	‡a Contributed articles presented at the Annual Academic Session of North East India Geographical Society on 9 February, 2008.
504	‡a Includes bibliographical references and index.
500	‡a Includes statistical tables.
700 1	‡a Deka, Sujit, ‡d 1971- ‡e editor of compilation.
710 2	‡a Pandu College (Guwahati, India). ‡b Department of Geography, ‡e host institution.

Authorized access points for all corporate bodies (including meetings) are constructed according to RDA chapter 11. See chapter 5 of this *Handbook* at 11.13 for more information.

18.4.2. CHANGE IN RESPONSIBILITY. Changes in responsibility affecting the identification of the work have been discussed in chapter 7 at 6.1.3. At issue there is whether a change in responsibility requires a new description (because the change causes a new work to be created) or not. RDA 6.1.3 tells us that if a change in responsibility occurs in a multipart monograph or an integrating resource, in most cases a new work is *not* considered to be created (but see exceptions under 6.1.3.1); a change in responsibility that affects the authorized access point of a serial work, however, *is* considered to trigger a new work.

RDA 18.4.2 gives instructions for recording the relationship between a resource and a newly responsible entity when identification of the work is *not* affected by the change in responsibility and a new description is *not* created, that is, when the cataloger is simply updating an existing record. The cataloger should link the new person, family, or corporate body to the resource by creating a new access point in a 7XX field *if* the cataloger considers that recording the relationship is important for access to the resource. In figure 9.15, a description of a serial, the issuing body changed several times. This change in responsibility did not affect the identification of the work. Because the cataloger considered the issuing body important for access to this resource, each time the body changed an access point for the newly responsible body was added in a 710 field.

Figure 9.15. Change in Responsibility

245 00	‡a Analecta papyrologica / ‡c Università degli studi di Messina, Facoltà di lettere e filosofia.	
264 1	‡a Messina : ‡b Sicania, ‡c 1991-	
300	‡a volumes : ‡b illustrations ; ‡c 24 cm	
310	‡a Annual	
336	‡a text ‡2 rdacontent	
336	‡a still image ‡2 rdacontent	
337	‡a unmediated ‡2 rdamedia	
338	‡a volume ‡2 rdacarrier	
362 1	‡a Began with I (1989).	
546	‡a Chiefly in Italian; some articles in English, German or French. Edited texts chiefly in Greek, Latin, or Coptic.	
550	‡a Volumes 1-7 issued by: Università degli studi di Messina, Facoltà di lettere e filosofia; 8/9 by: Università degli studi di Messina, Dipartimento di scienze dell'antichita; 10-17 by: Università degli studi di Messina, Dipartimento di filologia e linguistica; 18- by: Università degli studi di Messina, Dipartimento di studi sulla civiltà moderna e la tradizione classica, and Accademia fiorentina di papirologia e di studi sul mondo antico.	
588	‡a Description based on: IV (1992); title from title page.	
588	‡a Latest issue consulted: XVIII-XX (2006-2008).	
710 2	‡a Università di Messina. ‡b Facoltà di lettere e filosofia, ‡e issuing body.	
710 2	‡a Università di Messina. ‡b Dipartimento di scienze dell'antichità, ‡e issuing body.	
710 2	‡a Università di Messina. ‡b Dipartimento di filologia e linguistica, ‡e issuing body.	
710 2	‡a Università di Messina. ‡b Dipartimento di studi sulla civiltà moderna e la tradizione classica, ‡e issuing body.	
710 2	‡a Accademia fiorentina di papirologia e di studi sul mondo antico, ‡e issuing body.	

18.5. RELATIONSHIP DESIGNATOR. A relationship designator is a word or phrase associated with an authorized access point that clarifies the nature of the relationship of the person, family, or corporate body to the resource. The presence of an access point in 1XX or 7XX means there *is* a relationship between the resource and the entity in the access point, but in the absence of a relationship designator it is usually not clear what kind of relationship the entity has with the resource. Relationship designators were provided for in previous cataloging practice (see AACR2 21.0D) but were not widely used outside of specialist communities such as rare book cataloging because of an LC policy discouraging their use. This policy is not in force under RDA and the use of relationship designators to clarify the nature of the relationship is encouraged; they have been used throughout this *Handbook*.

Relationship designators may appear in either bibliographic or authority records. In bibliographic records designators for persons, families, or corporate bodies associated with a resource are recorded at the end of an access field (1XX or 7XX) in subfield ‡e. The subfield is normally preceded by a comma, except where the authorized access point for a person ends in a hyphen (i.e., an open date). Terms are drawn from RDA appendix I, which includes terms designating relationships to works, expressions, manifestations, and items. Appendix I is not a closed list and is not all-inclusive. According to 18.5.1.3, if none of the terms is appropriate or sufficiently specific to describe the relationship, another term may be used. This *Handbook* recommends using terms from RDA appendix I first and then turning to standard lists rather than just making up terms if no term in appendix I is appropriate. The most commonly used standard list of relationship designators outside RDA appendix I is the MARC code list for relators found at www.loc.gov/marc/relators/relaterm.html. Another commonly used list of relationship designators is that maintained by the Association of College and Research Libraries Rare Books and Manuscripts Section, available at www.rbms.info/committees/bibliographic_standards/controlled_vocabularies/relators/alphabetical_list.htm.

In this chapter, figures 9.1, 9.5, 9.6, and many others show relationship designators in bibliographic records. Relationship designators are also shown in numerous figures throughout this *Handbook*.

If more than one type of relationship to a resource applies to a single entity, subfield ‡e may be repeated. In figure 9.1, for example, Roger Green is the editor of one expression described and the translator of the other.

A relationship designator used in a 100, 110, or 111 field should be one of the relationship designators for creators (RDA appendix I.2.1). Note that there are many designators for creators in addition to "author." For example, the creator of a map is a "cartographer," and the creator of a musical work is a "composer." Any of these designators could appear in 1XX fields, as seen throughout this *Handbook*.

Relationship designators may appear in authority records as well. They are generally used to clarify the relationship of a person, family, or corporate body to a work or expression. In figure 9.2a, for example, a description of an expression—a person related to the expression (its translator)—is recorded in the 500 field. The relationship designator "Translator" is recorded in subfield ‡i (subfield ‡w with the code "r" is required when subfield ‡i is present in the field). This same relationship was recorded in the corresponding bibliographic record (see figure 9.1), but the link in the authority record is much clearer: in the bibliographic record it is not clear which expression Green edited and which he translated. In the authority record it is clear that he translated the English-language expression.

It is crucial to future entity-relationship or linked-data database structures that the nature of the relationships be known, so this *Handbook* strongly recommends that catalogers begin consistently recording relationship designators in bibliographic and authority records in order to help prepare MARC data for eventual migration to the new data structure.

CHAPTER 19. PERSONS, FAMILIES, AND CORPORATE BODIES ASSOCIATED WITH A WORK

19.2. CREATOR. The relationship of a work to its principal creator (or the creator named first in a resource embodying the work) is core in RDA. Recording the relationship to other creators (e.g., a joint author) is optional. Section 19.2 deals with recording this relationship.

In an important break with past cataloging practice, RDA has abandoned the term "main entry." The concept of main entry has its roots in alphabetized printed book catalogs and printed bibliographies where an item is given one complete "entry" at a particular place in the alphabetical arrangement, possibly with brief entries ("added entries") at other places in the arrangement, usually pointing to the main entry. In western bibliographic practice, the main entry in such a catalog or bibliography is usually alphabetized under the surname of the principal or first-named author of the work, or under the title if the work has no identifiable author.

In the context of a card catalog, "main entry" had reference to the "main" card created for the item, which was filed at a particular place in the catalog that was determined by the words at the top of the card, either the name of the principal or first-named creator or the title. "Added entries" were created by copying the main card one or more times and typing other access points at the top.

The concept of main entry continued to have relevance after the arrival of the electronic MARC environment, although that relevance was increasingly questioned as years went by. Main entry in an electronic environment was used to create browsable alphabetic lists of the contents of the catalog. However, in most catalog databases the full description could be found based on *any* access point, whether a main or added entry, so the distinction became blurred. But main entry rules were still used to determine the first element of the authorized access point for a work, so in this sense it remained important. In the MARC environment, the main entry in a bibliographic record was coded in a 100 (person), 110 (corporate body), 111 (meeting), or 130 (title) field. Added entries were recorded in 700, 710, 711, and 730 fields.

Although RDA has abandoned the term "main entry," a vestige of the concept remains in the core guidelines of 19.2, which read "If there is more than one creator responsible for the work, only the creator having principal responsibility named first in resources embodying the work or in reference sources is required." This particular creator is, generally speaking, the same entity that would have been chosen as main entry under previous cataloging codes, and in the initial MARC implementation of RDA the authorized access point for the "creator having principal responsibility named first" in a resource is coded in the MARC 100, 110, or 111 field. (The 130 field [title main entry], peculiarly, continues to be used in MARC implementations of RDA even though titles cannot in any way be said to be a "creator having principal responsibility" under 19.2.)

19.2.1.1. SCOPE. "Creator" is defined as a person, family, or corporate body responsible for the creation of a work. This may include writers of books, composers of music, preparers of bibliographies, artists, photographers, and cartographers. The principal or first-named creator of a resource is recorded in the 100, 110, or 111 field of the MARC bibliographic record. If there are more than one creator of a resource, other creators are recorded in 700, 710, or 711 fields. For example, in figure 9.1 George Buchanan is the creator of the original work realized by the English and Latin expressions published in the resource. Buchanan's status as principal creator of this work is signaled in the bibliographic record by recording his authorized access point in the 100 field and appending the relationship designator "author." In figure 9.6, the first-named creator is recorded in a 100 field, but there are other creators who have been recorded in 700 fields. All have the relationship designator "author." All are creators under 19.2, but only one is recorded as the principal or first-named creator in 100.

For a discussion of when a family is a creator, see the introductory paragraphs to chapter 4 of this *Handbook*.

19.2.1.1.1. CORPORATE BODIES CONSIDERED TO BE CREATORS. Corporate bodies may be considered to be creators under certain fairly restrictive circumstances. The first thing the cataloger must determine is if a corporate body is involved with a work. The definition of a corporate body given under 8.1.2 should be read carefully. The important thing to remember is that, for cataloging purposes, a corporate body must (1) be an organization or group of persons (2) that is identified by a particular name, and (3) that acts or may act as a unit. RDA 11.0 gives further guidance on what is meant by "particular name." For discussion, see chapter 8 at RDA 8.1.

If a corporate body is involved with a work, the cataloger must make two decisions under 19.2.1.1.1. First, is the corporate body responsible for originating, issuing, or causing the work to be issued? If so, does the nature of the work fall into one of the eight categories listed in 19.2.1.1.1? If both of these conditions are met, the corporate body will be considered the principal creator of the work.

Note that it makes no difference if a personal author is involved, even as the main author of the work. If the conditions of 19.2.1.1.1 are met, the corporate body is considered the principal creator (note the final example in 19.2.1.3 under Works Recording the Collective Thought of the Body in which Ann Mosely Lesch is clearly named as the principal author, but the Committee is deemed to be the creator of the work). For more information about this, see RDA 6.27.1.3, Collaborative Works, Exceptions: Corporate Bodies as Creators, in which the corporate body's authorized access point is used in combination with the preferred title to create the authorized access point for the work.

There are several ways a corporate body can be responsible for originating, issuing, or causing a work to be issued.

The corporate body may have published the work. In this case the body's name will normally appear in the resource as the publisher. Or, it may not actually be the publisher, but it may have arranged for the work's publication. A statement such as "Published for the Omohundro Institute of Early American History and Culture, Williamsburg, Virginia, by the University of North Carolina Press" means that Omohundro Institute of Early American History and Culture caused the work to be issued.

A corporate body might not actually be responsible for issuing or causing a resource to be issued and still qualify as responsible. An example given in the LC policy statement that accompanies RDA 19.2.1.1.1 is that of a commercial publisher that arranges to publish the card catalog of a library in book form. It cannot be said that the library issued the resource or caused it to be issued. However, because the content of the catalog was prepared by the library, the content of the work originates with the library.

The Library of Congress advises the cataloger to assume that the corporate body issued the resource if there is any doubt about this question, but in case of whether or not the work falls into any of the eight categories, the cataloger is advised not to consider the corporate body to be the work's creator (LC-PCC PS 19.2.1.1.1, July 2012, under "applicability" 1d and 2b). A corporate body will be considered to be the principal creator of a work it originated, issued, or caused to be issued *only* if its content falls under one of the categories listed in 19.2.1.1.1.

19.2.1.1.1a. Official reports, rules and regulations, and catalogs of an institution's resources are examples of "works of an administrative nature" dealing with the body itself. The corporate body is considered to be the creator of these. A newsletter reporting activities (i.e., the operations) of a corporate body is an example (see figure 9.16). An annual report is another example (see figure 9.17), as is a manual of procedure reflecting rules and regulations of a corporate body (see figure 9.18). Another example is the report of an official of a corporation, institution, or other corporate body dealing with administrative affairs, procedures, etc., of the corporate body (see figure 9.19).

Figure 9.16.
Work of an Administrative Nature Dealing with the Body Itself (Newsletter)

110 2	‡a American Book Collectors of Children's Literature, ‡e author, ‡e issuing body.
245 10	‡a ABC newsletter.
264 1	‡a [Hartford, Connecticut] : ‡b American Book Collectors of Children's Literature, ‡c 1989-
300	‡a volumes : ‡b illustrations ; ‡c 22 cm
310	‡a Semiannual
336	‡a text ‡2 rdacontent
337	‡a unmediated ‡2 rdamedia
338	‡a volume ‡2 rdacarrier
362 1	‡a Began with volume 1, number 1 (March 1989).
588	‡a Description based on: volume 1, number 1 (March 1989); title from cover.
588	‡a Latest issue consulted: volume 23, number 1 & 2 (25th anniversary issue 2011).

Figure 9.17.
Work of an Administrative Nature Dealing with the Body Itself (Annual Report)

110 1	‡a Great Britain. ‡b Metropolitan Police Service, ‡e author, ‡e issuing body.
245 10	‡a Commissioner's annual report to the Metropolitan Police Authority / ‡c Metropolitan Police.
264 1	‡a London : ‡b Metropolitan Police Service, Strategy and Improvement Department, Resources Directorate, ‡c [2010]-
300	‡a volumes : ‡b color illustrations ; ‡c 30 cm
310	‡a Annual
336	‡a text ‡2 rdacontent
337	‡a unmediated ‡2 rdamedia
338	‡a volume ‡2 rdacarrier
362 1	‡a Began with 2009/10.
500	‡a Title from cover.
588	‡a Identification of the resource based on: 2009/10.
710 1	‡a Great Britain. ‡b Metropolitan Police Authority.
780 01	‡a Great Britain. Metropolitan Police Service. ‡t Joint annual report.

Figure 9.18.
Work of an Administrative Nature Dealing with the Body Itself (Manual)

110 1	‡a Bhutan. ‡b Department of Survey & Land Records, ‡a author.
245 10	‡a Survey manual.
250	‡a 3rd edition.
264 1	‡a [Thimphu] : ‡b National Land Commission, ‡c 2009.
300	‡a 1 volume (various pagings) ; ‡c 30 cm
336	‡a text ‡2 rdacontent
337	‡a unmediated ‡2 rdamedia
338	‡a volume ‡2 rdacarrier
500	‡a Previously published: [Trashichhoedzong] : Surveyor General, 2004.
505 0	‡a Part 1. Organization, duties, general administration, field operations, and resposipilities -- part 2. Technical guidelines.
710 1	‡a Bhutan. ‡b Land Commission, ‡e issuing body.

Figure 9.19.
Works of an Administrative Nature dealing with the Body Itself (Report)

110 1	‡a United States. ‡b Office of Management and Budget, ‡e author.
245 10	‡a OMB final sequestration report to the President and Congress for fiscal year 2012 : ‡b communication from the Director, the Office of Management and Budget, transmitting OMB's final sequestration report for fiscal year 2012, pursuant to 2 U.S.C. 904.
264 1	‡a Washington : ‡b U.S. Government Printing Office, ‡c 2012.
300	‡a 1 online resource (15 pages)
336	‡a text ‡2 rdacontent
337	‡a computer ‡2 rdamedia
338	‡a online resource ‡2 rdacarrier
347	‡a text file ‡b PDF ‡2 rda
490 1	‡a House document / 112th Congress, 2d session ; ‡v 112-87
500	‡a Title from title screen (viewed on March 28, 2012).
500	‡a "February 17, 2012."
700 1	‡a Lew, Jacob J., ‡d 1955- ‡e author.
710 1	‡a United States. ‡b Congress. ‡b House, ‡e addressee.
830 0	‡a House document (United States. Congress. House) ; ‡v 112-87.
856 40	‡u http://purl.fdlp.gov/GPO/gpo20859

19.2.1.1.1b. A corporate body is deemed to be the creator of a work that records its "collective thought" (see figure 9.20). Works that fall into this category present official statements or position statements from a corporate body on matters other than those with which the body itself deals. However, the subject itself should be related to the corporate body's activities. It should contain recommendations for action, change, etc. If such a work simply gathers information, and does not include recommendations for action, this does not constitute the "collective thought" of the body.

19.2.1.1.1c. The body convening a hearing, whether legislative or otherwise, is deemed to be the creator of a work that records the hearing (see figure 9.21).

Figure 9.20. Collective Thought of the Body

020	ǂa 9783869280295
110 2	ǂa Gunda-Werner-Institut, ǂe author.
245 10	ǂa Peace and security for all : ǂb feminist positions and perspectives on peace and security policy : a position paper of the Gunda Werner Institute for Feminism and Gender Democracy / ǂc edited by the Heinrich Böll Foundation.
264 1	ǂa Berlin : ǂb Heinrich Böll Stiftung, ǂc [2010]
264 4	ǂc ©2010
300	ǂa 70 pages ; ǂc 24 cm.
336	ǂa text ǂ2 rdacontent
337	ǂa unmediated ǂ2 rdamedia
338	ǂa volume ǂ2 rdacarrier
490 1	ǂa Publication series of the Gunda Werner Institute ; ǂv volume 6
710 2	ǂa Heinrich-Böll-Stiftung, ǂe publisher.
830 0	ǂa Schriften des Gunda-Werner-Instituts. ǂl English ; ǂv v. 6.

Figure 9.21. Hearing

110 2	ǂa Human Rights Commission of San Francisco (San Francisco, Calif.), ǂe author.
245 10	ǂa Community concerns of surveillance, racial and religious profiling of Arab, Middle Eastern, Muslim, and South Asian communities and potential reactivation of SFPD intelligence gathering : ǂb September 23, 2010 hearing ; adopted February 24, 2011 / ǂc City and County of San Francisco Human Rights Commission.
264 1	ǂa [San Francisco] : ǂb City and County of San Francisco Human Rights Commission, ǂc [2011]
300	ǂa 44 leaves : ǂb color illustrations ; ǂc 28 cm
336	ǂa text ǂ2 rdacontent
337	ǂa unmediated ǂ2 rdamedia
338	ǂa volume ǂ2 rdacarrier
500	ǂa Testimony by Shirin Sinnar, a fellow at Stanford Law School, is described, and a report by the Asian Law Caucus and the Stanford Immigrant Rights Clinic entitled "Returning Home: How U.S. Government Practices Undermine Civil Rights at Our Nation's Doorstep" is cited.

19.2.1.1.1d. Conferences, expeditions, and events are considered corporate bodies. Such a body is the author of a work that reports its "collective activity." RDA 19.2.1.1.1d may *only* be applied to the three types of bodies stated in the guideline (conference, expedition, or event) (cf. LC-PCC PS 19.2.1.1.1, July 2012). See figure 9.13 for a report of a meeting, 9.22 for a report of an expedition, and 9.23 for a report of an event.

Figure 9.22. Expedition

111	2	‡a Antarctic Walk Environmental Research Expedition ‡d (1991-1993), ‡e author.
245	14	‡a Scientific results from the Antarctic Walk Environmental Research Expedition 1991-1993 / ‡c edited by K. Yoshikawa, K. Harada, S. Ishimaru.
264	1	‡a Tokyo : ‡b Antarctic Environmental Research Expedition Organizing Committee, ‡c 1995.
300		‡a 258 pages : ‡b illustrations, maps ; ‡c 27 cm
336		‡a text ‡2 rdacontent
336		‡a still image ‡2 rdacontent
336		‡a cartographic image ‡2 rdacontent
337		‡a unmediated ‡2 rdamedia
338		‡a volume ‡2 rdacarrier
504		‡a Includes bibliographical references.
700	1	‡a Yoshikawa, K. ‡q (Kenji), ‡e editor.
700	1	‡a Harada, K. ‡q (Koichiro), ‡e editor.
700	1	‡a Ishimaru, S. ‡q (Satoshi), ‡e editor.

Figure 9.23. Event

111	2	‡a Andean Nations/Central America Art Expo ‡d (2011 : ‡c Austin, Tex.), ‡e author.
245	10	‡a Artists' lecture, September 29, 2011.
264	1	‡a [Austin] : ‡b The University of Texas at Austin, Division of Diversity and Community Engagement, ‡c [2011]
300		‡a 1 CD-ROM : ‡b color ; ‡c 4 3/4 in.
336		‡a still image ‡2 rdacontent
337		‡a computer ‡2 rdamedia
338		‡a computer disc ‡2 rdacarrier
347		‡a image file ‡2 rda
520		‡a Series of color pictures commemorating the Andean Nations/Central America Art Expo held September 29, 2011 in Austin, Texas.
710	2	‡a University of Texas at Austin. ‡b Division of Diversity and Community Engagement, ‡e issuing body.

19.2.1.1.1e. A performing group is regarded as the creator of a work that results from its collective activity, as long as the group's responsibility goes beyond "mere performance, execution, etc." This guideline is most commonly applied to recordings of popular music, which frequently include a fair amount of improvisation (see figure 9.24).

Figure 9.24. Collective Activity of a Performing Group

028 02	‡a MTR 7357 2 US ‡b Music Theories Recordings
110 2	‡a Spock's Beard (Musical group), ‡e creator.
245 14	‡a The X tour / ‡c Spock's Beard.
246 1	‡i At head of title: ‡a SB
264　1	‡a New York : ‡b Music Theories Recordings, ‡c [2012]
264　4	‡c ©2012
300	‡a 1 audio disc (approximately 1 hr.) ; ‡c 4 3/4 in. + ‡e 1 insert (10 unnumbered pages ; 12 cm)
336	‡a performed music ‡2 rdacontent
337	‡a audio ‡2 rdamedia
338	‡a audio disc ‡2 rdamedia
344	‡a digital ‡b optical ‡g stereo ‡2 rda
347	‡a audio file ‡b CD audio ‡2 rda
500	‡a Title from insert.
518	‡a "Recorded in Downey, CA at the Downey Civic Theater on September 12, 2010"--Page 1 of insert.
505 0	‡a Edge of the in-between -- The emperor's clothes -- From the darkness -- The quiet house -- The man behind the curtain -- Kamikaze -- Jaws of heaven -- Drum duel -- On a perfect day -- Thoughts -- Ryo's solo -- The doorway -- June.
511 0	‡a Nick D'Virgilio: lead vocal, guitar, drums and keyboards ; Alan Morse: guitar vocals ; Dave Meros: bass keyboards, vocals ; Ryo Okumoto: keyboards, vocals ; Jimmy Keegan: drums, vocals ; Stan Ausmus: guitar on Man behind the curtain.

19.2.1.1.1f. A corporate body may be regarded as the creator of cartographic works, as long as it is not "merely responsible for their publication or distribution" (see figure 9.25).

Figure 9.25. Cartographic Work

110 1	‡a United States. ‡b Central Intelligence Agency, ‡e cartographer.
245 10	‡a Bhutan administrative divisions.
255	‡a Scale 1:1,750,000 ; ‡b transverse Mercator projection, central meridian 90°27′ E.
264　1	‡a [Washington, D.C.] : ‡b [Central Intelligence Agency], ‡c [2012]

300	‡a 1 map : ‡b color ; ‡c 17 x 22 cm
336	‡a cartographic image ‡2 rdacontent
337	‡a unmediated ‡2 rdamedia
338	‡a sheet ‡2 rdacarrier
500	‡a "803225AI (G00541) 2-12".
500	‡a Includes location map.

19.2.1.1.1g. A jurisdiction (or a subordinate body to a jurisdiction) is considered the creator of a legal work it issues, as long as the work is one of the types listed under 19.2.1.1.1f. The electoral law of Baja California Sur is an example of such a work (see figure 9.26).

Figure 9.26. Law

110 1	‡a Baja California Sur (Mexico), ‡e enacting jurisdiction.
245 10	‡a Ley electoral del estado de Baja California Sur.
264 1	‡a [La Paz, Baja California Sur] : ‡b Instituto Estatal Electoral Baja California Sur, ‡c [2010]
300	‡a 132 pages ; ‡c 21 cm
336	‡a text ‡2 rdacontent
337	‡a unmediated ‡2 rdamedia
338	‡a volume ‡2 rdacarrier
710 2	‡a Instituto Estatal Electoral Baja California Sur, ‡e publisher.

19.2.1.1.1h. A corporate body that consists of two or more artists acting together is considered the creator of a named individual work of art produced by the artists. The description of a painting illustrated in figure 9.27 was created by two artists who jointly call themselves FAILE.

Figure 9.27. Named Individual Work of Art

110 2	‡a FAILE (Artist collective), ‡e artist.
245 12	‡a Wrong end of the rainbow stories / ‡c FAILE.
264 0	‡c 2011.
300	‡a 1 painting : ‡b color ; ‡c 61 x 51 cm
336	‡a still image ‡2 rdacontent
337	‡a unmediated ‡2 rdamedia
338	‡a object ‡2 rdacarrier
340	‡a wood ‡c acrylic ‡c ink ‡d painting ‡d silkscreen
500	‡a Acrylic and silkscreen ink on wood, steel frame.

500	‡a Created by the artist collective FAILE, a Brooklyn-based collaboration between Patrick McNeil and Patrick Miller.
700 1	‡a McNeil, Patrick, ‡d 1975- ‡e artist.
700 1	‡a Miller, Patrick, ‡d 1976- ‡e artist.

19.2.1.1.2. GOVERNMENT AND RELIGIOUS OFFICIALS CONSIDERED TO BE CREATORS. Although in a different section from 19.2.1.1.1, this is in fact just another category of corporate body considered to be creator. Through an oddity in cataloging practice, in some cases government and religious officials acting in their official capacity are considered to be corporate bodies (see RDA 11.2.2.18 and 11.2.2.26, and discussion of these guidelines in chapter 5 of this *Handbook*). As corporate bodies, they are considered to be the creator of certain types of official communications as listed in 19.2.1.1.2. See figures 9.28 (government official) and 9.29 (religious official).

Figure 9.28. Proclamation of a Mayor

110 1	‡a Nacogdoches (Tex.). ‡b Mayor (2007- : Van Horn), ‡e author.
245 10	‡a Proclamation : ‡b Texas Society of the Sons of the American Revolution appreciation / ‡c City of Nacogdoches.
246 1	‡i Also known as: ‡a Texas Society of the Sons of the American Revolution appreciation proclamation, March 18, 2009
264 1	‡a [Nacogdoches, Texas] : ‡b [Office of the Mayor], ‡c [2009]
300	‡a 1 sheet ; ‡c 33 x 22 cm
336	‡a text ‡2 rdacontent
337	‡a unmediated ‡2 rdamedia
338	‡a sheet ‡2 rdacarrier
520	‡a Signed proclamation by Mayor Roger Van Horn on behalf of the City Commission proclaiming appreciation of the Texas Society Sons of the American Revolution for their "hard work and dedication to the memory of our Revolutionary War Pariots." Also signed by Lila Fuller, City Secretary.
700 1	‡a Van Horn, Roger, ‡e signer.
700 1	‡a Fuller, Lila, ‡e signer.

Figure 9.29. Pastoral Letter

110 2	‡a Catholic Church. ‡b Diocese of Saginaw (Mich.). ‡b Bishop (2005-2009 : Carlson), ‡e author.
245 10	‡a Jesus Christ, prince of peace : ‡b a pastoral letter on peace / ‡c Robert J. Carlson.
264 1	‡a Saginaw, Michigan : ‡b Office of the Bishop, Catholic Diocese of Saginaw, ‡c [2009]

```
264   4  ‡a ©2009
300      ‡a 45 pages ; ‡c 19 cm
336      ‡a text ‡2 rdacontent
337      ‡a unmediated ‡2 rdamedia
338      ‡a volume ‡2 rdacarrier
504      ‡a Includes bibliographical references.
700   1  ‡a Carlson, Robert J., ‡e author.
```

If a corporate body is responsible for originating, issuing, or causing a work to be issued but the work does not fit in one of the categories listed under 19.2.1.1.1 or 19.2.1.1.2, the corporate body is not considered to be the creator of the work. The relationship of the body to the work may still be recorded appropriately by creating an access point for it in the description of the resource as an "other corporate body associated with the work" (RDA 19.3; see discussion of this guideline below). Record the authorized access point for such a body in a 710 field (see figure 9.30).

Figure 9.30. Other Corporate Body Associated with the Work

```
245 02  ‡a A review of school community council election practices / ‡c Office of Legislative
        Auditor General, State of Utah.
264   1  ‡a [Salt Lake City, Utah] : ‡b Office of the Legislative Auditor General, ‡c 2012.
300      ‡a 16 pages ; ‡c 28 cm
336      ‡a text ‡2 rdacontent
337      ‡a unmediated ‡2 rdamedia
338      ‡a volume  ‡2 rdacarrier
490   1  ‡a Report to the Utah Legislature ; ‡v no. 2012-02
500      ‡a Title from cover.
500      ‡a "January 2012"
710   1  ‡a Utah. ‡b Legislature. ‡b Office of the Legislative Auditor General, ‡e issuing body.
830   0  ‡a Report to the Utah Legislature ; ‡v no. 12-02.
```

If a corporate body issues a work that is not of a type included in the categories of 19.2.1.1.1 or 19.2.1.1.2, it is not considered the creator, but the work may have a person or family associated with it (see the introductory discussion of 19.2.1.1.1, above). If so, the cataloger should consider whether the person or family is the creator. The example shown in figure 9.31 purports to be an official publication of the State of Arizona and is in fact a work issued by the Arizona Game and Fish Department (with the publisher Arizona Highways), but it does not fit any of the categories of 19.2.1.1.1. However, it also has a personal author, who will be recorded as the creator of the work.

Figure 9.31. Person as Creator of Work Issued by a Corporate Body

020	‡a 9780984570942
100 1	‡a Aikens, Rory, ‡e author.
245 10	‡a Arizona's official fishing guide : ‡b 181 top fishing spots, directions & tips / ‡c by Rory Aikens.
264 1	‡a Phoenix, Arizona : ‡b Arizona Highways in partnership with Arizona Game & Fish Department, ‡c [2011]
300	‡a 335 pages : ‡b color illustrations, color maps ; ‡c 23 cm
336	‡a text ‡2 rdacontent
336	‡a still image ‡2 rdacontent
336	‡a cartographic image ‡2 rdacontent
337	‡a unmediated ‡2 rdamedia
338	‡a volume ‡2 rdacarrier
500	‡a Includes index.
710 2	‡a Arizona. ‡b Game and Fish Department, ‡e issuing body.

19.2.1.1.3. PERSONS OR FAMILIES CONSIDERED TO BE CREATORS OF SERIALS. This guideline was added in 2012 to clarify when persons or families can be creators of serials. Serials are generally compilations of many works (the articles they contain) by different persons and thus are generally not assigned a principal creator (see 6.27.1.4) unless the serial is issued by a corporate body and falls under 19.2.1.1.1. However, if a person or family is responsible for the serial as a whole and is likely to continue to be responsible throughout the life of the serial, that person or family is considered the creator of the serial and this relationship will be recorded in the bibliographic record by giving the authorized access point for the person or family in a 100 field. Figure 9.10 is an example. The Chatman Family is clearly responsible for all of *Chatman's Family Reunion Chronicle* and is likely to continue to be responsible throughout the life of the serial.

19.2.1.3. RECORDING CREATORS. This treatment of chapter 19 has so far discussed recording relationships between a work and a creator within a bibliographic record using 1XX and 7XX fields. There is another situation where the relationship between a creator and a work is recorded in MARC practice and that is in the authorized access point for a work and its associated authority record. The authorized access point for a work is shown in figure 9.2b, in the 100 field of the authority record for the work "Psalmorum Davidis paraphrasis poetica." As explained in chapter 7 of this *Handbook,* the authorized access point for a work is formed by combining the authorized access point for the principal creator with the preferred title of the work (see, for example, this *Handbook*'s chapter 7 at 6.27.1.2). The authorized access point for the creator, found in subfields ‡a and ‡d of the 100 field in figure 9.2b, is *not* an attribute of the work. It is, rather, a *link* recording the relationship of the work to its creator, who is described in a separate record, figure 9.2c. Therefore, giving the authorized access point for the creator as the first part of the authorized access point for the work is another way in MARC of recording a relationship link between a work and its creator (see fuller discussion of this point in chapter 7 of this *Handbook* under 5.3, Core Elements).

A work may have more than one creator. As discussed above under 19.2.1.1, in a MARC bibliographic record the relationship of the principal or first-named creator of a resource is recorded in the 100, 110, or 111 field, and the relationships of other creators to the resource are recorded in 700, 710, or 711 fields. The distinction between principal or first-named creator and others also affects descriptions of the work in authority records. In an authority record representing the work, the access point for the creator chosen as the principal or first-named creator is given as the first part of the authorized access point for the work as described above and recorded in the 100, 110, or 111 MARC authority field, but the relationship of other creators to the work may be recorded as variant access points for the work and recorded in 400, 410, or 411 fields in the same record. The variant access point is created by combining the authorized access point for the other creator with the preferred title for the work (see figure 9.32).

Figure 9.32. Non-Principal Creator in Authority Record

046	‡k 1848
100 1	‡a Marx, Karl, ‡d 1818-1883. ‡t Manifest der Kommunistischen Partei
380	‡a Political work
400 1	‡a Engels, Friedrich, ‡d 1820-1895. ‡t Manifest der Kommunistischen Partei
400 1	‡a Marx, Karl, ‡d 1818-1883. ‡t Kommunistische Manifest
670	‡a Das kommunistische Manifest : Manifest der Kommunistischen Partei, 1995: ‡b (von Karl Marx und Friedrich Engels)
670	‡a Wikipedia, 26 July 2012 ‡b (The Communist Manifesto (Das Kommunistische Manifest), originally titled Manifesto of the Communist Party (German: Manifest der Kommunistischen Partei) is a short 1848 publication written by the German political theorists Karl Marx and Friedrich Engels)

19.3. OTHER PERSON, FAMILY, OR CORPORATE BODY ASSOCIATED WITH A WORK. There are cases where a person, family, or corporate body is not the creator of a work but nevertheless is associated with it in some other way. RDA lists some examples (note that this is not a closed list) in 19.3.1.1, and subsections of RDA 19.3 list others. These include a person honored by a festschrift, a director of a film, a body hosting an exhibition, a person prosecuted in a work reporting a criminal trial, and the judge at the trial. These are all related to the work (that is, they are not related to the expression, manifestation, or item) but cannot be said to be the creator of the work. The relationship of a work to a persons, families, or corporate bodies associated with a work who are not creators is generally recorded in a MARC bibliographic record in a 700, 710, or 711 field (for an exception, see discussion above of 18.3, with figure 9.7). For example, the various issuing bodies recorded in the 710 fields of figure 9.15 are "other corporate bodies associated with the work," as is the issuing body recorded in figure 9.31.

The relationship of an "other person, family, or corporate body associated with the work" can also be recorded in the authority record representing the work. This relationship is recorded in a 500, 510, or 511 field. A relationship designator may be recorded to specify the nature of the relationship in subfield ‡i. The first 500 field in figure 9.33 links the work "Abyss" with the person "James Cameron" and specifies that the relationship is that of the film director to the work.

Figure 9.33. Other Person Associated with the Work in Authority Record

046	‡k 1989
130 0	‡a Abyss (Motion picture)
380	‡a Motion picture
500 1	‡w r ‡i Film director: ‡a Cameron, James, ‡d 1954-
500 1	‡w r ‡i Novelization (work): ‡a Card, Orson Scott. ‡t Abyss
670	‡a The abyss, 1993: ‡b container (written and directed by James Cameron)
670	‡a IMDB, January 20, 2012 ‡b (The abyss, motion picture directed by James Cameron, released in USA 9 August 1989; novelization written by Orson Scott Card)

CHAPTER 20. PERSONS, FAMILIES, AND CORPORATE BODIES ASSOCIATED WITH AN EXPRESSION. RDA defines one large class of persons, families, and corporate bodies associated with expressions, and calls them "contributors" (see RDA 20.2). A contributor "realizes" an expression of a work. For example, a person who takes a text and translates it into another language is creating ("realizing") a new expression. The translator is called a contributor by RDA. Other common examples of contributors are illustrators, editors, and arrangers.

20.2.1.3. RECORDING CONTRIBUTORS. In the current MARC bibliographic environment, the relationship of a contributor to an expression is recorded by giving the authorized access point for the contributor in a 700, 710, or 711 field. A relationship designator may be added to the access point to specify the nature of the contributor relationship as explained above at 18.5. In figure 9.1, Roger Green edited one of the expressions in the resource and translated the other. His relationship to the resource is recorded in the third 700 field; a relationship designator for each of his relationships is included. Mack Wilberg contributed to the expression described in figure 9.5 by arranging the music. In figure 9.12, the relationship of the conductor and performers to a particular expression of Benjamin Britten's *War Requiem* is recorded in several 700 and 710 fields. See also other examples throughout this chapter.

The relationship of a contributor to an expression can also be recorded in the authority description of the expression. The authorized access point for the contributor is recorded in a 500, 510, or 511 field of the record for the expression; a relationship designator specifying the nature of the relationship may be recorded in subfield ‡i. See figure 9.2a, where the relationship of the translator Roger Green to an English expression of *Psalmorum Davidis Paraphrasis Poetica* is recorded in a 500 field.

CHAPTER 21. PERSONS, FAMILIES, AND CORPORATE BODIES ASSOCIATED WITH A MANIFESTATION. There can be numerous persons, families, or corporate bodies associated with manifestations, which are defined in RDA as "the physical embodiment of an expression of a work" (see the RDA glossary under "Manifestation"). This simply means the physical form the expression takes, for example, text on paper (a volume or a sheet), microfiche, videocassette, videodisc, or a digital form such as a computer disc or an online resource. Many entities can be involved in the production of these. Four are brought out specifically in chapter 21, producer of an unpublished work (RDA 21.2), publisher (RDA 21.3), distributor (RDA 21.4), and manufacturer (RDA 21.5), but there are also others such as book designers, lithographers, typographers, and engravers.

The relationship of an entity to a manifestation is recorded in a bibliographic record in the current environment. Throughout chapter 21 the cataloger is instructed to record the relationship following the instructions in RDA 18.4. Two methods are mentioned there, using an identifier or using an authorized access point for the entity. Of these two, only the authorized access point method is currently used in MARC bibliographic records. The relationship is recorded by giving the authorized access point for the person, family, or corporate body in a 700, 710, or 711 field; this may be accompanied by a relationship designator in subfield ‡e. Such relationships are frequently recorded in records for rare or special collections materials, but they may be recorded for any type of resource. In figure 9.34, the relationships between the manifestation and its publisher, book designer, and papermaker are recorded in 700 and 710 fields.

Figure 9.34. Relationships to a Manifestation

100 1	‡a Albee, Edward, ‡d 1928- ‡e author.
245 12	‡a A delicate balance / ‡c a play by Edward Albee ; introduction by David Littlejohn ; illustrations by Tom Holland.
264 1	‡a San Francisco : ‡b Arion Press, ‡c 2011.
300	‡a 169 pages : ‡b color illustrations ; ‡c 25 cm

336	‡a text ‡2 rdacontent
337	‡a unmediated ‡2 rdamedia
338	‡a volume ‡2 rdacarrier
520	‡a A drama which examines the lives and values of two middle-aged couples and two younger women.
500	‡a "The edition is limited to 300 numbered copies for sale ... All copies are signed by the playwright and the artist. ... The book was designed and produced by Andrew Hoyem ... This is the ninety-second Arion publication."--Colophon.
700 1	‡a Holland, Tom, ‡d 1936- ‡e illustrator.
700 1	‡a Hoyem, Andrew, ‡e book designer.
710 2	‡a Arion Press, ‡e publisher.
710 2	‡a Cartiere Enrico Magnani, ‡e papermaker.

Most generalist catalogers would not record these relationships formally by using authorized access points. However, the relationships are recorded in bibliographic records using a method not mentioned at RDA 18.4, but detailed in chapter 17 in a different context: the composite description (17.4.2.3). Figure 9.24, for example, records the relationship between the manifestation and its publisher simply by transcribing the publisher's name in subfield ‡b of the first 264 field. This may not be machine actionable (e.g., for reliable collation of all manifestations associated with this publisher) but it is a way of recording the relationship, and in fact is the method that is probably the most commonly followed to record relationships between persons, families, or corporate bodies and manifestations, especially producers, publishers, distributors, and manufacturers.

CHAPTER 22. PERSONS, FAMILIES, AND CORPORATE BODIES ASSOCIATED WITH AN ITEM. As with manifestations, there are many persons, families, or corporate bodies that might be associated with an item, defined as "a single exemplar or instance of a manifestation" (see the RDA glossary at "Item")—that is, a copy. RDA specifies two types of relationships, owner (RDA 22.2) and custodian (RDA 22.3), but acknowledges that there are many other kinds of possible relationships between entities and items (RDA 22.4) such as binders and signers.

Like chapter 21, chapter 22 directs the cataloger to RDA 18.4 for guidelines for recording the relationship between the item and another entity. The two methods outlined there are identifier and authorized access point.

Identifier is used in shared library databases such as OCLC to record some owner relationships to items (RDA 22.2.1.3). In such a database, it is important to know who actually owns items associated with bibliographic records (for example, for purposes of interlibrary loan) and the relationship between an item and its owning library is recorded by linking an identifier for the library to the record.

Within the context of a library's own database this owner-item relationship is not usually explicitly recorded by an identifier or authorized access point. The mere presence of a record in the database is usually considered to imply that the library owns the item, although this is becoming less true as libraries add more and more records for materials they have access to but do not own.

Relationships of persons, families, or corporate bodies to items can also be recorded using authorized access points, using 700, 710, or 711 fields. This is a common method used to record provenance relationships (former owners), one of the "owner" relationships (RDA 22.2). In figure 9.35, the book shows evidence of two former owners, Charles Dickens and Vincent Newton. The cataloger has chosen to record the relationship of the item (the book) to Charles Dickens by giving his authorized access point in a 700 field, with the appropriate relationship designator from appendix I and "‡5 UPB," which means this access point applies only to the Brigham Young University Library (the library's MARC code is UPB). Figure 9.35 also shows another way of recording the relationship of a person to an item. Although no access point was given for the other former owner, Vincent Newton, his relationship to the item is still recorded, through a note in the second 590 field.

Figure 9.35. Owner Relationship

100 1		‡a Trollope, Thomas Adolphus, ‡d 1810-1892, ‡e author.
245 10		‡a Marietta : ‡b a novel / ‡c by T. Adolphus Trollope.
250		‡a Second edition.
264	1	‡a London : ‡b Chapman & Hall, ‡c 1862.
264	3	‡a London : ‡b Printed by James S. Virtue, City Road
300		‡a 419 pages ; ‡c 19 cm
336		‡a text ‡2 rdacontent
337		‡a unmediated ‡2 rdamedia
338		‡a volume ‡2 rdacarrier
500		‡a "London: Printed by James S. Virtue, City Road"--Colophon.
590		‡a Two bookplates on inside upper cover. First: "Charles Dickens." Second: From the library of Charles Dickens, Gadshill Place, June 1870."
590		‡a Bookplate on first free flyleaf: "Vincent Newton." This bookplate and flyleaf annotated in pencil. Ink marks on endpapers, title page and half-title.
700 1		‡a Dickens, Charles, ‡d 1812-1870, ‡e former owner. ‡5 UPB

The book described in figure 9.36 has been specially bound by a bindery called "Riviere & Son" and is probably the only item within the manifestation so bound. The relationship of Riviere & Son to the item is recorded in a 710 field, with a relationship designator specifying the relationship in subfield ‡e. In a shared cataloging environment the institution to which the relationship applies is specified by recording the institution's MARC organization code in subfield ‡5 ("UPB" stands for Brigham Young University). This is because the bibliographic record represents the manifestation and might be used by other libraries to represent their copy, which would not have the same binding.

Figure 9.36. Other Relationship to an Item

100 1	‡aThackeray, William Makepeace, ‡d 1811-1863, ‡e author.	
245 10	‡a Unpublished verses / ‡c by William Makepeace Thackeray.	
250	‡a First edition.	
264 1	‡a London : ‡b Printed for W.T. Spencer, ‡c 1899.	
300	‡a 25 pages : ‡b illustrations, facsimiles ; ‡c 19 cm	
500	‡a "Twenty-five numbered copies only."	
500	‡a "With two original drawings and facsimiles of the original manuscripts, now printed for the first time."	
590	‡a Bound in full red levant, gilt top. Binder's stamp on front inside cover: "Bound by Riviere & Son."	
590	‡a B.Y.U. copy is number 16.	
710 2	‡a Riviere & Son, ‡e binder. ‡5 UPB	

RDA does not deal well with certain types of relationships that might apply to more than one of the primary FRBR entities (work, expression, manifestation, and item). For example, all items within the manifestation illustrated in figure 9.34 are signed by the playwright and the artist. Similarly, a cataloger might want to bring out the relationship to the binder of an entire manifestation. "Binder" and "Autographer" are, according to RDA appendix I.5.2, specifically associated with the item entity, but in these cases they are perhaps more appropriately associated with the manifestation.

RECORDING RELATIONSHIPS BETWEEN WORKS, EXPRESSIONS, MANIFESTATIONS, AND ITEMS

The title of section 8 of RDA may at first glance be a bit confusing because of its similarity to the title of section 5. Section 5 contains guidelines for recording *primary* relationships between works, expressions, manifestations, and items when they exist within the same "vertical" hierarchy, that is, the relationship between a work, the expression(s) that realize the work, the manifestation(s) that embody that expression, and the item(s) that exemplify that manifestation. Section 8 deals with "horizontal" relationships, that is, between different works, between different expressions, between different manifestations, and between different items.

CHAPTER 24. GENERAL GUIDELINES ON RECORDING RELATIONSHIPS BETWEEN WORKS, EXPRESSIONS, MANIFESTATIONS, AND ITEMS. Chapter 24 sets forth a few general guidelines for recording these relationships. Particularly important is the explanation of functional objectives and principles under 24.2. In an RDA environment, users should be able to find related works, expressions, manifestations, and items, and the relationship between them should be clear. Emphasis on the importance of relationships is one thing that sets RDA apart from previous cataloging codes. Although 24.3 states that recording non-primary relationships is not required, it is clear that RDA encourages recording them.

24.4. RECORDING RELATIONSHIPS BETWEEN WORKS, EXPRESSIONS, MANIFESTATIONS, AND ITEMS. RDA details three conventions for recording these relationships: identifier, authorized access point, and description.

An identifier is an alphanumeric character string uniquely associated with a work, expression, manifestation, or item. ISBN, for example, is an identifier associated with a manifestation (cf. RDA 2.15). In current MARC practice, identifiers for related resources are sometimes recorded, but are not used alone to record a relationship link between resources (see LC-PCC PS 24.4.1, February 2010).

An authorized access point is a standardized access point representing an entity. Among the entities treated in RDA section 8, it is currently only possible to assign authorized access points to work and expression (see chapters 7 and 8 of this *Handbook*), although guidelines for authorized access points for manifestations and items are in planning stages. Relationships between related works and related expressions can be recorded in a MARC environment by recording authorized access points in appropriate fields in bibliographic or authority records.

A description is a note in a record giving details about the relationship. They may be either structured (i.e., following a particular structure, such as ISBD order) or unstructured (free text).

24.5. RELATIONSHIP DESIGNATOR. A relationship designator is a word or phrase associated with an authorized access point for a work or expression that clarifies the nature of the relationship between that work or expression and the work or expression being described in the bibliographic or authority record containing the authorized access point. Relationship designators describing the relationships of persons, families, or corporate bodies to a resource are not new to RDA (see RDA 18.5 and discussion above), but relationship designators describing the relationship between works and other works, between expressions and other expressions, between manifestations and other manifestations, and between items and other items are new. They may be used in either authority records or bibliographic records, and in current practice they precede the authorized access point in the field.

The designators themselves are taken from a list in RDA appendix J, which divides the designators between those used with works, those used with expressions, those used with manifestations, and those used with items. According to RDA 24.5.1.3, if none of the terms in appendix J is appropriate, another term may be used. However, the Joint Steering Committee for Development of RDA is open to proposals for addition to appendix J (and all the relationship designator appendixes); therefore, this *Handbook* recommends that if a cataloger needs to describe a relationship not found in the list the needed designator be proposed as an addition. For an example see the 700 field in figure 9.8. This authorized access point links the record for the film *Sunday in New York* with the record (or records) for the novel it is based on. Figure 9.12 contains another example linking the musical work with the poems that part of its text is based on.

24.6. NUMBERING OF PART. Guidelines for recording the numbering of parts are found here in RDA's structure because they are part of recording a whole-part relationship between a work and a part of that work. Although RDA 24.6 can apply to any sort of work that exists in numbered parts, one important application is to series. A series is considered in FRBR and RDA to be a kind of work called an aggregate work, meaning it is composed of parts which are themselves works. When a work is part of a series the relationship between these two works is called a whole-part relationship and should be recorded. 24.6 does not give us complete instructions for recording that whole-part relationship, but it does give guidance on recording the numbering of a part.

The term "numbering" may be a bit misleading because it can include letters as well as numerals, and it also in this context includes a caption such as "volume" or "number" if present. It can also include a chronological designation such as a year instead of sequential number.

24.6.1.3. RECORDING NUMBERING OF PARTS. RDA instructs us to record the numbering of a part as it appears in the source. However, perhaps surprisingly given RDA's general preference for transcription, numbering is manipulated when recorded. First, the number itself may be manipulated. Following RDA 1.8, most numerals will be recorded "in the form preferred by the agency." LC policy is to record numerals in the form in which they appear on the source (LC-PCC PS 1.8.2, February 2010). Second, terms used as part of the numbering (including captions) are to be abbreviated according to appendix B.5.5. So "volume," for example, would be abbreviated to "v." For an example, see the 830 field in figure 9.13.

Caution: RDA 24.6 applies to numbering of parts that appears in access points, not transcribed elements. Contrast RDA 24.6 with RDA 2.12.9.3 (recording numbering within series), the guideline followed when recording a series statement in a MARC

490 field, and with RDA 2.3.1.7 (titles of parts, sections, and supplements), the guideline followed when recording parts in a title transcription (e.g., in a MARC 245 field). Neither of these guidelines call for abbreviating captions. For a good example of the differing practices outlined in the guidelines, compare the numbering recorded in the 490 field in figure 9.13, which is governed by RDA 2.12.9.3, with the numbering recorded in the 830 field of figure 9.13, which is governed by RDA 24.6. Figure 9.20 contains a similar example.

The authorized access point for a series is backed by an authority record for the series which, like any authority record, shows the authorized form of the series name in a 1XX field. Series authority records also contain several other fields, including 642, which gives the form the series numbering should appear in when used in conjunction with the authorized access point. Once the authority record for a series has been created, the form of numbering found in the 642 field, including the caption, should always be used when recording an authorized access point for the series in a bibliographic record. The series authority record illustrated in figure 9.37 corresponds to the series of the book described in figure 9.13. The 942 field in this record says to follow the pattern "Bd. 12." It so happens in this case that recording "Bd. 31" follows the instructions of RDA 24.6, but even if it did not (e.g., if the numbering on a particular part just said "32" with no caption) the pattern found in the authority record should be followed ("Bd. 32"). This promotes uniformity in indexing. This is not to say that RDA 24.6 should be disregarded. When the authority record for a series is first made, the pattern recorded in the 642 field should conform to the result of applying RDA 24.6 to the series numbering found in the resource being cataloged. Thereafter, however, the numbering in authorized access points for any further parts of the series should conform to the pattern recorded in the authority record.

Figure 9.37. Series Authority Record

046		‡k 1895
130	0	‡a Corpus papyrorum Raineri Archiducis Austriae
380		‡a Series (Publications) ‡a Monographic series ‡2 lcsh
430	0	‡a CPR
430	0	‡a Corpus papyrorum Raineri
642		‡a Bd. 12 ‡5 DLC
643		‡a Wien ‡b In Kommission bei Verlag Brüder Hollinek
644		‡a f ‡5 DLC
645		‡a t ‡5 DLC
646		‡a s ‡5 DLC
667		‡a Publisher varies.

> 670 ‡a Griechische Texte, 1895-1976: ‡b series title page (Corpus papyrorum Raineri Archiducis Austriae) cover (Corpus papyrorum Raineri)
>
> 670 ‡a Checklist of Greek, Latin, Demotic and Coptic papyri, ostraca and tablets, via WWW, 11 May 2011 ‡b (Corpus papyrorum Raineri, abbreviation CPR; first volume published 1895)

24.7. SOURCE CONSULTED. Just as the author of a scholarly paper justifies his or her assertions by citing sources, the creator of an RDA description must justify relationships recorded in an authority record by citing the source the information. In MARC authority work, this is done using the 670 field.[3] The source consulted element is not core in RDA, but justification of all information recorded as access points, elements, or relationships is required in LC/NACO practice. For example, figure 9.2a shows a relationship between an expression (100 field) and a person (its translator, 500 field). This relationship and the nature of the relationship are justified by the information copied from the title page and cited in the 670 field.

For a full discussion of LC/NACO practice in the source consulted element, see chapter 3 of this *Handbook* under 8.12.

24.8. CATALOGUER'S NOTE. The cataloguer's note element contains information about a relationship that might be helpful to persons using the authority record. The cataloguer's note element is not core in RDA, but it is useful when appropriate. It is recorded in the 667 field of the MARC authority format. Figure 9.37 contains a fairly common note of this type clarifying that the series is related to other publishers aside from the one recorded in the 643 field. For a fuller treatment of the cataloguer's note element, see chapter 3 of this *Handbook* under 8.13.

CHAPTER 25. RELATED WORK. There exist a vast number of ways works can be related to each other, but the relationships can generally be categorized as derivative, descriptive, whole-part, accompanying, and sequential relationships.[4]

Derivative Work Relationships. A derivative work relationship is the relationship between one work and another that is based on the first work, in which the original has been modified in some way. There are a range of possibilities, including such modifications as abridgement, adaptation, imitation, parody, paraphrase, and summary. Derivative work relationships are typically recorded in MARC bibliographic records using authorized access points or notes (called structured or unstructured descriptions in RDA), and in authority records using authorized access points.

When recording a derivative work relationship using an authorized access point in a bibliographic record, use a 7XX field. A relationship designator from RDA appendix J may be recorded in subfield ‡i to clarify the nature of the relationship. Figure 9.38 describes *Yes, Yes, Nanette*, a 1925 film parodying the musical comedy "No, No, Nanette." The relationship between the two is recorded in a 700 field.

Figure 9.38.
Derivative Work Relationship—Authorized Access Point in Bibliographic Record

245 00	‡a Yes, yes, Nanette / ‡c Hal Roach Studios ; directed by Stan Laurel and Clarence Hennecke ; produced by Hal Roach ; written by Carl Harbaugh.
264 1	‡a [United States] : ‡b Hal Roach Studios, ‡c 1925.
264 2	‡b Pathé Exchange
300	‡a 1 film reel (9 min., 822 ft.) : ‡b silent, black and white ; ‡c 35 mm
336	‡a two-dimensional moving image ‡2 rdacontent
337	‡a projected ‡2 rdamedia
338	‡a film reel ‡2 rdacarrier
508	‡a Supervised by F. Richard Jones ; assistant directed by Clarence Morehouse ; photography by Frank Young.
511 1	‡a Jimmie Finlayson, Lyle Tayo, Sue O'Neill, Babe Hardy, Jack Gavin, Grant Gorman.
500	‡a Full screen (1.33:1)
520	‡a Nanette writes home that she has found the man of her dreams, they have married and she will be bringing him home the next day. The family dresses up for the big day, but when Nanette and the new husband arrive, the family is none too impressed with the groom.
... [access points for directors, actors, etc.]	
700 1	‡i Parody of (work): ‡a Youmans, Vincent, ‡d 1898-1946. ‡t No, no, Nanette.
710 2	‡a Hal Roach Studios, ‡e film producer.
710 2	‡a Pathé Exchange, ‡e film distributor.

The description in figure 9.39 records the relationship between the work *Bloody Times* and the work *Bloody Crimes* using an unstructured description, the note in the 500 field. This same relationship could have been recorded as a structured description as follows:

> 500 ‡a Adaptation of: Bloody crimes : the chase for Jefferson Davis and the death pageant for Lincoln's corpse / James L. Swanson. New York : William Morrow/HarperCollins, [2010].

Figure 9.39. Derivative Work Relationship—Unstructured Description

020	‡a 9780061560897
100 1	‡a Swanson, James L., ‡d 1959- ‡e author.
245 10	‡a Bloody times : ‡b the funeral of Abraham Lincoln and the manhunt for Jefferson Davis / ‡c James L. Swanson.
250	‡a First edition.

264	1	‡a New York : ‡b Collins, ‡c [2011]
300		‡a 196 pages : ‡b illustrations, portraits ; ‡c 24 cm
336		‡a text ‡2 rdacontent
337		‡a unmediated ‡2 rdamedia
338		‡a volume ‡2 rdacarrier
500		‡a "James L. Swanson creates an adaptation for young people of his adult book Bloody crimes."--Jacket.
504		‡a Includes bibliographical references (pages 189-190).
520		‡a On the morning of April 2, 1865, Jefferson Davis receives a telegram from General Robert E. Lee: the Yankees are coming. That night Davis flees Richmond, setting off an intense manhunt for the Confederate president. Two weeks later, President Lincoln is assassinated, and the nation is convinced that Davis is involved in the conspiracy that led to the crime.

Alternatively (or additionally), the relationship could have been recorded in a 700 field containing the authorized access point for the related work:

> 700 1 ‡i Adaptation of (work): ‡a Swanson, James L., ‡d 1959- ‡t Bloody crimes.

Derivative work relationships can also be recorded in authority records representing works. The relationship is recorded by giving the authorized access point for the related work in a 5XX field. A relationship designator from RDA appendix J may be recorded in subfield ‡i to clarify the nature of the relationship. Figure 9.40 describes in authority records the same derivative relationship recorded in the bibliographic record shown in figure 9.39.

Figure 9.40.
Derivative Work Relationship—Authorized Access Point in Authority Records

046		‡k 2011
100	1	‡a Swanson, James L., ‡d 1959- ‡t Bloody times
380		‡a Historical work
500	1	‡w r ‡i Adaptation of (work): ‡a Swanson, James L., ‡d 1959- ‡t Bloody crimes
670		‡a Bloody times : the funeral of Abraham Lincoln and the manhunt for Jefferson Davis, 2011: ‡b jacket ("Swanson creates an adaptation for young people of his adult book Bloody crimes.")

046		‡k 2010
100	1	‡a Swanson, James L., ‡d 1959- ‡t Bloody crimes
380		‡a Historical work

500 1 ‡w r ‡i Adapted as (work): ‡a Swanson, James L., ‡d 1959- ‡t Bloody times

670 ‡a Bloody crimes : the chase for Jefferson Davis and the death pageant for Lincoln's corpse, 2010.

670 ‡a Bloody times : the funeral of Abraham Lincoln and the manhunt for Jefferson Davis, 2011: ‡b jacket ("Swanson creates an adaptation for young people of his adult book Bloody crimes.")

Descriptive Work Relationships. A descriptive work relationship is that between a work and another that describes it, including criticism, evaluations, and reviews. As with derivative work relationships, descriptive work relationships may be recorded in MARC bibliographic records using authorized access points or notes ("structured" or "unstructured descriptions"), and in authority records using authorized access points.

When recording a descriptive work relationship using an authorized access point in a bibliographic record, use a 7XX field. A relationship designator from RDA appendix J may be recorded in subfield ‡i to clarify the nature of the relationship. Figure 9.41 records the relationship between the work *Scholia Graeca in Odysseam* and Homer's *Odyssey* using an authorized access point (see the first 700 field).

Figure 9.41.
Descriptive Work Relationship—Authorized Access Point in Bibliographic Record

020 ‡a 8884984467 (v. 1)

020 ‡z 9788884984465 (v. 1 2008 reprint)

020 ‡a 9788863721621 (v. 2)

245 00 ‡a Scholia graeca in Odysseam / ‡c edidit Filippomaria Pontani.

264 1 ‡a Roma : ‡b Edizioni di storia e letteratura, ‡c 2007-<2010>

300 ‡a volumes ; ‡c 24 cm.

336 ‡a text ‡2 rdacontent

337 ‡a unmediated ‡2 rdamedia

338 ‡a volume ‡2 rdacarrier

490 1 ‡a Pleiadi ; ‡v 6

546 ‡a Notes and apparatus in Latin; text in Greek.

504 ‡a Includes bibliographical references.

505 1 ‡a I. Scholia ad libros 1-2 -- II. Scholia ad libros 3-4

700 0 ‡i Commentary on (work): ‡a Homer. ‡t Odyssey.

700 1 ‡a Pontani, Filippomaria, ‡d 1976- ‡e editor.

830 0 ‡a Pleiadi (Rome, Italy) ; ‡v 6.

The record illustrated in figure 9.42 uses an unstructured description (in the 520 field) to record the descriptive relationship between the lecture titled "The Grotesque

Imagination of Charles Dickens" and the topic of the lecture, Dickens's short story "Captain Murderer."

Figure 9.42. Descriptive Work Relationship—Unstructured Description

020	‡a 1890123374
100 1	‡a Engel, Elliot, ‡d 1948- ‡e author.
245 14	‡a The grotesque imagination of Charles Dickens : ‡b a light & enlightening literary program / ‡c by Professor Elliot Engel.
264 1	‡a Raleigh, NC : ‡b Authors Ink, ‡c [1997]
300	‡a 1 audio disc (54 min., 35 sec.) ; ‡c 4 3/4 in.
336	‡a spoken word ‡2 rdacontent
337	‡a audio ‡2 rdamedia
338	‡a audio disc ‡2 rdacarrier
344	‡a digital ‡b optical ‡g stereo ‡2 rda
347	‡a audio file ‡b CD audio ‡2 rda
520	‡a Professor Engel presents a lecture about Charles Dickens and the development of his imagination due to the terrifying bedtime stories that the family maid told him as a child. Includes a synopsis and discussion of the horror story by Dickens entitled Captain Murderer.

The descriptive relationship of Harry Blamire's *Word Unheard* to T. S. Eliot's *Four Quartets* is recorded in the pair of authority records shown in figure 9.43. Record the relationship by giving the authorized access point for the related work in a 5XX field. A relationship designator from RDA appendix J was recorded in figure 9.43 in subfield ‡i of the 500 field to clarify the nature of the relationship.

Figure 9.43.
Descriptive Work Relationship—Authorized Access Point in Authority Records

046	‡k 1969
100 1	‡a Blamires, Harry. ‡t Word unheard
380	‡a Analytical work
500 1	‡w r ‡i Analysis of (work): ‡a Eliot, T. S. ‡q (Thomas Stearns), ‡d 1888-1965. ‡t Four quartets
670	‡a Word unheard : a guide through Eliot's Four quartets, 1969

046	‡k 1943
100 1	‡a Eliot, T. S. ‡q (Thomas Stearns), ‡d 1888-1965. ‡t Four quartets
380	‡a Poems
500 1	‡w r ‡i Analysed in (work): ‡a Blamires, Harry. ‡t Word unheard

> 670   ‡a Four quartets, 1943
>
> 670   ‡a Word unheard : a guide through Eliot's Four quartets, 1969

Descriptive work relationships are inherently subject relationships, and this relationship can also be recorded in MARC bibliographic records by giving a subject access point for the work described. For example, the bibliographic record for *Word Unheard* would probably contain this subject access point:

> 600 10 ‡a Eliot, T. S. ‡q (Thomas Stearns), ‡d 1888-1965. ‡t Four quartets.

Whole-Part Work Relationships. The whole-part work relationship is that between a work and its parts. The relationship includes divisions of what are normally considered single works (e.g., the relationship of a preface or chapter to the entire work) as well as aggregate works and their parts (e.g., the relationship of a single monograph to its series, or the relationship of a collection of poems to a single poem in the collection).

The same methods used to record derivative and descriptive work relationships are used to record whole-part work relationships: whole-part work relationships may be recorded in MARC bibliographic records using authorized access points or notes ("structured" or "unstructured descriptions"), and in authority records using authorized access points.

If recording the relationship with authorized access points in bibliographic records, record the authorized access points for the related works in 7XX fields, accompanied by relationship designators from appendix J.2.4 if desired. The work *Riverworld* contains two novels by Philip José Farmer. The description shown in figure 9.44 records the relationship between the aggregate work *Riverworld* and the individual parts (the novels) in two 700 fields.

Figure 9.44.
Whole-Part Work Relationship—Authorized Access Point in Bibliographic Record

> 020   ‡a 9780765326522 (paperback)
>
> 100 1   ‡a Farmer, Philip José, ‡e author.
>
> 245 10 ‡a Riverworld / ‡c Philip José Farmer.
>
> 250   ‡a First edition.
>
> 264 1 ‡a New York : ‡b Tor, ‡c [2010]
>
> 300   ‡a 443 pages ; ‡c 21 cm
>
> 336   ‡a text ‡2 rdacontent
>
> 337   ‡a unmediated ‡2 rdamedia
>
> 338   ‡a volume ‡2 rdacarrier

500   ‡a "A Tom Doherty Associates book."

700 12 ‡i Contains (work): ‡a Farmer, Philip José. ‡t To your scattered bodies go.

700 12 ‡i Contains (work): ‡a Farmer, Philip José. ‡t Fabulous riverboat.

Whole-part relationships of monographic works to series are recorded in bibliographic records using authorized access points in 800, 810, 811, or 830 fields, depending on the nature of the authorized access point for the series. The work *Poetic Paraphrase of the Psalms of David,* illustrated in figure 9.1, has a whole-part relationship to the series *Travaux d'humanisme et Renaissance,* recorded in an 830 field. For other examples, see figures 9.5, 9.8, 9.13, and others throughout this chapter.

Figure 9.45 contains an example of an unstructured description of a whole-part relationship. The 520 field describes the stories contained in the aggregate work *Best of Hitopadesha* in very general terms.

Figure 9.45. Whole-Part Work Relationship—Unstructured Description

020   ‡a 9788175735903

100 1   ‡a Dua, Shyam, ‡e author.

245 10 ‡a Best of Hitopadesha / ‡c retold & edited by Shyam Dua.

246 3   ‡a Hitopadesha

264   1 ‡a Delhi, India : ‡b Tiny Tot Publications, ‡c 2007.

300   ‡a 144 pages : ‡b color illustrations ; ‡c 25 cm

336   ‡a text ‡2 rdacontent

336   ‡a still image ‡2 rdacontent

337   ‡a unmediated ‡2 rdamedia

338   ‡a volume ‡2 rdacarrier

520   ‡a A collection of stories in which the main characters are usually animals, but are meant to illustrate the nature and mentality of humans. The Hitopadesha was written in the 12th century and contains stories meant to provide gentle instruction.

730 0   ‡i Adaptation of (work): ‡a Hitopadeśa.

The whole-part relationship may also be recorded in a structured description. This method uses what was known in AACR2 as a "contents note." A contents note is recorded in a MARC bibliographic 505 field. If the cataloger is recording the complete contents of the item, the first indicator will be coded "0." If the cataloger is unable to record the complete contents, for example because a multivolume set is not yet finished, the first indicator will be coded "1" (see figure 9.41). Introductory terms or phrases such as "Contents:" should not be included, as these are system generated.

Record the titles proper and (optionally) other title information of individual works (or parts) contained in the resource. Add statements of responsibility that appear with these titles. Individual works or parts are separated by space-dash-space. If other title information is included, it is separated from its title proper by space-colon-space. If statements of responsibility are included, they are separated from their titles by space-slash-space. Contents can be recorded from anywhere, but are most commonly recorded from a table of contents.

Former LC practice set limits followed by most North American catalogers to the number of titles that should be recorded in a contents note. The LC policy statement accompanying RDA 25.1 reverses this: "There is no limit on the number of works in the contents note unless burdensome" (LCRI 25.1, December 2011; see also LC-PCC PS 25.1.1.3, January 2013, for detailed guidelines on forming contents notes).

Figure 9.46 includes a structured description of a whole-part relationship, also known as a contents note, in the 505 field. This note records the relationship of the individual articles to the work *Thucydides and Herodotus*. The record illustrated in figure 9.44 also could have recorded a structured description of the whole-part relationship either instead of or in addition to the authorized access points describing the relationship, as follows:

505 0   ‡a To your scattered bodies go -- The fabulous riverboat.

Figure 9.46.
Whole-Part Work Relationship—Structured Description (Contents Note)

020	‡a 9780199593262
245 00	‡a Thucydides and Herodotus / ‡c edited by Edith Foster and Donald Lateiner.
264 1	‡a Oxford, United Kingdom : ‡b Oxford University Press, ‡c 2012.
300	‡a xiv, 399 pages ; ‡c 23 cm
336	‡a text ‡2 rdacontent
337	‡a unmediated ‡2 rdamedia
338	‡a volume ‡2 rdacarrier
504	‡a Includes bibliographical references and indexes.
505 0	‡a Introduction / Edith Foster and Donald Lateiner -- Structure and meaning in epic and histori ography / Richard B. Rutherford -- Thucydides as reader of Herodotus / Philip A. Stadter -- Indirect discourse in Herodotus and Thucydides / Carlo Scardino -- The rationality of Herodotus and Thucydides as evidenced by their respective use of numbers / Catherine Rubicam -- Herodotus and Thucydides on blind decisions preceding military action / Hans-Peter Stahl -- Oaths : theory and practice in the Histories of Herodotus and Thucydides / Donald Lateiner -- Thermopylae and Pylos, with reference to the Homeric background / Edith Foster -- Thucydides on Themistocles : a Herodotean narrator? / Wolfgang Blösel -- Persians in Thucydides / Rosaria Vignolo Munson -- Aristotle's Rhetoric, the

Rhetorica ad Alexandrum, and the speeches in Herodotus and Thucydides / Christopher Pelling -- A noble alliance : Herodotus, Thucydides, and Xenophon's Procles / Emily Baragwanath -- Herodotus and Thucydides in Roman Republican historiography / Iris Samotta.

700 1	‡a Foster, Edith ‡q (Edith Marie), ‡e editor of compilation.
700 1	‡a Lateiner, Donald, ‡e editor of compilation.

Whole-part relationships can also be recorded in authority records by recording the related works in 5XX fields. The whole-part relationship for *Riverworld* (figure 9.44) might have been recorded using a set of authority records as shown in figure 9.47.

Figure 9.47.
Whole-Part Work Relationship—Authorized Access Point in Authority Records

046	‡k 2010
100 1	‡a Farmer, Philip José. ‡t Riverworld (Novel anthology)
380	‡a Anthologies ‡2 lcsh
380	‡a Novels ‡2 aat
381	‡a Novel anthology
500 1	‡w r ‡i Contains (work): ‡a Farmer, Philip José. ‡t To your scattered bodies go
500 1	‡w r ‡i Contains (work): ‡a Farmer, Philip José. ‡t Fabulous riverboat
670	‡a Riverworld, 2010: ‡b title page (To your scattered bodies go, The fabulous riverboat)

046	‡k 1971
100 1	‡a Farmer, Philip José. ‡t To your scattered bodies go
380	‡a Novels ‡2 aat
500 1	‡w r ‡i Contained in (work): ‡a Farmer, Philip José. ‡t Riverworld (Novel anthology)
670	‡a To your scattered bodies go, 1971
670	‡a Riverworld, 2010: ‡b title page (To your scattered bodies go, The fabulous riverboat)

046	‡k 1971
100 1	‡a Farmer, Philip José. ‡t Fabulous riverboat
380	‡a Novels ‡2 aat
500 1	‡w r ‡i Contained in (work): ‡a Farmer, Philip José. ‡t Riverworld (Novel anthology)
670	‡a The fabulous riverboat, 1971
670	‡a Riverworld, 2010: ‡b title page (To your scattered bodies go, The fabulous riverboat)

642 | CHAPTER 9

Analytics. Individual articles within journals or works within collections (e.g., in festschrifts) have a whole-part relationship to the aggregate work (the journal or monograph). Giving details about parts and recording their relationship to the larger work is called "analysis" or "analytical" description (see RDA 1.1.4). Relationship links between the whole and the parts that consist of access points are sometimes called "analytics."

All the techniques described above may be used to show whole-part links for serial or monographic analytics. The most common method for monographs is probably a structured description (contents note, MARC 505 field), or analytical authorized access points (in 7XX fields) (see figures 9.44 and 9.46; in either of these cases both techniques could have been used in the same bibliographic record). This method works well for monographs because they are cataloged on discrete records.

Conversely, individual issues of journals are almost never cataloged on discrete records, so the contents note plus analytical added access points technique would rarely if ever be used to show the whole-part relationship between an issue of a journal and its articles. Traditionally, this relationship is rarely brought out in library catalogs. For very practical reasons it was long ago decided that articles in journals would not usually be given individual descriptions—or indeed any notice at all—in library catalogs. However, an analytic technique does exist for the rare cases where individual descriptions for articles are desired, partly described in RDA 2.1.3 and 3.4.1.12. The analysis technique can be used for parts in monographs or articles in individual journal issues. When used, the individual work is linked to the aggregate using one of the MARC linking fields, usually 773.

To create an analytical description, follow the same procedures as for any other description. Choose a source of information following 2.1.3 and transcribe the title proper of the part following the guidelines in 2.3. If a statement of responsibility appears somewhere in the resource, record it following the guidelines in 2.4. Record the extent following 3.4.1.12. Include content type (6.9), media type (3.2), and carrier type (3.3). Include other elements (such as notes) as needed.

The relationship of the part being described in the analytical description to the whole is normally recorded in a 773 field. Although the field does not require using the authorized access point for the larger work, it is good practice to use this form in subfields ‡a (if a creator's authorized access point is part of the authorized access point for the work) and ‡t (for the preferred title). Information such as volume and issue number can be recorded in subfield ‡g following guidelines in 24.6. The indicators may be used to generate or suppress a label. Generally code the first indicator "0." Second indicator "1" will generate the label "In:". However, if a relationship designator from appendix J.2.4 is used (in subfield ‡i) the "In:" label should be suppressed by coding the second indicator "8." Figure 9.48 illustrates an analytical description of a part in a MARC bibliographic record. The cataloger has chosen to use an RDA relationship designator, so the 773 field is coded with indicators "08."

Figure 9.48. Whole-Part Work Relationship—Analytical Description of a Part

100 1	‡a Johnson, Kij, ‡e author.
245 10	‡a Schrödiger's cathouse / ‡c by Kij Johnson.
264 1	‡a Cornwall, Connecticut : ‡b Mercury Press, ‡c 1993.
300	‡a pages 25-30 ; ‡c 20 cm
336	‡a text ‡2 rdacontent
337	‡a unmediated ‡2 rdamedia
338	‡a volume ‡2 rdacarrier
773 08	‡i Contained in (work): ‡t The magazine of fantasy and science fiction, ‡g v. 84, no. 3 (March 1993)

Accompanying Work Relationships. An accompanying work relationship is that between a work and another that accompanies it or is intended to accompany it. This relationship is recorded in the same way as other work relationships in current MARC practice: authorized access points or notes.

There are two types of accompanying relationship: supplementary and complementary.

Supplementary Accompanying Work Relationships. Accompanying relationships are supplementary when one entity is predominant and the other is subordinate. An example of such a relationship is that between an index and its work. Wolfhard Steppe produced an index to James Joyce's *Ulysses* in 1985. Although the two works are widely separated chronologically they share an accompanying relationship because Steppe's work was intended to accompany Joyce's (see figure 9.49).

Figure 9.49. Supplementary Accompanying Work Relationship—Index

020	‡a 0824087534
100 1	‡a Steppe, Wolfhard, ‡e author.
245 12	‡a A handlist to James Joyce's Ulysses : ‡b a complete alphabetical index to the critical reading text / ‡c prepared by Wolfhard Steppe, with Hans Walter Gabler.
264 1	‡a New York ; ‡a London : ‡b Garland Publishing, Inc., ‡c 1985.
300	‡a x, 300 pages ; ‡c 29 cm
336	‡a text ‡2 rdacontent
337	‡a unmediated ‡2 rdamedia
338	‡a volume ‡2 rdacarrier
490 1	‡a Garland reference library of the humanities ; ‡v vol. 582
504	‡a Includes index.
700 1	‡a Gabler, Hans Walter, ‡d 1938- ‡e author.
700 1	‡i Index to (work): ‡a Joyce, James, ‡d 1882-1941. ‡t Ulysses.
830 0	‡a Garland reference library of the humanities ; ‡v vol. 582.

In the case of *Ulysses* and its index, the two works are independent of each other. Works with supplementary accompanying relationships can also be dependent. An index published with a text is an example of such a relationship. Another example is an illustrated text. The text and the illustrations can be considered separate works, each of which has a whole-part relationship with the aggregate work consisting of the text together with the illustrations. However, in relation to each other, the two works share an accompanying relationship, and in most (though not all) cases illustrations are considered supplementary to the text. A well-known example is Lewis Carroll's *Alice's Adventures in Wonderland,* published with illustrations by John Tenniel. In this case the relationship between the text and the illustrations is seldom explicitly recorded except inherently through the statement of responsibility or a note (see figure 9.50).

Figure 9.50. Supplementary Accompanying Work Relationship—Illustrations

020	9780451532008
100 1	‡a Carroll, Lewis, ‡d 1832-1898, ‡a author.
245 10	‡a Alice's adventures in Wonderland ; ‡b &, Through the looking-glass / ‡c Lewis Carroll ; illustrations by John Tenniel ; with an introduction Martin Gardner and a new afterword by Jeffrey Meyers.
246 3	‡a Through the looking-glass
264 1	‡a New York : ‡b Signet Classic, ‡c 2012.
300	‡a x, 239 pages : ‡b illustrations ; ‡c 18 cm
336	‡a text ‡2 rdacontent
336	‡a still image ‡2 rdacontent
337	‡a unmediated ‡2 rdamedia
338	‡a volume ‡2 rdacarrier
504	‡a Includes bibliographical references.
520	‡a Alice falls down a rabbit hole and discovers a world of nonsensical and amusing characters.
700 12	‡a Carroll, Lewis, ‡d 1832-1898. ‡t Alice's adventures in Wonderland.
700 12	‡a Carroll, Lewis, ‡d 1832-1898. ‡t Through the looking-glass.
700 1	‡a Tenniel, John, ‡c Sir, ‡d 1820-1914, ‡e illustrator.
700 1	‡a Gardner, Martin, ‡d 1914-2010, ‡e editor.

Naturally, it is possible to publish illustrations separately from the text, as sometimes happens when the illustrations become particularly famous. For example, Tenniel's illustrations were published without the text as *Tenniel's Alice.* Even though the illustrations were published separately, they still have an accompanying relationship to Carroll's text because they were intended to accompany it, and the accompanying relationship can be recorded (see the 700 fields in figure 9.51).

Figure 9.51. Supplementary Accompanying Work Relationship—Illustrations

100 1	‡a Tenniel, John, ‡c Sir, ‡d 1820-1914, ‡a artist.
245 10	‡a Tenniel's Alice / ‡c drawings by Sir John Tenniel for Alice's adventures in Wonderland and Through the looking-glass.
264 1	‡a [Cambridge, Massachusetts] : ‡b Department of Printing and Graphic Arts, Harvard College Library, ‡c [1978]
300	‡a 75 pages : ‡b illustrations ; ‡c 22 cm
336	‡a text ‡2 rdacontent
336	‡a still image ‡2 rdacontent
337	‡a unmediated ‡2 rdamedia
338	‡a volume ‡2 rdacarrier
500	‡a Drawings from the Harcourt Amory Collection in the Houghton Library, Harvard University.
504	‡a Includes bibliographical references.
700 1	‡i Illustrations for (work): ‡a Carroll, Lewis, ‡d 1832-1898. ‡t Alice's adventures in Wonderland.
700 1	‡i Illustrations for (work): ‡a Carroll, Lewis, ‡d 1832-1898. ‡t Through the looking-glass.

Other examples of supplementary accompanying relationships, any of which may be dependent (published with the primary work) or independent (published separately from the primary work), include guides, appendixes, supplements, etc.

Supplementary relationships between serial works are treated somewhat differently from those of monographic works. Rather than recording the authorized access points for related serial works in 700, 710, 711, or 730 fields, the MARC linking fields 770 and 772 are used.

The authorized access point for a serial that is a supplement to the serial being cataloged is recorded in the 772 field, first indicator "0," second indicator blank. This generates the relationship designator "Supplement to:". The 772 field in figure 9.52 would display:

Supplement to: College and research libraries

Figure 9.52. Supplementary Accompanying Work Relationship—Serial

022	‡a 0099-0086
245 00	‡a College & research libraries news.
246 3	‡a College and research libraries news
264 1	‡a Chicago : ‡b Association of College and Research Libraries, ‡c 1967-
300	‡a volumes : ‡b illustrations ; ‡c 24 cm
310	‡a Monthly (except July and August combined)

362 0   ‡a January 1967-December 1979 ; volume 41, no. 1 (January 1980)-

336   ‡a text ‡2 rdacontent

336   ‡a still image ‡2 rdacontent

337   ‡a unmediated ‡2 rdamedia

338   ‡a volume ‡2 rdacarrier

550   ‡a Issued by: Association of College and Research Libraries.

588   ‡a Description based on: January 1967; title from caption.

588   ‡a Latest issue consulted: Volume 73, number 7 (July/August 2012)

710 2   ‡a Association of College and Research Libraries, ‡e issuing body

772 0   ‡t College and research libraries, ‡x 0010-0870

780 00 ‡t ACRL news

The name of a serial that supplements the serial being cataloged is recorded in a 770 field, first indicator "0," second indicator blank, which generates the relationship designator "Has supplement." The 770 field is coded as follows:

770 0   ‡t Journal of the Royal Numismatic Society

This would display "Has supplement: Journal of the Royal Numismatic Society."

More complex situations are handled by combinations of 580 and 770 fields, first indicator "1." Using this combination the 580 field displays to the library user and the display of the 770 fields is suppressed, but the fields still serve a linking function between the records for the resources (see figure 9.53).

Figure 9.53. Supplementary Accompanying Work Relationship—Serial

022   ‡a 0010-0870

245 00 ‡a College and research libraries.

246 3   ‡a College & research libraries

264 1 ‡a Chicago : ‡b American Library Association, ‡c 1939-

300   ‡a volumes : ‡b illustrations ; ‡c 23-26 cm

310   ‡a Bimonthly, ‡b 1956-

321   ‡a Quarterly, ‡b 1939-1955

336   ‡a text ‡2 rdacontent

336   ‡a still image ‡2 rdacontent

337   ‡a unmediated ‡2 rdamedia

338   ‡a volume ‡2 rdacarrier

362 0   ‡a Volume 1, number 1 (December 1939)-

550   ‡a Official journal of: Association of College and Reference Libraries (U.S.), 1939-1957; Association of College and Research Libraries, 1958-

580	‡a Volume for 1966 has supplement: ACRL news; volumes for 1967- have supplement: College and research libraries news.
588	‡a Description based on: Volume 1, number 1 (December 1939); title from cover.
588	‡a Latest issue consulted: Volume 70, number 6 (November 2009)
710 2	‡a Association of College and Reference Libraries (U.S.), ‡e issuing body.
710 2	‡a Association of College and Research Libraries, ‡e issuing body.
770 1	‡t ACRL news
770 1	‡t College & research libraries news, ‡x 0099-0086

Complementary Accompanying Work Relationships. Accompanying relationships are complementary if entities are of equal status but have no chronological arrangement. These relationships are recorded in exactly the same way as supplementary accompanying work relationships.

Musical works frequently exhibit complementary accompanying relationships. An example considered to be complementary by RDA is the relationship of a cadenza to a concerto. Composers write concertos to showcase a solo instrument or voice; a typical feature of a concerto is a cadenza where the soloist performs without accompaniment. Sometimes the cadenza is written as part of the original composition, but the soloist may also be expected to improvise, or the cadenza may be written by a different composer than the composer of the concerto.

Figure 9.54 describes a resource containing five cadenzas written by Clara Schumann for two piano concertos by Beethoven and one by Mozart. The relationship of the cadenza to each work or part is recorded in the final 700 fields of the description.

Figure 9.54. Complementary Accompanying Work Relationship—Cadenza

028 30	‡a 3629 ‡b C.F. Peters
028 22	‡a 10118 ‡b C.F. Peters
100 1	‡a Schumann, Clara, ‡d 1819-1896, ‡e composer.
245 10	‡a Fünf Kadenzen für Klavier zu zwei Händen / ‡c Clara Schumann.
264 1	‡a Frankfurt ; ‡a London ; ‡a New York : ‡b C.F. Peters, ‡c [between 1970 and 1979?]
300	‡a 1 score (27 pages) ; ‡c 31 cm
336	‡a notated music ‡2 rdacontent
337	‡a unmediated ‡2 rdamedia
338	‡a volume ‡2 rdacarrier
546	‡b Staff notation.
500	‡a Originally published as Cadenzen zu Beethoven's Clavier-Concerten. Leipzig : J. Rieter-Biedermann, [1870] and as Zwei Cadenzen zu Mozart's Clavier-Concert in d Moll. Leipzig : J. Rieter-Biedermann, 1891.

505 0 ‡a Kadenz zu Beethoven, Konzert c-Moll op. 37 -- Kadenz zu Beethoven, Konzert G-Dur, op. 58. Erster Satz ; Dritter Satz -- Kadenz zu Mozart, Konzert d-Moll KV 466. Erster Satz ; Dritter Satz.

700 12 ‡a Schumann, Clara, ‡d 1819-1896. ‡t Cadenzen zu Beethoven's Clavier-Concerten.

700 12 ‡a Schumann, Clara, ‡d 1819-1896. ‡t Cadenzen zu Mozart's Clavier-Concert in d Moll.

700 1 ‡i Cadenza composed for (work): ‡a Beethoven, Ludwig van, ‡d 1770-1827. ‡t Concertos, ‡m piano, orchestra, ‡n no. 3, op. 37, ‡r C minor.

700 1 ‡i Cadenza composed for (work): ‡a Beethoven, Ludwig van, ‡d 1770-1827. ‡t Concertos, ‡m piano, orchestra, ‡n no. 4, op. 58, ‡r G major. ‡p Allegro moderato.

700 1 ‡i Cadenza composed for (work): ‡a Beethoven, Ludwig van, ‡d 1770-1827. ‡t Concertos, ‡m piano, orchestra, ‡n no. 4, op. 58, ‡r G major. ‡p Rondo.

700 1 ‡i Cadenza composed for (work): ‡a Mozart, Wolfgang Amadeus, ‡d 1756-1791. ‡t Concertos, ‡m piano, orchestra, ‡n K. 466, ‡r D minor. ‡p Allegro.

700 1 ‡i Cadenza composed for (work): ‡a Mozart, Wolfgang Amadeus, ‡d 1756-1791. ‡t Concertos, ‡m piano, orchestra, ‡n K. 466, ‡r D minor. ‡p Rondo.

Music written for an existing text usually has a complementary accompanying relationship with the text. Individual poems within Shakespeare's plays have frequently had music written for them (indeed, many were intended to be sung). An example is "Sigh No More, Ladies," from *Much Ado About Nothing*. A number of composers have written music for this poem, including Peter Warlock (see figure 9.55). Accompanying work relationships can also be recorded using authority records in RDA, and because so many composers have written music for this text it might be efficient to record the relationships there. The authority record illustrated in figure 9.56 records the relationships (in 500 fields) of just a few of the dozens of musical works related to this text. The situation can be reversed. In 1964 the comic team Michael Flanders and Donald Swann wrote words to be sung to the tune of the solo instrument in Mozart's fourth horn concerto (K. 495, movement III) (see figure 9.57).

Figure 9.55.
Complementary Accompanying Work Relationship—Music Written for Text

100 1 ‡a Warlock, Peter, ‡d 1894-1930, ‡e composer.

245 10 ‡a Sigh no more, ladies / ‡c Peter Warlock ; [words by] Shakespeare.

264 1 ‡a London : ‡b Oxford University Press, ‡c [1928]

300 ‡a 1 score (4 pages) ; ‡c 33 cm

336 ‡a notated music ‡2 rdacontent

336 ‡a text ‡2 rdacontent

337 ‡a unmediated ‡2 rdamedia

338 ‡a volume ‡2 rdacarrier

546	‡b Staff notation.
500	‡a For voice (range: E♭-F) and piano; English words.
500	‡a Title from caption.
700 1	‡i Musical setting of (work): ‡a Shakespeare, William, ‡d 1564-1616. ‡t Sigh no more, ladies.

**Figure 9.56. Complementary Accompanying Work Relationship—
Music Written for Text—Authority Record**

046	‡k 1598
100 1	‡a Shakespeare, William, ‡d 1564-1616. ‡t Sigh no more, ladies
400 1	‡a Shakespeare, William, ‡d 1564-1616. ‡t Much ado about nothing. ‡p Sigh no more, ladies
380	‡a Poem
670	‡a Songs from the plays of Shakespeare, 1923: ‡b page 20 (Sigh no more, ladies; from Much ado about nothing)
670	‡a Wikipedia, 31 July 2012 ‡b (Much ado about nothing; first performed 1598; includes Sigh no more, ladies)
670	‡a Sigh no more, ladies, 1928: ‡b caption (Peter Warlock)
670	‡a Sigh no more, ladies, song, 1950: ‡b caption (music by Walter Adrian)
670	‡a Sure on this shining night, 1997: ‡b container (Sigh no more, ladies / Thomson)
670	‡a Sigh no more, ladies : for women's voices : from the cantata In Windsor Forest, adapted from the opera Sir John in love: ‡b caption (R. Vaughan Williams)
670	‡a Spectra, 2002: ‡b label (Sigh no more, ladies (1983) for treble voices a cappella / E. Lauer)
500 1	‡w r ‡i Musical setting (work): ‡a Adrian, Walter, ‡d 1897-1963. ‡t Sigh no more, ladies, song
500 1	‡w r ‡i Musical setting (work): ‡a Lauer, Elizabeth. ‡t Sigh no more, ladies
500 1	‡w r ‡i Musical setting (work): ‡a Warlock, Peter, ‡d 1894-1930. ‡t Sigh no more, ladies
500 1	‡w r ‡i Musical setting (work): ‡a Thomson, Virgil, ‡d 1896-1989. ‡t Shakespeare songs. ‡p Sigh no more, ladies
500 1	‡w r ‡i Musical setting (work): ‡a Vaughan Williams, Ralph, ‡d 1872-1958. ‡t Sigh no more, ladies

**Figure 9.57.
Complementary Accompanying Work Relationship—Text Written for Music**

100 1	‡a Flanders, Michael, ‡e author.
245 10	‡a Ill wind / ‡c Flanders and Swann.
264 1	‡a [Place of publication not identified] : ‡b Thomas Bacon, ‡c [2009]
300	‡a 1 online resource

336	‡a text ‡2 rdacontent
337	‡a computer ‡2 rdamedia
338	‡a online resource ‡2 rdacarrier
347	‡a text file ‡b HTML ‡2 rda
500	‡a Text written to be sung to the tune of the rondo of Mozart's fourth horn concerto.
700 1	‡a Swann, Donald, ‡d 1923-1994, ‡e author.
700 1	‡i Musical setting (work): ‡a Mozart, Wolfgang Amadeus, ‡d 1756-1791. ‡t Concertos, ‡m horn, orchestra, ‡n K. 495, ‡r E♭ major. ‡p Rondo.
856 40	‡u http://www.hornplanet.com/hornpage/museum/articles/ill_wind.html

Sequential Work Relationships. Works or parts of works that continue or precede each other, or have a chronological or numerical relationship to each other, are said to have a sequential relationship.

A *sequel* has a sequential relationship with the work it follows. The relationship between a sequel and its prequel has traditionally been recorded in a MARC record by a simple note:

> 100   1 ‡a Collins, Suzanne.
> 245 10 ‡a Catching fire / ‡c Suzanne Collins.
> . . .
> 500   ‡a Sequel to: The hunger games.
> 500   ‡a Sequel: Mockingjay.

However, RDA chapter 25 allows this relationship to be recorded in a machine-actionable way, by recording the authorized access points for the sequel or prequel in 7XX fields (see figure 9.58a). This method allows for direct links between descriptions. This relationship can also be recorded in an authority record representing the work (see the 500 fields in figure 9.58b).

Figure 9.58a. Sequential Work Relationship—Sequel (Bibliographic Record)

020	‡a 9780439023498
100 1	‡a Collins, Suzanne, ‡e author.
245 10	‡a Catching fire / ‡c Suzanne Collins.
250	‡a First edition.
264 1	‡a New York : ‡b Scholastic Press, ‡c 2009.
300	‡a 391 pages ; ‡c 22 cm.
336	‡a text ‡2 rdacontent
337	‡a unmediated ‡2 rdamedia
338	‡a volume ‡2 rdacarrier

490 1	‡a The second book of The hunger games

490 1   ‡a The second book of The hunger games

520   ‡a By winning the annual Hunger Games, District 12 tributes Katniss Everdeen and Peeta Mellark have secured a life of safety and plenty for themselves and their families, but because they won by defying the rules, they unwittingly become the faces of an impending rebellion.

586   ‡a American Library Association Notables (2010); Booklist Editor's Choice/Books for Youth (2009)

700 1   ‡i Sequel to: ‡a Collins, Suzanne. ‡t Hunger games.

700 1   ‡i Sequel: ‡a Collins, Suzanne. ‡t Mockingjay.

800 1   ‡a Collins, Suzanne. ‡t Hunger Games ; ‡v bk. 2.

Figure 9.58b. Sequential Relationship—Sequel (Authority Record)

046   ‡a 2009

100 1   ‡a Collins, Suzanne. ‡t Catching fire

380   ‡a Novels ‡2 aat

500 1   ‡w r ‡i Sequel to: ‡a Collins, Suzanne. ‡t Hunger games

500 1   ‡w r ‡i Sequel: ‡a Collins, Suzanne. ‡t Mockingjay

670   ‡a Catching fire, 2009

670   ‡a Scholastic website, 13 August 2012 ‡b (Catching fire is a sequel to The hunger games, and its sequel is Mockingjay)

Individual works within a numbered monographic series or multipart monograph usually have a sequential relationship to each other, in addition to their whole-part relationship to the aggregate work. Both these relationships are recorded in bibliographic records by giving the authorized access point for the series in an 8XX field; the sequential relationship is recorded by giving the numbering of the individual item along with the authorized access point in subfield ‡v of the 8XX field (see discussion above at 24.6 for the formulation of the numbering of the part). The sequential relationship between parts may be shown by a database's series index, which may display in numerical order. The relationship between the parts of the multipart monograph *The Hunger Games* (see figure 9.58a) might be displayed to the user as follows:

Collins, Suzanne. Hunger games ; bk. 1
  The hunger games
Collins, Suzanne. Hunger games ; bk. 2
  Catching fire
Collins, Suzanne. Hunger games ; bk. 3
  Mockingjay

This display is generated from the 800 fields of the bibliographic records for the individual works and clearly shows the sequential relationship between them.

Individual issues of a serial have a sequential relationship to each other. They also have a whole-part relationship to the serial itself. For example, the October 2012 issue of *Scientific American* has a sequential relationship to the November 2012 issue. The sequential relationship between individual issues of a serial is usually shown in MARC cataloging by describing all the issues in a single record, with a numeration field describing the serial as a whole and a holdings record showing the issues owned by the library.

When a serial's title changes, a serial merges with another, or changes its identity an another way, a new serial is usually thought to be created, and the first has a sequential relationship with the next. Sequential serial relationships are recorded in bibliographic records using a pair of "linking entry" fields, MARC fields 780 and 785. These fields are intended to link records, may index, and the exact type of sequential relationship may be shown by the coding of the indicators. (Note: as of this writing the MARC format for 780 and 785 does not provide for suppressing the indicator-generated labels, so it is not currently possible to record the precise RDA relationship designators for sequential work relationships in appendix J.2.6.) This has the effect of linking all of the related serial works in sequential order.

The 780 field is used to record the title of the immediate predecessor of the serial described; the 785 field records its immediate successor. The coding of the first indicator should be "0." This will cause the local system to generate a note that will be visible to the patron. (In some cases the generation of a note is not wanted [see below]. In such cases, the first indicator is coded "1.") The second indicator depends on the nature of the sequential relationship. Its operation will be seen in the discussion below of specific situations.

In all cases, the related serial should be recorded in the linking field using the authorized access point for the serial work. For example, if the authorized access point combines the authorized access point for a corporate body with the preferred title of the serial, it should be so recorded in the linking field (‡a Corporate body. ‡t Preferred title); if the authorized access point is formed by using the preferred title alone, that is the form recorded in the linking field.

Continuation. Record a related previous serial in a 780 field with the indicators coded "00." This generates the relationship designator "Continues." The note generated from the 780 field of figure 9.59 for the serial Oregon Genealogical Society journal will appear to the patron:

Continues: Oregon Genealogical Society. Quarterly.

Figure 9.59. Sequential Work Relationship—Continuation

022	ǂy 0783-1891
110 2	ǂa Oregon Genealogical Society, ǂe author.
245 10	ǂa Oregon Genealogical Society journal.
264　1	ǂa Eugene, Oregon : ǂb Oregon Genealogical Society, ǂc 2011-
300	ǂa volumes : ǂb illustrations ; ǂc 28 cm
310	ǂa Semiannual
336	ǂa text ǂ2 rdacontent
336	ǂa still image ǂ2 rdacontent
337	ǂa unmediated ǂ2 rdamedia
338	ǂa volume ǂ2 rdacarrier
362 1	ǂa Began with Volume 49, number 1 (Spring 2011).
588	ǂa Description based on: Volume 49, number 1 (Spring 2011); title from cover.
588	ǂa Latest issue consulted: Volume 49, number 2 (Autumn 2011).
780 00	ǂa Oregon Genealogical Society. ǂt Quarterly ǂx 0738-1891

Record a related subsequent serial in a 785 field with the indicators coded "00." This generates the relationship designator "Continued by." The note generated from the 785 field of figure 9.60 for the Oregon Genealogical Society's *Quarterly* will appear to the patron:

Continued by: Oregon Genealogical Society journal.

Figure 9.60. Sequential Work Relationship—Continuation

022	ǂy 0783-1891
110 2	ǂa Oregon Genealogical Society, ǂe author.
245 10	ǂa Quarterly / ǂc Oregon Genealogical Society.
264　1	ǂa Eugene, Oregon : ǂb Oregon Genealogical Society, ǂc 1982-2010.
300	ǂa 27 volumes ; ǂc 28 cm
310	ǂa Quarterly
336	ǂa text ǂ2 rdacontent
337	ǂa unmediated ǂ2 rdamedia
338	ǂa volume ǂ2 rdacarrier
362 1	ǂa Began with Volume 21, number 1 (fall 1982); volume 48, number 4 (fall 2010).
588	ǂa Description based on: Volume 21, number 1 (fall 1982); title from cover.
588	ǂa Latest issue consulted: Volume 48, number 4 (fall 2010).
780 00	ǂa Oregon Genealogical Society. ǂt Bulletin ǂx 0738-1883
785 00	ǂt Oregon Genealogical Society journal ǂx 0738-1891

Merger. Because this situation is too complex for the indicators to generate the needed relationship designator and note, it is handled by a combination of a 580 field, which displays as a note, and 780 fields with indicators "14" (see figure 9.61). "Merged with" is handled in exactly the same way, except the related serial names are recorded in 785 fields with indicators "17" (see figure 9.62).

Figure 9.61. Sequential Work Relationship—Merger

022	‡a 0024-2527
245 00	‡a Library resources & technical services.
246 3	‡a Library resources and technical services
246 1	‡a Commonly known as: ‡a LRTS
264 1	‡a [Richmond, Virginia] : ‡b ALA Resources and Technical Services Division, ‡c 1957-
300	‡a volumes ; ‡c 24 cm
310	‡a Quarterly
336	‡a text ‡2 rdacontent
337	‡a unmediated ‡2 rdamedia
338	‡a volume ‡2 rdacarrier
362 1	‡a Began with Volume 1, number 1 (winter 1957).
550	‡a Official publication of: The American Library Association, Resources and Technical Services Division.
580	‡a Merger of: Serial slants, and: Journal of cataloging and classification.
588	‡a Description based on: Volume 1, number 1 (winter 1957); title from cover.
588	‡a Latest issue consulted: Volume 53, number 4 (October 2009).
710 2	‡a American Library Association. ‡b Resources and Technical Services Division.
780 14	‡t Serial slants ‡x 0559-5258
780 14	‡t Journal of cataloging and classification

Figure 9.62. Sequential Work Relationship—Merger

245 00	‡a Journal of cataloging and classification.
264 1	‡a [Richmond, Virginia] : ‡b American Library Association, Division of Cataloging and Classification, ‡c 1948-1956.
300	‡a 8 volumes ; ‡c 22 cm
310	‡a Quarterly
336	‡a text ‡2 rdacontent
337	‡a unmediated ‡2 rdamedia
338	‡a volume ‡2 rdacarrier
362 0	‡a Volume 5, number 1 (fall 1948)-volume 12, number 4 (Oct. 1956).

550	‡a Official publication of: The American Library Association, Division of Cataloging and Classification.
580	‡a Merged with: Serial slants, to form: Library resources & technical services.
588	‡a Description based on: Volume 5, number 1 (fall 1948); title from cover.
588	‡a Latest issue consulted: Volume 12, number 4 (October 1956).
710 2	‡a American Library Association. ‡b Division of Cataloging and Classification.
785 17	‡t Serial slants ‡x 0559-5258
785 17	‡t Library resources & technical services ‡x 0024-2527

Split. When a serial is the result of a previous serial splitting into more than one part, record this in a 780 field with indicators "01." This generates the relationship designator "Continues in part." The note generated from the 780 field in figure 9.17 will display:

> Continues in part: Great Britain. Metropolitan Police Service. Joint annual report.

The opposite situation, recording the names of the serials a "parent" serial has split into, requires a combination of 580 and 785 fields coded with indicators "16." The short-lived *Mobil Travel Guide. Southern California & Hawaii* was formed by a merger of separate guides for Southern California and Hawaii, and split after two years into *Forbes Travel Guides* for the same two states (see figure 9.63).

Figure 9.63. Sequential Work Relationship—Split

245 00	‡a Mobil travel guide. ‡p Southern California & Hawaii.
246 30	‡a Southern California & Hawaii
246 3	‡a Southern California and Hawaii
264 1	‡a Chicago, IL : ‡b Mobil Travel Guide, ‡c [2007-2008]
300	‡a 2 volumes : ‡b maps (some color) ; ‡c 23 cm
310	‡a Annual
336	‡a text ‡2 rdacontent
336	‡a cartographic image ‡2 rdacontent
337	‡a unmediated ‡2 rdamedia
338	‡a volume ‡2 rdacarrier
362 0	‡a 2008-2009.
580	‡a Merger of: Mobil travel guide. Southern California, and: Mobil travel guide. Hawaii.
580	‡a Split into: Forbes travel guide. Southern California, and: Forbes travel guide. Hawaii.
588	‡a Description based on: 2008; title from cover.

```
500      ‡a Latest issue consulted: 2009.
780 14  ‡t Mobil travel guide. Southern California
780 14  ‡t Mobil travel guide. Hawaii
785 16  ‡t Forbes travel guide. Southern California
785 16  ‡t Forbes travel guide. Hawaii
```

Absorption. The name of a serial that the serial being cataloged has absorbed is recorded in the 780 field with indicators "05." This generates the relationship designator "Absorbed." The example of an absorption in RDA 25.1.1.3 would be coded as follows:

780 05 ‡t Curriculum report (Reston, Va.)

and would display: "Absorbed: Curriculum report (Reston, Va.)."

To record a serial that absorbs the serial being cataloged, use a 785 field with indicators "04," which generates the relationship designator "Absorbed by." The example of this given under RDA 25.1.1.3 would be coded:

785 04 ‡t Bobbin (Colombia, S.C. : 1987)

and would display:

"Absorbed by: Bobbin (Colombia, S.C. : 1987)".

CHAPTER 26. RELATED EXPRESSION. There are many ways expressions can be related to each other, and as with works these relationships are generally categorized as derivative, descriptive, whole-part, accompanying, and sequential. Expression relationships are recorded in the same way as work relationships, that is, identifiers (not currently used in MARC cataloging), authorized access points, and descriptions (notes and other parts of the record). And like work relationships, they can be recorded both in bibliographic and authority records.

Because the recording of related expressions is so similar to recording related works, this section will just give a few examples of each type of relationship. For details on coding, etc., see the discussion of chapter 25, above.

Derivative Expression Relationships. Four common types of related expressions are translations, revisions, musical arrangements, and simultaneous editions of serial publications.

A translation is the conversion of an expression in one language into an expression in another language. In the resource illustrated in figure 9.64a, the Dutch original was translated into English. This was recorded in two ways: using a note (the 500 field), and using an authorized access point for the related (Dutch) expression. This same relationship can be recorded using an authority record (see figure 9.64b). Using an authorized access point to record this sort of relationship is new with RDA and may or may not be commonly used in the future.

Figure 9.64a.
Derivative Expression Relationship—Translation (Bibliographic Record)

020	‡a 9780374365172
100 1	‡a Heuvel, Eric, ‡d 1960- ‡e author.
240 10	‡a Zoektocht. ‡l English
245 14	‡a The search / ‡c Eric Heuvel, Ruud van der Rol, Lies Schippers ; English translation by Lorraine T. Miller.
250	‡a First American edition.
264 1	‡a New York : ‡b Farrar, Straus, Giroux, ‡c 2009.
300	‡a 61 pages : ‡b illustrations (chiefly color) ; ‡c 29 cm
336	‡a text ‡2 rdacontent
336	‡a still image ‡2 rdacontent
337	‡a unmediated ‡2 rdamedia
338	‡a volume ‡2 rdacarrier
500	‡a Translation of: De Zoektocht.
520	‡a After recounting her experience as a Jewish girl living in Amsterdam during the Holocaust, Esther, helped by her grandson, embarks on a search to discover what happened to her parents before they died in a concentration camp.
700 1	‡a Rol, Ruud van der, ‡e author.
700 1	‡a Schippers, Lies, ‡e author.
700 1	‡a Miller, Lorraine T., ‡e translator.
700 1	‡i Translation of: ‡a Heuvel, Eric, ‡d 1960- ‡t Zocktocht. ‡l Dutch.

Figure 9.64b.
Derivative Expression Relationship—Translation (Authority Record)

046	‡k 2009
100 1	‡a Heuvel, Eric, ‡d 1960- ‡t Zoektocht. ‡l English
377	‡a eng
400 1	‡a Heuvel, Eric, ‡d 1960- ‡t Search
500 1	‡w r ‡i Translator: ‡a Miller, Lorraine T.
500 1	‡w r ‡i Translation of: ‡a Heuvel, Eric, ‡d 1960- ‡t Zoektocht. ‡l Dutch
670	‡a The search, 2009: ‡b title page (English translation by Lorraine T. Miller)

A revised version creates a new expression and its relationship should be recorded either with a note or an authorized access point. The relationship of the resource described in figure 9.65 and the earlier version is recorded both as a structured description (775 field) and an unstructured description (500 field) (see RDA 24.4.3).

Figure 9.65. Derivative Expression Relationship—Revision

020	‡a 9780199600571
245 12	‡a A dictionary of plant sciences / ‡c edited by Michael Allaby.
250	‡a Third edition.
264 1	‡a Oxford : ‡b Oxford University Press, ‡c 2012.
300	‡a 565 pages : ‡b illustrations ; ‡c 20 cm.
336	‡a text ‡2 rdacontent
336	‡a still image ‡2 rdacontent
337	‡a unmediated ‡2 rdamedia
338	‡a volume ‡2 rdacarrier
490 1	‡a Oxford paperback reference
500	‡a Originally published in 1992 as: The concise Oxford dictionary of botany; Second edition, 1998, retitled: A dictionary of plant sciences; Revised edition, 2006.
700 1	‡a Allaby, Michael, ‡e editor of compilation.
775 08	‡i Revision of: ‡t A dictionary of plant sciences ‡b Revised edition. ‡d Oxford ; New York : Oxford University Press, 2006. ‡h 510 pages : illustrations ; 20 cm. ‡k Oxford paperback reference
830 0	‡a Oxford paperback reference.

The relationship of the musical arrangement described in figure 9.66 to the original expression for orchestra is recorded in an unstructured note (500 field).

Figure 9.66. Derivative Expression Relationship—Musical Arrangement

024 20	‡a M800015670
024 30	‡a 9790800015670
028 32	‡a GPL 167 ‡b Gems Music Publications
100 1	‡a Rolla, Alessandro, ‡d 1757-1841, ‡e composer.
240 10	‡a Concertos, ‡m viola, orchestra, ‡n Bl. 550, ‡r F major; ‡o arranged ‡s (Martinson)
245 10	‡a Concerto in fa maggiore, Bl. 550 : ‡b viola e orchestra / ‡c Alessandro Rolla ; piano reduction prepared by Kenneth Martinson.
264 1	‡a Gainesville, Florida : ‡b Gems Music Publications, ‡c 2011.
300	‡a 1 score (31 pages) + 1 part (13 pages) ; ‡c 28 cm
336	‡a notated music ‡2 rdacontent
337	‡a unmediated ‡2 rdamedia
338	‡a volume ‡2 rdacarrier

546	‡b Staff notation.
500	‡a Orchestral accompaniment arranged for piano. Edition based on an autograph set of parts held at the Archivo Musicale Noseda of the Milan Conservatory Library (G.I23.I.).
700 1	‡a Martinson, Kenneth, ‡e arranger of music.

The relationship of a serial to another edition of the same serial is recorded in a 580 field, which displays as a note. The name of the related edition is recorded in a 775 field, first indicator "1," second indicator blank (see figure 9.67).

Figure 9.67. Derivative Expression Relationship—Simultaneous Edition

022 0	‡a 1041-1410 ‡l 1041-1410 ‡y 0162-8399 ‡2 1
130 0	‡a Science world (New York, N.Y. : 1987)
210 0	‡a Sci. world ‡b (1987)
222 0	‡a Science world ‡b (1987)
245 00	‡a Science world.
264 1	‡a [New York, N.Y.] : ‡b Scholastic Inc., ‡c [1987]-
300	‡a volumes : ‡b illustrations ; ‡c 28 cm
310	‡a Biweekly (18 issues during school year)
336	‡a text ‡2 rdacontent
337	‡a unmediated ‡2 rdamedia
338	‡a volume ‡2 rdacarrier
362 1	‡a Began with Volume 44, number 4 (October 16, 1987)-
588	‡a Description based on: Volume 44, number 4 (October 16, 1987); title from cover.
588	‡a Latest issue consulted: Volume 68, number 14 (May 14, 2012).
580	‡a Issued also in a teachers' edition.
775 1	‡t Science world (New York, N.Y. : 1987). ‡b Teachers' edition
780 00	‡t Scholastic science world ‡x 0162-8399

Descriptive Expression Relationships. A descriptive expression relationship is that between a specific expression and another that describes it. Figure 9.68, a review of a specific expression of Lewis Carroll's *Alice in Wonderland,* is an example. Another example is a full-length study of a particularly famous translation (see figure 9.69).

Figure 9.68. Descriptive Expression Relationship—Review

100 1	‡a MacMillan, Kathleen Kelly, ‡e author.
245 10	‡a Alice in Wonderland / ‡c Kathleen Kelly MacMillan.
300	‡a page 85 ; ‡c 29 cm

336	‡a text ‡2 rdacontent
337	‡a unmediated ‡2 rdamedia
338	‡a volume ‡2 rdacarrier
500	‡a Review of Linda Hamilton's recording of Alice's adventures in Wonderland (NewStar Media, 1999)
700 1	‡i Review of (expression): ‡a Carroll, Lewis, ‡d 1832-1898. ‡t Alice's adventures in Wonderland. ‡l English. ‡h Spoken word ‡s (Hamilton)
773 08	‡i Contained in (work): ‡t School library journal, ‡g v. 45, issue 10 (October 1999)

Figure 9.69. Descriptive Expression Relationship—Analysis of an Expression

100 1	‡a Sohngen, Mary Way, ‡d 1916-2007, ‡e author.
245 10	‡a Alexander Pope's tolerable copy : ‡b a study of his translation of Homer's Iliad / ‡c by Mary Way Sohngen.
264 0	‡c 1973
300	‡a 2 volumes ; ‡c 28 cm
336	‡a text ‡2 rdacontent
337	‡a unmediated ‡2 rdamedia
338	‡a volume ‡2 rdacarrier
500	‡a Typescript (photocopy).
502	‡b Ph. D. ‡c Miami University (Oxford, Ohio) ‡d 1973
504	‡a Includes bibliographical references (leaves 412-419).
700 1	‡i Description of (expression): ‡a Homer. ‡t Iliad. ‡l English ‡s (Pope)

Whole-Part Expression Relationships. Whole-part relationships are usually work-level relationships, but they can also exist at the expression level. The 505 field in figure 9.70 contains a structured description of the whole-part relationship of the individual stories in the anthology *Obras Maestras* and the anthology as a whole. *Obras Maestras* is itself a translation of the English anthology *Masterpieces,* so the whole-part relationships recorded in figure 9.70 are between the Spanish-language expressions of the short stories and the Spanish-language expression of the anthology.

Figure 9.70. Whole-Part Expression Relationship

020	‡a 9788466633918
130 0	‡a Masterpieces (Anthology). ‡l Spanish.
245 10	‡a Obras maestras : ‡b la mejor ciencia ficción del siglo XX / ‡c selección y presentación de Orson Scott Card ; traducción: Pedro Jorge Romero.
250	‡a 1a edición.
264 1	‡a Barcelona : ‡b Ediciones B, ‡c 2007.
300	‡a 570 pages ; ‡c 23 cm.

```
336      ‡a text ‡2 rdacontent
337      ‡a unmediated ‡2 rdamedia
338      ‡a volume ‡2 rdacarrier
490 0    ‡a Nova ; ‡v 200
505 0    ‡a Llámame Joe / Poul Anderson -- "Todos vosotros zombis ..." / Robert A. Heinlein
         -- Componedor / Lloyd Biggle, Jr. -- Un platillo de soledad / Theodore Sturgeon
         -- Sueños de robot / Isaac Asimov -- Involución / Edmond Hamilton -- Los nueve
         mil millones de nombres de Dios / Arthur C. Clarke -- Una obra de arte / James
         Blish -- Tenían la piel oscura y los ojos dorados / Ray Bradbury -- ""Arrepiétete,
         Arlequín!", dijo el señor Tic Tac / Harlan Ellison -- La madre de Eurema / R. A.
         Lafferty -- Pasajeros / Robert Silverberg -- El túnel bajo el mundo / Frederik
         Pohl -- Quién puede reemplazar a un hombre? / Brian W. Aldiss -- Los que se
         van de Omelas / Ursula K. Le Guin -- Luna inconstante / Larry Niven -- Los reyes
         de la arena / George R.R. Martin -- El sendero descartado / Harry Turtledove --
         Comabe aéreo / William Gibson y Michael Swanwick -- Valor facial / Karen Joy
         Fowler -- Vasijas / C.J. Cherryh -- Nieve / John Crowley -- Rata / James Patrick
         Kelly -- Los osos descubren el fuego / Terry Bisson -- Una huida perfecta / John
         Kessel -- Turistas / Lisa Goldstein -- Uno / George Alec Effinger.
700 1    ‡a Card, Orson Scott, ‡e compiler.
700 1    ‡a Jorge Romero, Pedro, ‡d 1967- ‡e translator.
```

Accompanying Expression Relationships. A concordance to a particular expression of the Bible is an example of an accompanying expression relationship. The resource illustrated in figure 9.71 is a concordance to the New American Bible revised edition, an English-language expression of the Bible first published in 2011.

Figure 9.71. Accompanying Expression Relationship—Concordance

```
020      ‡a 9780199812530
100 1    ‡a Kohlenberger, John R., ‡c III, ‡d 1951- ‡e author.
245 04   ‡a The New American Bible, revised edition, concise concordance / ‡c John R.
         Kohlenberger III, editor.
264  1   ‡a New York : ‡b Oxford University Press, ‡c [2012]
300      ‡a viii, 308 pages ; ‡c 24 cm
336      ‡a text ‡2 rdacontent
337      ‡a unmediated ‡2 rdamedia
338      ‡a volume ‡2 rdacarrier
730 0    ‡i Concordance to (expression): ‡a Bible. ‡l English. ‡s New American. ‡f 2011.
```

Sequential Expression Relationships. The relationship between the translation of a sequel and the translation of its predecessor is an example of a sequential expression relationship. Figure 9.72a records the relationship of the Spanish translation of the first

Harry Potter book, *Harry Potter y la Piedra Filosofal,* to its sequel, *Harry Potter y la Cámera Secreta,* using an authorized access point (see the first 700 field). This relationship can also be recorded in an authority record (see figure 9.72b, second 500 field). Note that the authorized access point for the expression is used to record the relationship, which in this case does not include the Spanish-language title of the sequel.

Figure 9.72a.
Sequential Expression Relationship—Translation (Bibliographic Record)

020	‡a 9788478884452
100 1	‡a Rowling, J. K., ‡e author.
240 10	‡a Harry Potter and the philosopher's stone. ‡l Spanish
245 10	‡a Harry Potter y la piedra filosofal / ‡c J.K. Rowling ; traducción, Alicia Dellepiane.
250	‡a 1a edición.
264 1	‡a Barcelona : ‡b Salamandra, ‡c [1999]
300	‡a 254 pages ; ‡c 23 cm
336	‡a text ‡2 rdacontent
337	‡a unmediated ‡2 rdamedia
338	‡a volume ‡2 rdacarrier
500	‡a Sequel: Harry Potter y la cámera secreta.
520	‡a Rescued from the outrageous neglect of his aunt and uncle, a young boy with a great destiny proves his worth while attending Hogwarts School for Wizards and Witches.
700 1	‡i Succeeded by (expression): ‡a Rowling, J. K. ‡t Harry Potter and the Chamber of Secrets. ‡l Spanish.
700 1	‡a Dellepiane Rawson, Alicia, ‡e translator.

Figure 9.72b.
Sequential Expression Relationship—Translation (Authority Record)

046	‡k 1999
100 1	‡a Rowling, J. K. ‡t Harry Potter and the philosopher's stone. ‡l Spanish
377	‡a spa
400 1	‡a Rowling, J. K. ‡t Harry Potter y la piedra filosofal
500 1	‡w r ‡i Translator: ‡a Dellepiane Rawson, Alicia
500 1	‡w r ‡i Succeeded by (expression): ‡a Rowling, J. K. ‡t Harry Potter and the Chamber of Secrets. ‡l Spanish
670	‡a Harry Potter y la piedra filosofal, 1999: ‡b title page verso (traducción, Alicia Dellepiane)

CHAPTER 27. RELATED MANIFESTATION. Because RDA does not yet have any provisions for authorized access points for manifestations, the only ways to record relationships between manifestations are by using identifiers (RDA 24.4.1) or through structured or unstructured descriptions (RDA 24.4.3). Identifiers are not generally used alone in current MARC practice, although they may appear as part of a structured or unstructured description. Relationship designators are available in appendix J.4 to specify relationships between manifestations, and can be used with structured descriptions.

Manifestations can be related to each other in a number of ways; most of these may be formally categorized as equivalent, descriptive, whole-part, and accompanying relationships.

Equivalent Manifestation Relationships. An equivalent relationship is the relationship between a resource and a copy of a resource. In terms of FRBR, equivalent manifestations are those embodying the same expression of a work.

For example, Terry Pratchett's recent novel *Snuff* was first published in 2011 simultaneously in London by Doubleday and in New York by HarperCollins. These two "editions" have identical text and thus have an equivalent manifestation relationship to each other. The cataloger of the description illustrated in figure 9.73 chose to record the relationship using a structured description (775 field). The relationship could also have been recorded using an unstructured description, in this case quoting the title page verso:

500 ‡a "Published simultaneously in Great Britain by Doubleday"—title page verso.

Figure 9.73. Equivalent Manifestation Relationship—Simultaneous Publication

020	‡a 9780062011848 (hardback)
100 1	‡a Pratchett, Terry, ‡e author.
245 10	‡a Snuff : ‡b a novel of Discworld / ‡c Terry Pratchett.
250	‡a First edition.
264　1	‡a New York, NY : ‡b Harper, ‡c [2011]
300	‡a 398 pages ; ‡c 21 cm.
336	‡a text ‡2 rdacontent
337	‡a unmediated ‡2 rdamedia
338	‡a volume ‡2 rdacarrier
490 1	‡a The Discworld books
520	‡a Lady Sybil, wife of Sam Vimes, convinces him to travel to the countryside for a vacation. Sam soon finds various crimes to investigate, but he is out of his element and must rely on his instincts to bring the culprits to justice.
775 08	‡i Also issued as: ‡a Pratchett, Terry. ‡t Snuff. ‡d London : Doubleday, 2011. ‡z 9780385619264.
800 1	‡a Pratchett, Terry. ‡t Discworld books.

Audio recordings issued in different formats are also examples of equivalent manifestations. The description illustrated in figure 9.74 records the relationship between the described compact disc version and the LP and audiocassette versions by a simple unstructured description (500 field).

Figure 9.74. Equivalent Manifestation Relationship—Different Formats

028	00	‡a 415 122-2 ‡b London
100	1	‡a Tchaikovsky, Peter Ilich, ‡d 1840-1893, ‡e composer.
240	10	‡a Concertos, ‡m piano, orchestra, ‡n no. 1, op. 23, ‡r B♭ minor
245	10	‡a Konzert für Klavier und Orchester, no. 1 op. 23 = ‡b Piano concerto / ‡c Peter Tschaikowsky.
264	1	‡a Hamburg : ‡b Deutsche Grammophon, ‡c [1986]
264	4	‡a ℗1986
300		‡a 1 audio disc ; ‡c 4 3/4 in.
336		‡a performed music ‡2 rdacontent
337		‡a audio ‡2 rdamedia
338		‡a audio disc ‡2 rdacarrier
344		‡a digital ‡b optical ‡g stereo ‡2 rda
347		‡a audio file ‡b CD audio ‡2 rda
511	0	‡a Ivo Pogorelich, piano ; London Symphony Orchestra ; Claudio Abbado, conductor.
500		‡a Issued also as analog disc (415 122-1) and cassette (415 122-4).
518		‡a Recorded Watford Town Hall, London, June 1985.
700	1	‡a Abbado, Claudio, ‡e conductor.
700	1	‡a Pogorelich, Ivo, ‡d 1958- ‡e performer.
710	2	‡a London Symphony Orchestra, ‡e performer.

The description of an ink-on-paper resource is usually linked to the description of an electronic reproduction using a structured description in a 776 field (see figure 9.75).

Figure 9.75.
Equivalent Manifestation Relationship—Relationship to Digital Manifestation

100	1	‡a Páez, Ramón, ‡e author.
245	10	‡a Travels and adventures in South and Central America. ‡n First series, ‡p Life in the llanos of Venezuela / ‡c by Don Ramon Paez.
264	1	‡a New York : ‡b Charles Scribner & Co., ‡c 1868.
300		‡a xlviii, 473 pages : ‡b illustrations, maps ; ‡c 12 cm
336		‡a text ‡2 rdacontent
336		‡a still image ‡2 rdacontent

336	‡a cartographic image ‡2 rdacontent
337	‡a unmediated ‡2 rdamedia
338	‡a volume ‡2 rdacarrier
500	‡a A new and enlarged edition of the author's "Wild scenes in South America."
776 08	‡i Electronic reproduction: ‡a Páez, Ramón. ‡t Travels and adventures in South and Central America. ‡d [Provo, Utah] : ‡b [Harold B. Lee Library], ‡c [2011]

Descriptive Manifestation Relationships. A descriptive manifestation relationship is that between a specific manifestation and another that describes it. An example is a study of the *First Folio of Shakespeare,* a specific manifestation (see figure 9.76, in which the descriptive relationship is recorded as a structured description in a 787 field).

Figure 9.76. Descriptive Manifestation Relationship

020	‡a 0198187696 (volume 1)
020	‡a 0198187688 (volume 2)
100 1	‡a West, Anthony James, ‡e author.
245 14	‡a The Shakespeare first folio : ‡b the history of the book / ‡c Anthony James West.
264 1	‡a Oxford ; ‡a New York : ‡b Oxford University Press, ‡c 2001-<2005>
300	‡a volumes : ‡b illustrations ; ‡c 25 cm.
336	‡a text ‡2 rdacontent
336	‡a still image ‡2 rdacontent
337	‡a unmediated ‡2 rdamedia
338	‡a volume ‡2 rdacarrier
504	‡a Includes bibliographical references and index.
505 0	‡a volume 1. An account of the first folio based on its sales and prices -- volume 2. A new worldwide census of first folios.
787 08	‡i Analysis of (manifestation): ‡a Shakespeare, William, ‡d 1564-1616. ‡t Mr. William Shakespeares comedies, histories & tragedies : published according to the true originall copies. ‡d London : Printed by Isaac Iaggard and Ed. Blount, 1623. ‡o STC (2nd edition) 22273

Whole-Part Manifestation Relationships. Whole-part relationships, common at the work level, can also exist at the manifestation level. An example is a resource that contains a facsimile of another manifestation. In the example illustrated in figure 9.77, the Eduardo Chillida's first exhibition catalog is reproduced in facsimile as part of a 2002 exhibition catalog of his work. The relationship between the 2002 resource as a whole and the facsimile is expressed in this case both by an unstructured description (second 500 field) and a structured description (774 field). Another example of a whole-part manifestation relationship is the relationship of a special issue of a serial to the serial as a whole. A structured description of this relationship is recorded in a 770 field (see figure 9.78).

Figure 9.77. Whole-Part Manifestation Relationship

020	‡a 8448231732
100 1	‡a Chillida, Eduardo, ‡d 1924-2002, ‡e artist.
245 10	‡a Eduardo Chillida : ‡b elogio del hierro = praise of iron.
246 30	‡a Elogio del hierro
246 30	‡a Praise of iron
264 1	‡a [Valencia] : ‡b IVAM, Institut Valencià d'Art Modern, ‡c [2002]
300	‡a 229 pages : ‡b illustrations (some color) ; ‡c 31 cm
336	‡a text ‡2 rdacontent
336	‡a still image ‡2 rdacontent
337	‡a unmediated ‡2 rdamedia
338	‡a volume ‡2 rdacarrier
546	‡a Spanish and English.
500	‡a Exhibition catalog.
500	‡a Includes facsimile of Le cosmos du fer, the catalog of Chillida's first solo exhibition at Galerie Maeght, Paris (12 pages).
504	‡a Includes bibliographical references.
710 2	‡a Institut Valencià d'Art Modern.
774 08	‡i Contains facsimile of (manifestation): ‡a Bachelard, Gaston, 1884-1962. ‡t Le cosmos du fer. ‡d Paris : Éditions Pierre à Feu, 1956. ‡k Derrière le miroir ; no 90-91

Figure 9.78. Whole-Part Manifestation Relationship—Special Issue

020	‡a 0789005433
245 00	‡a Portraits in cataloging and classification : ‡b theorists, educators, and practitioners of the late twentieth century / ‡c Carolynne Myall, Ruth C. Carter, editors.
264 1	‡a New York : ‡b Haworth Press, ‡c [1998]
300	‡a 323 pages ; ‡c 23 cm
336	‡a text ‡2 rdacontent
337	‡a unmediated ‡2 rdamedia
338	‡a volume ‡2 rdacarrier
504	‡a Includes bibliographical references and index.
505 0	[Contents note omitted]

700 1 ‡a Myall, Carolynne, ‡d 1949- ‡e editor of compilation.

700 1 ‡a Carter, Ruth C., ‡e editor of compilation.

770 08 ‡i Special issue of: ‡t Cataloging & classification quarterly, ‡x 0163-9374, ‡g v. 25, no. 2-4 (1998)

Accompanying Manifestation Relationships. When a manifestation is issued with another manifestation, the two are said to have an accompanying manifestation relationship. The cataloger usually has the option to describe manifestations issued together in a single description, but if the manifestations are described separately the relationship between the two is recorded either by using a MARC 501 field for an unstructured description or a MARC 777 field for a structured description. The cataloger of the record shown in figure 9.79 chose to record the relationship with a structured description (777 field). An unstructured description of the same relationship might have looked something like this:

500   ‡a Issued with: A bookbinder's analysis of the first edition of The Wonderful Wizard of Oz / by Michael O. Riley (47 pages ; 31 cm)

Figure 9.79. Accompanying Manifestation Relationship

100 1 ‡a Hanff, Peter E., ‡e author.

245 10 ‡a Cyclone on the prairies : ‡b The wonderful Wizard of Oz and arts & crafts of publishing in Chicago, 1900 / ‡c Peter E. Hanff.

264 1 ‡a San Francisco : ‡b The Book Club of California, ‡c [2011]

300   ‡a 141 pages : ‡b illustrations (chiefly color) ; ‡c 32 cm

336   ‡a text ‡2 rdacontent

337   ‡a unmediated ‡2 rdamedia

338   ‡a volume ‡2 rdacarrier

490 1 ‡a Book Club of California publication ; ‡v number 228

500   ‡a Issued in a slip case.

777 08 ‡i Issued with: ‡a Riley, Michael O'Neal. ‡t A bookbinder's analysis of the first edition of The Wonderful Wizard of Oz. ‡d San Francisco : The Book Club of California, 2011. ‡h 47 pages ; 31 cm

830 0 ‡a Publication (Book Club of California) ; ‡v no. 228.

Caution: an accompanying manifestation relationship exists *only* when two manifestations were issued together, that is, all copies within the manifestation were issued in this way. Copies of manifestations that have been bound together after publication (for example, by a library) have an accompanying *item* relationship and the relationship is recorded differently (see below).

CHAPTER 28. RELATED ITEM. As is the case with manifestations, RDA does not yet have any provisions for authorized access points for items, so the only ways to record relationships between items are by using identifiers (RDA 24.4.1) or through structured or unstructured descriptions (RDA 24.4.3). Identifiers are not generally used alone in current MARC practice, although they may appear as part of a structured or unstructured description. Relationship designators are available in appendix J.5 to specify relationships between items, and can be used with structured descriptions.

Items can be related to each other in a number of ways; most of these may be formally categorized as equivalent, descriptive, whole-part, and accompanying relationships. Of these, the most commonly recorded in current cataloging practice are accompanying item relationships.

Accompanying Item Relationships. An accompanying item relationship exists when an item has been brought together with another subsequent to issuance. The most common example of this is two or more items bound together after publication. The accompanying relationship between the items is generally recorded using an unstructured description, using a MARC local note field. The usual field for recording local notes is 590, but many of the MARC note fields (5XX) can be made "local" by adding ‡5 and the institution's MARC symbol. Field 590 is used in figure 9.80. The same information might have been recorded using the 501 field with ‡5 ("UPB" is the Brigham Young University Library's MARC symbol):

> 501 ‡a 10th of 11 pamphlets bound with: An address to all classes and conditions of Englishmen / by the Duke of Newcastle. Third edition. London : T. and W. Boone, 1832. ‡5 UPB

Figure 9.80. Accompanying Item Relationship

245	00	‡a The Irish Church : ‡b important facts.
264	1	‡a London : ‡b Published by Rivingtons, St. Paul's Churchyard, ‡c MDCCCXXXV [1835]
264	3	‡b Printed by George Ellerton, Gough Square
300		‡a 12 pages ; ‡c 21 cm
336		‡a text ‡2 rdacontent
337		‡a unmediated ‡2 rdamedia
338		‡a volume ‡2 rdacarrier
590		‡a 10th of 11 pamphlets bound with: An address to all classes and conditions of Englishmen / by the Duke of Newcastle. Third edition. London : T. and W. Boone, 1832.

RECORDING RELATIONSHIPS BETWEEN PERSONS, FAMILIES, AND CORPORATE BODIES

RDA chapter 9 deals with the relationships between the FRBR Group 2 entities, that is, those entities capable of responsibility for the intellectual or artistic content, the physical production and dissemination, or the custodianship of Group 1 entities (works, expressions, manifestations, or items) (see FRBR 3.1.2). This chapter only deals with recording relationships; for details on describing persons, families, and corporate bodies and formulating authorized access points for them, see this *Handbook*'s chapters 2 through 5.

CHAPTER 29. GENERAL GUIDELINES ON RECORDING RELATIONSHIPS BETWEEN PERSONS, FAMILIES, AND CORPORATE BODIES. Chapter 29 sets forth a few general guidelines for recording these relationships. Particularly important is the explanation of functional objectives and principles under RDA 29.2. In an RDA environment users should be able to find persons, families, and corporate bodies that are related to other persons, families, or corporate bodies, and the relationship between them should be clear. Emphasis on the importance of relationships is one thing that sets RDA apart from previous cataloging codes. Although 29.3 states that recording relationships is not required, it is clear that RDA encourages recording them.

29.4. RECORDING RELATIONSHIPS BETWEEN PERSONS, FAMILIES, AND CORPORATE BODIES. RDA has two conventions for recording these relationships: identifier and authorized access point.

An identifier is an alphanumeric character string uniquely associated with a person, family, or corporate body. The Library of Congress Control Number (LCCN) associated with authority records for persons, families, and corporate bodies is a common type of identifier. In current MARC practice identifiers for related persons, families, or corporate bodies are sometimes recorded, but are not used alone to record a relationship link between these entities (see LC-PCC PS 29.4.1, February 2010).

An authorized access point is a standardized access point representing an entity. Relationships between related persons, families, and corporate bodies can be recorded in a MARC environment by recording authorized access points in appropriate fields in bibliographic or authority records. The most common place to record these relationships using authorized access points is in 500, 510, or 511 fields in MARC authority records. Although relationships between persons, families, and corporate bodies can be described in bibliographic records, it is uncommon and examples illustrating this section of RDA will show authority records.

29.5. RELATIONSHIP DESIGNATOR. A relationship designator is a word or phrase associated with an authorized access point for a person, family, or corporate body that clarifies the nature of the relationship between that person, family, or corporate body and another. Relationship designators describing these relationships are taken from RDA appendix K, and are recorded in subfield ‡i of 5XX fields in MARC authority records. RDA appendix K divides designators between those used with persons, those used with families, and those used with corporate bodies. Only terms found in appendix K should be used in LC/NACO authority records (see LC-PCC PS K.1, April 2012). At the time of writing of this edition of the *Handbook,* appendix K is rather short and inadequate to describe many kinds of relationships, but proposals have been received by the Joint Steering Committee (JSC) for expansion of the appendix, and the JSC is amenable to further proposals for designators as need arises. For an example, see figure 9.81. The relationship designators show the nature of the relationship between Goldwyn Pictures Corporation and the three persons recorded in the 500 fields (they were the founders of the company), and between Goldwyn Pictures Corporation and Metro-Goldwyn-Mayer (Metro-Goldwyn-Mayer was the product of a merger in which Goldwyn Pictures Corporation participated).

Figure 9.81. Relationship Designator

046	‡s 1916 ‡t 1924
110 2	‡a Goldwyn Pictures Corporation
370	‡e Fort Lee (N.J.) ‡2 naf
372	‡a Motion pictures--Production and direction ‡2 lcsh
368	‡a Motion picture studios ‡2 lcsh
500 1	‡w r ‡i Founder: ‡a Goldwyn, Samuel, ‡d 1879-1974
500 1	‡w r ‡i Founder: ‡a Selwyn, Edgar, ‡d 1875-1944
500 1	‡w r ‡i Founder: ‡a Selwyn, Archibald, ‡d 1877-1959
510 2	‡w r ‡i Product of a merger: ‡a Metro-Goldwyn-Mayer
670	‡a Polly of the circus, 1917 ‡b (name not given)
670	‡a Slide, A. The American film industry, 1986 ‡b (Goldwyn Pictures Corporation; formed December, 1916; in 1924, Goldwyn Pictures Corporation, Metro Pictures Corporation and independent producer Louis B. Mayer joined to form Metro-Goldwyn-Mayer)
670	‡a Wikipedia, January 28, 2011 ‡b (Goldwyn Pictures; founded by Samuel Goldfish, Edgar Selwyn, and Archibald Selwyn; headquarters in Fort Lee, New Jersey; production company)
678 1	‡a Goldwyn Pictures Corporation was a motion picture production company. The company was established in 1916 by Samuel Goldwyn, Edgar Selwyn, and Archibald Selwyn with headquarters in Fort Lee, New Jersey. In 1924 the company merged with Metro Pictures and Louis B. Mayer Pictures to form Metro-Goldwyn-Mayer.

29.6. SOURCE CONSULTED. See discussion of this element above at 24.7, and a fuller discussion in chapter 3 of this *Handbook* under 8.12. The second and third 670 fields in figure 9.81 are good examples.

29.7. CATALOGUER'S NOTE. See discussion of this element above at 24.8, and a fuller discussion in chapter 3 of this *Handbook* under 8.13. The cataloguer's note in figure 9.82 warns readers that a similarly named body is not the same as that described.

Figure 9.82. Cataloguer's Note

046	‡s 1878
110 2	‡a Brown Shoe Company
370	‡e Saint Louis (Mo.) ‡2 naf
372	‡a Shoes ‡a Retail trade ‡2 lcsh
377	‡a eng
500 1	‡w r ‡i Founder: ‡a Brown, George Warren, ‡d 1853-1921
510 2	‡w r ‡i Predecessor: ‡a Wohl Shoe Company
667	‡a Not related to: Hamilton, Brown Shoe Company, in which George Warren Brown's brother was a partner.
670	‡a Spring and summer, 1932, catalog no. 70, 1932: ‡b t.p. (Brown Shoe Company)
670	‡a Yahoo Finance company profile, viewed March 28, 2012 ‡b (Brown Shoe Company, Inc.; footwear retailer, operates retail shoe stores primarily under the brand names of Famous Footwear, Famous Footwear Outlet, Factory Brand Shoes, Mind Body Sole, Naturalizer, Brown Shoe Closet, F.X. LaSalle, Via Spiga, and Sam Edelman; also sells products online at Shoes.com; company founded in 1878 by George Warren Brown; based in St. Louis, Mo.)

CHAPTER 30. RELATED PERSONS. The relationship between a person and another person, a family, or a corporate body, is recorded by giving the authorized access point for the person in a 500 field in the authority record for the related person, family, or corporate body. Relationship designators from appendix K may be included in subfield ‡i (the "‡w r" coding is required whenever a relationship designator is given in subfield ‡i). Figures 9.81 and 9.82 are examples.

In LC/NACO practice an authorized access point can only be recorded in a 5XX field of an authority record if that access point has been authorized (or "established") in an authority record of its own. In the case of figure 9.81, for example, Samuel Goldwyn, Edgar Selwyn, and Archibald Selwyn have all been described in their own authority records, and the form in the 500 fields of figure 9.81 matches the form found in the 100 fields of those authority records.

As explained in chapter 3 of this *Handbook,* a human being may have more than one identity, and each of these may be defined as a separate "person" for purposes of RDA (see RDA 8.1). The most common example of this is a person writing under more than one name or pseudonym (see RDA 9.2.2.8 and the corresponding discussion in chapter 3 of this *Handbook*). Because each identity is usually considered a separate person in RDA, each will have its own description in an authority record. In these cases it is clear that these "persons" are related and their relationships should be recorded. The relationship between pseudonymous identities is recorded in the same way as any other relationship between persons: by recording the authorized access point in a 500 field of the description of the related person. This is simple enough when only two entities are involved: the two records are linked to each other by reciprocal 500 fields (see figure 9.83, in which the person has two identities, one identified by his real name and the other by a pseudonym).

Figure 9.83. Two Identities

046	ǂf 19700228
100 1	ǂa Snicket, Lemony
374	ǂa Authors ǂ2 lcsh
375	ǂa male
377	ǂa eng
500 1	ǂw r ǂi Real identity: ǂa Handler, Daniel
670	ǂa The bad beginning, 1999: ǂb title page (Lemony Snicket)
670	ǂa Wikipedia, 28 August 2012 ǂb (Lemony Snicket is the pen name of American novelist Daniel Handler (born February 28, 1970))
678 0	ǂa Lemony Snicket is a pseudonym of American author Daniel Handler (1970-)

046	ǂf 19700228
100 1	ǂa Handler, Daniel
370	ǂa San Francisco (Calif.) ǂ2 naf
374	ǂa Authors ǂa Screenwriters ǂa Accordionists ǂ2 lcsh
375	ǂa male
377	ǂa eng
500 1	ǂw r ǂi Alternate identity: ǂa Snicket, Lemony
670	ǂa The basic eight, 1999: ǂb CIP t.p. (Daniel Handler)
670	ǂa Wikipedia, 28 August 2012 ǂb (Daniel Handler (born February 28, 1970 in San Francisco) is an American author, screenwriter and accordionist. He is best known for his work under the pen name Lemony Snicket)
678 0	ǂa Daniel Handler (1970-) is an American author, screenwriter and accordionist.

Human beings can create more than two identities by using multiple pseudonyms. The more identities involved the more complex the descriptions might become. LC and PCC catalogers creating NACO authority records follow a process that simplifies the descriptions (see instructions in *Descriptive Cataloging Manual* Z1 at 663).

First, the cataloger chooses the predominant form as the "basic" description. The record for this description will include 500 fields containing the authorized access points of all the other identities, but they are coded "‡w nnnc" in order to suppress their display. It will also contain an "explanation of relationship" (RDA 30.2) recorded in a 663 field with the text "For works of this author written under other names, search also under [list names]." All other authority records created for the person will contain a single 500 field recording the authorized access point from the "basic" description, again coded "‡w nnnc," and an explanation of relationship in 663 with the text "Works by this author are identified by the name used in the item. For a listing of other names used by this author, search also under [form in the basic description]."

The result of this procedure will be that the user who searches for the "basic" name will be provided with a list of all the names; the user searching for one of the other names will not be given all the names, but will instead be directed to a description of the "basic" name for the list. The purpose of this procedure is simplification of authority database maintenance. Whenever a new pseudonym is used by an author, a new description will be created for the name, with a 500 and a 663 field linking the new name to the "basic" name, and the description of the "basic" name will be modified by the addition of the new name to its 663 field and one new 500 field. Without this procedure, the authorized access point for the new name would need to be added to all the descriptions created for the person rather than just to the basic description. This could become quite complex, and the LC-PCC procedure, although somewhat less helpful to the catalog user, is sensible and less prone to error on the part of the cataloger. An example of such an person is Charles Dickens, who wrote principally under his real name, but also used two pseudonyms. Figure 9.84 illustrates the three descriptions necessary for this situation.

Figure 9.84. More than Two Identities

046	‡f 18120207 ‡g 18700609
100 1	‡a Dickens, Charles, ‡d 1812-1870
370	‡a Portsea Island (England) ‡2 lcsh
370	‡b Higham (Kent, England) ‡2 naf
374	‡a Novelists ‡2 lcsh
375	‡a male
377	‡a eng
378	‡q Charles John Huffam
500 0	‡w nnnc ‡a Boz, ‡d 1812-1870
500 1	‡w nnnc ‡a Sparks, Timothy, ‡d 1812-1870

663	‡a For works of this author written under other names, search also under: ‡b Boz, 1812-1870 ‡a and ‡b Sparks, Timothy, 1812-1870
670	‡a David Copperfield, 2002: ‡b title page (Charles Dickens)
670	‡a Oxford dictionary of national biography, 28 August 2012 ‡b (Dickens, Charles John Huffam, novelist, was born on 7 February 1812 at 13 Mile End Terrace, Portsea, Portsmouth; died 9 June 1870 at Gad's Hill [Higham (Kent, England)]; some of his early works were written under the pseudonym Boz; also wrote Sunday under three heads under the pseudonym Timothy Sparks)
678 0	‡a Charles Dickens (1812-1870) was a British novelist.

046	‡f 18120207 ‡g 18700609
100 0	‡a Boz, ‡d 1812-1870
375	‡a male
377	‡a eng
500 1	‡w nnnc ‡a Dickens, Charles, ‡d 1812-1870
663	‡a Works by this author are identified by the name used in the item. For a listing of the names used by this author, search also under: ‡b Dickens, Charles, 1812-1870
670	‡a Sketches by Boz, 1836
670	‡a Oxford dictionary of national biography, 28 August 2012 ‡b (Dickens, Charles John Huffam, novelist, was born on 7 February 1812 at 13 Mile End Terrace, Portsea, Portsmouth; died 9 June 1870 at Gad's Hill [Higham (Kent, England)]; some of his early works were written under the pseudonym Boz; also wrote Sunday under three heads under the pseudonym Timothy Sparks)
678 0	‡a Boz is a pseudonym of Charles Dickens (1812-1870), a British novelist.

046	‡f 18120207 ‡g 18700609
100 1	‡a Sparks, Timothy, ‡d 1812-1870
375	‡a male
377	‡a eng
500 1	‡w nnnc ‡a Dickens, Charles, ‡d 1812-1870
663	‡a Works by this author are identified by the name used in the item. For a listing of the names used by this author, search also under: ‡b Dickens, Charles, 1812-1870
670	‡a Sunday under three heads, 1836: ‡b t.p. (Timothy Sparks)
670	‡a Oxford dictionary of national biography, 28 August 2012 ‡b (Dickens, Charles John Huffam, novelist, was born on 7 February 1812 at 13 Mile End Terrace, Portsea, Portsmouth; died 9 June 1870 at Gad's Hill [Higham (Kent, England)]; some of his early works were written under the pseudonym Boz; also wrote Sunday under three heads under the pseudonym Timothy Sparks)
678 0	‡a Timothy Sparks is a pseudonym of Charles Dickens (1812-1870), a British novelist.

CHAPTER 31. RELATED FAMILIES. The relationship between a family and another person, family, or corporate body is recorded by giving the authorized access point for the family in a 500 field (with first indicator coded "3") in the authority record for the related person, family, or corporate body. Relationship designators from appendix K may be included in subfield ‡i (the "‡w r" coding is required whenever a relationship designator is given in subfield ‡i). Figure 9.85 records the relationship between the Nibley family and Hugh Nibley.

Figure 9.85. Related Family

046	‡f 19100327 ‡g 20050224
100 1	‡a Nibley, Hugh, ‡d 1910-2005
370	‡a Portland (Or.) ‡b Provo (Utah) ‡2 naf
372	‡a Religion ‡2 lcsh
373	‡a Brigham Young University ‡2 naf
374	‡a College teachers ‡a Authors ‡2 lcsh
375	‡a male
377	‡a eng
510 2	‡w r ‡i Employer: ‡a Brigham Young University
500 3	‡w r ‡i Descendants: ‡a Nibley (Family : ‡g Nibley, Hugh, 1910-2005)
670	‡a Lehi in the desert, 1952: ‡b title page (Hugh Nibley)
670	‡a New York times, February 25, 2005: ‡b obituary (Hugh W. Nibley, Mormon religious scholar; d. Feb. 24, 2005 in Provo, Utah)
670	‡a Wikipedia, Nov. 9, 2010 ‡b (Hugh Nibley; Hugh Winder Nibley; b. Mar. 27, 1910 in Portland, Ore.; d. Feb. 24, 2005 in Provo, Utah; professor of Biblical and modern scripture at Brigham Young University, 1946-1975; apologist for the Church of Jesus Christ of Latter-day Saints; prolific author; earned Ph.D. at Univ. of Calif., Berkeley in 1938; served in intelligence during World War II)
678 0	‡a Hugh Nibley (1910-2005) was a religion professor and author in Utah. He is well known for his writings on the Church of Jesus Christ of Latter-day Saints.

Figure 9.86 illustrates a relationship between two families. The Zimmerman family changed its name to Carpenter around 1780. Because of the name change, RDA considers these to be different families, but they are clearly related.

In LC/NACO practice an authorized access point can only be recorded in a 5XX field of an authority record if that access point has been authorized (or "established") in an authority record of its own. In the case of figure 9.86, for example, the Carpenter family has been described in its own authority records, and the form in the first 500 field of figure 9.86 matches the form found in the 100 field of that authority record (see figure 4.13 in chapter 4 of this *Handbook*).

Figure 9.86. Related Family

046	‡s 1780
100 3	‡a Zimmerman (Family : ‡g Zimmerman, George, 1740-1779)
376	‡a Family
500 3	‡w b ‡a Carpenter (Family : ‡d 1780- : ‡c Carpenter's Station, Ky.)
500 1	‡w r ‡i Progenitor: ‡a Zimmerman, George, ‡d 1740-1779
667	‡a SUBJECT USAGE: This heading is not valid for use as a subject; use a family name heading from LCSH.
670	‡a The Carpenters of Carpenter's Station, Kentucky, 2001 ‡b (Carpenter family, founder of Carpenter's Station, Kentucky, in 1780; descendants of Swiss immigrant George Zimmerman, who arrived in Philadelphia in 1746; family changed its name to Carpenter some time around the Revolutionary War)

CHAPTER 32. RELATED CORPORATE BODIES. The relationship between a corporate body and another person, family, or corporate body is recorded by giving the authorized access point for the corporate body in a 510 field in the authority record for the related person, family, or corporate body. Relationship designators from appendix K may be included in subfield ‡i (the "‡w r" coding is required whenever a relationship designator is given in subfield ‡i).

Figure 9.85 records a relationship between a corporate body and a person: Brigham Young University was Nibley's employer. Another type of relationship between a corporate body and a person commonly recorded is the relationship between a performing group and persons in the group (see figure 9.87).

Figure 9.87. Related Body

046	‡f 19350216 ‡g 19980105
100 1	‡a Bono, Sonny
370	‡a Detroit (Mich.) ‡b South Lake Tahoe (Calif.) ‡2 naf
374	‡a Singers ‡a Composers ‡a Politicians ‡2 lcsh
375	‡a male
377	‡a eng
400 1	‡a Bono, Salvatore
510 2	‡w r ‡i Group member of: ‡a Sonny & Cher
670	‡a In case you're in love, 1967: ‡b label (Sonny Bono)
670	‡a International who's who in music, v. 2, popular music, 1st ed. ‡b (Bono, Sonny (Salvatore); born Feb. 16, 1935, Detroit, Mich.; singer, composer, mayor)
670	‡a USA today, Jan. 7, 1998: ‡b p. 1A, etc. (Salvatore "Sonny" Bono, 1935-1998; b. Salvatore Bono, Feb. 16, 1935, Detroit, d. Jan. 5, 1998, South Lake Tahoe, Nev., in skiing accident)

670	ǂa Washington post, 7 Jan. 1998: ǂb p. 1 (Sonny Bono, killed in ski crash; half of Sonny and Cher singing duo; U.S. Representative in 1990s; Rep. Sonny Bono (R-Calif.))
678 0	ǂa Sonny Bono (1935-1998) was an American singer and politician.

046	ǂf 19460520
100 0	ǂa Cher, ǂd 1946-
374	ǂa Singers ǂa Actresses ǂ2 lcsh
375	ǂa female
377	ǂa eng
400 1	ǂa Sarkisian, Cherilyn, ǂd 1946-
400 1	ǂa Bono, Cher, ǂd 1946-
510 2	ǂw r ǂi Group member of: ǂa Sonny & Cher
670	ǂa Cher, 1975
670	ǂa Wikipedia, April 18, 2009 ǂb (Cher, born Cherilyn Sarkisian on May 20, 1946; also known as: Cher Bono; in 1979 leagally changed her name to: Cher, no surname)
678 0	ǂa Cher (1946-) is an American singer and actress.

046	ǂs 1964 ǂt 1977
110 2	ǂa Sonny & Cher
368	ǂa Musical groups ǂ2 lcsh
410 2	ǂa Sonny and Cher
500 1	ǂw r ǂi Group member: ǂa Bono, Sonny
500 0	ǂw r ǂi Group member: ǂa Cher, ǂd 1946-
670	ǂa The best of Sonny & Cher, 1991: ǂb label (Sonny & Cher)
670	ǂa Wikipedia, 28 August 2012 ǂb (Sonny & Cher, American pop music duo, active 1964-1977)
678 1	ǂa Sonny & Cher was an American singing group active from 1964 to 1977.

Under cataloging theory, when a corporate body changes its name it becomes a new corporate body, and a new description is created for the body with the changed name. The two bodies are clearly related, and their relationship is one of the most commonly recorded relationships between corporate bodies. Figure 9.82 shows an example recording the relationship between the Brown Shoe Company and its predecessor, Wohl Shoe Company.

Another commonly recorded relationship between a corporate body and a person is the relationship between the corporate body representing a head of state or head of government and the person holding the office. The authorized access point for the corporate body is recorded in a 510 field within the description of the person (see figure 9.88).

Figure 9.88. Head of Government

046	‡f 19241001
100 1	‡a Carter, Jimmy, ‡d 1924-
370	‡a Plains (Ga.) ‡c United States ‡2 naf
374	‡a Politicians ‡a Farmers ‡2 lcsh
374	‡a Naval officer
375	‡a male
377	‡a eng
400 1	‡a Carter, James Earl, ‡c Jr., ‡d 1924-
510 1	‡w r ‡i Incumbent of: ‡a Georgia. ‡b Governor (1971-1975 : Carter)
510 1	‡w r ‡i Incumbent of: ‡a United States. ‡b President (1977-1981 : Carter)
670	‡a Jimmy Carter, 2011
670	‡a Encyclopaedia Britannica ‡b (Jimmy Carter; James Earl Carter, Jr.; born October 1, 1924 in Plains, Ga.; politician, peanut farmer, and naval officer; 39th president of the United States, 1977-1981; governor of Georgia, 1971-1975)
678 0	‡a Jimmy Carter (1924-) is an American politician. He served as the president of the United States (1977-1981) and as the governor of Georgia (1971-1975). He was previously a naval officer and peanut farmer.

In LC/NACO practice an authorized access point can only be recorded in a 5XX field of an authority record if that access point has been authorized (or "established") in an authority record of its own. In the case of figure 9.88, for example, the corporate bodies representing the offices of President and Governor have been described in their own authority records, and the forms in the 510 fields match the 110 fields of those bodies' authority records.

RECORDING RELATIONSHIPS BETWEEN CONCEPTS, OBJECTS, EVENTS, AND PLACES

RDA chapter 10, on recording relationships between concepts, objects, events, and places, has not been completed as of the date of this *Handbook*. However, relationships can be recorded between these entities in the same way as the relationships in chapter 9, "Recording Relationships between Persons, Families, and Corporate Bodies," by recording the authorized access point of the related entity in a 5XX field of the description. As an example using a place entity, the jurisdiction Ceylon changed its name to Sri Lanka in 1972. The relationship between Ceylon and Sri Lanka is recorded by giving the authorized access point for Ceylon in a 551 field in the description of Sri Lanka (and vice versa), together with a relationship designator (see figure 9.89).

Figure 9.89. Relationships between Places

046	‡s 197205
151	‡a Sri Lanka
451	‡a Lanka
451	‡a Serendib
451	‡a Serendip
451	‡a Taprobane
451	‡a Cellao
451	‡a Zeilan
451	‡a Sri Lanka Prajathanthrika Samajavadi Janarajaya
451	‡a Democratic Socialist Republic of Sri Lanka
551	‡w r ‡i Predecessor: ‡a Ceylon
670	‡a Fernando, N. Serendip to Sri Lanka, 1991: ‡b page 29 (Lanka, Serendib, Taprobane, Cellao, Zeilan)
670	‡a The statesman's year-book, 1995-1996: ‡b page 1213 (Sri Lanka; Sri Lanka Prajathanthrika Samajavadi Janarajaya (Democratic Socialist Republic of Sri Lanka)); 2005: page 1509 (Ceylon became republic and adopted name Sri Lanka, May 1972)
670	‡a GEONet, October 4, 2009 ‡b (Sri Lanka; Lanka; island; 07°30'00"N 080°30'00"E)

NOTES

1. See Charles A. Cutter, *Rules for a Dictionary Catalog,* 4th ed. (Washington, DC: Government Printing Office, 1904), 11–12. Cutter's objects have been reprinted many times, including in *Foundations of Cataloging: A Sourcebook,* edited by Michael Carpenter and Elaine Svenonius (Littleton, CO: Libraries Unlimited, 1985), 67.

2. For a fuller examination of relationships, see Robert L. Maxwell, *FRBR: A Guide for the Perplexed* (Chicago: American Library Association, 2008), 70–123.

3. Source information about certain elements may be recorded directly in the element's MARC field itself, in subfield ‡v, rather than in a 670 field. This technique is available for the 046 and 370–378 fields. This method has not yet found much favor in practice and is not used in this book.

4. See the discussion of relationships in chapter 4 of Robert L. Maxwell, *FRBR: A Guide for the Perplexed* (Chicago: American Library Association, 2008), 70–123; for a complete discussion, see also Barbara B. Tillett, *Bibliographic Relationships: Toward a Conceptual Structure of Bibliographic Information Used in Cataloging* (dissertation, UCLA, 1989) and her articles "A Taxonomy of Bibliographic Relationships," *Library*

Resources and Technical Services 35, no. 2 (April 1991): 150–58; "A Summary of the Treatment of Bibliographic Relationships in Cataloging Rules," *Library Resources and Technical Services* 35, no. 4 (October 1991): 393–405; "The History of Linking Devices," *Library Resources and Technical Services* v. 36, no. 1 (January 1992): 23–36; and "Bibliographic Relationships: An Empirical Study of the LC Machine-Readable Records," *Library Resources and Technical Services* 36, no. 2 (April 1992): 162–88.

APPENDIXES

HE FOLLOWING APPENDIXES GATHER TOGETHER in one place general guidelines for a number of commonly cataloged formats. They are intended to help catalogers unused to the organization of RDA by organizing the guidelines more or less in AACR2/MARC order. They are meant to be used independently, so there is a fair amount of repetition among the appendixes.

The appendixes primarily discuss the creation of bibliographic records, but authority issues are included and the record sets appended to each appendix include both bibliographic records and their associated authority records. The presence of authority records in the database matching the authorized access points in bibliographic records is crucial. In a system that links bibliographic records to authority records, this (1) allows linking between bibliographic records, (2) can help the cataloger to input the correct form when creating a bibliographic record, and (3) in many cases also allows global changes when the authorized access point for an entity changes. In systems that do not directly create links between bibliographic records and authority records, the presence of authority records is still important because it shows the cataloger the correct form of the authorized access point which he or she will then input manually into the bibliographic record.

This *Handbook* therefore recommends that all authorized access points present in bibliographic records within a library's database be backed up by corresponding authority records. Large numbers of authority records already exist in the LC/NACO Authority File (http://authorities.loc.gov) and other files such as those gathered together in the Virtual International Authority File (http://viaf.org). These can be easily downloaded into most library systems.

Details about creating authority records have been given in individual chapters of this *Handbook* for the person (chapter 3), family (chapter 4), corporate body (chapter 5), geographic (chapter 6), work (chapter 7), and expression (chapter 8) entities. Details about recording (and linking) related entities are given in chapter 9.

APPENDIX A

PRINTED BOOKS
AND SHEETS

THIS APPENDIX CONTAINS A RECOMMENDED PROCESS FOR CREATING BIBLIOGRAPHIC
records for published textual monographs. It covers bibliographic record creation for
these resources only in the most general of terms. Unusual situations are covered in
the body of this *Handbook*. As with the *Handbook* itself, this appendix does not cover
non-RDA related aspects of the bibliographic record, such as fixed-length data elements (the so-called fixed fields) or subject analysis. This appendix also contains three
sample record sets, consisting of bibliographic records and their associated authority
records, which illustrate many of the points described below.

1. DETERMINE THE MODE OF ISSUANCE

Consider the mode of issuance of the resource. Does it consist of a single unit? Is it
a multipart monograph? Is it a serial or integrating resource? Mode of issuance is
defined in RDA 1.1.3.

> A single-unit resource is a resource issued either as a single physical unit (e.g., a
> single volume book) or a single logical unit (e.g., a PDF file).
> A multipart monograph is a resource issued in two or more parts that is complete
> or is intended to be complete within a finite number of parts.
> A serial is a resource issued in successive parts, usually bearing numbering, that
> has no predetermined conclusion.
> An integrating resource is a resource that is added to or changed by means of
> updates that do not remain discrete but are integrated into the whole (includ-
> ing tangible resources such as loose-leaf publications, and intangible resources
> such as websites).

This appendix covers printed single units and printed multipart monographs. For serials or integrating resources in any format, see appendix K.

2. DECIDE ON THE TYPE OF DESCRIPTION

Consider the type of description you want to create. RDA 1.1.4 mentions three types of description: comprehensive, analytical, and hierarchical.

> A comprehensive description describes the resource as a whole.
> An analytical description describes a part of a larger resource.
> A hierarchical description combines a comprehensive description of a whole resource with analytical descriptions of one or more of its parts.

U.S. cataloging practice does not use hierarchical descriptions; therefore, these will not be described here. Analytical descriptions are described in appendix L. This appendix covers comprehensive descriptions.

3. CHOOSE THE BASIS FOR IDENTIFICATION AND SOURCES OF INFORMATION FOR THE RESOURCE

Examine the resource and choose a basis for identification following the instructions in RDA 2.1. If the resource is issued as a single-unit resource, the resource itself will be the basis for identification. If the resource is issued in more than one part, one of the parts will be chosen as the basis for identification. For a printed textual monograph, this will usually be the first volume. For details, see chapter 2 of this *Handbook* at 2.1.

Having chosen the part that will serve as the basis for identification, choose a "preferred source of information" within that part following the instructions in RDA 2.2. The preferred source of information for a printed textual monograph is the title page, title sheet, or title card (RDA 2.2.2.2). For details, see chapter 2 of this *Handbook* at 2.2.

4. DESCRIBE THE RESOURCE

Titles and Statements of Responsibility. Transcribe the title proper, other title information, and statement of responsibility in a MARC bibliographic 245 field. For information about transcription, see chapter 2 of this *Handbook* at 1.7.

Transcribe the title proper in subfield ‡a of the 245 field exactly as found on the preferred source of information, usually the title page (see RDA 2.3.2). Title proper is a core element and therefore must be included in the description. For details, see chapter 2 of this *Handbook* at 2.3.

Transcription of other title information is optional in RDA, although core for the Library of Congress. Most U.S. catalogers will follow LC practice and include other title information in the description. If including other title information, transcribe it after the title proper in subfield ‡b of the 245 field (see RDA 2.3.4). Other title information should be transcribed from the same source as the title proper. The first piece of other title information is separated from the title proper by space-colon-space. Subsequent pieces of other title information are separated from each other by space-colon-space. For details, see chapter 2 of this *Handbook* at 2.3.4.

The first statement of responsibility relating to the title proper is a core element in RDA. Other statements of responsibility are optional, although most catalogers will record them. If including statements of responsibility in the description, transcribe them after the title proper or other information in subfield ‡c of the 245 field (see RDA 2.4.1 and 2.4.2). Statements of responsibility may be transcribed from any source within the resource itself. In unusual situations, a statement of responsibility may be transcribed from outside the resource itself, in which case it should be bracketed. This will rarely be necessary. The first statement of responsibility is separated from the title proper (or other title information) by space-slash-space. Subsequent statements of responsibility are separated from each other by space-semicolon-space. For details, see chapter 2 of this *Handbook* at 2.4.

Variant Titles. Examine the resource for variant titles. Variant titles are not core in RDA, but if in your opinion a library user might attempt to find the resource using one of these titles, record it in subfield ‡a of a 246 field. Variant titles can be taken from any source (see RDA 2.3.6.2), including your own knowledge (e.g., you might record a variant to correct a misspelled word in the title). For economy's sake, most catalogers will not look beyond the resource itself for variant titles. For details, see chapter 2 of this *Handbook* at 2.3.6.

Edition Statement. Examine the resource for an edition statement. An edition statement can be taken from any source within the resource, but a statement found in the same source as the title proper is preferred. Edition statements may also be taken from outside the resource; if so, they should be bracketed.

Designation of edition is a core element, and therefore must be recorded if present in the resource. If found, transcribe a designation of edition (e.g., "Second revised edition") in subfield ‡a of a 250 field (see RDA 2.5.2).

Recording other elements of the edition statement is optional in RDA. The most common other element is a statement of responsibility relating to the edition. If you find such a statement and decide to include it in the description, record it following space-slash-space in subfield ‡b of the 250 field.

For details on recording an edition statement, see chapter 2 of this *Handbook* at 2.5.

Publication Statement. Examine the resource for publication information, including place of publication, publisher, and date of publication. Although information about publication can be taken from outside the resource itself, prefer information found inside the resource; within the resource, prefer information found in the same source as the title proper. Publication information is recorded in a MARC bibliographic 264 field, with the second indicator coded "1."

Record the first place of publication found in the resource in subfield ‡a of the 264 field. Transcribe the information exactly as found. This element is core. If no place is found in the resource either supply (in brackets) information from another source about the place of publication, or record "[Place of publication not identified]." If more than one place of publication is found in the resource, you may optionally record them all, but only the first is required. For details, see chapter 2 of this *Handbook* at 2.8.2.

Record the first publisher associated with the first place of publication found in the resource in subfield ‡b of the 264 field. Transcribe the information exactly as found. This element is core. If no publisher is found in the resource either supply (in brackets) information about the publisher from another source, or record "[Publisher not identified]." Separate the place of publication from the publisher's name with space-colon-space. If more than one publisher is found in the resource, you may optionally record them all, but only the first is required. For details, see chapter 2 of this *Handbook* at 2.8.4.

Record the date of publication. Record numerals in the form preferred by your cataloging agency (see RDA 1.8.2). Place a comma immediately after the publisher's name and record the date of publication in subfield ‡c of the 264 field. The date of publication element is core. If no explicit date of publication is found in the resource either supply (in brackets) information found in another source or inferred by the cataloger, or record "[Date of publication not identified]." Note that a copyright date is not a publication date. A copyright date can never be substituted for a publication date in RDA, but it may optionally be recorded in addition to the date of publication element. It may also be used as evidence for inferring the date of publication.

If the date of publication has not been identified, then either a date of distribution or a copyright date, if present in the resource, must be recorded (see discussion, however, in chapter 2 of this *Handbook* at 2.8.6.6 on ways to identify the date of publication). If recording a copyright date, include the copyright symbol (© or ℗) and record it in subfield ‡c of a separate 264 field, with the second indicator coded "4."

For details about publication statement and copyright date, see chapter 2 of this *Handbook* at 2.8 and 2.11.

Distribution and manufacture (printing) information may be recorded, but is optional if publication information has been recorded. For details, see chapter 2 of this *Handbook* at 2.9 and 2.10.

Describe the Carrier. A carrier is the physical medium in which the content of a resource is stored. Carriers for printed textual monographs include volumes and sheets. Examine the resource for physical details, including size and page numbering. Several carrier-related elements are required in an RDA record. Most are recorded in the 3XX block of the bibliographic record.

Extent. The extent of the resource is recorded in subfield ‡a of a MARC bibliographic 300 field. Extent is core if the resource is complete. Record the extent of a textual monograph following the instructions in RDA 3.4.5. Only the most basic procedures will be mentioned in this appendix. For details, see chapter 2 of this *Handbook* at 3.4.5.

If the resource consists of a single unit, look through the book for sequences of numbers. Record the last number in each sequence followed by "pages," "leaves," or "columns," as appropriate. Caution: a sequence is a consecutive run of numbers. The form of numbers can change within a sequence, for example, from roman numerals to arabic. A book whose pages are numbered i–xxx and then 1–500 is said to have two sequences; however, a book whose pages are numbered i-xxx and then 31–500 has only one sequence, because the only change has been from roman to arabic numerals in the same sequence. Only record the last number of a sequence.

If the resource consists of more than one volume, record the number of volumes followed by the term "volumes" (e.g., "15 volumes").

If the resource consists of a sheet or sheets, record the extent as "1 sheet," "4 sheets," etc.

Illustrative Content. Though not considered in RDA to be part of the carrier description, this element is treated here because it is recorded immediately after the extent element in the MARC bibliographic record. Examine the resource for illustrations, including maps. If found, and you think recording the information would help the library user to identify or select the resource (this element is not core), record the word "illustration" or "illustrations" in subfield ‡b of the 300 field (see RDA 7.15). Other terms may also be used, preferring terms found in the alternative list in RDA 7.15.1.3. Probably the most common of these is "map" or "maps." Record color content (e.g., "color illustrations") (see RDA 7.17). Separate this element from the preceding extent element with space-semicolon-space.

For details on illustrative content and color content, see chapter 8 of this *Handbook* at 7.15 and 7.17.

Dimensions. The dimensions element is not core in RDA, but it is core in descriptions of textual monographs for catalogers at the Library of Congress, except for online electronic resources (see LC-PCC PS 3.5, May 2012). Most U.S. catalogers will record this element. Dimensions are recorded in subfield ‡c of a MARC bibliographic 300 field. Separate the dimensions element from any preceding elements in the field with space-semicolon-space.

Record the dimensions of a printed book following the instructions in 3.5.1.4.14. Record the height of the volume, rounding up to the nearest centimeter. Also record the width in the form height x width (e.g., 31 x 10 cm) if it is less than half of the height of the volume, or greater than the height of the volume.

Record the dimensions of a sheet following the instructions in 3.5.1.4.11. Record the height x width of the sheet, rounding up to the nearest centimeter.

If the record has a series statement, record a period at the end of the field.

For details, see chapter 2 of this *Handbook* at 3.5.1.3, 3.5.1.4.11, and 3.5.1.4.14.

Content Type. Like the illustrative content element described above, the content type element is not part of the description of the carrier, but it is treated here because it is generally the next element after the dimensions recorded in the MARC bibliographic record. Content type is a core element, and is recorded in subfield ‡a of the MARC 336 field following the instructions in RDA 6.9. Record, as appropriate, one of the terms in the list found in RDA 6.9.1.3. End the field with "‡2 rdacontent":

336   ‡a text ‡2 rdacontent

The most common content type for a textual monograph is "text." If illustrations or maps are present, "still image" or "cartographic image" may also be appropriate. For details, see chapter 8 of this *Handbook* at 6.9.

Media and Carrier Type. Carrier type is core in an RDA description. Media type is not core, but most U.S. catalogers follow LC and PCC practice and record it (see LC-PCC PS 3.2, October 2012).

Media type is recorded in subfield ‡a of a MARC bibliographic 337 field. The term should be taken from the list in RDA 3.2.1.3. For a printed monograph, use "unmediated." End the field with "‡2 rdamedia":

337   ‡a unmediated ‡2 rdamedia

Carrier type is recorded in subfield ‡a of a MARC bibliographic 338 field. The term should be taken from the list in RDA 3.3.1.3. Most of the unmediated terms there might be used to describe a printed monograph, but the most common are "volume" (for a multipage printed monograph) or "sheet" (for a single-sheet publication). End the field with "‡2 rdacarrier":

338   ‡a volume ‡2 rdacarrier

For details, see chapter 2 of this *Handbook* at 3.2 and 3.3.

Series Statement. Examine the resource for a series statement. Although information about a series can be taken from outside the resource itself, prefer information found in the resource, and within the resource prefer information found on a series title page. Series information is recorded in a MARC bibliographic 490 field. The first indicator is coded "0" if the information is not indexed; it is coded "1" if the information is indexed (in which case an 8XX field will also be present in the bibliographic record; see below under Link the Resource to Related Entities).

Record the title proper of the series in subfield ‡a of the 490 field exactly as it appears in the resource. If series numbering is present, record it in subfield ‡v following the title proper of the series and any other elements (such as a statement of responsibility). Separate series numbering from preceding elements by space-semicolon-space.

The title proper of the series and numbering are core and therefore must be recorded if present. Other title information of the series and statements of responsibility relating to the series are not core and are not in most cases recorded. For details about recording series statements, see chapter 2 of this *Handbook* at 2.12.

Notes. Include any notes you consider necessary to help the library user contextualize, find, identify, or select the resource. No notes are core in an RDA description. Therefore, recording notes in a bibliographic record is entirely dependent on your judgment or the policies of your cataloging agency. Most notes are recorded in the 5XX block of the MARC bibliographic record. Some of the more common notes included in bibliographic records for printed textual monographs are notes giving summaries of the contents (see discussion in chapter 8 of this *Handbook* at 7.10), notes about bibliographical references or indexes contained in the resource (see discussion in chapter 8 of this *Handbook* at 7.16), and contents notes (see discussion in chapter 9 of this *Handbook* at RDA chapter 25, under Whole-Part Work Relationships). See the figures throughout this *Handbook* for many different kinds of notes.

Identifier for the Manifestation. Examine the resource for an identifier, defined as "a character string associated with a manifestation that serves to differentiate that manifestation from other manifestations." The identifier for the manifestation element is core (see RDA 2.15), and therefore an identifier must be recorded if present on the resource.

The most common identifier found in contemporary printed textual monographs is an ISBN (International Standard Book Number). Record an ISBN in subfield ‡a of the 020 field of the MARC bibliographic record. Copy it as found, but do not record hyphens. For details, see chapter 2 of this *Handbook* at 2.15.

5. LINK THE RESOURCE TO RELATED ENTITIES

Once the resource has been described, links should be made to related entities. These include works and expressions either contained in the resource or related to the work(s) or expression(s) described in the record, and related persons, families, corporate bodies, and geographic entities.

In the MARC bibliographic format these links are created by recording the authorized access point for the related entity in one of the access point fields, generally speaking, the 1XX, 7XX, and 8XX fields. This either (1) links the bibliographic record to an associated authority record, and via that record links the bibliographic record to other bibliographic records containing the same authorized access point (either by using the text string itself, or using an identifier); (2) directly links the bibliographic record to other bibliographic records containing the same authorized access point; or (3) at the least allows searches to retrieve all bibliographic records containing the same authorized access point.

RDA requires the cataloger to record at least one relationship: that between the resource and the principal creator of the work embodied in the manifestation being described (see discussion in chapter 9 of this *Handbook* at 18.3). Recording most other relationships is optional, but most catalogers will record many.

The relationship between the resource and the principal creator of the work is recorded in a 100 (persons or families), 110 (most corporate bodies), or 111 (meetings) field. If there is more than one work in the resource and they are by different creators, record these relationships in 700, 710, or 711. See chapter 9 of this *Handbook* at 19.2 for help in determining what entity is the principal creator of the work. With persons and families, the decision is usually fairly straightforward. Determining if a corporate body or meeting is the creator can be a little trickier, but reasonably clear guidelines are laid out at RDA 19.2.1.1.1 (see also corresponding discussion in chapter 9 of this *Handbook*).

Begin by recording the authorized access point for the principal creator of the work in a 1XX field. This form may be accompanied by a relationship designator to clarify the nature of the relationship. The use of relationship designators is optional but encouraged (see chapter 9 of this *Handbook* at 18.5).

Once the relationship to the principal creator has been recorded, think about other relationships that might be helpful. First consider other creators if there are more than one. Other commonly recorded relationships for textual monographs include those between the resource and its editors, translators, and illustrators. These relationships are all recorded by giving the authorized access point for the related entity in 7XX fields: 700 (persons and families), 710 (most corporate bodies), or 711 (meetings).

Consider also relationships to related works and expressions, or the relationship between the manifestation described in the bibliographic record and the work(s) or expression(s) embodied in the manifestation. Related works or expressions are recorded by giving the authorized access point for the work or expression in a 700, 710, 711, or 730 field, or in the case of a series, in an 800, 810, 811, or 830 field. Works or expressions embodied in the manifestation are recorded in a 1XX and 240 field combination or in 130 if there is only one; or if there are two or more, in the 700, 710, 711, or 730 fields as appropriate. For details, see discussion throughout chapter 9 of this *Handbook*.

6. SAMPLE RECORD SETS

RECORD SET A1
SINGLE UNIT

Bibliographic Record

020	‡a 9780470656808	[RDA 2.15]
245 00	‡a Blues, philosophy for everyone : ‡b thinking deep about feeling low / ‡c edited by Jesse R. Steinberg and Abrol Fairweather.	[RDA 2.3, 2.4]
264 1	‡a Chichester, West Sussex, UK ; ‡a Malden, MA, USA : ‡b Wiley-Blackwell, ‡c 2012.	[RDA 2.8]
300	‡a xxx, 211 pages : ‡b illustrations ; ‡c 23 cm.	[RDA 3.4.5.2, 7.15, 3.5.1.4.14]
336	‡a text ‡2 rdacontent	[RDA 6.9]
337	‡a unmediated ‡2 rdamedia	[RDA 3.2]

338	‡a volume ‡2 rdacarrier	*[RDA 3.3]*
490 1	‡a Philosophy for everyone	*[RDA 2.12]*
504	‡a Includes bibliographical references and index.	*[RDA 7.16]*
505 0	‡a Talkin' to myself again : a dialogue on the evolution of the blues Joel Rudinow -- Reclaiming the aura : B.B. King in the age of mechanicalreproduction / Ken Ueno -- Twelve-bar zombies : Wittgensteinian reflections on the blues / Wade Fox and Richard Greene -- The blues as cultural expression /Philip Jenkins -- The artistic transformation of trauma, loss, and adversity in the blues / Alan M. Steinberg, Robert S. Pynoos, and Robert Abramovitz -- Sadness as beauty : why it feels so good to feel so blue / David C. Drake.	*[RDA 25.1, 24.4.3a]*
700 1	‡a Steinberg, Jesse R., ‡e editor of compilation.	*[RDA 20.2, 18.4.1.2, 18.5]*
700 1	‡a Fairweather, Abrol, ‡e editor of compilation.	*[RDA 20.2, 18.4.1.2, 18.5]*
830 0	‡a Philosophy for everyone.	*[RDA 25.1, 24.4.2]*

Title page

Edited by Jesse R. Steinberg and Abrol Fairweather
BLUES
PHILOSOPHY FOR EVERYONE
Thinking Deep About Feeling Low
WILEY-BLACKWELL
A John Wiley & Sons, Ltd., Publication

Series title page
PHILOSOPHY FOR EVERYONE
Series editor: Fritz Allhoff
[List of titles in the series]
Title page verso
This edition first published 2012
©2012 John Wiley & Sons, Inc.
John Wiley & Sons, Ltd., The Atrium, Southern Gate, Chichester, West Sussex, PO 19 8SQ, UK
350 Main Street, Malden, MA 02148-5020, USA

Associated Authority Records

100 1	‡a Steinberg, Jesse R.	*[RDA 9.2.2, 9.19.1]*
372	‡a Philosophy ‡a Human ecology--Study and teaching ‡2 lcsh	*[RDA 9.15]*
373	‡a University of Pittsburgh at Bradford ‡2 naf	*[RDA 9.13]*
374	‡a College teachers ‡2 lcsh	*[RDA 9.16]*
375	‡a male	*[RDA 9.7]*
377	‡a eng	*[RDA 9.14]*
670	‡a Blues, philosophy for everyone, 2012: ‡b title page (Jesse R. Steinberg) cover page 4 (Jesse R. Steinberg is an assistant professor of philosophy and the director of the Environmental Studies Program at the University of Pittsburgh at Bradford)	*[RDA 8.12]*

100 1	ǂa Fairweather, Abrol	*[RDA 9.2.2, 9.19.1]*
372	ǂa Philosophy ǂ2 lcsh	*[RDA 9.15]*
373	ǂa San Francisco State University ǂ2 naf	*[RDA 9.13]*
373	ǂa University of San Francisco ǂ2 naf	*[RDA 9.13]*
374	ǂa College teachers ǂ2 lcsh	*[RDA 9.16]*
375	ǂa male	*[RDA 9.7]*
377	ǂa eng	*[RDA 9.14]*
670	ǂa Blues, philosophy for everyone, 2012: ǂb title page (Abrol Fairweather) page i ("Abrol Fairweather is an instructor at San Francisco State University and the University of San Francisco. He has published in the area of virtue epistemology.") *[RDA 8.12]*	

046	ǂk 2010	*[RDA 6.4]*
130 0	ǂa Philosophy for everyone	*[RDA 6.2.2, 6.27.1]*
380	ǂa Series (Publications) ǂa Monographic series ǂ2 lcsh	*[RDA 6.3]*
643	ǂa Chichester, West Sussex, UK ǂa Malden, MA, USA ǂb Wiley-Blackwell *[not RDA]*	
644	ǂa f ǂ5 NjBlaOCU	*[not RDA]*
645	ǂa t ǂ5 DPCC ǂ5 NjBlaOCU	*[not RDA]*
646	ǂa s ǂ5 NjBlaOCU	*[not RDA]*
670	ǂa Climbing--philosophy for everyone, 2010: ǂb series title page (Philosophy for everyone) *[RDA 5.8]*	
670	ǂa OCLC, 30 August 2012 ǂb (first publication in the series 2010)	*[RDA 5.8]*

RECORD SET A2
MULTIPART MONOGRAPH

Bibliographic Record

020	ǂa 9780205744206 (v. 1)	*[RDA 2.15]*
020	ǂa 9780205744213 (v. 2)	*[RDA 2.15]*
100 1	ǂa Stokstad, Marilyn, ǂd 1929- ǂe author.	*[RDA 18.3, 19.2, 18.4.1.2, 18.5]*
245 10	ǂa Art history / ǂc Marilyn Stokstad, Michael W. Cothren ; contributors, Frederick M. Asher, Douglass Bailey, David A. Brinkley, Claudia L. Brittenham, Claudia Brown, Patricia J. Darish, Patricka J. Graham, and D. Fairchild Ruggles. *[RDA 2.3, 2.4]*	
250	ǂa Fourth edition.	*[RDA 2.5]*
264 1	ǂa Boston : ǂb Prentice Hall, ǂc [2011]	*[RDA 2.8]*
300	ǂa 2 volumes (xli, 1182 pages) : ǂb color illustrations, maps, plans ; ǂc 28 cm. *[RDA 3.4.5.16, 3.4.5.17, 7.15, 3.5.1.4.14]*	
336	ǂa text ǂ2 rdacontent	*[RDA 6.9]*

336	‡a still image ‡2 rdacontent	*[RDA 6.9]*
336	‡a cartographic image ‡2 rdacontent	*[RDA 6.9]*
337	‡a unmediated ‡2 rdamedia	*[RDA 3.2]*
338	‡a volume ‡2 rdacarrier	*[RDA 3.3]*
500	‡a Also issued in a single volume hardcover edition.	*[RDA 27.1, 24.4.3b]*
504	‡a Includes bibliographical references (pages 1146-1157) and index.	*[RDA 7.16]*
700 1	‡a Cothren, Michael Watt, ‡e author.	*[RDA 19.2, 18.4.1.2, 18.5]*

Title page

VOLUME ONE | FOURTH EDITION
ART HISTORY

MARILYN STOKSTAD
Judith Harris Murphy Distinguished Professor of Art History emerita,
The University of Kansas
MICHAEL W. COTHREN
Scheuer Family Professor of Humanities, Department of Art, Swarthmore College
CONTRIBUTORS
Frederick M. Asher, Douglass Bailey, David A. Brinkley, Claudia L. Brittenham, Claudia Brown,
Patricia J. Darish, Patricka J. Graham, and D. Fairchild Ruggles
PRENTICE HALL
Boston Columbus Indianapolis New York San Francisco Upper Saddle River
Amsterdam Cape Town Dubai London Madrid Milan Munich Paris Montréal Toronto Delhi
Mexico City São Paulo Sydney Hong Kong Seoul Singapore Taipei Tokyo

Title page verso

Copyright © 2011, 2008, 2005 by Pearson Education, Inc., publishing as Prentice Hall, 1 Lake
St., Upper Saddle River, New Jersey, 07458. All rights reserved. Manufactured in the United
States of America.

ISBN: 978-0-205-74420-6

Associated Authority Records

046	‡f 19290216	*[RDA 9.3]*
100 1	‡a Stokstad, Marilyn, ‡d 1929-	*[RDA 9.2.2, 9.19.1]*
370	‡a Lansing (Mich.) ‡f Lawrence (Kan.) ‡2 naf	*[RDA 9.8]*
372	‡a Art--History ‡2 lcsh	*[RDA 9.15]*
373	‡a University of Kansas ‡2 naf ‡s 1958	*[RDA 9.13]*
373	‡a College Art Association of America ‡2 naf	*[RDA 9.13]*
374	‡a Art historians ‡a College teachers ‡a Medievalists ‡2 lcsh	*[RDA 9.16]*
375	‡a female	*[RDA 9.7]*
377	‡a eng	*[RDA 9.14]*
378	‡q Marilyn Jane	*[RDA 9.5]*

670	‡a The Pórtico de la Gloria of the cathedral of Santiago de Compostela, 1957: ‡b title page (Marilyn J. Stokstad)	*[RDA 8.12]*
670	‡a Art history, 2011: ‡b title page (Marilyn Stokstad, Judith Harris Murphy Distinguished Professor of Art History emerita, The University of Kansas)	*[RDA 8.12]*
670	‡a Dictionary of art historians (online), 31 August 2012 ‡b (Stokstad, Marilyn [Jane]; born February 16, 1929 in Lansing, Mich.; medievalist at University of Kansas since 1958)	*[RDA 8.12]*

046	‡f 19510409	*[RDA 9.3]*
100 1	‡a Cothren, Michael Watt	*[RDA 9.2.2, 9.19.1]*
372	‡a Art--History ‡2 lcsh	*[RDA 9.15]*
374	‡a Art historians ‡2 lcsh	*[RDA 9.16]*
375	‡a male	*[RDA 9.7]*
377	‡a eng	*[RDA 9.14]*
670	‡a The thirteenth and fourteenth-century glazing of the choir of the cathedral of Beauvais, 1980: ‡b title page (Michael Watt Cothren)	*[RDA 8.12]*
670	‡a Picturing the celestial city, 2006: ‡b ECIP title page (Michael Cothren) ECIP data view (born 9 April 1951)	*[RDA 8.12]*

RECORD SET A3
SINGLE SHEET

Bibliographic Record

100 1	‡a Bradbury, Ray, ‡d 1920-2012, ‡e author.	*[RDA 18.3, 19.2, 18.4.1.2, 18.5]*
245 10	‡a Once the years were numerous and the funerals few / ‡c Ray Bradbury ; design & illustration: Susan Makov & Patrick Eddington.	*[RDA 2.3, 2.4]*
264 1	‡a [Salt Lake City, Utah] : ‡b [Green Cat Press], ‡c [2004]	*[RDA 2.8]*
264 4	‡c ©2004	*[RDA 2.11]*
300	‡a 1 sheet : ‡b illustration ; ‡c 48 x 28 cm	*[RDA 3.4.5.14, 7.15, 3.5.1.4.11]*
336	‡a text ‡2 rdacontent	*[RDA 6.9]*
336	‡a still image ‡2 rdacontent	*[RDA 6.9]*
337	‡a unmediated ‡2 rdamedia	*[RDA 3.2]*
338	‡a sheet ‡2 rdacarrier	*[RDA 3.3]*
500	‡a Poem.	*[RDA 7.2]*
500	‡a Limited edition of 70 copies on Rives BFK paper.	*[RDA 2.20]*
590	‡a Library copy is no. 56/70. Signed by Bradbury, Makov, and Eddington.	*[RDA 3.21]*
700 1	‡a Makov, Susan, ‡e illustrator.	*[RDA 20.2, 18.4.1.2, 18.5]*
700 1	‡a Eddington, Patrick, ‡e illustrator.	*[RDA 20.2, 18.4.1.2, 18.5]*

Sheet face
Once
the Years were
Numerous and
the Funerals Few
Ray Bradbury
[text of poem]
©2004 text: Ray Bradbury   56/70   Design & Illustration: Susan Makov & Patrick Eddington
Publisher's catalog
Green Cat Press
915 S. McClelland
Salt Lake City, Utah 84105

Associated Authority Records

046	ǂf 19200822 ǂg 20120605	*[RDA 9.3]*
100 1	ǂa Bradbury, Ray, ǂd 1920-2012	*[RDA 9.2.2, 9.19.1]*
370	ǂa Waukegan (Ill.) ǂb Los Angeles (Calif.) ǂe Tucson (Ariz.) ǂ2 naf	*[RDA 9.8, 9.11]*
372	ǂa Science fiction ǂ2 lcsh	*[RDA 9.15]*
374	ǂa Authors ǂ2 lcsh	*[RDA 9.16]*
375	ǂa male	*[RDA 9.7]*
377	ǂa eng	*[RDA 9.14]*
400 1	ǂa Bradbury, Raymond Douglas, ǂd 1920-2012	*[RDA 9.2.3, 9.19.2]*
670	ǂa The last circus, 1980: ǂb title page (Ray Bradbury)	*[RDA 8.12]*
670	ǂa New York times WWW site, June 6, 2012 ǂb (Ray Bradbury; born Raymond Douglas Bradbury, August 22, 1920, Waukegan, Ill.; died Tuesday [June 5, 2012], Los Angeles, aged 91; lived in Tucson, Arizona and Los Angeles; master of science fiction whose lyrical evocations of the future reflected both the optimism and the anxieties of his own postwar America)	*[RDA 8.12]*
678 0	ǂa Ray Bradbury (1920-2012) was an American science fiction writer.	*[RDA 9.17]*

046	ǂf 19520821	*[RDA 9.3]*
100 1	ǂa Makov, Susan	*[RDA 9.2.2, 9.19.1]*
370	ǂe Salt Lake City (Utah) ǂ2 naf	*[RDA 9.11]*
372	ǂa Letterpress printing ǂ2 lcsh	
374	ǂa Printers ǂ2 lcsh	*[RDA 9.16]*
375	ǂa female	*[RDA 9.7]*
377	ǂa eng	*[RDA 9.14]*
670	ǂa Trading post guidebook, 1997: ǂb CIP title page (Susan Makov) data sheet (born 21 August 1952)	*[RDA 8.12]*
678 0	ǂa Susan Makov (1952-) is a letterpress printer in Salt Lake City, Utah.	*[RDA 9.17]*

046	‡f 19530107	*[RDA 9.3]*
100 1	‡a Eddington, Patrick	*[RDA 9.2.2, 9.19.1]*
374	‡a Illustrators ‡2 lcsh	*[RDA 9.16]*
375	‡a male	*[RDA 9.7]*
377	‡a eng	*[RDA 9.14]*
670	‡a Trading post guidebook, 1997: ‡b CIP title page (Patrick Eddington) data sheet (born 7 January 1953)	*[RDA 8.12]*
670	‡a Once the years were numerous and the funerals few, 2004: ‡b sheet (design & illustration, Susan Makov & Patrick Eddington)	*[RDA 8.12]*

CARTOGRAPHIC RESOURCES

THIS APPENDIX CONTAINS A RECOMMENDED PROCESS FOR CREAT-ing bibliographic records for published cartographic resources, including resources with content that represents the whole or part of the Earth, celestial bodies, and imaginary places (see RDA glossary under "Cartographic Content"). This appendix covers bibliographic record creation for these resources only in the most general of terms. Unusual situations are covered in the body of the *Handbook*. As with the *Handbook* itself, this appendix does not cover non-RDA related aspects of the bibliographic record, such as fixed-length data elements (the so-called fixed fields) or subject analysis. This appendix also contains three sample record sets consisting of bibliographic records and their associated authority records, which illustrate many of the points described below.

Many nonspecialist catalogers in general libraries find the vocabulary and techniques of cartography daunting. Such individuals will find much aid and comfort in a manual issued by the Anglo-American Cataloguing Committee for Cartographic Materials (AACCCM), *Cartographic Materials: A Manual of Interpretation for AACR2, 2002 Revision.*[1] Although the manual was written for AACR2 and not for RDA, it will still be useful until a version appears to accompany RDA. The manual consists of a discussion and elucidation of all AACR2 rules that apply to map cataloging; although some of these rules have changed, the principles underlying map cataloging practice have not and these are fully explained in *Cartographic Materials*. In addition, helpful appendixes discuss such mysteries as determination of the scale and coordinates of a map and treatment of map series. There are also sections on early cartographic resources and electronic resources.

1. DETERMINE THE MODE OF ISSUANCE

Consider the mode of issuance of the resource. Does it consist of a single unit? Is it a multipart monograph? Is it a serial or integrating resource? Mode of issuance is defined in RDA 1.1.3.

> A single-unit resource is a resource issued either as a single physical unit (e.g., a single map) or a single logical unit (e.g., a PDF file).
>
> A multipart monograph is a resource issued in two or more parts that is complete or is intended to be complete within a finite number of parts.
>
> A serial is a resource issued in successive parts, usually bearing numbering, that has no predetermined conclusion.
>
> An integrating resource is a resource that is added to or changed by means of updates that do not remain discrete but are integrated into the whole (including tangible resources such as loose-leaf publications, and intangible resources such as websites).

This appendix covers single units and multipart monographs. For serials or integrating resources in any format, see appendix K.

2. DECIDE ON THE TYPE OF DESCRIPTION

Consider the type of description you want to create. RDA 1.1.4 mentions three types of description: comprehensive, analytical, and hierarchical.

> A comprehensive description describes the resource as a whole.
>
> An analytical description describes a part of a larger resource.
>
> A hierarchical description combines a comprehensive description of a whole resource with analytical descriptions of one or more of its parts.

U.S. cataloging practice does not use hierarchical descriptions; therefore, these will not be described here. This appendix covers comprehensive descriptions. (See appendix L for more details about analysis.)

3. CHOOSE THE BASIS FOR IDENTIFICATION AND SOURCES OF INFORMATION FOR THE RESOURCE

Examine the resource and choose a basis for identification following the instructions in RDA 2.1. If the resource is issued as a single-unit resource, the resource itself will be the basis for identification. If the resource is issued in more than one part, one of the parts will be chosen as the basis for identification. For a printed cartographic resource, this will usually be the first sheet or volume. For details, see chapter 2 of this *Handbook* at 2.1.

Having chosen the part that will serve as the basis for identification, choose a "preferred source of information" within that part following the instructions in RDA 2.2. The preferred source of information for a printed cartographic resource is the title page (e.g., for an atlas), title sheet (e.g., for a series of sheet maps), or title card (RDA 2.2.2.2). For a digital cartographic resource, the preferred source of information is either a label bearing a title that is permanently printed or affixed to the resource (e.g., a DVD-ROM) or embedded textual metadata containing a title (e.g., for a PDF file). For details, see chapter 2 of this *Handbook* at 2.2.

4. DESCRIBE THE RESOURCE

Titles and Statements of Responsibility. Transcribe the title proper, other title information, and statement of responsibility in a MARC bibliographic 245 field. For information about transcription, see chapter 2 of this *Handbook* at 1.7.

Transcribe the title proper in subfield ‡a of the 245 field exactly as found on the preferred source of information, usually the title page or title sheet for printed cartographic resources (see RDA 2.3.2). Cartographic resources are somewhat more likely than other types of resources to lack a collective title. For such cases, see discussion in chapter 2 of this *Handbook* at 2.3.2.9, including a cartographic example in figure 2.31. Title proper is a core element and therefore must be included in the description. For details, see chapter 2 of this *Handbook* at 2.3.

Transcription of other title information is optional in RDA, although core for the Library of Congress. Most U.S. catalogers will follow LC practice and include other title information in the description. If including other title information, transcribe it after the title proper in subfield ‡b of the 245 field (see RDA 2.3.4).

If the title proper or other title information of the cartographic resource does not include any indication of the geographic area covered, the cataloger may supply as other title information a word or phrase describing the area covered. For discussion, see chapter 2 of this *Handbook* at 2.3.4.5.

Unless supplying information about the geographic area covered, the cataloger should transcribe other title information from the same source as the title proper. The first piece of other title information is separated from the title proper by space-colon-space. Subsequent pieces of other title information are separated from each other by space-colon-space. For details, see chapter 2 of this *Handbook* at 2.3.4.

The first statement of responsibility relating to the title proper is a core element in RDA. Other statements of responsibility are optional, although most catalogers will record them. If including statements of responsibility in the description, transcribe them after the title proper or other information in subfield ‡c of the 245 field (see RDA 2.4.1 and 2.4.2). Statements of responsibility may be transcribed from any source within the resource itself. In unusual situations, a statement of responsibility may be transcribed from outside the resource itself, but in that case it should be bracketed. This will rarely be necessary. The first statement of responsibility is separated from the title proper (or other title information) by space-slash-space. Subsequent statements of responsibility are separated from each other by space-semicolon-space. For details, see chapter 2 of this *Handbook* at 2.4.

Variant Titles. Examine the resource for variant titles. Variant titles are not core in RDA, but if in your opinion a library user might attempt to find the resource using one of these titles, record it in subfield ‡a of a 246 field. Variant titles can be taken from any source (see RDA 2.3.6.2), including your own knowledge (e.g., you might record a variant to correct a misspelled word in the title). For economy's sake, most catalogers will not look beyond the resource itself for variant titles. For details, see chapter 2 of this *Handbook* at 2.3.6.

Edition Statement. Examine the resource for an edition statement. An edition statement can be taken from any source within the resource, but a statement found in the same source as the title proper is preferred. Edition statements may also be taken from outside the resource; if so, they should be bracketed.

Designation of edition is a core element, and therefore must be recorded if present in the resource. If found, transcribe a designation of edition (e.g., "New world edition") in subfield ‡a of a 250 field (see RDA 2.5.2).

Recording other elements of the edition statement is optional in RDA. The most common other element is a statement of responsibility relating to the edition. If you find such a statement and decide to include it in the description, record it following space-slash-space in subfield ‡b of the 250 field.

For details on recording an edition statement, see chapter 2 of this *Handbook* at 2.5.

Scale. Examine the resource for statements about scale. Scale is "the ratio of the dimensions of an image or three-dimensional form contained or embodied in a resource to the dimensions of the entity it represents." Record the scale in subfield ‡a of a 255 field as a representative fraction, no matter how the statement appears in the source. The ratio is 1:X (e.g., 1:250 means that one inch on the resource represents 250 inches on the object represented by the resource). For details, see chapter 8 of this *Handbook* at 7.25.

Projection of the Cartographic Content. Projection is the method used to represent on a plane the surface of the Earth or another sphere. If the resource includes a statement of projection, it may be transcribed, as it appears, in subfield ‡b of the 255 field, separated from the scale statement by space-semicolon-space. For details, see chapter 8 of this *Handbook* at 7.26.

Coordinates of Cartographic Content. Record the coordinates (longitude and latitude) associated with the resource in parentheses in subfield ‡c of the 255 field. Coordinates are usually only recorded if found on the resource, although they may be supplied by the cataloger if desired. For details, see chapter 7 of this *Handbook* at 7.4.

Publication Statement. Examine the resource for publication information, including place of publication, publisher, and date of publication. Although information about publication can be taken from outside the resource itself, prefer information found inside the resource; within the resource, prefer information found in the same source as the title proper. Publication information is recorded in a MARC bibliographic 264 field, with the second indicator coded "1."

Record the first place of publication found in the resource in subfield ‡a of the 264 field. Transcribe the information exactly as found. This element is core. If no place is found in the resource either supply (in brackets) information from another source about the place of publication, or record "[Place of publication not identified]." If more than one place of publication is found in the resource, you may optionally record them all, but only the first is required. For details, see chapter 2 of this *Handbook* at 2.8.2.

Record the first publisher associated with the first place of publication found in the resource in subfield ‡b of the 264 field. Transcribe the information exactly as found. This element is core. If no publisher is found in the resource either supply (in brackets) information about the publisher from another source, or record "[Publisher not identified]." Separate the place of publication from the publisher's name with space-colon-space. If more than one publisher is found in the resource, you may optionally record them all, but only the first is required. For details, see chapter 2 of this *Handbook* at 2.8.4.

Record the date of publication. Record numerals in the form preferred by your cataloging agency (see RDA 1.8.2). Place a comma immediately after the publisher's name and record the date of publication in subfield ‡c of the 264 field. The date of publication element is core. If no explicit date of publication is found in the resource either supply (in brackets) information found in another source or inferred by the cataloger, or record "[Date of publication not identified]." Note that a copyright date is not a publication date. A copyright date can never be substituted for a publication date in RDA, but it may optionally be recorded in addition to the date of publication element. It may also be used as evidence for inferring the date of publication.

If the date of publication has not been identified, then either a date of distribution or a copyright date, if present in the resource, must be recorded (see discussion, however, in chapter 2 of this *Handbook* at 2.8.6.6 on ways to identify the date of publication). If recording a copyright date, include the copyright symbol (©) and record it in subfield ‡c of a separate 264 field, with the second indicator coded "4."

For details about publication statement and copyright date, see chapter 2 of this *Handbook* at 2.8 and 2.11.

Distribution and manufacture (printing) information may be recorded, but is optional if publication information has been recorded. For details, see chapter 2 of this *Handbook* at 2.9 and 2.10.

Describe the Carrier. A carrier is the physical medium (including digital media) in which the content of a resource is stored. Carriers for cartographic resources include volumes, sheets, and digital carriers such as computer discs or online. Examine the resource for physical details, including size. Several carrier-related elements are required in an RDA record. Most are recorded in the 3XX block of the bibliographic record.

Extent. The extent of the resource is recorded in subfield ‡a of a MARC bibliographic 300 field. Extent is core if the resource is complete. Record the extent of a cartographic resource following the instructions in RDA 3.4.2. Only the most basic procedures will be mentioned in this appendix. For details, see chapter 2 of this *Handbook* at 3.4.2.

Record the extent by giving the number of units followed by one of the terms listed in 3.4.2.2 (e.g., "2 maps", "1 atlas"). Specify the number of pages or volumes of an atlas within parentheses.

Colour Content. Though not considered in RDA to be part of the carrier description, this element is treated here because it is recorded immediately after the extent element in the MARC bibliographic record. If the resource is in color (other than black and white or shades of grey), record "color" in subfield ‡b of the 300. Separate this element from the preceding extent element with space-semicolon-space. For details on colour content, see chapter 8 of this *Handbook* at 7.17.

Dimensions. The dimensions element is not core in RDA, but it is core in descriptions of monographic cartographic resources for catalogers at the Library of Congress, except for online electronic resources (see LC-PCC PS 3.5, May 2012). Most U.S. catalogers will record this element. Dimensions are recorded in subfield ‡c of a MARC bibliographic 300 field. Separate the dimensions element from any preceding elements in the field with space-semicolon-space.

Record the dimensions of an atlas following the instructions in 3.5.1.4.14. Record the height of the volume, rounding up to the nearest centimeter. Also record the width in the form height x width (e.g., 31 x 10 cm) if it is less than half of the height of the volume, or greater than the height of the volume.

Record the dimensions of a map following the instructions in 3.5.2. Record the height x width of the area within the neat lines (the innermost of a series of lines that frame the map), rounding up to the nearest centimeter. In most cases do not record the size of the sheet itself.

If the record has a series statement, record a period at the end of the field.

For details, see chapter 2 of this *Handbook* at 3.5.1.3, 3.5.1.4.14, 3.5.2.2, 3.5.2.3, and 3.5.2.6.

Content Type. Like the colour content element described above, the content type element is not part of the description of the carrier, but it is treated here because it is generally the next element after the dimensions recorded in the MARC bibliographic record. Content type is a core element, and is recorded in subfield ‡a of the MARC 336 field following the instructions in RDA 6.9. Record, as appropriate, one of the terms in the list found in RDA 6.9.1.3. End the field with "‡2 rdacontent":

336   ‡a cartographic image ‡2 rdacontent

The most common content type for a cartographic resource is "cartographic image." For atlases "text" or "still image" may also be appropriate. For details, see chapter 8 of this *Handbook* at 6.9.

Media and Carrier Type. Carrier type is core in an RDA description. Media type is not core, but most U.S. catalogers follow LC and PCC practice and record it (see LC-PCC PS 3.2, October 2012).

Media type is recorded in subfield ‡a of a MARC bibliographic 337 field. The term should be taken from the list in RDA 3.2.1.3. For a printed cartographic resource, use "unmediated." For a digital resource, use "computer." End the field with "‡2 rdamedia":

337   ‡a unmediated ‡2 rdamedia

Carrier type is recorded in subfield ‡a of a MARC bibliographic 338 field. The term should be taken from the list in RDA 3.3.1.3. The most commonly used terms for a printed cartographic resource are "sheet" (for a sheet map) or "volume" (for an atlas). Digital cartographic resources use one of the "computer" carrier types, most commonly "computer disc" or "online resource." End the field with "‡2 rdacarrier":

338   ‡a sheet ‡2 rdacarrier

For details, see chapter 2 of this *Handbook* at 3.2 and 3.3.

Series Statement. Examine the resource for a series statement. Although information about a series can be taken from outside the resource itself, prefer information found in the resource. Series information is recorded in a MARC bibliographic 490 field. The first indicator is coded "0" if the information is not indexed; it is coded "1" if the information is indexed (in which case an 8XX field will also be present in the bibliographic record; see below under Link the Resource to Related Entities).

Record the title proper of the series in subfield ‡a of the 490 field exactly as it appears in the resource. If series numbering is present, record it in subfield ‡v following the title proper of the series and any other elements (such as a statement of responsibility). Separate series numbering from preceding elements by space-semicolon-space.

The title proper of the series and numbering are core and therefore must be recorded if present. Other title information of the series and statements of responsibility relating to the series are not core and are not in most cases recorded. For details about recording series statements, see chapter 2 of this *Handbook* at 2.12.

Notes. Include any notes you consider necessary to help the library user contextualize, find, identify, or select the resource. No notes are core in an RDA description. Therefore, recording notes in a bibliographic record is entirely dependent on your judgment or the policies of your cataloging agency. Most notes are recorded in the

5XX block of the MARC bibliographic record. Some of the more common notes included in bibliographic records for cartographic resources are described in RDA 7.27 (see also discussion in chapter 8 of this *Handbook* at 7.27).

Identifier for the Manifestation. Examine the resource for an identifier, defined as "a character string associated with a manifestation that serves to differentiate that manifestation from other manifestations." The identifier for the manifestation element is core (see RDA 2.15), and so an identifier must be recorded if present on the resource.

The most common identifier found in printed atlases is an ISBN (International Standard Book Number). Sheet maps sometimes have ISBNs, too. Record an ISBN in subfield ‡a of the 020 field of the MARC bibliographic record. Copy it as found, but do not record hyphens. For details, see chapter 2 of this *Handbook* at 2.15.

5. LINK THE RESOURCE TO RELATED ENTITIES

Once the resource has been described, links should be made to related entities. These include works and expressions either contained in the resource or related to the work(s) or expression(s) described in the record, and related persons, families, corporate bodies, and geographic entities.

In the MARC bibliographic format these links are created by recording the authorized access point for the related entity in one of the access point fields, generally speaking the 1XX, 7XX, and 8XX fields. This either (1) links the bibliographic record to an associated authority record, and via that record links the bibliographic record to other bibliographic records containing the same authorized access point (either by using the text string itself, or using an identifier); (2) directly links the bibliographic record to other bibliographic records containing the same authorized access point; or (3) at the least allows searches to retrieve all bibliographic records containing the same authorized access point.

RDA requires the cataloger to record at least one relationship: that between the resource and the principal creator of the work embodied in the manifestation being described (see discussion in chapter 9 of this *Handbook* at 18.3). For cartographic resources, the principal creator is most often a cartographer. Recording the majority of other relationships is optional, but most catalogers will record many.

The relationship between the resource and the principal creator of the work is recorded in a 100 (persons or families), 110 (most corporate bodies), or 111 (meetings) field. If there is more than one work in the resource and they are by different creators, record these relationships in 700, 710, or 711. See chapter 9 of this *Handbook* at 19.2 for help in determining what entity is the principal creator of the work. With persons and families the decision is usually fairly straightforward. Determining if a corporate body or meeting is the creator can be a little trickier, but fairly clear guidelines are laid out at RDA 19.2.1.1.1 (see also corresponding discussion in chapter 9 of the *Handbook*). Of particular importance to cartographic resources, a corporate body that originates or issues a cartographic work is considered to be the creator of the work, unless the body is "merely responsible for [its] publication or distribution" (RDA 19.2.1.1.1f).

Begin by recording the authorized access point for the principal creator (normally the cartographer) of the work in a 1XX field. This form may be accompanied by a relationship designator to clarify the nature of the relationship. The use of relationship designators is optional but encouraged (see chapter 9 of this *Handbook* at 18.5). A common relationship designator for the creator of a cartographic resource is "cartographer."

Once the relationship to the principal creator has been recorded, think about other relationships that might be helpful. First consider other creators if there are more than one. Other commonly recorded relationships for cartographic resources include those between the resource and editors, and the resource and its publishers. These relationships are all recorded by giving the authorized access point for the related entity in 7XX fields: 700 (persons and families), 710 (most corporate bodies), or 711 (meetings).

Consider also relationships to related works and expressions, or the relationship between the manifestation described in the bibliographic record and the work(s) or expression(s) embodied in the manifestation. Related works or expressions are recorded by giving the authorized access point for the work or expression in a 700, 710, 711, or 730 field, or in the case of a series, in an 800, 810, 811, or 830 field. Works or expressions embodied in the manifestation are recorded in a 1XX and 240 field combination or in 130 if there is only one; or if there are two or more, in 700, 710, 711, or 730 fields as appropriate. For details, see discussion throughout chapter 9 of this *Handbook*.

6. SAMPLE RECORD SETS

Other examples of cartographic resource cataloging in this *Handbook* include figures 2.30, 2.31, 2.37, 2.40, 2.79, 2.104, 2.109, 7.96, 7.97, 8.29 to 8.37, and 9.25.

RECORD SET B1
SHEET MAP

Bibliographic Record

110 2	‡a Survey of Kenya, ‡e cartographer.	*[RDA 18.3, 19.2.1.1.1f, 18.4.1.2, 18.5]*
245 10	‡a City of Nairobi, map and guide.	*[RDA 2.3]*
250	‡a Eighth edition.	*[RDA 2.5]*
255	‡a Scale 1:20,000.	*[RDA 7.25]*
264 1	‡a Nairobi, Kenya : ‡b Survey of Kenya, ‡c 1995.	*[RDA 2.8]*
300	‡a 1 map : ‡b color ; ‡c 49 x 80 cm, folded to 31 x 15 cm	*[RDA 3.4.2, 7.17, 3.5.2]*

336	‡a cartographic image ‡2 rdacontent	[RDA 6.9]
337	‡a unmediated ‡2 rdamedia	[RDA 3.2]
338	‡a sheet ‡2 rdacarrier	[RDA 3.3]
490 1	‡a SK ; ‡v 46	[RDA 2.12]
500	‡a Title from panel.	[RDA 2.20.2.3]
500	‡a Includes indexes.	[RDA 7.16]
500	‡a Map of central Nairobi, color illustrations, and textual information for tourists in English, French, and German on verso.	[RDA 7.2, 2.20]
505 0	‡a On verso: Ancillary map: Nairobi guide to city centre at 1:15,840, notes, charts and col. illustrations.	[RDA 25.1]
546	‡a Legend in English, French, German, and Italian. Text in English, French, and German.	[RDA 7.2]
810 2	‡a Survey of Kenya. ‡t SK (Series) ; ‡v 46.	[RDA 25.1]

Map panel

CITY OF NAIROBI
MAP AND GUIDE
TEXT IN ENGLISH/FRENCH/GERMAN
Published by
Survey of Kenya
Nairobi
1995

Map face
SCALE 1:20,000
3.168 inches = 1 mile - 5 centimetres = 1 kilometre
Eighth edition

Associated Authority Records

046	‡s 1903	[RDA 11.4]
110 2	‡a Survey of Kenya	[RDA 11.2.2, 11.13.1]
368	‡a Administrative agencies ‡2 lcsh	[RDA 11.7]
370	‡c Kenya ‡2 naf	[RDA 11.3]
372	‡a Surveying ‡2 lcsh	[RDA 11.10]
410 1	‡a Kenya. ‡b Survey of Kenya	[RDA 11.2.3, 11.13.2]
410 1	‡a Kenya. ‡b Department of Surveys	[RDA 11.2.3, 11.13.2]
410 1	‡a Kenya. ‡b Ministry of Lands and Housing. ‡b Survey of Kenya	
		[RDA 11.2.3, 11.13.2]
670	‡a Departmental bulletin (Survey of Kenya), March 1988: ‡b cover (Survey of Kenya; Ministry of Lands and Housing)	[RDA 8.12]
670	‡a Survey of Kenya Website, viewed 9 September 2008 ‡b (Survey of Kenya; The Department of Surveys is the official Government agency for land surveying and mapping. The Department came into inception in 1903; The role of the	

Department is therefore to survey land, collect data for research and production of topographical and thematic maps, plans, charts and aerial photographs required for use such as in public administration, defense, tourism, education, agriculture etc., and industrial development, planning and for registration of titles to land)

[RDA 8.12]

110	2	‡a Survey of Kenya. ‡t SK (Series)	[RDA 6.2.2, 6.27.1]
380		‡a Series (Publications) ‡a Monographic series ‡2 lcsh	[RDA 6.3]
430	0	‡a SK (Series)	[RDA 6.2.3, 6.27.4]
430	0	‡a Series SK	[RDA 6.2.3, 6.27.4]
642		‡a 71 ‡5 DPCC ‡5 CLU	[not RDA]
643		‡a Nairobi ‡b Survey of Kenya	[not RDA]
644		‡a f ‡5 CLU	[not RDA]
645		‡a t ‡5 DPCC ‡5 CLU	[not RDA]
646		‡a s ‡5 CLU	[not RDA]
670		‡a Nairobi National Park, map and guide, 1972: ‡b map recto (SK) panel (Series SK)	[RDA 5.8]

RECORD SET B2
ATLAS

Bibliographic Record

020		‡a 9780415433433 (hardcover)	[RDA 2.15]
020		‡a 9780415433440 (paperback)	[RDA 2.15]
100	1	‡a Gilbert, Martin, ‡d 1936- ‡e author.	[RDA 18.3, 19.2, 18.4.1.2, 18.5]
245	14	‡a The Routledge historical atlas of Jerusalem / ‡c Martin Gilbert.	[RDA 2.3, 2.4]
250		‡a 4th edition.	[RDA 2.5]
255		‡a Scales differ.	[RDA 7.25.1.4]
264	1	‡a London ; ‡a New York : ‡b Routledge, ‡c 2008.	[RDA 2.8]
264	4	‡a ©2008	[RDA 2.11]
300		‡a 1 atlas (133 pages) : ‡b illustrations, maps ; ‡c 26 cm	[RDA 3.4.2.5, 3.4.5, 7.15, 3.5.1.4.14]
336		‡a cartographic image ‡2 rdacontent	[RDA 6.9]
336		‡a text ‡2 rdacontent	[RDA 6.9]
337		‡a unmediated ‡2 rdamedia	[RDA 3.2]
338		‡a volume ‡2 rdacarrier	[RDA 3.3]
504		‡a Includes bibliographical references (pages 126-132).	[RDA 7.16]

Title page
THE ROUTLEDGE
HISTORICAL ATLAS OF
JERUSALEM
4th Edition
Martin Gilbert
Routledge
Taylor & Francis Group
London and New York
Title page verso
Fourth edition published 2008 by Routledge
©2008 by Martin Gilbert

Associated Authority Record

046	‡a f 19361025	*[RDA 9.3]*
100 1	‡a Gilbert, Martin, ‡d 1936-	*[RDA 9.2.2, 9.19.1]*
375	‡a male	*[RDA 9.7]*
377	‡a eng	*[RDA 9.14]*
670	‡a Israel, 1998: ‡b title page (Martin Gilbert)	*[RDA 8.12]*
670	‡a D-Day, 2004: ‡b CIP title page (Sir Martin Gilbert) CIP data sheet (born October 25, 1936)	*[RDA 8.12]*

RECORD SET B3
DIGITAL MAP

Bibliographic Record

Note: The 264 field follows RDA, not the PCC Provider-Neutral guidelines (see appendix I)

100 1	‡a Dodge, Grenville M., ‡d 1831-1916, ‡e cartographer.	*[RDA 18.3, 19.2, 18.4.1.2,18.5]*
245 10	‡a Map of location 11th hundred miles U.P.R.R. : ‡b [Utah] / ‡c G.M. Dodge, Chief Engr.	*[RDA 2.3, 2.4]*
255	‡a Scale 1:63,360. 1 mile = 1 inch.	*[RDA 7.25]*
264 1	‡a [Washington, D.C.] : ‡b [Library of Congress], ‡c [2010?]	*[RDA 2.8]*
300	‡a 1 online resource (1 map)	*[RDA 3.1.5, 3.4.1.7.5, 3.4.2]*
336	‡a cartographic image ‡2 rdacontent	*[RDA 6.9]*
337	‡a computer ‡2 rdamedia	*[RDA 3.2]*
338	‡a online resource ‡2 rdacarrier	*[RDA 3.1.5, 3.3]*
500	‡a "November 1868."	*[RDA 27.1]*
500	‡a Original pen-and-ink, colored ink, and watercolor on tracing linen., 61 x 186 cm.	*[RDA 27.1]*
500	‡a Relief shown by hachures.	*[RDA 7.27]*

500	‡a Shows the path of the Union Pacific Railroad in the Great Salt Lake region from the Weber River in the east to the Great Salt Lake in the west.	*[RDA 7.3]*
500	‡a Available also through the Library of Congress Web site as a raster image.	*[RDA 27.1]*
856 41	‡u http://hdl.loc.gov/loc.gmd/g4342g.ct003579	*[RDA 4.6]*

Map face

Map
of
LOCATION
11th Hundred Miles
U.P.R.R.
G.M. Dodge, Chief Engr.
Scale 1 Mile = 1 Inch
November 1868

Associated authority record

046	‡f 1831 ‡g 1916	*[RDA 9.3]*
100 1	‡a Dodge, Grenville M., ‡d 1831-1916	*[RDA 9.2.2, 9.19.1]*
372	‡a Railroads--Design and construction ‡2 lcsh	*[RDA 11.10]*
373	‡a Union Pacific Railroad Company ‡2 naf	*[RDA 9.13]*
374	‡a Railroad engineers ‡2 lcsh	*[RDA 9.16]*
375	‡a male	*[RDA 9.7]*
377	‡a eng	*[RDA 9.14]*
378	‡q Grenville Mellen	*[RDA 9.5]*
400 1	‡a Dodge, G. M., ‡d 1831-1916	*[RDA 9.2.3, 9.19.2]*
400 1	‡a Dodge, ‡c General, ‡d 1831-1816	*[RDA 9.2.3, 9.19.2]*
670	‡a Author's Personal recollections of Gen. William T. Sherman, 1902.	*[RDA 8.12]*
670	‡a NUCMC data from Texas Tech Univ. for Jones, M. Papers, 1877-1944 ‡b (Grenville Mellen Dodge)	*[RDA 8.12]*
670	‡a Railroads in the age of regulation, 1900-1980, c1988: ‡b p. 247 (Gen. Grenville M. Dodge, chief construction engineer of the Union Pacific Railroad)	*[RDA 8.12]*
670	‡a OCLC, 4 September 2012 ‡b (usage: Grenville M. Dodge; G.M. Dodge; General Dodge)	*[RDA 8.12]*

NOTE

1. Elizabeth U. Mangan, ed., *Cartographic Materials: A Manual of Interpretation for AACR2, 2002 Revision,* 2nd ed. (Chicago: American Library Association, 2003).

UNPUBLISHED MANUSCRIPTS AND MANUSCRIPT COLLECTIONS

THIS APPENDIX CONTAINS A RECOMMENDED PROCESS FOR CREAT-ing bibliographic records for unpublished manuscripts (including theses and dissertations) and manuscript collections. It covers bibliographic record creation for these resources only in the most general of terms. Unusual situations are covered in the body of the *Handbook*. Because online resources are considered published, this appendix does not treat digitized versions of unpublished resources published on the Internet. As with the *Handbook* itself, this appendix does not cover non-RDA related aspects of the bibliographic record, such as fixed-length data elements (the so-called fixed fields) or subject analysis. This appendix also contains three sample record sets consisting of bibliographic records and their associated authority records, which illustrate many of the points described below.

RDA is intended to provide cataloging guidelines for general materials and depends in part on the existence of specialized manuals for guidance on details. RDA can deal adequately with most manuscripts and manuscript collections, but catalogers with significant numbers of this type of resource should also consult two specialized cataloging manuals. While these publications have not yet been updated to take RDA into account, they still contain valuable information about manuscript and archival cataloging practice. For archival cataloging, see *Describing Archives: A Content Standard* (DACS).[1] For medieval and renaissance manuscripts, see *Descriptive Cataloging of Ancient, Medieval, and Early Modern Manuscripts*.[2] Appropriate supplemental instructions from either of these manuals can be incorporated into RDA records.

1. DETERMINE THE MODE OF ISSUANCE

Consider the mode of issuance of the resource. Does it consist of a single unit? Is it a multipart monograph? Is it a serial or integrating resource? Mode of issuance is defined in RDA 1.1.3.

> A single-unit resource is a resource issued as a single physical unit (e.g., a manuscript letter on one page).
>
> A multipart monograph is a resource issued in two or more parts that is complete or is intended to be complete within a finite number of parts (e.g., a diary in several volumes, a collection).
>
> A serial is a resource issued in successive parts, usually bearing numbering, which has no predetermined conclusion. Manuscript serials are rare and are not treated in this appendix.
>
> An integrating resource is a resource that is added to or changed by means of updates that do not remain discrete but are integrated into the whole (including resources such as loose-leaf publications). Manuscript integrating resources are rare and are not treated in this appendix.

2. DECIDE ON THE TYPE OF DESCRIPTION

Consider the type of description you want to create. RDA 1.1.4 mentions three types of description: comprehensive, analytical, and hierarchical.

> A comprehensive description describes the resource as a whole (including a collection).
>
> An analytical description describes a part of a larger resource (including parts of a collection).
>
> A hierarchical description combines a comprehensive description of a whole resource with analytical descriptions of one or more of its parts.

U.S. cataloging practice does not commonly use hierarchical descriptions; therefore, these will not be described here. Analytical descriptions are described in appendix L. This appendix covers comprehensive descriptions.

3. CHOOSE THE BASIS FOR IDENTIFICATION AND SOURCES OF INFORMATION FOR THE RESOURCE

Examine the resource and choose a basis for identification following the instructions in RDA 2.1. If the resource is issued as a single-unit resource, the resource itself will be the basis for identification. If the resource is issued in more than one part, one of the parts will be chosen as the basis for identification. For a multipart manuscript, this will usually be the first volume or part. For details, see chapter 2 of this *Handbook* at 2.1.

Having chosen the part that will serve as the basis for identification, choose a "preferred source of information" within that part following the instructions in RDA 2.2. Manuscripts can exist in a variety of formats, including text on paper, audio, visual, and computer formats. The preferred source of information for a text on paper manuscript, for example, is the title page, title sheet, or title card (RDA 2.2.2.2). Manuscripts, however, often do not have traditional preferred sources of information. RDA's fallback position is to use any source within the resource itself, preferring sources in which the information is formally given. For an archival collection, this might include documentation that comes with the collection.

4. DESCRIBE THE RESOURCE

Titles and Statements of Responsibility. Record the title proper, other title information, and statement of responsibility in a MARC bibliographic 245 field. For information about transcription, see chapter 2 of this *Handbook* at 1.7.

If the preferred source of information includes a presentation of the title (as may happen with single manuscripts, particularly formally presented ones such as theses), transcribe the title proper in subfield ‡a of the 245 field exactly as found on the preferred source of information (see RDA 2.3.2). Title proper is a core element and therefore must be included in the description. For details, see chapter 2 of this *Handbook* at 2.3.

Titles for collections are generally devised by the cataloger following the instructions in RDA 2.3.2.11 and 2.3.2.11.4. When devising a title, include information about the nature of the resource, its subject, its creator, or a combination of the three (e.g., "James Carter aerial photograph of the University of Michigan campus."). RDA 2.3.2.11 includes the instruction "If the resource is of a type that would normally carry identifying information, . . . make a note to indicate that the title has been devised." Archival resources are not considered to be of this type, and therefore this note is generally not included in the description, nor is the devised title presented in brackets (see RDA 2.2.4 exception).

Other title information is rare in descriptions of manuscript collections, but may occur with individual manuscripts, particularly theses. Recording other title information is optional in RDA, although core for the Library of Congress. Most U.S. catalogers will follow LC practice and include other title information in the description. If including other title information, transcribe it after the title proper in subfield ‡b of the 245 field (see RDA 2.3.4). Other title information should be transcribed from the same source as the title proper. The first piece of other title information is separated from the title proper by space-colon-space. Subsequent pieces of other title information are separated from each other by space-colon-space. For details, see chapter 2 of this *Handbook* at 2.3.4.

Like other title information, formal statements of responsibility are rare in descriptions of manuscript collections, but may occur with individual manuscripts, and almost invariably are present in theses. The first statement of responsibility relating to the title proper is a core element in RDA. Other statements of responsibility are optional, although most catalogers will record them. If including statements of responsibility in the description, transcribe them after the title proper or other information in subfield ‡c of the 245 field (see RDA 2.4.1 and 2.4.2). Statements of responsibility may be transcribed from any source within the resource itself. In unusual situations, a statement of responsibility may be transcribed from outside the resource itself, but in that case it should be bracketed. This will rarely be necessary. The first statement of responsibility is separated from the title proper (or other title information) by space-slash-space. Subsequent statements of responsibility are separated from each other by space-semicolon-space. For details, see chapter 2 of this *Handbook* at 2.4.

Variant Titles. Examine the resource for variant titles. Variant titles are not core in RDA, but if in your opinion a library user might attempt to find the resource using one of these titles, record it in subfield ‡a of a 246 field. Variant titles can be taken from any source (see RDA 2.3.6.2), including your own knowledge (e.g., you might record a variant to correct a misspelled word in the title). For economy's sake, most catalogers will not look beyond the resource itself for variant titles. For details, see chapter 2 of this *Handbook* at 2.3.6.

Edition Statement. Examine the resource for an edition statement. Although rare in unpublished resources, edition statements do sometimes occur. An edition statement can be taken from any source within the resource, but a statement found in the same source as the title proper is preferred. Edition statements may also be taken from outside the resource; if so, they should be bracketed.

Designation of edition is a core element, and therefore must be recorded if present in the resource. If found, transcribe a designation of edition (e.g., "Special prepublication private manuscript edition") in subfield ‡a of a 250 field (see RDA 2.5.2).

Recording other elements of the edition statement is optional in RDA. The most common other element is a statement of responsibility relating to the edition. If you find such a statement and decide to include it in the description, record it following space-slash-space in subfield ‡b of the 250 field.

For details on recording an edition statement, see chapter 2 of this *Handbook* at 2.5.

Production Statement. Examine the resource for production information, including place of production, producer, and date of production. Although information about publication can be taken from outside the resource itself (and this is common with unpublished resources), prefer information found inside the resource, and within the resource, prefer information found in the same source as the title proper. Production information is recorded in a MARC bibliographic 264 field, with the second indicator coded "0."

The place of production element is not core in RDA and, because the information is often difficult to determine, it is usually not recorded. However, if a place of production is found in the resource, you may record it in subfield ‡a of the 264 field. Transcribe the information exactly as found (see RDA 2.7.2).

Like place of production, the producer's name element is not core in RDA and, because the information is often difficult to determine, is usually not recorded. However, if a producer's name is found in the resource, you may record it in subfield ‡b of the 264 field. Transcribe the information exactly as found (see RDA 2.7.4).

Record the date of production. Record numerals in the form preferred by your cataloging agency (see RDA 1.8.2). The date of production element is core. If no explicit date of publication is found in the resource, either supply information found in another source or inferred by the cataloger, or record "Date of production not identified" (see RDA 2.7.6). Catalogers who work primarily with published materials should take note of 2.7.6.2, Sources of Information. Because the date of production can be taken from any source it is not bracketed even if the information is found outside the resource.

Because the place of production and producer's name elements are not core, the date of production will usually be recorded alone in subfield ‡c of the 264 field. However, if any preceding elements are present, place a comma immediately after the element, before the date of production element.

Describe the Carrier. A carrier is the physical medium in which the content of a resource is stored. Carriers for text on paper manuscripts include volumes and sheets, but as already mentioned manuscript resources can exist in nearly any physical medium. Examine the resource for physical details, including size and page numbering. Several carrier-related elements are required in an RDA record. Most are recorded in the 3XX block of the bibliographic record.

Extent. The extent of the resource is recorded in subfield ‡a of a MARC bibliographic 300 field. Extent is core if the resource is complete. Record the extent of an unpublished manuscript resource following the instructions in RDA 3.4 for the appropriate format. Only the most basic procedures will be mentioned in this appendix. For details, see chapter 2 of this *Handbook* at 3.4.

Text on paper manuscripts follow the instructions in RDA 3.4.5. If the resource consists of a single volume, look through the volume for sequences of numbers. Record the last number in each sequence followed by "pages," "leaves," or "columns," as appropriate. If the volume is unnumbered, follow the instructions in RDA 3.4.5.3 (e.g., "1 volume (unpaged)").

If the resource consists of more than one volume, record the number of volumes followed by the term "volumes" (e.g., "15 volumes").

If the resource consists of a sheet or sheets, record the extent as "1 sheet," "4 sheets," etc.

Record the extent of a collection following the instructions in RDA 3.4.1.11. Give the extent in terms of the number of items or containers in the collection ("43 boxes"), the storage space (libraries following LC practice will record this in terms of linear or cubic inches or feet, e.g., "12 linear ft."), the number and type of unit ("30 typescripts"), or a combination ("3 linear ft. (7 boxes)"). For details, see discussion in chapter 2 of this *Handbook* at 3.4.1.11.

Illustrative Content. Though not considered in RDA to be part of the carrier description, this element is treated here because it is recorded immediately after the extent element in the MARC bibliographic record. This element is not typically included in descriptions of archival collections, but may appear in descriptions of individual manuscripts. Examine the manuscript for illustrations, including maps. If found, and you believe that recording the information would help the library user to identify or select the resource (this element is not core), record the word "illustration" or "illustrations" in subfield ‡b of the 300 field (see RDA 7.15). Other terms may also be used, preferring terms found in the alternative list in RDA 7.15.1.3. Probably the most common of these is "map" or "maps." Record colour content (e.g., "color illustrations") (see RDA 7.17). Separate this element from the preceding extent element with space-semicolon-space.

For details on illustrative content and color content, see chapter 8 of this *Handbook* at 7.15 and 7.17.

Dimensions. The dimensions element is not core in RDA, and is not used in archival collection descriptions. However, it is usually recorded in descriptions of individual manuscripts. If recording this element, follow the instructions in RDA 3.5 for the appropriate format. Dimensions are recorded in subfield ‡c of a MARC bibliographic 300 field. Separate the dimensions element from any preceding elements in the field with space-semicolon-space.

Record the dimensions of a manuscript book following the instructions in 3.5.1.4.14. Record the height of the volume, rounding up to the nearest centimeter. Also record the width in the form height x width (e.g., 31 x 10 cm) if it is less than half of the height of the volume, or greater than the height of the volume.

Record the dimensions of a sheet following the instructions in 3.5.1.4.11. Record the height x width of the sheet, rounding up to the nearest centimeter.

For details, see chapter 2 of this *Handbook* at 3.5.1.3, 3.5.1.4.11, and 3.5.1.4.14.

Content Type. Like the illustrative content element described above, the content type element is not part of the description of the carrier, but it is treated here because it is generally the next element after the dimensions recorded in the MARC bibliographic record. Content type is a core element, and is recorded in subfield ‡a of the MARC 336 field, following the instructions in RDA 6.9. Record, as appropriate, one of the terms in the list found in RDA 6.9.1.3. End the field with "‡2 rdacontent":

336   ‡a text ‡2 rdacontent

Any of the content types listed in 6.9.1.3 are possible for manuscript resources. Some of the more common are "text" and "notated music." Multiple content types may be recorded if present in the manuscript or collection, although it is also permissible to record only the content type that applies to the predominant part of the resource. For details, see chapter 8 of this *Handbook* at 6.9.

Media and Carrier Type. Carrier type is core in an RDA description. Media type is not core, but most U.S. catalogers follow LC and PCC practice and record it (see LC-PCC PS 3.2, October 2012).

Media type is recorded in subfield ‡a of a MARC bibliographic 337 field. The term should be taken from the list in RDA 3.2.1.3. Most of the terms in 3.2.1.3 are possible for unpublished manuscript resources. End the field with "‡2 rdamedia":

337   ‡a unmediated ‡2 rdamedia

Carrier type is recorded in subfield ‡a of a MARC bibliographic 338 field. The term should be taken from the list in RDA 3.3.1.3. Most of the terms in 3.2.1.3 are possible for unpublished manuscript resources except for "online resource," because online resources are considered published. End the field with "‡2 rdacarrier":

338   ‡a volume ‡2 rdacarrier

For details, see chapter 2 of this *Handbook* at 3.2 and 3.3.

Production Method. Record the process used to create the manuscript (e.g., "typescript") in subfield ‡d of a 340 field if considered important. See chapter 2 of this *Handbook* at 3.9 for details.

System of Organization. If an archival collection is arranged in a particular way, record information about its system of organization in a MARC bibliographic 351 field. See discussion in chapter 7 of this *Handbook* at 7.8.

Series Statement. The title proper of a series and its numbering are core and therefore must be recorded if found in the resource. However, series information is very rare in manuscript resources and it is unlikely that this element will be present. For details about recording series statements, see chapter 2 of this *Handbook* at 2.12.

Notes. Include any notes you consider necessary to help the library user contextualize, find, identify, or select the resource. Notes are not core in an RDA description. Therefore, recording notes in a bibliographic record is entirely dependent on your judgment or the policies of your cataloging agency. However, bear in mind that while RDA does not require notes, other standards such as DACS or AMREMM may.

Most notes are recorded in the 5XX block of the MARC bibliographic record. Some of the more common notes included in bibliographic records for unpublished manuscripts include notes giving thesis or dissertation information (see discussion in chapter 7 of this *Handbook* at 7.9), restrictions on access (see discussion in chapter

2 of this *Handbook* at 4.4), summarization of the manuscript or scope of the collection's contents (see discussion in chapter 8 of this *Handbook* at 7.10); and custodial history (provenance) (see discussion in chapter 2 of this *Handbook* at 2.17).

Identifier for the Manifestation. Examine the resource for an identifier, defined as "a character string associated with a manifestation that serves to differentiate that manifestation from other manifestations." The identifier for the manifestation element is core (see RDA 2.15), and therefore an identifier must be recorded if present on the resource. However, it would be rare for an unpublished manuscript resource to have an identifier.

Contact Information. For archival resources, including collections, record the name of the repository, including its mailing address or other contact information, in an 852 field. For details, see chapter 2 of this *Handbook* at 4.3.

5. LINK THE RESOURCE TO RELATED ENTITIES

Once the resource has been described, links should be made to related entities. These include works and expressions that are either contained in the resource or related to the work(s) or expression(s) described in the record, and related persons, families, corporate bodies, and geographic entities.

In the MARC bibliographic format, these links are created by recording the authorized access point for the related entity in one of the access point fields, generally speaking the 1XX, 7XX, and 8XX fields. This either (1) links the bibliographic record to an associated authority record, and via that record links the bibliographic record to other bibliographic records containing the same authorized access point (either by using the text string itself, or using an identifier); (2) directly links the bibliographic record to other bibliographic records containing the same authorized access point; or (3) at the least allows searches to retrieve all bibliographic records containing the same authorized access point.

RDA requires the cataloger to record at least one relationship: that between the resource and the principal creator of the work embodied in the manifestation being described (see discussion in chapter 9 of this *Handbook* at 18.3). Recording other relationships is optional, but most catalogers will record many.

The relationship between the resource and the principal creator of the work is recorded in a 100 (persons or families), 110 (most corporate bodies), or 111 (meetings) field. If there is more than one work in the resource and they are by different creators, record these relationships in 700, 710, or 711. See chapter 9 of this *Handbook* at 19.2 for help in determining what entity is the principal creator of the work for individual manuscripts. With persons and families the decision is usually fairly straightforward. Determining if a corporate body or meeting is the creator can be a little trickier, but fairly clear guidelines are laid out at RDA 19.2.1.1.1 (see also corresponding discussion in chapter 9 of the *Handbook*).

Archival cataloging practice follows a slightly different philosophy from non-archival practice for determining the creator of a collection. The definition of creator in DACS is "a person, family, or corporate body that created, assembled, accumulated, and/or maintained and used records in the conduct of personal or corporate activity."[3] DACS chapter 9 further instructs that "for archival materials, the creator is typically the corporate body, family, or person responsible for an entire body of materials" (p. 89). This includes "artificially" collected materials: DACS gives as an example a collector of Vietnam War memorabilia (p. 89). This person, family, or corporate body is considered to be the creator of the collection.

Archival practice might seem to consider certain persons, families, or corporate bodies to be the creator of the collection that might not appear to qualify under RDA 19.2 (and especially RDA 19.2.1.1.1). RDA 19.2.1.1 brings archival practice into its scope, however, by stating:

> A person, family, or corporate body responsible for compiling an aggregate work may be considered to be a creator of the compilation if the selection, arrangement, editing, etc., of content for the compilation effectively results in the creation of a new work.

Archival collections are aggregate works of this kind. If the collection is considered as a whole and the person, family, or body responsible for assembling the collection (i.e., the intellectual activity involved in creation of the work) is thought of as the creator, archival practice may make more sense to a cataloger accustomed to the philosophy underlying non-archival practice on the question.

Begin providing links to related entities by recording the authorized access point for the principal creator of the work in a 1XX field. This form may be accompanied by a relationship designator to clarify the nature of the relationship. The use of relationship designators is optional but encouraged (see chapter 9 of this *Handbook* at 18.5).

Once the relationship to the principal creator has been recorded, think about other relationships that might be helpful. First consider other creators if there are more than one. Other commonly recorded relationships for manuscripts and archival collections include those between the resource and interviewers or transcribers. These relationships are all recorded by giving the authorized access point for the related entity in the 7XX fields: 700 (persons and families), 710 (most corporate bodies), or 711 (meetings).

Consider also relationships to related works and expressions, or the relationship between the manifestation described in the bibliographic record and the work(s) or expression(s) embodied in the manifestation. For example, an archival collection might have served as the basis for another work. Related works or expressions are recorded by giving the authorized access point for the work or expression in a 700, 710, 711, or 730 field, or in the case of a series, in an 800, 810, 811, or 830 field. Works or expressions embodied in the manifestation are recorded in a 1XX and 240 field combination or in 130 if there is only one; or if there are two or more, in 700, 710, 711, or 730 fields as appropriate. For details, see discussion throughout chapter 9 of this *Handbook*.

6. SAMPLE RECORD SETS

Other examples of manuscript cataloging in this *Handbook* include figures 2.35, 2.38, 2.62, 2.63, 2.101, 7.100, 7.101, 8.17, 8.28, 9.11, and 9.69.

RECORD SET C1
THESIS

Bibliographic Record

100 1	‡a Watry, Elizabeth A., ‡e author. *[RDA 18.3, 19.2, 18.4.1.2, 18.5]*
245 10	‡a More than mere camps and coaches : ‡b the Wylie Camping Company and the development of a middle-class leisure ethic in Yellowstone National Park, 1883-1916 / ‡c by Elizabeth Ann Watry. *[RDA 2.3, 2.4]*
264 0	‡c 2010. *[RDA 2.7.6]*
300	‡a v, 124 leaves ; ‡c 28 cm *[RDA 3.4.5.2, 3.5.1.4.14]*
336	‡a text ‡2 rdacontent *[RDA 6.9]*
337	‡a unmediated ‡2 rdamedia *[RDA 3.2]*
338	‡a volume ‡2 rdacarrier *[RDA 3.3]*
340	‡d Typescript. *[RDA 3.9.2.3]*
502	‡b MA ‡c Montana State University--Bozeman ‡d 2010 *[RDA 7.9]*
500	‡a Chairperson, Graduate Committee: Mary Murphy. *[RDA 19.3]*
504	‡a Includes bibliographical references (leaves 108-124). *[RDA 7.16]*
520	‡a This thesis examines the influences of tourism upon the American West and its relationship with Yellowstone National Park in the late nineteenth and early twentieth centuries. *[RDA 7.10]*

Title page

MORE THAN MERE CAMPS AND COACHES: THE WYLIE CAMPING COMPANY
AND THE DEVELOPMENT OF A MIDDLE-CLASS LEISURE ETHIC IN
YELLOWSTONE NATIONAL PARK, 1883-1916
by
Elizabeth Ann Watry
A thesis submitted in partial fulfillment
of the requirements for the degree of
Master of Arts in History
MONTANA STATE UNIVERSITY
Bozeman, Montana
April 2010

Associated Authority Record

100 1	‡a Watry, Elizabeth A.	*[RDA 9.2.2, 9.19.1]*
370	‡e Yellowstone National Park ‡2 lcsh	*[RDA 9.11]*
372	‡a History ‡2 lcsh	*[RDA 9.15]*
373	‡a Montana State University--Bozeman ‡2 naf	*[RDA 9.13]*
374	‡a Historians ‡2 lcsh	*[RDA 9.16]*
375	‡a female	*[RDA 9.7]*
377	‡a eng	*[RDA 9.14]*
378	‡q Elizabeth Ann	*[RDA 9.5]*
400 1	‡a Watry, Betsy	*[RDA 9.2.3, 9.19.2]*
670	‡a Whittlesey, Lee H. Yellowstone National Park, c2008: ‡b title page (Elizabeth A. Watry) page 4 of cover (Yellowstone resident and historian)	*[RDA 8.12]*
670	‡a Women in wonderland, 2012: ‡b title page (Elizabeth A. Watry) page 297 (Elizabeth "Betsy" Watry; researcher, author, speaker, independent scholar; women's historian; M.A., history, Montana State University; has written several books about Yellowstone)	*[RDA 8.12]*
670	‡a More than mere camps and coaches, 2010: ‡b title page (Elizabeth Ann Watry)	*[RDA 8.12]*

RECORD SET C2
MANUSCRIPT

Bibliographic Record

100 1	‡a Paisiello, Giovanni, ‡d 1740-1816, ‡e composer.	*[RDA 18.3, 19.2, 18.4.1.2, 18.5]*
245 12	‡a L'arabo cortese : ‡b drama giocosa / ‡c del Sigr. D. Giovanni Paisiello.	*[RDA 2.3, 2.4]*
264 0	‡a In Napoli, ‡c 1769?	*[RDA 2.7.2, 2.7.6]*
300	‡a 1 score (2 volumes) ; ‡c 23 x 31 cm	*[RDA 3.4.3, 3.4.5.16, 3.5.1.4.14]*
336	‡a notated music ‡2 rdacontent	*[RDA 6.9]*
337	‡a unmediated ‡2 rdamedia	*[RDA 3.2]*
338	‡a volume ‡2 rdacarrier	*[RDA 3.3]*
500	‡a Manuscript score.	*[RDA 2.20]*
546	‡a Italian words.	*[RDA 7.12]*
546	‡b Staff notation.	*[RDA 7.13]*
500	‡a Libretto by Pasquale Mililotti; Premiered in Naples, Winter 1769. See Robinson's Paisiello thematic catalogue, 1.22.	*[RDA 6.7, 25.1, 24.4.3b]*
561	‡a From the Collection of Marie-Louis-Fidèle de Talleyrand-Perigord.	*[RDA 2.17]*

Volume 1 title page

L'Arabo Cortese

Drama Giocosa

Del Sigr. D. Giovanni Paisiello

Atto primo

In Napoli

Associated Authority Record

046	‡f 17400509 ‡g 18160605	[RDA 9.3]
100 1	‡a Paisiello, Giovanni, ‡d 1740-1816	[RDA 9.2.2, 9.19.1]
370	‡a Roccaforzata (Italy) ‡b Naples (Italy) ‡2 naf	[RDA 9.8, 9.9]
372	‡a Opera ‡2 lcsh	[RDA 9.15]
374	‡a Composers ‡2 lcsh	[RDA 9.16]
375	‡a male	[RDA 9.7]
670	‡a 6 minuetti concertati, 1985: ‡b title page (Giovanni Paisiello)	[RDA 8.12]
670	‡a Grove Music online, 5 September 2012 ‡b (Paisiello, Giovanni; born 9 May 1740 at Roccaforzata, near Taranto; died 5 June 1816 in Naples; Italian composer. He was one of the most successful and influential opera composers of the late 18th century)	[RDA 8.12]

RECORD SET C3
COLLECTION

Bibliographic Record

110 2	‡a Combat Films and Research (Firm), ‡e creator.	[RDA 18.3, 19.2 and DACS, 18.4.1.2, 18.5]
245 10	‡a Combat Films and Research interviews on Helen Foster Snow.	[RDA 2.3.2.11.4]
264 0	‡c 1999-2000.	[RDA 2.7.6]
300	‡a 0.1 linear ft. ‡a (1 folder)	[RDA 3.4.1.11]
336	‡a two-dimensional moving image ‡2 rdacontent	[RDA 6.9]
337	‡a video ‡2 rdamedia	[RDA 3.2]
338	‡a videodisc ‡2 rdacarrier	[RDA 3.3]
506	‡a Open for public research.	[RDA 4.4]
520 2	‡a Contains six DVDs (three reference copies and three preservation copies) containing eight interviews with individuals who knew Helen Foster Snow. Individuals interviewed are An Wei, Huang Hua, Lu Cui, Gong Pusheng, Liu Lizhen, Lu Wanru, Israel Epstein, and Yu Jianting. Interviews were migrated from 16 mm film to DVD by Combat Films and Research and Dodge Billingsley, and were used in the production of the documentary Helen Foster Snow: Witness to Revolution (2000).	[RDA 7.10]

| 561 | ‡a Donated by Combat Films and Research in 2007. | *[RDA 2.17]* |
| 852 | ‡a L. Tom Perry Special Collections, Harold B. Lee Library, Brigham Young University, ‡e Provo, Utah 84602. | *[RDA 4.3]* |

Associated Authority Record

046	‡s 1997	*[RDA 11.4]*
110 2	‡a Combat Films and Research (Firm)	*[RDA 11.2.2, 11.13.1.1-2]*
370	‡e Salt Lake City (Utah) ‡2 naf	*[RDA 11.3]*
371	‡m info@combatfilms.com	*[RDA 11.9]*
372	‡a Documentation (Activity) ‡2 aat	*[RDA 11.10]*
377	‡a eng	*[RDA 11.8]*
410 2	‡a Combat Films (Firm)	*[RDA 11.2.3, 11.13.2]*
500 1	‡w r ‡i Founder: ‡a Billingsley, Dodge	*[RDA 30.1, 30.2, 29.4.2]*
670	‡a Immortal fortress, 1999: ‡b credits (Combat Films) cassette label (Combat Films and Research)	*[RDA 8.12]*
670	‡a Documentary Institute, College of Journalism and Communications, University of Florida resources page, January 5, 2004 ‡b (Combat Films and Research: "a small, conflict oriented, think-tank that uses film and video footage as its primary source for research. Sends camera crews throughout the world to document military and political conflicts")	*[RDA 8.12]*
670	‡a Combat Films and Research home page, December 6, 2011 ‡b (located in Salt Lake City, Utah; e-mail: info@combatfilms.com; founded in 1997 by Dodge Billingsley)	*[RDA 8.12]*
678 1	‡a Combat Films and Research is a documentary film production company in Salt Lake City, Utah.	*[RDA 11.11]*

NOTES

1. *Describing Archives: A Content Standard* (Chicago: Society of American Archivists, 2007).

2. Gregory A. Pass, *Descriptive Cataloging of Ancient, Medieval, and Early Modern Manuscripts* (Chicago: American Library Association, 2002).

3. DACS, 203.

NOTATED MUSIC

THIS APPENDIX CONTAINS A RECOMMENDED PROCESS FOR CREATING bibliographic records for published notated music. It covers bibliographic record creation for these resources only in the most general of terms. Unusual situations are covered in the body of the *Handbook*. As with the *Handbook* itself, this appendix does not cover non-RDA related aspects of the bibliographic record, such as fixed-length data elements (the so-called fixed fields) or subject analysis. This appendix also contains three sample record sets consisting of bibliographic records and their associated authority records, which illustrate many of the points described below.

1. DETERMINE THE MODE OF ISSUANCE

Consider the mode of issuance of the resource. Does it consist of a single unit? Is it a multipart monograph? Is it a serial or integrating resource? Mode of issuance is defined in RDA 1.1.3.

> A single-unit resource is a resource issued either as a single physical unit (e.g., a single score) or a single logical unit (e.g., a PDF file).
>
> A multipart monograph is a resource issued in two or more parts that is complete or is intended to be complete within a finite number of parts.
>
> A serial is a resource issued in successive parts, usually bearing numbering, that has no predetermined conclusion.
>
> An integrating resource is a resource that is added to or changed by means of updates that do not remain discrete but are integrated into the whole (including tangible resources such as loose-leaf publications, and intangible resources such as websites).

726 | APPENDIX D

This appendix covers single units and multipart monographs. For serials or integrating resources in any format, see appendix K.

2. DECIDE ON THE TYPE OF DESCRIPTION

Consider the type of description you want to create. RDA 1.1.4 mentions three types of description: comprehensive, analytical, and hierarchical.

> A comprehensive description describes the resource as a whole.
> An analytical description describes a part of a larger resource.
> A hierarchical description combines a comprehensive description of a whole resource with analytical descriptions of one or more of its parts.

U.S. cataloging practice does not use hierarchical descriptions; therefore these will not be described here. Analytical descriptions are described in appendix L. This appendix covers comprehensive descriptions.

3. CHOOSE THE BASIS FOR IDENTIFICATION AND SOURCES OF INFORMATION FOR THE RESOURCE

Examine the resource and choose a basis for identification following the instructions in RDA 2.1. If the resource is issued as a single-unit resource, the resource itself will be the basis for identification. If the resource is issued in more than one part, one of the parts will be chosen as the basis for identification. For printed notated music, this will usually be the first volume. For details, see chapter 2 of this *Handbook* at 2.1.

Having chosen the part that will serve as the basis for identification, choose a "preferred source of information" within that part following the instructions in RDA 2.2. The preferred source of information for printed notated music is the title page, title sheet, or title card (RDA 2.2.2.2). The preferred source of information for notated music in other formats (e.g., a CD-ROM) is a label bearing a title that is permanently printed on or affixed to the resource, embedded metadata, or another source forming part of the resource itself (RDA 2.2.2.4). For details, see chapter 2 of this *Handbook* at 2.2.

One type of title page unique to notated music is a "list" title page, a page that lists the composer's works issued by the publisher or lists related music from the publisher. Included in the list will be the title of the resource being cataloged. If this is the only source within the resource that bears a title, it may be used as the preferred source of information. Only record information from a list title page that pertains to the resource being described (e.g., do not transcribe other titles listed on the page as part of the title element).

4. DESCRIBE THE RESOURCE

Titles and Statements of Responsibility. Transcribe the title proper, other title information, and statement of responsibility in a MARC bibliographic 245 field. For information about transcription, see chapter 2 of this *Handbook* at 1.7.

Transcribe the title proper in subfield ‡a of the 245 field exactly as found on the preferred source of information (see RDA 2.3.2). Title proper is a core element and so must be included in the description. For details, see chapter 2 of this *Handbook* at 2.3.

If the title proper consists *only* of the name of a type of composition, such as "sonata," followed by a medium of performance (e.g., "for clarinet"), key (e.g., "in A major"), opus number (e.g., "no. 7"), etc., treat all this information as the title proper. On the other hand, if the title is not the name of a type of composition (e.g., "Don Giovanni" or "The Pastoral Symphony"), any mention of medium of performance, key, number, etc., on the preferred source will be treated as other title information (see RDA 2.3.2.8.1).

Transcription of other title information is optional in RDA, although core for the Library of Congress. Most U.S. catalogers will follow LC practice and include other title information in the description. If including other title information, transcribe it after the title proper in subfield ‡b of the 245 field (see RDA 2.3.4). Other title information should be transcribed from the same source as the title proper. The first piece of other title information is separated from the title proper by space-colon-space. Subsequent pieces of other title information are separated from each other by space-colon-space. For details, see chapter 2 of this *Handbook* at 2.3.4.

The first statement of responsibility relating to the title proper is a core element in RDA. Other statements of responsibility are optional, although most catalogers will record them. If including statements of responsibility in the description, transcribe them after the title proper or other information in subfield ‡c of the 245 field (see RDA 2.4.1 and 2.4.2). Statements of responsibility may be transcribed from any source within the resource itself. In unusual situations, a statement of responsibility may be transcribed from outside the resource itself, but in that case it should be bracketed. This will rarely be necessary. The first statement of responsibility is separated from the title proper (or other title information) by space-slash-space. Subsequent statements of responsibility are separated from each other by space-semicolon-space. For details, see chapter 2 of this *Handbook* at 2.4.

Variant Titles. Examine the resource for variant titles. Variant titles are not core in RDA, but if in your opinion a library user might attempt to find the resource using one of these titles, record it in subfield ‡a of a 246 field. Variant titles can be taken from any source (see RDA 2.3.6.2), including your own knowledge (e.g., you might record a variant to correct a misspelled word in the title). For economy's sake, most catalogers will not look beyond the resource itself for variant titles. For details, see chapter 2 of this *Handbook* at 2.3.6.

Edition Statement. Examine the resource for an edition statement. An edition statement can be taken from any source within the resource, but a statement found in the same source as the title proper is preferred. Edition statements may also be taken from outside the resource; if so, they should be bracketed.

Designation of edition is a core element, and so must be recorded if present in the resource. If found, transcribe a designation of edition (e.g., "Edition for two pianos") in subfield ‡a of a 250 field (see RDA 2.5.2).

Recording other elements of the edition statement is optional in RDA. The most common other element is a statement of responsibility relating to the edition. If you find such a statement and decide to include it in the description, record it following space-slash-space in subfield ‡b of the 250 field.

For details on recording an edition statement, see chapter 2 of this *Handbook* at 2.5.

Publication Statement. Examine the resource for publication information, including place of publication, publisher, and date of publication. Although information about publication can be taken from outside the resource itself, prefer information found inside the resource, and within the resource, prefer information found in the same source as the title proper. Publication information is recorded in a MARC bibliographic 264 field, with the second indicator coded "1."

Record the first place of publication found in the resource in subfield ‡a of the 264 field. Transcribe the information exactly as found. This element is core. If no place is found in the resource either supply (in brackets) information from another source about the place of publication, or record "[Place of publication not identified]." If more than one place of publication is found in the resource, you may optionally record them all, but only the first is required. For details, see chapter 2 of this *Handbook* at 2.8.2.

Record the first publisher associated with the first place of publication found in the resource in subfield ‡b of the 264 field. Transcribe the information exactly as found. This element is core. If no publisher is found in the resource either supply (in brackets) information about the publisher from another source, or record "[Publisher not identified]." Separate the place of publication from the publisher's name with space-colon-space. If more than one publisher is found in the resource, you may optionally record them all, but only the first is required. For details, see chapter 2 of this *Handbook* at 2.8.4.

Record the date of publication. Record numerals in the form preferred by your cataloging agency (see RDA 1.8.2). Place a comma immediately after the publisher's name and record the date of publication in subfield ‡c of the 264 field. The date of publication element is core. If no explicit date of publication is found in the resource (a common situation with notated music), either supply (in brackets) information found in another source or inferred by the cataloger, or record "[Date of publication not identified]." Note that a copyright date is not a publication date. A copyright date can never be substituted for a publication date in RDA, but it may optionally be recorded in addition to the date of publication element. It may also be used as evidence for inferring the date of publication. Caution, however: because notated music is often published by simply reproducing earlier publications photographically, a copyright date may not be good evidence for the publication date of notated music.

If the date of publication has not been identified, then either a date of distribution or a copyright date, if present in the resource, must be recorded (see discussion, however, in chapter 2 of this *Handbook* at 2.8.6.6 on ways to identify the date of publication). If recording a copyright date, include the copyright symbol (©) and record it in subfield ‡c of a separate 264 field, with the second indicator coded "4."

For details about publication statement and copyright date, see chapter 2 of this *Handbook* at 2.8 and 2.11.

Distribution Statement. The distribution statement element is not core if publication information has been recorded. However, information about distributors is considered important to users of records for notated music, so it is usually recorded if present. Record distribution information in the same way as publication information, but record it in a MARC bibliographic 264 field with the second indicator coded "2." For details, see chapter 2 of this *Handbook* at 2.9.

Describe the Carrier. A carrier is the physical medium in which the content of a resource is stored. Carriers for printed notated music include volumes and sheets. Examine the resource for physical details, including size and page numbering. Several carrier-related elements are required in an RDA record. Most are recorded in the 3XX block of the bibliographic record.

Extent. The extent of the resource is recorded in subfield ‡a of a MARC bibliographic 300 field. Extent is core if the resource is complete. Record the extent of notated music following the instructions in RDA 3.4.3. Record the number of units with a term for the format of the music from the list in 7.20.1.3. Then add, in parentheses, the number of volumes, pages, etc., following the instructions of 3.4.5. For details, see chapter 2 of this *Handbook* at 3.4.3.

Illustrative Content. Though not considered in RDA to be part of the carrier description, this element is treated here because it is recorded immediately after the extent element in the MARC bibliographic record. Examine the resource for illustrations. If found, and you think recording the information would help the library user to identify or select the resource (this element is not core), record the word "illustration" or "illustrations" in subfield ‡b of the 300 field (see RDA 7.15). Other terms may also be used, preferring terms found in the alternative list in RDA 7.15.1.3. One term from this list that will almost never be used in a description of notated music is "music." The fact that the resource contains music is specified by the content type "notated music" (see below).

Record colour content (e.g., "color illustrations") (see RDA 7.17). Separate this element from the preceding extent element with space-semicolon-space.

For details on illustrative content and color content, see chapter 8 of this *Handbook* at 7.15 and 7.17.

Dimensions. The dimensions element is not core in RDA, but it is core in descriptions of monographs (including notated music) for catalogers at the Library of Congress, except for online electronic resources (see LC-PCC PS 3.5, May 2012). Most U.S. catalogers will record this element. Dimensions are recorded in subfield ‡c of a MARC bibliographic 300 field. Separate the dimensions element from any preceding elements in the field with space-semicolon-space.

Record the dimensions of a resource containing notated music following the appropriate instruction in 3.5.1.4. The most common carriers for notated music are volumes and sheets.

Record the height of a volume, rounding up to the nearest centimeter. Also record the width in the form height x width (e.g., 31 x 10 cm) if it is less than half of the height of the volume, or greater than the height of the volume (see RDA 3.5.1.4.14).

Record the dimensions of a sheet following the instructions in 3.5.1.4.11. Record the height x width of the sheet, rounding up to the nearest centimeter.

If the record has a series statement, record a period at the end of the field.

For details, see chapter 2 of this *Handbook* at 3.5.1.3, 3.5.1.4.11, and 3.5.1.4.14.

Content Type. Like the illustrative content element described above, the content type element is not part of the description of the carrier, but it is treated here because it is generally the next element after the dimensions recorded in the MARC bibliographic record. Content type is a core element, and is recorded in subfield ‡a of the MARC 336 field following the instructions in RDA 6.9. Record, as appropriate, one of the terms in the list found in RDA 6.9.1.3. End the field with "‡2 rdacontent":

    336   ‡a notated music ‡2 rdacontent

The content type for this kind of resource is "notated music." If illustrations are present "still image" may also be appropriate and may be recorded in addition to "notated music." For details, see chapter 8 of this *Handbook* at 6.9.

Media and Carrier Type. Carrier type is core in an RDA description. Media type is not core, but most U.S. catalogers follow LC and PCC practice and record it (see LC-PCC PS 3.2, October 2012).

Media type is recorded in subfield ‡a of a MARC bibliographic 337 field. The term should be taken from the list in RDA 3.2.1.3. For printed notated music, use "unmediated." Other media types are possible depending on the format. End the field with "‡2 rdamedia":

    337   ‡a unmediated ‡2 rdamedia

Carrier type is recorded in subfield ‡a of a MARC bibliographic 338 field. The term should be taken from the list in RDA 3.3.1.3. Most of the unmediated terms there might be used to describe printed notated music, but the most common are "volume" (for a multipage printed monograph) or "sheet" (for a single-sheet publication). Most of the other carrier types are also possible, depending on the format of the notated music. End the field with "‡2 rdacarrier":

> 338   ‡a volume ‡2 rdacarrier

For details, see chapter 2 of this *Handbook* at 3.2 and 3.3.

Series Statement. Examine the resource for a series statement. Although information about a series can be taken from outside the resource itself, prefer information found in the resource, and within the resource prefer information found on a series title page. Series information is recorded in a MARC bibliographic 490 field. The first indicator is coded "0" if the information is not indexed; it is coded "1" if the information is indexed (in which case an 8XX field will also be present in the bibliographic record; see below under Link the Resource to Related Entities).

Record the title proper of the series in subfield ‡a of the 490 field exactly as it appears in the resource. If series numbering is present, record it in subfield ‡v following the title proper of the series and any other elements (such as a statement of responsibility). Separate series numbering from preceding elements by space-semicolon-space.

The title proper of the series and numbering are core and so must be recorded if present. Other title information of the series and statements of responsibility relating to the series are not core and are not in most cases recorded. For details about recording series statements, see chapter 2 of this *Handbook* at 2.12.

Notes. Include any notes you consider necessary to help the library user contextualize, find, identify, or select the resource. No notes are core in an RDA description. Therefore, recording notes in a bibliographic record is entirely dependent on your judgment or the policies of your cataloging agency. Most notes are recorded in the 5XX block of the MARC bibliographic record. Some of the more common notes included in bibliographic records for notated music resources are notes giving details about the form of composition (see discussion in chapter 7 of this *Handbook* at 6.3) or medium of performance (see discussion in chapter 8 of this *Handbook* at 7.21); the resource's musical notation (see discussion in chapter 8 of this *Handbook* at 7.13) or language (see discussion in chapter 8 of this *Handbook* at 7.12); the duration of a performance (see discussion in chapter 8 of this *Handbook* at 7.22); and contents notes (see discussion in chapter 9 of this *Handbook* at RDA chapter 25, under Whole-Part Work Relationships).

Identifier for the Manifestation. Examine the resource for an identifier, defined as "a character string associated with a manifestation that serves to differentiate that manifestation from other manifestations." The identifier for the manifestation element is core (see RDA 2.15) and so an identifier must be recorded if present on the resource.

A relatively common identifier found in contemporary printed notated music resources is an ISBN (International Standard Book Number). Record an ISBN in subfield ‡a of the 020 field of the MARC bibliographic record. Copy it as found, but do not record hyphens. The International Standard Music Number (ISMN), if present, is recorded in the MARC 024 field with the first indicator coded "3." For details, see chapter 2 of this *Handbook* at 2.15.1.4. Other common identifiers for notated music resources are publisher's numbers and plate numbers. These are recorded in the MARC 028 field. For details, see chapter 2 of this *Handbook* at 2.15.2 and 2.15.3.

5. LINK THE RESOURCE TO RELATED ENTITIES

Once the resource has been described, links should be made to related entities. These include works and expressions either contained in the resource or related to the work(s) or expression(s) described in the record, and related persons, families, corporate bodies, and geographic entities.

In the MARC bibliographic format these links are created by recording the authorized access point for the related entity in one of the access point fields, generally speaking the 1XX, 7XX, and 8XX fields. This either (1) links the bibliographic record to an associated authority record, and via that record links the bibliographic record to other bibliographic records containing the same authorized access point (either by using the text string itself, or using an identifier); (2) directly links the bibliographic record to other bibliographic records containing the same authorized access point; or (3) at the least allows searches to retrieve all bibliographic records containing the same authorized access point.

RDA requires the cataloger to record at least one relationship: that between the resource and the principal creator of the work embodied in the manifestation being described (see discussion in chapter 9 of this *Handbook* at 18.3). Recording most other relationships is optional, but most catalogers will record many.

The relationship between the resource and the principal creator of the work is recorded in a 100 (persons or families), 110 (most corporate bodies), or 111 (meetings) field. If there is more than one work in the resource and they are by different creators, record these relationships in 700, 710, or 711. See chapter 9 of this *Handbook* at 19.2 for help in determining what entity is the principal creator of the work. With persons and families the decision is usually fairly straightforward. Determining if a corporate body or meeting is the creator can be a little trickier, but fairly clear guidelines are laid out at RDA 19.2.1.1.1 (and see corresponding discussion in chapter 9 of the *Handbook*).

Begin by recording the authorized access point for the principal creator of the work in a 1XX field. This form may be accompanied by a relationship designator to clarify the nature of the relationship. The use of relationship designators is optional but encouraged (see chapter 9 of this *Handbook* at 18.5). A common relationship designator for creators of notated music resources is "composer." Note that in a change from U.S. practice under AACR2, the creator of a libretto in RDA is the author of the text, not the composer of the music (see discussion in chapter 7 of this *Handbook* at 6.27.4.2).

Once the relationship to the principal creator has been recorded, think about other relationships that might be helpful. First consider other creators if there are more than one. Other commonly recorded relationships for notated music resources include those between the resource and arrangers or editors. These relationships are all recorded by giving the authorized access point for the related entity in 7XX fields: 700 (persons and families), 710 (most corporate bodies), or 711 (meetings).

Consider also relationships to related works and expressions, or the relationship between the manifestation described in the bibliographic record and the work(s) or expression(s) embodied in the manifestation. Related works or expressions are recorded by giving the authorized access point for the work or expression in a 700, 710, 711, or 730 field, or in the case of a series, in an 800, 810, 811, or 830 field. Works or expressions embodied in the manifestation are recorded in a 1XX and 240 field combination or in 130 if there is only one; or if there are two or more, in 700, 710, 711, or 730 fields as appropriate. For details, see discussion throughout chapter 9 of this *Handbook*.

6. SAMPLE RECORD SETS

Other examples of cataloging of published notated music in this *Handbook* include figures 2.8, 2.26, 2.28, 2.29, 2.36, 2.46, 2.56, 2.57, 8.21, 8.26, 9.5, 9.54, 9.55, and 9.66.

RECORD SET D1
SINGLE UNIT

Bibliographic Record

024	1	‡a 680160582549	*[RDA 2.15.1.4]*
028	32	‡a 521-11 ‡b Peer Music	*[RDA 2.15.1.2]*
028	32	‡a HL00229283 ‡b Hal Leonard	*[RDA 2.15.1.2]*
100	1	‡a Saygun, Ahmed Adnan, ‡e composer.	*[RDA 18.3, 19.2, 18.4.1.2, 18.5]*
240	10	‡a Partitas, ‡m cello, ‡n op. 31	*[RDA 17.4.2.2]*
245	10	‡a Partita for violoncello alone / ‡c A. Adnan Saygun.	*[RDA 2.3, 2.4]*
264	1	‡a New York : ‡b Peer Music, ‡c [2012?]	*[RDA 2.8]*
264	2	‡a Milwaukee, WI : ‡b Hal Leonard	*[RDA 2.9]*
264	4	‡c ©1960	*[RDA 2.11]*
300		‡a 1 score (12 pages) ; ‡c 29 cm	*[RDA 3.4.3, 3.4.5.2, 3.5.1.4.14]*
336		‡a notated music ‡2 rdacontent	*[RDA 6.9]*
337		‡a unmediated ‡2 rdamedia	*[RDA 3.2]*
338		‡a volume ‡2 rdacarrier	*[RDA 3.3]*
546		‡b Staff notation.	*[RDA 7.13]*
500		‡a "Op. 31"--Caption.	*[RDA 2.20]*

Title page

A. Adnan Saygun
Partita
for Violoncello alone
peer music
CLASSICAL NEW YORK · HAMBURG

First page of music

©1960 by Southern Music

Back cover

peer music   Milwaukee WI
CLASSICAL NEW YORK · HAMBURG   Exclusively distributed by Hal Leonard

Associated Authority Records

046	ǂf 19070907 ǂg 19910106	[RDA 9.3]
100 1	ǂa Saygun, Ahmed Adnan	[RDA 9.2.2, 9.19.1]
370	ǂa İzmir (Turkey) ǂb Istanbul (Turkey) ǂ2 naf	[RDA 9.8, 9.9]
374	ǂa Composers ǂ2 lcsh	[RDA 9.16]
375	ǂa male	[RDA 9.7]
400 1	ǂa Saygun, A. Adnan ǂq (Ahmed Adnan)	[RDA 9.2.3, 9.19.2]
670	ǂa Yunus Emre, 1946: ǂb title page (Ahmed Adnan Saygun)	[RDA 8.12]
670	ǂa Musiki temel bilgisi, 1971- : ǂb volume 1, title page (A. Adnan Saygun)	[RDA 8.12]
670	ǂa Grove Music Online, WWW site, July 9, 2004: ǂb Opera (Saygun, Ahmed Adnan; born September 7, 1907, Izmir; died January 6, 1991, Istanbul. Turkish composer)	[RDA 8.12]
678 0	ǂa Ahmed Adnan Saygun (1907-1991) was a Turkish composer.	[RDA 9.17]

046	ǂk 1954	[RDA 6.4]
100 1	ǂa Saygun, Ahmed Adnan. ǂt Partitas, ǂm cello, ǂn op. 31	[6.14.2, 6.28.1]
380	ǂa Suites ǂ2 lcsh	[RDA 6.3]
382	ǂa cello	[RDA 6.15]
383	ǂb op. 31	[RDA 6.16]
670	ǂa Saygun, A. A. Partita for violoncello alone, c1960: ǂb title page (Partita for violoncello alone) caption (op. 31)	[RDA 5.8]
670	ǂa Wikipedia, 7 September 2012 ǂb (Op. 31, Partita for Cello, 1954)	[RDA 5.8]

RECORD SET D2
SINGLE UNIT

Bibliographic Record

020	‡a 0853608563	*[RDA 2.15]*
028 32	‡a NOV 890183 ‡b Novello	*[RDA 2.15.1.2]*
100 1	‡a Bainbridge, Simon, ‡d 1952- ‡e composer.	*[RDA 18.3, 19.2, 18.4.1.2, 18.5]*
245 10	‡a Ad ora incerta : ‡b four orchestral songs from Primo Levi, 1994 / ‡c Simon Bainbridge.	*[RDA 2.3, 2.4]*
250	‡a Study score.	*[RDA 2.5]*
264 1	‡a London : ‡b Novello, ‡c [1997?]	*[RDA 2.8]*
264 4	‡c ©1994	*[RDA 2.11]*
300	‡a 1 score (110 pages) ; ‡c 30 cm	*[RDA 3.4.3, 3.4.5.2, 3.5.1.4.14]*
336	‡a notated music ‡2 rdacontent	*[RDA 6.9]*
337	‡a unmediated ‡2 rdamedia	*[RDA 3.2]*
338	‡a volume ‡2 rdacarrier	*[RDA 3.3]*
500	‡a For mezzo-soprano, bassoon, and orchestra.	*[RDA 7.21]*
500	‡a "Received the 1997 Grawemeyer Award for musical composition."--Page iv.	*[RDA 7.28]*
546	‡a Italian words, printed also as text preceding score with parallel English translation.	*[RDA 7.12]*
546	‡b Staff notation.	*[RDA 7.13]*
500	‡a Duration: approximately 30 minutes.	*[RDA 7.22]*
505 0	‡a Il canto del corvo = The crow's song -- Il tramonto di Fossoli = Sunset at Fossoli -- Lunedì = Monday -- Buna.	*[RDA 25.1, 24.4.3a]*
700 1	‡i Musical setting of (work): ‡a Levi, Primo. ‡t Canto del corvo.	*[RDA 25.1, 24.4.2, 24.5]*
700 1	‡i Musical setting of (work): ‡a Levi, Primo. ‡t Tramonto di Fossoli.	*[RDA 25.1, 24.4.2, 24.5]*
700 1	‡i Musical setting of (work): ‡a Levi, Primo. ‡t Lunedì.	*[RDA 25.1, 24.4.2, 24.5]*
700 1	‡i Musical setting of (work): ‡a Levi, Primo. ‡t Buna.	*[RDA 25.1, 24.4.2, 24.5]*
700 1	‡a Levi, Primo, ‡e lyricist.	*[RDA 20.2, 18.4.1.2, 18.5]*

Title page
SIMON BAINBRIDGE
Ad Ora Incerta
four orchestral songs from Primo Levi
1994
Study score
NOVELLO
Order No: NOV 890183

Associated Authority Records

046	ǂf 19520830	*[RDA 9.3]*
100 1	ǂa Bainbridge, Simon, ǂd 1952-	*[RDA 9.2.2, 9.19.1]*
370	ǂa London (England) ǂ2 naf	*[RDA 9.8]*
374	ǂa Composers ǂ2 lcsh	*[RDA 9.16]*
375	ǂa male	*[RDA 9.7]*
378	ǂq Simon Jeremy	*[RDA 9.5]*
670	ǂa String quartet, 1974: ǂb title page (Simon Bainbridge)	*[RDA 8.12]*
670	ǂa Baker's biographical dictionary of musicians, 2001 ǂb (Bainbridge, Simon (Jeremy); born Aug. 30, 1952, London; English composer)	*[RDA 8.12]*
678	ǂa Simon Bainbridge (1952-) is an English composer.	*[RDA 9.17]*

046	ǂf 19190731 ǂg 19870411	*[RDA 9.3]*
100 1	ǂa Levi, Primo	*[RDA 9.2.2, 9.19.1]*
370	ǂa Turin (Italy) ǂb Turin (Italy) ǂ2 naf	*[RDA 9.8, 9.9]*
374	ǂa Chemists ǂa Poets ǂ2 lcsh	*[RDA 9.16]*
375	ǂa male	*[RDA 9.7]*
377	ǂa ita	*[RDA 9.14]*
378	ǂq Primo Michele	*[RDA 9.5]*
670	ǂa The collected poems of Primo Levi, 1988	*[RDA 8.12]*
670	ǂa Wikipedia, 8 September 2012 ǂb (Primo Michele Levi; born July 31, 1919 in Turin; died April 11, 1987 in Turin) was an Italian Jewish chemist and writer.	*[RDA 8.12]*
678	ǂa Primo Levi (1919-1987) was an Italian chemist and writer.	*[RDA 9.17]*

046	ǂk 19460109	*[RDA 6.4]*
100 1	ǂa Levi, Primo. ǂt Canto del corvo	*[6.2.2, 6.27.1]*
380	ǂa Poems ǂ2 aat	*[RDA 6.3]*
400 1	ǂa Levi, Primo. ǂt Ad ora incerta. ǂp Canto del corvo	*[RDA 6.2.3, 6.27.4]*
670	ǂa Bainbridge, S. Ad ora incerta : four orchestral songs from Primo Levi, 1997: ǂb page 1(Il canto del corvo)	*[RDA 5.8]*
670	ǂa Levi, P. Ad ora incerta, 1990: ǂb page 16 (Il canto del corvo; written 9 January 1946)	*[RDA 5.8]*

046	ǂk 19460207	*[RDA 6.4]*
100 1	ǂa Levi, Primo. ǂt Tramonto di Fossoli	*[6.2.2, 6.27.1]*
380	ǂa Poems ǂ2 aat	*[RDA 6.3]*
400 1	ǂa Levi, Primo. ǂt Ad ora incerta. ǂp Tramonto di Fossoli	*[RDA 6.2.3, 6.27.4]*

| 670 | ‡a Bainbridge, S. Ad ora incerta : four orchestral songs from Primo Levi, 1997: ‡b page 52 (Il tramonto di Fossoli) | *[RDA 5.8]* |

| 670 | ‡a Levi, P. Ad ora incerta, 1990: ‡b page 24 (Il tramonto di Fossoli; written 7 February 1946) | *[RDA 5.8]* |

046	‡k 19460117	*[RDA 6.4]*
100 1	‡a Levi, Primo. ‡t Lunedì	*[6.2.2, 6.27.1]*
380	‡a Poems ‡2 aat	*[RDA 6.3]*
400 1	‡a Levi, Primo. ‡t Ad ora incerta. ‡p Lunedì	*[RDA 6.2.3, 6.27.4]*
670	‡a Bainbridge, S. Ad ora incerta : four orchestral songs from Primo Levi, 1997: ‡b page 55 (Lunedi)	*[RDA 5.8]*
670	‡a Levi, P. Ad ora incerta, 1990: ‡b page 19 (Lunedì; written 17 January 1946)	*[RDA 5.8]*

046	‡k 19451228	*[RDA 6.4]*
100 1	‡a Levi, Primo. ‡t Buna	*[6.2.2, 6.27.1]*
380	‡a Poems ‡2 aat	*[RDA 6.3]*
400 1	‡a Levi, Primo. ‡t Ad ora incerta. ‡p Buna	*[RDA 6.2.3, 6.27.4]*
670	‡a Bainbridge, S. Ad ora incerta : four orchestral songs from Primo Levi, 1997: ‡b page 71 (Buna)	*[RDA 5.8]*
670	‡a Levi, P. Ad ora incerta, 1990: ‡b page 13 (Buna; written 28 December 1945)	*[RDA 5.8]*

RECORD SET D3
MULTIPART MONOGRAPH

Bibliographic Record

245 00	‡a Carols from around the world : ‡b for lever and pedal harp without exception / ‡c arranged by Ray Pool.	*[RDA 2.3, 2.4]*
264 1	‡a [New York] : ‡b Ray Pool, ‡c [2010-2011]	*[RDA 2.8]*
264 4	‡c ©2010-©2011	*[RDA 2.11]*
300	‡a 1 score (2 volumes) ; ‡c 28 cm	*[RDA 3.4.3, 3.4.5.16, 3.5.1.4.14]*
336	‡a notated music ‡2 rdacontent	*[RDA 6.9]*
337	‡a unmediated ‡2 rdamedia	*[RDA 3.2]*
338	‡a volume ‡2 rdacarrier	*[RDA 3.3]*
500	‡a Includes notes by the arranger.	*[RDA 7.16]*
500	‡a Lead sheets are provided for ensemble playing.	*[RDA 2.20]*
546	‡b Staff notation.	*[RDA 7.13]*

505 0	‡a volume 1. Austria: Still, still, still -- Czechoslovakia: Come, all ye shepherds ; Rocking -- England: Away in a manger ; In the bleak midwinter ; The holly and the ivy -- Ireland: The snow lay on the ground -- Poland: Infant holy, infant lowly ; Lullaby, Jesus ; O come rejoicing.	*[RDA 25.1, 24.4.3a]*
505 0	‡a volume 2. Canada: The Huron carol -- Germany: Good Christian men, rejoice -- O Christmas tree -- Italy: Tu scendi dalle stelle - France: The sleep of the infant Jesus ; Bring a torch Jeannette, Isabelle ; March of the three kings ; Pat-a-pan -- Spain: Fum, fum, fum ; The icy December.	*[RDA 25.1, 24.4.3a]*
700 1	‡a Pool, Ray, ‡e arranger of music.	*[RDA 20.2, 18.4.1.2, 18.5]*

Title page of volume 1

Carols from Around the World
Volume 1
for Lever and Pedal Harp
without exception
Austria, Czechoslovakia, England, Ireland, Poland
arranged by Ray Pool
©2010 by Ray Pool
All Rights Reserved International Copyright Secured
Printed in the USA

Associated Authority Record

046	‡f 1947	*[RDA 9.3]*
100 1	‡a Pool, Ray	*[RDA 9.2.2, 9.19.1]*
375	‡a male	*[RDA 9.7]*
400 1	‡a Pool, Raymond E.	*[RDA 9.2.3, 9.19.2]*
670	‡a South Pacific, 1997: ‡b title page (Ray Pool)	*[RDA 8.12]*
670	‡a Copyright history monograph file, 15 January 2006 ‡b (Access points: Pool, Ray; Pool, Raymond E., 1947-)	*[RDA 8.12]*

AUDIO RECORDINGS

THIS APPENDIX CONTAINS A RECOMMENDED PROCESS FOR CREAT-
ing bibliographic records for audio recordings. It covers bibliographic record creation for these resources only in the most general of terms. Unusual situations are covered in the body of the *Handbook*. As with the *Handbook* itself, this appendix does not cover non-RDA related aspects of the bibliographic record, such as fixed-length data elements (the so-called fixed fields) or subject analysis. This appendix also contains three sample record sets consisting of bibliographic records and their associated authority records, which illustrate many of the points described below.

1. DETERMINE THE MODE OF ISSUANCE

Consider the mode of issuance of the resource. Does it consist of a single unit? Is it a multipart monograph? Is it a serial or integrating resource? Mode of issuance is defined in RDA 1.1.3.

> A single-unit resource is a resource issued either as a single physical unit (e.g., a single cassette tape) or a single logical unit (e.g., a streaming audio file).
> A multipart monograph is a resource issued in two or more parts that is complete or is intended to be complete within a finite number of parts (e.g., an audiobook on ten compact discs).
> A serial is a resource issued in successive parts, usually bearing numbering, that has no predetermined conclusion.
> An integrating resource is a resource that is added to or changed by means of updates that do not remain discrete but are integrated into the whole.

This appendix covers single units and multipart monographs. For serials or integrating resources in any format, see appendix K.

2. DECIDE ON THE TYPE OF DESCRIPTION

Consider the type of description you want to create. RDA 1.1.4 mentions three types of description: comprehensive, analytical, and hierarchical.

> A comprehensive description describes the resource as a whole.
> An analytical description describes a part of a larger resource.
> A hierarchical description combines a comprehensive description of a whole resource with analytical descriptions of one or more of its parts.

U.S. cataloging practice does not use hierarchical descriptions; therefore, these will not be described here. Analytical descriptions are described in appendix L. This appendix covers comprehensive descriptions.

3. CHOOSE THE BASIS FOR IDENTIFICATION AND SOURCES OF INFORMATION FOR THE RESOURCE

Examine the resource and choose a basis for identification following the instructions in RDA 2.1. If the resource is issued as a single-unit resource, the resource itself will be the basis for identification. If the resource is issued in more than one part, one of the parts will be chosen as the basis for identification. For an audio recording, this will usually be the first unit (e.g., a disc or cassette). For details, see chapter 2 of this *Handbook* at 2.1.

Having chosen the part that will serve as the basis for identification, choose a "preferred source of information" within that part following the instructions in RDA 2.2. The preferred source of information for audio recordings is either a label bearing a title that is permanently printed on or affixed to the resource, or, for digital audio, embedded metadata in textual form that contains a title (RDA 2.2.2.4). If neither a label nor metadata are available, another source that is part of the resource itself may be used, including accompanying material or a container. For details, see chapter 2 of this *Handbook* at 2.2.

4. DESCRIBE THE RESOURCE

Titles and Statements of Responsibility. Transcribe the title proper, other title information, and statement of responsibility in a MARC bibliographic 245 field. For information about transcription, see chapter 2 of this *Handbook* at 1.7.

Transcribe the title proper in subfield ‡a of the 245 field exactly as found on the preferred source of information (e.g., the disc or cassette label) (see RDA 2.3.2). Title proper is a core element and therefore must be included in the description. For details, see chapter 2 of this *Handbook* at 2.3. For titles of musical works, see chapter 2 of this *Handbook* at 2.3.2.8.1.

Transcription of other title information is optional in RDA, although core for the Library of Congress. Most U.S. catalogers will follow LC practice and include other title information in the description. If including other title information, transcribe it after the title proper in subfield ‡b of the 245 field (see RDA 2.3.4). Other title information should be transcribed from the same source as the title proper. The first piece of other title information is separated from the title proper by space-colon-space. Subsequent pieces of other title information are separated from each other by space-colon-space. For details, see chapter 2 of this *Handbook* at 2.3.4.

Statements of responsibility for audio recordings are generally recorded just like those on any other type of resource. However, there are a couple of exceptions noted in the scope statement at RDA 2.4.1.1: (1) statements identifying performers of music who do no more than perform, execute, or interpret the music; (2) other persons or bodies who perform, narrate, or present; (3) or persons who have contributed to the artistic or technical production of the resource are omitted from the statement of responsibility and the information is instead recorded in a note (see below under Notes: Performer, Narrator, and/or Presenter, and Artistic and/ or Technical Credit).

The first statement of responsibility relating to the title proper is a core element in RDA. Other statements of responsibility are optional, although most catalogers will record them. If including statements of responsibility in the description, transcribe them after the title proper or other information in subfield ‡c of the 245 field (see RDA 2.4.1 and 2.4.2). Statements of responsibility may be transcribed from any source within the resource itself. In unusual situations, a statement of responsibility may be transcribed from outside the resource itself, but in that case it should be bracketed. This will rarely be necessary. The first statement of responsibility is separated from the title proper (or other title information) by space-slash-space. Subsequent statements of responsibility are separated from each other by space-semicolon-space. For details, see chapter 2 of this *Handbook* at 2.4.

Variant Titles. Examine the resource for variant titles. Variant titles are not core in RDA, but if in your opinion a library user might attempt to find the resource using one of these titles, record it in subfield ‡a of a 246 field. Variant titles can be taken from any source (see RDA 2.3.6.2), including your own knowledge (for example, you might record a variant to correct a misspelled word in the title). For economy's sake, most catalogers will not look beyond the resource itself for variant titles. For details, see chapter 2 of this *Handbook* at 2.3.6.

Edition Statement. Examine the resource for an edition statement. An edition statement can be taken from any source within the resource, but a statement found in the same source as the title proper is preferred. Edition statements may also be taken from outside the resource, but if so, they should be bracketed.

Designation of edition is a core element, and therefore must be recorded if present in the resource. If found, transcribe a designation of edition (for example, "Unabridged") in subfield ‡a of a 250 field (see RDA 2.5.2).

Recording other elements of the edition statement is optional in RDA. The most common other element is a statement of responsibility relating to the edition. If you find such a statement and decide to include it in the description, record it following space-slash-space in subfield ‡b of the 250 field.

For details on recording an edition statement, see chapter 2 of this *Handbook* at 2.5.

Publication Statement. Examine the resource for publication information, including place of publication, publisher, and date of publication. Although information about publication can be taken from outside the resource itself, prefer information found inside the resource, and within the resource, prefer information found in the same source as the title proper. Publication information is recorded in a MARC bibliographic 264 field, with the second indicator coded "1."

Record the first place of publication found in the resource in subfield ‡a of the 264 field. Transcribe the information exactly as found. This element is core. If no place is found in the resource either supply (in brackets) information from another source about the place of publication, or record "[Place of publication not identified]." The cataloger of audio resources must frequently search to find the place of publication because this information is often omitted from the resource. There are a number of useful reference sources that give this information, but the easiest way to find a place associated with a publisher is to search for the publisher's web page, which usually gives a location (often under "contact us").

If more than one place of publication is found in the resource, you may optionally record them all, but only the first is required. For details, see chapter 2 of this *Handbook* at 2.8.2.

Record the first publisher associated with the first place of publication found in the resource in subfield ‡b of the 264 field. Transcribe the information exactly as found. This element is core. If no publisher is found in the resource either supply (in brackets) information about the publisher from another source, or record "[Publisher not identified]." Separate the place of publication from the publisher's name with space-colon-space. If more than one publisher is found in the resource, you may optionally record them all, but only the first is required. For details, see chapter 2 of this *Handbook* at 2.8.4.

Record the date of publication. Record numerals in the form preferred by your cataloging agency (see RDA 1.8.2). Place a comma immediately after the publisher's name and record the date of publication in subfield ‡c of the 264 field. The date of publication element is core. If no explicit date of publication is found in the resource either supply (in brackets) information found in another source or inferred by the cataloger, or record "[Date of publication not identified]."

Note that a copyright (©) or phonogram (℗) date is not a publication date. For RDA copyright and phonogram are both referred to as "copyright." Phonogram is the copyright date of the *recording*, which is distinguished from the copyright of the underlying *work* (e.g., music or text). A copyright date can never be substituted for a publication date in RDA, but it may optionally be recorded in addition to the date of publication element. It may also be used as evidence for inferring the date of publication.

If the date of publication has not been identified, then either a date of distribution or a copyright date, if present in the resource, must be recorded (see discussion, however, in chapter 2 of this *Handbook* at 2.8.6.6 on ways to identify the date of publication). If recording a copyright date, include the copyright symbol (© or ℗) and record it in subfield ‡c of a separate 264 field, with the second indicator coded "4." Record the latest copyright date (e.g., if the resource has "℗2011, 2005," record "℗2011"). As of the 2013 revision of RDA, if the resource has multiple copyright dates that apply to various aspects of the resource (e.g., text and sound), the cataloger can record the latest copyright date that applies to each aspect. Both a copyright date and a phonogram date can be recorded, in separate 264 fields.

For details about publication statement and copyright date, see chapter 2 of this *Handbook* at 2.8 and 2.11.

Distribution Statement. The distribution statement element is not core if publication information has been recorded. However, information about distributors is often considered important to audio resource users, so it may be recorded if present. Record distribution information in the same way as publication information, but record it in a MARC bibliographic 264 field with the second indicator coded "2." For details, see chapter 2 of this *Handbook* at 2.9.

Describe the Carrier. A carrier is the physical medium in which the content of a resource is stored. Carriers for audio resources include discs and cassettes. Examine the resource for physical details, including size and page numbering. Several carrier-related elements are required in an RDA record. Most are recorded in the 3XX block of the bibliographic record.

Extent. The extent of the resource is recorded in subfield ‡a of a MARC bibliographic 300 field. Extent is core if the resource is complete. Record the extent of an audio resource following the instructions in RDA 3.4.1. Only the most basic procedures will be mentioned in this appendix. For details, see chapter 2 of this *Handbook* at 3.4. Record the number of units with a term from the carrier type list in 3.3.1.3 (in the plural, if appropriate). Record the extent of an online resource (such as a streaming audio file) as "1 online resource." For details, see chapter 2 of this *Handbook* at 3.4.1.3–3.4.1.5.

Optionally, record the duration of the recording in hours, minutes, and seconds in parentheses immediately following the main extent statement. Duration can be recorded in a number of other places in the MARC record as well. For details, see chapter 8 of this *Handbook* at 7.22.

Other Physical Details. There were a number of audio resource elements recorded in subfield ‡b of the 300 field under AACR2. While these elements may still be recorded there in an RDA record, this *Handbook* recommends that they be recorded in a new MARC field designed specifically for these RDA elements, 344 (see below under Sound Characteristic).

Dimensions. The dimensions element is not core in RDA, but it is core in descriptions of monographs (including audio resources) for catalogers at the Library of Congress, except for online electronic resources (see LC-PCC PS 3.5, May 2012). Most U.S. catalogers will record this element. Dimensions are recorded in subfield ‡c of a MARC bibliographic 300 field. Separate the dimensions element from any preceding elements in the field with space-semicolon-space.

Record the dimensions of an audio resource following the appropriate instructions in RDA 3.5.1.4. Audio carriers include cartridges (3.5.1.4.2), cassettes (3.5.1.4.3), and discs (3.5.1.4.4). For details, see chapter 2 of this *Handbook* under 3.5.1.4.3 and 3.5.1.4.4.

Content Type. The content type element is not part of the description of the carrier, but it is treated here because it is generally the next element after the dimensions recorded in the MARC bibliographic record. Content type is a core element, and is recorded in subfield ‡a of the MARC 336 field following the instructions in RDA 6.9. Record, as appropriate, one of the terms in the list found in RDA 6.9.1.3. End the field with "‡2 rdacontent":

336   ‡a spoken word ‡2 rdacontent

The most common content types for audio resources are "performed music," "sounds," and "spoken word." For details, see chapter 8 of this *Handbook* at 6.9.

Media and Carrier Type. Carrier type is core in an RDA description. Media type is not core, but most U.S. catalogers follow LC and PCC practice and record it (see LC-PCC PS 3.2, October 2012).

Media type is recorded in subfield ‡a of a MARC bibliographic 337 field. The term should be taken from the list in RDA 3.2.1.3. For most audio resources, use "audio." End the field with "‡2 rdamedia":

337   ‡a audio ‡2 rdamedia

For online audio resources, use "computer." Do not code both "computer" and "audio" in this element. The resource is either one or the other:

337　　‡a computer ‡2 rdamedia

Carrier type is recorded in subfield ‡a of a MARC bibliographic 338 field. The term should be taken from the list in RDA 3.3.1.3 from the group that corresponds to the media type chosen. Any of the audio carrier terms there may be used to describe an audio resource, but the most common are "audio disc" or "audiocassette." If appropriate, "online resource" may be used from the list of computer carriers (e.g., for a streaming audio file). End the field with "‡2 rdacarrier":

338　　‡a audio disc ‡2 rdacarrier

Do not "mix and match" media types and carrier types. The carrier type should correspond to the media type:

337　　‡a computer ‡2 rdamedia
338　　‡a online resource ‡2 rdacarrier

not

337　　‡a audio ‡2 rdamedia
338　　‡a online resource ‡2 rdacarrier

As many media and carrier types as necessary may be recorded (e.g., for a resource consisting of a book and a compact disc). In exceptional circumstances a single carrier may exhibit more than one media and carrier type, for example, a disc that contains both sound and video files. Best practices for this situation have not yet been established. This *Handbook* recommends, in the meantime, that both pairs of media/carrier types be recorded:

337　　‡a audio ‡2 rdamedia
337　　‡a video ‡2 rdamedia
338　　‡a audio disc ‡2 rdacarrier
338　　‡a videodisc ‡2 rdacarrier

For details, see chapter 2 of this *Handbook* at 3.2 and 3.3.

Sound Characteristic. The sound characteristic element (RDA 3.16) records details about the encoding of the sound in a resource. In previous cataloging practice as well as early implementation of RDA, this element was recorded in subfield ‡b of the 300 field. A new field has been incorporated into MARC for recording this RDA element, the MARC bibliographic 344 field. Not all sub-elements will be appropriate to all types of audio resources. Some of the more common sub-elements include: type of recording (analog or digital), recorded in subfield ‡a; recording medium (magnetic, magneto-optical, or optical), recorded in subfield ‡b; playing speed, recorded in subfield ‡c; and playback configuration (stereo, mono, etc.), recorded in subfield ‡g. For details and fuller explanation, see chapter 2 of this *Handbook* at 3.16.

Digital File Characteristic. Record specifications of the digital encoding of an audio resource (e.g., a compact disc) in the MARC bibliographic 347 field following the instructions in RDA 3.19. File type is recorded in subfield ‡a. For audio resources, this will always be "audio file." Record one of the terms from the audio encoding formats list in 3.19.3 in subfield ‡b.

Series Statement. Examine the resource for a series statement. Although information about a series can be taken from outside the resource itself, prefer information found in the resource. Series information is recorded in a MARC bibliographic 490 field. The first indicator is coded "0" if the information is not indexed; it is coded "1" if the information is indexed (in which case an 8XX field will also be present in the bibliographic record; see below under Link the Resource to Related Entities).

Record the title proper of the series in subfield ‡a of the 490 field exactly as it appears in the resource. If series numbering is present, record it in subfield ‡v following the title proper of the series and any other elements (such as a statement of responsibility). Separate series numbering from preceding elements by space-semicolon-space.

The title proper of the series and numbering are core and therefore must be recorded if present. Other title information of the series and statements of responsibility relating to the series are not core and are not in most cases recorded. For details about recording series statements, see chapter 2 of this *Handbook* at 2.12.

Notes. Include any notes you consider necessary to help the library user contextualize, find, identify, or select the resource. No notes are core in an RDA description. Therefore, recording notes in a bibliographic record is entirely dependent on your judgment or the policies of your cataloging agency. Most notes are recorded in the 5XX block of the MARC bibliographic record. Some of the more common notes included in bibliographic records for audio resources are contents notes (see discussion in chapter 9 of this *Handbook* at RDA chapter 25, under Whole-Part Work Relationships), notes giving summaries of the contents (especially for audiobooks) (see discussion in chapter 8 of this *Handbook* at 7.10), date and place of capture (see discussion in chapter 8 of this *Handbook* at 7.11) and notes giving the duration of the recording if not already recorded in 300 subfield ‡a (see discussion in chapter 8 of this *Handbook* at 7.22).

Performer, Narrator, and/or Presenter. A particularly important note in a record for an audio resource is that which records performers, narrators, and presenters. As mentioned above, statements found in the resource listing these persons, families, or corporate bodies are not recorded as part of a statement of responsibility, but are rather given in a note recorded in the MARC bibliographic 511 field. This is not transcribed information. Simply list the names as concisely as possible, with information about what they did if necessary. For more information, see chapter 8 of this *Handbook* at 7.23.

Artistic and/or Technical Credit. Another important and frequently encountered note in descriptions of audio resources is the artistic or technical credit note. Record information identifying persons who have contributed to the artistic or technical production of a resource not as a statement of responsibility, but as a note recorded in the MARC bibliographic 508 field. For more information, see chapter 8 of this *Handbook* at 7.24.

Identifier for the Manifestation. Examine the resource for an identifier, defined as "a character string associated with a manifestation that serves to differentiate that manifestation from other manifestations." The identifier for the manifestation element is core (see RDA 2.15) and therefore an identifier must be recorded if present on the resource.

An identifier commonly found with audiobooks is an ISBN (International Standard Book Number). Record an ISBN in subfield ‡a of the 020 field of the MARC bibliographic record. Copy it as found, but do not record hyphens. Other common identifiers for audio resources are issue numbers (also called publisher numbers), recorded in the MARC 028 field with first indicator coded "0"; and universal product codes (UPCs), recorded in the MARC 024 field with first indicator coded "1." For details, see chapter 2 of this *Handbook* at 2.15.

5. LINK THE RESOURCE TO RELATED ENTITIES

Once the resource has been described, links should be made to related entities. These include works and expressions either contained in the resource or related to the work(s) or expression(s) described in the record, and related persons, families, corporate bodies, and geographic entities.

In the MARC bibliographic format these links are created by recording the authorized access point for the related entity in one of the access point fields, generally speaking the 1XX, 7XX, and 8XX fields. This either (1) links the bibliographic record to an associated authority record, and via that record links the bibliographic record to other bibliographic records containing the same authorized access point (either by using the text string itself, or using an identifier); (2) directly links the bibliographic record to other bibliographic records containing the same authorized access point; or (3) at the least allows searches to retrieve all bibliographic records containing the same authorized access point.

RDA requires the cataloger to record at least one relationship: that between the resource and the principal creator of the work embodied in the manifestation being described (see discussion in chapter 9 of this *Handbook* at 18.3). Recording most other relationships is optional, but most catalogers will record many.

The relationship between the resource and the principal creator of the work (if there is only one work) is recorded in a 100 (persons or families), 110 (most corporate bodies), or 111 (meetings) field. If there is more than one work in the resource and they are by different creators, record these relationships in 700, 710, or 711. See chapter 9 of this *Handbook* at 19.2 for help in determining what entity is the principal creator of the work. With persons and families the decision is usually fairly straight-forward. Determining if a corporate body or meeting is the creator can be a little trickier, but fairly clear guidelines are laid out at RDA 19.2.1.1.1 (and see corresponding discussion in chapter 9 of the *Handbook*).

Note that for audio resources a performing group is the creator of works that result from the collective activity of the group where the group does more than "merely" perform (RDA 19.2.1.1.1e).

Caution: under previous cataloging practice (AACR2 21.23C), if an audio resource containing works by different persons or bodies had a collective title, the person or body represented as the principal performer was considered the creator of the resource (in AACR2 terms, was the "main entry"). This unprincipled approach was not carried over into RDA.

Begin by recording the authorized access point for the principal creator of the work (if there is only one work) in a 1XX field. This form may be accompanied by a relationship designator to clarify the nature of the relationship. The use of relationship designators is optional but encouraged (see chapter 9 of this *Handbook* at 18.5).

Once the relationship to the principal creator has been recorded, think about other relationships that might be helpful. First consider other creators if there are more than one. Other commonly recorded relationships for audio resources include those between the resource and its narrators, performers, and publishers. These relationships are all recorded by giving the authorized access point for the related entity in 7XX fields: 700 (persons and families), 710 (most corporate bodies), or 711 (meetings).

Consider also relationships to related works and expressions, or the relationship between the manifestation described in the bibliographic record and the work(s) or expression(s) embodied in the manifestation. Related works or expressions are recorded by giving the authorized access point for the work or expression in a 700, 710, 711, or 730 field, or in the case of a series, in an 800, 810, 811, or 830 field. Works or expressions embodied in the manifestation are recorded in a 1XX and 240 field combination or in 130 if there is only one; or if there are two or more, in 700, 710, 711, or 730 fields as appropriate. For details, see discussion throughout chapter 9 of this *Handbook*.

6. SAMPLE RECORD SETS

Other examples of cataloging of audio recordings in this *Handbook* include figures 2.22, 2.94, 2.95, 2.101, 2.107, 8.19, 8.27, 9.12, 9.24, 9.42, and 9.74.

RECORD SET E1
COMPACT DISC (MUSIC)

Bibliographic Record

024	1	‡a 675754028886	*[RDA 2.15.1.4]*
024	1	‡a 099925403829	*[RDA 2.15.1.4]*
028	02	‡a SU 4038-2 ‡b Supraphon	*[RDA 2.15.1.2]*
100	1	‡a Dvořák, Antonín, ‡d 1841-1904, ‡e composer.	*[RDA 18.3, 19.2, 18.4.1.2, 18.5]*
245	10	‡a String quartets in G major op. 106 : ‡b & in F major op. 96 "American" / ‡c Dvořák.	*[RDA 2.3, 2.4]*
264	1	‡a Praha, Czech Republic : ‡b Supraphon, ‡c [2010]	*[RDA 2.8]*
264	4	‡c ℗2010	*[RDA 2.11]*
300		‡a 1 audio disc (63 min., 3 sec.) ; ‡c 4 3/4 in.	*[RDA 3.4.1, 7.22, 3.5.1.4.4, 3.5.1.3 alternative]*
336		‡a performed music ‡2 rdacontent	*[RDA 6.9]*
337		‡a audio ‡2 rdamedia	*[RDA 3.2]*
338		‡a audio disc ‡2 rdacarrier	*[RDA 3.3]*
344		‡a digital ‡b optical ‡g stereo ‡2 rda	*[RDA 3.16]*
347		‡a audio file ‡b CD audio ‡2 rda	*[RDA 3.19]*
511	0	‡a Pavel Haas Quartet (Veronika Jarůšková, Eva Karová, violins ; Pavel Nikl, viola ; Peter Jarůšková, violoncello).	*[RDA 7.23]*
508		‡a Matouš Vlčinský, producer.	*[RDA 7.24]*
518		‡a Recorded at the Rudolfinum, Prague, on June 3, 6, 29 and 30, 2010.	*[RDA 7.11]*
500		‡a Durations: 36:37 ; 26:26.	*[RDA 7.22]*
546		‡a Booklet notes in Czech, English, French and German.	*[RDA 7.12]*
505	0	‡a String quartet no. 13 in G major Op. 106 (B. 192, 1895) -- String quartet no. 12 in F major Op. 96 "American" (B. 179, 1893)	*[RDA 25.1, 24.4.3a]*
700	12	‡a Dvořák, Antonín, ‡d 1841-1904. ‡t Quartets, ‡m strings, ‡n B. 192, ‡r G major.	*[RDA 25.1, 24.4.2]*
700	12	‡a Dvořák, Antonín, ‡d 1841-1904. ‡t Quartets, ‡m strings, ‡n B. 179, ‡r F major.	*[RDA 25.1, 24.4.2]*
710	2	‡a Pavel Haas Quartet, ‡e performer.	*[RDA 20.2, 18.4.1.2, 18.5]*

Disc face

DVOŘÁK
STRING QUARTETS
IN G MAJOR, OP. 106 &
IN F MAJOR, OP. 96 "AMERICAN"
PAVEL HAAS QUARTET
SU 4038-2 ℗ SUPRAPHON A.S.

Associated Authority Records

046	‡f 18410908 ‡g 19040501	[RDA 9.3]
100 1	‡a Dvořák, Antonín, ‡d 1841-1904	[RDA 9.2.2, 9.19.1]
370	‡a Nelahozeves (Czech Republic) ‡b Prague (Czech Republic) ‡2 naf [RDA 9.8, 9.9]	
374	‡a Composers ‡2 lcsh	[RDA 9.16]
375	‡a male	[RDA 9.7]
378	‡q Antonín Leopold	[RDA 9.5]
667	‡a Thematic-index numbers used in uniform titles for string quartets and works without opus numbers are from Burghauser, J. Antonín Dvořák, thematický katalog, 1960	[RDA 8.12]
670	‡a Cigánské melodie, 2010: ‡b title page (Antonín Dvořák)	[RDA 8.12]
670	‡a New Grove, 2nd ed. ‡b (Dvořák, Antonín (Leopold); born Sept. 8, 1841, Nelahozeves, near Kralupy, died May 1, 1904, Prague; Czech composer)	[RDA 8.12]
678 0	‡a Antonín Dvořák (1841-1904) was a Czech composer.	[RDA 9.17]

046	‡k 18951111- ‡l 18951209 ‡2 edtf	[RDA 6.4]
100 1	‡a Dvořák, Antonín, ‡d 1841-1904. ‡t Quartets, ‡m strings, ‡n B. 192, ‡r G major	[RDA 6.2.2, 6.27.1]
380	‡a String quartets ‡2 lcsh	[RDA 6.3]
382	‡a strings	[RDA 6.15]
383	‡c B. 192 ‡d Burghauser ‡2 mlati	[RDA 6.16]
383	‡a no. 13 ‡b op. 106	[RDA 6.16]
384	‡a G major	[RDA 6.17]
400 1	‡a Dvořák, Antonín, ‡d 1841-1904. ‡t Quartets, ‡m strings, ‡n no. 13, op. 106, ‡r G major	[RDA 6.2.3, 6.27.4]
400 1	‡a Dvořák, Antonín, ‡d 1841-1904. ‡t Quartets, ‡m strings, ‡n no. 8, op. 106, ‡r G major	[RDA 6.2.3, 6.27.4]
400 1	‡a Dvořák, Antonín, ‡d 1841-1904. ‡t Quartets, ‡m strings, ‡n op. 106, ‡r G major	[RDA 6.2.3, 6.27.4]
670	‡a Quartett, G dur, für 2 Violinen, Bratsche und Violoncell, op. 106, 1896	[RDA 5.8]
670	‡a Grove Music online, 10 January 2012 ‡b (B 192, S 128, Op. 106; String Quartet no. 13, G; composed before 11 Nov-9 Dec 1895, published Berlin, 1896, first performance, Prague, 20 Oct 1896)	[RDA 5.8]

046	‡k 18930608 ‡l 18930623	[RDA 6.4]
100 1	‡a Dvořák, Antonín, ‡d 1841-1904. ‡t Quartets, ‡m strings, ‡n B. 179, ‡r F major	[6.2.2, 6.27.1]
380	‡a String quartets ‡2 lcsh	[RDA 6.3]
382	‡a strings	[RDA 6.15]

383	‡c B. 179 ‡d Burghauser ‡2 mlati	*[RDA 6.16]*
383	‡a no. 12 ‡b op. 96	*[RDA 6.16]*
384	‡a F major	*[RDA 6.17]*
400 1	‡a Dvořák, Antonín, ‡d 1841-1904. ‡t Quartets, ‡m strings, ‡n op. 96, ‡r F major	
		[RDA 6.2.3, 6.27.4]
400 1	‡a Dvořák, Antonín, ‡d 1841-1904. ‡t Quartets, ‡mstrings, ‡n no. 12, op. 96, ‡r F	
	major	*[RDA 6.2.3, 6.27.4]*
400 1	‡a Dvořák, Antonín, ‡d 1841-1904. ‡t American	*[RDA 6.2.3, 6.27.4]*
670	‡a String quartet in F major, op. 96, 1979: ‡b container (Quartet no. 12 "American")	
		[RDA 5.8]
670	‡a Grove Music online, 10 September 2012 ‡b (B 179, S 118, Op. 96, String Quartet no. 12, F; composed 8-23 June 1893, published Berlin, 1894; 'The American,' 1st performance Boston, MA, 1 Jan 1894)	*[RDA 5.8]*

046	‡s 2002	*[RDA 11.4]*
110 2	‡a Pavel Haas Quartet	*[RDA 11.2.2, 11.13.1]*
368	‡a String quartets (Musical groups) ‡2 lcsh	*[RDA 11.7]*
410 2	‡a Kvarteto Pavla Haase	*[RDA 11.2.3, 11.13.2]*
410 2	‡a Pavel Haas Quartett	*[RDA 11.2.3, 11.13.2]*
410 2	‡a Quatuor Pavel Haas	*[RDA 11.2.3, 11.13.2]*
670	‡a Janáček, L. String quartet no. 2, 2006: ‡b label (Pavel Haas Quartet) container (Veronika Jarůšková, Kateřina Gemrotová, violins; Pavel Nikl, viola; Peter Jarůšek, violoncello) insert (Pavel Haas Quartett; Quatuor Pavel Haas; Kvarteto Pavla Haase)	*[RDA 8.12]*
670	‡a Pavel Haas Quartet, via WWW, 10 September 2012 ‡b (Pavel Haas Quartet; string quartet founded 2002 and named in honor of Pavel Haas (1899-1944))	
		[RDA 8.12]
678 1	‡a The Pavel Haas Quartet is a Czech string quartet founded in 2002.	
		[RDA 11.11]

RECORD SET E2
COMPACT DISC (AUDIOBOOK)

Bibliographic Record

020	‡a 9780307576439	*[RDA 2.15]*
028 02	‡a RHCD 6276 ‡b Random House Audio	*[RDA 2.15.1.2]*
100 1	‡a Bradley, C. Alan, ‡d 1938- ‡e author.	*[RDA 18.3, 19.2, 18.4.1.2, 18.5]*
245 12	‡a A red herring without mustard / ‡c Alan Bradley.	*[RDA 2.3, 2.4]*
250	‡a Unabridged.	*[RDA 2.5]*
264 1	‡a New York, N.Y. : ‡b Random House Audio, ‡c [2011]	*[RDA 2.8]*
264 4	‡c ℗2011	*[RDA 2.11]*

300	‡a 9 audio discs (11 hr.) ; ‡c 4 3/4 in.	*[RDA 3.4.1, 7.22, 3.5.1.4.4,*
		3.5.1.3 alternative]
336	‡a spoken word ‡2 rdacontent	*[RDA 6.9]*
337	‡a audio ‡2 rdamedia	*[RDA 3.2]*
338	‡a audio disc ‡2 rdacarrier	*[RDA 3.3]*
344	‡a digital ‡b optical ‡g stereo ‡2 rda	*[RDA 3.16]*
347	‡a audio file ‡b CD audio ‡2 rda	*[RDA 3.19]*
490 1	‡a Flavia de Luce mystery	*[RDA 2.12]*
500	‡a Title from disc label.	*[RDA 2.20]*
511 0	‡a Read by Jayne Entwistle.	*[RDA 7.23]*
520	‡a When a Gypsy caravan is passing through town, a local child is abducted and murdered. A young Gypsy woman is falsely accused by the townspeople, forcing Flavia to investigate the crime and find the real culprit.	*[RDA 7.10]*
700 1	‡a Entwistle, Jayne, ‡e voice actor.	*[RDA 20.2, 18.4.1.2, 18.5]*
800 1	‡a Bradley, C. Alan, ‡d 1938- ‡t Flavia de Luce mystery. ‡h Spoken word.	*[RDA 25.1, 24.4.2]*

Disc face of compact disc no. 1

A RED HERRING
Without
MUSTARD
Random House Audio
ALAN BRADLEY
©2011 by Alan Bradley
℗2011 Random House, Inc.
RHCD 6276 · Made in the U.S.A.

Associated Authority Records

046	‡f 19381010	*[RDA 9.3]*
100 1	‡a Bradley, C. Alan, ‡d 1938-	*[RDA 9.2.2, 9.19.1]*
370	‡a Toronto (Ont.) ‡f Saskatoon (Sask.) ‡c Malta ‡2 naf	*[RDA 9.8, 9.9]*
373	‡a University of Saskatchewan ‡2 naf ‡t 1994	*[RDA 9.13]*
374	‡a Authors ‡a Electronics engineers ‡a Teachers ‡2 lcsh	*[RDA 9.16]*
375	‡a male	*[RDA 9.7]*
377	‡a eng	*[RDA 9.14]*
400 1	‡a Bradley, Alan, ‡d 1938-	*[RDA 9.2.3, 9.19.2]*
670	‡a Ms. Holmes of Baker Street, 2004: ‡b title page (C. Alan Bradley) p. 204 (Alan Bradley) copyright statement (Alan C. Bradley)	*[RDA 8.12]*
670	‡a LAC database, March 30, 2005 ‡b (Bradley, C. Alan; born 10 October 1938)	*[RDA 8.12]*

670	‡a The sweetness at the bottom of the pie, 2009: ‡b title page (Alan Bradley) facing (also author of Ms. Holmes of Baker Street; The Shoebox Bible) *[RDA 8.12]*
670	‡a flaviadeluce.com, April 15, 2011 ‡b (born in Toronto and grew up in Cobourg, Ontario; an education in electronic engineering; has worked in radio and television, Director of Television Engineering at the Univ. of Saskatchewan in Saskatoon, SK for 25 years, until 1994; writes for children and adults; teaches script writing and TV production; lives in Malta) *[RDA 8.12]*
678 0	‡a C. Alan Bradley (1938-) is a Canadian author. *[RDA 9.17]*

100 1	‡a Entwistle, Jayne	*[RDA 9.2.2, 9.19.1]*
370	‡a Blackpool (England) ‡f Los Angeles (Calif.) ‡2 naf	*[RDA 9.8, 9.9]*
373	‡a Improvatorium	*[RDA 9.13]*
374	‡a Actresses ‡a Voice actors and actresses ‡a Teachers ‡2 lcsh	*[RDA 9.16]*
375	‡a female	*[RDA 9.7]*
377	‡a eng	*[RDA 9.14]*
670	‡a The sweetness at the bottom of the pie, 2009: ‡b container (Jayne Entwistle; Los Angeles based actress) *[RDA 8.12]*	
670	‡a IMDB, via WWW, 15 June 2011 ‡b (Jayne Entwistle, actress) *[RDA 8.12]*	
670	‡a Improvatorium, via WWW, 15 June 2011 ‡b (Jayne Entwistle, Associate Artistic Director; born Blackpool, England; Jayne has taken a circuitous rout through Canada, Tel Aviv and a good portion of America to land herself in L.A.; she teaches various levels of improv with Improvatorium. Outside the theater she is a professional voice actor, narrating audiobooks for Random House as well as voicing various commercials, video games and animations) *[RDA 8.12]*	

046	‡k 2010	*[RDA 6.10]*
100 1	‡a Bradley, C. Alan, ‡d 1938- ‡t Flavia de Luce mystery. ‡h Spoken word	*[RDA 6.27.3]*
336	‡a spoken word ‡2 rdacontent	*[RDA 6.9]*
377	‡a eng	*[RDA 9.14]*
430 0	‡a Flavia de Luce mystery	*[RDA 6.27.4]*
430 0	‡a Flavia de Luce novel	*[RDA 6.27.4]*
400 1	‡a Bradley, C. Alan, ‡d 1938- ‡t Flavia de Luce novel. ‡h Spoken word *[RDA 6.27.4]*	
500 1	‡w r ‡i Narrator: ‡a Entwistle, Jayne	*[RDA 30.1, 30.2, 29.4.2]*
643	‡a New York ‡b Random House ‡a Westminster, Md. ‡b Books on Tape	*[not RDA]*
644	‡a f ‡5 IlMpPL	*[not RDA]*
645	‡a t ‡5 DPCC ‡5 IlMpPL	*[not RDA]*
646	‡a s ‡5 IlMpPL	*[not RDA]*

670	‡a The weed that strings the hangman's bag, 2010: ‡b container (A Flavia de Luce mystery) (read by Jayne Entwistle)	*[RDA 5.8]*
670	‡a I am half-sick of shadows, 2011: ‡b container (A Flavia de Luce novel) (read by Jayne Entwistle)	*[RDA 5.8]*

RECORD SET E3
STREAMING AUDIO

Bibliographic Record

028 02	‡a 501 ‡b Victor	*[RDA 2.15.1.2]*
100 1	‡a Di Capua, Eduardo ‡d 1864-1917, ‡e composer.	*[RDA 18.3, 19.2, 18.4.1.2, 18.5]*
245 10	‡a O sole mio = ‡b My sunshine / ‡c composer, Eduardo Di Capua ; Lyricist, Giovanni Capurro.	*[RDA 2.3, 2.4]*
246 3	‡a My sunshine	*[RDA 2.3.6]*
246 3	‡a Neapolitan folk song	*[RDA 2.3.6]*
264 1	‡a [Washington, D.C.] : ‡b [Library of Congress], ‡c [2012?]	*[RDA 2.8]*
300	‡a 1 online resource (3 min., 12 sec.)	*[RDA 3.4.1, 7.22]*
336	‡a performed music ‡2 rdacontent	*[RDA 6.9]*
337	‡a computer ‡2 rdamedia	*[RDA 3.2]*
338	‡a online resource ‡2 rdacarrier	*[RDA 3.3]*
344	‡a digital ‡g mono ‡2 rda	*[RDA 3.16]*
347	‡a audio file ‡2 rda	*[RDA 3.19]*
500	‡a Digitized by the Library of Congress as part of the National Jukebox project.	*[RDA 2.20]*
546	‡a Sung in Italian.	*[RDA 7.12]*
518	‡a Originally recorded by Victor Talking Machine Company in Camden, New Jersey on February 5, 1916.	*[RDA 7.11]*
511 0	‡a Conductor: Walter B. Rogers; Tenor: Enrico Caruso.	*[RDA 7.23]*
534	‡p Originally published: ‡a Camden, New Jersey : ‡b Victor Talking Machine Company, ‡c [1916]	*[RDA 27.1]*
700 1	‡a Capurro, Giovanni ‡d 1859-1920, ‡e lyricist.	*[RDA 20.2, 18.4.1.2, 18.5]*
700 1	‡a Rogers, Walter B., ‡d 1865-1939, ‡e conductor.	*[RDA 20.2, 18.4.1.2, 18.5]*
700 1	‡a Caruso, Enrico ‡d 1873-1921, ‡e performer.	*[RDA 20.2, 18.4.1.2, 18.5]*
856 40	‡u www.loc.gov/jukebox/recordings/detail/id/4298	*[RDA 4.6]*

Title screen
Recording Details
Recording Title: O sole mio
Other Title(s):
 My sunshine (Parallel (translated) title)
 Neapolitan folk song (Title descriptor)

Composer: Eduardo Di Capua
Conductor: Walter B. Rogers
Lyricist: Giovanni Capurro
Tenor vocal: Enrico Caruso
Category: Vocal
Description: Tenor vocal solo, with orchestra
Language: Italian
Label Name/Number: Victor 501
Recording Date: 1916-02-05
Place of Recording: Camden, New Jersey
Size: 10"
Duration: 03:12

Associated Authority Records

046	‡f 18650512 ‡g 19171013	*[RDA 9.3]*
100 1	‡a Di Capua, Eduardo, ‡d 1864-1917	*[RDA 9.2.2, 9.19.1]*
370	‡a Naples (Italy) ‡b Naples (Italy) ‡2 naf	*[RDA 9.8, 9.9]*
374	‡a Composers ‡2 lcsh	*[RDA 9.16]*
375	‡a male	*[RDA 9.7]*
377	‡a ita	*[RDA 9.14]*
400 1	‡a Capua, Eduardo Di, ‡d 1864-1917	*[RDA 9.2.3, 9.19.2]*
670	‡a O sole mio, 1997: ‡b title page (Eduardo di Capua)	*[RDA 8.12]*
670	‡a Dizionario biografico degli Italiani, 1991: ‡b volume 39 (Di Capua, Eduardo; born in Naples 12 May 1865; died in Naples 3 October 1917; composer) *[RDA 8.12]*	

046	‡f 18590205 ‡g 19200118	*[RDA 9.3]*
100 1	‡a Capurro, Giovanni, ‡d 1859-1920	*[RDA 9.2.2, 9.19.1]*
370	‡a Naples (Italy) ‡b Naples (Italy) ‡2 naf	*[RDA 9.8, 9.9]*
374	‡a Poets ‡2 lcsh	*[RDA 9.16]*
375	‡a male	*[RDA 9.7]*
377	‡a ita	*[RDA 9.14]*
400 1	‡a Capurro, G. ‡q (Giovanni), ‡d 1859-1920	*[RDA 9.2.3, 9.19.2]*
670	‡a Carduccianelle, c1999: ‡b title page (Giovanni Capurro) front cover flap (born Naples, February 5, 1859; died Naples, Jan. 18, 1920; Neapolitan poet) *[RDA 8.12]*	
670	‡a Di Capua, E. O sole mio!, 1916?: ‡b title page (G. Capurro)	*[RDA 8.12]*

046	‡f 18651014 ‡g 19391224	*[RDA 9.3]*
100 1	‡a Rogers, Walter B., ‡d 1865-1939	*[RDA 9.2.2, 9.19.1]*
370	‡a Delphi (Ind.) ‡b Brooklyn (New York, N.Y.) ‡2 naf	*[RDA 9.8, 9.9]*
373	‡a Sousa Band ‡2 naf	*[RDA 9.13]*

373	‡a 7th Regiment Band ‡2 naf	*[RDA 9.13]*
374	‡a Cornet players ‡a Conductors (Music) ‡2 lcsh	*[RDA 9.16]*
375	‡a male	*[RDA 9.7]*
377	‡a eng	*[RDA 9.14]*
670	‡a Land of the free, 1976: ‡b insert (Walter B. Rogers)	*[RDA 8.12]*
670	‡a Encyclopedic discography of Victor recordings: matrix series, 1 through 4999, c1986: ‡b page 564 (Rogers, Walter B; cornetist, conductor)	*[RDA 8.12]*
670	‡a Allmusic, via WWW, 10 September 2012 ‡b (Walter B. Rogers, born October 14, 1865 in Delphi Indiana; died December 24, 1939 in Brooklyn, N.Y.; member of John Philip Sousa's Band; Capp's Seventh Regiment Band)	*[RDA 8.12]*

046	‡f 18730225 ‡g 19210802	*[RDA 9.3]*
100 1	‡a Caruso, Enrico, ‡d 1873-1921	*[RDA 9.2.2, 9.19.1]*
370	‡a Naples (Italy) ‡b Naples (Italy) ‡2 naf	*[RDA 9.8, 9.9]*
374	‡a Tenors (Singers) ‡2 lcsh	*[RDA 9.16]*
375	‡a male	*[RDA 9.7]*
377	‡a ita	*[RDA 9.14]*
670	‡a Caruso's book, being a collection of caricatures, 1906.	*[RDA 8.12]*
670	‡a Grove music online, 10 September 2012 ‡b (Caruso, Enrico, born Naples, 25 February 1873; died Naples 2 August 1921; Italian tenor)	*[RDA 8.12]*
678 0	‡a Enrico Caruso (1873-1921) was an Italian tenor.	*[RDA 9.17]*

MOVING IMAGE RESOURCES

THIS APPENDIX CONTAINS A RECOMMENDED PROCESS FOR CREAT-ing bibliographic records for moving image resources. It covers bibliographic record creation for these resources only in the most general of terms. Unusual situations are covered in the body of the *Handbook*. As with the *Handbook* itself, this appendix does not cover non-RDA related aspects of the bibliographic record, such as fixed-length data elements (the so-called fixed fields) or subject analysis. This appendix also contains three sample record sets consisting of bibliographic records and their associated authority records, which illustrate many of the points described below.

1. DETERMINE THE MODE OF ISSUANCE

Consider the mode of issuance of the resource. Does it consist of a single unit? Is it a multipart monograph? Is it a serial or integrating resource? Mode of issuance is defined in RDA 1.1.3.

> A single-unit resource is a resource issued either as a single physical unit (e.g., a single DVD) or a single logical unit (e.g., a streaming video file).
>
> A multipart monograph is a resource issued in two or more parts that is complete or is intended to be complete within a finite number of parts (e.g., a film on 2 discs).
>
> A serial is a resource issued in successive parts, usually bearing numbering, that has no predetermined conclusion.
>
> An integrating resource is a resource that is added to or changed by means of updates that do not remain discrete but are integrated into the whole.

This appendix covers single units and multipart monographs. For serials or integrating resources in any format, see appendix K.

2. DECIDE ON THE TYPE OF DESCRIPTION

Consider the type of description you want to create. RDA 1.1.4 mentions three types of description: comprehensive, analytical, and hierarchical.

> A comprehensive description describes the resource as a whole.
> An analytical description describes a part of a larger resource.
> A hierarchical description combines a comprehensive description of a whole resource with analytical descriptions of one or more of its parts.

U.S. cataloging practice does not use hierarchical descriptions; therefore, these will not be described here. Analytical descriptions are described in appendix K. This appendix covers comprehensive descriptions.

3. CHOOSE THE BASIS FOR IDENTIFICATION AND SOURCES OF INFORMATION FOR THE RESOURCE

Examine the resource and choose a basis for identification following the instructions in RDA 2.1. If the resource is issued as a single-unit resource, the resource itself will be the basis for identification. If the resource is issued in more than one part, one of the parts will be chosen as the basis for identification. For a moving image resource, this will usually be the first unit (e.g., a disc). For details, see chapter 2 of this *Handbook* at 2.1.

Having chosen the part that will serve as the basis for identification, choose a "preferred source of information" within that part following the instructions in RDA 2.2.2.3. The preferred source of information for moving image recordings is the title frame or frames, or the title screen or screens. If no title frame or screen is available, a label bearing a title that is permanently printed on or affixed to the resource, or, for digital moving image resources, embedded metadata in textual form that contains a title, may be used. If neither a label nor metadata are available, accompanying material or a container may be used. For details, see chapter 2 of this *Handbook* at 2.2.2.3.

4. DESCRIBE THE RESOURCE

Titles and Statements of Responsibility. Transcribe the title proper, other title information, and statement of responsibility in a MARC bibliographic 245 field. For information about transcription, see chapter 2 of this *Handbook* at 1.7.

Transcribe the title proper in subfield ‡a of the 245 field exactly as found on the preferred source of information (e.g., the title frame or the disc label) (see RDA 2.3.2). Title proper is a core element and therefore must be included in the description. However, pay close attention to RDA 2.3.1.6. Moving image resource title statement often include "words that serve as an introduction and are not intended to be part of the title," such as "Walt Disney presents a film by James Cameron." These are not transcribed as part of the title proper. For details, see chapter 2 of this *Handbook* at 2.3.

Transcription of other title information is optional in RDA, although core for the Library of Congress. Most U.S. catalogers will follow LC practice and include other title information in the description. If including other title information, transcribe it after the title proper in subfield ‡b of the 245 field (see RDA 2.3.4). Other title information should be transcribed from the same source as the title proper. The first piece of other title information is separated from the title proper by space-colon-space. Subsequent pieces of other title information are separated from each other by space-colon-space. For details, see chapter 2 of this *Handbook* at 2.3.4.

Statements of responsibility for moving image resources are generally recorded just like those on any other type of resource. However, there are a couple of exceptions noted in the scope statement at RDA 2.4.1.1. Statements identifying performers of music who do no more than perform, execute, or interpret the music; other persons or bodies who perform, narrate, or present; or persons who have contributed to the artistic or technical production of the resource are omitted from the statement of responsibility and the information is instead recorded in a note (see below under Notes: Performer, Narrator, and/or Presenter, and Artistic and/or Technical Credit).

The first statement of responsibility relating to the title proper is a core element in RDA. Other statements of responsibility are optional, although most catalogers will record them. If including statements of responsibility in the description, transcribe them after the title proper or other information in subfield ‡c of the 245 field (see RDA 2.4.1 and 2.4.2). Statements of responsibility may be transcribed from any source within the resource itself. In unusual situations, a statement of responsibility may be transcribed from outside the resource itself, but in that case it should be bracketed. This will rarely be necessary. The first statement of responsibility is separated from the title proper (or other title information) by space-slash-space. Subsequent statements of responsibility are separated from each other by space-semicolon-space. For details, see chapter 2 of this *Handbook* at 2.4.

Variant Titles. Examine the resource for variant titles. Variant titles are not core in RDA, but if in your opinion a library user might attempt to find the resource using one of these titles, record it in subfield ‡a of a 246 field. Variant titles can be taken from any source (see RDA 2.3.6.2), including your own knowledge (for example, you might record a variant to correct a misspelled word in the title). Typical sources of variant titles are disc labels and containers. For economy's sake, most catalogers will not look beyond the resource itself for variant titles. For details, see chapter 2 of this *Handbook* at 2.3.6.

Edition Statement. Examine the resource for an edition statement. An edition statement can be taken from any source within the resource, but a statement found in the same source as the title proper is preferred. Edition statements may also be taken from outside the resource, but if so, they should be bracketed.

Designation of edition is a core element, and therefore must be recorded if present in the resource. If found, transcribe a designation of edition (for example, "Remastered edition") in subfield ‡a of a 250 field (see RDA 2.5.2).

Recording other elements of the edition statement is optional in RDA. The most common other element is a statement of responsibility relating to the edition. If you find such a statement and decide to include it in the description, record it following space-slash-space in subfield ‡b of the 250 field.

For details on recording an edition statement, see chapter 2 of this *Handbook* at 2.5.

Publication Statement. Examine the resource for publication information, including place of publication, publisher, and date of publication. Although information about publication can be taken from outside the resource itself, prefer information found inside the resource, and within the resource, prefer information found in the same source as the title proper. Publication information is recorded in a MARC bibliographic 264 field, with the second indicator coded "1."

Note that for moving image resources, the production company is not usually the publisher of the manifestation you are describing. Information about production companies is recorded in a note (see below under Notes: Artistic and/or Technical Credit). Note also that the producer of a film is *not* a producer in the sense the term is used in RDA 2.7. RDA 2.7 production statements are statements relating to the production of an *unpublished* resource.

Record the first place of publication found in the resource in subfield ‡a of the 264 field. Transcribe the information exactly as found. This element is core. If no place is found in the resource either supply (in brackets) information from another source about the place of publication, or record "[Place of publication not identified]." The cataloger of moving image resources must frequently search to find the place of publication because this information is often omitted from the resource. There are a number of useful reference sources that give this information, but the easiest way to find a place associated with a publisher is to search for the publisher's web page, which usually gives a location (often under "contact us"). Full information about most commercially produced films is also available at the Internet Movie Database, www.imdb.com. Additionally, most major films now have their own websites which include much useful information about the film that may be used in the description.

If more than one place of publication is found in the resource, you may optionally record them all, but only the first is required. For details, see chapter 2 of this *Handbook* at 2.8.2.

Record the first publisher associated with the first place of publication found in the resource in subfield ‡b of the 264 field. Transcribe the information exactly as found. This element is core. If no publisher is found in the resource either supply (in brackets) information about the publisher from another source, or record "[Publisher not identified]." Separate the place of publication from the publisher's name with space-colon-space. If more than one publisher is found in the resource, you may optionally record them all, but only the first is required. For details, see chapter 2 of this *Handbook* at 2.8.4.

Record the date of publication. Record numerals in the form preferred by your cataloging agency (see RDA 1.8.2). Place a comma immediately after the publisher's name and record the date of publication in subfield ‡c of the 264 field. The date of publication element is core. If no explicit date of publication is found in the resource either supply (in brackets) information found in another source or inferred by the cataloger, or record "[Date of publication not identified]."

Note that a copyright date is not a publication date. A copyright date can never be substituted for a publication date in RDA, but it may optionally be recorded in addition to the date of publication element. It may also be used as evidence for inferring the date of publication.

If the date of publication has not been identified, then either a date of distribution or a copyright date, if present in the resource, must be recorded (see discussion, however, in chapter 2 of this *Handbook* at 2.8.6.6 on ways to identify the date of publication). If recording a copyright date, include the copyright symbol (© or ℗) and record it in subfield ‡c of a separate 264 field, with the second indicator coded "4."

For details about publication statement and copyright date, see chapter 2 of this *Handbook* at 2.8 and 2.11.

Distribution Statement. The distribution statement element is not core if publication information has been recorded. However, information about distributors is often considered important to moving image resource users; therefore, it may be recorded if present. Record distribution information in the same way as publication information, but record it in a MARC bibliographic 264 field with the second indicator coded "2." For details, see chapter 2 of this *Handbook* at 2.9.

Describe the Carrier. A carrier is the physical medium in which the content of a resource is stored. Carriers for moving image resources include videodiscs, videocassettes, and film reels. Examine the resource for physical details, including size and page numbering. Several carrier-related elements are required in an RDA record. Most are recorded in the 3XX block of the bibliographic record.

Extent. The extent of the resource is recorded in subfield ‡a of a MARC bibliographic 300 field. Extent is core if the resource is complete. Record the extent of a moving image resource following the instructions in RDA 3.4.1. Only the most basic procedures will be mentioned in this appendix. For details, see chapter 2 of this *Handbook* at 3.4. Record the number of units with a term from the carrier type list in 3.3.1.3 (in the plural, if appropriate). Record the extent of an online resource (such as a streaming video file) as "1 online resource." For details, see chapter 2 of this *Handbook* at 3.4.

Optionally, record the duration of the moving image resource in hours, minutes, and seconds in parentheses immediately following the main extent statement. Duration can be recorded in a number of other places in the RDA record as well. For details, see chapter 8 of this *Handbook* at 7.22.

Sound Content. Though not considered in RDA to be part of the carrier description, this element is treated here because it is recorded immediately after the extent element in the MARC bibliographic record. Record "sound" or "silent" as appropriate in subfield ‡b of the 300 field (see RDA 7.18). Separate this element from the preceding extent element with space-semicolon-space.

Colour Content. Like sound content, this element is not part of the carrier description, but it is treated here because it is recorded immediately after the sound content element in the MARC bibliographic record. Record "color" or "black and white" as appropriate in the same subfield ‡b as the sound content element (see RDA 7.17.3). Separate this element from the sound content element by preceding it with a comma.

Dimensions. The dimensions element is not core in RDA, but it is core in descriptions of monographs (including moving image resources) for catalogers at the Library of Congress, except for online electronic resources (see LC-PCC PS 3.5, May 2012). Most U.S. catalogers will record this element. Dimensions are recorded in subfield ‡c of a MARC bibliographic 300 field. Separate the dimensions element from any preceding elements in the field with space-semicolon-space.

Record the dimensions of a moving image resource following the appropriate instructions in RDA 3.5.1.4. Moving image carriers include cartridges (3.5.1.4.2), cassettes (3.5.1.4.3), discs (3.5.1.4.4), and reels (3.5.1.4.9). For details, see chapter 2 of this *Handbook* under 3.5.1.

Content Type. The content type element is not part of the description of the carrier, but it is treated here because it is generally the next element after the dimensions recorded in the MARC bibliographic record. Content type is a core element, and is recorded in subfield ‡a of the MARC 336 field following the instructions in RDA 6.9. Record, as appropriate, one of the terms in the list found in RDA 6.9.1.3. End the field with "‡2 rdacontent":

336   ‡a two-dimensional moving image ‡2 rdacontent

The most common content type for moving image resources is "two-dimensional moving image," but "three-dimensional moving image" may become more common in the future. "Performed music," "spoken word," and "cartographic moving image" are also possible content types for moving image resources. For details, see chapter 8 of this *Handbook* at 6.9.

Media and Carrier Type. Carrier type is core in an RDA description. Media type is not core, but most U.S. catalogers follow LC and PCC practice and record it (see LC-PCC PS 3.2, October 2012).

Media type is recorded in subfield ‡a of a MARC bibliographic 337 field. The term should be taken from the list in RDA 3.2.1.3. For most moving image resources, use "video." End the field with "‡2 rdamedia":

    337   ‡a video ‡2 rdamedia

Another possible media type is "projected," although this will be less common in most library catalogs.

For online moving image resources, use "computer." Do not code both "computer" and "video" in this element. The resource is either one or the other:

    337   ‡a computer ‡2 rdamedia

Carrier type is recorded in subfield ‡a of a MARC bibliographic 338 field. The term should be taken from the list in RDA 3.3.1.3 from the group that corresponds to the media type chosen. Any of the projected image or video carrier terms there may be used to describe a moving image resource, but the most common are "videodisc" or "videocassette." If appropriate, "online resource" may be used from the list of computer carriers (e.g., for a streaming video file). End the field with "‡2 rdacarrier":

    338   ‡a videodisc ‡2 rdacarrier

Do not "mix and match" media types and carrier types. The carrier type should correspond to the media type:

    337   ‡a computer ‡2 rdamedia
    338   ‡a online resource ‡2 rdacarrier
not
    337   ‡a video ‡2 rdamedia
    338   ‡a online resource ‡2 rdacarrier

As many media and carrier types as necessary may be recorded (e.g., for a resource consisting of a book and a DVD). In exceptional circumstances, a single carrier may exhibit more than one media and carrier type, for example, a disc that contains both sound and video files. Best practices for this situation have not yet been established. This *Handbook* recommends, in the meantime, that both pairs of media or carrier types be recorded:

    337   ‡a audio ‡2 rdamedia
    337   ‡a video ‡2 rdamedia

338   ‡a audio disc ‡2 rdacarrier
338   ‡a videodisc ‡2 rdacarrier

For details, see chapter 2 of this *Handbook* at 3.2 and 3.3.

Sound Characteristic. The sound characteristic element (RDA 3.16) records details about the encoding of the sound in a resource. In previous cataloging practice as well as early implementation of RDA this element was recorded in subfield ‡b of the 300 field. A new field has been incorporated into MARC for recording this RDA element, the MARC bibliographic 344 field. Not all sub-elements will be appropriate to all types of video resources. Some of the more common sub-elements include: type of recording (analog or digital), recorded in subfield ‡a; recording medium (magnetic, magneto-optical, or optical), recorded in subfield ‡b; and playback configuration (stereo, mono, etc.), recorded in subfield ‡g. For details and fuller explanation, see chapter 2 of this *Handbook* at 3.16.

Video Characteristic. Record the standard used to encode an analog video (e.g., Beta or VHS) in subfield ‡a of the MARC bibliographic 346 field. Record the broadcast standard of the resource, whether analog or digital (e.g., HDTV or NTSC), in subfield ‡b of the 346 field. Both of these pieces of information are most commonly recorded in MARC bibliographic records when the information appears on the resource itself, which it often does. For details and a fuller explanation, see chapter 2 of this *Handbook* at 3.18.

Digital File Characteristic. Record specifications of the digital encoding of a moving image resource (for example, a DVD) in the MARC bibliographic 347 field following the instructions in RDA 3.19. File type is recorded in subfield ‡a. For moving image resources, this will always be "video file." Record one of the terms from the video encoding formats list in 3.19.3 in subfield ‡b. If information about regional encoding is known, record it in subfield ‡e of the 347 field. Regional encoding information is quite important to users of moving image resources. For details on digital file characteristic, see chapter 2 of this *Handbook* at 3.19.

Series Statement. Examine the resource for a series statement. Although information about a series can be taken from outside the resource itself, prefer information found in the resource. Series information is recorded in a MARC bibliographic 490 field. The first indicator is coded "0" if the information is not indexed; it is coded "1" if the information is indexed (in which case an 8XX field will also be present in the bibliographic record; see below under Link the Resource to Related Entities).

Record the title proper of the series in subfield ‡a of the 490 field exactly as it appears in the resource. If series numbering is present, record it in subfield ‡v following the title proper of the series and any other elements (such as a statement of responsibility). Separate series numbering from preceding elements by space-semicolon-space.

The title proper of the series and numbering are core and therefore must be recorded if present. Other title information of the series and statements of responsibility relating to the series are not core and are not in most cases recorded. For details about recording series statements, see chapter 2 of this *Handbook* at 2.12.

Notes. Include any notes you consider necessary to help the library user contextualize, find, identify, or select the resource. No notes are core in an RDA description. Therefore, recording notes in a bibliographic record is entirely dependent on your judgment or the policies of your cataloging agency. Most notes are recorded in the 5XX block of the MARC bibliographic record. Some of the more common notes included in bibliographic records for moving image resources are information about intended audience, including rating (see discussion in chapter 7 of this *Handbook* at 7.7), notes giving plot summaries or other summaries of the contents (see discussion in chapter 8 of this *Handbook* at 7.10); notes about the language of the content (including original language, dubbed languages, subtitles, and closed captioning) (see discussion in chapter 8 of this *Handbook* at 7.12 and 7.14); awards (see discussion in chapter 8 of this *Handbook* at 7.28); aspect ratio (see discussion in chapter 8 of this *Handbook* at 7.19); and date and place of capture (see discussion in chapter 8 of this *Handbook* at 7.11).

Performer, Narrator, and/or Presenter. A particularly important note in a record for a moving image resource is the resource's performers, narrators, and presenters. As mentioned above, statements found in the resource listing these persons, families, or corporate bodies are not recorded as part of a statement of responsibility, but are rather given in a note recorded in the MARC bibliographic 511 field. This is not transcribed information. Simply list the names as concisely as possible, together with information about what they did if necessary. For more information, see chapter 8 of this *Handbook* at 7.23.

Artistic and/or Technical Credit. Another important and frequently encountered note in descriptions of moving image resources is the artistic or technical credit note. Record information identifying persons who have contributed to the artistic or technical production of a resource not as a statement of responsibility, but as a note recorded in the MARC bibliographic 508 field. For more information, see chapter 8 of this *Handbook* at 7.24.

Identifier for the Manifestation. Examine the resource for an identifier, defined as "a character string associated with a manifestation that serves to differentiate that manifestation from other manifestations." The identifier for the manifestation element is core (see RDA 2.15) and therefore an identifier must be recorded if present on the resource.

One identifier commonly associated with moving image resources, especially DVDs, is an ISBN (International Standard Book Number). Record an ISBN in subfield ‡a of the 020 field of the MARC bibliographic record. Copy it as found, but do not record hyphens. Other common identifiers for moving image resources are publishers' catalog numbers, recorded in the MARC 028 field with first indicator coded "4." For details, see chapter 2 of this *Handbook* at 2.15.

5. LINK THE RESOURCE TO RELATED ENTITIES

Once the resource has been described, links should be made to related entities. These include works and expressions either contained in the resource or related to the work(s) or expression(s) described in the record, and related persons, families, corporate bodies, and geographic entities.

In the MARC bibliographic format these links are created by recording the authorized access point for the related entity in one of the access point fields, generally speaking the 1XX, 7XX, and 8XX fields. This either (1) links the bibliographic record to an associated authority record, and via that record links the bibliographic record to other bibliographic records containing the same authorized access point (either by using the text string itself, or using an identifier); (2) directly links the bibliographic record to other bibliographic records containing the same authorized access point; or (3) at the least allows searches to retrieve all bibliographic records containing the same authorized access point.

RDA requires the cataloger to record at least one relationship: that between the resource and the principal creator of the work embodied in the manifestation being described (see discussion in chapter 9 of this *Handbook* at 18.3). Recording most other relationships is optional, but most catalogers will record many.

When considering whether or not a moving image resource has a principal creator, however, catalogers must consult the exceptions under 6.27.1.3, the guideline for creating authorized access points for collaborative works. The authorized access point for collaborative moving image works is formulated using just the preferred title for the work, without including an authorized access point for a creator in the authorized access point for the work. This means that, according to RDA, most moving image resources have no principal creator. RDA 6.27.1.3 does not say that a moving image resource cannot have a principal creator. If such a resource is a work created solely by one person, family, or corporate body, that person, family, or corporate body will be recorded as the principal creator. But such moving image resources are rare. Most will fall under 6.27.1.3.

In the rare case where a moving image resource is considered to have a principal creator, the relationship between the resource and that creator is recorded in a 100 (persons or families), 110 (most corporate bodies), or 111 (meetings) field. But most moving image resource records will record the relationship with creators in 700, 710, or 711.

Begin by recording the authorized access point for creators of the work, usually in 7XX fields. This form may be accompanied by a relationship designator to clarify the nature of the relationship. The use of relationship designators is optional but encouraged (see chapter 9 of this *Handbook* at 18.5). Creators of moving image resources include screenwriters, film directors, film producers, and production companies.

Other commonly recorded relationships for moving image resources include those between the resource and performers. These relationships are all recorded by giving the authorized access point for the related entity in 7XX fields: 700 (persons and families), 710 (most corporate bodies), or 711 (meetings).

Consider also relationships to related works and expressions, or the relationship between the manifestation described in the bibliographic record and the work(s) or expression(s) embodied in the manifestation. One common relationship of this type is the relationship between a fictional film and the textual work (e.g., a novel) it is based on. Related works or expressions are recorded by giving the authorized access point for the work or expression in a 700, 710, 711, or 730 field, or in the case of a series, in an 800, 810, 811, or 830 field. Works or expressions embodied in the manifestation are recorded in a 1XX and 240 field combination or in 130 if there is only one; or if there are two or more, in 700, 710, 711, or 730 fields as appropriate. For details, see discussion throughout chapter 9 of this *Handbook*.

6. SAMPLE RECORD SETS

Other examples of cataloging of moving image resources in this *Handbook* include figures 2.1, 2.4, 2.25, 2.48, 2.108, 7.99, 8.14, 8.18, 8.23, 8.25, 9.8, and 9.38.

RECORD SET F1
DVD

Bibliographic Record

020	‡a 1569388849	*[RDA 2.15]*
024 10	‡a 054961884995	*[RDA 2.15]*
028 42	‡a AMP-8849 ‡b Acorn Media	*[RDA 2.15]*
245 00	‡a PDQ Bach in Houston : ‡b we have a problem! / ‡c written by Peter Schickele.	*[RDA 2.3, 2.4]*
246 3	‡a P.D.Q. Bach in Houston	*[RDA 2.3.6]*
264 1	‡a Silver Spring, MD : ‡b Acorn Media, ‡c [2006]	*[RDA 2.8]*
300	‡a 1 videodisc (approximately 102 min.) : ‡b sound, color ; ‡c 4 3/4 in. *[RDA 3.4.1, 7.22, 7.18, 7.17.3, 3.5.1.3 alternative]*	
336	‡a a two-dimensional moving image ‡2 rdacontent	*[RDA 6.9]*
337	‡a video ‡2 rdamedia	*[RDA 3.2]*
338	‡a videodisc ‡2 rdacarrier	*[RDA 3.3]*
344	‡a digital ‡b optical ‡g stereo ‡g surround ‡2 rda	*[RDA 3.16]*
346	‡a NTSC ‡2 rda	*[RDA 3.18]*
347	‡a video file ‡b DVD video ‡e region 1 ‡2 rda	*[RDA 3.19]*
511 1	‡a Peter Schickele ; OrchestraX ; co-conductor Peter Jacoby ; O.K. Chorale.	*[RDA 7.23]*
508	‡a Producer, Peter Jacoby; directed for the stage, Buck Ross; directed for video, Alan Foster.	*[RDA 7.24]*

500	‡a Full screen (1.33:1).	*[RDA 7.19]*
520	‡a Concert of greatest hits by P.D.Q. Bach, 2005.	*[RDA 7.10]*

505 0	‡a "Desecration of the house" overture -- Schleptet : in E♭ major : S. 0 -- Iphigenia in Brooklyn : S. 52,162 -- "Unbegun" symphony. Minuet ; Andante/Allegro -- New horizons in music appreciation. Symphony no. 5 in C minor. Allegro con brio / Beethoven -- The musical sacrifice : S. 50% off. Fuga meshuga -- The seasonings : S. 1 1/2 tsp.	*[RDA 25.1, 24.4.3a]*

700 1	‡a Bach, P. D. Q., ‡d 1742-1807, ‡e composer.	*[RDA 19.2, 18.4.1.2, 18.5]*
700 1	‡a Schickele, Peter, ‡e performer.	*[RDA 20.2, 18.4.1.2, 18.5]*
700 1	‡a Jacoby, Peter, ‡e conductor.	*[RDA 20.2, 18.4.1.2, 18.5]*
710 2	‡a OrchestraX, ‡e performer.	*[RDA 20.2, 18.4.1.2, 18.5]*
710 2	‡a Acorn Media (Firm), ‡e publisher.	*[RDA 20.2, 18.4.1.2, 18.5]*

Title frames

PDQ Bach in Houston:
We have a Problem!
Professor Peter Schickele, Keeper of the Flame
OrchestraX
Peter Jacoby, Semiconductor

. . .

Written by Peter Schickele

Associated Authority Records

046	‡f [1742-03-31,1742-04-01] ‡g 1807-05-05 ‡2 edtf	*[RDA 9.3]*
100 1	‡a Bach, P. D. Q., ‡d 1742-1807	*[RDA 9.2.2, 9.19.1]*
370	‡a Leipzig (Germany) ‡2 naf	*[RDA 9.8, 9.9]*
374	‡a Composers ‡2 lcsh	*[RDA 9.16]*
375	‡a male	*[RDA 9.7]*
500 1	‡w r ‡i Real identity: ‡a Schickele, Peter	*[RDA 30.1, 30.2, 29.4.2]*
670	‡a P.D.Q. Bach in Houston, 2006	*[RDA 8.12]*
670	‡a The definitive biography of P.D.Q. Bach (1807-1742)?, 1976: ‡b page xiii (dates given on his tomb: 1807-1742) page 3 (born in Leipzig 31 March 1742) *[RDA 8.12]*	
670	‡a The Peter Schickele/P.D.Q. Bach web site, 11 September 2012 ‡b (P.D.Q. Bach was born on April 1, 1742 and died on May 5, 1807) *[RDA 8.12]*	
678 0	‡a P.D.Q. Bach (1742-1807 or 1807-1742) is a fictitious composer invented by musical satirist Peter Schickele. *[RDA 9.17]*	

046	‡f 19350717	*[RDA 9.3]*
100 1	‡a Schickele, Peter	*[RDA 9.2.2, 9.19.1]*
370	‡a Ames (Iowa) ‡2 naf	*[RDA 9.8, 9.9]*
374	‡a Composers ‡2 lcsh	*[RDA 9.16]*

375	‡a male	*[RDA 9.7]*
378	‡q Johann Peter	*[RDA 9.5]*
400 1	‡a Schickele, Johann Peter	*[RDA 9.2.3, 9.19.2]*
500 1	‡w r ‡i Alternate identity: ‡a Bach, P. D. Q., ‡d 1742-1807 *[RDA 30.1, 30.2, 29.4.2]*	
670	‡a The intimate P.D.Q. Bach (1807-1742?), featuring Professor Peter Schickele and the Semi-Pro Musica Antiqua, 1979 *[RDA 8.12]*	
670	‡a New Grove, 2nd ed. ‡b (Schickele, (Johann) Peter; born July 17, 1935, Ames, IA; American composer, arranger, and humorist) *[RDA 8.12]*	
678 0	‡a Peter Schickele (1935-) is an American composer, arranger, and humorist. *[RDA 9.17]*	

100 1	‡a Jacoby, Peter	*[RDA 9.2.2, 9.19.1]*
370	‡f Houston (Tex.) ‡2 naf	*[RDA 9.8, 9.9]*
373	‡a Moores Opera Center ‡2 naf	*[RDA 9.13]*
374	‡a Conductors (Music) ‡a College teachers ‡2 lcsh	*[RDA 9.16]*
375	‡a male	*[RDA 9.7]*
670	‡a Argento, D. Casanova's homecoming, 2004: ‡b disc label (Peter Jacoby, conductor) *[RDA 8.12]*	
670	‡a Peter Jacoby, Conductor, via WWW, 12 September 2012 ‡b (Music Director/ Principal Conductor, Moores Opera Center, University of Houston, Houston, Texas; visiting associate professor of music) *[RDA 8.12]*	

046	‡s 1996	*[RDA 11.4]*
110 2	‡a OrchestraX	*[RDA 11.2.2, 11.13.1]*
368	‡a Symphony orchestras ‡2 lcsh	*[RDA 11.7]*
370	‡e Houston (Tex.) ‡2 naf	*[RDA 11.3]*
410 2	‡a Orch. X	*[RDA 11.2.3, 11.13.2]*
500 1	‡w r ‡i Founder: ‡a Axelrod, John, ‡d 1966-	*[RDA 30.1, 30.2, 29.4.2]*
670	‡a P.D.Q. Bach in Houston, 2006: ‡b credits (OrchestraX) container (Orch. X) *[RDA 8.12]*	
670	‡a OrchestraX WWW site, Aug. 23, 2007 ‡b (OrchestraX; Orch. X; from Houston, TX, founded 1996 by John Axelrod) *[RDA 8.12]*	

110 2	‡a Acorn Media (Firm)	*[RDA 11.2.2, 11.13.1]*
370	‡e Bethesda (Md.) ‡2 naf	*[RDA 11.3]*
410 2	‡a Acorn Media Publishing, Inc.	*[RDA 11.2.3, 11.13.2]*
670	‡a The far pavilions, 1995: ‡b container (distributed . . . by Acorn Media, Bethesda, MD) *[RDA 8.12]*	
670	‡a Bernadette Peters in concert, 1999: ‡b title frames (Acorn Media Publishing, Inc.) *[RDA 8.12]*	

RECORD SET F2
STREAMING VIDEO

Bibliographic Record

245 02	‡a A day with Thomas A. Edison / ‡c General Electric Company presents ; Bray Productions, Inc.	*[RDA 2.3, 2.4]*
264 1	‡a [Washington, D.C.] : ‡b [Library of Congress], ‡c [2005?]	*[RDA 2.8]*
264 4	‡c 1922	
300	‡a 1 online resource (approximately 25 min.) : ‡b silent, black and white	*[RDA 3.4.1, 7.22, 7.18, 7.17.3]*
336	‡a two-dimensional moving image ‡2 rdacontent	*[RDA 6.9]*
337	‡a computer ‡2 rdamedia	*[RDA 3.2]*
338	‡a online resource ‡2 rdacarrier	*[RDA 3.3]*
347	‡a video file ‡b Quick Time ‡b RealVideo ‡b MPEG ‡2 rda	*[RDA 3.19]*
500	‡a Digitized as part of the Library of Congress's American Memory project.	*[RDA 2.20]*
500	‡a Duration: 3:37 (part 1), 4:13 (part 2), 4:02 (part 3), 4:02 (part 4), 4:15 (part 5), and 3:35 (part 6) at 16 fps.	*[RDA 7.22]*
518	‡a Originally produced by General Electric Co. in approximately 1922.	*[RDA 7.11]*
520	‡a A six-part documentary recording the 74-year-old Edison's collaborations with his staff, conversations with industrial leaders, and supervision of the factory's production line. The majority of the film (parts 3, 4, and 5) chronicles Edison's trip to the incandescent light bulb factory and details its manufacturing process.	*[RDA 7.10]*
710 2	‡a General Electric Company, ‡e film producer.	*[RDA 20.2, 18.4.1.2, 18.5]*
710 2	‡a Bray Productions, ‡e production company.	*[RDA 20.2, 18.4.1.2, 18.5]*
856 41	‡u http://hdl.loc.gov/loc.mbrsmi/edmp.4057	*[RDA 4.6]*

Title screen
AMERICAN MEMORY
Early Motion Pictures, 1897-1920
Movie 96 of 412
A day with Thomas A. Edison / General Electric Co. ; producer, Bray Studios
Title frame
GENERAL ELECTRIC COMPANY presents
A DAY WITH Thomas A Edison
BRAY PRODUCTIONS INC.

Associated Authority Records

046	‡s 1892	*[RDA 11.4]*
110 2	‡a General Electric Company	*[RDA 11.2.2, 11.13.1]*
370	‡e Fairfield (Conn.) ‡2 naf	*[RDA 11.3]*
410 2	‡a General Electric	*[RDA 11.2.3, 11.13.2]*

410 2	‡a GE	*[RDA 11.2.3, 11.13.2]*
410 2	‡a G.E.	*[RDA 11.2.3, 11.13.2]*
510 2	‡w r ‡i Mergee: ‡a Edison General Electric Company	*[RDA 32.1, 32.2, 29.4.2]*
510 2	‡w r ‡i Mergee: ‡a Thomson-Houston Electric Company	*[RDA 32.1, 32.2, 29.4.2]*
670	‡a A Power History of the Consolidated Edison System 1878-1900, 1940: ‡b page 13 (Edison General Electric Company succeeded as parent company in 1889 and was succeeded by the General Electric Company in 1892)	*[RDA 8.12]*
670	‡a A self-balancing capacitance bridge, 1947: ‡b t.p. (General Electric) p. 1 (General Electric Company)	*[RDA 8.12]*
670	‡a NFACT brings GE to light, c1988: ‡b t.p. (GE; General Electric)	*[RDA 8.12]*
670	‡a Wikipedia, July 21, 2011 ‡b (General Electric; General Electric Company; American multinational conglomerate; formed in 1892 in merger of Edison General Electric and Thomson-Houston Electric Company; headquarters, Fairfield, Conn.; founders, Charles Coffin, Edwin Houston, Elihu Thomson, Thomas Edison)	*[RDA 8.12]*
678 1	‡a General Electric Company (established 1892) is an American multinational conglomerate. The company was formed through a merger of Edison General Electric and the Thomson-Houston Electric Company.	*[RDA 11.11]*

046	‡s 1910~ ‡2 edtf	*[RDA 11.4]*
110 2	‡a Bray Productions	*[RDA 11.2.2, 11.13.1]*
510 2	‡a Bray Studios	*[RDA 32.1, 32.2, 29.4.2]*
510 2	‡a Bray Pictures Corporation	*[RDA 32.1, 32.2, 29.4.2]*
667	‡a All three companies are related, but unable to determine exact relationships between them.	*[RDA 8.13]*
670	‡a Reproductive system and human development, 1925: ‡b credit frame (Bray Productions, Inc.; New York City)	*[RDA 8.12]*
670	‡a The American film industry, 1986: ‡b page 48 (Bray Studios, Inc.; formed in early 1910s; Bray Studios enlarged and Bray Pictures Corporation founded in June, 1919; animation studio closed in 1927, continued to produce documentaries and educational filmstrips)	*[RDA 8.12]*
670	‡a Phone call to Bray Studios, 9 September 1992 ‡b (Bray Pictures Corporation might have been part of Bray Productions)	*[RDA 8.12]*

RECORD SET F3
FILM REEL

Bibliographic Record

130 0	‡a I wanted wings (Motion picture : 1941)	*[RDA 17.6, 17.4.2.2]*
245 10	‡a I wanted wings / ‡c a Paramount Picture ; produced by Arthur Hornblow, Jr. ; directed by Mitchell Leisen ; screen play by Richard Maibaum, Lieut. Beirne Lay, Jr., and Sig Herzig.	*[RDA 2.3, 2.4]*
264 1	‡a [Place of publication not identified] : ‡b [Publisher not identified], ‡c [1941]	*[RDA 2.8]*
264 2	‡a [United States] : ‡b Paramount Pictures	*[RDA 2.9]*

264	4	‡c ©1941	[RDA 2.11]

300	‡a 3 film reels (134 min., 4,860 ft.) : ‡b sound, black and white ; ‡c 36 cm, 16 mm [RDA 3.4.1, 7.22, 7.18, 7.17.3, 3.5.1.4.9]
336	‡a two-dimensional moving image ‡2 rdacontent [RDA 6.9]
337	‡a projected ‡2 rdamedia [RDA 3.2]
338	‡a film reel ‡2 rdacarrier [RDA 3.3]
344	‡a analog ‡g mono ‡2 rda [RDA 3.16]
500	‡a Based on a story by Eleanore Griffin and Frank Wead; from the book "I Wanted Wings" by Lieut. Beirne Lay, Jr. [RDA 25.1]
508	‡a Director of photography, Leo Tover ; music score, Victor Young ; art direction, Hans Dreier, Robert Usher ; editor, Hugh Bennett. [RDA 7.24]
511 1	‡a Ray Milland, William Holden, Wayne Morris, Brian Donlevy, Constance Moore, Harry Davenport, Veronica Lake. [RDA 7.23]
520	‡a Eighteen Army Air Corps bombers head toward Los Angeles to engage in a simulated air raid. At the completion of the air raid one of the bombers crashes in the desert and the body of a woman is found in the wreckage. [RDA 7.10]
586	‡a Academy Awards 1942: Best Effects, Special Effects for Farciot Edouart and Gordon Jennings (photographic effects) & Louis Mesenkop (sound effects) [RDA 7.28]
500	‡a Full screen (1.37:1). [RDA 7.19]
700 1	‡a Leisen, Mitchell, ‡d 1898-1972, ‡e film director. [RDA 19.3, 18.4.1.2, 18.5]
	... [access points for producer, writers, actors omitted]
710 2	‡a Paramount Pictures Corporation (1914-1927), ‡e film producer, ‡e film distributor. [RDA 19.3, 21.4, 18.4.1.2, 18.5]

Title frames

A Parmount Picture
I WANTED WINGS
COPYRIGHT MCMXLI BY PARAMOUNT PICTURES INC
STARRING
RAY MILLAND
WILLIAM HOLDEN
WAYNE MORRIS
BRIAN DONLEVY

. . .

PRODUCED BY Arthur Hornblow, Jr.
DIRECTED BY Mitchell Leisen
Screen Play by RICHARD MAIBAUM, LIEUT. BEIRNE LAY, JR. and SIG HERZIG

Associated Authority Records

046	‡k 1941	*[RDA 6.4]*
130 0	‡a I wanted wings (Motion picture : 1941)	*[6.2.2, 6.27.1.3, 6.27.1.9]*
380	‡a Motion pictures ‡2 lcsh	
500 1	‡w r ‡i Motion picture adaptation of (work): ‡a Lay, Beirne, ‡d 1909-1982. ‡t I wanted wings	*[RDA 25.1, 25.2, 24.4.2]*
670	‡a I wanted wings, 1941: ‡b title screen (from the book "I Wanted Wings" by Lieut. Beirne Lay, Jr.)	*[RDA 5.8]*
670	‡a Internet movie database, via WWW, Sept. 11, 2012 ‡b (I Wanted Wings; motion picture produced by Paramount Pictures and released in 1941)	*[RDA 5.8]*

046	‡f 18981006 ‡g 19721028	*[RDA 9.3]*
100 1	‡a Leisen, Mitchell, ‡d 1898-1972	*[RDA 9.2.2, 9.19.1]*
370	‡a Menominee (Mich.) ‡b Woodland Hills (Los Angeles, Calif.) ‡2 naf	*[RDA 9.8, 9.9]*
374	‡a Motion picture producers and directors ‡2 lcsh	*[RDA 9.16]*
375	‡a male	*[RDA 9.7]*
377	‡a eng	*[RDA 9.14]*
378	‡q James Mitchell	*[RDA 9.5]*
400 1	‡a Leisen, James Mitchell, ‡d 1898-1972	*[RDA 9.2.3, 9.19.2]*
670	‡a Artists and models abroad, 1938: ‡b credits (directed by Mitchell Leisen)	*[RDA 8.12]*
670	‡a International film necrology, 1981 ‡b (Mitchell Leisen; James Mitchell Leisen; born 6 October 1898, Menominee, Mich.; died 29 October 1972, Woodland Hills, Los Angeles, Calif.; director)	*[RDA 8.12]*
678 0	‡a Mitchell Leisen (1898-1972) was an American film director.	*[RDA 9.17]*

046	‡s 1914 ‡t 1927	*[RDA 11.4]*
110 2	‡a Paramount Pictures Corporation (1914-1927)	*[RDA 11.2.2, 11.13.1]*
368	‡Distributors (Commerce) ‡2 lcsh	*[RDA 11.7]*
410 2	‡a Paramount Pictures	*[RDA 11.2.3, 11.13.2]*
510 2	‡w r ‡ i Product of a merger: ‡a Paramount Famous Lasky Corporation	*[RDA 32.1, 32.2, 29.4.2]*
500 1	‡w r ‡ i Founder: ‡a Hodkinson, W. W. ‡q (William Wadsworth), ‡d 1881-1971	*[RDA 30.1, 30.2, 29.4.2]*
670	‡a Beggar on horseback, 1925: ‡b credits (Paramount Pictures)	*[RDA 8.12]*
670	‡a AFI catalog: features 1911-1920, index, 1988: ‡b page 246 (Paramount Pictures Corporation, a distribution company formed in 1914; in 1918 changed name to Paramount Pictures [1918-1927])	*[RDA 8.12]*

670 ‡a International motion pictures almanac, 1982: ‡b page 475 (Paramount Famous Lasky Corporation [1927-1930] formed in 1927 from a merger of Paramount Pictures and Famous Players-Lasky Corporation [1916-1927])   *[RDA 8.12]*

670 ‡a Wikipedia, January 20, 2011 ‡b (Paramount Pictures Corporation; established in 1914 by W.W. Hodkinson)   *[RDA 8.12]*

678 1 ‡a Paramount Pictures Corporation was a motion picture distributioncompany. Established in 1914 by W. W. Hodkinson, the company was acquired by Famous Players-Lasky Corporation in 1917. In 1927 it was merged with Famous Players-Lasky and reorganized as the Paramount Famous Lasky Corporation. *[RDA 11.11]*

TWO-DIMENSIONAL GRAPHIC RESOURCES

THIS APPENDIX CONTAINS A RECOMMENDED PROCESS FOR CREAT-
ing bibliographic records for two-dimensional graphic resources such as paintings and posters. It covers bibliographic record creation for these resources only in the most general of terms. Unusual situations are covered in the body of the *Handbook*. As with the *Handbook* itself, this appendix does not cover non-RDA related aspects of the bibliographic record, such as fixed-length data elements (the so-called fixed fields) or subject analysis. This appendix also contains three sample record sets consisting of bibliographic records and their associated authority records, which illustrate many of the points described below.

Elizabeth W. Betz's *Graphic Materials: Rules for Describing Original Items and Historical Collections* was designed to be used as a supplement to the rules contained in AACR2 chapter 8, but its concepts and principles are applicable to RDA.[1] A second edition is underway, which will take RDA into account.[2] Another important and useful supplement to general cataloging guidelines for graphic resources is the Visual Resources Association's *Cataloging Cultural Objects*.[3]

1. DETERMINE THE MODE OF ISSUANCE

Consider the mode of issuance of the resource. Does it consist of a single unit? Is it a multipart monograph? Is it a serial or integrating resource? Mode of issuance is defined in RDA 1.1.3.

> A single-unit resource is a resource issued either as a single physical unit (e.g., a mural) or a single logical unit (e.g., a PDF file of a work of art).

A multipart monograph is a resource issued in two or more parts that is complete or is intended to be complete within a finite number of parts.

A serial is a resource issued in successive parts, usually bearing numbering, that has no predetermined conclusion.

An integrating resource is a resource that is added to or changed by means of updates that do not remain discrete but are integrated into the whole.

This appendix covers single units and multipart monographs. For serials or integrating resources in any format, see appendix K.

2. DECIDE ON THE TYPE OF DESCRIPTION

Consider the type of description you want to create. RDA 1.1.4 mentions three types of description: comprehensive, analytical, and hierarchical.

A comprehensive description describes the resource as a whole.

An analytical description describes a part of a larger resource.

A hierarchical description combines a comprehensive description of a whole resource with analytical descriptions of one or more of its parts.

U.S. cataloging practice does not use hierarchical descriptions; therefore, these will not be described here. Analytical descriptions are described in appendix L. This appendix covers comprehensive descriptions.

3. CHOOSE THE BASIS FOR IDENTIFICATION AND SOURCES OF INFORMATION FOR THE RESOURCE

Examine the resource and choose a basis for identification following the instructions in RDA 2.1. If the resource is issued as a single-unit resource, the resource itself will be the basis for identification. If the resource is issued in more than one part, choose the earliest or first part if that is possible. Otherwise prefer a part containing a source of information that identifies the resource as a whole. As a last resort, treat all the parts as a collective source of information. For details, see chapter 2 of this *Handbook* at 2.1.

Having chosen the part that will serve as the basis for identification, choose a "preferred source of information" within that part following the instructions in RDA 2.2. The preferred source of information for a two-dimensional graphic materials resource is the title page, title sheet, or title card (RDA 2.2.2.2). For details, see chapter 2 of this *Handbook* at 2.2. Possible sources for graphic materials include text accompanying the image, lists of plates, and metadata (for digital resources).

4. DESCRIBE THE RESOURCE

Titles and Statements of Responsibility. Transcribe the title proper, other title information, and statement of responsibility in a MARC bibliographic 245 field. For information about transcription, see chapter 2 of this *Handbook* at 1.7.

Transcribe the title proper in subfield ‡a of the 245 field exactly as found on the preferred source of information (see RDA 2.3.2). Title proper is a core element and therefore must be included in the description. For details, see chapter 2 of this *Handbook* at 2.3.

If the resource does not contain a title (a common occurrence with two-dimensional graphic resources), devise a title and record it in square brackets, unless the resource is "of a type that does not normally carry identifying information" (RDA 2.2.4). Many unpublished two-dimensional graphic resources are of the type that do not normally carry identifying information (e.g., an oil painting), and therefore devised titles in their descriptions do not need to be recorded in square brackets. On the other hand, published graphic materials (such as posters) probably do not fall into this category; devised titles for these should usually be bracketed. This is a matter for the cataloger's judgment.

Transcription of other title information is optional in RDA, although core for the Library of Congress. Most U.S. catalogers will follow LC practice and include other title information in the description. If including other title information, transcribe it after the title proper in subfield ‡b of the 245 field (see RDA 2.3.4). Other title information should be transcribed from the same source as the title proper. The first piece of other title information is separated from the title proper by space-colon-space. Subsequent pieces of other title information are separated from each other by space-colon-space. For details, see chapter 2 of this *Handbook* at 2.3.4.

The first statement of responsibility relating to the title proper is a core element in RDA. Other statements of responsibility are optional, although most catalogers will record them. If including statements of responsibility in the description, transcribe them after the title proper or other information in subfield ‡c of the 245 field (see RDA 2.4.1 and 2.4.2). Statements of responsibility may be transcribed from any source within the resource itself. In unusual situations, a statement of responsibility may be transcribed from outside the resource itself, but in that case it should be bracketed. This will rarely be necessary. The first statement of responsibility is separated from the title proper (or other title information) by space-slash-space. Subsequent statements of responsibility are separated from each other by space-semicolon-space. For details, see chapter 2 of this *Handbook* at 2.4.

Variant Titles. Examine the resource for variant titles. Variant titles are not core in RDA, but if in your opinion a library user might attempt to find the resource using one of these titles, record it in subfield ‡a of a 246 field. Variant titles can be taken from any source (see RDA 2.3.6.2), including your own knowledge and reference sources. For economy's sake most catalogers do not look beyond the resource itself for variant titles, but given ambiguity about what the title of a two-dimensional graphic might be, graphic materials catalogers might do some research for variant titles. For details, see chapter 2 of this *Handbook* at 2.3.6.

Edition Statement. Examine the resource for an edition statement. An edition statement can be taken from any source within the resource, but a statement found in the same source as the title proper is preferred. Edition statements may also be taken from outside the resource, but if so, they should be bracketed.

Designation of edition is a core element, and therefore must be recorded if present in the resource. If found, transcribe a designation of edition (e.g., "New version") in subfield ‡a of a 250 field (see RDA 2.5.2).

Recording other elements of the edition statement is optional in RDA. The most common other element is a statement of responsibility relating to the edition. If you find such a statement and decide to include it in the description, record it following space-slash-space in subfield ‡b of the 250 field.

For details on recording an edition statement, see chapter 2 of this *Handbook* at 2.5.

Production Statement (Unpublished Materials). Examine unpublished resources for production information, including place of production, producer, and date of production. Although information about production can be taken from outside the resource itself (and this is common with unpublished resources), prefer information found inside the resource, and within the resource, prefer information found in the same source as the title proper. Production information is recorded in a MARC bibliographic 264 field, with the second indicator coded "0."

The place of production element is not core in RDA and, because the information is often difficult to determine, it is usually not recorded. However, if a place of production is found in the resource, you may record it in subfield ‡a of the 264 field. Transcribe the information exactly as found (see RDA 2.7.2). If the place of production is not found in the resource but is known, the cataloger may supply the information in square brackets.

Like place of production, the producer's name element is not core in RDA and, because the information is often difficult to determine, is usually not recorded. However, if a producer's name is found in the resource, you may record it in subfield ‡b of the 264 field. Transcribe the information exactly as found (see RDA 2.7.4). If the producer's name is not found in the resource but is known, the cataloger may supply the information in square brackets.

Record the date of production. Record numerals in the form preferred by your cataloging agency (see RDA 1.8.2). The date of production element is core. If no explicit date of publication is found in the resource either supply information found in another source or inferred by the cataloger, or record "Date of production not identified" (see RDA 2.7.6). Take note of RDA 2.7.6.2, sources of information. Because the date of production can be taken from any source it is not bracketed even if the information is found outside the resource.

Because the place of production and producer's name elements are not core the date of production will usually be recorded alone in subfield ‡c of the 264 field. However, if any preceding elements are present, place a comma immediately after the element, before the date of production element.

Publication Statement (Published Materials). Examine published resources for publication information, including place of publication, publisher, and date of publication. Although information about publication can be taken from outside the resource itself, prefer information found inside the resource, and within the resource, prefer information found in the same source as the title proper. Publication information is recorded in a MARC bibliographic 264 field, with the second indicator coded "1."

Record the first place of publication found in the resource in subfield ‡a of the 264 field. Transcribe the information exactly as found. This element is core. If no place is found in the resource either supply (in brackets) information from another source about the place of publication, or record "[Place of publication not identified]." If more than one place of publication is found in the resource, you may optionally record them all, but only the first is required. For details, see chapter 2 of this *Handbook* at 2.8.2.

Record the first publisher associated with the first place of publication found in the resource in subfield ‡b of the 264 field. Transcribe the information exactly as found. This element is core. If no publisher is found in the resource either supply (in brackets) information about the publisher from another source, or record "[Publisher not identified]." Separate the place of publication from the publisher's name with space colon space. If more than one publisher is found in the resource, you may optionally record them all, but only the first is required. For details, see chapter 2 of this *Handbook* at 2.8.4.

Record the date of publication. Record numerals in the form preferred by your cataloging agency (see RDA 1.8.2). Place a comma immediately after the publisher's name and record the date of publication in subfield ‡c of the 264 field. The date of publication element is core. If no explicit date of publication is found in the resource either supply (in brackets) information found in another source or inferred by the cataloger, or record "[Date of publication not identified]." Note that a copyright date is not a publication date. A copyright date can never be substituted for a publication date in RDA, but it may optionally be recorded in addition to the date of publication element. It may also be used as evidence for inferring the date of publication.

If the date of publication has not been identified, then either a date of distribution or a copyright date, if present in the resource, must be recorded (see discussion, however, in chapter 2 of this *Handbook* at 2.8.6.6 on ways to identify the date of publication). If recording a copyright date, include the copyright symbol (©) and record it in subfield ‡c of a separate 264 field, with the second indicator coded "4."

Because either the production statement or the publication statement is core, all RDA records must include one or the other (and RDA records coded in MARC will have at least one 264 field, with second indicator coded either "0" or "1"). For details about production statement, publication statement, and copyright date, see chapter 2 of this *Handbook* at 2.7, 2.8, and 2.11.

Distribution and manufacture (printing) information may be recorded, but is optional if production or publication information has been identified. For details, see chapter 2 of this *Handbook* at 2.9 and 2.10.

Describe the Carrier. A carrier is the physical medium in which the content of a resource is stored. Carriers for two-dimensional graphic resources are usually sheets, but other carriers are possible, especially for reproductions of resources (e.g., slides, computer discs, or online resources). Examine the resource for physical details, including size. Several carrier-related elements are required in an RDA record. Most are recorded in the 3XX block of the bibliographic record.

Extent. The extent of the resource is recorded in subfield ‡a of a MARC bibliographic 300 field. Extent is core if the resource is complete. Record the extent of a two-dimensional graphic resource following the instructions in RDA 3.4.4. Only the most basic procedures will be mentioned in this appendix. For details, see chapter 2 of this *Handbook* at 3.4.

Record the number of units together with an appropriate term from RDA 3.4.4.3. Note some of these terms represent a change from previous cataloging practice. Instead of AACR2's "art original," use "collage," "drawing," "icon," "painting," or "print." Instead of "art print" or "art reproduction," use "print." In some cases, "sheet" may be appropriate (see RDA 3.4.5.14 and 3.4.5.20), especially if the graphic resource includes text. Reproductions of graphics may use appropriate terms from the carrier type list (e.g., "slide" or "online resource"). If the graphics are contained in an album or portfolio, follow RDA 3.4.4.5.

Colour Content. Though not considered in RDA to be part of the carrier description, this element is treated here because it is recorded immediately after the extent element in the MARC bibliographic record. Examine the resource for color content. If the image is in black and white or shades of grey, record "black and white" in subfield ‡b of the 300 field. If the image is in more than two colors, record "color." If the image is in one or two colors, record the names of the colors (e.g., "yellow and green"). Digital still images may record "grayscale" if appropriate (see RDA 7.17.2.3). Separate this element from the preceding extent element with space-semicolon-space. For details on colour content, see chapter 8 of this *Handbook* at 7.17.

Note that under previous practice, other elements aside from colour content were recorded in subfield ‡b of the MARC 300 field. They may be recorded elsewhere in the RDA record. See below under Base Material and in the following sections.

Dimensions. The dimensions element is not core in RDA, but it is core in descriptions of monographs for catalogers at the Library of Congress, except for online electronic resources (see LC-PCC PS 3.5, May 2012). Most U.S. catalogers will record this element. Dimensions are recorded in subfield ‡c of a MARC bibliographic 300 field. Separate the dimensions element from any preceding elements in the field with space-semicolon-space.

Record the dimensions of a two-dimensional graphic resource following the instructions in 3.5.3. Record the measurements of the *pictorial area* (not the sheet itself). Record the height x width, diameter, or other appropriate dimensions, rounding up to the nearest centimeter (e.g., 31 x 10 cm). If the print includes a plate mark (e.g., a copper engraving), the measurement of the plate mark may be given separately. See RDA 3.5.3.2 for details.

If the measurement of the sheet is significantly greater than that of the pictorial area (i.e., more than twice as large), also record the dimensions of the sheet, preceding the measurements with the words "on sheet." Record the dimensions in the same way, height x width rounded up to the nearest centimeter (see RDA 3.5.3.3). If the dimensions of the sheet are considered important but they are not twice the size of the pictorial area, this information can be recorded in a note.

If the record has a series statement, record a period at the end of the field.

Content Type. Like the colour content element described above, the content type element is not part of the description of the carrier, but it is treated here because it is generally the next element after the dimensions recorded in the MARC bibliographic record. Content type is a core element, and is recorded in subfield ‡a of the MARC 336 field following the instructions in RDA 6.9. Record, as appropriate, one of the terms in the list found in RDA 6.9.1.3. End the field with "‡2 rdacontent":

336   ‡a still image ‡2 rdacontent

The most common content type for a two-dimensional graphic resource is "still image." More than one content type can be recorded, however; therefore, in some cases other terms from the list may also be appropriate. For details, see chapter 8 of this *Handbook* at 6.9.

Media and Carrier Type. Carrier type is core in an RDA description. Media type is not core, but most U.S. catalogers follow LC and PCC practice and record it (see LC-PCC PS 3.2, October 2012).

Media type is recorded in subfield ‡a of a MARC bibliographic 337 field. The term should be taken from the list in RDA 3.2.1.3. For a graphic on a medium such as paper, use "unmediated." End the field with "‡2 rdamedia":

337   ‡a unmediated ‡2 rdamedia

For a reproduction of a graphic, use the appropriate media type (e.g., "computer," "projected," or "microform").

Carrier type is recorded in subfield ‡a of a MARC bibliographic 338 field. The term should be taken from the list in RDA 3.3.1.3 corresponding to the chosen media type. Most of the unmediated terms found there might be used to describe a two-dimensional graphic resource, but the most common is probably "sheet." End the field with "‡2 rdacarrier":

> 338 ‡a sheet ‡2 rdacarrier

For details, see chapter 2 of this *Handbook* at 3.2 and 3.3.

Base Material. Record the underlying physical material of a resource (e.g., "paper" or "silk") if this is considered important. This element is recorded in subfield ‡a of the MARC bibliographic 340 field. For details, see chapter 2 of this *Handbook* at 3.6.

Applied Material. Record the substance applied to the base material (e.g., "ink" or "oil paint") if considered important. This element is recorded in subfield ‡c of the MARC bibliographic 340 field. For details, see chapter 2 of this *Handbook* at 3.7.

Mount. Record the physical material used to support or back the resource (e.g., "wood") if considered important. This element is recorded in subfield ‡e of the MARC bibliographic 340 field. For details, see chapter 2 of this *Handbook* at 3.8.

Production Method. Record the process used to produce the resource (e.g., "engraving," "daguerreotype," "blueprint") if considered important. This element is recorded in subfield ‡d of the MARC bibliographic 340 field. For details, see chapter 2 of this *Handbook* at 3.9.

Layout. Record the layout of the resource (e.g., "double sided" or "single sided") if this is considered important. This element is recorded in subfield ‡k of the MARC bibliographic 340 field. For details, see chapter 2 of this *Handbook* at 3.11.

Polarity. For photographs, record the polarity (e.g., "positive" or "negative") if considered important. This element is recorded in subfield ‡o of the MARC bibliographic 340 field. For details, see chapter 2 of this *Handbook* at 3.14.

Digital File Characteristic. For digital reproductions of graphic resources, record characteristics of the digital file in the MARC 347 field. For details, see chapter 2 of this *Handbook* at 3.19.

Series Statement. Examine the resource for a series statement. Although information about a series can be taken from outside the resource itself, prefer information found in the resource. Series information is recorded in a MARC bibliographic 490 field. The first indicator is coded "0" if the information is not indexed; it is coded "1" if the information is indexed (in which case an 8XX field will also be present in the bibliographic record; see below under Link the Resource to Related Entities).

Record the title proper of the series in subfield ‡a of the 490 field exactly as it appears in the resource. If series numbering is present, record it in subfield ‡v following the title proper of the series and any other elements (such as a statement of responsibility). Separate series numbering from preceding elements by space-semicolon-space.

The title proper of the series and numbering are core and therefore must be recorded if present. Other title information of the series and statements of responsibility relating to the series are not core and are not in most cases recorded. For details about recording series statements, see chapter 2 of this *Handbook* at 2.12.

Notes. Include any notes you consider necessary to help the library user contextualize, find, identify, or select the resource. No notes are core in an RDA description. Therefore, recording notes in a bibliographic record is entirely dependent on your judgment or the policies of your cataloging agency. Most notes are recorded in the 5XX block of the MARC bibliographic record. Some of the more common notes included in bibliographic records for two-dimensional graphic resources are notes giving summaries of the nature or scope of the content (see discussion in chapter 8 of this *Handbook* at 7.10), notes giving information about the attribution of the work to the creator if that is not clear from the context (see RDA 2.20.3.3 and discussion in chapter 2 of this *Handbook* at 2.20.3), notes giving details about the numbering of an individual copy (see discussion in chapter 2 of this *Handbook* at 3.21), and notes giving the source of the title (see discussion in chapter 2 of this *Handbook* at 2.20.2).

Identifier for the Manifestation. Examine the resource for an identifier, defined as "a character string associated with a manifestation that serves to differentiate that manifestation from other manifestations." The identifier for the manifestation element is core (see RDA 2.15) and therefore an identifier must be recorded if present on the resource. Two-dimensional graphic resources rarely have identifiers, but a published resource might have an ISBN (International Standard Book Number). Record an ISBN in subfield ‡a of the 020 field of the MARC bibliographic record. Copy it as found, but do not record hyphens. For details, see chapter 2 of this *Handbook* at 2.15.

5. LINK THE RESOURCE TO RELATED ENTITIES

Once the resource has been described, links should be made to related entities. These include works and expressions either contained in the resource or related to the work(s) or expression(s) described in the record, and related persons, families, corporate bodies, and geographic entities.

In the MARC bibliographic format these links are created by recording the authorized access point for the related entity in one of the access point fields, generally speaking the 1XX, 7XX, and 8XX fields. This either (1) links the bibliographic record to an associated authority record, and via that record links the bibliographic record to other bibliographic records containing the same authorized access point (either by using the text string itself, or using an identifier); (2) directly links the bibliographic record to other bibliographic records containing the same authorized access point; or (3) at the least allows searches to retrieve all bibliographic records containing the same authorized access point.

RDA requires the cataloger to record at least one relationship: that between the resource and the principal creator of the work embodied in the manifestation being described (see discussion in chapter 9 of this *Handbook* at 18.3). Recording most other relationships is optional, but most catalogers will record many.

The relationship between the resource and the principal creator of the work is recorded in a 100 (persons or families), 110 (most corporate bodies), or 111 (meetings) field. If there is more than one work in the resource and they are by different creators, record these relationships in 700, 710, or 711.

Although the creators of graphic resources are not usually creating texts, the same guidelines apply as to creators of texts. The artist is the creator of a painting. The photographer is the creator of a photograph, unless the photograph is a reproduction of another graphic (such as a painting). The creator of a work published in reproduction is the same as the creator of the original. This is because we are looking for the creator of the *work*, not the expression or manifestation of the work. A photographic reproduction of a two-dimensional graphic is usually simply a manifestation of the original work.

See chapter 9 of this *Handbook* at 19.2 for help in determining what entity is the principal creator of the work. With persons and families the decision is usually fairly straightforward. Determining if a corporate body or meeting is the creator can be a little trickier, but fairly clear guidelines are laid out at RDA 19.2.1.1.1 (and see corresponding discussion in chapter 9 of this *Handbook*). One provision, 19.2.1.1.1h, particularly applies to graphic resources: if two or more artists act together as a corporate body (i.e., the body has a name) to create an individual work of art, the corporate body is considered the creator of the work (see discussion in chapter 9 of this *Handbook* at 19.2.1.1.1h).

Begin by recording the authorized access point for the principal creator of the work in a 1XX field. This form may be accompanied by a relationship designator to clarify the nature of the relationship. The use of relationship designators is optional but encouraged (see *Handbook* chapter 9 of this *Handbook* at 18.5).

Once the relationship to the principal creator has been recorded, think about other relationships that might be helpful. First consider other creators if there are more than one. Other commonly recorded relationships for two-dimensional graphic resources include the relationship between the resource and a printer (e.g., of a woodcut created by another artist) or the relationship to a work the resource is based on. These relationships are all recorded by giving the authorized access point for the related entity in 7XX fields: 700 (persons and families), 710 (most corporate bodies), or 711 (meetings).

Consider also relationships to related works and expressions, or the relationship between the manifestation described in the bibliographic record and the work(s) or expression(s) embodied in the manifestation. Related works or expressions are recorded by giving the authorized access point for the work or expression in a 700, 710, 711, or 730 field, or in the case of a series, in an 800, 810, 811, or 830 field. Works or expressions embodied in the manifestation are recorded in a 1XX and 240 field combination or in 130 if there is only one; or if there are two or more, in 700, 710, 711, or 730 fields as appropriate. For details, see discussion throughout chapter 9 of this *Handbook*.

6. SAMPLE RECORD SETS

Other examples of two-dimensional graphic resource cataloging in this *Handbook* include figures 2.80 (print), 2.90 (photographs), 2.92 (card), 2.98 (flipchart), 2.100 (transparency), 2.103 (slide set), and 9.27 (painting).

RECORD SET G1
PAINTING

Bibliographic Record

100 1	‡a Le Blant, Julien, ‡d 1851-1936, ‡e artist.	*[RDA 18.3, 19.2, 18.4.1.2, 18.5]*
245 13	‡a Le bataillon carré / ‡c Julien Le Blant.	*[RDA 2.3, 2.4]*
264 0	‡a not after 1880.	*[RDA 2.7.6, 1.9.2.5]*
300	‡a 1 painting : ‡b color ; ‡c 2273 x 1511 cm	*[RDA 3.4.4, 7.17.2.3, 3.5.3]*
336	‡a still image ‡2 rdacontent	*[RDA 6.9]*
337	‡a unmediated ‡2 rdamedia	*[RDA 3.2]*
338	‡a sheet ‡2 rdacarrier	*[RDA 3.3]*
340	‡a canvas ‡c oil paint ‡d painting	*[RDA 3.6, 3.7, 3.9]*
586	‡a Silver medal, Paris Salon, 1880	*[RDA 7.28]*
586	‡a Gold medal, Paris World's Fair, 1889	*[RDA 7.28]*
500	‡a Title from paperwork received with the painting.	*[RDA 2.20.2]*
500	‡a Reproduced as a photogravure in: Walton, William, 1843-1915. Chefs-d'oeuvre de l'Exposition Universelle de Paris, 1889. -- Philadelphia : George Barrie and Son, Publishers, 1889.	*[RDA 27.1]*
500	‡a Reproduced as a black and white photograph in: Hook, Philip. Popular 19th century painting : a dictionary of European genre painters. -- London : Antique Collectors' Club, 1986.	*[RDA 27.1]*
520	‡a Oil painting depicting an ambush in La Vendée during an insurrection following the French Revolution.	*[RDA 7.10]*

Associated Authority Record

046	‡f 18510330 ‡g 19360228	*[RDA 9.3]*
100 1	‡a Le Blant, Julien, ‡d 1851-1936	*[RDA 9.2.2, 9.19.1]*

370	‡a Paris (France) ‡b Paris (France) ‡2 naf	*[RDA 9.8, 9.11]*
374	‡a Painters ‡a Illustrators ‡a Watercolorists ‡2 lcsh	*[RDA 9.16]*
375	‡a male	*[RDA 9.7]*
400 1	‡a Blant, Julien Le, ‡d 1851-1936	*[RDA 9.2.3, 9.19.2]*
670	‡a Catalogue des dessins originaux de Julien Le Blant, 1891	*[RDA 8.12]*
670	‡a Oxford art online, 19 September 2012 ‡b (Le Blant, Julien; French artist, male; born 30 March 1851 in Paris; died 1936; painter, illustrator, watercolorist) *[RDA 8.12]*	
670	‡a Julien Le Blant, via WWW, 19 September 2012 ‡b (born in Paris 30 March 1851; died in Paris 28 February 1936) *[RDA 8.12]*	

RECORD SET G2
POSTER

Bibliographic Record

110 2	‡a Harold B. Lee Library, ‡a author.	*[RDA 18.3, 19.2.1.1.1a, 18.4.1.2, 18.5]*
245 10	‡a [Cell phone being crushed by a fist].	*[RDA 2.3]*
264 1	‡a [Provo, Utah] : ‡b [Harold B. Lee Library], ‡c [2004]	*[RDA 2.8]*
264 4	‡c 2004	*[RDA 2.11]*
300	‡a 1 print : ‡b color ; ‡c 100 x 41 cm	*[RDA 3.4.4, 7.17.2.3, 3.5.3]*
340	‡a paper ‡c ink ‡d screen print	*[RDA 3.6, 3.7, 3.9]*
500	‡a Title supplied by cataloger.	*[RDA 2.20.2]*
520	‡a Poster depicting Library policy discouraging cell phone use in designated quiet reading areas, with images in the style of Soviet hammer, fist, and star iconography. *[RDA 7.10]*	

Associated Authority Record

046	‡s 1973	*[RDA 11.4]*
110 2	‡a Harold B. Lee Library	*[RDA 11.2.2, 11.13.1]*
368	‡a Libraries ‡2 lcsh	*[RDA 11.7]*
370	‡e Provo (Utah) ‡2 naf	*[RDA 11.3]*
377	‡a eng	*[RDA 11.8]*
410 2	‡a Lee Library	*[RDA 11.2.3, 11.13.2]*
410 2	‡a Brigham Young University. ‡b Harold B. Lee Library	*[RDA 11.2.3, 11.13.2]*
410 2	‡a HBLL	*[RDA 11.2.3, 11.13.2]*
510 2	‡w r ‡i Predecessor: ‡a J. Reuben Clark, Jr., Library	*[RDA 32.1, 32.2, 29.4.2]*
510 2	‡w r ‡i Hierarchical superior: ‡a Brigham Young University	*[RDA 32.1, 32.2, 29.4.2]*
670	‡a Harold B. Lee Library 1995 reaccreditation self-study, 1995	*[RDA 8.12]*

670 ‡a Brigham Young University campus map, via WWW, April 13, 2009 ‡b (Harold B. Lee Library; Lee Library; HBLL; originally named the J. Reuben Clark Library, but library name was changed) *[RDA 8.12]*

670 ‡a BYU Organizational History Project website, viewed on December 2, 2011 ‡b (Harold B. Lee Library; university library at Brigham Young University; previously known as J. Reuben Clark, Jr., Library, renamed 1973; library directors: Donald K. Nelson, 1973-1980; Sterling J. Albrecht, 1980-2002; Randy J. Olsen, 2002-2009; Julene Butler, 2010-) *[RDA 8.12]*

678 1 ‡a The Harold B. Lee Library is the university library at Brigham Young University. Previously known as the J. Reuben Clark, Jr., Library, it was renamed in 1973. Library directors have included Donald K. Nelson (1973-1980), Sterling J. Albrecht (1980-2002), Randy J. Olsen (2002-2009), and Julene Butler (2010-2012). *[RDA 11.11]*

RECORD SET G3
ONLINE REPRODUCTION OF PHOTOGRAPH

Bibliographic Record

100 1 ‡a Irvine, Edith, ‡e photographer. *[RDA 18.3, 19.2, 18.4.1.2, 18.5]*

245 10 ‡a Produce area, dead horses / ‡c Irvine, Edith, photographer. *[RDA 2.3, 2.4]*

264 1 ‡a [Provo, Utah] : ‡b L. Tom Perry Special Collections, Harold B. Lee Library, Brigham Young University, ‡c 2005. *[RDA 2.8]*

300 ‡a 1 online resource (1 photograph) : ‡b grey scale *[RDA 3.4.1.3, 3.4.1.7.5, 3.4.4, 7.17.2.3]*

336 ‡a still image ‡2 rdacontent *[RDA 6.9]*

337 ‡a computer ‡2 rdamedia *[RDA 3.2]*

338 ‡a online resource ‡2 rdacarrier *[RDA 3.3]*

340 ‡o positive ‡2 rda *[RDA 3.14]*

347 ‡a image file ‡b JPEG2000 ‡c 30930.201 KB ‡2 rda *[RDA 3.19]*

500 ‡a Original photograph taken April 1906. *[RDA 27.1, 24.4.3b]*

520 ‡a Produce area in the aftermath of the 1906 San Francisco earthquake, with at least four dead horses lying in a street that has overturned wagons and is filled with brick rubble. People in the back are blurred from movement. On both sides of the street are large buildings. *[RDA 7.10]*

856 40 ‡u http://contentdm.lib.byu.edu/cdm/singleitem/collection/EdithIrvine/id/813/rec/2 *[RDA 4.6]*

856 42 ‡z Finding aid: ‡u http://files.lib.byu.edu/ead/XML/MSSP585.xml *[RDA 4.6]*

Metadata
Title: Produce area, "Dead Horses"
Photographer: Irvine, Edith
Date original: 1906-04
Publisher digital: L. Tom Perry Special Collections, Harold B. Lee Library, Brigham Young
  University
Date digital: 2005-11
Place: San Francisco, California
Dimensions: 12.7 x 17.78 cm (5 x 7 in.)
Medium: gelatin dry plate negative
Collection: Edith Irvine Photograph Collection
Link to finding aid: http://files.lib.byu.edu/ead/XML/MSSP585.xml

Associated Authority Record

046	‡f 18840107 ‡g 19490814	*[RDA 9.3]*
100 1	‡a Irvine, Edith	*[RDA 9.2.2, 9.19.1]*
370	‡a Sheep Ranch (Calif.) ‡b Calaveras County (Calif.) ‡2 naf	*[RDA 9.8, 9.11]*
374	‡a Photographers ‡2 lcsh	*[RDA 9.16]*
375	‡a female	*[RDA 9.7]*
378	‡q Lizzie Edith	*[RDA 9.5]*
670	‡a Gregory, K. Earthquake at dawn, 1992: ‡b CIP galley (photographer Edith Irvine; 22 years old in 1906)	*[RDA 8.12]*
670	‡a FamilySearch, 16 September 2012 ‡b (Lizzie Edith Irvine; born 7 January 1884, Sheep Ranch, Calaveras, California, United States; died 14 August 1949, Calaveras, California, United States)	*[RDA 8.12]*
678 0	‡a Edith Irvine (1884-1949) was an California photographer.	*[RDA 9.17]*

NOTES

1. *Graphic Materials: Rules for Describing Original Items and Historical Collections* (Washington, DC: Library of Congress, 1982); an updated version is available in the *Cataloger's Desktop* at desktop.loc.gov.

2. The second edition will be part of the *Descriptive Cataloging of Rare Materials* suite, prepared by the ACRL Rare Books and Manuscript Section's Bibliographic Standards Committee. For information, see http://dcrmg.pbworks.com/w/page/6108102/ FrontPage.

3. Visual Resources Association, *Cataloging Cultural Objects* (Chicago: American Library Association, 2006).

THREE-DIMENSIONAL RESOURCES AND OBJECTS

THIS APPENDIX CONTAINS A RECOMMENDED PROCESS FOR CREATing bibliographic records for three-dimensional resources such as sculptures, games, etc., as well as manufactured and naturally occurring objects. It covers bibliographic record creation for these resources only in the most general of terms. Unusual situations are covered in the body of the *Handbook*. As with the *Handbook* itself, this appendix does not cover non-RDA related aspects of the bibliographic record, such as fixed-length data elements (the so-called fixed fields) or subject analysis. This appendix also contains four sample record sets consisting of bibliographic records and their associated authority records, which illustrate many of the points described below.

RDA was designed with generalist cataloging in mind, and although it is certainly possible to describe three-dimensional materials using RDA, it may fall short of the needs of some specialist communities. RDA envisions the use of specialist cataloging manuals to supplement the general guidelines.[1] The Visual Resources Association's *Cataloging Cultural Objects*[2] is one of the most important of these manuals for three-dimensional materials of all kinds. Although published before RDA's inception and therefore not designed with RDA in mind, it is heavily influenced by FRBR principles and structure, just as RDA is. The underlying principles and guidance in *Cataloging Cultural Objects* can profitably be applied by catalogers working within RDA.

1. DETERMINE THE MODE OF ISSUANCE

Consider the mode of issuance of the resource. Does it consist of a single unit? Is it a multipart monograph? Is it a serial or integrating resource? Mode of issuance is defined in RDA 1.1.3. The concept presupposes that a resource was in fact *issued*, perhaps excluding naturally occurring objects, but some of the distinctions remain relevant for all kinds of three-dimensional objects.

> A single-unit resource is a resource issued as a single physical unit (e.g., a statue or a building).
>
> A multipart monograph is a resource issued in two or more parts that is complete or is intended to be complete within a finite number of parts (e.g., a set of collectible glasses that came out once a month over a period of a year, or a kit).
>
> A serial is a resource issued in successive parts, usually bearing numbering, which has no predetermined conclusion.
>
> An integrating resource is a resource that is added to or changed by means of updates that do not remain discrete but are integrated into the whole.

This appendix covers single units and multipart monographs. Three-dimensional serials or integrating resources are rare. For serials or integrating resources in any format, see appendix K.

2. DECIDE ON THE TYPE OF DESCRIPTION

Consider the type of description you want to create. RDA 1.1.4 mentions three types of description: comprehensive, analytical, and hierarchical.

> A comprehensive description describes the resource as a whole.
>
> An analytical description describes a part of a larger resource.
>
> A hierarchical description combines a comprehensive description of a whole resource with analytical descriptions of one or more of its parts.

U.S. cataloging practice does not use hierarchical descriptions; therefore these will not be described here. Analytical descriptions are described in appendix L. This appendix covers comprehensive descriptions.

3. CHOOSE THE BASIS FOR IDENTIFICATION AND SOURCES OF INFORMATION FOR THE RESOURCE

Examine the resource and choose a basis for identification following the instructions in RDA 2.1. If the resource is issued as a single-unit resource, the resource itself will be the basis for identification. If the resource is issued in more than one part, choose the earliest or first part if that is possible. Otherwise, prefer a part containing a source of information that identifies the resource as a whole. As a last resort, treat all the parts as a collective source of information. For details, see chapter 2 of this *Handbook* at 2.1.

Having chosen the part that will serve as the basis for identification, choose a "preferred source of information" within that part following the instructions in RDA 2.2. The preferred source of information for a three-dimensional resource is a label bearing a title that is permanently printed on or affixed to the resource (RDA 2.2.2.4). Many three-dimensional resources and nearly all naturally occurring objects lack a such a label. If the resource does not contain such a source of information, another source may be used (see RDA 2.2.4). For a general discussion of sources of information, see chapter 2 of this *Handbook* at 2.2.

4. DESCRIBE THE RESOURCE

Titles and Statements of Responsibility. Transcribe or record the title proper, other title information, and statement of responsibility in a MARC bibliographic 245 field. For information about transcription, see chapter 2 of this *Handbook* at 1.7.

Transcribe the title proper in subfield ‡a of the 245 field exactly as found on the preferred source of information (see RDA 2.3.2). Title proper is a core element and therefore must be included in the description. For details, see chapter 2 of this *Handbook* at 2.3.

If the resource does not contain a title (a common occurrence with three-dimensional resources and nearly all naturally occurring objects), devise a title and record it in square brackets, unless the resource is "of a type that does not normally carry identifying information" (RDA 2.2.4). Many unpublished three-dimensional resources are of the type that do not normally carry identifying information (e.g., an installed art object), and therefore devised titles in their descriptions do not need to be recorded in square brackets. On the other hand, published three-dimensional materials (such as commercially produced reproductions or games) probably do not fall into this category; devised titles for these should usually be bracketed. This is, however, a matter for cataloger judgment.

Transcription of other title information is optional in RDA, although core for the Library of Congress. Most U.S. catalogers will follow LC practice and include other title information in the description. If including other title information, transcribe it after the title proper in subfield ‡b of the 245 field (see RDA 2.3.4). Other title information should be transcribed from the same source as the title proper. The first piece of other title information is separated from the title proper by space-colon-space. Subsequent pieces of other title information are separated from each other by space-colon-space. For details, see chapter 2 of this *Handbook* at 2.3.4.

The first statement of responsibility relating to the title proper is a core element in RDA. Other statements of responsibility are optional, although most catalogers will record them. If including statements of responsibility in the description, transcribe them after the title proper or other information in subfield ‡c of the 245 field (see RDA 2.4.1 and 2.4.2). Statements of responsibility may be transcribed from any source within the resource itself. In unusual situations, a statement of responsibility may be transcribed from outside the resource itself, but in that case it should be bracketed. This will be rarely be necessary. The first statement of responsibility is separated from the title proper (or other title information) by space-slash-space. Subsequent statements of responsibility are separated from each other by space-semicolon-space. For details, see chapter 2 of this *Handbook* at 2.4.

Variant Titles. Examine the resource for variant titles. Variant titles are not core in RDA, but if in your opinion a library user might attempt to find the resource using one of these titles, record it in subfield ‡a of a 246 field. Variant titles can be taken from any source (see RDA 2.3.6.2), including your own knowledge and reference sources. For economy's sake, most catalogers do not look beyond the resource itself for variant titles, but if there is ambiguity about what the title of some three-dimensional resources might be, it might be advisable to do some research for variant titles. For details, see chapter 2 of this *Handbook* at 2.3.6.

Edition Statement. Although edition statements are rare with three-dimensional resources, they do occur. Examine the resource for an edition statement. An edition statement can be taken from any source within the resource, but a statement found in the same source as the title proper is preferred. Edition statements may also be taken from outside the resource, but if so, they should be bracketed.

Designation of edition is a core element, and therefore must be recorded if present in the resource. If found, transcribe a designation of edition (e.g., "New version") in subfield ‡a of a 250 field (see RDA 2.5.2).

Recording other elements of the edition statement is optional in RDA. The most common other element is a statement of responsibility relating to the edition. If you find such a statement and decide to include it in the description, record it following space-slash-space in subfield ‡b of the 250 field.

For details on recording an edition statement, see chapter 2 of this *Handbook* at 2.5.

Production Statement (Unpublished Materials). Examine unpublished resources for production information, including place of production, producer, and date of production. Although information about production can be taken from outside the resource itself (and this is common with unpublished resources), prefer information found inside the resource, and within the resource, prefer information found in the same source as the title proper. Production information is recorded in a MARC bibliographic 264 field, with the second indicator coded "0."

The place of production element is not core in RDA and, because the information is often difficult to determine, it is usually not recorded. However, if a place of production is found in the resource, you may record it in subfield ‡a of the 264 field. Transcribe the information exactly as found (see RDA 2.7.2). If the place of production is not found in the resource but is known, the cataloger may supply the information in square brackets.

Like place of production, the producer's name element is not core in RDA and, because the information is often difficult to determine, is usually not recorded. However, if a producer's name is found in the resource, you may record it in subfield ‡b of the 264 field. Transcribe the information exactly as found (see RDA 2.7.4). If the producer's name is not found in the resource but is known, the cataloger may supply the information in square brackets.

Record the date of production. Record numerals in the form preferred by your cataloging agency (see RDA 1.8.2). The date of production element is core. If no explicit date of publication is found in the resource either supply information found in another source or inferred by the cataloger, or record "Date of production not identified" (see RDA 2.7.6). Take note of 2.7.6.2, sources of information. Because the date of production can be taken from any source it is not bracketed even if the information is found outside the resource.

Because the place of production and producer's name elements are not core the date of production will usually be recorded alone in subfield ‡c of the 264 field. However, if any preceding elements are present, place a comma immediately after the element, before the date of production element.

Publication Statement (Published Materials). Examine published resources for publication information, including place of publication, publisher, and date of publication. Although information about publication can be taken from outside the resource itself, prefer information found inside the resource, and within the resource, prefer information found in the same source as the title proper. Publication information is recorded in a MARC bibliographic 264 field, with the second indicator coded "1."

Record the first place of publication found in the resource in subfield ‡a of the 264 field. Transcribe the information exactly as found. This element is core. If no place is found in the resource either supply (in brackets) information from another source about the place of publication, or record "[Place of publication not identified]." If more than one place of publication is found in the resource, you may optionally record them all, but only the first is required. For details, see chapter 2 of this *Handbook* at 2.8.2.

Record the first publisher associated with the first place of publication found in the resource in subfield ‡b of the 264 field. Transcribe the information exactly as found. This element is core. If no publisher is found in the resource either supply (in brackets) information about the publisher from another source, or record "[Publisher not identified]." Separate the place of publication from the publisher's name with space-colon-space. If more than one publisher is found in the resource, you may optionally record them all, but only the first is required. For details, see chapter 2 of this *Handbook* at 2.8.4.

Record the date of publication. Record numerals in the form preferred by your cataloging agency (see RDA 1.8.2). Place a comma immediately after the publisher's name and record the date of publication in subfield ‡c of the 264 field. The date of publication element is core. If no explicit date of publication is found in the resource either supply (in brackets) information found in another source or inferred by the cataloger, or record "[Date of publication not identified]." Note that a copyright date is not a publication date. A copyright date can never be substituted for a publication date in RDA, but it may optionally be recorded in addition to the date of publication element. It may also be used as evidence for inferring the date of publication.

If the date of publication has not been identified, then either a date of distribution or a copyright date, if present in the resource, must be recorded (see discussion, however, in chapter 2 of this *Handbook* at 2.8.6.6 on ways to identify the date of publication). If recording a copyright date, include the copyright symbol (©) and record it in subfield ‡c of a separate 264 field, with the second indicator coded "4."

Because either the production statement or the publication statement is core, all RDA records for unpublished or published resources must include one or the other (and RDA records for such resources coded in MARC will have at least one 264 field, with second indicator coded either "0" or "1"). For details about production statement, publication statement, and copyright date, see chapter 2 of this *Handbook* at 2.7, 2.8, and 2.11.

Distribution and manufacture (printing) information may be recorded, but is optional if production or publication information has been identified. For details, see chapter 2 of this *Handbook* at 2.9 and 2.10.

Naturally Occurring Objects. In its discussion of core elements at 0.6.1, RDA states that "as a minimum, a resource description for a work, expression, manifestation, or item should include all the core elements *that are applicable* and readily ascertainable." Since naturally occurring objects do not have producers, publishers, distributors, or manufacturers, none of the core elements found in RDA 2.7–2.10 are applicable to them. Do not attempt to formulate a 264 field for a naturally occurring object unless it is part of a larger resource that is produced, published, distributed, or manufactured.

Describe the Carrier. A carrier is the physical medium in which the content of a resource is stored. There are many different carriers for three-dimensional resources, some of which are listed in RDA 3.4.6.2. Examine the resource for physical details, including size. Several carrier-related elements are required in an RDA record. Most are recorded in the 3XX block of the bibliographic record.

Extent. The extent of the resource is recorded in subfield ‡a of a MARC bibliographic 300 field. Extent is core if the resource is complete. Record the extent of a three-dimensional resource or object following the instructions in RDA 3.4.6. Only the most basic procedures will be mentioned in this appendix. For details, see chapter 2 of this *Handbook* at 3.4.6.

Record the number of units together with an appropriate term from RDA 3.4.6, or another term describing the carrier as concisely as possible. Note that some of these terms represent a change from previous cataloging practice. Instead of AACR2's "art original" or "art reproduction," use a specific term such as "sculpture." Subunits may be recorded in parentheses following the primary extent statement, if appropriate.

Colour Content. Though not considered in RDA to be part of the carrier description, this element is treated here because it is recorded immediately after the extent element in the MARC bibliographic record. Examine the resource for color content. If the resource is black and white, record "black and white" in subfield ‡b of the 300 field. If the image is in more than two colors, record "color." If the image is in one or two colors, record the names of the colors (e.g., "yellow and green") (see RDA 7.17.4.3). Separate this element from the preceding extent element with space-semicolon-space. For details on colour content, see chapter 8 of this *Handbook* at 7.17.

Dimensions. The dimensions element is not core in RDA, but it is core in descriptions of monographs for catalogers at the Library of Congress, except for online electronic resources (see LC-PCC PS 3.5, May 2012). Most U.S. catalogers will record this element. Dimensions are recorded in subfield ‡c of a MARC bibliographic 300 field. Separate the dimensions element from any preceding elements in the field with space-semicolon-space.

Record the dimensions of a three-dimensional resource following the instructions in 3.5.1.4.13. If recording only one dimension, give a word to indicate which dimension is given (e.g., "110 cm high"). If appropriate, you may record the height x width x depth, diameter, or other appropriate dimensions, rounding up to the nearest centimeter (e.g., 31 x 10 x 4 cm).

If the record has a series statement, record a period at the end of the field.

Content Type. Like the colour content element described above, the content type element is not part of the description of the carrier, but it is treated here because it is generally the next element after the dimensions recorded in the MARC bibliographic record. Content type is a core element, and is recorded in subfield ‡a of the MARC 336 field following the instructions in RDA 6.9. Record, as appropriate, one of the terms in the list found in RDA 6.9.1.3. End the field with "‡2 rdacontent":

336   ‡a three-dimensional form ‡2 rdacontent

The most common content type for a three-dimensional resource is "three-dimensional form." More than one content type can be recorded, however; therefore in some cases other terms from the list may also be appropriate. For details, see chapter 8 of this *Handbook* at 6.9.

Media and Carrier Type. Carrier type is core in an RDA description. Media type is not core, but most U.S. catalogers follow LC and PCC practice and record it (see LC-PCC PS 3.2, October 2012).

Media type is recorded in subfield ‡a of a MARC bibliographic 337 field. The term should be taken from the list in RDA 3.2.1.3. For a three-dimensional resource, use "unmediated." End the field with "‡2 rdamedia":

337   ‡a unmediated ‡2 rdamedia

Carrier type is recorded in subfield ‡a of a MARC bibliographic 338 field. The term should be taken from the list in RDA 3.3.1.3 corresponding to the chosen media type. RDA does not have a very rich supply of carrier type terms for three-dimensional resources or objects. The most commonly used term would be "object":

338   ‡a object ‡2 rdacarrier

For details, see chapter 2 of this *Handbook* at 3.2 and 3.3.

Base Material. Record the underlying physical material of a resource (e.g., "wood" or "marble") if this is considered important. This element is recorded in subfield ‡a of the MARC bibliographic 340 field. For details, see chapter 2 of this *Handbook* at 3.6.

Applied Material. Record the substance applied to the base material (e.g., "tempera") if considered important. This element is recorded in subfield ‡c of the MARC bibliographic 340 field. For details, see chapter 2 of this *Handbook* at 3.7.

Mount. Record the physical material use to support or back the resource (e.g., "wood") if considered important. This element is recorded in subfield ‡e of the MARC bibliographic 340 field. For details, see chapter 2 of this *Handbook* at 3.8.

Production Method. Record the process used to produce the resource (e.g., "continuous casting" or "lost-wax process") if considered important. This element is recorded in subfield ‡d of the MARC bibliographic 340 field. For details, see chapter 2 of this *Handbook* at 3.9.

Series Statement. Examine the resource for a series statement. Although information about a series can be taken from outside the resource itself, prefer information found in the resource. Series information is recorded in a MARC bibliographic 490 field. The first indicator is coded "0" if the information is not indexed; it is coded "1" if the information is indexed (in which case an 8XX field will also be present in the bibliographic record; see below under Link the Resource to Related Entities).

Record the title proper of the series in subfield ‡a of the 490 field exactly as it appears in the resource. If series numbering is present, record it in subfield ‡v following the title proper of the series and any other elements (such as a statement of responsibility). Separate series numbering from preceding elements by space-semicolon-space.

The title proper of the series and numbering are core and therefore must be recorded if present. Other title information of the series and statements of responsibility relating to the series are not core and are not in most cases recorded. For details about recording series statements, see chapter 2 of this *Handbook* at 2.12.

Notes. Include any notes you consider necessary to help the library user contextualize, find, identify, or select the resource. No notes are core in an RDA description. Therefore, recording notes in a bibliographic record is entirely dependent on your judgment or the policies of your cataloging agency. Most notes are recorded in the 5XX block of the MARC bibliographic record. Because the source of the title varies so much with three-dimensional resources, this note is almost always included (see discussion in chapter 2 of this *Handbook* at 2.20.2). Some other common notes include summaries of the nature or scope of the content (see discussion in chapter 8 of this *Handbook* at 7.10) and notes giving information about the attribution of the work to the creator if that is not clear from the context (see RDA 2.20.3.3 and discussion in chapter 2 of this *Handbook* at 2.20.3.

Identifier for the Manifestation. Examine the resource for an identifier, defined as "a character string associated with a manifestation that serves to differentiate that manifestation from other manifestations." The identifier for the manifestation element is core (see RDA 2.15) and therefore an identifier must be recorded if present on the resource. Three-dimensional resources rarely have identifiers, but a published resource such as a game or puzzle might have a publisher's catalog number or even an ISBN (International Standard Book Number). Record an ISBN in subfield ‡a of the 020 field of the MARC bibliographic record. Copy it as found, but do not record hyphens. For details, see chapter 2 of this *Handbook* at 2.15.

5. LINK THE RESOURCE TO RELATED ENTITIES

Once the resource has been described, links should be made to related entities. These include works and expressions either contained in the resource or related to the work(s) or expression(s) described in the record, and related persons, families, corporate bodies, and geographic entities.

In the MARC bibliographic format these links are created by recording the authorized access point for the related entity in one of the access point fields, generally speaking the 1XX, 7XX, and 8XX fields. This either (1) links the bibliographic record to an associated authority record, and via that record links the bibliographic record to other bibliographic records containing the same authorized access point (either by using the text string itself, or using an identifier); (2) directly links the bibliographic record to other bibliographic records containing the same authorized access point; or (3) at the least allows searches to retrieve all bibliographic records containing the same authorized access point.

RDA requires the cataloger to record at least one relationship: that between the resource and the principal creator of the work embodied in the manifestation being described (see discussion in chapter 9 of this *Handbook* at 18.3). Recording most other relationships is optional, but most catalogers will record many.

The relationship between the resource and the principal creator of the work is recorded in a 100 (persons or families), 110 (most corporate bodies), or 111 (meetings) field. If there is more than one work in the resource and they are by different creators, record these relationships in 700, 710, or 711.

Although the creators of three-dimensional resources are not usually creating texts, the same guidelines apply as to creators of texts. The sculptor is the creator of a sculpture. The designer is the creator of a puzzle.

Three-dimensional resources are somewhat less likely than other types of resources to have a discoverable creator. If this is the case, do not attempt to record one; inclusion of RDA core elements is only required for elements "that are . . . readily ascertainable" (see RDA 0.6.1).

See chapter 9 of this *Handbook* at 19.2 for help in determining what entity is the principal creator of the work. With persons and families the decision is usually fairly straightforward. Determining if a corporate body or meeting is the creator can be a little trickier, but fairly clear guidelines are laid out at RDA 19.2.1.1.1 (and see corresponding discussion in chapter 9 of the *Handbook*). One provision, 19.2.1.1.1h, particularly applies to three-dimensional art resources: if two or more artists act together as a corporate body (i.e., the body has a name) to create an individual work of art, the corporate body is considered the creator of the work (see discussion in chapter 9 of this *Handbook* at 19.2.1.1.1h).

Begin by recording the authorized access point for the principal creator of the work in a 1XX field. This form may be accompanied by a relationship designator to clarify the nature of the relationship. The use of relationship designators is optional but encouraged (see chapter 9 of this *Handbook* at 18.5).

Once the relationship to the principal creator has been recorded, think about other relationships that might be helpful. First consider other creators if there are more than one. Another type of relationship, for a non-creator, that could be recorded in a description of a three-dimensional resource, is the relationship between the resource and its manufacturer if it is not the same as the creator (e.g., the person who casts a sculpture someone else has created). These relationships are all recorded by giving the authorized access point for the related entity in 7XX fields: 700 (persons and families), 710 (most corporate bodies), or 711 (meetings).

Consider also relationships to related works and expressions, or the relationship between the manifestation described in the bibliographic record and the work(s) or expression(s) embodied in the manifestation. Related works or expressions are recorded by giving the authorized access point for the work or expression in a 700, 710, 711, or 730 field, or in the case of a series, in an 800, 810, 811, or 830 field. Works or expressions embodied in the manifestation are recorded in a 1XX and 240 field combination or in 130 if there is only one; or if there are two or more, in 700, 710,

711, or 730 fields as appropriate. For details, see discussion throughout chapter 9 of this *Handbook*.

6. SAMPLE RECORD SETS

Other examples of three-dimensional resource cataloging in this *Handbook* include figures 2.20 (naturally occurring object), 2.77 (silver pitcher set), and 8.15 (game).

RECORD SET H1
SCULPTURE

Bibliographic Record

100 0	‡a Khīan Yimsiri, ‡d 1922-1971, ‡e sculptor.	*[RDA 18.3, 19.2, 18.4.1.2, 18.5]*
245 10	‡a Thai sculpture of Phra Aphai Mani and his magic flute.	*[RDA 2.3]*
264　0	‡a between 1950 and 1971?	*[RDA 2.7.6, 1.9.2.4]*
300	‡a 1 sculpture ; ‡c 915 x 737 x 534 cm	*[RDA 3.4.4, 7.17.2.3, 3.5.3]*
336	‡a three-dimensional form ‡2 rdacontent	*[RDA 6.9]*
337	‡a unmediated ‡2 rdamedia	*[RDA 3.2]*
338	‡a object ‡2 rdacarrier	*[RDA 3.3]*
340	‡a bronze	*[RDA 3.6, 3.7, 3.9]*
500	‡a Title supplied by the cataloger.	*[RDA 2.20.2]*
520	‡a Sculpture depicting a Thai legend in which a flutist plays so sweetly that he is able to charm nuts out of their shells.	*[RDA 7.10]*

Associated Authority Record

046	‡f 1922 ‡g 1971	*[RDA 9.3]*
100 0	‡a Khīan Yimsiri, ‡d 1922-1971	*[RDA 9.2.2, 9.19.1]*
370	‡a Bangkok (Thailand) ‡2 naf	*[RDA 9.8]*
374	‡a Sculptors ‡2 lcsh	*[RDA 9.16]*
375	‡a male	*[RDA 9.7]*
400 1	‡a Yimsiri, Khīan, ‡d 1922-1971	*[RDA 9.2.3, 9.19.2]*
400 0	‡a Khien Yimsiri, ‡d 1922-1971	*[RDA 9.2.3, 9.19.2]*
400 1	‡a Yimsiri, Khien, ‡d 1922-1971	*[RDA 9.2.3, 9.19.2]*
670	‡a Nithatsakān sinlapānusŏn 'Āčhan Khīan Yimsiri . . . 1979: ‡b title page (Khien Yimsiri) page 5 (born 22 Phrứtsaphākhom 2465; died 18 Mīnākhom 2514)	*[RDA 8.12]*
670	‡a Khien Yimsiri, via WWW, 19 September 2012 ‡b (1922-1971; born in Bangkok; Thai sculptor)	*[RDA 8.12]*

RECORD SET H2
PUZZLE

Bibliographic Record

024 1	‡a 033500047886	*[RDA 2.15]*
245 00	‡a Marvel super-heroes fantasy jigsaw puzzle : ‡b a Marvel Comics family portrait featuring over 130 favorite characters.	*[RDA 2.3]*
264 1	‡a Racine, Wisconsin : ‡b Western Publishing Company, Inc., ‡c [1988]	*[RDA 2.8]*
264 4	‡c 1988	*[RDA 2.11]*
300	‡a 1 jigsaw puzzle (300 pieces) : ‡b color ; ‡c in box 30 x 32 x 7 cm	*[RDA 3.4.6, 7.17.4, 3.5.1.4.13 option, 3.5.1.5]*
336	‡a three-dimensional form ‡2 rdacontent	*[RDA 6.9]*
337	‡a unmediated ‡2 rdamedia	*[RDA 3.2]*
338	‡a object ‡2 rdacarrier	*[RDA 3.3]*
340	‡a cardboard	*[RDA 3.6]*
500	‡a Title from box.	*[RDA 2.20.2]*
500	‡a Size of completed puzzle: 57 x 83 cm.	*[RDA 3.22.4]*
500	‡a "This puzzle is produced under license from the Marvel Entertainment Group, Inc."	*[RDA 6.7]*
500	‡a "Golden 4788."	*[RDA 6.8]*
500	‡a Includes key giving the names of the characters and showing their location on the puzzle.	*[RDA 7.16]*
521	‡a Ages 8 to adult.	*[RDA 7.7]*

Box top
MARVEL
SUPER-HEROES
FANTASY JIGSAW PUZZLE
A Marvel® Comics Family Portrait featuring over 130 favorite characters
300 Extra large pieces fully interlocking

RECORD H3
NATURALLY OCCURRING OBJECT

Bibliographic Record

245 10	‡a Specimen scorpion.	*[RDA 2.3]*
300	‡a 1 scorpion ; ‡c 6 cm long	*[RDA 3.4.6, 3.5.1.4.13]*
336	‡a three-dimensional form ‡2 rdacontent	*[RDA 6.9]*
337	‡a unmediated ‡2 rdamedia	*[RDA 3.2]*
338	‡a object ‡2 rdacarrier	*[RDA 3.3]*
500	‡a Dried scorpion, obtained in the Arizona desert, August 1972.	*[RDA 7.2]*

RECORD SET H4
KIT

Bibliographic Record

245	00	ǂa Have fun reading backpack.	*[RDA 2.3]*
264	0	ǂc [2012]	*[RDA 2.7.6]*
300		ǂa 1 children's book, 1 graphic novel, 1 jigsaw puzzle, 10 vocabulary flash cards, 1 instruction manual : ǂb color ; ǂc in canvas backpack 40 x 31 x 10 cm *[RDA 3.4.6, 7.17.4,3.5.1.4.13 option, 3.5.1.5]*	
336		ǂa text ǂ2 rdacontent	*[RDA 6.9]*
336		ǂa three-dimensional form ǂ2 rdacontent	*[RDA 6.9]*
337		ǂa unmediated ǂ2 rdamedia	*[RDA 3.2]*
338		ǂa volume ǂ2 rdacarrier	*[RDA 3.3]*
338		ǂa object ǂ2 rdacarrier	*[RDA 3.3]*
500		ǂa Title supplied by the cataloger based on Library promotional campaign. *[RDA 2.20.2]*	
520		ǂa A kit assembled by Lincoln County Library, intended to encourage older children and teens to enjoy reading. *[RDA 7.10]*	
700	1	ǂi Contains (work): ǂa Card, Orson Scott. ǂt Ender's game.	*[RDA 25.1, 25.2]*
700	1	ǂi Contains (work): ǂa Card, Orson Scott. ǂt Ender's game (Graphic novel) *[RDA 25.1, 25.2]*	

Associated Authority Records

046		ǂk 1985	*[RDA 6.4]*
100	1	ǂa Card, Orson Scott. ǂt Ender's game	*[6.2.2, 6.27.1]*
380		ǂa Novels ǂ2 aat	*[RDA 6.3]*
500	1	ǂw r ǂi Novelization of (work): ǂa Card, Orson Scott. ǂt Ender's game (Short story) *[RDA 25.1, 25.2, 24.4.2]*	
500	1	ǂw r ǂi Adapted as (work): ǂa Card, Orson Scott. ǂt Ender's game (Graphic novel) *[RDA 25.1, 25.2, 24.4.2]*	
670		ǂa Ender's game, 1985	*[RDA 5.8]*

046		ǂk 2008	*[RDA 6.4]*
100	1	ǂa Card, Orson Scott. ǂt Ender's game (Graphic novel)	*[6.2.2, 6.27.1]*
380		ǂa Graphic novels ǂ2 lcsh	*[RDA 6.3]*
500	1	ǂw r ǂi Adaptation of (work): ǂa Card, Orson Scott. ǂt Ender's game	*[RDA 25.1, 25.2, 24.4.2]*
670		ǂa Ender's game, 2008-	*[RDA 5.8]*

NOTES

1. See discussion in the Joint Steering Committee document series 5JSC/ALA/3, at www.rda-jsc.org/working2.html#ala-3.

2. Visual Resources Association, *Cataloging Cultural Objects* (Chicago: American Library Association, 2006).

DIGITAL RESOURCES

THIS APPENDIX CONTAINS A RECOMMENDED PROCESS FOR CREAT-
ing bibliographic records for digital resources of all kinds, including resources with
physical carriers such as CD-ROMs as well as online digital resources. It covers
bibliographic record creation for these resources only in the most general of terms.
Unusual situations are covered in the body of the *Handbook*. As with the *Handbook*
itself, this appendix does not cover non-RDA related aspects of the bibliographic
record, such as fixed-length data elements (the so-called fixed fields) or subject analysis. This appendix also contains three sample record sets consisting of bibliographic
records and their associated authority records, which illustrate many of the points
described below.

Digital resources are defined in RDA as data or programs, or a combination of
the two, that are either stored on a physical carrier and accessible directly (e.g., via a
CD-ROM drive) or available by remote access (e.g., via the Internet) (see the RDA
glossary under Digital Resource). A "program" is a digital file containing a set of
instructions that tells the computer to perform certain tasks. "Data" comprise digital
information (which may be, for example, a set of numbers, blocks of alphabetic text,
or images) that is manipulated by a program. A program may stand alone (e.g., a
game); data always require an underlying program to be usable.

1. DETERMINE THE MODE OF ISSUANCE

Consider the mode of issuance of the resource. Does it consist of a single unit? Is it
a multipart monograph? Is it a serial or integrating resource? Mode of issuance is
defined in RDA 1.1.3.

A single unit resource is a resource issued either as a single physical unit (e.g., a single disc) or a single logical unit (e.g., a PDF file).

A multipart monograph is a resource issued in two or more parts that is complete or is intended to be complete within a finite number of parts.

A serial is a resource issued in successive parts, usually bearing numbering, that has no predetermined conclusion.

An integrating resource is a resource that is added to or changed by means of updates that do not remain discrete but are integrated into the whole (including among other things resources such as websites).

This appendix covers single units and multipart monographs. For serials or integrating resources in any format, see appendix K.

2. DECIDE ON THE TYPE OF DESCRIPTION

Consider the type of description you want to create. RDA 1.1.4 mentions three types of description: comprehensive, analytical, and hierarchical.

A comprehensive description describes the resource as a whole.

An analytical description describes a part of a larger resource.

A hierarchical description combines a comprehensive description of a whole resource with analytical descriptions of one or more of its parts.

U.S. cataloging practice does not use hierarchical descriptions; therefore, these will not be described here. Analytical descriptions are described in appendix L. This appendix covers comprehensive descriptions.

3. CHOOSE THE BASIS FOR IDENTIFICATION AND SOURCES OF INFORMATION FOR THE RESOURCE

Examine the resource and choose a basis for identification following the instructions in RDA 2.1. If the resource is issued as a single unit resource, the resource itself will be the basis for identification. If the resource is issued in more than one part, one of the parts will be chosen as the basis for identification. For a digital resource issued on disc, this will usually be the first disc. For details, see chapter 2 of this *Handbook* at 2.1.

Having chosen the part that will serve as the basis for identification, choose a "preferred source of information" within that part following the instructions in RDA 2.2. The preferred source of information for a digital resource is a label bearing a title that is permanently printed or affixed to the resource, or embedded metadata in textual form that contains a title (RDA 2.2.2.4). For details, see chapter 2 of this *Handbook* at 2.2.

4. DESCRIBE THE RESOURCE

Titles and Statements of Responsibility. Transcribe the title proper, other title information, and statement of responsibility in a MARC bibliographic 245 field. For information about transcription, see chapter 2 of this *Handbook* at 1.7.

Transcribe the title proper in subfield ‡a of the 245 field exactly as found on the preferred source of information, usually a label, a title screen, or embedded metadata (see RDA 2.3.2). One peculiarity of digital resources is that they may be given titles with unusual spelling or capitalization, and words are often run together (e.g., City-Engine or ArcGIS). Transcribe the information exactly as it appears. If you think that the user might attempt to find run-together words separately, record a variant title in a 246 field.

Title proper is a core element and so must be included in the description. For details, see chapter 2 of this *Handbook* at 2.3.

Transcription of other title information is optional in RDA, although core for the Library of Congress. Most U.S. catalogers will follow LC practice and include other title information in the description. If including other title information, transcribe it after the title proper in subfield ‡b of the 245 field (see RDA 2.3.4). Other title information should be transcribed from the same source as the title proper. The first piece of other title information is separated from the title proper by space-colon-space. Subsequent pieces of other title information are separated from each other by space-colon-space. For details, see chapter 2 of this *Handbook* at 2.3.4.

The first statement of responsibility relating to the title proper is a core element in RDA. Other statements of responsibility are optional, although most catalogers will record them unless they are unmanageably lengthy (as they can be with some digital resources). If including statements of responsibility in the description, transcribe them after the title proper or other information in subfield ‡c of the 245 field (see RDA 2.4.1 and 2.4.2). Statements of responsibility may be transcribed from any source within the resource itself. In unusual situations, a statement of responsibility may be transcribed from outside the resource itself, but in that case it should be bracketed. This will be rarely be necessary. The first statement of responsibility is separated from the title proper (or other title information) by space-slash-space. Subsequent statements of responsibility are separated from each other by space-semicolon-space. For details, see chapter 2 of this *Handbook* at 2.4.

Variant Titles. Examine the resource for variant titles. Variant titles are not core in RDA, but if in your opinion a library user might attempt to find the resource using one of these titles, record it in subfield ‡a of a 246 field. Variant titles can be taken from any source (see RDA 2.3.6.2), including your own knowledge (e.g., you might record a variant to correct a misspelled word in the title). For economy's sake, most catalogers will not look beyond the resource itself for variant titles. For details, see chapter 2 of this *Handbook* at 2.3.6.

Edition Statement. Examine the resource for an edition statement. An edition statement can be taken from any source within the resource, but a statement found in the same source as the title proper is preferred. Edition statements may also be taken from outside the resource; if so, they should be bracketed.

Be aware that edition statements for digital resources sometimes differ from edition statements for other types of resources. While the word "edition" is used, other words such as "issue," "release," "version," even "v," are used in edition statements associated with digital resources. Sometimes even words standing alone that designate a particular format can be interpreted as edition statements (see RDA 2.5.2.1e and discussion in this *Handbook* at 2.5.2.1). Be careful to distinguish between the name of the edition of the resource being described and the name of the edition of the operating system required to run the computer or program. Software often includes statements such as "requires Mac OSX" or "requires Adobe Acrobat Reader 7 or later." These are statements about the operating system or the underlying program, not the resource itself, and therefore are not an edition statement. This sort of information is recorded in a system requirements note (see RDA 3.20). On the other hand, if the statement distinguishes between versions written for different operating systems (e.g., Macintosh versus Windows), this may be recorded as an edition statement.

Designation of edition is a core element, and therefore must be recorded if present in the resource. If found, transcribe a designation of edition (e.g., "Second revised edition") in subfield ‡a of a 250 field (see RDA 2.5.2).

Recording other elements of the edition statement is optional in RDA. The most common other element is a statement of responsibility relating to the edition. If you find such a statement and decide to include it in the description, record it following space-slash-space in subfield ‡b of the 250 field.

For other details on recording an edition statement, see chapter 2 of this *Handbook* at 2.5.

Publication Statement. Like other types of resources, digital resources can be published or unpublished (see discussion in this *Handbook* at 2.7). Most digital resources described in libraries are published. All online resources are considered published, including digital reproductions of previously unpublished materials.

Examine the resource for publication information, including place of publication, publisher, and date of publication. Although information about publication can be taken from outside the resource itself, prefer information found inside the resource, and within the resource, prefer information found in the same source as the title proper. Publication information is recorded in a MARC bibliographic 264 field, with the second indicator coded "1."

Record the first place of publication found in the resource in subfield ‡a of the 264 field. Transcribe the information exactly as found. This element is core. If no place is found in the resource either supply (in brackets) information from another source about the place of publication, or record "[Place of publication not identified]." If more than one place of publication is found in the resource, you may optionally record them all, but only the first is required. For details, see chapter 2 of this *Handbook* at 2.8.2.

Record the first publisher associated with the first place of publication found in the resource in subfield ‡b of the 264 field. Transcribe the information exactly as found. This element is core. If no publisher is found in the resource either supply (in brackets) information about the publisher from another source, or record "[Publisher not identified]." Separate the place of publication from the publisher's name with space-colon-space. If more than one publisher is found in the resource, you may optionally record them all, but only the first is required. For details, see chapter 2 of this *Handbook* at 2.8.4.

Record the date of publication. Record numerals in the form preferred by your cataloging agency (see RDA 1.8.2). Place a comma immediately after the publisher's name and record the date of publication in subfield ‡c of the 264 field. The date of publication element is core. If no explicit date of publication is found in the resource either supply (in brackets) information found in another source or inferred by the cataloger, or record "[Date of publication not identified]." Note that a copyright date is not a publication date. A copyright date can never be substituted for a publication date in RDA, but it may optionally be recorded in addition to the date of publication element. It may also be used as evidence for inferring the date of publication.

If the date of publication has not been identified, then either a date of distribution or a copyright date, if present in the resource, must be recorded (see discussion, however, in chapter 2 of this *Handbook* at 2.8.6.6 on ways to identify the date of publication). If recording a copyright date, include the copyright symbol (© or ℗) and record it in subfield ‡c of a separate 264 field, with the second indicator coded "4."

For details about publication statement and copyright date, see chapter 2 of this *Handbook* at 2.8 and 2.11.

Distribution and manufacture information may be recorded, but is optional if publication information has been recorded. For details, see chapter 2 of this *Handbook* at 2.9 and 2.10.

Note on the PCC "provider-neutral record": As a response to the proliferation in databases such as OCLC of nearly identical records for online digital resources coming from different sources (e.g., dozens of libraries and vendors producing digital reproductions of the same book) a "provider-neutral" standard was developed as a model allowing a single bibliographic record to be used for all iterations of an online digital resource. In most respects the provider-neutral record follows RDA, but if the resource being described is an online reproduction of a physical format resource, the publication or distribution information will be that of the original physical format resource. This allows all iterations to share the same record, but it can lead to some odd juxtapositions, such as a description claiming that the digital resource was published in the nineteenth century or even earlier.[1]

Describe the Carrier. A carrier is the physical medium in which the content of a resource is stored. "Physical" comprises all media, including online digital media, which do in fact have a physical reality, consisting of electrons and other very small particles. Carriers for digital resources include cards, chips, discs, tapes, and online carriers (e.g., servers, the "cloud"). Examine the resource for physical details, including size and number of units. Several carrier-related elements are required in an RDA record. Most are recorded in the 3XX block of the bibliographic record.

Extent. The extent of the resource is recorded in subfield ‡a of a MARC bibliographic 300 field. Extent is core if the resource is complete. Record the extent of a digital resource following the instructions in RDA 3.4.1. Only the most basic procedures will be mentioned in this appendix. For details, see chapter 2 of this *Handbook* at 3.4.

Give the number of units and a term from the carrier type list in RDA 3.3.1.3. Choose a term from the "computer carriers" list, for example, "2 computer discs." The extent of an online resource is recorded as "1 online resource." Optionally, other terms "in common usage" may be used instead of terms from the carrier type list if the carrier is a newly developed format not yet covered by the list, or if an alternative such as "DVD-ROM" is preferred by the agency.

Optionally, record subunits in parentheses following the initial extent statement, if they are readily ascertainable and considered important. For digital resources, this might include the number of files or images, and the types of files. If the digital resource includes a cartographic resource, notated music, still images, or text, the subunit statement may follow the guidelines for those formats (e.g., "1 online resource (x, 134 pages)"). See RDA 3.4.1.7.1 and 3.4.1.7.5.

Illustrative, Color, and Sound Content. Though not considered in RDA to be part of the carrier description, this element is treated here because it is recorded immediately after the extent element in the MARC bibliographic record. Examine the resource for illustrations, including maps. If found, and you think recording the information would help the library user to identify or select the resource (this element is not core), record the word "illustration" or "illustrations" in subfield ‡b of the 300 field (see RDA 7.15). Other terms may also be used, preferring terms found in the alternative list in RDA 7.15.1.3. Probably the most common of these is "map" or "maps."

The illustrative content element is recorded for content designed to illustrate the primary content of the resource. It is not usually used to record the primary content of the resource (e.g., a digital map). The primary content is described elsewhere.

Also in subfield ‡b of the 300 field, record colour content (e.g., "color illustrations" or just "color") (see RDA 7.17). If the resource produces sound, record "sound" in the same subfield (see RDA 7.18).

Separate these elements from the preceding extent element with space-semicolon-space. For details on illustrative color and sound content, see chapter 8 of this *Handbook* at 7.15, 7.17, and 7.18.

Dimensions. The dimensions element is not core in RDA, but it is core in descriptions of monographs for catalogers at the Library of Congress, except for online digital resources (see LC-PCC PS 3.5, May 2012). Most U.S. catalogers will record this element. Dimensions are recorded in subfield ‡c of a MARC bibliographic 300 field. Separate the dimensions element from any preceding elements in the field with space-semicolon-space.

Record the dimensions of the physical carrier following the appropriate instructions under 3.5.1.4. In most cases use metric units, rounding up to the nearest centimeter. If following LC practice, however, record the diameter of a disc in inches (see LC-PCC PS 3.5.1.4.4, February 2010). The standard size of a computer disc is 4 ¾ inches, or 12 cm if recording in metric units. Measure the carrier itself, not a container such as a computer disc's jewel case.

If the record has a series statement, record a period at the end of the field.

Omit this element when describing an online resource.

For details, see chapter 2 of this *Handbook* under 3.5.1.4.

Content Type. Like the illustrative content element described above, the content type element is not part of the description of the carrier, but it is treated here because it is generally the next element after the dimensions recorded in the MARC bibliographic record. Content type is a core element, and is recorded in subfield ‡a of the MARC 336 field following the instructions in RDA 6.9. Record, as appropriate, one of the terms in the list found in RDA 6.9.1.3. End the field with "‡2 rdacontent":

> 336   ‡a text ‡2 rdacontent

Most of the content types listed in 6.9.1.3 are possible with digital resources. Digital resources often include more than one content type (e.g., text, still image, two-dimensional moving image). As many content types as needed may be recorded. Alternatively, record only the main applicable content type. For details, see chapter 8 of this *Handbook* at 6.9.

Media and Carrier Type. Carrier type is core in an RDA description. Media type is not core, but most U.S. catalogers follow LC and PCC practice and record it (see LC-PCC PS 3.2, October 2012).

Media type is recorded in subfield ‡a of a MARC bibliographic 337 field. The term should be taken from the list in RDA 3.2.1.3. For a digital resource, use "computer." End the field with "‡2 rdamedia":

> 337   ‡a computer ‡2 rdamedia

Carrier type is recorded in subfield ‡a of a MARC bibliographic 338 field. The term should be taken from the list in RDA 3.3.1.3. Any of the terms grouped under "computer carriers" may be used to describe digital resources. The most common are "computer disc" or "online resource." End the field with "‡2 rdacarrier":

> 338   ‡a computer disc ‡2 rdacarrier

Do not "mix and match" media types and carrier types. The carrier type should correspond to the media type:

> 337   ‡a computer ‡2 rdamedia
> 338   ‡a online resource ‡2 rdacarrier

not

> 337   ‡a audio ‡2 rdamedia
> 338   ‡a online resource ‡2 rdacarrier

As many media and carrier types as necessary may be recorded (e.g., for a resource consisting of a book and a computer disc). In exceptional circumstances a single carrier may exhibit more than one media and carrier type, for example, a single computer disc that contains computer files, sound files, and video files. Best practices for this situation have not yet been established. This *Handbook* recommends, in the meantime, that all appropriate pairs of media and carrier types be recorded:

> 337   ‡a audio ‡2 rdamedia
> 337   ‡a video ‡2 rdamedia
> 337   ‡a computer ‡2 rdamedia
> 338   ‡a audio disc ‡2 rdacarrier
> 338   ‡a videodisc ‡2 rdacarrier
> 338   ‡a computer disc ‡2 rdacarrier

For details, see chapter 2 of this *Handbook* at 3.2 and 3.3.

Sound Characteristic. It may be appropriate to record the sound characteristic element (RDA 3.16) in descriptions of digital resources. This element records details about the encoding of the sound in a resource. In previous cataloging practice as well as early implementation of RDA this element was recorded in subfield ‡b of the 300 field. A new field has been incorporated into MARC for recording this RDA element, the MARC bibliographic 344 field. Not all sub-elements will be appropriate to all types of digital resources. Some of the more common sub-elements include: type of recording (digital), recorded in subfield ‡a; recording medium (optical), recorded in subfield ‡b; and playback configuration (stereo, mono, etc.), recorded in subfield ‡g. For details and fuller explanation, see chapter 2 of this *Handbook* at 3.16.

Digital File Characteristic. Record specifications of the encoding of a digital resource in the MARC bibliographic 347 field following the instructions in RDA 3.19. File type is recorded in subfield ‡a. Digital resources could include any of the file types listed in 3.19.2.3. Encoding format is recorded in subfield ‡b. Record one of the terms listed under 3.19.3.3. If known, record the file size in subfield ‡c following the instructions in RDA 3.19.4. For image files, record resolution in subfield ‡d following the instructions of RDA 3.19.5 if it can be readily ascertained.

Series Statement. Examine the resource for a series statement. Although information about a series can be taken from outside the resource itself, prefer information found in the resource. Series information is recorded in a MARC bibliographic 490 field. The first indicator is coded "0" if the information is not indexed; it is coded "1" if the information is indexed (in which case an 8XX field will also be present in the bibliographic record; see below under Link the Resource to Related Entities).

Record the title proper of the series in subfield ‡a of the 490 field exactly as it appears in the resource. If series numbering is present, record it in subfield ‡v following the title proper of the series and any other elements (such as a statement of responsibility). Separate series numbering from preceding elements by space-semicolon-space.

The title proper of the series and numbering are core and therefore must be recorded if present. Other title information of the series and statements of responsibility relating to the series are not core and are not in most cases recorded. For details about recording series statements, see chapter 2 of this *Handbook* at 2.12.

Notes. Include any notes you consider necessary to help the library user contextualize, find, identify, or select the resource. No notes are core in an RDA description. Therefore, recording notes in a bibliographic record is entirely dependent on your judgment or the policies of your cataloging agency. Most notes are recorded in the 5XX block of the MARC bibliographic record.

Some of the more common notes included in bibliographic records for digital resources are notes giving the source of the title (see discussion in chapter 2 of this *Handbook* at 2.20.2), system requirements notes (see discussion in chapter 2 of this *Handbook* at 3.20), summaries of the contents (see discussion in chapter 8 of this *Handbook* at 7.10), and contents notes (see discussion in chapter 9 of this *Handbook* at RDA chapter 25, under Whole-Part Work Relationships). See the figures throughout this *Handbook* for many different kinds of notes.

Identifier for the Manifestation. Examine the resource for an identifier, defined as "a character string associated with a manifestation that serves to differentiate that manifestation from other manifestations." The identifier for the manifestation element is core (see RDA 2.15) and therefore an identifier must be recorded if present on the resource. Digital resources, especially online digital resources, rarely have identifiers, but a resource issued in a format such as CD-ROM might have an ISBN (International Standard Book Number). Record an ISBN in subfield ‡a of the 020 field of the MARC bibliographic record. Copy it as found, but do not record hyphens. For details, see chapter 2 of this *Handbook* at 2.15.

Uniform Resource Locator. A uniform resource locator (URL) is the address of a remote access resource, and it is crucial to the description if the user is to find the resource. Record a URL associated with the resource in subfield ‡u of an 856 field. For details, see chapter 2 of this *Handbook* at 4.6.

5. LINK THE RESOURCE TO RELATED ENTITIES

Once the resource has been described, links should be made to related entities. These include works and expressions either contained in the resource or related to the work(s) or expression(s) described in the record, and related persons, families, corporate bodies, and geographic entities.

In the MARC bibliographic format these links are created by recording the authorized access point for the related entity in one of the access point fields, generally speaking the 1XX, 7XX, and 8XX fields. This either (1) links the bibliographic record to an associated authority record, and via that record links the bibliographic record to other bibliographic records containing the same authorized access point (either by using the text string itself, or using an identifier); (2) directly links the bibliographic record to other bibliographic records containing the same authorized access point; or (3) at the least allows searches to retrieve all bibliographic records containing the same authorized access point.

RDA requires the cataloger to record at least one relationship: that between the resource and the principal creator of the work embodied in the manifestation being described (see discussion in chapter 9 of this *Handbook* at 18.3). Recording most other relationships is optional, but most catalogers will record many.

The relationship between the resource and the principal creator of the work is recorded in a 100 (persons or families), 110 (most corporate bodies), or 111 (meetings) field. If there is more than one work in the resource and they are by different creators, record these relationships in 700, 710, or 711. See chapter 9 of this *Handbook* at 19.2 for help in determining what entity is the principal creator of the work. With persons and families the decision is usually fairly straightforward. Determining if a corporate body or meeting is the creator can be a little trickier, but fairly clear guidelines are laid out at RDA 19.2.1.1.1 (and see corresponding discussion in chapter 9 of the *Handbook*).

Begin by recording the authorized access point for the principal creator of the work in a 1XX field. This form may be accompanied by a relationship designator to clarify the nature of the relationship. The use of relationship designators is optional but encouraged (see chapter 9 of this *Handbook* at 18.5).

Once the relationship to the principal creator has been recorded, think about other relationships that might be helpful. First consider other creators if there are more than one. Other commonly recorded relationships for digital resources include those between the resource and editors and compilers of data, publishers, and sponsoring bodies. These relationships are all recorded by giving the authorized access point for the related entity in 7XX fields: 700 (persons and families), 710 (most corporate bodies), or 711 (meetings).

Consider also relationships to related works and expressions, or the relationship between the manifestation described in the bibliographic record and the work(s) or expression(s) embodied in the manifestation. Related works or expressions are recorded by giving the authorized access point for the work or expression in a 700, 710, 711, or 730 field, or in the case of a series, in an 800, 810, 811, or 830 field. Works or expressions embodied in the manifestation are recorded in a 1XX and 240 field combination or the 130 if there is only one; or if there are two or more, in 700, 710, 711, or 730 fields as appropriate.

When describing a digital reproduction of a previously published resource (i.e., another manifestation), make a link to that manifestation using a MARC bibliographic 776 field, indicators coded "08." Begin by recording an appropriate relationship designator from appendix J in subfield ‡i (or, when following the provider-neutral standard, record "Print version"). Record the authorized access point for the principal creator in subfield ‡a, the title proper of the manifestation in subfield ‡t, edition statement in subfield ‡b, publication information in subfield ‡d, extent and dimensions in subfield ‡h, series statement in subfield ‡k, and ISBN in subfield ‡z. If necessary, the preferred title of the work and associated expression elements can be recorded in subfield ‡s.

For details on recording relationships, see discussion throughout chapter 9 of this *Handbook*.

6. SAMPLE RECORD SETS

Other examples of digital resource cataloging in this *Handbook* include figures 2.9b, 2.42, 2.58, 2.59, 2.61, 2.76, 2.109, 2.115, 7.95, 8.14, 8.32, 9.19, 9.23, and 9.57.

RECORD SET I1
UNPUBLISHED DIGITAL RESOURCE, COMPUTER DISC

Bibliographic Record

100 1	‡a Brown, Hugh B., ‡d 1883-1975, ‡e creator.	*[RDA 18.3, 19.2, 18.4.1.2, 18.5]*
245 10	‡a Hugh B. Brown scrapbook.	*[RDA 2.3.2.11.4]*
264 0	‡c 2010.	*[RDA 2.7.6]*
300	‡a 0.1 linear ft. ‡a (1 folder)	*[RDA 3.4.11.1]*
336	‡a still image ‡2 rdacontent	*[RDA 6.9]*
337	‡a computer ‡2 rdamedia	*[RDA 3.2]*
338	‡a computer disc ‡2 rdacarrier	*[RDA 3.3]*
347	‡a image file ‡b TIFF ‡b JPEG ‡2 rda	*[RDA 3.19]*
506	‡a Open for public research.	*[RDA 4.4]*
520 2	‡a Contains two digital copies of a scrapbook of Hugh B. Brown. The scrapbooks contain materials that document his mission for the Church of Jesus Christ of Latter-day Saints to Great Britain, with material dating from between 1937 and 1938.	*[RDA 7.10]*

538	‡a CD-ROM.	*[RDA 3.20]*
561	‡a Donated in 2011.	*[RDA 2.17]*
776 08	‡i Electronic reproduction of (manifestation): ‡a Brown, Hugh B., 1883-1975 ‡t Hugh B. Brown scrapbook ‡d 1937-1938 ‡h 70 pages	*[RDA 27.1, 24.5]*
852	‡a L. Tom Perry Special Collections, Harold B. Lee Library, Brigham Young University, ‡e Provo, Utah 84602.	*[RDA 4.3]*

Associated Authority Record

046	‡f 18831024 ‡g 19751202	*[RDA 9.3]*
100 1	‡a Brown, Hugh B., ‡d 1883-1975	*[RDA 9.2.2, 9.19.1]*
370	‡a Granger (Utah) ‡b Salt Lake City (Utah) ‡e Lethbridge (Alta.) ‡e Great Britain ‡2 naf	*[RDA 9.8, 9.9, 9.10]*
373	‡a Church of Jesus Christ of Latter-day Saints ‡2 naf	*[RDA 9.13]*
373	‡a Brigham Young University ‡2 naf	*[RDA 9.13]*
374	‡a Cowboys ‡a Farmers ‡a Soldiers ‡a Businessmen ‡a Lawyers ‡a Missionaries ‡a College teachers ‡2 lcsh	*[RDA 9.16]*
375	‡a male	*[RDA 9.7]*
377	‡a eng	*[RDA 9.14]*
378	‡q Hugh Brown	*[RDA 9.5]*
670	‡a An abundant life, 1988: ‡b CIP title page (Hugh B. Brown) galley (Hugh B. Brown (1883-1975) served in the First Presidency of the LDS Church; from 1961 to 1970)	*[RDA 8.12]*
670	‡a Utah history encyclopedia, via WWW, October 4, 2011 ‡b (Hugh B. Brown; Hugh Brown Brown; born October 24, 1883 in Salt Lake City, Utah; died December 2, 1975; married 1908 to Zina Young Card; served mission to England, 1904-1906; cowboy, farmer, soldier, businessman, lawyer, head of the Lethbridge Stake; moved to Salt Lake City, Utah in 1927; president of the British Mission, 1937-1940, 1944-1946; professor of religion at Brigham Young University, 1946-1949; assistant to the Quorum of the Twelve, 1953; member of the Quorum of the Twelve, 1958; member of the First Presidency, 1961-1970)	*[RDA 8.12]*
670	‡a Wikipedia, October 4, 2011 ‡b (b. in Granger, Utah; d. in Salt Lake City, Utah)	*[RDA 8.12]*
678 0	‡a Hugh B. Brown (1883-1975) was an attorney, educator, and ecclesiastical leader in Utah and Alberta. He served as an apostle in the Church of Jesus Christ of Latter-day Saints from 1958 to 1975.	*[RDA 9.17]*

RECORD SET I2
PUBLISHED DIGITAL RESOURCE, COMPUTER DISC

Bibliographic Record

110 2	‡a Utah Geological Survey, ‡e cartographer.	*[RDA 18.3, 19.2.1.1.1f, 18.4.1.2, 18.5]*
245 10	‡a Interim geologic map of the Rush Valley 30' x 60' quadrangle, Tooele, Utah, and Salt Lake Counties, Utah / ‡c by Donald L. Clark, Stefan M. Kirby, and Charles G. Oviatt.	*[RDA 2.3, 2.4]*
255	‡a Scale 1:62,500 ‡c (W 113°00'--W 112°00'/N 40°30'--N 40°00').	*[RDA 7.25, 7.4]*
264 1	‡a Salt Lake City, Utah : ‡b Utah Geological Survey, ‡c 2012.	*[RDA 2.8]*
300	‡a 1 computer disc ; ‡c 4 3/4 in.	*[RDA 3.4.1, 3.5.1.4.4]*
336	‡a cartographic image ‡2 rdacontent	*[RDA 6.9]*
336	‡a text ‡2 rdacontent	*[RDA 6.9]*
337	‡a computer ‡2 rdamedia	*[RDA 3.2]*
338	‡a computer disc ‡2 rdacarrier	*[RDA 3.3]*
347	‡a image file ‡a text file ‡b PDF ‡2 rda	*[RDA 3.19]*
490 1	‡a Open-file Report / Utah Geological Survey ; ‡v 593	*[RDA 2.12]*
500	‡a Relief shown by contours and shading.	*[RDA 7.27]*
504	‡a Includes bibliographical references.	*[RDA 7.16]*
538	‡a System requirements: Adobe Acrobat Reader and Microsoft Excel.	*[RDA 3.20]*
700 1	‡a Clark, Donald L., ‡d 1962- ‡e cartographer.	*[RDA 19.2, 18.4.1.2, 18.5]*
700 1	‡a Oviatt, Charles Gifford, ‡e cartographer.	*[RDA 19.2, 18.4.1.2, 18.5]*
700 1	‡a Kirby, Stefan M., ‡e cartographer.	*[RDA 19.2, 18.4.1.2, 18.5]*
830 0	‡a Open-file report (Utah Geological Survey) ; ‡v 593.	*[RDA 25.1, 24.4.2]*

Disc face

INTERIM GEOLOGIC
MAP OF THE RUSH VALLEY 30' x 60' QUADRANGLE,
TOOELE, UTAH, AND SALT LAKE COUNTIES, UTAH
by Donald L. Clark, Stefan M. Kirby, and Charles G. Oviatt
OPEN-FILE REPORT 593
UTAH GEOLOGICAL SURVEY
a division of Utah Department of Natural Resources
in cooperation with the U.S. Geological Survey
2012

Associated Authority Records

046	‡f 1962	*[RDA 9.3]*
100 1	‡a Clark, Donald L., ‡d 1962-	*[RDA 9.2.2, 9.19.1]*
374	‡a Cartographers ‡2 lcsh	*[RDA 9.16]*

375	‡a male	*[RDA 9.7]*
377	‡a eng	*[RDA 9.14]*
670	‡a Progress report geologic map of Dugway Proving Ground and adjacent areas, parts of the Wildcat mountain, Rush Valley, and Fish Springs 30′ x 60′ quadrangles, Tooele County, Utah (year 1 of 2), 2007: ‡b map recto (Donald L. Clark) *[RDA 8.12]*
670	‡a Phone call to author, September 14, 2007 (born in 1962) *[RDA 8.12]*

100 1	‡a Oviatt, Charles Gifford	*[RDA 9.2.2, 9.19.1]*
374	‡a Cartographers ‡2 lcsh	*[RDA 9.16]*
375	‡a male	*[RDA 9.7]*
377	‡a eng	*[RDA 9.14]*
400 1	‡a Oviatt, C. G. ‡q (Charles Gifford)	*[RDA 9.2.3, 9.19.2]*
670	‡a Lake Bonneville stratigraphy at the Old River Bed and Leamington, Utah, 1984: ‡b title page (Charles Gifford Oviatt) *[RDA 8.12]*
670	‡a Geologic map of the Honeyville quadrangle, Box Elder and Cache Counties, Utah, 1986: ‡b map recto (C.G. Oviatt) map envelope (Charles G. Oviatt) *[RDA 8.12]*

100 1	‡a Kirby, Stefan M.	*[RDA 9.2.2, 9.19.1]*
373	‡a Utah Geological Survey ‡2 naf	*[RDA 9.13]*
374	‡a Geologists ‡2 lcsh	*[RDA 9.16]*
375	‡a male	*[RDA 9.7]*
377	‡a eng	*[RDA 9.14]*
670	‡a Reconnaissance investigation of ground cracks along the western margin of Parowan Valley, Iron County, Utah, 2004: ‡b label (Stefan M. Kirby) *[RDA 8.12]*
670	‡a Utah Geological Survey, via WWW, 4 October 2012 ‡b (Stefan Kirby, within the Groundwater & Paleontology Program, specializes in geologic framework studies of hydrologic basins) *[RDA 8.12]*

046	‡s 1991	*[RDA 11.4]*
110 2	‡a Utah Geological Survey	*[RDA 11.2.2, 11.13.1]*
368	‡a Geological surveys ‡2 lcsh	*[RDA 11.7]*
410 1	‡a Utah. ‡b Geological Survey	*[RDA 11.2.3, 11.13.2]*
410 1	‡a Utah. ‡b Department of Natural Resources. ‡b Geological Survey	*[RDA 11.2.3, 11.13.2]*
510 2	‡w a ‡a Utah Geological and Mineral Survey	*[RDA 32.1, 32.2, 29.4.2]*
670	‡a Keaton, J.R. Assessing debris flow hazards, 1991: ‡b title page (Utah Geological Survey, a division of Utah Department of Natural Resources) *[RDA 8.12]*
670	‡a Information from Utah State Library, 22 August 1991 ‡b (Utah State Legislature changed the name of Utah Geological and Mineral Survey to Utah Geological Survey in 1991) *[RDA 8.12]*

046	ǂk 1991	*[RDA 6.4]*
130 0	ǂa Open-file report (Utah Geological Survey)	*[RDA 6.2.2, 6.27.1]*
380	ǂa Series (Publications) ǂa Monographic series ǂ2 lcsh	*[RDA 6.3]*
410 2	ǂa Utah Geological Survey. ǂt Open-file report	*[RDA 6.2.3, 6.27.4]*
530 0	ǂw a ǂa Open-file report (Utah Geological and Mineral Survey)	*[RDA 25.1, 24.4.2]*
642	ǂa 335 ǂ5 DLC	*[not RDA]*
643	ǂa Salt Lake City ǂb Utah Geological Survey	*[not RDA]*
644	ǂa f ǂ5 DLC	*[not RDA]*
645	ǂa t ǂ5 DLC	*[not RDA]*
646	ǂa s ǂ5 DLC	*[not RDA]*
670	ǂa Tar-sand resources of the Uinta Basin, 1996: ǂb title page (Open-file report)	*[RDA 5.8]*
675	ǂa Computerized resources information bank (CRIB), 1985: series title page (Open-file report / Utah Geological and Mineral Survey)	*[RDA 5.8]*

RECORD SET 13
BIBLIOGRAPHIC RECORD A: ONLINE RESOURCE, PROVIDER-NEUTRAL RECORD

100 1	ǂa Mason, Lowell, ǂd 1792-1872, ǂe composer.	*[RDA 18.3, 19.2, 18.4.1.2, 18.5]*
240 10	ǂa Nearer my God to Thee; ǂo arranged ǂs (Pinto)	*[RDA 17.4.2.2]*
245 10	ǂa Nearer my God to Thee : ǂb fantasia religiosa : harp solo, organ or orchestra accompaniment (ad libitum.) / ǂc A.F. Pinto.	*[RDA 2.3, 2.4]*
250	ǂa 2nd edition.	*[RDA 2.5]*
264 1	ǂa New York : ǂb International Music Pub. Co., ǂc [1911?]	*[Provider-neutral standard]*
264 4	ǂc ©1911	*[RDA 2.11]*
300	ǂa 1 online resource (1 score (11 pages))	*[RDA 3.4.1.7.5]*
336	ǂa notated music ǂ2 rdacontent	*[RDA 6.9]*
337	ǂa computer ǂ2 rdamedia	*[RDA 3.2]*
338	ǂa online resource ǂ2 rdacarrier	*[RDA 3.3]*
347	ǂa image file ǂb PDF ǂ2 rda	*[RDA 3.19]*
546	ǂb Staff notation.	*[RDA 7.13]*
500	ǂa Caption title.	*[RDA 2.20.2.3]*
588	ǂa Description based on print version record.	*[2.20.13]*
700 1	ǂa Pinto, A. F. ǂq (Angelo Francis), ǂe arranger of music.	*[RDA 20.2, 18.4.1.2, 18.5]*
776 08	ǂi Print version: ǂa Mason, Lowell, 1792-1872, composer. ǂs Nearer my God to Thee; arranged (Pinto) ǂt Nearer my God to Thee. -- ǂb 2nd edition. -- ǂd New York : International Music, [1911?] ǂh 1 score (11 pages) ; 35 cm ǂw (OCoLC)406422863	*[RDA 27.1, 24.4.3, 24.5]*
856 40	ǂu http://archive.org/details/nearermygodtothe00maso	*[RDA 4.6]*

BIBLIOGRAPHIC RECORD B:
ONLINE RESOURCE, RDA RECORD

100 1	‡a Mason, Lowell, ‡d 1792-1872, ‡e composer.	*[RDA 18.3, 19.2, 18.4.1.2, 18.5]*
240 10	‡a Nearer my God to Thee; ‡o arranged ‡s (Pinto)	*[RDA 17.4.2.2]*
245 10	‡a Nearer my God to Thee : ‡b fantasia religiosa : harp solo, organ or orchestra accompaniment (ad libitum.) / ‡c A.F. Pinto.	*[RDA 2.3, 2.4]*
250	‡a 2nd edition.	*[RDA 2.5]*
264 1	‡a [Provo, Utah] : ‡b [Harold B. Lee Library], ‡c 2011.	*[RDA 2.8]*
300	‡a 1 online resource (1 score (11 pages))	*[RDA 3.4.1.7.5]*
336	‡a notated music ‡2 rdacontent	*[RDA 6.9]*
337	‡a computer ‡2 rdamedia	*[RDA 3.2]*
338	‡a online resource ‡2 rdacarrier	*[RDA 3.3]*
347	‡a image file ‡b PDF ‡2 rda	*[RDA 3.19]*
546	‡b Staff notation.	*[RDA 7.13]*
500	‡a Caption title.	*[RDA 2.20.2.3]*
588	‡a Description based on PDF caption.	*[2.20.13]*
700 1	‡a Pinto, A. F. ‡q (Angelo Francis), ‡e arranger of music.	*[RDA 20.2, 18.4.1.2, 18.5]*
776 08	‡i Electronic reproduction of (manifestation): ‡a Mason, Lowell, 1792-1872, composer. ‡s Nearer my God to Thee; arranged (Pinto) ‡t Nearer my God to Thee. -- ‡b 2nd edition. -- ‡d New York : International Music, [1911?], ©1911. -- ‡h 1 score (11 pages) ; 35 cm	*[RDA 27.1, 24.4.3, 24.5]*
856 40	‡u http://archive.org/details/nearermygodtothe00maso	*[RDA 4.6]*

Caption

Inscribed to the Memory of Kathleen Keenan by request of my beloved wife.

2*nd* edition

Nearer my God to Thee.

Fantasia Religiosa

Harp Solo Organ or Orchestra Accompaniment (ad libitum.)

A.F. Pinto

Associated authority records

046	‡f 17920108 ‡g 18720811	*[RDA 9.3]*
100 1	‡a Mason, Lowell, ‡d 1792-1872	*[RDA 9.2.2, 9.19.1]*
370	‡a Medfield (Mass.) ‡b Orange (N.J.) ‡2 naf	*[RDA 9.8]*
372	‡a Music ‡2 lcsh	*[RDA 9.15]*
374	‡a Teachers ‡a Composers ‡a Conductors (Music) ‡2 lcsh	*[RDA 9.16]*
375	‡a male	*[RDA 9.7]*
377	‡a eng	*[RDA 9.14]*

670	‡a Pemberton, C.A. Lowell Mason, 1985. *[RDA 8.12]*
670	‡a New Grove dictionary of American music, 1986 ‡b (Lowell Mason; born January 8, 1792, Medfield, MA, died August 11, 1872, Orange, NJ; music educator, composer, anthologist, and conductor) *[RDA 8.12]*

046	‡k 1911 *[RDA 6.10]*
100 1	‡a Mason, Lowell, ‡d 1792-1872. ‡t Nearer my God to Thee; ‡o arranged ‡s (Pinto) *[RDA 6.18, 6.12, 6.28.3]*
336	‡a notated music ‡2 rdacontent *[RDA 6.9]*
381	‡a Pinto *[RDA 6.12]*
500 1	‡w r ‡i Arranger of music: ‡a Pinto, A. F. ‡q (Angelo Francis) *[RDA 20.2, 18.4.1.2, 18.5]*
670	‡a Mason, L. Nearer my God to Thee, 1911: ‡b caption ([arranged by] A.F. Pinto) *[RDA 5.8]*

046	‡g 1955 *[RDA 9.3]*
100 1	‡a Pinto, A. F. ‡q (Angelo Francis) *[RDA 9.2.2, 9.19.1]*
372	‡a Music ‡2 lcsh *[RDA 9.15]*
374	‡a Composers ‡2 lcsh *[RDA 9.16]*
375	‡a male *[RDA 9.7]*
400 1	‡a Pinto, Angelo Francis *[RDA 9.2.3, 9.19.2]*
670	‡a Berceuse, duo, organ, harp or piano, 1911: ‡b caption (A.F. Pinto) *[RDA 8.12]*
670	‡a Afghan Press Music for Harp website, 7 December 2012 ‡b (A.F. Pinto, born Angelo Francis Pinto was known as A. Francis Pinto. His birth date is unknown but he died in 1955) *[RDA 8.12]*

NOTE

1. For information about the provider-neutral standard, see www.loc.gov/aba/pcc/scs/documents/PCC-PN-guidelines.html.

MICROFORM RESOURCES

THIS APPENDIX CONTAINS A RECOMMENDED PROCESS FOR CREAT-ing bibliographic records for microform resources. It covers bibliographic record creation for these resources only in the most general of terms. Unusual situations are covered in the body of the *Handbook*. As with the *Handbook* itself, this appendix does not cover non-RDA related aspects of the bibliographic record, such as fixed-length data elements (the so-called fixed fields) or subject analysis. This appendix also contains two sample record sets consisting of bibliographic records and their associated authority records, which illustrate many of the points described below.

Microform is defined as "media used to store reduced-size images not readable to the human eye, designed for use with a device such as a microfilm or microfiche reader" and may be transparent or opaque (RDA glossary). They are generally issued on film or paper, but other media such as metals have been used. The rise of digital media, generally more convenient and accessible, has put a dent in library users' willingness to use microform, but the format has not been entirely supplanted (and in fact, from a preservation point of view, microform may be superior to digital media). A library collection is likely to include two types of microform: facsimile microform reproductions of works previously published in eye-readable format, and microforms that are original publications.

RDA treats microforms similarly to AACR2 chapter 11, but U.S. practice under AACR2 (following the Library of Congress's rule interpretation) was to ignore most of the AACR2 provisions when cataloging microreproductions of previously published materials. U.S. practice for these materials was to describe the microform as though it were the original, recording information about the microform in a note and selected additional elements, such as the general material designation and the MARC

007 field. Although there were practical reasons for this, it did result in descriptions that appeared to claim that a microform resource had been published, for example, in the 19th century or earlier, long before microform technology had been invented. The LC rule interpretation has not been incorporated into the Library of Congress Program for Cooperative Cataloging Policy Statements and catalogers are encouraged to apply RDA rather than follow previous practice.[1]

1. DETERMINE THE MODE OF ISSUANCE

Consider the mode of issuance of the resource. Does it consist of a single unit? Is it a multipart monograph? Is it a serial or integrating resource? Mode of issuance is defined in RDA 1.1.3.

> A single unit resource is a resource issued as a single physical unit (e.g., a single reel).
>
> A multipart monograph is a resource issued in two or more parts that is complete or is intended to be complete within a finite number of parts.
>
> A serial is a resource issued in successive parts, usually bearing numbering, that has no predetermined conclusion.
>
> An integrating resource is a resource that is added to or changed by means of updates that do not remain discrete but are integrated into the whole (including among other things resources such as websites).

This appendix covers single units and multipart monographs. For serials or integrating resources in any format, see appendix K.

2. DECIDE ON THE TYPE OF DESCRIPTION

Consider the type of description you want to create. RDA 1.1.4 mentions three types of description: comprehensive, analytical, and hierarchical.

> A comprehensive description describes the resource as a whole.
>
> An analytical description describes a part of a larger resource.
>
> A hierarchical description combines a comprehensive description of a whole resource with analytical descriptions of one or more of its parts.

U.S. cataloging practice does not use hierarchical descriptions, so these will not be described here. Analytical descriptions are described in appendix L. This appendix covers comprehensive descriptions.

3. CHOOSE THE BASIS FOR IDENTIFICATION AND SOURCES OF INFORMATION FOR THE RESOURCE

Examine the resource and choose a basis for identification following the instructions in RDA 2.1. If the resource is issued as a single unit resource, the resource itself will be the basis for identification. If the resource is issued in more than one part, one of the parts will be chosen as the basis for identification. For a microform resource this will usually be the first part. For details, see chapter 2 of this *Handbook* at 2.1.

Having chosen the part that will serve as the basis for identification, choose a "preferred source of information" within that part following the instructions in RDA 2.2. Microforms (as "images of one or more pages, leaves, sheets, or cards") are generally covered by RDA 2.2.2.2. The preferred source of information for a microform resource is the image of a title page, title sheet, or title card. Alternatively, an eye-readable label may be used, but catalogers following LC practice will not apply this alternative (see LC-PCC PS 2.2.2.2 alternative, February 2010). If the resource does not have an image of a title page, sheet, or card, use the image of a cover, caption, masthead, or colophon. If no such source is available, use another source within the resource that contains a title. For details, see chapter 2 of this *Handbook* at 2.2.

4. DESCRIBE THE RESOURCE

Titles and Statements of Responsibility. Transcribe the title proper, other title information, and statement of responsibility in a MARC bibliographic 245 field. For information about transcription, see chapter 2 of this *Handbook* at 1.7.

Transcribe the title proper in subfield ‡a of the 245 field exactly as found on the preferred source of information, usually a title frame or a label. Title proper is a core element and therefore must be included in the description. For details, see chapter 2 of this *Handbook* at 2.3.

Transcription of other title information is optional in RDA, although core for the Library of Congress. Most U.S. catalogers will follow LC practice and include other title information in the description. If including other title information, transcribe it after the title proper in subfield ‡b of the 245 field (see RDA 2.3.4). Other title information should be transcribed from the same source as the title proper. The first piece of other title information is separated from the title proper by space-colon-space. Subsequent pieces of other title information are separated from each other by space-colon-space. For details, see chapter 2 of this *Handbook* at 2.3.4.

The first statement of responsibility relating to the title proper is a core element in RDA. Other statements of responsibility are optional, although most catalogers will record them unless they are unmanageably lengthy. If including statements of responsibility in the description, transcribe them after the title proper or other information in subfield ‡c of the 245 field (see RDA 2.4.1 and 2.4.2). Statements of responsibility may be transcribed from any source within the resource itself. In unusual situations, a statement of responsibility may be transcribed from outside the resource itself, but in that case it should be bracketed. This will be rarely be necessary. The first statement of responsibility is separated from the title proper (or other title information) by space-slash-space. Subsequent statements of responsibility are separated from each other by space-semicolon-space. For details, see chapter 2 of this *Handbook* at 2.4.

Variant Titles. Examine the resource for variant titles. Variant titles are not core in RDA, but if in your opinion a library user might attempt to find the resource using one of these titles, record it in subfield ‡a of a 246 field. Variant titles can be taken from any source (see RDA 2.3.6.2), including your own knowledge (for example, you might record a variant to correct a misspelled word in the title). For economy's sake, most catalogers will not look beyond the resource itself for variant titles. For details, see chapter 2 of this *Handbook* at 2.3.6.

Edition Statement. Examine the resource for an edition statement. An edition statement can be taken from any source within the resource, but a statement found in the same source as the title proper is preferred. Edition statements may also be taken from outside the resource; if so, they should be bracketed.

When describing a microform reproduction of a previously published resource use caution: the edition statement recorded in this element must be that of the microform resource, not of the original resource. An edition statement associated with the original resource can be recorded as related manifestation information (see below).

Designation of edition is a core element, and therefore must be recorded if present in the resource. If found, transcribe a designation of edition (e.g., "Second revised edition") in subfield ‡a of a 250 field (see RDA 2.5.2).

Recording other elements of the edition statement is optional in RDA. The most common other element is a statement of responsibility relating to the edition. If you find such a statement and decide to include it in the description, record it following space-slash-space in subfield ‡b of the 250 field.

For other details on recording an edition statement, see chapter 2 of this *Handbook* at 2.5.

Publication Statement. Examine the resource for publication information, including place of publication, publisher, and date of publication. Although information about publication can be taken from outside the resource itself, prefer information found inside the resource, and within the resource, prefer information found in the same source as the title proper. Publication information is recorded in a MARC bibliographic 264 field, with the second indicator coded "1."

Caution: remember that for microform reproductions, the publication information recorded here is that of the *microform,* not of the original. This represents a change in practice for U.S. catalogers. The publication information of the original can be recorded as related manifestation information (see below).

Record the first place of publication found in the resource in subfield ‡a of the 264 field. Transcribe the information exactly as found. This element is core. If no place is found in the resource either supply (in brackets) information from another source about the place of publication, or record "[Place of publication not identified]." If more than one place of publication is found in the resource, you may optionally record them all, but only the first is required. For details, see chapter 2 of this *Handbook* at 2.8.2.

Record the first publisher associated with the first place of publication found in the resource in subfield ‡b of the 264 field. Transcribe the information exactly as found. This element is core. If no publisher is found in the resource either supply (in brackets) information about the publisher from another source, or record "[Publisher not identified]." Separate the place of publication from the publisher's name with space-colon-space. If more than one publisher is found in the resource, you may optionally record them all, but only the first is required. For details, see chapter 2 of this *Handbook* at 2.8.4.

Record the date of publication. Record numerals in the form preferred by your cataloging agency (see RDA 1.8.2). Place a comma immediately after the publisher's name and record the date of publication in subfield ‡c of the 264 field. The date of publication element is core. If no explicit date of publication is found in the resource either supply (in brackets) information found in another source or inferred by the cataloger, or record "[Date of publication not identified]." Note that a copyright date is not a publication date. A copyright date can never be substituted for a publication date in RDA, but it may optionally be recorded in addition to the date of publication element. It may also be used as evidence for inferring the date of publication.

If the date of publication has not been identified, then either a date of distribution or a copyright date, if present in the resource, must be recorded (see discussion, however, in chapter 2 of this *Handbook* at 2.8.6.6 on ways to identify the date of publication). If recording a copyright date, include the copyright symbol (©) and record it in subfield ‡c of a separate 264 field, with the second indicator coded "4." Remember, however, that for microform reproductions of previously existing resources, distribution and copyright dates should only be recorded here if they apply to the microform publication, not the original.

For details about publication statement and copyright date, see chapter 2 of this *Handbook* at 2.8 and 2.11.

Distribution and manufacture information pertaining to the microform may be recorded, but is optional if publication information has been recorded. For details, see chapter 2 of this *Handbook* at 2.9 and 2.10.

Describe the Carrier. A carrier is the physical medium in which the content of a resource is stored. Carriers for microform resources include cards, microfiches, microfilm reels, and other carriers. Examine the resource for physical details, including size and number of units. Several carrier-related elements are required in an RDA record. Most are recorded in the 3XX block of the bibliographic record.

Extent. The extent of the resource is recorded in subfield ‡a of a MARC bibliographic 300 field. Extent is core if the resource is complete. Record the extent of a microform resource following the instructions in RDA 3.4.1. Only the most basic procedures will be mentioned in this appendix. For details, see chapter 2 of this *Handbook* at 3.4.

Give the number of units and a term from the carrier type list in RDA 3.3.1.3. Choose a term from the "microform carriers" list, for example, "5 microfiches." Optionally, record subunits in parentheses following the initial extent statement if they are readily ascertainable and considered important. For microform resources, this might include the number of frames, or if the microform resource is a reproduction of a cartographic resource, notated music, still images, or text, the subunit statement may follow the guidelines for those formats (e.g., "1 microfilm reel (xvii, 207 pages)"). See RDA 3.4.1.7.4.

Illustrative Content. Though not considered in RDA to be part of the carrier description, this element is treated here because it is recorded immediately after the extent element in the MARC bibliographic record. Examine the resource for illustrations, including maps. If found, and you think recording the information would help the library user to identify or select the resource (this element is not core), record the word "illustration" or "illustrations" in subfield ‡b of the 300 field (see RDA 7.15). Other terms may also be used, preferring terms found in the alternative list in RDA 7.15.1.3. Probably the most common of these is "map" or "maps."

Separate this element from the preceding extent element with space-semicolon-space. For details on illustrative content, see chapter 8 of this *Handbook* at 7.15.

Dimensions. The dimensions element is not core in RDA, but it is core in descriptions of monographs for catalogers at the Library of Congress, except for online digital resources (see LC-PCC PS 3.5, May 2012). Most U.S. catalogers will record this element. Dimensions are recorded in subfield ‡c of a MARC bibliographic 300 field. Separate the dimensions element from any preceding elements in the field with space-semicolon-space.

Record the dimensions of the physical carrier following the appropriate instructions under 3.5.1.4 using metric units, rounding up to the nearest unit. Instructions for microform resources are 3.5.1.4.1 (cards), 3.5.1.4.2 (cartridges), 3.5.1.4.3 (cassettes), 3.5.1.4.7 (microfiches), 3.5.1.4.9 (reels), and 3.5.1.4.10 (rolls). Metal discs with microprinting or engraving also exist. If you are describing one of these, follow the instructions for discs in 3.5.1.4.4.

For details, see chapter 2 of this *Handbook* under 3.5.1.4.

Content Type. Like the illustrative content element described above, the content type element is not part of the description of the carrier, but it is treated here because it is generally the next element after the dimensions recorded in the MARC bibliographic record. Content type is a core element, and is recorded in subfield ‡a of the MARC 336 field following the instructions in RDA 6.9. Record, as appropriate, one of the terms in the list found in RDA 6.9.1.3. End the field with "‡2 rdacontent":

> 336   ‡a text ‡2 rdacontent

Many of the content types listed in 6.9.1.3 are possible with microform resources. Microform resources often include more than one content type (e.g., text, still image, or cartographic image). As many content types as needed may be recorded. Alternatively, record only the main applicable content type. For details, see chapter 8 of this *Handbook* at 6.9.

Media and Carrier Type. Carrier type is core in an RDA description. Media type is not core, but most U.S. catalogers follow LC and PCC practice and record it (see LC-PCC PS 3.2, October 2012).

Media type is recorded in subfield ‡a of a MARC bibliographic 337 field. The term should be taken from the list in RDA 3.2.1.3. For a microform resource, use "microform." End the field with "‡2 rdamedia":

> 337   ‡a microform ‡2 rdamedia

Carrier type is recorded in subfield ‡a of a MARC bibliographic 338 field. The term should be taken from the list in RDA 3.3.1.3. Any of the terms grouped under "microform carriers" may be used to describe microform resources. The most common are "microfiche" or "microfilm reel." If none of the terms applies (e.g., for a micro-engraved disc), record "other." End the field with "‡2 rdacarrier":

> 338   ‡a microfilm reel ‡2 rdacarrier

As many media and carrier types as necessary may be recorded (e.g., for a resource consisting of a book and a set of microfiches).

For details, see chapter 2 of this *Handbook* at 3.2 and 3.3.

Polarity. Record the polarity of the microform (positive or negative) in MARC field 340, subfield ‡o, if it is considered important. This element is probably more commonly recorded for negative polarity. For discussion and details, see chapter 2 of this *Handbook* at 3.14.

Series Statement. Examine the resource for a series statement. Although information about a series can be taken from outside the resource itself, prefer information found in the resource. Series information is recorded in a MARC bibliographic 490 field. The first indicator is coded "0" if the information is not indexed; it is coded "1" if the information is indexed (in which case an 8XX field will also be present in the bibliographic record; see below under Link the Resource to Related Entities).

Caution: remember that for microform reproductions, the series information recorded in this element is that of the *microform*, not of the original. This represents a change in practice for U.S. catalogers. A series statement associated with the original resource can be recorded as related manifestation information (see below).

Record the title proper of the series in subfield ‡a of the 490 field exactly as it appears in the resource. If series numbering is present, record it in subfield ‡v following the title proper of the series and any other elements (such as a statement of responsibility). Separate series numbering from preceding elements by space-semicolon-space.

The title proper of the series and numbering are core and therefore must be recorded if present. Other title information of the series and statements of responsibility relating to the series are not core and are not in most cases recorded. For details about recording series statements, see chapter 2 of this *Handbook* at 2.12.

Notes. Include any notes you consider necessary to help the library user contextualize, find, identify, or select the resource. No notes are core in an RDA description. Therefore, recording notes in a bibliographic record is entirely dependent on your judgment or the policies of your cataloging agency. Most notes are recorded in the 5XX block of the MARC bibliographic record.

Some of the more common notes included in bibliographic records for microform resources are notes giving summaries of the contents (see discussion in chapter 8 of this *Handbook* at 7.10), notes about bibliographical references or indexes contained in the resource (see discussion in chapter 8 of this *Handbook* at 7.16), and contents notes (see discussion in chapter 9 of this *Handbook* at RDA chapter 25, under Whole-Part Work Relationships), but most other kinds of notes can appear on records for microform resources. See the figures throughout this *Handbook* for many different kinds of notes.

Identifier for the Manifestation. Examine the resource for an identifier, defined as "a character string associated with a manifestation that serves to differentiate that manifestation from other manifestations." The identifier for the manifestation element is core (see RDA 2.15) and therefore an identifier must be recorded if present on the resource. Identifiers are uncommon in microform resources, but a resource might have an ISBN (International Standard Book Number). Record an ISBN in subfield ‡a of the 020 field of the MARC bibliographic record. Copy it as found, but do not record hyphens. For details, see chapter 2 of this *Handbook* at 2.15.

Caution: remember that for microform reproductions, the identifier recorded in this element is that of the *microform*, not of the original. This represents a change in practice for U.S. catalogers. An identifier (such as an ISBN) associated with the original resource can be recorded as related manifestation information (see below).

5. LINK THE RESOURCE TO RELATED ENTITIES

Once the resource has been described, links should be made to related entities. These include works and expressions either contained in the resource or related to the work(s) or expression(s) described in the record, and related persons, families, corporate bodies, and geographic entities.

In the MARC bibliographic format these links are created by recording the authorized access point for the related entity in one of the access point fields, generally speaking the 1XX, 7XX, and 8XX fields. This either (1) links the bibliographic record to an associated authority record, and via that record links the bibliographic record to other bibliographic records containing the same authorized access point (either by using the text string itself, or using an identifier); (2) directly links the bibliographic record to other bibliographic records containing the same authorized access point; or (3) at the least allows searches to retrieve all bibliographic records containing the same authorized access point.

RDA requires the cataloger to record at least one relationship: that between the resource and the principal creator of the work embodied in the manifestation being described (see discussion in chapter 9 of this *Handbook* at 18.3). Recording most other relationships is optional, but most catalogers will record many.

The relationship between the resource and the principal creator of the work is recorded in a 100 (persons or families), 110 (most corporate bodies), or 111 (meetings) field. If there is more than one work in the resource and they are by different creators, record these relationships in 700, 710, or 711. See chapter 9 of this *Handbook* at 19.2 for help in determining what entity is the principal creator of the work. With persons and families the decision is usually fairly straightforward. Determining if a corporate body or meeting is the creator can be a little trickier, but fairly clear guidelines are laid out at RDA 19.2.1.1.1 (and see corresponding discussion in chapter 9 of the *Handbook*).

Begin by recording the authorized access point for the principal creator of the work in a 1XX field. This form may be accompanied by a relationship designator to clarify the nature of the relationship. The use of relationship designators is optional but encouraged (see *Handbook* chapter 9 of this *Handbook* at 18.5).

Once the relationship to the principal creator has been recorded, think about other relationships that might be helpful. First consider other creators if there are more than one. Other commonly recorded relationships for digital resources include those between the resource and editors and compilers of data, publishers, and sponsoring bodies. These relationships are all recorded by giving the authorized access point for the related entity in 7XX fields: 700 (persons and families), 710 (most corporate bodies), or 711 (meetings).

Consider also relationships to related works and expressions, or the relationship between the manifestation described in the bibliographic record and the work(s) or expression(s) embodied in the manifestation. Related works or expressions are recorded by giving the authorized access point for the work or expression in a 700, 710, 711, or 730 field, or in the case of a series, in an 800, 810, 811, or 830 field. Works or expressions embodied in the manifestation are recorded in a 1XX and 240 field combination or in 130 if there is only one; or if there are two or more, in 700, 710, 711, or 730 fields as appropriate.

When describing a microform reproduction of a previously published resource (i.e., another manifestation), make a link to that manifestation using a MARC bibliographic 776 field, indicators coded "08." Begin by recording an appropriate relationship designator from appendix J in subfield ‡i. Record the authorized access point for the principal creator in subfield ‡a, the title proper of the manifestation in subfield ‡t, edition statement in subfield ‡b, publication information in subfield ‡d, extent and dimensions in subfield ‡h, series statement in subfield ‡k, and ISBN in subfield ‡z. If necessary, the preferred title of the work and associated expression elements can be recorded in subfield ‡s.

For details on recording relationships, see discussion throughout chapter 9 of this *Handbook*.

6. SAMPLE RECORD SETS

Other examples of microform resource cataloging in this *Handbook* include figures 2.93, 2.99, and 2.102.

RECORD SET J1
MICROFICHE, ORIGINAL PUBLICATION

Bibliographic Record

111 2	‡a Library History Seminar ‡n (4th : ‡d 1971 : ‡c Florida State University), ‡e author.	*[RDA 18.3, 19.2.1.1.1d, 18.4.1.2, 18.5]*
245 10	‡a Library history seminar, no. 4 : ‡b proceedings, 1971 / ‡c edited by Harold Goldstein, John M. Goudeau.	*[RDA 2.3, 2.4]*
264 1	‡a Tallahassee, Florida : ‡b Journal of library history, ‡c [1972]	*[RDA 2.8]*
264 4	‡a ©1972	*[RDA 2.11]*
300	‡a 4 microfiches (vi, 352 pages) ; ‡c 11 x 15 cm	*[RDA 3.4.1, 3.5.1.4.7]*
336	‡a text ‡2 rdacontent	*[RDA 6.9]*
337	‡a microform ‡2 rdamedia	*[RDA 3.2]*
338	‡a microfiche ‡2 rdacarrier	*[RDA 3.3]*
340	‡o negative ‡2 rda	*[RDA 3.14]*
700 1	‡a Goldstein, Harold, ‡d 1917- ‡e editor of compilation.	*[RDA 20.2, 18.4.1.2, 18.5]*
700 1	‡a Goudeau, John M. ‡q (John Milfred), ‡d 1915-1981, ‡e editor of compilation.	*[RDA 20.2, 18.4.1.2, 18.5]*

Frame 1
Library History Seminar
No. 4, Proceedings, 1971
Edited by Harold Goldstein, John M. Goudeau
The Journal of Library History
School of Library Science
Florida State University
Tallahassee, Florida

Frame 2
[blank]

Frame 3
Library History Seminar
No. 4, Proceedings, 1971
Copyright 1972 by the Journal of Library History

Associated Authority Records

046	‡s 1971	*[RDA 11.4]*
111 2	‡a Library History Seminar ‡n (4th : ‡d 1971 : ‡c Florida State University)	
		[RDA 11.2.2, 11.13.1]
368	‡a Congresses and conventions ‡2 lcsh	*[RDA 11.7]*
372	‡a Libraries--History ‡2 lcsh	*[RDA 11.10]*
373	‡a Florida State University ‡2 naf	*[RDA 11.5]*
377	‡a eng	*[RDA 11.8]*
670	‡a Library history seminar, no. 4, 1972: ‡b title frame (Library History Seminar, held 1971 at Florida State University)	*[RDA 8.12]*

046	‡f 191/	*[RDA 9.3]*
100 1	‡a Goldstein, Harold, ‡d 1917-	*[RDA 9.2.2, 9.19.1]*
372	‡a Library science ‡2 lcsh	*[RDA 9.15]*
373	‡a Florida State University. Library School ‡2 naf ‡t 1968	*[RDA 9.13]*
373	‡a Florida State University. School of Library Science ‡2 naf ‡s 1968 ‡t 1981	
		[RDA 9.13]
373	‡a Florida State University. School of Library and Information Studies ‡2 naf ‡s 1981	
		[RDA 9.13]
373	‡a Association for Library and Information Science Education ‡2 naf	*[RDA 9.13]*
374	‡a College teachers ‡2 lcsh	*[RDA 9.16]*
375	‡a male	*[RDA 9.7]*
377	‡a eng	*[RDA 9.14]*
670	‡a National Conference on the Implications of the New Media for the Teaching of Library Science, Chicago, 1963. Proceedings, c1963: ‡b title page (Harold Goldstein)	*[RDA 8.12]*

670	‡a School of Library and Information Studies, The Florida State University, via WWW, 5 October 2012 ‡b (Dr. Harold Goldstein, second dean of the FSU School of Library Training and Service from 1967; in 1968 the School changed its name to School of Library Science; in 1981 the name changed again to School of Library and Information Studies; Goldstein remained dean until 1985; The Goldstein Library at Florida State University is named after him.) *[RDA 8.12]*
670	‡a ALISE (Association for Library and Information Science Education), via WWW, 5 October 2012 ‡b (Harold Goldstein, Florida State University, president 1981-1982) *[RDA 8.12]*

046	‡f 19151030 ‡g 19811123	*[RDA 9.3]*
100 1	‡a Goudeau, John M. ‡q (John Milfred), ‡d 1915-1981	*[RDA 9.2.2, 9.19.1]*
370	‡b Leon (Fla.)	*[RDA 9.8]*
373	‡a Louisiana State University in New Orleans ‡2 naf ‡s 1958	*[RDA 9.13]*
374	‡a Librarians ‡2 lcsh	*[RDA 9.16]*
375	‡a male	*[RDA 9.7]*
377	‡a eng	*[RDA 9.14]*
378	‡q John Milfred	*[RDA 9.5]*
670	‡a Library history seminar no. 4, 1972: ‡b title page (John M. Goudeau, editor) *[RDA 8.12]*	
670	‡a RLIN, January 3, 2003 ‡b (access point: Goudeau, John Milfred, 1915-1981; usage: John M. Goudeau; John Milfred Goudeau (thesis)) *[RDA 8.12]*	
670	‡a University of New Orleans, via WWW, 6 October 2012 ‡b (John M. Goudeau, first librarian of the new Louisiana State University, New Orleans, appointed April 11, 1958) *[RDA 8.12]*	
670	‡a FamilySearch, 6 October 2012 ‡b (John Milfred Goudeau, born 30 October 1915; died 23 November 1981 at Leon, Florida) *[RDA 8.12]*	

RECORD SET J2
MICROFILM REEL, REPRODUCTION

Bibliographic Record

100 1	‡a Tuttle, John B. ‡q (John Betley), ‡d 1882- ‡e author.	*[RDA 18.3, 19.2, 18.4.1.2, 18.5]*
245 14	‡a The analysis of rubber / ‡c by John B. Tuttle.	*[RDA 2.3, 2.4]*
264 1	‡a Ann Arbor, Michigan : ‡b University Microfilms International, ‡c 1976.	*[RDA 2.8]*
300	‡a 1 microfilm reel (155 pages) ; ‡c 10 cm, 35 mm	*[RDA 3.4.1, 3.5.1.4.9]*
336	‡a text ‡2 rdacontent	*[RDA 6.9]*
337	‡a microform ‡2 rdamedia	*[RDA 3.2]*
338	‡a microfilm reel ‡2 rdacarrier	*[RDA 3.3]*

340	‡o positive ‡2 rda	*[RDA 3.14]*
504	‡a Includes bibliographical references (pages 121-138) and index.	*[RDA 7.16]*
776 08	‡i Reproduction of (manifestation): ‡a Tuttle, John B. (John Betley), 1882- author. ‡t The analysis of rubber. -- ‡d New York, U.S.A. : Book Department, The Chemical Catalog Company, Inc., 1922. -- ‡h 155 pages ; 24 cm. -- ‡k (Monograph series / American Chemical Society). *[RDA 27.1, 24.4.3, 24.5]*	

Associated Authority Record

046	‡f 18820525	*[RDA 9.3]*
100 1	‡a Tuttle, John B. ‡q (John Betley), ‡d 1882-	*[RDA 9.2.2, 9.19.1]*
370	‡a Philadelphia (Pa.) ‡2 naf	*[RDA 9.8]*
375	‡a male	*[RDA 9.7]*
377	‡a eng	*[RDA 9.14]*
378	‡q John Betley	*[RDA 9.5]*
400 1	‡a Tuttle, J. B. ‡q (John Betley), ‡d 1882-	*[RDA 9.2.3, 9.19.2]*
670	‡a The analysis of rubber, 1922: ‡b title page (by John B. Tuttle)	*[RDA 8.12]*
670	‡a RLIN, January 2, 2003 ‡b (access points: Tuttle, John Betley, 1882-; Tuttle, John B. ; Tuttle, John B. (John Betley), 1882- ; usage: John B. Tuttle; J.B. Tuttle)	*[RDA 8.12]*
670	‡a FamilySearch, 6 December 2012 ‡b (John Betley Tuttle, born 25 May 1882; birthplace Philadelphia, Pa.; residence Harrison, N.J. in 1942)	*[RDA 8.12]*

NOTE

1. For an LC discussion paper on the problem, see "Reconsidering the Cataloging Treatment of Reproductions," available at www.loc.gov/acq/conser/reproductions .pdf.

SERIALS AND INTEGRATING RESOURCES

THIS APPENDIX CONTAINS A RECOMMENDED PROCESS FOR CREATING bibliographic records for serials and integrating resources. It covers bibliographic record creation for these resources only in the most general of terms. Unusual situations are covered in the body of the *Handbook*. As with the *Handbook* itself, this appendix does not cover non-RDA related aspects of the bibliographic record, such as fixed-length data elements (the so-called fixed fields) or subject analysis. This appendix also contains three sample record sets consisting of bibliographic records and their associated authority records, which illustrate many of the points described below.[1]

1. DETERMINE THE MODE OF ISSUANCE

This appendix covers two modes of issuance, serials and integrating resources, as defined in RDA 1.1.3. It is important to think about the distinctions between the two, because they are treated slightly differently.

> A serial is a resource issued in successive parts, usually bearing numbering, which has no predetermined conclusion. This includes resources traditionally thought of as serials, such as newspapers and journals, and also monographic series.
>
> An integrating resource is a resource that is added to or changed by means of updates that do not remain discrete but are integrated into the whole (including tangible resources such as loose-leaf publications, and intangible resources such as websites).

2. DECIDE ON THE TYPE OF DESCRIPTION

Consider the type of description you want to create. RDA 1.1.4 mentions three types of description: comprehensive, analytical, and hierarchical.

> A comprehensive description describes the resource as a whole.
> An analytical description describes a part of a larger resource.
> A hierarchical description combines a comprehensive description of a whole resource with analytical descriptions of one or more of its parts.

U.S. cataloging practice does not use hierarchical descriptions, therefore these will not be described here. Analytical descriptions are described in appendix L. This appendix covers comprehensive descriptions.

3. CHOOSE THE BASIS FOR IDENTIFICATION AND SOURCES OF INFORMATION FOR THE RESOURCE

Examine the resource and choose a basis for identification following the instructions in RDA 2.1.

Follow RDA 2.1.2.3 for serials. For a serial, the basis for identification is the first part. For numbered serials, this part is the lowest numbered issue or part. For unnumbered serials (including unnumbered monographic series), this part is the issue or part with the earliest date. For details, see chapter 2 of this *Handbook* at 2.1. Because serial description is based in the *first* issue or part, this means that if a major change occurs somewhere along the way (e.g., the title changes) a new description may be required. Potential for change is also why 2.1.2.3 calls for a note identifying the part used as the basis for identification if the cataloger was unable to consult the first part.

Follow RDA 2.1.2.4 for integrating resources. The basis for identification for an integrating resource is "a source of information identifying the current iteration of the resources as a whole." The word "current" is important; because the basis for identification is the *current* iteration, the description may need to be changed if the current iteration changes (e.g., a change in title). The changeable nature of descriptions of integrating resources is why 2.1.2.4 calls for a note identifying the latest iteration consulted when the description was made.

Having chosen the part that will serve as the basis for identification, choose a "preferred source of information" within that part following the instructions in RDA 2.2. The preferred source of information for a serial or integrating resource depends on its presentation format. RDA 2.2.2.2 covers serial and integrating resources in traditional "book" formats. For these, use the title page as the preferred source of information, or other sources listed in 2.2.2.2 if there is no title page. If a serial or integrating resource consists of moving images, follow 2.2.2.3 and use the title frame(s) or screen(s), or other sources listed if there is no title frame or screen. For all other kinds of serials or integrating resources, follow 2.2.2.4 and choose either a label bearing a title permanently printed on or affixed to the resource, or embedded metadata that contains a title. If the resource does not contain either of those sources, choose another source within the resource itself. For details, see chapter 2 of this *Handbook* at 2.2.

4. DESCRIBE THE RESOURCE

Titles and Statements of Responsibility. Transcribe the title proper, other title information, and statement of responsibility in a MARC bibliographic 245 field. For information about transcription, see chapter 2 of this *Handbook* at 1.7.

Title Proper. Transcribe the title proper in subfield ‡a of the 245 field exactly as found on the preferred source of information (see RDA 2.3.2). However, take note of the exception under 2.3.1.4. In contrast to the general practice of transcribing inaccuracies found in resources (see RDA 1.7.9), when transcribing the title proper of a serial or integrating resource, correct an "obvious" typographic error and give the title as it appears (i.e., with the typographic error) in a note. This is a sensible guideline for serials and integrating resources, since such inaccuracies are likely to be corrected in a subsequent issue or iteration.

Omit dates, names, or numbers that vary from issue to issue when transcribing the title proper of a serial. Indicate that you left something out by using the mark of omission (...). Additionally, omit statements that mention an earlier title. These are not the title proper of the resource you are describing.

If the title proper of a serial or integrating resource is presented in a full form as well as an acronym, record the full form as the title proper. Record the acronym as other title information (see RDA 2.3.2.5 exception).

Title proper is a core element and therefore must be included in the description. For details, see chapter 2 of this *Handbook* at 2.3.

Changes Affecting the Title or Other Aspects of the Serial or Integrating Resource. One of the characteristics of serials and integrating resources is that they change over time in many ways. The most obvious way a serial changes is that it expands as new issues or volumes are published. Another way a serial or integrating resource changes is that the presentation of the title may change, the issuing body may change, or the format may change.

Serial title changes are treated in RDA 2.3.2.12.2 and 2.3.2.13. When you notice that a new issue of a serial has arrived with a change in the presentation of the title, consult RDA 2.3.2.13 to see if the change is considered "major" or "minor" (for a discussion of major and minor changes, see chapter 2 of this *Handbook* at 1.6.2.3). If the change is considered minor, nothing need be done. The existing description will be used to include the new issue as though there had been no change. If you think it is important for identification or access, record the later title in the description as a variant using a MARC 246 field (see RDA 2.3.8).

If the change of title is considered major, cataloging theory holds that a new work has been created, which means that a separate description must be created for the new work. Use the first issue with the changed title as the basis for identification of the resource in the new description (see discussion in chapter 2 of this *Handbook* at 1.6.2.3). The two descriptions will be linked by recording the relationship between the two works (see below under Link the Resource to Related Entities).

Changes in title proper of an integrating resource are treated differently, following RDA 2.3.2.12.3. A change of title in an integrating resource does not mean that a new work has been created; therefore, the same description will continue to be used. Simply revise the title proper in the description to reflect the current form. If in your opinion the previous title will remain important for identification or access, record it as a variant using a MARC 247 field (see RDA 2.3.7).

If you receive a new issue of a serial and notice that the corporate body responsible for the serial has changed, think about whether the earlier body appeared as part of the authorized access point for the serial, either because the authorized access point was created by combining the authorized access point for the body with the preferred title of the serial, or because the name of the body was used as a parenthetical qualifier to the preferred title of the serial. The authorized access point for the serial may appear in the bibliographic record either explicitly (in a 130 field or a 110/240 combination), or implicitly (when a body has been recorded in a 110 field without a 240 field, implying that the title proper recorded in 245 is the preferred title of the serial). If this is the case and the responsible body changes, the authorized access point for the work will no longer be the same, and under cataloging theory this means that a new work has been created, requiring that a separate description be created for the new work (see discussion in chapter 2 of this *Handbook* at 1.6.2.4). The two descriptions will be linked by recording the relationship between the two works (see below under Link the Resource to Related Entities).

Another similar change affecting the description of either a serial or an integrating resource is change in media type (format). If the format of a serial or integrating resource changes (e.g., a printed serial becomes an online serial, or a loose-leaf integrating resource becomes a database) a new description is required (see RDA 1.6.2.2 and 1.6.3.2). The two descriptions will be linked by recording the relationship between the two works (see below under Link the Resource to Related Entities).

Other Title Information. Transcription of other title information is optional in RDA. Because it tends to vary from issue to issue, most serials catalogers do not record other title information. However, if in the judgment of the cataloger other title information is important for identifying the resource, it may be recorded. One type of other title information that is usually included is an acronym that appears on the source when the full form of the acronym has been recorded as the title proper.

Words or phrases conveying only information about currency of contents ("including amendments through 2011") or frequency of updating ("updated daily") should not be considered other title information but should rather be recorded in the frequency element.

If including other title information transcribe it after the title proper in subfield ‡b of the 245 field (see RDA 2.3.4). Other title information should be transcribed from the same source as the title proper. The first piece of other title information is separated from the title proper by space-colon-space. Subsequent pieces of other title information are separated from each other by space-colon-space. For details, see chapter 2 of this *Handbook* at 2.3.4.

Statement of Responsibility. The first statement of responsibility relating to the title proper is a core element in RDA. Other statements of responsibility are optional. For serials, statements naming a corporate body that is the issuing body of the resource are usually recorded. However, statements naming an editor are only recorded if the name "is considered to be an important means of identifying the serial" (RDA 2.4.1.4 exception). An example where the name is considered to be an important means of identification is the case where one person edited the serial for all or most of its existence.

When deciding whether to include statements of responsibility, consider whether a statement on a particular issue is likely to be different in another issue. If including statements of responsibility in the description, transcribe them after the title proper or other information in subfield ‡c of the 245 field (see RDA 2.4.1 and 2.4.2). Statements of responsibility may be transcribed from any source within the resource itself. The first statement of responsibility is separated from the title proper (or other title information) by space-slash-space. Subsequent statements of responsibility are separated from each other by space-semicolon-space. For details, see chapter 2 of this *Handbook* at 2.4.

Variant Titles. Examine the resource for variant titles. Variant titles are not core in RDA, but if in your opinion a library user might attempt to find the resource using one of these titles, record it in subfield ‡a of a 246 field. Variant titles can be taken from any source (see RDA 2.3.6.2). For economy's sake, most catalogers will not look beyond the resource itself for variant titles. For details, see chapter 2 of this *Handbook* at 2.3.6.

Key Title and Abbreviated Title. Key title and abbreviated title are titles assigned to a serial by the ISSN Network. Do not attempt to create these titles; however, if they are known, record them in a 222 field (key title) or a 210 field (abbreviated title) (see discussion in chapter 2 of this *Handbook* at 2.3.9–2.3.10).

Edition Statement. Examine the resource for an edition statement. An edition statement can be taken from any source within the resource, but a statement found in the same source as the title proper is preferred. Edition statements may also be taken from outside the resource, but if so, they should be bracketed.

Be careful when you see wording on a serial resource that appears to be an edition statement. Sometimes the presence of words such as "edition" or "issue" on a serial is simply an enumeration of the parts (see RDA 2.5.2.5 and discussion in chapter 2 of this *Handbook* at 1.6.2.5).

Designation of edition is a core element, and therefore must be recorded if present in the resource. If found, transcribe a designation of edition (e.g., "East Coast edition") in subfield ‡a of a 250 field (see RDA 2.5.2).

Recording other elements of the edition statement is optional in RDA. The most common other element is a statement of responsibility relating to the edition. If you find such a statement and decide to include it in the description, record it following space-slash-space in subfield ‡b of the 250 field.

For details on recording an edition statement, see chapter 2 of this *Handbook* at 2.5.

Publication Statement. Examine the resource (beginning with the source chosen as the basis for identification) for publication information, including place of publication, publisher, and date of publication. Although information about publication can be taken from outside the resource itself, prefer information found inside the resource, and within the resource, prefer information found in the same source as the title proper. Publication information is recorded in a MARC bibliographic 264 field, with the second indicator coded "1."

Record the first place of publication found in the resource in subfield ‡a of the 264 field. Transcribe the information exactly as found. This element is core. If no place is found in the resource either supply (in brackets) information from another source about the place of publication, or record "[Place of publication not identified]." If more than one place of publication is found in the resource, you may optionally record them all, but only the first is required. For details, see chapter 2 of this *Handbook* at 2.8.2.

Record the first publisher associated with the first place of publication found in the resource in subfield ‡b of the 264 field. Transcribe the information exactly as found. This element is core. If no publisher is found in the resource either supply (in brackets) information about the publisher from another source, or record "[Publisher not identified]." Separate the place of publication from the publisher's name with space-colon-space. If more than one publisher is found in the resource, you may optionally record them all, but only the first is required. For details, see chapter 2 of this *Handbook* at 2.8.4.

As discussed above under titles, it is the nature of serials and integrating resources to change over time. One thing that can change is the publication statement. If a place of publication or publisher's name changes in a serial, make a note of the change if you think this would be important for identification of or access to the serial (see RDA 2.8.1.5.2 with 2.20.7.5.2). In contrast, if the place of publication or publisher's name changes in an integrating resource, *change* the information recorded in these elements to reflect the current iteration of the resource. If you think it is important for identification of or access to the resource, make a note of earlier places and names (see RDA 2.8.1.5.3 with 2.20.7.5.3).

Alternately, show changes in multiple 264 fields rather than notes. A 264 field with the first indicator coded blank represents the earliest publication statement associated with the resource. A 264 field with the first indicator coded 3 represents the latest or current statement. A 264 field with the first indicator coded 2 represents an intervening publication statement.

Record the date of publication. Record numerals in the form preferred by your cataloging agency (see RDA 1.8.2). Place a comma immediately after the publisher's name and record the date of publication in subfield ‡c of the 264 field. The date of publication element is core.

Note that a copyright date is not a publication date. A copyright date can never be substituted for a publication date in RDA, but it may optionally be recorded in addition to the date of publication element. It may also be used as evidence for inferring the date of publication. If recording a copyright date, include the copyright symbol (© or ℗) and record it in subfield ‡c of a separate 264 field, with the second indicator coded "4."

Because serials and integrating resources exist over time, their descriptions typically record both a beginning and ending date (if the resource has ended). However, these dates are to be recorded from the first and last issue or part. If these parts are not available the information may be supplied (in square brackets), but if they are not available and the information cannot be supplied, do not record this element (see RDA 2.8.6.5). Do not record "[Date of publication not identified]" as you might for other types of resources.

If changes in the publication statement have been recorded in multiple 264 fields, be aware that in current practice, the date element is only recorded in publication statements for serials in the 264 field with first indicator coded blank (the field containing the original publication statement); the date element is only recorded in publication statements for integrating resources in the 264 field with first indicator coded 3 (the field containing the latest publication statement).[2]

For details about publication statement, see chapter 2 of this *Handbook* at 2.8.

Describe the Carrier. A carrier is the physical medium in which the content of a resource is stored. Serials and integrating resources come in many kinds of carriers, including volumes (printed books), audio discs, microform carriers, video discs, and online. Examine the resource's carrier for physical details. Several carrier-related elements are required in an RDA record. Most are recorded in the 3XX block of the bibliographic record.

Extent. The extent of the resource is recorded in subfield ‡a of a MARC bibliographic 300 field. Extent is core if the resource is complete. Record the extent of a serial or integrating resource following the appropriate instructions in RDA 3.4. Only the most basic procedures will be mentioned in this appendix. For details, see chapter 2 of this *Handbook* at 3.4.5.

If a serial consists of printed text, record the number of *bibliographic* volumes (*not* physical volumes) followed by the term "volumes" (e.g., "15 volumes") (see RDA 3.4.5.16 exception). If the serial is not complete, either record "volumes" without a number, or do not record this element at all (see RDA 3.4.1.10, with its alternative).

For most other serial carriers, record the number of units followed by an appropriate term (given in the plural) from the carrier type list in 3.3.1.3 (e.g., "23 audio discs").

Illustrative Content. Though not considered in RDA to be part of the carrier description, this element is treated here because it is recorded immediately after the extent element in the MARC bibliographic record. Examine the resource for illustrations, including maps. If found, and you think recording the information would help the library user to identify or select the resource (this element is not core), record the word "illustration" or "illustrations" in subfield ‡b of the 300 field (see RDA 7.15). Other terms may also be used, preferring terms found in the alternative list in RDA 7.15.1.3. Probably the most common of these is "map" or "maps." Record colour content (e.g., "color illustrations") (see RDA 7.17). Separate these elements from the preceding extent element with space-semicolon-space.

When deciding whether to record these elements, consider the whole serial. If most issues contain illustrations, most catalogers would record the elements. If only an occasional issue contains an illustration, most catalogers would not record them.

For details on illustrative content and color content, see chapter 8 of this *Handbook* at 7.15 and 7.17.

Dimensions. The dimensions element is not core in RDA, nor is it core in serial descriptions or descriptions of online integrating resources prepared by the Library of Congress (see LC-PCC PS 3.5, May 2012). Most U.S. catalogers will not record this element for serials, and they will never be recorded for online serials or online integrating resources. The dimensions element is core for the Library of Congress for other types of integrating resources (e.g., a loose-leaf resource).

If you choose to record dimensions in a serial record, or if you are describing a non-online integrating resource, record the element in subfield ‡c of a MARC bibliographic 300 field. Separate the dimensions element from any preceding elements in the field with space-semicolon-space. For format-specific details, see chapter 2 of this *Handbook* beginning at 3.5. See also RDA 3.5.1.8.1 for special instructions for serials and 3.5.1.8.2 for special instructions for integrating resources.

Frequency. Although the frequency element is not part of the description of the carrier, it is treated here because it is generally the next element after the extent (or dimensions) recorded in a MARC serial or integrating resource record. Frequency refers to the intervals at which parts of a serial or updates to an integrating resource are issued. It is not a core element in RDA but is core for LC and PCC (LC-PCC PS 2.14, July 2012). Record frequency by giving one of the terms listed in RDA 2.14.1.3 in subfield ‡a of the MARC bibliographic 310 field (current frequency) or 321 field (former frequency). For details and examples, see chapter 2 of this *Handbook* at 2.14.1.3.

Content Type. Like the frequency element, the content type element is not part of the description of the carrier, but it is treated here because it is generally the next element after frequency recorded in a MARC serial or integrating resource bibliographic record. Content type is a core element, and is recorded in subfield ‡a of the MARC 336 field following the instructions in RDA 6.9. Record, as appropriate, one of the terms in the list found in RDA 6.9.1.3. End the field with "‡2 rdacontent":

336 ‡a text ‡2 rdacontent

The most common content type for a serial or integrating resource is "text," but nearly any of the content types could be used. More than one content type can be recorded. If illustrations or maps are present and prominent (that is, appearing more often that on just a few pages of an issue or two), "still image" or "cartographic image" may also be appropriate. For details, see chapter 8 of this *Handbook* at 6.9.

Media and Carrier Type. Carrier type is core in an RDA description. Media type is not core, but most U.S. catalogers follow LC and PCC practice and record it (see LC-PCC PS 3.2, October 2012).

Media type is recorded in subfield ‡a of a MARC bibliographic 337 field. The term should be taken from the list in RDA 3.2.1.3. For a printed resource, use "unmediated." However, any of the media types might be appropriate for a given serial or integrating resource. End the field with "‡2 rdamedia":

337 ‡a unmediated ‡2 rdamedia

Carrier type is recorded in subfield ‡a of a MARC bibliographic 338 field. The term should be taken from the list in RDA 3.3.1.3. Most of the terms there might be used to describe a printed monograph, but the most common are "volume" (for a printed resource) or "online resource." End the field with "‡2 rdacarrier":

338 ‡a volume ‡2 rdacarrier

For details, see chapter 2 of this *Handbook* at 3.2 and 3.3.

Numbering of Serials. Numbering of serials is defined in RDA 2.6.1.1 as "the identification of each of the issues or parts of a serial." This element is core. However, information about numbering must be taken from the first or last issue of the serial, and therefore the element is only recorded if one or both of those issues is available. Most serials catalogers, therefore, follow instead the alternative to RDA 2.6.2.3 and record this information as an unstructured note rather than in a formal numbering of serials element (see LC-PCC PS 2.6.2.3 alternative, September 2012). In either case numbering information is recorded in a MARC 362 field. If recording the numbering of serials element, code the first indicator "0." If recording the information as a note, code the first indicator "1." For a full explanation of numbering, with examples, see chapter 2 of this *Handbook* beginning at 2.6 (numbering of serials element) and at 2.20.5 (note on numbering).

Series Statement. Examine the resource for a series statement. Although information about a series can be taken from outside the resource itself, prefer information found in the resource, and within the resource prefer information found on a series title page. Series information is recorded in a MARC bibliographic 490 field. The first indicator is coded "0" if the information is not indexed; it is coded "1" if the information is indexed (in which case an 8XX field will also be present in the bibliographic record; see below under Link the Resource to Related Entities).

Record the title proper of the series in subfield ‡a of the 490 field exactly as it appears in the resource. If series numbering is present, record it in subfield ‡v following the title proper of the series and any other elements (such as a statement of responsibility). For serials, however, record numbering within the series *only* if all the parts of the serial carry the same series number (see RDA 2.12.9.8.2). Separate series numbering from preceding elements by space-semicolon-space.

The title proper of the series and numbering are core and therefore must be recorded if present (with the numbering exception for serials mentioned in the previous paragraph). Other title information of the series and statements of responsibility relating to the series are not core and are not in most cases recorded. For details about recording series statements, see chapter 2 of this *Handbook* at 2.12.

Notes. Include any notes you consider necessary to help the library user contextualize, find, identify, or select the resource. No notes are core in an RDA description. Therefore, recording notes in a bibliographic record is entirely dependent on your judgment or the policies of your cataloging agency. Most notes are recorded in the 5XX block of the MARC bibliographic record. Some of the more common notes included in bibliographic records for serials and integrating resources are notes detailing the basis for identification ("description based on" and "latest issue consulted" notes) (see chapter 2 of this *Handbook* at 2.20.13), notes naming bodies responsible for the resource (see chapter 2 of this *Handbook* at 2.20.3), and notes detailing peculiarities about the numbering (see RDA 2.20.5.4). See the figures illustrating serial or integrating resource descriptions throughout this *Handbook* for many different kinds of notes.

Identifier for the Manifestation. Examine the resource for an identifier, defined as "a character string associated with a manifestation that serves to differentiate that manifestation from other manifestations." The identifier for the manifestation element is core (see RDA 2.15); therefore an identifier must be recorded if present on the resource.

The most common identifier associated with serials is an ISSN (International Standard Serial Number). Record ISSN in subfield ‡a of an 022 field exactly as found, including the hyphen. An ISBN (International Standard Book Number) may be associated with an integrating resource. Record an ISBN in subfield ‡a of the 020 field of the MARC bibliographic record. Copy it as found, but do not record hyphens. For details, see chapter 2 of this *Handbook* at 2.15.

5. LINK THE RESOURCE TO RELATED ENTITIES

Once the resource has been described, links should be made to related entities. These include works and expressions either contained in the resource or related to the work(s) or expression(s) described in the record, and related persons, families, corporate bodies, and geographic entities.

In the MARC bibliographic format these links are created by recording the authorized access point for the related entity in one of the access point fields, generally speaking the 1XX, 7XX, and 8XX fields. This either (1) links the bibliographic record to an associated authority record, and via that record links the bibliographic record to other bibliographic records containing the same authorized access point (either by using the text string itself, or using an identifier); (2) directly links the bibliographic record to other bibliographic records containing the same authorized access point; or (3) at the least allows searches to retrieve all bibliographic records containing the same authorized access point.

RDA requires the cataloger to record at least one relationship: that between the resource and the principal creator of the work embodied in the manifestation being described (see discussion in chapter 9 of this *Handbook* at 18.3). Recording most other relationships is optional, but most catalogers will record many.

The relationship between the resource and the principal creator of the work is recorded in a 100 (persons or families), 110 (most corporate bodies), or 111 (meetings) field. If there is more than one work in the resource and they are by different creators, record these relationships in 700, 710, or 711. See chapter 9 of this *Handbook* at 19.2 for help in determining what entity is the principal creator of the work. With persons and families associated with integrating resources the decision is usually fairly straightforward. For serials, however, pay close attention to 19.2.1.1.3. A person or family will only be considered to be the creator of a serial under very limited circumstances (see corresponding discussion in chapter 9 of this *Handbook*). Determining if a corporate body or meeting is the creator of a serial or integrating resource can also be somewhat tricky, but fairly clear guidelines are laid out at RDA 19.2.1.1.1 (and see corresponding discussion in chapter 9 of the *Handbook*).

Begin by recording the authorized access point for the principal creator of the work in a 1XX field if there is one. This form may be accompanied by a relationship designator to clarify the nature of the relationship. The use of relationship designators is optional but encouraged (see *Handbook* chapter 9 at 18.5).

Once the relationship to the principal creator has been recorded, think about other relationships that might be helpful. First consider other creators if there are more than one. Other commonly recorded relationships for serials and integrating resources include those between the resource and prominent editors, and issuing or sponsoring bodies. These relationships are all recorded by giving the authorized access point for the related entity in 7XX fields: 700 (persons and families), 710 (most corporate bodies), or 711 (meetings).

Consider also relationships to related works and expressions, or the relationship between the manifestation described in the bibliographic record and the work(s) or expression(s) embodied in the manifestation. Related works or expressions are recorded by giving the authorized access point for the work or expression in a 700, 710, 711, or 730 field, or in the case of a series, in an 800, 810, 811, or 830 field. Works or expressions embodied in the manifestation are recorded in a 1XX and 240 field combination or in 130 if there is only one; or if there are two or more, in 700, 710, 711, or 730 fields as appropriate. For details, see discussion throughout chapter 9 of this *Handbook*.

Of particular importance to serial descriptions are relationships to related serials, particularly previous and later serials, results of mergers or splits, supplementary serial works, etc. These relationships are recorded in the MARC "linking" fields (760–787). For details, see the discussion of RDA chapter 25 in chapter 9 of this *Handbook*.

6. SAMPLE RECORD SETS

Other examples of serial and integrating resource cataloging in this *Handbook* include figures 2.9, 2.10 through 2.16, 2.50, 2.102, 9.10, 9.15 through 9.17, 9.52, 9.53, 9.59, 9.60, 9.61, 9.62 through 9.63, and 9.67.

RECORD SET K1
PRINT INTEGRATING RESOURCE

Bibliographic Record

020	‡a 9780838910931 (American Library Association)	*[RDA 2.15]*
020	‡a 9780888023553 (Canadian Library Association)	*[RDA 2.15]*
020	‡a 9781856047494 (CILIP)	*[RDA 2.15]*
022 0	‡a 2167-325X	*[RDA 2.15]*
210 0	‡a Resourc. descr. access	*[RDA 2.3.10]*
222 0	‡a Resource description & access	*[RDA 2.3.9]*
245 00	‡a Resource description & access : ‡b RDA / ‡c developed in a collaborative process led by the Joint Steering Committee for Development of RDA (JSC).	
		[RDA 2.3, 2.4]

246 3 ‡a Resource description and access   *[RDA 2.3.6]*

246 3 ‡a RDA   *[RDA 2.3.6]*

264 1 ‡a Chicago : ‡b American Library Association ; ‡a Ottawa : ‡b Canadian Library Association ; ‡a London : ‡b CILIP: Chartered Institute of Library and Information Professionals, ‡c 2010-   *[RDA 2.8]*

300   ‡a 1 volume (loose-leaf) ; ‡c 30 cm   *[RDA 3.4.1.10, 3.4.5.19, 3.5.1.4.14]*

310   ‡a Updated annually   *[RDA 2.14]*

336   ‡a text ‡2 rdacontent   *[RDA 6.9]*

337   ‡a unmediated ‡2 rdamedia   *[RDA 3.2]*

338   ‡a volume ‡2 rdacarrier   *[RDA 3.3]*

500   ‡a "Representing the American Library Association, the Australian Committee on Cataloguing, the British Library, the Canadian Committee on Cataloguing, CILIP: Chartered Institute of Library and Information Professionals, the Library of Congress."   *[RDA 2.20.3]*

504   ‡a Includes bibliographical references and index.   *[RDA 7.16]*

588   ‡a Description based on: 2010; title from title page.   *[RDA 2.20.13]*

710 2 ‡a Joint Steering Committee for Development of RDA, ‡e issuing body.   *[RDA 19.3, 18.4.1.2, 18.5]*

Title page

RDA
RESOURCE DESCRIPTION & ACCESS
Developed in a collaborative process led by the
Joint Steering Committee for Development of RDA (JSC), representing
The American Library Association
The Australian Committee on Cataloguing
The British Library
The Canadian Committee on Cataloguing
CILIP: Chartered Institute of Library and Information Professionals
The Library of Congress
AMERICAN LIBRARY ASSOCIATION, CHICAGO
CANADIAN LIBRARY ASSOCIATION, OTTAWA
CILIP: CHARTERED INSTITUTE OF LIBRARY AND
INFORMATION PROFESSIONALS, LONDON

Title page verso
PUBLISHED 2010 BY
American Library Association   *Canadian Library Association*
CILIP: Chartered Institute of Library and Information Professionals
...
ISBN: 978-0-8389-1093-1   ISBN: 978-0-88802-355-3   ISBN: 978-185604-749-4
...
©2011 American Library Association, Canadian Library Association, and CILIP: Chartered Institute of Library and Information Professionals

Associated Authority Record

110 2	‡a Joint Steering Committee for Development of RDA *[RDA 11.2.2, 11.13.1]*
372	‡a Cataloging standard development *[RDA 11.10]*
510 2	‡w a ‡ a Joint Steering Committee for Revision of AACR *[RDA 32.1, 32.2, 29.4.2]*
670	‡a Joint Steering Committee for Development of RDA WWW Home page, Oct. 26, 2007: ‡b (Joint Steering Committee for Development of RDA; new name of the Joint Steering Committee for Revision of AACR) *[RDA 8.12]*
670	‡a Resource description & access, 2010- : ‡b title page (Joint Steering Committee for Development of RDA (JSC), representing the American Library Association, the Australian Committee on Cataloguing, the British Library, the Canadian Committee on Cataloguing, CILIP--Chartered Institute of Library and Information Professionals, the Library of Congress) *[RDA 8.12]*

RECORD SET K2
PRINT SERIAL

Bibliographic Record

022	‡a 0075-4277 *[RDA 2.15]*
245 04	‡a The journal of juristic papyrology. *[RDA 2.3]*
264 1	‡3 1946: ‡a New York : ‡b Polish Institute of Arts and Sciences in America, ‡c 1946- *[RDA 2.8]*
264 21	‡3 1948-1952: ‡a Warsaw : ‡b Warsaw Society of Sciences and Letters *[RDA 2.8, 2.8.1.5.2]*
264 21	‡3 1953-1991: ‡a Warsaw : ‡b Polish Scientific Publishers *[RDA 2.8, 2.8.1.5.2]*
264 21	‡3 1992-1999: ‡a Warsaw : ‡b Wydawn. Uniwersytetu Warszawskiego *[RDA 2.8, 2.8.1.5.2]*
264 31	‡3 2000- ‡a Warsaw : ‡b Warsaw University, Institute of Archaeology, Department of Papyrology *[RDA 2.8, 2.8.1.5.2]*
300	‡a volumes ; ‡c 25 cm *[RDA 3.4.1.10, 3.5.1.4.14]*
310	‡a Annual *[RDA 2.14]*
336	‡a text ‡2 rdacontent *[RDA 6.9]*
337	‡a unmediated ‡2 rdamedia *[RDA 3.2]*
338	‡a volume ‡2 rdacarrier *[RDA 3.3]*
362 1	‡a Began with vol. 1, no. 1 (1946) *[RDA 2.6.2.3 alternative, 2.20.5.3]*
546	‡a Includes articles in English, French, German, and Italian. *[RDA 7.12]*
550	‡a Vols. 2-6 issued by: Warsaw Society of Sciences and Letters, Dept. II of Philosophy, History, and Sociology; vol. 7/8-11/12 by: Polish Academy of Sciences; vol. 13-22 by: University of Warsaw, Institute of Papyrology and Ancient Law; vol. 23- by: University of Warsaw, Institute of Archaeology, Department of Papyrology; vol. 31- with The Raphael Taubenschlag Foundation; v. 35- with University of Warsaw, Faculty of Law and Administration. *[RDA 2.20.3.6.2]*

588	‡a Description based on: Vol. 1, no. 1 (1946).	*[RDA 2.20.13]*
588	‡a Latest issue consulted: Vol. 40 (2010).	*[RDA 2.20.13]*
710 2	‡a Polish Institute of Arts and Sciences in America, ‡e issuing body.	
		[RDA 19.3, 18.4.1.2, 18.5]

... [access points for other issuing bodies omitted]

770 0	‡i Supplement (Work): ‡t Journal of juristic papyrology. Supplement.	
		[RDA 25.1, 24.4.2]

Title page of Vol. 1, no. 1

Vol. 1   No. 1

THE JOURNAL OF JURISTIC PAPYROLOGY

edited by Raphael Taubenschlag

Research Professor of Ancient Civilization, Columbia University

Professor of Roman Law, University of Cracow

1946

Published by POLISH INSTITUTE OF ARTS AND SCIENCES IN AMERICA

Distributed by HERALD SQUARE PRESS, INC.

New York

Title page of Vol. 40

University of Warsaw, Institute of Archaeology, Department of Papyrology

University of Warsaw, Faculty of Law and Administration

The Raphael Taubenschlag Foundation

The Journal of Juristic Papyrology

Founded by Raphael Taubenschlag

Edited by Tomasz Derda, Adam Łajtar, Jakub Urbanik

Assistant to the editors, Grzegorz Ochała

Vol. XI (2010)

Warsaw 2010

Title page verso

ISSN 0075-4277

Associated Authority Record

046	‡s 1942 ‡t 1978-12	*[RDA 11.4]*
110 2	‡a Polish Institute of Arts and Sciences in America	*[RDA 11.2.2, 11.13.1]*
368	‡a Cultural organization	*[RDA 11.7]*
370	‡e New York (N.Y.) ‡2 naf	*[RDA 11.3]*
377	‡a eng ‡a pol	*[RDA 11.8]*
410 2	‡a Polski Instytut Naukowy w Ameryce	*[RDA 11.2.3, 11.13.2]*
510 2	‡w b ‡a Polish Institute of Arts and Sciences of America	*[RDA 32.1, 32.2, 29.4.2]*
670	‡a The journal of juristic papyrology, 1946: ‡b vol. 1, no. 1 title page (Polish Institute of Arts and Sciences in America, New York)	*[RDA 8.12]*

670	‡a Telephone call to Institute ‡b (changed its name from Polish Institute of Arts and Sciences in America in December 1978)	*[RDA 8.12]*
670	‡a OCLC, 12 October 2012 ‡b (usage: Polish Institute of Arts and Sciences in America; Polski Instytut Naukowy w Ameryce)	*[RDA 8.12]*
670	‡a The Polish Institute of Arts and Sciences of America, via WWW, 12 October 2012 ‡b (cultural organization founded in 1942)	*[RDA 8.12]*

RECORD SET K3
ONLINE SERIAL

Bibliographic Record

022 0	‡a 2169-0685	*[RDA 2.15]*
245 00	‡a Journal for the evangelical study of the Old Testament.	*[RDA 2.3]*
246 1	‡a JESOT	*[RDA 2.3.6]*
264 1	‡a Eugene, OR : ‡b Wipf and Stock Publishers, ‡c 2012-	*[RDA 2.8]*
300	‡a 1 online resource	*[RDA 3.4.1.3]*
310	‡a Semiannual	*[RDA 2.14]*
336	‡a text ‡2 rdacontent	*[RDA 6.9]*
337	‡a computer ‡2 rdamedia	*[RDA 3.2]*
338	‡a online resource ‡2 rdacarrier	*[RDA 3.3]*
362 1	‡a Began with: Volume 1, issue 1 (2012)	*[RDA 2.6.2.3 alternative, 2.20.5.3]*
520	‡a "JESOT ... seeks to publish current academic research in the areas of ancient Near Eastern backgrounds, Dead Sea Scrolls, Rabbinics, Linguistics, Septuagint, Research Methodology, Literary Analysis, Exegesis, Text Criticism, and Theology as they pertain only to the Old Testament."	*[RDA 7.10]*
588	‡a Description based on: Volume 1, issue 1 (2012); title from PDF title page (jesot. org website, viewed November 15, 2012).	*[RDA 2.20.13]*
588	‡a Latest issue consulted: Volume 1, issue 1 (2012) (jesot.org website, viewed November 15, 2012).	*[RDA 2.20.13]*
856 40	‡u www.jesot.org	*[RDA 4.6]*

PDF cover

Volume 1, Issue 1
JOURNAL FOR THE EVANGELICAL
STUDY OF THE OLD TESTAMENT
[Table of contents]

PDF title page

Journal for the Evangelical Study
of the Old Testament
JESOT is published bi-annually online at www.jesot.org and in print
by Wipf and Stock Publishers
199 West 8th Avenue, Suite 3, Eugene, OR 97401, USA
©2011 by Wipf and Stock Publishers

NOTES

1. For a thorough overview of serials cataloging in RDA, including matters not covered in this *Handbook*, see Ed Jones, *RDA and Serials Cataloging* (Chicago: ALA Editions, 2013).

2. For details, see the PCC guidelines for the 264 field at www.loc.gov/aba/pcc/documents/264-Guidelines.doc.

ANALYTICAL DESCRIPTION

THIS APPENDIX DESCRIBES RECOMMENDED PROCESSES FOR CREAT-ing analytical descriptions using a MARC bibliographic record. It covers bibliographic record creation for these resources only in the most general of terms. Details are covered in the body of the *Handbook*. As with the *Handbook* itself, this appendix does not cover non-RDA related aspects of the bibliographic record, such as fixed-length data elements (the so-called fixed fields) or subject analysis. This appendix also contains two sample record sets consisting of bibliographic analytical descriptions and their associated authority records, which illustrate many of the points described below.

An analytical description is a description that describes a part of a larger resource (see RDA glossary). Analytical descriptions can be created for monographic resources (e.g., a single volume in a multipart monograph or a single chapter within a volume) and for serials or integrating resources (e.g., a single article within an issue of a serial, a single monograph within a monographic series). Most analytical descriptions are themselves monographic in nature, but they can also be serial (e.g., an analytical description of a regularly occurring column within a newspaper).

Analytical descriptions always describe a resource that has a whole-part relationship to another resource. There are many ways of doing this in RDA. It is possible to create an analytical description simply by recording links to individual works or expressions within the bibliographic record for the larger resource. This is done by recording the authorized access points for the individual works or expressions in 7XX fields, with the second indicator coded "2." Such access points are called "analytical access points." For example, a compilation of three Walt Whitman poems was published in 2011. While it would be possible to create a separate analytical description for each poem in separate bibliographic records, it is also possible to "analyze" the parts by recording each as an authorized access point in the description of the whole:

100　1　‡a Whitman, Walt, ‡d 1819-1892, ‡e author.

245　10　‡a Three poems / ‡c Walt Whitman.

264　1　‡a [Carrollton, Ohio] : ‡b Press on Scroll Road, ‡c 2011.

. . .

700　12　‡a ‡a Whitman, Walt, ‡d 1819-1892. ‡t I sing the body electric.

700　12　‡a ‡a Whitman, Walt, ‡d 1819-1892. ‡t Out of the cradle endlessly rocking.

700　12　‡a ‡a Whitman, Walt, ‡d 1819-1892. ‡t When lilacs last in the dooryard bloom'd.

This technique of analytical description simply records relationships by creating links to the parts within the description of the whole. An opposite technique is used when creating an analytical description of a part of a monographic series: the part is described exactly as any other monographic resource, recording a link in an 8XX field to the series as a whole. For example, the Alfred Hitchcock film *Rear Window* was released on DVD in 2008 in a series called "Universal legacy series":

245　00　‡a Rear window / ‡c a Paramount Pictures release ; produced by Alfred Hitchcock ; screenplay by John Michael Hayes ; directed by Alfred Hitchcock.

264　1　‡a Universal City, CA : ‡b Universal Pictures, ‡c [2008]

. . .

830　0　‡a Universal legacy series.

For more information on these two techniques as well as other methods of recording relationships between parts of resources and the whole, see the discussion in chapter 9 of this *Handbook* of RDA chapter 25, "Whole-Part Work Relationships"; chapter 26, "Whole-Part Expression Relationships"; and chapter 27, "Whole-Part Manifestation Relationships."

The remainder of this appendix will cover creation of bibliographic records for analytical descriptions of parts of monographs or serial issues. An example where such description might be useful would be the case of a library that has a comprehensive collection of a particular author and attempts to collect everything written by and about the author, including copies of articles in journals and encyclopedias.

1. DETERMINE THE MODE OF ISSUANCE

Consider the mode of issuance of the resource, the part to be analyzed. Does it consist of a single part? Is it more than one part of the whole? Is the analyzed part itself a serial? Is it an integrating resource? Analytical descriptions can be created for any of these.

2. CHOOSE THE BASIS FOR IDENTIFICATION AND SOURCES OF INFORMATION FOR THE RESOURCE

Examine the resource and choose a basis for identification following the instructions in RDA 2.1.3. If the resource to be analyzed is a single part, the resource itself will be the basis for identification. If the resource consists of more than one part, one of the parts will be chosen as the basis for identification following 2.1.2.3. Generally speaking, choose the first part.

Having chosen the part that will serve as the basis for identification, choose a "preferred source of information" within that part following the instructions in RDA 2.2. In analytical descriptions this source is often a caption, but it can be any part in which information (such as a title) is formally presented.

3. DESCRIBE THE RESOURCE

Titles and Statements of Responsibility. Transcribe the title proper, other title information, and statement of responsibility in a MARC bibliographic 245 field. For information about transcription, see chapter 2 of this *Handbook* at 1.7.

Transcribe the title proper in subfield ‡a of the 245 field exactly as found on the preferred source of information. Title proper is a core element and therefore must be included in the description. For details, see chapter 2 of this *Handbook* at 2.3.

Transcription of other title information is optional in RDA. If you decide recording other title information would be useful to the database user, transcribe it after the title proper in subfield ‡b of the 245 field (see RDA 2.3.4). Other title information should be transcribed from the same source as the title proper. The first piece of other title information is separated from the title proper by space-colon-space. Subsequent pieces of other title information are separated from each other by space-colon-space. For details, see chapter 2 of this *Handbook* at 2.3.4.

The first statement of responsibility relating to the title proper is a core element in RDA. Other statements of responsibility are optional, although most catalogers will record them. If including statements of responsibility in the description, transcribe them after the title proper or other information in subfield ‡c of the 245 field (see RDA 2.4.1 and 2.4.2). Statements of responsibility may be transcribed from any source within the resource itself. Note that in analyzed parts of resources a statement of responsibility is often far removed from the title (e.g., the author's name might appear only at the end of the article being analyzed).

The first statement of responsibility is separated from the title proper (or other title information) by space-slash-space. Subsequent statements of responsibility are separated from each other by space-semicolon-space. For details, see chapter 2 of this *Handbook* at 2.4.

Variant Titles. Examine the resource for variant titles. Variant titles are not core in RDA, but if in your opinion a library user might attempt to find the resource using one of these titles, record it in subfield ‡a of a 246 field. Variant titles can be taken from any source (see RDA 2.3.6.2). For details, see chapter 2 of this *Handbook* at 2.3.6.

Edition Statement. Examine the resource for an edition statement. An edition statement can be taken from any source within the resource, but a statement found in the same source as the title proper is preferred. Edition statements may also be taken from outside the resource; if so, they should be bracketed.

Edition statements for analyzed parts are rare. Only record an edition statement that applies to the part, not the whole resource. Designation of edition is a core element, and therefore must be recorded if present in the resource. If found, transcribe a designation of edition (e.g., "Second revised edition") in subfield ‡a of a 250 field (see RDA 2.5.2). For more details on recording an edition statement, see chapter 2 of this *Handbook* at 2.5.

Publication Statement. Examine the resource for publication information, including place of publication, publisher, and date of publication. Although information about publication can be taken from outside the resource itself, prefer information found inside the resource, and within the resource, prefer information found in the same source as the title proper (finding such a source is rare, however, when analyzing parts). Publication information for analyzed parts is often identical to the publication information for the whole resource. Publication information is recorded in a MARC bibliographic 264 field, with the second indicator coded "1."

Record the first place of publication found in the resource in subfield ‡a of the 264 field. Transcribe the information exactly as found. This element is core. If no place is found in the resource either supply (in brackets) information from another source about the place of publication, or record "[Place of publication not identified]." If more than one place of publication is found in the resource, you may optionally record them all, but only the first is required. For details, see chapter 2 of this *Handbook* at 2.8.2.

Record the first publisher associated with the first place of publication found in the resource in subfield ‡b of the 264 field. Transcribe the information exactly as found. This element is core. If no publisher is found in the resource either supply (in brackets) information about the publisher from another source, or record "[Publisher not identified]." Separate the place of publication from the publisher's name with space-colon-space. If more than one publisher is found in the resource, you may optionally record them all, but only the first is required. For details, see chapter 2 of this *Handbook* at 2.8.4.

Record the date of publication. Record numerals in the form preferred by your cataloging agency (see RDA 1.8.2). Place a comma immediately after the publisher's name and record the date of publication in subfield ‡c of the 264 field. The date of publication element is core. If no explicit date of publication is found in the resource either supply (in brackets) information found in another source or inferred by the cataloger, or record "[Date of publication not identified]." Note that a copyright date is not a publication date. A copyright date can never be substituted for a publication date in RDA, but it may optionally be recorded in addition to the date of publication element. It may also be used as evidence for inferring the date of publication.

If the date of publication has not been identified, then either a date of distribution or a copyright date, if present in the resource, must be recorded (see discussion, however, in chapter 2 of this *Handbook* at 2.8.6.6 on ways to identify the date of publication). If recording a copyright date, include the copyright symbol (© or ℗) and record it in subfield ‡c of a separate 264 field, with the second indicator coded "4."

For details about publication statement and copyright date, see chapter 2 of this *Handbook* at 2.8 and 2.11.

Describe the Carrier. A carrier is the physical medium in which the content of a resource is stored. Since any type of resource can be analyzed, they can be stored on any kind of carrier. Several carrier-related elements are required in an RDA record. Most are recorded in the 3XX block of the bibliographic record.

Extent. The extent of the resource is recorded in subfield ‡a of a MARC bibliographic 300 field. Extent is core if the resource is complete. Record the extent of an analyzed part following the instructions in RDA 3.4.1.12 as well as other instructions in RDA 3.4.

If the resource being described consists of a single part, record the position of the part within the larger resource (see RDA 3.4.1.12.2). For printed resources this usually appears in a form such as "pages 45–93." Alternately, following 3.4.1.12.1 simply record the number of units in the part ("150 pages"). RDA has no explicit guidance for recording the extent in an analytical description for a resource that consists of more than one part. Following the general logic of 3.4.1.12.1, however, this *Handbook* recommends following the general instructions for other types of resources, recording the number of units together with a carrier type term (e.g., "23 volumes").

Illustrative Content. Though not considered in RDA to be part of the carrier description, this element is treated here because it is recorded immediately after the extent element in the MARC bibliographic record. Examine the resource for illustrations, including maps. If found, and you think recording the information would help the library user to identify or select the resource (this element is not core), record the word "illustration" or "illustrations" in subfield ‡b of the 300 field (see RDA 7.15). Other terms may also be used, preferring terms found in the alternative list in RDA 7.15.1.3. Probably the most common of these is "map" or "maps." Record colour content (e.g., "color illustrations") (see RDA 7.17). Separate this element from the preceding extent element with space-semicolon-space.

For details on illustrative and color content, see chapter 8 of this *Handbook* at 7.15 and 7.17.

Dimensions. The dimensions element is not core in RDA, but it is core in descriptions of monographs for catalogers at the Library of Congress, except for online electronic resources (see LC-PCC PS 3.5, May 2012). If recorded, the dimensions of the part in an analytical description will generally be the same as those of the whole resource. Dimensions are recorded in subfield ‡c of a MARC bibliographic 300 field following instructions in RDA 3.5. Separate the dimensions element from any preceding elements in the field with space-semicolon-space. For details, see chapter 2 of this *Handbook* at 3.5.

Content Type. Like the illustrative content element described above, the content type element is not part of the description of the carrier, but it is treated here because it is generally the next element after the dimensions recorded in the MARC bibliographic record. Content type is a core element, and is recorded in subfield ‡a of the MARC 336 field following the instructions in RDA 6.9. Record, as appropriate, one of the terms in the list found in RDA 6.9.1.3. End the field with "‡2 rdacontent":

336   ‡a text ‡2 rdacontent

Any content type is possible in analytical descriptions, and more than one can be recorded. For details, see chapter 8 of this *Handbook* at 6.9.

Media and Carrier Type. Carrier type is core in an RDA description. Media type is not core, but most U.S. catalogers follow LC and PCC practice and record it (see LC-PCC PS 3.2, October 2012).

Media type is recorded in subfield ‡a of a MARC bibliographic 337 field. The term should be taken from the list in RDA 3.2.1.3. Any media type is possible in an analytical description. End the field with "‡2 rdamedia":

337   ‡a unmediated ‡2 rdamedia

Carrier type is recorded in subfield ‡a of a MARC bibliographic 338 field. The term should be taken from the list in RDA 3.3.1.3. Any carrier type is possible in an analytical description, but the term chosen should correspond to the term chosen to describe the media type. End the field with "‡2 rdacarrier":

338   ‡a volume ‡2 rdacarrier

For details, see chapter 2 of this *Handbook* at 3.2 and 3.3.

Notes. Include any notes you consider necessary to help the library user contextualize, find, identify, or select the resource. No notes are core in an RDA description.

Therefore, recording notes in a bibliographic record is entirely dependent on your judgment or the policies of your cataloging agency. Most notes are recorded in the 5XX block of the MARC bibliographic record.

Identifier for the Manifestation. Examine the resource for an identifier, defined as "a character string associated with a manifestation that serves to differentiate that manifestation from other manifestations." The identifier for the manifestation element is core (see RDA 2.15) and therefore an identifier must be recorded if present on the resource. However, remember that if you are describing a part of a resource, the identifier should correspond to that part, not to the resource as a whole. Finding such an identifier is very rare.

4. LINK THE RESOURCE TO RELATED ENTITIES

Once the resource has been described, links should be made to related entities. These include works and expressions either contained in the resource or related to the work(s) or expression(s) described in the record, and related persons, families, corporate bodies, and geographic entities.

In the MARC bibliographic format these links are created by recording the authorized access point for the related entity in one of the access point fields, generally speaking the 1XX, 7XX, and 8XX fields. This either (1) links the bibliographic record to an associated authority record, and via that record links the bibliographic record to other bibliographic records containing the same authorized access point (either by using the text string itself, or using an identifier); (2) directly links the bibliographic record to other bibliographic records containing the same authorized access point; or (3) at the least allows searches to retrieve all bibliographic records containing the same authorized access point.

RDA requires the cataloger to record at least one relationship: that between the resource and the principal creator of the work (or in the case of an analytical description, the principal creator of the part) embodied in the manifestation being described (see discussion in chapter 9 of this *Handbook* at 18.3). Recording most other relationships is optional, but most catalogers will record many.

The relationship between the resource and the principal creator of the work (including a part of a work) is recorded in a 100 (persons or families), 110 (most corporate bodies), or 111 (meetings) field. If there is more than one work in the resource and they are by different creators, record these relationships in 700, 710, or 711. See chapter 9 of this *Handbook* at 19.2 for help in determining what entity is the principal creator of the work. With persons and families the decision is usually fairly straightforward. Determining if a corporate body or meeting is the creator can be a little trickier, but fairly clear guidelines are laid out at RDA 19.2.1.1.1 (and see corresponding discussion in chapter 9 of the *Handbook*).

Begin by recording the authorized access point for the principal creator of the work in a 1XX field. This form may be accompanied by a relationship designator to clarify the nature of the relationship. The use of relationship designators is optional but encouraged (see chapter 9 of this *Handbook* at 18.5).

Once the relationship to the principal creator has been recorded, think about other relationships that might be helpful. First consider other creators if there are more than one. Such relationships might include those between the resource and editors, translators, and illustrators. These relationships are all recorded by giving the authorized access point for the related entity in 7XX fields: 700 (persons and families), 710 (most corporate bodies), or 711 (meetings).

Consider also relationships to related works and expressions, or the relationship between the manifestation described in the bibliographic record and the work(s) or expression(s) embodied in the manifestation. Related works or expressions are recorded by giving the authorized access point for the work or expression in a 700, 710, 711, or 730 field, or in the case of a series, in an 800, 810, 811, or 830 field. Works or expressions embodied in the manifestation are recorded in a 1XX and 240 field combination or in 130 if there is only one; or if there are two or more, in 700, 710, 711, or 730 fields as appropriate. For details, see discussion throughout chapter 9 of this *Handbook*.

Particularly important in analytical descriptions of parts of manifestations is the relationship between the part being described and the manifestation as a whole. This relationship is recorded by giving linking information to the manifestation in a 773 field. The first indicator is coded "0"; the second is coded "8" if you are including relationship information following RDA 24.5, otherwise it is left blank. Some of the more common subfields are ‡a (authorized access point of principal creator), ‡t (title), and ‡g ("related parts," where volume information can be recorded). Both of the examples in this appendix include 773 fields.

5. SAMPLE RECORD SETS

RECORD SET L1
SINGLE PART

Bibliographic Record

100 1	‡a Hamilton, William, ‡d 1924-2012, ‡e author.	*[RDA 18.3, 19.2, 18.4.1.2, 18.5]*
245 10	‡a Bartleby and he : ‡b the strange hermeneutic of Herman Melville / ‡c William Hamilton.	*[RDA 2.3, 2.4]*
264 1	‡a Glassboro, NJ : ‡b The Melville Society of America, ‡c 1989.	*[RDA 2.8]*
300	‡a pages 12-14	*[RDA 3.4.1.12.2]*
336	‡a text ‡2 rdacontent	*[RDA 6.9]*
337	‡a unmediated ‡2 rdamedia	*[RDA 3.2]*

338	‡a volume ‡2 rdacarrier	*[RDA 3.3]*
504	‡a Includes bibliographical references (pages 3-4).	*[RDA 7.16]*
773 08	‡i Contained in (manifestation): ‡t Melville Society extracts ‡g Number 78, September 1989	*[RDA 27.1, 24.4.3]*

Melville Society extracts, Number 78, September 1989 Page 12
[Text of previous article]

Bartleby and He:
The Strange Hermeneutic of Herman Melville
William Hamilton
Sarasota, Florida

[Text of article]
Melville Society extracts, Number 78, September 1989 Page 16
Melville Society Extracts is published quarterly by The Melville Society of America . . .
Glassboro, NJ.

Associated Authority Record

046	‡f 19240309 ‡g 20120228	*[RDA 9.3]*
100 1	‡a Hamilton, William, ‡d 1924-2012	*[RDA 9.2.2, 9.19.1]*
370	‡f Rochester (N.Y.) ‡f Sarasota (Fla.) ‡f Portland (Or.) ‡2 naf	*[RDA 9.11]*
373	‡a Colgate Rochester Divinity School ‡2 naf	*[RDA 9.13]*
373	‡a New College of Florida (Sarasota, Fla.) ‡2 naf	*[RDA 9.13]*
373	‡a Portland State University ‡2 naf	*[RDA 9.13]*
374	‡a Theologians ‡a Scholars ‡a College teachers ‡a Deans (Education) ‡2 lcsh	*[RDA 9.16]*
375	‡a male	*[RDA 9.7]*
377	‡a eng	*[RDA 9.14]*
378	‡q William Hughes	*[RDA 9.5]*
670	‡a The Christian man, 1956: ‡b title page (William Hamilton)	*[RDA 8.12]*
670	‡a Phone call to Portland State University, February 23, 1984 ‡b (William Hughes Hamilton, Dean, College of Liberal Arts & Sciences)	*[RDA 8.12]*
670	‡a Los Angeles times WWW site, March 7, 2012 ‡b (in obituary published March 3: William Hamilton; born March 9, 1924, Evanston, Ill.; died Tuesday [February 28, 2012], Portland, Or., aged 87; theologian; member of the Death of God movement of the 1960s. Taught at Colgate Rochester Divinity School (Rochester, N.Y.), New College (Sarasota, Fla.), Portland State University (Portland, Or.); in addition to theology, wrote on Shakespeare and Melville)	*[RDA 8.12]*
678 0	‡a William Hamilton (1924-2012) was an American theologian and scholar. He was a member of the Death of God movement in the 1960s, and also published on Shakespeare and Melville.	*[RDA 9.17]*

RECORD SET L2
MULTIPLE PARTS (SERIAL)

Bibliographic Record

100 1	‡a Card, Orson Scott, ‡e author.	*[RDA 18.3, 19.2, 18.4.1.2, 18.5]*
245 10	‡a Gameplay / ‡c Orson Scott Card.	*[RDA 2.3, 2.4]*
246 3	‡a Game play	*[RDA 2.3.6]*
264 1	‡a Greensboro, North Carolina : ‡b Compute, ‡c 1988-1992.	*[RDA 2.8]*
300	‡a 48 volumes	*[RDA 3.4.1.3]*
310	‡a Monthly	*[RDA 2.14]*
336	‡a text ‡2 rdacontent	*[RDA 6.9]*
337	‡a unmediated ‡2 rdamedia	*[RDA 3.2]*
338	‡a volume ‡2 rdacarrier	*[RDA 3.3]*
362 1	‡a Began with May 1988; ceased with October 1992.	
	[RDA2.6.2.3 alternative, 2.20.5.3]	
588	‡a Description based on: May 1988.	*[RDA 2.20.13]*
588	‡a Latest issue consulted: October 1992.	*[RDA 2.20.13]*
773 08	‡i Contained in (manifestation): ‡t Compute (Greensboro, N.C.) ‡g v. 10, no. 5 (May 1988)-v. 12, no. 12 (December 1990); v. 13, no. 2 (February 1991)-v. 13, no. 11 (November 1991); v. 14, no. 2 (February 1992)-v. 14, no. 3 (March 1992); v. 14, no. 5 (June 1992)-v. 14, no. 7 (August 1992), v. 14, no. 9 (October 1992)	
	[RDA 27.1, 24.4.3]	

Associated Authority Record

046	‡f 19510824	*[RDA 9.3]*
100 1	‡a Card, Orson Scott	*[RDA 9.2.2, 9.19.1]*
370	‡a Richland (Wash.) ‡e Greensboro (N.C.) ‡2 naf	*[RDA 9.8, 9.11]*
372	‡a Science fiction ‡a Fantasy fiction ‡a Computer games ‡2 lcsh	*[RDA 9.15]*
374	‡a Authors ‡2 lcsh	*[RDA 9.16]*
375	‡a male	*[RDA 9.7]*
377	‡a eng	*[RDA 9.14]*
670	‡a Characterization and viewpoint, 1988: ‡b title page (Orson Scott Card)	
	[RDA 8.12]	
670	‡a Contemporary authors, February 22, 2005 ‡b (Orson Scott Card; born August 24, 1951, Richland, Wash.; University of Utah, M.A., 1981; lives in Greensboro, N.C.)	
	[RDA 8.12]	

INDEX

names. *See also* corporate names; families;
    personal names; place names; preferred
    names
  changes in
    corporate names, 348–349
    personal names, 225
    place names, 381–383, 413–414
  not conveying the idea of
    corporate bodies, 388–389, 395, 401
    government bodies recorded
        subordinately, 357–358
    subordinate corporate bodies, 357–358
  of persons, families, and corporate bodies as
      title or integral part of title, 62–65
*Names of Persons: National Usages for Entry in
    Catalogues,* 287
narrators. *See* performers, narrators, and/or
    presenters
Natural Resources Canada's Canadian
    Geographical Names Data Base, 409
naturally occurring objects
  sample record sets, 800
  three-dimensional resources and objects,
      794
nature of the content, 531–532
New Grove, 480, 492
new works based on previously existing works.
    See adaptations or revisions of a work
non-Latin script variant access points
  for corporate bodies, 328
  for works, 438
Northern Ireland, place names, 418–419
notated music
  basis for identification, 726
  carrier, 729
  carrier type, 730–731
  colour content, 729
  content type, 730
  describing the resource, 727–732
  description, choosing type of, 726
  dimensions, 730
  distribution statement, 729
  edition statement, 728
  extent, 152, 729
  format, 577–578
  identifier for the manifestation, 731–732
  illustrative content, 729

media type, 730
mode of issuance, 725–726
notes, 731
principal creator of the work, 732–733
publication statement, 728–729
related entities, linking resource to, 732–733
sample record sets
  multipart monograph, 737–738
  single units, 733–737
series statement, 731
sources of information, 726
statement of responsibility, 727
title information, 727
title page, 726
variant titles, 727
note on the PCC "provider-neutral record,"
    807
notes. *See also* cataloguer's note; notes on
    manifestation or item
  analytical descriptions, 858–859
  audio recordings, 746
  cartographic resources, 703–704
  colour content, details of, 577
  digital resources, 811
  integrating resources, 844
  microform resources, 828
  moving image resources, 765
  notated music, 731
  printed books and sheets, 689
  serials, 844
  three-dimensional resources and objects,
      797
  two-dimensional graphic resources, 783
  unpublished manuscripts and manuscript
      collections, 717–718
notes on manifestation or item
  basis for identification of resource, 144
  carriers, 186
  frequency, 143–144
  general guidelines, 140
  numbering of serials, 141–142
  publication statement, 142–143
  statement of responsibility, 141
  titles
    general guidelines, 140
    other title information recorded as note,
        87, 88

CPSIA information can be obtained at www.ICGtesting.com
Printed in the USA
BVOW04s1247070616

451056BV00012B/43/P